AR

ARTIFICIAL LIFE VI

Proceedings of the Sixth International Conference on Artificial Life

edited by Christoph Adami, Richard K. Belew, Hiroaki Kitano, and Charles Taylor

A Bradford Book

The MIT Press
Cambridge, Massachusetts
London, England

This book was printed and bound in the United States of America.

Library of Congress Cataloging-in-Publication Data

International Conference on Artificial Life (6th : 1998 : UCLA)
Artificial Life VI : proceedings of the Sixth International Conference on Artificial Life / edited by Christoph Adami . . . [et al.].
p. cm.—(Complex adaptive systems)
Conference held at UCLA, June 27–29, 1998.
"A Bradford book."
Includes bibliographical references and index.
ISBN 0-262-51099-5 (pbk.: alk. paper)
1. Biological systems—Computer simulation—Congresses. 2. Biological systems—Simulation methods—Congresses. I. Adami, Christoph. II. Title. III. Series
QH324.2.I556 1998
570'.1'13—dc21

98-22859
CIP

CONTENTS

Invited Talks

Plenary Papers
(alphabetic)

Presented Papers

(alphabetic within topical area)

Artificial Chemistries

Molecular and Developmental Models

Locomotion

Adapting to Environmental Regularity

Evolutionary Dynamics

Evolutionary Themes

Social Dynamics

Language and Social Systems

Posters
(alphabetic)

Preface

It was fifty years ago in 1948, on the occasion of the Hixon Symposium at Caltech, that John von Neumann gave his celebrated lecture entitled "The General and Logical Theory of Automata" (von Neumann 1951), where he introduced to the public his thoughts on universal, self-reproducing machines. Von Neumann himself professed to have been inspired by Turing's theory of universal automata, which dates back another ten years. Also at the symposium was Warren McCullough, who five years earlier had introduced, with Pitts, the universal neuron which is at the center of almost all work on artificial neural networks. This work was also founded on Turing's ideas about universality.

For fifty years then, have researchers fought to capture the universality in Life, to transplant it into a different medium, and to study its "general and logical" characteristics. These intervening years have been sometimes quiet, sometimes punctuated by feverish activity. Clearly, Chris Langton's work and the Artificial Life conferences that he spawned in 1987, have ushered in a new epoch of Alife research (never mind having given us the umbrella term under which we all meet here!) Also, many consider Tom Ray's "tierra" system (introduced at the second Alife Workshop (Ray 1991)) another major milestone, arguably synthesizing a truly living system within a computer for the first time.

These are the Proceedings of the Sixth International Conference on Artificial Life. Like all things alive, the conference too has mutated and adapted over the years, from a "Workshop on the Synthesis and Simulation of Living Systems", attended by 150 researchers in a wide variety of fields, to the International Conference attended by many times more.

The theme of this year's conference, "Life and Computation: the Boundaries are Changing" addresses two of the topics touched upon above. First, von Neumann and Turing taught us that Artificial Life has its root in the universality of computation extended to the universality of life. But even these visionaries would be amazed at the stunning variations on computer/life interactions here represented: molecules used for computing, computers modeling molecules, self-assembly in thin films, resurrected fossils, evolving programs, statistical models of genetic populations, robotic crickets, developmental and immunological models, social and linguistic models, artificial architecture, and the economics of agents. What *would* they have thought?!

Indeed, the field does not stand still: it is itself evolving, and the boundaries are changing. For example, there are more papers dealing with computational molecular and cellular biology at this Alife meeting than ever before, providing new insights into developmental processes in the fruit fly, mechanisms for cell-differentiation, and the modeling of immune-response. And while the emergent properties of agents have always been a mainstay of the Alife field, today we are witnessing increasing applications to financial markets, trading, and even Internet transactions.

But we are also witnessing efforts at reshaping some of the staples of Artificial Life research. For example, Stuart Kauffman's NK-model (Kauffman and Levin 1987), has been used to model the "ruggedness" or "smoothness" of evolutionary landscapes for over a decade. In these proceedings, however, Barnett introduces an "NKp"-model with a form of *neutrality* that many believe essential to evolution (see (Eigen 1986) for a forceful argument). Similarly, Chris Langton's model of self-replication as virtual state machines on a Cellular Automaton (Langton 1984, 1986) is a second classic reference in Alife. Now, in these pages, Sayama introduces a form of "death" into Langton's model, transforming the crystalline but abiotic structures into much more life-like forms that even seem to evolve. Both of the latter presentations are outgrowths of Master theses: a sign that Alife is continually renewing.

As always, there is much more worthy work going on than we can publish in any one Proceedings volume. We received approximately 100 submissions, and 39 of those are presented as full papers. We have highlighted nine of these as examples of high-quality work crossing the entire spectrum of Alife topics; we recommend these especially to readers trying to see just what Alife is about in 1998. In addition, we include 21 shorter papers, presented as posters at the conference. Many of these extend Alife in exciting new directions, or bring a new student's or scientist's perspective to the field.

We are especially excited by the set of invited speakers that have agreed to participate in ALIFE VI. Christos Papadimitriou (MIT) and Len Adleman (USC) are seminal computer scientists, wrestling with many of the same issues that concerned Turing and von Neumann, but benefiting from the great progress in computational complexity theory developed in the interim. Gerald Joyce (UCSD) has been an active participant in Alife work for a number of years and combines an understanding of the computational issues with a practioner's insight into what is possible in a test-tube (even while succeeding at those which seemed impossible!)

Beyond the keynote speeches, the plenary talks, the parallel sessions and the posters which are covered in these proceedings, ALIFE VI sported events that remain undocumented, such as the Alife Art Show, workshops, demonstrations, and a robot contest, all occurring right at Hollywood's doorstep. In the shadow of a city that many brand 'artificial', the 'Alife experience' remains real and we have come full circle. Fifty years after Caltech hosted the Hixon Symposium, Southern California again provides a nurturing environment for Artificial Life. On to the next fifty years!

Pasadena, March 1998

Christoph Adami
Richard Belew
Hiroaki Kitano
Charles Taylor

References

Eigen, M. 1986. The physics of molecular evolution. In *Molecular Evolution of Life*, edited by H. Baltscheffsky, H. Jörnvall, and R. Rigler. Cambridge, MA: Cambridge Univ. Press, p. 13–26.

Kauffman, S. and S. Levin. 1987. Towards a general theory of adaptive walks on rugged landscapes. *J. Theor. Biol.* 128: 11–45.

Langton, C. G. 1984. Self-reproduction in cellular automata. *Physica* D 10: 135–144.

Langton, C. G. 1986. Studying artificial life with cellular automata. *Physica* D 22: 120–149.

Ray, T. 1991. An approach to the synthesis of life. In *Artificial Life II*, edited by C. G. Langton, C. Taylor, J. D. Farmer, and S. Rasmussen. Redwood City, CA: Addison-Wesley, p. 371–408.

von Neumann, J. 1951. The general and logical theory of automata. In *Cerebral Mechanisms in Behavior. The Hixon Symposium*, edited by L. A. Jeffress. New York: John Wiley and Sons, p. 1–41.

Acknowledgments

The organization of a conference as complex as this one is a work by committee, but even the present committee could not possibly have succeeded without the help of a number of key people. First and foremost among them is our conference secretary, Titus Brown, whose tireless, effective, and superb efforts have contributed immensely to a smooth development of the initial period of reviewing, the compilation of these proceedings, and the logistics of the conference itself.

Peary Brug, in expertly managing many of the local arrangements and acting as an interface between the Organizing Committee and the real world, was an immense help. In addition, Samantha Diosomito of the UCLA Conference Center was indispensable in putting the considerable resources of UCLA at our disposal. Bob Prior at MIT Press has made it possible to turn a pile of camera-ready pages into the bound volume in your hands. We would also like to thank Nicholas Gessler for arranging and curating the Alife Art Show. Barry Werger and Maja Mataric deserve our thanks for coordinating the robot contest. Jim Barry expertly and artistically rendered the artwork for the official poster. Taylor Kelsaw also contributed artwork and assisted in arranging entertainment during the conference.

Finally, we must thank the authors for contributing to these proceedings: without the high quality of their research, this conference could not have been successful.

Advisory Committee

David Ackley
Leonard Adelman
Ted Case
Daniel Dennett
Manfred Eigen
Jeffrey Elman
Tetsuyo Higuchi
Danny Hillis
David Hillis
Pauline Hogeweg
Gerald Joyce
Kunihiko Kaneko
Richard Lenski
John Roughgarden
J. W. Schopf
Peter Schuster
Terry Sejnowski
Luc Steels

Program Committee and Reviewers

Chris Adami
Takaya Arita
Jens Astor
Wolfgang Banzhaf
Mark Bedau
Randall D. Beer
Rik Belew
Rob de Boer
Hamid Bolouri
Eric Bonabeau
Rodney Brooks
C. Titus Brown
Leo Buss
Raffaele Calabretta
Duilio Cascio
Dave Cliff
Travis Collier
Gary Cottrell
Jim Crutchfield
Michael G. Dyer
Innes Ferguson
Kurt Fleischer
Dario Floreano
John Fry
William M. Hamner
Inman Harvey
Katherine Hayles
Paulien Hogeweg
Takashi Ikegami
Gerald Joyce
Brian Keeley
Hiroaki Kitano
Mark Land
Marc Lange
Rod Langman
Chris Langton
Blake LeBaron
Niles Lehman
Herbert Levine
Michael L. Littman
Pier Luigi Luisi
Henrik Hautop Lund
Carlo Maley
Maja Mataric
Craig Mautner
Filippo Menczer
Jean-Arcady Meyer
Stefano Nolfi
Charles Ofria
Una-May O'Reilly
Jordan Pollack
Chris Preist
Tom Ray
Mitch Resnick
Craig Reynolds
Chris Rosin
Nicol N. Schraudolph
Heinz Schuster
Moshe Sipper
Ed Stabler
Peter Stadler
Luc Steels
Chuck Taylor
Mark W. Tilden
Peter M. Todd
Yukihiko Toquenaga
Barbara Webb

Invited Talks

WHAT'S EVOLVING IN WET A-LIFE?

Gerald F. Joyce

The Scripps Research Institute

The principles of darwinian evolution can be applied to a large, heterogeneous population of RNA or DNA molecules to obtain particular molecules that have desired biochemical properties, including the ability to catalyze a target chemical reaction. A population of variant molecules is subjected to repeated rounds of selective amplification in the test tube. Only those individuals that perform a chosen catalytic task are amplified so that, through successive rounds, the population adapts to the task at hand.

Recently we developed the ability to carry out the in vitro evolution of RNA-based catalytic function in a continuous manner. The RNAs catalyze a ligation reaction that immediately makes them eligible for amplification and the newly-produced RNAs are immediately eligible to catalyze another reaction. This has enabled us to maintain laboratory "cultures" of evolving RNA enzymes, analogous to the way one maintains cultures of bacteria. The RNAs are perpetuated by a simple serial transfer procedure, amplifying indefinitely so long as an ongoing supply of substrate and other reaction materials is made available. During one run of continuous in vitro evolution, the RNA enzymes were amplified by a factor of 10E298 over 52 hours. By the end of this process, new "generations" of progeny RNA molecules were being produced approximately every 5 minutes.

COMPUTATIONAL COMPLEXITY IN THE LIFE SCIENCES

Christos H. Papadimitriou and Martha Sideri

UC Berkeley

The field of computational complexity has been investigating over the past three decades the reasons why some computational problems are so hard to compute. But it has more fascinating lessons to teach us than this, because many problems in science have latent algorithmic aspects.

Among those, the *protein folding problem* is one of the most intriguing. Proteins are polymer chains consisting of monomers of twenty different kinds, which tend to *fold*, presumably by dint of attraction or repulsion forces between monomers, to form a very specific and stable geometric pattern, known as the protein's *native state*. It is this geometric pattern that determines the macroscopic properties, behavior, and function of a protein. This surprising stability of the native state has led to the widespread belief that it must be the lowest-energy configuration of the chain. Thus Nature appears to be solving very rapidly an extremely complex combinatorial problem (a widely-studied discretized version of the protein folding problem has in fact recently proved NP-complete (cf. *Proceedings of the 1998 RECOMB Conference*). This conundrum is known as *Levinthal's paradox.* However, a simple explanation proceeds along these lines: Proteins must cooperate in order to function in an organism, and such cooperation often involves "locking" of their shapes. Hence, there is evolutionary pressure towards protein forms that have a unique stable native state, and this pressure could have resulted in proteins with very *flat energy landscapes.* Flat landscapes feature an overwhelmingly popular local optimum, which may not necessarily coincide with the global optimum. Computational experiments verify that such flat landscapes evolve very rapidly in a broad variety of optimization problems and circumstances.

Protein folding is only one of the mysterious steps in the map from genotype to phenotype. There have been exciting results in recent years linking certain human diseases to specific genes. Some geneticists envision a coming "last stage of the Mendelian revolution," in which all such macroscopic traits will be traced to their genetic causes. However, the vast majority of traits and diseases appear to be *polygenic*, in that they involve the complex interactions, as in a many-input Boolean circuit, of many genes. There seem to be unsurmountable obstacles of computational complexity lying in the path of this ambitious and important research project.

Plenary Papers

Evolution of Linguistic Diversity in a Simple Communication System

Takaya Arita and Yuhji Koyama

Graduate School of Human Informatics
Nagoya University
Furo-cho, Chikusa-ku, Nagoya 464-8601, JAPAN
ari@info.human.nagoya-u.ac.jp koyama@shiro.gs.human.nagoya-u.ac.jp

Abstract

This paper reports on the current state of our efforts to shed light on the origin and evolution of linguistic diversity by using synthetic modeling and artificial life techniques. We construct a simple abstract model of a communication system that has been designed with regard to referential signaling in nonhuman animals. The evolutionary dynamics of vocabulary sharing is analyzed based on these experiments. The results show that mutation rate, population size, and resource restrictions define the classes of vocabulary sharing. We also see a dynamic equilibrium, where two states, a state with one dominant shared word and a state with several dominant shared words, take turns appearing. We incorporate the idea of the abstract model into a more concrete situation and present an agent-based model to verify the results of the abstract model and to examine the possibility of using linguistic diversity in the field of distributed AI and robotics. It has been shown that the evolution of linguistic diversity in vocabulary sharing will support cooperative behavior in a population of agents.

Introduction

Chomsky's famous claim that from a Martian's-eye-view all humans speak a single language is surely plausible. However, in our view it is true that we have thousands of mutually unintelligible languages. Terrestrial scientists have no conclusive answer as to why this linguistic diversity exists (Pinker 1994). While the quest for the origin of diversity in languages is a challenging theme, diversity in species is also one of the most important themes in biology. Charles Darwin stressed the importance of language difference and linked the evolution of languages to biology (Darwin 1871).

The study of communication/language from an alife perspective has received a great deal of attention lately (Steels 1997). Some of the first experiments were conducted by MacLennan (1991) and Werner and Dyer (1991). MacLennan considered a population of simple organisms, represented genetically by truth tables, and created a shared environment through which the organisms could pass initially arbitrary signals. It was observed that effective communication evolved in the population based on their scoring function. The simulation experiment by Werner and Dyer successfully demonstrated the evolution of a system for signaling between members of opposite sexes to coordinate mating behavior. In their model, explicit scoring functions were not used, and instead effective communication allowed males to find females more rapidly, and thus increased the reproductive rate of the individuals that communicated effectively.

Concerning the evolution of grammar, Batali (1994) constructed a model for the evolution of grammar, and performed the simulations of evolution on populations of simple recurrent networks where the selection criterion was the ability of the networks to recognize strings generated by grammars. The results suggested a new explanation for the "critical period" effects observed in language acquisition. Hashimoto and Ikegami (1995) studied the evolution of grammar systems in networks using an agent model. In their model, the individual grammar was expressed by a symbolic generative grammar, and each agent was ranked explicitly by three scores in each round: speaking, recognizing and being recognized. It was observed that two processes, a module type evolution and a loop forming evolution, were significant. The number of recognized words rapidly increased when a module emerged in a grammar system, and many words could be derived recursively by a grammar processing a loop structure.

There have not been many studies concentrating on the issue of the linguistic diversity from an evolutionary perspective. Werner and Dyer (1991) showed that "dialects" that are bilingual (i.e., correctly interpret several signaling protocols) have an increased chance of dominating over time. Also, Hashimoto and Ikegami (1995) studied the diversity of spoken words produced by symbolic grammar systems in terms of the computational ability of automata, where their computational ability was the ratio of recognizable words to the total number of possible words.

The most straightforward explanation for the origin of linguistic diversity is based on spatial distribution of individuals (Arita, Unno, and Kawaguchi 1995). The following two studies have supported this view. Arita and Taylor (1996) constructed a simple communication model in which a population of artificial organisms with neural networks inhabited a lattice plane and each organism communicated information with neighbors by uttering words. The results of the experiments showed that the accumulation of mutation, propagation delay and the effects of inheritance produce very complex dynamics, while learning by neural networks and selection of parents have large effects on language unification. Through their experiments on naming games, Steels and McIntyre (1997) showed that agent interaction, which depends on spatial distribution, determines the degree of diversity in vocabulary. Their research takes the view that linguistic information evolves and is transmitted culturally, not genetically.

There have been other explanations of the origin of linguistic diversity. Hutchins and Hazlehurst (1995) presented simulations employing communities of simple agents in order to model how a lexicon could emerge from interactions between agents in a simple artificial world. Their models were not based on the evolutionary perspective, but on the connectionist approach. They occasionally observed that the random initial starting points of the networks in a community were incompatible with each other, and this led to divergence in the verbal representations of these individuals.

Recently, Werner and Todd (1997) have extended their previous model to focus on exploring the idea that the origin of diversity in communication signals is due to sexual selection. In their new model, communication signals were used to attract females as mates, and sexual selection drove the evolution of male songs and female song preferences. Each male had genes that directly encoded the notes of his songs, and females' genes encoded a transition matrix used to rate transitions from one note to another in male songs. Each entry in the transition matrix represented the female's expectation that one pitch would follow another in a song. They have adopted three methods for scoring the male songs, one of which is based on the idea in ethology that females exposed to the same song repeatedly will become bored and respond to that song less. They have shown that sexual selection could lead to maintenance of signal diversity, which was at its maximum in an initial population with many different male songs.

The first goal of our paper is to investigate the origin and evolution of linguistic diversity from an evolutionary perspective. To do this we construct minimal models that are designed with regard to referential signaling in nonhuman animals and analyze their evolutionary dynamics based on the synthetic experiments. The second goal is to examine the possibility of utilizing linguistic diversity in the fields of distributed AI and robotics, based on the results of the above experiments. We believe that a very simple communication system can continue to generate linguistic diversity in an environment without spatial distribution. This supports the hypothesis that in an environment with limited amounts of resources that contains individuals with poor linguistic facilities, linguistic unification is not necessarily adaptive.

Section 2 discusses the design of the abstract model based on the communication systems among the nonhuman animals, and shows the results of the experiments. Section 3 constructs an agent-based model by introducing the evolutionary mechanism of the abstract model into a concrete situation in order to verify the results obtained in Section 2. Section 3 also examines the possibility of utilizing the mechanism in engineering fields. Section 4 discusses several issues concerning the origin and evolution of linguistic diversity and its application, based on the results described in the previous Sections. Section 5 summarizes the paper.

Abstract Model

Background

Seyfarth, Cheney, and Marler's pioneering work (1980) on the vervet monkey's alarm call system revealed that they produce acoustically distinct and discrete alarm call types, and in response to hearing such calls, individuals respond with behaviorally appropriate escape responses. It is a remarkable point that vervet monkeys are born with the ability to respond appropriately to general predator categories (e.g. things up in the air, slithering things on the ground), where learning plays virtually no role in modifying signal structure, either during early development or later in life (Hauser 1996). A referential system is functionally significant because when an individual hears an alarm call, an appropriate antipredator response can be initiated without having to see what is going on. In fact, the vervet monkey's alarm call system is a beautiful illustration of how selection pressures might have favored signal diversification (Hauser 1996). An all-purpose alarm call would not work for vervet monkeys, because it would not provide sufficient information about the type of predator or escape response that would be most appropriate.

Since the work on the vervet monkey's alarm call system, several other studies have focused on the problem of referential signaling in nonhuman animals, including other simian primates (e.g., rhesus macaques), prosimians (e.g., ringtailed lemurs), and a few other species (e.g., domestic chickens). It has become clear that these signals are used in various contexts such as predator encounters, discovering food, and social relationships. For example, when a food call is given, listeners obtain information about the availability of alternative food sources, which can serve to guide their foraging decisions. Characteristics of these communication systems, especially in primates, are as follows:

- The communication systems are composed of speakers and listeners. Those who encounter the predators (or food) produce acoustically distinct and discrete alarm (or food) calls, and in response to hearing such calls, listeners behave appropriately.
- The signals are referential in the sense that they are reliably associated with objects and events in the environment.
- They don't react instinctively as a direct expression of their internal states. They send the signals with some primitive type of intention on the assumption of the existence of listeners.
- They are born with ability to respond appropriately to

general categories. Learning plays a relatively small role in modifying signal structure.

These types of communication systems illustrate how natural selection might have driven signal diversification.

The first steps toward human languages are still shrouded in mystery despite the studies and controversies in many fields, but the above described communication systems might be strong candidates for the immediate steps, in other words, the "protolanguages". This paper aims at exploring the origin and evolution of linguistic diversity using two different types of models (in Section 2 and Section 3) with a communication system which is constructed with regard to this type of communication system observed in nonhuman animals.

Definition

The communication system in our models is composed of N_{pop} individuals. Each has a simple vocabulary system that is represented by a table which relates words and meanings as shown in Fig. 1. Identical words can appear more than one time, which corresponds to homonyms (word 12 in this figure), while each meaning appears one time in this table. These tables describe innate information, and are transmitted to offspring by genetic operators.

Meaning	0	1	2	3	4
Word	87	12	34	60	12

Fig.1 An example of a vocabulary table.

First an initial population of N_{pop} individuals with randomly generated vocabulary tables is generated. A signaler and N_{rec} listeners are randomly selected in the beginning of each "conversation". In a conversation, a word is uttered by the signaler, and each listener is one of the following three types, based on the interpretation of the word:

- a listener that has the word in its vocabulary table, and its meaning is equal to the meaning in the signaler's vocabulary table ("right listener"),
- a listener that has the word in its vocabulary table, but its meaning is not equal to the meaning in the signaler's vocabulary table ("misunderstanding listener"),
- a listener that doesn't have the word in its vocabulary table ("ignorant listener").

In the case that the received word is a homonym in the listener's vocabulary table, one meaning is randomly selected as its interpretation. Fig. 2 shows an example where a signaler sends the word 5, which expresses the meaning 2.

Here, we divide the "right listeners" into "successful listeners" and "unsuccessful listeners", because it would be necessary to take these constraints into consideration in many situations investigated. For example, in the case of the food call, some of the listeners that wish to obtain the food might nonetheless fail to do so, because of feeding competition. In the case of the alarm call, some of the listeners that intend to respond with behaviorally appropriate escape responses might nonetheless fail in their effort to escape from the predator.

In every conversation each individual belongs to one of the following categories: signaler, successful listeners, unsuccessful listeners, misunderstanding listeners, ignorant listeners, or non-participants, as shown in Fig. 2, and they are rewarded with R_{send}, R_{share}, $R_{unshare}$, R_{wrong}, $R_{ignorant}$, or R_{out}, respectively. There can be positive, negative, and zero values. These rewards are genetic fitness scores for signaling.

Fig. 2 An example of a conversation.

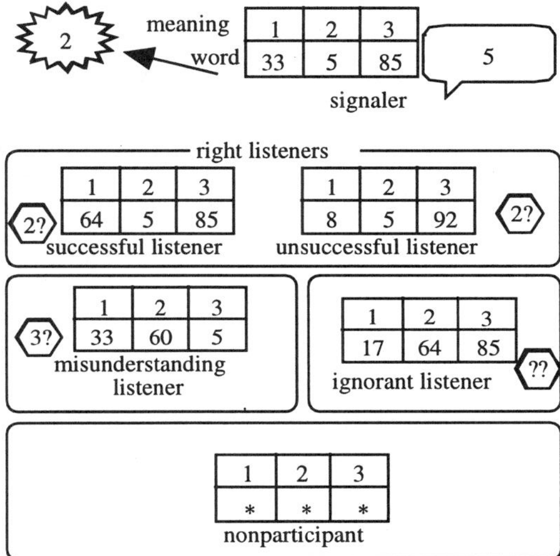

After this process of conversation is repeated N_{conv} times, the information in the vocabulary tables is passed on to offspring by genetic operations. The next generation that is composed of also N_{pop} individuals, is created by roulette selection based on the scores, where mated vocabulary tables cross over at a randomly-selected point of columns (Fig. 3). Then, mutation is performed on each word in the vocabulary tables with some probability P_{mut}, where the word is changed to a randomly selected word.

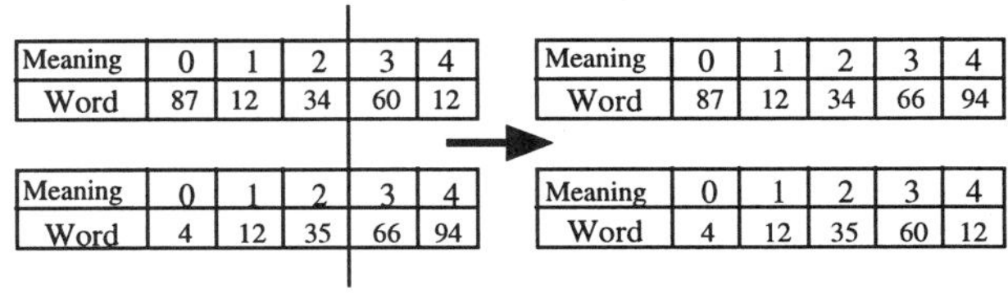

Fig. 3 An example of cross-over on a vocabulary table.

Experiments

We have conducted simulations following the procedure

described above. The abstract model is general in the sense that it can represent many situations depending on the values of the rewards. In this paper, we examine the communication system in the context that an individual finds a food source and utters the word for its meaning (the type of the food). We leave until later the case of alarm calls, though we see no reason why it should be different.

The number of the population (N_{pop}) was 64. If the number of the right listeners was not more than 4 in a conversation, all of the right listeners were considered to be successful and to obtain R_{share}. Otherwise, 4 successful listeners were randomly selected from the right listeners, and the remaining right listeners were considered unsuccessful because of competition. The individual that found the food source and successful listeners shared the food source equally, that meant $R_{send} = R_{share} = R_{food} / (n+1)$, where the amount of the food source was R_{food} and the number of the successful listeners was n. R_{food} was set to be an arbitrary constant, 20. The reward for the individuals that interpreted the uttered word correctly, but couldn't obtain the food source ($R_{unshare}$), was –3. The reward for the individuals that misunderstood the uttered word (R_{wrong}) was –2. The reward for the individuals which did not have the uttered word in their vocabulary tables ($R_{ignorant}$), and the reward for the individuals which didn't join the conversation (P_{out}), were –1 and 0, respectively. The number of the individuals which joined the conversation was always 20 (N_{rec}+1). Each generation had 500 conversations (N_{conv}). Each word was expressed by an integer I ($0 <= I <= 99$). In this paper, we have investigated the case that there is only one type of food source (the size of vocabulary table was one) for convenience of the analysis.

Fig. 4 a)-d) show the evolutionary dynamics in vocabulary sharing where mutation rates ($Pmut$) are 0.01, 0.015, 0.04, and 0.1 respectively. The horizontal axes represent the generations. The vertical axes represent the distribution of words corresponding to the meaning and each same gray level means that an identical word is dispatched to the meaning.

It has been shown overall, from these figures, that the lower the mutation rate becomes, the more individuals have the same word for the meaning. The states of how the meaning was typically shared among the population were classified into the following 4 classes (the threshold values are approximate numbers).

Class A (P_{mut} is less than 0.015, Fig. 4a)):

A dominant word emerges, and the state becomes stable.

Class B (P_{mut} is nearly 0.015, Fig. 4b)):

The state that 3-6 words coexist and the state that one word spreads, appear in turn.

Class C (P_{mut} is more than 0.015 and less than 0.07, Fig. 4 c)):

Several words coexist. New words appear and then disappear repeatedly.

Class D (P_{mut} is more than 0.07, Fig. 4d)):

The state changes in a chaotic manner.

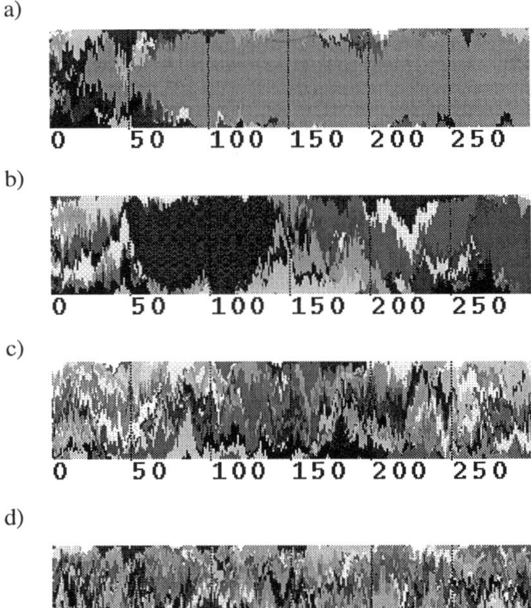

Fig. 4 Evolution of vocabulary sharing: R_{mut} = a) 0.01, b) 0.015, c) 0.04, d) 0.1.

In class B, the latter state was broken by an individual which had a new word generated by mutation. The reason this occurred is considered to be that the merit to the mutant of monopolizing the food sources it found was larger than the merit of sharing the sources found by the others by receiving the information of their existence at that moment. It is shown here that the unification of vocabulary tables in the population is not necessarily adaptive, which is a remarkable point.

We have conducted another series of experiments concerning the effects of the population size, and those concerning the effects of the amount of the source (R_{food}). Some of the results are shown in Fig. 5a)-b). It can be found from these figures that an increase (decrease) in population size has the similar effects to an increase (decrease) in mutation rate. One of the things that we notice is that there is a difference between those occasions where many words coexist generated by increasing the mutation rate, and those occasions where many words coexist because of increased population size. In the former, the individuals with a new word appeared repeatedly and the states are changing. However, in the latter, the state has a tendency to be stable without allowing the individuals with a new word to appear. The experiments on the effects of varying the amount of the food source have shown that the more the amount of the food source is, the more individuals have a same word for the meaning.

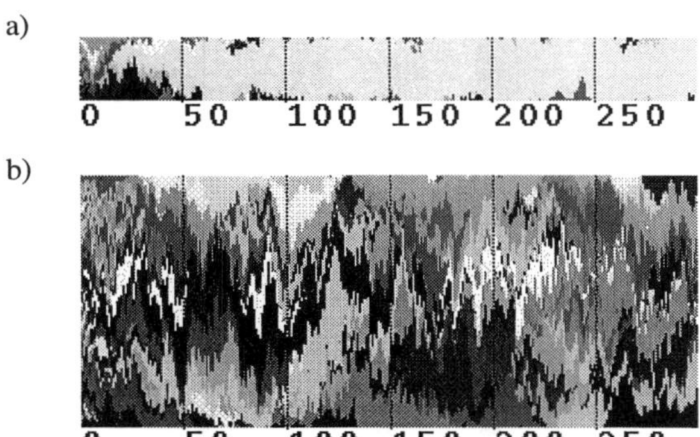

Fig. 5 Effect of varying population size:
N_{pop} = a) 32, b) 128.

Fig. 6 shows the relation between the state of vocabulary sharing and the scores of agents when P_{mut} = 0.015. The upper part of this figure shows the state of vocabulary sharing, the middle part shows the average score of individuals, and the lower part shows the number of the words shared by more than 3 agents. It is easy to make a distinction between the occasion where several words coexist and the occasion where there is only one dominant word in the middle graph. It is regarded as the cause of reduced scores in the state with a dominant word that a large number of individuals with the identical vocabulary obtained the reward (cost) $P_{unshare}$ frequently in this state.

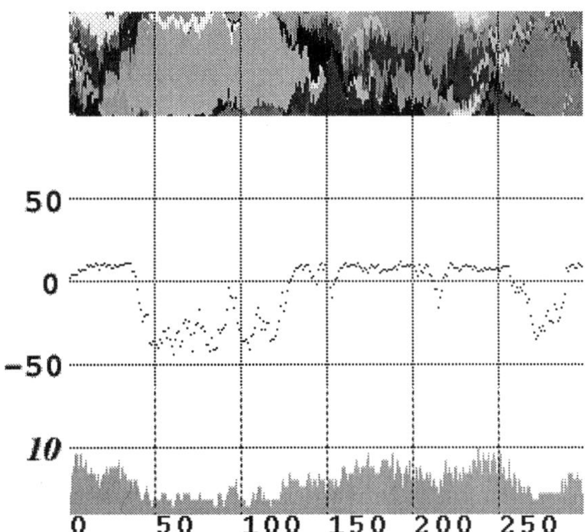

Fig. 6 Relations between average score and the number of shared words.

It has been assumed in all of the experiments to this point that any individual who has found the food source always signals. Here, we make a minor modification in the settings in order to investigate the motivation of signalers. We interpret that a specified word (the word 0 in this series of experiments) means being silent. If an individual who has found a food source has the word 0 corresponding to the food source, then it will not signal at all. Therefore, it could monopolize the food source, which will be a merit, but at the same time it can't obtain the information about the existence of the other food sources when the other individuals find them, which will be a demerit. The experiments have been conducted under the same conditions (P_{mut} = 0.015) but with this modification. The results are shown in Fig. 7a).
A silent individual, that is a mutant with this newly defined word 0, was generated by mutation at about the 180th generation, and then the silent group spread through the population rapidly. Communication died out in all experiments when silent individuals were allowed. The reason for this is estimated that the silent individuals have no need to pay the penalty when they can't obtain food sources, and at the same time, they have a slimmer chance to be sent signals from the individuals with a non-zero word, as the number of the silent individuals increases.

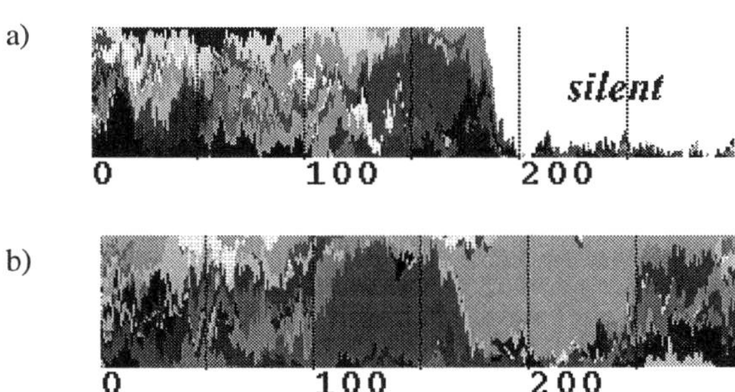

Fig. 7 Effects of allowing silent individuals:
full monopolization, b) half monopolization.

In the above described experiment, when a silent individual found a food source, it monopolized all of the food source if it could. We have modified this setting here to be that it could obtain half of the food source at most. The results are shown in Fig. 7b). In this case, the silent group does not become dominant. The reason is believed to be that the silent individuals made less efficient resource distribution than non-silent group in the sense that it sometimes happened that the silent individuals left food sources without transferring information of the source. The issues concerning the silent individuals are worth examining, and some of them will be discussed in Section 4.

Agent-Based Model

Definition

We have introduced the evolutionary mechanism of the abstract model generating the linguistic diversity into a concrete situation and have constructed an agent-based model. The first objective of its design and experiments is to verify the results of the experiments concerning the abstract model, which depend on the explicit reward setting, by defining a concrete task done by agents. The second objective is to explore the possibility of applying the evolutionary dynamics of the linguistic diversity to issues in various fields, such as robotics and distributed AI.

Foraging behavior in the population of simple mobile agents (robots) has been taken up as the theme of the agent-based model. The task described in this Section could be interpreted in many ways, as energy supply in robotics, or garbage collection in distributed AI, for example, since we have assumed a situation in which mobile agents move and gather food sources using the simple communication system.

The field has N_{pop} mobile agents and N_{food} food sources. Each agent has a vocabulary table and has an energy value as an internal state, which corresponds to a genetic fitness, though it could be negative. If the energy value of an agent is less than E_{hungry}, then the agent is "hungry". When the energy value is E_{full}, the agent is "full", and it cannot eat the food source any more. Each agent consumes one unit of energy every time step.

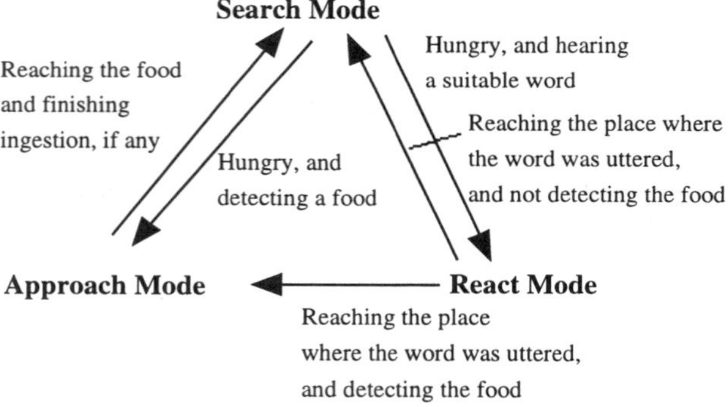

Fig. 8 Transitions among behavioral modes.

The behavioral state of each agent is one of the 3 modes: Search Mode, React Mode, or Approach Mode (Fig. 8). At the beginning of every generation, agents and the food sources are located at randomly selected positions in the field. All agents are in Search Mode, and the energy values are E_{full}. Each agent in Search Mode selects randomly and engages in one of the following five behaviors: halt, moving forward, moving backward, turning right, or turning left. The distance of moving forward/backward, D is randomly determined every time ($0 < D < L_{move}$, in pixels). The speed of moving in any mode is constant (V_{agent} pixel/step). The angle of turning right/left, X is randomly determined every time ($0 < X < A_{turn}$, in degrees). It takes 1 time step to turn right/left. Agents in Search Mode detect food sources within a distance of L_{detect}. When a hungry agent in Search Mode finds a food source, it utters the word for it, and its state changes into Approach Mode. This signaling process takes 1 time step.

An agent in Approach Mode approaches the food source. Each food source also has an energy level which is E_{food} initially. When an agent reaches a food source, it ingests the food until it becomes full or the energy of the food source becomes zero. If the energy of a food source becomes zero, it is removed from the field. Food sources are generated only when a new generation of agents is created. Other agents cannot get the information about the exhaustion of the food source. Therefore, when the food sources are removed, the agents which are in React Mode, in other words, which are devoting themselves to going for the location where the word was uttered, would generate loss of time and energy for themselves. This cost, which is represented implicitly and naturally in this agent-based model, is equivalent to the value expressed by $R_{unshare}$ in the abstract model.

Agents that are in Search Mode and are within a distance of L_{hear} can hear uttered word. If an agent is hungry and is a "right listener", its state changes into React Mode. Each agent in React Mode approaches the location where the word was uttered. When an agent in React Mode reaches the location, if it detects a food source, its state changes into Approach Mode, otherwise its state changes into Search Mode.

In this manner, the agents repeat searching for food, approaching food or the places the words were uttered, uttering words, and hearing the words, until N_{step} time steps pass from the beginning, or all food sources are consumed. Next, the information on vocabulary tables is passed on to offspring by genetic operations in the similar way as in the abstract model. The next generation that are composed of also N_{pop} agents, are created by roulette selection based on their energy values after scaling, where mated vocabulary tables cross over at a randomly-selected point of columns. Then, mutation is performed on each word in the vocabulary tables with some probability P_{mut}, where the word is changed to a randomly selected word. In this manner, these processes with a population of a new generation are repeated again and again.

Experiments

We have conducted some preliminary experiments with the following parameters.

$N_{pop} = 20$; $N_{food} = 20$; $N_{step} = 10000$; $L_{move} = 100$; $L_{detect} = 100$; $L_{hear} = 200$; $V_{agent} = 1$; $A_{turn} = 100$; $E_{hungry} = 3000$; $E_{full} = 5000$; $E_{food} = 4500$;

Also, only one meaning was set up in this series of

experiments. In other words, there was one type of food in the field. Evolution was observed for 300 generations.

Fig, 9 shows the evolutionary dynamics in vocabulary sharing for 300 generations, where *Pmut* was 0.01. We have observed the similar evolutionary dynamics to those in the abstract model, except that the effect of the mutation rate is slightly different. The threshold value is approximately 0.01 in this agent-based model which divides Class A and Class C, while P_{mut} around 0.015 is the threshold in the abstract model.

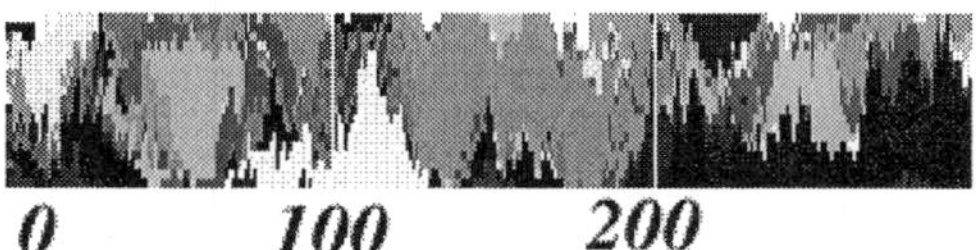

Fig. 9 Evolution of vocabulary sharing.

The following two additional methods were investigated for comparative evaluation:

Method 1:

All agents have the identical word-meaning relation (vocabulary table) a priori. Therefore, when an agent utters a word, each listener is either successful or unsuccessful, and cannot be a misunderstanding listener or an ignorant listener. No genetic operators are used, and there is no evolution.

Method 2:

There is no communication at all. All agents are silent all the time. There is also no evolution.

We have conducted 10 trials of the comparative experiments. The parameters have the same values as in the experiment shown in Fig. 9. Results are shown in Table 1. Table 1 shows the average energy value and the maximum energy value among all agents, and the number of the occurrences that all food sources were exhausted. We refer to the method based on the original agent-based model as Method 0 in this table. It is shown that the maximum energy value and the average energy value in the Method 0 are more than the ones in the Method 1 and Method 2. This means that the evolution of the vocabulary table contributed to the efficient task execution in these experiments. However, the number of the occurrences that all food sources were exhausted in Method 1, is slightly more than that in the Method 0. The cause of this seems to be that the communication with the identical word increased the cases that all food sources had been exhausted, although it made the agents that heard the word waste time and energy. It is also shown that Method 2 (no communication) shows poor performance as compared with the other two methods. These results mean that the role of the evolving communication system with linguistic diversity is significant for the foraging behavior in the population of agents.

Table 1 Results of the comparative experiments.

Trial No.	Method 0 Avg E. (max E.) Exhaustion	Method 1 Avg E. (max E.) Exhaustion	Method 2 Avg E. (max E.) Exhaustion
1	-1254 (4004) 175	-3608 (4354) 184	-4508 (4409) 131
2	-2667 (4529) 166	-2715 (4392) 179	-5016 (4634) 143
3	-3560 (4476) 166	-4096 (4200) 170	-5595 (4305) 140
4	-3654 (4242) 168	-3698 (3824) 171	-2219 (4193) 137
5	-3362 (4143) 162	-1908 (4319) 170	-3716 (3905) 145
6	-1039 (4680) 170	-4300 (3952) 175	-2052 (3953) 127
7	-2933 (4186) 165	-396 (3933) 177	-3764 (4195) 139
8	-2011 (4371) 168	-2601 (4676) 183	-5492 (3926) 147
9	-2239 (4427) 171	-3509 (4498) 169	-3531 (3675) 139
10	-2035 (4060) 161	-1759 (4174) 173	-4203 (3619) 122
Average	-2475 (4312) 167	-2859 (4232) 175	-4010 (3081) 137

Discussion

Observed linguistic diversity

The results of the experiments imply that the linguistic diversity grows when population size, mutation rate, or restriction on resources becomes greater. Fig. 10 shows this implication roughly. From another point of view, it can be said that the communication system adapts to the growth of population size, mutation rate, or restriction on resources by increasing its linguistic diversity. One extreme case is that there is no diversity. This corresponds to the case that all agents shared an identical vocabulary table in the experiments with small mutation rates, or the case that all agents were silent in the experiments allowing silent individuals. The other extreme case is that they share no stable and identical vocabularies at all, and they thus cannot transfer efficient information by communication systems. This corresponds to the case with a quite large mutation rate in the experiments. The results of the experiments on the agent-based model have shown that the evolutionary dynamics could maintain a proper level of linguistic diversity, and attain effective task execution.

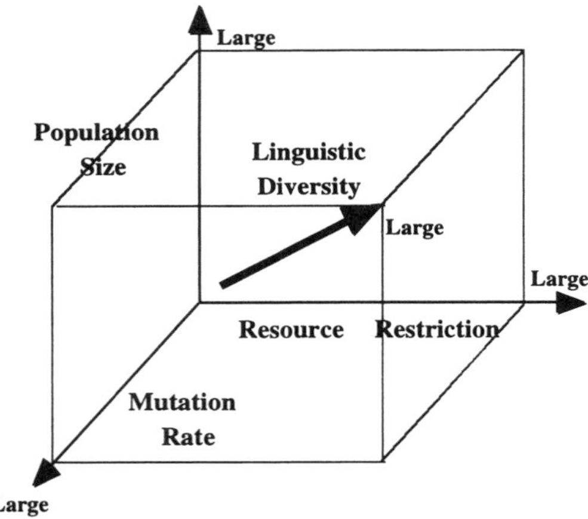

Fig. 10 Growth of linguistic diversity.

There was a tradeoff between the monopoly of the resources discovered by an agent itself and the sharing of the resources discovered by other agents (to be exact, sharing with risks of additional competition). When the former exceeded the latter, the linguistic diversity observed in the experiments was generated by the selection pressure. This selection pressure allowed the individuals with new words to increase in the population.

In other words, the individuals with new words can increase by making others respond with inappropriate reactions through misinterpreted words, which can be called functional deception, though cannot be called intentional deception (deception based upon manipulation of belief states). All agents became silent when we allowed the individuals to be silent. In this case, they withheld information about food sources and thereby increased their fitness relative to others. We can call it another primitive form of deception. This type of deceptive behavior in nonhuman animals has been reported. In Chimpanzees, food calls are given by individuals at relatively large food sources (implying that the costs of increased feeding competition may be negligible) (Wrangham 1977). Also, in some species, the probability of calling in the context of food call is less than 100%, suggesting the possibility that individuals sometimes suppress their calls (Hauser 1996).

The invasion of a silent population and the generation of linguistic diversity discussed in this paper are closely linked to the issue of the origin of altruism. Food calls would appear to be altruistic in general, because those who announce their discoveries are essentially inviting increased food competition and, consequently, potentially decreasing their own access to food. Kin selection and reciprocal relationships are strong candidates for its explanation. It has been also reported that there is social pressure making individuals call. Individual rhesus who found food but failed to call and were detected by other group members received more aggression than individuals who called upon discovery (Hauser 1992). The result that the silent population disappeared when we reduced the maximum amount of food sources which individuals could obtain to half, might be a candidate for its explanation at the lowest level.

The effects of incorporating a learning mechanism into these models would be worth investigating, though we have focused on the evolutionary dynamics of the linguistic diversity in this paper. It is clear that the effects depend on the adopted learning algorithm. If we would adopt a learning algorithm that uses the rewards in conversations as teacher signals in learning, and modifies the word-meaning relations gradually, the learning mechanism would be believed to simply accelerate the evolutionary dynamics observed in these experiments. However, the contributions of population size, resource restriction, and mutation rate to linguistic diversity could be rather complex.

Possibility of utilizing the diversity

Application of the results of alife studies has been investigated, and it has begun to bear fruits in various fields. One of the promising fields is robotics. We have conducted the experiments on the agent-based model, partly based on the idea that the communication system which evolves and maintains linguistic diversity would be beautifully fit to be used as the flexible mechanism for communication among population of autonomous robots that attain cooperative behavior. The results in the experiments concerning the agent-based model are encouraging in the sense that the communication system supported the cooperative task execution.

The complexity in the mechanism of the communication system is extremely reduced, because we have aimed to implement a minimal communication system that generates the linguistic diversity which could be utilized in engineering fields. Communication systems with far richer facilities, for example, those with which agents can negotiate on sharing the resources, would surely rank higher. On the other hand, slightly extended versions of the current communication system can be investigated, for example, as follows:

Version 1:

The agents which found the sources signal only when they finish feeding and there are food sources left. This modification of setting can reduce the cost of listener agents.

Version 2:

The volume of the food calls are set to be proportional to the amount of the food sources. This modification makes the number of the listening agents vary correspondingly to the amount of the food sources, which can reduce the cost of listener agents.

We expect both versions will rank higher than the results of our experiments, though we don't have enough evidence that in nonhuman animals there are such communication systems. Although, some species have a food call which refers to the quality of food sources.

One of the most difficult hurdles towards physical realization based on the evolutionary dynamics, in general, is the relationship between simulations and actual robot execution. Even the experiments on this simple communication system took a while to evolve in the agent-based model. It is very difficult and may take as much time for detailed simulations as it would take to build the actual robot systems. At the same time, it is also impractical to build and observe many actual robots during many generations. Therefore, we plan to adopt a hybrid simulated /embodied selection regime (Miglino, Nafasi, and Taylor 1995). Large numbers of simulated robots are examined in simulation, but only the promising subset of these are actually built and examined, thereby reducing the scope of the problem. Simulated evolution of communication systems will also be necessary for speeding up the adaptation in the physically realized robotic systems in the near future, and thereby the communication systems will be able to adapt to rapid changes in dynamic environments.

Summary

This paper reports on the current state of our efforts to shed light on the origin and evolution of linguistic diversity, using synthetic modeling and artificial life techniques. We have constructed a simple abstract model for a communication system that is designed with regard to referential signaling in nonhuman animals. The evolutionary dynamics of vocabulary sharing was analyzed based on these experiments.

The results have shown that only a subset of initial conditions leads to the unification of vocabulary, and the linguistic diversity evolves corresponding to the changes in population size, mutation rate and restriction of resources. We have also observed that unification of vocabulary causes the decrease in genetic fitness of the individuals.

We have incorporated the idea of the abstract model into a more concrete situation, and have presented an agent-based model to verify the results of the abstract model and to examine the possibility of utilizing the linguistic diversity in the field of distributed AI and robotics. It has been shown that selection pressure could explain the linguistic diversity in the cooperative behavior of multiple agents.

Acknowledgements.

This work is partially supported by the Artificial Intelligence Research Promotion Foundation and by the Hori Information Science Promotion Foundation. The authors would like to thank Charles Taylor for fruitful discussions.

References

Ackley, D. H.; Littman, M. L. 1994. Altruism in the Evolution of Communication. In *Proceedings of Artificial Life IV*, 40-48.

Arita, A.; Unno, K.; Kawaguchi, K. 1995. A primitive model for language generation by evolution and learning. In *Proceedings of the International* Workshop on Biologically Inspired Evolutionary Systems, p.181-186.

Arita, T., Taylor, C. E. 1996. A simple model for the evolution of communication. In *Evolutionary Programming V* (Proceedings of the Fifth Annual Conference on Evolutionary Programming), 405-409, The MIT Press.

Batali, J. 1994. Innate biases and critical periods: Combining evolution and learning in the acquisition of syntax. In *Proceedings of Artificial Life IV*, p. 160-171.

Darwin, C. 1871. *The Descent of Man and Selection in Relation to Sex*. London: John Murray.

Hashimoto, T., and T. Ikegami. 1995. Evolution of symbolic grammar systems. In *Proceedings of the Third European Conference on Artificial Life*, p. 812-823.

Hauser, M. D. 1992. Costs of deception: Cheater are punished in Rhesus monkey. *Proc. Nat. Acad. Sci.* 89: 12137-12139.

Hauser, M. D. 1996. *The Evolution of Communication*. Cambridge, MA: MIT Press.

Hutchins, E., and B. Hazelhurst. 1995. How to invent a lexicon: The development of shared symbols in interaction. In *Artificial Societies: The Computer Simulation of Social Life*, edited by N. Gilbertand R. Conte. UCL Press, p. 157-189.

MacLennan, B. 1991. Synthetic ethology: An approach to the study of communication. *In Proceedings of Artificial Life II*, p. 631-658.

Miglino, O., K. Nafasi, and C. E. Taylor. 1995. Selection for wandering behavior in a small robot. *Artificial Life* 2: 101-116.

Pinker, S. 1994. *The Language Instinct*. William Morrow and Company.

Seyfarth, R., D. L. Cheney, ans P. Marler. 1980. Monkey responses to three different alarm aalls: Evidence of predator classification and semantic communication. *Science* 210: 801-803.

Steels, L. and A. McIntyre.1997. Spatially distributed naming games. http://arti.vub.ac.be/www/steels/spatial.ps

Steels, L. 1997. The synthetic modeling of language origins. *Evolution of Communication* 1: 1-34.

Werner, G. M. and M. G. Dyer. 1991. Evolution of communication in artificial organisms. In *Proceedings of Artificial Life II*, p. 659-687.

Werner, G. M.; Todd, P. M. 1997. Too many love songs: Sexual selection and the evolution of communication. In *Proceedings of the Fourth European Conference on Artificial Life*, p. 434-443.

Wrangham, R. W. 1977. Feeding behaviour of chimpanzees in Gombe National Park, Tanzania. In *Primate Ecology: Studies of Feeding and Ranging Behaviour in Lemurs, Monkeys and Apes*, edited by T. H. Clutton-Brock. London: Academic Press, p. 504-538.

Ruggedness and Neutrality - The NKp family of Fitness Landscapes

Lionel Barnett

Centre for Computational Neuroscience and Robotics
Centre for the Study of Evolution
Department of Cognitive and Computing Sciences

University of Sussex, Brighton BN1 9QH, UK

lionelb@cogs.susx.ac.uk

Abstract

It has come to be almost an article of faith amongst population biologists and GA researchers alike that the principal feature of a fitness landscape as regards evolutionary dynamics is "ruggedness", particularly as measured by the auto-correlation function. In this paper we demonstrate that auto-correlation alone may be inadequate as a mediator of evolutionary dynamics, specifically in the presence of large scale neutrality. We introduce the NKp family of landscapes (a variant on NK landscapes) which possess the remarkable property that varying the degree of neutrality has minimal effect on the correlation structure. It is demonstrated that NKp landscapes feature *neutral networks* which have a "constant innovation" property comparable with the neutral networks observed in models of RNA secondary structure folding landscapes. We show that evolutionary dynamics on NKp landscapes vary dramatically with the degree of neutrality - at high neutrality the dynamics are characterised by population drift along neutral networks punctuated by transitions between networks. The relevance of these models to natural and artificial evolution is discussed.

Introduction

In attempting to address the dynamics of populations of genotypes evolving on fitness landscapes it appears that a specific scenario has become somewhat ingrained in the collective consciousness of researchers - that of a fitness landscape as a rugged, hilly terrain on which populations perform "hill-climbing". Selective pressure drags a population towards local peaks of relatively high fitness while mutation and recombination search the surrounding landscape by generating new genotypes. But this poses a problem which affects both the biologist and the GA specialist: if selective pressure is strong enough (relative to the disruptive effects of mutation and recombination) to drag a population up a hill, it is also likely to be strong enough to hold it there! How, then, is an evolving population to avoid becoming trapped on a local hilltop? For the GA worker seeking to optimise a multi-peaked function this is a practical issue and the literature abounds with schemes to avoid the dilemma (Goldberg 1989). For the biologist it is a serious theoretical conundrum, as populations in nature do not seem (at least on macro-evolutionary time-scales) to suffer this fate. It might be claimed that entrapment can be explained away by co-evolution and environmental change but another possibility must be considered - our picture of a fitness landscape as a rugged hilly terrain is misleading and in need of an overhaul.

In both natural and artificial systems a picture is emerging of populations engaged not in hill-climbing but rather drifting along connected networks of genotypes of equal fitness, with sporadic jumps between networks. These "neutral networks" are of particular significance if they have the "constant innovation" property (see below) - for this raises the possibility that (given enough time) almost *any* possible fitness value can ultimately be attained by the population. The scenario of a population trapped on a local hilltop vanishes. It is this new paradigm of evolutionary dynamics which we examine here. It has yet to make a significant impact on the scientific community.

It is, of course, reasonable to ask (both for natural and artificial evolutionary systems) whether such neutral networks actually occur. Comparatively recent developments in evolutionary theory and molecular biology all point to the importance of *selective neutrality* as a significant factor. This work includes Kimura's neutral theory of molecular evolution (Kimura 1983), Eigen's analysis of the molecular quasispecies (Eigen, McCaskill and Schuster 1989; Nowak and Schuster 1989) and recent developments in the understanding of RNA evolution both *in vitro*, in simulation and analytically (Reidys, Stadler and Schuster 1997; Schuster *et al.* 1994; Baskaran, Stadler and Schuster 1996; Grüner *et al.* 1996). Neutrality has also been detected in various protein models. In molecular biology it is clear that there is often a high degree of redundancy in the coding from genotype to phenotype - there may indeed be redundancy on several levels; e.g. many nucleotide sequences may code for the same amino acid, while many amino acid sequences may code for functionally equivalent proteins. Such coding redundancy will certainly imply the existence of selectively neutral mutation at the molecular level (Crow and Kimura 1970, Kimura 1983). Whether this takes the form of neutral networks with constant innovation is a (highly non-trivial) empirical question. Research into the structure of RNA folding landscapes suggests strongly that such networks may well be a feature of fitness landscapes in molecular biology.

There is also evidence that neutral networks can appear in the fitness landscapes of "difficult" artificial evolution problems; e.g. in the evolution of neural network robot control systems, on-chip hardware evolution (Thompson 1996; Harvey and Thompson 1996) and CA-based landscapes. Ironically it is customary among GA practitioners deliberately to avoid redundancy in the genetic coding of artificial evolution problems.

The NKp landscapes introduced in this paper have the property that altering the degree of neutrality has minimal effect on the ruggedness of the landscape (as measured by the auto-correlation function). They thus provide a useful test-bed for a comparative study of the effects of ruggedness and neutrality on evolutionary dynamics. We begin with some formal definitions.

Neutrality and Ruggedness

All fitness landscapes in this paper are based on fixed-length binary bit-string genotypes. We thus identify a ***fitness landscape*** of sequence length N with a ***fitness function*** f: $Q^N \to \mathbf{R}^+$ where Q^N denotes the binary N-hypercube and $\mathbf{R}^+$ is the set of real numbers ≥ 0. The ***fitness*** of a genotype $g \in Q^N$ is then given by f(g). There is a natural metric, ***Hamming distance***, on Q^N defined by: $h(g,g') \equiv$ number of loci (bit-positions) at which g and g' differ. Hamming distance is often referred to in terms of ***mutation***. If g, g' are hamming distance d apart we call g' a (d-bit) mutation of g (and vice-versa).

Neutrality

We call a (1-bit) mutation g' of g ***neutral*** iff f(g') = f(g). This relationship induces a partitioning of Q^N whereby g and g' are in the same equivalence class iff there is a sequence of neutral mutations connecting g and g'; i.e. there are genotypes $g \equiv g^{(0)}, g^{(1)}, g^{(2)}, \ldots, g^{(n)} \equiv g'$ such that $g^{(\alpha)}$ is a 1-bit mutation of $g^{(\alpha-1)}$ for $\alpha = 1, 2, \ldots, n$ and $f(g) \equiv f(g^{(0)}) = f(g^{(1)}) = f(g^{(2)}) = \ldots = f(g^{(n)}) \equiv f(g')$. The ***neutral networks*** of the fitness landscape are defined to be the equivalence classes of this partitioning. We can define a coarser partitioning of Q^N by specifying g and g' to be in the same equivalence class iff f(g) = f(g'). We refer to the equivalence classes of this partitioning as ***neutral sets***; the neutral networks are the connected components of the neutral sets. Although it is the neutral networks which are of direct relevance to evolutionary dynamics the neutral sets are generally easier to handle analytically; furthermore in many cases of interest the neutral sets consist of few connected components. A word of caution: the "network" terminology may well be misleading. If the frequency of neutral mutation is low there are likely to be very many neutral networks comprising a few, or even single genotypes. Even if there is high neutrality the neutral networks may not resemble networks as much as "clusters". The ***neutral degree*** of a genotype g, denoted by $\nu(g)$ is defined to be the number of neutral mutations of g.

We shall be interested in some notion of ***percolation*** for neutral networks. It is by no means obvious in what sense percolation may hold relevance for evolutionary dynamics. While it is feasible to transfer the graph-theoretical definition directly to neutral networks, it seems to this author that the related (but distinct) property of "constant innovation rate" introduced by (Huynen 1996) in the context of RNA folding landscapes is likely to be more pertinent; the reasons will hopefully become clear from the discussion of evolutionary dynamics in a later section. Random walks are performed on neutral networks ("neutral walks") and previously unseen phenotypes ("innovations") accumulated. The rate of discovery of innovations is then compared to the discovery rate for random walks on the landscape <u>not</u> constrained to a neutral network. Since we are not dealing with phenotypes (in the sense of an intermediate mapping between genotype and fitness) we identify phenotype directly with fitness and consider an innovation to be the discovery of a genotype of previously un-encountered *fitness*.

We thus say that a neutral network has the ***constant innovation property*** if: (I) the rate of discovery of innovations remains approximately constant for a reasonably large number of steps - what Huynen terms "perpetual innovation" - and (II) the rate of discovery is comparable with that of an unconstrained random walk. Below we investigate this property rather than conventional percolation. It should be noted that constant innovation is indeed distinct from percolation - it is not difficult to construct fitness landscapes with neutral networks that percolate in the graph-theoretical sense, but fail one or both of the above criteria (Jakobi 1996).

Ruggedness

The most frequently encountered measure of ruggedness of a fitness landscape is the ***auto-correlation function***. It is often defined in terms of fitness values at successive steps along random walks (Weinberger 1990; Kauffman 1993) but, as remarked in (Stadler 1996) "...it seems to be rather contrived to invoke a stochastic process in order to characterise a given function [i.e. the fitness function] defined on a finite set". We thus use the definition below, apparently first proposed in (Eigen, McCaskill and Schuster 1989).

Let f: $Q^N \to \mathbf{R}^+$ be a fitness landscape. We first define the mean fitness of the landscape:

$$\bar{f} \equiv 2^{-N} \sum_{g \in Q^N} f(g) \tag{1}$$

the fitness variance:

$$\sigma_f^{\,2} \equiv 2^{-N} \sum_{g \in Q^N} \left(f(g) - \bar{f}\right)^2 \tag{2}$$

and for d = 1, 2, ... N the set:

$$Q^N(d) \equiv \left\{(g, g') \in Q^N \times Q^N \mid h(g, g') = d\right\} \tag{3}$$

Thus $Q^N(d)$ is the set of pairs of genotypes in Q^N Hamming distance d apart. We now define the auto-correlation function to be:

$$\rho(d) \equiv \frac{1}{\sigma_f^{\,2}} \frac{1}{\left|Q^N(d)\right|} \sum_{(g,g') \in Q^N(d)} (f(g) - \bar{f})(f(g') - \bar{f}) \tag{4}$$

for d = 1, 2, ... , N. For consistency we also set $\rho(0) \equiv 1$.

Note: We stress that the quantities $\bar{f}$, σ_f^2 and $\rho(d)$ are not statistics but simply real numbers associated with a fitness landscape. There appears to be some confusion in the literature on this issue; auto-correlation is sometimes defined by averaging fitness, etc. over *ensembles* of landscapes, e.g. the family of all NKp landscapes with fixed N, K and p (Fontana *et. al.* 1993, Weinberger 1990). In this paper shall we use angle brackets exclusively to indicate that a mean (expectation) is to be taken of a quantity considered as a random variable defined on the sample space of all possible NKp landscapes with fixed N, K and p.

The NKp Family of Fitness Landscapes

We begin by reviewing the construction of an NK landscape (Kauffman 1993). Let N > 0 be the genotype length and let $0 \le K < N$. N and K are fixed during the construction. To each locus on the genotype (i.e. a position $1 \le i \le N$ on the bit-string) we assign independently and at random K distinct loci (excluding the locus under consideration). These loci, plus the locus i itself, are said to be ***epistatically linked*** to locus i. The idea is that a locus i makes a contribution to the total fitness of a genotype which depends on the value of the allele (0 or 1) at each of the K+1 loci epistatically linked to locus i. To each such combination of alleles (there are 2^{K+1} in all) a fitness contribution is assigned as a real number drawn independently and uniformly at random from the interval [0,1]. We can think of this as the association of a ***fitness table*** F_i with each locus i; for a genotype $g \in Q^N$, given the sequence of alleles $\varepsilon_i(g) = a_1 a_2 \ldots a_{K+1}$, say, at the loci epistatically linked to locus i the fitness contribution of locus i is given by $F_i(\varepsilon_i(g))$, which we also denote by $f_i(g)$.

Finally, to calculate the fitness of an entire genotype the fitness contributions of all loci are summed and the result divided by N to normalise the fitness to the range [0,1]. In the above notation:

$$f(g) \equiv \frac{1}{N} \sum_{i=1}^{N} f_i(g) \tag{5}$$

In summary, an NK landscape is fully specified by N, K, the particular assignment of epistatic links and the contents of the N fitness tables.

It is clear from the construction that there is (almost surely) *no* neutral mutation on an NK landscape - for if two genotypes differ at some locus the respective fitness contributions for that locus will be drawn from different fitness table entries which will (almost surely) be different. There is, however, a "natural" way to introduce neutrality into the model, via the following biologically-inspired argument: the NK model assumes that *every possible* combination of alleles at the loci epistatically linked to a given locus gives rise to a positive contribution to fitness. In nature, however, it seems plausible that many (if not most) combinations of alleles will make *no* contribution to fitness. We could reflect this in the NK model by specifying that the fitness table entry corresponding to such an allelic combination be equal to zero. Thus motivated we proceed as follows: a new parameter $0 \le p \le 1$ is introduced to represent the probability that an arbitrarily allelic combination makes no contribution to fitness. Explicitly, when assigning values to the fitness tables we set each entry to 0 independently with probability p. If an entry is not set to zero it is assigned uniformly randomly from the range [0,1] as before. We refer to the resulting landscape as an ***NKp landscape***. The case p = 0 corresponds to a normal NK landscape, while p = 1 corresponds to a completely flat landscape (all fitness table entries are zero).

Please note that due to space constraints most results in the following sub-sections are quoted without proof.

Neutral structure of NKp landscapes

Many of the results quoted below depend on the following observation (which holds almost surely):

(6) if g, g' $\in Q^N$ then f(g) = f(g') $\Leftrightarrow$ for all i such that $f_i(g) \neq 0$ we have $\varepsilon_i(g) = \varepsilon_i(g')$

It is evident that the possibility of neutral mutation arises on an NKp landscape. A calculation yields for the probability that an arbitrary mutation on an arbitrary NKp landscape be neutral:

$$(7) \qquad p_{\text{neutral}} = p^2\left(1 - \frac{K}{N-1}(1-p^2)\right)^{N-1}$$

For large sequence length N this is well approximated by:

$$(8) \qquad p_{\text{neutral}} \approx p^2 e^{-K(1-p^2)}$$

Thus for long genotypes the probability that a mutation is neutral is roughly independent of the genotype length and drops off exponentially with increasing epistasis K. A problem with p_{neutral} however, is that neutrality is not spread uniformly over the landscape - in fact an NKp landscape is by no means uniform in its structure, but may be decomposed naturally into subsets corresponding to genotypes with a particular number of zeroes in their fitness tables. Thus for an NKp landscape f: $Q^N \rightarrow \mathbf{R}^+$ and g $\in Q^N$ we define:

(9) $\zeta(g) \equiv$ number of loci i for which $f_i(g) = 0$

and for n = 0, 1, ... N we define:

(10) $Z_n(f) \equiv \{g \in Q^N \mid \zeta(g) = n\}$

Next we note that for g $\in Z_n(f)$ the fitness of g is the sum of N-n independent random variables uniformly distributed on [0,1]. Thus the expected fitness for a g $\in Z_n(f)$ for some NKp landscape is:

$$(11) \qquad \langle f(g)\rangle_{g \in Zn(f)} = \frac{N-n}{2N}.$$

A calculation gives for the expected neutral degree of a g $\in Z_n(f)$ with $1 \leq n \leq N$:

$$(12) \qquad \langle \nu(g)\rangle_{g \in Zn(f)} = np(1-q)^{N-n}[1-(1-p)q]^{n-1}$$

where we have set $q \equiv \frac{K}{N-1}$. Comparing (11) and (12) we find that for large N the neutral degree of genotypes in an NKp landscape drops off roughly exponentially with increasing fitness - the "higher up" the landscape we go the less neutrality we can expect to encounter. This can also be seen from the observation that for all g $\in Q^N$ we must have $\nu(g) \leq \zeta(g) \leq N(1 - f(g))$.

We also estimate the sizes of the sets $Z_n(f)$. A calculation yields:

$$(13) \qquad \langle |Z_n(f)| \rangle = 2^N \binom{N}{n} p^n (1-p)^{N-n}$$

It is easy to show that the subsets $Z_n(f)$ have the following useful property: if $\Gamma \subseteq Q^N$ is a neutral set (or indeed a neutral network) then $\Gamma \subseteq Z_n(f)$ for some n. We calculated the expected size of neutral sets contained in $Z_n(f)$ in the following sense: define the random variable S_n (for fixed N, K and p) to be the size of the (unique) neutral set containing a genotype uniformly randomly selected from $Z_n(f)$ for a randomly selected NKp landscape f: $Q^N \rightarrow \mathbf{R}^+$. [Note that S_n does *not* represent the size of a neutral set randomly selected from some $Z_n(f)$ - it will differ due to the variance of neutral set size within the $Z_n(f)$'s]. We have:

(14) $\langle S_n \rangle =$

$$\sum_{i=0}^{n}\sum_{j=0}^{i}\sum_{k=0}^{j}\sum_{m=0}^{k}(-1)^{i+j+k+m}\binom{n}{i}\binom{i}{j}\binom{j}{k}\binom{k}{m}\theta_{N,K,j,m}2^{j-k}p^i$$

where $\theta_{N,K,j,m} \equiv \left[\binom{N-1-(j-m)}{K}\Big/\binom{N-1}{K}\right]^{N-j}$

if j - m $\leq$ N - 1 - K and zero otherwise. If K is small compared to N it was found empirically that:

$$(15) \qquad \langle S_n \rangle \approx \exp\left(N\log(2p)\left(\frac{e^{2\frac{K}{p}\frac{n}{N}}-1}{e^{2\frac{K}{p}}-1}\right)\right)$$

This indicates that $\langle S_n \rangle$ scales roughly as $O\left(e^{e^n}\right)$ for small K. Fig 1a and 1b below plot the formula (14) for N = 30. In Fig 1a K = 4 and p is varied; in Fig 1b p = 0.9 and K is varied. The formula (14) may also be used to estimate the mean *number* of neutral sets in $Z_n(f)$.

It would appear to be difficult to derive analytically an estimate for the size, number and distribution of the neutral *networks* in NKp landscapes; in lieu the results on neutral sets are helpful - the author suspects that the neutral sets comprise, on the whole, few connected components. The reader is referred to (Barnett 1997) for an empirical analysis of neutral networks on "small" NKp landscapes. See also (Grüner *et al.* 1996) for a detailed analysis of neutral networks on RNA secondary structure folding landscapes.

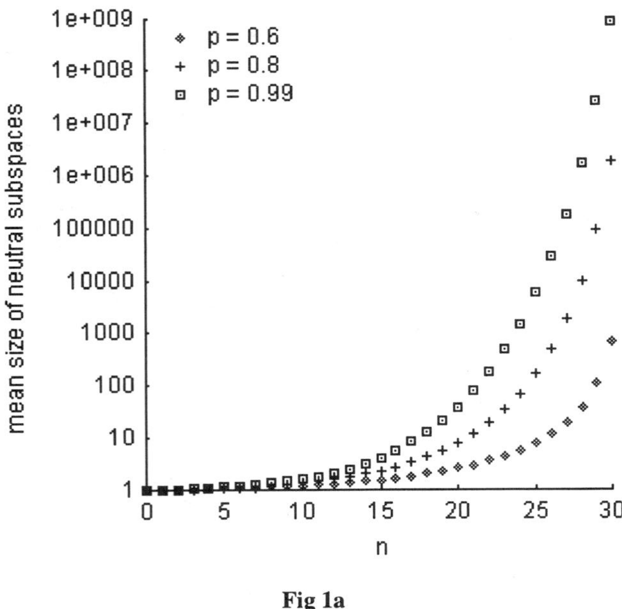

Fig 1a

Estimated mean sizes of neutral sets in $Z_n(f)$ as computed from (14) for N = 30, K = 4 and several values of p.

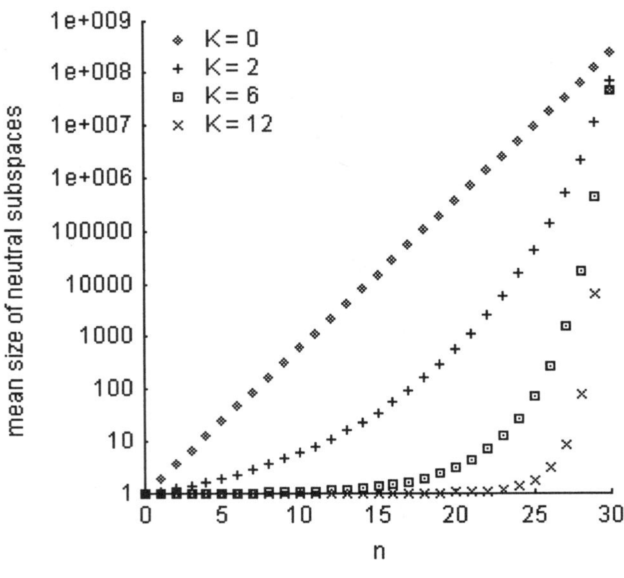

Fig 1b

Estimated mean sizes of neutral sets in $Z_n(f)$ as computed from (14) for N = 30, p = 0.9 and several values of K.

Correlation structure of NKp landscapes

The most surprising result regarding the correlation structure of NKp landscapes is the minimal effect of the neutrality parameter p on the auto-correlation function. The quantity $\langle\rho(d)\rangle$ (the auto-correlation ensemble mean) was estimated by sampling for a variety of N, K and p values. The results consistently indicated seemingly negligible dependence on p. Indeed, so small is the variation with p, that it was initially thought by the author that $\langle\rho(d)\rangle$ is invariant with respect to p. However more stringent statistical testing, in particular the Student's t-test (Press *et al.* 1992) which measures the significance of a difference of means, indicated a small but significant departure from invariance. The significance is smaller for large N and it may be the case that $\langle\rho(d)\rangle$ is invariant with respect to p in some sense "in the limit" of large N. The ensemble definition of auto-correlation, (as distinct from the ensemble mean - see note above), was also tested for p-invariance. The results suggest that it is a true invariant. The derivation of an analytical expression for the ensemble auto-correlation function in (Fontana *et. al.* 1993) suggests that this is indeed the case.

There is one particular class of NKp landscapes for which it is possible to calculate $\rho(d)$ explicitly: this is the case where, out of <u>all</u> the N fitness tables there is only a single entry of non-zero fitness. $\rho(d)$ for these "degenerate" NKp landscapes is given by:

$$\rho_{\deg}(d) = \frac{(P-1)^2\alpha(d) - 2(P-1)\beta(d) + \gamma(d)}{P(P-1)\binom{N}{d}} \tag{16}$$

where:

$$\alpha(d) \equiv \begin{cases} \binom{L}{d} & \text{if } d \le L \\ 0 & \text{otherwise} \end{cases} \tag{17}$$

$$\beta(d) \equiv \binom{N}{d} - \alpha(d) \tag{18}$$

$$\gamma(d) \equiv (P-1)\binom{N}{d} - \sum_{k=\mathrm{Max}(1,d-L)}^{\mathrm{Min}(d,K+1)} \binom{K+1}{k}\binom{L}{d-k} \tag{19}$$

and we have set $P = 2^{K+1}$ and $L = N-K-1$. See Appendix A.2 of (Barnett 1997) for details. Surprisingly, this turns out to be a remarkably good estimate for $\langle\rho(d)\rangle$. Fig 2 plots $\rho_{\deg}(d)$ for N=60 and a few K values.

It is also worth remarking that the *variance* of $\rho(d)$ (considered, for each d, as a random variable over the sample space of NKp landscapes with fixed N, K and p) is fairly small, particularly for small d. This implies in particular that $\rho_{\deg}(d)$ as defined by (16) is a useful estimate of the auto-correlation for a specific NKp

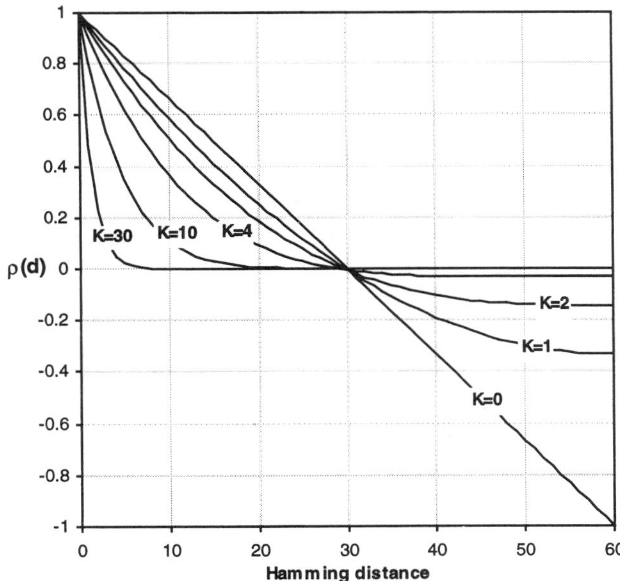

Fig 2
The function $\rho_{deg}(d)$ for N=60

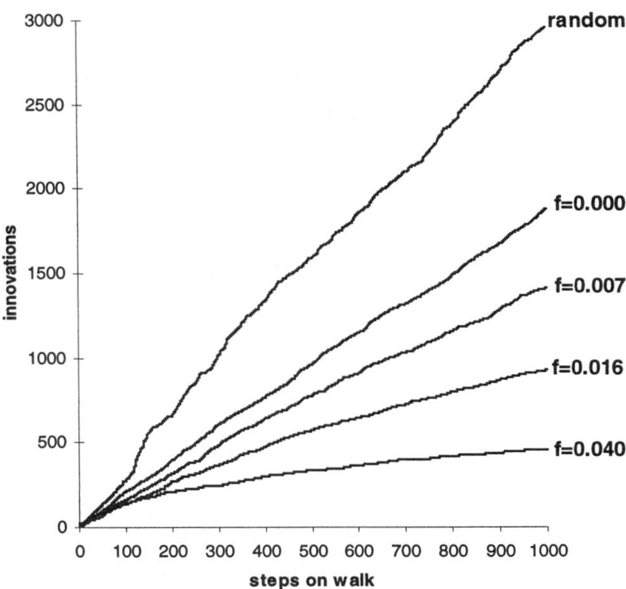

Fig 3
Cumulative innovations on an NKp landscape (N=60, K=14, p=0.99) for 1000-step random and neutral walks. f-values indicate the fitness of the corresponding neutral network.

landscape (and indeed for a specific NK landscape). These results appear at first sight to be paradoxical; we might expect that the high proportion of pairs of genotypes with equal fitness would tend to produce higher correlation with increasing p. However, in a certain sense, NKp landscapes actually become *more* rugged with increasing p. Genotypes of high fitness are comparatively rare; hence a near neighbour of a high fitness genotype is likely to be a genotype with more zeros in its fitness tables (particularly when epistasis is high), and hence of far smaller fitness. On average these effects seem to cancel each other out; it was found that the *covariance* of the fitness of pairs of genotypes Hamming distance d apart scales approximately the same as the fitness *variance*. More precisely, it was found empirically that for some function $\phi(d)$ which depends on N and K but not on p, the mean fitness "auto-covariance" of an NKp landscape is given to a high approximation by:

$$(20) \qquad \langle cov(d) \rangle \approx \phi(d)(1-p)(1+3p)$$

The fitness variance is just cov(0).

Constant innovation on NKp landscapes

Neutral walks were performed on NKp landscapes as previously described. One such test is plotted in Fig 3, which may be compared with the corresponding plot for an RNA folding landscape in (Huynen 1996). The approximate linearity and slope of the graphs indicate that the constant innovation property does indeed hold on NKp fitness landscapes, at least for neutral networks of modest fitness. As we climb higher up the landscape, however, the innovation rate falls and innovations "peter out" sooner; this is consistent with our earlier findings that the degree of neutrality and expected size of neutral networks fall as fitness increases.

This concludes our analysis of the structure of NKp landscapes. In the next Section we examine their evolutionary dynamics.

Evolutionary Dynamics on NKp Landscapes

Firstly note that in this paper we only consider fixed-size populations evolving under mutation and selection; recombination is not considered. The evolutionary algorithm employed is conventional "fitness-proportional with roulette-wheel selection", as follows: let population size be M. To construct the population at the next generation from the current population we perform M selections (with replacement) from the current population, such that the probability of a genotype being selected is proportional to its fitness. Every genotype in the new population is then mutated with a per-locus probability m, where m is the (fixed) mutation rate. Typically we take M

= 200 and m = 0.001.

A previous study (Barnett 1997) investigated in some detail the dynamics of adaptive evolution on several abstract fitness landscapes featuring neutral networks, including NKp landscapes. The picture that emerges is strikingly similar to that described in (Huynen, Stadler and Fontana 1996) for RNA secondary structure folding landscapes and we conjecture that such dynamics are generic for landscapes with neutral networks which have the constant innovation property. A brief summary is as follows: most of the time the population (at reasonably low mutation rates) is largely confined to a specific neutral network, (corresponding to Huynen *et al.*'s "dominant phenotype") on which it drifts at a characteristic rate which is related to the population size, mutation rate and degree of neutrality of the network (see below). During such "metastable" episodes (van Nimwegen, Crutchfield and Mitchell 1997) diffusion is qualitatively similar to diffusion on a flat (i.e. completely neutral) landscape; the latter situation is analysed mathematically in (Derrida and Peliti 1991), where it is found that stochastic effects of selection and mutation typically cause the population to fragment into clusters or sub-populations of genotypes, each cluster sharing a recent common ancestor. Such clustering is also a feature of populations diffusing on neutral networks in non-flat landscapes. Mutation generates new genotypes that explore neighbouring networks. If a genotype of higher fitness (i.e. on a higher-fitness neutral network) is discovered then, if selection pressure is strong enough relative to mutation, the population may, with a certain probability, transfer *en masse* to the higher neutral network. There is also the possibility that a population may, through stochastic effects, "fall off" its current network to a lower-fitness network. The probabilities of attaining or maintaining a given network are related to what has been termed the "phenotypic error threshold" (Forst, Reidys and Weber 1995) by analogy with the classical "genotypic" error threshold for single-peak fitness landscapes (Eigen, McCaskill and Schuster 1989).

NKp landscapes afford a unique opportunity to investigate the form of adaptive evolution with tuneable neutrality. Differences in dynamical behaviour observed for fixed N and K values, but different values of p, cannot be ascribed to the correlation structure as we know this to be virtually invariant under change of p. In this paper we concentrate on one particular aspect of the dynamics, that of population diffusion.

To this end we measured the *diffusion coefficient* of the population *centroid* at successive generations of an evolutionary run. The ***centroid*** of a population P of genotypes on an N-dimensional hypercube is a real-valued N-dimensional vector $\mathbf{c} \in \mathbf{R}^N$ defined by $c_i \equiv \frac{1}{N}\sum_{g \in P} g_i$ where $g_i = 0$ or 1 is the allele of g at locus i. **c** may be thought of as the centre of mass of the population, considered as a set of points (weighted by their multiplicity in the population) on the hypercube embedded in the vector space $\mathbf{R}^N$. The diffusion coefficient is defined as the square of the Euclidean distance (in $\mathbf{R}^N$) travelled by the population centroid per generation. It measures the rate at which the population drifts through the landscape. In practice this quantity tends to fluctuate rapidly from generation to generation; in the graphs below we plot a rolling average over the previous 100 generations to smooth it out. It is possible to estimate the diffusion coefficient by assuming that the diffusion rate will be similar to that on a *flat* landscape of dimension equal to the (mean) neutral degree of the current neutral network (Huynen, Stadler and Fontana 1996). For population size M, mutation rate m and neutral degree ν the estimated value is given by[1]:

$$D = \frac{\nu m}{1 + 2Mm} \tag{21}$$

In (Barnett 1997) this was found to be a good estimate for small values of m and a further refinement was suggested.

While the diffusion coefficient tells us about how "fast" the population is wandering about the landscape it does not tell us very much about how "far" it is wandering; e.g. on a single peaked landscape the centroid may move quite rapidly but remain in the locality of the peak. We will be especially interested in the actual distances travelled by the centroid when comparing population dynamics on low and high neutrality landscapes and thus have need for a measure of actual distances travelled by the centroid. To this end we also computed a "time-lagged" diffusion coefficient, which we define to be the square of the distance between the centroid "now" and its position t_{lag} generations previously. In all experiments $t_{lag} = 100$ was used and the time-lagged coefficient smoothed over 100 generations prior to plotting.

Figs 4 and 5 illustrate typical evolutionary runs over 3000 generations on NKp landscapes for N=60, K=12 and p=0.99 and 0 respectively. In both cases the population size was M = 200 and the mutation rate m=0.001. Apart from the population mean fitness we also plot the mean neutral degree (for the p=0.99 case), diffusion coefficient and time-lagged diffusion. In the p=0.99 case the graphs bears out the picture of evolutionary dynamics outlined above, with periods of metastability punctuated by transitions to higher fitness neutral networks clearly visible. In (Barnett 1997) it is demonstrated that during these periods the population is

[1] The formula given in (Huynen, Stadler and Fontana 1996) is for RNA sequences which have four allelic values (it also contains an error - the 5 should be replaced by a 6) and must be adjusted for the binary case. Furthermore, their definition of the centroid works out at twice the magnitude of ours so we must divide their diffusion coefficient by 2.

indeed largely confined to a specific neutral network and that the population drifts and clusters as described above. As we would expect the degree of neutrality falls as fitness increases. The apparently random fluctuations in the diffusion rate reflect the stochasticity of drift and clustering in the population, although overall there is a correlation between diffusion rate and neutral degree as suggested by (21).

During the transitions between neutral networks the time-lagged diffusion increases sharply. This may be ascribed to a "bottleneck effect" as the steep increase in selection pressure occasioned by the discovery of a fitter genotype strongly converges the population around the new genotype. This phenomenon, also known as "hitchhiking", has been studied in other fitness landscapes, particularly the so-called "Royal Road" landscapes (van Nimwegen, Crutchfield and Mitchell 1997). Mutation then reasserts itself and the population resumes neutral diffusion on the new network. Since (most) neutral networks have the constant innovation property it is unlikely that the drifting population will exhaust the supply of previously unseen (and thus potentially higher fitness) neighbouring genotypes. Evolutionary search may potentially continue unabated; the question is how long it is likely to take before neutral drift discovers a gateway to a higher network (van Nimwegen, Crutchfield and Mitchell 1997).

Fig 5 tells a different story. The landscape is now rugged and multi-peaked with many local optima (Kauffman 1993). The population climbs rapidly up the landscape until it reaches a local optimum at which still higher optima are too rare in the locality to be easily discovered by mutation. At this point the population is effectively trapped - the search for fitter genotypes becomes worse than random search, as the population is confined to the locality of a local optimum. This is indicated by the lagged diffusion, which is significantly lower than for the neutral case.

Conclusions

We have seen that the dynamics of adaptive evolution on fitness landscapes in the presence of neutral networks with the constant innovation property have a distinctly different flavour from the case of ruggedness without neutrality. The scenario of entrapment by local optima is evaded; adaptation is characterised by neutral drift punctuated by transitions between networks rather than local hill-climbing. Furthermore, the formation of sub-populations allows a population to search diverse areas of a fitness landscape in parallel.

Regarding natural evolution, as argued in the Introduction the issue of selective neutrality is becoming difficult to ignore. Even though the concerns of population geneticists and molecular biologists may often seem far removed from our abstract fitness landscapes it is pointed out in (Huynen, Stadler and Fontana 1996), for example, that one issue of prime interest to evolutionary biology, that of the fixation rate of nucleotide substitutions, is closely related to the population diffusion rate. One general approach that suggests itself is to "reverse engineer" theoretical results; thus a theoretical estimate of the diffusion rate might be deployed to determine the degree of neutrality in a natural evolving system.

There are also pungent implications for artificial evolution. The GA community has long been fixated on correlation structure as the primary factor in the efficacy of evolutionary search. It may be of benefit to GA practitioners to exploit the open-endedness and parallelism implicit in adaptation on neutral networks. One could, for example, envisage schemes whereby the mutation rate is optimised on-line for maximal rates of drift whilst staying below the (local) phenotypic error threshold. Perhaps, also, a change of attitude to the issue of coding of an optimisation problem may be fruitful. Whereas the instinct of many workers is to minimise coding redundancy as an extra burden on a search procedure, they may be thus dooming their search to the fate of entrapment by local optima. Of course it is not to be supposed that there is a "free lunch" involved - redundancy alone certainly does not imply neutral networks with constant innovation. However, it seems that some hard optimisation problems feature neutral networks in a natural way (Thompson 1996). A fascinating area for research would be to investigate in what sense neutral networks might be "intrinsic" to a search problem.

The NKp family of landscapes, aside from the intriguing near-invariance of the auto-correlation function, may hopefully prove to be a useful test-bed for the study of neutral evolution, given the combination of tuneable ruggedness and neutrality. Areas that suggest themselves for further research include the extension of results on neutral networks to include recombination, the issue of "nearly neutral" mutation and the effects of "noisy" fitness. It would also be of great interest to ascertain to what extent the pattern of evolutionary dynamics that emerges from RNA folding landscapes and NKp landscapes is in any sense "generic". A promising approach may be to employ techniques from statistical mechanics, as applied with some success by (van Nimwegen, Crutchfield and Mitchell 1997) to the Royal Road fitness landscapes, which feature neutrality, albeit without the constant innovation property.

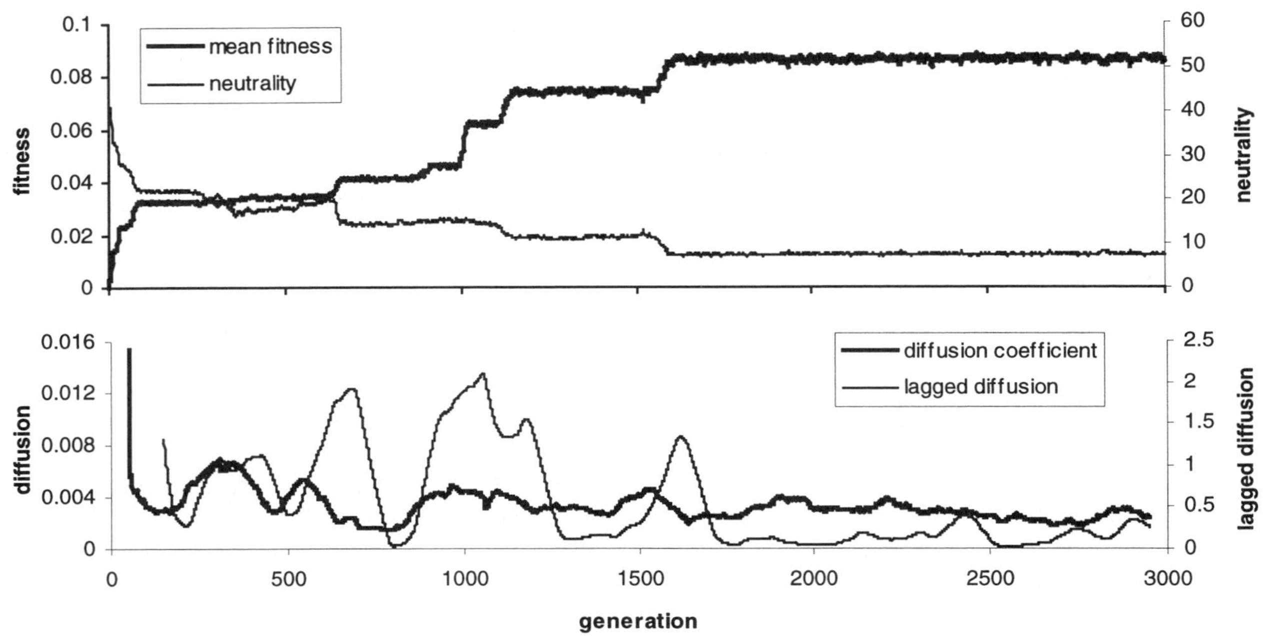

Fig 4

An evolutionary run on an NKp landscape (N=60, K=12, p=0.99) population size 200, mutation rate 0.001

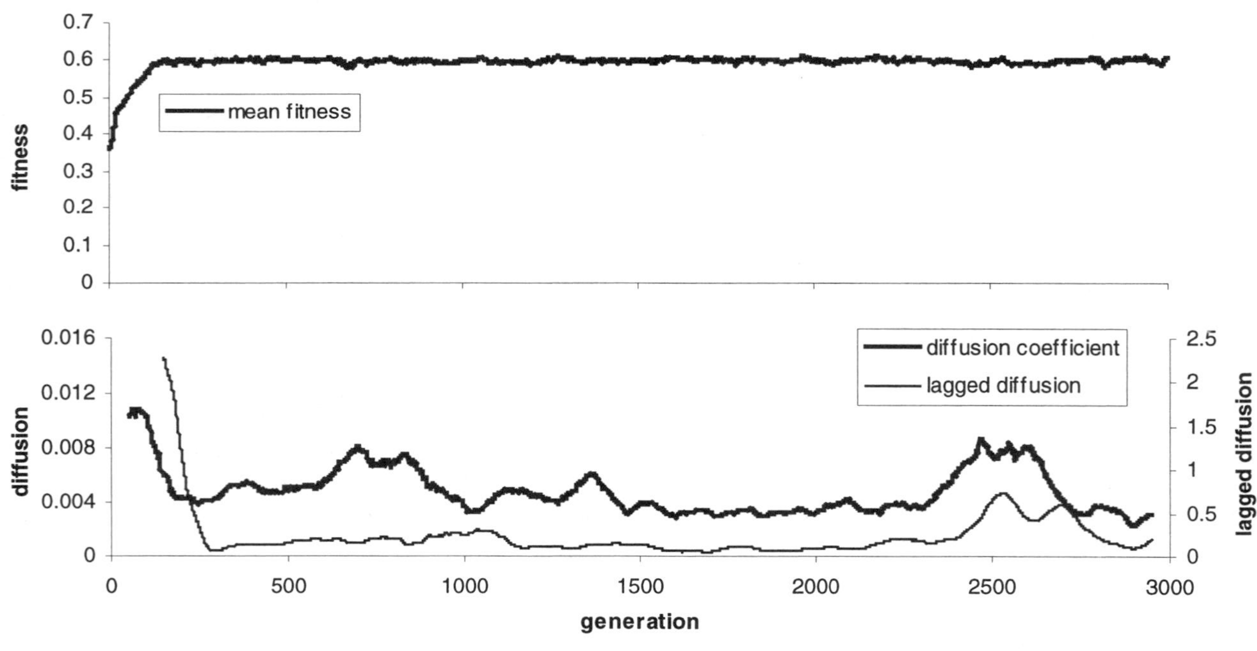

Fig 5

An evolutionary run on an NKp landscape (N=60, K=12, p=0) population size 200, mutation rate 0.001

Acknowledgements

The author would like to thank Inman Harvey and many others at the Sussex University CCNR for crucial discussions, and Dave Harper for invaluable assistance with statistical issues.

References

Barnett, L. C. 1997. *Tangled Webs - Evolutionary Dynamics on Fitness Landscapes with Neutrality*. MSc. diss., School of Cognitive and Computing Sciences, Sussex Univ. UK.

Baskaran, S., Stadler, P.F. and Schuster, P. 1996. Approximate scaling properties of RNA free energy landscapes. *J. Theor. Biol.* 181: 299-310.

Crow, J.F. and Kimura, M. 1970. *An Introduction to Population Genetics Theory.* , New York: Harper & Row.

Derrida, B. & Peliti, . 1991. Evolution in a flat landscape. *Bull.Math. Biol.* 53:355-382.

Eigen, M., McCaskill, J. & Schuster, P. 1989. The Molecular Quasispecies. *Adv. Chem. Phys.* 75:149-263.

Forst, C.V., Reidys, C. & Weber, J. 1995. Neutral networks as model-landscapes for RNA secondary-structure folding-landscapes. *Advances in Artificial Life, Lecture Notes in Artificial Intelligence, vol. 929*: edited by F. Morán, , A. Moreno, J.J. Merelo, and P. Chacón. Berlin: Springer-Verlag,

Goldberg, D.E. 1989. *Genetic Algorithms in Search, Optimization and Machine Learning*. Addison-Wesley.

Fontana, W., Stadler, P.F., Bornberg-Bauer, E.G., Griesmacher, T., Hofacker, I.L., Tacker, M., Tarazona, P., Weinberger, E.D. & Schuster, P. 1993. RNA folding and combinatory landscapes. *Phys. Review* E 47(3): 2083-2097.

Grüner, W., Giegerich, R., Strothman, D., Reidys, C., Weber, J., Hofacker, I. L., Stadler, P. F. and Schuster, P. 1996. Analysis of RNA sequence structure maps by exhaustive enumeration: I. Neutral networks. II. Structures of neutral networks and shape space covering. *Monathefte Chem.* 127: 355-374 & 375-389.

Harvey, I. and Thompson, A. 1996. Through the labyrinth evolution finds a way: A silicon ridge. In *Proc. 1st Internatl. Conf. Evol. Sys.: From Biology to Hardware* (ICES 96). Springer-Verlag.

Huynen, M.A 1996 Exploring phenotype space through neutral evolution. *J. Mol. Evol.* 43: 165-169.

Huynen, M.A., Stadler, P.F. & Fontana, W. 1996. Smoothness within ruggedness: The role of neutrality in adaptation. *Proc. Natl. Acad. Sci. (USA)* 93:397-401.

Jakobi, N. 1996. *In Proc. Parallel Processing in Nature,* edited by H.-M.Voigt, W. Ebeling,, I. Rechenberg, and H.-P. Schwefel. Berlin: Springer-Verlag, p. 52-61.

Kauffman, S. A., 1993. *The Origins of Order - Self-Organization and Selection in Evolution.* New York: Oxford University Press,.

Kimura, M. 1983. *The Neutral Theory of Molecular Evolution*. Cambridge, UK: Cambridge University Press.

van Nimwegen, E., Crutchfield, J.P. & Mitchell, M. 1997. Statistical dynamics of the Royal Road Genetic Algorithm. Santa Fe Institute preprint 97-04-035, Santa Fe, NM, USA.

Nowak, M. & Schuster, P. 1989. Error thresholds of replication in finite populations - Mutation frequencies and the onset of Muller's ratchet. *J. Theor. Biol.* 137:375-395.

Press, W.H., Teukolsky, S.A., Vetterling, W.T. & Flannery, B.P. 1992. *Numerical Recipes in C - The Art of Scientific Computing*. Cambridge,UK: Cambridge University Press.

Reidys, C.M., Stadler, P.F. & Schuster, P. 1997. Generic properties of combinatory maps - Neutral networks of RNA secondary structures. *Bull. Math. Biol.* 59: 339-397.

Schuster, P., Fontana, W., Stadler, P.F. & Hofacker, I.L. 1994. From sequences to shapes and back - A case study in RNA secondary structures. *Proc. Roy. Soc. (London)* B 255:279-284.

Stadler, P.F. 1996. Landscapes and their correlation functions. *J. Math. Chem.* 20: 1-45.

Thompson, A. 1996. Silicon evolution. In *Proc. Genetic Programming*, edited by J.R. Koza *et al.* 96:444-452. MIT Press.

Weinberger, E.D. 1990. Correlated and uncorrelated fitness landscapes and how to tell the difference. *Biol. Cybern.* 63:325-336.

Evolving Reaction-Diffusion Ecosystems with Self-Assembling Structures in Thin Films.

Jens Breyer, Jörg Ackermann and **John McCaskill**
Institute for Molecular Biotechnology, Beutenberg Straße 11, Jena 07745, Germany

Abstract

Recently, new types of coupled isothermal polynucleotide amplification reactions for the investigation of *in vitro* evolution have been established that are based on the multi-enzyme 3SR. Micro-structured thin-film open bioreactors have been constructed in our laboratory to run these systems spatially resolved in flow experiments. Artificial DNA/RNA chemistries close to the *in vitro* biochemistry of these systems have been developed which we have studied in computer simulations in configurable hardware (NGEN). These artificial chemistries are described on the level of individual polynucleotide molecules each with a defined sequence and their complexes. The key feature of spatial pattern formation provides a weak stabilization of cooperative catalytic properties of the evolving molecules. Of great interest is the step to include extended self-assembly processes of flexible structures — allowing the additional stabilization of cooperation through semi-permeable, flexible, self-organizing membrane boundaries. We show how programmable matter simulations of experimentally relevant molecular *in vitro* evolution can be extended to include the influence of self-assembling flexible membranes.

Introduction

Two complementary schools of thought have concentrated on fundamentally different properties of life: the primacy of self-replication (Eigen 1971) and the primacy of autopoieses (Varela 1979; Maturana & Varela 1980; McMullin & Varela 1997) in defining living systems. Within the self-replication based approaches, boundary formation or compartmentation appears necessary for the stable co-evolution of cooperative functional molecules (Boerlijst & Hogeweg 1991; McCaskill 1994; Cronhorst & Blomberg 1997; McCaskill 1997). Recently, several authors have shown that this move from independent replicators to cooperative molecular systems can also be fostered without boundaries in reaction-diffusion systems in two dimensions. This stabilization is relatively weak, however, so that the transition to cellular-like structures with distinct boundaries remains an important issue. However, the extension of reaction-diffusion modeling to include the processes of self-assembly and constrained diffusion of complex structures like membranes with internal degrees of freedom is far from trivial. In particular, when it comes down to parallel algorithms with local, possibly stochastic, update rules (as in the programmable matter paradigm) capable of dealing with extended flexible objects in a reasonable computer time, difficulties occur. Similar difficulties arise in the treatment of intramolecular conformational changes, so that the present work is relevant both to the dynamics of supra-molecular complexes and intramolecular folding (Zuker & Steigler 1981; McCaskill 1990).

Even local algorithms for parallel implementation of rigid-body motion of extended objects are non-trivial. Rasmussen and Smith (1994) have defined the problem of constrained collective motion and presented one class of solution in their lattice polymer automata. On the other hand, detailed molecular dynamics simulations of polymer motion capitulate to the problem of intramolecular constraints by moving to the femtosecond time scale: the separation of time scales between significant polymer motion and that of local bond relaxation allows the relatively rigid constraints of covalent bonds and hard-sphere contacts to be simulated at the cost of enormous computational effort. For the description of structural self-organization, this level of detail is inadequate, limited as it currently is to the nanosecond-microsecond time scale by computational resources. Rasmussen's solution is still relatively complex and requires the introduction of a large number of virtual particles to the lattice gas automata modeling platform. In this work, we make a simpler start on the discrete automata modeling of flexible structures and illustrate this by a complementary example of self-assembling boundaries for self-replicating molecular ecosystems. We leave the equally interesting example of template based self-assembly of dynamical structures to later work. The evolvable experimental ecosystems based on isothermal amplification of DNA and RNA, both the predator-prey (Wlotzka & McCaskill 1997) and the cooperative system (Ehricht, Ellinger, & McCaskill 1997; Ehricht *et al.* 1997), are modelled [see McCaskill (1997) for a review] in Section

Figure 1: The photograph shows the modular card of the massively parallel, hardware configurable Computer NGEN. The chips inserted on the card are Field Programmable Gate Arrays (FPGAs). FPGAs are user-configurable, i.e. the logic of the on-chip circuit can be programmed by the user in the hardware. 18 of these cards are connected to form a toroid of 144 configurable FPGAs together with 1296 8bit wide memory SRAM chips. Thus, NGEN combines massively parallel computing with application specific optimization. This allows us to make long term simulations of evolution with very large numbers of individuals. The second generation computer Polyp (Tangen, Schulte, & McCaskill 1997) uses micro-configurable FPGAs (XILINX XC6216) and an optical communication between the cards, making the step from user-configurable hardware to autonomous evolving hardware.

2. The major limitation of these studies is the restriction to limited size, whole molecule diffusion: prohibiting the study of intramolecular motion, diffusion and rearrangement of complexes and thereby multi-component self-assembly. In Section three, we discuss the problem of boundary formation within the above context and show how the abstract autopoietic models of Maturana and Varela (1980), and Ganti (1975) can be extended to include dynamical flexibility of the self-assembling membrane.

Programmable matter has been realized in our lab using massively parallel configurable hardware, NGEN (see Figure 1), enabling the study of complex reaction-diffusion systems involving combinatorial families of molecules as studied in *in vitro* evolution experiments. Because of the elegance and efficiency of this configurable digital logic and its closeness to the programmable matter ideal, we endeavor to make the above discussion concrete within the context of our configurable hardware. We first exhibit the evolutionary potential of modeling in this medium, with application to the modeling of experimental *in vitro* ecosystems, before outlining the extension to self-assembly in Section four. Special consideration has been made to allow very high population size and long-term simulations. The simulations include base-by-base processing of the reactions including strand hybridization in various alignments as stochastic processes. In our studies we focus on the effects of spatial distribution on the reaction and evolutionary dynamics of cooperative systems, with regard to the emergence of parasites through mutation. We show that stochastic spatial distributions stabilize cooperative systems which would otherwise go extinct under the pressure of parasitic mutants. On the basis of this stabilization, the systems can evolve to a level of higher complexity. The work has practical implications for real experiments with artificial molecular ecosystems.

In Vitro Molecular Ecosystems

To our knowledge, the first examples of *in vitro* molecular ecosystems are the predator-prey and symbiotic (CATCH) systems developed in our lab over the past few years based on the isothermal 3SR (Guatelli et al. 1990) or NASBA (Compton 1991) reaction. These systems provide a significant step forward in constructive evolution from the independent template evolution, describable by the quasispecies model (Eigen, McCaskill, & Schuster 1989), which form the basis of many biotechnological applications. The systems utilize several enzymes (extracted from bacteria) as catalysts to assist in the amplification process, but these are essentially constant and may be regarded as properties of a somewhat friendly chemical environment in assessing the self-replication capability of these systems. The systems are programmable in the sense that the choice of primer DNA sequences, which are buffered at high concentration and act as substrates for the polymerization reactions, strongly influence the type of system which can emerge. Very recently, symbiotic *in vitro* ecosystems on the basis of self-replicating peptides have also been created (Lee et al. 1997), and similar work is in progress on enzyme-free self-replication of nucleic acids (von Kiedrowski 1993) and organic molecules (Hong et al. 1992).

Simplified reaction schemes for both biochemical miniature ecosystems are shown in Figure 2. Kinetic analysis has shown that the predator-prey system oscillates at concentrations that should be detectable in experiments when placed in a flow reactor (Ackermann, Wlotzka, & McCaskill 1998). Spatial patch formation should then be observable with waves of pursuit and evasion in thin film reactors (McCaskill 1997). A micro-

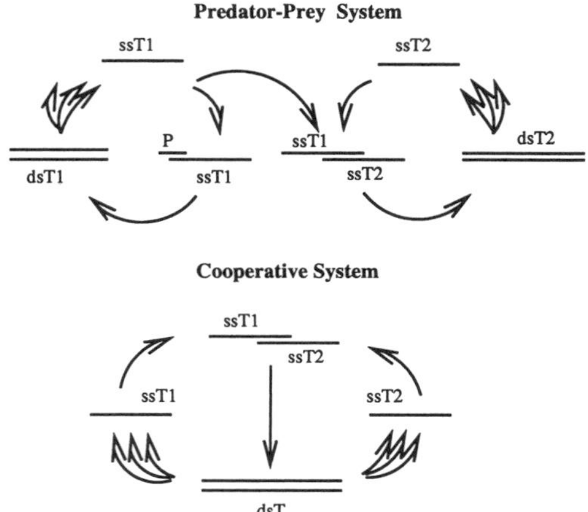

Figure 2: Simplified sketches of the *in vitro* molecular ecosystems of the predator–prey and the cooperative type. Both systems consist of coupled isothermal reaction systems for the amplification of polynucleotides (3SR). Each 3SR-reaction is performed by the concerted action of an RNA–polymerase and a reverse transcriptase, not shown in the sketch. The prey cycle (upper left) is provided by the primer P and can replicated without prey. The predator cycle (upper right), however, needs the prey template as a primer for its own replication. The single stranded prey template (ssT1) and single stranded predator template (ssT2) are annealed, reverse transcriptase can synthesize the double–stranded substrate (dsT2) for polymerase which can start the *in vitro* transcription of predator templates. In the cooperative system two templates (ssT1 and ssT2) must also hybridize to form a double stranded species capable to produce the two templates. This system exhibits a second order reaction step entailing the cooperation of the two different species.

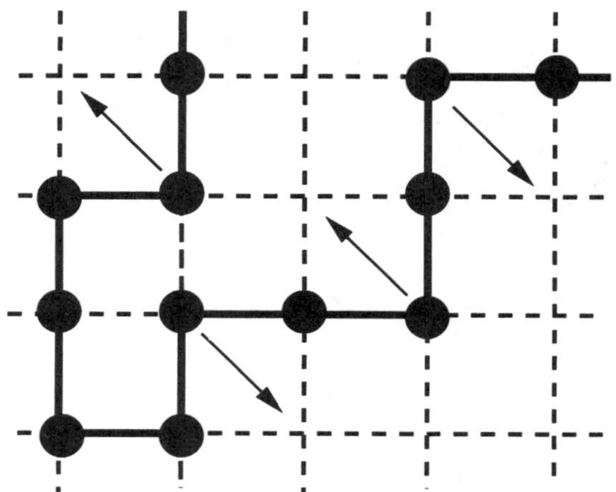

Figure 3: A part of a strand of L particles bound together to a linear chain, moving and folded on the rectangular grid. The arrows indicate the possible (random) motion of the L–particles in the chain. The movements are diagonal on the grid and restricted by the bonds to the next neighbour particles in the chain. In addition only those nodes are available which are either free or occupied by one substrate particle S.

reactor technology has been developed to study the other interesting aspects of spatially interacting populations, and is described elsewhere. In what follows we rather wish to focus on the cooperative system, as it provides important insight into the general structure of catalytic evolvable systems, and has provided us with an important testbed for the influence of spatial effects on evolution.

The CATCH kinetics may be radically simplified in a flow reactor to the following scheme, which displays the essential non-linearity of the bimolecular template-template hybridization step necessary to amplification:

$$\begin{aligned} X_1 + X_2 &\xrightarrow{k_1} Y \\ Y + R &\xrightarrow{k_2} Y + X_1 + X_2 \quad . \end{aligned}$$

Allowing diffusion in a thin film, this scheme, and indeed the full mechanism, shows the same phenomenon observed in the Scott-Gray kinetic model (McCaskill 1997): namely a spatial pattern formation similar in appearance to cellular division called self-replicating spots (Pearson 1993). The importance of such localized patterns in the evolution of cooperation has been outlined (McCaskill 1994; Cronhorst & Blomberg 1997; McCaskill 1997). This mechanism depends on a difference in diffusion constants between the substrates and templates of the reaction. In Section two we focus instead on the key process of complex formation which provides the basis for the cooperativity in amplification.

Self-Assembly of Flexible Structures by Diffusion and Autopoiesis

As clear from Section two, spatial isolation of cooperating molecules is a crucial feature of the step towards complex evolutionary stable organization of molecular systems. Motivated also by the desire to move in the direction of supra-molecular complexes in our description of molecular ecosystems, we decided as a first step to look at the comparatively simple abstract problem of membrane self-assembly, raised within the context of autopoietic systems (Maturana & Varela 1980; McMullin & Varela 1997; Luisi 1994) and also widely known in the form of Ganti's "Chemoton" (Ganti 1975). An effective simulation of the self-assembly processes involved in forming a chemical boundary will also prove useful in evolutionary simulations of self-organization based on self-replication.

Varela and coworkers (McMullin & Varela 1997; Maturana & Varela 1980) have constructed a simple computer simulation of an autopoietic system in which lipid-like monomers are produced with the assistance of a catalyst from freely diffusing substrates and assemble into a membrane which acts as a boundary for catalyst and lipid monomer diffusion. Catalysts within such a boundary can enrich the cellular space with monomers for membrane repair. Both Varela's original simulation (Varela 1979) and the more recent SWARM-based reimplementation (McMullin & Varela 1997) make the assumption that monomers bound into pieces of membrane are immediately thereafter immovable. This assumption has to do with the difficulties outlined above in implementing flexible or rigid body motion of extended objects in a local manner. In what follows we outline a simple solution to allow the simulation of flexible membranes and their self-assembly. This solution neatly circumvents the rather awkward discussion about mechanisms of catalytic inhibition necessary to avoid problems created by immovability. The solution has however a significant restriction in that it only applies to linear chain self-assembled structures and rigidifies with ternary interactions. We return to this problem further below.

In Varela's model, three chemical species are involved on a square cellular lattice: substrate S, catalyst K and lipid-like membrane monomers L. K catalysis the synthesis of S to L, the latter decaying slowly back to S. In Varela's model two proximal S are required for the synthesis and the decay is to $2S$. Proximal Ls can bind up to a valence of two per monomer. Bound Ls are immobile. Only S diffuses independently of the presence of L, the $NSEW$ random walk of other species requiring a free square to move into.

Because it is not essential for our purposes, we have reduced the order of the substrate catalysis by K to 1, with L correspondingly decaying to one S. The key feature of our model rests in a consistent local treatment of constrained bound membrane component diffusion. We have made use of an approach utilized by M. Go in the simulation of polymer chains on a square lattice. Backbone bonds are only allowed in $NSEW$ directions (not diagonally as in Varela's simulation), and monomers are allowed to move diagonally to an unoccupied (or S occupied) square as shown in Figure 3. Although individual monomers, like bishops on a chess board, are restricted to half the possible cells, this is not a serious restriction of the motion of the chain. This rule, at first implemented with a serial stochastic choice of cells to update, can readily be extended to a truly parallel algorithm using the alternating lattice approach used in other cellular simulations of diffusion for instance by Margolus (1984) and Toffoli (1984).

The result of such simulations are shown in Figure 4. It shows the temporary autopoietic stabilization of an initial loop surrounding a catalyst. Because of the

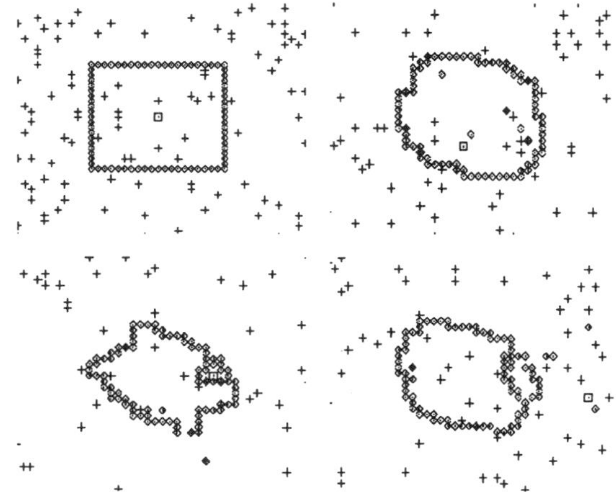

Figure 4: Snapshots from a simulation of the model described in the text. The diamonds are bound or free particles L, the crosses are substrate particles S and the square is a catalyst K for the reaction $S + K \rightarrow L + K$. L–particles may bond together, but the number of bond of each L–particle is restricted to less or equal two. The simulation starts with the configuration in the upper left corner. One catalyst K is surrounded by a closed chain of L particles. Substrate particles S may diffuse into the membrane and may be catalized to L–particles. Since L–particles are trapped in the closed chain of L–particles, this configuration is denoted as a two-dimensional "membrane" or "cell". The membrane structure is flexible and can diffuse through space, see upper right corner. Every L particle has a certain chance to be degraded to a S particle what leads to an instability of the membrane, see lower left corner. Such a defect can be repaired by binding new L particles. The catalyst may diffuse through such defects in the membrane to the outside, see lower right corner. This mechanism leads to the total degradation of the membrane. Instantaneous generation of cells is not observed for this configuration.

flexibility of the linear membrane segments, loop closing occurs statistically for much smaller loops than in the immobile case. Actually it seems sensible to introduce a limitation to the radius of curvature which can be supported by intact membranes, to allow parametric control of the generic size of loop structures. Two ways of doing this are.

1. To introduce an energetic cost of local bending and the Metropolis Monte Carlo choice of accepting moves with change to the net local binding curvature.

2. To introduce a curvature dependence to the decay of bound L to S.

A disadvantage of our dynamical chain model, applied to closed circular chains, is also that purely convex mem-

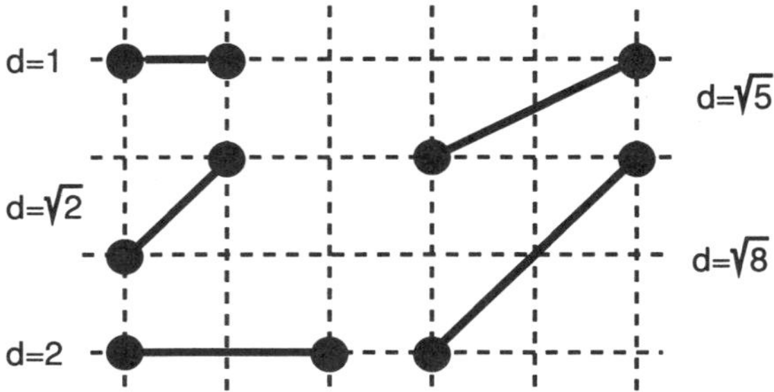

Figure 5: Possible bond distortions on a grid. Two molecules denoted by solid circles may be bond in various configurations. To ensure the locality of the update algorithm the bond length d should be less than a maximal value. The upper left configuration shows the bond of the two particles on neighboring nodes ($d = 0$). Examples of distortions are shown with increasing bond length.

branes without empty (or S filled) cells in their interior still cannot move.

The difficulty arises when ternary binding interactions are introduced. This would be the single most important extension for supramolecular self-assembly and intramolecular folding. The above approach does not allow rigid body motion, although it does allow translation of structures which are flexible. This would be the single most important extension for supramolecular self-assembly and intramolecular folding. The secondary structure of RNA (Zuker & Steigler 1981; McCaskill 1990), in particular the base-base pairing, provides a useful and prototypical example. It is not possible to allow flexible motion without changing the bond-lengths and bond-angles of a structure. The above lattice algorithm becomes immobile at the ternary interaction points. The hierarchy of possible bond distortions from simple proximity (in the von Neumann neighborhood on the square lattice) with increasing bond lengths are shown in Figure 5. We believe that the first four distance classes ($d \leq \sqrt{5}$) will be necessary to allow flexible motion of ternary structures on the two dimensional square lattice. Work in this direction is in progress, but involves relatively extended neighbourhoods. Using excitation energies of stretched or twisted bond configurations from the given (in general component–type dependent) ideal, would allow both structural conservation and limited flexibility with translation to be achieved with a Metropolis type probability weighting. The rotation and angle independent rigid body translation of extended structures remains a problem, probably like the problem of producing circular waves on cellular automata (Kapral, Lawniczak, & Masiar 1991) only solvable by assigning continuous coordinates to cells or using a fine sub-lattice.

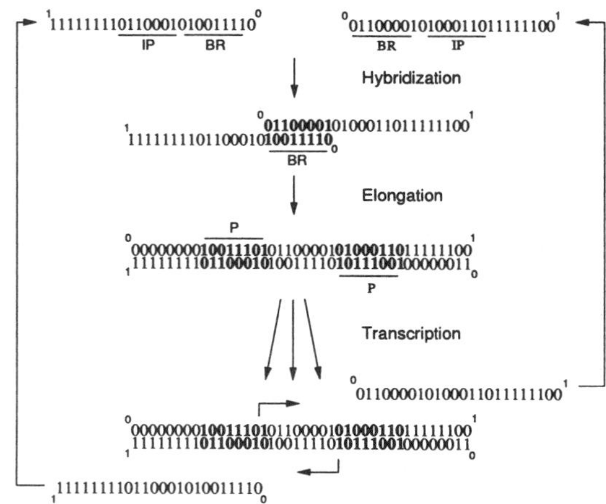

Figure 6: Example for the interaction and processing of bits strings on NGEN which correspond to the cooperatively coupled molecular amplification system. The amplification cycle is started with two single strands (or bit strings) of length 24. The strands hybridize with their complementary sequences. The enzyme for reverse transcription (HIV-RT in the experimental system) completes the strand complementary to the binding partner. The result is a fully double stranded molecule of length 40. Information encoded in the sequence may initiate a transcription process. The double strand above contains two so–called promoter sequences and the products of the transcriptions are the two single strands. The transcriptions can take place multiple times resulting in a non-linear growth.

Configurable Hardware Simulation of Spatial Molecular Evolution and Self-Assembly

In contrast with the *in vitro* molecular predator-prey ecosystem the CATCH system amplifies two molecular species trans–cooperatively (Ehricht, Ellinger, & McCaskill 1997), see Figure 2. A basic model has been developed capturing essential the biochemical aspects of the CATCH system, see Figure 6. Individual based modeling is necessary to include emergent aspects of the population genetics. Since very large population sizes are demanded to follow the systematic effects of evolution, the simulation of evolving molecular systems is a great numerical challenge that can only be performed by massively parallel computers. The model has been implemented in a large scale flow processor. The biopolymer molecules are encoded moving data. Biochemical reactions are realized through data processing. The flow processor consists of a large number of processing units connected to form a grid. The polymer molecules, each encoded in a data string, diffuse through this processor. Every grid point, i.e. processor, is able to perform an enzyme reaction, e.g. transcriptase, or a reaction between

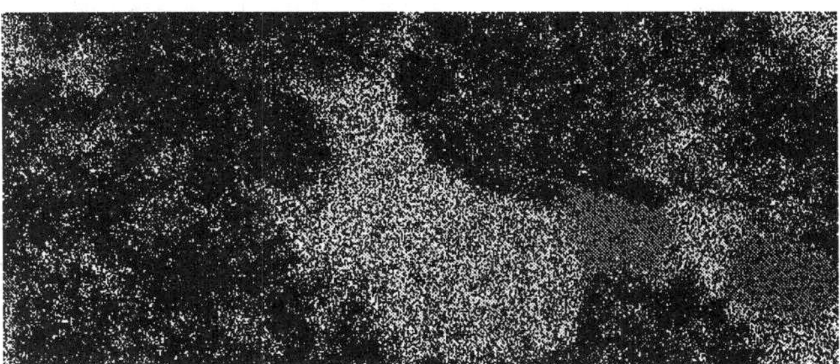

Figure 7: Snapshot from a stochastic, individual based simulation of the evolution in the experimental CATCH system, see text. At this stage the population has evolved away from the initial proliferation scheme of the CATCH system. The former dominating reaction network (white), becomes displaced by the more effective black one, which is an evolutionary descendent of it. The number of different open reaction networks at this stage is extremely high. The number of different molecules is in the order of 5×10^4. This variety is of central importance for the evolution and makes individual based, sequence dependent simulation indispensable.

two polymers, e.g. annealing.

Each molecule, single or double stranded, is represented by a 64×4 bit string. These molecules (or bit strings) are diffusing on a rectangular grid with 513×1152 nodes. Two single strands with complementary substrings may anneal when the enter the same node of the grid. Double stranded molecules are processed by processors for transcription and reverse transcription, producing more single stranded molecules. Point mutations are allowed during the transcription of new single stranded molecules.

The simulations, see a snapshot in Figure 7, show that spatial isolation plays a crucial role for the character of evolving open reaction networks. It favors the emergence and stability of complex cooperative reaction networks. Details will be reported elsewhere. The simulation currently includes self–assembly only by the formation of double stranded molecules and their processing. Including the bond between molecules on different grid nodes, describing the motion and action of such complexes in terms of local update rules would enable us to include the effects of extended self–assembly of supra–molecular template complexes.

Along the line of Section three we first plan to implement self–assembly boundaries in addition to complex self–replication in the hardware. The linear chain approach if Section three should be adequate for this. The implementation of two–dimensional diffusion allows a ready extention to diagonal exchanges, so that the model of Figure 3 should be achievable. NGEN will allow self–assembly to be long enough for component evolution to occur. We hope to be able to report first such results at the conference.

Conclusion

In this work, after outlining the interest in spatially resolved molecular ecosystems, partly stemming from their recent experimental realization, and their evolutionary simulation, we have proceeded to outline the extension of simulations to include self-assembly processes such as boundary formation. Such considerations must ultimately also be employed in general template based amplification via hybridization complexes with internal degrees of freedom. One aim of this research is to develop a high level description of these features of supramolecular dynamics in solution using the programmable matter paradigm in configurable hardware. This should enable a study of the evolution of replication processes involving multi-component complexes. These range from simple homogeneous aggregates such as globules and membranes to highly specific multimeric replicase complexes, spliceosomes, ribosomes etc.

The current approach aims at simulation on the time scale of entire self-organization processes and not on the nanosecond-microsecond time scale of molecular dynamics. The description is consequently vastly simplified and involves for example no inertial effects. The platform should allow a coarse grained analysis of self-assembly effects in the self-organization.

This work was supported by grants from the German Ministery of Education, Science and Technology (BMBF, grant no. 0310799-805).

References

Ackermann, J. B. Wlotzka, and J. McCaskill. 1998. In-vitro DNA-based predator-prey system with oscillatory kinetics. Bulletin of Mathematical Biology, to appear.

Boerlijst, M., and P. Hogeweg. 1991. Spiral wave structures in prebiotic evolution: Hypercycles stable against parasites. *Physica* D 48: 17.

Compton, J. 1991. Nucleic acid sequence–based amplification. *Nature* 350: 91.

Cronhorst, M., and C. Blomberg. 1997. Cluster compartmentalization may provide resistance to parasites for catalytic networks. *Physica* D 101: 289.

Ehricht, R.; T. Kirner, T. Ellinger, P. Foerster, and J. McCaskill. 1997. Monitoring the amplification of CATCH, a 3SR based cooperatively coupled isothermal amplification system, by fluorimetric methods. *Nucleic Acid Research* 25: 4697.

Ehricht, R., T. Ellinger, and J. McCaskill. 1997. Cooperative amplification of templates by cross–hybridization (CATCH). *Eur. J. Biochem.* 243: 358.

Eigen, M., J. McCaskill and P. Schuster. 1989. The molecular quasispecies. *Advances in Chemical Physics* 75: 149.

Eigen, M. 1971. The quasispecies model. *Naturwissenschaften* 58: 465.

Ganti, T. 1975. Organisation of chemical reactions into dividing and metabilizing units: the chemotons. *Biosystems* 7: 189.

Guatelli, J. C., K. M. Whitefield, D. Y. Kwoh, K. J. Barringer, D. D. Richman, and T. R. Gingeras. 1990. Isothermal, *in vitro* amplification of nuclei acids by a multienzyme reaction modeled after retroviral replication. *Proc. Natl. Acad. Sci.* 87: 1874.

Hong, J., Q. Feng, V. Rotello, V.; and J. Rebek. (1992). Competition, cooperation and mutation: Improving a synthetic replicator by light irridation. *Science* 255: 848.

Kapral, R., A. Lawniczak and P. Masiar. (1991). Oscillations and waves in a reactive Lattice–Gas Automaton. *Phys. Rev. Lett.* 66: 2539.

Lee, D., K. Severin, Y. Yokobayashi and M. Ghadiri. 1997. Emergence of symbiosis in peptide self–replicating through a hypercycle network. *Nature* 390: 591.

Luisi, P. L. 1994. The chemical implementation of autopoiesis. In *Self–Production of Supramolecular Structures,* edited by G. R. Fleischaker, S. Colonna, and P. L. Luisi. Kluwer Academic Publishers. p. 179.

Margolus, N. 1984. Physics–like Models of Computation. *Physica* D 10: 81.

Maturana, H. and F. Varela. 1980. *Autopoieses and Cognition: The Realization of the living* , volume 42. Dordrecht, Holland: Reidel Publishing Company.

McCaskill, J. 1990. The equilibrium partition function and base pair binding probabilities for RNA secondary structure. *Biopolymers* 29: 1105.

McCaskill, J. 1994. Ursprünge der Molekularen Kooperation: Theorie und Experiment. *Antrittsvorlesung an der Schiller Universität Jena* 27.

McCaskill, J. 1997. Spatially resolved *in vitro* Molecular Ecology. *Biophysical Chemistry* 66: 145.

McMullin, B., and F. Varela. 1997. Rediscovering Computational Autopoieses. In *Proceedings of the fourth European Conference on Artificial Life (ECAL),* edited by P. Husband and I. Harvey Cambridge:MIT Press/Bradford Books, p. 38.

Pearson, J. 1993. Complex patterns in simple systems. *Science* 261: 189.

Rasmussen, S., and J. R. Smith. 1994. Lattice Polymer Automaton. *Ber. Bunsenges. Phys. Chem.* 89: 1185.

Tangen, U., L. Schulte, and J. McCaskill. 1997. A parallel hardware evolvable computer POLYP. In *Proceedings of the IEEE Symposium on FBGAs for Custom Computing Machines,* edited by K. Pocek and J. Arnold, IEEE Computer Society, p. 238.

Toffoli, T. 1984. Cellular Automata as an alternative to (rather than an approximation of) differential equations in modeling physics. *Physica* D 10: 117.

Varela, F. 1979. *Principles of Biological Autonomy.* New York: North–Holland.

von Kiedrowski, G. 1993. Minimal replicator theory I: Parabolic versus exponential growth. *Biorgan. Chem. Front.* 3: 113.

Wlotzka, B. and J. McCaskill. 1997. A molecular predator and its prey: Coupled isothermal amplification of nucleic acids. *Biology & Chemistry* 4: 25.

Zuker, M., and P. Steigler. 1981. *Nucl. Acids. Res.* 9: 133.

Computational Models for the Formation of Protocell Structures

Linglan Edwards and **Yun Peng**
Computer Science and Electrical Engineering Department
University of Maryland, Baltimore County
1000 Hilltop Circle
Baltimore, MD 21250
email: linglan@cs.umbc.edu ypeng@cs.umbc.edu

Abstract

It is generally believed that during prehistoric evolution phospholipid molecules first self-assembled into protocell structures such as micelles, monolayer and bilayer structures, some of which eventually evolved into cell membranes. There have been various attempts to simulate the self-assembly process by computer. However, due to the computationally complex nature of the problem, previous simulations were often conducted with unrealistic simplifications of the molecules' morphology, intermolecular interaction, and the environment in which the molecules interact. In this paper, we present a new computational model to simulate the self-assembly of lipid aggregates. In this model, each lipid is simulated by a more realistic amphiphilic particle consisting of a hydrophilic head and a long hydrophobic tail. The intermolecular interactions are approximated by a set of simple forces reflecting physical and chemical properties (e.g., hydrophobicity and electrostatic) of lipids believed to be crucial for the formation of various aggregates. Special efforts have been made to reduce the model's computational complexity. With a set of carefully selected parameters, this model is able to successfully simulate the formation of micelles in an aqueous environment and reverse micelle structures in an oil solvent from an initially randomly distributed set of lipid-like particles. We believe that, compared with previous works, this model provides a more accurate computer simulation of the self-assembly of lipids in a more realistic prebiologic setting. This model can be used to study, at the microscopic level, the self-assembly of different protocell structures in the evolutionary process and the impact of environmental conditions on the formation of these structures. It may be further generalized to simulate the formation of other, more complex structures of amphiphilic molecules such as monolayer and bilayer aggregates.

Introduction

From the quest for the origins of life emerges this question: How did the first living cell form? This question leads to many speculations, including the origin of DNA, RNA, proteins, and also the origin of protocell structures such as micelles and membranes. Researchers have approached this problem from several different perspectives: finding clues about the processes involved in the origin of the cell, identifying underlying principles, constructing laboratory models, and more recently, creating computer simulations. The generally accepted assumptions are: first, that basic elements found in living systems were available on the primordial Earth; second, that as a result of various kinds of energy and catalytic effects, the simple molecules in the atmosphere, hydrosphere and lithosphere reacted to form a wide variety of small organic compounds; third, that condensation and polymerization reactions resulted in the formation of compounds of higher molecular weight and polymeric products; and finally, that selective interaction and association of these macromolecules resulted in the generation of a living cell (Oró et al. 1978). Researchers have been trying to verify these assumptions. The focus of our work is the development of computational models to simulate the formation of simple protocell structures from lipid-like amphiphilic particles. In this paper we present a new approach for computer modeling of the self-assembly process of protocell structures.

A Theory About the Formation of Protocell Structures

The general hypothesis about the origin of life on Earth is that an abundance of the simplest molecules existed in the prebiological period; these simple molecules eventually underwent chemical reactions to form more and more complex molecules, eventually forming all the elemental components of the first cell (Deamer and Oro 1980).

There is strong evidence that amphiphilic molecules such as phospholipids were abundant in the prebiotic Earth (Oró et al. 1990) These molecules can *self-associate* or *self-assemble* into small molecular aggregates such as monolayers, micelles, bilayers, vesicles and biological membranes (Figure 1). Unlike solid or rigid particles and macromolecules such as DNA, these aggregate structures are flexible and fluid-like. This is due to the fact that the amphiphilic molecules in micelles and bilayers are held together not by strong covalent and ionic bonds, but by weaker van der Waals, hydrophobic, hydrogen-bonding and screened electrostatic forces (Israelachvili 1991). The main forces governing the self-assembly of amphiphilic particles are believed to arise from the hydrophobic property of lipid tails at the hydrocarbon-water interface. Two opposing forces control the effective headgroup area exposed to the aqueous phase: The hydrophobic property of the lipid tails causes molecules to associate, while the hydrophilic property of the lipid headgroups tends to force the molecules to remain in contact with water (Is-

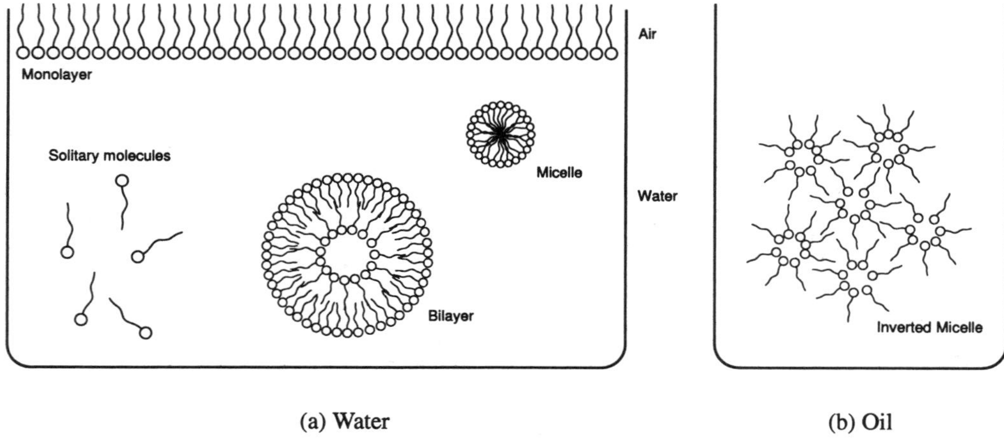

(a) Water

(b) Oil

Figure 1: Formations of lipids in water and oil environment (Jain 1988).

raelachvili 1991).

Computer modeling of biological systems

With the rapid development of computer and computing technology, computer modeling of biological systems has become more and more important in the study of prebiological evolution. The Earth is about 4.5 billion years old. The first living organisms appeared on the earth about 3.7 billion years ago. The formation of the first living cells as a result of possibly hundreds of millions of years of biochemical evolution is impossible to be completely simulated or reproduced in a biology lab. Realistic computer simulation of molecular compound interaction and formation can provide a distinctive insight of the biochemical synthesis at the microscopic level. Moreover, since the computer simulation is built upon our understanding of biological systems and hypotheses, it serves as a persuasive verification of the biological theories. Also, a well-defined computational model could be used as an important tool to investigate the interactions of more complex biological structures.

There have been a number of attempts by researchers to develop computational models for the formation of lipid structures. Each approached the problem differently, yielding different results. Some simulated the self-assembly of lipid aggregates, while others focused on the properties of such aggregates. Some of the major works are reviewed below.

Simulation of formation of micelles and monolayers

Smit et al. developed a computational model to simulate the dynamics of surfactants forming at an oil-water interface (Smit et al. 1990). This model works with two kinds of particles: oil (**o**) and water (**w**). A water molecule in the water region consists of one **w** particle, and an oil molecule in the oil region consists of one **o** particle. Each surfactant molecule is represented as a chain of 2 **w** particles followed by 5 **o** particles, each bound to its neighbor in the chain by a strong harmonic force. All surfactants are initially randomly distributed in the water region. The interactions between particles are determined by Lennard-Jones potential. The simulation yields formations of micelles in the water region and monolayers along the water-oil interface between the two regions. However, the model does have some serious drawbacks. First, this model does not take into account the actual biological structure of the lipid molecules, and the use of **w** and **o** particles to form surfactants cannot accurately capture the interactions of lipid-like molecules with water and oil solvents. Also, the micelles the simulation generates are somewhat different from the ones seen in actual biological experiments. Due to the geometrical packing properties of lipid molecules, lipids tend to form micelle structures when they are cone shaped, i.e. when they are single-chained lipids (surfactants) with large head-group areas and relatively thin tails (Israelachvili 1991). However, in Smit's experiments, the surfactants have large tails and small head-group areas, and thus should form inverted micelles.

Simulation of membrane-like structures

Drouffe et al. (1991) developed a model that simulates three-dimensional particles which self-assemble to form membrane-like objects. In this model, each particle, represented as a ball, is a combination of two lipid molecules with the two tails smashed into a intermediate layer across the center of the ball. A set of interaction forces was used to represent the properties of the particle. Starting from a randomly distributed set of 1,962 particles, the simulation ended with a membrane-like structure after 14 days of computation on a *Sun Sparc-1* workstation.

The main purpose of this model is to analyze the large-scale universal properties of membranes and vesicles, rather than a realistic formation of them. From the point of formation of protocell structures, several assumptions on which this model is based are questionable. First, the basic particle structure used in this model is not an actual stable biological structure. Such particles could not be present in abundance in the Prebiotic Earth. Also this model neglects the effect of the shape and structure of individual lipid molecules, which is generally considered essential to the self-assembly of lipid aggregates. Another major problem is that there is no biological evidence to suggest the existence of the "anisotropic" interaction, which is used in this model as the major interaction forcing the molecules to align in planar configurations.

Simulation of a membrane-water system

Heller et al. (1993) performed a molecular dynamics simulation of bilayer patch of 200 lipids in a water environment. The paper described a simulation of the dynamics of a rectangular patch of membrane over a time span of 263 ps ($1 \times 10^{-12} seconds$). The initial state of the system consists of a hand-constructed patch of a bilayer membrane with 200 molecules of 1-palmitoyl-2-oleoyl-sn-glycero-3-phosphatidylcholine (each containing 134 atoms) and of 5483 water molecules covering the head groups on each side of the bilayer. The simulation was done at the atomic level, with the total number of atoms about 27,000. The simulation took 14,640 hours or 20 months to reach thermal equilibrium on a 60-node MIMD (multiple instruction, multiple data) parallel computer with double ring architecture (equivalent to the computing power of a Cray 2 supercomputer).

This is undoubtedly an extraordinary effort. However, applying this approach (i.e., simulating the molecular dynamics at the atomic level) to the formation of protocell structures such as membranes is intractable. This is because the simulation of the formation of a membrane (or a patch of it) is computationally several orders of magnitude more complex than simulation of an already-formed membrane reaching equilibrium.

Cellular automata based simulation

Mayer et al. (1997) introduced a different type of self-assembly simulation, the lattice molecular automaton (LMA), which was able to simulate formation of small polymer clusters in a system of lipid-like pentamers in a polar environment. However, in order to simulate systems of larger scale, such as micelles and membranes, the level of description of automata will have to be redefined to make the computation feasible.

A New Computational Model

A good computational model for simulating lipid aggregates should have the following features: 1) the ability to simulate different types of protocell structures, 2) the ability to simulate formation of structures under different environmental conditions (different pH levels, presence of salt, etc.), 3) lipid molecule structures and their interactions modeled at a level of detail that is sufficient to be realistic, and 4) the system should be simple and computationally efficient. Deciding to what level of detail the model should simulate is crucial for a good compromise among these conflicting objectives.

Based on these considerations, we adopt a different approach from the simulation models mentioned in previous sections. This model is centered on what is believed to be the most important property of lipid molecules responsible for the formation of lipid aggregates, namely, the different hydrophobicity of the lipid's head and tail. First, to better reflect this amphiphilic property, lipids are modeled as *structured* particles of large heads and long, thin tails. Secondly, the inter-molecular interactions are approximated as a set of simple forces rather than summing up in energy function, with heads and tails of particles playing different roles in defining these interactive forces. This provides more details of the interactions during the biological process and reflects physical and chemical properties of the lipid particles believed to be crucial to the formation of various aggregates. These forces are then used to determine the linear and rotational movements of individual particles according to classical Newtonian mechanics. This is in contrast to models like that of Smit et al. (1990) where molecular interactions were coarsely modeled as energy functions and an energy-minimizing approach was used to determine the motion of particles. We do not attempt to model at the atomic level, but believe that Newtonian mechanics provides a reasonable approximation for the forces influencing the motion of the particles in this simulation.

Basic model and the interacting forces

In an aqueous environment, the hydrophobic effect will drive the phospholipid particles close to each other, with their tails pointing inward to squeeze the water out, forming structures like micelles. In order to simulate the hydrophobic effect, we define each particle in our model as an amphiphilic structure having a polar hydrophilic head group and a non-polar hydrophobic tail. These lipid-like particles are the basic elements of our simulation model. The head of a particle is defined as a sphere of radius r. The tail is represented as a thin, inflexible rod of length L (Figure 2).

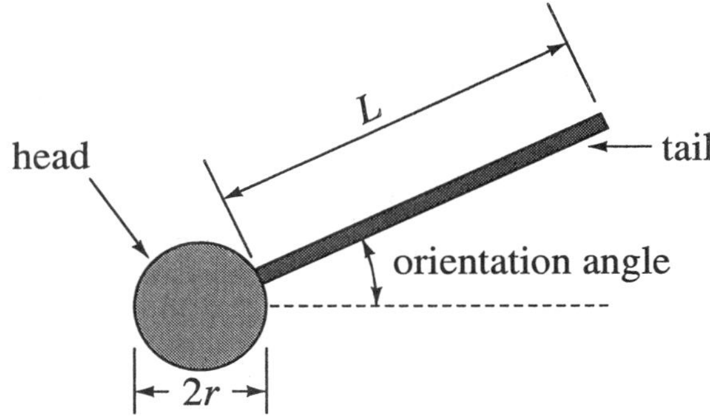

Figure 2: Lipid particle — The basic element in the simulation.

Based on biological properties of lipids, we define seven inter-particle interacting forces (Figure 3). These forces, outlined below, are defined for individual parts of any pair of particles in the system. Note that heads and tails play different roles in these definitions.

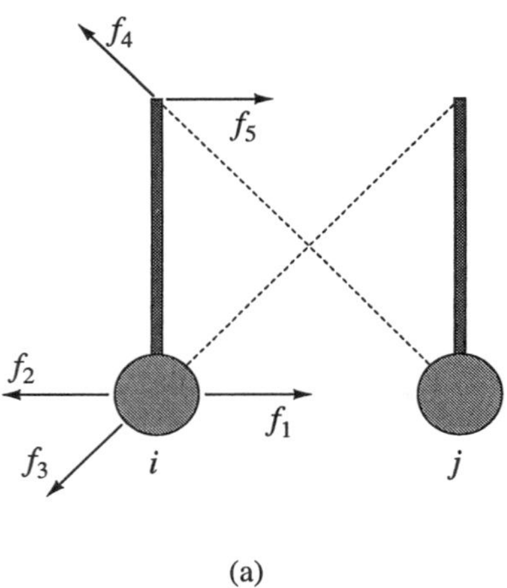

(a)

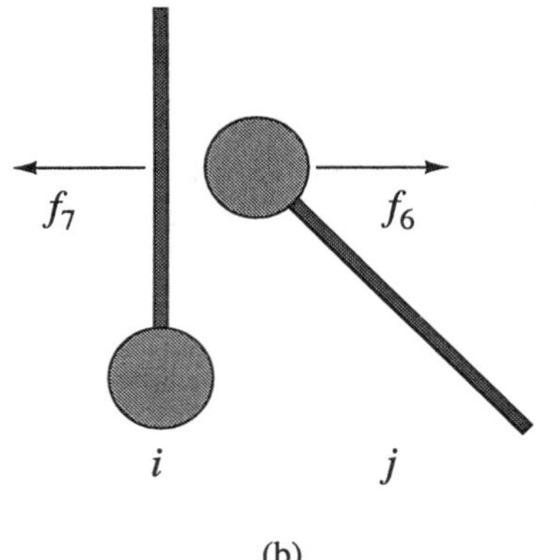

(b)

Figure 3: The interaction forces adopted in the simulation model.

1. The hydrophobic effect is the major driving force in this model. To realize hydrophobicity in the lipid tails and hydrophilicity in the lipid heads, we introduce the following group of forces:

- f_1: head-head attraction. The heads of the particles are hydrophilic, therefore they tend to move toward the direction of an aqueous environment. We interpret this as an attraction force between the heads of each pair of particles. This force has relatively long range.

- f_5: tail-tail attraction. The tails of particles are hydrophobic, meaning that in an aqueous environment, the tails will move toward each other, forming a structure to create an environment that does not contain water. In other words, they will try to squeeze water out of the compartment. We represent this effect as an attraction force between the tails of any pair of lipid particles.

- f_3 and f_4: tail-head and head-tail repulsion. The tails and heads of the lipid have opposite hydrophobicity. Therefore the head of a particle tends to repel the tail of another particle, and vice versa. We represent this property as a repulsive force between heads and tails of different particles.

2. Forces based on electrostatic charge and hydrophilicity.

- f_2: head-head repulsion. This force comes from the fact that heads are electrically charged but tails are not. When two particle heads are too close to each other, the hydrophilicity of the heads will try to maintain a distance between the lipid heads to ensure a water environment among them. This force has relatively short range.

3. Forces from incompressibility of molecules.

- f_6, f_7: repulsion force pair. These forces exist between two lipid particles due to the incompressibility of the molecules when they are close to each other. In our current simulation model, these forces are simplified by only considering the endpoints of the molecules (Figure 3b). Specifically, consider a pair of particles i and j: If the perpendicular distance from either the head or the end of the tail of particle i to any part of j is within a certain (very small) range, these repulsive forces take effect. f_6 and f_7 are a pair consisting of an applied force and a reacting force, having the same magnitude but opposite direction. Two pairs of such forces are computed for each pair of particles. They have very short range.

Computing the forces:

The directions and the points of actions of forces f_1 through f_7 are shown in Figure 3. The magnitudes of these forces are functions of their respective distances (e.g., f_1 depends on the distance between the centers of the heads of two particles, f_3 depends on the distance between the center of the head of particle i and the endpoint of the tail of particle j). They are constant within a distance and drop when the distance is beyond the given range. Currently we use two different ramp functions to specify the functional relations between the forces' magnitudes and the respective distances. The purpose of using such ramp functions is to simplify computation. One of the two ramp functions has a relatively smooth reduction of the force magnitude as the distance exceeds the given range. This function is used for the long-range forces f_1, f_3, f_4, and f_5 (Figure 4). The other ramp function, with a more abrupt reduction, is used for the short-range forces f_2, f_6, and f_7 (Figure 5). The magnitude of each force f_k is determined by the distance d and the three function parameters r_k, a_k, and b_k, where r_k is the radius of the range of force f_k with maximum magnitude, a_k is the maximum magnitude of force f_k, and b_k is the residual or minimum magnitude of force f_k.

The forces are calculated via the relation

$$f_k = a_k * ramp$$

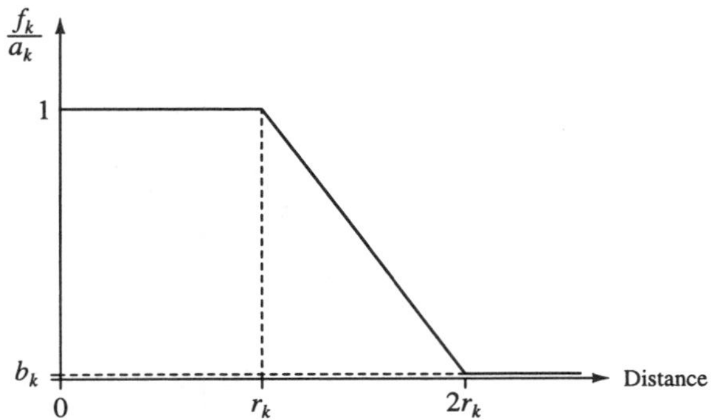

Figure 4: Ramp function for the interacting forces f_1, f_3, f_4, and f_5.

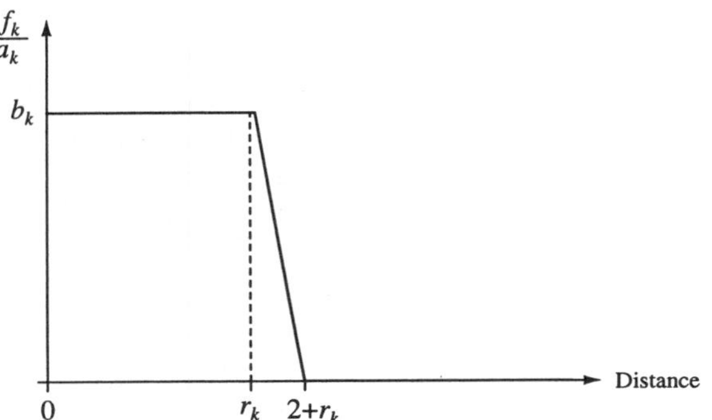

Figure 5: Ramp function for the interacting forces f_2, f_6 and f_7.

. Each force produces a torque relative to the center of mass of the particle:

$$\tau_k = f_k * d$$

where d is the distance from the point of action of force f_k to the geometric center of the particle.

Function of movement

We compute two types of movement, linear and rotational, for each particle. The linear movement of particle i is determined by the following:

- The movement of the center of mass of molecule i is determined by the compound force on i from all other molecules j.

$$F_i(t) = \left(\sum_{j \neq i} \sum_k f_k(t) \right) + rand_1(t) - c_1 * v_i(t)$$

where k ranges over all forces from j to i, and

  - $f_k(t)$ is the force placed on particle i at time t,
  - $rand_1(t)$ is a small random force placed on particle i,
  - $v_i(t)$ is the current velocity of particle i, and
  - $c_1 > 0$ is the friction coefficient.

- Assuming each particle has an unit mass, we then have:

$$\Delta v_i(t + \delta t) = F_i(t) \cdot \delta t \quad (1)$$

$$\Delta S_i(t + \delta t) = \frac{1}{2} F_i(t) \delta t^2 + v_i(t) \delta t \quad (2)$$

where ΔS_i is the linear displacement.

For rotational movement, the compound torque of particle i can be computed by

$$T_i(t) = \left(\sum_{j \neq i} \sum_k \tau_k(t) \right) + rand_2(t) - c_2 \omega_i(t)$$

where k ranges over all forces from j to i, and

  - $\tau_k(t)$ is the torque generated by force f_k at time t,
  - $rand_2$ is a small random torque,
  - $\omega_i(t)$ is the current rotational velocity, and
  - $c_2 > 0$ is rotational friction coefficient.

The rotational inertia I can be computed by assuming each particle to be a uniform thin rod of length $2r + l$:

$$I = \frac{1}{12}(2r + l)^2$$

The rotational movement will then be

$$\Delta \omega(t + \delta t) = \frac{T_i(t)}{I} \delta t \quad (3)$$

$$\Delta \theta_i(t + \delta t) = \frac{1}{2} \frac{T_i(t)}{I} \delta t^2 + \omega_i(t) \delta t \quad (4)$$

where $\Delta \theta_i$ is the angular displacement.

Implementation and Simulation Results

Based on the computational model described in the previous section, we built a system to simulate the interactions between the lipid particles and the formation of micelle structures. We have obtained some very promising results. The major effort in the implementation has been the adjustment and final selection of the parameters a_k, b_k and r_k. We have made various efforts to reduce the computation. They include using the ramp functions to simplify the computation of forces, calculating inter-particle interactions only for those particle pairs whose distance is within a certain range, and restricting the simulation to two spatial dimensions.

The simulation is divided into two parts. The first part is the simulation computation, which generates a data file recording the position of each particle at each time step. The second part is the interactive animated display which reads the data file generated from the computation in the first part and graphically displays the movement of lipid particles.

The results shown here are simulations of a system in an aqueous environment. The size of the environment is 900 × 900 (normalized) units. Each lipid particle has a sphere head of radius 5, and a tail of length 30. There are 200 lipid-like

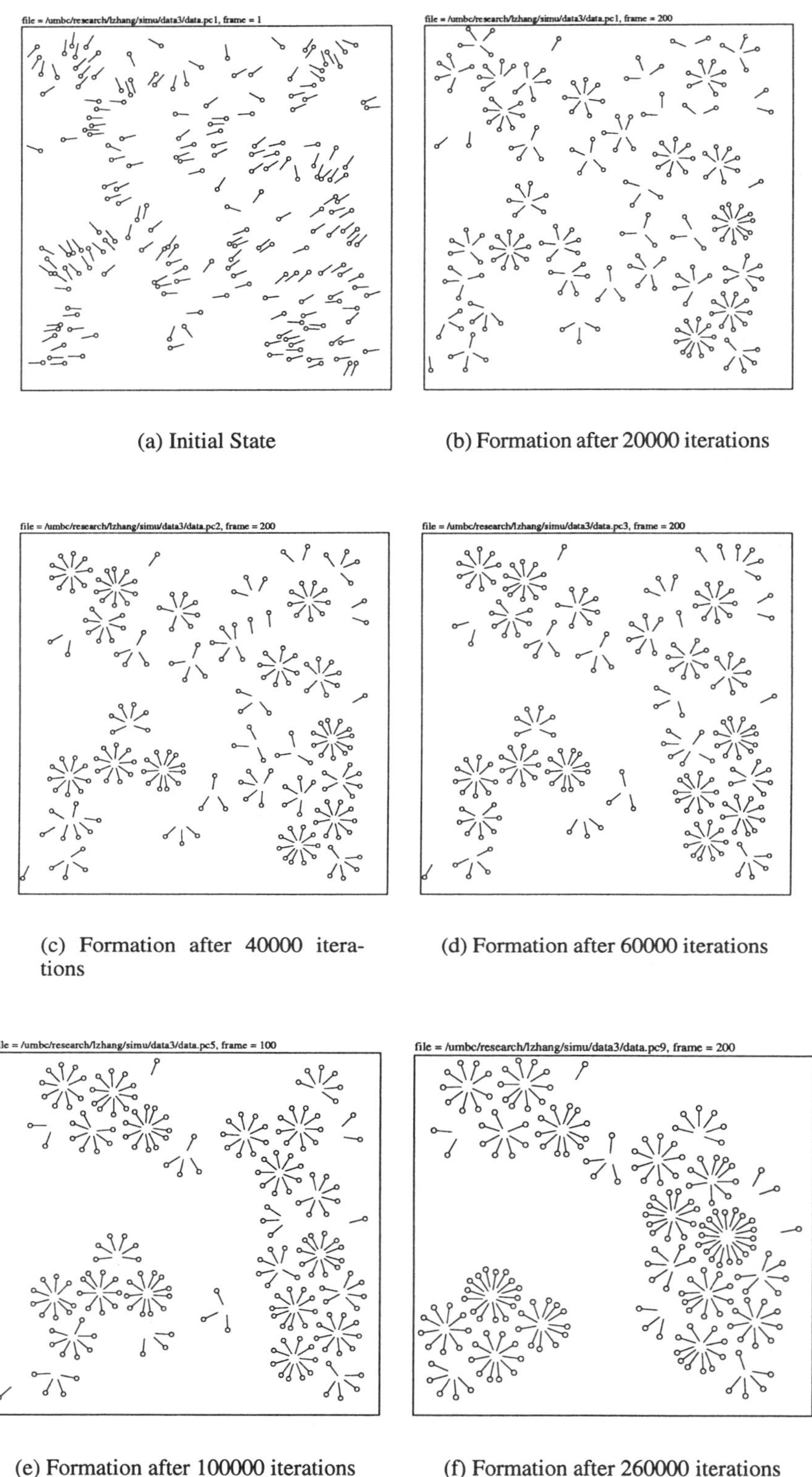

(a) Initial State

(b) Formation after 20000 iterations

(c) Formation after 40000 iterations

(d) Formation after 60000 iterations

(e) Formation after 100000 iterations

(f) Formation after 260000 iterations

Figure 6: System of 200 lipid particles, Simulation 1.

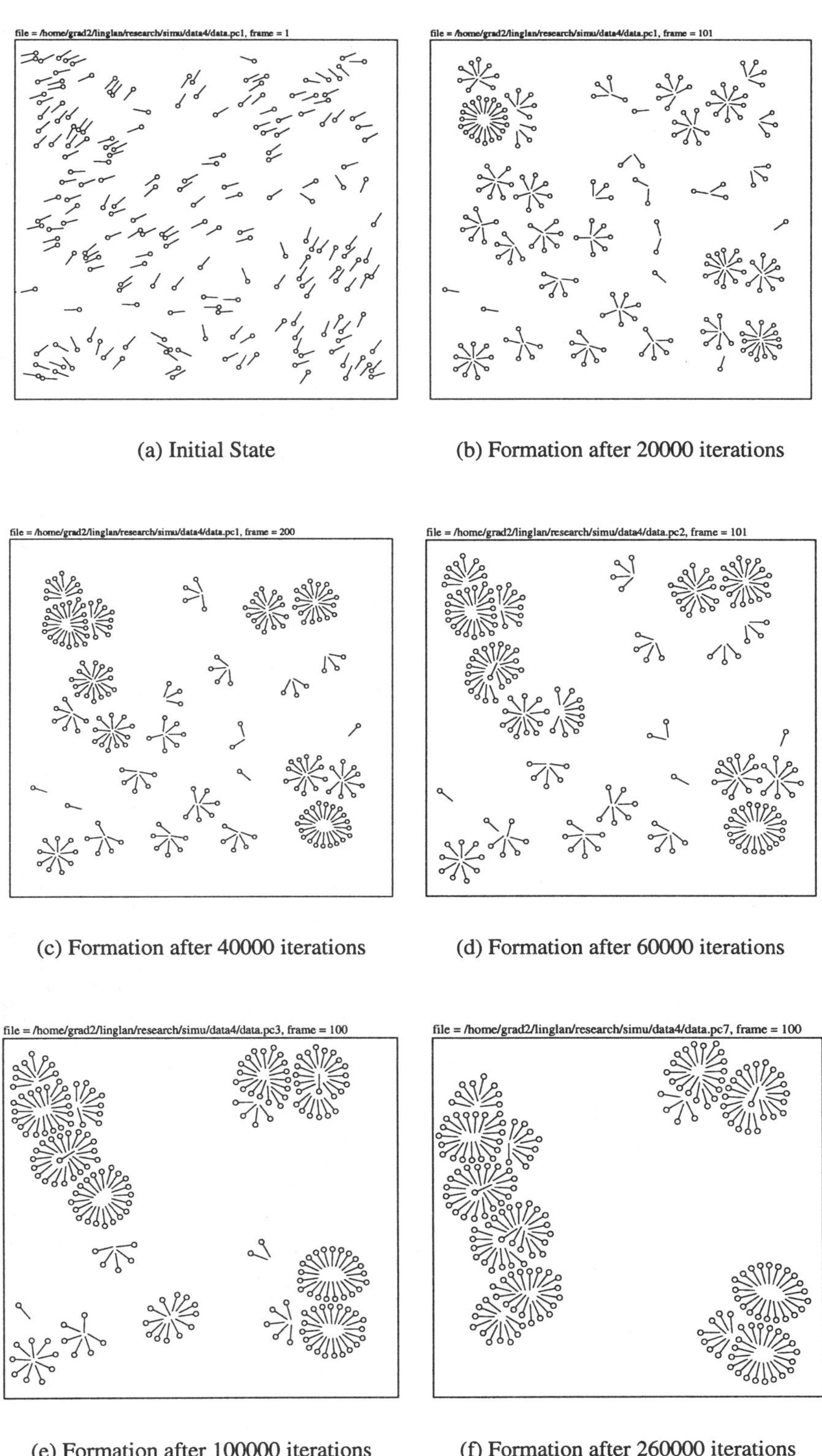

(a) Initial State

(b) Formation after 20000 iterations

(c) Formation after 40000 iterations

(d) Formation after 60000 iterations

(e) Formation after 100000 iterations

(f) Formation after 260000 iterations

Figure 7: System of 200 lipid particles, Simulation 2.

particles randomly distributed in the initial state of the system. A series of snapshots for different stages of two simulations is shown in Figure 6 and Figure 7, each starting from a different randomized initial state, and reaching a relatively stable state after 260,000 iterations.

Micelle-like structures can be seen forming eventually during the process. The difference between the two simulations is that the range of repulsive forces f_3 and f_4 in simulation 2 is 30% less than that in simulation 1. It can be observed that larger sized micelle structures are formed in simulation 2. Simulation 1 was performed on an *SGI R4400* platform. The total running time for 260,000 iterations was about 76 hours. Simulation 2 was performed on an *SGI R8000* platform, with a total running time of about 57.5 hours for the same number of iterations.

Conclusions

We presented a new computational model for simulations of the self-assembly of lipid-like particles into well-formed protocell structures. We believe this model is a demonstration of a more accurate computer simulation of the self-assembly of lipids in a more realistic prebiologic setting than found in previous efforts. By adopting a structural particle model and using a set of simple forces as an approximation to model the inter-molecular interaction between lipid molecules, this computational model provides a more accurate reflection of the biological properties and a more detailed simulation for the actual biological process. The effectiveness and efficiency of this model was demonstrated by successful simulations of the formation of simple structures such as micelles from a pool of randomly distributed lipid-like particles.

We are currently extending the computational model to simulate the formation of reversed micelle structures in an oil environment. We have obtained very promising initial results which provide further support for our model. Our next immediate objective is to simulate the formation of monolayer structures in an oil-water interface environment, and develop computer programs for a three-dimensional simulation.

We expect this simulation model to be able to reveal some underlying principles on which different lipid structures (monolayers, micelles, reversed micelles, and bilayers) are formed. It may also provide a new approach and be useful as a tool for other artificial life simulations. We hope that this simulation system can be used to investigate the effects of changes in the environment (such as pH values and temperature in the solvent, the density of the lipids, etc.) on the formation of lipid aggregates, as well as the dynamic (fluid-like) property of those aggregates. This model can be used to study, at the microscopic level, the self-assembly of different protocell structures in the evolutionary process and the impact of environmental conditions on the formations of these structures. It may be further generalized to simulate the formation of other, more complex structures of amphiphilic molecules such as mono-layer and bilayer aggregates. We are also exploring the possibility of further extending this model to simulate the formation of membrane-like bilayer structures. We hope that the completion of this research will provide substantial insight into the process of protocell structure formations as well as provide a useful tool for further study of the properties and functions of biological membranes.

References

Bachmann, P. A., P. Walde, P. L. Luisi, and J. Lang. 1991. Self-replicating micelles: Aqueous micelles and enzymatically driven reactions in reverse micelles. *J. Am. Chem. Soc.* 113: 8204–8209.

Bachmann, P. A., P. L. Luisi, and J. Lang. 1992. Autocatalytic self-replicating micelles as models for prebiotic structures. *Nature* 357: 57–59.

Deamer, D. W. and J. Oro. 1980. Role of lipids in prebiotic structures. *BioSystems* 12: 167–175.

Drouffe, J. M., A. C. Maggs, and S. Leibler. 1991. Computer simulations of self-assembled membranes. *Science* 254: 1353–1356.

Haile, J. M. 1992. *Molecular Dynamics Simulation — Elementary Methods*. New York: John Wiley.

Hargreaves, W. R. and D. W. Deamer. 1978. Origin and early evolution of bilayer membranes. In *Light Transducing Membranes*, edited by D. W. Deamer. New York: Academic Press, p. 23-59.

Harrison, R. and G. G. Lunt. 1980. *Biological Membranes*. New York: John Wiley.

Heller, H., M. Schaefer, and K. Schulten. 1993. Molecular dynamics simulation of a bilayer of 200 lipids in the gel and in the liquid-crystal phases. *J. of Phys. Chem.* 97: 8343–8360.

Israelachvili, J. N. 1991. *Intermolecular and Surface Forces*. London, San Diego: Academic Press.

Jain, M. K. 1998. *Introduction to Biological Membranes*. New York: John Wiley.

Mayer, B., G. Köhler, and S. Rasmussen. 1997. Simulation and dynamics of entropy-driven, molecular self-assembly processes. *Physical Review* E 55: 4489–4499.

Oró, J., and A. Lazcano. 1984. A minimal living system and the origin of a protocell. *Adv. Space Res.* 4: 167–176.

Oró, J., E. Sherwood, J. Eichberg, and D. Epps. 1978. Formation of phospholipids under primitive earth conditions and the role of membranes in prebiological evolution. In *Light Transducing Membranes*, edited by D. W. Deamer. New York: Academic Press, p. 1-23.

Oró, J., S. L. Miller, and A. Lazcano. 1990. The origin and early evolution of life on earth. *Annu. Rev. Earth Planet. Sci.* 18: 317–356.

Smit, B., P. A. J. Hilbers, K. Esselink, L. A. M. Rupert, N. M. van Os, and A. G. Schlijper. 1990. Computer simulations of a water/oil interface in the presence of micelles. *Nature* 348: 624–625.

Emergence of Multicellular Organisms with Dynamic Differentiation and Spatial Pattern

Chikara Furusawa and Kunihiko Kaneko
Department of Pure and Applied Sciences
University of Tokyo, Komaba, Meguro-ku, Tokyo 153, JAPAN

Abstract

The origin of multicellular organisms and the mechanism of development in cell societies are studied by choosing a model with intracellular biochemical dynamics allowing for oscillations, cell–cell interaction through diffusive chemicals on a 2-dimensional grid, and state-dependent cell adhesion. Cells differentiate due to a dynamical instability, as described by our "isologous diversification" theory (Kaneko and Yomo 1994, 1997, Furusawa and Kaneko 1998). A fixed spatial pattern of differentiated cells emerges, where spatial information is sustained by cell–cell interactions. This pattern is robust against perturbations. With an adequate cell adhesion force, active cells are released which form the seed of a new generation of multicellular organisms, accompanied by death of the original multicellular unit as a halting state. It is shown that the emergence of multicellular organisms with differentiation, regulation, and life-cycle is not an accidental event, but a natural consequence in a system of replicating cells with growth.

Introduction

The development of multicellular organisms is one of the most elegant and interesting processes in biology. Cells which contain the same set of genomes differentiate to several types with exact order and exact location. The determination of cell type is quite robust, even though the development process occurs in a thermodynamic environment with molecular fluctuations. Three mechanisms are necessary to sustain a robust developmental process in multicelluar organisms. First, an external field, which provides information to control differentiation and proliferation must be maintained through the interaction among cells. Second, each cell must detect and interpret such external information. Finally, the internal state of each cell must be changed according to this interpreted information, leading to differentiation. Recent advances in molecular biology provide us with a molecular basis for these mechanisms. The gradient of morphogen concentration giving positional information can be identified experimentally, the existence of a signaling pathway from receptor protein on the membrane to the nucleus is verified, and the internal states of cells are reduced to regulations of protein synthesis from DNA molecules.

However, when we focus on the emergence of multicellular organisms in the evolutionary process, it is hard to argue that such elaborate mechanisms appear independently at the same time. On the other hand, the fossil record shows that the transition to multicellularity has occurred at least three times in fungi, plants and animals (Maynard-Smith and Szathmary, 1995). This suggests that the evolution to multicellularity is not a chance event but a *necessity* in evolution. The three mechanisms mentioned above must be tightly incorporated, at least at the first stage of multicellularity. Thus, to understand the transition to multicellular organisms, the interplay between interactions among cells and intracellular dynamics must be studied.

The motivation behind this work is not restricted to the origin of multicellularity. Even if it might be possible to describe all detailed molecular processes of the present organism, this does not answer why such a developmental process is robust in spite of the considerable thermodynamic fluctuations occurring at the molecular level, which seems to make machine-like functions such as a 'clock' almost impossible. Any rule with a threshold given by a signal molecule's concentration is accompanied by fluctuations, and therefore cannot proceed correctly. We need to construct a logic for the development process that, in general, works even under molecular fluctuations. Such a logic is relevant to understanding the level of multicelluarity in present organisms, from primitive structures such as Dictyostelum discoideum and Volvox, to higher organisms.

To understand the emergence of multicellularity as a general consequence of the interplay between inter- and intra-dynamics of cell societies, we have earlier proposed the "isologous diversification" theory (Kaneko and Yomo 1994, 1997, Furusawa and Kaneko 1998). This theory is rooted in the "dynamic clustering" observed in globally coupled chaotic systems (Kaneko 1990, 1992). It provides a general mechanism of spontaneous differentiation of replicating biological units, where the cells (which have oscillatory chemical reactions within) differentiate through interaction with other cells, as their number increases through divisions. This differentiation is due to the separation of orbits in phase space which is not attributed to a specific chemical substance, but rather is represented through the dynamic relationships of several chemicals. While the differentiation is triggered by the instability of a nonlinear system, the differentiation process as a whole is shown to be robust against fluctuations.

In this paper, we extend previous work to incorporate the formation of *spatial patterns* on a 2-dimensional grid. At first glance, our framework may appear similar to previous work (Fleischer and Barr 1994, Mjolsness, Sharp, and Reinitz 1991, Eggenberger 1997), in which cells with internal states are placed on a 2-dimensional grid and interact with each other through this environment. In the latter approaches, intra-cellular dynamics are mainly governed by a set of 'if-then'-like (conditional) rules which are specified in advance as genetic control. Although this implementation simplifies the description of the simulation in terms of logical chains, there are three problems which we think will be overcome only by our approach. First, such if-then–like rules are based on the response to signals with some threshold. However, as mentioned above, given the fluctuations in the number of signal molecules, such rules cannot work as anticipated. Second, from the implementation of the rules, one cannot deduce how such a set of rules appears at the first stage of multicellularity. Third, the rules have to be tuned externally to fashion a stable development process.

As mentioned, we propose that the interplay between interactions among cells and intracellular dynamics leads to the emergence of such conditional rules. The rule is found to be tuned spontaneously depending on cell–cell interactions rendering the development process robust against molecular fluctuations, and maintaining a degree of order in the cell society. In contrast with previous studies, the rules of our cell society are not given in advance, but emerge as a consequence of interactions among cells.

We have studied numerically several models consisting of cells with internal chemical reaction networks and interactions among them through the environment. Three basic problems are discussed: **fixation of a spatial pattern of differentiated cells, robustness in the developmental process, and the emergence of a replicating cluster of cells**. The first problem is answered by the formation of a **ring pattern of differentiated cells**, and the second by **regeneration of a damaged cell cluster**. The solution of the last problem is also given, which is essential to the origin of multicellularity since it treats recursive generation of an ensemble of cells at a higher level than cell replication. It will be shown that the dynamic order of the cell society is a natural consequence of interacting cells with oscillatory dynamics and cell–cell adhesion forces. Hence, the emergence of multicellularity should occur as a necessity in the course of evolution.

Model for Differentiation

Our model for differentiation consists of

- Internal biochemical reaction dynamics in each cell
- Cell–cell interactions through media
- Cell division
- Cell adhesion

In essence we assume a network of catalytic reactions for internal dynamics that also allows chaotic oscillations of chemical concentrations, while the interaction process is just a diffusion of chemicals through media.

We represent the internal state of a cell by k chemicals' concentrations as dynamical variables. Cells are assumed to be surrounded by the medium, where the same set of chemicals is given. Hence, the dynamics of the internal state is represented by a set of variables $c_i^{(m)}(t)$, the concentration of the m-th chemical species at the i-th cell, at time t. The corresponding concentration of the species in the medium is represented by a set of variables $C^{(m)}(x, y, t)$, where x and y denote the position on the 2-dimensional grid.

Internal reaction dynamics

As internal chemical reaction dynamics we choose a catalytic network among the k chemicals. Each reaction from chemical i to j is assumed to be catalyzed by chemical ℓ, determined by a matrix (i, j, ℓ). To represent this reaction-matrix we adopt the notation $Con(i, j, \ell)$ which takes on unity when the reaction from the chemical i to j is catalyzed by ℓ, and 0 otherwise. Each chemical has several paths to other chemicals, which act as a substrate to create several enzymes for other reactions. In addition, we assume that all chemicals have the potential to catalyze a reaction to generate itself from another chemical, besides the ordinary reaction paths determined randomly. Due to this auto-catalytic reaction, positive feedback to amplify external signals is made possible, which often leads to oscillatory reaction dynamics[1]. This reaction matrix $Con(i, j, \ell)$, generated randomly, is fixed throughout the simulation.

Still there can be a variety of choices in the enzymatic chemical kinetics. In this paper, we assume quadratic effects of enzymes. Thus, the reaction from chemical m to ℓ aided by chemical j leads to the term $e_1 c_i^{(m)}(t)(c_i^{(j)}(t))^2$, where e_1 is a coefficient for chemical reactions, taken to be identical for all paths.

[1]For a more detailed discussion of the role of auto-catalytic reactions, see Furusawa and Kaneko (1998).

Of course, the real biochemical mechanisms within cells are very much more complicated. We do not take such details into account here, as our purpose is to show how the differentiation process appears as a general consequence of interacting cells with internal nonlinear dynamics. What is essential here is a biochemical reaction that allows for nonlinear oscillation, which is generally expected as long as there is a positive feedback process. It should be noted that in real biological systems, oscillations are observed in chemical substrates such as Ca, cyclic AMP, and so on (Hess and Boiteux 1971, Tyson et al. 1996, Goodwin 1963, Goldbeter 1996).

Besides the change in chemical concentrations, we take into account the change in the volume of a cell. The volume is now treated as a dynamical variable, which increases as a result of transportation of chemicals into the cell from the environment. As a first approximation, it is reasonable to assume that the cell volume is proportional to the sum of chemicals in the cell. We note that the concentrations of chemicals are diluted as a result of an increase in the volume of the cell. With the above assumption, this dilution effect is tantamount to imposing the restriction $\sum_\ell c_i^{(\ell)} = 1$, that is, the normalization of chemical concentrations at each step of the calculation, while the volume change is calculated from the transport as described later.

Cell–cell interaction through diffusion to media

Each cell communicates with its environment through the transport of chemicals. Thus, cells interact also with each other via the environment. Here we consider only indirect cell–cell interactions via diffusive chemical substances, as a minimal form of interaction. We assume that the rates of chemicals transported into a cell are proportional to differences of chemical concentrations between the inside and the outside of the cell.

The transportation or diffusion coefficient should depend on the chemical. Here, we assume that there are two types of chemicals, one which can penetrate the membrane and one which can not. We use the notation σ_m, which takes the value 1 if the chemical $c_i^{(m)}$ is penetrable, and 0 otherwise.

To sum up all these process, the dynamics of chemical concentrations in each cell is represented as follows:

$$dc_i^{(\ell)}(t)/dt = \Delta c_i^{(\ell)}(t) - (1/k)\sum_{l=1}^{k} \Delta c_i^{(\ell)}(t) \,, \qquad (1)$$

with

$$\Delta c_i^\ell(t) = \sum_{m,j} Con(m,\ell,j)\; e_1\; c_i^{(m)}(t)\; (c_i^{(j)}(t))^2 - \sum_{m',j'} Con(\ell,m',j')\; e_1\; c_i^{(\ell)}(t)\; (c_i^{(j')}(t))^2 + \sigma_\ell D_m(C^{(\ell)}(p_i^x, p_i^y, t) - c_i^{(\ell)}(t)) \,. \qquad (2)$$

where the terms with $\sum Con(\cdots)$ represent paths coming into and out of ℓ, respectively. The variables p_i^x and p_i^y denote the location of the i-th cell on the $x-y$ grid. The term $\Delta c_i^{(\ell)}$ gives the increment of chemical ℓ, while the second term in Eq. (1) summarizes the constraint $\sum_\ell c_i^{(\ell)}(t) = 1$ due to growth of volume (Eigen and Schuster 1979). The third term in Eq. (2) describes the transport in the medium, where D_m denotes the diffusion constant of the membrane, which we assume to be identical for all chemicals.

The diffusion of penetrable chemicals in the medium is governed by a partial differential equation for the concentration of chemical $C^{(\ell)}(x,y,t)$. For each chemical $C^{(\ell)}$, at a particular location:

$$\partial C^{(\ell)}(x,y,t)/\partial t = -D_e \nabla^2 C^{(\ell)}(x,y,t) + \sum_i \delta(x-p_i^x, y-p_i^y)\sigma_\ell D_m(C^{(\ell)} - c_i^{(\ell)}(t)) \,. \qquad (3)$$

We assume the following boundary condition:

$$C(0,y,t) = C(x_{max},y,t) = C(x,0,t) = C(x,y_{max},t) = \text{const.} \quad (0 < x < x_{max}, 0 < y < y_{max}) \,, \qquad (4)$$

where D_e is the diffusion constant of the environment, x_{max} and y_{max} denote the extent of the lattice, and $\delta(x,y)$ is Dirac's delta function. This boundary condition can be interpreted as a chemical bath outside of the medium, which supplies those penetrable chemicals that are consumed to the medium via a constant flow to the cell. In practice, the variable $C^{(\ell)}(x,y,t)$ is discretized on an $n \times n$ grid, to reduce the diffusion equation to n^2 differential equations.

Cell division

Each cell takes penetrable chemicals from the medium as the nutrient, while the reaction in the cell transforms them to unpenetrable chemicals which construct the body of the cell such as membrane and DNA. As a result of these reactions, the volume of the cell is increased by a factor $(1 + \sum_\ell \Delta c_i^\ell(t))$ per dt. In this paper, the cell is assumed to divide into two almost identical cells when the volume of the cell is doubled.

The chemical composition of two divided cells are almost identical with their mother's, with slight differences between them due to random fluctuations. In other words, each cell has $(1+\epsilon)c^{(l)}$ and $(1-\epsilon)c^{(l)}$, respectively, with a small "noise" ϵ given by a random number with a small amplitude, say from $[-10^{-6}\ ,\ 10^{-6}]$. Although the existence of this imbalance is essential to differentiation in our model and in nature, the mechanism or the degree of imbalance is not important for the differentiation itself. The important feature of our model is the amplification of microscopic differences between the cells through the instability of the internal dynamics.

Cell adhesion

In cell biology, each cell adheres to its neighbor cells through binding to proteins on its membrane surface. The nature of membrane proteins depends on the internal state of the cell, and it is natural to assume that whether adhesion occurs or not is determined by a combination of the cell types of the two neighbors. As a minimal model for adhesion, we assume that cells within a given threshold distance have a 'connection', where a 'spring' is put between them so that they adhere within the natural length of the spring if the combination of the two cell types satisfies a given condition. For example, cells with the same cell type will be connected by the same spring (with the same strength and natural length) if a distance condition is satisfied, while pairs with any combination of two different cell types do not adhere.

In addition to the adhesion force, a random fluctuation force is applied to all cells that is expected from molecular Brownian motion. We seek a configuration that is stable against perturbations including these fluctuations. When a cell divides, two daughter cells are placed at randomly chosen positions close to the mother cell, and each daughter cell makes new connections with the neighbor cells.

Results Without Spatial Information

We have performed several simulations of our model with different chemical networks and different parameters. Since typical behaviors are rather common as long as nonlinear oscillatory dynamics are included, we present our results by taking a specific chemical network with $k = 20$ chemicals. First we show some results of simulation without spatial information, to demonstrate the essence of our differentiation process based on dynamical instabilities.

In this section, we assume that the medium is well stirred and all cells interact through an identical environment[2]. Later, simulations with spatial information and diffusive chemicals are shown to discuss pattern formation and the emergence of multicellularity. As initial condition, we take a single cell with randomly chosen chemical concentrations $c_i^{(\ell)}$ satisfying $\sum_\ell c_i^{(\ell)} = 1$. In Fig. 1, we have show the time series of concentration of the chemicals in a cell, when only a single cell is in the medium. We call this state "type-0" in this paper. This is the only attractor of internal cellular dynamics, detected from randomly chosen initial conditions.

With diffusion, external chemicals flow into the cell which leads to an increase in the volume of the cell. Thus, the cell is divided into two, with almost identical chemical concentrations. The chemicals within the

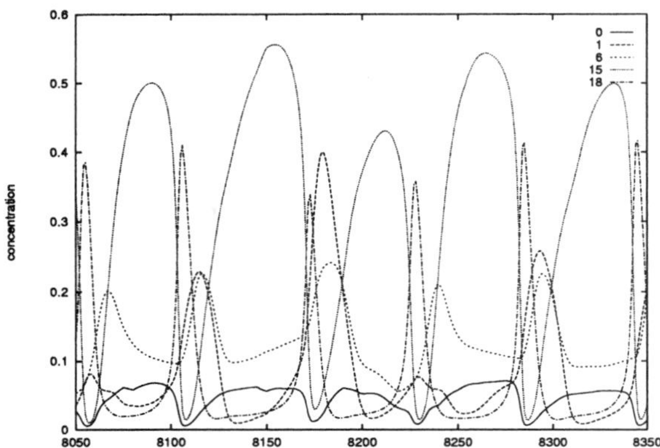

Figure 1: Overlaid time series of $c^{(m)}(t)$ in the type-0 cell, obtained from a network with 20 chemicals and seven connections in each chemical. We have plotted only the time series of 5 internal chemicals out of 20 to avoid a crowded figure. Each line with number m=0,1,6,15,18 represents the time series of concentration of the corresponding chemical $c^{(m)}(t)$. The parameters are set as $e_1 = 0.7$, $D_m = 0.1$, $D_e = 0.2$, chemicals $c^{(\ell)}(t)$ for $\ell \le 3$ are penetrable(i.e., $\sigma_\ell = 1$), while the others are not. The reaction network $Con(i, j, \ell)$ is randomly chosen, and is fixed throughout the simulation results of the present paper.

two daughter cells oscillate coherently, with the same dynamical behavior as their mother cell (i.e., attractor-0). As the number of cells increases by a factor of two (i.e., $1-2-4-8\cdots$) with further divisions, the coherence of oscillations is easily lost. Such loss of synchrony is expected from the studies of coupled nonlinear oscillations. The microscopic differences introduced at each cell division are amplified to a macroscopic level through interaction, which destroys the phase coherence.

Differentiation

When the number of cells exceeds a threshold value, some cells start to display differing types of dynamics. In Figs. 2(a) and (b), the time series of chemicals in these cells are plotted. We call these states "type-1" and "type-2" cells, respectively. Note that these states are not an attractor of the internal dynamics of a single cell. Rather, these states are stabilized by the coexistence of cells with a *different* type. In Fig. 3, orbits of chemical concentrations at the transition from type-0 to type-1 are plotted in phase space. It shows that each attractor occupies a distinct regime in phase space. These two types of cells are clearly distinguishable as "digitally" separated states, so that they can be identified computationally[3]. Hence, this phenomenon is regarded

[2]Here, the results are described only briefly. More detailed accounts are given in prior publications (Furusawa and Kaneko 1998), where we adopted a different biochemical network.

[3]In practice, each cell type is distinguished by computing the average of concentrations $c^{(m)}(t)$ over a certain period to

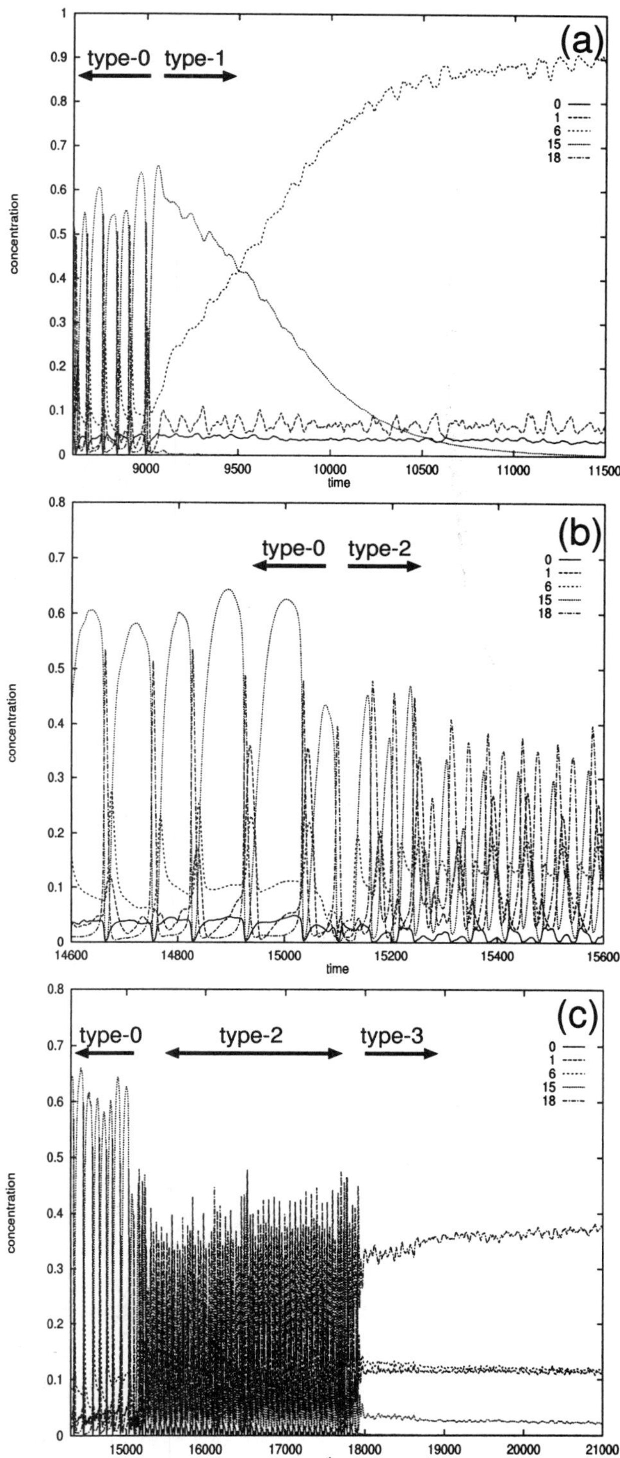

Figure 2: Time series of $c^{(m)}(t)$, overlaid for the 5 chemicals (as given in Fig. 1) in a cell. (a)-(c) represent the course of differentiation to type-1,2, or type-3 cells respectively. The differentiation to type-3 always occurs starting from type-2 cells. Note the difference in scale of the x-axes.

as differentiation. Here, the type-0 cells can potentially differentiate to either "1" or "2", while some of the type-0 cells remain the same type after division.

As the cell number further increases, some type-2 cells further differentiate to another distinct cell type, which is called type-3 here (Fig. 2(c)). At this stage, hierarchical differentiation occurs. The type-2 cells also can potentially differentiate back to type-0 cell. Thus, type-2 cells have three choices at division: to replicate, and to differentiate to a type-0 or type-3 cell. All in all, four distinct cell types coexist in this system. In addition, there is a limitation on the number of cells to allow for the diversity in cell types. When the number of cells exceeds this limit, all cells turn into type-1 or type-3 cells, where the chemical dynamics is described by fixed points.

Note that this differentiation is not induced directly by the tiny differences introduced at the division. The switch from one cell-type to another does not occur precisely at cell division, but occurs later through the interaction among the cells. This phenomenon is caused by an instability in the full dynamical system consisting out of all the cells and the medium. Thus, tiny differences between two daughter cells are amplified to a macroscopic level through the interaction. Only when the instability exceeds a threshold, does differentiation occur. Then, the emergence of another cell type stabilizes the dynamics of each cell again. The cell differentiation process in our model is due to the amplification of tiny differences by orbital instability (transient chaos), while the coexistence of different cell types stabilizes the system.

Emergence of rules for differentiation and global stability

The switch from type to type by differentiation follows specific rules. These rules originate in a constraint on the transient dynamics between attractor states corresponding to each cell type. In Fig. 4, we show an automaton-like representation of these rules. As mentioned earlier, cell-type "0" can undergo three transitions: to reproduce itself, and to differentiate to types "1" or "2". A cell of type-2 also has three possibilities. Cell-types "1" and "3" replicate without any further differentiation.

When there are multiple choices of differentiation processes (as in "0" $\rightarrow$ "0", "1", "2", "3"), the probability to choose a particular path is neither fixed nor random, but is governed by the distribution of coexisting cell types in the system.

Information about the distribution of cell types in the cell society is embedded in each internal dynamics.

obtain the average position of each orbit. With this average, temporal fluctuations from oscillatory dynamics are smeared, and the average positions form clusters clearly separated in phase space, which correspond to the cell types. See Furusawa and Kaneko (1998) for details.

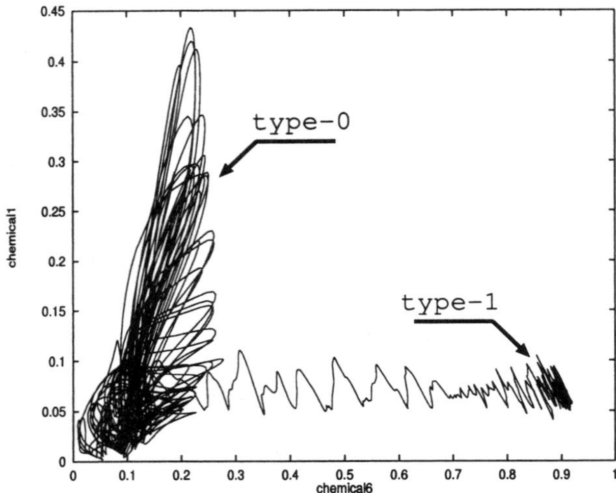

Figure 3: Orbit of internal chemical dynamics in phase space. The orbit of chemical concentrations at a transient process from type-0 to type-1 cells is plotted in the projected space $(c^{(6)}(t), c^{(0)}(t))$. Each cell type is clearly distinguishable in phase space.

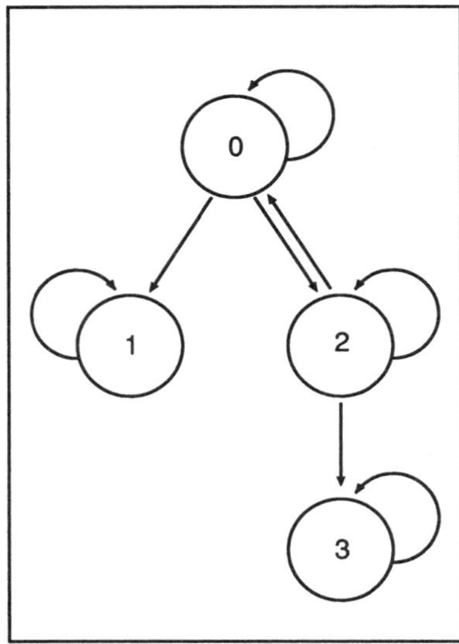

Figure 4: Automaton-like representation of the rules of differentiation. The path back to the own node represents the reproduction of type, while the paths to other nodes represent the potential of differentiation to the corresponding cell type.

Here, each attracting state of internal dynamics is gradually modified by a changing distribution of the states of other cells. This modulation of internal dynamics is much smaller than the differences between different cell types, but it is found that this modulation controls the rate at which differentiation to those cell types occurs. On the other hand, differentiations change the distribution of cell types, whose information is embedded again into the intra-cellular dynamics (Furusawa and Kaneko 1998).

Simulation Results with Spatial Information

Here, we present results of simulations including the motion of cells and diffusive chemicals on a 2-dimensional grid. The reaction matrix and the parameters of internal dynamics are the same as those in the previous section, while the parameters related to the dynamics on the surrounding medium are tuned so that the same set of cell types are obtained with almost identical reaction dynamics and rules for differentiation. For cell types, the same nomenclature is adopted as in the previous section.

Spatial pattern of differentiated cells

In this subsection, we assume that all cells adhere to each other with the same strength, irrespective of their type, when their distance is within a given threshold.

The first cell, initially placed in the medium, shows type-0 dynamics and divides into two almost identical daughter cells, in the manner described in the previous section. These two daughter cells then make a new connection and adhere. With further divisions, a cluster of type-0 cells is formed (Fig. 5(a)).

When the size of the cell cluster exceeds a threshold value, some cells located at the inside of the cluster start to differentiate to type-1 and type-2 cells (Fig. 5(b)). As the cell number further increases, type-2 cells at the inside differentiate to type-3 cells, to form the inner core of the cluster shown in Fig. 5(c). At this stage, a ring pattern consisting of three layers is formed. The ring of type-2 cells lies between peripheral cells with type-0 dynamics and an inner core consisting of type-1 and 3 cells. Positional information giving rise to such a spatial pattern naturally appears through competition for nutrients, without any sophisticated programs implemented in advance. Note that the pattern formation originates from temporal differentiation. It is not a diffusion-induced pattern like Turing's mechanism.

At this stage, the growth of cell clusters is only due to divisions of peripheral type-0 cells. The cell division of type-1 or 3 cells located at the inner core has stopped, due to their slower growth speed and the limited nutrients therein. As the size of the cell cluster increases, the size of the inner core also increases through differentiations from type-0 to type-1 or 3 cells. Finally, the growth of the inner core by differentiation overcomes the growth by divisions. At this stage, the ring structure is broken and all cells differentiate to type-1 or 3 cells. The growth of cell clusters almost stops and the internal dynamics of all cells fall into fixed points.

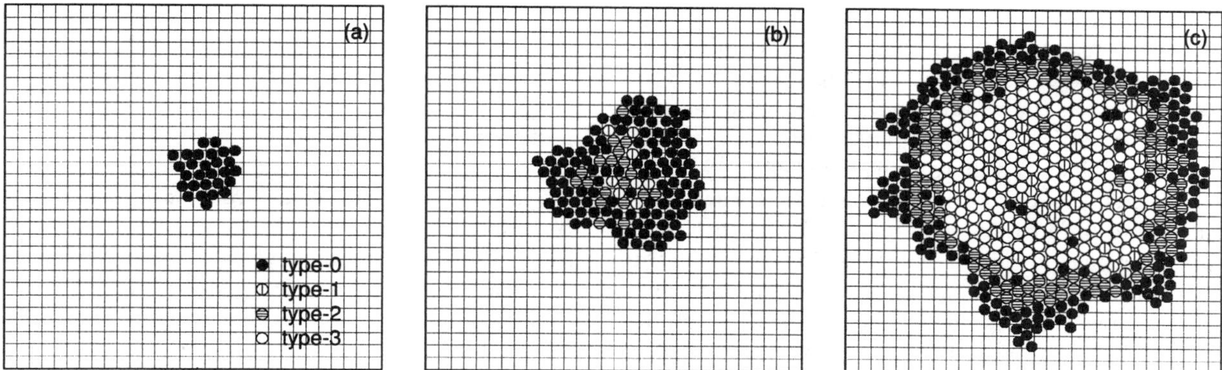

Figure 5: Development of cell cluster on a 2-dimensional grid. Each mark corresponds to a particular cell-type determined by differing internal dynamics. The grid indicates the unit of discretization on the diffusive chemicals $C^{(\ell)}(x, y, t)$.

Regeneration of damaged structure

A biological system often has robustness against some perturbations, such as for example the processes in regulative egg. Such robustness is difficult to realize only by successive execution of pre-programmed 'commands' on DNA. The mechanism for robustness must include the interplay between intra-cellular dynamics and interactions among cells. As an example of such robustness, we discuss the regeneration of a damaged cell cluster, which is a natural consequence of our dynamic differentiation process.

When a cluster develops into the stage with ring pattern as Fig. 5(c), we remove a quarter of the cells from this cluster externally (see Fig. 6(a)), and see what happens later with our model dynamics. After this operation, the division of peripheral cells at the damaged part is enhanced because they receive more nutrition than other cells. Besides this increase, cells also differentiate towards the original pattern, and the damaged part is gradually recovered (Fig. 6(b)).

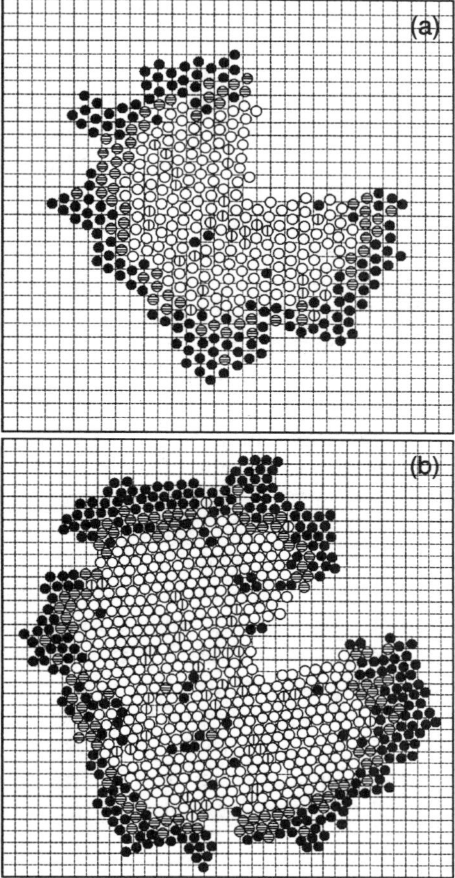

Figure 6: Regeneration of a cell cluster. (a): A fourth of the cell cluster is purposefully removed during the developmental process. (b): The growth in the damaged part is enhanced, and this part is gradually recovered. Note that the layer of peripheral cells at the damaged part becomes thicker.

Emergence of multicellularity

In this section, we change the condition of adhesion between the cells, to see continuous growth in our cell society. As is mentioned, the ring pattern with three layers is formed when all cell types can connect to each other. The growth, however, stops at a certain stage, and new cell clusters are not formed. Thus, such a cellular system cannot be sustained for long. If a change in the adhesion properties allows for the continuous growth and formation of a new generation of cell clusters, such cellular systems will come to dominate.

To study this problem we introduce a dependence of the adhesion force on cell types. Since the force of adhesion should depend on the membrane proteins on the cell surface, it is natural to include dependence of adhesion on the relative internal states of two adjacent cells.

As a simple example, we assume that no connection is allowed between a type-2 cell and a type-3 cell, while the connections for all other combinations are preserved. This restriction on the connection implies that the second layer of type-2 cells and the inner core in Fig. 5(c) lose their capability to adhere to each other.

We have made several simulations with these adhesion rules, and found that cell clusters divide into multiple parts during development. The first stage of the developmental process is unchanged from the previous example. A cluster of type-0 cells grows through cell divisions, and type-1 and type-2 cells appear at the inside of this cluster by differentiations until the inner core is formed as a result of further differentiations. When the growth of the inner core that consists mainly of type-3 cells reaches the edge of the cell cluster, however, a small cluster of cells, or a solitary cell, is released from the periphery of the mother cluster, as shown in Fig. 7(c). This figure depicts the process which gives rise to the fourth generation from the third generation of our multicellular organism. As will be shown, the formation of the second generation proceeds in the same way. The peripheral layer of type-0 and type-2 cells is cut off by the growth of the inner core, and the type-2 and type-3 cells at the contact surface of these layers do not adhere any more by our model assumption.

The released small clusters move away by the force of random fluctuations. They encounter a new environment with rich chemical substances, and start to divide actively. The increase in cell number in these clusters makes their random motion slower, because the fluctuation force is added to each cell independently, and thus tend to cancel out when the cell number is larger. In the new clusters, development proceeds as in their mother-cluster: The cells at the inside of a type-0 cluster differentiate to type-1 and type-2 cells, while the type-3 core is formed through further differentiations, until their peripheral cells are released again (Fig. 7(c)). Hence a life-cycle of multicellular replicating units is observed, which emerges without explicit implementation. Thus, we observe the emergence of a replicating unit on a higher hierarchical level than individual cell replication. Note that this emergence of replicating cell societies is a natural consequence of a system with internal cellular dynamics with nonlinear oscillation, cell–cell interaction through media, and cell-type dependent adhesion.

Death of multicellular organism

After the release of peripheral cells, the remnant core with type-1 and type-3 cells stops cell divisions after intra-cellular chemical oscillations cease (Fig. 7(b)). This determines the lifetime of the replicating multicellular unit, given by its cell configurations and the deficiency of nutrition. This fact provides an interesting point of view with respect to the death of multicellular organism. As is well known, the death of a multicellular organism is not identical with the death of cells in the organism, but rather coincides with the death of the organism as a 'system'. For example, cells in a dead body often survive for a while. Thus, the emergence of multicellularity must be accompanied with such a 'halting' state of the system. This halting state limits the size and the lifetime of an organism, which is required to complete a life-cycle and to give rise to a new generation. Indeed it is expected that when the size reaches a critical value, such a halting state is brought about by the lack of nutrition, at the first stage of multicellularity, where no special organ for transportation of nutrition is developed yet. In fact, our results show that there is a halting state in a cell cluster when it reaches a size where even cells at the boundary of the cluster lose their activity and stop reproducing.

At the first stage of multicellularity in evolution, two daughter cells fail to separate after division, and a cluster of identical cell types is formed first. To survive as a unit, differentiation of cells has to occur, and subsequently the multicellular cluster needs to release their active cells before the system falls into the halting state. Hence, germ cell segregation and a closed life-cycle is expected to emerge simultaneously with a multicellular organism, as our simulation have demonstrated.

Summary and Discussion

In the present paper, we have studied a dynamical model to show that a prototype of cell differentiation occurs as a result of internal dynamics, interaction, and division. We have made several simulations choosing several chemical networks, with a different number of chemical species, and were able to observe the same scenario for cell differentiation. With the same parameters as used in the previous example, approximately 40% of randomly chosen chemical networks show oscillatory behavior in our system, while others fall into fixed points. Furthermore, approximately 20% of these oscillatory dynamics are destabilized through cell divisions, where some of the cells differentiate following specific rules such as those shown in Fig. 4.

Let us summarize the consequences of our simulations. First, cells differentiate, caused by a dynamical instability due to cell–cell interactions when the cell number exceeds a threshold value. The initial state is destabilized for some cells, and changes into another state. Several discrete cell states appear, whose coexistence restabilizes the overall cellular dynamics. The differentiated states are transmitted to the daughter cells or switch to a different state, obeying a set of hierarchical rules (depicted in Fig. 4) which are not pre-programmed but rather emerge from the cell–cell interactions. In addition, the rate of differentiation is modulated by the distribution of different cell types. Information about this distribution is embedded into the dynamics of each cell as a slight (ana-

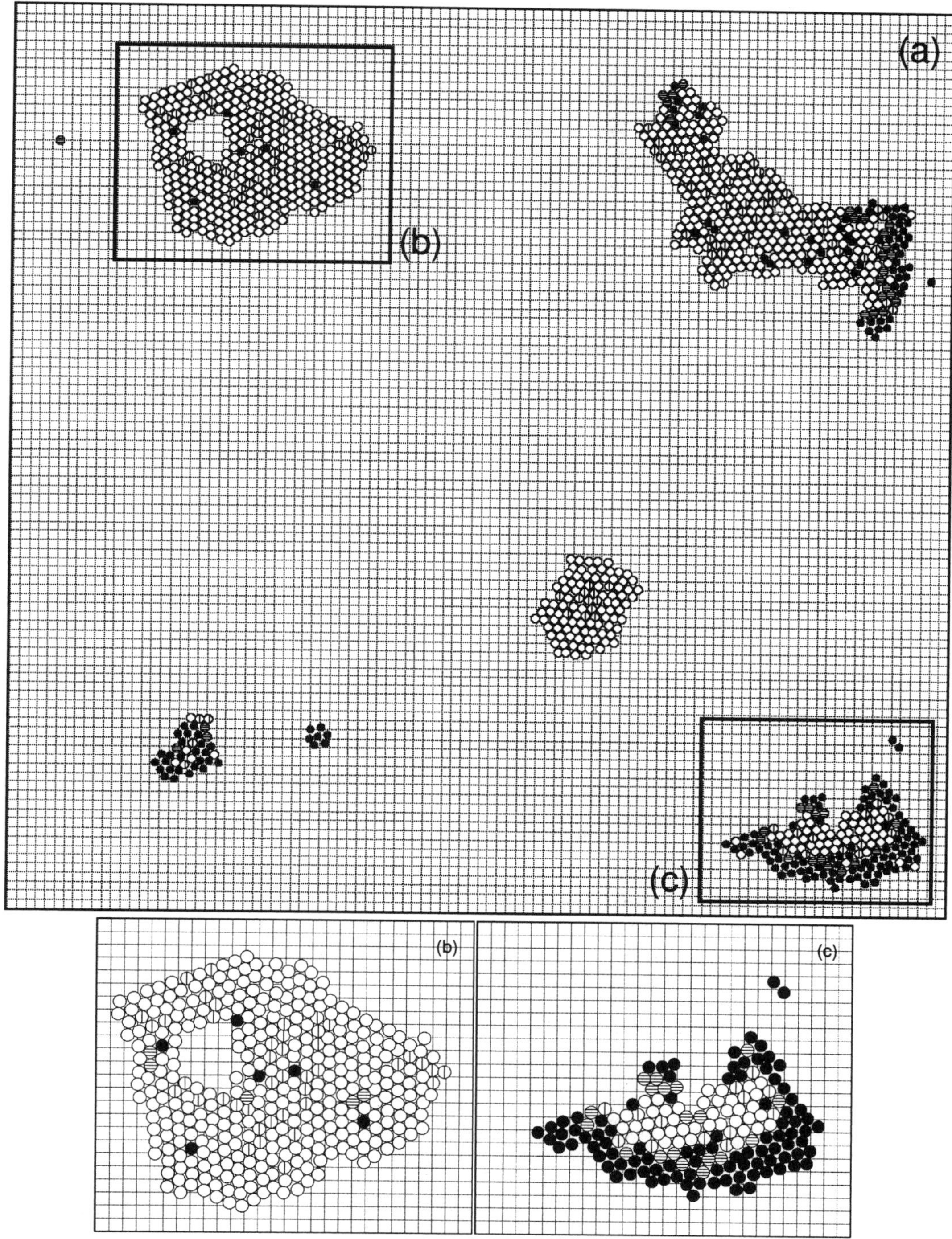

Figure 7: Emergence of a life-cycle in multicellular organism. (a) gives a part of snapshot pattern of our model, while each of Fig.(b) and (c) is an expansion of the corresponding area in Fig.(a). The cluster in (b) has already fallen into a halting state, where the oscillation and the growth of almost all cells have stopped. The cluster in (c) is the second-next generation from the cluster in (b). It is just releasing its peripheral cells (the two type-0 cells at the upper part of (c)), which will lead to the next generation.

log) modulation of the intra-cellular dynamics for each type.

During simulations on a 2-dimensional grid with diffusive chemicals, we have found ring patterns of differentiated cells such as shown in Fig. 5(c). This positional information is not imposed on the system from the outside, but is sustained by cell–cell interactions through competition for nutrients. Each cell can detect information about this external "field" by modulating its own internal dynamics. This modulation controls the rate of transitions among cellular states, and the transitions in turn change the external field. This feedback maintains the spatiotemporal order of the cell society, and also provides the robustness of the multicellular system. As can be seen in Fig. 6(b), a damaged structure is recovered both by an increase in cell divisions at the damaged part, and cell differentiations to recover the original pattern. It should be noted that this overall stability is an intrinsic feature of our dynamic differentiation process. No external regulation mechanisms are required, rather, this robustness is a feature of the differentiation mechanism itself.

Our results also suggest a novel view of the emergence of multicellularity. With an adequate cell–cell adhesion force, active peripheral cells are released when the process of development reaches a particular stage through divisions and differentiations. These released cells start to develop in the same manner as their mother cluster, and release their peripheral cells again. On the other hand, a cluster which has lost the peripheral cells stops its growth, and all the intra-cellular dynamics fall into fixed points. At the level of the cluster, this inactive state can be regarded as death of the multicellular system. Thus, a life-cycle emerges for these multicellular organisms, alternating replication and death of cell clusters. We would like to stress again that this ordered cell society with a closed life-cycle appears not from a particular implementation of internal reaction dynamics, but from the interplay between inter- and intra- cell dynamics.

Still, one might ask in which way multicellularity carries an advantage in natural selection. At this stage, this question is unimportant for our scenario of the emergence of multicellularity. Our results show that when the number of cells increases and the interactions among cells become tight, the diversity of cell types naturally emerges. The tight coupling between cells can easily appear, for example, when the cell separation after division fails due to an adhesive force. Then, it is found that only cell clusters that have a diversity of cell types and adequate cell-type dependent adhesion forces can avoid death as a cluster, and keep on growing to give rise to new generations. Thus, the emergence of multicellularity appears to be a natural consequence of an evolutionary process with never ending reproduction.

It is often believed that the rules which determine when, where, and what type of cells appear in a multicellular organism, should be precisely specified beforehand as a successive switching of genes in the DNA, depending on external signals. Our scenario is not necessarily inconsistent with such a switching mechanism, since our biochemical dynamics and the emergent regulation mechanisms can include those associated with DNA. However, the essential point of this theory is not the formation of rules consistent with such an explanation. Note that a rule-based explanation cannot answer important questions in the development process such as: Why did a particular development process evolve? Why is such a process robust with respect to thermodynamic fluctuations at a molecular level? Why does a multicellular organism have cell differentiation and death? The mechanism proposed here giving rise to ordered cell societies is able to answer such questions simultaneously.

Acknowledgments

The authors are grateful to T. Yomo for stimulating discussions. The work is partially supported by Grant-in-Aids for Scientific Research from the Ministry of Education, Science, and Culture of Japan.

References

Eggenberger, P. 1997. *In Fourth European Conference on Artificial Life*, edited by P. Husbands and I. Harvey. Cambridge, MA: MIT Press, pp. 205-213.

Eigen, M. and P. Schuster. 1979. *The Hypercycle.* Berlin: Springer-Verlag.

Fleischer, K. and A. H. Barr. 1994. In *Artificial Life III*, edited by C. G. Langton. Redwood City: Addison-Wesley, pp. 389-416.

Furusawa and Kaneko. 1998. *Bull. Math. Biol.* in press.

Goldbeter, A. 1996. *Biochemical oscillations and cellular rhythms.* New York: Cambridge University Press.

Goodwin, B. 1963. *Temporal Organization in Cells.* London: Academic Press.

Hess, B. and A. Boiteux. 1971. *Ann. Rev. Biochem.* 40: 237.

Kaneko, K. 1990. *Physica* D 41: 137.

Kaneko, K. 1992. *Physica* D 55: 368.

Kaneko, K. and T. Yomo. 1994. *Physica* D 75: 89–102.

Kaneko, K. and T. Yomo. 1997. *Bull. Math. Biol.* 59: 139.

Maynard-Smith, J. and E. Szathmary. 1995. *The Major Transitions in Evolution.* Oxford: W. H. Freeman.

Mjolsness, E., D. H. Sharp, and J. Reinitz. 1991. *J. Theor. Biol.* 152: 429.

Tyson, J.J., B. Novak, G. M. Odell, K. Chen, and C. D. Thron. 1996. *Trends in Biochem. Sci.* 21: 89–96.

Price-War Dynamics in a Free-Market Economy of Software Agents

Jeffrey O. Kephart, James E. Hanson and Jakka Sairamesh
IBM Thomas J. Watson Research Center
P.O. Box 704, Yorktown Heights, NY 10598

Abstract

One scenario of the future of computation populates the Internet with vast numbers of software agents providing, trading, and using a rich variety of information goods and services in an open, free-market economy. An essential task in such an economy is the retailing or *brokering* of information: gathering it from the right producers and distributing it to the right consumers. This paper investigates one crucial aspect of brokers' dynamical behavior, their price-setting mechanisms, in the context of a simple information filtering economy.

We consider only the simplest cases in which a broker sets its price and product parameters based solely on the system's current state, without explicit prediction of the future. Analytical and numerical results show that the system's dynamical behavior in such "myopic" cases is generically an unending cycle of disastrous competitive "wars" in price/product space. These in turn are directly attributable to the existence of multiple peaks in the brokers' profitability landscapes, a feature whose generality is likely to extend far beyond our model.

Introduction

We envisage the evolution of the Internet into a free-market *information economy* in which billions of software agents exchange a rich variety of information goods and services with humans and amongst themselves (Chavez & Maes 1996; Eriksson, Finne, & Janson 1996; Tsvetovatyy *et al.* 1997; White 1996). This will inevitably occur as agents assume an ever more pervasive and responsible role in electronic commerce. Even more fundamentally, the proven ability of a free-market economy to adjudicate and satisfy the conflicting needs of billions of *human* agents recommends it as a decentralized organizational principle for billions of *software* agents as well (Miller & Drexler 1988). However, given that software agents can make decisions several orders of magnitude faster than humans, and are vastly less flexible and complex, it is quite conceivable that an agent economy would behave in ways that are entirely unfamiliar. It is thus legitimate to ask whether a free-market information economy is inherently capable of facilitating the interactions of billions of software agents; and if so, what are the minimal requirements on the infrastructure of such an economy and on the agents that populate it.

An unequivocal answer cannot be found in the literature. Previous research suggests that large systems of interacting, self-motivated software agents can be susceptible to the emergence of wild, unpredictable, disastrous collective behavior (Kephart, Hogg, & Huberman 1989; 1990). On the other hand, a large body of work on market mechanisms in distributed multi-agent environments suggests that efficient resource allocation or other desirable global properties may emerge from the collective interactions of individual agents (Kurose, Schwartz, & Yemini 1985; Huberman 1988; Clearwater 1995).

Much of the latter work falls under the rubric of "market-based control", in which economic transactions are used to bring about some predefined, desired end (Birmingham *et al.* 1996; Wellman 1993; Stonebraker & others 1994; Clearwater 1995). Agents may be designed to cooperate (Huberman, Lokose, & Hogg 1996) or to compete (Hogg & Huberman 1991), but so long as the aggregate evolves toward a globally defined optimum, the system as a whole is deemed successful. But in an open system like the Web, there is no global purpose being served by the collective of agents; in a sense, *there is no collective.* Agents' goals may be harmonious, conflicting, or unrelated, as the case may be (Rosenschein & Zlotkin 1994). One cannot prescribe a universal medium of exchange, a universal ontology of goods and services, or a universal set of agent types or algorithms. Rather, these must *emerge* as the system evolves.

All of this motivates a general, wide-ranging study of economically motivated autonomous agents. In this paper, we focus on one uniquely "economic" property, the price of information, and investigate the consequences of different price-setting algorithms in a simple model of a multi-agent news filtering economy inspired by information dissemination services that can be found on the Internet today. In Section 2, we describe the details of the model. Section 3 delineates the system's state space and presents a baseline analysis of its dynamical behavior under an idealized price-setting algorithm, in the case of direct competition between two brokers offering a single type of information good. Section 4 presents numerical results for a more complex situation in which three brokers may choose freely among three types of information good. We close by discussing the generality of our results and indicating some future directions.

Model of a News Filtering Economy

Our model of an information filtering economy consists of a *source* agent that publishes news articles, C *consumer* agents that want to buy articles they are interested in, B *broker* agents that buy selected articles from the source and resell them to consumers, and a *market infrastructure* that provides communication and computation services to all agents. Figure 1 illustrates part of the model system. The ellipse at the top represents the source agent, brokers are in the middle, and consumers are at the bottom. Each agent's internal parameters (defined below) appear inside its ellipse. The infrastructure is represented by the rectangle on the left. Solid lines represent the propagation of a sample article through broker 1. Broken lines indicate payment, and are labeled with symbols (explained below) for the amount paid.

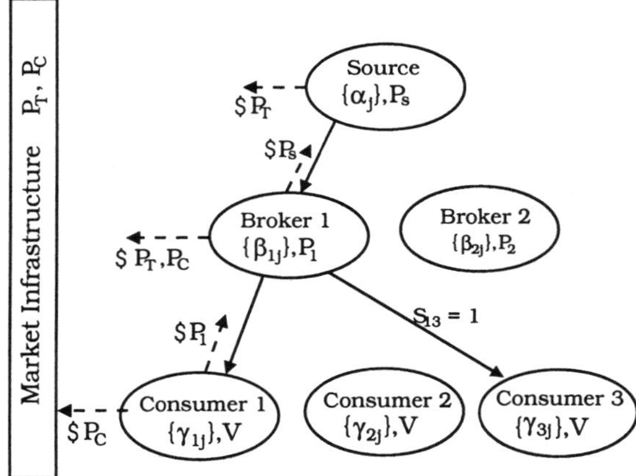

Figure 1: Part of an idealized news filtering economy. Only a subset of agents is shown. See text for interpretation of symbols.

The source agent publishes one article at each time step t, and waits until that article has propagated through the system before publishing the next. It classifies articles according to its own internal categorization scheme, assigning each a *category index* j. The nature of the categories, and the number J of them, do not change. We represent this (hidden) classification scheme by a random process in which an article is assigned category j with fixed probability α_j. The set of all α_j is the source's *category prevalence* vector α. Each article is labeled with its category index and offered for sale to all brokers at a fixed price P_S. For each article sold to each broker, the source pays a fixed *transport cost* P_T.

Upon receiving an offer, each broker b decides whether or not to buy the article using its own evaluation method to select which categories it is "interested" in. The broker's evaluation method is approximated by an *interest vector* β_b, where β_{bj} represents the probability for b to purchase an article labeled with category j. Analysis (Kephart *et al.* 1998) shows that it is in broker b's best interest to set the β_{bj} individually to either 0 or 1.

When broker b purchases an article, it immediately sends it to a set of *subscribing* consumers, paying tranportation cost P_T for each. Subscribers may examine the article, but must pay the broker P_b if they want the right to use ("consume") it. The broker's internal parameters β_b and P_b are under its direct control.

Subscriptions are represented by a *subscription matrix* S, where $S_{bc} = 1$ if consumer c subscribes to broker b, and $S_{bc} = 0$ if not. Subscriptions are maintained only with the consent of both parties and may be cancelled by either. For example, a broker b might reject c if the cost of sending articles exceeds the expected payment from c, or c might reject b if the cost of sifting through lots of junk outweighs the benefit of receiving the rare interesting article. The bilateral nature of the agreement is represented by setting $S_{bc} = \sigma_{bc}^{(b)}\sigma_{bc}^{(c)}$, where $\sigma_{bc}^{(b)} = 1$ if broker b wants consumer c as a subscriber and 0 if not; analogously, $\sigma_{bc}^{(c)}$ represents consumer c's wishes.

Each consumer waits for articles to arrive from the brokers it subscribes to. If a consumer receives at least one copy of an article, it pays the computation cost P_C to evaluate whether it is *interested* in the article, then decides whether (and from whom) to buy it. Like the brokers, the consumers' evaluation function is approximated by a stochastic process parametrized by an interest vector γ_c: consumer c will be interested in an article labeled with category j with fixed probability γ_{cj}. If a consumer is interested in an article, it then selects from the set of brokers it subscribes to the one broker b^* with the most attractive offer; we shall assume this to be the cheapest one. The consumer then decides whether its interest justifies paying P_{b^*} for that article. For simplicity, we model this decision process as follows: each consumer assigns a universal *anticipated value* V to each article it is interested in. If $V > P_{b^*}$, it purchases the usage rights; otherwise it discards the article unused.

Each broker's or consumer's decision-making process may be expressed as an attempt to optimize its *utility function*, defined as the amount of net "value" or "utility" gained by making that particular decision. In the system described here, the expected utility per article for each broker and consumer may be explicitly formulated from the system variables. For consumers, the anticipated value V provides the fundamental benchmark for measuring utility. For brokers, the appropriate measure of utility is *profit*, defined in the usual way as revenue less expenses. General expressions for consumer utility and broker profit may be found in (Kephart *et al.* 1998).

Profit Landscapes; A Simple Price War

We define the *state* of the system at time t, $\mathcal{Z}(t)$, as the collection of broker prices p_b, broker interest vectors β_{bj}, and subscription matrix elements S_{bc} at time t. Our goal is to understand the evolution of $\mathcal{Z}(t)$, given

1. an initial configuration $\mathcal{Z}(0)$,
2. the values of the various extrinsic (possibly time-varying) variables, comprising the category prevalences α^j, the costs P_S, P_T, and P_C, the consumer value V, and the consumer interest vectors γ_c, and
3. a specification of the utility-maximization algorithms used by each agent to dynamically change its own parameters, including
   (a) the state information accessible to the agent (and its accuracy and timeliness), and
   (b) the times or conditions when the agent updates its own state.

Even in systems of modest size (e.g., $J = 10$ categories, $B = 10$ brokers, $C = 1000$ consumers), the state space can be quite large: its dimension is $(J + 1 + C)B$, or more than 10^4 for the numbers just quoted. This is mainly due to the $C \times B$ elements of the subscription matrix S. However, it is possible to reduce the dimensionality by factoring out the degrees of freedom associated with S. This is done by assuming that each broker and consumer instantly adapts to changes in its environment by selecting *its* optimal set of subscribers or subscriptions. Recall, however, that both broker and consumer must consent to a subscription. The conflicting opinions on what constitutes "optimal" may be resolved via a game-theoretic analysis. Thus the subscription matrix becomes a function of the remaining system variables β_{bj} and p_b. Note that, by factoring out the subscription matrix, we have in effect factored out the consumer population, so that the "reduced" system's state is expressed entirely in terms of the brokers' states. We will denote the reduced state space by $\mathcal{Y}$, and the subspace associated with broker b by $\mathcal{Y}_b$. Thus $\mathcal{Y} = \mathcal{Y}_1 \times \mathcal{Y}_2 \times \ldots \times \mathcal{Y}_B$, where $\mathcal{Y}_b$ is the space of possible values of the $(J + 1)$ broker variables $y_b \equiv \{p_b, \beta_{bj}\}$.

In the reduced system, the broker utility function $W_b(\mathcal{Y})$ defines broker b's *profit landscape*, and the system dynamics is a *co-evolutionary* process in which each broker b attempts to maximize its profit $W_b(\mathcal{Y})$ by setting the values of y_b, *given* the values of y_i for all the other brokers i.

The remainder of this section is devoted to an analysis of the simplest possible multi-broker system, in which two brokers compete in a large consumer market in which there is only one type of information good. Thus $B = 2$, $J = 1$, and $C \to \infty$. For the moment, assume that broker 1 charges less than broker 2 for the good ($p_1 < p_2$). In this case, we can apply the definition of the system given in the last section to get an expected utility per article for consumer c of

$$\begin{aligned} U_c &= \beta_1 S_{1c}\left[(V - P_1)\gamma_c - P_C\right] + \\ &\quad \beta_2 S_{2c}(1 - \beta_1 S_{1c})\left[(V - P_2)\gamma_c - P_C\right] \end{aligned} \tag{1}$$

The expected profit per article for the brokers is

$$\begin{aligned} W_1 &= \beta_1 \left(\sum_{c=1}^{C} S_{1c}\left[p_1\gamma_c - P_T\right] - P_S \right) \\ W_2 &= \beta_2 \left(\sum_{c=1}^{C} S_{2c}\left[p_2\gamma_c(1 - \beta_1 S_{1c}) - P_T\right] - P_S \right) \end{aligned} \tag{2}$$

From equation 2, it is readily seen that, independent of any other choices it may make, broker i can maximize its expected profit by setting its interest level β_i equal to 1 if the quantity in parentheses is positive, and 0 otherwise. In other words, a self-interested broker will never have a negative expected profit, because it always has the option of pulling out of the market by setting its interest level to 0. In all that follows, we shall assume that $\beta_1 = \beta_2 = 1$, and if the resulting expected profit per article for broker i is negative we shall override this, setting $\beta_i = W_i = 0$. This reduces the dimensionality of the landscape, nominally 4, to 2.

Having established the optimal setting of interest levels by the brokers, now consider the subscription matrix elements $S_{1c} = \sigma_{1c}^{(b)}\sigma_{1c}^{(c)}$ and $S_{2c} = \sigma_{2c}^{(b)}\sigma_{2c}^{(c)}$. First, note that each term in the expression for broker 1's expected utility in Eq. 2 can be maximized independently by setting $\sigma_{1c}^{(b)} = \Theta(\gamma_c - P_T/p_1)$, where Θ represents the step function: $\Theta(x) = 1$ for $x > 0$, and 0 otherwise. In other words, it is only worthwhile to send articles to consumer c if c's interest level γ_c is sufficiently high that c's expected payment for interesting articles exceeds the cost of sending articles to c. Broker 2 is in a different situation. If c is already subscribed to broker 1, it will never purchase articles from broker 2 because it charges a higher price for the same good. Under such circumstances, broker 2 should not attempt to send articles to c because it will be paying for article transport with no hope of reimbursement. However, if c is not subscribed to broker 1, then broker 2 should set $\sigma_{2c}^{(b)} = \Theta(\gamma_c - P_T/p_2)$ in order to maximize each term of the sum over consumers in the expression for W_2. Putting all of this together, we have

$$\begin{aligned} \sigma_{1c}^{(b)} &= \Theta(\gamma_c - P_T/p_1) \\ \sigma_{2c}^{(b)} &= \Theta(\gamma_c - P_T/p_2)\,(1 - S_{1c}) \end{aligned} \tag{3}$$

Now consider the situation from the consumer's perspective, using Eq. 1. The consumer c will choose the optimal setting of $(\sigma_{1c}^{(c)}, \sigma_{2c}^{(c)})$ from among the four possible choices: (0,0), (0,1), (1,0) and (1,1).

First, suppose that $\sigma_{1c}^{(b)} = 1$. If c chooses to set $\sigma_{1c}^{(c)} = 1$, then $S_{1c} = 1$ and therefore $S_{2c} = 0$, so that $U_c = (V - p_1)\gamma_c - P_C$. Alternatively, if c chooses to set $\sigma_{1c}^{(c)} = 0$, then $S_{1c} = 0$, and so $U_c = S_{2c}\left[(V - p_2)\gamma_c - P_C\right]$. Which is the better choice? If $(V - p_1)\gamma_c - P_C > 0$, then this quantity always exceeds $S_{2c}\left[(V - p_2)\gamma_c - P_C\right]$ because $p_1 < p_2$. In this case, $\sigma_{1c}^{(c)}$ should be set to 1, and the value of $\sigma_{2c}^{(c)}$ is immaterial because $S_{1c} = 1$ substituted into Eq. 3 shows that $\sigma_{2c}^{(b)} = 0$. However, if $(V - p_1)\gamma_c - P_C < 0$, then $(V - p_2)\gamma_c - P_C < 0$ as well, and both $\sigma_{1c}^{(c)}$ and $\sigma_{2c}^{(c)}$ should be set to zero.

Now consider the other alternative: $\sigma_{1c}^{(b)} = 0$. In this case the value of $\sigma_{1c}^{(c)}$ is immaterial, $S_{1c} = 0$, and $U_c = S_{2c}\left[(V - p_2)\gamma_c - P_C\right]$. The value of $\sigma_{2c}^{(c)}$ matters only if $\sigma_{2c}^{(b)} = 1$, in which case the optimal value for $\sigma_{2c}^{(c)}$ is 1 if $(V - p_2)\gamma_c - P_C > 0$ and 0 otherwise.

Assembling all of the above analysis, we obtain:

$$
\begin{aligned}
S_1(\gamma; p_1) &= \Theta\left(\gamma - \frac{P_T}{p_1}\right)\Theta\left(\gamma - \frac{P_C}{V - p_1}\right) \\
S_2(\gamma; p_1, p_2) &= S_1(\gamma; p_2)\left(1 - S_1(\gamma; p_1)\right)
\end{aligned}
\tag{4}
$$

In the expression for S_1, the step function on the left represents the veto power of the brokers, and the one on the right represents the veto power of the consumers. The expression for S_2 is similar, except that it is automatically zero if the consumer already subscribes to the lower-priced broker.

Having established the subscription matrix elements, and the brokers' interest levels, the only remaining decisions to be considered are the optimal brokers' prices p_1 and p_2. Since the number of consumers $C \to \infty$, we may replace the sums in Eq. 2 with integrals over a consumer population with a distribution of interest levels given by $\Gamma(\gamma)$, with the result:

$$
\begin{aligned}
W_1(p_1) &= C I_1(p_1) - P_S \\
W_2(p_1, p_2) &= C I_2(p_1, p_2) - P_S
\end{aligned}
\tag{5}
$$

where

$$
\begin{aligned}
I_1(p_1) &= \int_0^1 d\gamma\, \Gamma(\gamma)\, (p_1\gamma - P_T)\, S_1(\gamma; p_1) \\
I_2(p_1, p_2) &= \int_0^1 d\gamma\, \Gamma(\gamma)\, (p_2\gamma - P_T)\, S_2(\gamma; p_1, p_2)
\end{aligned}
\tag{6}
$$

Suppose that $\Gamma(\gamma)$ is the uniform distribution, i.e. $\Gamma(\gamma) = 1$ for all values of γ. Then substitution of Eq. 4 into Eq. 6, and some integration by parts and other algebra lead to analytic solutions for the integrals I_1 and I_2. In the interval $P_T \leq p \leq (V - P_C)$,

$$
\begin{aligned}
I_1(p_1) = {} & \\
& \frac{p_1}{2} - P_T + \frac{{P_T}^2}{2p_1} + \\
& \left[\frac{P_C P_T}{(V - p_1)} - \frac{p_1 P_C^2}{2\,(V - p_1)^2} - \frac{{P_T}^2}{2p_1}\right]\Theta(p_1 - \frac{P_T V}{P_C + P_T})
\end{aligned}
\tag{7}
$$

and outside this interval $I_1(p_1) = 0$. (Despite the step function, $I_1(p_1)$ is *not* discontinuous at $p_1 = \frac{P_T V}{P_C + P_T}$.) The solution for I_2 is:

$$
\begin{aligned}
I_2(p_1, p_2) = {} & \\
& \frac{p_2 {P_T}^2}{2{p_1}^2} - \frac{{P_T}^2}{p_1} + \frac{P_T^2}{2p_2} + \\
& \left[\frac{P_C P_T}{(V - p_2)} - \frac{p_2 {P_C}^2}{2\,(V - p_2)^2} - \frac{P_T^2}{2p_2}\right]\Theta(p_2 - \frac{P_T V}{P_C + P_T})
\end{aligned}
\tag{8}
$$

in the region satisfied by the constraints $0 \leq p_1 < p_2 \leq 1$, $p_1 < \frac{P_T V}{(P_T + P_C)}$, and $p_2 < V - \frac{p_1 P_C}{P_T}$. Beyond this region, $I_2(p_1, p_2) = 0$. Again, $I(p_1, p_2)$ contains no real discontinuity, despite the step function.

The restriction $p_1 < p_2$ can be removed by exploiting the symmetry arising from the fact that there is no inherent difference between the two brokers. We obtain the *profit landscapes* for brokers 1 and 2 as a function of the prices p_1 and p_2:

$$
\begin{aligned}
W_1(p_1, p_2) &= C I(p_1, p_2) - P_S \\
W_2(p_1, p_2) &= W_1(p_2, p_1)
\end{aligned}
\tag{9}
$$

where $I(p_1, p_2)$ is given by:

$$
I(p_1, p_2) = I_1(p_1)\Theta(p_2 - p_1) + I_2(p_2, p_1)\Theta(p_1 - p_2) \tag{10}
$$

Each broker's profit landscape describes the dependence of its expected profitability as a function of the price vector (all of the brokers' prices, including its own). For any given price vector, the myriad self-interested decisions of the consumers and brokers about subscriptions and interest levels are taken into account.

The profit landscape W_1 is illustrated for the case $P_C = P_T = 0.3$, $V = 1$ in Fig. 2. Note that there are two distinct humps, the one on the right corresponding to $I_1(p_1)\,\Theta(p_2 - p_1)$ in Eq. 10 and the one on the left corresponding to $I_2(p_1, p_2)\,\Theta(p_1 - p_2)$. The "cheap" hump on the right corresponds to a situation in which broker 1 is cheaper ($p_1 < p_2$). The "expensive" hump on the left corresponds to the case in which broker 1 is more expensive than broker 2, but is still able to find customers. This comes about when broker 2 charges so little that it cannot afford to keep marginal customers (those with low interest levels γ_c) as subscribers. (Recall that a broker pays P_T for each article it sends to each of its subscribers, but receives payment only for those articles a subscriber is interested in.) Broker 1 can make money by serving the marginal customers that were rejected by the lower-priced broker 2.

Suppose that brokers use the profit landscape itself to periodically update their parameters so as to maximize their profitability. Assume further that the updates are asynchronous, and that the entire agent population adjusts its subscription matrix elements in a selfishly optimal way. Such an update strategy is guaranteed to produce the optimal profit in the very short term — up until the moment when the next broker updates *its* parameters. Thus we call such a strategy "myopically optimal", or "myoptimal" for short.

If broker 1 is myoptimal, it could derive from its profit landscape a function $p_1^*(p_2)$ that gives the value of p_1 that maximizes $W_1(p_1, p_2)$ for each possible p_2[1]. Figure 3 shows a contour plot of W_1 on which $p_1^*(p_2)$ is overlaid as a heavy solid line. (As before, $P_C = P_T = 0.3$, $V = 1$.) For $0.3 < p_2 < 0.388709$, $p_1^*(p_2)$ is given by the solution to a cubic equation involving cube roots of square roots of p_2; in this region it looks fairly linear. The "vertical" segment at $p_2 = 0.388709$ is a discontinuity as the optimal price jumps from the I_2 peak to the I_1 peak. In the region $0.388709 < p_2 < 0.589511$, $p_1^* = p_2 - \epsilon$, where ϵ is a price quantum — the minimal amount by which one price can exceed another. For $0.589511 < p_2 < 0.7$, $p_1^* = 0.589511$. This is the value of p_1 that maximizes $I_1(p_1)$, i.e. it is the price that would be established by a monopolist. Any further increase in p_1 would cut consumer demand by too much.

If broker 2 also uses a myoptimal strategy, then by symmetry its price-setting function is identical to that of broker 1 with p_1 and p_2 interchanged. The profit landscape $W_2(p_1, p_2)$ and optimal price $p_2^*(p_1)$ are likewise identical under an interchange of p_1 and p_2.

Now the evolution of both p_1 and p_2 can be obtained simply by alternate application of the two price optimization functions. I.e., first broker 1 sets its price $p_1(t+1) = p_1^*(p_2(t))$, then broker 2 sets its price $p_2(t+2) = p_2^*(p_1(t+1))$, and so forth. The time series may be traced graphically on a plot of both $p_1^*(p_2)$ and $p_2^*(p_1)$ together, as shown in Fig. 4. Assume *any* initial price vector (p_1, p_2), and suppose broker 1 is the first to move. Then the graphical construction starts by holding p_2 constant while moving horizontally to the curve for $p_1^*(p_2)$. Then, p_1 is held constant while moving vertically to the curve $p_2^*(p_1)$. Alternate horizontal moves

[1] Analytically, this curve is composed of solutions to cubic equations involving P_C, P_T, V and the prices.

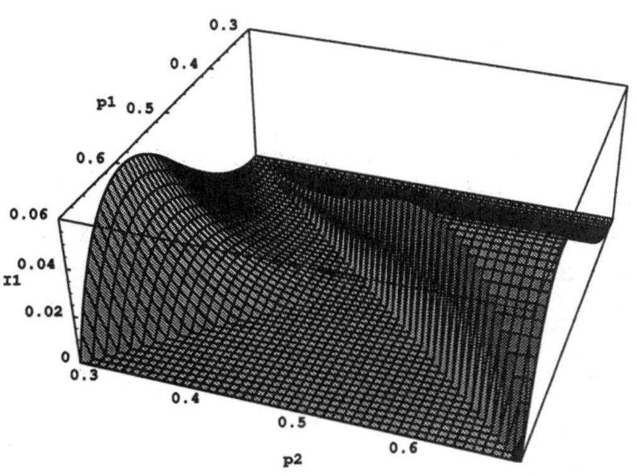

Figure 2: Double-peaked rofit landscape W_1/C for broker 1 when $P_C = P_T = 0.3$, $V = 1$.

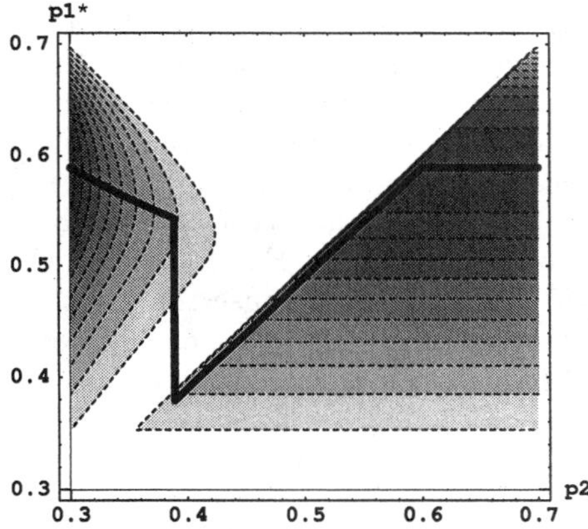

Figure 3: Contour map of profit landscape, with overlaid optimal price function $p_1^*(p_2)$ for $P_T = P_C = 0.3, V = 1$.

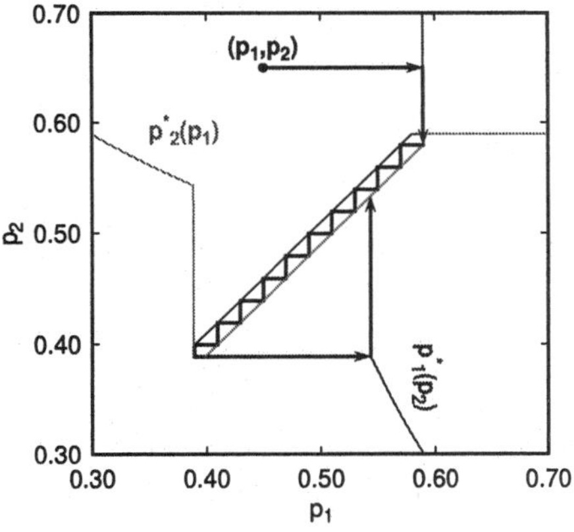

Figure 4: Iterative graphical construction of price-war time series, using functions $p_1^*(p_2)$ and $p_2^*(p_1)$. See text.

to $p_1^*(p_2)$ and vertical moves to $p_2^*(p_1)$ always lead to a price war during which the brokers successively undercut each other, corresponding to zig-zagging between the diagonal segments of the curves. The horizontal or vertical offset between the diagonals, equal to the amount by which a broker's price drops on every other iteration, is 2ϵ. Eventually, the price gets driven down to 0.388709, at which point the other broker (say broker 1) opts out of the price war, switching to the high-priced peak I_2 in its profit landscape. Raising the price to $p_1^*(0.388709) = 0.543376$ breaks the price war, but unfortunately, as Fig. 4 shows, it triggers the immediate start of another one. The brokers are caught in a never-ending (and, as we shall see, disastrous) limit cycle of price wars punctuated by abrupt resets.

Classic models of price wars, including those introduced by Cournot and Bertrand (Tirole 1988), typically have the feature that prices are driven down to a stable value (e.g. the marginal cost in Bertrand's model). However, limit-cycle price wars have been observed previously in a simple model introduced by Edgeworth, in which it assumed that no single firm is able to satisfy the entire aggregate consumer demand (Shubik 1980). On constructing the profit landscape for Edgeworth's model, we find that it has two peaks that are qualitatively similar to those of Figure 2. In our case, the "expensive" hump arises because the low-priced broker may reject some consumers; this can be regarded as a sort of self-induced capacity constraint.

Complex Price Wars

In this section, we shall demonstrate the existence of complex analogs of limit-cycle price wars in systems with more brokers and categories. In this case, exact analysis or computation of the profit landscape $W_b(\mathcal{Y})$ for a given broker b becomes very difficult. For each point y in the $(J+1)B$-dimensional state space $\mathcal{Y}$, a game-theoretic analysis must be performed to compute BC subscription matrix elements S_{bc}. W_b must then be computed from y and the matrix elements using a generalization of Eq. 2 (see (Kephart *et al.* 1998)).

Consider for example what would be involved in computing the landscape for a system with $B = 3$ brokers, $J = 3$ categories, and 10,000 consumers. The reduced state space $\mathcal{Y}$ is 12-dimensional, as compared to the full state space $\mathcal{Z}$, which is 30,012-dimensional. Suppose that the set of allowed prices is quantized, such that it runs from 0 to 1 in increments of 0.002. The optimal interest level in each category is known to be either 0 or 1, so broker 1 can be in any of $2^3 * 501 = 4008$ distinct discrete states, as can brokers 2 and 3. For each of the resulting several billion discrete states in $\mathcal{Y}$, computation of the landscape W_1 would require a game-theoretic computation of $BC = 30,000$ subscription matrix elements — an absolutely monstrous task.

A reasonable alternative to computing the entire landscape is to start the system in some initial configuration, and simulate its evolution as follows. At any given time step t, a broker b is randomly selected, and it attempts to maximize $W_b(t)$ by setting its own parameters to $y_b(t)$, resulting in a new system state in which the parameters of all brokers other than b are equal to what they were at time $t-1$. For example, in the three-broker system, suppose that broker 1 is selected at time t. It will try to choose $y_1(t)$ such that $W_1(y_1(t), y_2(t-1), y_3(t-1))$ is optimized. The myoptimal strategy introduced in the previous section can be implemented as an exhaustive search over all 4008 possibilities at each time step — still a lot of computation, but (just barely) feasible.

Figure 5 shows the resulting price dynamics for the system just described, with 3 myoptimal brokers, 3 goods, and 10,000 consumers. The interest levels γ_{cj} are generated independently for each category j and consumer c from a uniform distribution between 0 and 1. The computational and transport costs are the same as in the example of the previous section: $P_C = P_T = 0.3$, $V = 1$. The set of possible prices is quantized in increments of 0.002, and each broker performs an exhaustive search among the 4008 possible states. If a consumer perceives two brokers to be equally attractive, the broker with the lower index is preferred.

Expressing an individual broker's state b using the notation $y_b = (p_b, \beta_{b1}\beta_{b2}\beta_{b3})$, we can now follow the dynamics, starting from an initial configuration in which each broker is in the state (0.480,111) (i.e. each has price 0.48 and is interested in all three categories). In the simulation run depicted in Fig. 5, broker 3 moves first, and chooses to set its state to (0.560,100). Broker 2 follows, choosing (0.564,010). Broker 1 is selected next. By choosing (0.586,001), broker 1 would make a profit $W_1 = 183.6$. However, the random generation of consumer interests yields a very slight bias in favor of category 1, and it turns out that broker 1 can do even better ($W_1 = 183.8$) by choosing (0.560,100), undercutting broker 3 and triggering a price war over the interest vector (100). Meanwhile, broker 2, in the absence of any other competition for category 2, increases its price to the optimal single-category-monopoly value: (0.584,010). Note that this is very close to the price that optimizes $I_1(p)$ in a system with an infinite number of consumers, as computed by maximizing Eq. 7 in the previous section: $p^* = 0.589511$ (see also Fig. 3).

Now the high price for category 2 increases its attractiveness, and broker 3 immediately gives up its fight over (100) with broker 1, and now undercuts broker 2 with (0.582,010). With brokers 2 and 3 now specializing in category 2, broker 1 finds it most profitable to offer both categories 1 and 3: (0.564,101). Immediately thereafter, all three brokers join in a price war over the 101 configuration, during which the price is ultimately driven

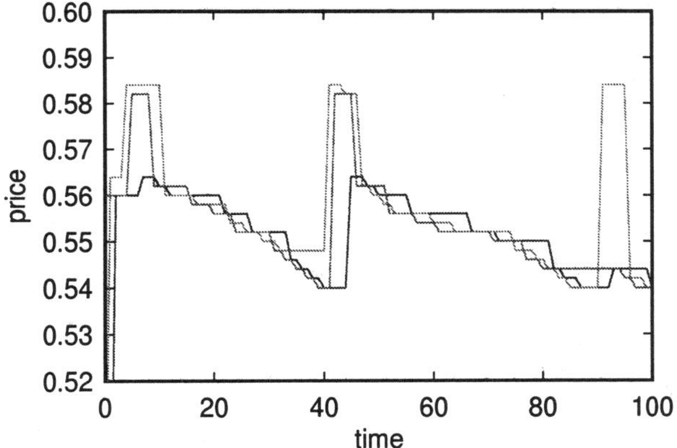

Figure 5: Price war time series for 3 myoptimal brokers, 3 categories, with $P_C = P_T = 0.3$, $V = 1$. See text for other parameters.

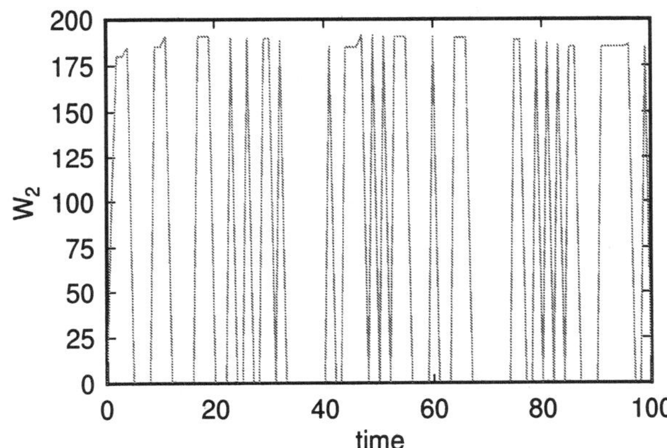

Figure 6: Profit for broker 2 as a function of time; same simulation run as in Fig. 5.

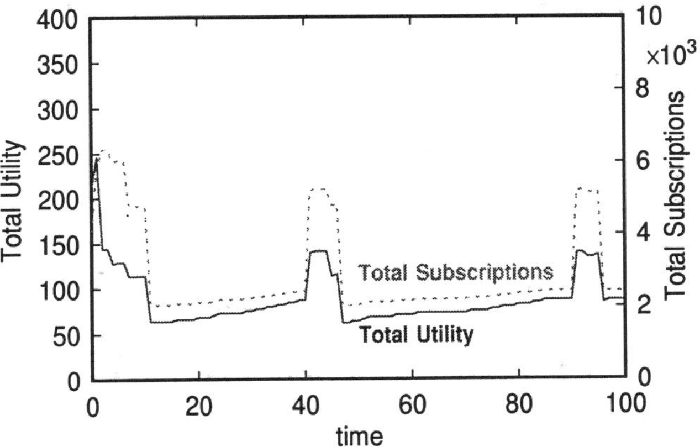

Figure 7: Sum over all consumer's utilities and total number of subscriptions; same simulation run as in Fig. 5.

down to 0.540. Now it becomes most profitable to specialize purely in category 2, with price 0.584 (0.584,010). Immediately, a second broker joins into the battle over category 2, causing the remaining broker at (0.540,101) to raise its price, resulting in (0.564,101), instigating yet another price war over the 101 configuration. Although the stochasticity of the order in which brokers make decisions causes some variation in the exact details, the price war cycle continues in this fashion indefinitely.

In summary, after a short initial transient, the system alternates between two price wars: a short-lived one between two brokers vying for the 010 configuration, and a longer-lived one in which all three brokers vie for the 101 configuration. A broker participating in the 010 price war receives its expected profit when it undercuts its competitor, and zero when it is being undercut. During the long 101 price war, a broker will be undercut two thirds of the time, and will thus receive just one third of what it expects. This is illustrated in Fig. 6, which tracks the profit of broker 2 as a function of time.

Price wars are clearly harmful to brokers. In this particular model, they hurt the consumers as well, as illustrated in Fig. 7. During the 010 price war, a single broker is left to offer both categories 1 and 3, which is unsatisfactory to consumers who are highly interested only in one of the two categories. During the long 101 price war, category 2 is completely unavailable to consumers, so the total consumer utility is even lower during this phase than during the 010 price war. Generally, when some or all of the brokers are competing for the same interest vector, a gap is created in the coverage of categories, adversely affecting some consumers.

As the number of brokers and consumers in the system grows, the myoptimal strategy becomes completely impractical because of the tremendous demands it makes upon on exact knowledge of the system state, the strategies used by other agents, and computational power. Consider a second strategy that still assumes full knowledge of the system state, but requires less computational power. Instead of performing an exhaustive search for the optimal state y_b^*, the *random-explorer* strategy randomly selects a few candidate states, computes the expected profit for each using a generalization of Eq. 2, and chooses the candidate that provides the maximal expected profit. The candidates are biased towards incremental changes in the prices, but occasional large random jumps in price and interest vector are permitted.

Figure 8 shows a simulation run for such a system. The consumer population and the intial conditions are identical to those in Fig. 5. Price wars are still in evidence, but now there are metastable periods during which configurations and prices hold steady. During one such metastable period, lasting from roughly time 283 until time 413, the brokers have specialized into separate monopolistic niches: $y_1 = (0.585, 100)$,

$y_2 = (0.585, 010)$, and $y_3 = (0.587, 001)$. The corresponding profits per unit time are $W_1 = 191.35, W_2 = 185.20, W_3 = 183.68$. At time 414, broker 2 discovers that it can improve its profitability from $W_2 = 185.20$ to 190.88 by switching from (0.585,010) to (0.580,100), which undercuts broker 1. A brief battle between brokers 1 and 2 over category 1 ensues, with broker 1 finally giving up and settling for category 2 at time 424. But just when it looks as though order is going to be restored, brokers 2 and 3 start to fight over category 1. This quickly evolves into a price war in which broker 2's interest vector (101), overlaps partially with broker 3's interest vector (100). As the brokers undercut each other in price, their profits shoot up and down, never going to zero because the sets of consumers served by the two brokers do not overlap perfectly. Finally, at time 473, broker 2 cedes category 1 to broker 3, and the three brokers are once again fully specialized, one to each category. (Note, however, that the brokers have switched roles since the previous period of full specialization.) Brokers 2 and 3 now proceed to raise their prices independently with no interference from one another, eventually reaching near-optimal prices that persist until the next price war.

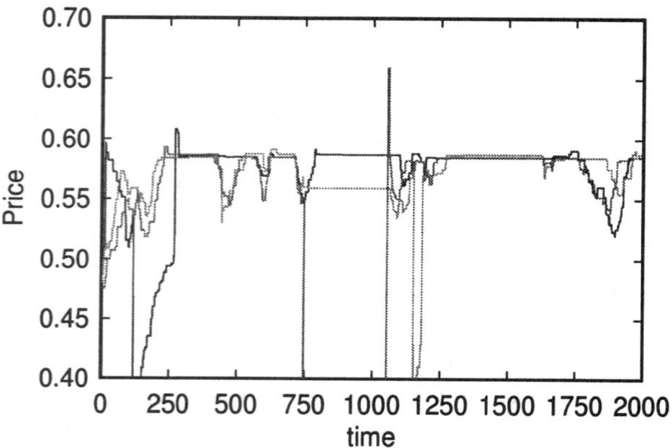

Figure 8: Price war time series for 3 random-explorer brokers and 3 categories. All other parameters are as in Fig. 5.

Figure 9 shows a close-up of a somewhat different price war that starts near time 1750. At first, brokers 1 and 3 vie for category 1, leaving category 3 uncovered. At time 1803, the price has dropped to roughly 0.565, at which point brokers 1 and 3 both switch to the interest vector (101). Prices continue to drop. At time 1829, broker 1 cedes category 1 to broker 3, and the price war continues with broker 1 at (001) and broker 3 at (101). Eventually, at time 1860, broker 2 gets drawn into a price war with broker 1 when broker 1 switches to (011) and broker 2 remains at (010). At this point, the system is in the state ((0.547,011),(0.584,010),(0.547,101)). No two brokers share the same interest vector, yet appar-

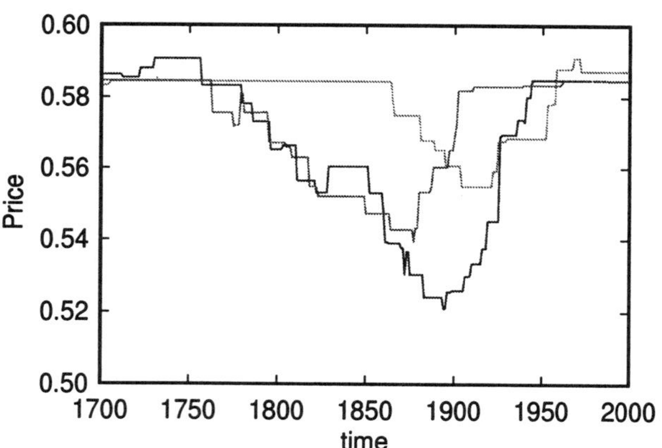

Figure 9: Close-up of Fig. 8.

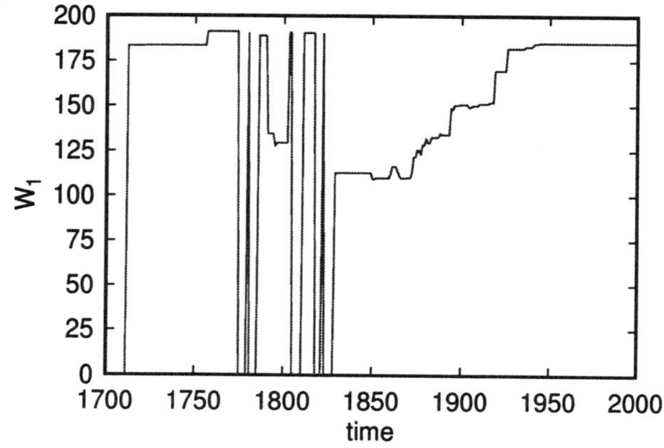

Figure 10: Broker 1's profit for time interval of Fig. 9.

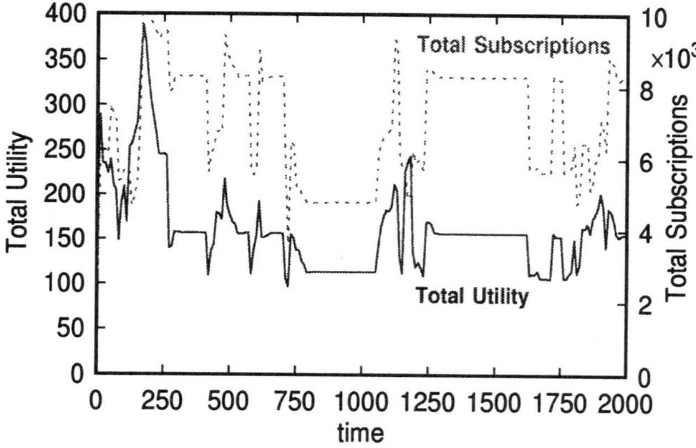

Figure 11: Total consumer utility and number of subscriptions; same simulation run as in Fig. 8.

ently the partial overlap between their interest vectors provides sufficient coupling to sustain a price war! At time 1878, broker 3 finds that it can drop its competition with broker 1 by dropping category 3, leaving it a specialist in category 1. While brokers 1 and 2 are fighting it out, broker 3's price drifts back to the single-category-monopoly level. Meanwhile, it is interesting to note that the price war between brokers 1 and 2 does *not* involve undercutting: broker 1's price is consistently lower than broker 2's price. A quantitative analysis of this coupling would be valuable, and appears to be feasible. After some further switches in broker 1's interest vector, brokers 1 and 2 eventually specialize in categories 2 and 3 respectively, their prices drift up towards the monopolistic optimal point, and the brokers are once again in specialized niches.

On average, a universally-adopted random-explorer strategy is more advantageous to the brokers than a universally-adopted myoptimal strategy, as can be seen by comparing Figs. 6 and 10. During the metastable regimes, each broker has a single-category monopoly. The monopoly is inherently unstable because eventually a broker specializing in a slightly less profitable category will undercut a broker that is better off. Since all brokers have this tendency, price wars are still inevitable, but less frequent because it takes random explorers longer to find a good opportunity for undercutting. On the whole, the price wars tend not to be quite as devastating as they are in societies consisting entirely of myoptimals, because they often involve brokers that are only partially in competition with one another, so a broker that is being undercut in price may still retain some customers.

Likewise, the consumers tend to be better off on the whole, as seen by comparing Figs. 7 and 11. For the most part, customers are happiest when the brokers are specialized, because this allows them to receive any articles that they desire without being forced to receive much junk. There are some conditions under which the consumer population as a whole is even better off than during the metastable regime, namely, after a price war, when the brokers are fully specialized but their prices are still rising back towards the equilibrium monopolistic levels. This accounts for the blips in overall utility and subscription rate just prior to the reestablishment of each metastable period, for example at (approximately) times 480 and 610.

Conclusion

Cyclical price wars are an undesirable but fundamental mode of collective behavior in our model economy of information filtering agents that optimize (or nearly optimize) their short-term utility. When the agents are permitted to simultaneously optimize both their price *and* their product (i.e. the categories they offer to consumers), a more complex cycle in price/product space is typically observed. The natural tendency of agent economies to self-organize into non-competitive niches (Hanson & Kephart 1998) is thwarted, and agents tend to compete for the same (possibly narrow) market, leaving consumer demand in other niches unsatisfied. Less optimal but equally myopic policies may actually lead to better collective behavior in the sense that both the brokers and the consumers have higher average utilities overall. However, the underlying myopia still makes the system inherently unstable, and periods of relative calm and prosperity will necessarily be punctuated sporadically with price wars.

Three main ingredients drive these instabilities: the multi-peaked nature of the profit landscape, the ability of well-informed agents to discover and jump nimbly to better peaks in that landscape, and the inability of myopic agents to anticipate the retaliatory response of other agents. These characteristics appear to be generic enough to raise the concern that many types of software agent economies will be plagued with such instabilities.

Consider the first of these three factors. In our model, a broker's ability to unilaterally reject unprofitable customer relationships helped to create the "expensive" hump in Figures 2 and 3. The capacity constraint in Edgeworth's model also leads to multiple peaks. Our own study of an entirely different model involving a vertically differentiated product reveals multi-peaked landscapes as well. The existence of so many different mechanisms for creating them leads us to suppose that multi-peaked landscapes may actually be the norm.

In realistic large-scale distributed agent systems, no single agent will have perfect information about the system, and even an omniscient agent might find it infeasible to compute the profit landscape perfectly. However, the present study shows that instabilities can persist even when decisions are made imperfectly. For the economy to be unstable, it is only necessary that agents be able to jump to *better* (not necessarily *optimal*) peaks in the landscape. Note that agents will be strongly motivated to obtain the best possible information and to employ the best possible decision algorithms, and this selfish pursuit of individual optimality will threaten the overall stability of the agent economy.

The third factor, myopia, may be curable. One possibility is to endow agents with a predictive algorithm based on some form of machine learning. The agent could base its decisions on its estimation of what will happen over some discounted future horizon. Our preliminary (unpublished) efforts in this area indicate that, under some conditions, price wars can be eliminated in two-broker systems. However, strict application of our particular method to larger systems would be computationally infeasible. The collective dynamics of an economy of co-evolving machine learners are certain to be fascinating, and an important topic for further research.

If we believe that agent economies are susceptible to price-war instabilities, how can we explain the relative infrequency of price wars in human economies? The economics literature provides several possible explanations (Tirole 1988), including explicit or tacit collusion (based upon foresight), and a variety of frictional effects. The latter include the cost to sellers of updating prices or modifying products, the cost to consumers of shopping for good bargains, and spatial or informational differentiation of products (i.e. different consumers might value the same good differently, depending on their physical location or knowledge).

We believe that these and other mitigating factors that may hold price-war instabilities in check in human economies are likely to be weaker in agent-based economies. Humans are almost certainly more accurate than software agents in predicting the likely effect of their actions upon others. In agent-based information economies, frictional effects like consumer inertia are likely to be much less when agents rather than people are doing the shopping, and updates to prices and products of information goods and services can be made and advertised much more quickly. Localization effects should be much smaller for information goods and services than they are for carrots and carwashes.

Perhaps some unanticipated effect will naturally hinder price wars in information economies. But even if no such factor presents itself, we hope that our continued efforts to understand price wars and related instabilities will lead to methods for controlling them.

Acknowledgments

We thank Steve White, David Levine, Benjamin Grosof, and Richard Segal for stimulating discussions about information economies, and Gerald Tesauro for sharing early results on endowing agents with foresight.

References

Birmingham, W. P.; Durfee, E. H.; Mullen, T.; and Wellman, M. P. 1996. The distributed agent architecture of the University of Michigan Digital Library. In *AAAI Spring Symposium on Information Gathering in Heterogeneous, Distributed Environments.* AAAI Press.

Chavez, A., and Maes, P. 1996. Kasbah: an agent marketplace for buying and selling goods. In *Proceedings of the first international Conference on the Practical Application of Intelligent Agents and Multi-Agent Technology.*

Clearwater, S., ed. 1995. *Market based control: a paradigm for distributed resource allocation.* Singapore: World Scientific.

Eriksson, J.; Finne, N.; and Janson, S. 1996. Information and interaction in MarketSpace — towards an open agent-based market infrastructure. In *Proceedings of the Second USENIX Workshop on Electronic Commerce.*

Hanson, J. E., and Kephart, J. O. 1998. Spontaneous specialization in a free-market economy of agents. Submitted to Workshop at Autonomous Agents 98.

Hogg, T., and Huberman, B. A. 1991. Controlling chaos in distributed systems. *IEEE Transactions on Systems, Man, and Cybernetics* 21:1325.

Huberman, B. A.; Lokose, R. M.; and Hogg, T. 1996. An economics approach to hard computational problems. *Science* 275:51–54.

Huberman, B. A., ed. 1988. *The Ecology of Computation.* Amsterdam: North-Holland.

Kephart, J. O.; Hanson, J. E.; Levine, D. W.; Grosof, B. N.; Sairamesh, J.; Segal, R. B.; and White, S. R. 1998. Dynamics of an information-filtering economy. To be published in Workshop on Cooperative Information Agents at the International Conference on Multi-Agent Systems.

Kephart, J. O.; Hogg, T.; and Huberman, B. A. 1989. Dynamics of computational ecosystems. *Physical Review A* 40:404–421.

Kephart, J. O.; Hogg, T.; and Huberman, B. A. 1990. Collective behavior of predictive agents. *Physica D* 42:48–65.

Kurose, J. F.; Schwartz, M.; and Yemini, Y. 1985. A microeconomic approach to optimization of channel access policies in multiaccess networks. In *Proc. of 5th Int. Conf. Distrib. Comput. Syst.*

Miller, M. S., and Drexler, K. E. 1988. Markets and computation: agoric open systems. In Huberman, B. A., ed., *The Ecology of Computation.* Amsterdam: North-Holland.

Rosenschein, J., and Zlotkin, G. 1994. *Rules of Encounter.* Cambridge, Massachusetts: The MIT Press.

Shubik, M. 1980. *Market Structure and Behavior.* Cambridge, Massachusetts: Harvard University Press.

Stonebraker, M., et al. 1994. An economic paradigm for query processing and data migration in Mariposa. In *Proc. of Parallel and Distributed Information Systems,* 58–67.

Tirole, J. 1988. *The Theory of Industrial Organization.* Cambridge, MA: The MIT Press.

Tsvetovatyy, M.; Gini, M.; Mobasher, B.; and Wieckowski, Z. 1997. MAGMA: an agent-based virtual market for electronic commerce. *Applied Artificial Intelligence.*

Wellman, M. P. 1993. A market-oriented programming environment and its application to distributed multicommodity flow problems. *Journal of Artificial Intelligence Research* 1:1.

White, J. 1996. Mobile agents white paper. General Magic, Inc.

Physical and Temporal Scaling Considerations in a Robot Model of Cricket Calling Song Preference

Henrik Hautop Lund
The Danish National Centre for IT-Research
University of Aarhus
Ny Munkegade bldg. 540
8000 Aarhus C., Denmark
hhl@daimi.aau.dk
http://www.daimi.aau.dk/~hhl

Barbara Webb
Department of Psychology
University of Nottingham
Nottingham NG7 2RD, UK
Barbara.Webb@nottingham.ac.uk

John Hallam
Department of Artificial Intelligence
University of Edinburgh
5 Forrest Hill
Edinburgh EH1 2QL, Scotland, UK
john@dai.ed.ac.uk

Abstract

Behavioural experiments with crickets show that female crickets respond to male calling songs with syllable rates within a certain band-width only. We have made a robot model in which we implement a simple neural controller that is less complex than the controllers traditionally hypothesised for cricket phonotaxis and syllable rate preference. The simple controller, which had been successfully used with a slowed and simplified signal, is here demonstrated to function, using songs with identical parameters to those found in real male cricket song, using an analog electronic model of the peripheral auditory morphology of the female cricket as the sensor. We put the robot under the same experimental conditions as the female crickets, and it responds with phonotaxis to calling songs of real male Gryllus bimaculatus. Further, the robot only responds to songs with syllable rates within a band-width similar to the band-width found for crickets. By making polar plots of the heading direction of the robot, we obtain behavioural data that can be used in statistical analyses. These analyses show that there are statistical significant differences between the behavioural responses to calling songs with syllable rates within the band-width and calling songs with syllable rates outside the band-width. This gives the verification that the simple neural control mechanism (together with morphological auditory matched filtering) can account for the syllable rate preference found in female crickets. With our robot system, we can now systematically explore the mechanisms controlling recognition and choice behaviour in the female cricket by experimental replication.

Introduction

Taxis, or approach to a sensory source, is frequently modelled in animat simulations, as a basic behaviour of animals in seeking food, mates or nests. The task is commonly abstracted as a source signal whose value decreases with distance (smoothly or as a step function) and an animat that can sense the value and use it to control movement to the source. Braitenberg's (1994) "vehicle 2" is the prototype.

It is often argued that such simulations model the "essence" of the behaviour - as such they should illuminate the understanding of any specific example of the behaviour. However, what these abstractions generally ignore are the real physics of signal propagation and detection. The abstract model is a reasonable representation of light, and thus translating simulation results to robot photo-taxis is quite often successful. But the model is less adequate for other modalities, many of which are more salient to real animals. For example, in chemotaxis, the properties of the odour plume are critical determinants of the problem (Bell, Kipp and Collins 1995). Braitenberg-type control is not appropriate in a task where the signal is highly dispersed (eliminating local gradients) and carried in specific directions by currents in the environment (for example around obstacles).

We have argued previously that the common abstraction is positively misleading when applied to the specific example of phonotaxis behaviour in crickets. Here the sensors do not respond exclusively to the relevant signal - bursts of sound of a characteristic frequency and repetition rate. However, rather than first filtering for the signal properties and subsequently comparing strength to control turns, the directionality of the sensors and the motor control mechanism are dependent on signal characteristics. For example, a tube connecting the ears transfers a phase-delayed signal from one to the other, thus modifying the negliable amplitude difference between the sensors of this small animal in a noisy environment. Thus we can only understand this system through consideration of the physical properties of the task and agent, which we believe are best investigated through building a physical model.

The same considerations suggest that the physical and temporal scales of the model are likely to be influential in the success of certain controllers for the behaviour. Our original implementation of a robot model (a LEGO robot

[0]The first author provided the extended neural model, made the experiments and analysis described in the paper, and wrote Sections 3, 4, 5, 6 and parts of 2 and 7. The second author provided the original hypotheses and wrote Sections 1, parts of 2, and 7. The third author designed the auditory circuit.

prototype) of the cricket suffered from a number of limitations in this regard, particularly in that the processing of sound was relatively slow compared to the speed of movement (Webb 1995). While this model nevertheless sufficed to demonstrate the viability of basic mechanisms, it was difficult to make strong comparisons with data from the animal.

These limitations, and details of the construction of a new robot addressing them have been described in detail in (Lund, Webb and Hallam 1997). We showed there that the re-implementation enabled us to experimentally verify assumptions that had been made, but not tested, about how the cricket responds selectively to carrier frequency of the signal. Here, we report on how the new robot led to a revised model of neural control of phonotaxis, to explain the band-pass selectivity for repetition rate, using signals that were temporally identical to those used in cricket experiments.

Neural Model

The original neural model was based on two properties of identified interneurons (AN1) known to be involved in phonotaxis in the cricket (Schildberger and Horner 1988). First, the long time constant of these neurons means that they act as low-pass filters for the temporal pattern of the signal: given repeated inputs they can only code distinct syllables (bursts of sound) below a certain repetition rate (for calling song structure, see Figure 1). Second, the latency to onset of firing for each syllable is dependent on the amplitude of the sound. Thus which side fires first can be used to generate a turn towards the sound. However this mechanism has two features: it will not work when syllables repeat too fast for the low-pass filtering to track the onsets; and if the syllables repeat slowly, signals to turn will come less often. Thus there should be a band of repetition rates for which this mechanism works best.

We were able to demonstrate an effective "preference" for certain syllable rates using this mechanism in the old robot. However, this depended partly on the fact that the robot could move a significant distance between slow syllables, which because of the auditory processing speed lasted a second or more in the LEGO robot. Real cricket song has repetition rates in the order of 30Hz, and "slow syllables" to which they no longer respond may last only 50ms. With the new robot able to process song at comparable rates to the cricket, slowing the song to 10Hz or less was not sufficient to interfere with taxis because it was still making 10 corrections a second which was quite adequate to get it to the sound source. Consequently we had to produce a more complex neural control model than the one suggested in (Webb 1995) and used to show the robot's phonotaxis to male *Gryllus bimaculatus* calling song in (Lund, Webb and Hallam 1997). Especially, it has been extended to include an extra neuron on each side that performs integration over syllables. This simple neural system can account for much of the biological data that show a band-pass in crickets' phonotaxis to calling songs with different syllable rates.

The structure of the extended neural model is as follows: input from the auditory sensors is fed into a neuron on each side (N1), activation can flow from N1 to another neuron (N2), that in turn feeds activation directly to the motor on that side. The activation within a neuron is modeled with a leaky integrator specific for that neuron, so that the activation, A, at time t is calculated as

$$A(t) = \alpha * A(t-1) + I(t) \quad , \quad 0 < \alpha < 1$$

where I is the input to that neuron and α is the decay rate. If A reaches an upper threshold, T_{high}, it will fire activation on in the network. After having fired, neural activation (A) has to decay below a lower threshold, T_{low}, before the neuron can fire once again. As in natural systems, different groups of neurons can have different decay rates (α) and thresholds (T_{high} and T_{low}).

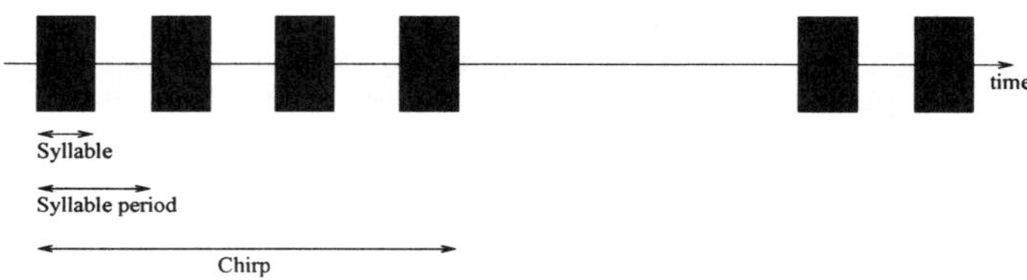

Figure 1: The song structure of the cricket calling song. The calling song consists of chirps, each with a number of syllables (bursts of sound with the species specific carrier frequency). In this case, with equal syllable length and gap length, the syllable duty-cycle (within a chirp) is 50%.

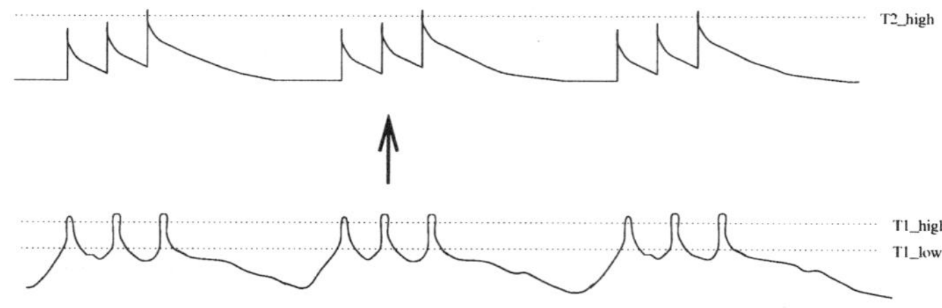

Figure 2: The neural model implemented in the robot. The figure shows the neural activation of neuron N1 at the bottom and of neuron N2 at the top over the same time scale. Three chirps each with three syllables is imagined as input to neuron N1.

Figure 2 shows the activation of N1 and N2 over time when three chirps with three syllables each is given as input to N1. For each syllables, the activation of N1 exceeds $T1_{high}$, so N1 fires for each syllable, since the activation drops below $T1_{low}$ in between the syllables. When N1 fires, it sends activation directly to N2. In the example in Figure 2, this activation from N1 by itself is not enough for N2 activation to reach $T2_{high}$, so N2 will not fire given only one input from N1. However, if the firing rate from N1 is high enough, N2 activation will reach $T2_{high}$ after a while and will be able to fire. In Figure 2, it takes 3 firings at the right rate from N1 for N2 to reach $T2_{high}$ and fire. N2 is able to fire for each chirp since it reaches $T2_{high}$ at the third syllable.

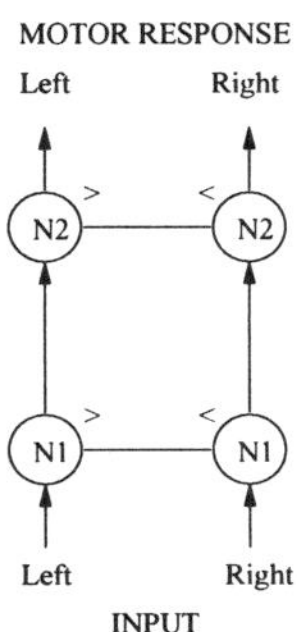

Figure 3: The structure of the neural control mechanism. Activation from the ears is fed into N1. If N1 activation on either left or right reaches $T1_{high}$, it is compared with the activation on the contralateral side. If it is higher, the neuron will fire activation on to N2 on the same side. N2 neurons work in a similar way.

The neural model suggested here is somewhat similar to the one suggested by Schildberger (1984) who found low-pass and high-pass neurons in neurophysiological experiments with *Gryllus bimaculatus.* Based on this, Schildberger suggested a neural model with low-pass and high-pass neurons that process in parallel and then is ANDed together in order to produce the band-pass filtering observed in behavioural experiments (see Figure 4). However, the model suggested here is simpler, since it directly produces the motor behaviour, and not only recognition of the right syllable rate. The reason for this is the processing contained in the auditory pathway. As we have argued in (Webb 1995), the peripheral auditory system of the cricket might provide directional cues through its structure, and we showed in (Lund, Webb and Hallam 1997) that this was indeed so when presenting such a system with male *Gryllus bimaculatus* calling song.

Robot Implementation

The female cricket has four auditory openings: an ear (tympanum) located on each upper foreleg, and an auditory spiracle (or hole) on each side of the frontal section of her body. The four are linked internally by means

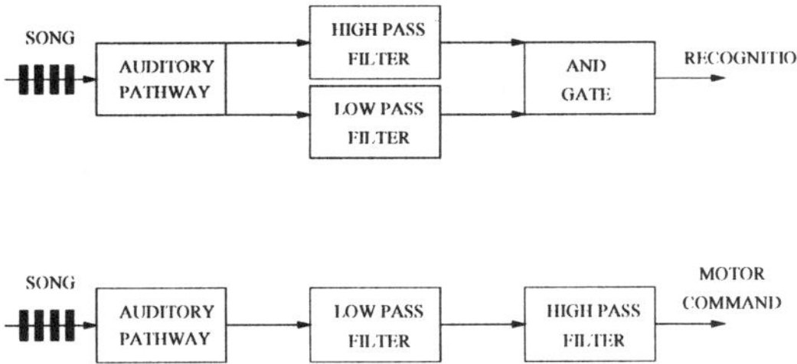

Figure 4: Top: Diagram of Schildberger's hypothesised mechanism for recognition of syllable rates. Bottom: Diagram of our hypothesised mechanism for both recognition and motor response for syllable rates in the right band-width.

of tracheal tubes. Sound reaches the tympani directly through the air and, after propagation through the internal tubes, from the other auditory openings. The sound transduced from each tympanum by the cricket's auditory receptors is thus a combination of delayed and filtered signals from the other tympanum and the spiracles arriving at the back of the tympanum with the direct sound arriving at its outer face.

The delays and filtering performed by the auditory morphology improve the cricket's ability to discriminate the arrival direction of the conspecific song since the phased combination of sounds from the different sources induces a strong directional sensitivity into the response of each tympanum. Essentially, sounds arriving from the same side as the tympanum are delayed by the internal structures to arrive in anti-phase with respect to the direct path at the ipsilateral ear and in phase at the contralateral ear. Since the sounds arriving by the two paths are subtracted (being on opposite sides of the tympanum), the stimulus intensity at the ipsilateral ear is enhanced while at the contralateral ear it is diminished.

In the cricket, the delays and filter characteristics of the internal auditory structures are species-specific. To model the auditory morphology of the cricket, we have built an electronic emulation of some of these characteristics (see Figure 5 and 6). Sound is collected by two or four microphones whose spacing is carefully controlled. After amplification and initial filtering three delayed copies of the sound are generated with programmable relative delays, which are then scaled and added together to construct a tympanal response. The intensity of the resultant signal is transduced using an analogue-to-digital conversion system for use by the control program. This hardware allows us to approximate the auditory morphology of various crickets by adjusting the programmable delays and the summing gains. It is not a perfect emulation of the insect, however: two programmed delays allow us to sum signals from each tympanum and both spiracles, but not from all auditory openings; and the summation system allows us to program relative gains, but not frequency dependent gains.

Figure 5: The Khepera robot with the auditory sensors. © Lund, Hallam & Webb, 1997.

Phonotaxis Experiments

In (Lund, Webb and Hallam 1997), we used the robot with the auditory system described above to verify that the simple neural control mechanism could account for frequency selectivity, since the robot did phonotaxis to male cricket *Gryllus bimaculatus* calling song, and preferred calling songs with the right carrier frequency. Here, we will first replicate some of these experiments with the extended model, and then go on to the syllable rate experiments.

In the present experiments, for N1 neurons, the decay rate, $\alpha 1$, is set to 7/8, upper threshold, $T1_{high}$, to 900, and lower threshold, $T1_{low}$, to 600. For N2 neurons, the decay rate, $\alpha 2$, is set to 63/64, upper threshold, $T2_{high}$, to 1725. These are empirical settings.

The robot has its auditory sensory system's parameters set as in (Lund, Webb and Hallam 1997) (i.e. the two microphones are placed 18mm apart since 18mm corresponds to 1/4 wavelength of the carrier frequency, 4.7kHz, of male *Gryllus bimaculatus* calling song, the delays are set to $53\mu s$ (the time sound propagates the

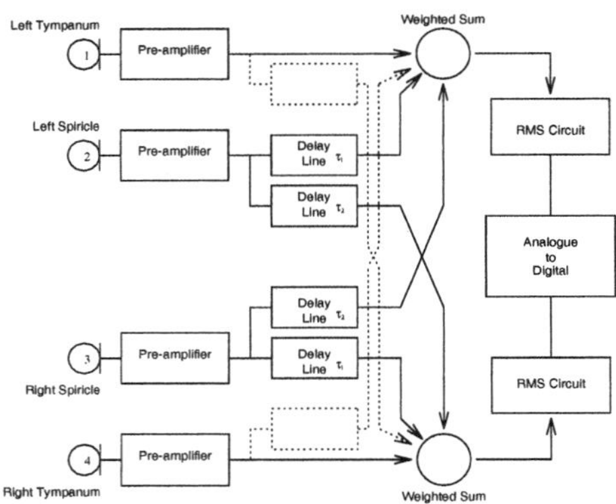

Figure 6: Simplified diagram of the ears circuit. When sound arrives at each microphone (the analogue of the cricket's tympanum), the received signal is pre-amplified. The signal is then sent with a 'through delay' to the mixer at the same side, and with a 'cross delay' to the mixer at the opposite side. The mixed signal is sent through an RMS and an A/D converter to one of the Khepera's input channels. The same happens on the opposite side. © Lund, Hallam & Webb, 1997.

length of 1/4 wavelength of 4.7kHz), and the mixers subtract the delayed signal from the contralateral side from the signal from the lateral side). When we play male *Gryllus bimaculatus* calling song to the robot, the empirical settings of neural activation decay and thresholds described above result in the neural effect drawn on Figure 2.

We have replicated the data from (Lund, Webb and Hallam 1997) with the extended neural model. The results are shown in Figure 7. It shows that the robot with the extended neural models performs phonotaxis to male cricket *Gryllus bimaculatus* calling song[1] emitted from a loud speaker in the arena. The figure shows 10 different runs with the robot's starting point alternating between 45 degrees left or right to the sound source. Both starting points are 150cm away from the sound source. In all cases, the robot moves forward a bit, then it reacts to the calling song by turning towards the loud speaker and moves directly towards it.

[1] The calling song was recorded at Life Science Department, University of Nottingham. The adult male cricket was sitting in a sand-floored arena and was recorded using a Maplin uni-directional dynamic microphone (YU-34) on a Marantz Stereo cassette recorder (CP230) from a distance of about 20cm. A 30s part of these recordings is played through a host Pentium computer with SB AWE32 sound card and was repeated twice for each experiment. The sound was fed through an amplifier to a loud speaker that was placed on a 240*240cm arena in our robot lab. It should be noted that we did nothing to control echos from the surrounding environment

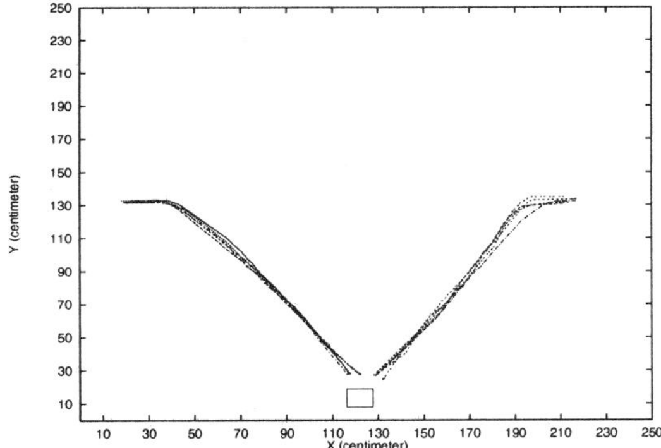

Figure 7: The robot's behaviour when male cricket Gryllus bimaculatus calling song is emitted from the loud speaker at the bottom of the arena.

Hence, the robot with this neural model is attracted to male *Gryllus bimaculatus* calling song. As was the case with the robot with the previous neural model, this robot also discriminates between calling songs with the right carrier frequency (4.7kHz) and those with other carrier frequencies (e.g. 6.7kHz). (The data is not shown here because of space limitation and emphasis on syllable rate preference. For frequency selectivity, see (Lund, Webb and Hallam 1997).)

Syllable Rate Experiments

Syllable rate experiments with crickets have shown that the female cricket responds only to calling songs with syllable rates within a certain band-pass. Weber and Thorson (1989) report that *Gryllus campestris* females do "tracking almost perfectly near 30 syllables per second but [are] revealing reduced performance or [are] stopping entirely at rates below 20Hz or above 40Hz" (Weber and Thorson 1989) p. 321. These data were found using trills, but Weber and Thorson also report that in performance tests for chirps with different syllable numbers, "we have uniformly found that the females' response increases as the number of syllable increases, as long as syllables are delivered at the natural (30-Hz) rate" (Weber and Thorson 1989) p. 318. Doherty (1985a) also found that *Gryllus bimaculatus* failed to discriminate between calling songs having a 45ms syllable period and an alternative syllable period until the alternative syllable period was 30ms or shorter, or 55ms or longer.

Though Popov and Shuvalov's (1977) arena experiments suggests that *Gryllus campestris* are more attracted by the four-syllable calling song than those with three or five or more syllables, other experiments (Doherty 1985b; Weber and Thorson 1989) show that chirps can be dispensed with entirely and females can "track continuous trills of syllables delivered at rates near 30Hz. Our recent tests indicate that this ability increases with the age of the animal" (Weber and Thorson 1989) p. 318. Regarding the change over age, Stout and McGhee (1988) also conclude that adult female *A. domestica* were more attracted to calling songs with a much wider range of syllable periods than were attractive to younger females, and thus "for *A. domestica* females, a central filter for SP [syllable period] would at least need a variable band-pass width that could be influenced by other stimuli, age, and other variables" (Stout and McGhee 1988) p. 287.

In the following experiments, we will show how the simple neural model suggested above together with the auditory mechanism implemented in the auditory sensor circuit can account for this data on cricket band-pass filtering of syllable rates. Further, the band-width is dependent only on the characteristics of the N1 and N2 neurons (namely the decay rate and the firing threshold) that might change over age in natural nervous systems.

We made computer generated trills of a carrier frequency of 4.7kHz (the carrier frequency of the *Gryllus bimaculatus* calling song) with different syllable rates. The trills had syllable periods of 10ms, 20ms, 30ms, 40ms, 50ms, 60ms, 70ms, and 80ms. The duty cycle was kept constant at 50% (i.e. the syllables were 50% of the syllable period), and since we were using trills, also the chirp duration and chirp rate were kept constant.

As in the previous experiment, we replicated each experiment ten times by placing the robot at the two starting positions five times each (alternating between them). Figure 8 shows the result of these experiments. When the robot was presented with the 10ms syllable period trill, it did not react at all, but just moved with the default forward movement. With the 20ms syllable period trill, the robot would react very few times and would not perform successful phonotaxis. However, with both 30ms, 40ms, and 50ms syllable period trills, the robot performed phonotaxis by reacting to the trill and moving to the source. With 60ms syllable period trills, the robot reacted to the trill very few times, and managed to reach the sound source only once out of the ten runs. With neither 70ms nor 80ms syllable period trills did the robot react to the sound at all. Hence, the simple neural model provides an effective syllable rate band-pass filter that allowed the robot to perform phonotaxis only with a narrow band-pass. In this case, the neural band-pass filtering was such that the robot could not perform succesful phonotaxis below a syllable period of 30ms or above 50ms.

Statistical Analyses

In order to analyse the trajectories of the robot and whether there are statistical significant differences be-

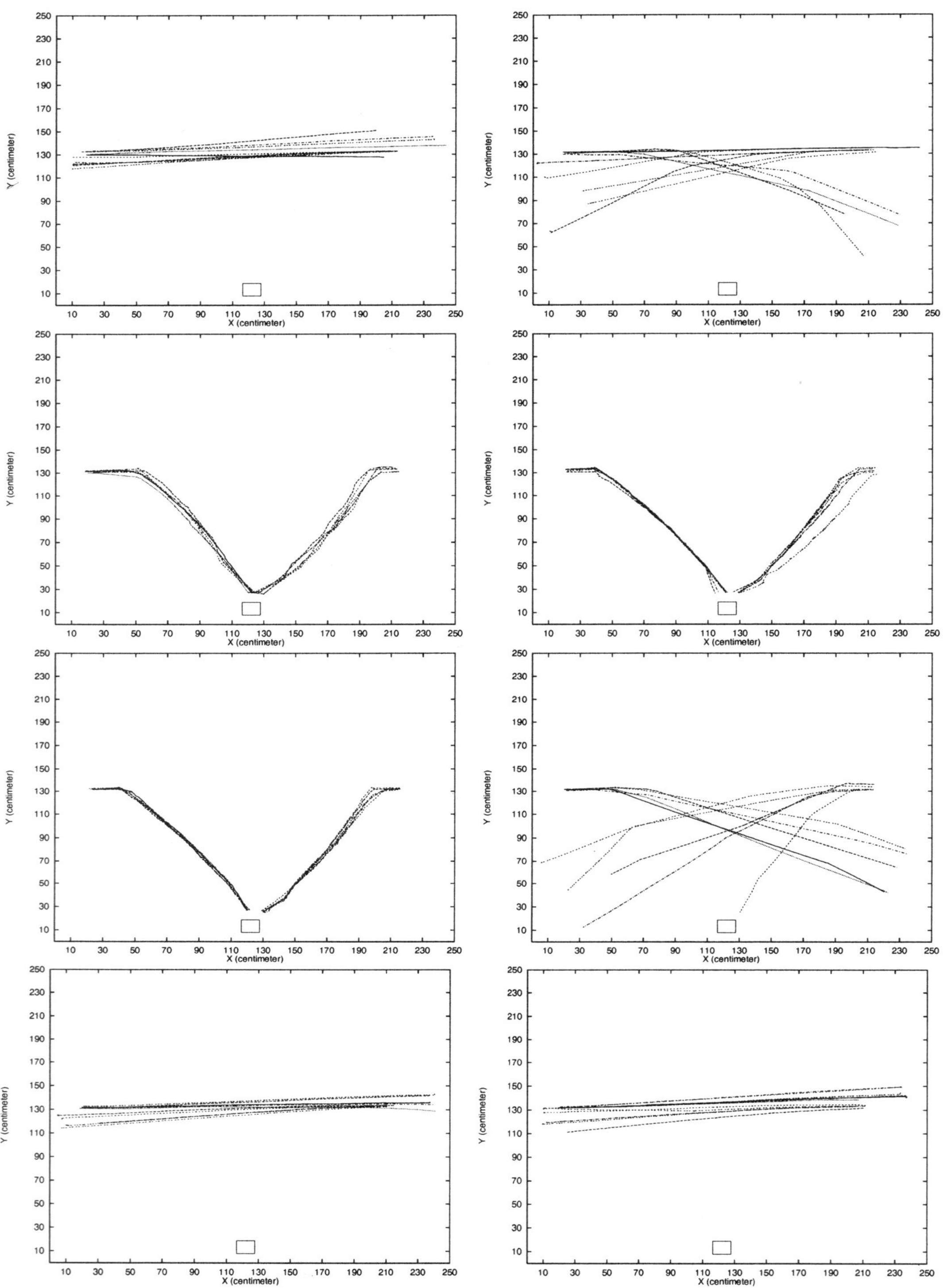

Figure 8: The robot's behaviour when trills are emitted from the loud speaker at the bottom of the arena. The duty cycle is 50% in all experiments, while the syllable rate changes. The experiments are with syllable intervals of 10ms, 20ms, 30ms, 40ms, 50ms, 60ms, 70ms, and 80ms (ordered left,right from top to bottom). © Lund, Hallam & Webb, 1998.

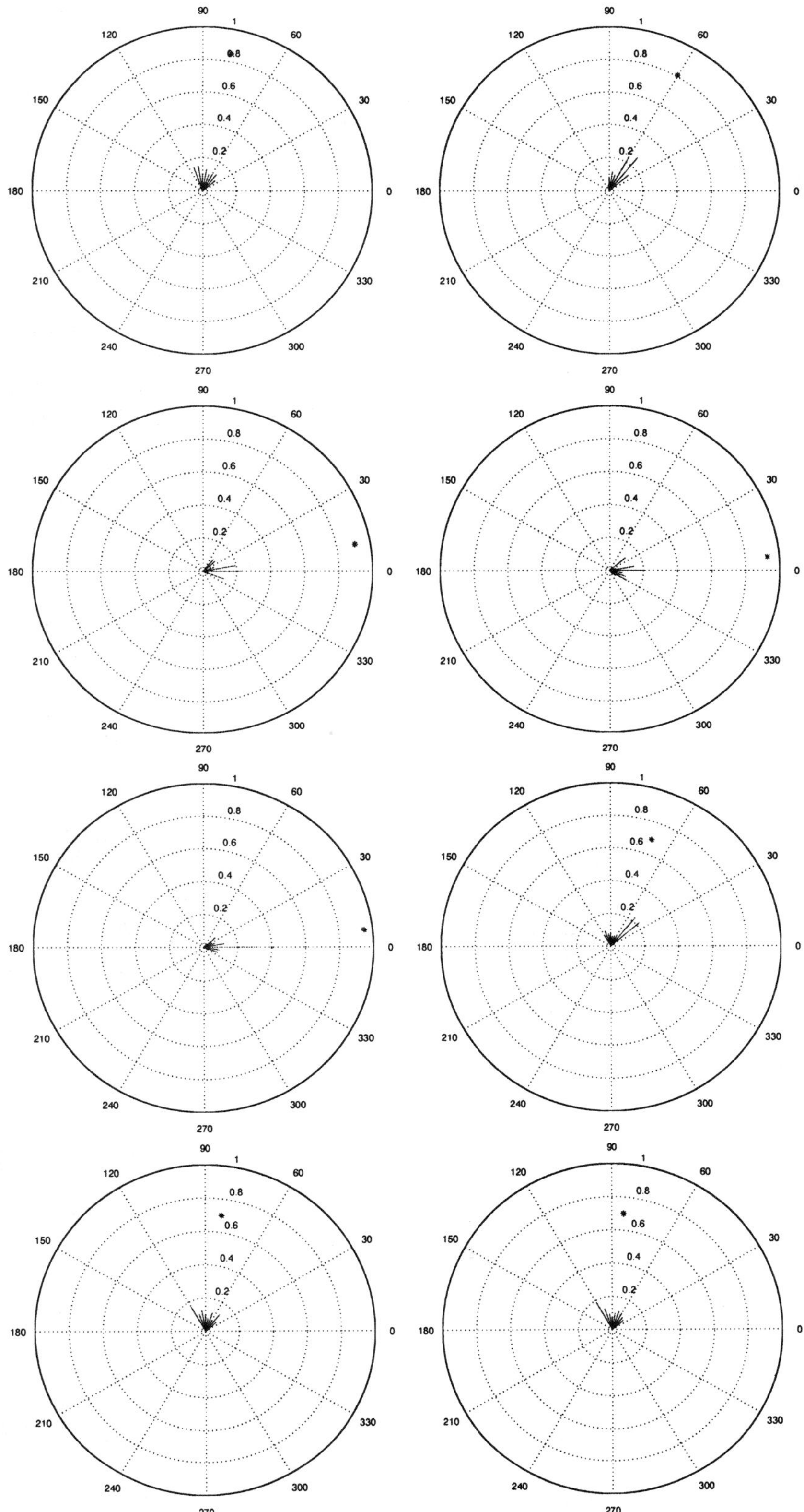

Figure 9: The robot's heading in experiments with songs with different syllable rates. The experiments are with syllable intervals of 10ms, 20ms, 30ms, 40ms, 50ms, 60ms, 70ms, and 80ms (ordered left, right from top to bottom). Here, we show data from only one of the ten runs for each syllable rate. © Lund, Hallam & Webb, 1998.

tween the performance under the different experimental set-ups, we plot the robot's heading in polar coordinates with the origin at the loud speaker position. Approximately each 0.3sec, we record the robots position and find the vector connecting the previous position of the robot with the present position. After one run, the vector mean is calculated and the vectors with their (summed) length is used for the plots in Figure 9. The mean heading angle (towards the speaker) and directionality of the path is plotted as a dot (*). A direct path from starting position to the loud speaker would therefore be plotted as (0,1) — the angle would be 0 and the directionality of the path would be 1.

We can then perform statistical tests on the vector means in the different groups of experiments in order to achieve statistical evidence of the phonotaxis behaviour (discrimination between sounds with different syllable rates). Here, we use the statistical U-test and obtain the table shown in Table 1.

syllable period	10	20	30	40	50	60	70	80
10			S	S	S	S		
20			S	S	S			
30	S	S				S	S	S
40	S	S				S	S	S
50	S	S				S	S	S
60	S		S	S	S		S	S
70			S	S	S	S		
80			S	S	S	S		

Table 1. Analysis of difference between mean heading direction in polar coordinates between experiments with computer generated trills with syllable periods of 10ms, 20ms, 30ms, 40ms, 50ms, 60ms, 70ms, and 80ms. 'S' indicates that there is a statistical significant difference (significance level 0.01) between heading direction under the corresponding two conditions. Each experimental set-up was repeated 10 times to achieve the mean heading direction. Notably, there is no statistical significant difference within 30-50ms, and statistical significant difference between 30-50ms and experiments with syllable periods lying outside this interval.

For the experiments with songs with varying syllable rates, the statistical analysis shows that there is a statistical significant difference in the robot's performance between experiments with syllable periods in the interval 30-50ms and all other syllable periods. This is a verification of the biological data — but here we show it with a much simpler control system than has been hypothesised by most biologists (e.g. Schildberger).

Discussion

We have hypothesised a model for explaining the band-pass filtering found in crickets.The model is an extension of the simpler one with which we previously showed frequency selectivity. The experiments presented here show that the extended model result in a behaviour similar to the behaviour resulted from the previous model, but most importantly, the syllable rate experiments show that the model results in band-pass filtering similar to the one found in biological experiments. The statistical analysis of the heading directions shows that there is a statistical difference in heading direction between the conditions where 30-50ms syllable rate songs are presented and the conditions with syllable rates outside this interval.

Although we have described this as a neural model, it is more properly a 'neuron-like' algorithm. N1 and N2 are not intended to correspond explicitly to specific neurons in the cricket but represent processes we believe are carried out by small numbers (3-10) of neurons in the cricket prothoracic ganglion and brain. In (Webb and Scutt 1997) we have described how these processes might be mapped onto specific neurons, and we are currently working on implementing the spiking neuron controller described there on the new robot base.

Nevertheless, the way in which our model controls the band-pass response to syllable rates is a plausible 'high-level' model of the cricket controller and provides a number of useful insights for interpreting behavioural and physiological cricket research. In particular, it is the simple interactions of decay rates and thresholds in our model that determine the effectiveness of different signals.

The neural band-pass filtering is dependent on the neural characteristica, namely the decay rate and firing thresholds of N1 and N2, and the correspondence between the two. If $T1_{low}$ is lowered, then the syllable period has to be increased for the N1 activation to drop below $T1_{low}$ in between syllables, so the robot would respond only to trills with a larger syllable period. If $T1_{low}$ is set higher, then N1 would be able to fire on trills with a lower syllable period. However, this also depends on the decay rate. On the other hand, N2 allows only trills with syllable period up to a certain level to pass. If the syllable period is too long, N2 activation will drops too much in between activation from N1 and it will never be able to reach $T2_{high}$.

With the decay rates and thresholds set in these experiments, N1 works as a low-pass filter, while N2 works as a high-pass filter of syllable rates.

This also provides a simple method by which the variation in syllable rate preference can be explained. Small parameter changes in decay rates and thresholds can set the preference of the cricket at different values, thus genetic predisposition to species specific rates can evolve. Adaptation in these parameters during the cricket's life-time can explain the age-related change in bandwidth of preference reported in (Stout and McGhee 1988; Weber and Thorson 1989).

A more complex issue is raised by the biological data regarding the syllable duty-cycle: "one can alter the duty cycle [...] of the syllables from very small values to ca. 90%; the song remains attractive as long as the syllable repetition rate is near 30Hz." (Weber and Thorson 1989) pp. 319. At first glance our model suffices to explain this effect because it is only the onset of syllables that controls behaviour and the length of syllable is irrelevant. In fact the issue is more complex. For a short duty-cycle, our model will produce taxis behaviour provided the amplitude of the signal is sufficient to sum to threshold ($T1_{high}$) before the short syllable ends (this depends on details of the summation rate and the value of $T1_{high}$). Consequently it is interesting to note that short syllables do need to be louder to be equally attractive to female crickets. For long duty-cycles our current model is more problematic, because the decay rate and $T1_{low}$ set a minimum length of gap between syllables. If we increase $T1_{low}$ to decrease the length of gap required (e.g. for a 90% duty cycle the gap would be around 5ms) we also change the low-pass filtering properties such that songs with syllable periods of 10ms should be easily trackable. We believe this points to an important experiment for cricket neuroethology: no-one has (to our knowledge) explored the response of auditory interneurons to long duty-cycle songs. Unless these neurons have a more complex characteristic than low-pass filtering, the ability to track 90% duty cycle songs is an anomaly.

Our new robot should enable us to explore a variety of other interesting questions in cricket behaviour. One is the evolutionarily interesting issue of choice by female crickets between differing males. Our preliminary tests in this area suggest that sensory bias may play a significant role. Another issue is the interaction of taxis with the auditory escape response.

Our exploration of the phonotaxis system has reemphasised the close relationship of physical and temporal scales with the control systems underlying behaviour. A generic simulation approach may tell us little about real problems in approach behaviour. By investigating a specific biological system and modelling it at a level of detail driven by biological questions, we gain more sophisticated insights into the real problems of sensorimotor control.

Acknowledgements

This work was supported by EPSRC grant nr. GR/K 78942 and The Danish National Research Councils. Facilities were provided by the Danish National Centre for IT Research, and the Universities of Edinburgh and Nottingham.

References

Bell, W. J., L. R. Kipp, and R. D. Collins. 1995. The role of chemo-orientation in search behaviour. In *Chemical Ecology of Insects 2*, edited by R. T. Carde and W. J. Bell, Chapman and Hall.

Braitenberg, V. 1984. *Vehicles: Experiments in Synthetic Psychology*. Cambridge, MA: MIT Press.

Doherty, J. A. 1985a. Phonotaxis in the cricket *Gryllus bimaculatus* degeer: comparison of choice and no-choice paradigms. J. Comp. Physiol. A 157: 279–289.

Doherty, J. A. 1985b. Temperature coupling and trade-off phenomena in the aucustic communication system of the cricket, *Gryllus bimaculatus* degeer (gryllidae). J. Exp. Biol. 114: 17–35.

Lund, H. H., B. Webb, and J. Hallam. 1997. A Robot Attracted to the Cricket Species *Gryllus bimaculatus*. In *Proceedings of Fourth European Conference on Artificial Life*, edited by P. Husbands and I. Harvey, Cambridge, MA: MIT Press, p. 246–255.

Popov, A. V. and V. F. Shuvalov. Phonotactic behaviour of crickets. J. Comp. Physiol. 119: 111–128.

Schildberger, K. Temporal selectivity of identified auditory neurons in the cricket brain. J. Comp. Physiol. 155: 171–185.

Schildberger, K. and M. Horner. 1988. The function of auditory neurons in cricket phonotaxis I Influence of hyperpoloarization of identified neurons on sound localization. J. Comp. Physiol. A 163: 621–631.

Stout, J. F. and R. W. McGhee. 1988. Attractiveness of the male *Acheta domesticus* calling song to females II. The relative importance of syllable period, intensity, and chirp rate. J. Comp. Physiol. A 164: 277–287.

Webb, B. Using robots to model animals: A cricket test. Robotics and Autonomous Systems 16: 117–134.

Webb, B. and T. Scutt. 1997. A simple latency-dependent spiking-neuron model of cricket phonotaxis. University of Nottingham, submitted.

Weber, T and J. Thorson. 1989. Phonotactic Behavior of Walking Crickets. In *Cricket Behaviour and Neurobiology*, edited by F. Huber, T. E. Moore, and W. Loher, Ithaca, NY: Cornell University Press, pp. 310–339,

A Method to Reconstruct Genetic Networks Applied to the Development of *Drosophila*'s Eye

Mineo Morohashi
Keio University
3-14-1 Hiyoshi Kohoku-ku Yokohama,
Kanagawa 223 Japan
moro@aa.cs.keio.ac.jp

Hiroaki Kitano
Sony Computer Science Laboratory
3-14-13 Higashi-Gotanda, Shinagawa-ku,
Tokyo 141 Japan
kitano@csl.sony.co.jp

Abstract

In this paper, we describe a method for reconstructing and predicting a possible gene network based on partial information of gene expression data. We have applied the method to identify a gene network involved in the formation of the *Drosophila melanogaster* eye. In particular, the experiment developed a gene network which determines the differentiation of photo receptor cells in the ommatidia, or eye segment. We used a classifier system to generate a set of rules describing a gene network. For each photoreceptor cell (R1–R8 cell) within the ommatidia, a unique classifier system computes the genetic interaction cascade within the cell, and is optimized to reproduce the spatio-temporal dynamics of a gene expresion pattern. During this process rules are added or deleted; this process models the development of hypothetical gene interactions. The classifier system's fitness function is based on the actual gene expresion patterns of *Drosophila* photo receptor cells during ommatidia formation. Our results predict a novel interaction between the *atonal* and *rough* genes.

Introduction

Understanding biological processes, such as the developmental process, is one of the ultimate goals of modern biology. Rapid progress in molecular biology and related instrumentation technologies has made available massive amounts of data on the DNA sequence, genes and their enhancer structures, protein functions, and metabolic cascades. Nevertheless, these biological systems are so complex that mere collection of data does not lead to real understanding. In this paper, we present an attempt to understand biological systems using a synthetic approach, which constructs a detailed simulation model of actual biological systems, and a method of identifying unknown genes and genetic interactions using computer simulations and an automated learning scheme. The goal of this research is to establish a methodology to systematically predict unknown genes and their interactions, as well as establish detailed simulation models of actual biological systems so that various virtual biological experiments can be carried out. This approach leads to a clear division of labor between theoretical biology and experimental biology, just as there is in particle physics. The main task of theoretical biology, therefore, is to establish a model of biological systems from which powerful predictions may be derived.

In this paper, we report one of our early attempts to accomplish this goal. The specific biological process discussed in this paper is the eye formation of *Drosophila melanogaster*. Currently we are working on a project called the "**Virtual Drosophila Project**" (Kitano 1997), which aims to create a detailed model of *Drosophila melanogaster*. We chose *Drosophila melanogaster* because it, along with *C. elegans*, is one of the most well investigated animals in all of biology. Eye formation is particularly interesting because it involves creation of large numbers of repetitive structures, each of which has a complex internal structure. Eye formation is also interesting because it is an example of the development of sensory systems joined to neural systems.

Because of the biological significance of eye formation, a large number of molecular biologists are working on identifying the genes involved, and trying to determine the mechanism behind eye formation. Nevertheless, the system is so complex and the gene expression patterns so dynamic that no systematic model of eye formation has yet been proposed. One reason for this is that not all genes and gene interactions have been identified. This paper presents our attempt to create a simulation model of gene interactions in eye formation, and predict unknown genes and their interactions.

Eye Formation in *Drosophila*

The *Drosophila* retina is an especially useful model system for examining cell fate induction (Bate 1993). It is a simple micronervous system consisting of several hundred identical 'ommatidia', each of which contains eight photoreceptor neurons. The determination of cell fate within an ommatidium is not dictated by lineage (Ready 1976). Instead, it is believed that cell differentiation takes place based on cell-cell interaction. Cells are initially undifferentiated, and could be differentiated into any cell type; such cells are called *omnipotent precursor cells* (Tomlinson 1987). Most ommatidial cell fates are considered determined by short-range cell-to-cell inductive signaling.

The eye is derived from the eye-antennal disc. The disc itself arises from approximately 20 cells from the optic primordium in the embryonic blastoderm. The disc is formed by invagination at stage 12, to produce a flattened sac of epithelium. By the third instar larva, the disc contains about 2,000 cells.

The morphogenetic furrow

During the middle of the third instar phase, a dorsal ventral furrow forms, sweeping from the posterior to the anterior (Figure 1). This furrow is called the *morphogenetic furrow* (MF), and it is the site where each photoreceptor cell commits to a different cell fate. The area anterior to the furrow is rich in synchronously dividing cells, but lacks any pattern. The furrow itself is caused by a shortening of cells at its center. The area posterior to the furrow shows *preclusters* of cells, each with a recognizable core of five cells, corresponding to cells 2, 3, 4, 5 and 8 of the photoreceptor.

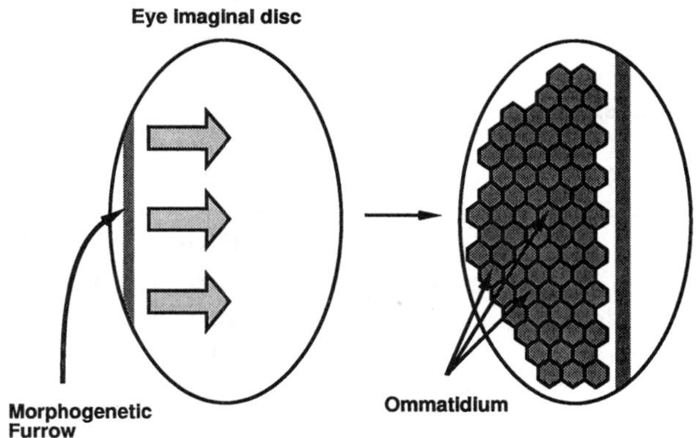

Figure 1: Morphogenetic furrow

Figure 2 shows a simulated expression level of the *atonal* and *rough* genes triggered by the MF. It clearly illustrates that the MF triggers expression of several genes which affect eye formation later on. Simulation of MF progression will be discussed elsewhere.

Ommatidia formation

Each ommatidium contains eight photoreceptor cells, each containing a *rhabdomere*, a rod-like element which holds the cell's photoreceptor machinery. In the ommatidium, photoreceptor cells R1 through R6 surround cells R7 and R8, forming an irregular trapezoid. The rhabdomeres of R7 and R8 center themselves, R7 above R8. Each ommatidium is surrounded by two primary pigment cells; these in turn are surrounded by six secondary pigment cells shared with adjacent ommatidia. Thus each ommatidium contains a total of 22 cells, making the total number of cells in each eye over 16,000. The R8 photoreceptor neuron is the first terminally differentiated cell type in the neuroepithelium and therefore must arise from a different mechanism than the other cells. Mutations in several different genes give rise to multiple R8s within a single ommatidium (Cagan 1989; Baker 1990), suggesting R8 emerges from a larger cluster of 'R8 candidate' cells. A process of selection between initially equivalent cells leads to the formation of one single R8 neuron in each ommatidium.

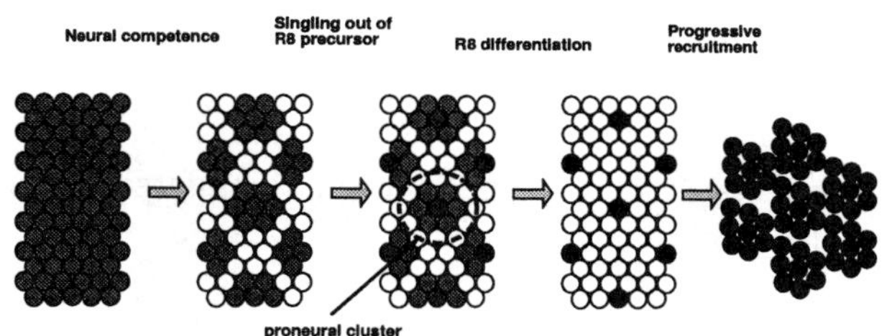

Figure 3: R8 selection

Three cell pairs are then differentiated in succession: R2/R5, R3/R4, and R1/R6. Following this, R7 and the surrounding four cone cells become differentiated. After pupation, pigment cells are established, and excess cells are eliminated by apoptosis.

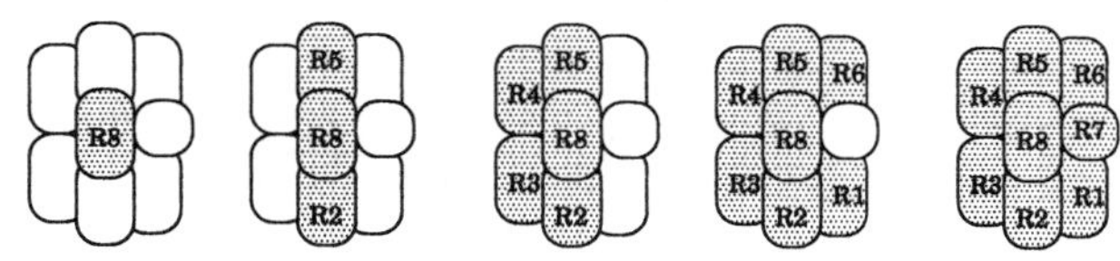

Figure 4: R-cell differentiation

Communication between cells has emerged as a theme underlying many of the mechanisms by which cells in a developing organism acquire their specific fate. A cell may receive information from its neighbors, causing it to adopt a specific identity and thereby follow a particular developmental pathway. These cell–cell interactions can be limited to adjacent cells, or can range over a larger area, mediated by some diffusible factor. Inductive interactions have been extensively studied in the *Drosophila* compound eye. Within the imaginal disc, a cell's fate is believed to be determined only through interaction with other cells (Wolff 1991; Cagan 1993).

During the development of complex multi-cellular organisms, numerous local cell signaling events are required for proper cell fate determination (Artavanis-Tsakonas 1995). Among a group of initially equivalent cells, *lateral inhibition* allows an individual cell or a group of cells to be singled out from the surrounding cells (Figure 5).

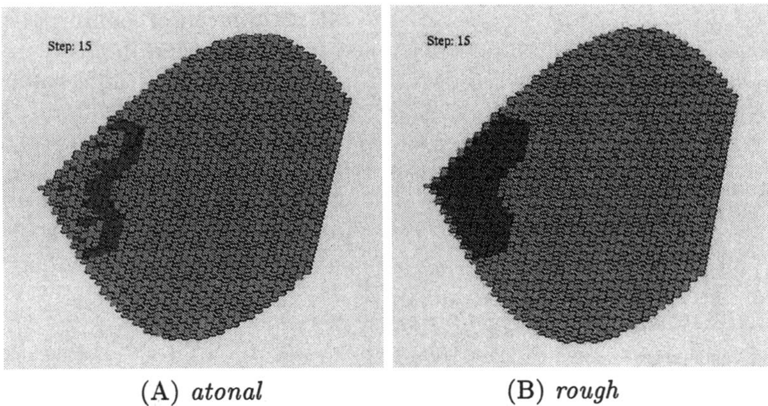

(A) *atonal* (B) *rough*

Figure 2: Simulated expression patterns of atonal and rough

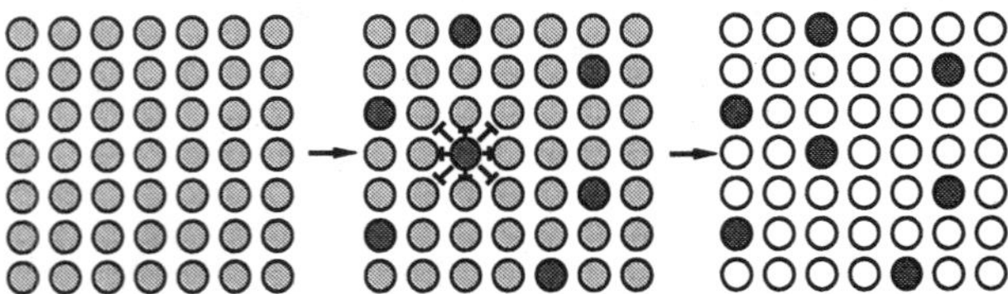

Figure 5: Lateral Inhibition

Genetic Networks for Ommatidia Formation

A large number of genes are involved in eye formation. The interactions and cascades of gene products have not been fully identified. Nevertheless, there is a substantial body of experimental data from which we can reconstruct possible genetic interactions. Figure 6 represents a possible genetic cascade during the development of the *Drosophila* eye after the precluster has emerged. Nodes in the graph are genes, and edges are the genes' inhibition or activation of each other. This diagram is based on various papers' experimental data, and represents what is believed to be the major genetic interactions involved in ommatidia formation. Table 1 shows properties of the major genes involved.

It should be noted, however, that the genetic interaction shown in the diagram is not confirmed to be fully accurate nor complete. The challenge now is to verify whether the interaction described in the diagram is correct and complete. If it is not correct, we may inquire about other possible interactions and unknown genes which can reproduce the gene expression patterns during the eye formation.

The Simulator Architecture

The simulator architecture is composed of three layers: the Classifier System Layer, the Interaction Layer, and the Diffusion Layer (Figure 7). Since the simulation re-

Gene	Cellular Location
atonal(ato)	nuclei
Enhancer of split complex (*E(spl)*-C)	nuclei
Delta(Dl)	transmembrane
Notch(N)	transmembrane
EGF receptor(DER)	transmembrane
spitz(spi)	diffusive
rough(ro)	nuclei
rhomboid(rho)	transmembrane
seven-up(svp)	nuclei
argos	diffusive
bride of sevenless(boss)	transmembrane
sevenless(sev)	transmembrane
rolled(rl)	nuclei, cytoplasm
Supressor of Hairless(Su(H))	nuclei, cytoplasm

Table 1: List of genes

ported in this paper focuses on the differentiation of photorecpetor cells in a single ommatidia, the simulation is restricted to only eight cells. However, the system can be extended to simulate an arbitarily large number of cells.

The classifier system layer

The simulator's classifier system is applied in the classifier system layer. A classifier system is a learning mechanism based on message matching, bidding, and reinforcement (Holland 1995). The classifier system layer contains eight classifier systems, each corresponding to one of the ommatidia's cells, simulating each cell's internal genetic cascade. The eight classifier systems run concurrently. Whenever there is interaction with other cells via cell–cell contact or diffusion, the interaction layer and the diffusion layer will mediate this process, and propagate the resultant information as environment status. In our classifier system, each rule set is regarded as a

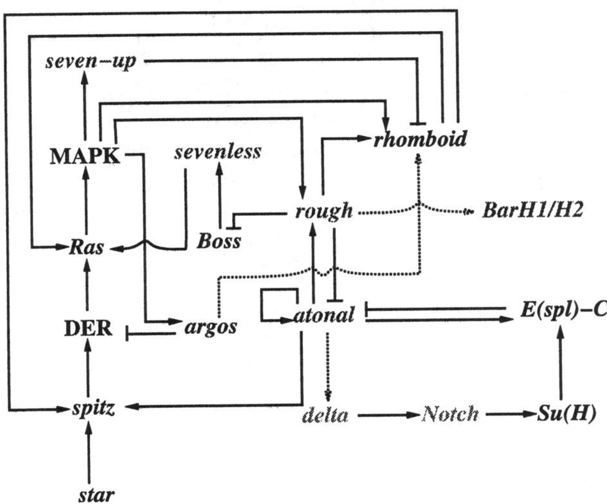

Figure 6: Gene regulation pathways. Some pathways are abbreviated. For example, the Ras1 →MAPK pathway has intermediate components not shown here, such as MAPKK and MAPKKK.

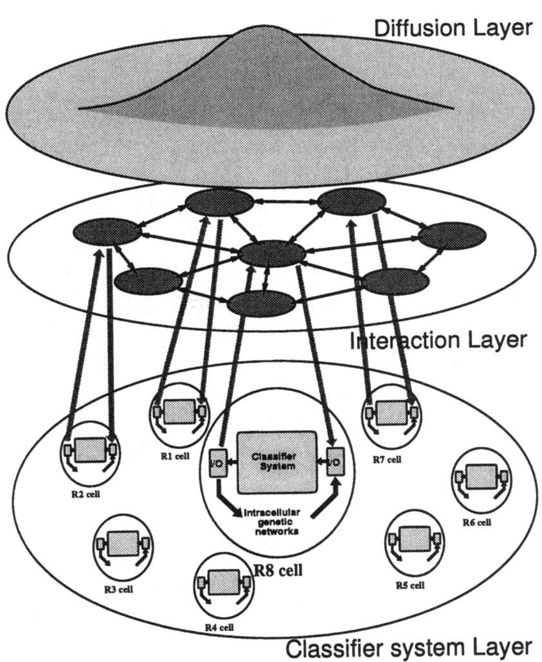

Figure 7: System architecture

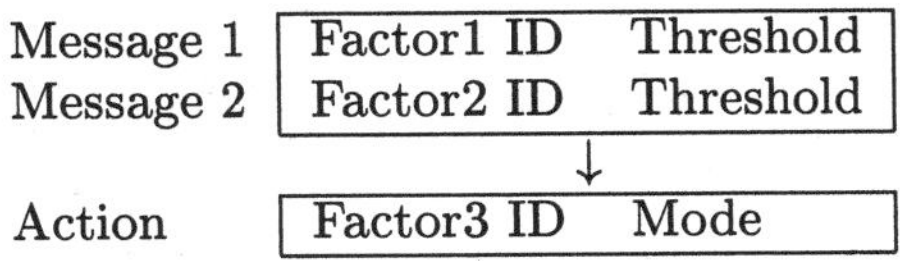

Figure 8: A classifier structure

separate individual.

The basic execution cycle of the classifier system consists of an iteration of the following steps:

1. Messages from the environment are placed on the message list.
2. Each condition of each classifier is checked against the message list to see if it is satisfied by (at least one) message thereon.
3. All satisfied classifiers participate in a *competition*, and the winner posts its messages to the message list.
4. All messages directed to effectors are executed (causing actions in the environment).
5. All messages on the message list from the *previous* cycle are erased (i.e., message persist for only a single cycle, unless they are repeatedly posted).

The format of classifier is shown in Figure 8. For this preliminary study, we used a rather simple classifier structure. The "condition" part of the classifier consists of two matching templates, each of which has Factor ID and its concentration threshold. A Factor ID is a unique identifier for a particular kind of protein, produced by the transcription of some corresponding gene.

Figure 9 shows a classifier which represents the following rule: *when both proteins ("Factors") A and B, produced by genes A and B, are at a concentration of more than 0.5 units (the threshold), the transcription of gene C is activated.*

This can be written as: `CS1: A 0.5, B 0.5 → C A`, where CS1 is a rule identifier. Notice that the action part and the condition part of the classifier is different. In this simulation, the expression of a gene produces a predefined amount of gene products, and there are other factors involved, such as diffusion, protein decay, and cell–cell interaction. These factors are taken into consideration to convert the classifier's active messages into a set of messages to post to the message list.

The interaction layer

The interaction layer is the layer in which cell–cell interaction is simulated, especially signal transduction in the ligand-receptor channel. Depending on the amount and position of ligands and receptors (calculated in the classifier system layer), the interaction layer determines

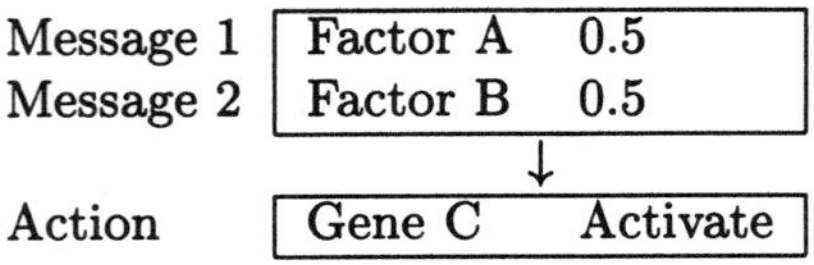

Figure 9: A classifier structure

a receptor's signalling intensity. A *signal* is a concentration level of chemicals which causes effects downstream in the cascade; in this model, signals are presented as messages to the classifier in the classifier layer.

To accurately simulate the cell–cell interaction, it is essential to accurately simulate cell shape and topology. Although the topology of cells in the wild-type ommatidia is strictly determined, cell shapes are not identical. Furthermore, during the process of morphogenesis, cell division takes place, and cells change their shape. Based on (Sun 1996), we use a Voronoi diagram to simulate cell topology and shapes.

The diffusion layer

The diffusion layer is where the diffusion of paracrine substances is simulated. The basic equation used in the model is:

$$\frac{\partial U_i}{\partial t} = D_i \frac{\partial^2 U_i}{\partial x^2} \quad (1)$$

U_i: concentration of protein i
D_i: diffusion coefficient of protein i

Parameter Search and Hypotheses Generation

While the simulator architecture reproduces gene expression patterns at sufficient accuracy for this research, it assumes that each parameter is set appropriately and that the gene interactions (represented by the set of classifiers) are complete and accurate.

There are two major challenges in the simulation of gene expression in biological systems. The first is to identify a set of parameters which enable the model to reproduce individual gene expression patterns consistent with the actual data. This can be a Herculean task, as the number of parameters involved easily exceeds 100, and can even be over a few thousand.

The second issue is to find all correct and complete gene interactions. To do this, we need to introduce a sophisticated method of hypotheses generation and testing.

The approach we haved tested in this paper is to use classifiers for both issues. Parameter identification can be done through the adaptation capability of the classifier system. For the photoreceptor cell differentiation, we assumed that the very existence of a particular gene expression is more important than some subtle difference in expression level. Accordingly, the parameter set is limited to just gene expression thresholds. This assumption holds only for this specific process, and does not generalize to other processes, such as R8 selection.

In finding the appropriate set of threshold levels for each gene, we used the credit assignment mechanism of the classifier. Credit assignment in classifier systems is based on competition. There are several ways to do this: we used the "Pittsburgh" approach. That is, we regard a rule set as an individual, and the assembly of the rule sets generate a cluster. Within the Pittsburgh approach, credit assignment is performed over an entire rule set. However, we also need to have adapation within a generation to efficiently identify threshold level. Accordingly, we also use the "Michigan" approach.

The procedure is as follows:

1. At the end of time t, the error between the concentration of a sample pattern and that of simulation pattern is calculated with each gene. This is calculated with least squares as follows:

$$Diff_t = \sum_{i \in genes} (C(i,t)_{sample} - C(i,t)_{simulation})^2 \quad (2)$$

where $C(i,t)$ represents the concentration of gene i products at time t.

2. This is compared with the difference at time *t-1*.

3. If $Diff_{t-1} < Diff_t$, then the *strength* of the active rule is updated.

Thus, the credit assigment is done for each time step so that classifiers which made appropriate rule-firing are reinforced, and the strength of each classifier changes.

Besides the identification of parameters, the use of classifier systems combined with genetic algoreithms to alter a classifier set enables the system to predict unknown genes and their interactions. Using crossover and mutation, new classifiers are introduced and some existing rules may be elimiated. After obtaining optimum fitness, we can investigate resultant classifier sets and decode them to see if any new gene or the removal of a cascade contributes to improving the accuracy of expression pattern reproduction.

Experiments

To evaluate the validity of the system, we conducted a simulation on an ommatidia which consists of eight photoreceptor cells, four cone cells and eight pigment cells. The rule set embedded in the system is based on knowledge accumulated so far from real biological experiments. For this experiment, we collected the genetic data from a number of papers in the literature, and from this formed the regulation pathway map shown previously in Figure

6. Each gene classification in the simulation is shown in Figure 1.

Our experiment is summarized as follows.

1. Create an initial rule set, and initialize the strength to 100.
2. Execute the system for 150 steps.
3. For each step, perform credit assignment in order to estimate threshold paramters.
4. Goto step 2.

After each cycle, we alter the strengths. In the first run, all strengths were initialized to the same value: 100. In the second run, all values were initialized except for the strengths.

At the begining of the simulation, the *atonal* gene is expressed in all cells; this is an initial condition assumed in this simulation. Figure 10 and Figure 11 show the simulated expression patterns for the *atonal* and *rough* genes in the R8 and R2 cells, averaged over ten trials. Changes in the strength of each classifier is shown in Figure 12 and Figure 13, based on gene interactions shown in Figure 6. In an actual ommatidium, soon after differentiation begins, *atonal* is expressed only in R8, and *rough* is expressed in R2 and R5 after a short delay. There are other genes involved in photo-receptor cell-fate determination, such as *spitz*, *star*, and *sca*, but we focus on *atonal* and *rough* in this paper.

The problem of the results shown here is that the *rough* expression level is too high in the R8 cell, which should never express *rough*.

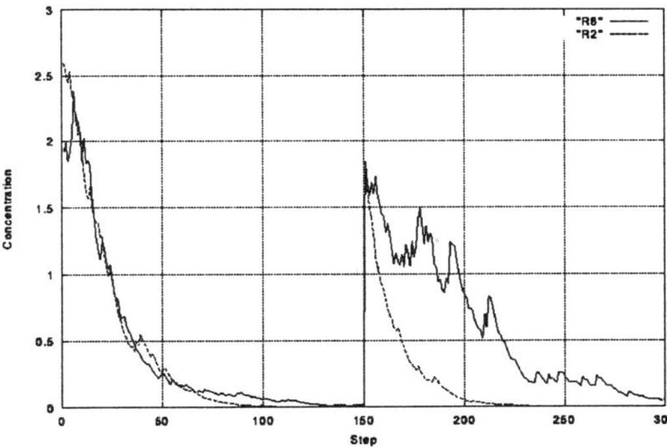

Figure 10: Dynamics of *atonal* expression in R8 and R2 cells

Figure 12 and Figure 13 show changes in the strength of the classifiers. Note the strength changes in R8 and R2. This reflects changes in the concentration of gene products in R8 and R2.

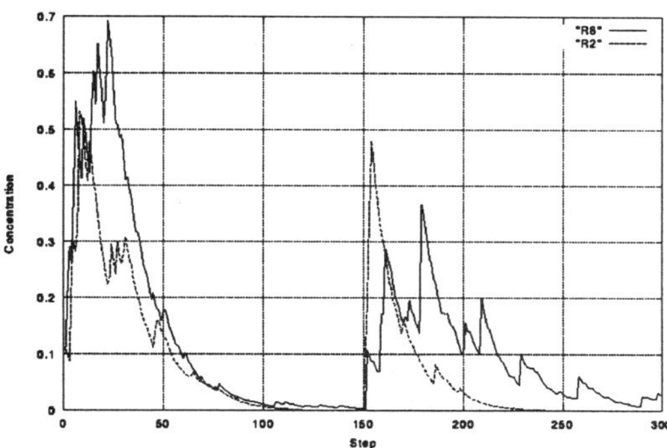

Figure 11: Dynamics of *rough* expression in R8 and R2 cells

The different run allows the system to change classifiers which encode genetic interaction now believed to be correct.

A new set of classifiers which removed the intracellular *atonal* to *rough* activation is shown in Figure 15 and Figure 14. With this set, *rough* is not expressed in R8, which is consistent with actual data. Also, the *atonal* expression level in R8 and R2 is better distiguished than original rule set.

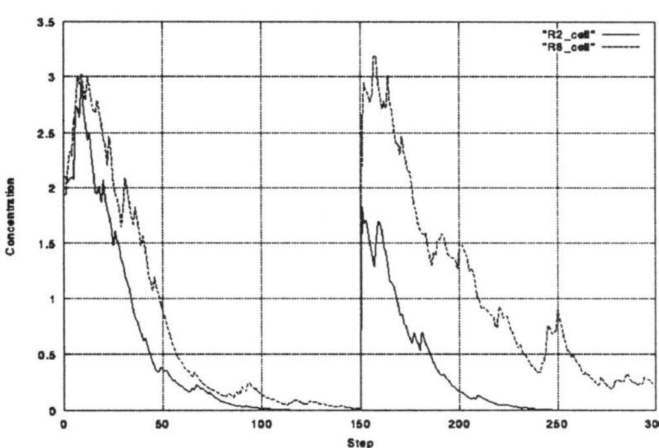

Figure 14: *atonal* expression dynamics in the R8 and R2 cells

Discussion

In this work, we have used a classifier system to investigate the genetic networks in the development of *Drosophila*'s eye. From Figure 10 and Figure 11 it can be seen that expression patterns within the second cycle are quite similar to those of actual experimental data.

These data implies that the rules seem to adapt to the

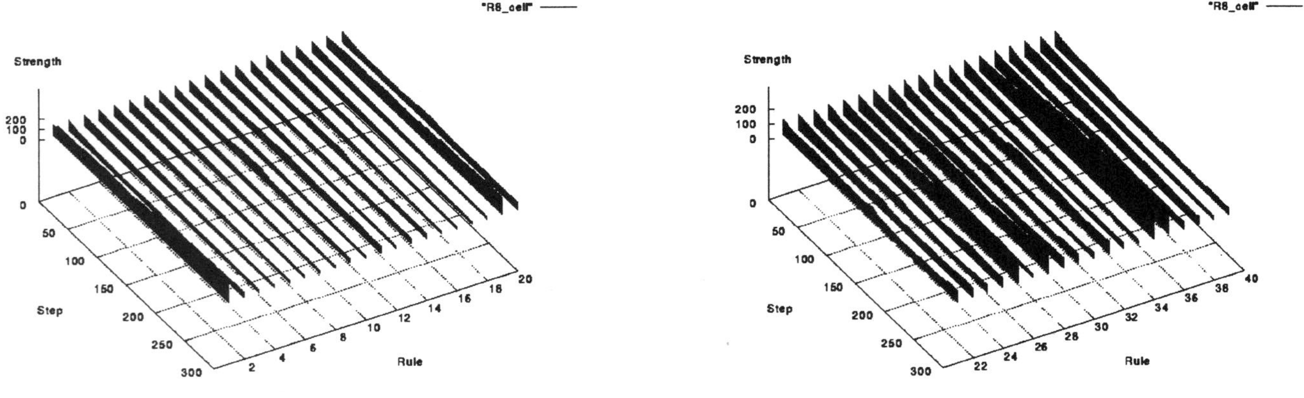

Figure 12: Dynamics of strength of rules 1–40 in the R8 cell

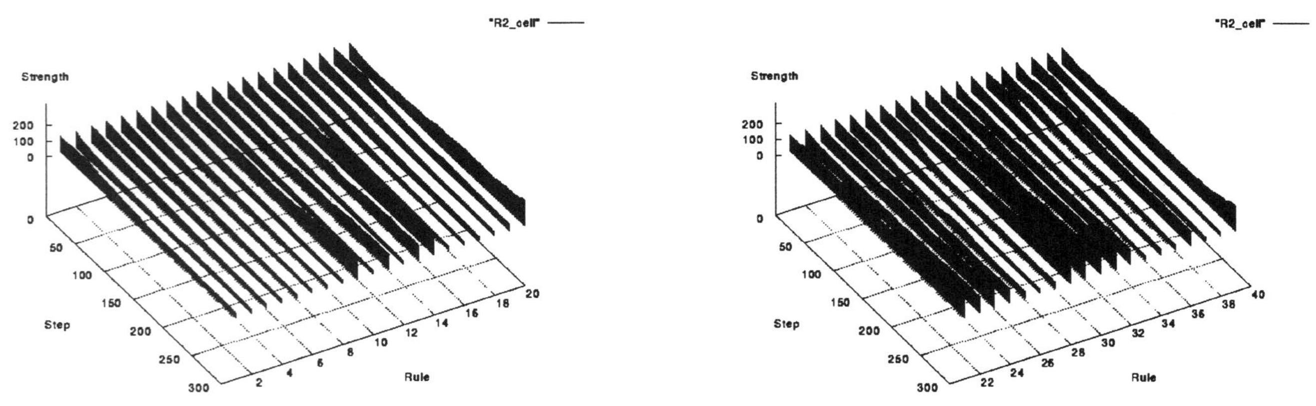

Figure 13: Dynamics of strength of rules 1–40 in the R2 cell

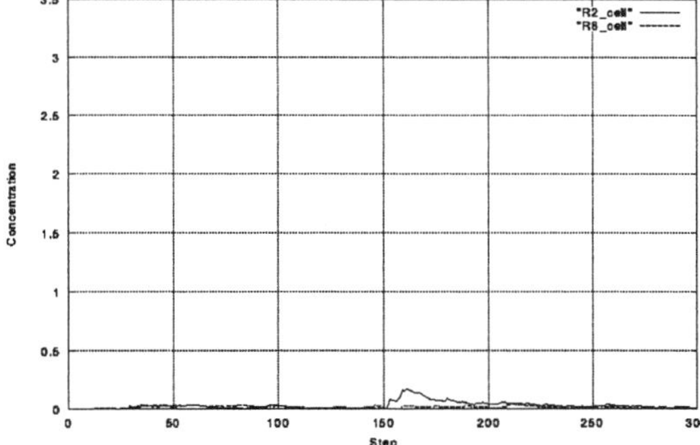

Figure 15: *rough* expression dynamics in the R8 and R2 cells

environment.

In addition, the results provide suggestions about the interaction between *atonal* and *rough*. As seen in Figure 11, within both R8 and R2 cells, *rough* gene products appear just after the simulation begins. In actual biological data, *rough* is never expressed in the R8 cell, but is expressed in the R2 cell. And the *rough* gene product is generated after some delay. From experimental biological observation, *atonal* and *rough* expression appear to complement each other (Dokucu 1996). In contrast with real experimental data, the simulation data exhibits different dynamics, with respect to *rough* expression data. These differences are partly due to a rule describing some of the interaction between *atonal* and *rough*. The rule was originally defined as follows:

if (*atonal* is expressed) then activate (*rough*)

This rule allows *atonal* to both activate *rough* directly inside the cell, or activate *rough* in neighboring cells. The use of this rule, therefore results in the expression of *rough* in *both* the R8 and R2 cells. However, this is not the case in a real expression pattern, where *rough* is expressed in *R2*, but not in *R8*. From this we can predict a hypothetical interaction mechanism between *atonal* and *rough*: *atonal* does not activate *rough* directly inside the cell where *atonal* exists, but instead it activates *rough* in adjacent cells, possibly mediated by transmembrane factors, or some other unknown factor **X** (Figure 17). One plausible mediating pathway is the Ras1→MAPK pathway.

There may also be other unknown mechanisms controlling the activation of *rough* expression; without these mechanisms it would be difficult to maintain the expression of *rough* over time. According to the regulation pathway shown previously, MAPK activates *rough*, yet the results tend to show a decrease in concentration of *rough* gene products. In particular, Rule 23's strength

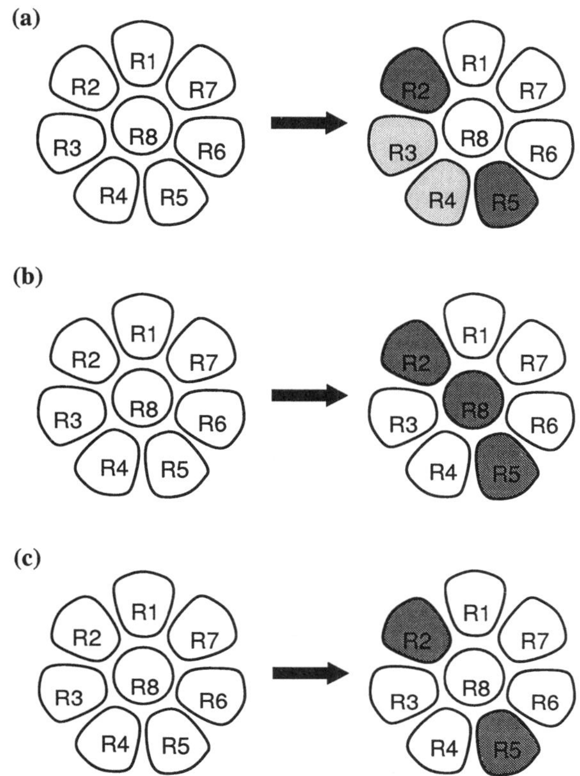

Figure 16: Expression Patterns of *atonal*

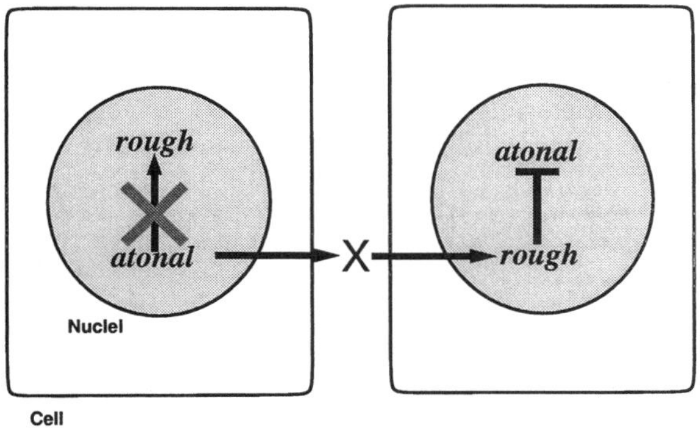

Figure 17: Hypothetical interaction between *atonal* and *rough*

in Figure 12 rises less than in Figure 13. Rule 23 is the MAPK→*rough* promoting function. As such, the expression of *rough* is less than expected from the actual data. Three possibilities may explain this:

- self-activation of *rough*
- relatively strong activation of Ras1→MAPK pathway prior to *rough*
- activation by external factors

We have not yet identified which one of these mechanisms is the most biologically plausible. Further extension of our simulation may be able to narrow down the hypotheses, but actual biological experiments will be needed to verify whether our predictions are correct.

Conclusion

In this paper, we report our initial attempts to develop a methodology for reproducing gene expression patterns involved in *Drosophila* eye formation. We have concentrated on the identification of genes and the interactions involved in photoreceptor differentiation in ommatidia. Our simulator is based on three layer architecture consisting of the classifier layer, the interaction layer, and the diffusion layer. A classifier system is used to identify a set of parameters, and to find unknown genes and their cascades, in order to produce correct expression patterns. As a result we have made several predictions about unknown genes and their interactions with other genes. We also propose that *atonal* may only activate *rough* in neighbour cells, but not in the same cell where *atonal* is being expressed. We have also proposed three possible mechanisms which may maintain *rough* expression; without these mechanisms, *rough* decreases rapidly in our simulation. This is not in accordance with actual biological data. While we believe that there is a considerable need to make more precise predictions, still this research exemplifies the possiblities of a new approach to computational biology.

Acknowledgments

The authors would like to express their gratitude to Professor Yuichiro Anzai at Keio University for his thoughtful advice. Special thanks to Dr. Frank Nielsen at Sony CSL, and to members of the Virtual Biology Laboratory. Sean Luke was especially helpful in providing us critical comments in the final version of this paper, in both scientific and linguistic contents.

References

Artavanis-Tsakonas, S., K. Matsuno, and M. E. Fortini. 1995. Notch Signaling. *Science* 268: 225-232.

Baker, N. E., M. Mlodzik, and G. M. Rubin. 1990. Spacing differentiation in the developing *Drosophila* eye: a fibrinogen-related lateral inhibitor encoded by scabrous". *Science* 250: 1370-1377.

Bate, M., and A. M. Ariase, editors. 1993. *The Development of Drosophila melanogaster, Vol.2.* Cold Spring Harbor Laboratory Press.

Cagan, R. 1993. Cell fate specification in the developing *Drosophila* retina. *Development* Supplement: 19–28.

Cagan, R.L., and D. F. Ready. 1989. Notch is required for successive cell decisions in the developing *Drosophila* retina". *Genes & Development* 3: 1099–1112.

Dokucu, M. E., L. Zipursky and R. L. Cagan. 1996. Atonal, Rough and the resolution of proneural clusters in the developing *Drosophila* retina. *Development* 122: 4139–4147.

Holland, J. H. 1995. *Adaptation in Natural and Artificial Systems.* Cambridge, MA: MIT Press, 4th Edition.

Kitano, H. et al. '997. Virtual biology laboratories: A new approach of computational biology", *Proc. of the 4th European Conference on Artificial Life (ECAL-97)*, edited by P. Husbands and I. Harvey. Cambridge, MA: MIT Press, p. 274–283.

Ready, T. F., T. E. Hanson, and S. Benzer. 1976. Development of the *Drosophila* retina, a neurocrystalline lattice. *Developmental Biology* 53: 217–240.

Sun, X., and S. Artavanis-Tsakonas. 1996. The intracellular deletions of DELTA and SERRATE define dominant negative forms of the *Drosophila* Notch ligands. *Development* 122: 2465–2472.

Tomlinson, A., D. F. Ready. 1987. Neuronal differentiation in the *Drosophila* ommatidium. *Developmental Biology* 120: 366–376.

Wolff, T., and D. F. Ready. 1991. The beginning of pattern formation in the *Drosophila* compound eye: The morphogenetic furrow and the second mitotic wave. *Development* 113: 841–850.

Computational Coevolution of Antiviral Drug Resistance

Christopher D. Rosin[1,2], Richard K. Belew[2], Garrett M. Morris[1], Arthur J. Olson[1], David S. Goodsell[1]

[1] The Scripps Research Institute; La Jolla, CA 92037

[2] Computer Science & Engineering Department; University of California, San Diego; La Jolla, CA 92093-0114

Email contact: `crosin@scripps.edu`

Abstract

An understanding of antiviral drug resistance is important in the design of effective drugs. Comprehensive features of the interaction between drug designs and resistance mutations are difficult to study experimentally, because of the very large numbers of drugs and mutants involved. We describe a computational framework for studying antiviral drug resistance. Data on HIV-1 protease are used to derive an approximate model that predicts interaction of a wide range of mutant forms of the protease with a broad class of protease inhibitors. An algorithm based on competitive coevolution is used to find highly resistant mutant forms of the protease, and effective inhibitors against such mutants, in the context of the model. We use this method to characterize general features of inhibitors that are effective in overcoming resistance, and to study related issues of selection pathways, cross-resistance, and combination therapies.

Introduction

Drug resistance is a major obstacle to the effectiveness of many antiviral drugs. Through the selection of mutations that reduce the efficacy of antiviral drugs, viruses such as HIV are very adept at evolving resistance. Comprehensive features of the interaction between drug designs and resistance mutations are difficult to study experimentally, because of the very large numbers of drugs and mutants involved. Computational modelling offers one approach to the study of the drug/mutant dynamic. Other authors have also proposed viral evolution as a rich domain for artificial life studies (Moya, Domingo, & Holland 1995).

We use *competitive coevolution* to search for highly resistant mutants, and for drug designs that are effective against these resistant mutants. Our computational framework depends on a model that predicts the effectiveness of specific antiviral drug designs against specific mutants of targeted viral enzymes. In this paper, we use a simple model that is based on the interaction of HIV-1 protease mutants with peptidomimetic protease inhibitors. We consider several classes of resistance mutations and inhibitors, and analyze the results of coevolution to study a variety of questions about drug design in the face of resistance.

The following section gives basic descriptions of our simple computational model of inhibitor interaction with HIV-1 protease mutants, and of the coevolutionary algorithms we use to analyze this model. Technical details of the model and algorithms are in the Appendixes. The "Experiments and Results" section gives an overview of a diverse set of experimental results. We consider strategies for effective inhibitor design, cross-resistance against a range of inhibitors, the design of combination therapies, and restrictions imposed by the evolutionary trajectories of a mutating virus.

Methods

Model

We model the interaction of HIV-1 protease with protease inhibitors. The HIV-1 protease enzyme serves an essential role during HIV-1 maturation by cleaving polyproteins manufactured from viral genetic material into the individual proteins required by HIV-1. Cleavage takes place at a localized active site in the protease. Protease inhibitors bind to this active site, preventing the normal function of HIV-1 protease and interrupting the life cycle of the virus. The emergence of resistance limits the effectiveness of such drugs. Mutants of HIV-1 protease that are resistant to an inhibitor have a modified shape that reduces binding by the inhibitor, while retaining the ability to bind and cleave the viral polyprotein.

Nine polyprotein sites must be be cleaved by HIV-1 protease during maturation. These sites are represented here as octapeptides, consisting of eight amino acids with four on either side of the cleavage site. These peptides are the *natural substrates* that every active mutant of HIV-1 protease must be able to bind and cleave. We consider inhibitor designs from the class of peptidomimetic inhibitors, which includes many of the drugs currently being tested (Wlodawer & Erickson 1993; Darke & Huff 1994). Such inhibitors closely resemble a peptide, with the central bond replaced by an uncleavable bond. In our model, these inhibitors are represented as octapeptides, just like the natural substrates.

The fitness computation for a mutant in the presence of an inhibitor is based on the strength of binding between the mutant protease and the inhibitor, and the rate at which the mutant cleaves its natural substrates. Both of these contributions to fitness are calculated using a binding model that predicts protease binding to peptides. A full atomic simulation is computationally unfeasible: current methods incorporating the necessary flexibility in the peptide inhibitors and in the protease active site would require minutes to hours for evaluation of each pair (Rosenfeld, Vajda, & DeLisi 1995). Since we need to consider the interaction of many pairs of peptides and protease mutants, the computational model must be very fast.

For this work, we use a simple binding model that is derived empirically from data on HIV-1 protease, and captures the effect of mutations in the active site. Such active site mutations have the most direct effects on protease specificity, and form a sizable fraction of the known resistance responses to protease inhibitors (Schinazi, Larder, & Mellors 1997). While the accuracy and generality of this binding model is limited, it should still be useful for studying the general qualitative features of resistance and drug design that concern us here.

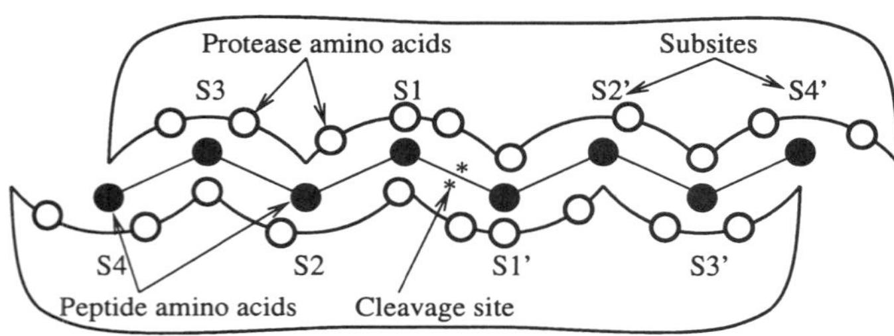

Figure 1: Schematic of HIV-1 Protease Active Site

Figure 1 shows a schematic of the active site of HIV-1 protease, with a bound peptide substrate. Subsites are numbered S4, S3, S2, S1, S1', S2', S3', S4', with the cleavage site between S1 and S1'. Each subsite is in contact with several amino acids in the protease, and each protease amino acid in the active site may contact several subsites. Since HIV-1 protease is a homodimer (i.e., made up of two identical subunits), a change in any amino acid of a subunit affects the active site at two positions. In our model, there are ten distinct mutable amino acids that affect the active site at twenty positions.

The viral fitness function used for coevolution evaluates the likelihood that a given virus may reproduce when challenged by a given inhibitor. The mutant virus must retain the ability to cleave its polyprotein processing sites at a sufficient rate, so we have defined the fitness function as the ratio of: (i) the reaction velocity of the mutant protease cleaving its worst substrate (i.e. its rate-limiting substrate) when challenged by the inhibitor, to (ii) that of the wild type (unmutated) enzyme, uninhibited, cleaving *its* worst substrate. For inhibitor i and protease mutant m this ratio will be referred to as $A(m, i)$, the relative *activity* of the the protease mutant in the presence of the inhibitor. A simple volume-based model is used to approximate the binding free energy of substrates and inhibitors, and mutation is incorporated by a simple modification of this binding model based on crystallographic structures of protease-inhibitor complexes. A detailed description of the model is given in Appendix B.

Model fitness values larger than one indicate mutants that are more active than wild type, even in the presence of inhibitor, whereas values less than one are proteases that are effectively inhibited. It has been estimated that reduction of protease activity to 2% that of the wild type is sufficient to block viral maturation (Rose, Babe, & Craik 1995) and that restoration of protease activity to about 26% that of the wild type will yield a viable resistant strain (Tang & Hartsuck 1995). We consider changes of this order of magnitude to be significant in our simulations. Since the absolute level of activity obtained from the model depends on the chosen concentrations of substrate and inhibitor, for which there is a wide range of reasonable values, experiments below emphasize comparison of the relative magnitude of different activities, rather than their absolute level.

Coevolution

Given this model, the basic problem we wish to solve is the design of minimax-optimal inhibitors. Given a mutant protease $m \in \mathcal{M}$, where $\mathcal{M}$ is the set of all allowed mutant proteases; an inhibitor $i \in \mathcal{I}$, where $\mathcal{I}$ is the set of all allowed inhibitors; and our model $A(m, i)$ that evaluates the activity of the protease when challenged by the inhibitor, we seek the particular i with the minimax-optimal activity:

$$\min_{i \in \mathcal{I}} \max_{m \in \mathcal{M}} A(m, i)$$

i.e., the inhibitor that *minimizes* the activity of the best protease, while that protease itself retains the *maximal* activity when inhibited.

Since the quality of an inhibitor is defined in terms of the entire (possibly very large) set of mutant proteases, we do not have an efficient objective function that allows us to search directly for good inhibitors. Instead, we use *coevolutionary* algorithms (Hillis 1991; Rosin & Belew 1997) that simultaneously anticipate specific resistance mutations while searching for inhibitors that overcome this resistance. These algorithms are based on the biological concept of an arms race (Dawkins & Krebs 1979); in our context, inhibitors drive the evolution of resistance, which in turn drives the evolution of inhibitors that are effective against a broader range of resistance mutations, and so on.

The experiments here use a genetic algorithm to continually search for new protease mutants and inhibitors that are effective against inhibitors and mutants that arose during earlier search. The particular method used is based on prior work (Rosin & Belew 1996; 1997) adapted for this problem. Technical details about the method are given in Appendix A. Note that coevolution is used here only as a computational technique (albeit biologically inspired); we are not attempting to model a physically realizable coevolutionary process.

This genetic algorithm-based coevolutionary method is a heuristic that cannot be guaranteed to return a minimax-optimal inhibitor. The inhibitor that results from coevolution, however, *can* be tested exhaustively to guarantee that it is minimax-optimal. This is an advantage of the computationally simple model used in these experiments. We take the final best inhibitor produced by coevolution, and the set of protease mutants that were sufficient to test the candidate inhibitors that arose during coevolution. By enumerating all inhibitors against this set of protease mutants, we verify that there does not exist an inhibitor better than the one found. By enumerating all protease mutants against the final inhibitor, we guarantee that there does not exist a mutant with higher activity against the final inhibitor than the activity found during coevolution. These methods are used to verify that all results found here are, in fact, exactly optimal.[1] The coevolutionary heuristics proved to be reliable: a single run on each problem was adequate to produce an optimal inhibitor.

Experiments and Results

Strategies for Designing Resistance-Evading Inhibitors

Any viable protease mutant must retain its natural cleavage ability. One common strategy for the design of inhibitors is to model them after natural substrates (Wlodawer & Erickson 1993): since the enzyme must retain some binding to the natural substrates, such an inhibitor may perform well against a broad range of mutants. Such mimics of natural substrates are one class of inhibitors that we consider here.

Most enzymes are highly specific for a single substrate and their active sites have evolved to complement perfectly the shape and chemical nature of the reaction transition state associated with this substrate. Natural substrate mimics are ideal inhibitors for these enzymes: they bind tightly to the active site and block substrate binding. They are also fairly robust in the face of resistance mutations: because of the close similarity of inhibitor and transition state of the natural substrate, mutant enzymes that evade the inhibitor while retaining activity may be difficult to find.

There may, however, exist better inhibitors than these substrate mimics. This issue is particularly important for retroviral proteases such as HIV-1 protease. Retroviral proteases have a large, cylindrical active site that binds and cleaves a diverse set of protein sequences required for viral maturation (Pettit *et al.* 1991; Dunn *et al.* 1994). The modular nature of substrate recognition in HIV-1 protease, with eight substrate residues binding to eight protease subsites, and the lack of absolute specificity of each site together provide a mechanism for mutation and drug resistance: the active site may mutate slightly to widen the energetic difference between inhibitor binding and substrate binding.

With coevolution, we can search for inhibitors from a much larger class than the nine substrate mimics. Here, we consider general-sequence octapeptides composed of fifteen amino acids.[2] There are about 2.6 billion such inhibitors. By comparing the performance of minimax-optimal inhibitors obtained from this large class, with that of minimax-optimal inhibitors drawn from the nine substrate mimics, we can evaluate these two design strategies in terms of ability to overcome resistance.

Inhibitors are coevolved against increasingly diverse sets of protease mutants. We start by considering single point mutations, then proteases with up to two mutations from wild type, then up to three, and so on up to any set of mutations at the ten mutable protease sites. The size of these sets increases exponentially with the allowed number of mutations, from 119 single-point mutants up to about 41 billion arbitrary mutants. These sets allow us to see trends as the possibilities for resistance increase.

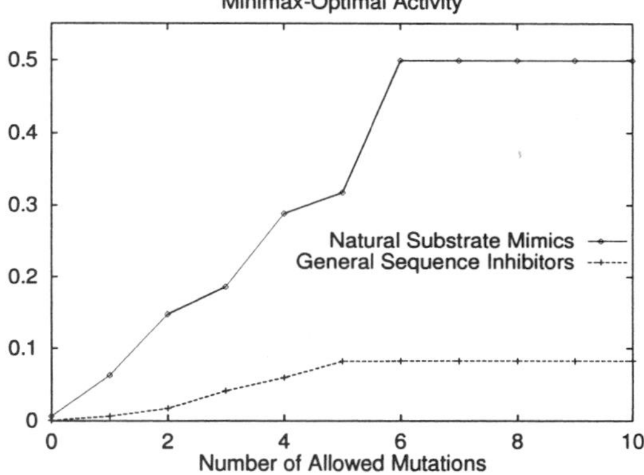

Figure 2: Natural Substrate Mimics vs. General-Sequence Inhibitors

[1]The one exception to this arises in the "Combination Therapies" section: there are too many inhibitor pairs to enumerate all and verify that none are better than the one found during coevolution. But proteases are enumerated against the inhibitor pair found to verify that it is as good as it appears to be during coevolution; this is the most important test for the comparison made in that section.

[2]The uncharged amino acids: all except D, E, H, R, K.

Figure 2 shows the minimax-optimal activity obtained against each class of protease mutants. As the number of allowed mutations increases, resistance increases and the minimax-optimal activity goes up. Both inhibitor binding and substrate binding contribute to the activity of a mutant; in general, resistant mutants in these experiments display both improved substrate binding and reduced inhibitor binding. Both modes of resistance have been observed in HIV-1 protease (Schock, Garsky, & Kuo 1996).

The experiment reveals several features of resistance in this model. First, there do exist inhibitors with a significant capability to limit resistance: even allowing any set of mutations, the best inhibitor forces a protease activity that is below 10% that of the uninhibited wild type. Second, there are large differences in the relative abilities of different inhibitors to limit resistance: the difference in activity between the two lines is a factor of 5-10. Finally, there exist inhibitors that fare much better than the substrate mimics in the face of resistance mutations. The natural substrates do not seem to provide a completely adequate model for inhibitor design. A more extensive discussion of these features, in the context of an earlier version of this experiment, is given in (Rosin *et al.* 1998).

Cross-Resistance

In clinical trials, it has been observed that resistance mutations that arise in a patient using one protease inhibitor often confer resistance to a large number of different protease inhibitors that the patient has never used (Condra *et al.* 1995). This is called *cross-resistance*, and it is problematic because it limits the number of distinctly useful drugs available to treat patients that have developed resistance to one drug.

In our context, we can consider cross-resistance by enumerating the best inhibitor designs, then finding the mutant most resistant to *one* of them and seeing how it fares against the rest of these designs. Most inhibitors currently being tested have been designed to inhibit the wild type protease. This is most closely modelled in our context by choosing inhibitors that are best against the wild type protease. Consider the best inhibitor designed against the wild type in our model. We find the mutant (from the set of all mutants, with any number of allowed mutations) that is most resistant to this inhibitor, and check the activity of this mutant against other inhibitor designs that performed well against the wild type. We can also consider the best inhibitor designs obtained by coevolution against larger pools of mutants than the single wild type, and compare cross-resistance results on these.

More specifically, we take the minimax-optimal inhibitor design i_n against the set of mutants with at most n mutations. We then find the optimal mutant m_n against i_n. To obtain a set of "reasonably good" inhibitor designs against proteases with at most n mutations, let S_n be the set of all inhibitors with worst-case activity that is at most twice the minimax-optimal activity. S_n is found by enumeration, and typically has several thousand members. Finally, we test the cross-resistance of m_n by evaluating its activity against each member of S_n, and computing the fraction of S_n against which it achieves an activity of at least a desired threshold T. Results are shown for $T = 0.25$ and $T = 0.0825$. Results at other thresholds typically resemble one of these graphs.

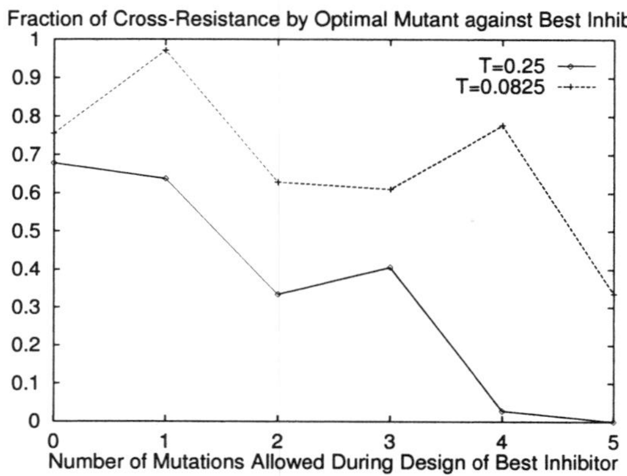

Figure 3: Cross-Resistance

In Figure 3, n is allowed to range from 0-5, where n is defined as above to be the maximum number of mutations allowed in the set of proteases against which inhibitors are initially designed. The graph shows the fraction of S_n to which m_n is cross-resistant at the $T = 0.25$ and $T = 0.0825$ levels of activity. The lack of smoothness in the graphs is partly due to the use of a *single* mutant m_n at each point. The exact properties of this particular mutant are somewhat arbitrary and may not entirely reflect the average behavior of other mutants resistant to a single inhibitor chosen from S_n.

A high level of cross-resistance is displayed against inhibitors that are designed against the wild type protease: only about 25-30% of such inhibitors remain successful against the mutant most resistant to i_0. Since most existing protease inhibitor drugs have been targeted to inhibit the wild type enzyme, these cross-resistance results for S_0 are the most relevant comparison with clinical data on cross-resistance. Existing data reveals a high degree of cross-resistance by HIV-1 against protease inhibitors in clinical trials (Condra *et al.* 1995), so the model is in general agreement with this data. Such agreement is an encouraging feature of the model, because cross-resistance is one of the few comprehensive features of the interaction between drug design and resistance where data is available.

Cross-resistance displays a general decreasing trend as inhibitors are designed against larger sets of mutants. These inhibitors tend to remain robust in the face of unrestricted mutations, despite the fact that they were not designed against such unrestricted mutants. While this is interesting in itself, it indicates that substantial resistance cannot emerge against such inhibitors. This limits the degree of cross-resistance that could be seen in this experiment.

Combination Therapies

The most effective therapies against HIV-1 in current use consist of combinations of multiple drugs. Resistant mutants may be less likely to arise if they must be simultaneously effective against several different drugs with varying properties (Condra & Emini 1997). Such combination therapies are typically chosen to be diverse, containing drugs that target multiple viral enzymes. Here, we consider more limited combinations consisting of two protease inhibitors.

The activity of a protease mutant in the presence of a combination of protease inhibitors is modelled by taking the minimum of its activities against each inhibitor separately. Thus, if any member of a combination is effective against a particular mutant, the whole combination is considered to be effective. This makes sense since all inhibitors in the combination are simultaneously present. This type of action by inhibitor combinations allows them to split up the work of covering the set of possible resistant mutants: each inhibitor needs only to be effective against a subset of the mutants, while the other inhibitors pick up the slack on the remaining mutants.

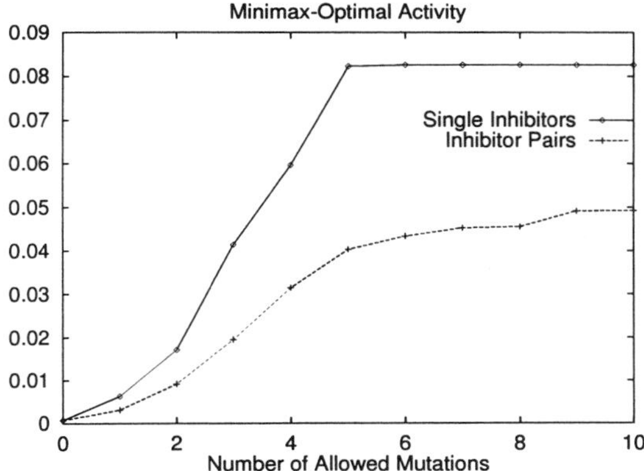

Figure 4: Single Inhibitors vs. Combinations

We coevolve pairs of inhibitors against the mutant pools, and compare these results to those obtained for single inhibitors. Figure 4 shows minimax-optimal activities at 0-10 allowed mutations. Against the single wild type protease, combination therapies offer no advantage over single inhibitors. This follows from the definition of protease activity against a combination of inhibitors: the minimum over activities obtained by each member of a combination against the wild type can be no better than the activity obtained by the best single inhibitor against the wild type. With mutations allowed, inhibitor pairs perform better than single inhibitors, yielding a minimax-optimal activity that is almost a factor of 2 smaller at 2-10 allowed mutations. Thus, even with the limited range of inhibitor diversity available in our model, combination therapies can limit resistance to a greater degree than single inhibitors.

Coevolved inhibitor pairs reflect features of the energy potentials that form the basis for the fitness function. Most importantly, the energy in subsite S1' has two minima, reflecting a preference for both large and small amino acids in this subsite. A single inhibitor must choose some compromise between these two minima, but resistance mutations have substantial freedom in increasing binding energy away from these minima. The coevolved pairs of inhibitors contains one inhibitor that has a small amino acid in S1', and another inhibitor that has a large amino acid in S1'. This greatly constrains the range of feasible resistance mutations.

Selection Pathways

One of the reasons for the rapid rise of drug resistance in HIV-1 is its high turnover rate and high mutation rate: every point mutation is likely to be tried over the course of a few days in an infected individual (Coffin 1995). Point mutations that yield increased fitness are selected, and can form the basis for further mutations. Resistance arises through a *selection pathway*: an ordered sequence of mutations, each of which yields a viable mutant (Molla *et al.* 1996).

In experiments above, protease mutants with multiple point mutations from the wild type were not constrained to have arisen by any particular sequence of mutations. We assumed that the worst-case mutant would arise, without considering how it would arise. To contrast this permissive model, we use here a very restrictive model of virus evolution. Resistant mutants against a particular inhibitor are constrained to arise by a sequence of point mutations, each of which must confer increased activity. Since such mutations are genetic, we consider only those amino-acid substitutions that may be achieved by some single point change in the genetic sequence. Beyond this restriction, however, we allow *any* sequence of mutations that yields increasing activity, without attempting to model the likelihood that such a pathway would actually be followed under biological conditions.

We consider classes of mutants of increasing size, as the maximum allowed selection pathway length (the maximum number of sequential mutations) is increased. A restriction is also placed on inhibitors: we only allow inhibitors against which there are no pathways that continue to increase activity out to the maximum allowed number of mutations. This restriction is natural in these experiments because the allowed inhibitors are fully tested: no resistance can evolve (within the confines of our model) beyond the selection pathways that are explicitly tested.

Note that, as a result of this restriction on inhibitors, increasing numbers of allowed mutations actually help the inhibitors rather than the virus. When selection pathways are restricted to be short, inhibitors are limited to those against which resistance cannot evolve much beyond the fitness of the wild type. When selection pathways are permitted to be longer, inhibitors have more freedom to allow viral evolution. This freedom may help if there exist longer selection pathways that have increasing fitness that nonetheless remains low in absolute terms. This benefit to inhibitors stands in contrast to experiments above, where increasing numbers of allowed mutations could only benefit the protease mutants.

Table 1: Minimax-Optimal Activity Against Selection Pathways

Max Path Length	Activity
1	0.0129
2	0.0117
3	0.0092
4	0.0092
5	0.0092

Results for minimax-optimal inhibitors against selection pathways are shown in Table 1. Activity is reduced to about 1% that of the uninhibited wild type. This is substantially better than the minimax-optimal activity of about 8% that was obtained without restricting mutants to selection pathways. This shows that there exist highly-resistant mutants that cannot be reached through a series of single-mutation improvements. Restrictions on viral evolution allow much more effective inhibition than is possible against unconstrained mutants.

It should be noted that the advantages in reduced activity that are seen here cannot obtained with arbitrary inhibitor designs. For example, allowing selection pathways of length at most 5, the best substrate mimic yields an activity of 0.15; about 15 times worse than that for the best inhibitors seen here. The minimax-optimal general-sequence inhibitors that were obtained in the initial experiment also fare relatively poorly. Against selection pathways of length at most 5, the best inhibitor designs against pools of mutants with at most 1,2, and 3 mutations fail to terminate all selection pathways. Such inhibitors allow continued increases in viral fitness. Beyond this, the minimax-optimal inhibitors designed against unrestricted mutants obtain an activity of 0.034 against selection pathways of length at most 5.

Evolutionary constraints on resistance appear to place important restrictions on the mutations that need to be considered. Inhibitor designs that cut off viral evolution before it has a chance to get very far are highly effective. Such inhibitors are also obtained at a relatively low design cost: only proteases with a small number of mutations from wild type need to be considered, as opposed to the vast search space that must be considered in finding inhibitors that are minimax-optimal against unrestricted mutants. Future work will consider such design strategies in more realistic models of virus evolution, between the permissive and restrictive regimes discussed here.

Conclusion

We have presented a computational framework that allows a broad range of issues in the interaction of resistance and drug design to be readily addressed. Within the scope of a simple model of HIV-1 protease interaction with inhibitors, competitive coevolution is able to find inhibitors that optimally limit the emergence of resistance. Due to the limited accuracy of the current model, we do not place much confidence in specific predictions concerning resistance mutations or good inhibitor designs. Our basic framework does, however, allow the exploration of several qualitative features of drug design and resistance.

We find that there exist inhibitors with a substantial ability to limit resistance. While mimics of the natural substrates of the targeted enzyme have some ability to limit resistance, much more effective designs are found from a broader class of inhibitors. As inhibitor designs are forced to compete against larger and larger sets of possible resistance mutations, the possibilities for the emergence of resistance and cross-resistance are greatly reduced. Also, even in our limited domain, combination therapies offer an advantage in limiting resistance over single inhibitors. Finally, constraining viral evolution to mutants reached by an ordered sequence of mutations of increasing fitness prevents some highly-resistant mutants from being discovered. Inhibitors designed to exploit these constraints can greatly limit the ability of the virus to evolve resistance.

Future work will focus on improving the model and the coevolutionary algorithms used to analyze it. The present model is quite simple: it captures only basic geometric features of binding, does not attempt to model separately differences in binding and catalysis, and is calibrated using only data on the wild type HIV-1 protease. Current work is exploring the improvement of accuracy with additional features such as hydrophobicity, explicit modelling of changes in catalytic efficiency, and the incorporation of experimental data on the interaction of mutants of HIV-1 protease with peptides. Beyond such empirically-derived models, we hope eventually to use more accurate predictions of binding based on molecular docking (Morris *et al.* 1996) for important evaluations during coevolution. As more and more data becomes available on observed mutations to the HIV virus, both across patients and within a single patient during the course of the disease, we aspire to model gross features of its evolution.

Coevolution is successful in finding minimax-optimal inhibitors under the current model. This problem is a good test case for coevolutionary algorithms, because it permits exact testing of results. Still, the vast number of potential drug designs and HIV mutants means it is not an easy problem for coevolutionary methods. These preliminary results raise important issues such as the difficulty of dealing with large, diverse test sets in coevolving populations. A more detailed understanding of these issues may help improve the coevolutionary algorithms used in this work. Such improvements will become important as we consider more computationally intensive models of molecular interaction.

Problems of drug resistance involve evolutionary questions that are difficult to address directly with experiments. However, data is available at the molecular level, and this allows us to build computational models that permit easy exploration. As these models become more accurate, we hope to reach a point where some results from these computational models, such as specific inhibitor designs, will be experimentally verifiable. Drug resistance provides a domain where both artificial life models and real-life experiments can contribute to an understanding of evolutionary questions.

Acknowledgments

This work was supported by NIH grant P01 GM48870, and Burroughs Wellcome LJIS grant APP #0842 (C.D.R.). This is publication #11417-MB from The Scripps Research Institute.

Appendix A: Coevolution Algorithm Details

A number of coevolutionary algorithms were tested on this problem. Methods that employ two competing populations that evolve simultaneously (Rosin & Belew 1997) encounter difficulties. This is partly because of the large number of mutants required to test adequately the inhibitors that arise during coevolution: even with niching methods, it is difficult for a single panmictic population to maintain simultaneously such a large number of tests and continue successfully searching for new protease mutants. Modifications such as subpopulation schemes (Mühlenbein, Schomisch, & Born 1991) might improve results, but for now we use a more computationally intensive coevolutionary method that succeeds reliably using our model of inhibitor/protease interaction.

We adapt a method for minimax problems that directly forces progress in an arms race (Rosin & Belew 1996; Rosin 1997). In this context, the method maintains sets I and M of inhibitors and mutants, respectively. I begins empty, and M begins with the unmutated wild type protease. At each step, the inhibitor i, whose worst-case activity over M is optimal, is found and is added to I. Then, against each member of I, the highest activity obtainable against it by any allowed mutant is found. The minimum of these activities sets the threshold v at which I may be covered: we find a minimal set S of mutants, such that for each member $i \in I$, at least one $m \in S$ obtains activity at least v against i. S is then added to M.

This procedure is guaranteed eventually to find the minimax-optimal inhibitor. The exact search, that is required each step to find inhibitors optimal against M and mutants optimal against I, seems to be too inefficient for the full version of this problem (despite savings over complete enumeration obtained by a branch-and-bound technique). So, we use a genetic algorithm (GA) instead in most of the experiments described here. The exception to this is that optimal selection pathways against each inhibitor in I are found with breadth-first search in the "Selection Pathways" section; the increasing-activity constraint makes this search reasonably efficient.

Inhibitor and mutant genetic algorithms are restarted each step. During evolution against M, each member of the inhibitor population is tested against each member of M. An inhibitor is scored with the worst-case (max) activity over M (Barbosa 1997). Inhibitor evolution proceeds until the population stagnates (defined here to be 20 successive generations without improvement in best fitness), at which point the best inhibitor in the population is added to I.

Each step, a separate population is initialized and run against each individual member of I. These separate runs are not much more costly than a single run against all of I, because each run does only a $\frac{1}{|I|}$ fraction of the fitness testing that would be done in a single large run, and fitness testing dominates the run time. Once each of these runs stagnates, an equal number of the best individuals from each of the separate runs are used to seed a final population that is evolved directly against all of I. This helps compress the size of the resulting cover (the importance of this is discussed in (Rosin & Belew 1996)), and sometimes makes further progress against I when the results of one run against one member of I are helpful against a different member of I. Fitness during this phase is calculated using an extension of *competitive fitness sharing* (Rosin & Belew 1997): against each inhibitor, a unit of fitness is divided up among all proteases that obtain the best activity against it that was obtained by any protease in that generation. Thus, if there is a single best protease against the inhibitor this generation, it receives the entire unit of fitness. But if many proteases obtain maximal activity against it, each only receives a small amount of fitness. This is a niching method (Goldberg & Richardson 1987) that has the effect of focusing selection on proteases that are resistant to inhibitors to which few other proteases in the population are resistant. This large GA is run to stagnation, and a greedy set-covering algorithm (Chvatal 1979) is used on the final population to choose a small cover that achieves the best activity currently possible against I, as described above. This cover is added to M. After each step, minimax-optimal activity is estimated from the current I and M. Coevolution terminates when this activity is unchanged for five successive steps.

GA parameters were chosen with minimal experimentation, and may not be optimal. A large population size of 3000 is used to give reliable results in all experiments. The inhibitor population uses a single elitist, and the mutant population uses 50 elitists; elitists are chosen using the same fitness used for selection. Tournament selection is used, with each parent chosen in an independent tournament of size 3 in the inhibitor population, and of size 2 in the mutant population. Offspring are created via crossover with 75% probability in the inhibitor population, and with 25% probability in the mutant population. Mutation[3] occurs in each child with 80% probability in the inhibitor population, and 90% probability in the protease population.

The inhibitor population uses fairly simple operators: 2-point crossover, and a mutation probability of 0.15 at each site (0.075 in the "Combination Therapies" experiment) of an inhibitor chosen for mutation. Mutant protease search is complicated by the restrictions placed on the total number of mutations allowed from wild type, and the fact that viable mutants are sparse in the entire space of mutants. A 2-point crossover operator is used, with crossover points chosen repeatedly until the resulting child does not violate the constraint on the total number of mutations. The protease mutation operator chooses a single site to mutate, and chooses a random allowed allele for it. If the resulting protease exceeds the total number of allowed mutations from the wild type, one of the other sites is chosen randomly and is back mutated to restore this condition. Finally, a *repair* operator (Hart, Kammeyer, & Belew 1995) is applied to the protease. If it fails to bind to one of the natural substrates, each possible single-site change is tried (preserving the original mutated site, so that this site is not simply back mutated). For each, if the constraint on total mutational distance from the wild type is violated, each possible back mutation is tried (again, excluding the originally chosen mutated site). If any of these attempted repairs is successful in yielding a protease that binds to all natural substrates, one of the successful repairs is chosen at random. If none is successful, a new mutation is randomly chosen and the repair attempt begins again. Such complex mutations seem to be required to prevent the population from getting stuck on suboptimal individuals from which successful changes are very difficult to find. The initial population is prepared using the repair operator: to generate a random protease, one site is chosen and fixed randomly, a random number of additional mutations from wild type are chosen (up to the total number allowed), and the repair operator is then applied, preserving the initially fixed site. This helps obtain an initial population with sufficient diversity in each gene of GA's representation.

[3]Note that this is mutation in the genetic algorithm, not natural mutation of the protease.

Appendix B: Model Details

Fitness Calculation

The reaction velocity of the wild type protease with a given substrate, $\nu(wt)$, is calculated using Michaelis-Menten kinetics (Stryer 1995):

$$\nu(wt) = V_{max}(wt)\frac{[S]}{[S] + K_M(wt)}$$

where $[S]$ is the substrate concentration, $V_{max}(wt)$ is the maximal velocity, and $K_M(wt)$ is the Michaelis constant. To define the velocity of the rate-limiting step, we evaluate $\nu(wt)$ using the substrate with the lowest velocity, making two assumptions: (i) V_{max} is identical for each of the substrates, and (ii) K_M may be approximated by the binding constant K_d, such that $K_M \approx K_d = e^{\Delta G/RT}$, where ΔG is the energy evaluated by the volume-based method described below. Nine native substrates are tested for the $\nu(wt)$ evaluation: RGANFLGK, AETFYVDR, SQNYPIVQ, RKILFLDG, ATIMMQRG, PGNFLQSR, TLNFPISP, SFNFPQIT, and ARVLAEAM (the cleavage site is at the center of each octapeptide).

The reaction velocity of a given mutant protease with a competitive inhibitor is calculated similarly:

$$\nu(m,i) = V_{max}(m)\frac{[S]}{[S] + K_M(m) + \frac{[I]K_M(m)}{K_I(m,i)}}$$

where $[I]$ is the concentration of inhibitor, K_I is the inhibition constant, and m and i indicate that the values are taken for a given mutant protease and inhibitor, respectively. Again, the velocity is evaluated for the worst substrate of the nine. Michaelis and inhibition constants are evaluated using the volume-based method modified for mutations (see below), with $K_I = e^{\Delta G(m,i)/RT}$.

We define the fitness $A(m,i)$ as the ratio $\nu(m,i)/\nu(wt)$, assuming that V_{max} and the concentrations of all substrates are identical between wild type and mutant proteases. The concentration of substrate in the HIV-1 virion has been estimated variously from 10 mM (Gulnik *et al.* 1995) to 80 mM (Tang & Hartsuck 1995), and K_M values for wild type protease with peptide substrates are in the high mM range (Darke *et al.* 1988). We set the concentration of substrate to a value ten times less than $K_M(wt)$, and the inhibitor concentration to a value ten times more than the substrate concentration. Qualitatively similar results were obtained for different ratios of $[I]$ and $[S]$ versus $K_M(wt)$ (data not shown). Higher values of $[I]$ generally reduce the fitness of the entire set of mutant proteases, while retaining similar ordering and relative effectiveness among the set of inhibitors.

Volume-based Binding Free Energy Model

The free energy of binding of inhibitors and substrates to wild type protease is estimated using a simple measure of volume complementarity. A potential of mean force was calibrated using a data set of 63 cleaved sequences and 239 uncleaved sequences (Chou *et al.* 1996), and adding a set of 1488 uncleaved octapeptides taken from the gag and pol proteins of HIV-1 BRU isolate (SWISS-PROT accession codes P03348 and P03367). First, two tables of abundances were created, one for the cleaved amino acid sequences and the other for the uncleaved peptides, with subsites from S4 to S4' along one axis and amino acid sidechain volumes (Chothia 1975) in bins of 20Å^3 along the other axis. These tables were populated by averaging over a moving window of 10Å^3, to minimize artifacts from the discrete binning. We then used the uncleaved sequence table to define the reference state, to normalize the effects of the distribution of the twenty amino acids within the volume bins. Probabilities, P, were obtained by normalizing all volume values at a given subsite. The probabilities were used to calculate the free energy of binding of substrate to protease by assuming Boltzmann-type statistics using the relation $\Delta G = -RT\ln(P)$ (Sippl 1995). An arbitrary high energy of 100 kcal/mol was assigned to bins that had probability zero.

The volume-based binding model was tested by cross-validation. Each sequence in the training set was removed in turn, new potentials calculated, and the binding energy calculated for the omitted sequence using the new potentials. Choosing a threshold value of 44 kcal/mol, 80% of the cleaved sequences showed binding stronger than the threshold and 77% of the uncleaved sequences showed weaker binding. The discriminant function method (Chou *et al.* 1996), from which much of our training set was taken, performs somewhat better than this: using their reported threshold of 0.8 on data not included in their training set, the method yields proper prediction of 89% of a set of 55 sequences known to be cleaved. However, the discriminant function method, and other methods that deal with amino acids as "symbols" without physical properties, are incompatible with the scheme by which we evaluate mutations, described below.

These potentials reflect many of the qualitative features previously reported for protease-substrate recognition (Griffiths *et al.* 1992). Low free energies are observed for large amino acids in S1 and medium-sized amino acids in S2'. High free energies disallow large amino acids in S2 and S2', and S1' shows two minima, one for large amino acids, reflecting substrates with aromatic groups flanking the cleavage site, and one for small amino acids, reflecting substrates cleaved between aromatic amino acids and proline.

Modelling of Protease Mutation

Protease mutation was modelled by assuming that changes in volume of amino acids in contact with the substrate add linearly, and may be used with the volume-based model described above. For example, mutation V32L increases the size of the amino acid by 26Å^3, decreasing the size of the S2 and S2' protease subsites. In order to evaluate the free energy of binding, we then shift the potentials for S2 and S2' 1.3 bins towards the smaller volumes. The shifted potentials disfavor larger sidechains in the substrates and inhibitors even more strongly than the original potentials. Sites of mutation were limited to amino acids judged to be in contact with substrate, determined using structures of 12 protease-inhibitor complexes with inhibitors that are peptidomimetics (Brookhaven Protein Data Bank accession codes: 1aaq, 1hef, 1heg, 1hih, 1hiv, 1hvi, 1hvj, 1hvk, 1hvs, 7hvp, 8hvp, 9hvp). The protein chains were overlapped, and average values for the Cβ positions of protein and inhibitor residues determined. Distances between inhibitor and protein Cβ atoms were calculated (the RMSD of these distances was $\sim$ 0.5Å), and protein residues within 6Å of an inhibitor were added to the list of residues contacting that given subsite. The 12 structures did not contain inhibitors with a Cβ position at S4', so we assumed that this site is symmetrical with the S4 site, and is contacted by the symmetry-related residues. In the final model, ten protease amino acids were allowed to mutate: G27, A28, V32, I47, G48, G49, I50 and I84 were allowed to mutate to uncharged amino acids, and D29 and D30 were allowed to mutate conservatively to E, N or Q. The subsites they contact are: G27-S1; A28-S2; D29-S3,S4; D30-S2,S4; V32-S2; I47-S2,S3,S4; G48-S3; G49-S1,S2,S3; I50-S2'; I84-S1'; G127-S1'; A128-S2'; D129-S3',S4'; D130-S2',S4'; V132-S2'; I147-S2',S4', G148-S3'; G149-S1',S2'; I150-S2; I184-S1.

References

Barbosa, H. 1997. A coevolutionary genetic algorithm for a game approach to structural optimization. In *Proceedings of the Seventh International Conference on Genetic Algorithms*, edited by T. Bäck. Morgan Kaufmann, p. 545–552.

Chothia, C. 1975. Structural invariants in protein folding. *Nature* 254: 304–306.

Chou, K.; Tomasselli, A.; Reardon, I.; and Heinrikson,

R. 1996. Predicting human immunodeficiency virus protease cleavage sites in proteins by a discriminant function method. *Proteins* 24: 51–72.

Chvatal, V. 1979. A greedy heuristic for the set-covering problem. *Math. Oper. Res.* 4:233–235.

Coffin, J. 1995. HIV population dynamics in vivo: implications for genetic variation, pathogenesis, and therapy. *Science* 267: 483–489.

Condra, J., and Emini, E. 1997. Preventing HIV-1 drug resistance. *Science & Medicine.*

Condra, J.; Schleif, W. A.; et al. 1995. In vivo emergence of HIV-1 variants resistant to multiple protease inhibitors. *Nature* 374: 569–571.

Darke, P., and Huff, J. 1994. HIV protease as an inhibitor target for the treatment of AIDS. *Advances in Pharmacology* 25: 399–454.

Darke, P., et al. 1988. HIV-1 protease specificity of peptide cleavage is sufficient for processing of gag and pol polyproteins. *Biochemical and Biophysical Research Communications* 156:297–303.

Dawkins, R., and Krebs, J. 1979. Arms races between and within species. *Proc. Roy. Soc. London* B 205: 489–511.

Dunn, B.; Gustchina, A.; Wlodawer, A.; and Kay, J. 1994. Subsite preferences of retroviral proteinases. *Methods in Enzymology* 241: 254–278.

Goldberg, D., and Richardson, J. 1987. Genetic algorithms with sharing for multimodal function optimization. In *Proceedings of the Second International Conference on Genetic Algorithms*, edited by J. J. Grefenstette. L. Erlbaum Assoc.

Griffiths, J., et al. 1992. Different requirements for productive interaction between the active site of HIV-1 proteinase and substrates containing -hydrophobic*hydrophobic- or -aromatic*pro- cleavage sites. *Biochemistry* 31: 5193–5200.

Gulnik, S., et al. 1995. Kinetic characterization and cross-resistance patterns of HIV-1 protease mutants selected under drug pressure. *Biochemistry* 34: 9282–9287.

Hart, W.; Kammeyer, T.; and Belew, R. 1995. The role of development in genetic algorithms. In *Foundations of Genetic Algorithms 3*,edited by D. Whitley and M. Vose. Morgan Kaufmann, p. 315–332.

Hillis, W. D. 1991. Co-evolving parasites improve simulated evolution as an optimization procedure. In *Artificial Life II*, edited by C. G. Langton et al. Addison-Wesley.

Molla, A., et al. 1996. Ordered accumulation of mutations in HIV protease confers resistance to ritonavir. *Nature Medicine* 2:760–766.

Morris, G.; Goodsell, D.; Huey, R.; and Olson, A. 1996. Distributed automated docking of flexible ligands to proteins– Parallel applications of autodock 2.4. *Journal of Computer-Aided Molecular Design* 10: 293–304.

Moya, A.; Domingo, E.; and Holland, J. 1995. RNA viruses: a bridge between life and artificial life. In *Advances in Artificial Life. Third European Conference on Artificial Life*, p. 170–178.

Mühlenbein, H.; Schomisch, M.; and Born, J. 1991. The parallel genetic algorithm as function optimizer. *Parallel Computing* 17: 619–632.

PDB: Brookhaven protein data bank. Available online at http://www.pdb.bnl.gov.

Pettit, S.; Simsic, J.; Loeb, D.; Everitt, L.; Hutchison, C.; and Swanstrom, R. 1991. Analysis of retroviral protease cleavage sites reveals two types of cleavage sites and the structural requirements of the p1 amino acid. *J. of Biol. Chem.* 266: 14539–14547.

Rose, J.; Babe, L.; and Craik, C. 1995. Defining the level of human immunodeficiency virus type 1 (HIV-1) protease activity required for HIV-1 particle maturation and infectivity. *J. of Vir.* 69: 2751–2758.

Rosenfeld, R.; Vajda, S.; and DeLisi, C. 1995. Flexible docking and design. *Annual Review of Biophysics and Biomolecular Structure* 24: 677–700.

Rosin, C., and Belew, R. 1996. A competitive approach to game learning. In *Proc. Ninth Ann. Conf. on Computational Learning Theory*, p. 292–302.

Rosin, C., and Belew, R. 1997. New methods for competitive coevolution. *Evol. Comp.* 5: 1–29.

Rosin, C.; Belew, R.; Morris, G.; Olson, A.; and Goodsell, D. 1998. Coevolutionary analysis of resistance-evading HIV-1 protease inhibitors. *Submitted to Proceedings of the National Academy of Sciences.*

Rosin, C. 1997. *Coevolutionary Search Among Adversaries.* Ph.D. Diss., Univ. of California, San Diego.

Schinazi, R.; Larder, B.; and Mellors, J. 1997. Mutations in retroviral genes associated with drug resistance. *International Antiviral News* 5: 129–142.

Schock, H.; Garsky, V.; and Kuo, L. 1996. Mutational anatomy of an HIV-1 protease variant conferring cross-resistance to protease inhibitors in clinical trials. compensatory modulations of binding and activity. *Journal of Biological Chemistry* 271: 31957–31963.

Sippl, M. 1995. Knowledge-based potentials for proteins. *Current Opinion in Structural Biology* 5: 229–235.

Stryer, L. 1995. *Biochemistry.* San Franciso: W.H. Freeman.

SWISS-PROT protein sequence database. Available online at http://www.expasy.ch/sprot/sprot-top.html.

Tang, J., and Hartsuck, J. 1995. A kinetic model for comparing proteolytic processing activity and inhibitor resistance potential of mutant HIV-1 proteases. *FEBS Letters* 367: 112–116.

Wlodawer, A., and Erickson, J. 1993. Structure-based inhibitors of HIV-1 protease. *Annual Review of Biochemistry* 62: 543–585.

Presented Papers

Artificial Chemistries

Mesoscopic Analysis of Self-Evolution in an Artificial Chemistry

Peter Dittrich, Jens Ziegler, and **Wolfgang Banzhaf**
University of Dortmund, Dept. of Computer Science, D-44221 Dortmund, Germany
http://ls11-www.informatik.uni-dortmund.de
dittrich || ziegler || banzhaf@LS11.informatik.uni-dortmund.de

Abstract

In an algorithmic artificial chemistry the objects (molecules) are data and the interactions (reactions) among them are defined by an algorithm. The same object can appear in two forms: (1) as a machine (operator) or (2) as data (operand). Thus, the same object can, on the one hand, process other objects or, on the other hand, it can be processed. This dualism enables to implicitly define a constructive artificial chemistry which exhibits quite complex behavior. Remarkably, even evolutionary behavior emerged in our experiments, without defining any explicit variation operators or fitness-function. In addition to microscopic methods (e.g., monitoring the actions of single molecules) and macroscopic measures (e.g., diversity or complexity) we developed a stepwise mesoscopic analysis method based on classification and dynamic clustering. Knowledge about the system is accumulated by an iterative process in which measuring tools (classificators) extract information which in turn is used to create new classificators.

Keywords:

self-organization, evolution, computational chemistry, constructive dynamical systems, algorithmic chemistry, chemical computing, cluster analysis, binary string system, automata reaction

Motivation

The construction of artificial life systems with complex behaviors is surprisingly easy (Ray, 1992). Analysis is often much harder, especially in population-based systems with a huge number of diverse and interacting individuals. In this case the reduction of experimental data is necessary. Measuring macroscopic parameters only (i.e., temperature, diversity or complexity) allows to see that something is happening, but does not provide insight into how or what. Microscopic tracing of an experiment and understanding every single step is possible in principal. But with growing computational resources, this becomes more and more difficult, probably iqmpossible, because time complexity for the generation of n microscopic events (e.g., $O(n)$) is lower than time complexity needed for analysis (e.g., $O(n \log(n)$ for sorting the population). Therefore, methods for analysis in between macroscopic and microscopic methods are required.

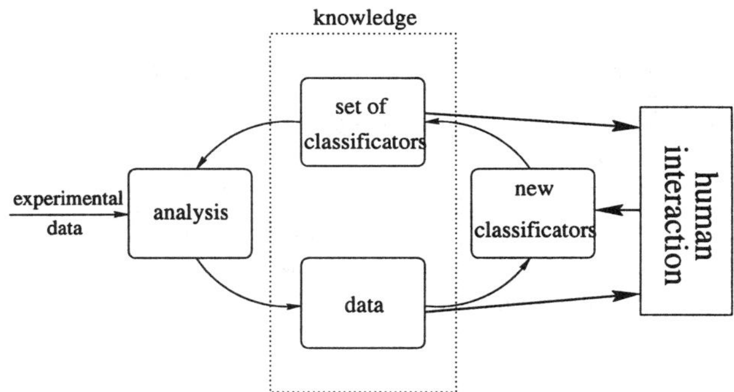

Figure 1: Iterative increase of knowledge.

In this paper we present a stepwise mesoscopic analysis method for artificial chemistries, which might be applied to other population-based systems as well. In this mesoscopic analysis the population is decomposed into groups. The decomposition is based on so-called **classifiers**[1]. A classifier represents a property p of an object. A first-order classifier is simply a function $C : S \longrightarrow [0, 1]$. The value $C(s) = p$ represents the strength of a property C of a string s and is used for a separation of the population into partial quantities with a cluster algorithm. Data produced by the classifiers as well as the collection of classifiers themselves represent knowledge about the system. This knowledge will grow by creating and collecting more and more classifiers. It is then possible to gain more information about the system by classifying the classifiers, i.e., by analyzing the basic properties of classifiers with, for example, the same clustering procedure that separated the population. This can be done in an iterative process (Fig. 1).

Mesoscopic Analysis

The mesoscopic analysis is a tool to find groups in data. The field of data analysis provides an overwhelming

[1]The classifiers introduced here are not to be confused with Holland's classifier systems.

amount of methods, ranging from classical statistical methods (e.g., correlation analysis, c-means clustering) to modern adaptive methods from the fields of computational intelligence (e.g., neural networks, genetic programming). Furthermore, many more complex methods exist that are specialized for certain problem domains.

We do not present a new classification or clustering method here, but we suggest a method how to apply available data analysis methods on artificial chemistries or on other population-based evolutionary artificial life systems. Our method will allow the integration of different available data analysis tools in an uncomplicated way.

First-Order Classifier: Property

A **first-order classifier** C relates an object s to a property p by indicating to what extend s has the property p.

A first-order classifier is defined as a map $C : S \longrightarrow [0,1]$. Without loss of generality and for simplification the output of a classifier is normalized. If the output of $C(s) = p$ is either 0 (s does not have the property p) or 1 (p is property of s) we call the classifier **binary**. If p is continuous the classifier C might be called **fuzzy**.

There are different ways of constructing a classifier: (1) manually by estimating the classifying property by an apriori analysis of the data, and (2) automatically by learning of the mapping C. Typical examples are artificial neural networks, evolutionary algorithms or any other supervised or unsupervised algorithm with the ability to learn the classifying function C.

A typical example for a manually defined classifier is a detector C_s for a certain subsequence s. For the binary case $C_s(s')$ is equal to 1 if the subsequence s can be found in s' otherwise $C_s(s')$ is 0.

Second-Order Classifier: Distance

A **second-order classifier** is defined as a mapping $C : S \times S \longrightarrow [0,1]$. It relates two objects. A classifier of this type is called a **distance measure** or shortly **distance**. If the conditions

$$\begin{aligned} C(s,s'') &\leq C(s,s') + C(s',s''), \\ C(s,s') &= C(s',s) \\ C(s,s) &= 0 \end{aligned} \tag{1}$$

are valid, the classifier C is a metric. As mentioned in the previous section we can define C manually. Hamming distance, for instance, is a well known distance measure. Using an evolutionary algorithm for the automatic generation of classifiers of any order is an appropriate method. Its fitness function then relies on the phenotypic/genotypic behavior of the objects or is given explicitly by user interaction (Banzhaf, 1997).

It is also possible to construct a second-order classifier C_F based on first-order classifiers $C_1, \ldots C_n$ by using the Euclidean distance

$$C_F(s,s') = \sqrt{\sum_i (C_i(s) - C_i(s'))^2} \tag{2}$$

or by methods taken from fuzzy set theory, i.g. (Miyamoto and Nakayama, 1986):

$$C_F(s,s') = \frac{\sum_{i=1}^{n} min(C_i(s), C_i(s'))}{\sum_{i=1}^{n} max(C_i(s).C_i(s'))} \tag{3}$$

Application and Integration of Classifiers

In this section we shall describe and demonstrate how classifiers may be integrated into a mesoscopic analysis of an evolutionary population-based system. The development of the population $P = (s_1, \ldots, s_M)$ in time requires the analysis of $P(t)$ (population at time t) for every single time step. The results of consecutive analyses have to be compared and correlated.

Clustering

The task of a cluster analysis procedure is to classificate a set $P = \{s_1, \ldots, s_n\}$ into c partial quantities (Bacher, 1996; Dunn, 1974). Each of these quantities is represented by a so-called **prototype** v_i, $(i = 1, \ldots, c)$. The degree of affiliation u_{ik} of object s_i to cluster c_k is computed and quantifies the probability of s_i to belong to c_k. In the case of fuzzy clustering u_{ik} is $\in [0,1]$..

The partition of P should obey the following rules:

- similar data should be partitioned into similar clusters: **homogeneity**.
- different data should be separated into different clusters: **heterogeneity**.

The first step in a mesoscopic analysis could be a clustering based on a manually designed first-order classifier. The separating feature is, to what extend the objects have this property.

The second step could be a second-order classificator-based clustering. The number of clusters now depends on the internal structure of the population and the used classifier. The minimum of the objective function

$$J(U,V) = \sum_{k=1}^{n} \sum_{i=1}^{c} u_{ik} \cdot d_{ik}^2 \tag{4}$$

with d_{ik}^2 symbolizing the distance between s_k and prototype v_i according to the used distance measure (a second-order classifier) is then the optimal clustering. Our distance measure for the following experiments is the Hamming distance, a natural choice given the binary nature of strings used as individuals here.

Distance

Classification of a population with a clustering algorithm thus depends crucially on the structure and dimension(s) of the sequence space.

The genotypic Hamming distance measures the number of different bits between two individuals represented by binary strings. Therefore the clustering only uses structural information to separate the population into different clusters. But the use of the genotypic information only causes in fact a loss of information.

Cluster algorithms using distance measures depending on both, genotypic and phenotypic information may be able to represent the internal structure of the population more accurately. The phenotypic distance between two individuals could be quantified by taking their functional behavior into account or by determining the difference between their fitness values according to a globally defined fitness function. If this global fitness function furthermore changes with an evolving population, it may be considered an **environmental distance**. This distance measure is a classifier of an order equal to the population size M.

Both, phenotypic and environmental distance are still under investigation. The following experimental results use genotypic distance only.

Tracing of Cluster Development

The development of a population is traced by analyzing its state after every generation (about 10^6 reactions). Each resulting cluster is represented by its specific prototype v_c which is the center of a hypersphere in distance space. The relationship between clusters at t_i and t_{i+1} is determined by the distances between their prototypes v_{c,t_i}, $v_{c,t_{i+1}}$.

An analysis of the development of properties of an artificial chemistry using the above explained techniques is the main object of the following sections.

Artificial Chemistry

Our mesoscopic analysis method will be applied to a static and dynamic analysis of an artificial chemistry (Varela, 1978; Lugowski, 1989; Rasmussen et al., 1990; Bagley et al., 1992; Fontana, 1992; Thürk, 1993; Bagley and Farmer, 1992; Banzhaf, 1993; Fontana and Buss, 1994). Usually, an artificial chemistry consists of at least two parts: 1.) a set of objects (molecules, substances) S and 2.) a set of collision rules. In addition, a simulation of the artificial chemistry requires a third component: an algorithm, which models the reaction vessel and is therefore called **reactor algorithm**.

In our case the objects are binary strings of fixed length $S = \{0,1\}^{32}$ (Banzhaf, 1993; Banzhaf, 1995). The collision rules are all second-order catalytic reactions of the form $s_1 + s_2 + X \longrightarrow s_1 + s_2 + s_3$, shortly $s_1 + s_2 \Longrightarrow s_3$. All collisions of two objects s_1, s_2 will have a unique outcome s_3. Therefore the set of collision rules can be represented as a function $r : S \times S \longrightarrow S$.

The following reactor algorithm operates on a population $P = \{s_1, \ldots, s_M\}$ which is a multiset on S.

Reactor algorithm

The development of the population P is realized by iteratively applying steps 2, 3, and 4 of the following reactor algorithm:

1. Initialize the population P with M objects selected randomly from S.

2. Select two objects s_1, s_2 from the population P randomly, without removing them.

3. If there exists a reaction $s_1 + s_2 \Longrightarrow s_3$ and the filter condition $f(s_1, s_2, s_3)$ holds, replace a randomly selected object of the population by s_3.

4. Goto step 2.

The filter condition $f : S \times S \times S \longrightarrow \{true, false\}$ is used to introduce elastic collisions easily, without changing the reaction mechanism. In our case f is defined as

$$f_1(s_1, s_2, s_3) = (s_1 \neq s_2 \wedge s_1 \neq s_3). \qquad (5)$$

This filter condition inhibits the reaction if, on the one hand, operator s_1 and operand s_2 are the same and, on the other hand, if the operator string s_1 is an active replicator. (See Sec. *Automata Reaction* for more details.)

The reactor algorithm simulates mass-action kinetics of second-order catalytic reactions which allows hypercyclic dynamics (Eigen and Schuster, 1979; May, 1991). For a large population size M the system can be modeled by coupled ordinary differential equations (Hofbauer and Sigmund, 1984; Stadler et al., 1993).

The following macroscopic measurements are used in the diagrams:

The **diversity** is the number of different strings in P divided by the population size M for normalization.

The **productivity** is the probability, that a collision of two strings is reactive, The term **collision** refers to one execution of steps (2) and (3) of the reactor algorithm. A collision is called **reactive** if a product s_3 is inserted into the population. So, a collision of two objects s_1, s_2 is reactive, if a product is defined by the reaction rule and if the filter condition allows the insertion of the product.

The **innovativity** is the probability of a collision producing an object that has never been in the system before.

We will use the the following 32-bit automata reaction as a reaction mechanism.

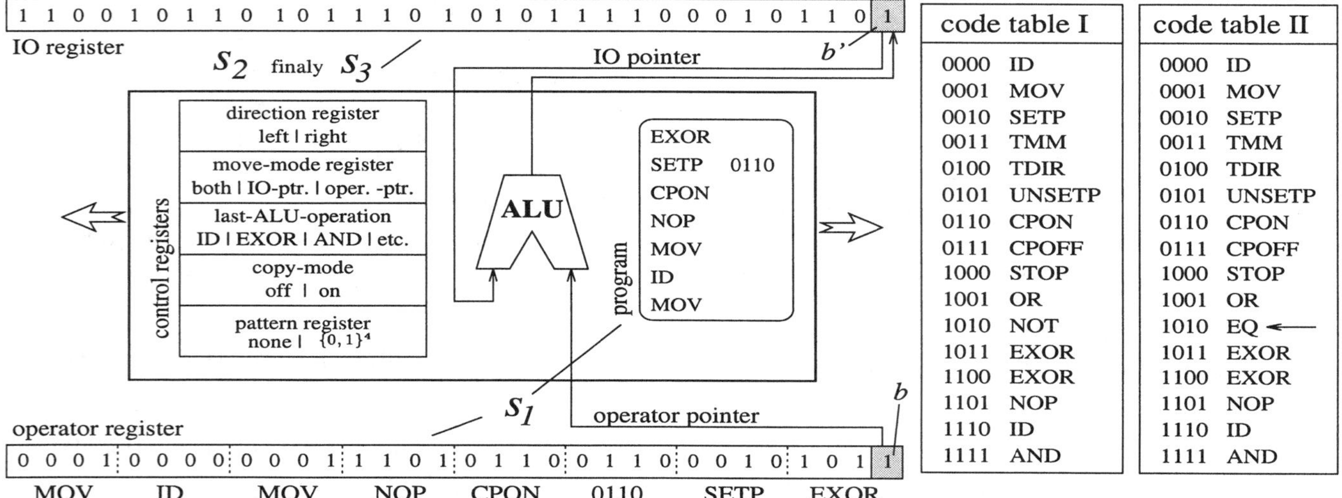

Figure 2: Automaton, resulting by folding s_1. It carries out the reaction $s_1 + s_2 \Longrightarrow s_3$. s_1 is written into the operator register and specifies the program. The IO register is initialized with s_2 and contains the result s_3 after running the program.

Automata Reaction

The **automata reaction** is based on a finite state automaton which is a mixture of a Turing-machine and a register machine. It has also been inspired by Hofstadter's (Hofstadter, 1985; Morris, 1989) Typogenetics.

The **automata reaction** instantiates a deterministic reaction $s_1 + s_2 \Longrightarrow s_3$, with $s_1, s_2, s_3 \in \{0,1\}^{32}$. In order to calculate the product s_3, string s_1 is "folded" into an automaton A_{s_1}, which gets s_2 as an input. The construction of A_{s_1} ensures that the automaton will halt after a finite number of steps. Because A_{s_1} is a deterministic finite automaton, the automata reaction defines a functions $\{0,1\}^{32} \times \{0,1\}^{32} \longrightarrow \{0,1\}^{32}$. Figure 2 shows the structure of the automaton. It contains two 32-bit registers, the **IO register** and the **operator register**. At the outset operator string s_1 is written into the operator register and operand s_2 into the IO register. The program is generated from s_1 by simply mapping successive 4-bit segments into instructions. The resulting program is executed sequentially, starting with the first instruction. There are no control statements for loops or jumps in the instruction set[2].

Each 32-bit register has a pointer, referring to a bit location, the **IO pointer**, referring to bit b' in the IO register and the **operator pointer**, referring to bit b in the operator register. Bit b and b' are inputs to the **ALU**. The result of the execution of one instruction of the operator register is stored at the IO pointers location, therefore replacing b'.

[2]The instruction set used here is ID, MOV, SETP, TMM, TDIR, UNSETP, CPON, CPOFF, STOP, OR, EQ, EXOR, NOP, ID, AND. The resulting reaction is usually called a2-reaction

Instead of going into more details here we point the reader to a precise formal specification of the automata reaction as source code, available from (Dittrich, 1997) and a discussion of self-evolution in artificial chemistries based on the automata reaction in (Dittrich and Banzhaf, 1998).

As a short summary the following basic properties of the automata reaction should be noted:

- The probability of producing a string s_3 similar to one of the colliding strings is high.
- The product of two randomly generated strings s_1, s_2 is likely ($p \approx 30\%$) equal to s_2. This is called **passive replication**, because the operator string s_1 does not modify the operand string s_2.
- A string s_1 for which $\forall x \in S : s_1 + x \Longrightarrow s_1$ is called **active replicator**, because it copies the operator string (itself) into the IO register. Active self-replicatiors are rare and have to be evolved during the development of the population. Due to their proliferation, they are the strings for which part two of the filter condition holds.

The structure of the population thus changes with the replicating ability of its individuals. Passive replicators may survive if the population is small ($M << 1000$) but they are displaced if active replicators evolve during a run. Due to the starting position of the register-pointers during a collision, the center positions of the string are likely to remain nearly unchanged while the possibility of changing the margins is higher.

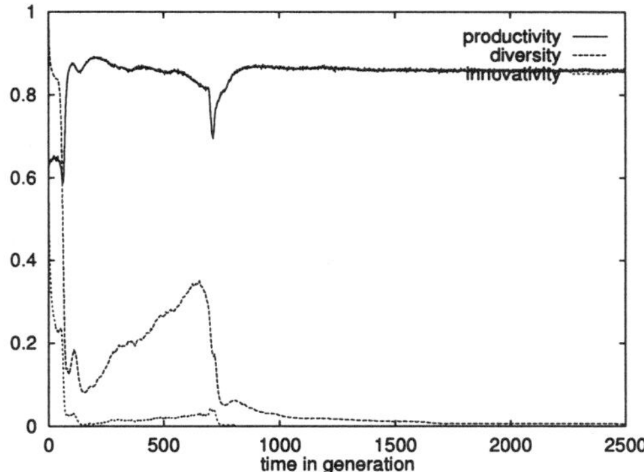

Figure 3: Diversity, productivity and innovativity of experiment A4-23 with the automata reaction a2. Parameters: $M = 100000$, reaction a2, no replication, full system seeding.

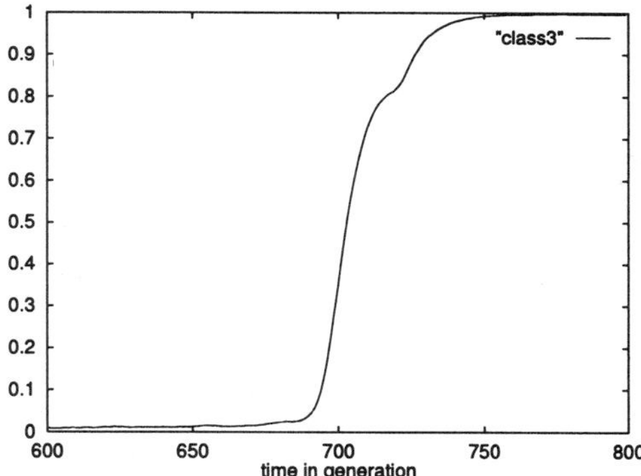

Figure 4: Normalized sum of classifier C_1 over time. Run A4-23.

Application

We will now demonstrate the application of the mesoscopic analysis method with data obtained from an artificial chemistry.

Figure 3 shows run A4-23 out of a series of 100 experiments all with the following parameter setting: population size: $M = 10^5$ (constant), reaction: automata reaction, reaction type: catalytic second-order, filter condition: active replication disabled (elastic), initialization: random strings (full system seeding). The observed behaviors in the series were very diverse ranging from early stabilization with short transients to complex, oscillating dynamics (Fig. 10). In (Dittrich and Banzhaf, 1998) we have identified two different evolutionary phases. The first one is characterized by high constructive activity which creates many new strings per generation. The second evolutionary phase begins with the emergence of a very stable, self-replicating core-set of cooperating strings dominating the system. This stable core-set keeps evolving by detachment of sub reaction pathways, by integration of totally new molecules or by emergence of new substrings which proliferate in almost every string. Here we will concentrate on one phenomenon in run A4-23: The sudden decrease and sudden increase of productivity around $t = 700$. The macroscopic observables in Fig. 3 are indicating that something is happening. The increasing diversity and the decreasing productivity indicate an interesting developmental phase. Even looking at the innovativity does not elucidate the process. So what happens and why? In principle we can reconstruct every single step and thus may be able to understand the phenomenon. But reducing the interval of interest to $t = 600$ until $t = 800$ still leaves about $16 * 10^6$ collisions between $3 \cdot 10^5$ different strings at $t = 600$.

We now start our mesoscopic analysis by asking the question:

(Q1)*Does the structure of the population change from $t = 600$ to $t = 800$?*

To answer this question we generated automatically (using genetic programming (GP) (Koza, 1992; Banzhaf et al., 1998)) a first-order classifier C_1 which is able to discriminate strings at $t = 600$ from strings at $t = 800$.

The training cases for the GP fitness function are the 400 most frequent strings of both, generation 600 and generation 800: $C_1(s)$ should be 0 if s is a string of gen. 600 and 1 if s is a member of the population at gen. 800.

The GP system has been used with the following settings: Operator set: conventional boolean functions, two ADFs (automatically defined functions) allowed. Random constants out of $\{0, 1, \ldots, 32\}$. $(\mu + \lambda)$ selection (Schwefel, 1995) with $\mu = 500$ (population size) and $\lambda = 350$ (number of descendants), finite life span: 5 generations. Program structure: tree and linear.

Among many other programms, GP created a short program which only tests bit 14 of the input string. Surprisingly, this bit discriminates not only the test cases but nearly every string in gen. 600 from any string in gen. 800. Thus, with the automatically generated classifier C_1 we are able to visualize the moment when the population is beginning to change its structure (Fig. 4).

We have now identified a structural change, but

(Q2)*Does the functional property of strings change?*

To answer this question we define a first-order classifier C_2 manually:

$$C_2(s) = 1 - \frac{d_{Ham}((s \oplus s_0), s) + d_{Ham}((s \oplus s_f), s)}{64} \quad (6)$$

where s_0 =**0000000** and s_f =**fffffff**. This classifier estimates the self-replicating ability by testing s against the s_0 and the s_f string. The string s is the operator processing both, s_0 and s_f. The number of bit flips, either from 0 to 1 ($d_{Ham}((s \oplus s_0), s)$) or from 1 to 0

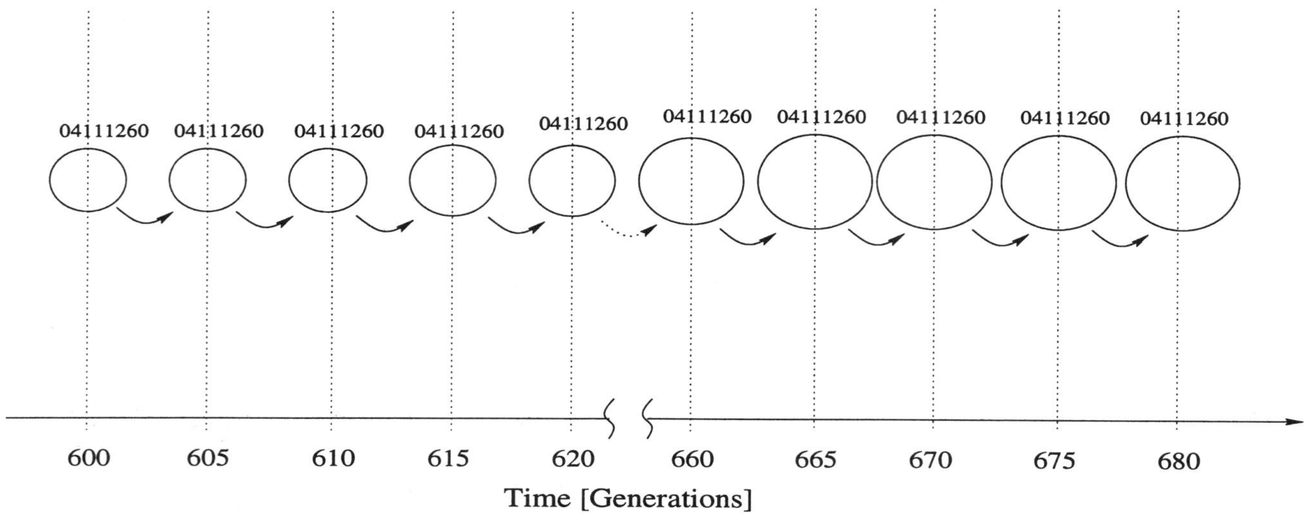

Figure 5: Clusterdevelopment of cluster **04111260**. Cluster method: fuzzy c-means. Run A4-23. 1 cm diameter $\approx$ 30 % of population.

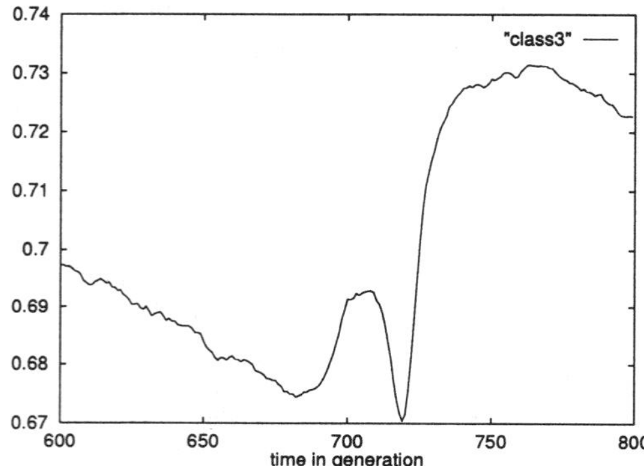

Figure 6: Normalized sum of classifier C_2 over time (self-replication ability). Run A4-23.

$(d_{Ham}((s \oplus s_f), s))$ caused in s_0 and s_f indicate the replicating ability of s. $C_2(s)$ is at maxixmum if s causes as many bit flips in s_0 (and s_f) as necessary to reproduce its bit pattern. $C_2(s)$ is 0, if s does not change neither s_0 nor s_f. Indeed, Fig. 6 shows that there is a functional change. The replicating ability of strings in the population decreases until $t \approx 690$. There is a strong increase in C_2 from $t = 720$ until $t = 750$, the point in time at which the restructuring of P seems to be finished. The questions to answer are now:

(Q3) *How is the population structured at* $t = 600$*?*
(Q4) *What happens at* $t = 690$*?*

The structure of the population in experiment A4-23 at about $t = 600$ until $t = 680$ is shown in Fig. 5. All strings present belong to cluster **04111260**, so their genotypic structure is almost the same. There is a slight increase in volume which indicates that more and more individuals are replaced by one of the most frequent 400 strings. Figure 7 shows a second-order cluster analysis of these 400 most frequent strings from $t = 693$ to $t = 699$, the moment of the supposed restructuring. At $t = 695$ the single cluster **0c211260** (**04111260** of Fig. 5 slightly changed its center) splits into two clusters **4b0112d6** and **4b1412d6**. The former disappears after two generations while the latter quickly grows and changes its center (in $t = 699$ almost half of the population is in **4b1432d4**). Analysis shows that the center of the shrinking cluster has almost the same structure as in previous generations but the second cluster has an obviously different bit pattern on the left side. Further development of the remaining cluster shows that now both, individuals with modified and unmodified left and right sides belong to the same cluster. The point of interest is now:

(Q5) *Is there a change in the way genotypic information is reproduced or conserved ?*

Looking at the clusters obtained from (Q3) and (Q4) reveals that strings in the displaced cluster have high diversity on the left side. Strings in the new cluster are much more homogeneous on the left side. This raises the question whether the members of the new cluster have acquired the ability to replicate their left side more accurately. To validate this assumption we have defined a first-order classifier C_{s_m} which checks for replicating activity at certain bit positions specified by the substring s_m:

$$C_{s_m}(s) = 1 \quad - \quad \frac{d_{Ham}(((s \oplus s_0) \wedge s_m), s \wedge s_m)}{2\#ones(s)}$$

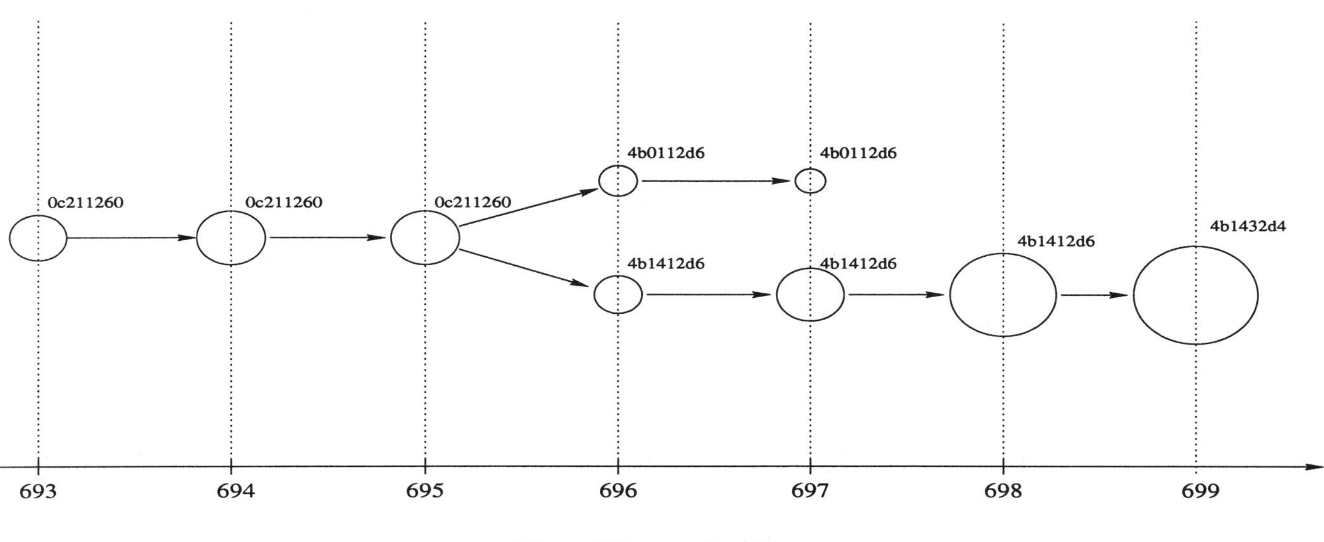

Figure 7: Clusterdevelopment. Clustering performed on the 400 most frequent strings per generation. 1 cm diameter $\approx$ 20% of population. Cluster method: fuzzy c-means. Run A4-23.

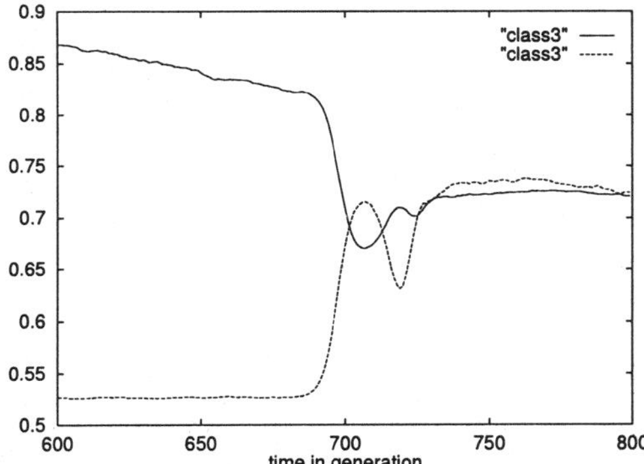

Figure 8: Normalized sum of classifier $C_{0000ffff}$ and $C_{ffff0000}$ over time. Run A4-23.

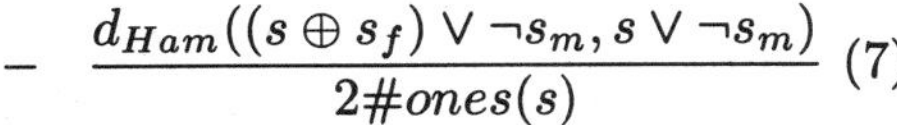

$$- \quad \frac{d_{Ham}((s \oplus s_f) \vee \neg s_m, s \vee \neg s_m)}{2\#ones(s)} \quad (7)$$

with $s_m \in S$ and $\#ones(s)$ denotes the number of ones in s. (Note that $C_2 = C_{s_m}$ with $s_m =$ **ffffffff**.)

The change of replication from right-oriented to left and-right-oriented is shown in Fig. 8 by showing the development of $C_{0000ffff}$ and $C_{ffff0000}$.

Another very interesting experiment is shown in Fig. 10. Obviously, there is an oscillating behavior of the the macroscopic parameters from $t = 1000$ to $t = 2000$. A zoom into the interval from $t = 1200$ to $t = 1600$ is shown in Fig. 11. This run is remarkable because its complex behavior is an exception. Most of the exper-

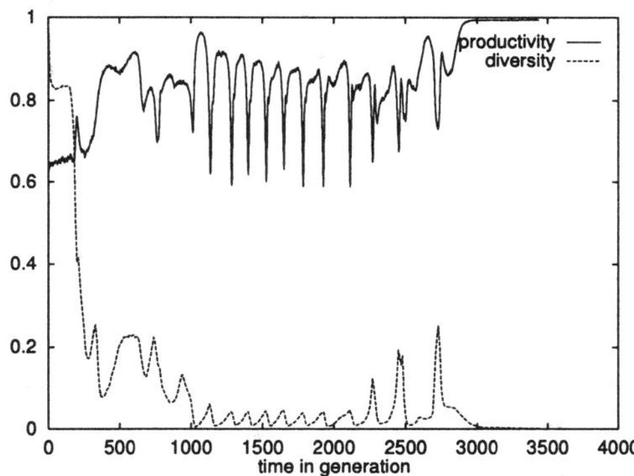

Figure 10: Diversity, productivity and innovativity of experiment A4-49 with the automata reaction. Parameters: $M = 100000$, no replication.

iments are similar to run A4-23, about 20% are even simpler. The result of a cluster analysis of A4-49 is shown in Fig. 9. Here, an oscillating separation and merging of two clusters with stable centers (**ee10526a** and **effff26a**) is the dominating phenomenon.

Discussion

A new mesoscopic step-wise analysis method for evolutive population-based systems has been suggested. Knowledge about the system is gained by decomposing it with the help of classifiers. The application of classifiers generates information which can be used to generate new classifiers which in turn can be applied to the

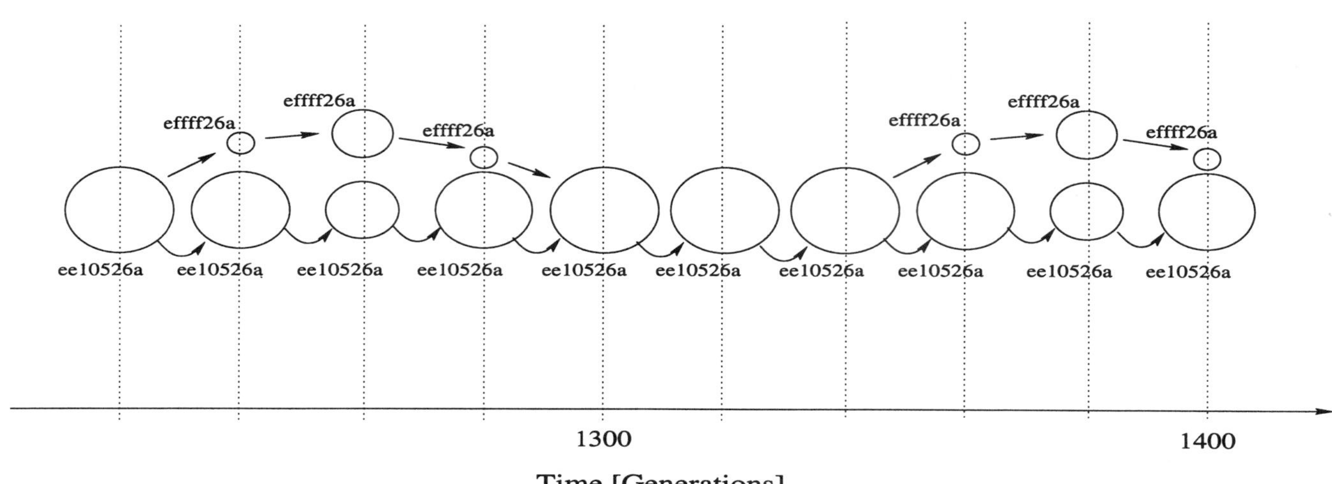

Figure 9: Time development of clusters **ee10526a** and **effff26a** in run A4-49. 1 cm diameter ≈ 20% of population. Cluster method: fuzzy c-means.

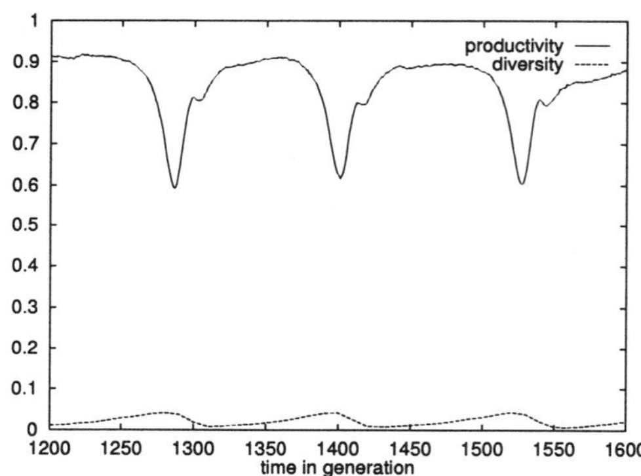

Figure 11: Magnification of Fig. 10.

system. This concept allows the integration of different automatic and manual analysis techniques. The method has been successfully applied to an articial chemistry. A sudden decrease and increase of a macroscopic quantity (productivity) has been identified as the indication of the appearance of a new organization (cluster). Its development has been visualized and investigated by dynamic cluster analysis. The resulting clusters motivated the definition of more specialized classifiers which confirmed the assumption that the new organization has acquired the ability to replicate the left side of a string.

Future Work

Classifiers can be generated automatically (i.e., C_1), may be parameterized (i.e., C_{s_m}) or may be combined into a huge number of new classifiers. To ease the handling of classifiers we can assign a "meaning" to each classifier, e.g., a text describing the properties of the classifier, and set up a data base containing the classifier name, its formal definition (program) and its meaning (text). We are then able to combine and integrate formal descriptions with more intuitive, linguistic descriptions. In a second step the classifiers may be correlated.

If we also allow classifiers to be discarded (for instance, because they are redundant measures), the resulting process seems to become an evolutionary process, now on the level of classifiers. So, we can apply the same techniques as described here not only to the primary population system but also to the system of evolving classifiers.

Acknowledgements

This project is supported by the DFG (Deutsche Forschungsgemeinschaft), grant Ba 1042/2-2. We would like to thank Christian Düntgen, Ahmet Koç, Andre Skusa, Markus Brameier and Wolfgang Kantschik.

References

Bacher, J. 1996. *Clusteranalyse.* München, Wien: Oldenbourg.

Bagley, R. J. and Farmer, J. D. 1992. Spontaneous emergence of a metabolism. In *Proceedings of the 2nd Workshop on Artificial Life*, edited by C. G. Langton, C. Taylor, J. D. Farmer, and S. Rasmussen. Redwood City, CA: Addison-Wesley, p 93–140.

Bagley, R. J., Farmer, J. D., and Fontana, W. (1992). Evolution of a metabolism. In *Proceedings of the 2nd Workshop on Artificial Life*, edited by C. G. Langton,

C. Taylor, J. D. Farmer, and S. Rasmussen. Redwood City, CA: Addison-Wesley, p 141–158.

Banzhaf, W. 1993. Self-replicating sequences of binary numbers – Foundations i and ii: General and strings of length n = 4. *Biological Cybernetics* 69: 269–281.

Banzhaf, W. 1995. Self-organizing algorithms derived from RNA interaction. In *Evolution and Biocomputation: Computational Models of Evolution*, edited by W. Banzhaf and F. H. Eeckman. Berlin-Heidelberg-New York: Springer-Verlag, p 69–102.

Banzhaf, W. 1997. Interactive evolution. In *Handbook of Evolutionary Computation*, edited by T. Bäck, D. B. Fogel, and Z. Michalewicz. IOP Publishing.

Banzhaf, W., Nordin, P., Keller, R. E., and Francone, F. D. 1998. *Genetic Programming - An Introduction.* Morgan Kaufmann and dpunkt Verlag.

Dittrich, P. (1997). Source code of the automata reaction. Internet FTP server at the Chair of Systems Analysis, Dept. of Comp. Science, Univ. of Dortmund, file name: *ftp://lumpi.informatik.uni-dortmund.de/pub/biocomp/src/autoreac-1.0.tar.gz.*

Dittrich, P. and Banzhaf, W. 1998. Self-evolution in a constructive binary string system. Artificial Life, in press.

Dunn, J. C. 1974. Well separated clusters and optimal fuzzy-partitions. *Journal of Cybernetics* 4: 95–104.

Eigen, M. and Schuster, P. 1979. *The Hypercycle.* Berlin: Springer.

Fontana, W. 1992. Algorithmic chemistry. In *Proceedings of the 2nd Workshop on Artificial Life*, edited by C. G. Langton, C. Taylor, J. D. Farmer, and S. Rasmussen. Redwood City, CA: Addison-Wesley, p 159–209.

Fontana, W. and Buss, L. W. 1994. "The arrival of the fittest": Toward a theory of biological organisation. *Bull. Math. Biol.* 56: 1–64.

Hofbauer, J. and Sigmund, K. 1984. *Evolutionstheorie und Dynamische Systeme.* Berlin: Paul Parey.

Hofstadter, D. R. 1985. *Gödel, Escher, Bach:.* New York: Basic Books.

Koza, J. R. 1992. *Genetic Programming: On the Programming of Computers by Natural Selection.* Cambridge, MA: MIT Press.

Lugowski, M. W. 1989. Computational metabolism: Towards biological geometries for computing. In *Artificial Life*, edited by C. G. Langton. Redwood City, CA: Addison-Wesley, p. 341–368.

May, R. M. 1991. Hypercycles spring to life. *Nature* 353: 607–608.

Miyamoto, S. and Nakayama, K. 1986. Similarity measures based on a fuzzy set model and application to hieracical clustering. *IEEE Trans., Syst., Man and Cybernetics* 16(3): 479–482.

Morris, H. C. 1989. Typogenetics: A logic for artificial life. In *Artificial Life*, edited by C. G. Langton, Redwood City, CA: Addison-Wesley, p. 369–395.

Rasmussen, S., Knudsen, C., Feldberg, R., and Hindsholm, M. 1990. The coreworld: Emergence and evolution of cooperative structures in a computational chemistry. *Physica D* 42: 111–194.

Ray, T. S. (1992). An approach to the synthesis of life. In *Proceedings of the 2nd Workshop on Artificial Life*, edited by C. G. Langton, C. Taylor, J. D. Farmer, and S. Rasmussen. Redwood City, CA: Addison-Wesley, p 371-408.

Schwefel, H.-P. 1995. *Evolution and Optimum Seeking.* Sixth-Generation Computer Technology Series. New York: John Wiley.

Stadler, P. F., Fontana, W., and Miller, J. H. 1993. Random catalytic reaction networks. *Physica D* 63: 378–392.

Thürk, M. 1993. *Ein Modell zur Selbstorganisation von Automatenalgorithmen zum Studium molekularer Evolution.* PhD thesis, Universität Jena, Naturwissenschaftliche Fakultät.

Varela, F. 1978. On being autonomous: The lessons of natural history for systems theory. In *Applied General Systems Research*, edited by G. Klir, p. 77–84.

Emergent Structures in Sparse Fields of Conway's "Game of Life"

Nicholas Mark Gotts* and **Paul B. Callahan**
Department of Computer Science, University of Wales Aberystwyth

Abstract

A new approach to the study of "complex" cellular automata is described, and applied to Conway's "Game of Life". It is shown that in infinite and very large finite fields of the Game of Life, emergent structures will eventually dominate the dynamics of initially random configurations, provided the initial density of "live" cells is sufficiently low. It is also shown that many quite simple structures will self-replicate under these conditions, although none are known to do so efficiently enough to increase their numbers indefinitely. The application of the approach to other cellular automata is discussed.

Introduction

A cellular automaton or CA, as the term is used here, is a discrete state system consisting of a countable network C of identical cells. Each cell is, at any "step", in one of k states (k finite); all are updated synchronously. The state of a cell c at time step $t+1$ depends on the states at step t of a finite set of *in-neighbors* (usually we just say *neighbors*). This may or may not include c, in-neighborhood may or may not be symmetric, and different neighbors may have different roles in determining c's next state. For every possible combination of states of a cell's in-neighbors, the "transition rule" R specifies the possible states at the next step – a single state in the deterministic case, to which we limit our attention. R is the same for each cell and at each step. There is an automorphism of C mapping any cell onto any other. For a k-state CA with network C there are $k^{|C|}$ possible configurations or *fields*; a maximal set of fields which map onto each other by automorphisms of C we call a *layout*. The *distance* between two cells is the minimum number of *links* between neighboring cells traversed on any path between the two.

CA can be classified structurally by their network topology. Most work has been done on 1-dimensional arrays and square lattices, finite or infinite. For finite networks, periodic boundary conditions are used (or edge cells given special treatment, but this falls outside our definition). In-neighbors are most commonly the cell itself and the r cells to each side in the 1-d case. The common 2-d in-neighborhoods are the cell itself plus the four orthogonally adjacent cells (von Neumann neighborhood), and these plus the diagonally adjacent cells (Moore neighborhood).

The Game of Life (henceforth GoL) is a two-dimensional Moore neighborhood binary ($k = 2$) CA. We call the states 0 and 1. $C_{x,y}$ is in state 1 at step $t+1$ iff either of the following is true at step t:
1) $C_{x,y}$ is in state 0, and exactly three of its neighbors are in state 1.
2) $C_{x,y}$ is in state 1, and either two or three of its other ("non-self") neighbors are in state 1.
State 0 is *quiescent*: if all cells are in state 0 they will remain so. Any layout having a finite number of state 1 cells we call a "pattern". Since the transition rule is spatially symmetric, spatial symmetries cannot be lost as a pattern evolves; they may be gained.

In (Berlekamp et al. 1982, p.849), GoL's discoverer John Conway, and his co-authors, sketch proofs that it is computationally universal, and can support self-reproducing patterns. They then say that:

> Inside any sufficiently large random broth, we expect *just by chance*, that there will be some of these self-replicating creatures... It's probable... that after a long time, intelligent self-reproducing animals will emerge and populate some parts of the space.

Poundstone (Poundstone 1985, pp.175-6) says:

> Speculation about "living" Life patterns focuses on infinite, low-density random fields... If there are self-reproducing Life patterns, they would have room to grow in such a field.

What *does* happen in infinite (and large finite), "low-density random fields" of GoL is the main topic of this paper. The work resembles "computational mechanics" (Hanson and Crutchfield 1997) in its detailed investigation of a particular CA.

By "infinite, low density random field", Poundstone means an infinite lattice, in which each cell *independently*

*Email: nmg@aber.ac.uk

has a small probability, p, of being initially in state 1. Consider the set of all cells within a distance d from a given cell (we could equally use cell-sets of other shapes). Probabilities of particular arrangements of cell-states in this set depend only on the number of cells in each state, and on p. Taking increasingly large finite chunks of an infinite array, or averaging over increasingly large ensembles of finite arrays, frequencies of such arrangements will tend toward these probability values. The quoted statements will thus hold for sufficiently large arrays of any binary CA[1] capable of supporting self-reproducing patterns, whatever the value of p (so long as $0 < p < 1$). However, it may be that for some or all such p values, the density of self-reproducing patterns tends to zero for almost all initial fields (including all those for which the frequencies of arrangements are as expected given independently assigned cell-states).

Would "intelligent, self-reproducing, animals", or other very complex structures and processes, emerge from simpler elements in infinite or very large finite random fields of GoL or any other CA? If so, would they persist and evolve through anything like mutation and selection? What properties must the CA have? These questions are largely unexplored — but see (Chou and Reggia 1997). This paper does not answer them, but demonstrates that the medium-term dynamics of large random GoL fields with sufficiently low p will be dominated by emergent structures, and will include simple kinds of self-replication. The meanings given to "medium-term", "dominated", "emergent" and "self-replication" are made clear below.

Very sparse fields are good places to look for the emergence of complexity from disorder for two reasons. First, most "complex" CAs, like GoL, tend to develop local structures which occasionally interact: there is substantial but not complete decoupling between local and global scales of activity. Very sparse fields emphasise the features of such CAs that make them interesting. Second, much can be discovered about the history of such fields by combining local computation using CA-simulating software with global analysis.

Classification of Cellular Automata

There are numerous ways to classify CA in terms of their computational and dynamic properties. The most relevant classifications here are those describing the histories of classes of initial layouts.

Wolfram (Wolfram 1984) describes classes based on the evolution of "disordered" fields. He initially considers the left-right symmetric 1-d CA with r=2, k=2, a quiescent state 0, and a totalistic rule (all in-neighbors have equivalent effect on a cell's state), but conjectures that his classes apply across all types of CA:

Class 1: Evolution leads to a homogeneous state.
Class 2: Evolution leads to a set of separated simple stable or periodic structures.
Class 3: Evolution leads to a chaotic pattern.[2]
Class 4: Evolution leads to complex localized structures, sometimes long-lived.

These are not precise definitions: how "complex" and "long-lived" must structures be before a CA is class 4? Wolfram conjectures that class 4 CA are capable of universal computation. (Dhar et al. 1995), exhibiting computationally universal CA apparently of classes 2 and 3, argue that different classifications arise according to the set of initial configurations considered.

Among refinements or modifications to Wolfram's scheme, that of (Braga et al. 1995) is most relevant here. They define a 3-way classification of infinite 1-d CA, concentrating on the "elementary" CA (those with $k = 2$, $r = 1$), with 0 a quiescent state. Their class $\mathcal{C}_1$ includes CA where all patterns (they use the word as we do) disappear. Class $\mathcal{C}_2$ includes all CA for which no patterns increase their length without limit, and $\mathcal{C}_3$ is the complement of $\mathcal{C}_2$. Membership of these three classes is decidable for the 128 CA they consider.

There are obvious ways to refine their classification. We find it convenient first to modify it to consist of mutually exclusive and jointly exhaustive classes:

1. All patterns disappear.
2. There is a pattern that persists indefinitely, but no patterns grow indefinitely.
3. There is a pattern that grows indefinitely.

Two types of refinement are possible. First, we can refine classification of individual patterns. For patterns that neither disappear nor grow without limit, we can ask about periodicity and movement across the network. For those that grow without limit, we can ask whether the number of cells does so, or just the diameter (maximum distance between any two cells). The latter implies the former for the 128 CA Braga *et al.* consider, but not in general. In either case, we can ask *how fast* this quantity increases. Second, we can ask whether some property holds for *all*, *some* or *no* patterns. If it holds for some but not all, we can ask for the minimal size of pattern (in terms of cell number or diameter) for which it holds. This paper shows the relevance of such classifications to the dynamics of layouts other than patterns.

Previous Work on GoL

Since its discovery in 1970, GoL has generated widespread popular interest (Wainwright 1971; Gardner 1983; Poundstone 1985). It was not designed for a specific task; Conway wanted simple patterns' histories to be hard to predict. Recent work on GoL includes:

1. Design of layouts (mostly patterns) with particular properties, by "Life hackers". Occasional papers are

[1] We can extend the idea of an infinite random field to cases where $k > 2$, but $k - 1$ probabilities must be specified.

[2] A configuration or field, not a pattern in our sense.

published, e.g. (Buckingham and Callahan forthcoming), but most results appear on Internet newsgroups and WWW pages. Some ideas presented here were independently arrived at by this community. We used GoL freeware from sources within it.

2. Numerical studies of GoL fields' histories. (Bagnoli et al. 1991) found final densities of state 1 cells to be around 2.85% if the initial density is 15% – 75%, falling off beyond these limits. The results of (Gibbs and Stauffer 1997), using 50% initial density on lattices up to 204384×204384, agree closely with this. Studies including (Garcia *et al.* 1993; Sales et al. 1993) examine the number and size distribution of "clusters"[3] of cells in the final state of small (150×150) lattices, finding power-scaling laws for 15% – 75% initial densities. (Hof and Knill 1995), in a study of infinite fields, describe the first 100 steps of some almost periodic layouts defined in terms of circle-shifts, but do not try to interpret their results.

3. Studies concerned with the idea that some CA, and GoL in particular, may be poised on the "edge of chaos". A finite random field with 50% density is run until it becomes periodic. A single cell-state is then flipped, and the ensuing disturbance is measured. (Bak et al. 1989; Alstrøm and Leão 1994) claim that GoL shows "self-organized criticality", with the distribution of disturbance sizes governed by a power law, but (Bennett and Bourzutschky 1991; Hemmingsson 1995) claim this finding is an artifact of small lattice sizes and GoL is subcritical.

Our work differs from type 1 in concentrating on GoL's "natural" behavior rather than on esthetically-guided engineering. It differs from types 2 and 3 in concentrating on the behavior of *low-density* infinite random fields, and in deducing features of such fields' evolution from the proved existence (or non-existence) of particular types of finite pattern and process.

Infinite Sparse Random GoL Fields

Random fields

We call the layout arising after t steps from an infinite random CA field, with initial state 1 probability p for each cell, $\mathsf{C}_{p,t}$. For GoL, we use $\mathsf{L}_{p,t}$. The reciprocal of p we call N. For infinite CA, specifying C, R, t and p determines the expected frequency of any finite arrangment of cell-states. We can expect sufficiently large ensembles of finite arrays to approximate these frequencies as closely as desired.

There are two values of p for which, given any infinite deterministic binary CA, $\mathsf{C}_{p,t}$ can readily be characterised for all t: $p = 0$ and $p = 1$. If both states are quiescent[4], $\mathsf{C}_{0,t}$ will consist entirely of 0s, $\mathsf{C}_{1,t}$ of 1s. If only one is quiescent, $\mathsf{C}_{0,t}$ and $\mathsf{C}_{1,t}$ will consist entirely of cells in that state for all $t > 0$. If neither is quiescent, uniform fields of the two states will alternate.

For all other values of p we can calculate exact frequencies for any finite arangement of states, but in many cases, including GoL, the effort required appears to grow very rapidly with t. For GoL, we can make some definite statements without detailed analysis:

(1) The density, $D(\mathsf{L}_{p,t})$ will be > 0 but < 1 for all $t > 0$. Initially, there will be both arbitrarily large empty areas, and oscillators (see below) surrounded by such areas. Effects cannot propagate faster than one link per step, so both will survive at any finite t.

(2) In $\mathsf{L}_{p,0}$ where $0 < p < 1$, all finite subfields will appear infinitely often. However, some of these have no possible predecessor in GoL (Berlekamp et al. 1982, pp.828-9), and will not appear at any $t > 0$.

(3) $D(\mathsf{L}_{p,1})$ is $28(3-p)p^3(1-p)^5$ (calculated from the transition rule). We cannot reiterate the computation to get $D(\mathsf{L}_{p,2})$: the probabilities of neighboring cells being in state 1 are not independent for $t > 0$.

Most CA studies of random fields concentrate on $p = 1/2$. Here we assume that p is *arbitrarily low*, but non-zero: whenever the value of p makes a difference to our analysis, we assume it to be in the lowest distinguishable range of values.

Clusters

If p is very low, most 1s will be far from each other. Only $\sim p$ of them will be near any others; only $\sim p^2$ of them will have two others near, and so on ("near" means within some fixed distance $\ll N$). We will use "cluster" rather than "pattern" for a finite group of state 1 cells surrounded by a non-empty field.

A "0-cluster" is a maximal set of 1s such that any two members are joined by a continuous path of neighborhood links going through no state 0 cells. A "d-cluster" is a maximal set of 1s such that the corresponding paths never pass through more than d successive 0 cells. A 1-cluster's future depends only on itself, for the next step, but of course that step may merge or split 1-clusters. The number of state 1 cells in a cluster is its "size", s. "Cluster" without a numerical prefix means a set of 1s which form a d-cluster for some d. A *pattern* is necessarily a cluster.

For any infinite binary CA, there is a p below which there will only be finite 0-clusters in random fields. The critical value of p will be $\geq 1/(z-1)$, where z is the number of neighbors a cell has (Shante and Kirkpatrick 1971, p.332). For CAs on square lattices we can extend the result to any value of d by dividing the lattice into $(d+1) \times (d+1)$ "macrocells" (square sub-arrays of cells).

[3] Their use of "cluster" overlaps with, but differs from ours, given below.

[4] We use "quiescent" for *any* state of a CA such that a homogeneous field of cells in that state does not change.

A d-cluster in the original network must occupy a contiguous set (i.e. a 0-cluster) of these macrocells. The probability that a macrocell contains at least one 1 can be derived from p, and can be made as low as we please for any given d by reducing p. Thus if p is low enough, all d-clusters will be finite.

Consider GoL cluster-types defined so that two clusters are of the same type iff a translation maps one onto the other. The *exact* frequency of such a cluster-type in $\mathsf{L}_{p,0}$ depends on how many cells must be in state 0 for a cluster of that type to exist, as well as how many must be in state 1. However, with p very low, considering just the number of 1s the cluster contains gives a very good approximation. All translation-defined cluster-types of size s will be almost equal in frequency in $\mathsf{L}_{p,0}$, if $s \ll N$ and $d \ll N$.

We will need terms for some types of cluster defined in behavioral terms.

- An *oscillator* is a cluster which, if it were a pattern, would show periodicity: the CA's configuration would be the same at t_{x+r} as at t_x, where r is the period (which may be 1).

- A *repeater* would also show periodicity if it were a pattern, but the definition is wider: the CA's *layout* would be the same at t_{x+r} as at t_x. A repeater which is not an oscillator is a *spaceship* (i.e., it moves).

- A *quiet cluster* consists of a set of repeaters, no two of which overlap the same 1-cluster, or would ever do so in an otherwise empty array. (This ensures that no two of the repeaters interact.)

- An *indefinite growth cluster* would increase its number of cells without limit if it were a pattern; by definition, it would never become quiet.

A *cs-cluster*, intuitively, is a cluster extended through some time-span. If we envisage a succession of CA fields "stacked" vertically[5], with the earliest at the base, each "slice" of the structure represents a time step and each "cell", a cell of the CA field at a particular step: a "cell-slice". Two cell-slices are "cs-neighbors" iff they belong to the same or adjacent steps, and their cells are neighbours in the CA concerned. We can define d-cs-clusters for any d. Two cell-slices are in the same d-cs-cluster with start and end steps t_s, t_e, iff there is a path between the two along cs-neighbor links, which always passes from one state 1 cell to another when moving up or down a slice, and which never goes through more than d successive state 0 cell-slices within a slice. If $t_s = t_e$, d-cs-clusters correspond 1-1 with d-clusters. If we increase t_e by 1 without changing t_s, each of the d-clusters of the new t_e may act as a "bridge" between two or more previously separate d-cs-clusters, but cs-clusters can never split. The t_j *slice* of a cs-cluster is the set of cell-slices (c_i, t_j) belonging to that cs-cluster. We say a cs-cluster is quiet, or has indefinite growth, iff its top slice does.

Cs-clusters with $t_s = 0$ are *rooted* cs-clusters; we will be most interested in rooted 1-cs-clusters. If we removed all state 1 cells from an initial field, except those belonging to the $t = 0$ slice of a rooted 1-cs-cluster with end step t_e, that 1-cs-cluster would be unaffected up to t_e.

Statement of results

Very sparse CA fields provide us with a logarithmic time scale of "eras" expressed in terms of p or its reciprocal N. "In era 1", for example, means "after $\sim N$ steps"; "in era 3" means "after $\sim N^3$ steps". All isolated clusters without indefinite growth become quiet during era 0 (the "very short term"). The "short term" lasts until interactions between initially distant clusters become important dynamically. For GoL, the "medium term" certainly begins by era 5/2. "Long term" refers to what happens in the temporal limit; here, we do not go beyond era 3.

Our specific claims concern the growing importance of "emergent" indefinite growth clusters after era 5/2 and before era 3. If $p > 0$ but is low enough, a time will come when almost all 1-cs-clusters with indefinite growth have gained it through mergers of quiet 1-cs-clusters, with roots distant from each other. Also, the top slices of such 1-cs-clusters will contain almost all state 1 cells which were in state 0 up to $t = 1$, and the *nearest* such cell in an orthogonal or diagonal line from almost all points. These "emergent structures" thus "dominate" the dynamics of the field by providing most of the centres of growth in the state 1 population, *and* almost all state 1 cells — except those in minimal size original clusters which have remained isolated.

Preparing to state our results, we first note that all $t = 0$ clusters of ≤ 5 cells become quiet by $t = 1105$; all of ≤ 9 cells, with an exception detailed later, by $t = 17410$. We now define two conditions on indefinite growth 1-cs-clusters. Those meeting condition A are created by merging at least 2 clusters (each starting from < 10 cells), all of which become quiet before the merger begins. Those meeting condition B (stricter than A), are created by merging at least 3 clusters (one starting from 5 cells, the rest from 3) which all become quiet before the merger begins. In both cases, the quiet clusters that merge do *not* constitute the whole of a larger cluster at the time the last of them becomes quiet.

(A) There is a t_j slice, $t_j \leq 17410$, consisting of 2 or more quiet clusters which do *not* all belong to the same rooted 1-cs-cluster with end step t_j, and each of which developed from a $t = 0$ cluster of < 10 cells.

(B) There is a t_j slice, $t_j \leq 1105$, consisting of 3 or more quiet clusters, which do *not* all belong to the same rooted

[5] We need not assume the CA is 1-d or 2-d — "stacking" is simply an aid to visualization.

1-cs-cluster with end step t_j. One of these quiet clusters develops from a $t = 0$ cluster of 5 cells, the rest from $t = 0$ clusters of 3 cells.
The following then hold:

1. For any $E > 2\frac{181}{190}$, and any $w < 1$, there is a p such that there is a step t_e ($t_e < p^{-E}$) at which a proportion $> w$ of the indefinite growth rooted 1-cs-clusters meet condition A.

2. For any $E > 2\frac{94}{95}$ and any $x, y < 1$ there is a p such that there is a step t_e ($t_e < p^{-E}$) at which:
   (a) A proportion $> x$ of all state 1 cells which were in state 0 up to $t = 1$ belong to rooted 1-cs-clusters which meet condition A.
   (b) For a proportion $> y$ of all cells, the nearest state 1 cells (along an orthogonal or diagonal line) which were in state 0 up to $t = 1$ belong to rooted 1-cs-clusters which meet condition B.

3. For any $E > 2\frac{189}{190}$ and any $z < 1$, there is a p such that there is a step t_e ($0 < t_e < p^{-E}$) at which a proportion $> z$ of the indefinite growth rooted 1-cs-clusters meet condition B.

The first 17410 time steps

In this subsection, when we say a quantity or ratio approaches or tends to some value, it is to be understood that this occurs as $p \to 0$.

At $t = 1$, all clusters of size ≤ 2 will vanish (and some larger ones). The formula $28(3-p)p^3(1-p)^5$ given for $D(\mathsf{L}_{p,1})$ tends to $84p^3$. By $t = 2$, all initial size 3 3-clusters will have vanished except blinkers and those producing blocks (see the leftmost patterns in Figure 1). The same will be true of a proportion of size 3 1-clusters approaching 1. The ratio of blocks to blinkers tends to 2:1 and $D(\mathsf{L}_{p,2})$ tends to $22p^3$. From $t = 2$ onward, the layout will, for a number of steps $\to \infty$ as $p \to 0$, contain mostly these blocks and blinkers, with the proportion of other cells approaching 0 as p does. (Collectively blocks and blinkers are "blonks"; those derived from 3 cells at $t = 0$ are "original blonks"; and we extend "original" to other clusters derived from minimal size clusters at $t = 0$.)

By $t = 11$, all the initial size 4 clusters which have not interacted with other clusters (approaching all of them as $p \to 0$) will reach a stable state or a 2-cycle, producing "debris" in the form of oscillators scattered thinly among the original blonks: additional blonks, plus "beehives", "traffic lights", "ponds" and "tubs" (see Figure 1) in ratios approaching 58:12:4:1 (reflecting the numbers of cluster-types leading to each).

Size 5 clusters give rise to two new kinds of oscillator. More significantly, some are or become "gliders" — the smallest GoL spaceship, which moves 1 link diagonally in 4 steps — and others "r-pentominos", each of which produces six gliders, plus some oscillators. These two forms will be produced in a ratio approaching 8:9. Some of the r-pentomino predecessors take 1105 steps to become quiet.

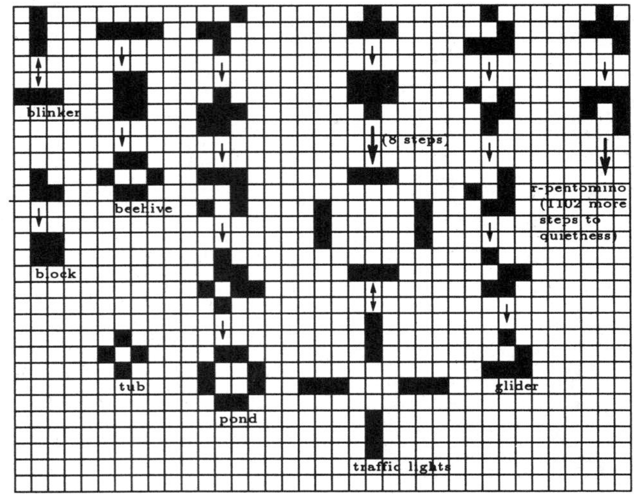

Figure 1: Life-histories of some small patterns

All clusters with 6, 7, 8 or 9 cells become quiet by $t = 17410$, except for some consisting of two sub-clusters, one of which emits a glider that later hits the other. In all these cases, the two *sub-clusters* both become quiet before $t = 17410$.

Minimal patterns in GoL

In analyzing very sparse CA fields, we are interested in the *smallest* clusters with particular dynamic properties. We have seen the smallest persistent GoL clusters (3 cells), and the smallest spaceships and clusters with indefinite growth in diameter (5 cells). We recently found three 10-cell patterns that increase their number of cells without limit (linearly)[6]. These patterns grow into "switch engines": patterns with a "head" which moves 8 cells diagonally in 96 steps, and an ever-lengthening "tail" of oscillators. Two grow into the "block-laying switch engine" (see Figure 2, showing the head, going NW, and part of the tail, consisting wholly of blocks); the third into the "glider-stream switch engine", with a more complex tail, and a stream of gliders the head "fires" ahead of itself.

We also found the smallest *known* patterns with indefinite superlinear (in fact quadratic) growth. These have 130 cells, and use 16 interacting switch engines to build further switch engines indefinitely (the latter do not interact to produce a third generation).

[6]Outlines of the techniques used to show there are none smaller are available from Gotts, along with patterns mentioned in the paper and software to run them.

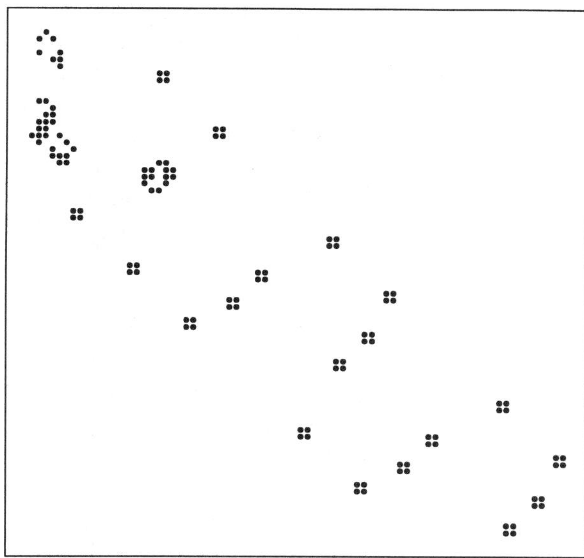

Figure 2: Block-laying Switch Engine

In the long run, a GoL pattern's number of cells can at most grow quadratically; its diameter (as for any CA) at most linearly. Thus in very sparse fields, the total density contribution of any type of original cluster at most grows $\propto t^2$ (interaction between clusters cannot overcome this limit, although it might produce new quadratic growth clusters). The linear limit on diameter growth means that an original cluster's distance from a given cell, or a straight strip of cells (such as a glider's prospective path) cannot *shrink* faster than $\propto t$. Even if there were 10-cell quadratic growth patterns (which seems highly implausible, but an exhaustive check has not been made), their total density contribution could not reach $\sim p^4$ until era 3.

Collision sequences

Consider the future of an original glider in a very sparse, random, infinite GoL field. The *expected* distance to the first original blonk so placed that the glider would interact with it is $\sim N^3$ links, but for $\sim p^2$ of them it will be $< N$ links, and in general $\sim p^{3-E}$ of them will have one at $< N^{3-E}$ links. While original blonks remain much commoner than anything else, the rough proportion of original gliders that will have collided with one is easily calculated. In the first $\lfloor N \rfloor$ time steps, $\sim p^2$ of the original gliders will have hit a blonk ($\sim p^3$ of them will have hit something else instead). The same calculations apply to the gliders emitted by an original r-pentomino (a single glider going in one direction, and "fleets" of two and three in two others).

The result of such an glider or fleet hitting a blonk depends on precisely how the collision occurs. Two of the 12 glider/blinker collisions, and some of those between r-pentomino derived fleets and a blinker, produce further gliders (plus clusters of oscillators). If, contrary to fact, one of these collisions produced a cluster with indefinite linear growth, this process could have a significant effect on the overall field density by era 5/2. By this era, $\sim p^{1/2}$ of the original gliders would have taken part in such a collision, meaning that overall such a collision would have occurred "near" (within some small fixed distance of) $\sim p^{11/2}$ of the cells in the field. Almost all such collisions would have generated a pattern containing $\sim N^{5/2}$ cells, for a total density contribution of around $\sim p^3$ — the same order as for the original blonks. If the cluster were linear in shape as well as growth rate, an original fleet (we allow "fleet" to cover the case of a single glider) would be roughly as likely to hit such a resulting cluster as to hit an original blonk: the expected distance to either kind of obstacle would be $\sim N^3$.

If a cluster with indefinite *quadratic* growth could be produced in this way, the same density contribution would be reached in era 5/3, when $\sim p^{4/3}$ of the gliders would have taken part in such a collision, and almost all would have produced $\sim N^{10/3}$ cells. However, an original fleet would not be likely to hit such a cluster until era 5/2. A cluster must spread across a fleet's path to be hit by it; the number of glider paths a cluster obstructs can at most grow linearly. To challenge the preponderance of fleet collisions with original blonks, the number of paths each member of a cluster type can be expected to obstruct, multiplied by the density of their starting points, must be $\sim p^3$.

Of the two glider/blinker collisions mentioned above, one produces two new gliders, the other ("glider/blinker 6") produces five (two travelling parallel to the incoming glider but shifted sideways, one antiparallel to it, two at right angles). The "onward" pair follow the same path, 52 "half-diagonals" from the path of the incomer (a "half-diagonal" is the least by which two parallel but distinct glider paths can differ). The "sideways" pair both travel in the same direction, but their paths are 53 half-diagonals apart.

If one of the fleets produced by a "first generation" collision itself hits something, then with probability almost 1 this will be an original blonk, assuming indefinite growth clusters remain sufficiently rare. This collision may itself produce further fleets and another collision — on the same assumption, almost certain to be with either an original blonk, or the oscillators left by the first collision. (The second possibility depends on exact details of the collisions, but the path of any backward glider from the second collision must at least pass *close* to the debris from the first, and prior to era 3, that debris is almost certain to be closer to the second collision than any original blonk in the path of any gliders produced.)

We call a collision sequence involving only a single glider or r-pentomino, and a set of original blonks, a "standard collision sequence". The number of possible standard collision sequences grows rapidly with the number of original blonks involved; the probability of any given sequence occurring falls correspondingly.

Prior to era 3, and retaining our assumption about the rarity of indefinite growth clusters, the proportion of original gliders and r-pentominos taking part in standard collision sequences involving at least b original blonks by era E (after $\sim N^E$ steps) is $\sim (p^{3-E})^b$, or $\sim p^{b(3-E)}$. We can neglect factors due to variation in the number of output gliders different collisions produce, as p is taken to be much smaller than any finite probability that occurs in the analysis.

Collision sequences and self-replication

Successive collisions with blonks can reduce any fleet to a single glider, and there is a 3-collision sequence leading from a single glider to an r-pentomino. Hence any cluster produced by a collision sequence *starting* from an original glider or r-pentomino, and which itself produces any gliders, can start a collision sequence leading to a copy of itself. Gliders, r-pentominos, and the glider fleets and other clusters produced by such collision sequences could all be considered to replicate themselves in sparse GoL fields, using the original blonks as raw material.

There are a number of possible objections to this description of affairs. First, none of these patterns replicate "autonomously": all require interaction with objects in a non-uniform environment. However, the same is true of real organisms; it is replication in an otherwise empty environment, as in (von Neumann 1966; Langton 1984) that is unnatural!

Second, it could be said that this form of replication is "trivial". It does not use a universal computer, as in (von Neumann 1966), nor even have a "genome" which is both copied and read (Langton 1984). Some might therefore prefer a term such as "auto-catalysis" rather than "self-replication". At any rate, it is clearly different from the kind of replication found in Fredkin's parity-rule CA (Gardner 1983), where *any* pattern self-replicates: only certain clusters can replicate, and different ones replicate themselves (and produce each other), with different probabilities.

Third and most convincingly, no cluster is known to be able to replicate itself in this way with sufficient efficiency to increase its numbers indefinitely. Such a process could not in any case become self-sustaining until era 3, and other processes may radically alter the environment before then. Before turning to these, we show that fleets of any finite size can arise.

Glider/blinker 6, as noted, produces a 2-glider fleet with a 53 half-diagonal sideways separation. One of these can collide with a blinker to produce two forward gliders one half-diagonal to the side of (and somewhat behind) the other member of the fleet. The first two of *this* fleet (the third neither helps nor hinders) can react successively with a block and another blinker to give a 3-fleet, of which two again follow paths a half-diagonal apart. The process can then be repeated indefinitely, adding one glider to the fleet every two collisions. The extra gliders can also, with the right sequence of collisions, produce further half-diagonal pairs, giving a further kind of replication, of sub-fleets within a fleet.

Switch engine construction/destruction

If there is a standard collision sequence which produces an indefinite growth cluster, its products would meet conditions A and B in the "Statement of Results" subsection, and could dominate the dynamics of sparse GoL layouts before era 3 arrives. Collision sequences producing indefinite growth clusters *could* make use of original clusters of > 5 cells, and/or of more than one cluster with > 3 cells at $t = 0$, but these would meet only condition A, and would occur much less often than standard collision sequences. We recently found a 96-blonk standard collision sequence producing a block-laying switch engine. The first collision is glider/blinker 6. The next 94, making use of the fleet-growing sequence described above, convert the sideways 2-fleet into a final 5-fleet. This collides with a final blinker to produce the switch engine.

For a standard collision sequence producing a linear growth pattern and involving collisions with b original blonks, a first calculation suggests a density contribution of $\sim p^3$ in era $2\frac{b}{b+1}$. In this era, $\sim p^{b/(b+1)}$ of original gliders and r-pentominos will have produced standard collision sequences involving at least b original blonks. Some fraction of these (*not* dependent on p and $\gg p$, if p is sufficiently low) will be the desired sequence. The pattern concerned will therefore have begun to grow near $\sim p^{5\frac{b}{b+1}}$ of the cells in the array. Each one will reach a size of $\sim N^{2\frac{b}{b+1}}$ during the era $2\frac{b}{b+1}$, for a total density contribution of $\sim p^3$.

This calculation neglects the fact that, at characteristic diameter $\sim N^{5/2}$, the rate at which clusters such as switch engines are struck by gliders will reach ~ 1 per step. This is *before* they would be expected to run into an obstacle, so long as the expected distance to such an obstacle is $\gg N^{5/2}$. As a switch engine grows past a particular point, the nearest glider moving toward it will usually be $\sim N^5$ links away, but for $\sim p^{5/2}$ cases it will be $\sim N^{5/2}$ links away, and will hit the switch engine tail after $\sim N^{5/2}$ steps. (This process will affect *original* indefinite growth clusters significantly in era 5/2.) Some infinite growth clusters are easily "killed" (their growth is halted). The glider-stream switch engine can be killed by a single glider hitting the glider stream, creating an obstruction in the switch engine's path. The block-laying switch engine cannot be killed by a single glider, or fleet from an r-pentomino, but may be vulnerable to multiple collisions of this kind. If so, both original switch engines and those produced by collision sequences will "die" when they reach $\sim N^{5/2}$ cells. Moreover, it is conceivable that some sequence of collisions with the tail could "ignite" it and burn it away.

We will show here that all the results claimed in the "statement of results" subsection will hold, even under the following conservative assumptions:

1. Block-laying switch engines ignite and burn away at size $\sim N^{5/2}$.

2. Block-laying switch engines cannot be produced from a standard collision sequence involving fewer than 96 original blonks.

3. Collision sequences can make no other indefinite growth clusters from < 10 cell quiet clusters.

In fact, we believe none of these assumptions hold, and that it is feasible to disprove the last two at least. We show in the next subsection that their failure to hold could not undermine our claims, but might enable us to strengthen them.

The rate per step at which the 96 collision sequence produces switch engines, if nothing else interferes, depends on the *product* of the densities of original blonks, and of copies of the fleet produced by the first 95 collisions: $\sim p^3 \times (p^5 \times p^{95(3-E)})$ where E is the era. In era $2\frac{181}{190}$ this will be $\sim p^{25/2}$; in era $2\frac{94}{95}$, $\sim p^9$; in era $2\frac{189}{190}$, $\sim p^{17/2}$. If block-laying switch engines burn away at size $\sim 5/2$, we can expect, in any era after era 5/2, that a proportion ~ 1 of those created in the last $N^{5/2}$ steps will survive, but few others. Most will have a size of $\sim N^{5/2}$ cells. (In the eras of interest, and with p low, rate of production will be nearly constant over a period of $N^{5/2}$ steps. The process of burning away must itself take $\sim N^{5/2}$ steps.) The head of such a cluster will therefore be found near $\sim p^{10}$ cells in era $2\frac{181}{190}$ (see claim 1) and $\sim p^6$ in era $2\frac{189}{190}$ (claim 3).

In any era after $2\frac{94}{95}$ the density contribution of switch engines from the 96 collision sequence would be $> p^4$. The commonest *original* indefinite growth clusters begin to grow near $\sim p^{10}$ cells, and even with quadratic growth would only produce a density contribution of $\sim p^4$ in era 3. Original 3 cell clusters that do not interact create *no* new state 1 cells after $t = 1$. Original clusters of > 3 cells that do not help to produce indefinite growth can never contribute more than $\sim p^4$. After era $2\frac{94}{95}$ the 96 collision sequence switch engines would therefore meet claim 2a. The expected distance to the tail of a 96 collision sequence switch engine in a diagonal or orthogonal line would be $< p^4$, so claim 2b would also be met.

The nearest cells to the quiet clusters of conditions A and B can safely be taken to belong to original blonks that do *not* take part in the collision sequences producing the switch engines. We lose a negligible proportion of clusters that would otherwise meet these conditions by assuming this, as the nearest original blonk to almost all initial clusters at any $t \leq 17410$ will be $\sim N^{3/2}$ away. On the assumptions above, our 96-collision sequence will therefore produce indefinite growth rooted 1-cs-clusters meeting all our claims.

Possibilities for preemption

If we assume that the block-laying switch engine would not burn away when it reached a size of $\sim N^{5/2}$, or even more strongly, that its growth would not be halted at that size, the growth targets set by our claimed results would be met sooner than under our pessimistic assumption. In the case that growth is not halted (retaining our assumption that no faster construction processes are operating), we could make much stronger claims: in era $2\frac{96}{97}$, the density contribution of these switch engines would be $\sim p^3$. In any subsequent era, the density could surpass Kp^3 for any desired constant K if we took p sufficiently low. (If glider bombardment from the side does not halt a switch engine's growth, it will continue to grow until it runs into something. Here, this would typically be another switch engine, in era $2\frac{97}{98}$, when the length of such clusters and the expected straight-line distance from a given cell to one of them are comparable.)

If there are standard collision sequences using *fewer* than 96 blonks which lead to indefinite growth clusters (as is very likely), then again the targets set will be reached earlier than required. It would be surprising if the shortest such sequence produced anything other than a switch engine: experiments with various kinds of random pattern produced a switch engine once in around 300,000 tries, and never produced any other indefinite growth pattern. Nevertheless, it is not impossible. Furthermore, a sequence producing some *other* type of indefinite linear growth cluster could preempt the minimal switch engine producing sequence, if this cluster did not burn away at size $\sim N^{5/2}$ (assuming the switch engine does), or did not have its growth halted (and the switch engine does). Such indefinite growth clusters are most likely to have heads that move *orthogonally*: many are known with heads that move at one link every two steps — and no finite pattern can move or grow faster than that indefinitely. If there are *any* indefinite growth clusters which can arise from a standard collision sequence, and which do not have their growth halted at $\sim N^{5/2}$ cells, then all our claims will be met, *and* the overall density of a sparse GoL field will exceed p^3 before era 3.

Whether or not they die, switch engines may also reproduce at size $\sim N^{5/2}$ cells. Sequences of collisions between gliders and the tail may produce further switch engines, headed in any direction. This would be another form of self-replication, and might be efficient enough to produce quadratic growth of a "mycelium" in which the threads are individual switch engines. Alternatively, glider collisions with the tail could produce some other form of superlinear growth. Neither possibility undermines our claims.

Also possible is the production of superlinear infinite growth clusters directly from quiet clusters. These could make an important density contribution even if they arose only from non-standard collision sequences. (But recall that no cluster of size ≥ 10 could be involved in a sequence producing a density contribution of $\sim p^4$ before era 3.) Non-standard collision sequences involve either an original cluster of ≥ 6 cells, or the $\sim p$ (or worse) chance of an original cluster other than a blonk being hit by a fleet from a sequence beginning with a 5 cell cluster. They could not therefore produce indefinite growth clusters starting near as many as $\sim p^6$ cells before era 3. This means that no non-standard collision sequence could interfere significantly with the 96-collision sequence. Moreover, superlinear growth rates cannot change the rate of growth of cluster diameter, so no non-standard collision sequence could rival a standard collision sequence in producing the nearest state 1 cell (not counting original blonks) on an orthogonal or diagonal line from almost any point.

Looking back at the "statement of results" subsection, we are now in a position to affirm the claims made there. The 96-collision sequence could be prevented from bringing about the fulfillment of the conditions listed, but only if other processes that also build indefinite growth clusters from sets of small, quiet clusters do so first. In the case of claims (2b) and (3), only standard collision sequences (using at least two blonks) could do so; for claims (1) and (2a), the possibilities are wider, but still limited as required in those claims.

Discussion

We have shown that the medium-term dynamics of sparse random GoL fields will be dominated, in ways we can make precise, by emergent structures, and that some simple forms of self-replication will occur. So far as GoL itself is concerned, considerable further progress may be possible. It is certainly feasible to check whether the two switch engines are indeed the only 10 cell indefinite growth patterns. It may be possible to find the minimal collision sequence that produces indefinite growth clusters, to discover whether the block-laying switch engine is vulnerable to glider bombardment when it reaches size $\sim N^{5/2}$, and to prove that there are other indefinite growth clusters which can be produced by collision sequences and which are not vulnerable.

So far as other CA are concerned, work is already in progress both on the "elementary" 1-d CA (for example, the smallest indefinite growth pattern for that generally called ECA 120 (Braga et al. 1995) grows $\propto t^{1/2}$, which does not appear to have been noted before), and on CA closely related to GoL. Of these, the most interesting may be "HighLife" (Bell 1994), which differs from GoL only in that a cell switches from 0 to 1 iff either 3 *or* *6* of its non-self neighbours are in state 1. Many GoL patterns "carry over" to HighLife, but there are two major differences. First, no standard collision sequence can get going: the glider carries over, but its collisions with blonks produce no new gliders, and there is nothing corresponding to the r-pentomino. Second, there is a 6 cell cluster with indefinite growth, of a kind which is difficult (though possible) to produce in GoL: at ever-increasing intervals, the number of cells returns to a fixed figure (20), then rises to new heights. The effect is to "embed" copies of the 1-d CA known as ECA 18 into the HighLife field. It turns out that when these copies reach a size $\sim N^{5/2}$ in a very sparse field, a single glider can cause them to self-replicate.

This raises a wider point. Both these CA show complex behavior, but the two are very different, and how the differences manifest themselves depends on the range of initial conditions tested. Also, the features displayed in very sparse random fields are the outcome of interplay between patterns whose behavior depends on details of the transition rule, and can be radically changed by small changes in the rule. The relative sizes of the smallest clusters with crucial dynamic properties are important, as are the interactions of these minimal clusters. The approach taken, like the work of (Dhar et al. 1995; Hanson and Crutchfield 1997) and others, casts doubt on claims that CA fall into a few "universality classes" within which the details of rules do not matter much. Whether this is so appears to depend on how you look at them.

Acknowledgements

Comments from two anonymous reviewers, and discussions with the late Robert G. Norman and several "Life hackers", are gratefully acknowledged.

References

Alstrøm, P. and J. Leão. 1994. Self-organized criticality in the "game of life". Physical Review E 49: R2507–8.

Bagnoli, F., R. Rechtman, and S. Ruffo. 1991. Some facts of life. Physica A 171: 249–264.

Bak, P., K. Chen, and M. Creutz. 1989. Self-organized criticality in the "game of life". Nature 342: 780–1.

Bell, D. I. Highlife: An interesting variant of life. Available from David Bell's web page: http://www.tip.net.au/ dbell/, May 1994.

Bennett, C and M. S. Bourzutschky. 1991. "Life" not critical. Nature 350: 468.

Berlekamp, E., J. H. Conway, and R. Guy. 1982. *Winning Ways (vol.2)*. New York: Academic Press.

Braga, G, G. Cattaneo, P. Flocchini, and C. Quaranta Vogliotti. 1995. Pattern growth in elementary cellular automata. Theoretical Computer Science 145: 1–26.

Buckingham, D. J. and P. B. Callahan. 1998. Tight bounds on periodic cell configurations in life. Experimental Mathematics, forthcoming.

Chou, H. H. and J. A. Reggia. 1997. Emergence of self-replicating structures in a cellular automata space. Physica D 110: 252–276..

Dhar, A., P. Lakdawala, and G. Mandal. 1995. Role of initial conditions in the classificiation of the rule-space of cellular-automata dynamics. Physical Review E 51: 3032–3037.

Garcia, J. B. C., M. A. F. Gomes, T. I. Jyh, T. I. Ren, and T. R. M. Sales. 1993. Nonlinear dynamics of the cellular-automaton "game of life". Physical Review E 48: 3345–3351.

Gardner, M. *Wheels, Life And Other Amusements.* New York: Freeman.

Gibbs, P. and D. Stauffer. 1997. Search for asymptotic death in game of life. International Journal of Modern Physics C 8: 601–604.

Hanson, J. E. and J. P. Crutchfield. 1997. Computational mechanics of cellular automata: An example. Physica D 103: 169–189.

J Hemmingsson. 1995. Consistent results on "life". Physica D 80: 151–3.

Hof, A. and O. Knill. 1995. Cellular automata with almost periodic initial conditions. Nonlinearity 8: 477–491.

Langton, C. G. 1984. Self-reproduction in cellular automata. Physica D 10: 134–144, 1984.

Poundstone, W. 1985. *The Recursive Universe.* New York: William Morrow and Company.

Sales, T. M., J. B. C. Garcia, T. I. Jyh, T. I. Ren, and M. A. F. Gomes. 1993. On the game of life: population and its diversity. Physica A 197: 604–612.

Shante, V. K. S. and S. Kirkpatrick. 1971. An introduction to percolation theory. Advances in Physics 20: 325–357.

von Neumann. J. 1966. *The Theory of Self-Reproducing Automata.* Urbana, IL: University of Illinois Press, edited by A.W. Burks.

Wainwright, R. T. (ed). 1971. Lifeline: A quarterly newsletter for enthusiasts of John Conway's Game of Life. 11 issues published 1971-73. Now available from Wainwright at Lifeline, 12 Longvue Avenue, New Rochelle, N.Y. 10804.

Wolfram, S. 1984. Universality and complexity in cellular automata. Physica D 10: 1–35.

Introduction of Structural Dissolution into Langton's Self-Reproducing Loop

Hiroki Sayama
Department of Information Science, University of Tokyo
sayama@is.s.u-tokyo.ac.jp

Abstract

The phenomenon of death, or disappearance of life, has two aspects. One is failure in the function of life and the other is dissolution of the structure of life. In order to examine the significance of the latter aspect, the author contrived a "structurally dissolvable self-reproducing (SDSR) loop" by introducing the capability of structural dissolution into Langton's self-reproducing (SR) loop in which death as functional failure has already been installed. To be more specific, a *dissolving state* '8' was introduced into the set of states of the CA, besides other modifications to Langton's transition rules. Through this improvement, the SDSR loop can dissolve its own structure when faced with difficult situations such as a shortage of space for self-reproduction. This mechanism (disappearance of a subsystem of the whole system) induces, for the first time, dynamically-stable and potentially evolvable behavior into the colony of SDSR loops.

Introduction

This study is an attempt to introduce death as *structural dissolution* into Langton's self-reproducing loop (abbreviated as "SR loop" in the following) in which death as *functional failure* is already featured. While it was motivated simply by the author's desire to allow SR loops to continue with their characteristic behavior semi-permanently within finite memory space, it also creates a means to investigate the significance of a death-process for the dynamics of life.

What is life? How does a living system behave? To answer any of these basic questions, so far many kinds of behavior characteristic of life have been studied, such as self-reproduction, metabolism, physical motion, perception, learning, immunity, inheritance, evolution, emergent behavior of population, death, and so forth. According to these studies, life has been defined many times in many ways. We temporarily and simply define life here only via its behavioral aspects, as a complex system which adapts to and affects the external environment, and also has the capability of self-reproduction and evolution. Among these characteristics of life, it may be no exaggeration to say that death is one of the phenomena which are examined relatively less than the others.

What is death? What kind of behavior do we call death? At least we can say as a trivial definition that death is a state transition of a system from a living state to a non-living one. Though we also need definitions for the living state and the non-living state in order to complete this statement, we do not want to consider it too deeply here. For the time being, here we will define the living state to be a state in which a system functions correctly and shows the above-mentioned behavior characteristic of life. "Death of life" as a state transition from the living state to the non-living caused by loss of sound function of the system is, for now, referred to as *death as functional failure* in this article.

In practice, however, there are many cases in which we view the cessation of life not only as functional failure but also by the disorganization of the physical structure of a system. Here, we shall refer to this, again for the time being, as *death as structural dissolution.* For example, all terrestrial creatures including human beings will be decomposed into organic compounds by their own function and other microorganisms after death due to functional failure, unless a special treatment for preservation is applied to their corpses. Moreover, it is clearly understood that in the engineering techniques represented by genetic algorithms, e.g., or in artificial ecosystem simulations like *Tierra*, death of an individual implies not only their functional termination but also removal of them from the memory space of computers. Thus, it is obvious that the value of death for a system in a finite environment would not only be functional failure, but in fact in the structural dissolution associated with it. However, death has never been discussed while drawing a distinct line between these two aspects.

Therefore, we aim here at elucidating the significance of death as structural dissolution by introducing it into a system in which it was previously absent, and chose Langton's SR loop for the subject matter. A new state '8' was introduced into the set of states of the CA, while states '0'–'7' and Langton's transition rules were preserved in order to completely emulate the properties of the SR loop. Transition rules governing the behavior of the new state '8' were designed in such a manner as

Figure 1: Configuration of Langton's SR loop. Six signal states '7' (each of which make the arm grow straight for one cell) and two signal states '4' (which make the arm turn left) are set in the 'Q'-shaped tube enclosed by sheath states '2'. The right chart indicates the correspondence between states of cells and shades of pixels in the figure. The following figures are also drawn according to this chart.

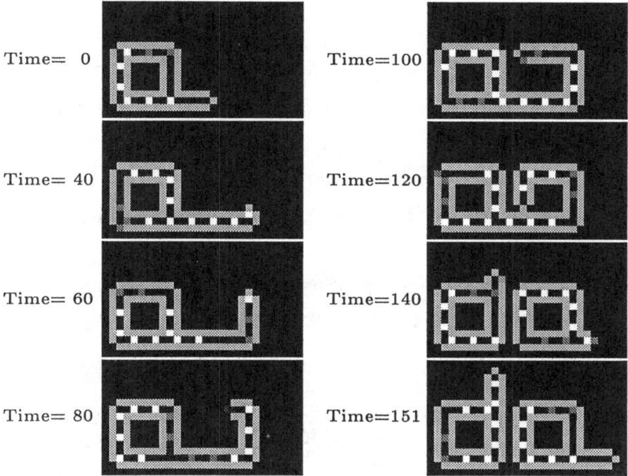

Figure 2: Self-reproduction of the SR loop. As signals in the loop propagate counterclockwise, copies of them are made and sent toward the tip of the arm. The arm grows through repetition of straight growth and left turning (time=40–100). When the tip reaches its own root after three left turns, they bond together to form a new offspring loop. Then the connection between parent and offspring disappears (time=120–140). In such a way, the loop reproduces its offspring which has a structure identical to its parent's in the right area, in 151 updates (time=151).

to give state '8' the meaning of a *dissolving state* which can propagate along the tube of the loop and dissolve the neighboring structure. Such an improved loop was termed "structurally dissolvable self-reproducing loop" ("SDSR loop".) Through experiments with the SDSR loop, several interesting phenomena never previously seen in the world of SR loops were observed.

This article consists of five parts: Review of Langton's SR loop, explanation of a concrete method for implementation of the SDSR loop, observation of results of experiments using the SDSR loop, several discussions about them, and a brief conclusion.

Langton's Self-Reproducing Loop

Langton's SR loop (Langton 1984) is one of the most famous models of self-reproduction constructed by means

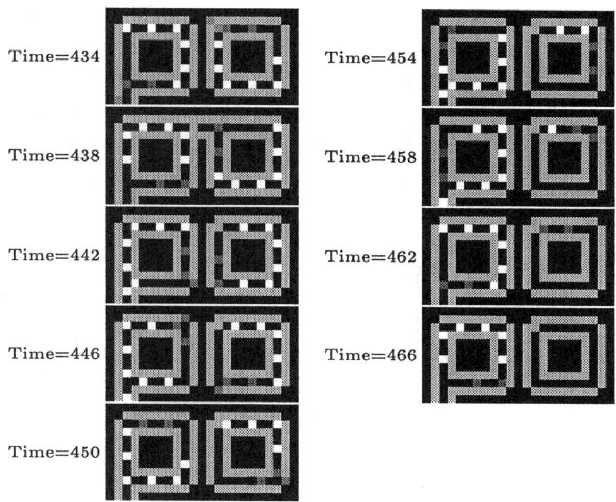

Figure 3: Death as functional failure of the SR loop. The right loop tries to thrust its arm to the left (time=438). Since the left area is already occupied by another loop, however, a sheath fragment is generated on the pathway of signals at the upper left part of the right loop (time=442). Signals propagating in the loop are absorbed one after another by the generated fragment (time=446–462). Eventually, all the signals have been extinguished, and only a circular tube filled with core states are left (time=466).

of cellular automata (CA). Langton invented it in order to reveal that universality of construction is not necessary for self-reproduction. The SR loop is implemented in an 8-state 5-neighbor CA. Its configuration is shown in Figure 1. Signal states '4' and '7' are set to float in the 'Q'-shaped tube enclosed by sheath states '2'. Signals propagate along the tube in the direction of the neighboring core state '1'. When a signal reaches the tip of a construction arm which is thrust outward from the loop, translation from genotype to phenotype will occur, such as straight growth or left turning of the arm. When the tip of the arm reaches its own root after it turned left three times, tip and arm bond together to form a new offspring loop, and then the connection between parent and offspring—which Langton called the "umbilical cord"—disappears. In such a way, the SR loop is ingeniously designed to reproduce itself in just 151 updates. This method of self-reproduction is shown in Figure 2. Since the specifications of the SR loop are described at length in Langton's paper, details are omitted here.

When the SR loop finishes self-reproduction, it will try to do the same again in the same way but rotated by ninety degrees counterclockwise. It repeats this action forever while there is enough space for self-reproduction. If an area in which the loop wants to place its offspring is already occupied by others, it generates a new sheath fragment in the tube to obstruct the pathway of signals. Then, signals in the loop become extinct one after another, being absorbed by the obstacle fragment. Finally, only a circular tube filled with core states is left, by itself. The manner by which this proceeds is shown in Figure 3. Thus, death as functional failure is certainly present in the SR loop. However, it is not equipped with the capability of death as structural dissolution, except for partial dissolution: the disappearance of the umbilical cord.

A Structurally Dissolvable Self-Reproducing Loop

In order to accomplish at the same time the following two tasks—to completely emulate the above-mentioned properties of the SR loop and to introduce the capability of structural dissolution, it was decided to introduce a new *dissolving state* '8' into the set of states of the CA, while exactly preserving the states '0'–'7' and all the transition rules proposed by Langton[1]. We expected that structural dissolution would be realized through propagation of this dissolving state along the tube of the loop. Details of this implementation are described in below.

First, we need to address a technical problem inherent in the rules published by Langton, as those were limited to an *indispensable* rule set for simple self-reproduction only, while many situations ("neighborhoods") still remained undefined. We suppose that Langton implicitly assumed that the environment in which the loops would expand was itself infinite, so that the loops would not encounter any irregular situation not previously defined in the transition rules. However, if space is designed to be finite by imposing periodic, or free, boundary conditions at the edges, it is obvious that those inhabitants will eventually face the limitation of space and the appearance of irregular situations will cause their activities to halt. To avoid this inconvenience, before introducing the possibility of structural dissolution, the transition rules needed to be extended to redefine rules which had been left undefined in Langton's SR loop, by a natural extension of the ideas of Codd and Langton (Codd 1968; Langton 1984) as follows:

1. A background state '0' in the tube next to a core state '1' will turn to '1'. All other '0's will remain as is.
2. A core state '1' in the tube next to a signal state '7' will turn to '7'. Or, a '1' in the tube next to a signal state '6' will turn to '6'. Or, a '1' in the tube next to a signal state '4' will turn to '4'.
3. Signal states '4', '6' and '7' in the tube next to '0' will turn to '0'.
4. A sheath state '2' next to a signal state '3' will turn to '1'. Or, a '2' next to another '2' will remain as is.

[1]As we remark later, there is *one* exception to this complete preservation.

Extensions 1, 2 and 3 define general rules for propagation of signals in the tube, and extension 4 defines general rules for the connection of two tubes. The criterion for judgment whether a cell is in the tube or not was taken to be whether at least two cells in the state '1', '2', '4', '6' or '7' are included in the four cells neighboring itself.

Second, a new *dissolving state* '8' was introduced into the set of states of the CA with the following transition rules:

1. A state '8' will unconditionally turn to '0'.
2. When neighboring an '8',
   (a) both background states and core states ('0' and '1') will turn to '8' if there is a sheath state or a signal state in the four cells next to themselves. This rule represents *infection* of dissolving states. Otherwise, they will remain unchanged.
   (b) a sheath state and several signal states ('2', '3' and '5') will turn to '0'. This rule represents dissolution of tube structure.
   (c) the remaining signal states ('4', '6' and '7') will turn to '1'. This rule represents dissolution of signals in the tube.

Owing to these rules, the dissolving state acquires the ability to propagate along the tube and dissolve a neighboring tube structure. The direction of propagation of a dissolving state is the same as that of the signals' flow in the tube, because, if it propagates against the signals' flow, it is blocked by the sequence of signals. This behavior of the dissolving state is shown in Figure 4.

Third, only *one* alteration was made in the transition rules inherited from Langton as follows:

$$\frac{\texttt{CTRBL I}}{\texttt{11152 2}} \longrightarrow \frac{\texttt{CTRBL I}}{\texttt{11152 8}}$$

Here, CTRBL and I stand for the states of neighbor cells and the image of transition, respectively. This alteration implies that the SDSR loop will generate a dissolving state in itself for the situation in which the SR loop will generate a sheath fragment in itself at the beginning of death process.

Fourth, finally, it was decided that all the rules left undefined after the above definitions are implemented are uniformly directed to the dissolving state '8'.

Via the previous definitions, once a site takes on the dissolving state, a continuous structure which includes that site will be extinguished quickly by the dissolving state propagating in the tube. Thus, the SDSR loop acquires the capability of structural dissolution in addition to self-reproduction.

The SDSR loop designed here can dissolve itself in the manner depicted in Figure 5. This can be regarded as a phenomenon similar to programmed death of biological cells, such as apoptosis. However, it is important to

```
signals' flow ⟶                 ⟵ signals' flow

2 2 2 2 2 2                     2 2 2 2 2 2 2
8 1 0 7 1 1 2                   8 1 7 0 1 7 0
2 2 2 2 2 2                     2 2 2 2 2 2 2

     ⇓                                ⇓

  2 2 2 2 2                         2 2 2 2 2 2
  8 1 0 7 1 2                       8 0 1 7 0 1
  2 2 2 2 2                         2 2 2 2 2 2

     ⇓                                ⇓

    2 2 2 2                           2 2 2 2 2
    8 1 0 7 2                         8 7 0 1 7
    2 2 2 2                           2 2 2 2 2

     ⇓                                ⇓

      2 2 2                             2 2 2 2
      8 1 1 1                           1 1 7 0
      2 2 2                             2 2 2 2

     ⇓                                ⇓

        2 2 2                           2 2 2 2
        8 1 1 2                       2 1 7 0 1
        2 2 2                           2 2 2 2

     ⇓                                ⇓

          2 2                           2 2 2 2
          8 1 2                       2 7 0 1 7
          2 2                           2 2 2 2

     ⇓                                ⇓

            2                           2 2 2 2
            8 2                       1 1 1 7 0
            2                           2 2 2 2

     ⇓                                ⇓

                                      2 2 2 2 2
                                    2 1 1 7 0 1
                                      2 2 2 2 2
```

Figure 4: Behavior of the dissolving state '8'. Cells not explicitly specified are in background state '0'. When a dissolving state propagates in the same direction as the signal flows (left), it can completely dissolve the structure to the tip of the tube. However, when a dissolving state propagates against the direction of flow (right), it is blocked by the sequence of signals. For these reasons, a dissolving state will extinguish the tube structure along the same direction as the signals' flow.

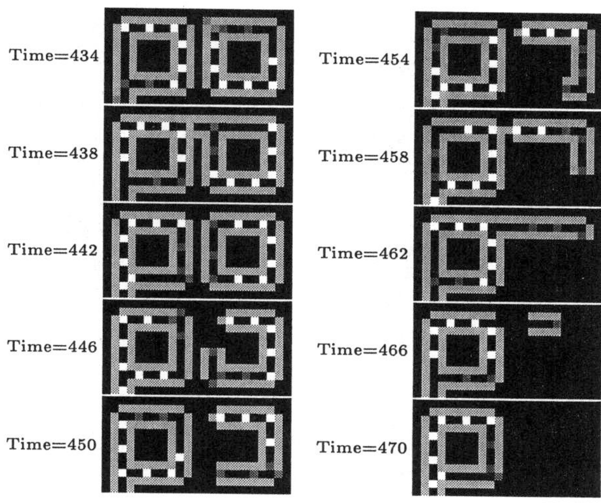

Figure 5: Death as structural dissolution of the SDSR loop. The right loop tries to thrust its arm to the left (time=438). Since the left area is already occupied by another loop, however, a dissolving state is generated on the pathway of signals at the upper left part of the right loop (time=442). The dissolving state propagates counterclockwise along the tube and dissolves neighboring sheaths one after another (time=446–462). Eventually, the structure of the right loop has been completely dissolved (time=466–470).

point out the fact that structural dissolution of the SDSR loop is programmed not in the genes of a living organism, but into the transition rules, the natural laws of the very world.

In addition, the SDSR loop also acquires some ability to overcome external difficulties. For example, when several obstacles are placed in front of the loop, it is possible that the loop eliminates them by dissolving its organ (i.e., the tip of the arm) together with obstacles and reproduces itself correctly, as shown in Figure 6. This can be regarded as a phenomenon similar to the cutting of a lizard's tail, or the vomiting of internal organs of sea cucumbers, that is, the action of disposing partial organs of an individual in order to overcome external difficulties and achieve survival of the individual.

Experiment

In this section, several experiments using SR loops and SDSR loops are reported. The SR loop is provided with the same extension of transition rules as the SDSR loop except for the rules concerned with the dissolving state '8'. All sites under undefined situations in the SR loop are set to remain as they are.

Self-reproduction in infinite space

The first experiment is to breed loops with no restriction due to finite space. Figure 7 shows the development of the spatial distribution of SR loops and SDSR loops in infinite space, compared with each other. One genera-

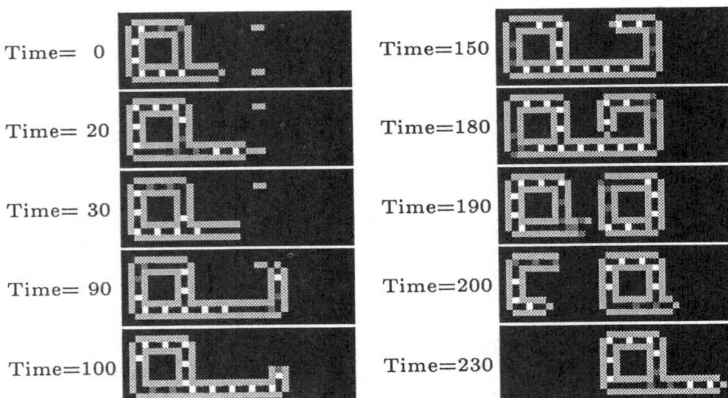

Figure 6: Structural dissolution of organs of the SDSR loop. Two sheath fragments are placed in the area in which the loop intends to reproduce its offspring (time=0). As the loop thrusts an arm, a dissolving state appears because of collision of a tip of the arm with a sheath fragment. The dissolving state extinguishes the fragment together with the tip (time=20–100). After the loop has managed to eliminate obstacles in such a way, it reproduces the offspring correctly into the right area (time=150–190). However, because the length of the arm is changed in the process of elimination of fragments, an inconsistent situation with the mechanism of the loop has developed in the parent, and the structure of the parent loop is consequently dissolved (time=190–230).

tion takes 151 CA updates, which the loop needs for one complete self-reproduction.

The behavior of SDSR loops at the edge of the colony is identical to that of SR loops at the same location, because there is no deficit in space so that no dissolving states appear in the SDSR loops at that point. However, at the core of the colony, it is observed that many SDSR loops dissolve their own structure and provide new space for neighbor loops to reproduce themselves, while corpses of SR loops which died because of functional failure remain at the same location in the "control" world of SR loops. Thus the colony of SDSR loops appears more sparse.

Figure 8 shows the temporal development of the number of living individuals in the process of self-reproduction of both SR loops and SDSR loops. We can see from this figure that the number of living SDSR loops is much larger than that of living SR loops. Since SDSR loops can reproduce into the central area of the colony (which is filled with corpses in the world of SR loops,) they arrange themselves into the shape of a collapsing spiral. We can therefore estimate that the number of living individuals of SDSR loops approaches $O(\text{Generation}^2)$ as time proceeds, substantially different from the number of living individuals of SR loops, which is estimated to be $O(\text{Generation})$ as they can reproduce only at the edge of the colony.

Self-reproduction in finite space

The second experiment involves breeding loops in *finite* space. Under this condition, the advantage of SDSR

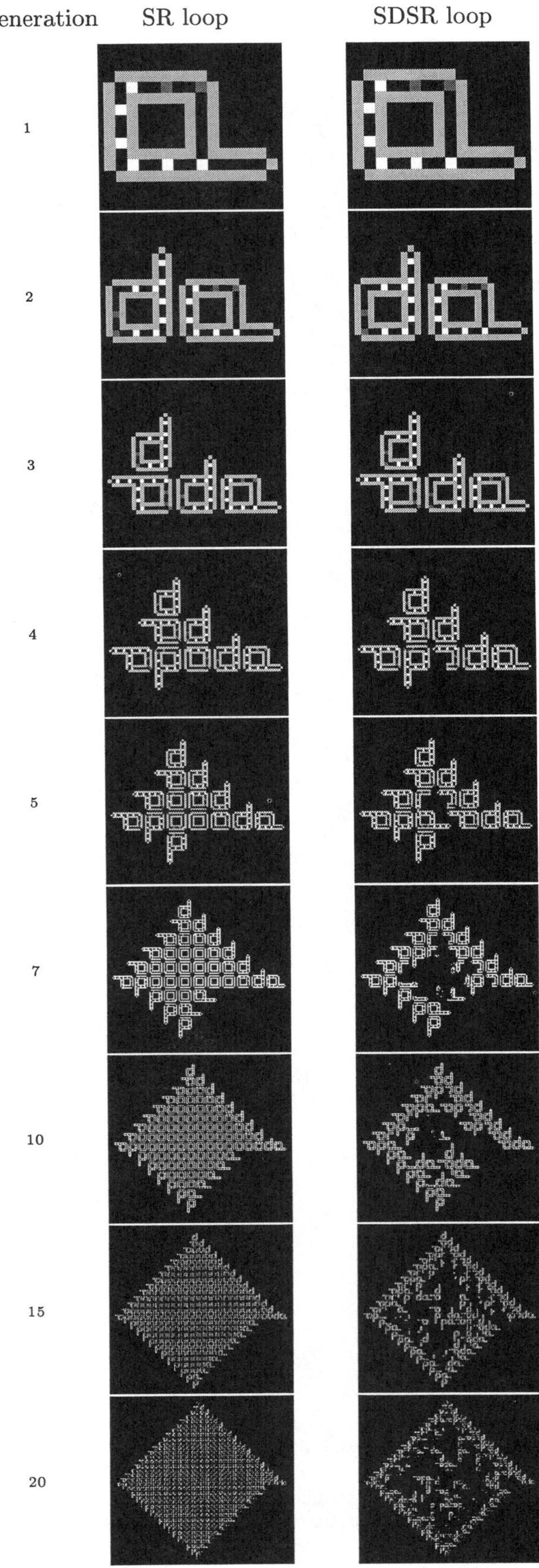

Figure 7: Development of spatial distribution of SR/SDSR loops in infinite space. Each picture is scaled differently to the size of the colony.

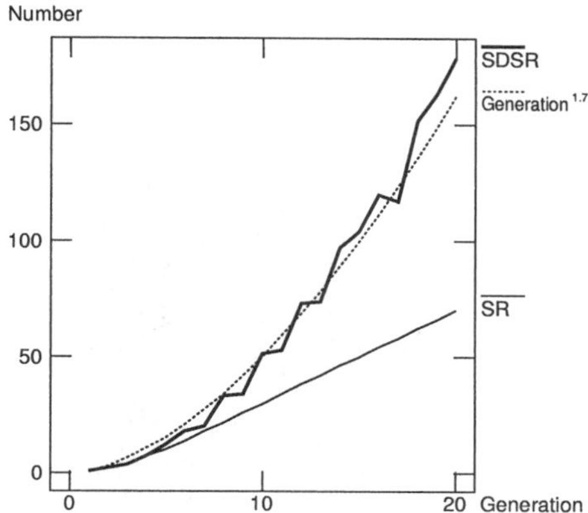

Figure 8: Development of the number of living loops in Figure 7. The curve of Generation$^{1.7}$ is drawn for reference.

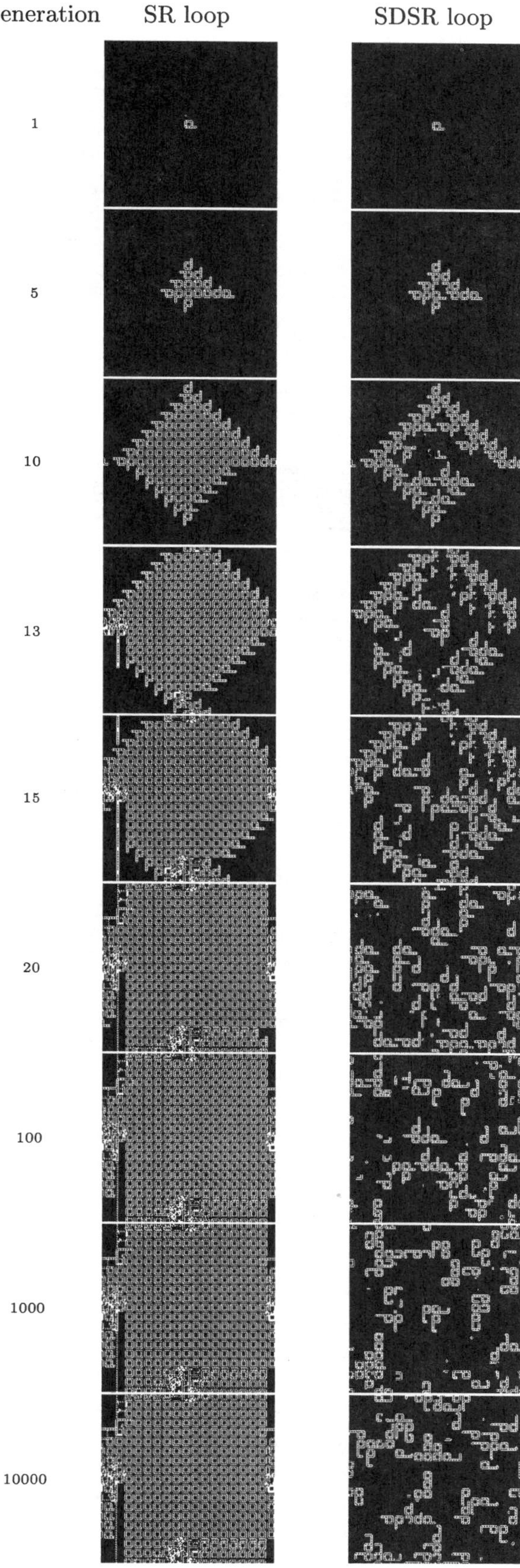

Figure 9: Development of spatial distribution of SR/SDSR loops in finite space. Each picture is scaled to 200×200 cells.

loops will become even more apparent than in the former experiment. Figure 9 shows the evolution of the spatial distribution of SR loops and SDSR loops in finite space, just as in Figure 7. The size of the space is restricted to 200×200 sites, where wrapping (periodic) boundary conditions have been applied in both x and y directions.

In the world of SR loops, when the opposite edges of the colony collide with each other due to the periodicity of space, the irregularity of the emerging situation leads to a failure of the loops' function, so that their self-reproductive behavior halts. Eventually, the entire space is filled with static patterns including corpses of loops. After that, no changes can happen in this world ever more. On the other hand, in the SDSR loops' world, as new regions, which can be used for self-reproduction of new loops, are produced continuously by structural dissolution, the self-reproduction of loops is actively maintained. Although SDSR loops have a probability of accidental extinction of species caused by structural dissolution, they continue self-reproduction for a significantly longer period longer of time, at least ten thousand generations in this experiment. Thus, there can be no doubt that SDSR loops have attained a semi-permanent state of dynamic stability, while SR loops tend to fall into a static state without living behavior.

In addition, we observed a number of *merged* loops, strange configurations shown in Figure 10, which were produced in the course of self-reproduction of SDSR loops. Because SDSR loops can continue their self-reproductive behavior for a long period owing to structural dissolution, they are faced many times by rare situations which can produce these merged loops by *direct interaction of phenotypes.* However, since they are generated by bonding arms of more than one loop, they are destined to lose their construction arms which are necessary for self-reproduction. In this sense, they can be regarded as corpses having lost the capability of self-

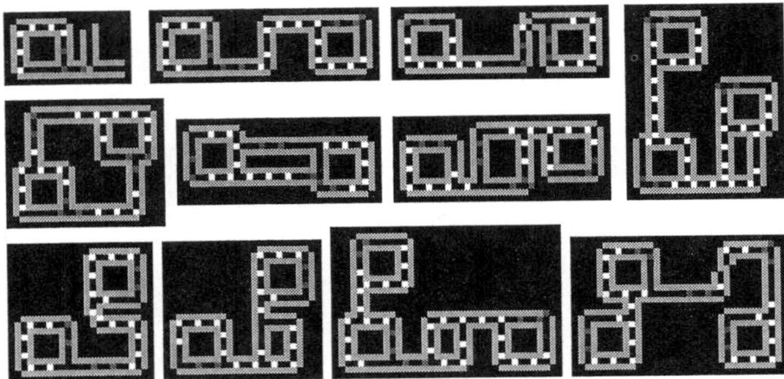

Figure 10: Examples of merged loops produced through the interaction of phenotypes of SDSR loops in the course of self-reproduction in Figure 9.

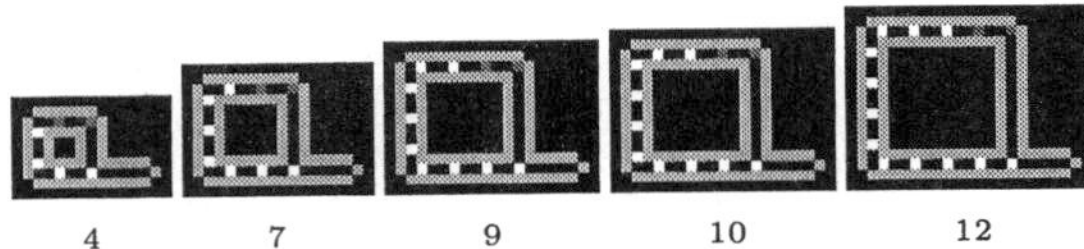

Figure 11: Examples of loops of different species. The name for each species is (temporarily) the number of signal states '7' contained in the loop of that species.

reproduction because of functional failure.

Struggle for existence in finite space

The third experiment is to observe the struggle for existence among SDSR loops of different species in finite space. Even though Langton's loop contains exactly six signal states '7', we can construct loops of arbitrary size using extended transition rules, as long as no less than four signal states '7' are contained in the loop. Figure 11 shows examples of loops of different species.

When loops of two different species were placed and bred in the same finite space, we observed that in the SDSR loops' world one species drove the other into extinction in less than ten thousand updates. Figure 12 shows an example of competition between species 4 and 6. It is observed that small species generally fit this world better than big ones. This is a trivial result as the smaller the size of loops, the faster they can reproduce themselves (as the gestation time is shorter) and the slighter the damage due to structural dissolution for the entire colony.

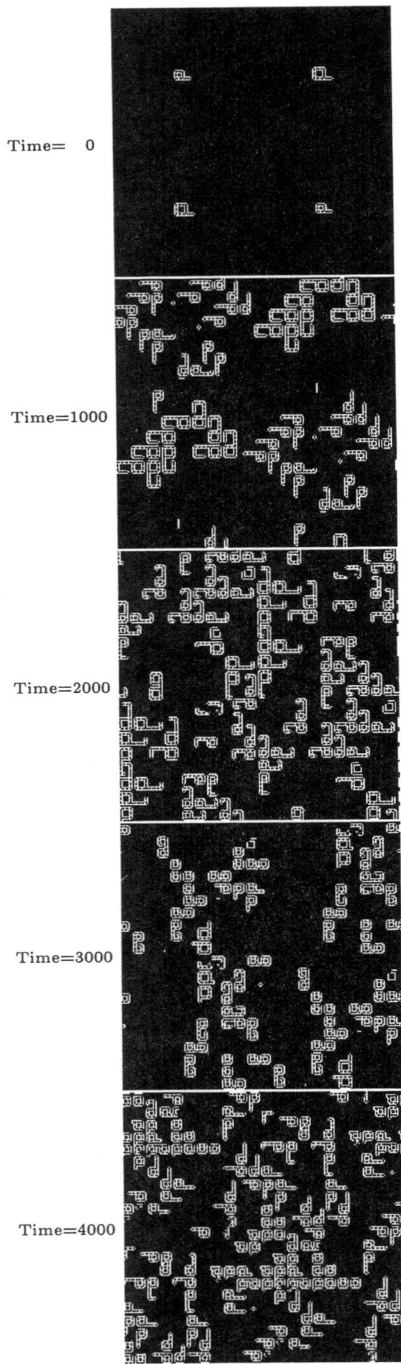

Figure 12: Example of struggle for existence between loops of species 4 and 6. At the beginning, loops of species 4 are placed in the upper left and lower right regions of the space, and loops of species 6 in the upper right and lower left regions (time=0). As time proceeds, loops of species 4 show that they are superior to those of species 6 (time=1000–3000). Eventually all loops of species 6 are exterminated (time=4000). Each picture is scaled to 200×200 cells.

Discussion

Significance of structural dissolution

In the previous sections, we compared the behavior of SDSR loops to that of SR loops. Both loops are identical to each other except for the rules concerned with the dissolving state '8'. As a result, SDSR loops show several unique phenomena never observed in the world of SR loops, such as (1) an ability to overcome external difficulties by means of organic dissolution, (2) significant increase in the number of living loops when bred in infinite space, (3) continuous self-reproduction in finite space, (4) production of many merged loops in the course of self-reproduction, and (5) competitive exclusion acting between loops of different species.

Because the phenomena (2), (4) and (5) can be regarded as by-products of (3), the substantial meaning of structural dissolution lies in (1) and (3). The difference between them is the level at which structural dissolution occurs: the organic, or the individual, level. Even though we usually view the latter as the cessation of life, the level of dissolution is actually not essential to the consideration of the behavior of the whole system. The important fact is that both (1) and (3) have a common point in being a phenomenon of *disappearance of a subsystem which becomes inconsistent with the environment.*

Thus, it is evident that structural dissolution functions as a kind of negative feedback mechanism. Resources having been owned by the dissolved subsystem will be re-utilized by the other subsystem. Repetition of such processes provides the whole system with dynamic and adaptive stability, and furthermore, probability of evolution. For instance, an individual can secure its living state by dissolution of partial organs, and a colony can continue its dynamic behavior by dissolution of individuals.

Strategic death based on structural dissolution

Note again here that the mechanism of structural dissolution in this study is not described in the "genes" of the loops, but rather is embedded in the transition rules which govern the dynamics of the CA. In contrast, as was pointed out by Todd (Todd 1993), if death is genetically programmed in individuals, those individuals are subject to being driven into extinction in the course of natural selection by the emergence of *immortal* individuals which have lost their genes of death. Still, many genes concerned directly with aging and death have recently been discovered and discussed in the field of molecular genetics. These discoveries teach us that death is effectively preprogrammed in real creatures by genetic means. What, then, should we conclude from the fact that genetic programs implying aging and death actually exist while avoiding being eliminated through natural selection?

We would like to offer the guess that death programmed by genetic means can be effective and remain in the population *if a primitive mechanism of structural dissolution is embedded in the basic laws of Nature,* such as the transition rules of CA adopted in this study. In other words, if the world is furnished with the rule that *everything will change sometime no matter how much you invest to preserve it,* the strategy of dynamic development of structures with positive dissolution of them will be more efficient than the strategy of static maintenance of fixed structures, and as a consequence death programmed in genes can be selected by living organisms. The other extreme of self-preservation is to force continuation of existence by constructing extra-strong structures in a static equilibrated system without dissolution, such as the structure of carbon atoms in diamond. However, such structures are generally simple, regular and static, and cannot be the source of complex and dynamic behavior characteristic of life. Because life is a structure which emerges in a system far from equilibrium, there may always be an essential probability of it changing its phase. Then, it is much more likely that strategic death has an advantage over other strategies and becomes the substantial characteristic of life.

Primitive evolution in SDSR loops' world

Before concluding this article, let us briefly consider here the evolvability of SDSR loops. The fact that both alteration of phenotypes caused by their direct interaction and competitive exclusion acting between loops of different species are observed in the world of SDSR loops suggests that the SDSR loop is potentially evolvable with mutations caused by the *interaction of phenotypes.* It is easy to imagine that, if a self-reproducing offspring different from its parent loop appears through a situation such as the merger of parent loops, and if it fits the laws of the world better than its parents, that it would spread through space and drive the parent species into extinction.

On the other hand, we usually think that the phenotype of life develops mostly according to its genotype, so that the evolution of life is caused by accidental changes which might occur to its genotype. This principle is based on the idea that a biological cell is regarded as a universal constructor which can control external/internal environments well and faithfully construct another cell according to DNA 'tapes.' Of course, this is almost certainly true with respect to sophisticated life forms such as eukaryotic organisms including human beings.

However, as mentioned by Langton (Langton 1984), there can be little doubt that life at the ancient dawn was *not* a universal constructor. At that time, the genotypes of living objects may have been physical structures at the *same* scale as their phenotypes, so that the genotype may have had some phenotypical character, and *vice versa.* Thus, it is very likely that evolution of life at that time was accomplished not only by change of genotypes but also by such environmental factors as direct interaction of phenotypes—in other words, such environmental factors could alter how the genotype is interpreted into a phenotype. Production of merged loops in the world of SDSR loops resembles the beginning of such a process of primitive evolution. Since both genotype and phenotype of the SDSR loop are configurations of the same scale which can affect each other, the SDSR loop (after some further development) will be a useful model for investigating the primitive evolution of life.

Conclusion

In this study, the SDSR loop which has the capability of structural dissolution was implemented through an improvement in Langton's SR loop. According to the results of several experiments using SDSR loops, remarkable behavior of dynamic stability and potential evolvability was observed, which has never been seen in the world of SR loops.[2]

We believe that, through the extension of rules given in this study, Langton's SR loop having been no more than a simple model of self-reproduction has begun to step toward an entity which could well contribute to the elucidation of the dynamics and history of life. With this conviction, we are now tackling the question *how the SDSR loop can be made to actually evolve.* This effort would represent the basis for the process of natural selection and evolution by means of a set of interacting *virtual state machines* embedded in CA, as foretold by Langton (1986).

Acknowledgments

I would like to express my deep respect for Christopher G. Langton and his work. I also thank the following for valuable advice in proceding with this study: Yoshio Oyanagi, Chris Adami, Tsutomu Oohashi, Tadao Maekawa, and especially Mari Sayama.

References

Codd, E. 1968. *Cellular Automata.* ACM Monograph Series. Academic Press.

Langton, C. 1984. Self-reproduction in cellular automata. *Physica* D 10: 135–144.

Langton, C. G. 1986. Studying artificial life with cellular automata. *Physica* D 22: 120–149.

Todd, P. 1993. Artificial death. In *Proceedings of the Second European Conference on Artificial Life Vol. 2*, edited by J. L. Deneubourg, H. Bersini, S. Goss, G. Nicolis, and R. Dagonnier. p. 1048–1059.

[2]A WWW server which provides information about the SDSR loop is open on the following place:

http://proton.is.s.u-tokyo.ac.jp/~sayama/sdsr/

This site contains color movies of SDSR loops in action which are inserted as figures in this article. They may be useful for the reader in helping to understand the behavior of SDSR loops.

Self-Reproduction of Dynamical Hierarchies in Chemical Systems

Bernd Mayer[a] and **Steen Rasmussen**[b,c]
[a]Institute for Theoretical Chemistry and Radiation Chemistry,
University of Vienna, UZAII, Althanstrasse 14, A-1090 Vienna, Austria.
bernd@asterix.msp.univie.ac.at; http://asterix.msp.univie.ac.at/local-link
[b]EES-5 MS D407 and T-CNLS MS B258, Los Alamos National Laboratory,
Los Alamos, New Mexico, 87545, U.S.A., steen@lanl.gov.
[c]Santa Fe Institute, 1399 Hyde Park Road, Santa Fe, New Mexico, 87501, U.S.A., steen@santafe.edu.

Abstract

In biological systems higher order hyperstructures seem to occur both in an intuitive and a formal sense. Starting at a molecular level of description we have: molecules, polymers, supramolecular structures, organelles, cells, tissues, organs, etc. But in models and simulations of these systems it has turned out to be difficult to produce higher order emergent structures from first principles.
We demonstrate how monomers (first order structures) compose polymers (second order structures) which in turn can assemble into ordered, micellar (third order) structures, which in turn can self-reproduce as they catalyse the formation of additional amphiphilic molecules. Processes of this particular kind have probably been important for the origins of life.
Our molecular system is defined on a 2-D lattice and the dynamics is modeled as a discrete automaton. In this system all interactions (electromagnetic forces) are decomposed and communicated via propagating information particles. Each lattice site has an associated data structure where molecules are represented by information particles and their associated force fields (excluded volumes, kinetic energies, bond forces, attractive and repulsive forces) are decomposed and propagated as information particles as well. The propagation- and interaction rules are derived from Newton's Laws.
Based on this self-assembly and self-reproduction example it is possible to extract some of the principles involved in the generation of higher order (hyper-) structures and relate them to dynamical systems. An Ansatz for generating higher order structures in formal dynamical systems is given.

Introduction

One of the key steps in the origin of life and also one of the key elements in making a proto-cell is the emergence of a protecting 'shell' within which a more stable and controlled environment can be maintained (Schnur 1993). Such a shell must be able to self-reproduce together with a templating molecular complex (a primitive genome) and a simple aggregate that is able to harness external energy (a proto-metabolism), presumably of chemical nature (Deamer 1997). The most primitive, known self-reproducing shell-aggregate is a micelle. Luisi and his group pioneered this experimental work in 1990 (Bachmann et al. 1990) and have later elaborated on this scenario to include self-replicating RNA within a self-reproducing liposome yielding simultaneous core- and shell-replication (Oberholzer et al. 1995) as well as specific shell-shell recognition (Berti et al. 1997). The main topic of the present paper is to study the self-assembly of micelles and concomittant micelle self-reproduction in simulation using realistic models for the relevant physico-chemical interactions.

A step by step aggregation of molecular elements can lead to the emergence of novel functionalities as it must have happened in the processes that eventually lead to the origin of life. However, the same phenomenon is found in contemporary living systems as they also have clear functionalities to emerge at different levels:

molecules → organells → cells → tissues → etc.

At each of these levels of description we can observe distinct properties which only have a meaning at this particular level and where each of the levels is generated by the levels below. A dynamical system organized in this manner defines a *dynamical hierarchy* (Baas et al. 1996). The above identification of levels of course has many sub-levels. It should also be noted that it does not define a strict hierarchy. Communication can and does indeed occur between, e.g., level 1 and level 5. In this paper we demonstrate how a 3-level dynamical hierarchy can be generated in a formal system and show how our Ansatz to do this also works in the general case for even higher order systems. A more detailed discussion of these issues can also be found in Baas et al. (1996).

There are two significant reasons why it is not trivial to generate a dynamical hierarchy in a formal system : (i) It involves multilevel dynamics–that is simultaneous dynamics on several time- and length scales–which requires large computational resources. (ii) The natural, conceptual framework for such a system seems to be a set of interacting objects and not a closed form model as, e.g., a differential equation system. How to form the higher oder structures from the bottom up becomes simple in systems of interacting objects. For example, starting with objects that are models of monomers it is trivial that the monomer objects can form polymers as they are combined into a string. Now the polymers can form membranes as they are aggregated in a particular fashion, and so forth. A systematic study of systems of interacting objects, including cellular automata, is a relatively recent scientific activity (Wolfram 1986, Langton etal. 1989).

It turns out that a formulation of a dynamical hierarchy can be made conceptually simple if the interacting objects are defined on a lattice. Furthermore, the most promising results on modeling macroscopic effects in chemical systems based on a fine grained system representation are based on lattice-type simulation methods (Chen et al. 1992, Ostrovsky et al. 1995, Coveney et al. 1996, Emerton et al. 1997). Thus, we introduce a lattice gas style (Frisch et al. 1986), discrete field simulation concept (Rasmussen and Smith 1994, Baas et al. 1996, Mayer et al. 1997, Mayer and Rasmussen 1998) which allows to simulate micelle formation and self-reproduction as well as demonstrate some of the fundamental formal properties of a dynamical hierarchy.

Emergence of Dynamical Hierarchies

We have just discussed the notion of dynamical hierarchies in the context of chemical and biological systems. In order to understand them better, i.e., their use as well as their synthesis, it is important also to have formal systems in which such structures can be generated. In general when higher order structures occur, new properties arise at each level–for example through aggregation. This means that in this context we will be looking for objects or aggregates with new properties. An obvious question is then what *new* really means? This brings us into the basic discussion of emergence and the notion of an observer. For a general discussion of emergence and higher order structures we refer to Baas (1993) where a suitable framework is given in which these concepts can be discussed. How this connects to dynamics we refer to Rasmussen and Barrett (1995). Let us just recall briefly a few basic notions (Baas 1993). We consider families of objects or structures S_r^1 of *first order*

$$S_r^1 = S_r^1(f_{rs}, s_r, \tau_r), \quad r, s = 1, 2, \ldots, n \tag{1}$$

where s_r is the state of the object, f_{rs} defines the object-object interactions, and τ_r is the local object time. In addition we need to define an update functional U which schedules the object updates (e.g., parallel, random, event driven), which together with the interaction rules–given by f_{rs}–defines the dynamics. Also the important notion of an observer O^1 needs to be introduced. With O^1 we can measure explicit system properties as for instance internal object states. The system dynamics may now generate a new structure S^2 through the interactions

$$S^2 = R(S_r^1), \quad r = 1, 2, \ldots, n \tag{2}$$

where R is the process that generates S^2. This is what we call a *second order* structure which may be subjected to a possible new observer O^2. Then we say that a property P is *emergent* iff

$$P \in O^2(S^2), \ and \ P \ \notin O^2(S_r^1). \tag{3}$$

Clearly emergence depends on the observer in use which may be *internal* or *external*. An external observer can be the experimenter, but it can also be a mechanism (given by an algorithm) encoded in the system to detect patterns, regularities, aggregates, correlations, etc.

Part of the dynamics may actually be viewed as an internal observer. For example, each object will typically receive information about its neighborhood and act accordingly following an algorithm as an experimenter would have done from the outside. Also note that the emergent properties may be *computable* or *non-computable* (Baas 1993, Rasmussen and Barrett 1995).

The above process can be iterated in a *cumulative*, not necessarily a *recursive*, way to form higher order emergent structures which we shall call *hyperstructures* of, e.g., order N:

$$S^N = R(S_{r_{N-1}}^{N-1}, S_{r_{N-2}}^{N-2}, \ldots). \tag{4}$$

It should be noted that the definition of an observation function is no more–or just as–arbitrary as the definition of the objects and their interactions. For more details we refer to Baas (1993) and Rasmussen and Barrett (1995), where the concept of emergence and the relation between emergence and dynamics are discussed.

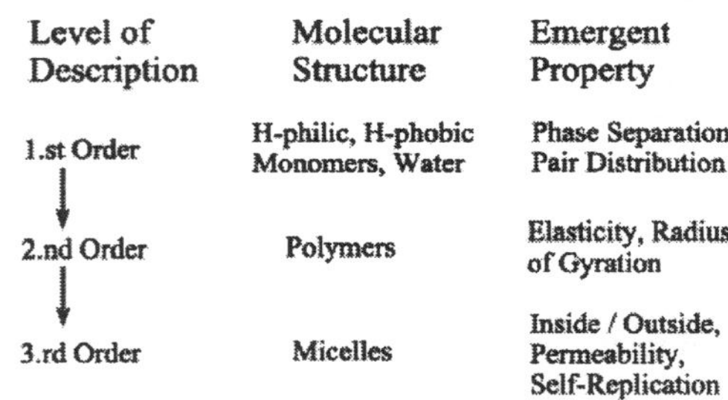

Level of Description
Molecular Structure
Emergent Property
1.st Order
H-philic, H-phobic Monomers, Water
Phase Separation, Pair Distribution
2.nd Order
Polymers
Elasticity, Radius of Gyration
3.rd Order
Micelles
Inside / Outside, Permeability, Self-Replication

Figure 1: Dynamical hierarchy in a chemical system.

As we use this conceptual framework to interpret how self-assembling processes form micelles which again self-reproduce we obtain the following picture (see Figure 1). At each level of description the physical structures; the monomers (level 1), the polymers (level 2), and the micelles (level 3), 'carry', or more correctly, through their interactions, generate, properties that cannot be observed at the levels below. They are emergent properties. At the fundamental level 1 (water and monomers) we can, e.g., observe the generation of water structures as well as phase separation between water and hydrophobic monomers. At the polymer level, level 2, we can, e.g., observe elasticity. At the micelle level, level 3, we can observe an outside and an inside as well as permeability which does not have any meaning at the level below. Also, the micelles (the third order structures) can under certain conditions self-reproduce [assuming a distinct chemical reactivity at the water-membrane interphase (Oberholzer et al. 1995)] which none of the objects at the lower levels can. Thus, the interactions of the molecules (water and monomers) in this relatively simple, chemical system, generate higher order structures which carry non-trivial (e.g., life-like), emergent properties.

It should be stressed that the encoded functional properties of the basic, first order objects does not change during this process. It is only the *context* within which these objects are arranged that changes. Thus, the operational semantics of the information, the forces each object receives from its environment, is *context sensitive.* For example the accessible states for a hydrophobic monomer in bulk polar phase are distinctively different from the states in a non-polar phase and again different from the states of a hydrophobic monomer in an amphiphilic polymer (Baas et al. 1996, Mayer et al. 1997.) This fact defines a downwards causality as the higher order structures modulate or restrict the dynamics of the lower order structures by which they are made up. This phenomenon of observed downwards causality in dynamical hierarchies is related to the 'slaving principle' as originally suggested by Haken (1987).

The next section introduces the principles of a lattice gas style simulation concept, the Lattice Molecular Automaton (LMA) (Rasmussen and Barrett 1994, Mayer et al. 1997, Mayer and Rasmussen 1998), which is capable of generating higher order, chemical structures, as self-replicating micelles, in a simulation.

The Discrete Field Automaton Concept

The basic idea behind the discrete field automaton is to model both, matter and forces, as mediating information particles. Three main steps determine the molecular dynamics: (*i*) rules that propagate force information particles, (*ii*) rules that evaluate the received information together with the local state, and (*iii*) rules that move molecules on the lattice and transform the system into the next time-step. All rules are directly derived from the laws of physics.

Our simulation takes place on a square, 2-D lattice, but the general formalism holds for arbitrary lattice topologies as, e.g., a triangular lattice (Rasmussen and Smith 1994, Baas et al. 1996, Mayer et al. 1997, Mayer and Rasmussen 1998). The simulation objects (i.e., molecular entities) and vacuum are encoded as data structures, located at each site of the lattice (see Figure 2A). A Boltzmann distribution of kinetic energies as well as potential energies (based on discrete force fields) are

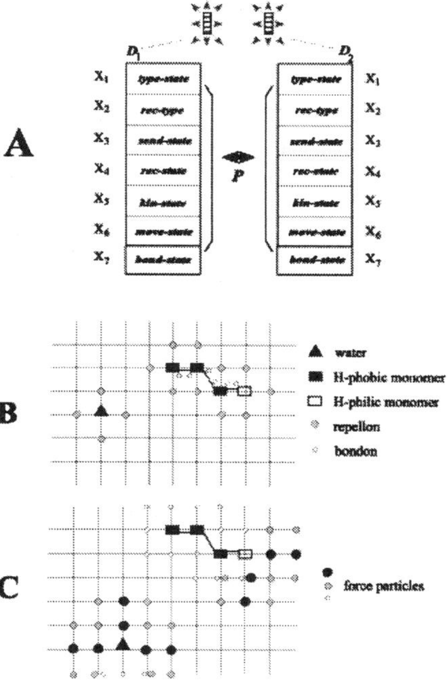

Figure 2: A: The LMA data structure concept; B: Propagation of repellons ensuring excluded volume and *bondons* to maintain bonds in polymers; C: Force particle propagation to construct a type-specific force field.

implemented to describe the molecular dynamics. Kinetic energies are distributed between colliding molecules following a hard sphere model conserving the overall momentum. The total potential energy V_{total} of our model system with n molecules on a lattice with q neighbors is described by:

$$V_{total} = \sum_{i=1}^{n}\sum_{j=1}^{q} V^{i,j}_{dip.-dip.,charge-charge,H-bond} + \sum_{i=1}^{n}\sum_{j=1}^{q} V^{i,j}_{dip.-ind.dip.} + \sum_{i=1}^{n}\sum_{j=1}^{q} V^{i,j}_{ind.dip.-ind.dip.} + \sum_{i=1}^{n}\sum_{j=1}^{q} V^{i,j}_{coop.} \quad (5)$$

These potential energy terms are implemented to account for specific physico-chemical properties of our molecular objects as, e.g., dipoles, induced dipoles, hydrogen bond donor and acceptor sites, or polarizability volumes, all crucial parameters for the micelle formation in polar environment. This set of weak intermolecular interactions given in the above equation, commonly summarized as Van der Waals forces, has generally proven to be suitable for a description of macromolecular systems (Privalov et al. 1998, Browman 1975) as well as responsible for the emergence of bulk phase phenomena as the structured hydrogen-bond network in water or the hydrophobic effect (Mayer et al. 1997). Kinetic energy terms drive the molecular system into local minima on the potential energy hypersurface. The overall setup corresponds to a microcanonical ensemble, conserving mass, momentum and the total energy.

The dynamical system that defines our LMA is of the form

$$\{S_r(t+1)\} = U\{S_r(t)\}, r = 1, \ldots, n. \quad (6)$$

where

$$S_r = S_r(f_{rs}, x_r, \tau_r), \quad (7)$$

denotes the interacting objects defined on the 2-D, square lattice. Each object has an internal state x_r, an object-object interaction function f_{rs} (which has its own state x_r as an argument together with the state(s) of the object(s) that it is interacting with $x_s, s = 1, 2 \ldots$), and local time τ_r. To generate the dynamics the object-object interactions have to be scheduled by an update functional U, which is random sequential for this version of our LMA.

A data structure $\mathcal{D}_t^{(i,j)}$ at the lattice location (i,j), at time t, denoting an object S_r–e.g., vacuum if it is empty and a molecule if it is occupied–with k variables x_h, $h = 1, \ldots k$

$$\mathcal{D}_t^{(i,j)} = (x_1{}^{(i,j)}(t), \ldots, x_k{}^{(i,j)}(t)), \quad (8)$$

is updated to time $t+1$ by an only implicitely given local interaction function F in the following way:

$$\mathcal{D}_{t+1}^{(i,j)} = F(\mathcal{D}_t^{(i,j)}, \mathcal{D}_t^{1(i,j)}, \ldots, \mathcal{D}_t^{q(i,j)}), \quad (9)$$

where the other data structures are located at the q neighboring lattice positions. The different variables within each data structure indicate which molecular type a given object is, which force particles (variables) are emitted from the current object (and received from neighboring sites), what the local potential energy gradient is as well as the value of the kinetic energy of the current object as well as of colliding objects.

The principal structure of each step in the update cycle is a function that updates one of the data structure variables x_h. The function, denoted by formal compositions "$\circ$" for the individual elements x_h on a square lattice is of the form

$$\begin{aligned} x_h^{(i,j)}(t+1) \quad = \quad & f'_0(x_1^{(i,j)}, \ldots, x_k^{(i,j)})(t') \circ \\ & f'_1(x_1^{1,(i,j)}, \ldots, x_k^{1,(i,j)})(t') \circ \ldots \circ \\ & f'_4(x_1^{4,(i,j)}, \ldots, x_k^{4,(i,j)})(t'), \end{aligned} \quad (10)$$

which means that the new value of a given variable at a given lattice site is a composed function of the variables at the site (i,j) itself and of the variables $h = 1, \ldots k$ (where k defines the number of variables in the data structure) at the neighboring sites (in the four principal directions). For a more detailed discussion of the formal proporties of such a dynamical system we refer to Baas et al. (1996) and Rasmussen et al. (1997).

A data structure $\mathcal{D}$ is defining all (lattice) objects through the $q = 7$ variables $x_1 - x_7$, which are elements in the 7 sets $\mathcal{X}_1$ - $\mathcal{X}_7$ (see Figure 2A). These sets define the local object's state space. Below is the list of variables associated with every lattice location (data structure) (i,j) in the LMA:

$\mathcal{X}_1 = \{x_1\}$; $x_1 \in N_0$; *type-state*:
molecular types (including vacuum) at site (i,j).
$\mathcal{X}_2 = \{x_{2,1}, \ldots, x_{2,8}\}$; $x_{2,l} \in N_0$; *rec-type*:
molecular types (including vacuum) in the neighborhood of site (i,j).
$\mathcal{X}_3 = \{x_{3,1}, \ldots, x_{3,4}\}$; $x_{3,l} \in Z$: *send-state*:
outgoing force particles along q lattice directions.
$\mathcal{X}_4 = \{x_{4,1}, \ldots, x_{4,8}\}$; $x_{4,l} \in Z$; *rec-state*:
incoming force particles from q lattice directions.
$\mathcal{X}_5 = \{x_{5,1}, \ldots, x_{5,4}\}$; $x_{5,l} \in N_0$; *kin-state*:
local kinetic energy at location (i,j) in q directions.
$\mathcal{X}_6 = \{x_{6,1}, \ldots, x_{6,4}\}$; $x_{6,l} \in Z$; *move-state*:
list of net energetic states (including potential and kinetic energies).
$\mathcal{X}_7 = \{x_{7,1}, \ldots, x_{7,8}\}$; $x_{7,l} \in \{0,1\}$; *bond-state*:
maintain bonds within polymers.

The $type - state$ defines vacuum and the molecular type at the monomer level, e.g., as water, a hydrophilic or a hydrophobic object. Associated with the $type - state$ is the $send - state$ list denoting the respective force field, e.g., describing dipoles and hydrogen bond sites. The information particles in the $send - state$ list are propagated to the neighborhood and stored in the respective $rec - state$ list. The $rec - type$ stores the $type - state$ entries from the neighboring molecules and is used to interpret the force particle data received in the $rec - state$. Thus the entries in the $send - state$, $rec - state$ and $rec - type$ lists are used to calculate the potential and respective forces following a Coulomb potential. The $kin - state$ list holds the kinetic energy state of the object and the $bond - state$ encodes the bonds formed within a polymer. The individual information particle propagation steps are schematically shown in Figure 2B (propagation of 'repellons' to maintain excluded volume, of 'bondons' to keep the configuration of polymers) and Figure 2C (propagation of force particles 'forceons' capable of representing the potential energy surface given in Equation (5)). A water molecule is characterized by three hydrogen-bond sites, hydrophilic monomers show two hydrogen bond sites (e.g., a COOH group) and all molecular objects furthermore interact based on various dipole contributions. Finally, the calculated potential energy as well as the kinetic energy determine the $move - state$ of the object, i.e., which lattice site will be occupied in the next update cycle, considering constraints as the excluded volume and bonds between monomers in polymers.

It should be noted that as we include more details about the physics of the interactions it becomes possible to generate higher and higher order structures (Baas et al. 1996, Mayer et al. 1997). For example, if we as here require that these objects need to be able to generate third order structures (micelles) which are able to self-reproduce and that the molecular interactions are based on known physical principles, then it cannot be done with much less object complexity (variable and interaction functions) than given here. A detailed discussion of the notion of object complexity and what it means in connection to a system's ability to generate higher order (≥ 3) emergent structures is given in Baas et al. (1996) and Rasmussen et al. (1997).

The full LMA update cycle holds the following individual steps:
(1) propagation of molecular types
(2) construction of type-specific force fields
(3) calculation of potential energies
(4) calculation of the most proper move direction
(5) random update of the individual objects transfering the system into the time step $t+1$
A detailed description of the update cycle is given in Mayer and Rasmussen (1998).

Simulation of Dynamical Hierarchies and Self-Reproduction in a Chemical System

A central molecule in biomolecular structure and dynamics is water. The strong polarity of water and concomittant ability to form hydrogen bonds allows to form large, hydrogen-bonded water networks that continuously break up and reform due to thermal noise. It is the entropic and enthalpic balance associated with joining these networks of water molecules that is responsible for the hydrophobic effect (Mayer et al. 1997). An example of a water network generated by the LMA is shown in Figure 3A, which is a detail of a 100 × 100 lattice.

When hydrophobic monomers are present in water we observe a phase separation of the molecular types (see Figure 3B). The hydrophobic effect is responsible for this separation phenomenon, but it should be noted that the mechanics of the separation is as follows: The water - hydrophobic- and the hydrophobic-hydrophobic attractions are of the same magnitude in this simulation: The enthalpic loss due to hydrogen bond breakage is counteracted by various dipole interactions (dipole - induced dipoles between water and hyrophob. monomers and ind. dipoles - ind. dipoles between hydrophob. monomers) giving a comparable enthalpy for bulk water and the mixture. This is set according to experimental results on changes of enthalpy, entropy and resulting free energy of such mixtures. In our LMA model mixtures, the phase separation is generated by the complex dynamics of solvating hydrophobic surfaces and maintaining the hydrogen bond network, which results in an entropy-driven phase separation process (Mayer et al. 1997). This process is commonly refered to as the hydrophobic effect, clearly an emergent property.

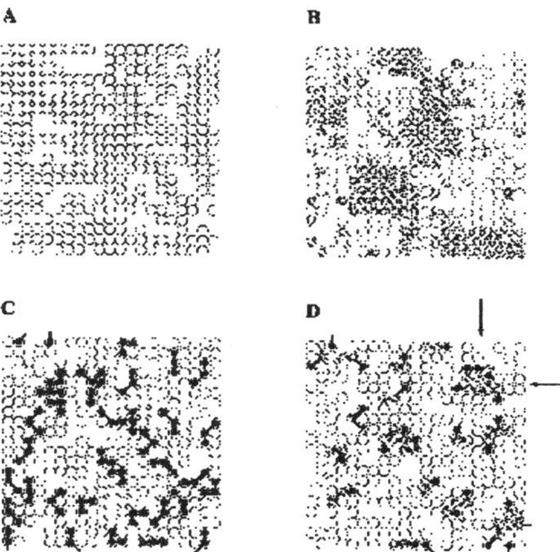

Figure 3: LMA simulation of molecular systems (empty circle: water; grey circle: hydrophobic monomer; black circle: hydrophilic monomer):
A: bulk water phase
B: mixture of water and hydrophobic monomers
C: mixture of water and hydrophilic trimers
D: mixture of water and amphiphilic trimers. The arrows indicate the location of a micellar structure.

As monomers polymerize they form 'strings' or polymers. As we discussed in the previous section the dynamics of the polymer generates properties which are not observable at the level of the individual monomer. The polymer has its own (lower) diffusion constant, a radius of gyration, an elasticity constant, just to mention a few. In Figure 3C we see how hydrophilic polymers stay solvated in water (contrary to hydrophobic objects) as they can participate in the ever changing water networks (as the hydrophilic model polymers can participate in the hydrogen bond network, too). When the polymers are amphiphilic (hydrophilic head and a hydrophobic tail) the hydrophobic effect together with the structure of the polymers generate a structurally well defined aggregate, a micelle, which we can identify as a third order structure (see Figure 3D).

A micelle carries properties: like inside / outside, permeability, has another (much lower) diffusion constant and defines a new interface chemistry. In fact, the particular chemical properties at the hydrophilic heads organized in the surface can hydrolyze one end of a hydrophobic polymer as demonstrated in a oleic acid / oleate system experimentally (Oberholzer et al. 1995). The resulting polymer is amphiphilic. This amphiphilic

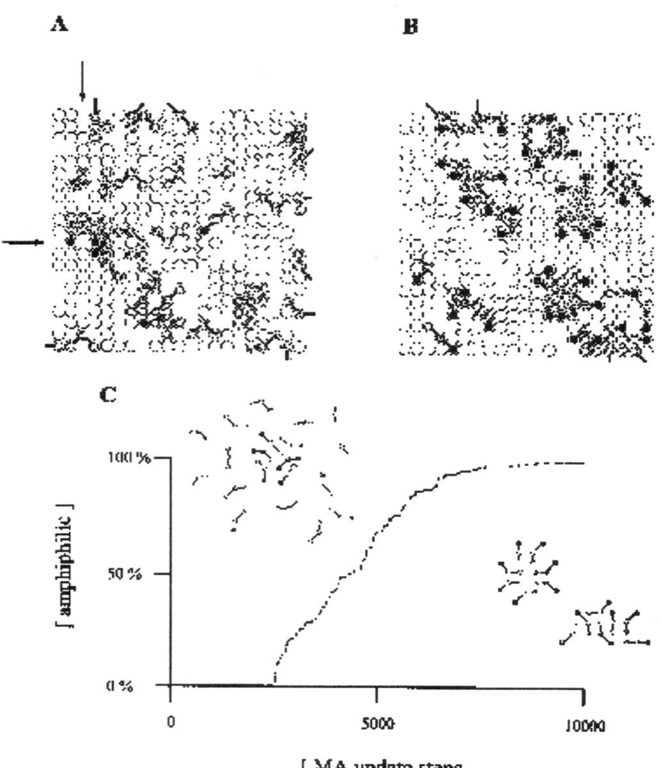

Figure 4: LMA micelle self-replication (empty circle: water; grey circle: hydrophobic monomer; black circle: hydrophilic monomer):
A: Early stage mixture of water, amphiphilic and hydrophobic trimers. The arrows indicate a chemically active site to convert a hydrophobic into an amphiphilic trimer.
B: Final state of a micelle self-replication simulation.
C: Kinetics of the hydrophobic trimer - amphiphilic trimer conversion process. The concentration of amphiphilic trimers is plotted versus the LMA update steps.

polymer now seeks, with a certain probability, into the micelle that catalyzed it in the first place and as many such processes occur the micelle continues to grow until it becomes unstable and divides.

Thus, we have an autocatalytic self-reproduction of micelles as long as the system has a surplus of hydrophobic polymers which can be hydrolyzed. Figure 4A shows an initial condition of a mixture of access hydrophobic and some amphiphilic polymers in aqueous solution, where one micellar structure is formed. If one head group of a hydrophobic polymer faces the polar surface of the micelle (i.e., at least two hydrophilic head groups in our simulation) it is 'hydrolyzed', forming an amphiphilic polymer. After the hydrolysis of all the available hydrophobic polymers the initial micelles have replicated many times (see Figure 4B). The dynamics of this process is reflected in the concentration of amphiphilic polymers which grows rapidly until it runs out of fuel (hydrophobic polymers). The kinetics of this process is shown in Figure 4C.

This demonstrates how we can within our LMA concept (i): generate a dynamical hierarchy of chemical nature, which carries distinct properties at each level, (ii) including the ability for the generated third order structures to self-reproduce in an autocatalytic fashion.

Conclusion and Outlook

By defining a formal system of interacting (molecular) objects on a 2-D lattice we demonstrate how a dynamical hierarchy can be generated in simulation. All interactions are derived from first principles and are thus representing a simplified, but still realistic picture of the actual physico- chemical nature of the system. At each level of description (monomers, polymers, micelles) distinct emergent properties are being generated by the dynamics, which are also observable in the corresponding real system. The system's ability to generate higher order structures depends in a nontrivial way on the object complexity. The more details of the physics we include, the higher order structures the system can generate. We demonstrate how a generated third order structure, a micelle, can self-reproduce in an autocatalytic fashion, as has been shown *in vitro*.

This approach is neither limited to 2-D nor to generate third order structures. We are in the process of extending the simulation to 3-D and by including more details of the physics in the first order objects it is possible to have the system generate fourth or higher order emergence, e.g., allowing a templating molecule to cooperate with the self-reproducing micelles. This Ansatz has opened an avenue where we in a formal system can have objects interact with objects to generate higher order objects which in turn can interact with yet other objects which again can generate higher order objects, etc, without any principal limit.

This leaves us with many unanswered questions including: At which level of object complexity can we in a formal system generate a dynamical hierarchy which supports, say what corresponds to a proto-organism? Such a limit probably exists, since only a limited set of biological precursor molecules are in turn combined into a limited number of biomolecules, which in turn seem to constitute a universal 'tool kit' from which all cellular organelles are assembled. This is also in fine agreement with the existence of neutral networks for RNA secondary structures, and a very limited number of actual RNA shapes (Reidys et al. 1997), as well as the possibly limited number of actual folds of proteins (Rost et al. 1996).

Acknowledgements

B. M. thanks the Austrian Academy for Sciences for generous financial support within APART (Austrian Programme for Advanced Research and Technology).

References

Bachmann, P. A., P. Walde, P. L. Luisi, and J. Lang. 1990. *J. Amer. Chem. Soc.* 112: 8200.

Baas, N. A. 1993. Emergence, hierarchies and hyperstructures. In *Artificial Life III, Proceedings of SFI Studies in the Science of Complexity*, edited by C. G. Langton. Reading, MA: Addison-Wesley, p. 515.

Baas, N. A., M. W. Olesen, and S. Rasmussen. 1996. Generation of higher order emergent structures. Los Alamos National Laboratory preprint, LA-UR 96-2921.

Berti, D., L. Franchi, P. Baglioni and P. L. Luisi. 1997. Molecular recognition in monolayers. Complementary base pairing in dioleoylphosphatidyl derivatives of adenosine, uridine, and cytidine. *Langmuir* 13: 3438.

Browman, M. J. 1975. ECEPP: Empirical conformational energy programs for peptides. QCPE 11:286 (1975).

Chen, S.-H., J. S. Huang, and P. Tartaglia, eds. 1992. *Structure and Dynamics of Strongly Interacting Colloids and Supramolecular Aggregates in Solution.* Dordrecht: Kluwer, and references cited therein.

Coveney, P., A. Emerton, and B. Boghosian. 1996. Simulation of self-reproducing micelles using a lattice gas automaton. Oxford U. TP 96-13S.

Deamer, D. W. 1997. The first living systems: A bioenergetic perspective. *Microbiol. Rev.* 61: 239.

Emerton, A., P. Conveney and B. Boghosian B. 1997. Applications of a lattice-gas automation model for amphiphilic systems. *Physica* A 239: 373.

Frisch, U., B. Hasslacher and Y. Pomeau. 1986. Lattice gas automata for the Navier Stokes equation. *Phys. Rev. Lett.* 56: 1722.

Haken, H. 1987. Information compression in biological systems. *Biol. Cybern.* 56: 11.

Langton C. G., ed. 1989. *Artificial Life* SFI Studies in the Science of Complexity, and later volumes about the Artificial Life activities.

Mayer, B., G. Köhler, and S. Rasmussen. 1997. Simulation and dynamics of entropy-driven, molecular self-assembly processes . *Phys. Rev. E* 55: 4489.

Mayer, B. and S. Rasmussen S. 1998. The Lattice Molecular Automaton (LMA): A simulation system for constructive molecular dynamics. *Int. J. Mod. Phys.* C. In press.

Oberholzer, T., R. Wick, P. L. Luisi, and Ch. Biebricher. 1995. Enzymatic RNA replication in self-reproducing vesicles: An approach to a minimal cell. *Biochem. Biophys. Res. Comm.* 207: 250.

Ostrovsky, O., M. A. Smith, and Y. Bar-Yam. 1995. Applications of parallel computing to biological problems. *Annu. Rev. Biophys. Biomol. Struct.* 24: 239.

Privalov, P. and S. J. Gill. Stability of protein structure and hydrophobic interaction. *Adv. Prot. Chem.* 39: 191.

Rasmussen, S. and J. R. Smith. 1994. Lattice polymer automata. *Ber. Bunsenges. Phys. Chem.* 98: 1185.

Rasmussen, S. and Ch. L. Barrett. 1995. Elements of a theory of simulation. In *Advances in Artificial Life*, Lecture Notes in Artificial Intelligence 929:515, edited by F. Moran, A. Moreno, J. J. Merelo, and P. Chacon. Berlin: Springer Verlag.

Rasmussen, S., N. Baas, C. Barrett, and M. Olesen. 1997. A note on simulation and dynamical hierarchies. In *Self-Organization in Complex Structures - From Individual to Collective Dynamics*, edited by F. Schweitzer. Gordon & Breach Publishing, p. 83–90.

Reidys, C., P. F. Stadler, and P. Schuster. 1997. Generic properties of combinatory maps: Neutral networks of RNA secondary structures. *Bull. Math. Biol.* 59: 339.

Rost, B. and C. Sander. 1996. Bridging the protein sequence-structure gap by structure predictions. *Annu. Rev. Biophys. Biomol. Struct.* 25: 113.

Schnur, J. 1993. Lipid tubules: A paradigm for molecular engineered structures. *Science* 262: 1669.

Wolfram, S. 1986. *Theory and Applications of Cellular Automata.* Singapore: World Scientific.

Order Parameter for a Symbolic Chemical System

Yasuhiro Suzuki and Hiroshi Tanaka
Department of Bio-informatics
Medical Research Institute,
Tokyo Medical and Dental University
Yushima 1-5-45, Bunkyo, Tokyo 113 JAPAN

Abstract

We develop an abstract computational model (ARMS) to deal with systems with many degrees of freedom (such as liquids) and confirm that it can simulate the emergence of oscillations. Furthermore, by a theoretical investigation of ARMS, we propose an order parameter which reflects the qualitative dynamics of the system. We examine and confirm the effectiveness of this parameter in describing macroscopic aspects of our simulations.

Introduction

Life can be considered as a system in a specific class of chemical reaction systems, but real biochemical systems are so complex that it is difficult to reconstruct the precise dynamics in the system. Thus, it is important to abstract the essential properties of biochemical systems in order to obtain insights into its dynamical properties. We develop an abstract computational model (ARMS), which can deal with systems with many degrees of freedom and confirm that it can simulate the emergence of complex cycles such as chemical oscillations that are often found in the emergence of life. We also study mathematical properties of the model by using a computational algebra and propose an order parameter to describe the global behavior of the system.

Model

In this section, we describe an abstract chemical system in terms of an abstract rewriting system. Before describing the system in detail, we introduce abstract rewriting systems in general.

Abstract Rewriting System (ARS)

An abstract rewriting system models the algebraic characteristics of calculation. By introducing this formal structure, several characteristics of calculation can be discussed in a common framework. This concept is applied to various formal methods in mathematics and computer science, for example in proof theory, the algebraic description of computer software, and automated deduction.

The principle of calculation within an ARS is simple. A calculation is performed by rewriting using rules as in formal grammar: $a \to Sa$.

Definition 1 (Abstract Rewriting System) *An abstract rewriting system is defined as a pair $(A, \mathcal{R})$, where A and $\mathcal{R}$ denotes a finite alphabet and a finite set of pairs of words over the alphabet A, respectively. A rule which transforms $b \in A$ into $a \in A$ is written as $a \to b$ and we say that $a \to b$ is a "rewriting step".*

An abstract rewriting system is a string-replacing system. If the left hand side of a rule matches a string, it is replaced with the right hand side of the rule. The final result of a calculation is called a normal form:

Definition 2 (Normal Form) *If there does not exist b such as $a \to b$ and $b \in A$, then $a \in A$ is called a normal form.*

Multiplication, for example, can be viewed as an abstract rewriting model. Let us define a set of rewriting rules, Ru as: $Ru = \{2 \times 2 \to 4, 4 \times 2 \to 8\}$. Using Ru, $2 \times 2 \times 2$ is calculated as shown in Figure 1,

$$\mathbf{2 \times 4} \leftarrow 2 \times 2 \times 2 \to 4 \times 2 \to \mathbf{8}.$$

Figure 1: An example of rewriting calculus

In the first step, since only the rule $2 \times 2 \to 4$ can be used on $2 \times 2 \times 2$, the string $2 \times 2 \times 2$ is rewritten into 4×2, for example. This string on the other hand can be transformed into 8 using the rule $4 \times 2 \to 8$. Because there are no rules that apply to 8, the latter is a normal form. However, as the first step we can also transform $2 \times 2 \times 2$ into 2×4, which turns out to be another normal form. In this calculation, we see that two normal forms exist (see Figure 1).

ARMS

Extending the concepts of the abstract rewriting system, we introduce an abstract rewriting system on multi-sets (ARMS). Intuitively, ARMS is like a chemical solution in which floating *molecules* can interact with each other according to reaction rules. Technically, a chemical solution is a finite multi-set of elements denoted $A^k = \{a, b, \ldots, \}$; these elements correspond to *molecules*, and reaction rules are specified in terms of rewrite rules. As to the intuitive meaning of an ARMS, we refer to the study of chemical abstract machines (Bellin and Boudol 1992). In fact, rewrite rule systems can be thought of as reflecting an underlying *algorithmic chemistry*:

Algorithmic Chemistry Fontana (1994) introduces an abstract model, called the λ-gas, where a new chemical is generated by interactions between existing chemicals, using the λ-calculus. This model is described by a set of functions which correspond to *molecules*. Two functions are randomly selected and interact with each other, which is represented as a compound function $f(g)$. Although this model also focuses on the characteristics of chemical reactions, the main difference between the λ-gas and ARMS is that we focus on *temporal* aspects and the emergence of cycles. Let us now continue with the definition of ARMS.

We denote the empty set by ϕ, and the *base number* of a multi-set (size of a multi-set) by $|S|$ (where S is a multi-set), respectively. Then we define:

Definition 3 (Multi-set) *A "multi-set" is an element $t \in A^k$ $(1 \leq k \leq n) \in \Sigma$, where n is a finite number, and A^k is a Cartesian product $A_1 \ldots A_k$. $A^k = A_1 \times A_2 \ldots \times A_k$, Σ denotes the set of multi-sets, and n is called the "maximal multi-set size."*

The multi-sets correspond to possible states of *chemical solution*. The set of multi-sets corresponds to the space of transitions of an ARMS.

Definition 4 (Rewriting rule) *A "rewriting rule" is a relation $l\ \mathcal{R}\ r$ $(l,\ r \in \Sigma)$, $|l|, |r| \leq$ maximal multi-set size, n. A rewriting rule $l\ \mathcal{R}\ r$ is denoted as $l \rightarrow r$.*

A rewriting rule such as

$$a \rightarrow a \ldots b, \qquad (1)$$

is called a *heating rule* and denoted as $r_{\Delta > 0}$; it is intended to contribute to the stirring solution. It breaks a complex *molecule* into smaller ones: *ions*. On the other hand, a rule such as

$$a \ldots c \rightarrow b, \qquad (2)$$

is called a *cooling rule* and denoted as $r_{\Delta < 0}$; it rebuilds *molecules* from smaller ones. In this paper, reversible reactions, i.e., $S \rightleftharpoons T$, are not considered. We shall not formally introduce the refinement of *ions* and *molecules* though we use refinement informally to help intuition.

Definition 5 (ARMS) *An "Abstract Rewriting System on Multi-sets" (ARMS) is a pair (T, Ru) consisting of a multi-set T and a set Ru of rewriting rules.*

Definition 6 (Rewriting on ARMS) *Let (T, Ru) be an ARMS. We write $s \overset{Ru}{\rightarrow} t$ if there exists a rewriting rule $l \rightarrow r \in Ru$ such that $l \subseteq s$ and $t = (\mathbf{s} - l) \cup r$.*

The ARMS can construct input by such a rule, for example, $\phi \rightarrow a$.

Definition 7 (Normal Form in ARMS) *If no rule in Ru can be applied to a multi-set and no symbols can be inputted to the multi-set without the resulting base number exceeding the limit on the multi-set, then the multi-set is called Normal Form (final state).*

Normal forms correspond to a steady state.

The reader will notice that the method of rewriting of ARMS is different from that of the abstract rewriting system. Since the abstract rewriting system is a string-replacing system, the string *ab* and the string *ba* are treated as different strings on rewriting. On the other hand, since ARMS is a multi-set replacing system, the system regards *ab* and *ba* as multi-sets of symbols, $\{ab\}$ and $\{ba\}$. Thus, they are treated the same. Hence, e.g., ARS cannot rewrite *ab* using the rule $ba \rightarrow c$, while ARMS, however, can rewrite *ab* into *c* using this rule.

How ARMS works

In ARMS, we assume that one randomly selected rule is applied in each rewriting step, unless no input is allowed. An algorithm for rewriting steps in ARMS is described in Figure 2.

```
procedure ARMS (Rewriting Step)
begin
  count-step ← 0;
  while count-step ≠ n do
    begin
      if the multi-set reached Normal Form then
        count-step:= n;
      else
        Input string(s) to the multi-set;
        Select a rule;
        if the rule can rewrite the multi-set then
          Rewrite the multi-set;
          count-step := count-step + 1;
        end if
      end if
    end
  end while
end.
```

Figure 2: An algorithm for ARMS (for the first n steps)

Example In this example, we assume that a will be inputted on each rewriting step, the maximal multi-set size is 4 and the initial state is given by $\{a, a, f, a\}$. The set of the rewriting rules, Ru_1 is $\{r_1, r_2, r_3, r_4\}$, where each rule is described by the following:

$$aaa \rightarrow b : r_1,\ b \rightarrow a : r_2,\ b \rightarrow c : r_3,\ a \rightarrow bb : r_4.$$

In this example, we assume that rules are selected as following the order $\{r_4 \Rightarrow r_1 \Rightarrow r_3 \Rightarrow r_2\}$. Then, each rule is applied in the following way. First, r_4 is applied. Next, as steps 2 and 3, r_1 and r_3 are applied, respectively. Finally, as step 4, r_2 is applied.

$\{aafa\}$	$\subseteq a$ (the left hand side of r_4)
$\downarrow$	.... can not input a and can not apply r_4,
$\{aafa\}$	$\subseteq aaa$ (the left hand side of r_1)
$\downarrow$	.... can not input a but can apply r_1
$\{ba\}$	

Figure 3: Example of rewriting steps of ARMS

Figure 3 illustrates two rewriting steps of the calculation from the initial state.

As the first step, since the base number of the multi-set is 4, the system can not input a. On the left hand side of r_4, a is included in $\{aafa\}$, however, r_4 can not be used. If a is replaced with bb, the base number of the multi-set becomes 5 and it exceeds the maximal multi-set size, 4.

In the next step, the system can not input a, however, r_1 can apply to the multi-set and $\{aafa\}$ is rewritten into $\{ba\}$ (because if aaa is replaced with b, the base number of the multi-set does not exceed the maximal multi-set size, see Figure 3).

In step 3, ARMS inputs a to the multi-set and transforms it to $\{c, a, a\}$ with r_3.

$$\text{Step } 3 : \{c, a, a\}.$$

In step 4, the system inputs a, but r_2 can not apply to it. Thus $\{c, a, a\}$ becomes $\{c, a, a, a\}$.

$$\text{Step } 4 : \{c, a, a, a\}.$$

Typical Examples In this paragraph, we shall present two examples. Let us assume a set of rewriting rule Ru_1 and a maximal multi-set size of 4. The first example is a case where ARMS generates two cycles. This example has the following rule order:

$$\{r_4 \Rightarrow r_3 \Rightarrow r_2 \Rightarrow r_4 \Rightarrow r_1 \Rightarrow r_2 \Rightarrow r_1 \Rightarrow r_3 \Rightarrow r_4\},$$

whose state transition is shown in Figure 4. After 8 steps, the system forms two cycles, whose periods are of 3 steps.

The next example is a case where ARMS terminates. Although ARMS applies the same rules, the obtained result is completely different (Figure 5). This example has the following rule order:

$$\{r_4 \Rightarrow r_1 \Rightarrow r_2 \Rightarrow r_4 \Rightarrow r_3 \Rightarrow r_1 \Rightarrow r_2\}.$$

The state transition is shown in Figure 5:

0.	$\{f\}$	
1.	$\{a, f\}$	
2.	$\{a, a, f\}$	
3.	$\{a, a, a, f\}$	
4.	$\{b, f\}$	$\uparrow$
5.	$\{a, b, f\}$	a cycle
8.	$\{a, a, a, f\}$	$\downarrow$
9.	$\{b, f\}$	$\uparrow$
10.	$\{a, b, f\}$	a cycle
11.	$\{a, a, a, f\}$	$\downarrow$
12.	$\{b, f\}$	

Figure 4: Example of a system that generates cycles

0.	$\{f\}$
1.	$\{a, f\}$
2.	$\{a, a, f\}$
3.	$\{a, a, a, f\}$
4.	$\{b, f\}$
5.	$\{a, b, f\}$
6.	$\{a, a, b, f\}$
7.	$\{a, a, c, f\}$.

Figure 5: Example of a system that halts

Experimental Results of the Simulation of ARMS

We simulated ARMS with various different setups; in this paper we shall discuss two of them as follows:

- Simple setup
- Brusselator model.

Through these experiments, we confirmed that the system is capable of generating complex patterns.

A simulation with a simple setup

Computational experiments were made under the following initial conditions:

(1) only five symbols $\{a, b, c, d, e\}$ were used to describe the rewriting rules,

(2) $\{a\}$ was the only input symbol,

(3) the maximal multi-set size was 10,

(4) six rules were used for rewriting steps, and

(5) two important parameters, namely the frequency of inputs and randomness of rule application, were given for each simulation, where the former four conditions were fixed and two parameters in the last condition were set to variables.

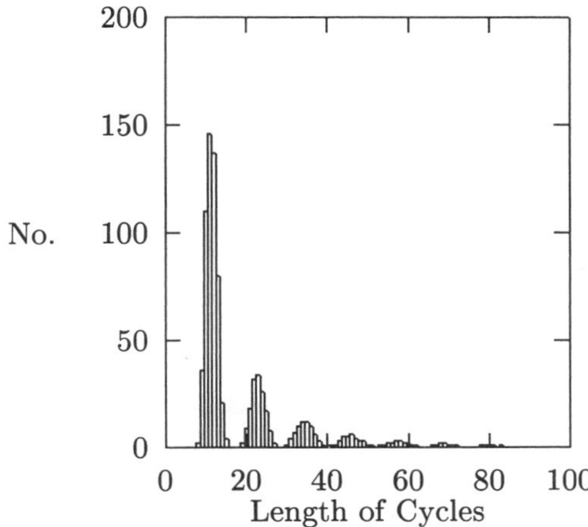

Figure 6: Example of period-doubling

Although these are clearly very simple settings, the experiments led to the following two interesting results. The first one showed the emergence of a *cycle* even under simple initial conditions, compared with Kauffman's network model (Kauffman 1993) or Fontana's λ-calculus (Fontana and Buss 1994), which both need large-scale computation to generate cyclic structures from a given system. The second result showed the complex behavior of cycles. Fusion of several cycles and period-doubling were observed easily, when randomness in the input was introduced. Figure 6 shows a system undergoing period-doubling. (For more details, the reader should refer to Suzuki and Tanaka 1998).

The Brusselator model of ARMS

In order to confirm that ARMS works as an abstract chemical system, we performed an experiment implementing the Brusselator model (Nicolis and Prigogine 1989) within ARMS. The Brusselator is a well-known mathematical model of chemical oscillations of the Belousov-Zabotinsky reaction (Field and Burger 1985) (see Figure 7.)

$$\begin{array}{lllll} & \mathrm{A} & \xrightarrow{k_1} & \mathrm{X} & \\ \mathrm{B} & +\mathrm{X} & \xrightarrow{k_2} & \mathrm{Y} & +\mathrm{D} \\ 2\mathrm{X} & +\mathrm{Y} & \xrightarrow{k_3} & 3\mathrm{X} & \\ & \mathrm{X} & \xrightarrow{k_4} & \mathrm{E} & . \end{array}$$

Figure 7: Abstract chemical model of the Brusselator.

We can view the abstract chemical reaction equations as rewriting rules, as Figure 8 shows:

In this simulation, the reaction rate corresponds to the frequency of rule application. If r_1 has the highest reaction rate, then r_1 is applied at the highest frequency.

$$\begin{array}{llllllll} & & \mathrm{A} & \longrightarrow & \mathrm{X} & & & : r_1 \\ & \mathrm{B} & \mathrm{X} & \longrightarrow & \mathrm{Y} & \mathrm{D} & & : r_2 \\ \mathrm{X} & \mathrm{X} & \mathrm{Y} & \longrightarrow & \mathrm{X} & \mathrm{X} & \mathrm{X} & : r_3 \\ & & \mathrm{X} & \longrightarrow & \mathrm{E} & & & : r_4. \end{array}$$

Figure 8: Rewriting rules for the Brusselator model.

Simulation of the Brusselator model Let us examine the relationship between the frequency of rule application (reaction rate) and the concentration X and Y in the multi-set. The concentration of X and Y in the multi-set is indicated by the number of X and Y present in the multi-set.

As to the initial condition, we assume that the maximal multi-set size is equal to 5000 and the initial state of the multi-set is an empty multi-set. We assume that the system makes inputs A and B continually. Hence this model can be regarded as a continuously-fed stirred tank reactor (CSTR).

In this simulation, we confirmed that oscillations between the number of X and Y in the multi-set emerged. Furthermore, we discovered three types of oscillations as follows: (1) quasi-stable oscillations (Figure 10), (2) unstable oscillations (Figure 11) and (3) divergence and convergence (Figure 9). For further details of this simulation, see (Suzuki and Tanaka 1997).

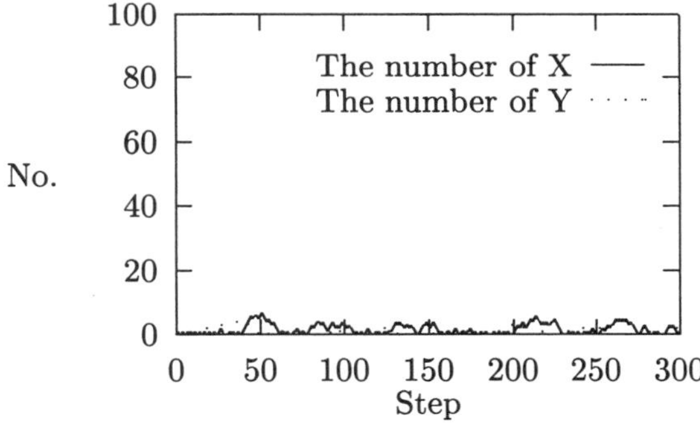

Figure 9: Example of convergence

Classification of the behavior pattern of ARMS

Up to now, we have been studying the formal properties of ARMS, based on our experimental results. Throughout the investigation we made a conjecture that the global behavior of ARMS is closely related to two essential properties: termination and confluence. Before entering into a detailed discussion of classifying the behavior patterns of ARMS, we shall describe the confluence termination properties.

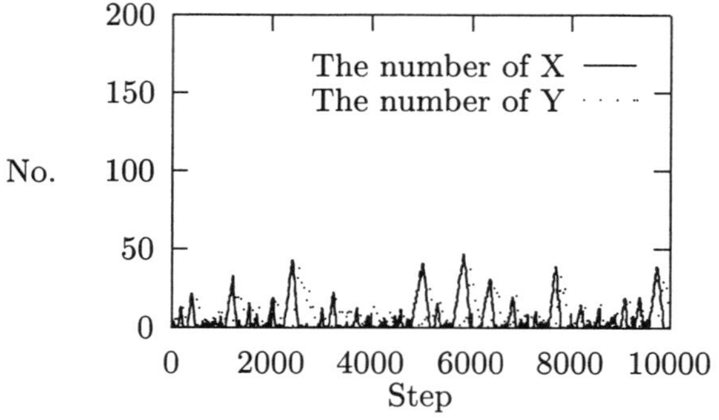

Figure 10: Example of (quasi) stable oscillation

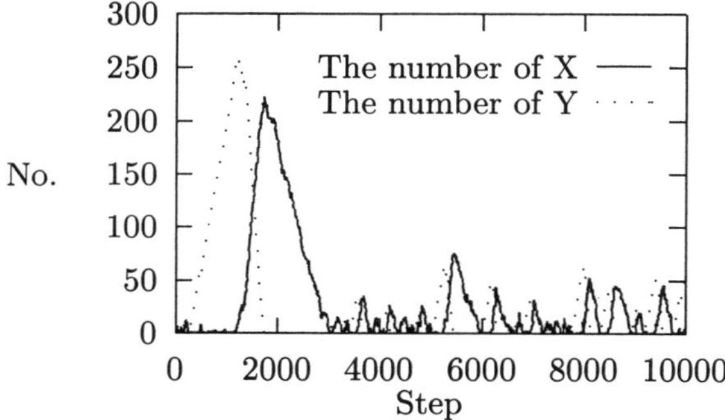

Figure 11: Example of unstable oscillation

Termination property The "termination property" can be related to the *halting* of a computation. There are two types of terminations:

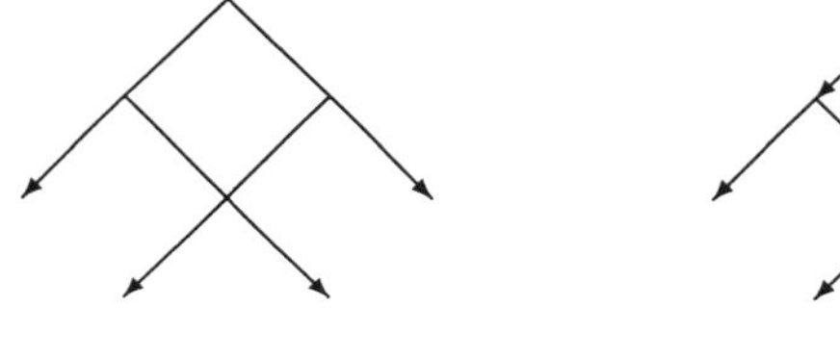

Strongly terminating **Weakly terminating**

Figure 12: Types of terminations

Weakly terminating We classify as "weakly terminating", chemistries where some calculations reach a normal form while other do not (see the right hand side of Figure 12.)

Strongly terminating "Strongly terminating" implies that *any* calculation reaches a normal form. Note that this property does not ensure a *unique* normal form (see the left hand side of Figure 12.)

Confluence property The "confluence property" is related to the particulars of the pathway of rewriting calculus. We distinguish two types as follows:

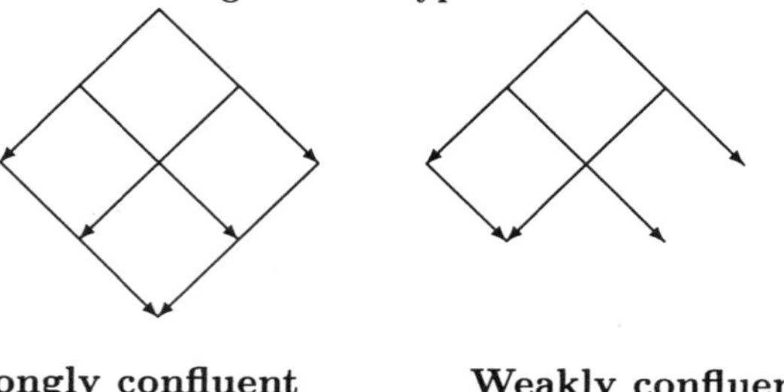

Figure 13: Confluence property

Weakly confluent "Weakly confluent" means that some calculations reach the same forms, while others do not (see the right side of Figure 13.)

Strongly confluent "Strongly confluent" implies that every calculation reaches the same form. This property ensures that the system has a unique normal form (see the left side of Figure 13.)

Classification table of ARMS behavior

We can classify the behavior of ARMS using the above characteristics of ARS.

		Terminating		
		Strong (I)	Weak (II)	Non (III)
Conflu-ent	Strong	$\perp$	$\perp$ or $\odot$	$\odot$
	Weak	$\perp$	$\perp$ or $\bigodot$	$\bigodot$
	Non	$\perp$	$\perp$ or ∞	∞

Table 1: Classification table of ARMS behavior

Table 1 illustrates the behavioral pattern with respect to the termination and confluence properties. The columns indicates the characteristics of confluence property while the rows show the characteristics of termination.

In this table, $\perp$ denotes the case where the system does not generate any cycles, while $\odot$ denotes the case where the system generates several kinds of cycles. Further, $\bigodot$ denotes the case where the system generates many kinds of cycles, and ∞ stands for the case where the system generates a great many kinds of cycles.

The most important feature of this table is that the confluence property determines the *complexity* of cycles while the termination property determines the *number* of cycles.

Effect of termination property

As we just mentioned, the termination property is related to the number of cycles. If an ARMS is strongly terminating, every calculation must reach the normal form. Consequently, the system can not generate any cycles. When this property becomes weak, the system is apt to generate cycles. When the calculation does not terminate, the ARMS must generate cycles because the transitional space of ARMS is finite (Suzuki and Tanaka 1998).

Effect of confluence

The confluence property determines the *spatial* behavior of ARMS. If an ARMS does not have this property, the trajectory of the system resembles a spiral. Once a rewriting sequence branches away from a state, the rewriting sequence can never return to it.

When this property becomes strong, even if a rewriting sequence branches away from a state, the rewriting sequence is apt to return to the former state and the trajectory of the system becomes a complex *cycle*. When entering such a complex cycle, many kinds of cycles emerge (Suzuki and Tanaka 1998).

Order parameter for ARMS

From an examination of the effectiveness of the termination property, we obtained the λ_e parameter as an order parameter for the qualitative behavior of ARMS.

We define "order" here as being given by the *diversity* of cycles. Thus, in this paper, "ordered state" refers to a case where the system yields simple cycles (such as the limit cycle), while "disordered state" refers to the case where the system yields chaotic or complex cycles.

The λ_e parameter

Let us define the λ_e parameter as follows:

$$\lambda_e = \frac{\Sigma r_{\Delta S>0}}{1 + (\Sigma r_{\Delta S<0} - 1)} \tag{3}$$

where $\Sigma r_{\Delta S>0}$ corresponds to the number of *heating rules* used, and $\Sigma r_{\Delta S<0}$ to the number of *cooling rules* used. This parameter is defined when the number of rules used is greater than 1.

When the ARMS only uses rules of the type $r_{\Delta S<0}$, λ_e is equal to 0.0. On the contrary, if the ARMS uses rules of the type $r_{\Delta S>0}$ and $r_{\Delta S<0}$ with the same frequency, λ_e is equal to 1.0. Finally, when the ARMS only uses rules of the type $r_{\Delta S>0}$, λ_e is greater than 1.0.

Simulation

We confirmed the appropriateness of the λ_e parameter through a simulation of the ARMS, and verified that the parameter reflects the diversity of cycles that are generated by the system.

Setup A simulation was carried out under the following environment:

```
procedure ARMS (Rewriting Step)
begin
  count-step ← 0;
  while count-step ≠ n do
    begin
      if the multi-set reached Normal Form then
        count-step:= n;
      else
        .... not assuming any inputs ...
        Select a rule;
        if the rule can rewrite the multi-set then
          Rewrite the multi-set;
          count-step := count-step + 1;
        end if
      end if
    end
  end while
end.
```

Figure 14: An algorithm for the simulation (until n-th step)

Rule set The length of the left- or right-hand-side of a rule was between one and five. Both sides of the rules were obtained by sampling with replacement of two symbols a and b. A set of rewriting rules was constructed as the overall permutation of both sides of the rules. The number of rules is given by Equation (4), where n corresponds to the kinds of symbols that we take and m is the range of lengths of strings.

$$\Big\{\sum_{k=1}^{m} \binom{n+k-1}{k}\Big\}^2 \tag{4}$$

As Equation (4) illustrates, if many kinds of symbols are used, the number of rules increases rapidly. Hence we use two symbols in this simulation. We assume that the string's length can range between 1 and 5. Then, the number of rules for this simulation is equal to 30976.

Algorithm of ARMS In this simulation, we intend to focus on qualitative features of the rewriting rule, while not assuming any inputs. The algorithm of ARMS (Figure 14) is therefore slightly different from the previous one (Figure 2).

A rule was selected randomly according to the following protocol: the probability of selecting a $r_{\Delta S>0}$ rule is given by the probability $0 \le p \le 1$, while a $r_{\Delta S<0}$ rule is selected with probability $(1 - p)$.

Method We assume that the maximal multi-set size is 10. At the beginning of a simulation, the value of p is set to 0 and it increased by steps of 0.01. At each value of p, 100 new initial states with base number between 1 and 10 are generated by selecting the symbol a or b randomly.

The base number of the initial state of a multi-set is decided randomly. For each initial state the simulation is performed for 1000 steps.

Experimental results

Let us present the experimental results, focusing on the following two points:

(1) the correlation between the system's terminating property and the value of p,

(2) the correlation between the diversity of periods of the generated cycles and the value of p.

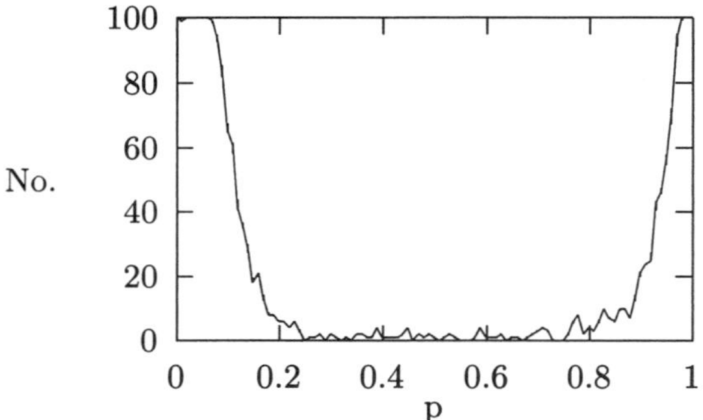

Figure 15: The correlation between the number of terminating calculations and p

Termination Figure 15 illustrates the correlation between p and the number of terminating calculations. In Figure 15, the vertical axis corresponds to the number of terminating calculations and the horizontal axis corresponds to p.

In this simulation, before p exceeded 0.1, most calculations terminated. When p exceeded 0.1, the number of terminating calculations decreased rapidly, while when p was greater than 0.2, this decrease leveled off. Then, for p between 0.3 and 0.85, only a few calculations terminated, while with p greater than 0.85, the number of terminating calculations increased rapidly again. In other words, for p near 0 or 1, the system strongly terminated, while with when p away from 0 or 1, the termination property became weak.

The number of generated cycles Figure 16 illustrates the relationship between the number of generated cycles and p.

As p increases, the number of generated cycles also increases rapidly. This rise levels off when p exceeds 0.3. For p between 0.3 and 0.8, the number of generated cycles remains at the same level, however, when p exceeds 0.75, this number rapidly decreased again.

This result indicates that the termination property indeed is related to the number of generated cycles. As we mentioned in the previous subsection, when p was close to 1 or 0, the system strongly terminated while for p away from 0 or 1, this property became weak. Also, for p near 1 or 0, only a few cycles were generated while for p away from 1 and 0, the system generated many cycles. We may thus conclude that the degree of termination influences the number of cycles generated by the system.

It is interesting that once the number of generated cycles reaches around 450, it remains at the same level, even while p was changed from 0.3 continuously up to 0.8. We believe that for p between 0.3 and 0.8, the system is in an equilibrium state.

To investigate the system's behavior in this equilibrium state, let us examine the relationship between the kinds of periods generated by the cycles and the value of p.

The kinds of periods generated by the cycles The experimental result indicates that even if the system is in an equilibrium state, the kinds of periods are different for each value of p. Figure 17 displays the average number of different kinds of periods. As we can see in this figure, when p reaches about 0.5, the number of different kinds of periods is maximal. In other words, when *cooling rules* and *heating rules* are used at the same frequency, many kinds of periods are generated.

Discussion

In this section, we shall show that the λ_e parameter is related to the termination property, which implies that Langton's λ parameter is also related to termination.

Before discussing this issue, let us describe cellular automata, Langton's λ parameter (Langton 1991) and Wolfram classes (Wolfram 1984b) in more detail. Then, we display the relation among these parameters and Wolfram classes.

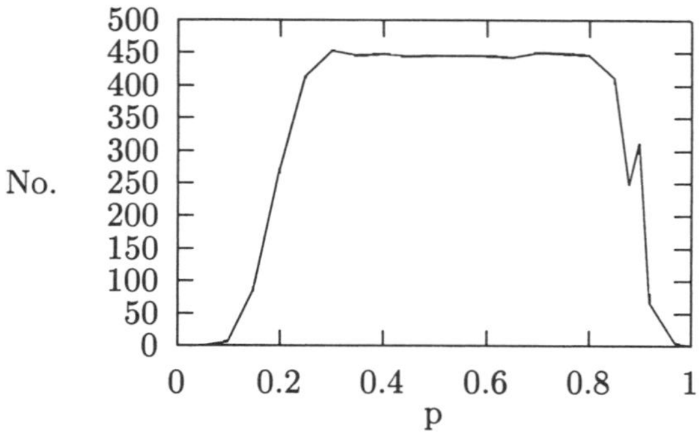

Figure 16: Correlation between the number of generated cycles (vertical axis) and p (horizontal axis).

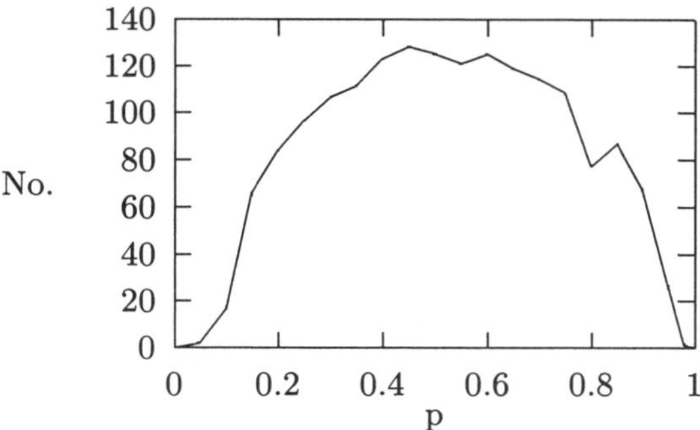

Figure 17: Correlation between the kinds of periods of generated cycles (vertical axis) and p (horizontal axis).

Cellular Automata

A Cellular Automaton (CA) is a discrete mathematical model (Wolfram 1984a) whose behavior is caused by the interactions among neighbor sites. This model can be applied to various fields to model, for example, statistical mechanics, mathematical biology, public hygiene (as a model of infectious disease, for example), in medicine and so on.

Formally, a cellular automaton is a D-dimensional lattice automaton. Each lattice site is updated by a deterministic rule involving a local neighborhood of sites, in discrete time steps.

The possible state of a site is chosen from the alphabet $K = \{0, 1, \ldots, k-1\}$, and the value of site i at step t is denoted by $a_i^{(t)}$. At each time step, each site value is updated according to the particular neighborhood of N sites around it by a local rule

$$\phi : K^N \to K, \tag{5}$$

of the form

$$pa_i^{(t)} = \phi\{a_{1-r}^{(t-1)}, a_{1-r+1}^{(t-1)}, \ldots, a_{1+r}^{(t-1)}\}. \tag{6}$$

This local rule leads to a global mapping

$$\Phi : K^N \to K^N \tag{7}$$

on all cellular automata configurations. Then, in general

$$\Omega^{(t+1)} = \Phi\Omega^{(t)} \subseteq \Omega^{(t)}, \tag{8}$$

where

$$\Omega^{(t+1)} = \Phi^t N^K \tag{9}$$

is the set of configurations generated after t iterated applications of Φ (Wolfram 1984a, Langton 1991).

For example, a local rule for the one dimensional cellular automaton with neighborhood two is:

000	001	010	011	100	101	110	111
0	1	0	0	1	0	0	0.

By using this rule, a step of global mapping is;

000101011011100
0100000000001.

Qualitative characterizations of CA

Wolfram's classification and Langton's λ parameter as qualitative characterizations of the behavior of cellular automata are well known.

Wolfram classes

Wolfram (1984b) proposed four classes of qualitative behavior patterns of cellular automata based on his investigation of a large sample of CA rule tables. He maintained that any cellular automata would fall into one of the four basic classes':

- **Class 1**: Evolution leads to a homogeneous state.
- **Class 2**: Evolution leads to a set of separated simple stable or periodic structures.
- **Class 3**: Evolution leads to a chaotic pattern.
- **Class 4**: Evolution leads to chaotic, localized structures, sometimes long-lived.

These four classes are obtained in an analogy between the CA's behavior and the classification of dynamical systems:

- **Class 1**: Limit points.
- **Class 2**: Limit cycles.
- **Class 3**: Chaotic behavior of the kind associated with strange attractors.
- **Class 4**: No direct analogue.

With respect to Class 4, Wolfram suspected that CA in this class are capable of universal computation, so that properties of its infinite-time behavior would be undecidable (Wolfram 1984b).

Langton's λ parameter

Langton criticized Wolfram's classification by saying: "it is obvious that such a classification can only serve as rough approximations to the more subtle, underlying structure (Langton 1991, p.46)" and proposed his λ parameter to describe CA rules, to obtain "a deeper understanding of the structure of cellular automata rule spaces, one that provides an explanation for their relationships to one another"(Langton 1991, p. 46). The λ parameter is defined as follows:

$$\lambda = \frac{K^N - n_q}{K^N}, \tag{10}$$

where K corresponds to the number of symbols used, N to the size of the neighborhood, and n_q to the number of local rules which transform cellular automata to the *quiescent* state, respectively. The quiescent state is picked arbitrarily, and is usually associated with a "special" state, such as the "zero" state. If all rules transform to the quiescent state, $K^N = n_q$, and the the λ parameter is equal to 0. When no rules transform to the quiescent state on the other hand, λ is equal to 1.

The values $\lambda = 0$ and $\lambda = 1 - \frac{1}{K}$ represent the most homogeneous and the most heterogeneous rule tables. As the value of the λ parameter increases, the dynamical activity of cellular automata becomes chaotic. The correspondence between the value of the λ parameter and dynamical activity of cellular automata is as follows:

fixed point → periodic → "complex" → chaotic.

In terms of the Wolfram classes, the sequence is:

$$\text{Class 1} \Rightarrow \text{Class 2} \Rightarrow \text{Class 4} \Rightarrow \text{Class 3}. \qquad (11)$$

Langton (1991) demonstrated that the complex rules are located in between the periodic and the chaotic rules, and that there is a clear phase-transition between periodic and chaotic behavior.

Computational algebraic characteristics of λ parameter

We demonstrate here that the λ parameter indicates a degree of *termination* and that when cellular automata yield complex or chaotic behavior, this termination property of the system becomes weak. When λ is close to 0, the dynamical activity of the cellular automaton quickly dies out or reaches a uniform fixed point. In this regime, thus, the termination property of cellular automata is strong. As the value of the λ is increasing, cellular automata evolve to periodic structures or chaotic aperiodic patterns. As the value of the λ increases even more, the termination property becomes weak. The larger the parameter becomes, the later the calculation terminates. Since the transitional space of cellular automata is finite, if a calculation does not terminate or is difficult to stop, cyclic structure must emerge in the process of the computation.

When λ is equal to 0.125, for example, we could find the following rule:

000	001	010	011	100	101	110	111
0	0	1	0	0	0	0	0.

As this parameter increases, the rule might change to that given below:

000	001	010	011	100	101	110	111
1	0	1	0	0	0	0	1 .

The λ parameter of this rule is equal to 0.375. As the value of λ parameter increases, the number of rules such as,

$$\begin{matrix} * & * & * \\ & 0 & \end{matrix} \quad (* = 0 \text{ or } 1) ,$$

termina -ting	λ_e	λ	Wolfram classes
Strong	$\lambda_e \cong 0.0$, $\lambda_e \gg 1.0$	$\lambda \cong 0.0$	I or II
Fair strong	$1.0 > \lambda_e > 0.0$, $\lambda_e > 1.0$	$0.0 < \lambda < 1 - \frac{1}{K}$	II or IV
Weak	$\lambda_e \cong 1.0$	$\lambda \cong 1 - \frac{1}{K}$	III

Table 2: Relation among parameters, complexity classes

decreases while, on the other hand, the number of rules such as,

$$\begin{matrix} * & * & * \\ & 1 & \end{matrix} \quad (* = 0 \text{ or } 1) ,$$

increases. The CA rule yields a complex or chaotic pattern when λ is near $1 - \frac{1}{K}$, and rules that lead to the quiescent state are used at the same frequency as rules that lead *away* from said state.

Relation between λ_e, λ, Wolfram classes, and the termination property

The qualitative dynamics of CA and ARMS that we have described is summarized in Table 2. It suggests that each parameter and class indicate a degree of terminating.

Comments on the 'edge of chaos'-regime

We have demonstrated that an equal frequency of $r_{\Delta S>0}$ rules to $r_{\Delta S<0}$ rules yields dynamical patterns for both cellular automata and ARMS. We can now see that the principle of "edge of chaos" (Langton 1991, Kauffman 1993), according to the dynamics just described, results from a biased ratio of $r_{\Delta S>0}$ rules to $r_{\Delta S<0}$ rules.

If these two types of rules are used at the same frequency, the system yields a chaotic pattern. However, when the ratio changes slightly, the "edge of chaos" regime emerges. Thus, a lack of symmetry in the application of rules generates the diversity of cycles in these systems.

Finally, we close with a quote of Fontana (1994), who addresses the difference between his λ-calculus and abstract rewriting systems, and their importance for simulating chemistry:

> *With some ingenuity the observer will further derive all laws supplied by the uncovered group structure [...]. If read as rewrite rules, the equations thus obtained will enable the observer to exactly describe (and predict) each and every collision product in the system - without any knowledge about λ-calculus. The observer will, then, have discovered a perfectly valid theory of that organization, without reference to its underlying micro-mechanics. (from: Fontana and Buss 1994, p. 22)*

References

Langton, C. G. 1991. Life at the edge of chaos. In *Artificial Life II*, edited by C. G. Langton, C. Taylor, J. D. Farmer, and S. Rasmussen. Redwood City, CA: Addison Wesley.

Field, R. J. and M. Burger. 1985. *Oscillations and Traveling Waves in Chemical Systems.* New York: John Wiley and Sons.

Fontana, W. and L. W. Buss. 1994. The arrival of the fittest: Toward a theory of biological organization. *Bulletin of Mathematical Biology* 56: 1–64.

Bellin, G. and G. Boudol. 1992. The chemical abstract machine. *Theoretical Computer Science* 96: 217–248.

Kauffman, S. A. 1993. *The Origins of Order.* Oxford: Oxford University Press.

Nicolis, G. and I. Prigogine. 1989. *Exploring Complexity, An Introduction.* San Francisco: Freeman and Company.

Suzuki, Y. and H. Tanaka. 1997. Chemical oscillation on symbolic chemical system and its behavioral pattern. In *Proceedings of the International Conference on Complex Systems*, Nashua, NH, 21-26 Sept 1997.

Suzuki, Y. and H. Tanaka. 1998. Symbolic chemical system based on abstract rewriting system and its behavior pattern. *Journal of Artificial Life and Robotics.* In press.

Wolfram, S. 1984a. Computation theory of cellular automaton. *Commun. Math. Phys.* 96: 15–57.

S. Wolfram. 1984b Universality and complexity in cellular automata. *Physica D* 10: 1–35.

Molecular and Developmental Models

Modeling Thymic Selection and Concomitant Immune Responses on $CD4^+$ T Lymphocyte Sub-Populations

Artur Caetano, António Grilo and **Agostinho Rosa**

Instituto Superior Técnico, Technical University of Lisbon
Av. Rovisco Pais, 1, 1096 Lisboa Codex Portugal

Abstract

The behavior and type of immune responses are currently believed to be the result of cross regulation of $CD4^+$ T lymphocyte populations. Many debates have arisen concerning the way the immune system is able to provide an immune response and tolerate self simultaneously. Classical theories try to explain these phenomena through the specificity of T cell receptors. Nevertheless, observations show us that the specificity of the immune system cells can be quite degenerated, providing a different scope on the understanding of the immune system's balance. We propose a computational model for the dynamics of Th_1 and Th_2 $CD4^+$ T lymphocyte sub-populations, aiming the study of diversity and multiple responses. Using this model we are able to identify some experimental observations which are poorly understood. Some of the results show us that the immune system's balance can be related to a measure of locality, helping to explain the paradigm of concomitant responses and tolerance.

Introduction

The behavior of the immune system as well as the type of immune responses is believed to be set by the cross regulation of $CD4^+$ T lymphocyte populations (Fitch, McKisic, Lancki and Gajewski 1993).

This is especially the case of the Th_1 and Th_2 classes, as demonstrated in several experimental situations (Bottomly 1989; Mosmann and Coffman 1989). In these situations, the murine immune response to certain pathogens and antigens can be strongly biased to either a Th_1 or Th_2 dominant phenotype, suggesting that these cells do exist and are important *in vivo*. Therefore, it is strongly sustained that the differentiation pathway between Th_1 and Th_2 plays a major role in the immune system ontogeny, since the entire organism can be compromised if the wrong pathway is taken.

The theories around these mechanisms rely mostly on features that have no relation with the intrinsic properties of the Th populations themselves. Hence the suggestion that the bias towards a specific pathway is determined by the nature of the antigen, its route of presentation or its density to the Th cell population (Gajewski, Pinnas, Wong, Fitch 1991). However, it is implausible that the immune system could identify such extrinsic features *per se*. The system will engage with different antigens, and it may be useful to classify them based on a set of extrinsic features. At the level of the Th population, it is required to identify what mechanisms direct the system either to a Th_1 or Th_2 mode. Thus, this feature is likely to be established *a priori*, due to the way antigen engages Th populations dynamics. Only incidentally, this feature would be related with the extrinsic features of the antigens (Carneiro and Stewart 1995; Murray, Madri, Tite, Carding, and Bottomly 1989). Today, most immunologists considered that the activity of the immune system reflects both its own dynamics and ontogeny, and that the Th populations themselves are probably the major determinant in their own role and development.

The importance of studying the development of Th populations is broadly justified by current research on auto-immunity, since the immune system's regulation and tolerance mechanisms are strongly sustained to be a result of cross-regulation between Th cells. However, experiments concerning the study of cross-regulatory points are centered on homogeneous and isolated populations within *in vitro* environments, aiming towards a broad extrapolation between the observed qualitative results and *in vivo* observations. Nevertheless, this operation neglects two primary factors: the ontogenesis of cell population *in vitro* and the fact that simultaneous and concurrent immune responses do occur *in vivo*. In Carneiro, Stewart, Coutinho and Coutinho 1995, the question of cell ontogeny is studied and mathematically modeled, but no attempts are made in order to establish results concerning multiple and concomitant responses. The model presented here enables the analysis of cross-regulatory points in a system capable of providing simultaneous antigenic immune responses and yet upholding tolerance.

Method

This section describes the model for the population dynamics of multiple Th lymphocyte sub-populations. The basic concept concerning such a model for the sub-populations of $CD4^+$ T lymphocytes, as well as the cross-regulatory and tolerance mechanisms, is based on the work of Institut Pasteur's Unité d'Immunobiologie (Carneiro, Stewart, Coutinho and Coutinho 1995; Carneiro and Stewart 1995; Carneiro, Coutinho, Faro and Stewart 1996).

We have defined a model to study multiple responses and cross-regulatory points using a complex adaptive system's emergent behavior analysis. We will first describe the underlying postulates of the model and then explain its formulation.

The sub-populations of CD4$^+$ T lymphocytes

The CD4+ T lymphocyte population can be distinguished by the pattern of T Cell Receptors (TCR) and through cytokine expression and cross-regulation mechanisms of the population. We will focus on the differentiation pathway into Th_1 and Th_2 cells. First, these pathways seem mutually exclusive due to the intrinsic dynamics and cross-regulatory mechanisms. Second, two poles can be associated to each sub-population: the inflammatory or Th_1 pole, associated with cell-mediated immunity; and the Th_2 or helper pole, which promotes B cell growth and antibody production. However, we emphasize that these poles do not define a single pattern of cytokine expression a dominant state instead. The intermediate states, i.e., non Th_1 and non Th_2 states, are depicted through a neutral compartment, the Th_0 compartment. This compartment can derive from thymic output and by differentiation of resting Th_2 lymphocytes as we will discuss shortly. Furthermore, both Th_1 and Th_2 poles can be assigned one of two modes: resting and activated. A Th cell is said to be activated when successfully bound to a specific antigen, therefore able to express its dominant pole, whether inflammatory or tolerant.

The Th sub-populations are expressed by a set of agents, each representing a single Th cell. At any given time, each agent will be in one of five states: activated in Th_1 pole (aTh_1), resting in Th_1 pole (rTh_1), resting in neutral state (rTh_0), resting in Th_2 pole (rTh_2) or activated in the Th_2 pole (aTh_2). The model comprises the definition of multiple lineages of CD4$^+$ T cells, along with the required mechanisms for the analysis of binding affinity towards several antigenic niches. The dynamics of a Th lymphocyte cell are depicted in Figure 1.

1.1. The concept of antigenic niche

The activation of Th cells is essentially local and involves immune system cell-to-cell cooperation. In the same way, the cross-regulatory mechanisms mediated by cytokines are short ranged, and require either direct contact or interference within close vicinity. Furthermore, TCR binding is required to maintain a stable interaction in order to keep Th cells activated (Dustin and Springer 1991, Fiorentino, Zlotnik, Vieira, and Mosmann 1991).

In this model, the antigenic niche designates the set of local conditions which are required to activate and cross regulate a Th cell population, whether they are the morphogenic mechanisms in the lymphoid organs or the artificial conditions sustained in *in vitro* experiments. The term 'antigenic' derives from a major condition required to activate those cells: the availability of antigen presenting cells (APC) and MHC/peptide complex. However, other components will modulate the driving capacity of the niche such as regulatory cells or molecules, or specific clonal positive/negative stimuli.

In the general case, a given T cell clone may be associated with several antigenic niches. The distribution depends on the affinity between clones and the corresponding niches, and on the size of competing sub-populations. However, in this model we assume that each T cell clone can be associated with only one antigenic niche. Each antigenic niche can be associated with more than one T cell clone depending on its driving capacity, and different niches are independent of each other. These simplifying assumptions, although probably unrealistic, are nevertheless useful since they enable us to focus on the basic phenomena, which arise from the cross regulation of Th sub-populations.

Differentiation pathways and population dynamics

The basic differentiation pathway is activated when the whole population is in resting state, i.e., when no antigenic niche is present in the system to successfully activate the Th cells. In the absence of any activation, the dynamics of the Th cell population are characterized by a set of main features:

- Input of thymic migrants into the Th_2 and Th_0 compartments;
- Spontaneous flow by differentiation from resting the Th_2 into the resting Th_0 compartment, and from the latter to the resting Th_1 compartment;
- Output dominated by an exponential decay of each compartment by cell death.

When in the presence of an antigenic niche with a significant driving capacity, the activation of resting Th lymphocytes results in a flow from all the resting compartments to the activated Th_1 and Th_2 compartments. Both the Th_1 and Th_2 compartments are poles with effector functions and regulatory potential that ensure the population expansion by cell division.

In Bendelac and Schwartz 1992 it is suggested that a considerable fraction - if not all Th lymphocytes - come out of the thymus committed to an IL-4 expressing pathway of differentiation. However, it is observed that IFN-γ expression dominates IL-4 expression after 3 to 6 days.

Two different processes could explain this change in proportions:

- Each differentiation state is irreversibly committed, but individual cells have very short lived IL-4 expressions;
- There exists a differentiation from IL-4 to IFN-γ expression in recent thymic migrant, i.e., a spontaneous flow from the resting Th_2 compartment to the resting Th_0, and thence to the Th_1 compartment.

Accordingly to some recent work on immunology, the second alternative seems more likely since the precursors of both types of activated cells expressed IL-4, corresponding to the resting Th_2 cells of the model.

Cross-regulatory mechanisms in the antigenic niche

The cytokines produced by each of the activated polar compartments tend to work in such a way as to increase the relative importance of their own differentiation pathway. In order to capture the main features of cross-regulation in Th populations, we have identified three main regulatory mechanisms:

- Down-modulation of expansion potentials;
- Access modulation of the resting sub-populations to the driving niche;
- Biasing of the commitment step.

See Carneiro, Stewart, Coutinho and Coutinho 1995 for further details on cytokine modulation effects on CD4⁺ T cells.

Model description and formulation

The dynamics of both resting and activated Th_1 and Th_2 sub-populations are governed by following postulates. The simulation parameters, the rate constants k, the thymic source terms s, and the cytokine mediated effects c, are indicated along.

1. Resting Th_2 and resting Th_0 cells are produced by thymic output with constant rates, (s_2 and s_0, respectively).
2. The resting Th_2 sub-population decreases exponentially by death (k_4) and by spontaneous differentiation (k_5) into the rTh_0 compartment, or by niche-driven activation into the aTh_2 compartment (k_6); it increases as activated Th_2 cells revert to resting Th_2 state, with (k_3) or without (k_2).
3. The resting Th_0 population decreases exponentially by death (k_7) and by spontaneous differentiation into the resting Th_1 compartment; it also decreases by following niche-driven activation into aTh_2, through (k_8), and/or to aTh_1 compartment through (k_9).
4. The resting Th_1 sub-population decreases exponentially by death (k_{11}) and by activation into the aTh_1 compartment (k_{12}); it increases as activated Th_1 cells revert to resting Th_1 state, with (k_{15}) or without (k_{14}) going through the mitotic cycle.
5. Only activated Th_2 and activated Th_1 cells produce cytokines with regulatory effects. These cytokines are assumed to have effective concentrations in the niche and are directly proportional to the sizes of the activated Th_1 compartment (c_1 and c_2) and activated Th_1 compartment (c_3).
6. All three resting compartments compete in the driving capacity of the antigenic niche, being the share of each sub-population proportional to its size.
7. Cytokines produced by aTh_2 cells inhibit the capacity of the niche to drive aTh_1 cells. The force of this inhibition depends on the relative size of aTh_2 sub-population with the niche's driving capacity.
8. Resting Th_0 cells will differentiate into activated Th_1 cells after their activation in the niche (k_9). The differentiation into aTh_2 cells can be redirected through cytokines produced by the same compartment (c_2), however the Th_1 sub-population will inhibit the same differentiation (c_3). Therefore, the proportion of rTh_0 cells that will commit into aTh_2 cells depends on the balance between activated Th_1 and Th_2 cells.
9. The driving capacity of the niche can be dynamically changed in order to study cross-regulation under such conditions as well as the corresponding emergent behaviors.

We have explained the dynamics of Th lymphocyte sub-populations, the concept of antigenic niche and driving capacity. The rules enumerated above describe the global dynamics of the system.

The simulation model includes one or more Th cell lineages and a set of antigenic niches with a specific binding affinity, comprehended within a bi-dimensional lattice. The parameters k_n, c_n and s_n, which guide population dynamics, are the values that enable an output in agreement with experimental results. They remain constant for every simulation. Since the spatial location within the lattice, especially the Hamming distance between niches modify the emergent behavior, it is considered as another variable.

Th cells and APCs

To control the binding mechanism between MHC/peptide molecules on the antigenic niche and the Th cell TCR molecule, two additional independent variables are introduced: TCR and MHC/peptide 'length' and the binding affinity value for each sub-population element.

The Th sub-populations are mapped into a mutually exclusive five-element space state. The transition functions, TCR pattern expression and the state of a T cell clone are modeled by a single agent, which allows heterogeneous agent populations (Smith, Forrest, Perelson 1994).

This population is distributed over an object oriented cellular automaton, comprising a set of sites arranged in a two-dimensional lattice. This same lattice is used to depict the data concerning the antigenic niches and cell mediated cytokines.

Binding mechanisms

To model the TCR molecules on the Th cell clones and the MHC/peptide pairs we have used a bit-string matching procedure (Hightower, Forrest, and Perelson 1993). In this bit-string universe, molecular binding takes place when a TCR bit-string and an antigenic one match each other in a complementary fashion. The match score between two bit-strings is the number of complementary bits, computed by applying the exclusive-or operator. The binding value, derived from the match score, represents how well two molecules bind. Actually, molecular binding requires a

Figure 1: Th cell dynamics and state transition flows. The boxes represent the Th sub-populations: aTh_2 (activated Th_2), rTh_2 (resting Th_2), aTh_1 (activated Th_1), rTh_1 (resting Th_1) and rTh_0 (resting in Th_0 state). Plain arrows stand for the flow between sub-populations. Decay by death is indicated by arrows into a cross. The thin arrows depict spontaneous flows between compartments, while the thick ones correspond to flows, which are activated by the driving capacity of the niche. Dashed arrows from one compartment to a transfer arrow indicate the modulation effect of cytokines on the target: inhibitory effects are depicted by a crossed line, while stimulatory effects are given by a ⊕ sign. Cell division is indicated by a double arrow from the source compartment to the target one. The parameters s_n (thymic output rate), k_n (rate constants) and c_n (cytokine effects) are affixed to the corresponding process.

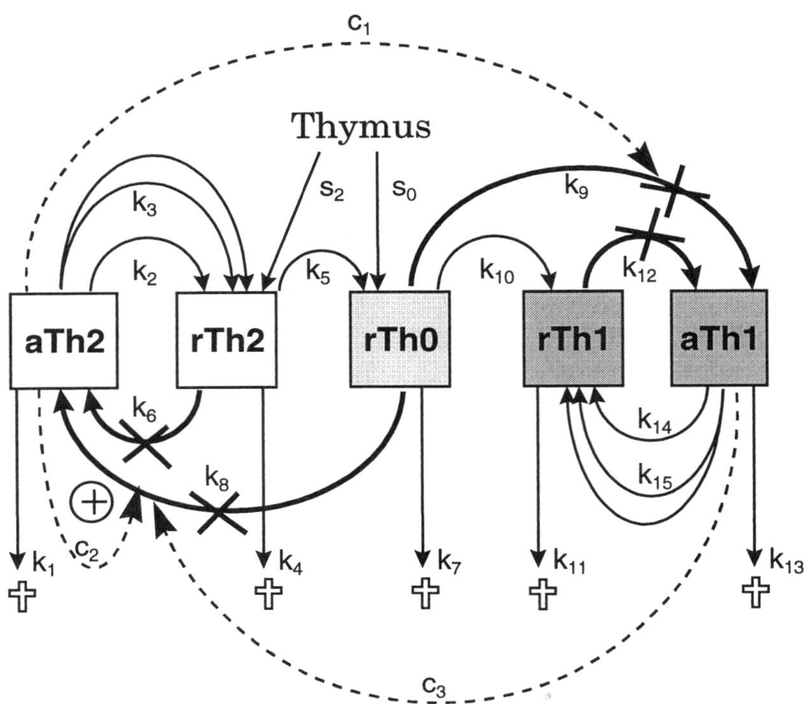

sufficiently large surface area match, essential to form a stable bond. This feature is emulated by requiring the match score to exceed a certain threshold before binding takes place. For match scores below the threshold the binding value is essentially zero. For match scores above the threshold, the value approaches one. The binding function makes a smooth transition on either side of the threshold, rather than an abrupt shift (Hinton and Nowlan 1987, Hightower, Forrest, and Perelson 1994).

State transition functions

The basic parameter values, k_1, ... k_{15}, c_1, c_2 and c_3, have been automatically determined with a genetic algorithm whose fitness function was based on an agent population attaining the three basic steady state configurations, SS0, SS1 and SS2. See the Results section for details on Th_1 and Th_2 steady states.

The parameters values used to obtain the presented results are: $s_0 = 8000$; $s_2 = 1000$; $c_1 = 100$; $c_2 = 100$; $c_3 = 45$; $k_1 = 0$; $k_2 = 48$; $k_3 = 41$; $k_4 = 57$; $k_5 = 29$; $k_6 = 55$; $k_7 = 40$; $k_8 = 21$; $k_9 = 52$; $k_{10} = 47$; $k_{11} = 30$; $k_{12} = 53$; $k_{13} = 0$; $k_{14} = 23$; $k_{15} = 17$.

The transition functions define the agent's behavior based upon internal and environmental criteria. Hence, each of the possible five states holds a specific transition function.

Every state relies in a stochastic decision function. Depending on the agent's state, two situations can be considered: the resting and activated modes. In resting mode it is required to test the binding affinity to choose either the activation or the spontaneous flow pathways. It is clear that only the spontaneous flow requires testing for the binding affinity, since the activation pathway assumes a stable molecular bond.

The binding result θ, depends on the agent's type, the TCR and the target antigenic molecule. This value is obtained by comparing the binding value of the two molecules with the agent's binding affinity threshold.

The Th sub-population space state is represented by the set $\Sigma_{Th} = \{aTh_1, rTh_1, rTh_0, rTh_2, aTh_2\}$. Set upon this, a global decision space state $\Sigma_A = \Sigma_{Th} \cup \{✞\}$ is defined to identify the possible transition space state of every agent. The transition function, σ, is defined by $\sigma: \Sigma_{Th} \rightarrow \Sigma_A$ and is evaluated by all agents on every simulation step. Any element of Σ_{Th} can be overloaded with the symbol ✧, denoting state transition and simultaneous cell division or cloning. The Σ_A element {✞} depicts the agent's death.

The value of $\rho(c_n)$ describes the cytokine absolute density value within the site where the evaluated agent currently is. The value of c_n can be one of c_1, c_2 or c_3.

Finally, the operator α depicts the competitive stochastic selection among the parameter space of an element of Σ_{Th}, and is defined as: $\alpha: N_0 \otimes N_0 \rightarrow$ Bool. The operator $\alpha[n, m]$ can be interpreted as: given a value n and a maximum discriminating boundary m, if $s(n)$ is outside the boundary ceiling m, α returns a Boolean true value, otherwise a false one. $s(n)$ is a stochastic function which returns a value within the range [0, n]. With this operator it is possible to select a single transition state from a n-dimensional parameter space on each evaluation of α.

The state transition functions for every element of Σ_{Th} provide a complete description of the function σ. Every state has been divided into a set of independent groups (depicted by I, II,...), each confining the scope of the α operator to the same group.

$\sigma(\boldsymbol{rTh_0})$

I. ✞ $\Leftarrow \alpha[(1-\theta)k_7, 200]$

$rTh_1 \Leftarrow \alpha[(1-\theta)k_{10}, 200]$

II.

$$aTh2 \Leftarrow \alpha\left[\frac{\theta(k_8(1+c_2\rho(c_2)))}{k_8(1+c_3\rho(c_3))+k_9(1+c_1\rho(c_1))}+200-k_7-k_8, \frac{k_8(1+c_2\rho(c_2))}{(1+c_3\rho(c_3))}\right]$$

$$aTh1 \Leftarrow \alpha\left[\frac{\theta(k_8(1+c_2\rho(c_2)))}{k_8(1+c_3\rho(c_3))+k_9(1+c_1\rho(c_1))}+200-k_7-k_8, k_9(1+c_1\rho(c_1))\right]$$

III. $rTh_0 \Leftarrow$ otherwise

$\sigma(\boldsymbol{rTh_1})$

I. ✞ $\Leftarrow \alpha[(1-\theta)k_{11}, 100]$

II. $aTh_1 \Leftarrow \alpha[\theta(k_{12}(1 + c_1\rho(c_1)) + 100 - k_{12}), k_{12}(1 + c_1\rho(c_1)) + 100]$

III. $rTh_1 \Leftarrow$ otherwise

$\sigma(\boldsymbol{aTh_1})$

I. ✞ $\Leftarrow \alpha[(1-\theta)k_{13}, 300]$

$rth_1 \Leftarrow \alpha[(1-\theta)k_{14}, 300]$

$rth_1^{\diamond} \Leftarrow \alpha[(1-\theta)k_{15}, 300]$

II. $ath_1 \Leftarrow$ otherwise

$\sigma(\boldsymbol{rTh_2})$

I. ✞ $\Leftarrow \alpha[(1-\theta)k_4, 200]$

$rTh_1 \Leftarrow \alpha[(1-\theta)k_5, 200]$

II. $aTh_2 \Leftarrow \alpha[\theta(k_6(1 + c_3\rho(c_3)) + 100 - k_6), k_6(1 + c_3\rho(c_3))]$

III. $rTh_2 \Leftarrow$ otherwise

$\sigma(\boldsymbol{aTh_2})$

I. ✞ $\Leftarrow \alpha[(1-\theta)k_1, 300]$

$rTh_2 \Leftarrow \alpha[(1-\theta)k_2, 300]$

$rTh_2^{\diamond} \Leftarrow \alpha[(1-\theta)k_3, 300]$

II. $ath_2 \Leftarrow$ otherwise

Results

The obtained results concern:

- Basic steady states for the canonical conditions of antigen presentation;
- Concomitant responses to the same antigen;
- Concomitant responses towards skin grafts.

In Carneiro, Stewart, Coutinho and Coutinho (1995), the attained system responses considered unary diversity, i.e. a Th cell population with similar TCRs. Since this model allows diversity, both of cell population and antigen, we are able to extrapolate some results to complex *in vitro* observations and even to conditioned *in vivo* environments.

Depending on the development conditions, the system can reach different steady state responses. In the present model, the driving capacity of the antigenic niches does not change with Th cell activity throughout the simulation, meaning that the achieved steady states are highly dependent on it. Nevertheless, they are also dependent on the way the system develops, i.e., on the timing and type of antigen presentation. With a homogeneous population and antigen as described in Carneiro, Stewart, Coutinho and Coutinho 1995 these states are easier to identify. When diversity is considered, some complex behaviors occur, as different responses to different antigens can be achieved simultaneously. As a basic experiment to identify the possible states, we tried the system with a diverse population but only one type of antigen. Three main equilibrium states were identified. SS0 equilibrium corresponds to a complete absence of antigen, featuring no activated cells and the dominance of Th_1 and Th_0 population compartments (v. Figure 2). SS1 equilibrium corresponds to antigen rejection and is typically achieved through the presentation of antigen to a system in SS0 state. It's main feature is the clear dominance of the inflammatory or Th_1 compartment (v. Figure 3). Finally, SS2 equilibrium is reached when the system develops from its onset on the presence of antigen, featuring a dominant Th_2 population, which corresponds to a tolerant response of self antigen (v. Figure 4).

The protocol of this simulation requires the system to evolve its population in the presence of an antigen patch, which occupies a small fraction of the available space, yet big enough to promote a SS2 response. After the system reaches equilibrium, another patch of the same antigen is inserted, somewhat distant from the initial one (v. Figure 5). The initial patch keeps promoting a SS2 response while the second promotes a concomitant SS1 response. This result can be easily explained. As the system evolves, the SS2 response is obtained in the area occupied by the initial patch. Nevertheless, as the remaining space is empty, the flux of cells from resting Th_2 state towards Th_0 and thence to Th1, promotes a SS0 equilibrium. The antigen which was later inserted in the SS0 dominant area leads to a new and local SS1 response. As there is still an unoccupied physical space between the two patches, the SS0 pole keeps offering a boundary that stops any influence between the antigenic clusters.

Figure 2: SS0 equilibrium is reached in the absence of antigen.

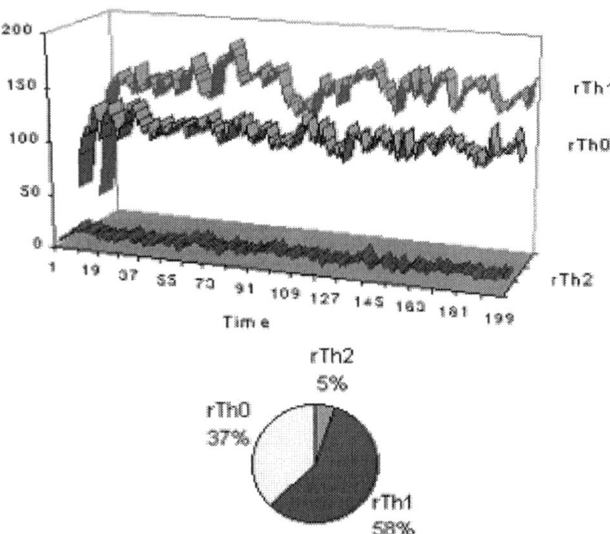

The study of concomitant tolerant and rejection responses has special interest to understand the observations on skin graft experiments, whether *in vitro* or *in vivo*. The main issue concerns the immune response, which eliminates the pathogenic agents without interfering with the tolerant response to self. In other words, why the rejection of a skin graft does not propagate to the self tissues in the vicinity? A possible explanation relies on a set of different responses from the cells promoting rejection and those who lead to self-tolerance, with no interference between both compartments. This theory has been classically accepted, however, current research holds that lymphocyte specificity is quite degenerated. In the light of those observations, concomitant responses would depend on a balance between regulatory and inflammatory cells through the definition of boundaries in both physical space and specificity.

This model considers the latter theory. The following experiments concern tolerance towards skin grafts. Firstly, a diverse Th population develops in the presence of MHC/peptide molecule *A* homogeneously distributed throughout the available physical space, leading to the tolerance of antigen *A*, identified by a global SS2 steady state. Next, a small area is cleared of *A*, and replaced with a patch of MHC/peptide molecule *B* with the same average density. The obtained immune response is studied for both molecules, *A* and *B*, allowing the identification of the cell compartments and populations which responded to each peptide. We take into account the ratio of *B* in the global system, as well as the similarity between both antigens. The similarity degree is the factor of equivalence of the TCR receptors. The results are shown on Table 1 and Table 2.

The SS2 response to peptide *A* is the same after the graft attachment, meaning overall self recognition. Moreover, we can observe that the response increases in proportion to the graft's fraction of the total driving capacity of the system, enabling the identification of the graft either as self or as allogeneic material. Keeping this fraction constant, we note that *B* is more likely to be rejected as its similarity towards *A* decreases. Note that the less similar self and non-self are, the more orthogonal the responding populations.

Table 1: average relative density of Th1 or Th2 active cells per antigenic niche occupied by antigen A before grafting.

Initial response to antigen A	
Th_1	Th_2
1	7

The interpretation of these observations leads to a possible explanation on the way the immune response eliminates pathogenic agents and simultaneously tolerates self. Once the peptide *A* is added to the system, the population which positively binds to it develops a SS2 response, enabling the recognition of *A* as self. Nevertheless, the remaining cells evolves as if there was no initial antigen in the system, thus developing a response of type SS0. When the graft is added, tolerance to A is maintained no matter what the response is towards B, thanks to the overwhelming c_1 and c_2 cytokine action. If the B peptide is similar to *A*, the response is essentially created by cells that are reactive to the antigen, and thus the SS2 response propagates to the graft, inducing tolerance. On the other hand, when the similarity is low enough (at least below or equal 50%), the response is mainly created by the cells which do not match peptide *A* and thus in SS0 state. The addition of antigen in a SS0 state system promotes the inflammatory SS1 response. Acceptance of small grafts is related to the fact that the cell population matching *A*, already in a SS2 state and therefore in larger global concentration, easily overwhelms the remaining cells to promote tolerance. This result is consistent with the observations described in Carneiro, Stewart, Coutinho and Coutinho 1995.

Discussion

Concomitant responses towards a single antigen are a somewhat unusual result that might occur in some *in vivo* experiments. An example can be given by the experiments made on transgenic animals whose beta cells of the pancreas express an antigen *A* of viral origin. Those animals also express an anti-*A* transgenic TCR. When those animals are infected with the virus from which the gene was imported, the virus is rejected while the pancreas shows no sign of disease. This model can explain this by the simultaneous existence of both SS2 and SS0 equilibrium states towards a given antigen in different areas of the same organism, depending on its concentration and density.

Responses to skin grafts were achieved through an active mechanism that keeps a balance between regulatory and inflammatory cells. There is experimental evidence that the diversity within in the immune system alone is several times greater than that in the rest of the body. This is consistent with the described results. Cytokine mediated regulation, especially IL-4 and IL-10, was found to have a significant role on local graft rejection and effector function restraint on neighbor tissues. Although the proposed model considers a population with low diversity, we believe that the achieved results can be extrapolated to a broader domain of diversity.

Figure 3: After the SS0 state, the addition of peptide in moment A causes a SS1 type response to develop.

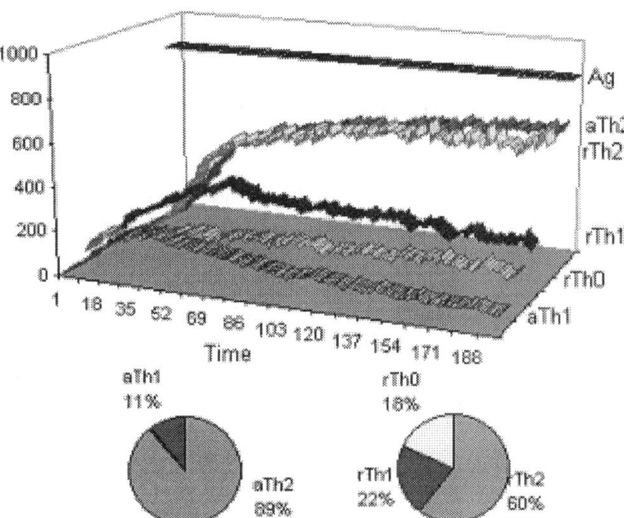

These results depict immune responses upon local steady states and well-defined boundaries. The major interrogation concerns the way local interactions are considered, in other words, the spatial scale of the model. Each *in vitro* culture can be regarded as a single antigenic niche, since the antigenic stimulus are homogeneously distributed by all antigen presenting cells, and cytokines are usually added from the outside and distributed consistently. However, *in vivo* environments provide a set of additional problems. In a pragmatic way, we have considered to interpret the neighborhood between antigenic niches as the probability of a cell to change between the niches, additionally representing a boundary for cytokine modulation.

Figure 4: SS2 state reached in the presence of peptide.

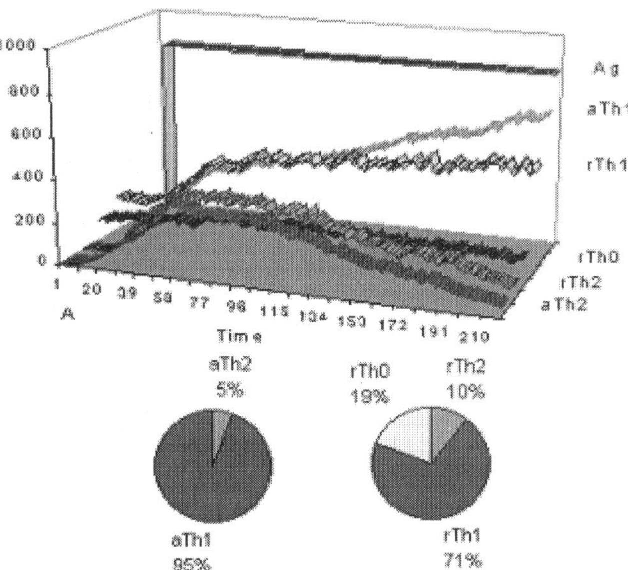

Figure 5: Antigen presence is indicated by a white dot. The first patch o f antigen *A*, can be seen on the top left corner. Its color indicates that the cell majority is Th2 (tolerant state). On the bottom right corner, we have a majority of Th1 cells, a synonym of rejection.

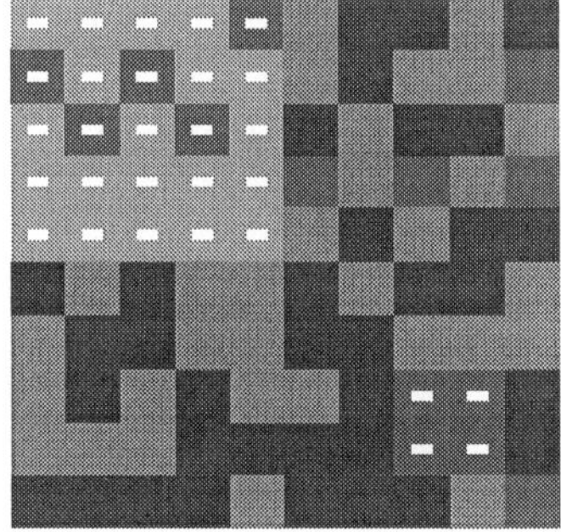

Table 2: Values represent the average relative density of active Th1 and Th2 cells per antigenic niche A and B after grafting. Darker areas indicate convergence towards an inflammatory SS1 local state. Lighter areas indicate dominant tolerance, towards SS2 local state.

		Similarity between molecules B and A											
		62.5%		50%		37.5%		25%		12.5%		0%	
MHC peptide	Graft Area	Th_1	Th_2	Th_1	Th_2	Th_1	Th_2	Th_1	Th_2	Th_1	Th_2	Th_1	Th_2
A	16%	1	7	1	7	1	7	1	7	1	7	1	7
	9%	1	7	1	7	1	7	1	7	1	7	1	7
	4%	1	7	1	7	1	7	1	7	1	7	1	7
B	16%	1	5	2	2	3	2	4	1	5	1	5	1
	9%	1	6	3	2	3	0	4	0	5	1	5	0
	4%	1	7	3	1	3	0	4	0	5	0	5	0

Conclusion

We have presented a model for the ontogeny and concomitant immune responses on $CD4^+$ T lymphocytes sub-populations. The model enables both TCR and MHC/peptide diversity considering different matching coefficients with the same antigen, which makes it suitable for simulations concerning *in vitro* and *in vivo* test protocols. Moreover, the ontogeny and the dynamics of Th lymphocytes appear to be one of the major regulatory mechanisms that upholds the tolerance and rejection of the immune system. We note that the establishment and maintenance of local equilibrium states, a process in which cytokines appear to have a decisive role, may help to understand one of the many important phenomena in the immune system.

The proposed model gives interesting clues on the learning process the immune system is submitted during its ontogeny and on how a population that presents a very degenerated specificity can recognize both self and allogeneic antigen. These results somewhat contradict the more orthodox theories which put exclusive specificity as the main factor for immune regulation and immunity.

Acknowledgments

We would like to thank Jorge Carneiro and António Coutinho from the Unité d'Immunobiologie, Institut Pasteur, whose collaboration was essential to this research.

References

Bendelac, A., P. Matzinger, R. Seder, W. Paulm, and R. H. Schwartz. 1992. *J. Exp. Med.* 175:731.

Bendelac, A. and R. Schwartz. 1992. *Nature* 353:68-76.

Bottomly, K. 1989. *Sem. Immunol.* 1:21-35.

Carneiro, J., J. Stewart, A. Coutinho, G. Coutinho. 1995. *Int. Immunol.* 7: 1265-1277.

Carneiro, J., and J. Stewart. 1995. *Lect. Notes Artf. Int. 929*: 406-424.

Carneiro, J., A. Coutinho, J. Faro, and J. Stewart. 1996. A model of the immune network with B-T cell co-operation. *J. Theor. Biol.* 182: 513-529; (E) 183: 119.

Dustin, M. and T. Springer. 1991. *Annu. Rev. Immunol.* 9:27.

Fiorentino, D., A. Zlotnik, P. Vieira, and T. Mosmann. 1991. *J. Immunol.* 146: 3444.

Fitch, F., M. McKisic, D. Lancki, and T. Gajewski. 1993. *Annu. Rev. Immunol.* 11: 29.

Gajewski T., M. Pinnas, T. Wong, and F. Fitch. 1991. *J. Immunol.* 146: 1750.

Hightower R., S. Forrest, and A. Perelson. 1993. In *Proc. of Second European Conference on Artificial Life.*

Hightower R., S. Forrest, and A. Perelson. 1994. The Baldwin effect in the immune system: learning by somatic hypermutation. In *Adaptive Individuals in Evolving Populations: Models and Algorithms.* Addison-Wesley.

Hinton G., and S. Nowlan. 1987. *Complex Systems.* 1: 495-502.

Holland, J. 1992. *Adaptation in Natural and Artificial Systems.* Cambridge MA: MIT Press.

Modigliani, Y., A. Coutinho, et al. 1996. Establishment of tissue-specific tolerance is driven by regulatory T-cells selected by thymic epithelium. *Eur. J. Immununol.* 26: 1807-1815.

Mosmann, T. and R. Coffman. 1989. *Annu. Rev. Immunol.* 7:145.

Murray, J., J. Madri, S. Tite, S. Carding, and K. Bottomly. 1989. *J. Exp. Med.* 170:2135

Smith R., S. Forrest, and A. Perelson. 1994. *Evolutionary Computation,* 1: 127-149.

Simulation of *Drosophila* Embryogenesis

Shugo Hamahashi *†
shugo@mt.cs.keio.ac.jp

Hiroaki Kitano †
kitano@csl.sony.co.jp

*Department of Computer Science
Keio University
3-14-1, Hiyoshi, Kohoku-ku
Yokohama, Kanagawa, 223 Japan

†Sony Computer Science Laboratory
3-14-13, Higashi-Gotanda
Shinagawa-ku, Tokyo, 141 Japan

Abstract

Drosophila is one of the most well investigated animals in molecular and developmental biology. However, the process of embryogenesis is still a complex phenomenon in biological studies. Due to its complexity, it is almost impossible to understand intuitively what is going on during embryogenesis. In this paper, we replicated *Drosophila* embryogenesis in a computational model. The system successfully reproduced the patterns of gene expression compared to the actual staining patterns of *Drosophila*'s embryo. In this system, we use a genetic algorithm to determine the parameter set for the development of *Drosophila*'s early segmentation. As the result of the simulation, we found that some phenomena taking place in *Drosophila*'s early embryogenesis are understandable. We propose that computer simulation can become a useful new method for biological experimentation.

Introduction

Current biological studies on *Drosophila* have revealed much about its genetics and development. *Drosophila* is a fruit fly, which is very popular experimental material in traditional genetics, experimental embryology, and molecular biology. These fields have been combined to build a blueprint of its developmental mechanisms. Due to their efforts, *Drosophila* has yielded a large map of genes which is far more complete than that of any other complex organism (Lawrence 1992).

Computer simulations have also contributed to studies of *Drosophila*, especially about the formation of gene expression during early embryo genesis. In 1990, Axel Hunding simulated the *hairy* gene expression pattern (Hunding et al. 1990) by using reaction-diffusion theory (Turing 1952). John Reinitz performed the simulation of several gene expressions and found the diffusion constant of *even-skipped* product is uniquely smaller than those of other genes (Reinitz and Sharp 1995). Masanori Arita simplified Reinitz's model to propose Simfly (Arita 1995) the same year.

For *Drosophila*, quite a large amount of data is available about early embryogenesis, a number of mutants have been identified, and detailed expression patterns of genes have been studied. However, *Drosophila* is still complex animal. There may be unknown mechanisms, genes, regulational pathways, etc. yet to discover. The morphogenesis of *Drosophila* is still quite complex and it also has a substantial central nervous system. In addition, recent biological studies have reported that the mechanisms of development (such as the specification of the anterior-posterior axis of the body) between mammals and *Drosophila* are very similar. *Drosophila* is quite a simple animal, but it is a significant animal. That is why *Drosophila* is a most suitable animal for the computational modeling (Kitano et al. 1997). Thus we chose *Drosophila*, especially its early embryogenesis, for our computational model.

The goal of this paper is to make a detailed model of *Drosophila* early embryogenesis, mainly its segmentation along the anterior-posterior axis of the body, to predict unknown mechanisms in its development, and to propose a new methodology called *computational biology*. This goal is part of the Virtual *Drosophila* Project (Kitano et al. 1997) at Sony Computer Science Laboratory Inc.

Drosophila

Early Segmentation

During the past decade, a model has emerged (Figure 1) which synthesizes much existing the data to show how the polarity of the *Drosophila* egg gives rise to the polarity of the fly body with its repetitive individual segments (Gilbert 1994). The basis of the establishment of segment polarity and homeotic stripes is the anterior-posterior distribution of maternal genes. These genes are maternally localized at different regions of the embryo. The two major such genes, *bicoid* and *nanos*, are believed to be very important in specifying the anterior-posterior polarity of the embryo. The *bicoid* protein and the *nanos* protein respectively regulate the formation of the anterior and posterior parts of the embryo. These maternal genes regulate zygotic genes called *gap genes* which form bands along the anterior-posterior axis of the embryo. These bands roughly determine the position of body segments. The various concentrations of gap gene products also regulates the expression of pair-rule genes.

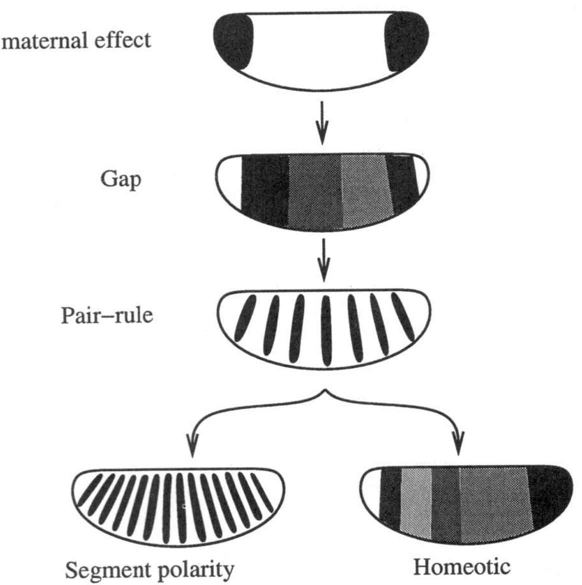

Figure 1: Generalized model of *Drosophila* pattern formation (Gilbert 1994)

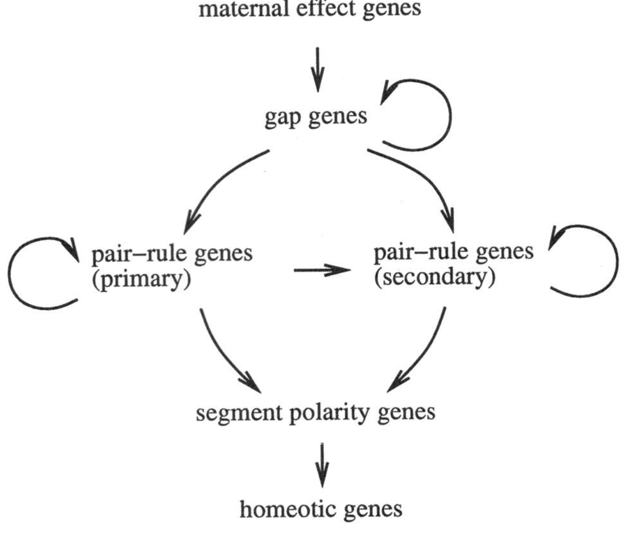

Figure 2: Hierarchical structure of gene regulation

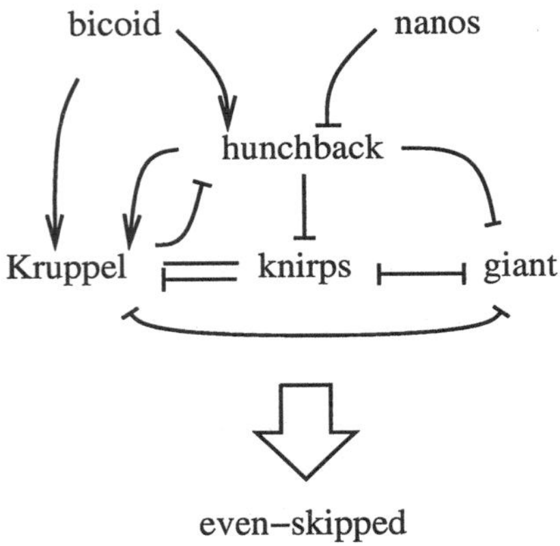

Figure 3: Gene Regulation Circuit

The expression of pair-rule genes forms the pattern of seven vertical bands along the anterior-posterior axis. The pair-rule gene proteins regulate the expression of segment polarity genes and homeotic genes. Segment polarity genes create 14 bands which divide the embryo into 15 segments. The homeotic genes determine the developmental fate of each segment.

In *Drosophila*, nuclei division occurs rapidly every 9 minutes. At the stages of embryogenesis during the 13th nucleic division cycle, the embryo is not cellularized and forms a syncytial blastoderm (that is, it consists of one large cell with many nuclei). This is different from the embryos of many other organisms, which perform cellular division every time a nucleus divides. The *Drosophila* embryo thus allows the free diffusion of proteins within the egg, while in many other embryos this is not feasible.

Gene Regulation

Early in segmentation, *Drosophila* forms seven vertical "bands" of concentration of gene products along the anterior-posterior axis of the embryo. These stripes lead to the body segments which are formed in latter stages of embryogenesis. The gene expression patterns are determined by the distribution of concentrations of regulational gene products.

As shown in Figure 2, genes are hierarchically regulated from upstream genes to downstream genes.

One of the maternal genes is *bicoid*, whose mRNA (from the mother's *bicoid* gene) is placed into the anterior region of the embryo by the mother's ovarian cells. The product of the *bicoid* gene controls anterior development. The *bicoid* protein binds to the promoter of the *hunchback* gene and activates its expression. It does likewise to the *Krüppel* gene. Another maternal gene is *nanos*, whose mRNA is placed into the posterior region of the embryo and product plays a role in posterior development. Both of the *bicoid* and *nanos* genes produce proteins soon after fertilization. The protein product of the *nanos* gene represses the translation of *hunchback* mRNA. The members of the gap gene group are *hunchback*, *Krüppel*, *knirps*, and *giant*. The *hunchback* protein activates the expression of *Krüppel* and inhibits *knirps giant*. The *Krüppel* protein activates *knirps* expression but inhibits *hunchback* and *giant* expression. The *knirps* protein inhibits both *Krüppel* and *giant* expression. The giant protein inhibits the expression of *Krüppel* and *knirps*. In this way, gap genes regulate one another and form

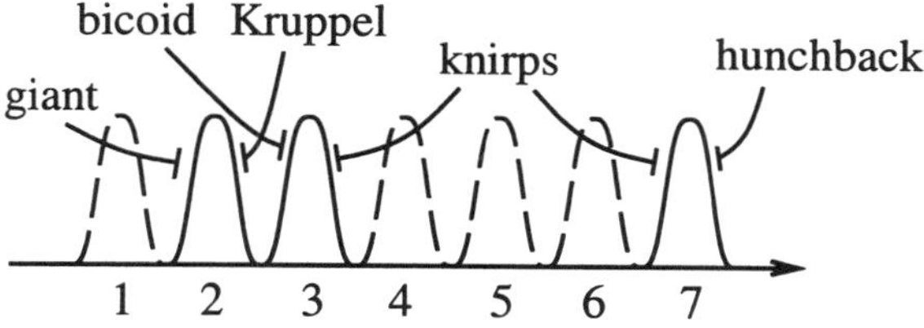

Figure 4: The regulation of *even-skipped* gene

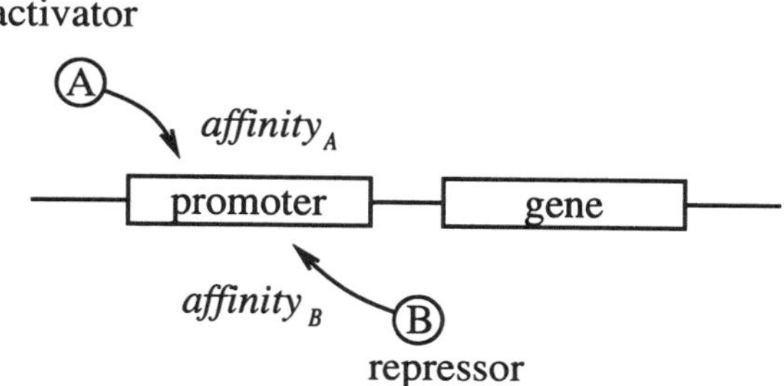

Figure 5: Transcription Model

various distributions of protein concentration along the anterior-posterior axis.

The seven vertical bands of the *even-skipped* protein are formed by the various concentration distributions of the maternal and gap proteins. Formerly, as the expression pattern looked like a wave, it was assumed that it was under the control of some chemical reaction-diffusion system. However, current biological efforts have shown that this is not the case for *even-skipped* expression. Each stripe of *even-skipped* expressions are regulated by unique regulational factors, as shown in Figure 4.

Stripe 2 of *even-skipped* has been quite extensively investigated and its regulation is well understood. The anterior border of stripe 2 is determined by the inhibition of the *giant* protein and its posterior border is determined by the inhibition of the *Krüppel* protein. Stripe 3 is refined by anterior *bicoid* inhibition and posterior *knirps* inhibition. Stripe 7 is refined by anterior *knirps* inhibition and posterior *hunchback* inhibition. The posterior border of stripe 7 is believed to be determined by another gene:*tailless*.

Modeling

In this paper, we have modeled *Drosophila* embryogenesis from fertilization to the 14th cleavage cycle. During these cycles, the embryogenesis involves the interaction of maternal genes, gap genes, and pair-rule genes. Table 1 shows the set of genes which have been modeled in current version of our simulator. Note that we do not include any pathways other than those known to exist from real biological data.

Class	Genes
Maternal Effect Genes	bicoid (bcd) nanos (nos) torso (tor)
Gap Genes	hunchback (hb) Krüppel (Kr) knirps (kni) giant (gt) tailless (tll) huckebein (hkb)
Pair-Rule Genes	even-skipped (eve)

Table 1: A list of genes implemented in the simulation

For a detailed simulation, the simulator needs to model the shape of the embryo, genetic processes, and the behavior of the gene products. Genetic processes include transcription and translation. The chief behavior of the products is diffusion.

Transcription

Gene transcription can be modeled by a stochastic process where activators and repressors compete for a binding site on the promoter of the target gene. As shown in figure 5, for example, when two proteins compete for one binding site, a simple way to approximate the probability that protein A can bind to the site can be described by the following formula:

$$P_A = \frac{U_A}{U_A + U_B + \beta_A} \tag{1}$$

In formula (1), U_A and U_B are protein A and B concentrations surrounding the target binding site, and the constant value β_A is introduced to adjust the probability as deemed appropriate. However, this approximation assumes that both binding affinities of protein A and B are equal. If the binding affinities are different from one another, formula (1) does not make sense. In that case, we have to extend the formula (1) to:

$$P_A = \frac{\alpha_A U_A}{\alpha_A U_A + \alpha_B U_B + \beta_A} \tag{2}$$

In Eq. (2), α_A and α_B are the binding affinity of the activator or repressor of protein A and B. In this paper, we consider that the probability of transcription is given by Eq. (2). In reality, the situation can be even more complex, and in the future we may extend this model even further.

Whether gene A is transcribed or not can be determined if the following inequality holds:

$$P_A > \text{Threshold}_A \tag{3}$$

The same threshold determines the expression of each gene. The amount of mRNA which is transcribed from

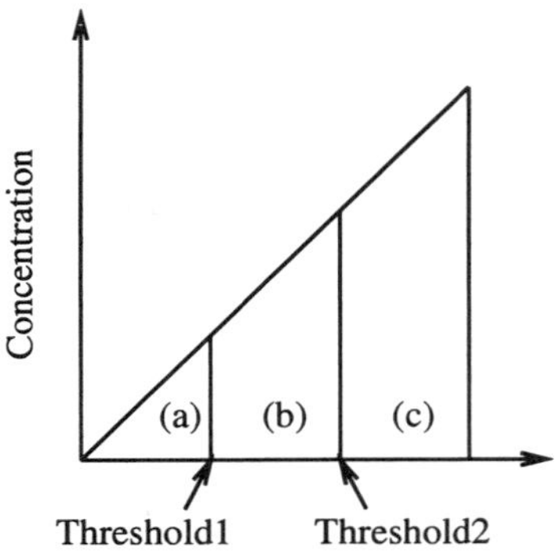

Figure 6: Two-threshold model

gene A is described as follows:

$$amount_A = \begin{cases} T_A & \text{if inequality (3) is true} \\ 0 & \text{otherwise} \end{cases} \quad (4)$$

In Eq. (4), T_A is a constant value representing the amount of mRNA which is transcribed at each step. However, this model can be used only in the case that activation occurs when the amount of activator is higher than some threshold level. For example, the *hunchback* protein acts as an activator or repressor under unusual conditions. In particular, *knirps* is activated only by low values of *hunchback*, while *Küppel* is activated only by medium levels of *hunchback*, but inhibited again by high levels. Also, *giant* is activated *only* by high or low levels of *hunchback*, (but not medium levels!). This case is modeled with two thresholds in our system. Figure 6 shows how the two-threshold model works. In Figure 6, the horizontal axis indicates the activation levels of thresholds and the vertical axis indicates the levels of concentration of protein, for both activator and repressor. This model can describe two opposing situations. Different concentrations (low, medium, high) can individually activate, inhibit, or not affect gene expression. Because this model is more flexible in various situations, we chose to implement it.

Translation

In the translational process, messenger RNA is translated into protein. Biologically, the process of translation is also regulated by "regulational factors" (other proteins). For example, the translation of the mRNA of the *hunchback* gene is inhibited by the *nanos* protein. Due to the lack of available data, however, we perform the translational process without regulatory inhibition except in the case of *hunchback* translation.

Embryo shape

We approximate the shape of *Drosophila*'s embryo with a cylindrical coordinate system, instead of the exact oval

(i) Original embryo shape

(ii) Abstracted embryo shape

Figure 7: Approximation of *Drosophila* embryo shape

shape, as shown in Figure 7. With such an approximation, when the distribution of proteins along the anterior-posterior axis is taken into account, the three dimensional embryo shape can be regarded as just a line; only the anterior-posterior distribution is considered. This model breaks down near the poles of the egg, and could be improved if more accuracy is needed in the simulation.

Diffusion

In the process of diffusion, proteins produced by the translation of genes diffuse within the embryo. During the first two hours or so, there are no partitions in the egg to prevent the proteins from diffusing freely. Because of the abstraction of the shape described above, the transition of the protein along the dorsal-ventral and lateral axes need not be calculated. Therefore, the diffusion can be described by a simple differential equation. For example, the diffusion of the protein of gene A is described as follows:

$$\frac{\partial U_A}{\partial t} = D_A \frac{\partial^2 U_A}{\partial x^2} \quad (5)$$

U_A : concentration of protein A
D_A : diffusion parameter

In Eq. (5), x denotes the position along the anterior-posterior axis and U_A describes the concentration of protein A at position x. The diffusion constant for the protein of gene A is D_A. For such a diffusion process, diffusion constants are individually determined for each gene product.

Behavior of components

During early embryogenesis, many components interact with one another to form seven stripe patterns of protein concentration within the egg. The interactions involve genes, mRNAs, and proteins. In the simulation, the behavior of the items must be considered.

- Protein production through transcription and translation process
- Diffusion of proteins
- Deletion of proteins

Deletion occurs when a protein breaks down or is removed through a process such as methylation. In summary, the behavior of the proteins are described by the following equation:

$$\frac{\partial U_i}{\partial t} = D_i \frac{\partial^2 U_i}{\partial x^2} + g \cdot U_i + f(\mathbf{U}) \quad (6)$$

U_i	:	concentration of protein i
x	:	position on axis
t	:	time
D	:	diffusion parameter
g	:	deletion parameter ($g = -0.2$)
f	:	protein production function
$\mathbf{U}$	:	concentration vector

Equation (6) is derived from (5) and involves diffusion, deletion, and production of the proteins. It is consistent with a model proposed by Reinitz and Sharp (1995).

Optimization

A number of parameters (protein diffusion constants, binding affinity, ratio of transcription, etc.) are optimized using a genetic algorithm. At each time step, the result of the simulation is compared with the desired pattern. The details of the optimization processes is described elsewhere.

Simulator

Outlines

Simulation cycle The simulation covers about two hours of *Drosophila* segmentation development, in which the genes interact with one another, mRNA and proteins are produced through the process of transcription and translation, and proteins diffuse throughout the embryo to form the striped patterns of the *even-skipped* gene product. In the current version of the simulator, only stripes 2, 3, and 7 of the *even-skipped* protein are implemented because the mechanisms of the other stripes remain unknown.

The simulation has four stages per run, which are shown in table 2. At the first stage of the simulation, maternal mRNA of *bicoid* and *nanos* genes is localized at the anterior pole and posterior pole of the embryo. Their amounts are predetermined. At the second stage, mRNAs of maternal genes start to be translated, respectively, into proteins and diffuse within the embryo. At the beginning of the third stage, the downstream genes such as gap and pair-rule genes begin to be transcribed into mRNA, which is translated into proteins. These proteins also diffuse in the embryo and form their own gradients of protein concentration. Finally, the fitness of the resultant protein distribution is determined by comparing it to the ideal "wild-type" distribution.

Stage	Operation
Stage 1	Localization of maternal mRNAs
Stage 2	Start translations
Stage 3	Gap and pair-rule gene start to be operated
Stage 4	Fitness evaluation

Table 2: A chart of simulation flow

The experiment has two steps:

1. Determination of a parameter set by using genetic algorithm optimizing fitness compared to the *wild-type* embryo
2. Simulation for the mutants by adjusting the optimized parameter set obtained from step 1

Mutant analysis We only generate mutants through major changes in gene interaction, not subtle changes to parameter settings. The simulator can perform the usual kinds of mutant analysis: loss-of-function knock out, over-expression of a gene product, and site-directed mutagenesis. The loss-of-function knock out experiments can be replicated by simply disabling the transcription of a target gene through the simulation. In the over-expression experiment, the amount of the product transcribed from the target gene is artificially increased. This method can be replicated by increasing a parameter which determines the amount transcribed in one time step. Site-directed mutagenesis is where a specific binding site on the promoter of the target gene is altered, to disable the activator or the repressor to bind to it.

Simulator interface

A whole screen capture of the simulator interface is shown in Figure 8. There are three different kinds of windows on the screen. At the top of the screen is the protein concentration graph along the anterior-posterior axis of the egg. In the middle of the screen, there are embryo shaped maps for each gene product, which show the image of the staining patterns of respective proteins. Below these windows, there is a control panel for all of the operations of the simulator.

The simulator also has other control panels which can enable or disable gene transcription, the diffusion constants for the respective proteins, and assign values to the strength of transcription, the levels of threshold which determine the gene transcription sensitivity, and the binding affinities between any two genes. While the simulation is running, all of the parameters can be changed quickly to see the effect of such a change.

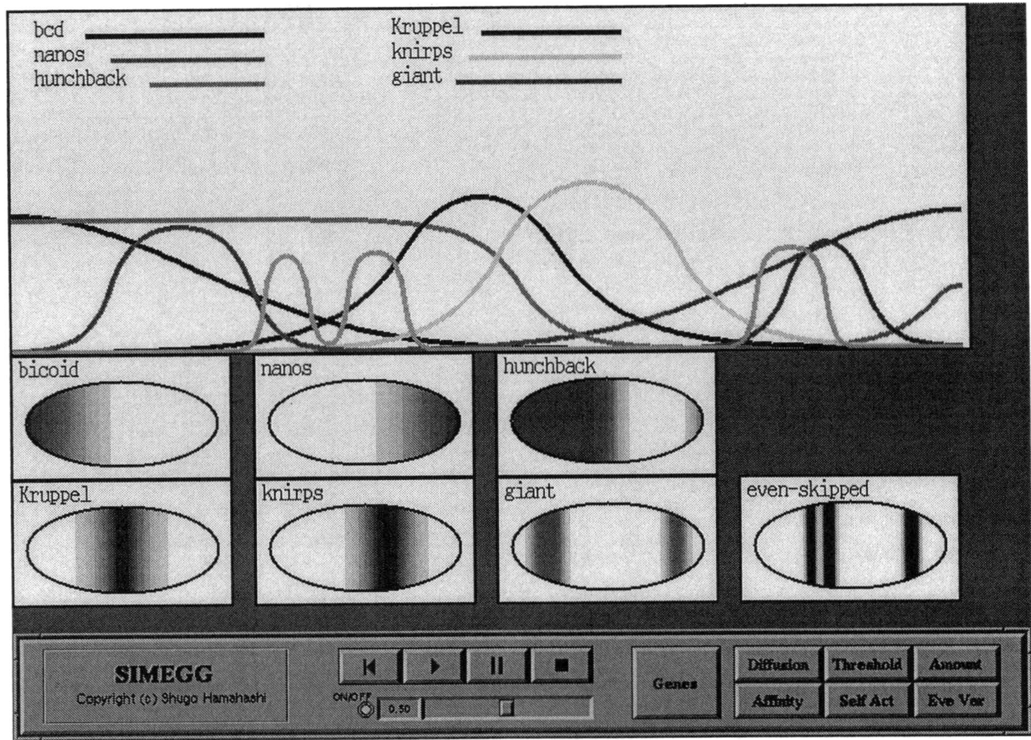

Figure 8: Screen capture

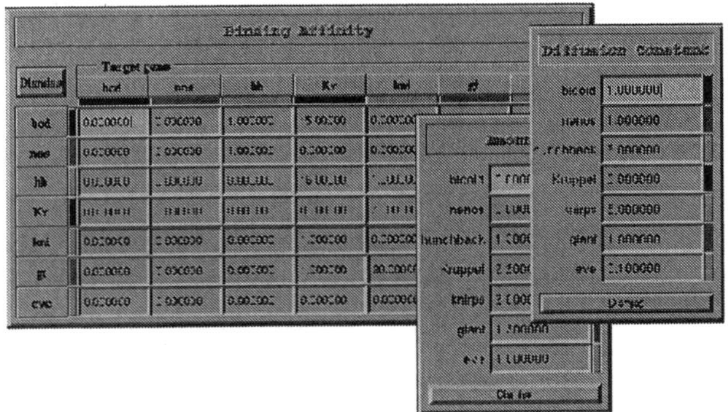

Figure 9: Interfaces

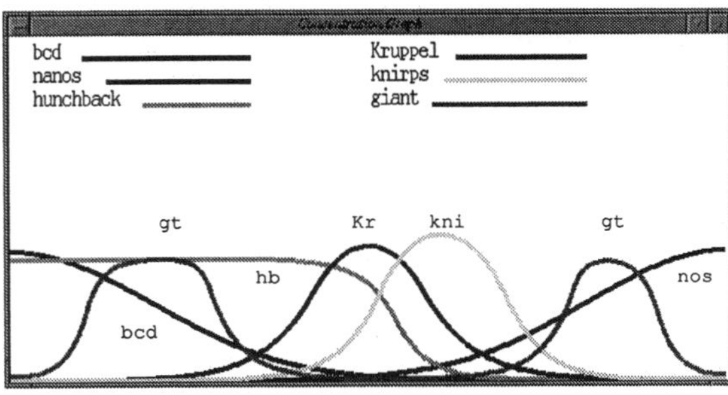

Figure 10: Simulated expression patterns of gap genes

Result

At the early stages of the simulation, the embryo shows the non-characteristic mixture of proteins along the anterior-posterior axis except the two gradients of the maternal proteins from *bicoid* mRNA and *nanos* mRNA. They are localized at the anterior and posterior pole at the beginning of the simulation. As the simulation proceeds, the gap proteins form unique gradients through their interaction with one another. The formation of gap proteins refines the expression bands of the *even-skipped* protein.

We have examined various situations in embryogenesis. For example, we artificially changed the transcription amount of a target gene. This simulation corresponds to the over-expression experiments in biology. In addition, we have tested loss-of-function knock-out mutation simulations and site-directed mutagenesis simulations. Later in this paper, we report some of the results of simulations such as wild-type embryo and loss-of-function mutants of *giant*– (gt–). Also, we record the temporal dynamics of the gap gene expression patterns during their development.

Wild-type

Figure 10 shows the simulated expression patterns of gap genes for the wild-type embryo. The figure is drawn with the left side as the anterior pole and the right side as the posterior pole of the egg along the horizontal axis. The vertical axis indicates the level of concentration of proteins.

Figure 11 shows the embryo images for embryo-shaped concentration maps for both the result of simulation and the actual staining pictures of the wild-type embryo. These are the pictures of the final stages of the wild-type simulation. The left column in Figure 11 shows the simulated result and the right column shows the actual staining pattern of the specific protein of the wild-type embryo.

Comparing the result images the with actual staining patterns, each expression pattern has been reproduced consistent with the actual one.

Loss-of-function mutants

The result of a simulation of the loss-of-function mutation of *giant* is shown in Figure 12. In this embryo, the transcription of *giant* is strictly cut off, while the other properties of the simulation are preserved from the wild-type simulation. Therefore no *giant* protein is in the egg. As the *giant* protein determines the anterior border of the *even-skipped* stripe 2 by is inhibition, without *giant* protein, *even-skipped* is broadly expressed in the anterior region. Because *giant* is not the regulational factor for stripes 3 and 7, they do not suffer the effects from the lack of *giant* protein, which is described as "gt–". The result of the simulation of gt– is quite consistent with the actual experimental data.

If the *knirps* protein does not exist in the middle of the egg, (it works as the inhibitor against the posterior border of stripe 3 and the anterior border of stripe 7 of the *even-skipped* gene), the *even-skipped* protein can express broadly in the region between stripes 3 and 7 while stripe 2 is expressed normally at the anterior region of the egg.

Figure 14 shows the expression patterns of the *Krüppel* and *giant* proteins in an embryo with a loss-of-function mutation of the *bicoid* gene. The *Krüppel* protein occupies the anterior region, inhibiting the transcription of the *giant* gene, while in the posterior region of the egg the *giant* protein is strongly expressed.

Compared with the actual staining patterns of biological experiments, Figures 13 and 14 are also highly consistent with the biological data. In this manner, we have tried various mutants of *Drosophila* and confirmed the expression patterns for the mutants respectively.

Discussion

Expression dynamics

We recorded a series of temporal dynamics of gene expression from the beginning of the simulation to the final stage where the transitions of the expression are converged. In series (i), the *knirps* and *giant* protein competitively express at the posterior half of the egg, as shown in the second and third pictures of Figure 15. Series (ii) finished similarly to series (i) but the path taken there is quite different. At the early stage of the simulation, the *giant* protein increased because of inhibition from the *knirps* protein. Then, *giant* begins to appear near the posterior pole of the egg. As the expression of *giant* protein becomes wider, it pushes the expression of the *knirps* gene toward the anterior side. The difference is that the binding affinity in the series (i) is only $10^{-6}\%$ larger than that in the series (ii). Even though this difference is very small, the expression processes have changed dramatically.

Verification of the simulator

In this paper, we have reported simulation results of the wild-type and the loss-of-function mutant of the *giant* gene. In fact, the simulator can examine the gene expression of many gene mutants. Because of a lack of real biological data, our comparisons are limited at this time. This happens a lot in biology. We hope that much more biological data will improve our simulation accuracy and verify the correctness of our simulator parameters.

Additionally, we hope to use the simulator and GAs or other global search methodologies to predict (currently unknown) mechanisms behind known biological results. For example, the unknown mechanisms behind stripes 1, 4, 5, and 6 of the *even-skipped* protein, the posterior band of the *hunchback* expression, etc., are exciting areas for prediction. We think that simulated computational biology may be able to predict a variety of unknown mechanisms behind *Drosophila* development.

Lastly, we are careful not to reject out-of-hand the inconsistencies between some simulator results and actual experimental data. We think many of these inconsistencies are due to oversimplifications in our simulator model. For example, consider one inconsistency we found in the loss-of-function mutant arising from the lack of the *Krüppel* gene. Our initial explanation was simply simulation inaccuracy. However, we now think a more plausible explanation is *binding competition.* Binding competition occurs where more than two regulational factors competitively bind to the same binding site or

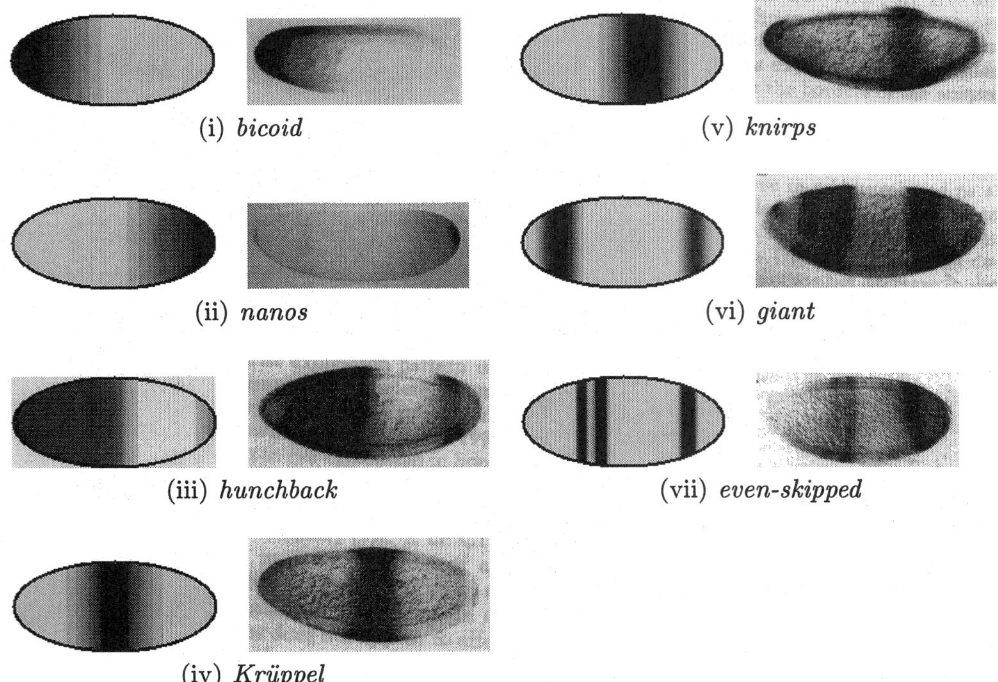

Figure 11: Pictures of a wild-type simulation. The picture of the actual staining patterns of (i) is from (Curtis et al. 1995), (ii) is from (Driever and Nüsslein-Volhard 1988), (iii)—(vi) are from (Binari and Perrimon 1994), and (vii) is from (Goto et al., 1989).

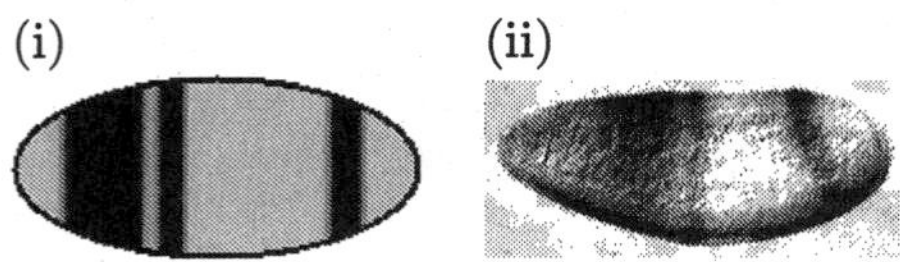

Figure 12: Expression patterns of *even-skipped* for gt− mutant. The actual staining pattern on the right side is from (Goto et al., 1989).

Figure 13: Expression patterns of *even-skipped* in kni− embryo

to neighboring sites which both can locally determine whether a target gene is activated or not. We believe that inconsistencies may be arising between the simulator and biological data because the simulator does not model binding competition at all; however, binding competition is believed to exist in real organisms. As the simulator improves, we hope to add more details to our model to eliminate such inconsistencies.

When the *knirps* transcription is prevented, the expression of the *even-skipped* has drastically changed in formation, as shown in Figure 13.

Figure 15 shows two different series of temporal dynamics. Both of the simulations had the same parameter set, except for the binding affinity of the *giant* protein toward the site of the *knirps* promoter.

Conclusion

Our simulator successfully reproduced gene expression patterns of *Drosophila* embryogenesis by comparing them with actual expression patterns. We have shown that current biological knowledge is sufficient to reproduce the gene expression patterns of early segmentation during wild-type *Drosophila* development. However, because actual experimental data about mutants and the transition of gene expressions during the development of *Drosophila* are still not complete, currently we can not make completely convincing arguments about mutants or the temporal dynamics of gene expression patterns. On the other hand, the work reported in this paper suggests that the prediction of unknown mechanisms in biology might be possible by using such a simulator. We have confirmed that computational biology can be a useful experimental tool in biological studies.

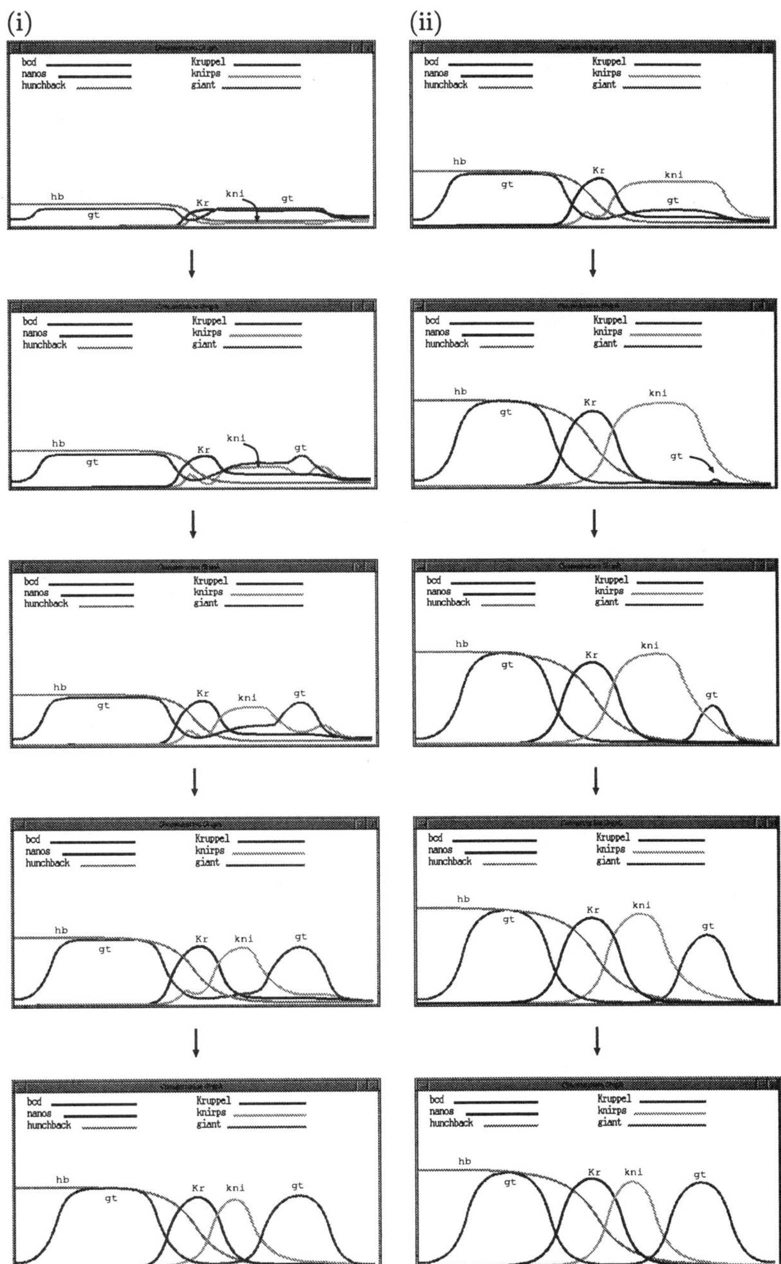

Figure 15: Temporal Dynamics of Gene Expression

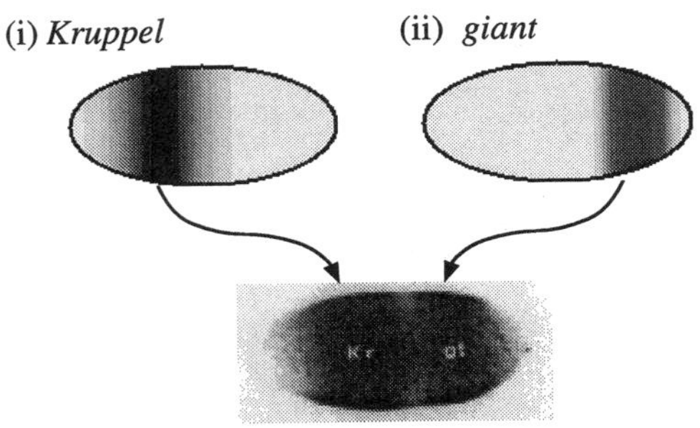

Figure 14: Expression patterns of *Krüppel* and *giant* in an embryo where *bicoid* is knocked out. Pictures (i) and (ii) are the result of a simulation while (iii) is an actual staining pattern from (Struhl et al. 1992). In (iii), the anterior side of expressions shows the *Krüppel* protein and the other side of the expression shows the *giant* protein.

Acknowledgment

This research was carried out under the Virtual *Drosophila* Project at Sony Computer Science Laboratory Inc. We would like to express our sincere thanks to Dr. Mario Tokoro of Keio University for his useful advice. We also want to extend our sincere gratitude to Sean Luke for his demi-godlike power in correcting our English.

References

Arita, M. 1995. Simfly. Master's thesis, University of Tokyo.

Curtis, D., J. Apfeld and R. Lehmann. 1995. *nanos* is an evolutionarily conserved organizer of anterio-posterior polarity. *Development* 121: 1899–1910.

Driever, W. and C. Nüsslein-Volhard. 1988. A gradient of *bicoid* protein in drosophila embryos. *Cell* 54: 83–93.

Gilbert, S. F. 1994. *Developmental Biology*, Chapter 15. Sinauer Associates Inc., fourth edition.

Goto, T., P. Macdonald and T. Maniatis. 1989. Early and late periodic patterns of *even-skipped* expression are controlled by distinct regulatory elements that respond to different spatial cues. *Cell* 57: 413–422.

Kitano, H., S. Hamahashi, J. Kitazawa, K. Takao, and S. Imai. 1997. Virtual Biology Laboratories: A New Approach of Computational Biology. In *Proceedings of Fourth European Conference on Artificial Life*, edited by P. Husbands and I. Harvey. Cambridge, MA: MIT Press, p. 274–283.

Hunding, A., S. A. Kauffman, and B. C. Goodwin. 1990. Drosophila segmentation: Supercomputer simulation of prepattern hierarchy. *J. theor. Biol.* 145: 369–384.

Lawrence, P. A. 1992. *The Making of a Fly*. Blackwell Science.

Reinitz, J. and D. H. Sharp. 1995. Mechanism of *eve* stripe formation. *Mechanisms of Development* 49: 133–158.

Struhl, G., P. Johnston, and P. A. Lawrence. 1992. Control of drosophila body pattern by the hunchback morphogen gradient. *Cell* 69: 237–249.

Turing, A. M. 1952. The chemical basis of morphogenesis. *Philos. Trans. R. Soc. Lond.* B 237: 37–72.

Probing the Dynamics of Cell Differentiation in a Model of *Drosophila* Neurogenesis

George Marnellos
Sloan Center for Theoretical Neurobiology,
The Salk Institute, La Jolla, CA 92037, USA

Eric Mjolsness
Machine Learning Systems Group,
Jet Propulsion Laboratory,
Pasadena, CA 91109, USA

Abstract

We have formulated a computational model of *Drosophila* early neurogenesis, the process by which neuroblasts and sensory organ precursor (SOP) cells differentiate from within proneural clusters of cells. The model includes intracellular gene regulatory interactions as well as lateral cell-cell signalling. It makes predictions about how the interplay of factors like proneural cluster shape and size, gene expression levels, and strength of cell-cell signalling determines the timing and position of appearance of neuroblasts and SOP cells; and about the robustness of this process and the effects of gene product level perturbations on cell differentiation.

Introduction

One of the very early steps in neural development is the generation of neuronal precursor cells in appropriate numbers and their precise positioning, which to a large extent determines the identity of their progeny. In *Drosophila*, neuroblasts and sensory organ precursor (SOP) cells differentiate from epithelia to give rise to the central nervous system in the fly embryo and to epidermal sensory organs in the peripheral nervous system of the adult fly, respectively. Neuroblasts are precursor cells that divide to form neurons and glia; they segregate from the ventral neuroectoderm of the embryo in a regular segmental pattern (Bate 1976). SOPs appear at stereotypical positions on imaginal discs (which are primordia giving rise to appendages like wings, legs, eyes and antennae) during late larval and early pupal stages and divide to produce a neuron and three other cells that form *Drosophila*'s sensory organs, like the bristles on its thorax (Hartenstein & Posakony 1989).

The activities of two main sets of genes working in opposite directions are thought to underlie this differentiation process: one promoting neural development and the other preventing it and favoring epidermal development. Cell-cell signalling is believed to be an essential part of this specification of cell fate and thus *Drosophila* neurogenesis is an example of many such related processes of cell differentiation in epithelia both in invertebrate and vertebrate organisms — see recent reviews (Campuzano & Modollel 1992; Muskavitch 1994; Artavanis-Tsakonas, Matsuno, & Fortini 1995).

More specifically, neuroblasts and SOPs differentiate from clusters of apparently equivalent cells which at some stage all have the potential to adopt the neural fate (Stern 1954), as ablation studies have shown (Doe & Goodman 1985a; 1985b). These cell clusters express genes of the *achaete-scute* complex, so called *proneural* genes, which all encode transcription activators and confer to cluster cells the potential to adopt the neural fate (Romani *et al.* 1989; Cubas *et al.* 1991; Skeath & Carroll 1991; 1992); the clusters are therefore called proneural clusters (see Fig. 1).

The other set of genes involved in neurogenesis includes a number of genes also encoding nuclear proteins, for instance genes of the *Enhancer-of-split* (*E(spl)*) complex and *hairy*, as well as other genes for membrane and cytoplasmic proteins; all these tend to suppress neurogenesis and promote epidermal development. In this paper we refer to this set of genes as *epithelial* genes — in the literature they are called "neurogenic" genes, because loss-of-function mutations of these genes lead to overproduction of neurons (Poulson 1940; Lehmann *et al.* 1983; Skeath & Carroll 1992), but we have avoided this term as it might create confusion with proneural genes.

Expression of proneural genes in embryonic neuroectoderm and imaginal disc clusters eventually gets restricted to a single cell per cluster, in the case of the neuroectoderm, or very few cells per cluster, in the case of imaginal discs (clusters in the discs are typically larger than those in the neuroectoderm); in these cells, the future neuroblasts or SOPs, proneural expression increases, whereas in the remaining cluster cells it ceases and those cells become epidermal (Cubas *et al.* 1991; Martin-Bermudo *et al.* 1991; Skeath & Carroll 1991; 1992); the whole process is referred to as "cluster resolution". Cluster resolution and the singling out of neural precursors from within proneural clusters is brought

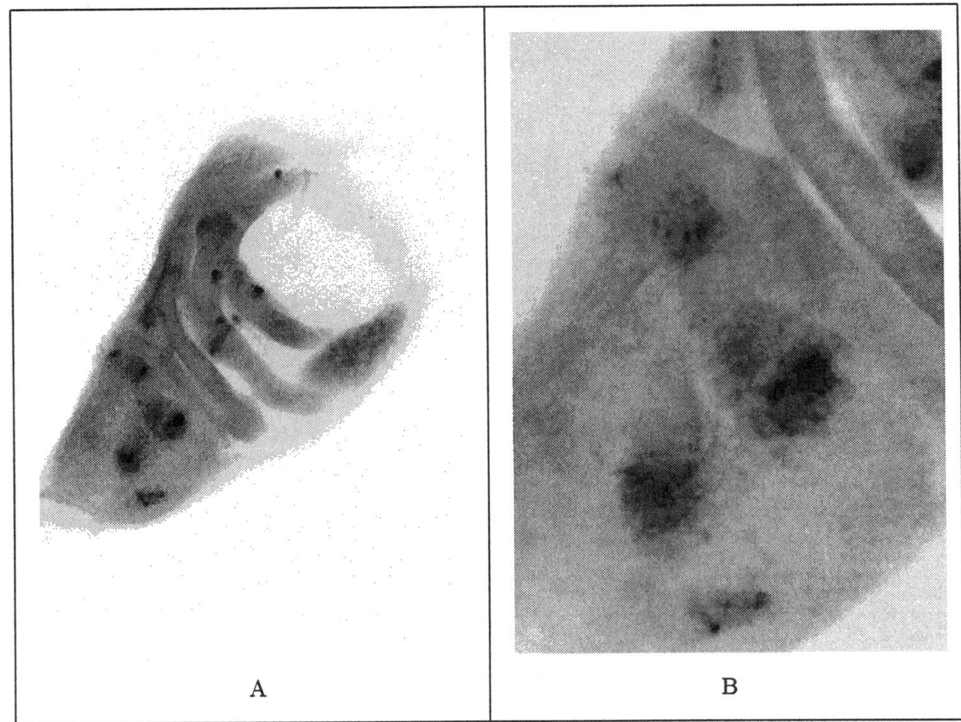

Figure 1: (A) Proneural gene expression in clusters in a *Drosophila* wing disc (the appendage of the fly larva that gives rise to the wing and the back of the adult). The *lacZ* reporter indicates *achaete* expression (*achaete* is one of the proneural genes). (B) Detail of (A), note cluster on lower left that has not yet resolved; other clusters appear to be at a more advanced stage of resolution. We have used the enhancer-trap line A1-1, which expresses the reporter *lacZ* gene under the influence of *cis*-elements in the promoter of *achaete* (van Doren *et al.* 1992); we have stained with anti β-gal antibody and secondary fluorescent antibody; images were obtained with a Bio-Rad MRC1000UV confocal microscope and processed with the NIH-Image program.

about by inhibitory lateral signalling between adjacent cells, through which the neural fate is promoted in the future neuroblasts and SOPs and suppressed in other cells (Wigglesworth 1940; Stern 1954; Doe & Goodman 1985a; 1985b). The lateral signal is transmitted by the product of *Delta* which is a ligand of the receptor encoded by *Notch* (Fehon *et al.* 1990; Heitzler & Simpson 1991; Struhl, Fitzgerald, & Greenwald 1993). The signal is relayed from Notch to epithelial genes through a protein that has been shown to directly activate *E(spl)* transcription (Fortini & Artavanis-Tsakonas 1994; Jarriault *et al.* 1995; Bailey & Posakony 1995)

Despite the amount of experimental data that have been gathered, several features of the neural fate determination process remain unexplained. A precise characterization of the function of lateral signalling is still lacking. Some researchers have described the singling out of neural precursors from equivalence groups as a process in which one of the cells in the group receives an initial push to become a neural precursor, in an unspecified, perhaps stochastic, manner, and this cell then extinguishes the neural potential in the other cells of the proneural cluster through "lateral inhibition" (Wigglesworth 1940; Stern 1954), possibly amplifying its own inhibitory power and weakening that of its neighbors through a feedback mechanism (Heitzler & Simpson 1991). Other researchers have favored a scheme of "mutual inhibition", in which all cells in a proneural cluster, including the future neural precursor, are subject to inhibition by other cells in the cluster, but the future precursor has additional means to shield itself from inhibition (Goriely *et al.* 1991; Muskavitch 1994; Bang, Bailey, & Posakony 1995). There are also questions about how important interactions of range longer than that of lateral signalling are: it is not clear, for instance, how crucial diffusible factors are for the resolution of proneural clusters.

Dynamical aspects of cluster resolution are poorly understood. It is not known, for example, whether and how the shape and size of proneural clusters can determine how cluster resolution proceeds: although there have been some observations regarding shapes of clusters, and descriptions of subsets of cells (often centrally located) in the clusters from which future neural precursors are more likely to emerge (Goriely *et al.* 1991; Cubas *et al.* 1991) as well as some work on the temporal sequence of neural precursor emergence (Huang, Dambly-Chaudière, & Ghysen 1991), there has been no systematic study of how shape or size of clusters might affect the position and timing of neural precursor emergence.

In order to address questions like these and investigate the interplay between proneural and epithelial genes and the genes that mediate cell-cell signalling, we have constructed a model which is presented below; it is an extension of a model that was first described in Marnellos (1997).

Model

In our model, cells are represented as overlapping circles in a 2-dimensional hexagonal lattice; the extent of overlap determines the strength of interaction between neighboring cells (see Fig. 2). Cells in the model express a small number of genes corresponding to genes that are involved in neuroblast and SOP differentiation. In the work presented here we have used networks with four genes (one corresponding to the proneural group, another for the epithelial group and two for the ligand and receptor, respectively, mediating cell-cell signalling). The model has been based on a framework introduced in Mjolsness *et al.* (1991) to simulate developmental processes through the use of regulatory gene networks; a framework very similar to this in scope and structure, but with some differences in how state changes in cells are represented, has also been proposed by Fleischer and Barr (Fleischer & Barr 1994; Fleischer 1995).

Genes interact as nodes in recurrent neural nets: A gene a sums inputs from genes in the same cell or in neighboring cells at time t according to the following equation

$$u_a(t) = \sum_b T_{ab} v_b(t) \tag{1}$$

where T is the matrix of gene interactions and $v_b(t)$ gene product concentrations within the cell; the T matrix has the structure depicted in the table below; columns in this table are for input genes and rows for genes affected (empty boxes signify zero interaction strength. i.e. no interaction):

Intracellular Interactions				
	Proneural	Epithelial	Receptor	Ligand
Proneural	◆	◆		
Epithelial	◆	◆		
Receptor	◆	◆		
Ligand	◆	◆		

This table shows that we have allowed only proneural and epithelial gene products to directly regulate the expression of other genes (themselves included), since these two genes correspond to transcription factors in the real biological system.

Concentration $v_a(t)$ of the product of gene a then changes according to

$$\frac{dv_a}{dt} = R_a g(u_a(t) + h_a) - \lambda_a v_a(t) \tag{2}$$

where $u_a(t)$ is the linear sum of Eq. 1, g a sigmoid function, R_a the rate of production of gene a's product, h_a the threshold of activation of gene a and λ_a the rate of decay of gene a product. We integrate these differential equations using Euler's method (we use 150 time steps).

We have modeled lateral interactions between cells by the binding of ligand to the receptor in the neighboring cell and subsequent regulation of the epithelial gene by the active ligand-receptor complex — this corresponds to the signal relayed from activated Notch receptor to epithelial gene *E(spl)*, as was mentioned in the Introduction. In more detail, the ligand-receptor reaction is taken to be of the following form:

$$L + R \leftrightarrows L \circ R \tag{3}$$

where L is ligand (on one cell), R receptor (on a neighboring cell) and $L \circ R$ the active receptor-ligand complex; the rate of the reaction to the right is k_1 and to the left k_2. If v_L is ligand concentration, v_R receptor concentration and $[L \circ R]$ concentration of the receptor-ligand active complex, we have that

$$\frac{d[L \circ R]}{dt} = k_1 v_L v_R - k_2 [L \circ R] \tag{4}$$

$$\frac{dv_L}{dt} = \frac{dv_R}{dt} = -k_1 v_L v_R + k_2 [L \circ R]. \tag{5}$$

This reaction is assumed to take place at a much faster timescale than gene expression and to have reached a steady state before influencing gene expression. From Eqs. 4 and 5, at this steady state we have

$$[L \circ R] = k v_L v_R \tag{6}$$

where $k = \frac{k_1}{k_2}$. Thus the epithelial gene in a cell receives input from receptor-ligand complexes activated by ligand in the six surrounding cells (the lattice is hexagonal); this can be represented as an extra term $\hat{u}_E$ that is added to u_E (which is the sum of inputs u for the epithelial gene, see Eq. 1) before Eq. 2 is calculated

$$\hat{u}_E = \sum_{i \in N} \Lambda^i \hat{T}_E [L \circ R]^i \tag{7}$$

where N is the set of six surrounding cells, Λ^i a factor depending on the overlap of the cell with neighboring cell i (as measured for instance by the common chord of the two circles), $\hat{T}_E$ the strength of the action of the receptor-ligand complex on the epithelial gene (k of Eq. 6 has been included in $\hat{T}_E$), and finally $[L \circ R]^i$ is the concentration of receptor-ligand complex due to ligand on cell i. Because of Eq. 6, we can write this as

$$\hat{u}_E = \sum_{i \in N} \Lambda^i \hat{T}_E v_L^i v_R \qquad (8)$$

where v_L^i is ligand concentration in neighboring cell i.

We optimize on gene interaction strengths, i.e. $\hat{T}_E$ of Eq. 7 and the eight T's of Eq. 1 (the other parameters in the equations above are kept constant) in order to fit gene expression patterns described in the literature; the cost function optimized is

$$E = \sum_{cells, genes, times} (v^i_{aMODEL}(t) - v^i_{aDATA}(t))^2, \qquad (9)$$

which is the squared difference between gene product concentrations in the model and those in the dataset, summed over all cells and over all gene products and times for which data is available. We have used a stochastic algorithm, simulated annealing, for this optimization. For more details on the model and the optimization method used see Marnellos (1997).

Simulation Results

Design of optimization and test runs. The gene expression datasets we optimize on, the *training* datasets, are adapted from schematic results described in the experimental literature (Cubas *et al.* 1991; Skeath & Carroll 1992; Jennings *et al.* 1994); they specify the initial pattern of concentrations of gene products (i.e. the proneural clusters), the desired intermediate pattern, and the desired final pattern when the proneural clusters have resolved to single cells expressing the proneural gene at high levels (see Fig. 2); it is left to the optimization to find the right model parameters so that the system develops from the initial state through the intermediate one to the desired final one. The initial concentrations of receptor and ligand are uniform for all cells and their subsequent concentrations are not constrained by the dataset (in this respect, they are comparable to hidden units in neural nets).

All cells in a proneural cluster have initially the same gene expression levels. The size and cluster arrangement of the training datasets do not have any particular biological significance; the datasets have been designed in such a way as to keep the number of cells low while including as many clusters as possible, since optimization is very expensive computationally and so optimization runs on datasets with more cells than we have used would be impractical. We have used torus topology in our runs, although this does not appear to be a crucial factor in the results described here.

Robustness of solutions. We have tried to limit the number of parameters we optimize on (as was mentioned above, we optimize only on gene interaction strengths), in order to avoid overfitting our rather small datasets. The optimization procedure used (simulated annealing) has produced very good and consistent fits to the training datasets. For instance, out of the eight (8) good solutions obtained for the dataset in Fig. 2, six were very similar in their parameter values (same signs, similar orders of magnitude); so all these solutions probably come from the same optimum of the cost function, which may be one of very few large optima, or even the global optimum. Also, successful optimization runs have yielded solutions that not only perform well on the training dataset shown in Fig. 2 (see top row of Fig. 3) but also work for other datasets with clusters like those in the training dataset but with greater numbers of such clusters in various spatial arrangements (data not shown). This indicates that optimization does not just find parameter values that only work for the specific size and cluster arrangement of the training dataset, but rather produces solutions incorporating "rules" for cluster resolution.

In order to further evaluate these solutions and determine how robust they are and what they can tell us about the biological system under consideration, we have also run these solutions with different initial conditions, changes of solution parameter values, perturbations of gene expression during a run, as well as on *test* datasets containing novel, bigger or smaller, proneural clusters.

In Fig. 3, for instance, we have the same optimization solution parameters in both rows, but in the run of the top row initial concentrations of proneural and epithelial gene products are identical for all cells in a cluster, while in the bottom row initial proneural concentrations vary and differ between cells by about 10-15%. Despite this and despite the fact that, in this particular example, the future neural precursors start out with lower proneural concentrations than other cluster cells (even the lowest in the cluster), the pattern of cluster resolution remains identical as the end result shows (compare right panels of top and bottom rows of Fig. 3). So the optimization solutions are robust to small changes in initial conditions. Such robustness is a feature that a biological system would need during development.

Test datasets specify only initial concentrations and contain many more cells than training ones (since we do not optimize on them). An example appears in Fig. 4: it contains several clusters of various shapes and sizes, both smaller (4-cell clusters) and bigger (cluster in top right

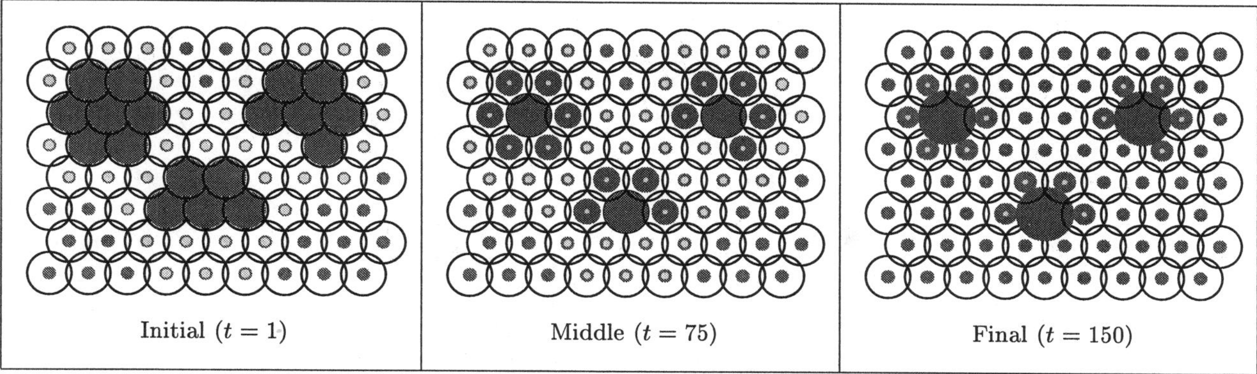

Figure 2: Cells are modeled as circles on a hexagonal lattice. Gene expression is represented by disks, proneural expression in brown, epithelial in green, and where the two overlap in yellow-green (dark, medium and light gray, respectively, in black-and-white); disk radius is proportional to level of expression. This figure shows the training dataset: on the left, the initial concentrations of the gene products — there is only proneural gene expression in three symmetrical clusters; in the middle, the desired intermediate pattern of expression; on the right, the desired final pattern of gene expression — proneural expression is retained only in the central cell of each cluster, the future neuroblast or SOP, whereas all other cells express the epithelial gene. Times (t) indicate the points in the run when the desired expression pattern is compared with the actual one (see Eq. 9); at $t = 1$ there is of course only initialization and no comparison. Initial concentrations of ligand and receptor are not shown.

corner of panels in Fig. 4) than in the training dataset of Fig. 2. The test datasets could in principle have been used as training datasets, if it were not for the practical considerations mentioned above.

The optimization solution presented in Fig. 3 works well on the dataset of Fig. 4 too and resolves almost all clusters apart from the small, 4-cell ones; this is something we have observed in previous work with a model of similar structure to the one presented here and similar optimization procedures (Marnellos 1997; Marnellos & Mjolsness 1998): it is probably due to the fact that 4-cell clusters do not have a cell that is much more encircled than the others (as 5,6 and 7-cell of Fig. 4 do), but all cells are almost equally exposed. The optimization solution also resolves the big cluster in Fig. 4, for which it was not optimized; this is another aspect of the robustness of the solution.

Changes in initial proneural concentrations, as in the bottom row of Fig. 3, can be also studied in the dataset of Fig. 4 and usually do not alter the final outcome in the resolution of the big cluster, but in rare cases the big cluster does not resolve to a single cell but to two or three cells. This is consistent with experimental observations (Huang, Dambly-Chaudière, & Ghysen 1991) and provides an illustration of the interplay between position in cluster and level of proneural expression in determining whether a cell becomes a neural precursor or not.

A feature of our simulations that becomes apparent in Fig. 4 is that proneural expression in differentiated neural precursors decreases with time after they have been selected (see last panel, $t = 256$, in Fig. 4). This does not mean that the model diverges from biological observations at this point, but is simply a result of the fact that our model was not meant to deal with what happens after clusters resolve; in any case, in the actual biological system, neural precursors do not stay around expressing high levels of proneural proteins either, but, soon after they differentiate, they divide to give rise to neurons and glia and other cell types (Doe & Goodman 1985a; Hartenstein & Posakony 1989).

Dynamics of cluster resolution The parameters of the simulation in Fig. 4 are identical to those of the runs in Fig. 3, apart from one: the strength of lateral interactions through the receptor-ligand complex, i.e. $\hat{T}_E$ of Eqs. 7 and 8. Since lateral interactions are crucial for cluster resolution, we have varied their strength to see the effects on the dynamics of the whole process. In Fig. 4 the value of $\hat{T}_E$ is 25% higher than in Fig. 3; the stronger lateral interaction makes cluster resolution faster, as can be observed, for instance, when comparing the stage of resolution at $t = 76$ of the symmetrical, 7-cell clusters in Figs. 3 and 4: resolution has clearly progressed more in clusters of Fig. 4. The effect is much more pronounced for the big cluster of Fig. 4, which takes about 200 timesteps longer to resolve when lateral interaction strengths are 20-30% lower (not shown). At even higher values of $\hat{T}_E$, clusters start to fail to resolve and proneural expression is extinguished (not shown). When $\hat{T}_E = 0$, i.e. when lateral interactions are abolished, clusters do not resolve but all cells in them retain proneural gene expression. This parallels the effect of the neurogenic mutations in the real biological system; these mutations disrupt lateral communication between cells

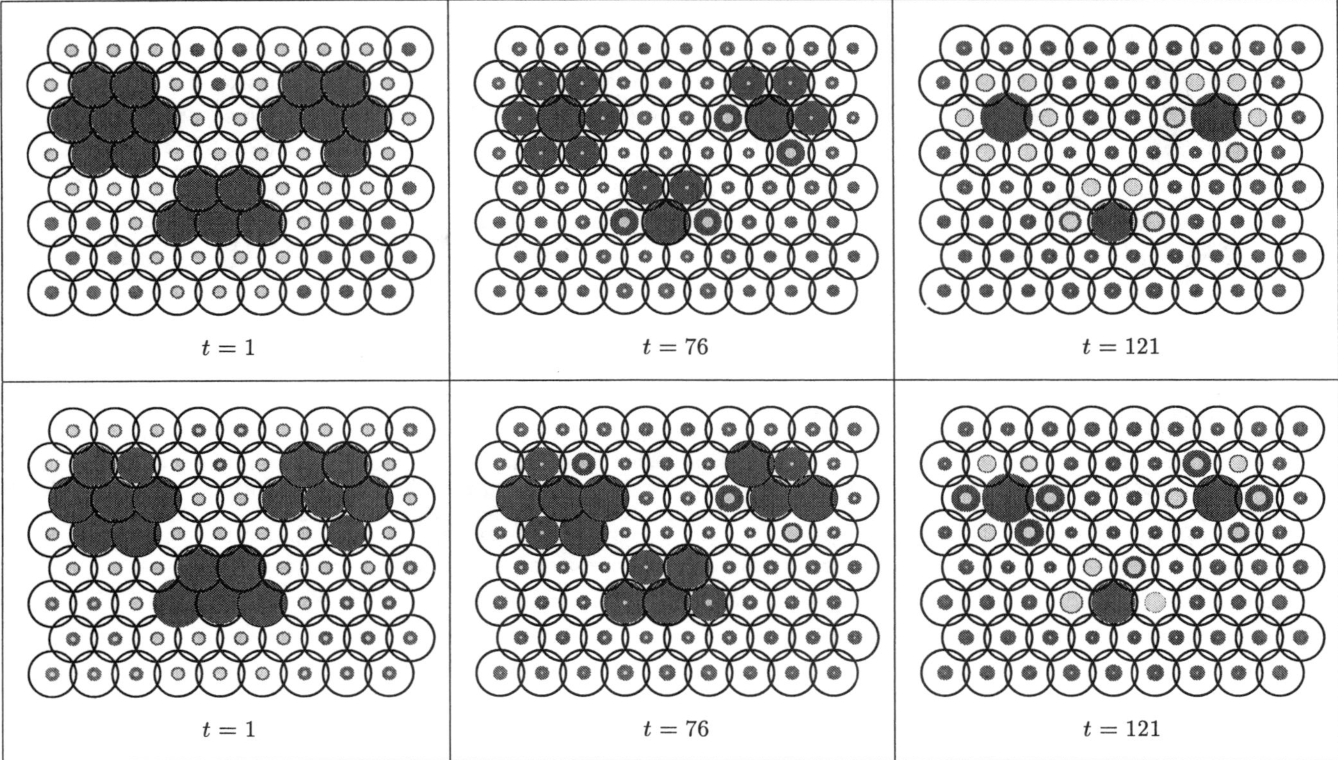

Figure 3: Computer simulation of neural precursor differentiation with parameter values in the model derived by optimization on the dataset of Fig. 2. From left to right, different time frames of the evolution of gene product concentrations. Top row: run with identical initial gene product concentrations for all cells in each proneural cluster. Bottom row: initial proneural concentrations vary by about 10-15% between cells in each cluster. In both runs the clusters resolve in the same way, as the comparison of the two panels at $t = 121$ shows (the only difference being that in the bottom run the clusters take slightly longer to resolve). This illustrates the robustness of cluster resolution to small changes in initial gene expression levels in proneural clusters. Conventions as in Fig. 2.

and lead to overproduction of neurons (Poulson 1940; Lehmann *et al.* 1983; Skeath & Carroll 1992). Thus variation in the value of a single parameter, $\hat{T}_E$, can produce this "heterochronic" change in the process of cluster resolution or even prevent neural precursor differentiation. This is an interesting and testable prediction of the model.

The timing of cluster resolution also depends on the size of the cluster; bigger clusters take longer to resolve, which is something we have observed in previous work (Marnellos 1997; Marnellos & Mjolsness 1998), but which is much more evident in the example of Fig. 4.

To further probe the dynamics of cluster resolution, we have perturbed the levels of expression of proneural and epithelial genes in specific cells during a run, as illustrated in Fig. 5. In this simulation (which has the same initial concentrations as the one in Fig. 4 and uses the same parameter values, including $\hat{T}_E$) we instantaneously increased at $t = 60$ the level of epithelial expression in the central cell of a symmetrical, 7-cell cluster and also the level of proneural expression in a peripheral cell of a different symmetrical cluster. Whereas the first perturbation prevents normal resolution of the cluster involved, (as can be observed at $t = 121$ for instance), the second one has no effect on resolution and the cluster involved resolves normally (see Fig. 5). The effects of such perturbations will vary depending on the time and cell in which they are carried out, and on whether they occur singly, as in the two examples of Fig. 5, or in various combinations. Such manipulations are therefore a rich source of predictions of the model.

Discussion

In this paper we have extended and slightly modified a *Drosophila* neurogenesis model introduced in Marnellos (1997), in order to make it more biologically realistic. The previous model had only proneural and epithelial genes that could interact with each other across cells; this afforded much greater flexibility in cell-cell signalling than has been experimentally observed in this system. In the work presented here we have included genes for a receptor and a ligand that gate communica-

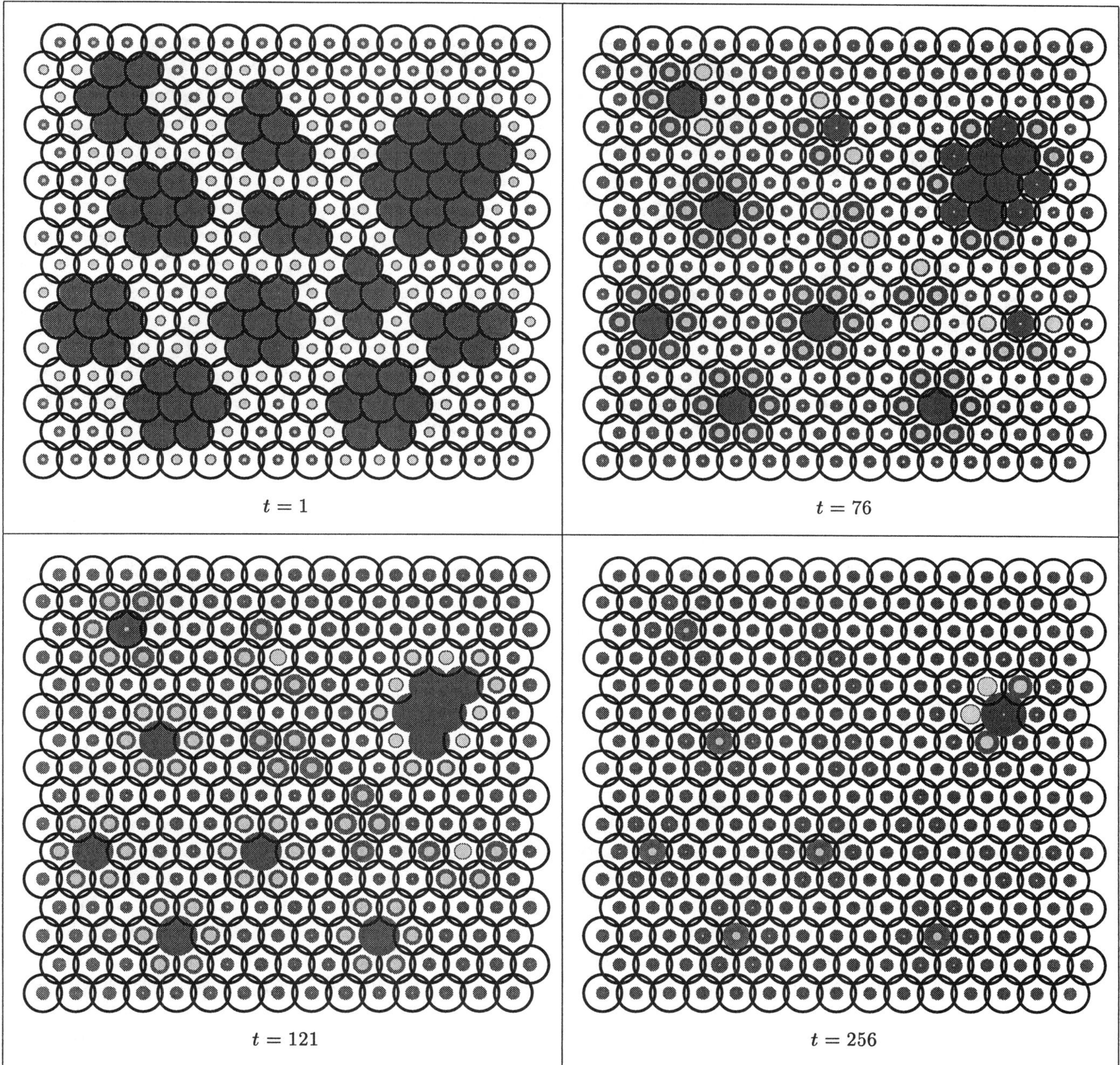

Figure 4: Simulation using a test dataset with clusters of various shapes and sizes. The parameter values are almost all identical to those of the simulations in Fig. 3. All clusters, except for the 4-cell ones, successfully resolve. The big cluster takes much longer than other clusters to resolve. The strength of the lateral interaction, $\hat{T}_E$ of Eqs. 7 and 8, is greater in this simulation than in those of Fig. 3. This has a "heterochronic" effect: it makes clusters resolve faster, as can be seen by comparing the degree of resolution of symmetrical, 7-cell clusters at $t = 76$ in this Figure with those of Fig. 3. Same conventions as in Fig. 2.

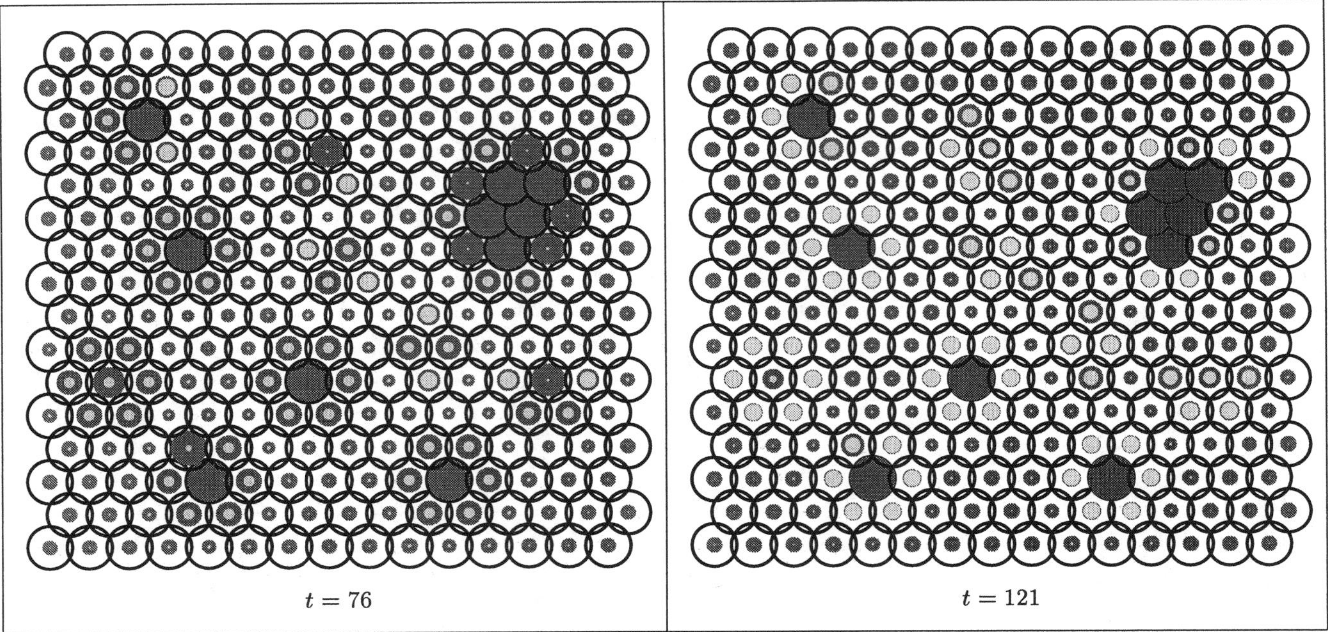

Figure 5: Simulation with perturbations of gene expression in individual cells of two symmetrical, 7-cell clusters. The clusters are the two ones in the lower left corner of the dataset. At $t = 60$ the level of epithelial expression in the central cell of the upper one of these two clusters was instantaneously increased, while in the lower cluster proneural expression was increased in a peripheral cell. Both perturbations can be detected in the left panel ($t = 76$). The first perturbation abolishes cluster resolution, while the second has no effect on resolution, as can be seen in the right panel (and also in comparison with the corresponding panel of Fig. 4).

tion across cells; such communication can now occur only through the interaction of an activated receptor-ligand complex with the epithelial gene, as has been described in the literature (Fortini & Artavanis-Tsakonas 1994; Jarriault *et al.* 1995; Bailey & Posakony 1995). The increase in the number of genes has been accomplished without an accompanying increase in the number of optimized parameters. The size of the training datasets has also increased with the addition of desired intermediate concentrations: performance is now scored in the middle and at the end of a run, instead of only at the end. This more constrained optimization has yielded many good and consistent solutions. The training datasets now have one 7-cell, one 6-cell and one 5-cell cluster, instead of only symmetrical 7-cell clusters, and this may have made the optimization solutions better at resolving novel types of clusters.

In the present model the strength of lateral signalling during a run is modulated by changes in receptor and ligand concentrations, whereas in the original model similar but less flexible modulation was afforded by the inclusion of cell delamination (absent here) which changed the area of contact between adjacent cells and contributed to the resolution of larger clusters. Although neuroblast delamination accompanies cluster resolution in the central nervous system of the *Drosophila* embryo, delamination does not occur during cluster resolution in imaginal discs and may not be necessary for resolution; the present model is therefore more consistent with experimental evidence.

Our results here have reconfirmed findings of the previous model (Marnellos 1997; Marnellos & Mjolsness 1998): for instance, that smaller clusters generally resolve faster than larger ones (Fig. 4); that lateral signalling is crucial for cluster resolution and when it is abolished clusters do not resolve (which parallels the neurogenic mutant phenotype in the biological system); or that cell-cell interactions involving just the immediate neighborhood of any given cell can bring about cluster resolution, without the need of other longer range processes like diffusion (even though the existence of such processes cannot be ruled out). This last conclusion is even stronger in the context of the present model, as lateral interactions now depend on a single optimized parameter; this indicates that even rather limited cell-cell signalling is sufficient for cluster resolution.

Investigation of our present model has also revealed that variations in the strength of lateral signalling have a heterochronic effect on cluster resolution (Fig. 4). This may have some bearing upon issues such as the differences in bristle number between different fly species. Researchers have considered these differences as the result of altered patterns of expression of genes that set up proneural clusters (Simpson 1996). Our work suggests that variation in the strength of lateral signalling may also contribute to bristle number phenotypes.

Our optimization solutions have also been shown to be robust to small changes in initial conditions (Fig. 3). Of course one might argue that, since through our training dataset we look for solutions that result in the most central and most encircled cell of each cluster becoming the neural precursor, it is not surprising that with slightly different initial conditions the same cell is still selected. This is true, but the point is that, if in the biological system the same selection rule occurs, then our results show that this is a robust process. This point relates to questions raised in the literature about "lateral inhibition" versus "mutual inhibition" explanations of cluster resolution (see Introduction above). Our results would favor mutual inhibition as the most likely explanation, with position in cluster and degree of encirclement being the properties that shield the prospective neural precursor from inhibition from other cells.

Finally, perturbations of gene expression in individual cells in the model (Fig. 5) are a rich source of quantitative predictions about how cells would respond to externally imposed changes. Such predictions are now testable in *Drosophila* (Halfon *et al.* 1997).

In conclusion, the model described in this paper, sufficiently simple and faithful to experimental observations, can produce biologically intepretable results. With more quantitative data to optimize its parameters on and with experimental testing of its various predictions, it could become a good tool to probe the dynamics of developmental processes like neurogenesis.

Acknowledgements

We wish to thank Anne Bang, Chris Kintner and John Thomas for discussions, Jim Posakony for discussions and fly stocks, Terry Sejnowski for use of the confocal microscope in his lab, and Larry Carter (UCSD and SDSC) and the Yale Center for Parallel Supercomputing for use of their computers. This work was supported in part by Office of Naval Research grant N00014-97-1-0422.

References

Artavanis-Tsakonas, S.; Matsuno, K.; and Fortini, M. 1995. Notch signaling. *Science* 268:225–232.

Bailey, A., and Posakony, J. 1995. Suppressor of Hairless directly activates transcription of *Enhancer of split* complex genes in response to Notch receptor activity. *Genes and Development* 9:2609–2622.

Bang, A.; Bailey, A.; and Posakony, J. 1995. *Hairless* promotes stable commitment to the sensory organ precursor cell fate by negatively regulating the activity of the *Notch* signaling pathway. *Developmental Biology* 172:479–494.

Bate, C. 1976. Embryogenesis of an insect nervous system. I. A map of the thoracic and abdominal neuroblasts in *Locusta migratoria. Journal of Embryology and Experimental Morphology* 35:107–123.

Campuzano, S., and Modollel, J. 1992. Patterning of the *Drosophila* nervous system - the *achaete-scute* gene complex. *Trends in Genetics* 8:202–208.

Cubas, P.; de Celis, J.-F.; Campuzano, S.; and Modolell, J. 1991. Proneural clusters of *achaete-scute* expression and the generation of sensory organs in the *Drosophila* imaginal wing disc. *Genes and Development* 5:996–1008.

Doe, C., and Goodman, C. 1985a. Early events in insect neurogenesis. I. Development and segmental differences in the pattern of neuronal precursor cells. *Developmental Biology* 111:193–205.

Doe, C., and Goodman, C. 1985b. Early events in insect neurogenesis. II. The role of cell interactions and cell lineage in the determination of neuronal precursor cells. *Developmental Biology* 111:206–219.

Fehon, R.; Kooh, P.; Rebay, I.; Regan, C.; Xu, T.; Muskavitch, M.; and Artavanis-Tsakonas, S. 1990. Molecular interactions between the protein products of the neurogenic loci *Notch* and *Delta*, two EGF-homologous genes in *Drosophila*. *Cell* 61:523–534.

Fleischer, K., and Barr, A. 1994. A simulation testbed for the study of multicellular development: The multiple mechanisms of morphogenesis. In Langton, C., ed., *Artificial Life III : Proceedings of the Workshop on Artificial Life, held June 1992 in Santa Fe, New Mexico.* Reading, MA: Addison-Wesley.

Fleischer, K. 1995. *A Simulation Testbed for the Study of Multicellular Development: Multiple Mechanisms of Morphogenesis.* Ph.D. Dissertation, California Institute of Technology.

Fortini, M., and Artavanis-Tsakonas, S. 1994. The Suppressor of Hairless protein participates in Notch receptor signaling. *Cell* 79:273–282.

Goriely, A.; Dumont, N.; Dambly-Chaudière, C.; and Ghysen, A. 1991. The determination of sense organs in *Drosophila*: Effect of the neurogenic mutations in the embryo. *Development* 113:1395–1404.

Halfon, M.; Kose, H.; Chiba, A.; and Keshishian, H. 1997. Targeted gene expression without a tissue-specific promoter: Creating mosaic embryos using laser-induced single-cell heat shock. *Proceedings of the National Academy of Sciences USA* 94:6255–6260.

Hartenstein, V., and Posakony, J. 1989. Development of the adult sensilla on the wing and notum of *Drosophila melanogaster. Development* 107:389–405.

Heitzler, P., and Simpson, P. 1991. The choice of cell

fate in the epidermis of *Drosophila*. *Cell* 64:1083–1092.

Huang, F.; Dambly-Chaudière, C.; and Ghysen, A. 1991. The emergence of sensory organs in the wing disc of *Drosophila*. *Development* 111:1087–1095.

Jarriault, S.; Brou, C.; Logeat, F.; Schroeter, E.; Kopan, R.; and Israel, A. 1995. Signalling downstream of activated mammalian Notch. *Nature* 377:355–358.

Jennings, B.; Preiss, A.; Delidakis, C.; and Bray, S. 1994. The Notch signalling pathway is required for *Enhancer of split* bHLH protein expression during neurogenesis in the *Drosophila* embryo. *Development* 120:3537–3548.

Lehmann, R.; Jiménez, F.; Dietrich, U.; and Campos-Ortega, J. 1983. On the phenotype and development of mutants of early neurogenesis in *Drosophila melanogaster*. *Wilhelm Roux's Archives of Developmental Biology* 192:62–74.

Marnellos, G., and Mjolsness, E. 1998. A gene network approach to modeling early neurogenesis in Drosophila. In *Pacific Symposium on Biocomputing*, volume 3, 30–41.

Marnellos, G. 1997. *Gene Network Models Applied to Questions in Development and Evolution*. Ph.D. Dissertation, Yale University.

Martin-Bermudo, M.; Martinez, C.; Rodriguez, A.; and Jimenez, F. 1991. Distribution and function of the *lethal of scute* gene product during early neurogenesis in *Drosophila*. *Development* 113:445–454.

Mjolsness, E.; Sharp, D.; and Reinitz, J. 1991. A connectionist model of development. *Journal of Theoretical Biology* 152:429–453.

Muskavitch, M. 1994. Delta-Notch signalling and *Drosophila* cell fate choice. *Developmental Biology* 166:415–430.

Poulson, D. 1940. The effect of certain X-chromosome deficiencies on the embryonic development of *Drosophila melanogaster*. *Journal of Experimental Zoology* 83:271–318.

Romani, S.; Campuzano, S.; Macagno, E.; and J., M. 1989. Expression of *achaete* and *scute* genes in *Drosophila* imaginal discs and their function in sensory organ development. *Genes and Development* 3:997–1007.

Simpson, P. 1996. *Drosophila* development: A prepattern for sensory organs. *Current Biology* 6:948–950.

Skeath, J., and Carroll, S. 1991. Regulation of *achaete-scute* gene expression and sensory organ pattern formation in the *Drosophila* wing. *Genes and Development* 5:984–995.

Skeath, J., and Carroll, S. 1992. Regulation of proneural gene expression and cell fate during neuroblast segregation in the *Drosophila* embryo. *Development* 114:939–946.

Stern, C. 1954. Two or three bristles. *American Scientist* 42:213–247.

Struhl, G.; Fitzgerald, K.; and Greenwald, I. 1993. Intrinsic activity of the Lin-12 and Notch intracellular domains *in vivo*. *Cell* 74:331–345.

van Doren, M.; Powell, P.; Pasternak, D.; Singson, A.; and Posakony, J. 1992. Spatial regulation of proneural gene activity: Auto- and cross-activation of *achaete* is antagonized by *extramacrochaetae*. *Genes and Development* 6:2592–2605.

Wigglesworth, V, B. 1940. Local and general factors in the development of "pattern" in *Rhodnius prolixus*. *Journal of Experimental Zoology* 17:180–200.

Locomotion

Reconstruction of Extinct Animals in the Computer

Yoshiyuki Usami*, **Hirano Saburo**, **Satoshi Inaba** and **Masatoshi Kitaoka**

*Institute of Physics, Kanagawa University
* "Form and Function", PRESTO
Department of Industrial Engineering, Kanagawa University
Rokkakubashi 3-27-1, Kanagawa-ku, Yokohama 221, Japan
*usami@phsu1.phsc.kanagawa-u.ac.jp
*http://www.phsc.kanagawa-u.ac.jp

Abstract

We report on our attempts at reconstructing a lost ecosystem through computer simulation. The Cambrian explosion is known as the time when various body forms appeared during a relatively short period of geological time. One of the largest predatory species of the period, which swam with other curious animals in the ancient seas of 530 million years ago, was *Anomalocaris*, characterized by a series of lateral flaps. We study their behavior based on a theoretical framework. A 3D virtual model of the extinct animal is constructed within a computer graphics environment. The possible behavior of the animal is calculated by simple hydro-dynamics modeling and an evolutionary computation approach, showing that *Anomalocaris* probably swam by waving its flaps like a stingray. We also introduce a rule-based system which creates a basic body plan of swimming animals with flaps. The swimming ability of those creatures was evaluated and the results show that *Anomalocaris* or similar body-typed animals have a considerable swimming ability. The goal of our work is to reconstruct an ecosystem–that was lost 530 million years ago–by computer simulation. Based on theoretical considerations we are constructing a system in which virtual creatures live in a virtual world with the ability to interact with the real world through additional inputs by us.

Introduction

The Cambrian explosion has drawn attention recently because of the appearance of animals with a large variety of body forms at the early stage of evolution (Morris 1994). The largest predator, *Anomalocaris*, swam with a series of flaps, and possessed two big limbs and a mouth beneath its head. In this paper we investigate possible swimming motions in water using a theoretical framework. In the field of ALife, Sims (1994a-c) developed a computational approach to studying swimming and walking motions of artificial creatures in a three-dimensional space. Terzopoulos, Tu, and Grzeszczuk (1994) studied the swimming motion of realistic models of tropical fish. Also, Ngo and Marks (1993) studied ground-locomotion, while Hamner (1998) also studied swimming motion. In this paper, we model a virtual creature by a composition into blocks in a 3D-space, according to the structure of *Anomalocaris*. We then study how such a creature might swim in a water medium. In the second part of this paper, we introduce a rule-based system which creates the basic body structure of swimming animals with flaps. The swimming ability of each virtual creature is studied, and it is found that *Anomalocaris*-type animals are remarkably adept at swimming. This may explain why *Anomalocaris* became the largest predator during this early period of animal evolution on earth.

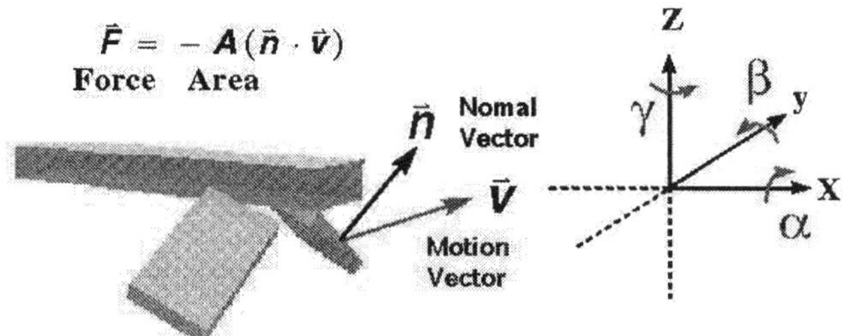

Figure 1: Model creature and its coordinate system.

Computational Method

In this part we investigate swimming for a model animal using evolutionary computation. Suppose that the creature is constructed out of a main body and lateral flaps. When the creature waves its flaps, the flaps receive a force from the water

$$\vec{F} = -A\vec{n} \cdot \vec{v} \,,$$

where $\vec{v}$ denotes the velocity relative to the fixed frame, $\vec{n}$ is the normal vector of the surface of the flap and A its surface area. The flaps are assumed to rotate around the x, y and z axis, according to the following Fourier-series–like time-series:

$$\alpha = a_1^1\cos(\omega_1^1 t + \delta_1^1) + a_2^1\cos(\tfrac{1}{2}\omega_2^1 t + \delta_2^1)$$
$$\beta = a_1^2\cos(\omega_1^2 t + \delta_1^2) + a_2^2\cos(\tfrac{1}{2}\omega_2^2 t + \delta_2^2)$$
$$\gamma = a_1^3\cos(\omega_1^3 t + \delta_1^3) + a_2^3\cos(\tfrac{1}{2}\omega_2^3 t + \delta_2^3)$$

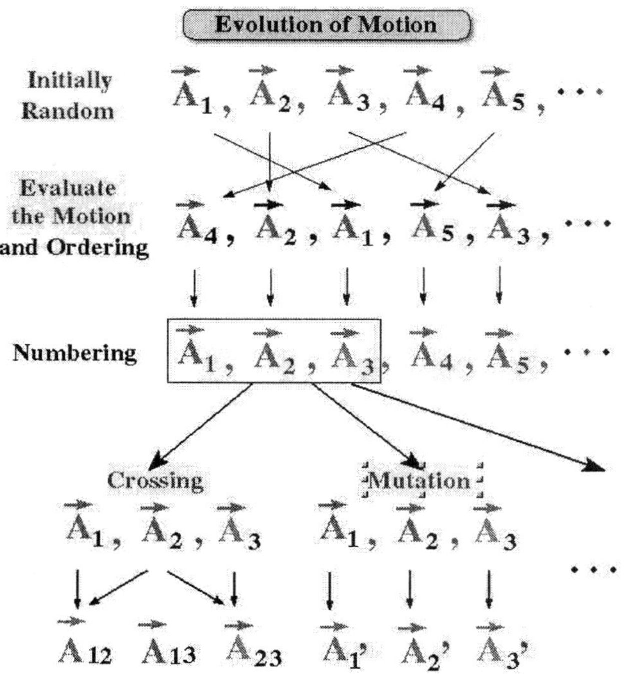

Figure 2: Diagrammatic representation of evolution algorithm.

A set of parameters

$$\vec{A} \equiv a_1^1, \omega_1^1, \delta_1^1, a_1^2, \omega_1^2, \ldots$$

describe the creature's motion, which is determined by an evolutionary algorithm. In this algorithm, each parameter is initially chosen randomly. and 12 sets of candidates are generated:

$$\vec{A_1}, \vec{A_2}, \vec{A_3}, \vec{A_4}, \vec{A_5}, \cdots, \vec{A_{12}}\ .$$

Next, the swimming ability is evaluated in a 3-D calculation. The top three sets among 12 samples were selected. Crossing and mutation of parameters are applied. The three sets give rise to three sets of offspring by parameter crossing, said crossing being achieved by simply taking the average of two species. The top three sets create 9 offspring by mutation of parameters. Again, the swimming ability of the 12 offspring are evaluated. This procedure is repeated through many generations.

We construct our *Anomalocaris* model by combining blocks as shown in Fig. 3. Nearest neighbor flaps are assumed to rotate with a phase difference given by δ and θ, where δ can be adjusted for each individual flap while θ is an overall phase difference. The emergent behavior of the swimming motion is then determined by the evolutionary algorithm.

$$\alpha_i = a_1^1 \cos(\omega_1^1 t + \delta_1^1 - i \cdot \theta) + a_2^1 \cos(\frac{1}{2}\omega_2^1 t + \delta_2^1 - i \cdot \theta)$$

Figure 3: The structure of a model of *Anomalocaris*.

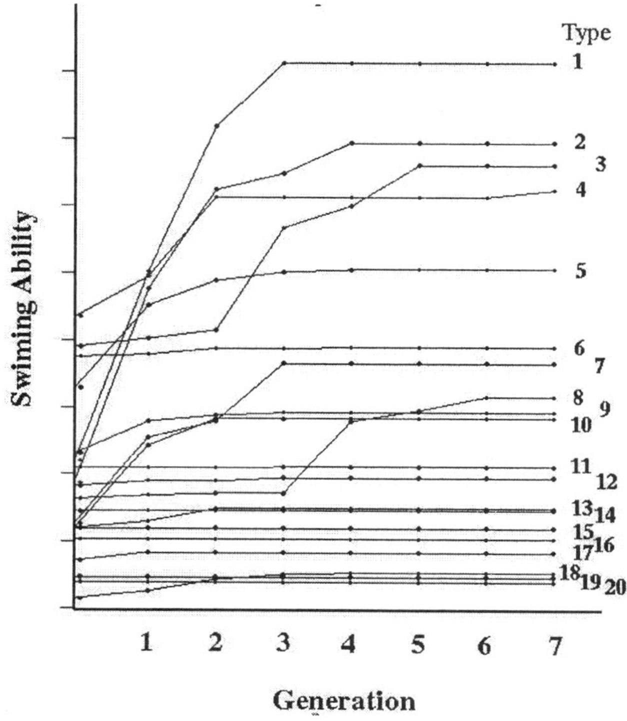

Figure 4: Development of swimming ability.

In addition to the mathematical evolution scheme, we introduce physiological conditions on the rotation speed of flaps of the virtual creature. We assume that the frequency has an upper limit so that the sum of the force does not exceed a certain constant value C, which is set to about 1/3 of the maximum force we experienced through all the simulation. If C is set large enough, the best swimmer rotates each fin without any phase difference.

Possible Motion of Model *Anomalocaris*

Figure 4 displays the increase in swimming ability of our *Anomalocaris* model during evolution using this algorithm. We ran 20 sets of calculations with different initial conditions, in which each calculation contains 12

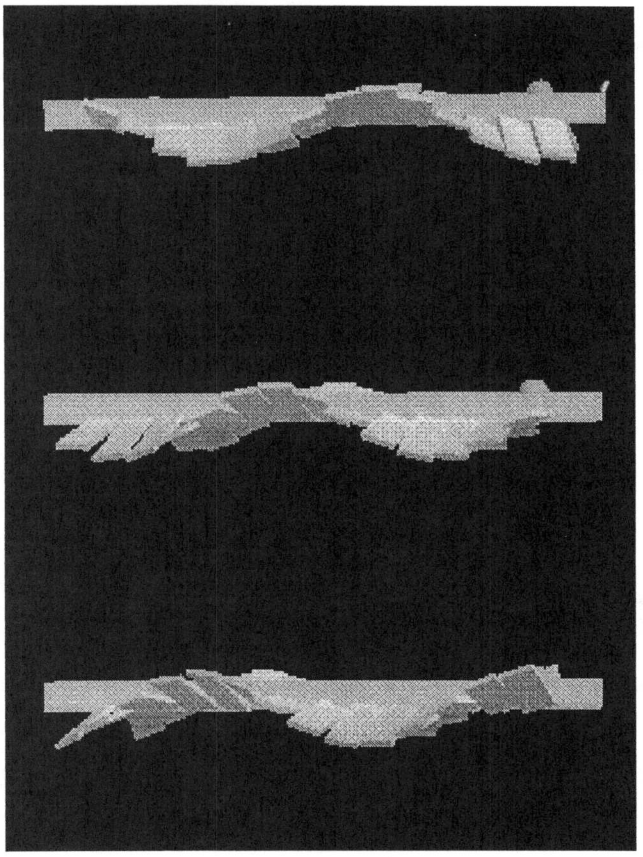

Figure 5: Swimming style of type 1.

species $(\vec{A_1}, \vec{A_2}, \vec{A_3}, \cdots, \vec{A_{12}})$. The best candidate's ability among those 12 is plotted in the figure. Looking at Fig. 4, we observe that a certain trajectory grows from generation to generation and finally attains No. 1. We call it type 1, and similarly we call the second type 2 and so forth. We display the swimming motion of type 1 in Fig. 5. As we can see, type 1's motion smoothly waves each fin with a certain phase. At first glance, the waving motion is reminiscent of a stingray. From these simulations, we suggest that *Anomalocaris* swam like this in the sea of 530 million years ago.

Elementary Forms and Motion

As we mentioned in the Introduction, the Cambrian explosion is known as an interesting and mysterious event. The fossil record shows a short time range to develop various body forms of animals. From a biological point of view, the question could be summarized as to how and why the explosion occurred. Both questions are hard to answer at present, especially from a biological basis such as genetics. In the second part of our work, we introduce a simple rule-based form system. The structure of a creature is created by a composition of simple rules. A comparison of swimming ability for each body form will be made. The authors believe that such a calculation may help clarify certain mechanisms in evolution.

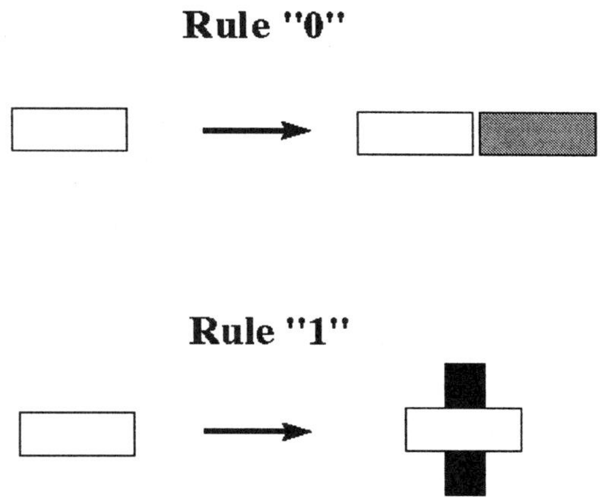

Figure 6: The basic rule to produce basic body plan.

To create various body forms, we introduce a system to create forms from rules. Each form is constructed out of 3D blocks. For example, rule "0" gives rise to the same element as the parent, as shown in Fig. 6. On the other hand, rule "1" produces a branch from the parent element, also shown in Fig. 6.

In Fig. 7, we show the branch tree of the rule system, and the body structure created from the rule. Once each body plan is determined from the rule-form system, we evaluate its moving ability. In order to simplify the calculation, we make an approximation such that a branch occurs only from the main body. Examples of such approximations are shown in Fig. 8.

Actually, we have never observed an animal having a multi-branched structure such as "1111..", except for plants in the real world. In future publications, we plan to present work on the behavior of agents having such complex structures.

In Fig. 9, we display the swimming ability of virtual creatures created from the rules. Roman numbers indicate the rule-type while italic numbers below show the swimming ability of the best among the simulations for each body form. For example, we created a virtual creature from rule "101", then searched for the best swimming form and determined its ability. On the right of Fig. 9, we show the species which scored highest in swimming ability. As we can see from the figure, we found that creatures with high swimming ability are generated from rule "00001", etc. We can see from Fig. 7 that such rules create *Anomalocaris*-type structures. From the result of these calculations, we conclude that *Anomalocaris*-type structures result in the best swimming ability among all the structures created from the present rule-form system.

It is well known that *Anomalocaris* was the largest

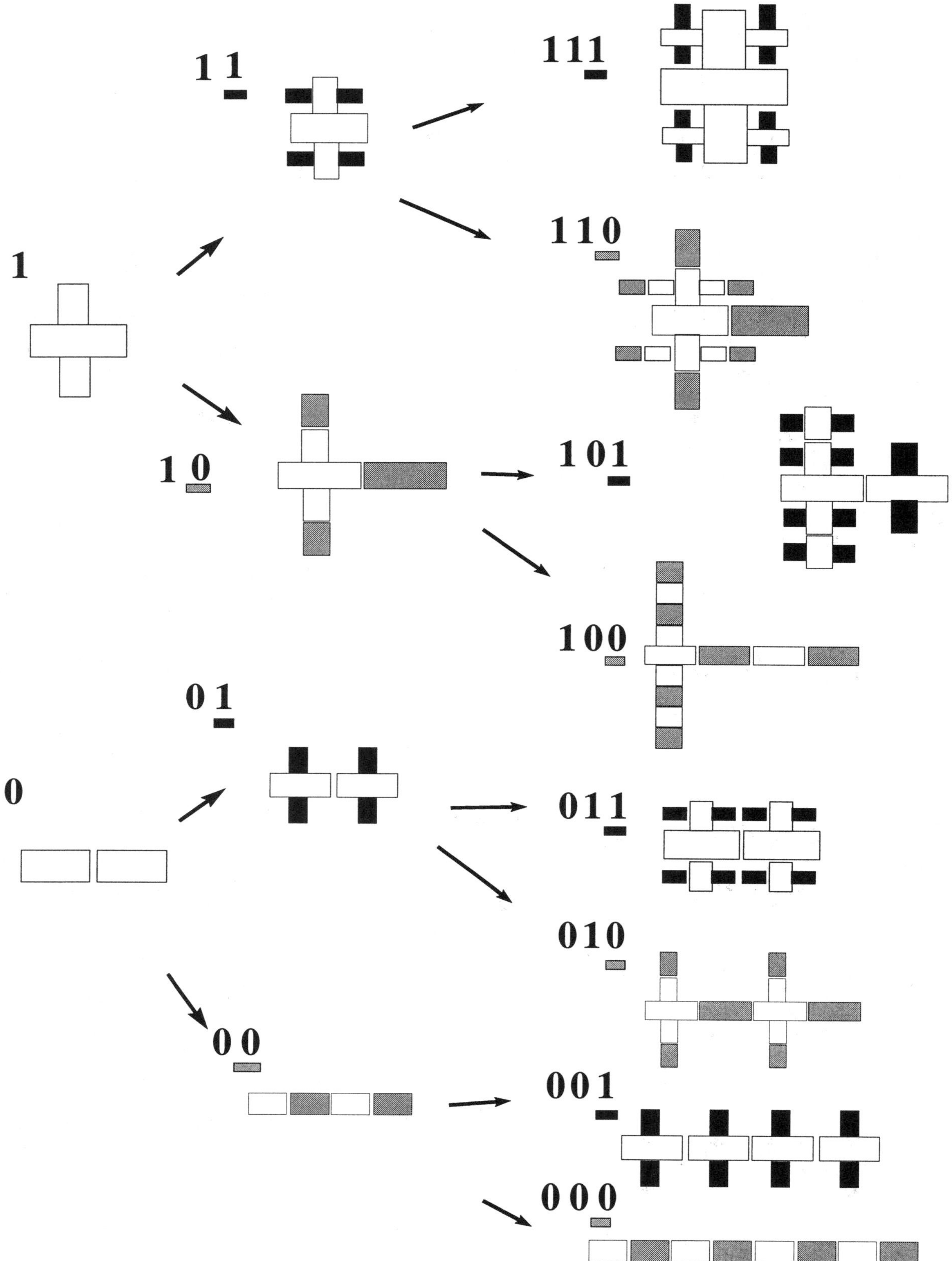

Figure 7: Branch tree of rules, and the forms created using the rule. Rule "0" gives rise to the same element as the parent, shown here as a gray block. Rule "1" creates a branch of the parent element, shown as a black block.

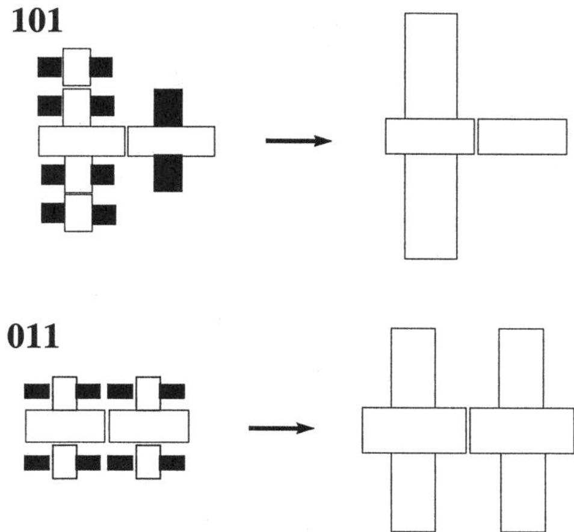

Figure 8: Examples of the result of the approximation. Complicated branching structure is approximated as the main body and the branch from it shown on the right hand side.

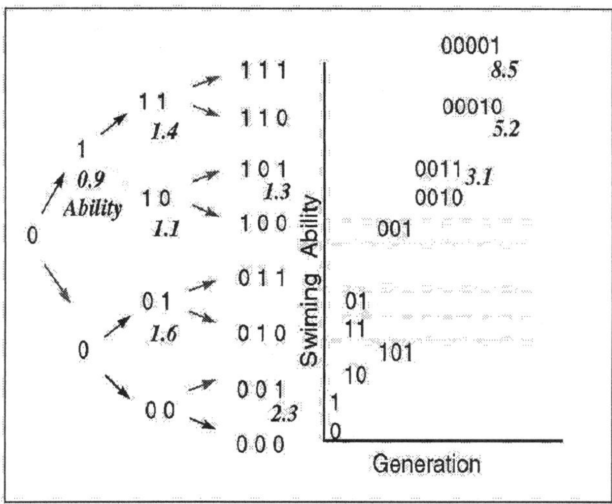

Figure 9: Swimming ability of virtual creature created from rule.

predator among Burgess shale animals that lived in early Cambrian period. Our calculations suggest that *Anomalocaris* may have had enough food by the benefit of its outstanding swimming ability.

An Attempt at Reconstructing a Lost Ecosystem in the Computer

The goal of our work is to reconstruct lost ecosystems in computer graphics on the basis of theoretical consideration. In Fig. 10, we display a prototype of such a system. There, a lost animal such as *Anomalocaris* is reconstructed as a realistic 3D object within computer graphics. The virtual creature swims based on the result of the simulations presented here. We are constructing an interactive system in which agents have neural systems allowing them to react to video input. While *Anomalocaris* was lost 530 millions years ago, we plan to resurrect it in its own virtual world in the future.

Figure 10: The lost animal *Anomalocaris* is reconstructed in the computer.

Acknowledgments

This work is supported by the Grant-in Aid for Encouragement of young Scientists (Grant No.09740321). The authors thank Prof. K. Nagata and Prof. N. Konno for continual encouragement throughout this work. The authors would also like to thank Prof. C. Adami for helpful comments on the manuscript.

References

Hamner, W. 1998. Personal communication.

Grzeszczuk, R. and D. Terzopoulos. 1995. Automated learning of muscle-actuated locomotion through control abstraction. SIGGRAPH 95 Conference Proceedings Los Angeles. Addison Wesley.

Morris, S.C. 1994. Fossils of the Burgess shale. Geological survey of Canada Miscellaneous Report, p. 43.

Ngo, J. T. and J. Marks. 1993. Physically realistic motion synthesis in animation. *Evolutionary Computation* 1: 235–268.

Sims, K. 1994a. Evolving 3D morphology and behavior by competition. In Proc. of *Artificial Life IV*, edited by R. A. Brooks and P. Maes. Cambridge, MA: MIT Press, p. 28–39.

Sims, K. 1994b. Evolving virtual creatures. Computer Graphics Annual Conference Series, 7/1994, p. 43-50.

Sims, K. 1994c. Evolving virtual creatures. Proceedings of SIGGRAPH '94. New York: ACM Press, p. 24–29.

Terzopoulos, D., X. Tu, and R. Grzeszczuk. 1994. Artificial fishes with autonomous locomotion, perception, behavior, and learning in a simulated physical world. In Proc. of *Artificial Life IV*, edited by R. A. Brooks and P. Maes. Cambridge, MA: MIT Press, p. 17–27.

Attractiveness vs Efficiency

(How Mate Preference Affects Locomotion in the Evolution of Artificial Swimming Organisms)

Jeffrey Ventrella
jeffrey@ventrella.com
http://www.ventrella.com

Abstract

This paper describes a unique simulation in which a population of physically-based organisms evolves morphology and motor control for fluid locomotion, through competition for mates and food. Preference for mates exhibiting specified phenotypic features has an affect on the evolution of locomotion which is sometimes inhibitory, sometimes advantageous, and at times amusing. Reproduction of genotypes is autonomous and local in this spatial model, occurring among organisms which are able to approach critical proximity to a desired mate. An organism's energy level dictates whether it will seek mates or pursue food. Thus, an organism whose motions expend excessive amounts of energy will eat more, and reproduce less. The simulation was set up to determine whether mate preferences for arbitrary features can inhibit optimization of locomotion. While the general evolutionary trend is towards energy-efficient locomotion, the inclusion of mate preference causes a bias towards arbitrary anatomy and motion within the population. It was found that certain preferences indeed counter the trend for efficient swimming. A delicate balance between two forces (representing natural selection and sexual selection) is demonstrated.

Introduction

In the natural world, there are particular instances of form and motion which are the direct result of a phenomenon known as sex. The exuberant display of colored feathers during courtship in some bird species is an example. Much of the amazing variety of form and motion in nature which has become such a basic part of our aesthetic lives can be traced to the need for organisms to reproduce sexually.

Many fish species possess body plans and coloration strongly adapted for sexual attraction. Some species exhibit elaborate displays of dance, often causing risk to their own safety, in order to attract mates (i.e., the widely-studied African rift valley *cichlids*). The need to attract mates in some species may be demanding enough on the evolution of a body plan to greatly affect other characteristics, such as locomotion.

What is the importance of "attractiveness" in evolution? In what ways does mate preference affect the overall fitness of individuals or species? While this paper does not attempt to address the deep questions concerning the subtle interactions between natural selection and sexual selection, it does offer a context in which to explore this subject, by describing a simulation which produces intriguing forms and motions, resulting from a simple form of mate choice. The hypothesis is that mate preferences for arbitrary features in phenotypes can inhibit the evolution of energy-efficient locomotion.

In this simulation, a population of coexistent organisms evolves optimized morphology and motor control for locomotion in a viscous fluid, through competition for mates and food. There is no distinction between male and female in this simulation–it is not meant to model sex, but simply to introduce mate preference as a factor in the evolution of physically-based locomotion.

In a preliminary version of this model, the criteria for choosing mates involved a minor genetic component. But for the sake of clarity in observing results, the genetic component was replaced with a set of pre-defined criteria for attractiveness, so that the results of different kinds of mate preferences could be studied and compared. The simulation demonstrates how preferences for specific phenotypic features in the bodies of potential mates can alter, and sometimes inhibit the optimization of energy-efficient locomotion in the population. The emergence of peculiar motions and forms is then observed qualitatively, compared with results of simulations in which organisms choose mates randomly.

Background

Computer animation techniques which complement traditional animated scripting with autonomous agents have made possible complex life-like systems composed of many distributed elements (Reynolds, 1987). Physically-based modeling techniques and virtual motor control systems inspired by real animals are used to automate many of the subtle, hard-to-design nuances of animal motion (Badler, 1991). In task-level animation, (Zeltzer, 1991), and the space-time constraints paradigm, (Witkin and Kass, 1988), these techniques allow an animator to direct a character on a higher level.

The idea to use the genetic algorithm (GA) for automation of animated motion follows naturally. One application in using the GA for evolution of goal-directed motion in physically-based animated figures includes evolving stimulus-response mechanisms for locomotion (Ngo and Marks, 1993).

While the work described in this paper bears a resemblance to the virtual creatures of Sims (1994a), it continues a previous line of explorations, using a GA for optimizing locomotion in physically-based figures. The first example is a 2-legged walking figure (Ventrella, 1990) which evolves locomotion through pursuit of food, continuing with an unpublished 1992 project in evolving morphology and locomotion in 2D swimming creatures, and later, including evolution of 3D morphology as well as anatomy for locomotion (Ventrella 1994).

Sims (1994a, 1994b) has developed techniques for the evolution of morphology and locomotion most comprehensively and impressively, using the genetic programming paradigm (Koza 1992), and includes extensive 3D physical modeling. A holistic model of fish locomotion, with perception, learning, and group behaviors, has been developed by Terzopoulos, Tu, and Grzeszczuk (1994), which generates beautifully realistic animations.

Evolutionary modeling of situated organisms which reproduce spontaneously takes evolutionary modeling a step closer to nature (Ray 1991). "Electronic primordial soups" involving spatiality, such as Yaeger's Polyworld (1994), demonstrate artificial ecosystems in which mating, eating, learning, and even social behaviors, evolve within the simulated world.

In a prior paper (Ventrella 1996), it was demonstrated that swimming skills in physically-based figures could evolve without the use of an explicit fitness function, by delegating reproductive freedom to the organisms in the simulation such that locomotive skill emerged through competition for mates and food. (Throughout this paper I refer to this work as "the previous simulation"). A commercial product was derived from this work (RSG 1997) which enables users to manipulate the organisms and conduct experiments.

Ijspeert, Hallam, and Willshaw (1997) have developed artificial neural controllers which evolve through a GA for optimizing swimming locomotion in simulated lampreys, which can produce complex oscillations for undulating-style locomotion.

Todd and Miller (1991) developed a model which demonstrates how the forces of sexual selection can drive a population to have arbitrary phenotypic features, above and beyond the features resulting from natural selection.

The current project is motivated in part by Todd and Miller, and explores mate preference, building upon the previous simulation. As an extension of the previous simulation, the current simulation includes:

1) a more comprehensive physical model with a larger phenotype space

2) a set of pre-defined mate preference criteria

3) a means of measuring the effects of mate preference on evolution of locomotion skills

Fitness

Genetic algorithm-based systems for optimizing motor control in physically-based articulated figures typically update a population of genotypes in discrete generations, and use a pre-defined fitness function to control reproduction. This simulation places each organism of the population in a common spatial domain and allows mate selection to be local and autonomous. It does not use a pre-defined fitness function: fitness is instead considered as a property of the simulation: defined as the rate at which the population reproduces. Now, what is required for a higher reproductive rate in the population is a set of necessary emergent properties in individuals, such as: swimming quickly and efficiently towards mates or food; turning efficiently; and, of course, being attractive.

Physics and genetics are linked

In this simulation, the physically-based model is intimately tied to, in fact, *drives*, the genetic algorithm, and vice versa. Genotypes are housed in physically-based phenotypes, which in time become better at transporting their genotypes. Phenotypes which are better at transporting their genotypes to other phenotypes get to reproduce more genotypes. High reproduction of genotypes is rewarded naturally–the selfish gene at work.

The problem of reproduction is tied-in with the means for organisms to attain energy, as follows: organisms who waste energy at a high rate fall below a hunger threshold frequently. They must therefore spend more of their lives pursuing food than mating, and so they reproduce less. This creates evolutionary pressure for relatively rapid locomotion which expends relatively little energy.

In addition to selection for energy-efficient locomotion, mate preference encourages stylized motion and form. Each organism consists of a collection of body parts which move in relation to each other. Organisms can be set to respond to specific phenotypic features in other organisms, such as movement, size, length, etc. Selective pressure to flaunt these features encourages the emergence of non-locomotion-based motions and anatomy among body parts within the population. Existence of these features may not benefit locomotion in an individual, but does however increase its chances of having offspring, thereby making it more fit within the context of the population. Whether or not efficient swimming is affected by this is what provided the central inquiry behind the project.

The Simulation

A simulation was designed to test the hypothesis. It models a continuous two-dimensional square area representing a fluid medium. In the model, distances and sizes are measured in abstract world units. The size of the square domain is 6000 by 6000. Nothing can pass beyond its boundary–it is like an aquarium tank.

Organisms in this simulation are called "swimbots", due to a slight machine-like, or *robot*-like appearance. In addition to swimbots, there are food bits, and the medium in which they exist, called, the *fluid*. Time is measured in discrete units of 1, with each time step corresponding to an update of physical forces, swimbot states, and an animation frame. Food is regenerated periodically (one bit every 20 steps) in the fluid, and eaten by swimbots. Swimbots eat, mate, give birth to new swimbots, and die.

Energy

Global energy is set to 150,000 (abstract units), and remains constant. Throughout the simulation it is exchanged between fluid, food, and swimbots, as shown in Figure 1.

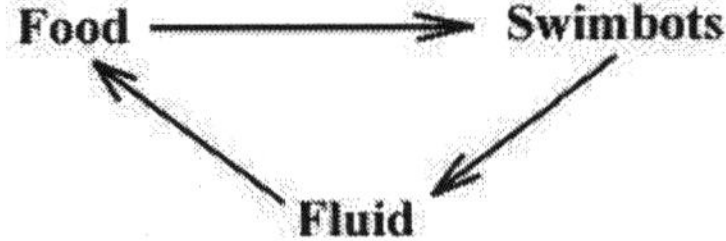

Figure 1. Energy exchange

The fluid contains ambient energy which is gradually converted into new food bits which appear in random locations of the fluid. Each food bit contains 50 units of energy and remains stationary until eaten by a swimbot, which then acquires this energy. Energy is expended in the swimbot from the work of moving body parts. This expended energy is then converted back into ambient energy and stored in the fluid.

Swimbots

A Swimbot is a two-dimensional object consisting of a set of rectangular parts connected in a tree-like topology. Parts can have varying thicknesses (rectangular heights) and lengths (rectangular widths), as shown in Figure 2.

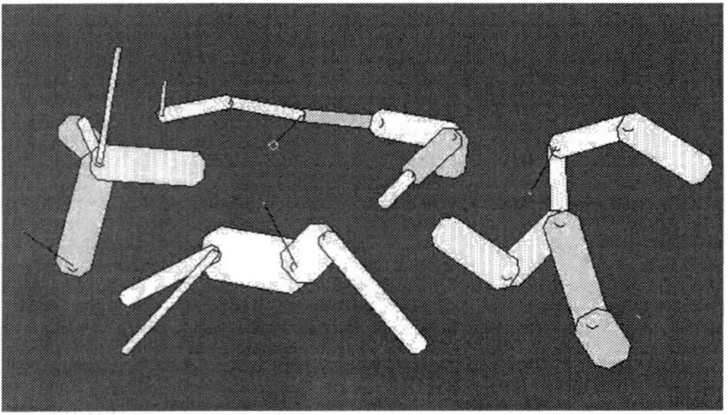

Figure 2. Swimbot anatomies

In this illustration, the ends of the parts are rounded for cosmetics, and bumps are shown to indicate joints. Parts range in length from 5.0 to 20.0, and in thickness from 0.3 to 4.0. Each part has two ends, labeled 0, and 1. Body parts are organized hierarchically, such that each part, as *child*, has an associated *parent* part (except for part 0 which has no physical extension but provides the original parent node for all other parts). End 0 of each part is rigidly connected to end 1 of its parent part at a resting angle ranging from -90 to 90 degrees, and is free to rotate about the joint. In the physical model, parts are permitted to intersect other parts (as if they were thin slabs overlapping in the third dimension). Similarly, the model does not recognize collisions between swimbots: they overlap freely with each other as well. Parts come in six colors: red, orange, yellow, green, blue, and violet. Part colors are genetically determined but are not perceivable by other swimbots as a factor in mate choice, and thus are not evolutionarily relevant. They are however useful in visualization, and help in detecting the emergence of distinct local gene pools within the fluid field, since coloration gets reproduced along with other traits.

These various physical attributes among parts do not represent any explicit bodily functions, although the parts of swimbots in evolved populations often exhibit qualitative locomotive or mate-attracting functions.

Part 1 is functionally special in one respect: it possesses the *genital* and the *mouth*. The genital is located at end 0, and the mouth is located at end 1. These regions are the foci for mating and eating. They are seen in Figure 2. as short black line segments of length 10, with each segment directed towards the swimbot's goal. For instance, if a swimbot is interested in food, a segment is seen originating from its mouth and aiming at a food bit, with a dot at the end. If it is interested in mating, a segment is seen originating from the genital and aiming at a potential mate, with a small circle at the end. These graphical elements are used to help visualize the swimbots' goals and thus to enhance comprehension and intuition while observing the animated simulation.

Motor control

Swimbots are assumed to have absolute strength to bend parts as their motor control systems dictate, without resistance from friction or torque. They bend their joints in a predetermined, predictable manner, using sine functions as controllers. The angles in the joints of a swimbot change by small increments at each time step. Over extended time, every swimbot part rotates about the end of its parent part in pendulum fashion–back and forth, driven by its associated sine function. Within a single swimbot, all the parts' sine functions have the same frequency, but overall frequency can vary among different swimbots.

While frequency remains fixed within a single swimbot, amplitudes and phases of these sine functions vary among the parts. The resulting accumulation of this hierarchy of motions (along with variation in anatomy) gives rise to a large variety of complex periodic rhythms, and hence, a large phenotypic space of possible swimming strategies.

The physics of swimming

A forward dynamics model is used to generate linear and angular momentum of a swimbot's body, resulting from body parts moving within a fixed fluid frame, with high viscosity. No fluid dynamics are modeled. Proportional to a friction constant, the motion of each part creates a force in the direction of the normal to the main axis of the part, which is proportional to the sine of the angle between the main axis of the part and the part's velocity. Part forces are summed to determine the linear and angular forces on the whole body, at each time step of the simulation.

Moving around burns off virtual calories: energy is expended by bending joints and by stroking the fluid. Energy expenditure is proportional to the combined torques required for each joint to rotate the masses of parts on either side, plus friction from parts sweeping through the fluid, times a caloric burn constant.

Energy efficiency in a swimbot is defined to be equal to *speed* divided by *energy expenditure*, where *speed* and *energy expenditure* are equal to the change in position and energy level, respectively, after each period of 100 time steps.

Mental states

Swimbots have simple brains to accompany their simple goals in life (to eat food and have sex). They do not learn from experience, but just change from state to state, triggered by a few stimuli. The mental states of a swimbot, and their transitions, are borrowed directly from the previous simulation, as shown in Figure 3.

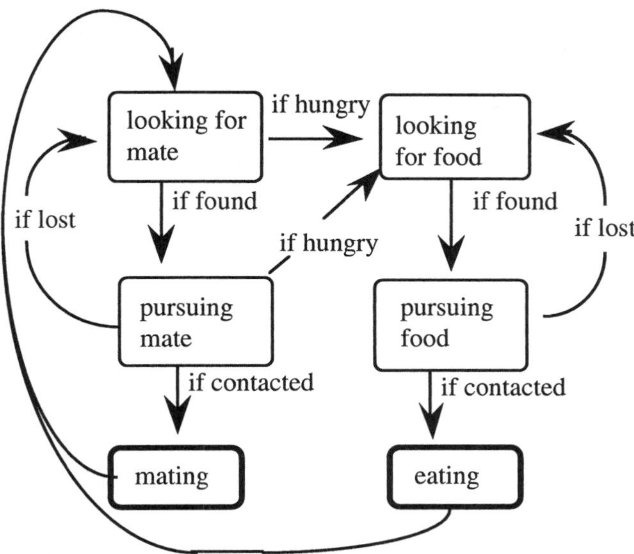

Figure 3. The states of a swimbot and the transitions between them.

All states persist through time until their associated conditions are met, except for the mating and eating states, which are instantaneous. These two states are accomplished when the distance between the swimbot and its goal reaches a distance less than 10.

A *looking* state transitions to its associated *pursuing* state when the swimbot has chosen its goal (a food bit or a potential mate). While in a *pursuing* state, this goal does not change unless a) the swimbot swims away in the wrong direction and loses sight of it, or b) the goal disappears (the food is eaten or the potential mate dies).

Perception

Swimbots can see in all directions–a complete 360 degrees, but cannot see further than a distance of 300 units. Although they are two-dimensional creatures, living in a world analogous to Abbot's Flatland creatures (Abbott, 63), they can interpret a few properties of the 2D anatomies and motions of companion swimbots as if viewed from outside of the 2D plane. The things a swimbot can perceive are:

1 the direction from its genital to another swimbot's genital in relation to its own axis of orientation (i.e., the degree it would have to turn in order to orient itself).
2 the direction of a coveted food bit (similar to above)
3 various features of the bodies of other swimbots, such as part sizes, distances between parts, and amounts of movement.

Perceptions 1 and 2 are used to modulate the swimbot's part amplitudes and phases (as explained in the next section). Perception 3 goes into affect when the swimbot is sizing up potential mates.

Reactivity

This model uses a straightforward stimulus-response mechanism: a swimbot responds to the direction of its current goal (represented by focus vector F in Figure 4) relative to its own orientation (vector O).

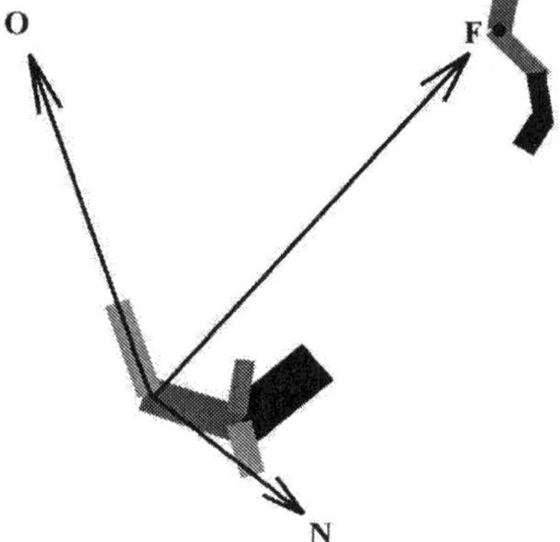

Figure 4. Focus direction compared to orientation

A swimbot's orientation is set equal to the main axis of one of its parts (part #1 in the hierarchy). The swimbot's focus vector continually adapts in order to aim towards its current goal, rotating (as in the hands of a clock) as the relative positions of the swimbot and its goal change. While the actual direction of the goal may sometimes change rapidly in relation to the swimbot's own orientation (i.e., when the swimbot is near its goal, and both are mobile), its focus vector must not change too rapidly since this provides a stimulus which directly modulates the motions of its parts. Thus, to avoid occasional jolts in the body as a result of quick changes in the direction of the goal, a maximum rotation rate is imposed on the focus vector so that it cannot rotate more than 1 degree per time step. This lag in adjusting focus is analogous to a lag in visual tracking of a moving target in real animals.

If a swimbot is searching for a mate or food, there is no specific goal and thus no goal direction. In this case, the focus vector wanders randomly, rotating by small amounts, as if searching. This behavior enables the swimbot to avoid swimming off in a straight line when there is no specific goal.

The dot product *d* of the normalized direction vectors O and N (N being the normal to vector F) is used to modulate the amplitudes and phases of the motions of each body part, so as to affect a turning mechanism. For example, if a swimbot's goal is to its left, *d* dictates that it will move its parts in a different rhythm than if its goal is to the right. If vectors O and F are aligned, then *d* is zero and there is no modulation added to the already existing motions. The amplitude and phase modulators associated with each parts' motion are genetically-determined (from genes 8 and 9 below). These modulators are multiplied by the dynamically-changing *d* as the simulation runs, to affect part motions for the sake of turning. The farther away from zero *d* is, the greater the modulation. Since these modulator genes are randomized at initialization, it is up to the forces of evolution to select for a set of modulations which affect better turning to orient towards a goal, as *d* changes dynamically.

It is interesting to note that, since a swimbot's overall direction of motion may not necessarily be aligned with its orientation, it does not necessarily have to align vectors O and F in order to move towards its goal.

As noted in the previous simulation, in tracking the overall trajectories of un-evolved swimbots, we get a mixed bag: some spiraling outwards away from the goal, some spiraling in, and many tracing spirals within spirals. These paths, caused by a combination of locomotion style and the stimulus-response mechanism, are reminiscent of the wanderings of Braitenberg creatures [Braitenberg, 84]. Over evolutionary time, these paths become more direct and purposeful.

Genetics

Swimbot genes are represented in fixed-length arrays, consisting of real number values ranging from 0 to 1. In expression from genotype to phenotype, these values are converted into real and integer values, each existing within a pre-determined phenotype-specific range, and used as parameters for building the body and controlling motions. Each swimbot's genotype consists of 74 values: 2 over-all values (see below), and 72 values controlling 8 possible body parts (with 9 values associated with each of the 8 parts: `9*8=72`). Swimbots with fewer than 8 parts still possess latent gene values for a full 8, and can continue their reproduction.

The phenotypic effects of each of the genes are:

(for whole swimbot)
1 number of parts (2-8)
2 frequency of motion

(for each possible part)
1 parent part (for connectivity)
2 color
3 resting angle (relative to parent)
4 length
5 thickness
(for sine wave bending)
6 amplitude
7 phase
8 turning amplitude modulator
9 turning phase modulator

Many genetic algorithm techniques have been described in the literature pertaining to the ordering of values within a genotype, and its relation to the problem domain. This model uses a straightforward approach: each set of 9 genes associated with a part are ordered in sequence from 1 to 8. So each part is represented in the genotype by a set of adjacent genes.

Mate choice

If a swimbot's energy level is above the hunger threshold (50), and it has not already chosen a mate, it begins looking for one. From the set of potential mates within its circular view horizon, it chooses one whose body provides the most attractive stimuli. The choice is made by ranking the set of potential mate according to one of the following measurements:

Massiveness
the sum of all the parts' sizes
Movement
the sum of all the parts' instantaneous speeds
Openness
the sum of all the parts' distances from the centroid
Length
the largest distance between any two parts

When attractiveness is set to equal Massiveness, swimbots choose mates exhibiting comparatively larger bodies than the others within view. When it is set to equal Openness, swimbots choose mates whose parts tend to be splayed outward the most. Attraction to the inverse of these features can also be set. For instance, if attractiveness is set to equal the inverse of Movement, swimbots choose mates who exhibit the least motion.

Reproduction

If swimbots could sing, half the population would be singing the Blues. Mate choice is not necessarily reciprocal in this world: a swimbot's chosen mate is not guaranteed to have also chosen the chooser, and in fact it is more likely to be concerned with eating a food bit or pursuing its own (possibly indifferent) chosen mate. This simulation does not require mutual consent for reproduction to occur. The inclusion of this requirement was tested briefly, and it was found that the resulting low birth-rate could not sustain the population, given the model settings. While comparing evolutionary dynamics of reproduction with and without mutual consent would be interesting, it is not the central inquiry in this project, and will likely be explored in a subsequent simulation.

When swimbots reproduce, they have exactly one offspring, which is initialized midway between its parents. It inherits a mixture of genes from each parent, using genetic crossover. The offspring genotype is subject to chance mutation (mutation rate = 0.01).

The energy level of each parent is halved during reproduction and the remaining energy is donated to the offspring swimbot. The offspring is born as an "adult" and immediately begins looking for a mate or food. Since parental energy is halved, it sometimes dips below the hunger threshold, and so the parents often begin immediately pursuing food.

Reproduction is rewarded to those swimbots who possess one or more of the following characteristics: they are good enough at swimming to reach a desired mate; they are lucky enough to have found an attractive mate in immediate range (uncommon); and they are attractive enough to have been chosen by a good swimbot as a mate

Results

In all simulations, swimbot count is initialized at 1000, and food count at 2000.

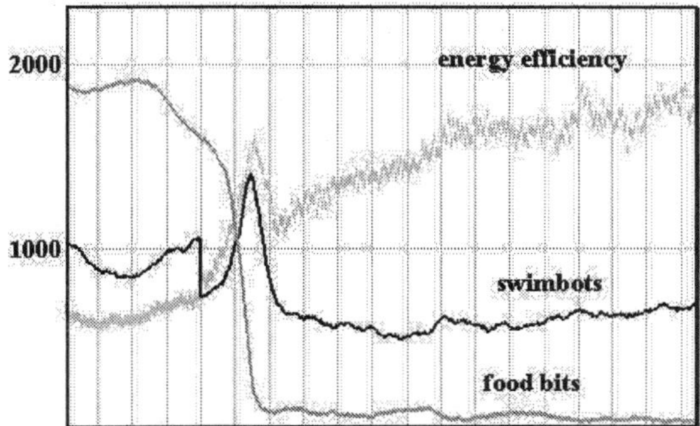

Figure 5. Swimbot vs. food population, superimposed with energy efficiency, from a typical simulation

Figure 5 illustrates swimbot and food population from a simulation over a span of 184900 time steps. Each vertical register is equal to 10000 time steps. The sudden drop in swimbot population at time 40000 is the result of surviving members of the first generation of swimbots dying of old age (swimbots are initialized at age 0, and cannot live longer than 40000 time steps).

The increase in swimbot population around 50000 is the result of swimbots multiplying in local regions, spreading out, and consuming large amounts of food, giving them energy to reproduce. Food population plummets as a result, followed by a decrease in swimbot population. Most simulations exhibit this characteristic spike.

The jagged light gray line indicates average energy efficiency in the population. This graph element uses a different scaling than population, and is superimposed to show correlation of efficiency with population dynamics. In most simulations run without mate preference, energy efficiency continues to rise for another 100000 to 500000 steps before leveling off. Figure 6 shows 3 macroscopic views of the state of a typical simulation in which there is no mate preference. The states at time steps 0, 50000, and 100000 are shown. In the top panel, random swimbots and food bits are seen distributed randomly in the fluid. In the middle panel, local gene pools of swimbots have begun reproducing and

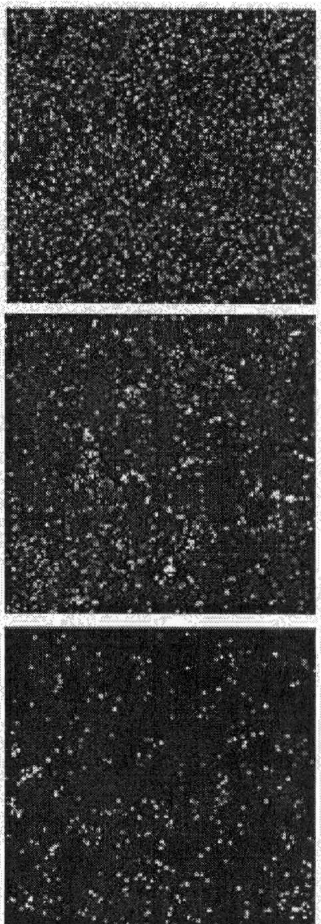

Figure 6. initialization, foraging, stasis

foraging through regions rich in food, leaving food-sparse areas in their wake. The bottom panel represents the general appearance of the simulation after food and swimbot populations have become more stable.

An exemplary swimming strategy which emerged from this simulation is illustrated in Figure 7.

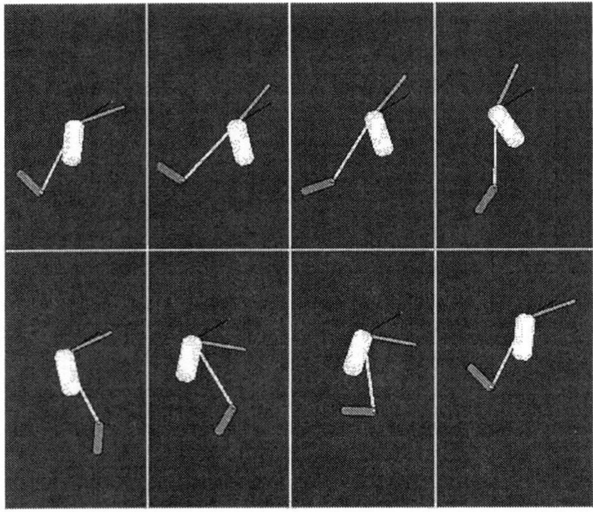

Figure 7. An evolved swimming strategy

The sequence is ordered from top-left to bottom-right. Each image in this illustration is separated by 4 time steps. It shows approximately one swim cycle. The swimbot is moving towards the upper-right. The two "paddle" parts are responsible for most of the swimming work.

Preliminary mate preference runs

In preliminary experiments, preferences were modeled with a genetically-inherited factor. These experiments were inspired by the work of Todd and Miller (91), whose model demonstrated how mate preferences can evolve to exploit existing phenotypic features. Each swimbot was given a "favorite color" gene. When sizing up potential mates, swimbots would seek out those individuals having this color in any of their parts. And they were especially attracted if these parts were more massive, and moved more than any other parts encountered. The idea was to model a form of stimulus in which organisms respond simply to the amount of colored movement in their visual fields.

In running these simulations, it was hoped that such criteria would inhibit swimming performance. In simulations run with mate preference, isolated body parts became larger and exhibited more motion, as expected, yet energy efficiency increased at the same rate as simulations run without mate preference, and the population flourished. It appears as if mate preferences had evolved to exploit attractive features existing in swimbots who were already efficient swimbots. In fact, these attractive characteristics actually correlate with many efficient swimming strategies (of an aggressive, flamboyant nature).

Observations

For the sake of more controlled experiments and predictable results, the choice of what is attractive was taken out of the hands (or *genes*, as it were) of the swimbots. The "favorite color" gene was removed, and the criteria for attractiveness were set up as the objectively-defined features (as described earlier). When attractiveness was set to equal *Massiveness*, the simulation produced thick-bodied swimbots which moved slowly, as expected. When it was set to equal *Movement*, large motions became the norm, and consequent swimming strategies became aggressive and bold. *Openness* resulted in bodies which were spread-out more, as illustrated in Figure 8, where each image represents 3 time steps. The population represented in this illustration exhibited a curious behavior: the stroke recovery (at the beginning and end of this sequence) appears more exaggerated than what would normally be expected.

It is as if the swimbots had overshot the motion, and *opened-up* inside-out. This behavior might have given some swimbots a slight advantage in being chosen. A pursuing swimbot sizing up mates can take a snapshot of a potential mate at any stage of its swim cycle to measure its attractiveness. Therefore, exhibiting open features through the majority of the swim cycle creates an advantage.

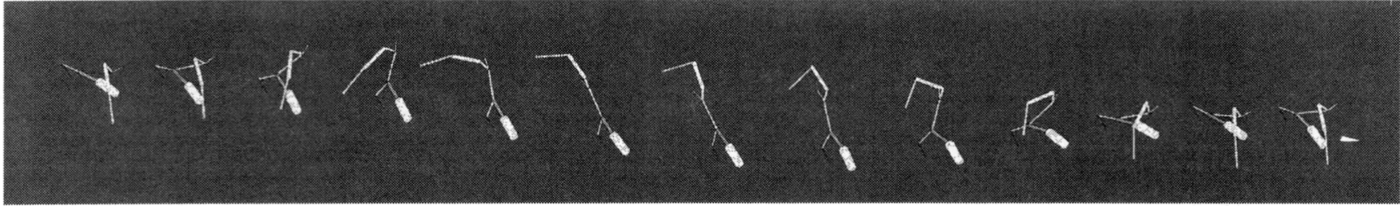

Figure 8. Locomotion exhibiting "open" features

Attraction to *Length* resulted in unique behavior: bodies became long, with few branches in their topology. The "parent" genes (for part connectivity) had adapted to become more sequential. Figure 9 illustrates a group of swimbots from a population which evolved with this criteria. These swimbots exhibit very rigid postures, using a small paddle-like part at the end to propel forward. Over evolutionary time these paddling behaviors were replaced by graceful undulating motions in straight bodies.

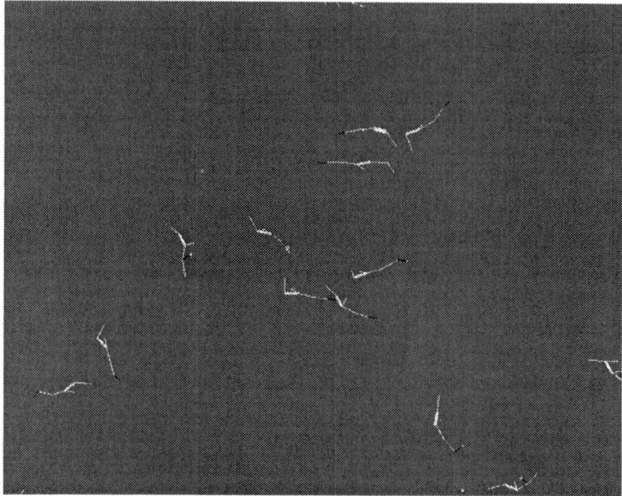

Figure 9. A group of long swimbots

The virtues of vegetating

Setting attraction to be the inverse of these features revealed interesting results. For instance, in a simulation run in which attractiveness was set to equal *lack of movement*, the simulation produced a population of swimbots with sparse anatomy, and with very little motion.

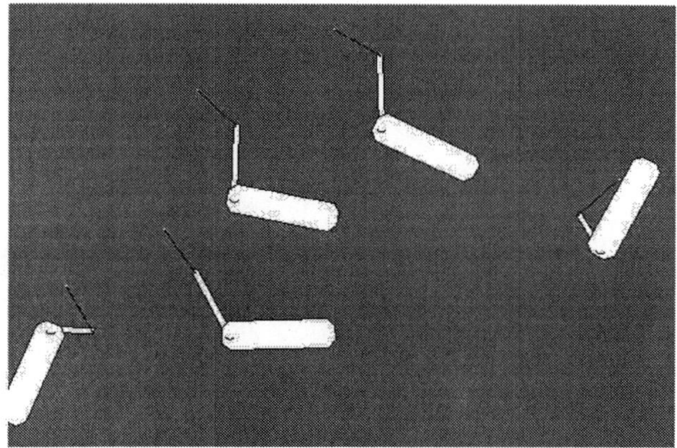

Figure 10. A family of slow swimbots from a population attracted to lack of movement

This simulation resulted in lower average energy efficiency than most other simulation runs (the time series graph which is not illustrated here reveals a relatively low, uneventful energy efficiency trend). A few qualitative observations were made from this simulation.

Since the simulation had produced swimbots who moved slowly, the fluid field exhibited a great patchwork quilt of phenotypes (indicated by coloration), since genotypes mixed at such a slow rate. Mating remained predominantly local. All swimbots however were very simple in anatomy, possessing only two parts, as shown in Figure 10.

Another observation was made: although swimming was slow, swimbot population rose dramatically. The explanation may be that since swimbots expended little energy, they were able to live long lives: a lower death rate. This large population then offered those few swimbots who were slightly mobile a wealth of potential mates within close proximity. Locomotion required for reproduction was not demanding of energy or time.

Conclusion

The results indicate that mate preferences for arbitrary features may not necessarily inhibit evolution of energy efficiency in all cases, but in some experiments, energy efficiency was inhibited, as in the experiment in which attractiveness was set to equal lack of movement. In addition to this conclusion, a wealth of discoveries and surprises have resulted, as the populations discovered ways to adapt their phenotypes to increase reproduction.

It is hoped that this paper inspires further, more in-depth explorations in similar artificial worlds, where the search for the perfect mate has an impact on how things evolve.

Future Developments

Now that a simple scheme has been built into the model, enabling swimbots to evaluate a few phenotypic features in potential mates, it would be useful to add more extensive motion feature detectors. For instance, swimbots could respond to features such as uniformity of movement, possibly giving rise to symmetrical swimming styles and anatomies. Pattern-matching could also be used, whereby swimbots generate archetypal periodic motions from a parameter set, which they then compare to motion trajectories detected in potential mates.

Many other developments could be easily envisioned, including the addition of gender to the model, extending the physics to 3 dimensions, and adding motor modulators which respond to additional mental states (such as courting).

Acknowledgements

Special thanks goes to Dr. Will Harvey for his support and suggestions. Thanks also to Michael Kaplan for technical help and fruitful conversations. Much appreciation also goes to Brian Dodd and Bryan Galdrikian for their many insights. Thanks to Frey Waid and Mike Rosenzweig, Ph.D. for helpful suggestions.

References

Abbott, E.A. 1963. *Flatland, A Romance of Many Dimensions*. Barnes & Noble.

Badler, N. I., B. A. Barsky, and D. Zeltzer, eds. 1991. *Making Them Move*. San Mateo, CA: Morgan Kaufmann.

Braitenberg, V. 1984. *Vehicles: Experiments in Synthetic Psychology*. Cambridge, MA: MIT Press.

Goldberg, D. 1989. *Genetic Algorithms in Search, Optimization, and Machine Learning*. Addison-Wesley.

Holland, J. 1975. *Adaptation in Natural and Artificial Systems*. Ann Arbor: University of Michigan Press.

Ijspeert, A.J., Hallam, J., and Willshaw, D. 1997. Artificial lampreys: Comparing naturally and artificially evolved swimming controllers. In *Proceedings of the Fourth European Conference on Artificial Life*, edited by P. Husbands and I. Harvey. Cambridge, MA: MIT Press/Bradford Books, p. 256-265.

Koza, J. 1992. *Genetic Programming: on the Programming of Computers by Means of Natural Selection*. MIT Press.

Ngo, T. J. and J. Marks. 1993. Spacetime constraints revisited. *Computer Graphics*, p. 343-350.

Ray, T. S. 1991. An approach to the synthesis of life. In *Proceedings of Artificial Life II*, edited by C. G. Langton, J. D. Farmer, C. Taylor, and S. Rasmussen. Redwood City, CA: Addison-Wesley, p. 371-408.

Reynolds, C. 1987. Flocks, herds, and schools: A distributed behavioral model. *Computer Graphics* 21(4): 25.

RSG (Rocket Science Games, Inc., producer) 1997. *Darwin Pond*, software product, designed by Jeffrey Ventrella, (contact: jeffrey@ventrella.com or visit `http://www.ventrella.com`)

Sims, K. 1994a. Evolving virtual creatures. *Computer Graphics. SIGGRAPH Proceedings* p. 24-29.

Sims, K. 1994b. Evolving 3D morphology and behavior by competition. In *Proceedings of Artificial Life IV*, edited by R. A. Brooks and P. Maes. Cambridge, MA: MIT Press, p. 28-39.

Terzopoulis, D., Tu, X., and Grzeszczuk, R. 1994. Artificial fishes with autonomous locomotion, perception, behavior, and learning in a simulated physical world. In *Proceedings of Artificial Life IV*, edited by R. A. Brooks and P. Maes. Cambridge, MA: MIT Press, p. 17-27.

Todd, P.M., and Miller, G.F. 1991. The sympatric origin of species: Mercurial mating in the Quick-silver model. In *Proceedings of the Fourth International Conference on Genetic Algorithms,* edited by R.K. Belew and L.B. Booker. Morgan Kaufmann, p. 547-554.

Ventrella, J. 1990. *Walker* video demonstrated at Artificial Life III conference, and an unpublished paper, produced at the Advanced Graphics Research Lab of Syracuse University, NY (contact: `jeffrey@ventrella.com`)

Ventrella, J. 1994. Explorations in the emergence of morphology and locomotion behavior in animated figures. In *Proceedings of Artificial Life IV*, edited by R. A. Brooks and P. Maes. Cambridge, MA: MIT Press.

Ventrella, J. 1996. Sexual swimmers (Emergent morphology and locomotion without a fitness function). In *From Animals to Animats*. MIT Press, p. 484-493.

Witkin, A. and M. Kass. 1988. Spacetime constraints. *Computer Graphics.* 22(4): 159-168.

Yaeger, L. 1994. Computational genetics, physiology, metabolism, neural systems, learning, vision, and behavior or PolyWorld: Life in a new context. In *Proceedings of Artificial Life III*, edited by C. G. Langton. Redwood City, CA: Addison-Wesley.

Zeltzer, D. 1991. Task level graphical simulation: Abstraction, representation, and control. In *Making Them Move*, edited by N. I. Badler, B. A. Barsky, and D. Zeltzer. San Mateo, CA: Morgan Kauffman, p. 3-24.

Adapting to Environmental Regularity

Effect of Environmental Structure on Evolutionary Adaptation

Jeffrey A. Fletcher, Mark A. Bedau, and Martin Zwick

Systems Science Ph.D. Program, Portland State University, Portland, Oregon 97207-0751, jeff@sysc.pdx.edu
Department of Philosophy, Reed College, 3203 SE Woodstock Boulevard, Portland, Oregon 97202, mab@reed.edu
Systems Science Ph.D. Program, Portland State University, Portland, Oregon 97207-0751, zwick@sysc.pdx.edu

Abstract

This paper investigates how environmental structure, given the innate properties of a population, affects the degree to which this population can adapt to the environment. The model we explore involves simple agents in a 2-d world which can sense a local food distribution and, as specified by their genomes, move to a new location and ingest the food there. Adaptation in this model consists of improving the genomic sensorimotor mapping so as to maximally exploit the environmental resources. We vary environmental structure to see its specific effect on adaptive success. In our investigation, two properties of environmental structure, conditioned by the sensorimotor capacities of the agents, have emerged as significant factors in determining adaptive success: (1) the information content of the environment which quantifies the diversity of conditions sensed, and (2) the expected utility for optimal action. These correspond to the syntactic and pragmatic aspects of environmental information, respectively. We find that the ratio of expected utility to information content predicts adaptive success measured by population gain and information content alone predicts the fraction of ideal utility achieved. These quantitative methods and specific conclusions should aid in understanding the effects of environmental structure on evolutionary adaptation in a wide range of evolving systems, both artificial and natural.

Adaptation as a Function of Environmental Structure

An evolving system consists of a population of agents adapting their behavior to an environment through the process of natural selection. The difficulty of the adaptive challenge obviously depends upon the population, the environment, and the interaction between the two. In this paper, we adopt an environment-centered view, that is, we examine how environments vary in the adaptive challenge which they present. This orientation reflects a kind of figure/ground reversal. One commonly takes the environment as ground and the adapting population as figure. That is, one treats the adaptive challenge as fixed and examines the resulting dynamics of adaptation, e.g., as a function of different adaptive capabilities of the population. Here, we treat the population as relatively given and study how varying the environment affects the difficulty of the adaptive task to be solved. This reversal of focus is found in some other recent studies (e.g., Wilson 1991; Littman 1993; Todd and Wilson 1993; Todd et al. 1994, Todd and Yanco 1996, and Menczer and Belew 1996) and it recalls the earlier work of Emery and Trist (1965) on the causal texture of environments of social organizations. These studies tend to pursue one of two projects: either providing an abstract categorization of environments, or gathering experimental evidence about how artificial agents actually adapt in different simulated environments. Here and in a previous paper (Fletcher, Zwick, and Bedau 1996) we pursue both projects simultaneously; we experimentally study how the adaptation of given (possibly sub-optimal) agents varies in response to environmental structure. Since our characterization of environmental structure is quantitative, we can seek evidence for general laws relating adaptive success and environmental structure.

We intentionally have made our model quite simple. In this way we can more easily develop quantitative methods and results which can then be applied to more complicated evolving systems. In particular, our model encompasses the following simplifications:

- simple environment
    1. agents do not affect the environmental structure, which is static
    2. agents randomly sample the entire environment
- simple agents
    1. simple internal representation of the environment (implicit in the genome)
    2. no genotype/phenotype difference (every gene encodes a response to a unique sensory condition)
    3. simple behavior: movement (and food ingestion)
    4. no temporal organization of behavior
- simple evolutionary process
    1. minimal inter-agent interactions
    2. no sexual recombination

The following complex features of agent-environment interaction were, however, retained in our model:

- differences between objective environment and an agent's sensory discrimination
- uncertain consequences of action (an agent's sensory horizon is smaller than its movement horizon)
- no explicit fitness function

The population in our model consists of sensorimotor agents. Each agent responds to limited sensory input from the environment with a single behavioral output specified by the agent's genome. The adaptive task consists of finding an output to associate with each possible input. The difficulty of the adaptive task, therefore, involves at least the following aspects of environmental structure:

- the quantity of sensory information, i.e., the variety of sensed environmental conditions with which behaviors must be associated (a "syntactic" aspect)
- the utility of the information, i.e., the benefit of adaptive behaviors over non-adaptive behaviors (a "pragmatic" aspect)

The first draws upon the information theory of Shannon and Weaver (1949); the second draws upon game theory (sometime referred to as decision theory) of von Neumann and Morgenstern (1944). Both aspects are needed to characterize the evolutionary challenge. We refer to them jointly as *environmental structure*.

In terms of these aspects, an adaptive task is difficult if the environment sends many messages requiring an adaptive response, or if they have little utility. The syntactic aspect is central to Ashby's (1956) conceptualization of adaptation, according to which environmental variety poses a problem to which behavioral variety is the response. Agents also experience the second aspect of environmental structure directly as they gain the resources yielded by particular responses to particular sensory inputs. In our previous paper (1996) we began to explore these issues. Here we extend that work by quantitatively measuring both aspects of environmental structure and showing their relationship to our quantitative measures of adaptive success.

Modeling Adaptation in Diverse Environments

Our observations are from computer simulations of adaptation in a series of constructed environments. The model consists of many agents that sense their local environment, move as a function of what they sense, and ingest what resources they find where they move. This model is a modification of those previously studied by Bedau and Packard (1992), Bedau, Ronneburg and Zwick (1992), Bedau (1994), Bedau and Bahm (1994), Bedau (1995), Bedau, Giger and Zwick (1995), and Fletcher, Zwick, and Bedau (1996). All of these models are extensions of one originally developed by Packard (1989).

Agent and environment interactions

The world is a grid of 128 x 128 sites with periodic boundary conditions, i.e., a toroidal lattice. All that exists in the world besides the agents is a resource field, which is spread over the lattice of sites. The resource level at a given site is set at a value chosen from the interval [0-*R*], where *R* is the maximum resource level (chosen arbitrarily as 255). In the framework of Emery and Trist (1965), our model is a type-II ("placid, clustered") rather than type-III ("disturbed, reactive") environment, because the principal consideration is location rather than actual or potential inter-agent interactions.

Here we consider only *static* resource fields, i.e., fields in which resources are immediately replenished whenever they are consumed, so that the spatiotemporal resource distribution, i.e., structure, is constant. In static resource models the population has no effect on the distribution of resources. Nevertheless, since the agents constantly extract resources and expend them by living and reproducing, the agents function as the system's resource sinks and the whole system is dissipative.

Adaptation is resource driven since the agents need a steady supply of resources in order to survive and reproduce. Agents interact with the resource field at each time step by ingesting all of the resources (if any) found at their current location and storing it in their internal resource reservoir. Agents must continually replenish this reservoir to survive for they are assessed a constant resource tax at each time step. If an agent's internal resource supply drops to zero, it dies and disappears from the world. As a practical expedient for speeding up the simulation, each agent also runs a small risk, proportional to population size, of randomly dying.

Each agent moves each time step as dictated by its genetically encoded sensorimotor map: a table of behavior rules of the form: IF (environment *j* sensed) THEN (do behavior *k*). Only one agent can reside at a given site at a given time, so an agent randomly walks to the first unoccupied site near its destination if its sensorimotor map sends it to a site which is already occupied. (Population sizes range from about 2% to 10% of the number of sites in the world, so at the larger population sizes these collisions will occur with a non-negligible frequency.) An agent receives sensory information about the resources (but not the other agents) in its von Neumann neighborhood of the five sites above, below, to the left, to the right, and at its present location. An agent can discriminate only four resource levels (evenly distributed over the [0-*R*] range of objective resource levels) at each site in its von Neumann neighborhood. Thus, each sensory state *j* corresponds to one of 4^5 = 1024 different detectable local environments. Each behavior *k* is a jump vector between zero and fifteen sites in any one of the eight compass directions (north, northeast, east, etc.). The behavioral repertoire of these agents thus consists of 8 x 16 = 128 different possible behaviors. This sensorimotor map, consisting of a movement genetically hardwired for each detectable environmental condition, is the agent's "genotype." These genotypes are extremely simple, amounting to nothing more than a lookup table of 1024 sensorimotor rules. On the other hand, the space in which adaptation occurs is vast, consisting of 128^{1024} distinct possible genotypes. (As the next section explains, in some environments some von Neumann neighborhoods do not exist and so the corresponding sensorimotor rules cannot ever be used; this lowers the number of *effectively* different genotypes in these environments.)

An agent reproduces (asexually) if its resource reservoir exceeds a certain threshold. The parent produces one child, which starts life with half of its parent's resource supply. The child also inherits its parent's sensorimotor map, except that mutations may replace the behaviors associated with some sensory states with randomly chosen behaviors. The mutation rate parameter determines the probability of a mutation at a single locus, i.e., the probability that the behavior associated with a given sensory state changes. At the extreme case in which the mutation rate is set to one, a child's entire sensorimotor map is chosen at random.

Sensorimotor strategies evolve over generations. A given simulation starts with randomly distributed agents containing randomly chosen sensorimotor strategies. The model contains no *a priori* fitness function (Packard 1989), so the population's size and genetic constitution fluctuates with the contingencies of extracting resources. Agents with maladaptive strategies tend to find few resources and thus to die, taking their sensorimotor genes with them; by contrast, agents with adaptive strategies tend to find sufficient resources to reproduce, spreading their sensorimotor strategies (with mutations) through the population. The basic components of our model have some similarities to the LEE model studied by Menczer and Belew (1996) including: varying the adaptive challenge by varying the patterns in a resource grid, movement in the grid as the adaptable behavior, asexual reproduction, and no explicit fitness function.

During each time step in the simulation, each agent follows this sequence of events: it senses its present von Neumann neighborhood, moves to the new location dictated by its sensorimotor map, consumes any resources found at its new location, and then goes to a new location chosen at random from the entire lattice of sites. This repositioning constantly scatters the population over the entire environment, exposing it to the entire range of detectable environmental conditions. Since the resource field is static, the set of detectable environmental conditions remains fixed throughout a given simulation. Agents never have the opportunity to put together unbroken sequences of behaviors, since each behavior is followed by a random relocation. And since all agents are taxed equally, rather than being taxed according to distance moved, all that matters to an agent in a given detectable local environment is to jump to the site most likely to contain the most resources. Thus, the adaptive challenge the agents face is to make the best possible single move given specific sensory information about the local environment. Adaptation occurs through multiple instances of these one-step challenge-and-response trials.

Varying environmental structure

We want to study adaptation in a variety of environments that differ only in their environmental structure. At the same time, to make population size a measure of adaptability that can be meaningfully compared across the different environments, we want all of these environments to have the same total quantity of resources. If we let R be the maximal possible resource level at a site (in the present simulation $R = 255$), we can achieve this goal by engineering the environments so that the average resource level at a site is $R/2$. (Although a site can have any of 256 different objective resource levels, recall that the agents can discriminate only four resource levels.) The following suite of environments meets these desiderata:

1. Flat: Each site in this environment has a resource level set to $R/2$.
2. Random: Resource levels in this environment are chosen at random with equal probability from the interval [0-R], thus ensuring that the average level is $R/2$.
3. Sine waves: Resource are assigned by two sine waves, one along the x-axis and the other along the y-axis. The amplitude of these waves is scaled in such a way that when both are maximal and overlapping the site has the maximum resource level, when both are minimal the site has no resources, and the average resource level is $R/2$. The frequencies of the two sine waves can be varied independently and are expressed in the number of sine-wave periods which cover the x- or y-axes.
4. Substituting Flat or Random levels in Sine waves. In these environments the sine wave-generated resource level is substituted at randomly chosen sites with either constant or random values. Since the constant resource level is set equal to $R/2$, and the random resource levels are chosen with equal probability from the interval [0-R], the average resource level per site remains $R/2$ regardless of the density of sites. The density of substituted sites is a model parameter.

In a previous paper (Fletcher, Zwick, and Bedau 1996) we provided several figures illustrating the various patterns generated in our suite of environments. We also discussed how these environments apply to Wilson's (1991) and Littman's (1993) environment classification schemes.

Quantitative Measures

To study how adaptability depends on environmental structure, we define separate measures of environmental structure and adaptive success. We then observe how adaptive success (our dependent variable) responds when we manipulate environmental structure (our independent variable). The measures we propose illuminate how adaptation and environmental structure interact.

Two aspects of environmental structure

Adaptation is sensitive to those aspects of environmental structure that the agents perceive and act upon. One such aspect is the variety of the environmental conditions which the agents can discriminate; a second is the utility provided by the environment for adapting to these environmental conditions. These two aspects correspond to the syntactic information content in the environment and pragmatic value of the information, respectively.

Information. A natural way to quantify the former is with the information-theoretic uncertainty or Shannon entropy (Shannon and Weaver 1949) of the distribution of detectable local conditions:

$$H(E) = -\sum_i F_E(v_i)\log_2 F_E(v_i)$$

where v_i is the ith detectable local environmental condition (in this case, a distinct resource distribution in the von Neumann neighborhood), and $F_E(v_i)$ is the frequency of occurrence, across all sites in environment E, of v_i.

$H(E)$ measures the information content of the environmental conditions that the agents can detect, i.e., the reduction in uncertainty about v when an agent detects a local environmental condition. This measure is a particular way of integrating two aspects of the distribution $F_E(v)$: its width (number of different v) and flatness (constancy of $F_E(v_i)$). Everything else being equal, the wider or the flatter $F_E(v)$ is, the more uncertain an agent will be about which neighborhood it will detect, the more information an agent will get when it does detect its neighborhood, and the higher $H(E)$ will be. We can equivalently refer to $H(E)$ as the detectable environment's uncertainty, Shannon entropy, or information content.

Since the environments studied here all have static resource distributions, in every case $H(E)$ is constant over time. $H(E)$ would change in environments with dynamic resource distributions and thus would apply to a wide variety of environments in addition to those studied here.

Utility. To measure the pragmatic differences among environments, we calculate what the expected utility would be for a perfectly adapted population in each environment. We measure this ideal expected utility, $U^*(E)$, as how much resources on average each agent would receive per time step in a perfectly adapted population in excess over what the average agent would receive in a randomly behaving, non-adapted, population.

Like $H(E)$, $U^*(E)$ is a property of the environment, given the innate capacities of the agents, and it can be calculated *a priori*—before any simulation is run. For each distinct von Neumann neighborhood in the environment, the utility (above the average utility of random action) of all moves from each instance of the von Neumann neighborhood is tallied. The highest tally gives the best average expected utility for this neighborhood. The average of all the best expected utilities, weighted by the frequency of each neighborhood type in the environment, is $U^*(E)$. This would be the result of successful application of a Maximum Expected Value strategy in a game against nature (von Neumann and Morgenstern 1944).

Given that the objective resource levels are the same in all our environments, it might seem that the ideal utility, $U^*(E)$, should be equal for all environments. There are two reasons why this is not the case:

1. The limited jump range of agents (15 sites) makes it impossible in some environments for agents to jump to a maximal resource hill from some environmental locations.
2. Even if an environment always contains a close by resource hill, agents can only have one behavior mapping per distinct von Neumann neighborhood type. Therefore, if the best action in different instances of that neighborhood is different, even a perfectly adapted agent could not move to a maximum benefit site from each environmental location.

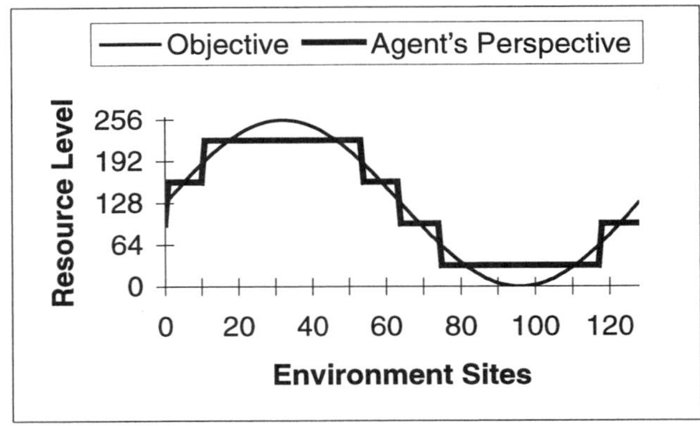

Figure 1 Side view of the 1 x 1 sine-wave environment in a 128 x 128 toroidal lattice of sites, showing both the objective resource field and the agents' perspective of it. Note that, although the objective resource level at a site can have 1 of 256 possible values, the agents can distinguish only 4 resource levels.

Figure 1 shows a cross-section of the 1 x 1 environment and illustrates both cases above. An agent sitting at position 80 jumping 15 sites to the left makes the best move possible, but still does not reach the resource maximum located at position 32. In this same environment, an agent sitting at position 5 would sense a resource plateau—the same resource level in each of the 5 sites that makes up the von Neumann neighborhood centered on its position. The ideal behavior from position 5 would be a jump 15 to the *right*, but at position 60 the agent senses the same von Neumann neighborhood and the ideal behavior is a jump 15 to the *left*.

The agent's coarse sensory discrimination and limited jump range make the $U^*(E)$ value for the 1 x 1 environment only 11.5. On the other hand, some high frequency, regularly patterned environments always have a maximum resource site unambiguously located within an agent's jump range, e.g. in the 64 x 64 sine-wave environment, the $U^*(E)$ value is 127.3 (very close to the maximal value of $R / 2$ or 127.5).

Note that $U^*(E)$ does not capture environmental utility *completely*. It says nothing about the distribution of benefits for sub-optimal behaviors. Nevertheless, it gives a rough measure of the differences in expected utility among a wide variety of environments.

To develop a feel for aspects of the detectable environmental structure measured by *H(E)* and *U*(E)* consider our suite of environments:

1. If E is the flat environment, all local environmental conditions *are* identical, so they all *look* identical to the agents in the population. Thus, *H(flat)* = 0. Also, *U*(flat)* = 0 since there is no structure to adapt to.
2. If E is the random environment, all detectable environments occur with (approximately) equal frequency, which makes *H(random)* close to its maximal value, which is $\log_2$ of the number of different v. Since the agents in our model can detect two bits of information about resource levels at each site in their von Neumann neighborhood, there are $4^5 = 2^{10}$ detectable environmental conditions, so *H(random)* ≈ 10. (In the random environments we generated, typically *H(random)* = 9.95.) In a random environment, the best behavior varies among different instances of each von Neumann neighborhood. The *U*(random)* value is about 85.
3. Sine-wave environments vary in the x and y frequency of the sine waves, and the number and frequency of detectable neighborhoods varies with these frequencies. Thus, $F_E(v)$ can have a variety of shapes, and both *H(E)* and *U*(E)* can take a variety of values, as shown in the table below:

Environment	*H(E)*	*U*(E)*
1 x 1	2.65	11.5
4 x 4	3.99	73.3
64 x 64	2.00	127.3
34 x 42	7.09	119.1

4. If some fraction of the sites in a sine-wave environment are replaced with flat or random resource levels, *H(E)* and *U*(E)* values can vary quite a bit. Low density of replaced sites tend to make $F_E(v)$ slightly flatter, which makes *H(E)* slightly higher, regardless of whether the resource levels in the new sites are flat or random. As the density of replaced sites approaches one however, depending on whether the substituted levels are flat or random, $F_E(v)$ approaches the shape of $F_{flat}(v)$ or $F_{random}(v)$, so *H(E)* approaches the value of *H(flat)* or *H(random)* and *U*(E)* approaches *U*(flat)* or *U*(random)*.

Finally, we wish to reiterate that both *H(E)* and *U*(E)* do not simply reflect the objective properties (i.e., the resource field) of the environment; they reflect this field *as perceived by* agents of the population. In this respect, it is like the ways in which Wilson (1991) and Littman (1993) characterize environments.

Measures of adaptation

We have developed two different measures of adaptive success: an external one that is based on the gain in population size due to adaptation, and a more internal view of adaptation based on the degree to which agents achieve the ideal expected utility.

External measure of adaptation. The model we study here is resource driven, and a population's size reflects its ability to locate the resources found in the environment. Although, in all the environments we studied, objective resource levels were roughly equal, we cannot assume in general that observed population size *by itself* is an accurate indication of the degree to which adaptation has taken place. Given the resources available in the environment and given the agents' existence taxes, even non-adapting randomly behaving agents might still survive by accidentally "bumping into" resources. To factor this out, we compare equilibrium population size in a given environment with the equilibrium size of a "reference" population in exactly the same kind of environment. The reference population has exactly the same set of internal features (sensory and behavioral capacities, existence tax, etc.) as the observed population, *except* that its behaviors are always chosen at random instead of being based on sensory input. We denote this reference population size $P_R(E)$, while *P(E)* denotes the actual equilibrium population size of population P in environment E. Thus $A_P(E)$, the adaptive success of population P in environment E is the proportion of increase above the reference population size:

$$A_P(E) = \frac{P(E) - P_R(E)}{P_R(E)}$$

Internal measure of adaptation. $A_P(E)$ gives us a way to compare the adaptive success of our standard population among different environments, but we can also look more closely at the internal causes of the observed population differences. That is, we can also express adaptive success in terms of *U(E)*: how much utility agents receive compared to non-adapting agents. As we will see, *U(E)* and $A_P(E)$ are highly correlated.

Consider two environments that result in the same $A_P(E)$ and also result in the same *U(E)* of 25 resource units per agent per time step. If *U*(E)* of one environment is 100 and *U*(E)* of the second is 50, then the population in the first environment achieved 25% of the ideal expected utility and in the second the population achieved 50% of the expected utility. The behaviors, and therefore the agents' genomes, are closer to the ideal in the second environment. Since the $A_P(E)$ values were the same, the $A_P(E)$ measure does not capture this adaptation difference. We capture this more internal view of adaptive success with the ratio of *U(E)* to *U*(E)*:

$$A_U(E) = \frac{U(E)}{U^*(E)}$$

We use the subscript U to distinguish adaptive success

measured using the utility ratios from $A_r(E)$ which is our measure of adaptation based on population size.

Measures of diversity in adaptive behavior

Finally, we can study another internal aspect of adaptation by measuring the change in Shannon entropy of the population's alleles (weighted by gene usage) as adaptation takes place. Three different measures are relevant. First, we can simply calculate the total Shannon entropy (diversity) of alleles used by a population. We periodically sample the population for a small time interval and calculate the Shannon entropy of all alleles used during this interval. We designate this by $H(L)$ where L stands for alleles. Second, we can bin this same data by gene and calculate the diversity of alleles within each gene (von Neumann neighborhood), and then average these results (weighted by gene usage) to calculate an overall within-gene allelic diversity. This we designate as $H(L|G)$: the diversity of allele, L, given the gene (or von Neumann neighborhood), G. Because there are 128 = 2^7 different alleles, the maximum $H(L)$ or $H(L|G)$ value is 7. Third, the difference

$$I(L:G) = H(L) - H(L \mid G)$$

is the mutual information which can also be considered the "between-gene" diversity. In our present simple environments, variation increases $H(L|G)$ while selection reduces it; successful adaptation is reflected in an increase in $I(L:G)$. For more details on these information-theoretic measures, see Bedau, Zwick, and Bahm (1995).

NB: For notational simplicity, we now will drop the argument E for measures U, U^*, A_p, and A_U. H without an argument will always refer to environmental information, but we will write $H(E)$ explicitly where we need to differentiate it from other Shannon entropy measures.

Environmental Structure and Adaptation

We studied adaptation in a total of 70 different distinct environments with environmental information content, H, values ranging from 0.00 to 9.95 (10 is maximum) and ideal expected utility, U^*, values ranging from 0.00 to 127.25 (127.50 is maximum). For all of these runs we used a mutation rate of 0.001 and allowed population size to reach equilibrium. Our task is to understand the relationship between our independent environmental variables H and U^*, and our dependent variable, adaptive success, measured using either A_P or A_U.

Observations using A_P

We first note a very high correlation between A_P values and the actual average utility, U. Figure 2 shows this relationship, which holds very well across the whole range of environments tested. This gives us confidence that average resource consumption is directly proportional to population size gain, and therefore factors such as the chance of random death do not significantly affect population size results.

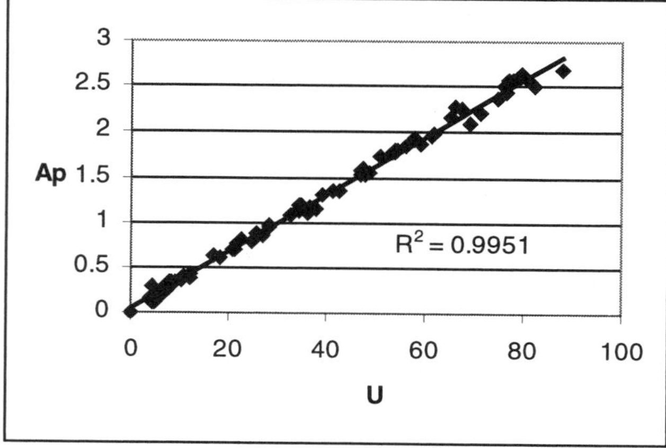

Figure 2 Adaptive success (measured using population) as a function of actual equilibrium utility per agent per time step. The relationship is proportional and shows that other factors besides U do not significantly contribute to A_P.

Next we examine how A_P depends on our environmental parameters. We expect that it will be inversely dependent on H and directly dependent on the ideal utility, U^*. In other words, increased adaptive success will be associated with less uncertainty of sensory inputs to adapt to, and higher utility for adapting. Figure 3 shows the relationship between A_P and U^*. We can see that A_P tends to increase with U^*, but this relationship is weak. This "fuzziness" may be partially due to our other environmental parameter H.

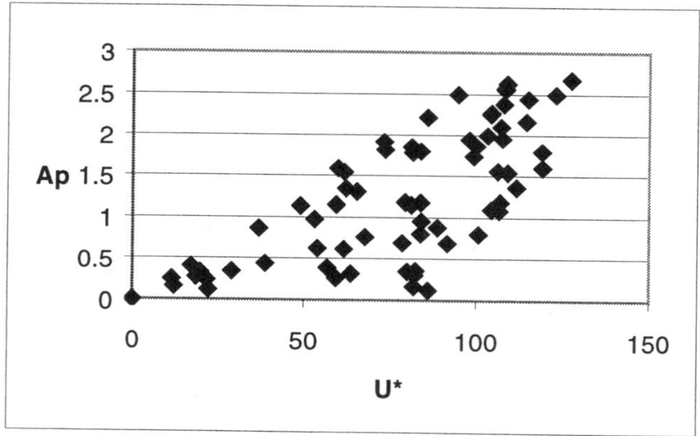

Figure 3 Adaptive success (measured using population) as a function of average ideal utility per agent per time step. This shows a weak relationship.

Figure 4 plots the relationship between A_P and $1 / H$. Again, there is an indication of the expected relationship, but we observe two notable exceptions. First, there is a series of points that show a low A_P across the whole range of $1/H$ values. These tend to be environments with very low U^* values (typically less than 30). Second, there is series of environments where A_P is flat for high A_P values. We discuss this leveling off of adaptive success for environments with low H values (high $1 / H$) in the next section.

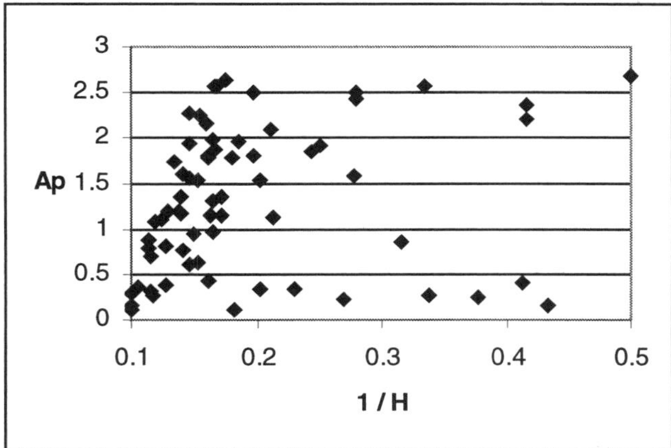

Figure 4 Adaptive success (measured using population) as a function of the inverse of environmental information content. This shows a weak relationship with notable exceptions for low and high A_P values.

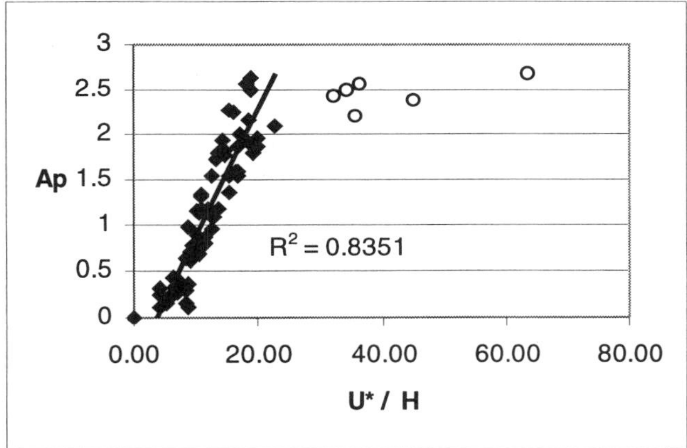

Figure 5 Adaptive success (measured using population) as a function of ideal utility divided by environmental information content (utility per bit of environmental information). This shows a significant relationship for U^* / H less than 30. A linear fitting of all data gives an R^2 value of 0.5846.

In Figure 5 we combine our two measures of environmental structure by dividing U^* by H. The relationship between this combined measure and A_P is strikingly improved over the relationship with A_P of either individually. There are six points that do not fit well into the linear relationship. There appears to be a hard upper limit to A_P of about 2.5 where neither raising the utility nor lowering the uncertainty of sensory inputs raises A_P. We discuss possible reasons for this in the next section. We should note that U^* / H is only one of many possible ways to model our data. We have used other models, such as exponential and polynomial models, to fit the entire range of data, but since the number of points in the non-linear range is small, we restrict ourselves here to the linear model. The rational for a linear dependence of U^* / H is compelling. It is a measure of the utility of perfect adaptation per bit of environmental sensory information to be adapted to. Across all the environments we studied with U^* / H less than 30, this ratio predicts how well the population will adapt (as measured by population size gain). For U^* / H less than 30 there is a linear relationship with A_P (R^2 = 0.8351). For U^* / H greater than 30, A_P is maximal at roughly 2.5.

We have also obtained reasonable fits of the data using simple linear regressions of A_P against U^* and H (or $1 / H$), but the dependence of A_P on the composite U^* / H is more compact and readily interpretable.

Observations using A_U

Although population size is a traditional way of measuring adaptive success, A_U has the advantage of having a hard upper limit defined by U^*. Also, it gives us an internal view of how behaviors (genomes) are changing as adaptation takes place. Figure 6 plots A_U against the ratio U^* / H. Although the general trends are the same as seen in Figure 5, the relationship is rather weaker.

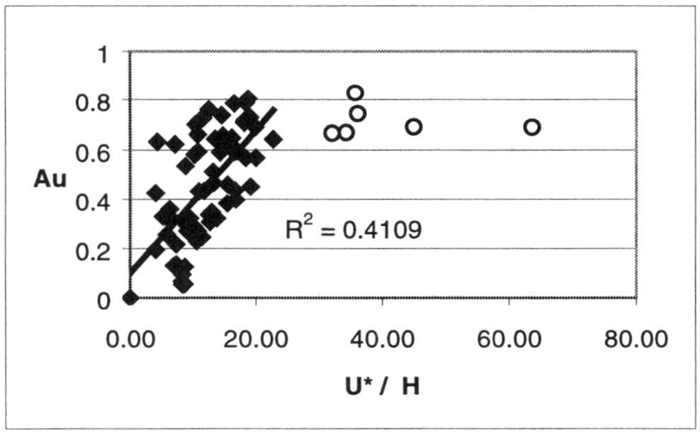

Figure 6 Adaptive success (measured using achieved fraction of ideal utility) as a function of ideal utility divided by environmental information content (utility per bit of environmental information). This relationship using this measure of adaptive success is much less significant than the one using A_P (shown in Figure 5). A linear fitting of all data gives an R^2 value of 0.3088.

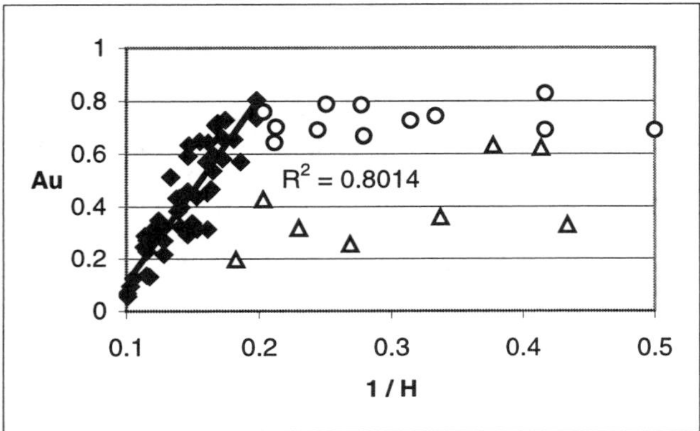

Figure 7 Adaptive success (measured using achieved fraction of ideal utility) as a function of the inverse of environmental information content. This shows a linear relationship with two notable exceptions: 1) very low U^* values (less than 30) shown with empty triangle; and 2) H values less than 5 ($1 / H$ values less than 0.2) shown with empty circles. This shows that for environments with moderate to high U^* values and H values greater than 5, the degree of utility achieved is inversely proportional to the diversity of sensory inputs. For H values less than 5 ($1 / H$ greater than 0.2), A_U is fairly flat at about 60-80%. A linear fitting of all data gives an R^2 value of 0.3007.

Figures 7 shows A_U plotted against $1 / H$. This shows a relationship between the syntactic information content of environments, H, and the degree to which ideal utility is achieved. This relationship appears to be approximately linear with two notable exceptions. First, the points shown with empty triangles represent environments with very low U^* values (less than 30). For these environments, the degree of ideal utility achieved, A_U, appears to be not well correlated with $1 / H$ values. The second exception occurs for H less than 5 ($1 / H$ greater than 0.2). These points are shown with empty circles. In this region A_U appears to level off at about 60-80%. In other words, even as the adaptive task becomes easier (less uncertainty of sensory inputs), the degree of utility achieved though adaptation does not appear to improve appreciably. We would not expect a population to ever reach 100% perfect adaptation. The mutation rate alone would keep this from happening. Additionally, as mentioned before, as environments become more crowded, agents are more likely to land on each other and be diverted to another nearby site. In this case, even if agents' genomes were ideal, the utility gain would not be the ideal value since they were being "bumped" from their target site. Our measure depends on the actual utility and we would expect U to level off below the ideal, U^*, at least in part due to the reasons above. For the environments studied here and a mutation rate of 0.001, A_U plateaus at around 60-80% and lowering H (raising $1 / H$) does not improve A_U. This plateau appears to begin for $1 / H$ greater than 0.2 (or H less than 5). There was no discernable relationship for U^* vs. A_U—not shown.

Relationship between A_P and A_U

We can tie our two measures of adaptive success together by deriving the relationship depicted in Figure 5 (which uses A_P) from the relationship depicted in Figure 7 (which uses A_U). The four steps below are intended to illustrate a hypothesized relationship, rather than to prove a mathematical one.

1. $1 / H \propto A_U$ [relationship shown in Figure 7]
2. $1 / H \propto U / U^*$ [definition of A_U]
3. $U^* / H \propto U$ [multiply both sides by U^*]
4. $U^* / H \propto A_P$ [$U \propto A_P$ by Figure 2]

We have, thus, $A_P \propto (A_U) \bullet (U^*)$. A_P measures the increase in population size due to adaptation and is dependent on the utility of adapting per bit of environmental sensory information to be adapted to (except for high values of this ratio where A_P is maximal). A_U measures the fraction of ideal *utility* achieved due to adaptation and indirectly the degree to which ideal *behaviors* are achieved. A_U is inversely dependent on the uncertainty of sensory inputs (with two exceptions: (1) where expected utility is quite low—in which case A_U is variable, and (2) where the diversity of sensory inputs is low, in which case A_U is maximal).

In retrospect, if we had constructed our environments with constant U^* rather than constant total resources, we would expect A_U and A_P to show the same dependence on environmental information.

Ashby's law of requisite variety

Another indication that a population is adapting to an environment is that the variety of alleles across different genes matches the variety of sensory inputs and at the same time the variety of alleles for any particular gene is small. In other words, full adaptation to the static environments we are studying calls for the existence of a unique allele for each sensory input—that allele being the best behavioral response to the particular environmental condition.

At the start of a run, the distribution of alleles across all genes in the population is random and thus the overall allele uncertainty is maximal at $H(L) \approx 7$. Within each particular gene, the uncertainty, $H(L|G)$, over the population is similarly random and maximal, i.e., is also close to 7. By contrast, the between-gene diversity, which is the mutual information, $I(L:G)$, between allele and environmental condition is near zero.

Figure 8 illustrates what then happens as the population becomes well adapted. The between-gene diversity of the alleles, $I(L:G)$, which represents also the tightness of constraint between alleles and environmental conditions, approaches the uncertainty of the environment, H(E), which equals 4. At the same time, the within-gene diversity, $H(L|G)$, drops to near zero., i.e., there is no allelic diversity not coupled to environmental diversity.

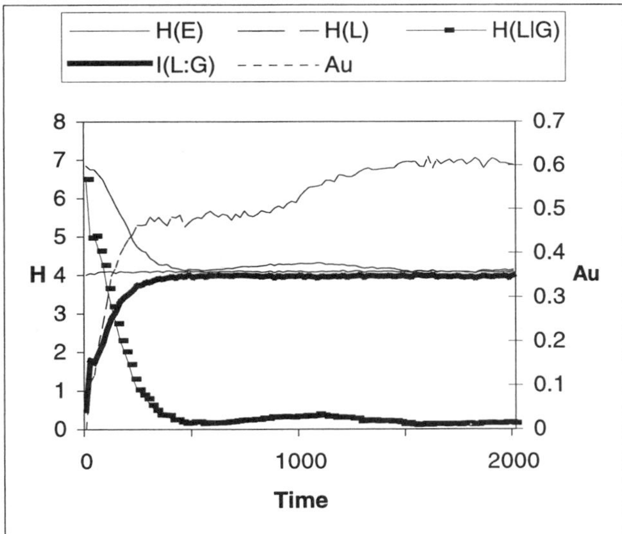

Figure 8 Time series showing the allelic diversity changes as adaptation takes place. A_U is also shown on the same graph. This shows that as adaptation takes place the overall allelic diversity, *H(L),* and the mutual information, between alleles and genes, *I(L:G),* matches that of the environment, in this case 4.0. At the same time the diversity of alleles within genes, *H(L|G),* drops to almost zero.

Both of these changes exemplify Ashby's "Law of Requisite Variety" (1956). Ashby's Law states that for optimal regulation a system needs to have a variety of responses to match the variety of environmental conditions it encounters, and second that this variety should not be mere randomness. This second point specifies that the "regulator of the system", here the genomic sensorimotor mapping, should be deterministic and not stochastic: for a particular environmental condition, there should be in the population only *one* response, namely the optimal one, not a mixture of responses. In Ashby's language, the uncertainty of the regulator state, given the disturbance, should be zero. This applies to the very simple evolving system studied here. For more complex evolutionary contexts (where resource levels are dynamic and inter-agent interactions are significant), there may well be advantages for non-zero *H(L|G)*. Both of these conditions are satisfied as adaptation approaches its maximal value: *H(L)* matches *H(E)* and *H(L|G)* is near zero. It is interesting also to observe the slight bump in *H(L|G)* at approximately *Time = 1000*. Here a temporary slight stochasticity of allelic response reflects the introduction through mutation of new and improved alleles, which as they spread, generate an increase in adaptive behaviors, A_U.

Conclusions

Our observations support two kinds of conclusions:

1. methodological conclusions about how to quantify major aspects of environmental challenge and adaptive success
2. substantive conclusions, based on experimental data, about how variations in these aspects of environmental challenge influence the degree to which populations in them adapt

Our measures of environmental structure have been applied to this simple evolutionary model, but we have defined them in general terms so that they can be applied across a wide range of evolving systems. Concepts such as the diversity of sensory inputs, *H,* and the utility for adaptive behaviors, *U*,* are relevant to both artificial and natural systems where natural selection occurs. In addition, measuring external adaptive success by comparing population size to a non-adapting population in the same environment, A_P, and internal adaptive success by measuring the degree to which ideal utility is achieved, A_U, can also be applied to many other adapting systems. We have also demonstrated how, for artificial systems where genome information is readily available, the diversity of alleles both across genes and within genes can illuminate the internal workings of the adaptive process.

On the substantive side, although there are certainly facets of environmental structure and adaptive success not captured by our measures, we have clear and testable indications about how environmental structure influences adaptation. For a wide range of environments, adaptive success depends upon both the syntactic (information-theoretic) and pragmatic (game-theoretic) aspects of environmental structure. In our work these two aspects are effectively integrated as utility per bit of sensory information. We expect that this measure will be useful in other studies of evolving systems. At the very least, both aspects of environmental structure will still need to be considered. When adaptive success is measured "internally" as the fraction of ideal utility gained, the utility aspect is encompassed implicitly. Adaptive success then depends simply (but less accurately) on sensory information content alone. Lastly, we have demonstrated explicitly Ashby's Law of Requisite Variety by showing that evolutionary adaptation is accomplished by the genomic representation of environmental information.

Acknowledgements

We would like to thank three anonymous reviewers for their detailed and thoughtful suggestions.

References

Ashby, W. R. 1956. *An Introduction to Cybernetics.*

London: Chapman & Hall.

Bedau, M. A. 1994. The evolution of sensorimotor functionality. In *From Perception to Action*, edited by P. Gaussier and J. D. Nicoud. New York: IEEE Press.

Bedau, M. A. 1995. Three illustrations of Artificial Life's working hypothesis. In *Evolution and Biocomputation—Computational Models of Evolution*, edited by W. Banzhaf and F. Eeckman. Berlin: Springer.

Bedau, M. A., and A. Bahm. 1994. Bifurcation structure in diversity dynamics. In *Proceedings of Artificial Life IV*, edited by R. Brooks and P. Maes. Cambridge, MA: Bradford/MIT Press.

Bedau, M. A., M. Giger, and M. Zwick. 1995. Adaptive diversity dynamics in static resource models. *Advances in Systems Science and Applications* 1: 1-6.

Bedau, M. A., and N. H. Packard. 1992. Measurement of evolutionary activity, teleology, and life. In *Proceedings of Artificial Life II*, edited by C. G. Langton, C. Taylor, J. D. Farmer, and S. Rasmussen. Redwood City, CA: Addison-Wesley.

Bedau, M. A., F. Ronneburg, and M. Zwick. 1992. Dynamics of diversity in an evolving population. In *Parallel Problem Solving from Nature, 2*, edited by R. Manner and B. Manderick. Amsterdam: North-Holland.

Bedau, M. A., M. Zwick, and A. Bahm. 1995. Variance and uncertainty measures of population diversity dynamics. *Advances in Systems Science and Applications,* Special Issue I, 1-000.

Emery, F. E., and E. L. Trist. 1965. The causal texture of organizational environments. *Human Relations* 18: 21-32.

Fletcher, J. A., M. Zwick, and M. A. Bedau. 1996. Dependence of adaptability on environmental structure in a simple evolutionary model. *Adaptive Behavior* 4: 275-307.

Littman, M. L. 1993. An optimization-based categorization of reinforcement learning environments. In *From Animals to Animats 2*, edited by J. A. Meyer, H. L. Roiblat, and S. W. Wilson. Cambridge, MA: Bradford/MIT Press.

Menczer, F., and R. K. Belew. 1996. From complex environments to complex behaviors. *Adaptive Behavior* 4: 309-355.

Packard, N. H. 1989. Intrinsic adaptation in a simple model for evolution. In *Proceedings of Artificial Life*, edited by C. G. Langton. Redwood City, CA: Addison-Wesley.

Shannon, C. E., and W. Weaver. 1949. *The Mathematical Theory of Communication*. Urbana, IL: University of Illinois Press.

Todd, P. M., and S. W. Wilson. 1993. Environment structure and adaptive behavior from the ground up. In *From Animals to Animats 2*, edited by J. A. Meyer, H. L. Roiblat, and S. W. Wilson. Cambridge, MA: Bradford/MIT Press.

Todd, P. M., S. W. Wilson, A. B. Somayaji, and H. A. Yanco. 1994. The blind breeding the blind: Adaptive behavior without looking. In *From Animals to Animats 3*, edited by D. Cliff, P. Husbands, J. A. Meyer, and S. W. Wilson. Cambridge, MA: Bradford/MIT Press.

Todd, P. M., and H. A. Yanco. 1996. Environmental effects on minimal behaviors in the Minimat world. *Adaptive Behavior* 4: 365-413.

von Neumann, J., and O. Morgenstern. 1944. *Theory of Games and Economic Behavior.* Princeton, N.J.: Princeton University Press.

Wilson, S. W. 1991. The animat path to AI. In *From Animals to Animats*, edited by J. A. Meyer and S. W. Wilson. Cambridge, MA: Bradford/MIT Press.

Comparison Between Off-Line Model-Free and On-Line Model-Based Evolution Applied to a Robotics Navigation System Using Evolvable Hardware

Didier Keymeulen, Masaya Iwata, Yasuo Kuniyoshi, and Tetsuya Higuchi

Electrotechnical Laboratory, Tsukuba, Ibaraki 305 Japan

Abstract

Recently there has been great interest in the idea that evolvable systems based on the principles of Artificial Life can be used to continuously and autonomously adapt the behavior of physically embedded systems such as mobile robots, plants and intelligent home devices. At the same time, we have seen the introduction of *evolvable hardware*(EHW): new integrated circuits that are able to adapt their hardware autonomously and almost continuously to changes in the environment (Higuchi *et al.* 1992). This paper describes how a navigation system for a physical mobile robot can be evolved using a dynamic Boolean function approach implemented on evolvable hardware. The task of the mobile robot is to track a moving target represented by a colored ball, while avoiding obstacles during its motion in a *non-deterministic* and *not stationary* environment. Our results show that a dynamic Boolean function approach is sufficient to produce this navigation behavior. Although the classical *model-free* evolution method is often infeasible in the real world due to the number of possible interactions with the environment, we demonstrate that a *model-based* evolution method can reduce the interactions with the real world by a factor of 250, thus allowing us to apply the evolution process *on-line* and to obtain an *adaptive* tracking-avoiding system, provided the implementation can be accelerated by the utilization of evolvable hardware.

Introduction

Robotics has, until recently, consisted of systems able to automate mostly simple, repetitive and large scale tasks. These robots, e.g., arm manipulators, are mostly programmed in a very explicit way and in a well-defined environment. However, for mobile robot applications, the environment must be perceived via sensors and is usually not fully specified. This implies that a mobile robot must be able to learn to deal with an unknown and possibly changing environment.

In this paper we tackle the navigation task for a mobile robot which must reach a goal, from any given position in an environment while avoiding obstacles. The robot is regarded as a *reactive system* described by a dynamic Boolean function which is represented by a disjunctive normal form. The dynamic Boolean function can easily be implemented by evolvable hardware and change with the environment.

Unfortunately, the classical *model-free* evolution method, where the robot behavior is learned by evolution without learning a model of the environment, is infeasible in the real world due to the number of required fitness evaluations in the real world which may need several hours (Floreano & Mondada 1996). To avoid this problem, most of the model-free evolution methods use *off-line evolution*, e.g., the robot behavior is trained off-line using the training data. The robot's behavior will be fixed after training. However, good training data are very difficult to obtain, especially for real-world environments where we have little prior knowledge about them. A simulated environment has often been used instead in training. This raises the issue of how close the simulated environment might be of the real one. The main objective of the off-line model-free evolution method is to find a robust behavior to maintain the robot performance in the real world despite the gap between the simulated and real world.

We have shown in this paper that a *model-based* evolution method can alleviate this problem significantly. In this method, a robot tries to build a model of the environment while learning by *on-line evolution* how to navigate in this environment. Such simultaneous learning of the environment and navigation within the environment can reduce the number of fitness evaluations in the real physical environment since the robot can use the environment it builds progressively. Our experiments have shown that we can reduce the number of fitness evaluations in the real environment by a factor of 250 for the navigation task we considered. Fitness evaluations can be done extremely fast in the internal environment because they are done at electronic speed in hardware.

The paper first defines the robot task and its environment. In Section 3, it describes the reactive navigation system based on a Boolean function controller represented in its disjunctive normal form. In Section 4 it presents the implementation of the evolution mechanism on the Evolvable Hardware. In Section 5 it describes and compares the model-free and the model-based evolution

Figure 1: Real robot.

methods implemented using Evolvable Hardware.

Robot Environment and Task

The shape of the robot is circular with a diameter of 25 cm (Fig.1). It has 10 infra-red sensors mapped into 6 Boolean variables indicating the presence of objects at a distance smaller than 30 *cm*. It is equipped with a bumping sensor to detect when the robot hits an obstacle and with two cameras able to identify and track a colored object (the ball in Fig. 1). The cameras return one of the 4 sectors, covering 90 degrees each, in which the target is located. The robot is driven by two independent motor wheels, one on either side. This allows the robot to perform 8 motions: 2 translations, 2 rotations and 4 combinations of rotation and translation. The robot is controlled by a PC mother board connected to two transputers: one dealing with the infra-red sensors, the vision sensor and the motor wheels, and the other controlling two EHWs which respectively, execute the robot behavior and simulate the evolutionary process. The environment is a world with low obstacles such that the colored target can always be detected by the robot. The obstacle shapes are such that using only a reactive system the robot will not become stuck. In other words, these are no overly complex shapes such horseshoes. For the off-line evolution approach, we built a robot simulation to generate and evaluate the performance of the model-free method.

The task assigned to the robot is to reach the target without hitting obstacles within a minimum number of motions and from any position in the real world. To perform its task, the robot must learn two basic behaviors, obstacle avoidance and going to the target, and coordinate these two behaviors to avoid becoming stuck due to repetition of an identical sensor-motor sequence.

Reactive Navigation System

To describe our evolutionary approach, we consider a model of robot-world interaction widely used in robot learning (Wilson 1987). In this model the robot and the world are represented by two synchronized processes interacting in a discrete time cyclical process. At each time point, (i) the robot directly observes the world state, (ii) based on this current world state, the robot chooses a motion to perform, (iii) based on the current world state and the motion selected by the robot, the world makes a transition to a new state and generate a reward, and (iv) finally the reward is passed back to the robot.

One way to specify a robot's behavior is in terms of a controller, which prescribes, for each world state, a motion to perform. For the tracking-avoiding task in a *non-deterministic*[1] and *not stationary*[2] environment (Kaelbling & Moore 1996) we considered, a dynamic Boolean function control system will be used. The system can change or evolve its function with time. It assumes neither knowledge of the necessary behaviors nor the high level primitives of each behavior. It is well suited for an evolutionary search algorithm and is easily implementable in hardware. However to perform more complex tasks such as navigation in an environment with obstacles of arbitrary shape (e.g., horseshoe shape) or where the target is not always visible, it may be necessary to exploit properties of the task, the sensor configurations, the environment and to change the existing control structure.

Formally, the controller is a function $\mathcal{F}$ from world states to motions. The Boolean function approach describes the function $\mathcal{F}$ as m Boolean functions of n Boolean variables which represents the desired reactive behavior. The input domain of the function $\mathcal{F}$ is $\{0,1\}^n$ where 2^n is the number of possible world states directly observable by the robot. It is encoded by 8 Boolean variables in our study: 6 bits for the infra-red sensors and by 2 bits for the vision sensor. It represents 256 world states observable by the robot. The output range of the function is $\{0,1\}^m$ where 2^m is the number of possible motions. It is encoded by 3 bits to represent 8 possible motions.

A possible representation of function $\mathcal{F}$ is a look-up table. But the look-up table is generally impractical for real-world applications due to its space and time requirements and that it completely separates the information they have about one input situation without influencing what the robot will do in similar input situations. We chose to represent function $\mathcal{F}$ by m Boolean formula in *k-term* DNF[3] which consists of a disjunction of at most k terms ($k = 50$ in our study), each term being the conjunction of Boolean variables or their complement, such that function $\mathcal{F}$ can easily be implemented in LSI hardware which has a limited number of logic gates. The function controller represents function $\mathcal{F}$ by m Boolean functions f_i in their k-term DNF.

[1]The environment is *non-deterministic* if taking the same action in the same state on two different occasions may result in different next states and/or reward.

[2]The environment is *not stationary* if the probabilities of making state transitions and/or receiving reward change over time.

[3]f_i in k-term DNF: $f_i = (x_0 \wedge \cdots \wedge x_{n-1})_0 \vee \cdots \vee (x_0 \wedge \cdots \wedge x_{n-1})_{k-1}$

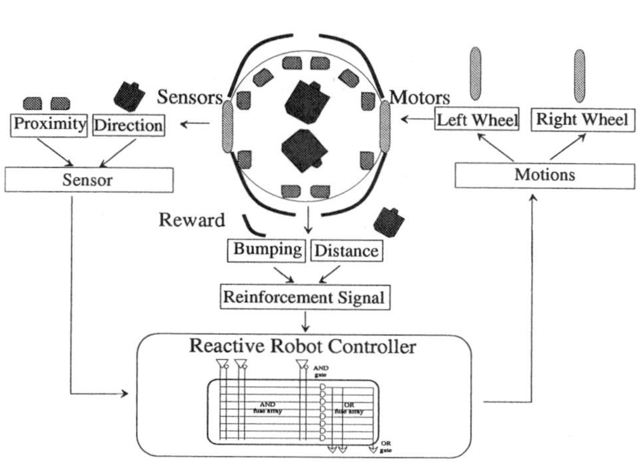

Figure 2: Reactive navigation system.

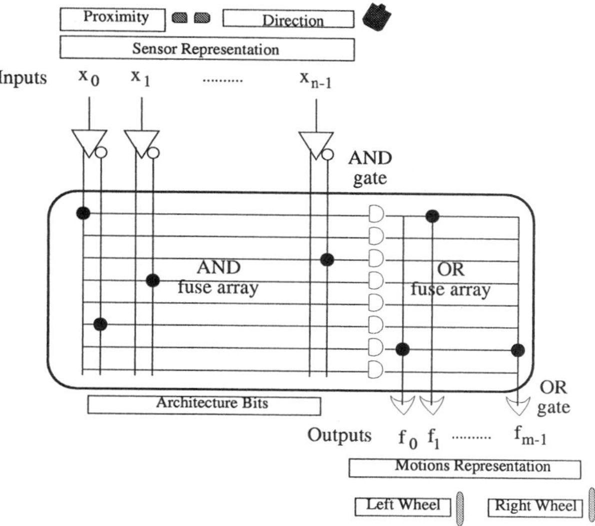

Figure 3: Evolvable Hardware Controller (EHW).

To increase the computation speed by one order of magnitude, function $\mathcal{F}$ described by m Boolean functions in their k-term DNF is executed with an EHW. The EHW structure suited for the execution of function $\mathcal{F}$ consists of an AND-array and an OR-array (Fig.3). Each row in the AND array calculates the conjunction of the inputs connected to it, and each column of the OR-array calculates the disjunction of its inputs (Keymeulen *et al.* 1998). In our experimental set-up with $n = 8$ Boolean input sensors (6 bits for the infra-red sensors and 2 bits for the vision sensor) and 3 Boolean outputs, the AND-OR array has $2*n+3 = 19$ columns and needs a maximum number of $2^n = 256$ rows. However to force the Boolean function to generalize, the number of rows can be reduced by merging rows with the same output. In our experiments, we were able to reduce the number of rows to $k = 50$. In this way, on average, $\frac{256}{50} \simeq 5$ input states are mapped to the same output.

Evolvable Reactive Navigation System

From a machine learning perspective, the tracking-avoiding *control* task where the motions performed by the robot influence its future input situations (Kaelbling & Moore 1996) is an *associative delayed reinforcement* problem where the robot must learn the best motion for each world state from a *delayed* reward signal (Watkins & Dayan 1992). For learning this robot task in *unknown* and *non-deterministic* environments, researchers have applied evolution-based learning algorithms (Mataric & Cliff 1996) to low level control architecture such as LISP-like programming languages (Koza 1992)(Brooks 1992)(Reynolds 1994), finite state automata (Thompson 1995), production rules (classifier systems) (Wilson 1987) (Dorigo & Colombetti 1994) (Grefenstette & Schultz 1994), process network (Steels & Brooks 1995) and neural networks (Floreano & Mondada 1996) (Beer & Gallagher 1992)(Parisi, Nolfi, & Cecconi 1992)(Husbands *et al.* 1995)(Hoshino, Mitsumoto, & Nagano 1998).

In our experiments, the learning task consists to find the function $\mathcal{F}$, mapping 256 inputs (world states) to 8 outputs (motions), in a search space of 8^{256} functions from a given set of observable input-output pairs and a reward signal. For learning pure, instantaneous Boolean functions of the inputs from a delayed reinforcement signal, we chose the evolutionary approach. It is better suited for not stationary environments and large search spaces when a large number of inputs and motions make $\mathcal{Q}$ learning impractical (Watkins & Dayan 1992). The evolutionary algorithm performs a parallel search in the space of Boolean functions in a genetically inspired way. The algorithm is implemented in hardware where the 950 architecture bits of the EHW are regarded as the chromosome for the genetic algorithm (Keymeulen *et al.* 1998). We built specific mutation and cross-over operators for the k-term DNF representation to change the architecture bits and to reduce the learning time (Keymeulen *et al.* 1998).

Evolvable Hardware Methods

To learn the tracking-avoiding task, the robot must interact with the real world environment (*on-line*) or its simulation (*off-line*) to obtain information which can be processed to produce the desired controller. There are two ways to proceed to obtain the controller (Kaelbling & Moore 1996):

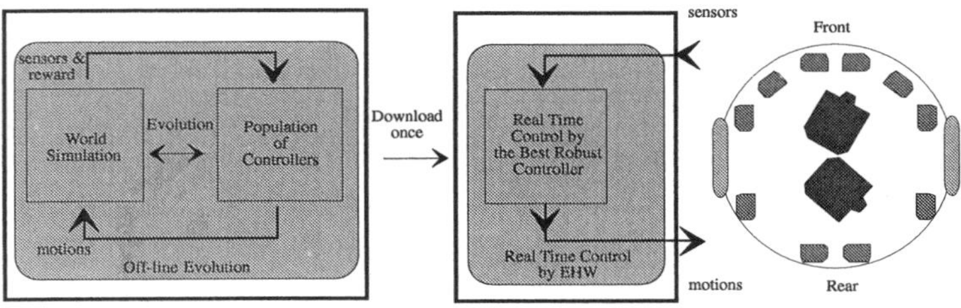

Figure 4: Off-line Model-free evolution schema.

- **Model-free**: learn a controller without learning a model of the environment.

- **Model-based**: learn a model of the environment, and use it to derive a controller.

The next sections discuss and compare the model-free and model-based evolution. But for both methods, in order to give leverage to the learning process we incorporate 3 biases:

- **reflexes**: we have programmed a reflex that moves the robot toward the ball when no obstacle is perceived around the robot. In this way the robot finds interesting parts in the environment but it is still hitting obstacles and becoming stuck.

- **shaping**: we present very simple environments to the robot first and then gradually expose it to more complex environments. For the *model-free* method, once the robot reaches the target it is moved to new positions (selected in a deterministic way). For the *model-based* method, the robots are evolved in a growing and changing world model.

- **local reinforcement signals**: for the *model-based* method, we give a reinforcement signal that is local, helping the robot to step up a gradient in he space of the learning parameters.

Off-line model-free evolvable hardware

The off-line model-free evolution simulates the evolutionary process of the robot controller in an artificial environment, simulating the real environment known a priori (Fig. 4). In this approach both the EHW and the environment are simulated to find the controller able to track a colored object and avoid the obstacles (left box in Fig. 4). Then the best controller found by evolution is used to control the real robot: the EHW architecture bits defining the best behavior are downloaded into the robot evolvable hardware board and control the robot in the real world (right box in Fig.4).

In this model-free approach, the evolutionary algorithm is used as an *optimization strategy* to find the optimal controller for a given simulated environment known

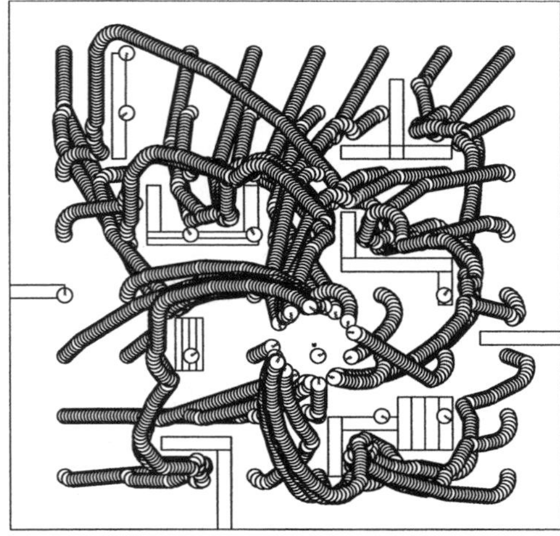

Figure 5: Simulation of the motion of a real robot controlled by the best individual at generation 285 obtained by off-line model-free evolution.

a priori. The population size is 20 individuals. For the selection scheme, we have used a tournament selection with tournament size $s = 5$ and the elitist strategy to maintain the best individual. The main objective of the off-line evolution is to find a *robust controller* because the robot's controller cannot change during robot's life time. To obtain a robust controller, we first improve the generalization ability of the controller by limiting the number of disjunctive terms in the k-term DNF representation.Second we force the robot, during its evolution, to encounter many different situations.

Evaluation Each robot is evaluated in the simulated environment. It fails when it cannot reach the target within a long period of time. It can fail for two reasons:

- It hits an obstacle.

- It reaches the maximum number of steps it is allowed to move in the environment. This situation occurs when the robot is stuck in a loop.

The fitness Φ of a controller is represented by a scalar between 0 (worst) and 64 (best) through combining three factors:

- $\mathcal{R}_1$: The number of times the robot has reached the target. When it reaches the target, it will be assigned to a new position in the environment. There are 64 new positions. This forces the robot to encounter many different world situations.

- $\mathcal{R}_2$: The distance to the target $D(robot, target)$, which forces the robot to reach the target. It is normalized using the dimension L of the simulated environment.

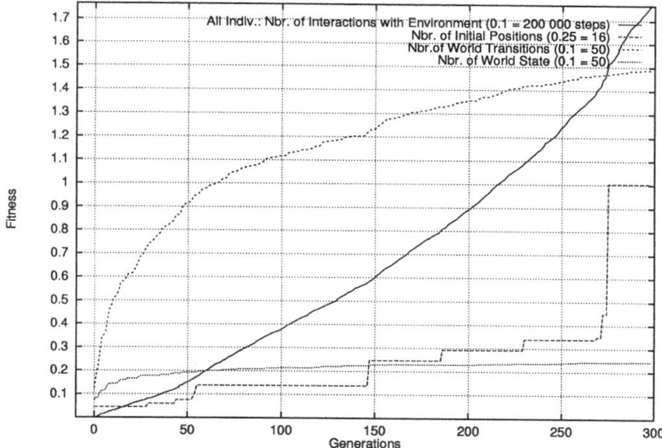

Figure 6: Number of new positions of best individual (1 = 64 new positions) and interactions of all the individuals with the environment (1 = 2,000,000 interactions) throughout generations.

- $\mathcal{R}_3$: The number of steps used to reach its actual position from its initial position. This forces the robot to choose a shorter path and to avoid becoming stuck in a loop. An arbitrary large *Maximum Nbr. Steps* is used for normalization.

In our experiment the distance and the number of steps evaluations had an equal contribution to the fitness:

$$\Phi = \underbrace{Nbr.\ of\ New\ Positions}_{\mathcal{R}_1} + \underbrace{0.5\left(1 - \frac{D(robot, target)}{L}\right)}_{\mathcal{R}_2} + \underbrace{0.5\left(1 - \frac{Nbr.\ Steps}{Maximum\ Nbr.\ Steps}\right)}_{\mathcal{R}_3}$$

Experiments We have conducted experiments with an environment containing 9 obstacles of different shapes except for horseshoes. The target is situated in the center of the environment (Fig.5).

During evolution and for each individual evaluation, the robot is always placed at the same initial position in the environment: the upper left corner. At the beginning of evolution, the controllers are initialized at random. The behavior of each individual is then simulated until it hits an obstacle or becomes stuck in a loop. When an individual reaches the target position, it is moved to a new position in the environment and its fitness is increased by 1. There are 64 new positions which are distributed equally in the environment and selected in a

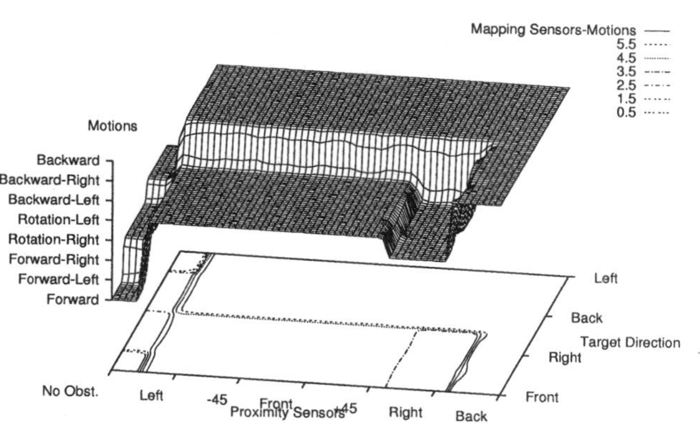

Figure 7: Learning Off-line: sensor-motion mapping of best individual at generation 0.

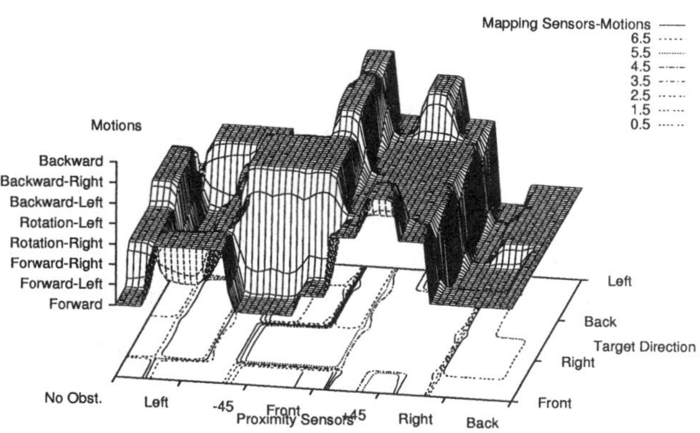

Figure 8: Learning Off-line: sensor-motion mapping of the best individual at generation 285.

deterministic careful way introducing a *shaping bias* in the learning process. The important point is that during its evolution, all individuals start from the same initial position and that the sequence of new positions is always the same for all individuals.

The behavior of the best individual in the population at generation 285 is shown in Figure 5. It demonstrates that the best individual coordinates the obstacle avoidance and the target tracking behaviors very well. For example, it discovers that a robust strategy is to turn clockwise around the obstacle until there is no obstacle in the direction of target.

Figure 6 shows the number of steps and the fitness of the best individual with generations. First and most importantly, figure 6 shows the number of interactions (nbr. of generations $*$ nbr. of individuals $*$ nbr. of steps) with the environment of all the individuals is $3,283,269$. It shows also that although there are 256 possible world states and 2048 possible transitions, the individuals in the population have encountered 122 world states and 744 transitions during their evolution. The number of genetic operations is 5700 (nbr. of individuals $*$ nbr. of generations).

Figures 7 and 8 show the sensor-motion mappings for 52 world states of the best controller at generation 0 and 285 respectively. The 52 world states represent, for the 4 possible target directions (Front, Right, Back, Left), the situation without obstacle (No Obst.) and 12 situations with 1 obstacle around the robot. Both figures show the reflexes that map the 4 world states with no obstacle around the robot to 4 pre-programmed motions. Figure 8 illustrates the ability of Evolvable Boolean Controller to generalize. For example, the best individual at generation 285 executes a Rotation-Left motion independently of the target direction when there is an obstacle at its right side.

Once the best individual reaches the target 64 times, we download the controller of the best individual in generation 285 into the EHW. Although the real world differs from the simulated world in diverse aspects, the controller was robust enough to work well in the real world *known a priori*. In this *model-free* experiment the computation speed obtained by the hardware implementation of the Boolean function controller is not crucial for the real-time robot controller.

On-line model-based evolvable hardware

The off-line model-free approach assumes that the simulated world is designed carefully and that the Boolean controller is robust enough to deal with the uncertainty and inaccuracy of the sensor values and the motors. Unfortunately, this approach cannot take into account any failures of the robot hardware, e.g. *not stationary* environment, and does not allow the controller to be adaptive, e.g. changing its structure while performing its task. But simply replacing training in the simulated

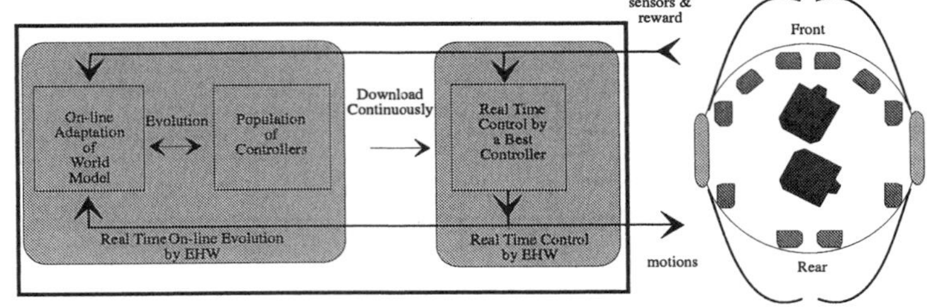

Figure 9: On-line Model-based Evolution schema.

Figure 10: On-line model-based evolvable hardware board with 2 EHW's.

world with training in the real world presents two problems. First, it decreases considerably the efficiency of the evolutionary approach due to the number of interaction with the environment needed (10 days if an interaction takes 0.25 second) to learn an effective behavior. Second, it doesn't maintain good on-line performance because the off-line evolutionary approach is only interested in the end-result.

To learn with fewer interactions with the physical environment and maintain good on-line performance, the robot can do some experiments in an "approximated" world model of the environment (Mahadevan 1992)(Booker 1988). This approach is especially important in applications in which computation is considered to be cheap and real-world experience costly. It has been explored in reinforcement learning and extended to deal with unknown environments by learning the world model during robot's interaction with its environment (Whitehead & Ballard 1989) (Sutton 1990). In the evolutionary approach, Grefenstette et al. use a world model known a priori (a parameterized quantitative model) and calibrate it during robot's life time (Grefenstette & Schultz 1994). Nordin et al. propose an on-line control method using genetic programming and a memory of the past experiences but designed for problems in which reward is not delayed in the sense that reward occurs at each decision steps (Nordin & Banzhaf 1997).

On-line model-based learning Our method learns a model continually through robot's life time and, at each step, the current model is used to compute an optimal controller (Fig. 9).

In order to keep the world model simple, adaptive and without bias, it is predictive model built using the experiences encountered by the robot (Lin 1992). It is represented by a deterministic state transition function where the states are the past world states observed by the robot, the transition are the motion generated by the robot and the outcome is the resulting world state observed by the robot. In the non-deterministic real world environment, each motion can have multiple possible outcomes. To model the environment we decide that the world model generates only the most recent outcome. There is one exception: the transitions which cause the robot to hit an obstacle are never erased from the world model. The world model is learned during the robot's life and is continuously changing to represent the non-deterministic and not stationary real world in a locally deterministic way (Zhivotovsky, Bergman, & Feldman 1996).

The on-line model-based approach works as follows: at each time step, the on-line model-based evolution simulates the evolutionary process of the robot controllers in the current world model of the environment to compute the optimal controller (left box on Fig. 9). After a few generations (around 10), the best controller found by evolution is downloaded to the EHW to control the robot in the real world (right box on Fig. 9). Moreover, while the robot executes the behavior of the best controller, the model is updated. In this approach the learning phase and motion phase are concurrent: while searching a new optimal controller, the robot, controlled by the last optimal controller, continue to track the ball and gather environmental data.

In this model-based approach, the evolutionary algorithm is used as an *adaptive strategy* to find continuously an optimal controller for an approximated world model changing slightly but continuously. The population size is increased to 500 individuals to maintain diversity in the population. For the selection scheme, we have used a tournament selection with tournament size $s = 20$ and the elitist strategy.

In order to accelerate the entire evolutionary process by one order of magnitude, this process is implemented in a special-purpose hardware including an evolvable hardware located next to the evolvable hardware controlling the robot (Fig10). The special purpose hardware evaluates a population of controllers, implemented by an evolvable hardware, with the world model, implemented by a look-up table.

On-line model-based evolution Each controller is evaluated in the world model using an *experience replay* strategy (Lin 1992). Although the learning and the execution phase may be concurrent, we use them in a sequence to simplify the comparison between the two methods. The learning phase starts when the robot fails to reach the target during the execution phase in the real world as described for the off-line model-free evolution approach.

The fitness Φ of each individual controller is obtained by testing the controller for each world state of the world model. Each world state of the world model is presented to the controller which returns the corresponding motion. Then the transition found in the world model predicts the next world state. The process continues until (i) no such world state exists in the actual world model, (ii) the transition causes the robot to hit an obstacle, (iii) this world state was already tested previously and (iv) an infinite loop is detected.

The fitness Φ is represented by a scalar between 0 (worst) and 1 (best) obtained by combining three factors:

- $\mathcal{R}_1$: The number of crashes when the robot hits an obstacle.
- $\mathcal{R}_2$: The number of infinite loops detected.
- $\mathcal{R}_3$: The total distance covered by the robot for each world state. For this measure, we know the distances covered by the real robot for each of the 8 motions and its $Max.\ Distance$..

In our experiment, limiting the number of crashes and the number of infinite loops are the most important and has a greater contribution to the fitness than the distance:

$$\Phi = \underbrace{0.5\left(1 - \frac{Nbr.\ of\ Crash}{Nbr.\ of\ World\ States}\right)}_{\mathcal{R}_1} + \underbrace{0.4\left(1 - \frac{Nbr.\ of\ Infinite\ Loop}{Nbr.\ of\ World\ States}\right)}_{\mathcal{R}_2} + \underbrace{0.1\left(\frac{Distance\ Covered}{Max.\ Distance\ *\ Nbr.\ of\ World\ States}\right)}_{\mathcal{R}_3}$$

Using these three factors and the reflexes, the real robot is able to reach the target by searching and switching controllers in the population every time the world model changes.

Experiments Although the method is dedicated to real world robots, we analyze the advantage of the on-line model-based evolution by simulating the real robot and conducting the same experiments in the same environment as that for the off-line evolution. The target is situated in the center of the environment (Fig.11).

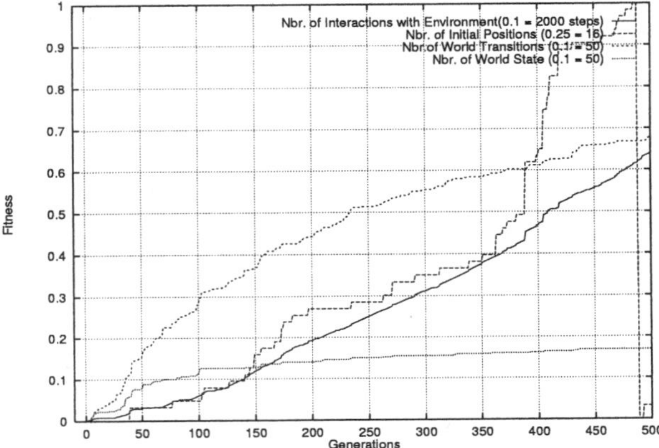

Figure 12: Number of new positions of real robot (1 = 64 new positions) and of world interactions of real robot (1 = 20,000 interactions) throughout generations.

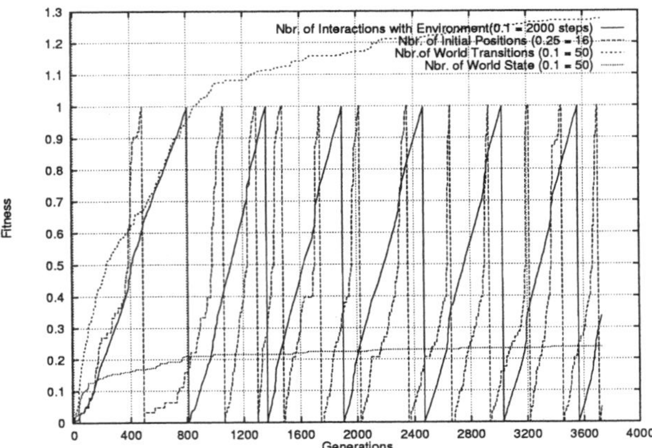

Figure 13: Number of new positions (1 = 64 new positions) and of world interactions (1 = 20,000 interactions) executing 12 times 64 positions throughout generations.

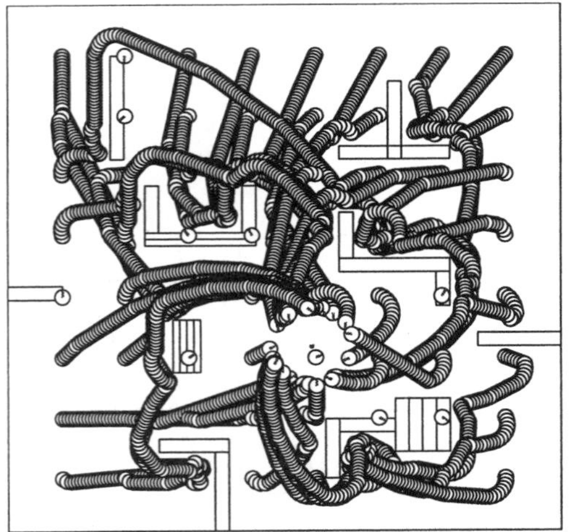

Figure 11: Simulation of the motion of a real robot using on-line model-based evolution and adapting continuously its controller.

At the beginning of evolution, all controllers (individuals) are initialized at random and the world model is empty. One of the controllers in the population is chosen at random to control the behavior of the robot. The real robot gathers data and builds the world model by memorizing the experiences, until it hits an obstacle or reaches a maximum number of steps. Then the evolution phase starts for a few generations (around 10) to find a controller which doesn't hit an obstacle and is not stuck in a loop. The execution and gathering process resumes with the new best controller after the evolution phase. When the robot reaches the target position, the robot is moved to a new position in the environment. There are 64 new positions and are identical as for the off-line evolution.

The behavior of the robot during its life time is shown in Figure 11. It demonstrates that the robot behavior changes its strategy during its life. For example, the way it follows a vertical obstacle: sometimes it strictly follows the wall (vertical wall of the bottom left obstacle) other times it follows by bouncing on the wall (vertical wall of the obstacle at the left side of the target).

Figure 12 shows the relation between the execution and evolution process by plotting the number of times the robot reached the target versus the number of generations. Also it shows the number of world state and transitions during the execution of the robot. It reached 84 world states and 334 transitions when the robot reached the target 64 times. But the world model was continuously changing, modifying the deterministic transition. The number of genetic operations is around 50 times larger than that for the model-free method: $242,500$ genetic operations. Finally and most importantly, it shows that the number of interactions of the robot with the environment is $12,280$, which is a factor of 250 smaller than the model-free evolution. It makes the model-based method using EHW, feasible in the real world.

Figure 13 is the extension of Figure 12 when we continue to assign new positions to the robot after 64 positions have already been assigned. It shows that although the robot needs less interactions (around 30 percent less) to reach the target 64 times, the on-line model-based evolution is a weak approach as an optimization strategy for a *stationary* environment because it is unable to find an optimal robust controller even after more than 120,000 interactions and 3,600 generations with the environment because its world model is local and continually changing. Figures 14 and 15 illustrate, using the same 52 world states defined for the model-free experiment, the adaptation of the sensor-motion mapping of the controller executed by the robot at generation 3500 and 3600. It first shows that the mapping is still changing with time and second that parts of the sensor-motion mapping are conserved through generations.

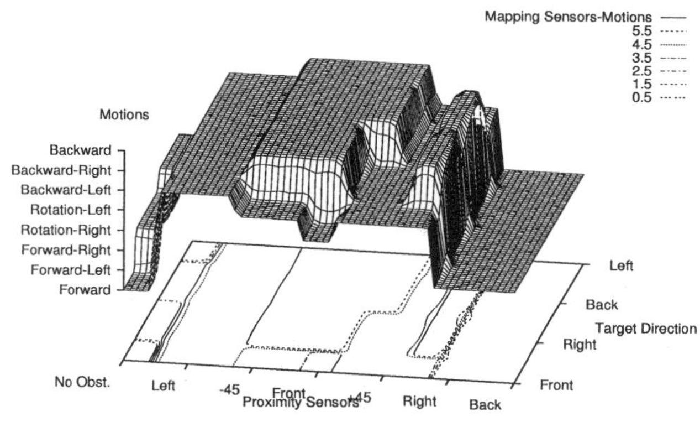

Figure 14: Learning on-line sensor-mapping of the best individual at generation 3500.

The on-line model-based approach has been tested in the real world for an environment with only one obstacle. The robot was able to avoid it in less than 5 *min* and to adapt to the *non-stationary* environment when one of the sensor was blinded. These first experiments first show that as a result of the on-line learning of world models, the number of interactions with the real world can be reduced by a second order of magnitude and second that as a result of the evolvable hardware implementation the computation time to derive the controller can be reduced by a first order of magnitude. These results are encouraging. But many problems remain, such as how detailed the world model must be, whether it must include internal states and whether it must be probabilistic. All these questions are topics for future research.

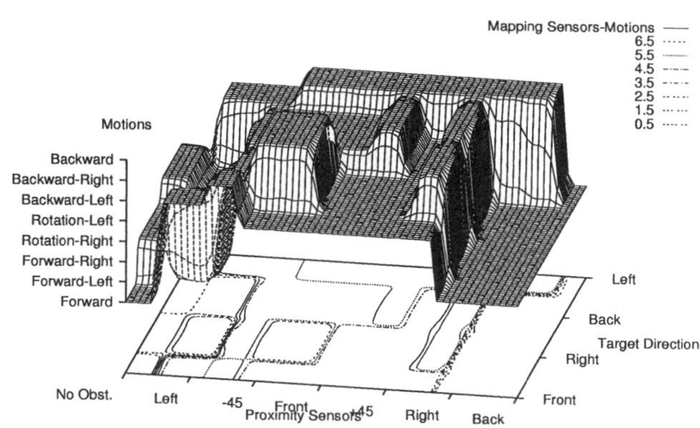

Figure 15: Learning on-line sensor-motion mapping of the best individual at generation 3600.

Conclusion

We have demonstrated how EHW can be used to produce an on-line, model-based evolutionary navigation system for a mobile robot in a *non-deterministic* and *not stationary* environment. The specific navigation task we addressed was the tracking of a colored target while avoiding obstacles. Our EHW produces dynamic reactive navigation control for this task by executing a dynamic Boolean function in its disjunctive normal form. Thus, we have demonstrated (1) that a dynamic reactive navigation system is able to perform the task of tracking and avoiding, (2) that the model-based approach allows us to build highly adaptive behaviors on-line, and (3) that a hardware implementation using EHW can maintain real-time robot performance.

Other tasks for which model-based on-line evolution with EHW is currently being investigated are data compression for ultra high precision images (Salami *et al.* 1998) and digital mobile communication (Murakawa *et al.* 1997). Our research can be seen as part of this ongoing attempt to apply EHW to real world problems.

Acknowledgments

This research was supported by MITI Real World Computing Project (RWCP). The authors would like to express great thanks to Dr. Otsu and Dr. Ohmaki of ETL for their support and encouragement, Prof. Yao of New South Wales University for his invaluable comments, Dr. Frank for his helpful remarks and to Prof. Hoshino of Tsukuba University for his valuable discussions and his visionary thinking on artificial life.

References

Beer, R. D., and Gallagher, J. 1992. Evolving dynamic neural networks for adaptive behavior. *Adaptive Be-*

havior 1(1):91–122.

Booker, L. B. 1988. Classifier systems that learn internal world models. *Machine Learning* 3(2–3):161–192.

Brooks, R. 1992. Artificial life and real robots. In Varela, F. J., and Bourgine, P., eds., *Proceedings of the First European Conference on Artificial Life*, 3–10. Cambridge, MA: MIT Press / Bradford Books.

Dorigo, M., and Colombetti, M. 1994. Robot shaping: developing autonomous agents through learning. *Artificial Intelligence* 71:321–370.

Floreano, D., and Mondada, F. 1996. Evolution of homing navigation in a real mobile robot. *IEEE Transactions on Systems, Man and Cybernetics - part B* 26(3).

Grefenstette, J. J., and Schultz, A. 1994. An evolutionary approach to learning in robots. In *Proceedings of the Machine Learning Workshop on Robot Learning, Eleventh International Conference on Machine Learning*. New Brunswick, NJ.

Higuchi, T.; Niwa, T.; Tanaka, T.; Iba, H.; de Garis, H.; and Furuya, T. 1992. Evolvable hardware with genetic learning: A first step towards building a darwin machine. In Meyer, J.-A.; Roitblat, H. L.; and Wilson, S. W., eds., *Proceedings of the 2nd International Conference on the Simulation of Adaptive Behavior*, 417–424. MIT Press.

Hoshino, T.; Mitsumoto, D.; and Nagano, T. 1998. Fractal fitness landscape and loss of robustness in evolutionary robot navigation. *Autonomous Robots* 5:1–16.

Husbands, P.; Harvey, I.; Cliff, D.; and Miller, G. 1995. The use of genetic algorithms for the development of sensorimotor control systems. In Moran, F.; Moreno, A.; Merelo, J.; and Chacon, P., eds., *Proceedings of the third European Conference on Artificial Life*, 110–121. Granada, Spain: Springer.

Kaelbling, L. P., and Moore, A. W. 1996. Reinforcement learning: A survey. *Journal of Artificial Intelligence Research* 4:237–277.

Keymeulen, D.; Iwata, M.; Konaka, K.; Kuniyoshi, Y.; and Higuchi, T. 1998. Evolvable hardware: a robot navigation system testbed. *New Generation Computing* 16(2).

Koza, J. 1992. Evolution of subsumption using genetic programming. In Varela, F. J., and Bourgine, P., eds., *Proceedings of the First European Conference on Artificial Life*, 3–10. Cambridge, MA: MIT Press / Bradford Books.

Lin, L.-J. 1992. Self-improving reactive agents based on reinforcement learning, planning and teaching. *Machine Learning* 8(3-4):297–321.

Mahadevan, S. 1992. Enhancing transfer in reinforcement learning by building stochastic models of robot actions. In *Proceedings of the Ninth International Conference on Machine Learning*, 290–299.

Mataric, M., and Cliff, D. 1996. Challenges in evolving controllers for physical robots. *Robotics and Autonomous Systems* 19(1):67–83.

Murakawa, M.; Yoshizawa, S.; Kajitani, I.; and Higuchi, T. 1997. Evolvable hardware for generalized neural networks. In Pollack, M. E., ed., *Proc. of Fifteenth International Joint Conference on Artificial Intelligence*, 1146–1151. Morgan Kaufmann Publishers.

Nordin, P., and Banzhaf, W. 1997. Real time control of a khepera robot using genetic programming. *Cybernetics and Control* 26(3).

Parisi, D.; Nolfi, S.; and Cecconi, F. 1992. Learning, behavior and evolution. In *Proceedings of the First European Conference on Artificial Life*, 207–216. Cambridge, MA: MIT Press / Bradford Books.

Reynolds, C. W. 1994. An evolved, vision-based model of obstacle avoidance behavior. In *Artificial Life III*, Sciences of Complexity, Proc. Vol. XVII. Addison-Wesley. 327–346.

Salami, M.; Sakanashi, H.; Tanaka, M.; Iwata, M.; Kurita, T.; and Higuchi, T. 1998. On-line compression of high precision printer images by evolvable hardware. In *Proceedings of the 1998 Data Compression (DCC'98)*. Los Alamitos, CA, USA: IEEE Computer Society Press.

Steels, L., and Brooks, R., eds. 1995. *The Artificial Life Route to Artificial Intelligence: Building Embodied, Situated Agents*. Lawrence Erlbaum Assoc.

Sutton, R. S. 1990. Integrated architectures for learning, planning, and reacting based on approximating dynamic programming. In *Proceedings of the Seventh International Conference on Machine Learning*, 216–224.

Thompson, A. 1995. Evolving electronic robot controllers that exploit hardware resources. In Moran, F.; Moreno, A.; Merelo, J.; and Chacon, P., eds., *Advances in Artificial Life: Proceedings 3rd European Conference on Artificial Life*, 640–656. Granada, Spain: Springer-Verlag.

Watkins, C. J., and Dayan, P. 1992. Q-learning. *Machine Learning* 8(3):279–292.

Whitehead, S. D., and Ballard, D. H. 1989. A role for anticipation in reactive systems that learn. In *Proceedings of the Sixth International Conference on Machine Learning*, 354–357.

Wilson, S. 1987. Classifier systems and the animat problem. *Machine Learning* 2:199–228.

Zhivotovsky, L. A.; Bergman, A.; and Feldman, M. W. 1996. A model of individual adaptive behavior in a fluctuating environment. In *Adaptive Individuals in Evolving Populations*. Addison-Wesley Publishing. 131–153.

The Evolution of Complexity and the Value of Variability

Anil K Seth

Centre for Computational Neuroscience and Robotics
and School of Cognitive and Computing Sciences,
University of Sussex, Brighton BN1 9SB, UK
anils@cogs.susx.ac.uk

Abstract

The hypothesis that environmental variability promotes the evolution of organism complexity is explored and illustrated, in two contexts. A co-evolutionary 'Iterated Prisoner's Dilemma' (IPD) ecology, populated by strategies determined by variable length genotypes, provides a quantitative demonstration, and an example from evolutionary robotics (ER) provides a more qualitative and naturalistic exploration. In the ER example, the above hypothesis is illustrated in real environments, and the organism complexity is seen in robots exhibiting relatively complex behaviours and neural dynamics.

Implications are drawn for the emergence of complexity in general, and also for artificial evolution as a design methodology.

Introduction

The general principle that there is organism complexity by virtue of environmental complexity, has a substantial historical pedigree. This is prominent in the work of Ashby (1952), and, earlier, Dewey (1929), and has enjoyed more recent attention from Godfrey-Smith (1996). The present work empirically explores this idea, firstly by taking environmental variability to be one measure of environmental complexity (there may, of course, be others), and secondly by postulating that the process of *evolution* can serve to link this environmental complexity with organism complexity. Thus, the hypothesis under test is that environmental variability promotes the evolution of organism complexity.

Two methodologies are employed, both based on the principles of artificial evolution. The first example quantitatively analyses the dynamics of co-evolutionary artificial ecologies with specifiable degrees of environmental variability. These ecologies were constructed on the basis of the 'Iterated Prisoner's Dilemma', with complexity and simplicity charted by the 'memory' of the strategies (instantiated with variable length genotypes) deployed by the constituent agents. A second example is based on the artificial evolution, in simulation, of neural network controllers for mobile 'Khepera' robots. Again, by controlling the levels of environmental variability present during evolution, differences in the behavioural and neural dynamics of the evolved robots can be examined. This is a more qualitative test. Conclusions are drawn from the analysis of simulations, and some of the results are confirmed in the real world.

Background

The context

Broadly speaking, there are two frameworks for understanding the emergence of complexity; internalist and externalist (see Godfrey-Smith 1996). Internalist explanations, ranging from the rationalist tradition in philosophy and psychology to (albeit to a lesser extent) the 'self-organising' theories of Kauffman (1993) and his colleagues, give explanatory privilege to mechanisms *internal* to the agent. In contrast, externalist theories (from the empiricist tradition and, for example, adaptationist biology) locate causal mechanisms and explanatory precedence primarily in external (environmental) influences[1].

This research, with its emphasis on the evolutionary effects of environmental variability on organism complexity, resides within the externalist camp. However, it in no way intends to refute or argue against internalism; indeed, the internal structures of both the robotic and IPD agents are crucial for the development and deployment of behaviour. So, whilst exploring the value of externalism, this work is in fact a manifestation of an *interactionist* viewpoint, which allows that both internal and external factors have explanatory currency. This research is also not to be set in exclusive competition with other accounts of externalist explanation. For example, 'predator-prey' situations provide useful explanations of certain *specific* competences of organisms[2] (see, for example, Dawkins (1986)). In another example, Schuster (1996) has argued for environmental resource abundance

[1] There is, of course, a case for arguing that all divisions between 'internal' and 'external' are artificial. Nevertheless, for the purposes of explanatory expediency, 'internal' here is taken to refer only to the *control structure* of the agent (that is to say, the robot body in the ER example is taken to be part of the environment).

[2] Though not all; for example, algae have not evolved sophisticated 'fish-avoidance mechanisms'.

as a spur for 'radical innovation' in the evolution of complexity.

Godfrey-Smith (1996) makes a strong case for what he terms the 'environmental complexity thesis', arguing that 'the function of cognition is to enable the agent to deal with environmental complexity'. The present research takes considerable inspiration from this position, which itself draws inspiration from the earlier work of Dewey (see, for example, Dewey 1929). However, less stress is laid on the meaning of 'cognition', with other, more empirical measures of organism complexity being preferred. And more emphasis is placed on *variability* as a measure of environmental complexity. Indeed, Dewey himself proposed that only environments containing both variable *and* predictable elements would lead to the emergence of 'cognition'. Without variability, he argues, cognition would have no value, and without regularity, could not engage with the world. To quote:

> The incomplete and the uncertain give point and application to the ascertainment of regular relations and orders.
>
> Dewey (1929) p. 160

This valuable proposal will be discussed in terms of the evolutionary robotics model.

The meaning of complexity

In the present research, complexity in the *environment* is measured in terms of variability, or noise. However, this definition is far from rigorous, and does not apply in such an obvious way to considerations of *organism* complexity.

Information theory provides a quantitative and specific, yet narrow definition of complexity in terms of 'minimum description size', or 'Kolmogorov complexity' (Kolmogorov 1965). This measure is only applicable to *finitely presented languages,* such as the genotypes employed in genetic algorithms (GAs). It cannot be applied to behaviours, nor neural dynamics, nor even notions of environmental variability. It *can* be applied to the variable length genotypes of the agents in the IPD example, but it is not clear, even then, that such a measure would always be appropriate.

The idea of minimum description size suggests that the complexity of a given expression is determined by its minimum length following compression, whilst still retaining all the original information. This certainly allows that mere duplications of expressions do not augment complexity, but also (implausibly) awards maximal complexity to purely random expressions.

Therefore, in the IPD example, both straightforward genotype length (indicating strategy 'memory') and the Kolmogorov complexities of the genotypes were used as quantitative metrics of organism complexity[3].

No such quantitative basis exists for assessing the complexity of the behavioural and neural dynamics exhibited by evolved robots (or indeed, living creatures). Therefore, measurements of organism complexity in the evolutionary robotics (ER) example must rely more on common sense than on rigour. However, the lack of specificity is compensated by the natural context of the evolved robots. Behavioural complexity can be assessed in terms much less arbitrary than 'minimum description size', and, furthermore, can be related to the functional complexity of the underlying neural dynamics.

The IPD ecology

Introduction

In this section, the Iterated Prisoner's Dilemma (IPD) is used to found a co-evolutionary artificial ecology, whose constituent members can evolve from being simple to being complex. This complexity is charted through the memory of the strategies deployed, reflected in genotype length. By studying the changes in mean genotype length in populations evolving in both variable and non-variable environments, it is demonstrated that more complex individuals evolve readily in the variable case, but not in the non-variable[4].

The Prisoner's Dilemma

The Prisoner's Dilemma has enjoyed substantial popularity in co-evolutionary investigations, (Axelrod 1984, Langton 1995). Essentially, it provides a framework for modelling interactions between agents where the maximisation of individual short term gain minimises the collective welfare, as illustrated in the following anecdote:

Imagine that you and an alleged accomplice have both been arrested, accused of a terrible crime. You are held in separate cells, and upon interrogation you can either *cooperate* by denying all knowledge, or *defect* by implicating your accomplice. You have no idea what your accomplice will do, but if you both cooperate, you will both be released (the reward, **R**), and if you both defect, then both of you will be jailed (the punishment, **P**). However, if you defect and she cooperates, then you will receive a payoff (the temptation, **T**) and she will go to jail for longer (the sucker, **S**). But if she defects and you cooperate, then you yourself are the sucker. The paradox is thus evident, in a single meeting you will always do best to defect, in doing so either receiving the monetary payoff or avoiding being the sucker. But of course the logic is the same for your alleged accomplice, and if

[3]Some contact with the variability as a measure of complexity is maintained here; high Kolmogorov complexity can also be interpreted in terms of high variability.

[4]A more detailed exploration of this example appears in Seth (1997).

	player 2 cooperates	*player 2 defects*
player 1 cooperates	1:R=3 2:R=3	1:S=0 2:T=5
player 1 defects	1:T=5 2:S=0	1:P=1 2:P=1

Table 1: Prisoner's Dilemma Scoring Table

you both defect then you will both do worse than if you had both cooperated (see Table 1). Note that the actual scores don't really matter so long as $T > R > P > S$ and $2R > T + S$.

Cooperation is thus unlikely to arise in a one-shot case, but in the *Iterated* Prisoner's Dilemma (IPD) cooperation on any given move *can* become a rational strategy, and indeed many researchers have used GAs to evolve cooperating strategies to play the IPD (see e.g. Axelrod 1984, Langton 1995). In these studies, as in the present model, the fitness function (evaluated for each individual) is simply the score over a number of iterations of the game, and the genotypes comprise of binary character strings representing the strategies, with the length of the genotype determining the number of preceding moves (the game history) upon which each individual can base it's moves. Genotype length thus has a direct interpretation as 'memory'. In the present example, the evolution of cooperation *per se* is not of primary interest. Rather, the co-evolution of a cooperating population provides a good platform for the subsequent investigation of the evolution of complexity.

Variable length genotypes and the Iterated Prisoner's Dilemma

By introducing variable length genotypes (VLGs) into an IPD ecology, Lindgren (1991) demonstrated the evolution of longer and increasingly complex strategies (with longer memories) in variable (noisy) environments, but did not rigorously address the possibility of a causal role for variability in this process. The variability was introduced by invoking a certain probability for the opposite move to that specified by the genotype being made - this can be interpreted as 'environmental variability' since the environment for any given individual consists simply of the moves made by the other members. VLG's were instantiated by Lindgren by allowing *splitting* and *doubling* mutations (in addition to point mutation and crossover), which would increment or decrement the potential memory (and hence potential complexity) of the strategy in question by one game iteration.

The present study employs splitting and doubling mutations, and variability, in the same way as Lindgren in order to provide a quantitative method for following the evolution of complexity. This method is particularly attractive because the phenotypical strategy is not directly affected by a doubling mutation. By itself, an increase in memory doesn't change behaviour. Changes will only occur if the extra memory is subsequently used

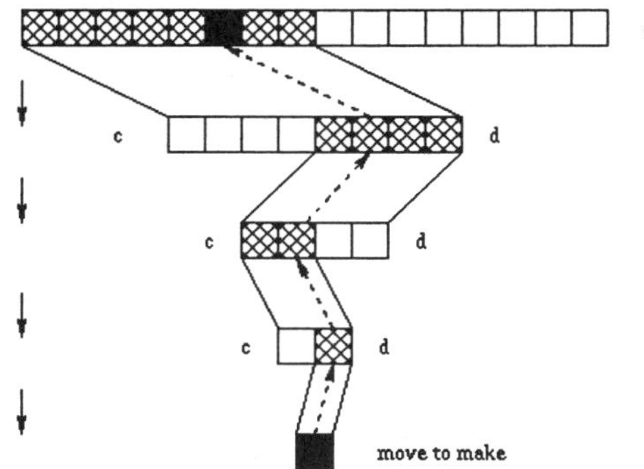

Figure 1: Genotype encoding scheme; see text for details.

(through further mutations/crossover in the new genotype segment) to discriminate between possible courses of action (cooperation or defection). Thus, evolution of longer memories cannot simply be ascribed to some phenotypical side-effect of having a longer genotype, and must be attributed to some employment of the extra memory provided; thus a more complex strategy.

Genotype encoding scheme

Each individual in the ecology consists of a genotype, comprising of a string of `c`'s and `d`'s, determining the strategy of that individual for playing the IPD. The longer the genotype, the more it can be influenced by the history of the game, thus the longer the 'memory' of the individual.

Fig 1 illustrates how the genotype can code for a particular strategy. Each time a previous move in the game history (between two particular agents) is considered, half of the genotype is (temporarily) discarded (the non-shaded area in Fig 1) - one half if the move had been cooperative, or the other if it had been a defection. In this way, the genotype in Fig 1 (of length 16) can encode a strategy with a memory of 4 prior interactions (after cutting a string of 16 characters in half 4 times, you are left with just a single character). The black square in Fig 1 indicates which allele would be accessed for a `[c,d,c,d]` history.

The genotype must actually be even longer in order to specify the initial moves up until this memory limit is reached. The genotype in Fig 1 would require an extra 9 alleles to code for the initial 3 moves before the final 16 alleles can be used[5]. The maximum genotype length employed was (somewhat arbitrarily) 127 alleles, allowing for a maximum memory of 6 iterations[6].

[5]Doubling mutations were therefore instantiated by copying the latter half of the genotype twice again onto its own end, thereby preserving an appropriate section for initial move specification and also incrementing the memory by one.

[6]The crossover rate was set at 0.95, and all mutation rates were set at 0.005 (per bit for point mutations).

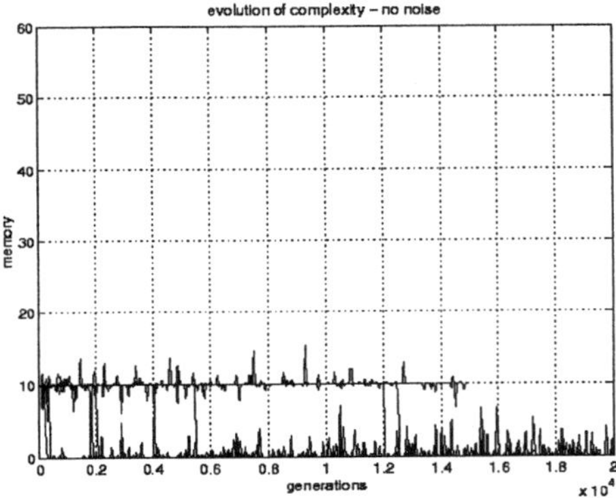

Figure 2: Evolution of complexity without variability; complexity does not evolve (results from 12 evolutionary runs overlayed).

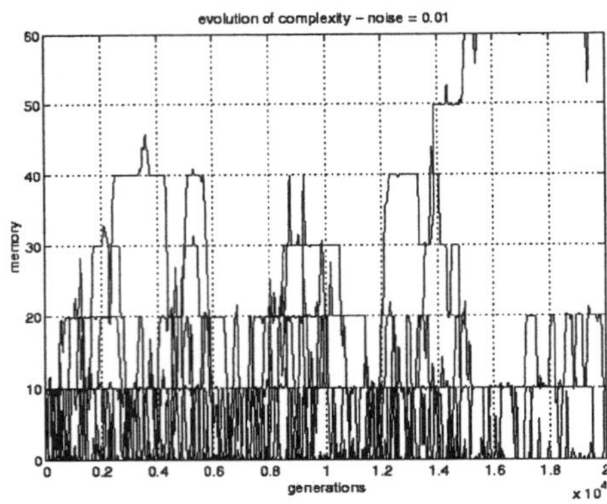

Figure 3: Evolution of complexity with variability; complexity does evolve (results from 12 evolutionary runs overlayed).

IPD Results

In the first experiment, ecosystems were populated with 30 strategies of memory length one, each playing 20 rounds of IPD with every other member, and were allowed to evolve over 20,000 generations. Twelve evolutions were followed in non-variable, non-noisy ecologies, and 12 in ecologies with a noise level of 1 percent. Fig 2 illustrates that, without environmental variability, complexity does not evolve, but Fig 3 illustrates that, with such variability, complexity *does* evolve[7]. Not monotonically, nor often to the maximum possible. But it is evident that noise (or environmental variability) does promote the evolution of agent complexity.

To confirm this result, a test was performed with populations evolving with a *cost* placed on complexity, in both variable and non-variable environments[8]. This cost was set at 0.25 percent of fitness score per memory unit of the strategy in question. Twelve runs were performed without noise, and 12 with 1 percent noise. Fig 4 and Fig 5 clearly illustrate that the presence of environmental variability (noise) promotes the evolution of complexity, even given an explicit fitness penalty imposed on such complexity.

Evolutionary Robotics Example

Introduction

In this example, a distributed GA was used to evolve weights and thresholds for a simple neural network to

[7]For clarity, the Kolmogorov complexity metric is omitted; it followed the same pattern as the memory metric.

[8]A further change in this experiment was the introduction of 'partner choice mechanisms' for each individual, based on an algorithm from Stanley, Ashlock, & Smucker (1995), and discussed in detail in Seth (1997). The effect of this mechanism was to further facilitate the evolution of complex strategies, even to the extent that a small fitness cost on long genotypes could be overcome.

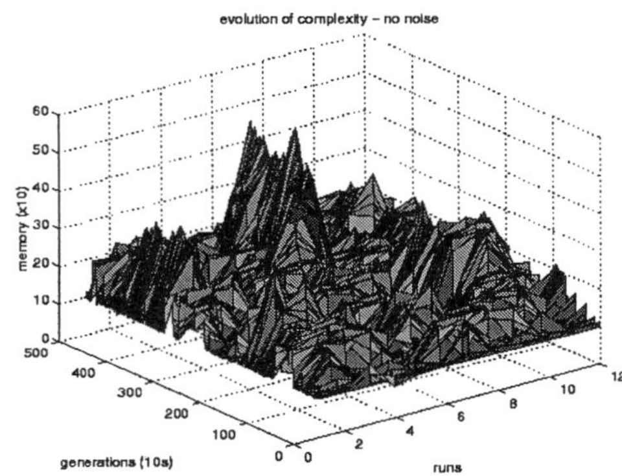

Figure 4: Evolution of complexity without variability, and a medium cost on complexity; complexity does not evolve.

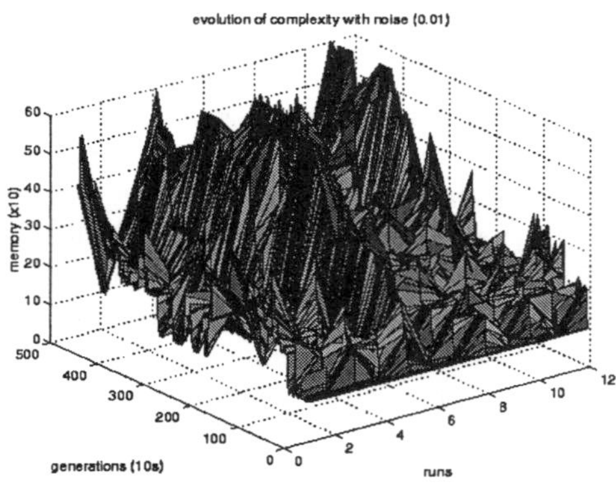

Figure 5: Evolution of complexity with variability, and a medium cost on complexity; complexity does evolve.

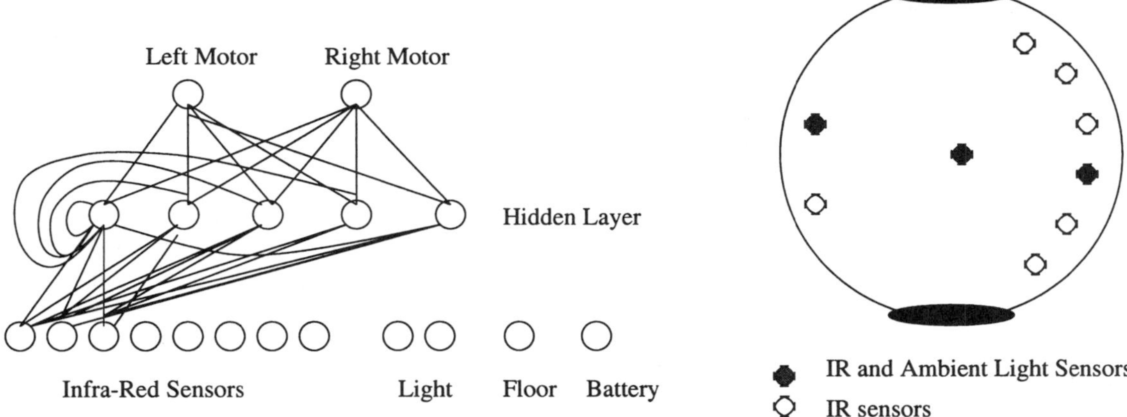

Figure 6: Khepera network architecture and sensor layout; for clarity, not all connections are shown. All input units are connected to all hidden units, and all hidden units are connected to themselves and to every other hidden unit, as well as to both motors. The central floor sensor is located beneath the robot base.

control a Khepera (K-Team (1993)) mobile robot[9]. The context used for this study was drawn from a 'homing behaviour' experiment by Floreano & Mondada (1996) in which a 40cm by 45cm walled arena was employed, situated in a dark room, but with a small light tower at one corner. This corner (denoted the 'charging area') also had black paint on the floor out to a radius of 8cm (the floor was otherwise white). The Khepera robot was equipped with an extra sensor attached to its undercarriage (a 'floor sensor') which was thresholded so to be able to detect this difference in floor reflectivity. This sensor was in addition to the usual array of 8 infra-red proximity sensors (which also independently detect ambient light levels).

The robot had a simulated battery of 50 'actions', but if it happened to pass over the recharging area, the battery would be instantaneously recharged and the robot could carry on for another 50 actions, up to a maximum of 150. Each action corresponded to one update of the controlling neural network, taking place about every 300ms.

The fitness function was very simple, calculated incrementally at every step (except when the robot was directly over the charging area, where no score was awarded), and maximised by speed and IR avoidance (V is the linearly scaled average wheel speed, and i the (linearly scaled) highest IR activation level):

$$\theta = V(1-i), \qquad 0 \leq V \leq 1, \quad 0 \leq i \leq 1$$

Under this fitness function, robots evolved to roam around the arena at high speed, avoiding the walls, and periodically returning to the charging area at suitable intervals to maintain a viable battery level. It is important to note that this 'homing' behaviour is only specified *implicitly* by this function. Candidate robots that tend to return to the charging area will tend to live longer, and since the (simple) fitness function is incremental, will tend to accrue higher fitness scores. This is important because it means that the way in which the robot evolves to perform the homing behaviour is not subject to indirect experimenter preconception expressed through an overly specific fitness function. And this is important because evolution then has the potential to explore many different kinds of organism architecture, according to the degree of variability in the environment.

Floreano & Mondada (1996) pursued artificial evolution in the real world, actually downloading candidate control networks onto real Kheperas and evaluating their performance, taking ten whole days (about 150 generations) to evolve fit individuals. The approach taken in the present work, in contrast, was to perform the evolution in *simulation*, with subsequent testing of the evolved controllers in the real world. The simulation techniques used were based on Jakobi's (1997) 'minimal simulation' methodology, which enables the transference from simulation to real world with sufficient amounts of noise in the right places in the simulation. Of central interest in the present context is that these noise levels (ie. the degree of environmental variability) can be adjusted, and the resulting differences in behaviour and neural mechanism can be explored.

The simulation

The experimental set up, as described above, was simulated using a number of look-up tables to deliver appropriate values for the robot sensors in any given situation (distance from wall or corner, angle to wall or light, ori-

[9]For a detailed introduction to the approach of evolutionary robotics see Harvey et al. (1997).

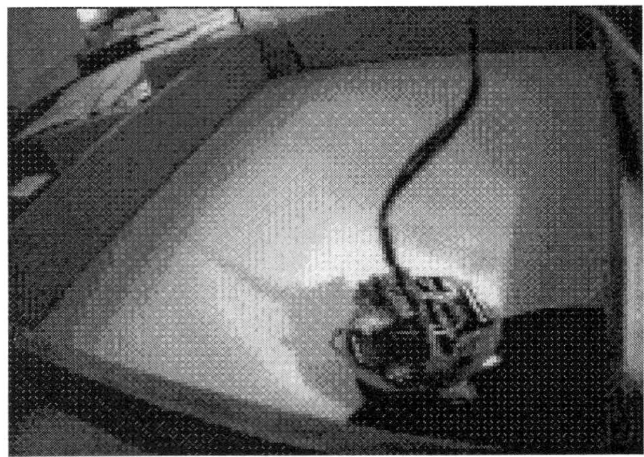

Figure 7: A real Khepera going about its business, controlled by a network evolved in a very noisy simulation.

entation of robot, and so on) in the environment. These sensor values were then fed into the candidate control network and a further look-up table was used to calculate the position and orientation change of the robot given the wheel speeds (as specified by the activations of the output units). The neural net controller (Fig) was a three layer perceptron of exactly the same architecture as that employed by Floreano & Mondada (1996). Thus, 12 input units corresponding to the 8 IR sensors, the ambient light sensors number 2 and 6 (front and back), and one input unit each for the floor sensor and battery level. These inputs pass through a 5 unit internally recurrent hidden layer, which in turn is connected to the two unit output layer, setting the wheel speeds. Sigmoid activation functions were employed in all layers apart from the input layer, which scaled the sensory inputs to range linearly from -0.5 to 0.5.

The other important aspect of the simulation was, of course, that a lot of *noise* or *variability* could be employed, both during each trial and between trials (each individual was evaluated over twelve separate trials in the GA). *Intra-trial* noise could be applied to all input sensor readings, the robot position, wheel speeds, orientation, the rate of orientation change during turning, and to the effects of wall collision; following collision the robot was randomly repositioned within about 2-3cm of the wall, with a large and random orientation and speed change. *Inter-trial* noise could be applied to the angle of acceptance of the light sensors, the dimensions of the arena, the radius of the charging zone, and the levels of IR, background IR, and ambient light noise. These loci of variability are all external to the control structure of the robot and therefore are aspects of *environmental* noise.

The experiment proceeded using a distributed GA, with a population of 100, to evolve the weights and thresholds for the network (this structure remained fixed for the duration of each individual). The weights and thresholds were specified as floating point numbers on a 102 allele genotype, with mutation and crossover being the only genetic operators employed.[10]

With this simulation, evolutionary runs of about 100 generations always produced very fit individuals. These runs took about 1 hour on a single user Sun SparcUltra (143 MHz) workstation, considerably faster than the real world evolution reported in Floreano & Mondada (1996). Many runs were performed, either with high levels of inter- and intra-trial noise, or with no inter-trial noise and very low intra-trial noise levels (see Appendix 1 for details of these noise levels). Successful transfer to reality was consistently observed when networks from the fittest robots, evolved in noisy conditions, were downloaded onto real Kheperas[11]. Fig 7 illustrates a real Khepera (powered externally, but with all processing onboard) just leaving the recharging area halfway through a demonstration.

Behavioural analysis

Twelve evolved robots were analysed - six evolved in noisy environments (type A robots), and six in non-noisy environments (type B robots), with all analysis taking place in simulation. Three environmental conditions were analysed for each robot; a normal (NO) condition (with light source and charging area), a 'no charging area' (NC) condition, where the black paint is removed and the robot cannot recharge, and a 'no-light-source' (NL) condition where, although the charging area is present, the light source at the corner is removed[12]. The robots were all evolved in the NO condition, with the NC and NL conditions deployed only for test purposes. Low noise levels were used in all these test conditions.

Figs. 8 (a-c) illustrates typical overhead trajectory plots for the robots evolved in noisy environments (type A) in the three conditions, and (d-f) illustrate the same for robots evolved in non-noisy environments (type B). The behaviours are evidently different. Both A and B robots can repeatedly find the charging area (situated in the lower left hand corner), in normal conditions, and their trajectories are not obviously different. However in the NC and NL conditions, there are clear differences. The B robots maintain a behaviour pattern qualitatively similar to that displayed in normal conditions, but the

[10] Crossover probability was set at 0.95, with a 0.03 probability of point mutation per genotype bit.

[11] Robot controllers evolved in non-noisy conditions did *not* transfer effectively to the real world. This was to be expected from Jakobi (1997), but does not affect the present arguments, since we are considering the emergence of complexity at a primarily abstract level.

[12] These tests were also performed by Floreano & Mondada (1996), who observed similar results to those of the type A robots in the present study.

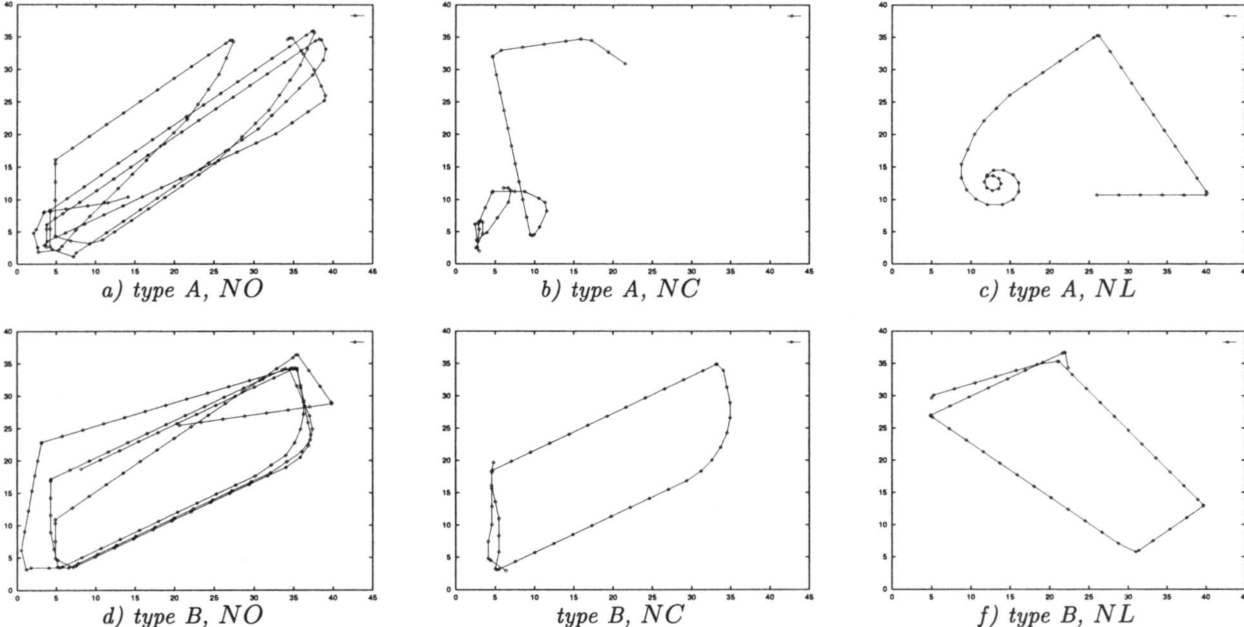

Figure 8: Trajectory plots of robots evolved under noisy (a-c) or non-noisy (d-f) conditions in either normal (a,d), no charging area (b,e), or no light (c,f) conditions. The charging area is located in the bottom left-hand corner of each plot, out to a radius of $8cm$. The type B robots maintain a simple trajectory regardless of the environmental manipulations, but the type A robots clearly deploy more complex 'searching' and 'circling' behavioural strategies.

A robots present a much more interesting picture. In the NC condition, these robots head towards the charging area and remain in the vicinity, as if 'confused' by the absence of charging. We can call this a *searching* behaviour. In the NL condition, the robots begin, as in normal conditions, with a semilinear trajectory, but after a while begin to circle. This *circling* behaviour makes good sense if the robot is thought of as trying to orient to a light source using front and rear light detectors.

Thus, the B robots seem only to have evolved to move in straight lines and to turn upon encountering walls; a strategy which does indeed periodically return the robot to the charging area (in non-variable environments). However, the A robots are clearly affected by the presence (or absence) of the black charging area and the light source. This results in the qualitatively more complex behaviours of searching and circling when these environmental features are tampered with (these searching and circling behaviours were also observed in real-world Khepera behaviour, when the environment in Fig. 7 was manipulated in the appropriate way). All six A robots presented qualitatively similar searching and circling behaviours, and all six B robots displayed the simple behaviour (as in Figs. 8 (d-f)). Therefore, it seems sensible to conclude that artificial evolution in variable environments has led to the evolution of more complex behaviours than artificial evolution in non-variable environments.

One final example of how the A robots are behaviourally more complex can be seen in a competition between an A robot and a B robot in a condition (in a low-noise simulation) in which the walls are removed, and the charging area extends in a complete circle around the light source. Fig. 10 illustrates that the B robots was completely impotent in such circumstances, hinting at reliance on IR stimulation (one typical run is shown, and out of 40 test runs the robot only managed a single visit to the charging area, most probably due to sheer chance). On the other hand, the A robot could cope to some extent, although performance was still seriously prejudiced. Fig. 9 illustrates a particularly impressive trajectory, and out of 40 test runs, 10 resulted in the robot reaching the charging area, and in 4 cases it returned more than once. This considerably greater success rate suggests that the A robots are taking account of a greater range of environmental stimuli than the B robots, and are thereby deploying a more complex behaviour.

Neural analysis

The purpose of this section is to show that the neural dynamics of the robots evolved in noisy conditions are more complex (this again has to be a qualitative judgement, as in the behavioural case) than those of robots evolved in non-noisy conditions. Furthermore, that the enhanced neural complexity of the robots in the noisy case makes sense in terms of the more complex behaviour displayed by these robots.

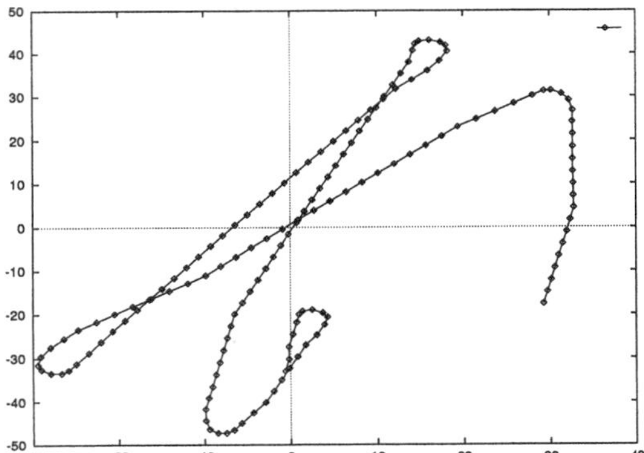

Figure 9: Type A robot in no-wall test; the edge of the graph does not represent a wall, and the charging area is situated in a circle around the origin (0,0 point). The robot is able to find the charge area.

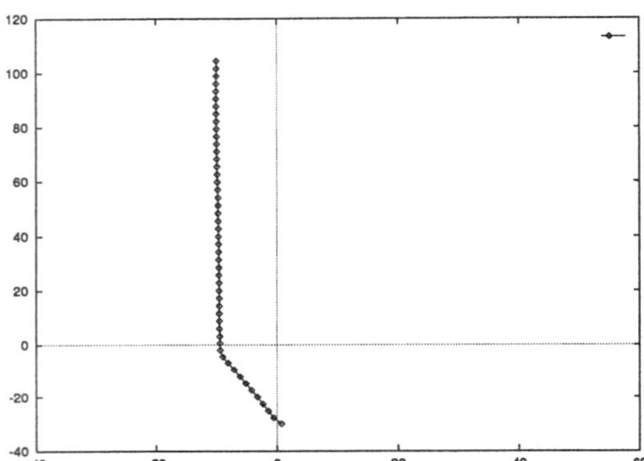

Figure 10: Type B robot in no-wall test; the edge of the graph does not represent a wall, and the charging area is situated in a circle around the origin (0,0 point). The robot is not able to find the charge area.

An initial analysis was undertaken by examining plots of neural activations for all 19 neurons in all three conditions (NO, NC, and NL) for all of the 12 robots (6 A, and 6 B). Although this data is too extensive to be shown here, the main initial conclusion was that whereas for the B robots, the vast majority of the hidden units appeared to respond primarily to IR activity, for the type A case neural activation displayed much more activity *not* correlated with IR activity, but instead with some combination of light/battery/floor sensor input.

To explore this in a non-behavioural context, short periods (spikes) of activity were injected into six combinations of input units, with the activations of the hidden and motor units being recorded. What became immediately clear from this was firstly that only in the type A robots did the battery input unit have any direct influence on the motor layer, in the absence of any IR input.

A set of six input conditions were tested; the first two

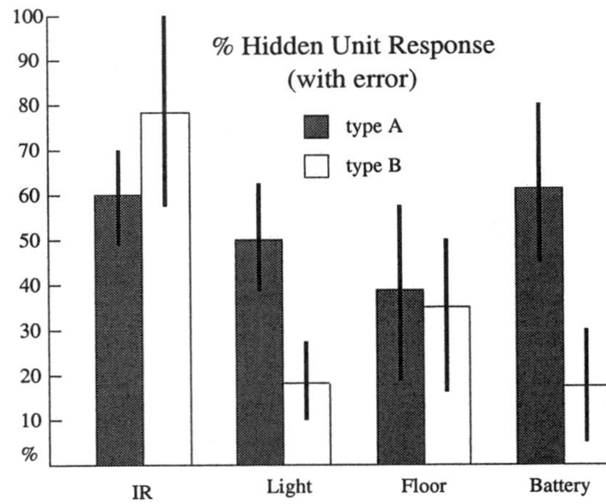

Figure 11: Hidden unit response patterns for both type A and type B robots; see text for details.

consisted of IR inputs only, with either all 8 inputs active, or all except the rear two. The next 2 conditions tested combinations of ambient light inputs in the absence of IR input. The final 2 conditions injected either a negative floor sensor input (as if the robot were over the charging area), or a negative battery input (signifying an empty battery), both in the absence of IR.

These six conditions were tested on each of the 12 robots. Fig 11 presents summary data for all 12 robots over all the six conditions, in terms of the hidden unit activity elicited by the various inputs. For example, for the condition involving battery unit activation, 60 percent of the type A robot hidden units responded strongly, compared to 20 percent of the type B robot hidden units. Thus, Fig 11 makes it clear that the A robots take greater account than the B robots of the light and battery sense data. These conditions were statistically significant according to Mann-Whitney U tests (($U = 57.0; df = 6,6; p < 0.01$), ($U = 56.5; df = 6,6; p < 0.01$) respectively). And although the statistical test is not significant, the B robots appear to rely more heavily on IR input than the A robots.

This extra reliance on light data for the A robots is particularly clear in the 'no-wall' condition discussed beforehand, only the A robots display any significantly varying neural activity, and what there is, is strongly correlated with the light, floor, and battery sense data (see Fig 12 and Fig 13).

The neural dynamics of the A robots are therefore taking into account a wider variety of environmental stimuli and forging them into a coherent and complex behaviour. This is not the case for the B robots, and so, again, it seems sensible to conclude that at both the neural and behavioural levels, evolution in variable environments has delivered organisms of greater complexity than evolution in non-variable environments.

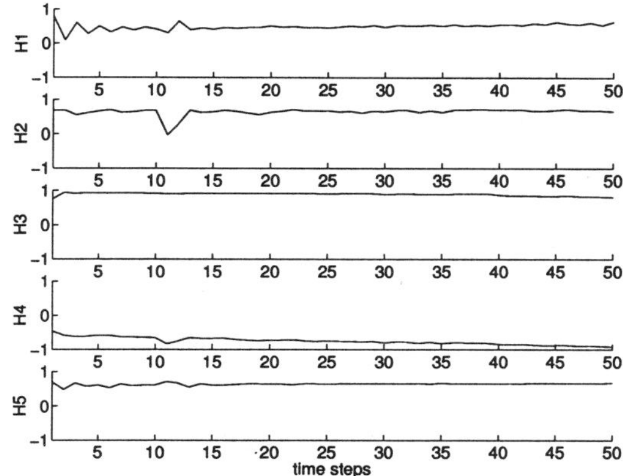

Figure 12: Type B robot hidden unit activation in no-wall test; very little changing activation in any units.

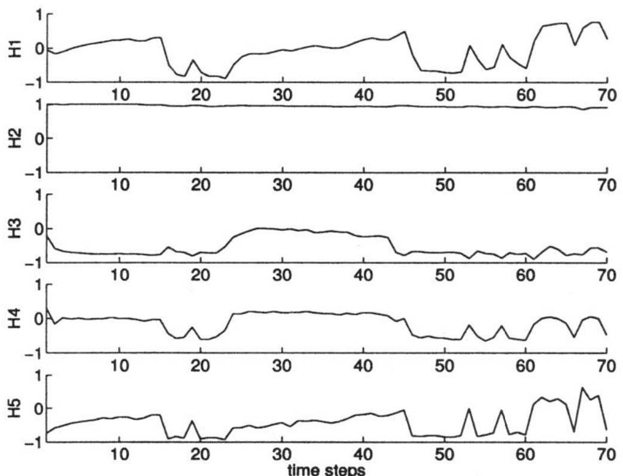

Figure 13: Type A hidden unit activation in no-wall test; significantly changing levels of activation; (only first 70 time steps shown).

Discussion

Two examples of environmental variability promoting the evolution of organism complexity have been illustrated; a model based on the IPD, and a model employing evolutionary robotics (ER).

The IPD example provides a quantitative illustration of the environmental variability principle, with 'noise' in the responses generated by individuals engaged in the IPD providing the environmental variability. It is worth noting that what was observed was a *population* of mostly equally complex individuals, rather than a *complex* population of individuals (which would comprise of individuals of many different levels of complexity). In the natural world, population complexity *and* individual complexity require explanation. The position taken here is that, in nature, there are (or were) many different drives towards complexity, not all of which are (or have been) available to all organisms. And this diversity in drives could have led to the emergence of population complexity. It may be possible to extend the present IPD model to include differential drives to complexity to further investigate this question.

The ER example provides a more qualitative exploration, illustrating that environmental variability can lead to the artificial evolution of both behavioural and neural complexity. Contact here is made with a central aspect of Dewey's philosophy; that 'cognition' will arise in environments characterised by a *mixture* of predictable and unpredictable elements[13]. In the ER case certain properties of the environment were indeed variable, and others (properties necessary for the survival of the robot, for example, the presence of a charging area) did not vary. Whether the more complex robots are in any sense 'more cognitive' is, however, more a matter of semantics than of substance.

Dewey's insight also makes sense in terms of evolutionary dynamics. With a mixture of variability and reliability, then certain local maxima (which depend on the environmental features that are rendered excessively variable) will be eliminated, whilst others (which depend on the still-reliable environmental features) will be preserved. In the ER case, variability has been applied such that the simple, type B, strategy is infeasible, and so the local maxima corresponding to that solution will not be present in the landscape. Evolution is then free to migrate towards the more complex solution.

It should be emphasised once again that this paper does lack a rigorous definition of complexity applicable to both the IPD and ER experimental contexts. Unfortunately, such a definition does not yet exist. Nevertheless, the notion of *variability* as an intuitive metric for complexity does provide a common thread throughout the present work. This is most apparent in the use of noise as an indicator of environmental complexity (in both the IPD and ER examples). But the 'complex' behaviours in the ER example are indeed more variable than the simple behaviours, and the longer memories evolved in the IPD example also provide the potential for increased variation in the strategies that are deployed.

Some useful alternative definitions of complexity are now beginning to appear. For example, Adami & Cerf (1997) provide a metric for the complexity of symbolic strings that is grounded in the information about an environment that is coded in the string, and which does not suffer from the problems associated with Kolmogorov complexity[14]. Future research could apply this metric to the IPD experiment, and could provide empirical guid-

[13] In the IPD case, since environmental complexity is one-dimensional (just noise) then Dewey's idea boils down to the observation that with either zero noise, or too much noise, complex strategies do not arise.

[14] The present 'memory' metric is similar to Adami's metric in that strategies with longer memories can potentially store more information about their environment.

ance for constructing a definition of complexity that remains useful beyond the confines of information theory.

In conclusion; the hypothesis that environmental variability promotes the evolution of organism complexity is presented as an empirically-testable elaboration of the general (externalist) principle that environmental complexity leads to organism complexity. It is, however *not* an argument against internalism[15]. The hypothesis is illustrated in both quantitative and qualitative contexts, but of course these contexts are quite specific to particular computational models and methods of artificial evolution. Nevertheless, empirical approaches to such general questions as the 'emergence of complexity' must necessarily start from simple examples, and this paper has illustrated that such simple examples are possible.

Furthermore, given that these examples employ artificial evolution as a methodology, it is also possible that the use of selective variability to engineer fitness landscape structure will become of practical importance in the application of genetic algorithms.

Appendix 1

The noise levels used in the homing navigation (evolutionary robotics) example are given below:

	noisy levels	*non-noisy levels*
IR	±50	±10
background IR	±10	0
ambient light	±50	±5
floor sensor	±50	±5
robot position	±0.1*cm*	0
robot orientation	±0.02*rad*	0
turning noise	±0.2*rads*	0
friction	±3*cm*	0
arena size	±5*cm*	0
charge radius	±1*cm*	0
light angle of acceptance	±0.25*rad*	0

Acknowledgements

Thanks to Nick Jakobi for help with the code, Adrian Thompson for help with the robots, and Phil Husbands, Hilary Buxton, Matt Quinn, Tom Smith, Andy Philippides, and my anonymous reviewers for helpful comments. Financial support was provided by the EPSRC award no. 96308700.

[15]Godfrey-Smith (1996) notes a possible internalist challenge to his 'environmental complexity thesis', which argues that it is the internal structure of the organism that *makes it the case* that the environment contains relevant (to the organism) complexity, or that it does not. Environmental complexity is then dependent upon internal structure. Perhaps an empirical approach can begin to address this challenge: an evolutionary process acting in a complex environment leads to the evolution of mechanisms, that then make it the case that certain kinds of environmental complexity, (such as ambient light information, for example), are relevant to the organism. This change in 'relative complexity' will then further influence the evolutionary process.

References

Adami, C., and N. J. Cerf. 1997. A practical lower bound on the complexity of symbolic sequences. eprint adap-org/9605002. Physica D, to be published.

Ashby, W. R. 1952. *Design for a Brain: The Origin of Adaptive Behaviour.* Chapman Hall.

Axelrod, R. 1984. *The Evolution of Cooperation.* New York: Basic Books.

Dawkins, R. 1986. *The Blind Watchmaker.* Longman.

Dewey, J. 1929. *Experience and Nature.* New York: Dover (rev. edn.).

Floreano, D., and F. Mondada. 1996. Evolution of homing navigation in a real mobile robot. *IEEE transactions on systems, man, and cybernetics: part B; cybernetics* 26: 396–407.

Godfrey-Smith, P. 1996. *Complexity and the Function of Mind in Nature.* Cambridge: Cambridge University Press.

Harvey, I., P. Husbands, D. Cliff, A. Thompson, and N. Jakobi. 1997. Evolutionary robotics: the sussex approach. *Robotics and Autonomous Systems* 20: 205–224.

Jakobi, N. 1997. Evolutionary robotics and the radical envelope of noise hypothesis. *Journal of Adaptive Behaviour* 6(2). (forthcoming).

K-Team. 1993. Khepera: the user's manual. Technical report, LAMI-EPFL.

Kauffman, S. 1993. *The Origins of Order. Self-Organisation and Selection in Evolution.* Oxford: Oxford University Press.

Kolmogorov, A. 1965. Three approaches to the definition of the concept 'quantity of information'. *Problems Inform. Transmission* 1: 1–7.

Langton, C. G., ed. 1995. *Artificial Life; an Overview.* MIT : Bradford Books.

Lindgren, K. 1991. Evolutionary phenomena in simple dynamics. In *Artificial Life II*, edited by C. G. Langton, C. Taylor, J. D. Farmer, and S. Rasmussen. Redwood City: Addison-Wesley, p. 295.

Schuster, P. 1996. How does complexity arise in evolution? Technical report, TBI working paper 96-05-026.

Seth, A. 1997. Interaction, uncertainty, and the evolution of complexity. In *Proceedings of the 4th European Conference on Artificial Life*, edited by P. Husbands and I. Harvey. Cambridge, MA: MIT Press, p. 521–530.

Stanley, E., D. Ashlock, and M. Smucker. 1995. Iterated prisoner's dilemma with choice and refusal of partners: Evolutionary results. In *Advances in Artificial Life* Lecture Notes in Artificial Intelligence, edited by F. Moran, A. Moreno, J. J. Merelo, and P. Chacon. Heidelberg, New York: Springer-Verlag.

Evolutionary Dynamics

Critical Exponent of Species-Size Distribution in Evolution

Chris Adami[1], **Ryoichi Seki**[1,2] and **Robel Yirdaw**[2]

[1]California Institute of Technology, Pasadena, CA 91125
[2]California State University, Northridge, CA 91330

Abstract

We analyze the geometry of the species– and genotype-size distribution in evolving and adapting populations of single-stranded self-replicating genomes: here programs in the Avida world. We find that a scale-free distribution (power law) emerges in complex landscapes that achieve a separation of two fundamental time scales: the relaxation time (time for population to return to equilibrium after a perturbation) and the time between mutations that produce fitter genotypes. The latter can be dialed by changing the mutation rate. In the scaling regime, we determine the critical exponent of the distribution of sizes and strengths of avalanches in a system without coevolution, described by first-order phase transitions in single finite niches.

Introduction

Power law distributions in Nature usually signal the absence of a scale in the region where the scaling is observed, and sometimes point to critical dynamics. In Self-Organized-Criticality (SOC) (Bak, Tang, and Wiesenfeld 1987, 1988), for example, power law distributions reveal the dynamics of an unstable critical point, brought about by slow driving and a feed-back mechanism between order parameter and critical parameter. The critical dynamics is usually described within the language of second-order phase transitions in condensed matter systems (Sornette, Johansen and Dornic 1996), but it can be shown that SOC-type behavior also occurs within a dual description in terms of the Landau-Ginzburg equation as *first-order* transitions (Gil and Sornette 1996). Indeed, it was shown that a power law distribution of *epoch-lengths*, that is, the time a particular species dominates the dynamics of an adapting population, is explained by a self-organized critical scenario (Adami 1995) that carries the hallmark of first-order phase transitions. Here, we measure the distribution of abundances of *species* and genotypes in an artificial chemistry, (the Avida Artificial Life system, Adami and Brown 1995, Ofria, Brown and Adami 1998) and show that the distribution is scale-free under a broad class of circumstances, confirming the results reported in Adami (1995). In the next section, we discuss the first-order dynamics in more detail and examine "avalanches of invention" from the point of view of a thermodynamics of information. In Section III, we measure the critical exponent of the power law of genotype abundances in the limit of infinitesimal driving, i.e., infinitesimal mutation rate, and discuss the role of the fitness landscape in shaping the distribution. In Section IV, we repeat the analysis for a higher taxonomic level (that of species) and discuss its relation to the geometric distributions found by Burlando (1990, 1993). Conclusions about the evolutionary process drawn from the data obtained in this paper are presented in Section V.

Self-Organization in Evolution

The idea that the evolutionary process occurs in spurts, jumps, and bursts rather than gradual, slow and continuous changes has been around for over 75 years (Willis 1922), but has gained prominence as "punctuated equilibrium" through the work of Gould and Eldredge (1977, 1993). The general idea is that evolutionary innovations are not bestowed upon an existing species as a whole, gradually, but rather by the emergence of *one* better adapted mutant which, by its superiority, serves as the seed of a new breed that sweeps through an ecological niche and supplants the species previously occupying it. The global dynamics thus has a microscopic origin, as shown experimentally, e.g., in populations of *E. Coli* by Elena, Cooper and Lenski (1996).

Such avalanches can be viewed in two apparently contradictory ways. On the one hand we may consider the wave of extinction touching all species that are connected by their ecological relations, a process akin to percolation and therefore suitably described by the language of second-order critical phenomena (Bak and Sneppen 1993). Such a scenario relies on the *coevolution* of species (to build their ecological relations) and successfully describes power-law distributions obtained from the fossil record (Solé and Bascompte 1996, Bak and Paczuski 1996). There is, on the other hand, a description in terms of *informational* avalanches that does not require coevolution and leads to the same statistics, as we show here. Rather than contradicting the aforementioned picture (Newman et al. 1997), we believe it to be complementary.

In the following, we set up a scenario in which *information* is viewed as the agent of self-organization in evolving and adapting populations. Information is, in the strict sense of Shannon theory, a measure of correlation between two ensembles: here a population of genomes and the environment it is adapting to. As described elsewhere (Adami 1998), this correlation grows as the population stores more and more information about the environment via random measurements, implementing a very effective *natural Maxwell demon.* Any time a stochastic event increases the information stored in the population, a wave of extinction removes the less adapted genomes and establishes a new era. Yet, information cannot leave the population as a whole, which therefore may be thought of as protected by a *semi-permeable membrane* for information, the hallmark of the Maxwell demon. Let us consider this dynamics in more detail.

The simple living systems we consider here are populations of self-replicating strings of instructions, coded in an alphabet of dimension $\mathcal{D}$ with variable string length ℓ. The total number of possible strings is exponentially large. Here, we consider the subset of all strings currently in existence in a finite population of size N, harboring N_g different types, where $N_g \ll \mathcal{D}^\ell$. Each *genotype* (particular sequence of instructions) is characterized by its replication rate ϵ_i, which depends on the sequence only, while its survival rate is given by $\epsilon_i/\langle\epsilon\rangle$, in a "stirred-reactor" environment that allows a mean-field picture. This average replication rate $\langle\epsilon\rangle$ characterizes the fitness of the population as a whole, and is given by

$$\langle\epsilon\rangle = \sum_i^{N_g} \frac{n_i}{N}\epsilon_i \,, \tag{1}$$

where n_i is the *occupation number*, or frequency, of genotype i in the population. As N_g is not fixed in time, the average depends on time also, and is to be taken over all genotypes currently living. The total abundance, or size, of a genotype is then

$$s_i = \int_0^\infty n_i(t)\,dt = \int_{T_c}^{T_e} n_i(t)\,dt \,, \tag{2}$$

where T_c is the time of creation of this particular genotype, and T_e the moment of extinction. Before we obtain this distribution in Avida, let us delve further into the statistical description of the extinction events.

At any point in time, the fate of every string in the population is determined by the craftiness of the best adapted member of the population, described by $\epsilon_{\rm best}$. In this simple, finite, world, which does not permit strings to affect other members of the population except by replacing them, not being the best reduces a string to an ephemeral existence. Thus, every string is characterized by a *relative* fitness, or *inferiority*

Figure 1: "Energies" (inferiorities) of strings in a first-order phase transition with latent heat $\Delta\epsilon$.

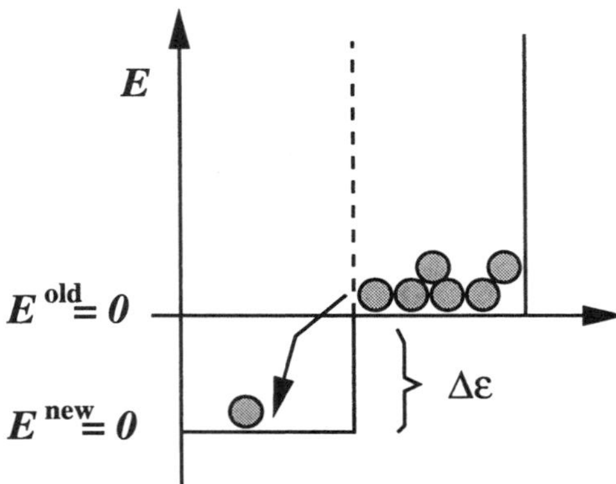

$$E_i = \epsilon_{\rm best} - \epsilon_i \tag{3}$$

which plays the role of an *energy* variable for strings of information (Adami 1998). Naturally, $\langle E\rangle = 0$ characterizes the *ground state*, or vacuum, of the population, and strings with $E_i > 0$ can be viewed as occupying *excited* states, soon to "decay" to the ground state (by being replaced by a string with vanishing inferiority). Through such processes, the dynamics of the system tend to minimize the average inferiority of the population, and the fitness landscape of replication rates thus provides a Lyapunov function. Consequently, we are allowed to proceed with our statistical analysis. Imagine a population in equilibrium, at minimal average inferiority as allowed by the "temperature": the rate (or more precisely, the probability) of mutation. Imagine further that a mutation event produces a new genotype, fitter than the others, exploiting the environment in novel ways, replicating faster than all the others. It is thus endowed with a new best replication rate, $\epsilon_{\rm best}^{\rm new}$, larger than the old "best" by an amount $\Delta\epsilon$, and redefining what it means to be inferior. Indeed, all inferiorities must now be *renormalized*: what passed as a ground state ($E = 0$) string before now suddenly finds itself in an excited state. The seed of a new generation has been sown, a phase transition must occur. In the picture just described, this is a first-order phase transition with latent heat $\Delta\epsilon$ (see Fig. 1), starting at the "nucleation" point, and leading to an expanding *bubble* of "new phase". This bubble expands with a speed given by the Fisher velocity

$$v \sim \sqrt{D\Delta\epsilon} \,, \tag{4}$$

where D is the diffusion coefficient (of information) in this medium, until the entire population has been converted (Chu and Adami 1997). This marks the end of the phase transition, as the population returns to equilibrium via mutations acting on the new species, creating new diversity and restoring the *entropy* of the population to its previous value. This prepares the stage for a new avalanche, as only an equilibrated population is vulnerable to even the smallest perturbation. The system has returned to a critical point, driven by mutations, self-organized by information.

Thus we see how a first-order scenario, without coevolution, can lead to self-organized and critical dynamics. It takes place within a single, finite, ecological niche, and thus does not contradict the dynamics taking place for populations that span many niches. Rather, we must conclude that the descriptions complement each other, from the single-niche level to the ecological web. Let us now take a closer look at the statistics of avalanches in this model, i.e., at the distribution of genotype sizes.

Exponents and Power Laws

The size of an avalanche in this particular system can be approximated by the size s of the genotype that gave rise to it, Eq. (2). We shall measure the distribution of these sizes $P(s)$ in the Artificial Life system Avida, which implements a population of self-replicating computer programs written in a simple machine language-like instruction set of $\mathcal{D} = 24$ instructions, with programs of varying sequence length. In the course of self-replication, these programs produce mutant off-spring because the copy instruction they use is flawed at a rate R errors per instruction copied, and adapt to an environment in which the performance of *logical* computations on externally provided numbers is akin to the catalysis of chemical reactions (Ofria, Brown and Adami 1998). In this *artificial chemistry* therefore, successful computations accelerate the metabolism (i.e., the CPU) of those strings that carry the *gene* (code) necessary to perform the trick, and any program discovering a new trick is the seed of another avalanche.

Avida is not a stirred-reactor environment (although one can be simulated). Rather, the programs live on a two-dimensional grid, each program occupying one site. The size of the grid is finite, and chosen in these experiments to be small enough that avalanches are generally over before a new one starts. As is well-known, this is the condition *sine qua non* for the observation of SOC behavior, a separation of time scales which implies that the system is driven at infinitesimal rates.

Let τ denote the average duration of an avalanche. Then, a separation of time scales occurs if the average time between the production of new seeds of avalanches is much larger than τ. New seeds, in turn, are produced with a frequency $\langle\epsilon\rangle P$, where $\langle\epsilon\rangle$ is again the average replication rate, and P is the mutation probability (per replication period) for an average sequence of length ℓ,

$$P = 1 - (1 - R)^{\ell} \; . \tag{5}$$

Figure 2: Fitness of the dominant genotype in the population, $\epsilon_{\rm best}$ as a function of time (in updates).

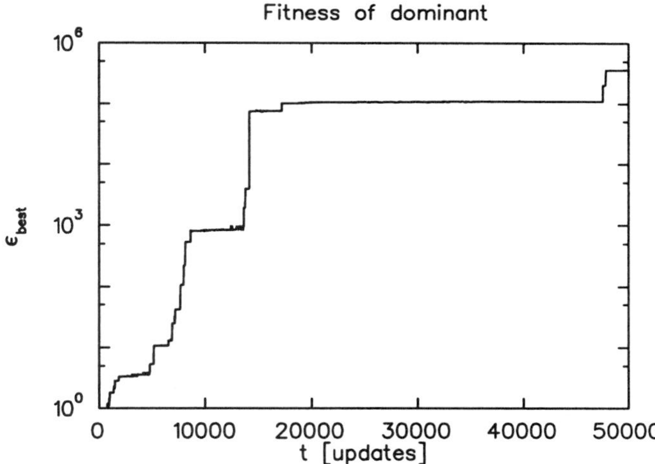

For small enough R and not too large ℓ (so that the product $R\ell$ is smaller than unity) we can approximate $P \approx R\ell$, and infinitesimal driving occurs in the limit

$$\langle\epsilon\rangle R\ell \ll \frac{1}{\tau} \; . \tag{6}$$

Furthermore

$$\tau \sim \frac{L}{v} \tag{7}$$

with L the diameter of the system and v a typical Fisher velocity. The fastest waves are those for which the latent heat is of the order of the new fitness, i.e., $\Delta\epsilon \sim \epsilon$, in which case $v \approx \epsilon$ (because $D \sim \epsilon$ in Eq. (4), see Chu and Adami 1995) and a separation of time scales is assured whenever

$$\frac{1}{R\ell} \gg L \, , \tag{8}$$

that is, in the limit of vanishing mutation rate or small population sizes. For the $L = 60$ system used here, this condition is obeyed (for the fastest waves) only for the smallest mutation rate tested and sequence lengths of the order of the ancestor.

In the following, we keep the population size constant (a 60×60 grid) and vary the mutation rate. From the previous arguments, we expect true scale-free dynamics only to appear in the limit of small mutation rates. As in this limit avalanches occur less and less frequently, this is also the limit where data are increasingly difficult to obtain, and other finite size effects can come into play. We shall try to isolate the scale-free regime by fitting the distribution to a power law

$$P(s) \sim s^{-D(R)} \tag{9}$$

and monitor the behavior of D from low to high mutation rates.

In Fig. 2, we display a typical history of ϵ_{best}, i.e., the fitness of the dominant genotype[1]. Note the "staircase" structure of the curve reflecting the "punctuated" dynamics, where each step reflects a new avalanche and concurrently an extinction event. Staircases very much like these are also observed in adapting populations of *E. Coli* (Lenski and Travisano 1994).

As touched upon earlier, the Avida world represents an environment replete with information, which we encode by providing bonuses for performing logical computations on externally provided (random) numbers. The computations rewarded usually involve two inputs A and B, are finite in number and listed in Table 1. At the end of a typical run (such as Fig. 2) the population of programs is usually proficient in almost all tasks for which bonuses are given out, and the genome length has grown to several multiples of the initial size to accommodate the acquired information.

Table 1: Logical calculations on random inputs A and B rewarded, bonuses, and difficulty (in minimum number of nand instructions required). Bonuses b_i increase the speed of a CPU by a factor $\nu_i = 1 + 2^{b_i - 3}$.

Name	Result	Bonus b_i	Difficulty
Echo	I/O	1	–
Not	$\neg A$	2	1
Nand	$\neg(A \wedge B)$	2	1
Not Or	$\neg A \vee B$	3	2
And	$A \wedge B$	3	2
Or	$A \vee B$	4	3
And Not	$A \wedge \neg B$	4	3
Nor	$\neg(A \vee B)$	5	4
Xor	A xor B	6	4
Equals	$\neg(A$ xor $B)$	6	4

Because the amount of information stored in the landscape is finite, adaptation, and the associated avalanches, must stop when the population has exhausted the landscape. However, we shall see that even a 'flat' landscape (on which evolution is essentially neutral after the sequence has optimized its replicative strategy) gives rise to a power law of genotype sizes, as long as the programs do not harbor an excessive amount of "junk" instructions[2]. A typical abundance distribution (for the run depicted in Fig. 2) is shown in Fig. 3. As mentioned

Figure 3: Distribution of genotypes sizes $P(s)$ fitted to a power law (solid line) at mutation rate $R = 0.004$.

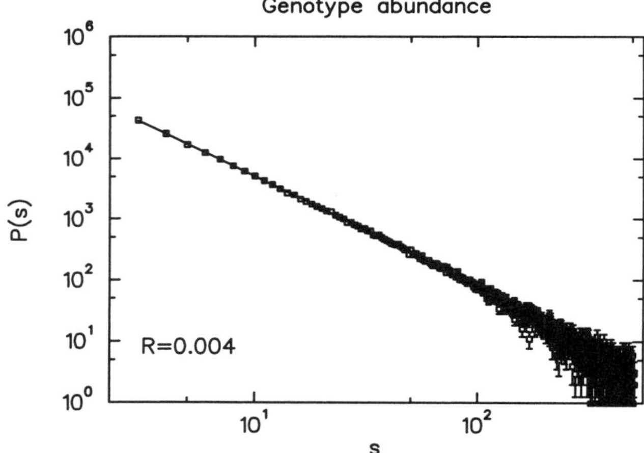

earlier, we can also turn *off* all bonuses listed in Tab. 1, in which case fitness is related to replicative abilities only. Still, avalanches occur (within the first 50,000 updates monitored) due to minute improvements in fitness, but the length of the genomes typically stays in the range of the ancestor, a program of length 31 instructions. We expect a change of dynamics once the "true" maximum of the local fitness landscape is reached, however, we did not reach this regime in the experiments presented here. The distribution of genotype sizes for the flat landscape is depicted in Fig. 4. Clearly then, even such landscapes (flat with respect to all other activities except replication) are not neutral. Indeed, it is known that neutral

Figure 4: Distribution of genotypes sizes $P(s)$ for a landscape devoid of the bonuses listed in Tab. 1, at mutation rate $R = 0.003$.

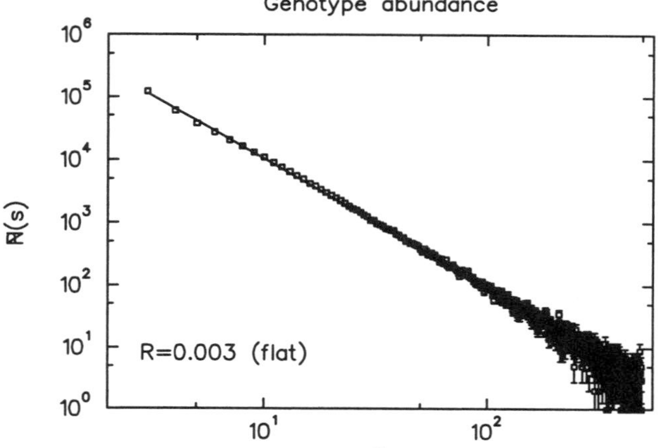

[1] As the replication rate ϵ is exponential in the bonus obtained for a successful computation, ϵ_{best} increases exponentially with time.

[2] "Junk" instructions do not code for any information, and do not affect the fitness of their bearer. Consequently, programs with excessive amounts of junk code will give rise to many "degenerate" genotypes with no competitive advantage. In this regime, the genotype abundance distribution is exponential rather than of the power-law type, due to a violation of condition (6).

Figure 5: Fitted exponent of power law for 34 runs at mutation rates between $R = 0.0005$ and $R = 0.01$ copy errors per instruction copied. The error bars reflect the standard deviation across the sample of runs taken at each mutation rate. The solid line is to guide the eye only.

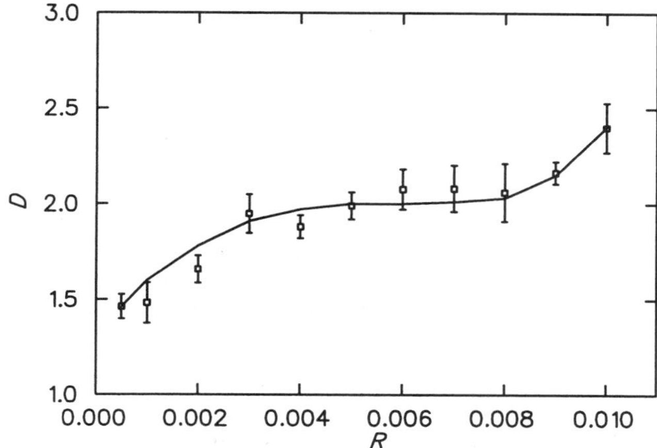

evolution, where the chance for a genotype to increase or decrease in number is even, leads to a power law in the abundance distribution with exponent $D = 1.5$ (Adami, Brown, and Haggerty, 1995).

In order to test the dependence of the fitted exponent $D(R)$ [Eq. (9)] on the mutation rate, we conduct a set of experiments at varying copy-mutation rates from 0.5×10^{-3} to 10×10^{-3} and take data for 50,000 updates. Again, a "best" genotype is not reached after this time, and we must assume that avalanches were still occurring at the end of these runs. Furthermore, in some runs we find that a genotype comes to dominate the population (usually after most 'genes' have been discovered) which carries an unusual amount of junk instructions. As mentioned earlier, such species produce a distribution that is exponentially suppressed at large genotype sizes (data not shown). To avoid contamination from such species, we stop recording genotypes after a plateau of fitness was reached, i.e., if the population had discovered most of the bonuses. Furthermore, in order to minimize finite size effects on the determination of the critical exponent, we excluded from this fit all genotype abundances larger than 15, i.e., we only fitted the smallest abundances. Indeed, at larger mutation rates the higher abundances are contaminated by a pile-up effect due to the toroidal geometry, while at lower mutation rates a scale appears to enter which prevents scale-free behavior. We have not, as yet, been able to determine the origin of this scale.

In the results reported here, we show the dependence of the fitted exponent D as a function of the mutation rate R used in the run, which, however, is a good measure of the mutation probability P only at small R and if the sequence length is not excessive. As a consequence, data points at large R, as well as runs where an excessive sequence length developed, carry a systematic error.

For the 34 runs that we obtained, the power D was measured for each run (for the low abundances), and an average was calculated for all the runs at a particular mutation rate. This data is plotted in Fig. 5 and shows a plateau in the fitted exponent only at intermediate mutation rates, with $D = 2.0 \pm 0.05$. A fit of the middle abundances (10-100) produces a critical coefficient more or less independent of mutation rate, around $D = 2.0$, but with less accuracy (data not shown). At high R, we witness a deviation from scale-free behavior (reflected in the rising D for small abundances) which is most likely due to pile-up, i.e., a finite toroidal lattice. This effect may be avoided by using absorbing rather than periodic boundary conditions. We also see a violation of scaling at small R, which is due to the emergence of some other scale. While it is most likely a finite-size effect, the exact origin of this scale is as yet unclear. We comment on the significance of these results in Section V.

Still, more control over the spread in exponents for fixed mutation rate would be desirable. This can obviously be achieved by plotting D versus P, rather than R, for example, and by better keeping track of the coding percentage within a genotype, a variable that we know significantly affects the shape of the distribution. Such experiments are planned for the near future.

Distribution of Species Sizes

In Avida, it is possible to monitor groups of programs that display the same "phenotype", while differing in genotype. Even though programs in this world are haploid (single-stranded) and do not reproduce sexually, it is convenient to label such groups taxonomically, i.e., we refer to them as "species". Strictly speaking, a species consists out of all those genotypes that, when executed, give rise to the same "chemistry", i.e., such programs differ only in instructions that are either unexecuted, or else are *neutral*. Algorithmically, the determination whether two genotypes belong to the same species is complicated by the fact that sequence length is *not* constant in these experiments. Thus, we need to be able to compare strings with differing lengths, which is achieved by lining them up in such a manner that they are identical in the maximum number of corresponding sites. Subsequently, a *cross-over* point is chosen randomly and the genomes above and below this point are *swapped*. In other words, we construct a *hybrid* program from the two candidates and test it for functionality, but without introducing it in the population (see Adami 1998.) In the experiments reported here, we actually test *two* cross-over points in order to rule out accidental matches. In retrospect, we find that almost all those strings classified as belonging to the same species by this method differ only in "silent", or at least inconsequential, instructions.

Figure 6: Distribution of genotypes within species at $R = 0.004$, fitted to a power law with $D = 2.44 \pm 0.05$.

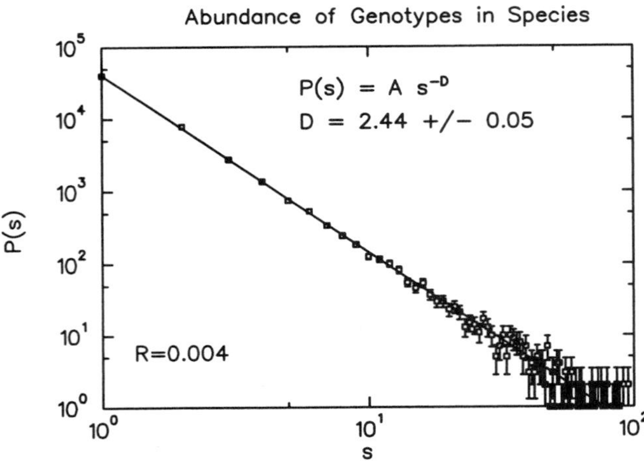

The abundance distribution of genotypes within species more closely corresponds to the kind of geometric distributions investigated by Willis (1922) as well as Burlando (1990, 1993). Indeed, Burlando found, in an analysis of distributions of subtaxa within taxa obtained from the fossil record as well as recorded flora and fauna, that these distributions appear to be scale-free across taxonomic hierarchies, with critical coefficients between $2.0 < D < 2.5$. This distribution can also be viewed as a distribution of avalanches sizes, if avalanches are redefined as events that spawn different genotypes of the same species. Indeed, in this manner it is possible to investigate hierarchies of avalanches, each higher level presumably sporting a higher critical coefficient.

In the experiments reported here, we found species coefficients closer to $D \approx 2.5$, but we also found violations of power-law behavior which are most likely due to the contribution of species of different lengths to the abundance distribution. Indeed, the amount of "junk" instructions in a species most likely governs the steepness of the distribution, and several different such species may give rise to a *multifractal* distribution rather than a pure power law. In the future, we expect to disentangle such distributions by appealing to a an even higher level in taxonomy, reuniting all species of the same sequence length within a *genus*. The latter taxonomic level could, for example, be entirely phenotypic, by keeping track of which tasks a genus executes (irrespective of its genotype).

Still, even though changing sequence lengths affect the distribution of genotypes within species, those experiments in which the sequence length does *not* change significantly can give rise to power laws with single exponents, as shown below in Fig. 6. The data for this experiment were obtained from the same run as gave rise to Figs. 2 and 3.

Conclusions

The distribution of avalanche sizes in evolving systems, which is quite clearly related to the distribution of extinction events, can reveal a fair amount of information about the dynamics of the adapting agents. For example, purely random systems in which there are no fitness advantages, and where selection does not occur, can still show power law behavior, as extinction events are governed by the return-to-zero probability of random walks (Adami, Brown and Haggerty 1995). In Avida, we observe a scaling exponent $D = 2.0$ in an intermediate regime of mutation rates. While it is still unclear whether the *mixing of scales* that we have observed at small and large mutation rates is due to the finite size of the lattice or the emergence of another scale, we can conclude with confidence that scale-free dynamics does occur. Scaling violations should be investigated by a thorough finite lattice-size analysis, and this is planned for the future along with more refined methods for dealing with explicit neutrality (i.e., "junk" code.)

An interesting hint at what the distribution might be like in Nature comes from Raup's analysis of a data set prepared by Sepkoski (Raup 1991): genera of marine invertebrates from the fossil record. Raup's "kill-curve" can be transformed into a distribution of sizes of extinction evens (as shown by Newman 1996) governed by a critical exponent close to $D = 2.0$. This is tantalizingly close to the coefficient we found in our genotype abundance distribution, but we must be careful in comparing these distributions.

The avalanche-size distribution of genotypes gives us a good indication of the strength of an evolutionary shock, but also about the length of time the particular species dominates the dynamics, and therefore, of the time *between* evolutionary transitions. Also, each evolutionary transition brings with it a wave of extinction, as all previously extant genotypes and species of lower fitness must disappear on the heels of the new "discovery". The size of extinction events proper, however, is not measured by the "epoch-length" distribution reflected in the avalanche sizes, but rather by the abundance of genotypes within species (or any higher taxonomic abundance distribution) because each species appearing in this distribution must eventually go extinct, and thus this distribution must equal the distribution of extinction sizes. The latter distribution (measured in Section IV), appears to have a critical exponent around $D \approx 2.5$, higher than the corresponding one from the fossil record. Furthermore, we must keep in mind the simplicity of the model treated here when comparing to actual fossil data. As mentioned in the introduction, coevolution does not play a role in the dynamics controlling the size of avalanches in this model, while we must assume that extinctions in Earth history have some coevolutionary component. On the other hand, the abundance distribution of genotypes within species is consistent with those obtained by Burlando (1990, 1993), who argued that they represented evidence for a "fractal geometry of Nature".

From the present analysis, it is clear that there is as yet no reason to jump to conclusions from the evidence extracted either from the fossil record, theoretical models of extinctions (Newman 1997), or else direct implementation of the dynamics of adaptive avalanches as we have done here. We do, however, see clear evidence that avalanches not reigned in by any scale can and do develop in evolving and adapting systems *without* co-evolutionary pressures, via first-order transitions in populations occupying single ecological niches. Not only do we find scale-free dynamics for the time between transitions (as evidenced by the genotype abundance distribution) but also for the *strength* of these transitions, measured by the distribution of species-sizes. It is left for future experiments to determine how such dynamics, taking place in *interacting* ecological niches, gives rise to power laws for co-evolutionary systems, and how the description in terms of first-order transitions is *ipso facto* transmutated into a second-order scenario.

This work was supported by NSF grant No. PHY-9723972.

References

Adami, C. 1995. Self-organized criticality in living systems. *Phys. Lett.* A 203: 23.

Adami, C. 1998. *Introduction to Artificial Life.* Santa Clara: TELOS Springer-Verlag.

Adami, C. and C. T. Brown. 1994. Evolutionary learning in the 2D Artificial Life system 'Avida'. In *Artificial Life IV*, edited by R.A. Brooks and P. Maes. Cambridge, MA: MIT Press, p. 377.

Adami, C., C. T. Brown and M. R. Haggerty. 1995. Abundance distributions in Artificial Life and stochastic models: 'Age and Area' revisited.*Lect. Notes in Artif. Intell.* 929: 503.

Bak, P. and M. Paczuski. 1996. In *Physics of Biological Systems.* Heidelberg: Springer-Verlag.

Bak, P. and K. Sneppen. 1993. Punctuated equilibrium and criticality in a simple model of evolution. *Phys. Rev. Lett.* 71: 4083.

Bak, B., C. Tang, and K. Wiesenfeld. 1987. Self-organized criticality: An explanation of $1/f$ noise. *Phys. Rev. Lett.* 59: 381.

Bak, B., C. Tang, and K. Wiesenfeld. 1988. Self-organized criticality. *Phys. Rev.* A 38: 364.

Burlando, B. 1990. The fractal dimension of taxonomic systems. *J. Theor. Biol.* 146: 99.

Burlando, B. 1993. The fractal geometry of evolution. *J. Theor. Biol.* 163: 161.

Chu, J. and C. Adami. 1997. Propagation of information in populations of self-replicating code. In Proc. of *Artificial Life V*, edited by C. G. Langton and K. Shimohara. Cambridge, MA: MIT Press, p. 462.

Elena, S. F., V. S. Cooper and R.E. Lenski. 1996. Punctuated evolution caused by selection of rare beneficial mutations. *Science* 272: 1802.

Gil, L. and D. Sornette. 1996. Landau-Ginzburg theory of self-organized criticality. *Phys. Rev. Lett.* 76: 3991.

Gould, S. J. and N. Eldredge. 1977. Punctuated equilibria: The tempo and mode of evolution reconsidered. *Paleobiology* 3: 115.

Gould, S. J. and N. Eldredge. 1993. Punctuated equilibrium comes of age. *Nature* 366: 223.

Lenski, R. and M. Travisano. 1994. Dynamics of adaptation and diversification–A 10,000 generation experiment with bacterial populations. *Proc. Nat. Acad. Sci.* 91: 6808-6814.

Newman, M. E. J. 1996. Self-organized criticality, evolution, and the fossil extinction record. *Proc. Roy. Soc.* B 263: 1605–1610.

Newman, M. E. J. 1997. A model of mass extinction. Eprint adap-org/9702003.

Newman, M. E. J., S. M. Fraser, K. Sneppen, and W.A. Tozier. 1997. Self-organized criticality in living systems—Comment. *Phys. Lett.* A 228: 202.

Ofria, C., C. T. Brown and C. Adami. 1998. *The Avida User's Manual.* In Adami (1998). The Avida software is publicly available at ftp.krl.caltech.edu/pub/avida.

Raup, D. M. 1991. A kill curve for phanerozoic marine species. *Paleobiology* 17: 37–48..

Sornette, D., A. Johansen, and I. Dornic. 1995. Mapping self-organized criticality to criticality. *J. de Phys.* I 5: 325.

Solé, R. V. and J. Bascompte. 1996. Are critical phenomena relevant to large-scale evolution? *Proc. Roy. Soc.* B 263: 161–168.

Willis, J. C. 1922. *Age and Area.* Cambridge: Cambridge University Press.

A Classification of Long-Term Evolutionary Dynamics

Mark A. Bedau[†], Emile Snyder[†], Norman H. Packard[‡]
[†]Reed College, 3203 SE Woodstock Blvd., Portland OR 97202, USA, {mab, emile}@reed.edu
[‡]Prediction Company, 236 Montezuma St., Santa Fe NM 87501, USA, n@predict.com

Abstract

We present empirical evidence that long-term evolutionary dynamics fall into three distinct classes, depending on whether adaptive evolutionary activity is absent (class 1), bounded (class 2), or unbounded (class 3). These classes are defined using three statistics: diversity, new evolutionary activity (Bedau & Packard 1992), and mean cumulative evolutionary activity (Bedau *et al.* 1997). The three classes partition all the long-term evolutionary dynamics observed in Holland's Echo model (Holland 1992), in a random-selection adaptively-neutral "shadow" of Echo, and in the biosphere as reflected in the Phanerozoic fossil record. This classification provides quantitative evidence that Echo lacks the unbounded growth in adaptive evolutionary activity observed in the fossil record.

Why Classify Evolutionary Dynamics?

We present and illustrate a classification of long-term evolutionary dynamics. Classifications of complex dynamical behavior are reasonably familiar, with Wolfram's classification of cellular automata rules being one well-known example (Wolfram 1984), but there are few attempts to classify the dynamics specifically of adaptive evolution. Nevertheless, such a classification is at least implicitly presupposed by the debates in biology about such issues as the evolution of clay crystallites (Cairns-Smith 1982; 1985), the evolution of "memes" (Dawkins 1976), and the increasing complexity of life on Earth (Gould 1989; McShea 1996; Gould 1996). Likewise for claims in artificial life about systems exhibiting "open-ended evolution" or "perpetual novelty" or operating "far from equilibrium" (Lindgren 1992; Ray 1992; Holland 1992; 1995; Bedau *et al.* 1997). Indeed, the defining focus of the field of artificial life—simulating and synthesizing systems that behave essentially like living systems—implies such a classification. How can we tell whether artificial systems behave relevantly like real living systems without using at least an implicit classification of system behavior?

The classification question arises sharply only when we have many concrete instances to classify, so our inattention to the classification question was understandable when we had a sample size of only one—the biosphere. But the advent of artificial life changes this. Scores of artificial evolving systems are now generating many thousands of instances of long-term evolutionary dynamics. So we now have ample empirical data to tackle the classification question rigorously.

On the basis of studying data from a variety of artificial life models and from the biosphere, we have concluded that long-term evolutionary dynamics fall into three different classes. Our procedure here is to define statistics characterizing evolutionary dynamics and then use them to define three classes of long-term evolutionary trends. We then illustrate these classes of evolutionary dynamics in three systems: Holland's Echo model (Holland 1992; 1995), a random-selection model that shadows Echo's dynamics, and the Phanerozoic biosphere as reflected in the fossil record. We choose these systems to illustrate the kinds of dynamics because (i) Echo, among artificial life models, is an especially promising candidate for exhibiting complex adaptive evolutionary dynamics, (ii) Echo's random-selection shadow provides an adaptively-neutral null case which highlights adaptations in Echo, and (iii) the Phanerozoic fossil record presents our best evidence about long-term dynamics in natural evolving systems. We are in the process of classifying many other artificial and natural evolving systems.

Evolutionary Activity Statistics

Our classification of evolutionary dynamics is based on statistics for quantifying adaptive evolutionary phenomena. These statistics have already been applied to various evolving systems in various ways for various purposes (Bedau & Packard 1992; Bedau 1995; Bedau *et al.* 1997; Bedau & Brown 1997). This section describes these statistics with maximal generality and then explains how they are applied here.

Our evolutionary activity statistics are computed from data obtained by observing an evolving system. In our view an evolving system consists of a population of components, all of which participate in a cycle of birth, life and death, with each component largely determined by inherited traits. (We use this "component" terminology to maintain enough generality to cover a wide variety of entities, ranging from individuals alleles to taxonomic families.) Birth, however, creates the possibility of innovations being introduced into the population. If the innovation is adaptive, it persists in the population with a beneficial effect on the survival potential of the components that have it. It persists not only in the component which first receives the innovation, but in all subsequent components that inherit the innovation, i.e., in an entire lineage. If the innovation is not adaptive, it either disappears or persists passively.

Our idea of evolutionary activity is to identify innovations that make a difference. Generally we consider an innovation to "make a difference" if it persists and continues to be used. Counters are attached to components for bookkeeping purposes, to update each component's current activity as the component persists and is used. If the components are passed along during reproduction, the corresponding counters are inherited with the components, maintaining an increasing count for an entire lineage. Two large issues immediately arise:

1. What should be counted as a component, and what counts as the addition or subtraction of a component from the system? In most evolving systems components may be identified on a variety of levels. Previous work has studied components on the level of individual alleles (Bedau & Packard 1992; Bedau 1995) as well as genotypes (Bedau *et al.* 1997; Bedau & Brown 1997) and taxonomic families (Bedau *et al.* 1997).

   Here we study entire genotypes and taxonomic families. The addition or subtraction of a given component consists of the origination or extinction of a given genotype or taxonomic family. It's natural to choose genotypes and taxonomic families as components because adaptive evolution can be expected to affect the dynamics of those entities.

2. What should be a new component's initial contribution to the evolutionary activity of the system and how should it change over time? To measure activity contributions we attach a counter to each component of the system, $a_i(t)$, where i labels the component and t labels time. These activity counters are purely observational devices. A component's activity increases over time as follows, $a_i(t) = \sum_{k \leq t} \Delta_i(k)$, where $\Delta_i(k)$ is the activity increment for component i at time k. Various activity incrementation functions $\Delta_i(t)$ can be used, depending on the nature of the components and the purposes at hand.

   Since genotypes and taxonomic families are components in the present context, it's natural to measure a component's contribution to the system's evolutionary activity simply by its age. Everything else being equal, the more adaptive an innovative genotype or taxonomic family continues to be, the longer it will persist in the system. So we choose an activity incrementation function that increases a component's activity counter by one unit for each time step that it exists:

$$\Delta_i(t) = \begin{cases} 1 & \text{if component } i \text{ exists at } t \\ 0 & \text{otherwise} \end{cases} . \qquad (1)$$

   Though there are ways to refine this simple counting method (Bedau & Packard 1992; Bedau 1995; Bedau *et al.* 1997), this version facilitates direct comparison with many other systems.

   In some contexts activity statistics indicate a system's *adaptive* evolutionary dynamics only after the activity increment $\Delta_i(t)$ is normalized with respect to a "neutral" model devoid of adaptive dynamics (Bedau 1995; Bedau *et al.* 1997; Bedau & Brown 1997). Here we address this issue in two different ways. With respect to taxonomic families in the Phanerozoic biosphere, we consider this normalization to be accomplished *de facto* by the fossil record itself. In our view, the mere fact that a family appears in the fossil record is good evidence that its persistence reflects its adaptive significance. Significantly maladaptive taxonomic families would likely go extinct before leaving a trace in the fossil record. But measuring evolutionary activity in Echo data is another matter, because we know maladaptive genotypes contribute to Echo's activity data. So, to screen off the activity of maladaptive Echo genotypes, we measure evolutionary activity in a "neutral shadow" of Echo. Then, by comparing the Echo and neutral shadow data we can tell how much (if any) of Echo's evolutionary activity is due to the genotypes' adaptive value. The details of this neutral screening are explained in subsequent sections.

Now, we can define various statistics based on the components in a system and their activity counters. Perhaps the simplest statistic—because it ignores activity information—is the system's *diversity*, $D(t)$, which is simply the number of components present at time t,

$$D(t) = \#\{i : a_i(t) > 0\} , \qquad (2)$$

where $\#\{\cdot\}$ denotes set cardinality.

The values of the activity counters of each component in the system over all time can be collected in the *component activity distribution*, $C(t, a)$, as follows:

$$C(t, a) = \sum_i \delta(a - a_i(t)) , \qquad (3)$$

where $\delta(a - a_i(t))$ is the Dirac delta function, equal to one if $a = a_i(t)$ and zero otherwise. Thus, $C(t, a)$ indicates the number of components with activity a at time t. (Normalizing the component activity distribution by the diversity, $\frac{C(t,a)}{D(t)}$, gives the *fraction* of components in the population with activity a at time t.)

A measure of the continual adaptive success of the components in the system at a given time is provided by the *total cumulative evolutionary activity*, $A_{\text{cum}}(t)$, which simply sums the evolutionary activity of all the components at a given time:

$$A_{\text{cum}}(t) = \sum_i a_i(t) \quad (4)$$

$$\rightarrow \int_0^\infty aC(t,a)\,da \ . \quad (5)$$

(In practice, we compute activity statistics using the sum; the integral indicated is obtained in the limit when activity takes on a continuum of values.) As the integral shows, you can think about $A_{\text{cum}}(t)$ as the mass in the component activity distribution weighted by its level of activity. So, the cumulative activity per component, or *mean cumulative evolutionary activity*, $\bar{A}_{\text{cum}}(t)$, is simply the cumulative evolutionary activity $A_{\text{cum}}(t)$ divided by the diversity $D(t)$:

$$\bar{A}_{\text{cum}}(t) = \frac{A_{\text{cum}}(t)}{D(t)} \ . \quad (6)$$

We sometimes refer to mean cumulative evolutionary activity simply as "mean activity."

Adaptive innovations correspond to new components flowing into the system and proving their adaptive value through their persistent activity. Let a_0 and a_1 define a strip through the component activity distribution function, $C(t,a)$, such that activity values a in the range $a_0 \leq a \leq a_1$ are among the lowest activity values that can be interpreted as evidence that a component has positive adaptive significance. Then, one reflection of the rate of the evolution of adaptive innovations is the *new evolutionary activity*, $A_{\text{new}}(t)$, which sums the evolutionary activity per component with values between a_0 and a_1:

$$A_{\text{new}}(t) = \frac{1}{D(t)} \sum_{i,a_0 \leq a_i(t) \leq a_1} a_i(t) \quad (7)$$

$$\rightarrow \frac{1}{D(t)} \int_{a_0}^{a_1} C(t,a)\,da \ . \quad (8)$$

We sometimes refer to new evolutionary activity per component just as "new activity."

Since we view any appearance in the fossil record as evidence of a taxonomic family's positive adaptive significance (recall above), we measure new activity in the fossil record in a strip right along the bottom of the component activity distribution. To screen off the low activity values which might reflect maladaptive genotypes in Echo, we use a "neutral shadow" of Echo to determine that activity level, a', at which we can begin to have confidence that a component's activity reflects its positive adaptive value, and we let a_0 and a_1 define a small window surrounding a'.

There is more than one way to quantify diversity and evolutionary activity. For example, another useful measure of diversity is the Shannon entropy of the distribution of sizes of components in the system. In addition, the choice of what to count as a system's components affects a system's diversity as measured by $D(t)$. Likewise, the activity statistics are affected by choices about, among other things, what the system's components are, how to define the component activity incrementation function, $\Delta_i(t)$, where to set a_0 and a_1, how to define a "neutral" model, etc. Furthermore, there are other kinds of activity statistics besides those defined here (Bedau & Packard 1992; Bedau 1995; Bedau & Brown 1997). Our specific choices of diversity and evolutionary activity statistics here is motivated by the desire to directly compare the adaptive evolutionary dynamics in Echo and in the Phanerozoic biosphere.

Classes of Evolutionary Dynamics

On the basis of observing evolutionary dynamics from a variety of artificial and natural evolving systems, we have concluded that there are three fundamentally different kinds of long-term evolutionary dynamics:

Class 1. No adaptive evolutionary activity: diversity D is bounded, new activity A_{new} is zero, and mean activity $\bar{A}_{\text{cum}}$ is zero.

Class 2. Bounded adaptive evolutionary activity: diversity D is bounded, new activity A_{new} is positive, and mean activity $\bar{A}_{\text{cum}}$ is bounded.

Class 3. Unbounded adaptive evolutionary activity: diversity D is unbounded, new activity A_{new} is positive, and mean activity $\bar{A}_{\text{cum}}$ is bounded. Evolutionary activity is growing because D is unbounded, $\bar{A}_{\text{cum}}$ is bounded, and total cumulative evolutionary activity, A_{cum}, is their product.[1]

(The Appendix precisely defines what we mean by a statistic being positive or bounded.) The three classes of evolutionary dynamics apply equally well to artificial and natural evolving systems. Although we sometimes lack sufficient evidence for an unambiguous classification, and although the available evidence sometimes is misleading, we have found that the evolutionary dynamics of any evolving system in which our statistics can be defined will eventually be seen to fall into one of these three classes.

The classification of a system's evolutionary dynamics depends on certain decisions made when defining the

[1] Unbounded $\bar{A}_{\text{cum}}$ and bounded (or unbounded) D would also yield unbounded A_{cum}, but we have never observed such dynamics.

statistics. In particular, diversity and activity statistics can be implemented only after the components of a system are identified and the activity incrementation function, $\Delta_i(t)$, is defined. Thus, a system could exhibit different classes of evolutionary dynamics at different levels of analysis (say, the genetic and the phenotypic levels).

The three classes of evolutionary dynamics are not logically exhaustive. Other classes of long-term evolutionary dynamics can be defined, such as a system showing bounded diversity, zero new activity, and unbounded mean activity, or a system showing bounded diversity, positive new activity, and unbounded mean activity. And, in fact, some evolving systems do *appear* to exhibit these two kinds of dynamics. However, when a system has evolved long enough to reveal its long-term evolutionary dynamics, and when its evolutionary activity data is appropriately normalized with a neutral model, we have always found its behavior to fall into one of the classes 1-3. (If further study were to reveal the need for additional classes of evolutionary dynamics, they should be definable with our statistics.)

In the first instance, our classification applies to the evolutionary dynamics in a given run of a given system. But if different runs of the same system at the same spot in parameter space all exhibit the same class of evolutionary dynamics, then the classification is a generic property of that system at that place in parameter space. Further, if the same class of evolutionary dynamics is exhibited by a system across a large area of parameter space, then the classification is even more generic. When adjacent regions in parameter space have different kinds of generic evolutionary dynamics, an important question is to identify and explain the line demarking these dynamics. Finally, a class of evolutionary dynamics might be shared as a generic feature across a large area of parameter space by a wide class of evolving systems, including both those found naturally and those constructed artificially.

The Echo Model

John Holland created Echo in the attempt to produce a model that would illustrate the creation of complex structures by natural selection (Holland 1995). Echo's central explicit focus is to allow natural selection to shape the strategies by which a population of agents engage in various kinds of interactions. Detailed information about the Echo model is available elsewhere (Holland 1992; Jones & Forrest 1993; Holland 1994; Forrest & Jones 1994; Holland 1995; Hraber, Jones, & Forrest 1997; SFI 1998).

An Echo world consists of a toroidal lattice of sites, each site having a resource fountain and a population of agents. (The Echo runs we describe here consist of worlds with only one site.) Different letters of the alphabet represent different types of resources available in the world. A fixed amount of resources is distributed to each site at each time step, and unconsumed resources accumulate at a site up to a fixed ceiling.

An Echo agent consists of a "chromosome" that is composed of eleven sub-strings of the world's resources (letters of the alphabet) together with a reservoir storing excess resources. The sub-strings of the chromosome constitute an agent's *external tags* and *internal conditions* together with an uptake mask which specifies what resources the agent can take up from the environment. An agent's tags are external in the sense that other agents have access to them, while an agent's conditions are inaccessible to other agents. The tags and conditions are used to determine the outcome of the three types of interactions that Echo agents can engage in—combat, trade, and mating. Whether two agents interact and, if so, what type of interaction they have is determined by comparing the agents' tags and conditions. A string match of the appropriate tag and condition causes the interaction to take place. External tags and internal conditions allow complex (e.g. non-transitive) relationships to exist between the agents, and it is central to Echo's endogenous fitness function (a fitness function that is an emergent property of the environment and the other agents (Packard 1989)).

The combat interaction gives a good illustration of how tags and conditions are used. Two individuals engage in combat provided there is a prefix match between their combat conditions and the other individuals' offense tag. Each individual's payoff of the combat interaction is determined by a calculation based on the letters in the two individuals' offense and defense tags, and the winner of the combat is chosen probabilistically, based on the two individuals' relative payoffs. The losing agent gets a chance to flee, and otherwise is killed and loses it resources to the winner.

Trading and mating interactions use tags and conditions in a related way. Trading takes place if there is a prefix match between the trading condition of the first agent and the offense tag of the other agent. A trading interaction between two agents results in each agent transferring the excess of its trading resource (the amount of resources in the agent's reservoir over and above what the it needs for reproduction) to the other agent. The mating interaction takes place if a bilateral match is found between the mating tags and conditions of two agents chosen to interact. The result of a successful mating interaction is more analogous to the types of genetic exchange seen in bacteria as opposed to sexual reproduction. The two participating agents exchange genetic material via crossover (at a random point in the chromosome) and replace their "parents" in the population.

Agents that have acquired enough resources in their reservoir to copy their chromosome reproduce asexually.

Asexual reproduction is subject to a probability, μ, of a point mutation as well as probabilities of mutation by crossover and by insertion-deletion within the parent chromosome. As a part of asexual reproduction, parents give a fixed percentage of the resources remaining in their reservoir to their offspring. In addition to gathering resources from the environment, agents lose resources through a metabolic tax τ, as well as by asexual reproduction, and they gain and loose resources by fighting and trading. The interaction probability, ι, determines the probability that nearby agents will engage in the interactions that affect their resource levels. It is mutation together with the selection pressure due to competition for resources that drives the evolution of Echo's population.

One time step in the Echo model consists of the following cycle of events: A proportion of the agents are selected to undergo interactions and the interactions take place. Resources at a site are distributed to those agents that can accept them. Agents are taxed probabilistically. Some agents are randomly killed and their resources returned to the environment. Agents that have not collected resources migrate to a randomly chosen neighboring site (in multi-site worlds). Finally, agents that have acquired sufficient resources reproduce asexually.

Echo's Neutral Shadow

In order to discern which features of Echo's genotype statistics can be attributable to the genotypes' adaptive significance, we created a "neutral shadow" of Echo. The crucial property of Echo's neutral shadow is that its evolutionary dynamics are like Echo's *except* that a genotype's presence or concentration or longevity in the shadow population cannot be due to its adaptive significance.

Echo's neutral shadow consists of a population of nominal "creatures" with nominal "genotypes." A shadow "creature" has no spatial location and it cannot ingest resources or interact with other "creatures." All it ever does is come into existence, perhaps reproduce (perhaps many times), and go out of existence; its only properties are its genotype and the times of its birth, reproductions (if any), and death.

Each Echo run has its own corresponding neutral shadow run. Changes in the Echo run sometimes cause corresponding changes in its neutral shadow, but changes in the neutral shadow never affect the run (hence the "shadow" terminology). The timing and number of birth and death events in the neutral shadow are directly copied from those in the normal Echo run, as is the neutral shadow's mutation rate.

When some creature is born in the normal Echo run, it is time for a birth event in the shadow model, so a shadow parent chosen at random (with equal probability) from the shadow population reproduces. The new shadow child inherits its parent's genotype unless a mutation gives the child a new, unique genotype. When some creature dies in the normal Echo run, it is time for a death event in the shadow model and a "creature" is chosen at random (with equal probability) from the shadow population and killed. Thus, all selection in the neutral shadow is random.

The evolutionary dynamics in a neutral shadow is a neutral diffusion process in genotype space. Genotypes arise and go extinct, and their concentrations change over time, but the genotype dynamics are at best weakly linked to adaptation through the birth and death rates determined by adaptation in the normal Echo model. The birth, reproduction and death statistics that drive a neutral model "shadow" those of the Echo model, and those in the Echo model are (typically) affected by adaptation. Still, properties like the relative longevity and concentration of a genotype in the neutral shadow cannot be due to the genotype's adaptive significance. All selection in the shadow model is random so no genotype has any adaptive significance. At the same time, by precisely mimicing the births, deaths, and mutation rate in a normal Echo run, the neutral shadow's behavior helps us to determine which aspects of the behavior of the normal Echo run can be attributed to the adaptive significance of genotypes and which might reflect nothing more than the system's underlying architecture or chance.

Figure 1 illustrates the difference between Echo and its neutral shadow. The Figure shows a "side view" of component activity distributions (from the Echo run and neutral shadow shown in Figure 4). These distributions have been collapsed (summed) along the temporal dimension and then divided by the total number of counts in both distributions. There is no guarantee that an Echo run and it's neutral shadow will have the same number of genotypes. In fact, often the neutral shadow has more genotypes, since natural selection does not preferentially preserve those that are well adapted. By dividing the distributions by the total number of activity counts in both distributions, the value of each distribution at a given activity value a reflects the fraction of activity counts in each distribution that have activity a.

Note that, on average, the activity counters in the neutral shadow's collapsed activity distribution are lower than those in Echo's collapsed activity distribution; i.e., the distribution is squashed to the left. This is just how one would expect the neutral shadow's random selection to affect a component activity distribution. By construction, individuals in Echo and its neutral shadow have the same birth, reproduction, and death rates, and their mutation rates are the same (indeed, all model parameters are identical). But while the selective force in the neutral shadow is entirely random, natural selection can pref-

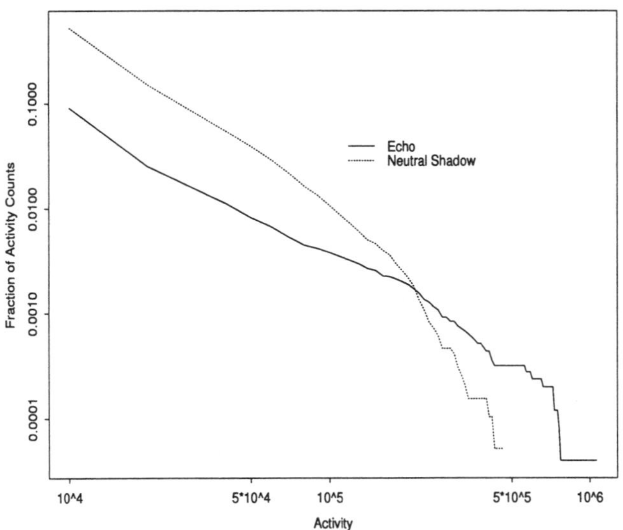

Figure 1: Log-log plot of the component activity distributions for the Echo run shown and neutral shadow shown in Figure 4, where these distributions have been collapsed (summed) along the temporal dimension. As one would expect, the neutral shadow's genotypes show relatively lower activity. The point at which the distributions are equal is the activity value at which an activity count has the same probability of having occurred in the Echo and neutral shadow distributions. Since these distributions are equal at activity $a' = 2.1 \times 10^5$, we set a_0 and a_1 (used to calculate new activity, A_{new}) slightly above and below this value, specifically, $a_0 = 1.7 \times 10^5$ and $a_1 = 2.5 \times 10^5$.

erentially cull poorly adapted genotypes and preserve well adapted genotypes in Echo. This squashes the low-activity end of Echo's collapsed distribution and inflates its high-activity end. The difference between the two collapsed distributions quantifies *how much* natural selection affects the activity counts in Echo's component activity distribution.

The point at which the two distributions have the same value (i.e., cross) reveals the activity value, a', at which an activity count is equally likely to have been chosen from either distribution. Thus, to calculate new activity, A_{new}, we set a_0 and a_1 slightly above and below a'. (Recall our discussion of evolutionary activity statistics above.) Specifically, if we let a_{max} be the highest activity value at which either collapsed distribution is positive and if we let a' be the lowest value at which the two collapsed distributions cross, then we set a_0 and a_1 to be $a' \pm (0.05 \times (a_{\text{max}} - a'))$.

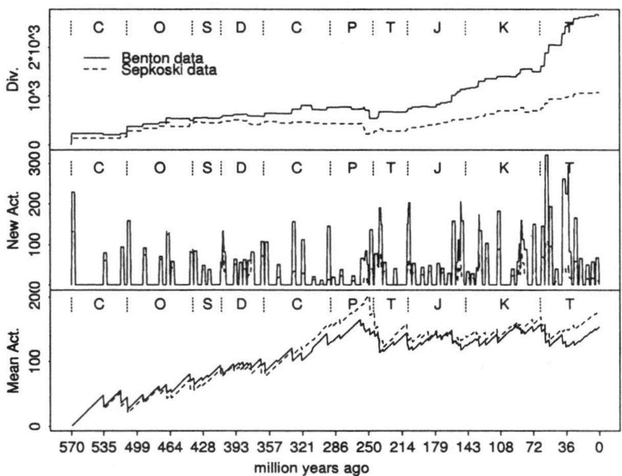

Figure 2: Diversity, new activity, and mean cumulative activity in the fossil data of Benton and Sepkoski. The labels at the top of each graph show the boundaries between the standard geological periods, thus: Cambrian, Ordovician, Silurian, Devonian, Carboniferous, Permian, Triassic, Jurassic, Cretaceous, Tertiary.

The Fossil Data

We used two fossil data sets, each of which indicates the geological stages or epochs with the first and last appearance of taxonomic families. Benton's data (Benton 1993) covers all families in all kingdoms found in the fossil record, for a total of 7111 families. Sepkoski's data (Sepkoski 1992) indicates the fossil record for 3358 marine animal families. The duration of different stages and epochs varies widely, ranging over three orders of magnitude. In order to assign a uniform time scale to the fossil data, we used Harland's time scale (Harland *et al.* 1990) to convert stages and epochs into time indications expressed in units of millions of years before the present.

We are most interested in classifying long-term trends among fossil species, but we study fossil families because much more complete data is available at this level of analysis (Valentine 1985; Sepkoski & Hulver 1985). Although fossil family data is certainly no precise predictor of fossil species data, there is evidence that species-level trends in the fossil record are reflected at the family level (see (Valentine 1985) and the references cited therein). Sepkoski and Hulver ((Sepkoski & Hulver 1985), p. 14) summarize the situation thus: 'Although families do not display all of the detail of the fossil record, they should be sufficiently sensitive to show major evolutionary trends and patterns with characteristic time scales of fives to tens of millions of years.' The trends we use to classify evolutionary dynamics occur in the fossil data on time scales at least that long.

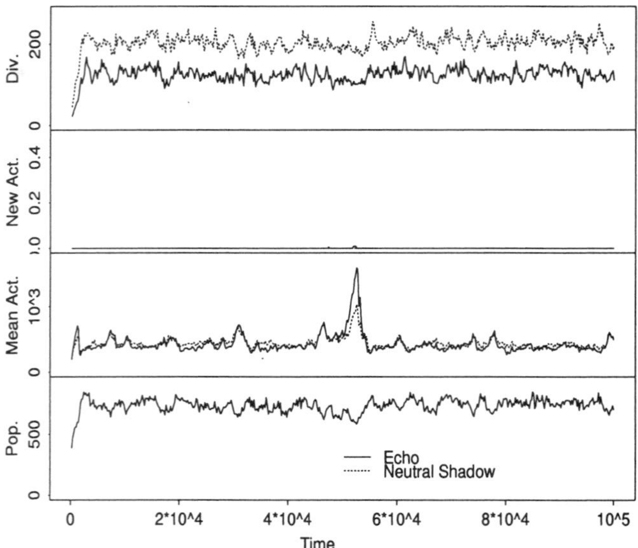

Figure 3: Typical diversity, new activity, and mean cumulative activity data from Echo and a neutral shadow when mutation rate $\mu = 10^{-2}$, interaction probability $\iota = 0.05$, and metabolic tax $\tau = 0.01$. Note that $A_{\text{new}} = 0$ for both Echo and the neutral shadow and that $\bar{A}_{\text{cum}}$ is not significantly higher in Echo than in the neutral shadow. (Here, $a_0 = 6.4 \times 10^3$ and $a_1 = 6.8 \times 10^3$.)

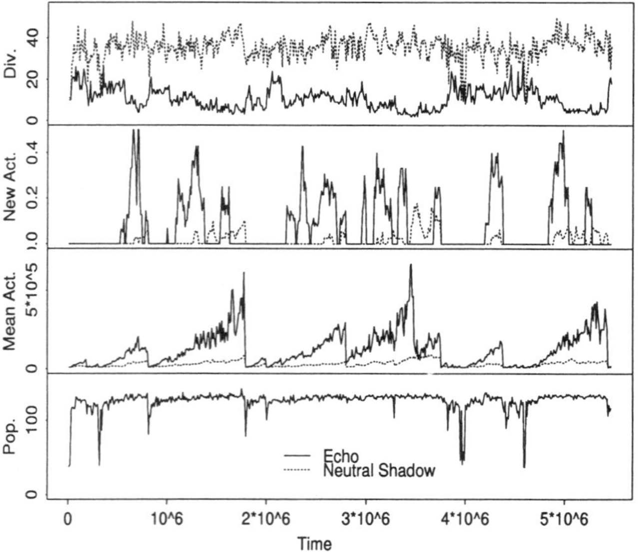

Figure 4: Typical diversity, new activity, and mean cumulative activity data from a Echo and a neutral shadow when mutation rate $\mu = 10^{-2}$, interaction probability $\iota = 0.85$, and metabolic tax $\tau = 0.15$. Note that A_{new} and $\bar{A}_{\text{cum}}$ are significantly higher in Echo than in the neutral shadow. (Here, $a_0 = 1.7 \times 10^5$ and $a_1 = 2.5 \times 10^5$.)

Results

We computed diversity, new activity, and mean cumulative activity in the Benton and Sepkoski fossil data sets (see Figure 2). We also computed these statistics from data produced by the Echo model and its neutral shadow at a variety of places in Echo's parameter space (see Figures 3 and 4). Comparing the data from Echo and its neutral shadow allows us to normalize Echo's evolutionary activity statistics.

The paucity of earlier fossil data lead us to restrict our attention to the Phanerozoic fossils, which start with the Cambrian explosion. The major extinction events, such as the mammoth one which ends the Permian period, and the famous K/T extinction which ended the age of the dinosaurs, are visible in the data. The overall trends in the fossil statistics are pretty unambiguous: D is unbounded, A_{new} is positive, and $\bar{A}_{\text{cum}}$ is bounded. Thus the evolutionary dynamics of the Phanerozoic biosphere is in class 3.

We examined the evolutionary dynamics of Echo and its neutral shadow while varying three crucial parameters across their entire viable range. The per-locus mutation rate, μ, ranged over $0 \leq \mu \leq 1$; the interaction probability, ι, ranged over $0 \leq \iota \leq 1$; and the metabolic tax (metabolic tax), τ, ranged over $0 \leq \tau \leq 0.45$. All other Echo parameters were held constant across all runs. (The CD available with this volume contains the Echo source code we used, including the parameter files, as well as evolutionary activity analysis software.)

To normalize the Echo data by a "neutral" model, we compare activity data from Echo and its neutral shadow. Not all of the activity generated by Echo reflects adaptive innovations. In fact, the neutral shadow's activity shows how much "raw" activity accumulates in a non-adaptive analogue of Echo. So, we normalize Echo's activity data by subtracting the neutral shadow's new or cumulative activity from that of Echo. If the result is negligible or negative, then Echo's normalized activity is nil. Since that level of raw activity has been observed in the neutral shadow, it is not evidence of the adaptive value of Echo's components. On the other hand, if Echo's level of raw activity is significantly higher than its neutral shadow, then we have good evidence that this residue—the normalized new or cumulative activity—indicates significant new and cumulative adaptive success of the system's components.

After making sure that we were observing long-term trends and properly normalizing the activity data, we found that Echo's evolutionary dynamics fell into either class 1 or class 2. Since long-term diversity dynamics were always bounded, class 3 dynamics never materialized.

If the mutation rate was very low (at or near zero), Echo and its neutral shadow show virtually identical evolutionary dynamics. Except for fleeting exceptions caused by a mutation, only one genotype exists at a time, so the indefinite trend is $D(t) = 1$ and $A_{\text{new}}(t) = 0$. This causes the "raw" mean activity to increase with a slope of unity in both Echo and its neutral shadow, so the normalized mean activity is zero. Thus, the evolutionary dynamics of Echo when $\mu \approx 0$ falls into class 1.

When the mutation rate is very high (at or near zero), the evolutionary dynamics of Echo and its neutral shadow are again virtually identical. A child's genotype is virtually guaranteed to differ from that of its parent, so virtually every genotype has only one instance and $D(t)$ remains very high. Furthermore, those genotypes that by chance have some adaptive significance have no chance to leave an imprint on the population, which means that the collapsed component activity distributions of Echo and the neutral shadow are virtually identical. Thus, a_0 is set so high that $A_{\text{new}}(t) \approx 0$ in both Echo and the neutral shadow. In addition, the two models have such similar "raw" mean activity dynamics that after normalization the consistent trend is $\bar{A}_{\text{cum}}(t) \approx 0$. Thus, the evolutionary dynamics of Echo when $\mu \approx 1$ falls into class 1.

If the mutation is between these extremes, then the long-term evolutionary dynamics depend on other system parameters. Here we focus on two other parameters: interaction probability, ι, and metabolic tax, τ. Previous work has shown that these parameters are key determinants of evolutionary activity in Echo (Smith 1998). For example, when both ι and τ are very low, then even at moderate mutation rates Echo exhibits behavior reminiscent of what happens when the mutation rate is very high. For example, Figure 3 shows typical long-term statistical trends in Echo and its neutral model with $\iota = 0.05$ and $\tau = 0.01$. The long-term trend is clearly that diversity is bounded and new activity is zero. Furthermore, since "raw" mean activity is about the same in Echo and the neutral shadow, normalized mean activity is approximately zero. This illustrates how, at very low interaction probability and metabolic tax, Echo has class 1 evolutionary dynamics regardless of the mutation rate.

On the other hand, at intermediate mutation rates, evolutionary activity in Echo increases significantly within a certain range of interaction probabilities and metabolic taxes, specifically, when $0.5 \leq \iota \leq 1.0$ and $0.15 \leq \tau \leq 0.4$ (Smith 1998). Some qualitative features of the evolutionary dynamics vary with the mutation rate, as one would expect, but those features of the statistics that determine long-term evolutionary dynamics remain the same. Figure 4 shows typical dynamics of the statistics from an Echo run and its neutral shadow within this region of parameter space. First, diversity is bounded (and significantly higher in the neutral shadow, as one would expect). Second, both new and mean activity are positive. Moreover, both are significantly higher in Echo than in the neutral shadow, so Echo's normalized new and mean activity are positive. Thus, Echo's long-term evolutionary dynamics fall into class 2.

Finally, it is worth noting that, when normalized, the neutral shadows themselves have no new or cumulative evolutionary activity. Since data from a neutral shadow and *its* neutral shadow would look alike, subtracting one from the other would yield nothing. Thus, its normalized new and cumulative activity will be zero. In addition, since the qualitative shape of a neutral shadow's diversity dynamic follows that of the Echo run which it shadows, and since all observed Echo runs show bounded diversity dynamics, so do all of Echo's neutral shadows. For this reason, the long-term evolutionary dynamics of all observed neutral shadows of Echo falls into class 1.

Table 1 summarizes the three classes of evolutionary dynamics and the examples of each we have observed.

Discussion

Our classification of long-term evolutionary dynamics in Echo, the neutral shadow, and the biosphere suggests three main conclusions:

Conclusion 1: New evolutionary activity measures the flow of adaptive innovations into an evolving system and mean cumulative evolutionary activity measures the continual adaptive success of such innovations. The primary evidence for this is the comparison between Echo and its neutral shadow and the effect of varying key Echo parameters (mutation rate, probability of interaction, metabolic tax) governing the process of adaptation. Further evidence supporting this conclusion comes from comparisons between other artificial evolving models and their neutral shadows (Bedau 1995; Bedau *et al.* 1997; Bedau & Brown 1997).

Conclusion 2: Comparison of the long-term evolutionary dynamics observed in Echo, its neutral shadow, and the Phanerozoic biosphere reveals these to be partitioned into three distinct classes: no adaptive evolutionary activity (class 1), bounded adaptive evolutionary activity (class 2), and unbounded adaptive evolutionary activity (class 3). All neutral shadow dynamics and some Echo dynamics fall into class 1, the rest of Echo dynamics fall into class 2, and only the biosphere dynamics fall into class 3.

Conclusion 3: If we accept conclusions 1 and 2, then Echo and the biosphere exhibit qualitatively different kinds of evolutionary dynamics. In particular, Echo lacks the unbounded growth in adaptive activity observed in the fossil record.

Classes 1-3 provide a classification of the evolutionary dynamics in artificial models and natural evolving systems. These classes have internal quantitative structure and they can be further subdivided, but we think that these three classes mark the most fundamental distinction among adaptive evolutionary dynamics. To be

CLASS	EVOLUTIONARY ACTIVITY	STATISTICAL SIGNATURE D	A_{new}	$\bar{A}_{\text{cum}}$	EXAMPLES
1	none	bounded	zero	zero	$\text{Echo}_{\mu\approx 0}$ $\text{Echo}_{\mu\approx 1}$ $\text{Echo}_{\iota\approx 0,\, \tau\approx 0}$ all neutral shadows of Echo
2	bounded	bounded	positive	bounded	$\text{Echo}_{10^{-4}\leq\mu\leq 10^{-1},\ 0.5\leq\iota\leq 1.0,\ 0.15\leq\tau\leq 0.4}$
3	unbounded	unbounded	positive	bounded	Phanerozoic biosphere

Table 1: Classes of evolutionary dynamics and their statistical signatures observed in Echo, Echo's neutral shadow, and data from the fossil record. The Echo parameters varied in these examples are mutation rate, μ, interaction probability, ι, and metabolic tax, τ.

sure, detecting these classes requires surmounting some practical problems. A system must be observed long enough for long-term trends to reveal themselves, and seeing a system's specifically adaptive evolutionary activity might require normalization with a suitable "neutral" model. Nevertheless, the payoff of surmounting these obstacles is the ability to classify an evolving system by reference to an elusive and controversial (Gould & Lewontin 1979) but central property: the extent to which adaptations are being created by the process of evolution.

A weakness with the statistics we use to define classes 1-3 is the "emergence" problem: The statistics can be applied only after settling what a system's components are and what counts as their activity, so the statistics would not directly reflect the evolutionary innovation of genuinely novel kinds of system components. The emergence problem does not arise when classifying the fossil data, because *post hoc* analysis has identified the relevant system components. Furthermore, with existing artificial life models, our understanding the system usually allows us to identify the relevant components confidently. Anyway, it's unclear how serious the emergence problem will prove in practice. On the one hand, as discussed earlier, evolutionary activity statistics are always defined at a given level of analysis, and we should not expect to see the evolutionary activity at *all* levels with statistics defined at *one* level. On the other hand, we *would* often expect to see significant adaptive innovations echoed in activity statistics across many levels. For example, activity statistics defined at the level of individual cell types in the biosphere would show marked activity at the origination of multicellular life. So, activity statistics defined at one level will often indirectly indicate the emergence of higher levels of adaptive activity. The fact that we do not see this sort of signature in the Echo data indicates that higher levels of adaptive innovation are probably not occurring.

There are special problems and pitfalls inherent in using the fossil record to study long-term trends (Raup 1988). In particular, the "pull of the present" is a well-known sampling bias due to the fact that there are simply more recent fossils to study than older fossils. Future work will investigate the extent to which our classification of the evolutionary dynamics evident in the fossil record can be supported more rigorously.

Although we focus here only on Echo, its neutral shadow, and the Phanerozoic biosphere, our methodology and conclusions have quite broad import. Some natural evolving systems probably have class 2 dynamics. For example, space and time constraints might bound the adaptive activity of bacterial evolution in a chemostat. Other natural evolving systems probably show class 3 dynamics. Class 3 dynamics might even be detectable in systems like the global economy or internet traffic. We also suspect that no existing artificial evolving system has class 3 dynamics. In our opinion, creating such a system is among the very highest priorities of the field of artificial life. From one perspective, this is a negative result: Echo, and perhaps all other existing artificial evolutionary systems, apparently lack some important characteristic of the biosphere—whatever is responsible for its unbounded growth of adaptive activity. But at the same time this conclusion calls attention to the important constructive and creative challenge of devising an artificial model that succeeds where all others have failed. Here, again, classes 1-3 show their value, for they provide a feasible, objective, quantitative test of success.

Acknowledgements. Thanks to M. J. Benton and J. J. Sepkoski, Jr., for making their fossil data available. For help with Echo, thanks to Terry Jones, Simon Fraser, and Richard Smith. Thanks to Andreas Rechtsteiner and Richard Smith for on-going discussions about Echo and neutral models. Thanks for helpful comments to the anonymous reviewers for Artificial Life VI. Thanks also to the Santa Fe Institute for the hospitality, financial support, and computation resources which initiated and helped sustain this work.

Appendix: Definitions

In this paper our operational definitions of what it is for a function $f(t)$ to be unbounded or positive are as follows: The function $f(t)$ is unbounded *iff*

$$\lim_{t \to \infty} \left(\frac{\sup(f(t))}{t} \right) > 0 \ , \tag{9}$$

where $\sup(\cdot)$ is the supremum function. The function $f(t)$ is positive *iff*

$$\lim_{t \to \infty} \left(\frac{\int_0^t f(t)dt}{t} \right) > 0 \ . \tag{10}$$

References

Bedau, M. A., and Brown, C. T. 1997. Visualizing evolutionary activity of genotypes. *Adaptive Behavior.* Submitted.

Bedau, M. A., and Packard, N. H. 1992. Measurement of evolutionary activity, teleology, and life. In Langton, C.; Taylor, C.; Farmer, D.; and Rasmussen, S., eds., *Artificial Life II.* Addison-Wesley.

Bedau, M. A.; Snyder, E.; Brown, C. T.; and Packard, N. 1997. A comparison of evolutionary activity in artificial evolving systems and in the biosphere. In Husbands, P., and Harvey, I., eds., *Proceedings of the Fourth European Conference on Artificial Life.* MIT Press/Bradford Books.

Bedau, M. A. 1995. Three illustrations of artificial life's working hypothesis. In Banzhaf, W., and Eeckman, F., eds., *Evolution and Biocomputation—Computational Models of Evolution.* Springer.

Benton, M. J., ed. 1993. *The Fossil Record 2.* London: Chapman and Hall.

Cairns-Smith, A. G. 1982. *Genetic Takeover and the Mineral Origins of Life.* Cambridge: Cambridge University Press.

Cairns-Smith, A. G. 1985. *Seven Clues to the Origin of Life.* Cambridge: Cambridge University Press.

Dawkins, R. 1976. *The Selfish Gene.* New York: Oxford University Press.

Forrest, S., and Jones, T. 1994. Modeling complex adaptive systems with echo. In Stonier, R. J., and Yu, X. H., eds., *Complex Systems: Mechanisms of Adaptation.* IOS Press.

Gould, S. J., and Lewontin, R. C. 1979. The spandrals of san marco and the panglossian paradigm: a critique of the adaptationist programme. *Proceedings of the Royal Society of London Series B* 205:581–598.

Gould, S. J. 1989. *Wonderful Life: The Burgess Shale and the Nature of History.* New York: Norton.

Gould, S. J. 1996. *Full House: The Spread of Excellence from Plato to Darwin.* New York: Harmony Books.

Harland, W. B.; Armstrong, R. L.; Cox, A. V.; Craig, L. E.; Smith, A. G.; and Smith, D. G. 1990. *A Geological Time Scale 1989.* Cambridge: Cambridge University Press.

Holland, J. H. 1992. *Adaptation in Natural and Artificial Systems: An Introductory Analysis with Applications to Biology, Control, and Artificial Intelligence.* MIT Press/Bradford Books, 2 edition.

Holland, J. H. 1994. Echoing emergence: objectives, rough definitions, and speculations for echo-class models. In Cowen, G. A.; Pines, D.; and Meltzer, D., eds., *Complexity: Metaphors, Models and Reality.* Addison-Wesley.

Holland, J. H. 1995. *Hidden Order: How Adaptation Builds Complexity.* Helix Books.

Hraber, P. T.; Jones, T.; and Forrest, S. 1997. The ecology of echo. In *Artificial Life 3.* 165–190.

Jones, T., and Forrest, S. 1993. An introduction to sfi echo. Technical Report 93-12-074, Santa Fe Institute, Santa Fe NM.

Lindgren, K. 1992. Evolutionary phenomena in simple dynamics. In Langton, C.; Taylor, C.; Farmer, D.; and Rasmussen, S., eds., *Artificial Life II.* Addison-Wesley.

McShea, D. W. 1996. Metazoan complexity and evolution: is there a trend? *Evolution* 50:477–492.

Packard, N. 1989. Intrinsic adaptation in a simple model for evolution. In Langton, C., ed., *Artificial Life.* Addison-Wesley.

Raup, D. M. 1988. Testing the fossil record for evolutionary progress. In Nitecki, M. H., ed., *Evolutionary Progress.* Chicago: The University of Chicago Press.

Ray, T. S. 1992. An approach to the synthesis of life. In Langton, C.; Taylor, C.; Farmer, D.; and Rasmussen, S., eds., *Artificial Life II.* Addison-Wesley.

Sepkoski, J. J., and Hulver, M. L. 1985. An atlas of phanerozoic clade diversity diagrams. In Valentine, J. W., ed., *Phanerozoic Diversity Patterns: Profiles in Macroevolution.* Princeton: Princeton University Press. 11–39.

Sepkoski, Jr., J. J. 1992. *A Compendium of Fossil Marine Animal Families*, volume 61. 2 edition. Milwaukee Public Museum Contributions in Biology and Geology.

SFI. 1998. Echo home page. http://www.santafe.edu/projects/echo.

Smith, R. 1998. Personal communication.

Valentine, J. W. 1985. Diversity as data. In Valentine, J. W., ed., *Phanerozoic Diversity Patterns: Profiles in Macroevolution.* Princeton: Princeton University Press. 3–8.

Wolfram, S. 1984. Cellular automata as models of complexity. *Nature* 311:419–424.

Challenges in Coevolutionary Learning: Arms-Race Dynamics, Open-Endedness, and Mediocre Stable States

Sevan G. Ficici and **Jordan B. Pollack**
DEMO Lab
Computer Science Department
Volen National Center for Complex Systems
Brandeis University
Waltham, Massachusetts USA
http://www.demo.cs.brandeis.edu

Abstract

Coevolution has been proposed as a way to evolve a learner and a learning environment simultaneously such that open-ended progress arises naturally, via a competitive arms race, with minimal inductive bias. Nevertheless, the conditions necessary to initiate and sustain arms-race dynamics are not well understood; mediocre stable states frequently result from learning through self-play (Angeline & Pollack 1994), while analysis usually requires closed domains with known optima, like sorting-networks (Hillis 1991). While intuitions regarding what enables successful coevolution abound, none have been methodically tested. We present a game that affords such methodical investigation. A population of deterministic string generators is coevolved with two populations of string predictors, one "friendly" and one "hostile"; generators are rewarded to behave in a manner that is simultaneously predictable to the friendly predictors and unpredictable to the hostile predictors. This game design allows us to employ information theory to provide rigorous characterizations of agent behavior and coevolutionary progress. Further, we can craft agents of known ability and environments of known difficulty, and thus precisely frame questions regarding learnability. Our results show that subtle changes to the game determine whether it is open-ended, and profoundly affect the existence and nature of an arms race.

Introduction

Most machine learning (ML) systems operate by optimizing to a fixed fitness function, or learning environment, and typically require considerable inductive bias in order to succeed; this inductive bias takes the form of either a learner that is *pre-adapted* to the learning environment, or a carefully *gradient-engineered* fitness landscape that provides the learner with a clear path towards a global optimum. In both cases, however, the onus inevitably falls upon the human user of ML technology to imbue the learning system with the appropriate bias. Thus, results are often attributable to inductive bias as much as, or more than, the ML methods used. As learning domains become more intricate and demanding of ML systems, however, both methods of bias engineering quickly become infeasible: gradient engineering turns overwhelmingly complex, and, following the observation that "you can only learn what you almost already know," pre-adaptation requires the learning problem to be already substantially solved.

To address these problems, *coevolution* has been proposed as a way to evolve a learner and learning environment simultaneously such that progress arises naturally with minimal inductive bias. In coevolution, however, the terms 'learner' and 'environment' no longer denote absolute roles, but relative ones; each participant in a coevolutionary system is both a learner as well as an environment against which other participants learn — the conventional asymmetry between learner and environment does not exist.

The key to successful coevolutionary learning is a *competitive arms race* between opposed participants. Competitors must be sufficiently well-matched in skill to force each other to improve. The difference between what participants already know and what they must learn is critical: if one competitor becomes relatively expert such that the opponent is "overpowered," then the opponent will fail to find a gradient towards improvement and be subsequently unable to offer continued challenge, thereby breaking the arms race. If a balance in the arms race is maintained, on the other hand, coevolution is hypothesized to provide a way to gradually evolve opposing forces such that each is always suitably pre-adapted to learn against the other while, at the same time, offering a suitably engineered gradient against which the other can learn. In *open-ended* domains, coevolutionary progress can, theoretically, continue indefinitely.

Nevertheless, the precise conditions necessary to initiate and sustain such arms-race dynamics are neither definitively known nor well understood; *mediocre stable-states* (MSS) (Angeline & Pollack 1994; Pollack, Blair, & Land 1997) are a common result in coevolutionary systems, where the agents in the evolving population(s), to anthropomorphise, discover a way to *collude* to give the impression of competition without actually forcing each other to improve in any "objective" sense. This phenomenon is analogous to that found in accounts of World-War I trench warfare (Axelrod 1984), where opposing forces established ritualized acts of aggression meant to appear genuine to their respective commanders that were, nevertheless, completely predictable to each other, and thus of no real threat.

Complicating research into the arms-race mechanism is the fact that analysis of coevolutionary systems usually requires domains with known optima, like sorting-networks (Hillis 1991), and simple differential games (Isaacs 1965), so that an objective metric of performance is available. Unfortunately, these domains are closed-ended, and are thus categorically less interesting than open-ended domains. Without quantitative metrics of agent behavior, researchers in open-ended coevolutionary domains can do no better than use qualitative language to describe agent behavior and system progress. Indeed, this problem has been recognized by researchers in the pursuer-evader domain (Cliff & Miller 1996).

Thus, while current research is rich with insights and intuitions regarding what enables coevolution, there is, at the same time, a paucity of domains that can serve as systematic testbeds for these intuitions; we present a game that affords such methodical investigation. Our game involves three agents: one bitstring generator, and two string predictors — one "friendly" and one "hostile"; the generator is to behave in a manner that is simultaneously predictable to the friendly predictor partner yet unpredictable to the hostile predictor opponent. The two predictor roles produce a tension between cooperative and competitive pressures, respectively. Because agent behavior is expressed as a binary time series, we can use information theory to quantitatively assess agent behavior and coevolutionary progress. Further, we are able to hand-build agents of known ability, which implies that we can also build environments of known difficulty. We may thus pose precisely-framed questions regarding learnability, arms-race dynamics, mediocre stable-states, and open-endedness.

Our results demonstrate the expressiveness of our domain in investigating coevolution; many different dynamics can be produced by simple changes to our game. While our substrate is capable of representing both good generators and predictors, we find that high-quality players are not an inevitable outcome of coevolution; the obvious competitive approach to coevolution in our game (one that omits the friendly partner) does not produce an open-ended arms-race. Rather, a mediocre stable-state or closed-ended system is the result, depending on a seemingly minor change in how the game is scored. Mediocre stable-states result from a variety of causes in coevolutionary research. Due substantially to our rigorous metric of behavior, we can refine the notion of MSS and begin a taxonomy of such causes. All three players in our game are found required to enable an arms-race. The viability of an arms race relies on the sustained *learnability* (Pollack, Blair, & Land 1997) of environments; we are able to construct environments that are too easy and too difficult for learning to take place, and quantitatively demonstrate the poorness of these environments.

This paper is organized as follows: we first explain our game in detail, discuss the recurrent artificial neural network substrate used for our experiments, and describe the evolutionary algorithm. Next, key concepts from information theory that are relevant to this work are introduced. These concepts are then integrated into the framework of arms-race dynamics. Results are presented and analyzed. Finally, we summarize our work and present concluding remarks.

Game Setup, Substrate, and Evolutionary Algorithm

Illustrated in Figure 1, our game is played by three agents that operate in discrete time and space. The generator, $\mathcal{G}$, is an agent that ballistically produces a binary time series. That is, its behavior is determined solely by its own internal dynamics; at each time step, the generator simply outputs a single new bit. The predictors, $\mathcal{F}$ and $\mathcal{H}$, are agents that simultaneously try to predict the generator's output for the current time step; given their own internal state and the generator's output from the previous time step as input, the predictors also output a single bit in synchrony with the generator. The generator's job is to behave in a manner that is both predictable to the friendly predictor, $\mathcal{F}$, and unpredictable to the hostile predictor, $\mathcal{H}$. The purpose of having both friendly and hostile predictors in our game is to explore how the opposed needs for predictability and unpredictability affect coevolutionary dynamics. Each match lasts one thousand time steps.

Agents are coevolved in three distinct populations, one population for each role (represented by $\mathcal{F}$, $\mathcal{G}$, and $\mathcal{H}$) in our game. The three populations are all of a fixed size of 75 agents. For each generation of evolution, all generators are played against all friendly and hostile predictors. Agent performance is measured strictly in terms of the number of correct and incorrect predictions made. Scores across all games are averaged to derive fitness values. Game scores for all agents range between [0, 1]. The exact formulas used for scoring predictors are discussed below in the experiment descriptions. A generator's score is computed by subtracting the average score of its hostile opponents from the average score of its friendly partners and normalizing the result to fall within the range [0, 1]; values above 0.5 thus indicate that a generator is able to make itself more predictable to friendly predictors than hostile ones.

The substrate used for the agents is an enhanced version of the deterministic, discrete-time recurrent artificial neural network used in the *GNARL* system (Angeline, Saunders, & Pollack 1994); the network enhancement consists of a set of nine new transfer functions, *min*,

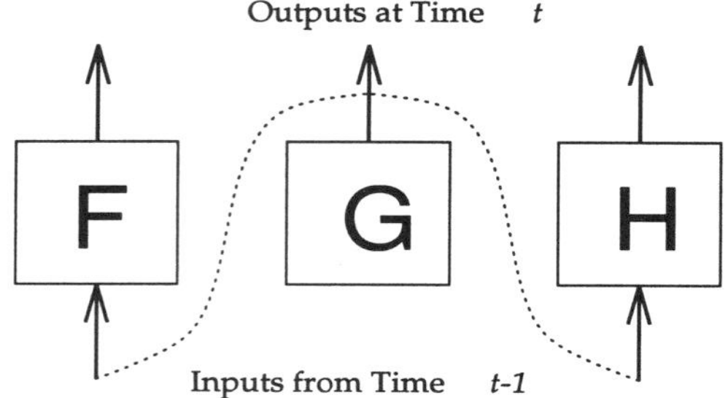

Figure 1: Game Setup.

max, *sum*, *product*, *sig-prod* (sigmoid applied to product), *unit-time-delay*, *sign*, *uni-linear-truncate* (truncate outside range [-1, 1]), *dec-linear-truncate* (truncate outside range [-10, 10]), in addition to the traditional sigmoid function. Though these supplementary transfer functions increase the range of behavior significantly, they by no means guarantee successful coevolution, as we will see. Unfortunately, the new functions also make network analysis much more difficult.

GNARL is used to coevolve networks' internal architectures and weights. Generators are allowed to have as many as 60 hidden nodes and 400 weights. Because the prediction task is more difficult, predictors are allowed to have as many as 150 hidden nodes and 700 weights. These values merely reflect intuition and are not known to be optimal; indeed, actual network sizes fall far below these limits.

Mutation is the only genetic operator used by the GNARL algorithm — crossover is not used. Five forms of mutation are implemented: *change-weights*, *add-hidden-nodes*, *remove-hidden-nodes*, *add-weights* (connections), and *remove-weights* (connections). When a hidden node is removed, all efferent and afferent connections from and to that node are removed as well. New nodes are added with no connections. Network weights are modified by adding a gaussian to each weight. Only a single form of mutation is applied to a network when it is modified. The overall severity of mutation performed to a network is determined by its *temperature*, which is an inverse function of its fitness. The higher the temperature of a network, the more severe the mutation will be.

The input and output layers of the networks are fixed. Generators and predictors have a single, real-valued output that is thresholded to a binary value. Though the game formally defines predictors to have a single input, our current experiments provide predictors with a small buffer to enhance performance: the predictors have five binary-valued inputs, corresponding to the last five outputs of the generator at times $t-1, ..., t-5$. Note that this predictor enhancement in no way obviates the need for a recurrent network architecture: generator behavior can be induced only by observation over time.

Metric of Behavior

Introduction

In this section we introduce two key notions from the field of information theory that provide our game with a rigorous and quantitative metric of agent and system behavior, namely *entropy* and *order*. Rather than give their formal mathematical definitions, we emphasize a more intuitive explanation of these concepts and their implications as they relate to our domain. Readers interested in more formal detail are referred to (Hamming 1980).

Entropy

Information theory is concerned with characterizing signals and their transmission. A signal *source* produces some symbol, which is passed through a channel to a *receiver*. We assume, for our purposes, that the channel does not distort the signal. The *entropy*, h, of a source reflects the receiver's uncertainty as to what it will receive. The higher the entropy, the less certain the receiver is, and the more it learns once the symbol is actually received. Thus, entropy is a measure of the amount of *information* in a signal. More precisely, the entropy of a source is equal to the average number of bits of information produced (conveyed) per generated symbol.

By indicating the uncertainty of the receiver, entropy inversely indicates the degree to which the source can be *predicted* by the receiver, that is, the receiver's certainty. We must be careful to point out that the receiver's opinion of what the next symbol will be is based exclusively upon the *observed behavior* of the source — assumptions about the source's internal dynamics are not made.

Order

If the receiver's certainty is based upon observation of the source, we can ask "How much observation is required to maximize the receiver's certainty?" For example, let us consider some binary source, $\mathcal{S}$. If the receiver only tallies the number of occurrences of *0* and *1*, this source may be found to produce each 50% of the time. With this amount of behavioral context, the receiver's certainty is zero and entropy is measured at $h = 1.0$. Nevertheless, it may be that if the receiver keeps track of the previous symbol received, then the source will be found simply to be alternating between *0* and *1*; in this case, a behavioral context of one symbol makes the source completely predictable. Measured entropy would now be $h = 0.0$. If the receiver keeps track of yet another symbol, now the previous two, no additional advantage is gained with respect to source $\mathcal{S}$.

The minimal amount of behavioral context needed to maximize a receiver's certainty of a source is the *order* of the source. The order is equal to the number of symbols that must be tracked, that is, the size of the history *window* needed to maximize receiver certainty. The entropy measured when using a window size equal to a source's order is the ***true entropy*** of the source; window sizes larger than a source's order will produce measurements equal to the source's true entropy, but not lower. Thus, a receiver cannot increase its certainty of a source by using a window size larger than the source's order.

Order Statistics and Measured Entropy

With our example source, $\mathcal{S}$, above, we first measured entropy without keeping track of the previously generated symbol; this is equivalent to measuring entropy with a window size of zero, or, alternatively, measuring entropy with zero-order statistics. Our second measurement, then, used a window size of one, or first-order statistics. Our zero-order measurement gave us an entropy of $h = 1.0$, but the first-order measurement fell to the true entropy of $h = 0.0$. Indeed, measured entropy will always monotonically decrease as window size is increased, and eventually reach a source's true entropy, as illustrated in Figure 2.

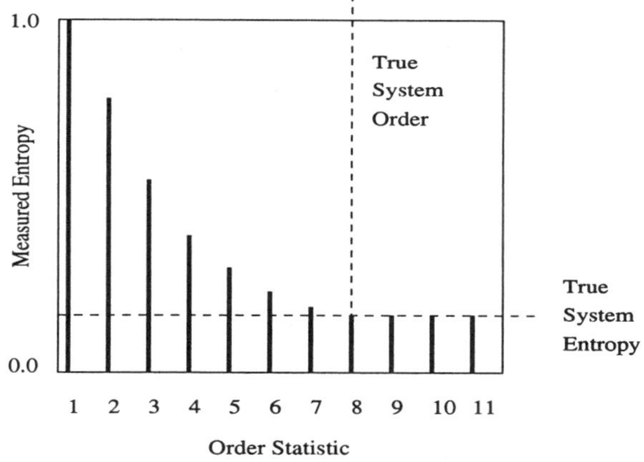

Figure 2: Measured vs. True System Entropy and Order.

A source with true entropy $h = 0.0$, such as S, is completely predictable and regular. In contrast, a binary source with maximum true entropy of $h = 1.0$ entirely lacks structural regularity and cannot be predicted better than random, on average, without specific knowledge of its internal works. For a source with true entropy somewhere in between, $0.0 < h < 1.0$, there exists both a *regular component* and an *irregular component* to the source's signal. The regular component is that portion of the signal that can be reliably predicted, while the irregular component is that portion that cannot. By definition, the information content of a source must reside exclusively in the irregular component.

Order as Complexity

System order is also equal to the logarithm of the maximal number of states required for a Markov model to reproduce behavior statistically identical to a source; entropy reflects the degree of certainty in the model's state transitions. Consider a randomly behaving binary source, with true entropy of $h = 1.0$. We find that the minimal window size needed to maximize a receiver's certainty of this source is *zero*! Since the order of such a source is zero, the equivalent Markov model requires $2^0 = 1$ state to reproduce statistically identical behavior. This result is understandable since there exists no signal structure to capture through state. This view of system complexity thus considers random sources to be simpler than completely predictable sources of higher order; the size and structure of the Markov model is what counts, not the compressibility of the produced signal (Kolen & Pollack 1994).

Where's the Arms Race?

When considered together, order and entropy form the nexus between generator complexity and predictor power: if a signal has a regular component, then that component can be predicted assuming the power of the predictor is sufficient; that is, the predictor must use an order statistic, i.e., history window, of size $m \geq n$, where n is the order of the signal being predicted. If the predictor's window size is m, such that $m < n$, then it will be able to predict only that portion of the signal's regular component that is detectable when measuring the signal's entropy with m^{th}-order statistics. Recall that as window size decreases, measured entropy increases; thus, predictors using smaller windows will necessarily be weaker than those using larger windows.

Because irregular signal components are inherently unpredictable, and our three-player game requires generators to be predictable to friendly predictors, generators must maintain substantial regular components in order to succeed. Nevertheless, generators need to be unpredictable to the hostile predictors. The only way both goals can be effectively met is for the generators and friendly predictors to evolve system order and predictive power that are closely matched, yet greater than the predictive power of the hostile predictors.

Regular signals allow for a general solution to the prediction task. A predictor of power n can predict any generator of order $m \leq n$; to escape prediction, therefore, a generator has no choice but to increase its order above n. The amount by which the generator increases its order and the unpredictability it exhibits at lower order-statistics determines how much the predictor's performance degrades. Of course, a generator may increase its true entropy instead; doing so, however, will also defeat any hopes of being predicted by the friendly predictor.

The assumption up to now has been that predictors will actually evolve such a general prediction algorithm and evolve the functional equivalent of ever-growing history windows. Of course, this represents an idealized solution; in reality, the issue of generalization vs. specialization is intimately tied to that of diversity and domain "physics." Nevertheless, having some notion of what idealized predictors can and cannot do, and what an idealized arms race looks like, provides a useful framework in which to examine empirical results.

Experiments and Results

Testing the Search Space

Our concern here is to verify that the combination of our substrate and problem domain yields a search space rich enough to support an arms race. Our first question is whether the substrate is capable of representing irregular generators and regular, high-order generators. As recurrent networks are known to produce chaotic behavior with ease, this question is partly rhetorical. Nevertheless, we seek to evolve generators in an environment that closely mimics our game. Using hand-built (non-network) predictors that employ a variety of window sizes, we evolve generators to become minimally predictable to weaker predictors while remaining maximally predictable to more powerful ones. The hand-built predictors are used as the basis of a boot-strapping process: predictors of known power are used to evolve generators of specific order complexity. Seventy generators, predominantly of orders two through eight, are thus evolved. Our second question is whether, given these generators of known order, predictors can be evolved to predict them. Evolving against this fixed population of generators, we are able to produce predictors that perform at an average rate of 75% to 85% correct prediction, or 50% to 70% better than random. The nominal range of behaviors demonstrated by our networks suggest a non-trivial solution space.

The Two Half-Games

We begin our analysis of game results by looking at the two possible *half-games.* These are versions of the game where generators coevolve only with friendly predictors or hostile predictors, but not both. The purpose of the half games is to explore convergent and competitive pressures in isolation such that we may compare and contrast results with those that include all three players.

In the first half-game, we coevolve generators with friendly predictors only. The system is asked, essentially, to establish a convention of behavior. This version of the game quickly converges in less than twenty generations. Generators and predictors alike display static behaviors of all ones or zeros, depending on which the system settles on. All agents receive perfect scores. Simply, there is no pressure for complexity and none is observed.

The second half-game, coevolving generators against hostile predictors, is more illuminating. A reasonable intuition would expect an arms race to develop between ever more complex generators and ever more powerful predictors. The actual outcome depends strongly on how the game is scored. One scoring method (A) gives predictors a point for each correct prediction. The tallies are then normalized to the percentage of correct or incorrect predictions. Another scoring method (B) tallies correct predictions, like method A, but predictors are now rewarded only to the extent that they perform better than random; predictors that get less than or equal to 50% correct prediction receive a score of zero. Method A gives maximal reward to a generator when a predictor is unable to make any correct predictions, whereas method B gives maximal reward when a predictor performs no better than random. No other experiment parameters are modified between these two scoring methods.

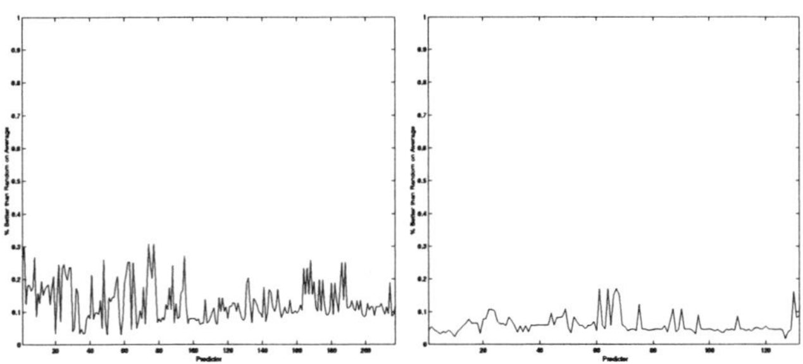

Figure 3: Performance of Best Predictors vs. Best Generators (Methods A, left, and B, right). The champion predictors are arranged along the X axis in the order in which they appear in evolutionary time. The Y axis is prediction performance as percent better than random guessing.

With each scoring method, we collect the champion predictor and generator from each generation and play the two sets of champions against each other. Predictors perform considerably worse than in the fixed-environment substrate tests described above. With method A the average prediction rate is 13% better than random (56.5% correct), though many predictors perform 20%–30% better than random, as shown in Figure 3a. Method B gives an average prediction rate of 6% better than random (53% correct); these data, shown in Figure 3b, have a standard deviation of 0.03 — less than half that of Figure 3a. The predictor scores alone are not particularly informative. We must look at the generators to discover why these scores are so low and whether they are low for the same reason.

Our principle method of measuring generator behavior is to take entropy measurements over a range of window sizes; Figures 4 and 5 graph these *entropy contours* for the best generators that arise over evolutionary time in sample runs for scoring methods A and B, respectively. These contour graphs indicate the extent to which the generators can be predicted when observing their behavior with various window sizes.

Neither figure suggests the presence of an arms race — generator characteristics do not change during the runs. The contours produced by method A drop rapidly; this indicates that the generators are substantially predictable and regular. In contrast, the contours produced by method B decline gradually and consume a much greater volume of space, indicating considerably more irregular (unpredictable) generator behavior. This difference results simply from the change in scoring method.

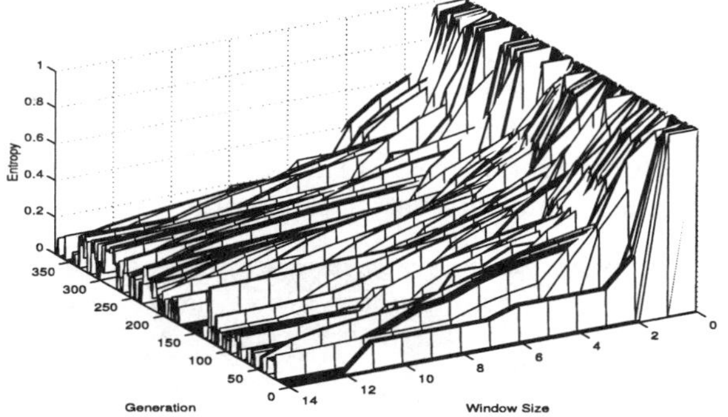

Figure 4: Generator Behavior by Scoring Method A.

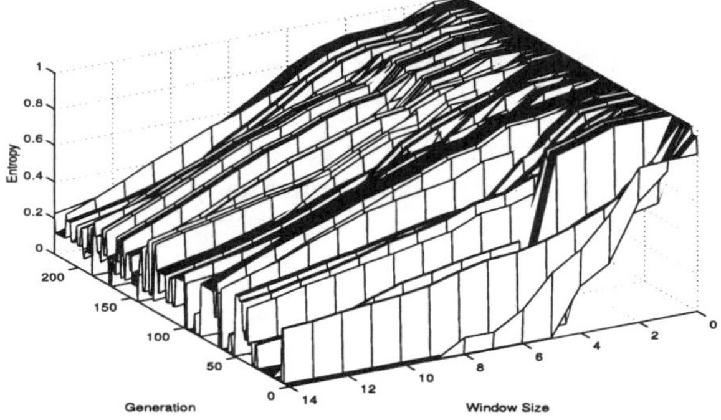

Figure 5: Generator Behavior by Scoring Method B.

Significantly, Figure 5 shows that the best generator from the initial population is already of relatively high order and entropy, while Figure 4 does not — not because such generators do not exist within the initial population of this run, but rather because they are not as adaptive to scoring method A. That low-order, regular generators out-score irregular ones by method A indicates that simple prediction strategies can be elicited from the initial predictor population — prediction strategies against which the most adaptive generators act as potent *anti-signals*, sequences that make predictors perform worse than random (Zhu & Kinzel 1997). Since the generators are ballistic, they require some homogeneity amongst the predictors in order to be viable as anti-signals. Consequently, the selected-for generators must reflect this homogeneity and thus do not provide a suitably diverse environment for subsequent predictor evolution: the predictors do evolve to counter the generators, but through specialization instead of generalization. At this point, much of the evolutionary turnover is due to exploitation of peculiar weaknesses in the agents. Rather than enter an arms race, the two populations form loose food-chain relationships and fall into a circular pattern of *convention chasing* — a mediocre stable-state.

Much like the *CIAO* graphs of (Cliff & Miller 1995), Figure 6 shows the results of playing the champion predictors against the champion generators that were evolved by scoring method A. Each position on the axes represents a moment in evolutionary time when a change in champion occurred. A column (going up) thus shows a particular predictor champion playing against all the generator champions in the order in which they reigned during the run; similarly, a row (going right) shows a particular generator champion playing against all predictor champions in the order in which they reigned. The data are thresholded such that a white point represents a prediction score of $\geq 40\%$ better than random, and black points $< 40\%$.

The important details are the many prominent horizontal and vertical lines. The pattern of a line serves to characterize an individual predictor or generator with respect to the opposing population. For example, champion generators #61, #100, and #129 have very similar (horizontal) profiles regarding which champion predictors can predict them. The gaps in these lines indicate periods where the predictor champion has lost some ability to predict this class of generator behavior. This repeated appearance and loss of particular generator and predictor behaviors is the manifestation of convention chasing.

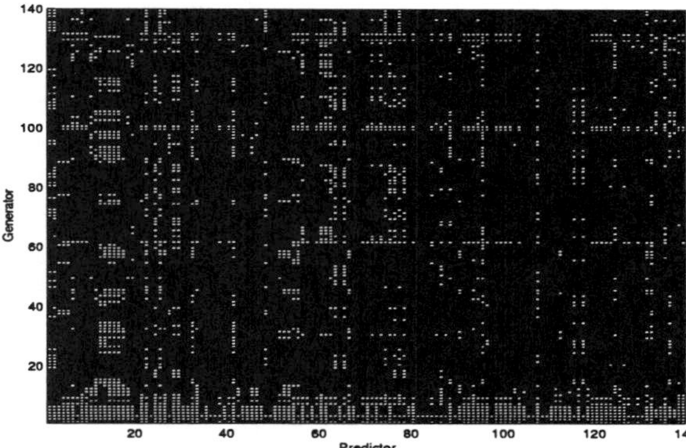

Figure 6: Evidence of Convention Chasing.

A frequently effective prediction behavior seen with scoring method A is to simply predict all ones or zeros; this strategy is general in the sense that it provides performance similar to random guessing, on average. Nevertheless, this strategy also dampens any tendency to evolve generator complexity or irregularity: because a random generator can cause it to do no worse than a simple oscillator, there is nothing to be gained by evolving or maintaining irregular generators. In contrast, irregular generator behavior is clearly adaptive by scoring method B because it guarantees a minimal predictor score, regardless of what the predictor does, short of specialized memorization. Thus, method B defines an optimal generator strategy and makes the game closed-ended. The anti-signal behavior from method A does not represent an optimal generator solution, however, because its effectiveness depends entirely upon the simplicity and homogeneity of the predictor population.

The key observations of our analysis result from being able to characterize the nature of adaptiveness with respect to a known environment, and are independent of the mechanics of evolution, due to the evolutionary algorithm (GNARL). The utility of isolating the contributions made by these two components to an evolutionary system's operation is considerable. Historically, much more attention is paid to the algorithmics than to the environment. This imbalance is perhaps due to the inherent opaqueness of most problems domains with regard to adaptiveness. Because information theory provides tools to analyze and synthesize agents, our domain allows detailed exploration of adaptiveness in isolation from the vagaries of mutation operators, reproduction schemes, and so on.

The Full Game

For the *full-game*, where all three populations participate, we keep scoring method B, to provide a pressure to evolve irregular generators. The tension between the opposed requirements of being unpredictable to hostile opponents while being predictable to friendly partners is the feature of interest in the full-game. In this case, a reasonable intuition might expect these opposing forces to stifle any possibility of an arms race; to the contrary, we believe this tension to be a necessary ingredient. Two particular runs of the full-game are discussed below; the first run displays features of an arms race, while the second run exhibits a phenomenon more typical of the full-game setup, one that likely subsumes the arms race dynamic.

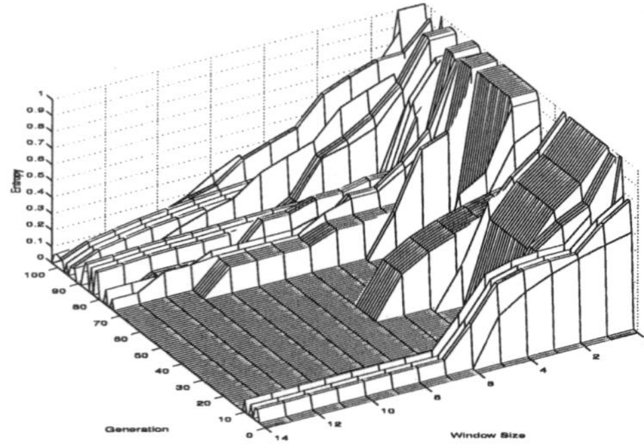

Figure 7: Generator Behavior in First Full-Game Run.

Evidence of the arms race is found first through entropy contour graphs. Figure 7, unlike Figures 4 and 5, shows a general increase in the order and entropy of the best generators over evolutionary time; that is, higher-order generators are eventually required to keep the hostile predictors at bay while remaining predictable to the friendly predictors, ostensibly because the hostile predictors have mastered simpler generator behaviors.

From each generation of the run we save the best generator, friendly predictor, and hostile predictor and play these champions against each other to look for evidence of such skill accumulation in predictors. Figure 8 shows how well hostile predictor champions perform against generator champions. The shade of the data point refers to the success of the predictor in the match; lighter shades indicate better prediction.

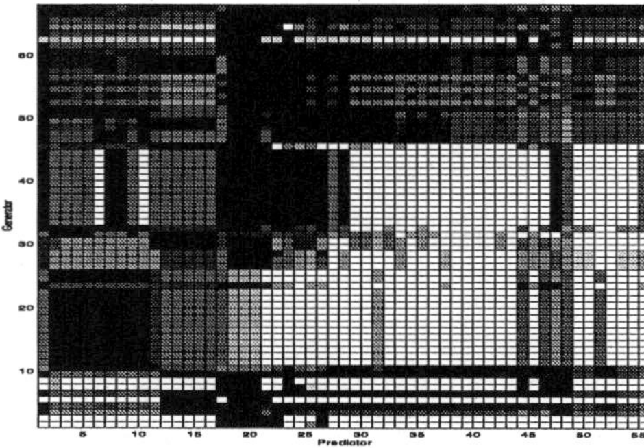

Figure 8: Champion Hostile Predictors vs. Champion Generators. Lighter shade indicates greater predictor success.

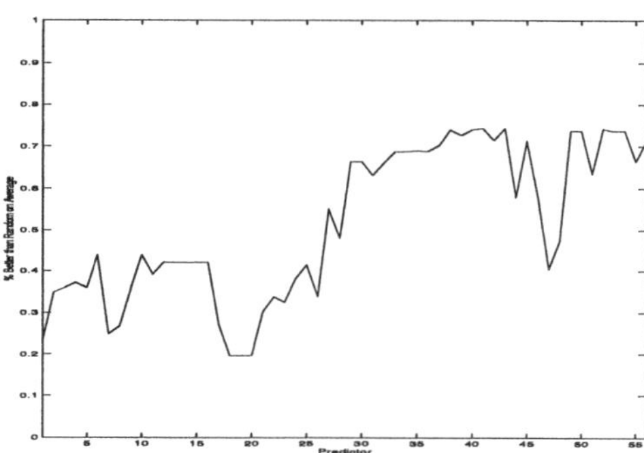

Figure 9: Average Scores of Champion Hostile Predictors against Champion Generators.

Figure 9 graphs the average performance of each champion predictor against the entire set of champion generators, that is, the average value of each column of Figure 8. Starting approximately with predictor #18, we see a clear accumulation of skill as the predictors evolve. The first group of generators to be mastered is the set #11–#25, then generators #26–#31 (starting around predictor #23), and finally generators #32–#45 (starting with predictor #27). The generators numbered #46 and higher come to be predicted, on the whole, with moderate success (up to about 50% above random).

Paradoxically, Figure 8 appears to show that predictors #1–#17 already predict a rather wide range of generators. This seems to contradict the view that predictors require evolution to generalize. If we look at Figure 9, we see that predictor #15, for example, performs no better on average than predictor #25. But, predictors #15 and #25 have very different characteristics, according to Figure 8; predictor #15 scores 40%–50% above random against most generators, whereas predictor #25 does no better than random against many, but near perfect against others. Thus, predictor #25 is specialized. Yet, predictor #15 is a generalist only in a weak sense because it does not effectively adapt its behavior to match different generators. In contrast, predictors that arise later in the run (e.g., #40) actually master a variety of generators, and exhibit a more substantive form of generalization.

In summary, these data suggest a decomposition of the arms-race notion into finer-grained events. Figures 8 and 9 suggest that predictor ability increases through accumulation of specific and distinct skills rather than a more diffuse improvement of a monolithic prediction strategy. Figure 7 allows us to see how generators evolve in response.

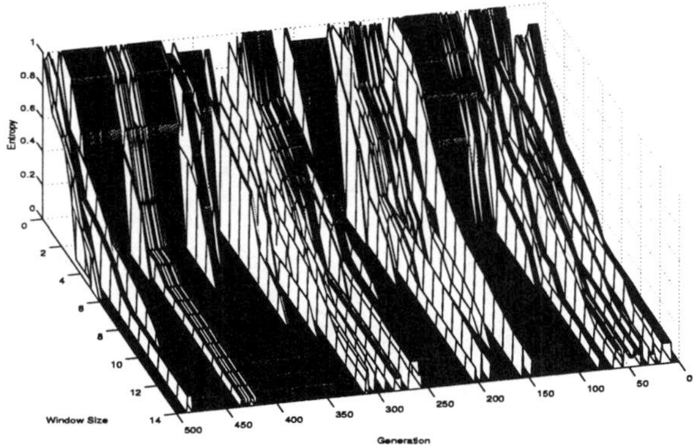

Figure 10: Punctuated Shifts in Generator Behavior from Second Full-Game Run.

More typically, however, the full-game exhibits punctuated shifts in generator behavior, from simple to complex and back again, rather than the monotonic increase in complexity indicative of an arms race. Figure 10 shows one such example; indeed, Figure 7, used to argue for the presence of an arms race above, also shows abrupt retreats in generator complexity. To help us discover the adaptive utility of these sudden behavioral changes, Figure 11 plots, from top to bottom, average population fitness of the friendly predictors, hostile predictors, and generators, and order of the most fit generator over evolutionary time. We see that, on average, generators are able to behave more predictably to their friendly partners than to their hostile opponents almost throughout the run, as generator scores rarely fall below 0.5; average generator fitness increases, by definition, with increased difference between average friendly and hostile predictor fitness.

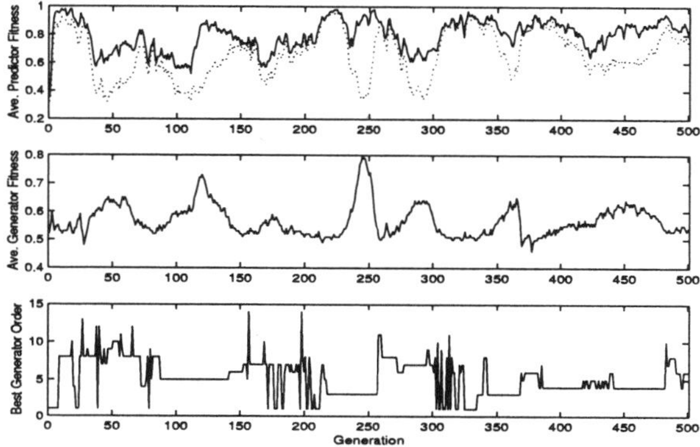

Figure 11: Fitness Averages and Best Generator Order.

We can develop an intuition of the dynamics in this run if we consider how generator order corresponds to fitness; particularly, we wish to pay attention to when, and how frequently, generator order changes. The periods of greatest stability in generator order always span the onset and duration of a period of generator success, that is, a period during which generators and their friendly predictor partners are most easily and effectively able to cooperate without falling prey to the hostile opponents. Generators stably maintain relatively low-order behavior during these periods.

Nevertheless, this very stability allows the hostile predictors to eventually learn the current behavioral convention, as evidenced by their fitness values. Once both populations of predictors are of comparable ability, generator fitness is minimal. Empirically, this tends to be the moment at which the order of champion generators becomes unstable, often alternating between very high-order and low-order behaviors. We conjecture that this period of generator instability injects noise into the evolutionary process of the predictor populations such that the two, presumably similar, populations once again diverge. When the two predictor populations become suitably differentiated, some medium-order generator is found that only the friendly predictors can predict. Thus, we enter a period of renewed generator stability and success. While further analysis is required to confirm this model of generator and predictor interaction, Figures 10 and 11 clearly show that rather than continuously improve predictor ability over the entire run, the system achieves mediocrity by repeatedly initiating short-lived arms races — a particularly interesting MSS.

We must recognize, however, that the desired arms race does not simply involve competition, but also enculturation towards convention. Presently, the generators and friendly predictors have no opportunity to develop their convention of cooperative behavior in isolation; once hostile predictors latch onto their current convention, the opportunity to evolve a more complex convention is long past. This issue may very well require a richer model of coevolution that encompasses both "public" and "private" interactions. Giving the generators the ability to distinguish friend from foe does not solve this problem, as a private sign of species "membership" must still be evolved.

The Question of Learnability

The central tenet of coevolution deems that an environment must be neither too difficult, nor too easy, for learning to take place. But, what precisely constitutes an extreme environment for a particular learner in a particular domain is a question usually left unasked out of faith that coevolutionary dynamics will correctly maintain a balanced environment, thus obviating the need to know. More seriously, most domains do not provide an obvious method of characterizing environment learnability, nor of constructing environments of arbitrary hardness. Our domain suggests ways in which to investigate not only the question of learnability, but also the question of what is really learned: to what extent might learning in one environment confer knowledge that is applicable in another? This kind of investigation is enabled only by the existence of a behavioral metric.

What's Too Easy? If a learner is not sufficiently challenged, nothing will be learned. The friendly predictors coevolved with the generators in the first half-game described above had such an impoverished environment. This half-game merely converged onto the simplest of conventions. When we play these predictors against the generators evolved in the full-game, they perform very poorly — 12% better than random, or roughly 56% prediction. Curiously, the generators frequently cause the predictors to behave very differently than they do against their "native" half-game opponents. Yet, the performance the predictors do achieve above random stems from games where they predict all *0*s and the generator has slightly more *0*s than *1*s.

What's Too Hard? If a learner is overwhelmed, nothing will be learned. Recall that, in the competitive half-game with scoring method B, the generators become reasonably complex and the hostile predictors perform only 6% better than random. The predictors do not appear to learn at all over the run. Consequently, we might assume that the environment provided by the generators is too hard. Yet, when we play these very same predictors against the generators from the full-game depicted in Figure 7, we are surprised to see that the predictors have, in fact, learned *something*. Figure 12a shows that some of these predictors actually perform as well as those coevolved in the full-game itself, though the skill displayed by the group of half-game predictors is very inconsistent.

This result begs the question of how well the best full-game predictors fare against the complex generators of the half-game. Indeed, they perform very poorly. This time we are not surprised, however, because we know from comparing Figures 5 and 7 that the full-game did not produce generators as complex as those seen in the competitive half-game. The full-game predictors cannot reasonably be expected to perform well versus generators much harder than those against which they evolved. Thus, the half-game generators confer adaptiveness to the full-game generators, but not vice versa.

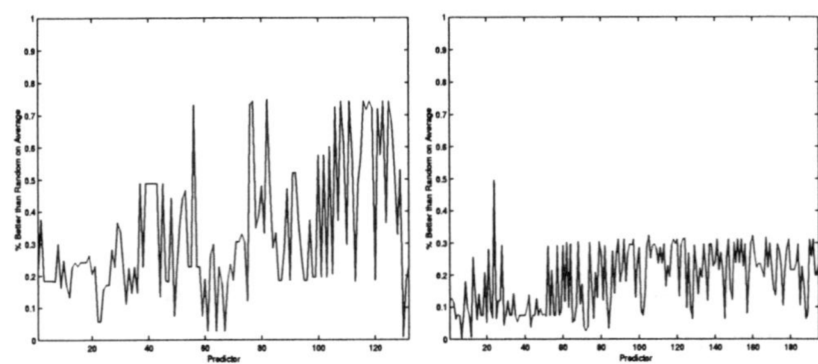

Figure 12: A (left): Performance of champion predictors of competitive half-game vs. champion generators of full-game; B (right): Predictors evolved against hand-built, chaotic generator show no improvement over evolutionary time against champion generators of first full-game.

Can we construct an environment that is too difficult for substantial learning to occur? To find out we use the logistic function as the sole sequence generator (instead of a population of neural networks) against which we evolve predictors. When the logistic function's constant is set to 4.0 and its output values are thresholded, it yields a binary sequence of true entropy $h = 1.0$. Since this generator will cause, on average, predictors to perform no better than random guessing, predictors will all receive the minimum fitness of zero with scoring method B. This makes the system behave equivalently to random search. Figure 12b shows that predictors thus evolved generally perform no better than 30% above random (65% prediction) when played against the full-game generators. Indeed, the lion's share of this 30% stems from predicting the single band of similar generators numbered 11 through 25 in Figure 8. Therefore, this pathological control is a significantly harder environment for evolving general prediction ability than the complex generators of the half-game. The prediction task is nontrivial and does not yield to simple random search.

Maintaining the Balance That cooperative half-game predictors are ill-prepared to play against full-game generators is not a particularly compelling result.

But, we also find that competitive half-game predictors perform inconsistently against full-game generators, and predictors evolved against the logistic function do poorly. Finally, predictors evolved from a different run of the full-game do relatively well against the full-game generators of Figure 7, ranging mostly from 30% to 60% above random prediction. We now see a picture consistent with the hypothesis of learnability — coevolutionary progress is heightened when a balance of skill can be maintained between participants.

Conclusions

The information-theoretic tools described in this paper allow us to measure the complexity of an evolved generator and construct a predictor that uses an arbitrarily large order statistic. Conspicuously, we do not directly build generators of known complexity, but rather we evolve them. Further, in this paper the power of evolved predictors is measured only indirectly, with respect to the evolved generators. We have recently built new tools that will allow us to directly measure predictor power and construct regular generators of arbitrary complexity.

The experiments described here are suggestive of the wide variety of questions our domain allows to be expressed. Our game provides not only a powerful metric of behavior, but also the ability to explore convergent and competitive dynamics and their interaction. The domain allows us to begin refining key notions in coevolutionary learning, namely arms-race dynamics, mediocre stable-states, and learnability.

By hand-building agents and environments we can artificially create situations that may arise during coevolution. This allows us to systematically test our game, our substrate, and coevolutionary dynamics. We discover, for example, that the ability of the substrate to successfully perform the opposing roles of our game does not guarantee that coevolution will find these solutions; just because a substrate can do X and Y does not mean that both will arise automatically when the substrate is placed in a coevolutionary framework.

We find that open-ended coevolution is not necessarily synonymous with a purely competitive framework; our game requires a mixture of cooperative and competitive pressures to avoid simple mediocre stable-states and closed-endedness. In this sense, our result agrees substantially with (Akiyama & Kaneko 1997).

Finally, because our domain allows us to characterize the difficulty of an environment, we can identify arms races that have broken because a participant has become too good. Indeed, we can begin to tease apart the many possible causes of system disfunction. While every domain has unique peculiarities, we believe the parsimony of our prediction game extends the validity and applicability of our results to other domains.

Acknowledgements

The authors gratefully acknowledge the many hours of conversation that have contributed to this work provided by Alan Blair, Marty Cohn, Paul Darwen, Pablo Funes, Greg Hornby, Ofer Melnik, Jason Noble, Elizabeth Sklar, and in particular Richard Watson. Thanks also to an anonymous reviewer for many helpful comments.

References

Akiyama, E., and Kaneko, K. 1997. Evolution of communication and strategies in an iterated three-person game. In Langton and Shimohara (1997), 150–158.

Angeline, P. J., and Pollack, J. B. 1994. Competitive environments evolve better solutions for complex tasks. In Forrest, S., ed., *Proceedings of the Fifth International Conference on Genetic Algorithms*, 264–270. Morgan Kaufmann.

Angeline, P. J.; Saunders, G. M.; and Pollack, J. B. 1994. An evolutionary algorithm that constructs recurrent neural networks. *IEEE Transactions on Neural Networks* 5:54–65.

Axelrod, R. 1984. *The Evolution of Cooperation.* New York: Basic Books.

Cliff, D., and Miller, G. F. 1995. Tracking the red queen: Measurments of adaptive progress in co-evolutionary simulations. In Moran, F., et al., eds., *Third European Conference on Artificial Life*, 200–218. Berlin; New York: Springer Verlag.

Cliff, D., and Miller, G. F. 1996. Co-evolution of pursuit and evasion 2: Simulation methods and results. In Maes, P., et al., eds., *From Animals to Animats IV*, 506–515. MIT Press.

Hamming, R. W. 1980. *Coding and Information Theory.* Englewood Cliffs, NJ: Prentice-Hall, Inc.

Hillis, D. 1991. Co-evolving parasites improves simulated evolution as an optimization procedure. In Langton, C.; Taylor, C.; Farmer, J.; and Rasmussen, S., eds., *Artificial Life II (1990).* Addison-Wesley.

Isaacs, R. 1965. *Differential Games.* New York: John Wiley and Sons.

Kolen, J. F., and Pollack, J. B. 1994. The observer's paradox: Apparent computational complexity in physical systems. *The Journal of Experimental and Theoretical Artificial Intelligence* (Summer).

Langton, C. G., and Shimohara, K., eds. 1997. *Artificial Life V (1996).* MIT Press.

Pollack, J. B.; Blair, A.; and Land, M. 1997. Coevolution of a backgammon player. In Langton and Shimohara (1997).

Zhu, H., and Kinzel, W. 1997. Anti-predictable sequences: Harder to predict than a random sequence. *(Submitted).*

Energy Dependent Adaptation of Mutation Rates in Computer Models of Evolution

Jan T. Kim
Max-Planck-Institut für Züchtungsforschung
Carl-von-Linné-Weg 10, 50829 Köln, Germany

Abstract

The evolutionary adaptation of mutation rates is known to play an important role in the molecular evolution of life as well as in evolutionary algorithms (such as evolution strategies). In molecular life, active adaptation of mutation rates is associated with an energy cost. However, there is a lack of computer models of evolution which include such an energy cost.

In this contribution, energy dependent mutation rate adaptation in computer models and evolutionary algorithms is explored. A general modelling concept is introduced and demonstrated with LindEvol-GA, a computer model of plant evolution. As an extension of the basic modelling concept, the energy cost of mutation rate adaptation can be represented as a fitness penalty. This allows the application of energy dependence to mutation rate adaptation in all types of evolutionary algorithms which operate by using fitness values. It is shown that the use of such fitness penalties can prevent premature convergence resulting from the evolution of excessively small mutation rates.

Introduction

Mutations are the source of new variations and diversity in molecular evolution as well as in Artificial Life models of evolution and evolutionary algorithms. However, mutation limits the genetic complexity of organisms by imposing an error threshold (Schuster & Swetina 1988; Maynard Smith 1989). In molecular biology, it is known that mutation rates are reduced by several orders of magnitude through various mechanisms such as DNA proofreading (Watson et al. 1987, p. 340). Without these mechanisms, which require energy, error thresholds would prevent life forms of the genetic complexity observed today from being evolutionarily stable.

Artificial Life simulations of evolution and evolutionary algorithms frequently use random perturbations such as adding Gaussian noise or flipping bits for modelling mutation. In simple systems, these operations are applied using fixed control parameters (e.g. fixed parameters for Gaussian noise or constant mutation rates). More advanced approaches use various types of adaptation of mutation rates (Bäck 1992a; 1993; Ostermeier 1992). In evolution strategies, mutation rates are typically subject to evolution themselves (Rechenberg 1994). This approach has also been applied to genetic algorithms (Bäck 1992b). A variety of other Artificial Life models with adaptive mutation rates (Maley 1995) or evolvable mutation mechanisms (Ray 1992; Ikegami & Hashimoto 1995; Ofria, Brown, & Adami 1998) also exists. However, energy dependence of mutation rate adaptation is not captured by these models.

Artificial Life models of evolution are appropriate test systems to investigate the effects of energy dependence of mutation rate adaptation on the course of evolutionary processes. For evolutionary algorithms, coupling mutation rate adaptation to an energy cost may be interesting as an approach to prevent simulated evolutionary processes from evolving excessively low mutation rates and converging prematurely. In this contribution, some support for this hypothesis are presented.

Concept

The basic approach for extending computer models of evolution in order to allow for individual based, energy dependent adaptation of mutation rates consists of the following steps:

- A scalar (real valued or integer) component, called the mutation modificator is added to the phenotype description of individuals and initialized to zero upon creation of an individual. Let $\mu(i)$ denote the mutation modificator of individual i.
- Two new control parameters, called the mutation modification factor denoted by q, and the mutation modification penalty denoted by p, are introduced.
- Individuals are enabled to change their mutation modificator. Changing the value of the mutation modificator by one unit is associated with an energy cost of p (i.e. the mutation modification penalty).
- The effective individual mutation rates are calculated by

$$m(i) = m \cdot q^{\mu(i)} \tag{1}$$

where m denotes the global mutation rate and $m(i)$ denotes the effective mutation rate for individual i. After mutating the genome with this individual mutation rate, the mutation modificator of the individual is reset to zero. The global mutation rate is typically given as a control parameter, but it could also be computed according to arbitrary rules built into the simulation.

The method for calculating effective individual mutation rates (eq. 1) was designed to enable the evolution of all individual mutation rates greater than zero while not allowing the evolution of zero mutation, which would freeze evolution or negative individual mutation rates, which would make no sense. Other functions with these properties may in principle also be used in place of eq. 1.

The mutation modification factor q can be used to perform control runs in which q is set to 1, which effectively disables mutation rate modification and thus allows to compare results with and without this feature.

Many evolutionary algorithms do not include an explicit energy representation. However, in a large array of evolutionary algorithms, fitness values are assigned to individuals. In models with explicit energy representation, an individual's ability to allocate energy usually implicitly determines its fitness and reproductive success. Explicit fitness values serve the same purpose in a more direct way. Thus, associating mutation rate modification with a fitness penalty is a logical extension of the concept of energy dependent mutation rate adaptation.

The following section illustrates the application of the concept of energy dependent mutation rate adaptation using two models as examples.

Models

LindEvol-GA

LindEvol-GA is a model in which simulated plants grow in a two dimensional lattice world (see (Kim 1996; 1997) for details). Plant cells obtain energy units by absorbing light. Each plant has a genome consisting of several genes. Gene activation is triggered by the local structure surrounding a cell, resulting in the cell carrying out an action specified by the activated gene. Plant growth takes place by cells performing `divide` n actions, where the parameter n, which determines the position of the new cell being produced, is also encoded in the activated gene. Division is only possible at the expense of an energy unit. All genes which are activated during the growth of a plant are collectively called the developmental program of the plant. Plants grow from single germ cells for a finite vegetation period, at the end of which the number of energy containing cells in a plant is assigned as a fitness value to the corresponding genome. The subsequent generation is then assembled by a genetic algorithm procedure.

There are three types of mutation in LindEvol-GA, replacement, insertion and deletion. The rates with which they occur per site and time step are control parameters, labelled m_{repl}, m_{ins} and m_{del}, respectively.

Following the concept described above, the set of parameters describing a plant was extended to include an integer valued mutation modificator. Two new actions, called `mut-` and `mut+`, were introduced. These can be performed by cells, their effect is to decrement or increment the mutation modificator, respectively. Both actions consume one energy unit; thus, the mutation modification penalty is implicitly fixed to be one and is not specified as a control parameter. The mutation modification factor q was added to the control parameters of LindEvol-GA. All three mutation rates are modified according to eq. 1:

$$m_{repl}(i) = m_{repl} \cdot q^{\mu(i)} \quad (2)$$

$$m_{ins}(i) = m_{ins} \cdot q^{\mu(i)} \quad (3)$$

$$m_{del}(i) = m_{del} \cdot q^{\mu(i)} \quad (4)$$

Evolutionary algorithms

In evolution strategies, mutation is traditionally implemented by adding Gaussian noise to the real valued genome components. Additionally, genomes contain values for the standard deviation of Gaussian noise for each individual component. These standard deviation values are themselves subject to mutation and thus to evolutionary adaptation. This adaptation of standard deviations has been modified to be "energy dependent" by associating it with a fitness penalty.

A genome in this evolution strategy with fitness dependent standard deviation adaptation (EFDSA for short) consists of a vector of d real valued components denoted by $\vec{x} = (x_0, \ldots, x_{d-1})$ and a vector of d mutation modificators, denoted by $\vec{\mu} = (\mu_0, \ldots, \mu_{d-1})$, where d is the dimensionality of the fitness landscape. The selection scheme used in EFDSA is tournament selection, only asexual reproduction was employed. EFDSA has these control parameters:

symbol	meaning
d	Dimensionality of the fitness function
m	Global standard deviation for mutation, subject to energy dependent modification
M	Global standard deviation for mutating the mutation modificators, cannot be modified
q	Mutation rate modification factor
p	Mutation rate modification penalty
n	Population size

The penalty associated with mutation rate modification is introduced by converting "raw" fitness value $F_{raw}(i) = F(\vec{x}(i))$ (i.e. the fitness value calculated for genome i by the fitness function) into an effective fitness

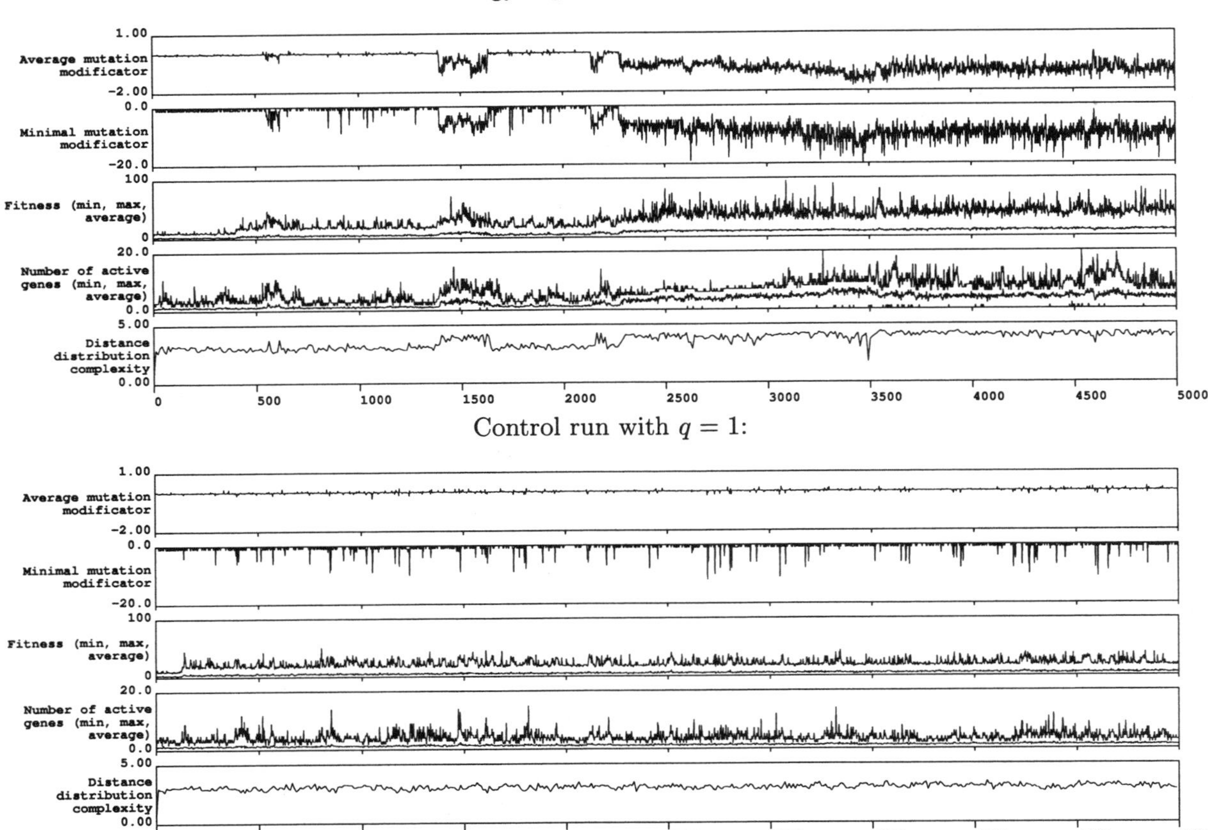

Figure 1: Results of a LindEvol-GA with energy dependent mutation rate adaptation and of a control run where mutation rate adaptation is disabled by setting the modification factor to 1.

value which is used during selection:

$$F_{\mathit{eff}}(i) = \frac{F_{raw}(i) - F_{min}}{F_{max} - F_{min}} + p \cdot \sum_{j=0}^{d-1} |\mu_j(i)| \qquad (5)$$

Here, F_{max} denotes the maximal and F_{min} denotes the minimal fitness value in the population at the current generation. EFDSA minimizes the fitness function, therefore the penalty is applied by increasing effective fitness. If p is set to zero, this conversion simply rescales the fitness values to the interval [0, 1]. This rescaling allows application of the penalty such that it is independent of the absolute raw fitness values.

The fitness function used in this contribution are:

$$f_1 = ||\vec{x}|| \qquad (6)$$

$$f_{10} = -\cos(2\pi||\vec{x}||) + 0.1 \cdot ||\vec{x}|| + 1 \qquad (7)$$

$$f_6 = \sum_{j=0}^{d-1} (x_j^2 - 10\cos(2\pi x_j) + 10) \qquad (8)$$

These are known as the sphere function (eq. 6), Salomon's function (eq. 7), and Rastrigin's function (eq. 8); their definition and their indexing was taken from (Salomon 1996).

Mutation is performed by replacing each component of $\vec{x}$ by $x_j + \text{Gauss}(0, m \cdot q^{\mu_j})$. Subsequently, the components of $\vec{\mu}$ are replaced by $\mu_j + \text{Gauss}(0, M)$. $\vec{\mu}$ is not reset to $\vec{0}$, its value is inherited because $\vec{\mu}$ is considered to belong to the genetic, and not to the phenotypic description of individuals in EFDSA. A mutation modification vector in the phenotype would be an identical copy of the $\vec{\mu}$ created in each generation at the cost implied by eq. 5, therefore, the vector $\vec{\mu}$ can directly be taken from the genome for mutation rate modification as well as for penalty calculation and there is no need for an explicit representation of a phenotypic mutation modification vector.

Results and discussion

LindEvol-GA

Fig. 1 shows results from runs of LindEvol-GA with a selection rate of $s = 0.8$ (i.e. 80% of the genomes in the population are replaced in each generation) and mutation rates set to $m_{repl} = m_{ins} = m_{del} = 0.1$. With these settings, only rather simple developmental programs can evolve without modification of mutation rates (see be-

World at generation 1400:

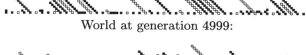

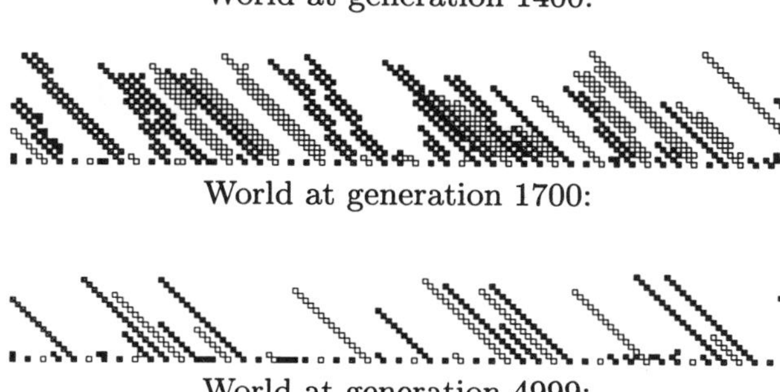

World at generation 4999:

Figure 2: Pictures of plant communities observed in the LindEvol-GA run with energy dependent mutation rate adaptation. The entire lattice worlds (150 * 30 sites) are shown. Plant cells are shown as boxes. Cells with different gray shades belong to different plants.

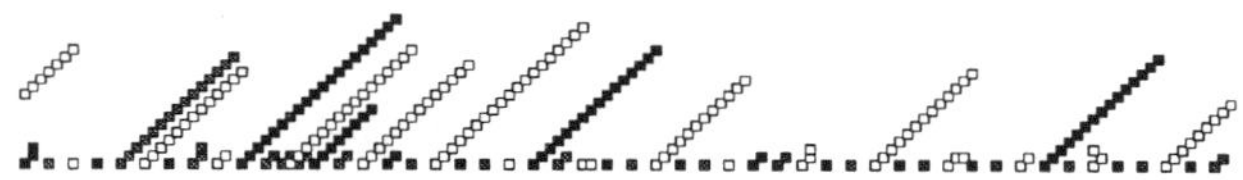

Figure 3: Picture of plant community observed in the LindEvol-GA control run at generation 4999.

low). In the run with energy dependent mutation rate modification enabled, the mutation modification factor was set to $= 2$, the control was run with $q = 1$.

For the run with mutation rate adaptation, the time series of mutation modificator values immediately reveal that the run can be divided into phases in which no relevant mutation rate modification takes place and other phases in which effective individual mutation rates are significantly lowered (the latter extending approximately from generation 1400 to 1600, a short period around generation 2100 and from generation 2300 until the end of the run). During times with mutation rate reduction, both average and maximal fitness values are significantly higher than in phases without mutation rate modification. Likewise, the number of active genes, which is an indicator of complexity at the level of developmental programs, increases in phases of mutation rate reduction. Furthermore, distance distribution complexity, which was introduced as a measure of structured diversity in (Kim 1996), exhibits elevated levels strongly correlated to phases with mutation rate reduction. Finally, the pictures of plant communities shown in Fig. 2 demonstrate that complex phenotypes are abundant in phases with mutation rate reduction whereas they are seen only rarely in phases without mutation rate modification.

In the control run, no evolution of negative mutation modificators takes place. Fitness values and number of active genes remain at lower levels, as does distance distribution complexity. Fig. 3 shows that the phenotypes also remain simple. Thus, adaptation of mutation rates can be identified as necessary for the evolution of complexity which is evidenced by the observations listed above.

In (Kim 1996), it was discussed that a developmental program consisting of r genes can only be evolutionarily stable at a given selection rate s if the mutation rates are below the error threshold $t_D(s, r)$, and an estimation for the critical error threshold was derived for the case that only replacement mutations are used. For the case that all three mutation rates are set to the same value, $m_{repl} = m_{ins} = m_{del} = m$, an estimation for the critical error threshold of m can be derived in a similar way:

$$m_{crit} = 1 - \sqrt[6r]{1 - s} \tag{9}$$

If m exceeds m_{crit}, no developmental programs with r or more genes can be evolutionarily stable (because even at maximal reproductive success, the statistically expected number of descendants inheriting the developmental program without alterations is lower than one). Equation 9 can be rewritten to estimate the maximal length of developmental programs (in genes) that can be evolutionarily stable at given values for m and s:

$$r_{max} = \frac{\log(1 - s)}{6 \log(1 - m)} \tag{10}$$

For $m = 0.1$ and $s = 0.8$, the setting in the run shown in Fig. 1, this estimation yields $r_{max} = 2.55$, thus, developmental programs with more than 2 genes cannot evolve without mutation rate reduction in this run. This estimation correlates well to the observed average numbers of active genes which never exceeds 2 in phases without mutation rate modification. However, in phases where mutation rates are lowered, the average number of used genes substantially exceeds the threshold of 2.55. These observations prove that the energy dependent mutation rate reduction which takes place in the run presented here is indeed necessary for the evolution of developmental programs with a complexity above the threshold imposed by the unmodified mutation rates.

EFDSA

The effects of mutation rate adaptation in the EFDSA system were explored by simulation series with the following control parameters:

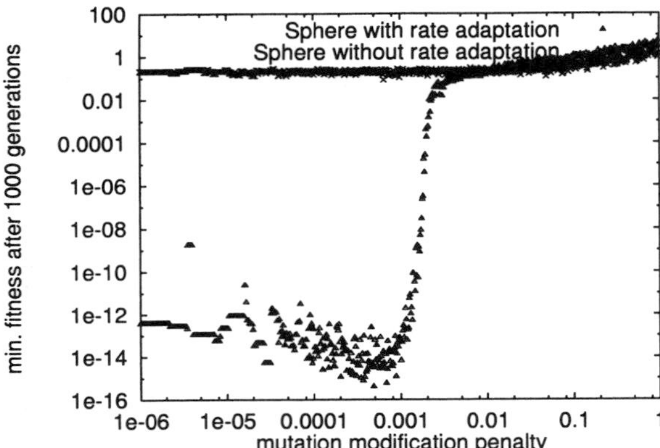

Figure 4: Minimal fitness values obtained after 1000 generations with the sphere function with energy dependent standard deviation adaptation (triangles) and without it (crosses). Both axes have a logarithmic scale.

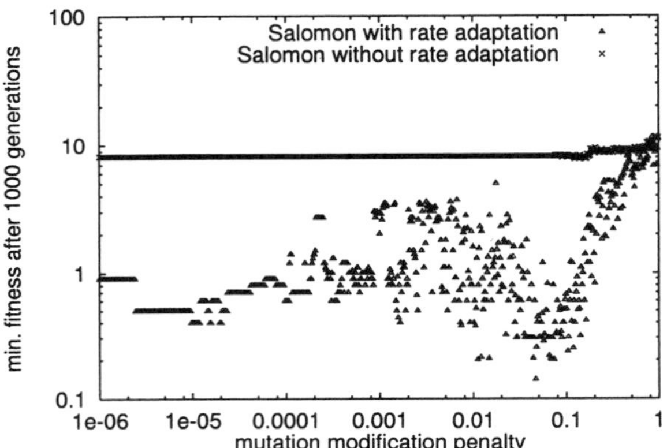

Figure 5: Minimal fitness values obtained after 1000 generations with Salomon's function with energy dependent standard deviation adaptation (triangles) and without it (crosses). Both axes have a logarithmic scale.

parameter	value
Genome space dimensionality	$d = 8$
Global standard deviation for mutation	$m = 0.1$
Standard deviation for mutating μ values	$M = 1.0$
Mutation modification factor	$q = 2$
Mutation modification penalty	$p = 10^{-6} \ldots 1.0$
Population size	$n = 500$

The first simulation in a series was performed with $p = 10^{-6}$ and for each subsequent simulation, the penalty was increased by 2% (with respect to the preceding run). Each simulation was run for 1000 generations. For each penalty setting, a control with the mutation factor set to 1 was also performed. Other variations of the mutation

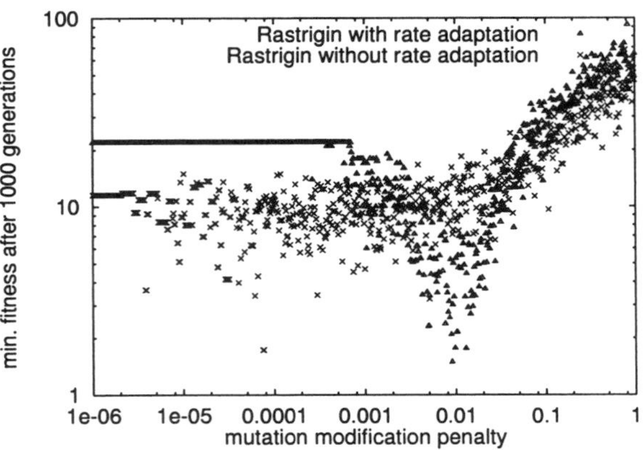

Figure 6: Minimal fitness values obtained after 1000 generations with Rastrigin's function with energy dependent standard deviation adaptation (triangles) and without it (crosses). Both axes have a logarithmic scale.

modification factor were not tested because for any $y > 0$, keeping q constant and changing p to $y \cdot p$ results in the same penalty / modification table as keeping q constant and setting p to p^y. (Notice, however, that this does not mean that a simulation run with q and $y \cdot p$ is identical to one run with p and p^y unless M is also adjusted).

Series were run using the three fitness functions given in equations 6, 7 and 8. The results are shown in Figures 4, 5 and 6. Common features seen in these three Figures are:

1. Optimal minimization results are achieved with intermediate settings of the mutation modification penalty.

2. As the penalty increases above this optimal range, minimization levels approach those observed in the controls.

3. At penalty settings below the optimal range, minimization results are significantly suboptimal. (In the case of Rastrigin's function, they are even worse than the controls.)

The controls exhibit some deterioration at high penalty values. The reason is that disabling adaptation has no effect on the penalty term $p \cdot \sum_{j=0}^{d-1} |\mu_j|$ in the effective fitness (see eq. 5). Thus, in the control runs minimization of this term takes place simultaneously with minimization of the fitness function. When the penalty is set to large values, minimization of the penalty term dominates over the optimization of the fitness function resulting in the observed deterioration. This phenomenon can be interpreted as hitch-hiking, where a suboptimal $\vec{x}$ hitch-hikes on top of a $\vec{\mu}$ that minimizes the penalty term well.

With Rastrigin's function (Fig. 6), lower penalty settings (ranging approximately from $5 \cdot 10^{-5}$ to 10^{-2}) result

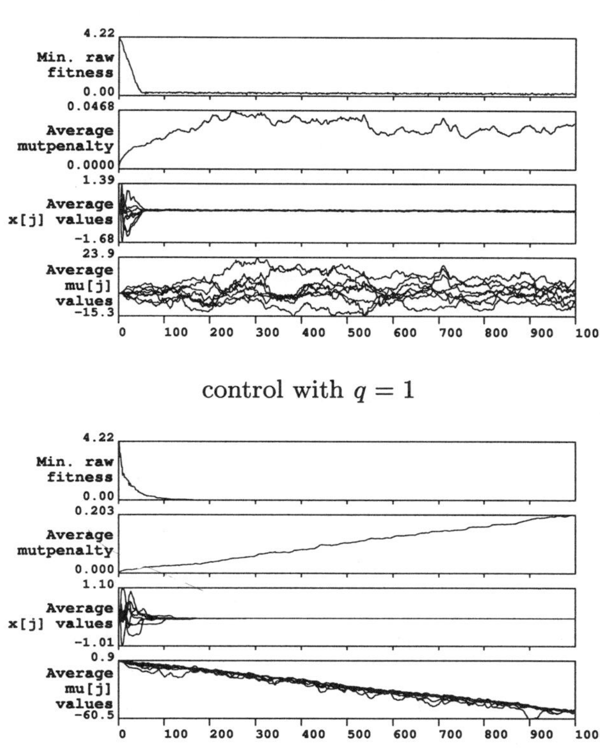

Figure 7: Time series from an individual simulation using the sphere function and from the corresponding control simulation. p was set to 0.0004822 in both runs. The x and μ values are averaged over the entire population.

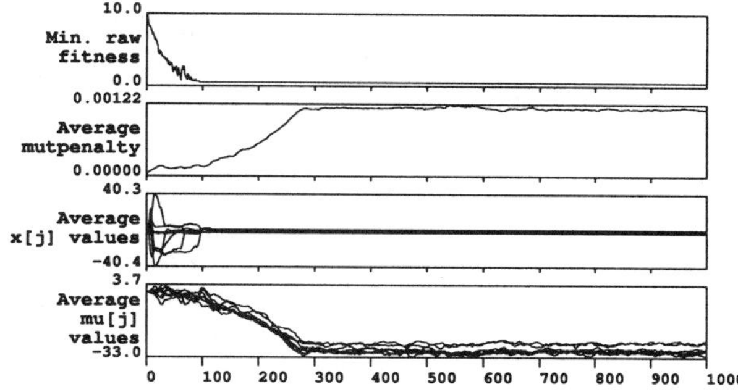

simulation with $p = 0.04676$

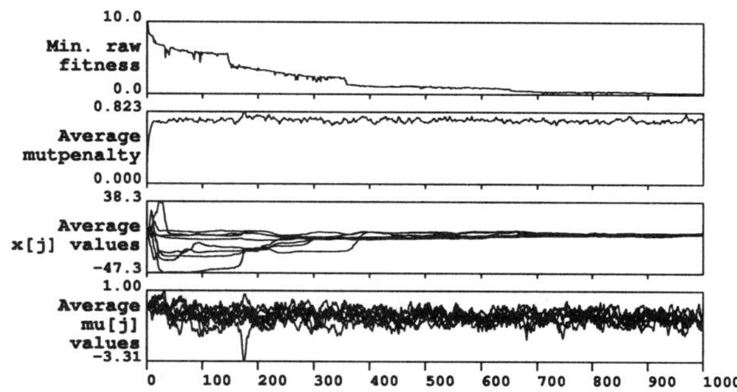

Figure 8: Time series from two individual simulations using Salomon's fitness function. With $p = 0.04676$, the best minimization result was observed within the series, whereas the evolutionary process converges prematurely with $p = 5 \cdot 10^{-6}$.

in substantially improved results in some cases. Rastrigin's function has a large number of local minima, and here, some amount of hitch-hiking turns out to be beneficial by allowing for hitch-hiking out of these minima.

The sphere function has only a global minimum and no additional local minima, so the EFSDA algorithm converges towards the global minimum until arrives at an equilibrium where mutation prevents further convergence. The control simulation shown in Fig. 7 demonstrates that the system reaches this equilibirium within the 1000 generations that were run. It can be concluded that the improvement of minimization seen at appropriate penalty settings is a result of mutation rate adaptation, allowing closer approximations to the global minimum to be evolutionarily stable, as it is described for LindEvol-GA above. It should be noted that the simulation with adaptation enabled shown in Fig. 7 does not reach equilibrium within 1000 generations. This means that the optimization results shown in Fig. 4 do not necessarily reflect equilibrium minimization levels.

Salomon's fitness function can be thought of as a variant of the sphere function in which suboptimal minima are layered in spherical surfaces around the global minimum which is located at the coordinate origin. Thus, the algorithm can prematurely converge and become stuck in a suboptimal minimum of this fitness function. Fig. 8 shows time series from two individual runs with Salomon's function which demonstrate that such premature convergence occurs when the mutation modification penalty is set too low. In the simulation performed with $p = 5 \cdot 10^{-6}$, the system reaches an equilibrium state in which the chance for further progress in minimization is extremely diminished by strongly negative average μ values. In the simulation run with $p = 0.04676$ (the optimal value identified in the series shown in Fig. 5), the average μ values also reach an equilibrium, but in this case, the equilibrium values allow the system to cross some barriers between the local minima. As a result, the minimization achieved after 1000 generations is substantially better than the one observed after 1000 generations with $p = 5 \cdot 10^{-6}$. The phenomenon of premature convergence explains why the best minimization results are achieved with intermediate penalty settings for Salomon's function.

Rastrigin's function differs from the sphere function

and Salomon's function in that it is not rotationally invariant, and it was chosen for this contribution to demonstrate that optimal minimization at intermediate penalty settings is not a feature specific for sphere-like fitness functions. Rastrigin's function has a large number of local minima, and as a consequence simulations run with low penalty settings converge at local minima which are even worse than the minimization levels achieved by the controls, as can be seen in Fig. 6. However, at intermediate penalty settings, minimization results with adaptation are substantially better than in the controls, and also, the best simulation of the series is found in this range.

Since the sphere function has no local optima, the observation of the best minimization results at intermediate penalty settings cannot be explained by premature convergence, as it was done above for Salomon's and for Rastrigin's function. With the sphere function, this phenomenon is due to differential speed of minimization, combined with the fact that equilibrium is not reached in all simulations, particularly in those with low penalty values, during the first 1000 generations. With low penalty settings, negative μ values tend to evolve quickly, resulting in a slowdown of minimization speed. Imposing a mutation modification penalty reduces the rate at which negative μ values evolve, resulting in faster progress of fitness function minimization over the first 1000 generations.

In summary, the EFDSA results demonstrate that fitness dependent standard deviation adaptation allows for optimization beyond the error threshold which is implied by the global standard deviation without the adaptation mechanism. Small penalty settings render the system prone to premature convergence. High penalty values make mutation rate adaptation so costly that it does not evolve at significant levels and consequently, results obtained using such penalty settings are not significantly different from the controls. For all three fitness functions that were explored, intermediate penalty values at which optimal minimization takes place were identified. With these intermediate settings, on the one hand the cost of adaptation is sufficient to counterbalance the tendency of evolving increasingly negative μ values and thereby to prevent or at least delay premature convergence and premature slowdown in evolutionary speed, while on the other hand, this cost is not so high that it prevents any significant adaptation.

Conclusions and Ideas for Future Work

It is a typical approach in Artificial Life to develop abstract methods to represent key principles of molecular life in order to investigate these principles using computer models (cf. (Langton et al. 1992, preface)). The principle investigated in this contribution is that mutation rate adaptation is coupled to an energy cost. The formal method proposed to represent this principle is suitable for integration ito a large class of evolutionary algorithms and simulations. The application of this formal method was demonstrated using two systems, firstly LindEvol-GA, an Artificial Life model of plant evolution and secondly a simple evolution strategy.

The LindEvol-GA results show that extending a simulation of evolution with the proposed method can indeed fundamentally change the evolutionary process. With energy dependent mutation rate adaptation, evolution of elevated complexity levels with respect to the control can be observed using various indicators. The experiments with an evolution strategy with fitness dependent standard deviation adaptation demonstrate that coupling mutation rate adaptation with a fitness cost can prevent premature convergence which occurs with unconstrained mutation rate adaptation. This suggests that energy dependence of mutation rate adaptation in molecular evolution may be more than a random feature that just inevitably results from the underlying physics, but that it may be important to keep evolution open-ended by preventing it to freeze at some locally stable state. This idea can be further investigated by additional experiments with LindEvol and other models.

Preventing premature convergence is a potentially very useful property of energy dependent mutation rate adaptation for optimization by evolutionary algorithms, and it would be interesting to further explore this possibility. For Salomon's and Rastrigin's functions, which have local, suboptimal minima, the best penalty values are larger than those for the sphere function. One may therefore speculate that rugged fitness landscapes can be minimized better with larger mutation rate modification penalties. Using e.g. NK fitness landscapes (Kauffman & Weinberger 1989), this issue may be systematically addressed. It would also be interesting to evaluate the performance of evolutionary algorithms more extensively, e.g. as suggested in (Whitley et al. 1996) and (Salomon 1996).

Finally, it was seen that μ values may arrive at equilibria in which fitness penalties counterbalance the evolution of further mutation rate reduction (Fig. 8). It would be interesting to find out how these equilibrium levels are related to the setting of the control parameters, and to possibly extend the theory of critical error thresholds to systems with energy dependent mutation rate modification.

References

Adami, C. 1998. *Introduction to Artificial Life.* Santa Clara: TELOS, Springer-Verlag.

Bäck, T. 1992a. The interaction of mutation rate, selection, and self-adaptation within a genetic algorithm. In *Parallel Problem Solving from Nature, 2*, edited by R. Männer, and B. Manderick, Amsterdam: Elsevier

Science Publishers, p. 85–94.

Bäck, T. 1992b. Self-adaptation in genetic algorithms. In *Toward a Practice of Autonomous Systems*, edited by F. Varela and P. Bourgine, Cambridge, MA: MIT Press, p. 263–271.

Bäck, T. 1993. Optimal mutation rates in genetic search. In *Proceedings of the Fifth International Conference on Genetic Algorithms*, edited by S. Forrest, San Mateo, CA: Morgan Kauffmann Publishers, p. 2–8.

Ikegami, T., and Hashimoto, T. 1995. Active mutation in self-reproducing networks of machines and tapes. *Artificial Life* 2: 305–318.

Kauffman, S. A., and Weinberger, E. W. 1989. The NK model of rugged fitness landscapes and its application to maturation of the immune response. *J. Theor. Biol.* 141: 211–245.

Kim, J. T. 1996. Distance distribution complexity: A measure for the structured diversity in evolving populations. In *Artificial Life V*, edited by C. G. Langton and K. Shimohara, Cambridge, MA: MIT Press, p. 281–288.

Kim, J. T. 1997. Lindevol: Models for investigating the interplay between development, ecology and evolution. *Bayreuther Forum Ökologie* 52: 17–33.

Langton, C. G., C. Taylor, J. D. Farmer and S. Rasmussen, eds. 1992. *Artificial Life II.* Redwood City, CA: Addison-Wesley.

Maley, C. 1995. The coevolution of mutation rates. In *Advances in Artificial Life*, edited by F. Morán, A. Moreno, J. J. Merelo, and P. Chacón, Berlin Heidelberg: Springer Verlag, p. 219–233.

Maynard Smith, J. 1989. *Evolutionary Genetics.* Oxford: Oxford University Press.

Ofria, C.; Brown, C.T.; and Adami, C. 1998. Avida User's Manual. In Adami, C. (1998).

Ostermeier, A. 1992. An evolution strategy with momentum adaptation of the random number distribution. In *Parallel Problem Solving from Nature, 2*, edited by R. Männer and B. Manderick, Amsterdam: Elsevier Science Publishers, p. 197–206.

Ray, T. S. 1992. An approach to the synthesis of life. In (Langton et al. 1992).

Rechenberg, I. 1994. *Evolutionsstrategie '94.* Stuttgart-Bad Cannstadt: Fromann-Holzboog.

Salomon, R. 1996. Re-evaluating genetic algorithm performance under coordinate rotation of benchmark functions. a survey of some theoretical ans practical aspects of genetic algorithms. *BioSystems* 39: 263–278.

Schuster, P., and Swetina, J. 1988. Stationary mutant distributions and evolutionary optimization. *Bull. Math. Biol.* 50: 635–660.

Watson, J. D., N. H. Hopkins, J. W. Roberts, and J. Argetsinger Steitz. 1987. *Molecular Biology of the Gene.* Menlo Park, CA: Benjamin/Cummings.

Whitley, D., S. Rana, J. Dzubera, and K. E. Mathias. 1996. Evaluating evolutionary algorithms. *Artificial Intelligence* 85: 245–276.

Replaying the Tape: An Investigation into the Role of Contingency in Evolution

Tim Taylor and **John Hallam**
Department of Artificial Intelligence, University of Edinburgh
5 Forrest Hill, Edinburgh EH1 2QL, U.K.
timt@dai.ed.ac.uk

Abstract

The role of contingency (random events) in an artificial evolutionary system is investigated by running the system a number of times under exactly the same conditions except for the seed used to initialize the random number generator at the beginning of each run. Twelve different measures were used to track the course of evolution in each run, and "activity wave diagrams" were also produced (Bedau & Brown 1997). The results of 19 runs are presented and analyzed. The performance of every run was compared with each of the others using a non-parametric test (a randomization version of the paired-sample t test). When comparing absolute values of the measures between the runs, some significant differences were found. However, looking at the *difference* in values between adjacent sample points for a run, no run was significantly different to any other for any of the measures. This suggests that the general behaviour is the same in all runs, but the accumulation of differences results in significantly different outcomes. The results lead us to propose a rule of thumb for future experiments with the system: *to check whether the outcome of any particular experiment is robust to contingency in the evolutionary process, at least nine runs should be conducted using different seeds for the random number generator, to be confident of seeing a variety of results.* The results are likely to be applicable to other A-Life platforms of self-replicating computer programs, but at this stage can probably tell us little about the role of contingency in biological evolution.

Introduction

There is much debate in the field of evolutionary biology over the role of contingency ("historical accidents") in determining the course of evolution (see, for example, (Gould 1989), and, for a flavour of the ensuing debate, (Ridley 1993; Gould 1993; McShea 1993)). If evolution were to be re-run on Earth, starting from the same initial conditions and proceeding for another 4 billion years, encountering the same sorts of perturbations from the physical environment that it encountered the first time around, what sort of a world would exist today? Would *homo sapiens* evolve again, or might life not even make the transition from prokaryotic to eukaryotic cells, or maybe not even reach the cellular stage at all? What, in other words, would happen if "the tape were played twice"?

The same question arises when considering artificial evolutionary systems, where we have the advantage of being able to "replay" evolution under experimental control. Indeed, in considering the performance of *any* evolutionary system, we generally wish to disentangle the relative influence of three factors: (1) contingency, (2) performance due to the particular design of the system, and (3) performance which may be general to a wide class of evolutionary systems (Taylor & Hallam 1997). However, considering the importance of these questions, very little has been published to date on the role of contingency in artificial systems. Fontana and Buss have done some excellent work on the subject, choosing to focus on self-maintaining organizations in an artificial chemistry, rather than presupposing the existence of self-replicating entities (Fontana & Buss 1994b; 1994a). Their results suggest that a number of generic organizational features may be expected to emerge in any comparable system.

Fontana and Buss have not, as yet, witnessed the emergence of high-level self-reproducing entities in their work (and that was not their primary goal). There do, however, exist a growing number of A-Life systems which *presuppose* the existence of self-replicators (e.g. Ray's Tierra (Ray 1991), Adami et al.'s Avida (Adami & Brown 1994), Skipper's Computer Zoo (Skipper 1992), and our own platform, Cosmos (Taylor & Hallam 1997; Taylor 1997)). Most publications relating to these systems mention in passing that the results being presented were typical of a large number of runs, but details are rarely given, and, to our knowledge, no systematic study of the role of contingency in such systems has yet been published. One factor that may have contributed to this omission is the difficulty of dealing sensibly with the huge amounts of data that such simulations can produce, which can make it difficult to usefully compare one run with another. However, Bedau et al. have recently been developing a number of techniques for visualizing evolutionary activity, and have also proposed some quantitative measures of evolution (Bedau & Packard 1991;

Bedau *et al.* 1997; Bedau & Brown 1997). These analysis tools provide some fairly straightforward ways of comparing the results of a number of evolutionary runs, both qualitatively and quantitatively.

The purpose of this paper is twofold: (1) to report an experiment that runs an artificial life system a number of times, varying just the random number seed between runs, in order to compare how each run evolves and therefore get some idea of the role of contingency in the system; and (2) to use a variety of measures and visualization techniques to compare the runs, and hopefully to ascertain which are the most useful measures for such comparisons. The paper ends with a discussion of the results, including the extent to which they may be generalized to other evolutionary systems.

The A-Life System

Cosmos is a Tierra-like platform that supports a population of self-replicating computer programs living in an environment. Its design differs from Tierra in a number of ways, the most relevant of which, for the present discussion, are described below. For more details about Cosmos, refer to (Taylor 1997; Taylor & Hallam 1997), or look on the worldwide web at `http://www.dai.ed.ac.uk/daidb/people/homes/timt/research.html`. The source code is available from the authors.

Spatial organization For the runs reported in this paper, the environment was configured as a two-dimensional toroidal grid. There is evidence that such spatial organization, where interactions between programs are restricted to a program's local neighbourhood, can promote heterogeneity and prevent premature convergence (Adami & Brown 1994).

Energy collection At each time step, energy is distributed throughout the grid. Programs must collect energy from the environment in order to execute their instructions. If a program's internal energy level falls below a certain threshold, it dies. In addition, a maximum population size can be specified for the system. If this is the case, when the population maximum is reached, a fraction of the programs are killed off stochastically, but those with low internal energy have a higher probability of being killed. Programs therefore have to concern themselves with energy collection as well as reproduction, and thus have some degree of control over their own lifespans (i.e. those that collect more energy are less likely to be killed).

Communication Unlike in Tierra, programs in Cosmos can *not* directly read the code of other programs. However, any program can compose an arbitrary message (a string of bits) and transmit it to the local environment, and any program can issue instructions to receive such messages from the environment and interpret them how it wishes. However, in the experiments reported here, such communication did not evolve, so the programs generally had fewer ecological interactions than, for example, Tierran parasites that execute the code of other programs.

Mutations and flaws As a run proceeds, variation may begin to appear amongst the programs in the environment, caused by the action of two different mechanisms: (1) *Mutations* can affect any program, by the random flipping of one or more bits in the program's code or associated structures. The mutation rate is a system-wide parameter, and does not vary throughout the run; (2) *Flaws.* While a program in running, a flaw may occur in its execution. If this happens, the instruction which was about to be executed will, with equal probability, either be executed *twice* consecutively, or not at all. The rate at which flaws occur is determined by a parameter owned by each individual program. Being a part of the program, it is therefore possible for the flaw rate to evolve over time (by being changed by mutations) in a lineage of individuals.

On a technical note, as this paper is concerned with the role of chance events in evolution, the choice of random number generator (RNG) is particularly relevant, as different types of RNG have different properties. Cosmos uses the `bsd_random()` RNG, which uses the linear feedback shift register generation technique. `bsd_random()` does not suffer from some of the deficiencies of many versions of the standard `random()` RNG.

Measurement Techniques

In any population of self-replicating entities which are competing against each other for resources required for replication (e.g. energy and materials), there are three factors which determine the rate at which any particular type of replicator will spread throughout the population (Dawkins 1989). These are the life-span or *longevity* of the replicator, the rate at which it replicates (its *fecundity*), and the number of errors in makes while producing copies of itself (its *copy-fidelity*). A number of measures were chosen to track changes in each of these three factors through an evolutionary run.

For *longevity*, we looked at the age at death of each program. Specifically, for time slice windows of equal width from the start to the end of the run, we plotted the age at death of each program that died within that time slice window. Example plots are shown in Figure 2. The plots for measures of fecundity and copy-fidelity, described below, also used this windowing technique. For the plots for all three of these factors, the data is pruned by only plotting values for individual programs of types which achieved a concentration of at least two individuals at some time during the run. In the plots, the darkness displayed at any point reflects the number of individual programs taking that particular value at that particular time.

For *fecundity*, we looked at two measures: the number of time slices between the first and second successful replication of each program (the *replication period*) (this could obviously only be applied to programs that successfully replicated at least twice in their lifetime), and the length of programs. Example plots for replication period are shown in Figure 9.

For *copy-fidelity*, we looked at three measures: the flaw rate, the number of faithful (error-free) replications made by individual programs over their lifetime, and the number of unfaithful replications. Example plots of these three measures are shown in Figures 3 and 4.

In addition to these six measures, the population size throughout the run was also recorded, as was the population diversity (the number of *different types* of program in the population).

Four measures suggested by Bedau et al. were used: the Activity (presence), Mean Activity (presence), Activity (concentration), and Mean Activity (concentration), along with their visualization technique of plotting "activity distribution functions" (also referred to as "activity waves"). The basic idea behind all of these techniques is the same, involving the notion of the *evolutionary activity* of each genotype (type of program) in the population:

> "the *evolutionary activity* $a_i(t)$ of the ith genotype at time t [is] its concentration integrated over the time period from its origin up to t, provided it exists:
>
> $$a_i(t) = \begin{cases} \int_0^t c_i(t)dt & \text{if genotype } i \text{ exists at } t \\ 0 & \text{otherwise} \end{cases}$$
>
> where $c_i(t)$ is the concentration of the ith genotype at t. A genotype's evolutionary activity ... reflects its adaptedness (relative to the other genotypes in the population) throughout its history in the system." (Bedau & Brown 1997)

Activity (concentration) is defined at time t as $\sum_i a_i(t)$. *Activity (presence)* is defined similarly, but with $c_i(t)$ defined to simply reflect whether genotype i *exists* at time t, rather than being a measure of concentration (i.e. $c_i(t)$ is 1 if genotype i exists at t, and 0 otherwise). *Mean Activity (concentration)* and *Mean Activity (presence)* are defined as their respective Activity measures divided by the diversity (number of different genotypes) of the population at t.

For a fuller explanation of these measures and the reasons they are defined as they are, refer to (Bedau *et al.* 1997; Bedau & Brown 1997; Bedau & Packard 1991).

To end this section, we acknowledge that paleobiologists have developed their own suite of measures of biological evolution. Daniel McShea has recently published some particularly interesting work on tests for evolutionary trends (McShea 1994), and definitions of complexity (McShea 1996; 1991). Ideally, we would like to be able to use the same set of measures for studying both natural and artificial evolution. Unfortunately, the amount of evolutionary change occurring in Cosmos in the runs reported here is really *very* small compared to the sorts of macroscopic trends that McShea's measures were designed to track, so it is not clear that these measures can usefully be applied to artificial evolutionary systems (or at least to Cosmos) at present.

Method

Nineteen runs of Cosmos were initialized, each with exactly the same ancestor programs, and exactly the same parameter values except for the seed for the random number generator.

Most of the parameters took on the system's default values; those that did not are listed in the Appendix. The most salient of these are `grid_size`, set to 40 (i.e. a 40 x 40 square environment), `max_cells_per_process`, set to 800, and `number_of_timeslices`, set to 300,000.

For each completed run, the measures described in the previous section were investigated. To recapitulate, these measures were as follows:

1. Program age at death
2. Replication period (time between 1st and 2nd faithful replication)
3. Program length
4. Flaw rate
5. Number of faithful replications per program
6. Number of unfaithful replications per program
7. Population size
8. Population diversity
9. Activity (presence)
10. Mean activity (presence)
11. Activity (concentration)
12. Mean activity (concentration)
13. Activity waves

Results

For each measure, the results from each of the 19 runs were compared. (In the following, the pairs of run results displayed in Figures 1–9 and Figure 15 were generally chosen because they illustrate noticeably different results.)

Population size, age at death, flaw rate, number of faithful replications, number of unfaithful replications.

In each run, the *population size* rose rapidly from the initial value (64 ancestors) up to 800, the maximum number

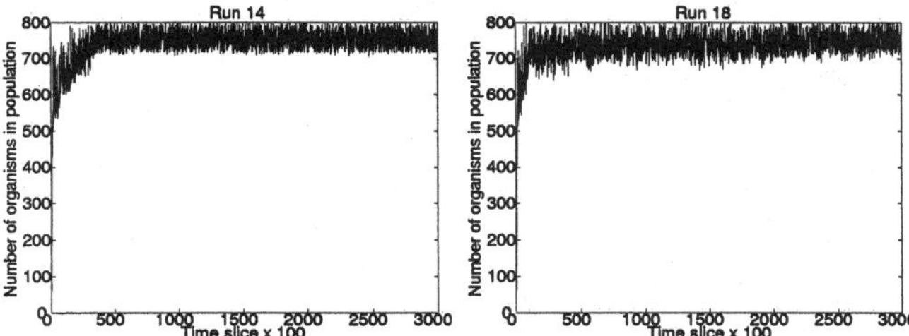

Figure 1: Population size, Runs 14 (*left*) and 18 (*right*)

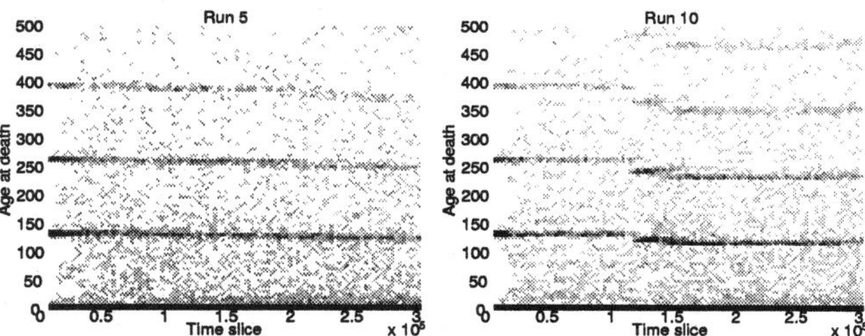

Figure 2: Age at Death, Runs 5 (*left*) and 10 (*right*)

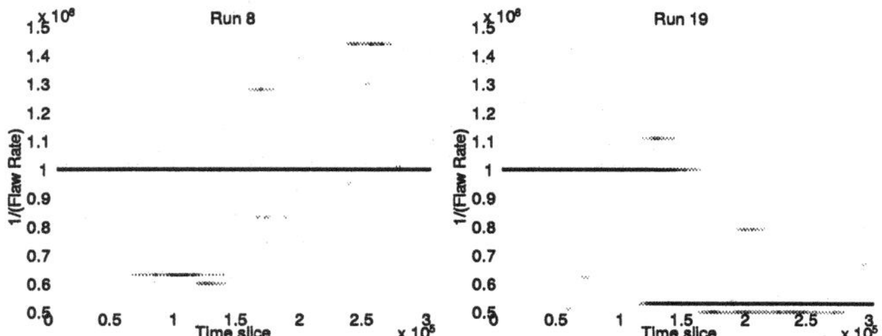

Figure 3: $\frac{1}{FlawRate}$, Runs 8 (*left*) and 19 (*right*). The vertical axis is scaled by a factor of 10^6.

allowed. Whenever this ceiling was reached, 10% of the population was killed off stochastically, but according to each program's internal energy levels (as described earlier). After the ceiling had first been reached, the population size fluctuated in the region of around 700-800 programs for the rest of the run. Typical population size graphs are shown in Figure 1.

No trends were found for program *age at death*, *flaw rate*, *number of faithful replications per program*, and *number of unfaithful replications per program*. That is, for each of these measures, the distribution of values across the population showed no change right through the run. In addition to showing no trends, the *absolute* values of the measures were generally very similar in different runs. Example graphs for these measures are shown in Figures 2 (age at death), 3 (flaw rate), and 4 (faithful and unfaithful replications per program). In Figures 2 and 3, the plot on the left hand side shows a representative graph of the measure, as observed in the majority of the runs. The plots on the right hand side of Figures 2 and 3 show slightly unusual or noteworthy cases.

For *Age at Death* (Figure 2), there are a couple of points to note. Most obviously, there is considerable structure in the distribution of ages at which organisms die. This is interpreted as indicating that the cycle of births and deaths in the population is well synchronized throughout the run. The figure shows that the majority of programs live for some multiple of a little over 130 time slices, with fewer programs surviving for each successive multiple. This figure of 130 time slices corresponds very well with the time it takes the programs to replicate (see Figure 9). The obvious explanation is that each time the population size reaches the ceiling of 800 programs, a number of programs die, creating space for the remaining programs to reproduce. Once this reproduction stage occurs, the population size is soon at the ceiling again, so the cycle repeats. The extinctions triggered by the population size hitting the ceiling are therefore periodic, resulting in the observed distribution of ages, with most organisms surviving for an integral multiple of the period of this cycle. The second point about the *Age at Death* plots is that, in some runs, a slight kink in seen in them (e.g. in the middle section of the plot for Run 10, on the right hand side of Figure 2). Having just discovered that age of death is related to the replication period of the programs, it is not surprising to see that these kinks are associated with times of significant change in the replication period of the programs. For the graph of replication period for run 10, corresponding to the *Age at Death* plot on the right hand side of Figure 2, see the right hand side of Figure 9.

For flaw rates (Figure 3), in 16 out of the 19 runs, very few programs with flaw rates different to that of the ancestor programs appeared throughout the run. However, in three runs (3, 11 and 19), the whole population moved to a higher rate during the run (the figure effectively shows the reciprocal of the flaw rate, so the increase in flaw rate appears as a downward trend). If these changes in flaw rate were adaptive, one might expect to see corresponding changes in other measures, particularly the number of faithful and unfaithful reproductions per organism. However, no such trends were observed (the graph of number of unfaithful reproductions per organism for Run 3, for example, is shown on the right hand side of Figure 4). It therefore appears that these changes in flaw rate were the result of random (genetic) drift.

Activity (presence), mean activity (presence), activity (concentration), mean activity (concentration), diversity, program length, replication period.

To recap, the measures just discussed generally showed no trends, and their absolute values were very similar across different runs. In contrast, trends *were*

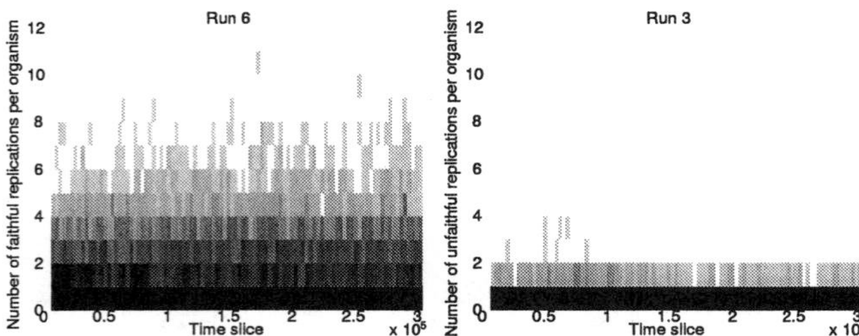

Figure 4: Number of Faithful Replications per Program, Run 6 (*left*). Number of Unfaithful Replications per Program, Run 3 (*right*)

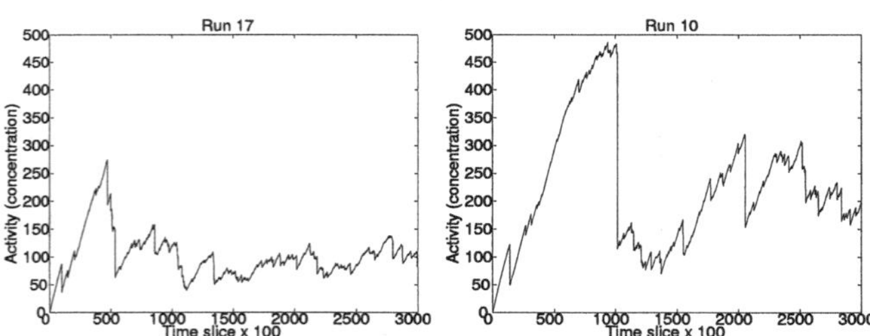

Figure 5: Activity (concentration), Runs 17 (*left*) and 10 (*right*)

observed in seven of the other measures (i.e. Activity (presence), Mean Activity (presence), Activity (concentration), Mean Activity (concentration), Diversity, Program Length and Program Replication Period—discussion of the wave plots will be left until the end of the section), with noticeable differences between some of the runs. Plots for some of these measures are presented for two example runs (17 and 10) in Figures 5–9.

Ideally, we would like to know whether the differences in these measures between any of the runs are statistically significant. Such differences would indicate that evolution might genuinely be treading a different path, for no other reason than the different seed used for the random number generator when the runs commenced. The choice of a statistical test for this task was not immediately obvious. We wished to avoid parametric tests, as we did not want to make assumptions about the population parameters (for example, there is no reason to suspect that any of the measures we are looking at are normally distributed across all possible evolutionary runs).

We therefore chose a non-parametric method—a randomization version of the paired sample t test (see, for example, (Cohen 1995)). For each measure of interest, this test will tell us, for each run, which other runs produced significantly different results. The test can indicate whether two samples are related without any reference to population parameters. The procedure used was as follows:

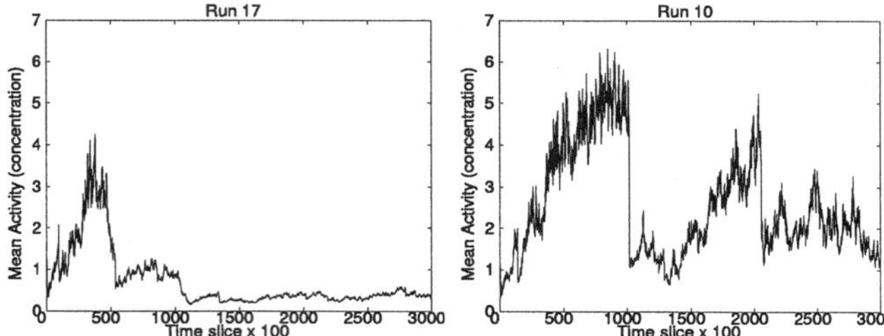

Figure 6: Mean Activity (concentration), Runs 17 (*left*) and 10 (*right*)

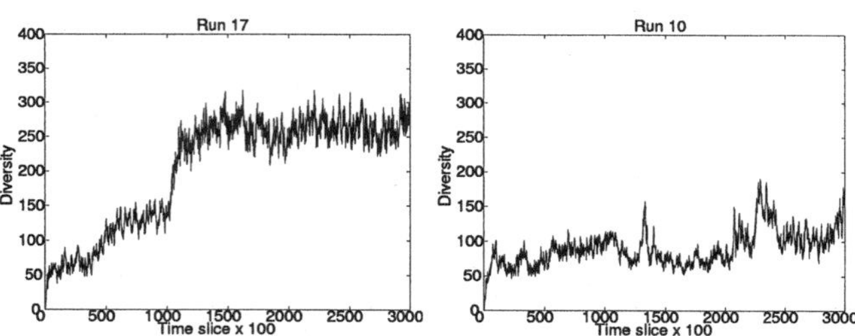

Figure 7: Diversity, Runs 17 (*left*) and 10 (*right*)

Procedure: randomization version of the paired-sample t test For each run, 10 sample data points were extracted, each one representing the value of the measure in question at one of 10 equally spaced times throughout the run.

The basic idea of the paired sample t test in this case is to consider the 10 sample points for pairs of runs in turn. By doing pairwise tests at 10 sample points we are comparing the measures at a number of points through the run, with no point having more significance than any other. For each pair of runs, the difference between corresponding samples is calculated, together with the mean value for the 10 differences. We then ask what the likelihood is of achieving this mean difference under the null hypothesis that the two runs are statistically equivalent. The method by which this is done will be explained shortly.

Obtaining Raw Sample Points In the case of measures which are already statistics of the whole population at any given time (i.e. both forms of the Activity measure, both forms of the Mean Activity measure, and Diversity), these 10 sample points could be taken directly from the value of the measure at the appropriate time. However, to prevent high-frequency changes in these measures from producing aberrant results, the measures were first smoothed before the samples were taken (using median-smoothing with a window of 10,000 time slices).

In the case of the measures where the existing data consisted of multiple values at each time slice, each rep-

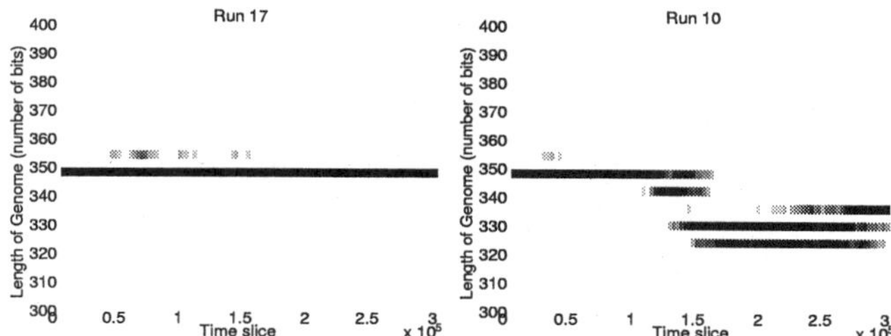

Figure 8: Program Length, Runs 17 (*left*) and 10 (*right*)

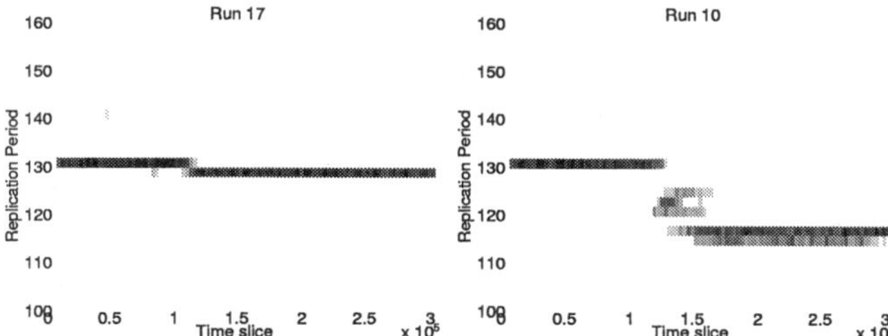

Figure 9: Replication Period (interval between first and second faithful replications), Runs 17 (*left*) and 10 (*right*)

resenting individual programs (i.e. the Program Length and Replication Period measures), each of the 10 sample points was produced by taking the median value of all values lying within a window of 1000 time slices around the time slice being sampled.

Obtaining Differenced Sample Points Because of the cumulative nature of evolution, it is possible that a small difference in the sampled value of a measure early on in a pair of runs will be magnified into a large difference later on, even if the two runs are actually proceeding in a fairly similar fashion. In order to gauge the magnitude of this effect, a duplicate set of tests was run, which used the *difference* in value between adjacent sample points as the figure to compare between runs, rather than the *absolute* value of the sample points. Using differenced data should reduce the influence of any cumulative disparity between runs.

Testing for Significance We are considering the difference in values between corresponding sample points in a pair of runs. Under the null hypothesis that the two runs are equal, however, it is equally likely that these values would be reversed (i.e. for sample point n for runs A and B, the null hypothesis is that the values A_n from run A and B_n from run B are just as likely to have come from the other run—A_n from run B and B_n from run A). If this were the case, the difference between the values would be the same as before, but with the sign reversed. We can test for the significance of the observed mean difference by constructing the distribution of all mean differences obtained from looking at each possible combination of each of the paired samples into one or other of the runs. As there are 10 paired samples, there are 2^{10} (1024) such combinations. The exact procedure is listed below (adapted from (Cohen 1995)), which may make things clearer:

1. For run I and J, if S_I and S_J are lists of the 10 sample data points for each run, construct a list D of the differences between these values, $D = S_I - S_J$. Denote the mean of these differences $\bar{x}_D$.

2. *if* $\bar{x}_D = 0$

   $p = 0.5$

   else

   (a) Set a counter C to zero.

   (b) for $i = 0..1023$

   - Construct a list D^* such that $D_j^* = D_j$ if $b_{ij} = 0$, or $D_j^* = -D_j$ if $b_{ij} = 1$, for $j = 1..10$, where b_{ij} is the jth digit of i in base 2.
   - denote the mean of the new list $\bar{x}_{D^*}$
   - *if* $\bar{x}_D > 0$

     if $\bar{x}_{D^*} \geq \bar{x}_D$, then increment C by one

     else if $\bar{x}_D < 0$

     if $\bar{x}_{D^*} \leq \bar{x}_D$, then increment C by one

     endif

   (c) $p = (C/1024)$

p is the (one-tailed) probability of achieving a result greater than or equal to $\bar{x}_D$ (or less than or equal to $\bar{x}_D$ if $\bar{x}_D < 0$) by chance under the null hypothesis. That is, p is the probability of incorrectly rejecting the null hypothesis that systems I and J have equal population mean scores for the measure in question.

For each of the seven measures being considered (Activity (presence), Mean Activity (presence), Activity (concentration), Mean Activity (concentration), Diversity, Program Length and Replication Period), this procedure was followed for each of the $19(19-1)/2 = 171$ pairwise comparisons between runs, for both the raw sample data and the differenced sample data.

The p values for each pairwise comparison are shown graphically in Figures 10–14. These figures show one histogram for p values obtained using raw sample data, and another for p values obtained using differenced sample data. In all of the histograms, any p value less than 0.05 is plotted as zero. Bars of non-zero height on the histograms therefore represent pairs of runs which are not significantly different from each other for the measure in question at the $p = 0.05$ level.

(Note that, in order to emphasize the formation of various clusters of runs in these histograms, the runs in each histogram are arranged along the x and y axes in increasing order according to the mean of their 10 sample values. While this emphasizes clusters in any one histogram, it means that clusters occurring in similar positions in the histograms of different measures do not necessarily represent the same runs.)

The randomization version of the paired-sampled t test has some advantages over other methods of investigating pairwise comparisons (e.g. it is non-parametric), but it has the disadvantage that it is "virtually certain to produce some spurious pairwise comparisons" (Cohen 1995) (p.203). Cohen suggests one way, not to get around this problem, but at least to have some idea of the reliability of a particular set of pairwise comparisons (Cohen 1995) (p.204). The idea is to first calculate, at the 0.05 level, how many runs, on average, each run differed from (call this $\bar{n}_{0.05}$). Then calculate a similar figure at a much more stringent level. As we have 1024 numbers in our distribution of mean differences, the 0.001 level is appropriate. Finally, calculate the *criterion differential*, $C.D. = \bar{n}_{0.05} - \bar{n}_{0.001}$. If $C.D.$ is large, this indicates that many significant differences at the 0.05 level did not hold up at the 0.001 level. A small $C.D.$ value indicates that the experiment differentiates runs unequivocally, therefore lending more weight to the validity of the results at the 0.05 level. Table 1 shows $\bar{n}_{0.05}$, $\bar{n}_{0.001}$ and $C.D.$ for each measure, and for both raw and differenced sample data.

Table 1 reveals a number of interesting results. The most striking is the difference in the results of using raw sample points compared with differenced sample points.

Using raw data, the average number of runs that any particular run was significantly different to at the 0.05 level ranged from 3.89 for Activity (presence) to 13.26 for Diversity. However, the criterion differential for all of these measures is high (ranging from 3.68 for Activity (presence) to 12.32 for Program Length). This suggests that the validity of the figures at the 0.05 level are questionable, and the true figures are probably somewhat lower than those calculated. Having said this, the average number of runs that any particular run was significantly different to even at the 0.001 level was non-zero for the five measures suggested by Bedau et al. (ranging from 0.21 for Activity (presence) to 6.32 for Diversity).

Using differenced data, the results have a very different look. In only two measures were any runs significantly different from any others even at the 0.05 level (0.11 for Activity (concentration) and 0.42 for Diversity), and both of these vanished at the 0.001 level. In other words, these figures suggest that, for *all* of these measures, starting off at any point during any of the runs, the amount the measure *changed* over a given period was not significantly different compared to any of the other runs.

Activity wave diagrams

Whereas the Activity and Mean Activity measures produce a summary figure for a whole population of geno-

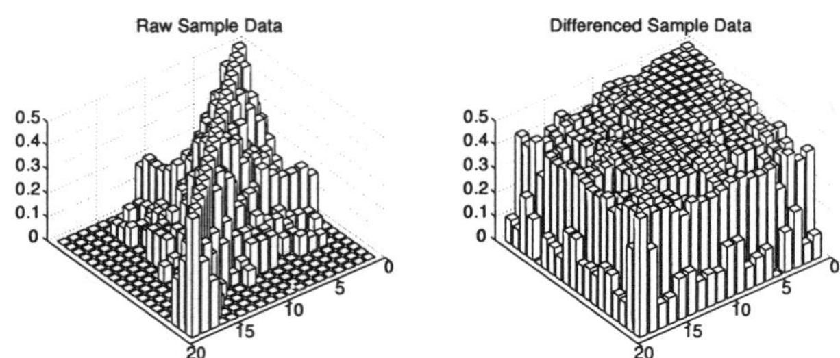

Figure 10: **Activity (concentration)**: Pairwise comparisons (p values) between runs. Raw Sample Data (*left*). Differenced Sample Data (*right*). p values below 0.05 are plotted as zero, so bars of non-zero height indicate pairs of runs that are not significantly different at the 0.05 level. See text for details.

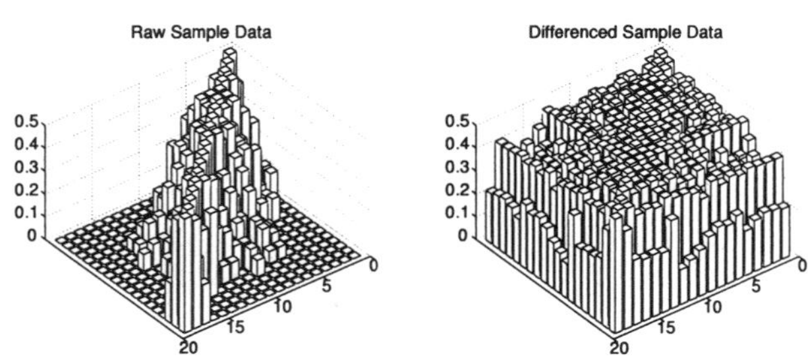

Figure 11: **Mean Activity (concentration)**: Pairwise comparisons between runs. See text and caption of Figure 10 for details.

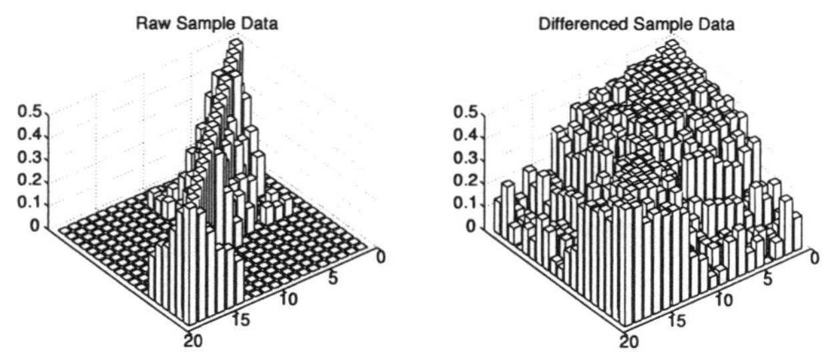

Figure 12: **Diversity**: Pairwise comparisons between runs. See text and caption of Figure 10 for details.

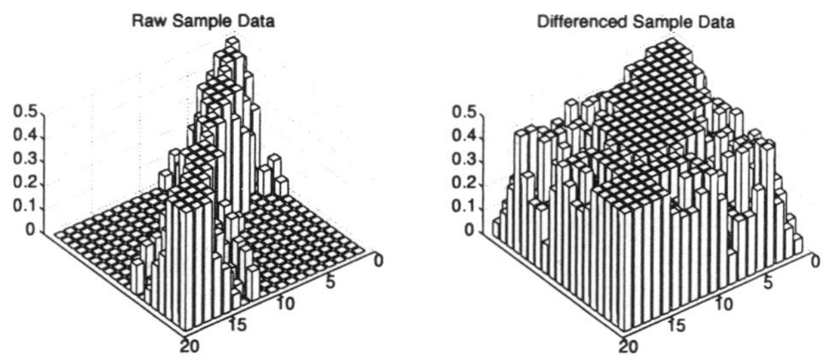

Figure 13: **Program Length**: Pairwise comparisons between runs. See text and caption of Figure 10 for details.

Measure	Data Type	$\bar{n}_{0.05}$	$\bar{n}_{0.001}$	$C.D.$
Activity (presence)	raw	3.89	0.21	3.68
	differenced	0.00	0.00	0.00
Mean Activity (presence)	raw	12.00	4.53	7.47
	differenced	0.00	0.00	0.00
Activity (concentration)	raw	8.42	2.11	6.32
	differenced	0.11	0.00	0.11
Mean Activity (concentration)	raw	10.32	4.11	6.21
	differenced	0.00	0.00	0.00
Diversity	raw	13.26	6.32	6.95
	differenced	0.42	0.00	0.42
Program Length	raw	12.32	0.00	12.32
	differenced	0.00	0.00	0.00
Replication Period	raw	10.21	0.00	10.21
	differenced	0.00	0.00	0.00

Table 1: Mean number of runs that each run is significantly different from at the 0.05 level ($\bar{n}_{0.05}$) and 0.001 level ($\bar{n}_{0.001}$), and the criterion differential ($C.D.$). See text for details.

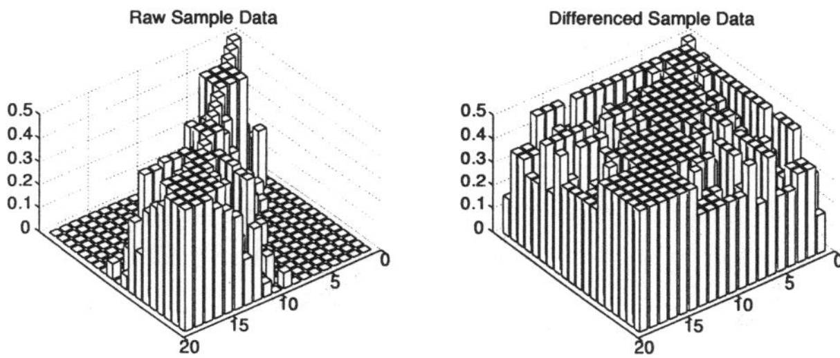

Figure 14: **Replication Period**: Pairwise comparisons between runs. See text and caption of Figure 10 for details.

Figure 15: Activity Wave Diagram, Runs 17 (*left*) and 10 (*right*)

types at time t, activity wave diagrams plot the success of every genotype in the population at every stage of the run (Bedau & Brown 1997). They are therefore a useful visualization technique for competition between genotypes, and the shape of an individual wave can also suggest the level of adaptive value of the corresponding genotype relative to its competitors.

The activity wave diagrams for most of the runs looked surprisingly different, although it is hard to quantify these differences (the Activity and Mean Activity measures do quantify some aspects of them, but no single measure captures all of the important information that the diagrams can tell us). Example activity wave diagrams (for runs 17 and 10) are presented in Figure 15.

One way in which the activity wave diagrams can be very useful is in evaluating the effectiveness of different measures of evolution at highlighting the important adaptive events during a run. In particular, in the runs reported here it was observed that the Activity and Mean Activity measures based purely upon the *presence* of genotypes in the population bear little resemblance to the salient features of the wave diagrams. Indeed, these measures were introduced mainly so that they could be applied to fossil data as well as to data from artificial systems (the concentration data for fossil taxa being unknown) (Bedau *et al.* 1997). The measures based upon the *concentrations* of genotypes should be better, and the results of these runs indicate that this is indeed the case. Activity (concentration) usually seems to give a better reflection of the wave diagram than does Mean Activity (concentration). This is possibly because the latter measure is defined as Activity divided by Diversity, but diversity, by its very nature, does not take account of the *concentrations* of different genotypes, but merely their presence.

Discussion

As discussed earlier in the paper, the three factors that are fundamental to the success of genotypes in an evolving population are the longevity, fecundity and copy-fidelity of the individuals. The measures chosen to track these factors in the runs reported here were *Age at Death*, *Replication Period*, *Program Length*, *Flaw Rate*, *Number of Faithful Replications* and *Number of Unfaithful Replications*. Very little change was observed in any of these measures except Program Length and Replication Period throughout the course of any of the runs. It therefore appears that, under the set of parameters used in these runs, the programs are only able to evolve along one of the three axes (fecundity) theoretically available to them. Studying some of the programs that evolved during the runs suggests that most adaptive events involved either making the program shorter by removing (what turned out to be) redundant instructions, or by adding energy collection instructions to reduce the chance of the program being culled.

For Program Length and Replication Period, significant differences (at the 0.05 level) were observed in the raw data values between some runs. For these measures, the mean number of runs that each run is significantly different from at this level was calculated as 12.3 for Program Length and 10.2 for Replication Period, but the high criterion differential on these scores suggests that the true value should be somewhat lower (looking at Figures 13 and 14, probably somewhere in the range of 6 to 10).

Looking at the derived measures suggested by Bedau et al. (Activity (presence), Mean Activity (presence), Activity (concentration), Mean Activity (concentration) and Diversity), significant differences were found between runs which did hold up even at the 0.001 level. Again, the true value of each of these differences probably lay in the range of roughly 6 to 10.

These results indicate that each run, on average, performed significantly differently to between a third and a half of the other runs. One of the main reasons for doing these experiments was to understand how we should deal with contingency when conducting further experiments with Cosmos. If we assume that at least the finding that each run is statistically different to more than a third of the others is a general result, then we can use the following rule of thumb: For each re-run of a trial with a different seed for the RNG, the probability of its outcome being statistically equivalent (at the $p = 0.05$ level) to the original one is, at most, about $\frac{2}{3}$. Therefore, the number of *re*-runs that should be conducted to be confident (at the 95% level) of at least seeing one statistically different type of behaviour is n, where $(\frac{2}{3})^n \leq 0.05$, i.e. $n \geq 7.388$, or, in round figures, $n \geq 8$. This is the number of *re*-runs *after* the original, so, finally, we can say that *any trial should be conducted nine times with different seeds for the RNG.*

Having said that each run performed significantly differently to at least a third of the other runs, precisely *which* runs were significantly different depended upon the particular measure being looked at. This emphasizes the fact that one should be clear about exactly what measure is being used when talking about comparisons between evolutionary runs.

The fact that *no* significant differences were found between any of the runs for any of the measures when looking at *differenced* sample data is of great interest. It suggests that the significant differences observed in *raw* sample data may be caused (at least in part) by the cumulative magnification of initially small differences as a run proceeds. If this effect is controlled for (which was the purpose of using differenced data), the behaviour of the runs in terms of the *change* in values of the measures over a given time period would seem to be very similar in all of the runs. However, because of the cumulative magnification of small differences, the *absolute* outcomes of the runs *do* differ significantly in some cases, so contingency *does* play a big role.

Finally, we can ask to what extent these results can be generalized to other evolutionary systems. Considering biological evolution first, it is clear that even just in terms of population size and the length of runs, the system is completely trivial. Also, the role of contingency may be different in systems which have rich ecological interactions (of which Cosmos programs have very little). It would therefore be unwise to claim that these results can tell us much about the role of contingency in biological evolution, but they may be relevant in specific cases. As for other artificial evolutionary systems, Cosmos is of comparable design, so the results, and the rule of thumb about the number of trials that should be run, should be broadly applicable to these platforms as well. The extent to which ecological interactions affect the results may be investigated by running similar trials on systems that display stronger interactions of this kind (such as Tierra).

Acknowledgements

Thanks to Chris Adami and four anonymous reviewers for helpful comments on a draft of this paper, and also to Mark Bedau and Emile Snyder for supplying software for producing evolutionary activity data from the raw data of a run. One of the authors [TT] is supported financially by EPSRC grant number 95306471. The facilities used for this work were provided by the University of Edinburgh.

Appendix:Non-default parameter values

ancestor=user_defined number=64 rng_seed=[*variable*] limited_run=yes number_of_timeslices=300000 grid_size=40 horizontal_wrap=yes vertical_wrap=yes max_cells_per_process=800 x_delta=0.025 et_value_constant=0.025 et_value_power=1.0 max_energy_tokens_per_cell=50 apply_flaws=yes max_energy_tokens_per_grid_pos=25 mutation_period=1000000 mutation_application_period=1 default_flaw_period=1000000 neighbouring_genomes_readable=yes

References

Adami, C., and C. T. Brown. 1994. Evolutionary learning in the 2D artificial life system 'Avida'. In *Artificial Life IV*, edited by R. Brooks and P. Maes, Cambridge, MA: MIT Press, p. 377–381.

Bedau, M. A., and C. T. Brown. 1997. Visualizing evolutionary activity of genotypes. (preprint).

Bedau, M. A., and N. H. Packard. 1991. Measurement of evolutionary activity, teleology and life. In *Artificial Life II*, edited by C. G. Langton, C. Taylor, J. D. Farmer and S. Rasmussen. Redwood City, CA: Addison-Wesley, p. 431–461.

Bedau, M. A., E. Snyder, Brown, C. T. and N. H. Packard. 1997. A comparison of evolutionary activity in artificial evolving systems and in the biosphere. In *Fourth European Conference on Artificial Life*, edited by P. Husbands and I. Harvey. Cambridge, MA: MIT Press/Bradford Books, p. 124–134.

Cohen, P. 1995. *Empirical Methods for Artificial Intelligence.* Cambridge, MA: MIT Press.

Dawkins, R. 1989. *The Selfish Gene.* Oxford: Oxford University Press, 2nd edition.

Fontana, W., and L. W. Buss. 1994a. 'The arrival of the fittest': Toward a theory of biological organization. *Bull. Math. Biol.* 56: 1–64.

Fontana, W., and L. Buss. 1994b. What would be conserved if "the tape were played twice"? *Proc. Nat. Acad. Sci. USA* 91: 757–761.

Gould, S. 1989. *Wonderful Life: The Burgess Shale and the Nature of History.* Penguin Books.

Gould, S. J. 1993. How to analyze the Burgess disparity—a reply to Ridley. *Paleobiology* 19: 522–523.

McShea, D. W. 1991. Complexity and evolution: What everybody knows. *Biology and Philosophy* 6: 303–324.

McShea, D. W. 1993. Arguments, tests, and the Burgess Shale—a commentary on the debate. *Paleobiology* 19: 399–402.

McShea, D. W. 1994. Mechanisms of large-scale evolutionary trends. Evolution 48: 1747–1763.

McShea, D. 1996. Metazoan complexity and evolution: Is there a trend? *Evolution* 50: 477–492.

Ray, T. 1991. An approach to the synthesis of life. In *Artificial Life II*, edited by C. G. Langton, C. Taylor, J. D. Farmer and S. Rasmussen. Redwood City, CA: Addison-Wesley, p. 371–408.

Ridley, M. 1993. Analysis of the Burgess Shale. *Paleobiology* 19: 519–521.

Skipper, J. 1992. The computer zoo—evolution in a box. In *Toward a Practice of Autonomous Systems: Proceedings of the First European Conference on Artificial Life*, edited by F. Varela and P. Bourgine. Cambridge, MA: MIT Press, p. 355–364.

Taylor, T., and Hallam, J. 1997. Studying evolution with self-replicating computer programs. In *Fourth European Conference on Artificial Life*, edited by P. Husbands and I. Harvey. Cambridge, MA: MIT Press/Bradford Books, p. 550-559.

Taylor, T. 1997. The COSMOS artificial life system. Working Paper 263, Department of Artificial Intelligence, University of Edinburgh. Available from `http://www.dai.ed.ac.uk/daidb/people/homes/timt/papers/`.

Large-Scale Evolution and Extinction in a Hierarchically Structured Environment

C. Wilke, S. Altmeyer and **T. Martinetz**
Ruhr-Universität Bochum
D-44780 Bochum, Germany
e-mail: Claus.Wilke@neuroinformatik.ruhr-uni-bochum.de

Abstract

A class of models for large-scale evolution and mass extinctions is presented. These models incorporate environmental changes on all scales, from influences on a single species to global effects. This is a step towards a unified picture of mass extinctions, which enables one to study coevolutionary effects and external abiotic influences with the same means. The generic features of such models are studied in a simple version, in which all environmental changes are generated at random and without feedback from other parts of the system.

Introduction

In the history of the Earth, there have been several catastrophic events which in a short period of time have wiped out large parts of the existing species. The amount of species annihilated in such events has been up to 96% of the biodiversity at that time (Raup 1986). It has often been argued that these mass extinctions must have been caused by some disastrous abiotic incidences like extraterrestrial impacts. Evidence in favor of that has been put forward (Alvarez 1987), but on the other hand, only 5% of the total loss of biodiversity in the fossil record can be connected to mass extinctions. The rest are the so-called background extinctions, which happen on much smaller scales. Interestingly, the two types of extinction cannot clearly be distinguished from another in the frequency distribution of extinction event sizes. The event sizes' distribution forms a smooth curve, very close to a power-law (Solé & Bascompte 1996).

In order to explain a single smooth distribution, the idea of coevolutionary avalanches has been developed (Kauffman 1992). The extinction of a single species might cause another species to die out, which might drive a third species into extinction and so on, producing an avalanche that in principle could span the whole system. Because of the diverging mean avalanche size, the distribution of extinction events would then be a power-law, similar to the situation of thermodynamical systems at the point of a phase-transition. Nevertheless, this mechanism, called self-organized criticality, completely neglects external influences that certainly are present.

On the contrary, as it has recently been shown, a power-law distribution of extinction events can appear even in a system in which species are wiped out solely because of external influences (Newman 1996). However, this effect depends crucially on influences that are imposed on all species coherently.

From the point of view of a single species it does not really matter whether it has to struggle with bad conditions imposed externally, e.g., a global shift in temperature, or with bad conditions due to heavy competition with other species. All that counts for a single species is whether it can keep up with its environment or not.

A species goes extinct when its population decreases to zero. This can happen for several reasons. One is a loss of habitat. Climatic or tectonic changes affect the location and the size of a species' habitat. If the size decreases rapidly, the species may not be able to adapt fast enough to find a new niche. Then the population will drop below a level at which it can sustain itself and the species will die out. Another reason for species' extinction is the invasion of new competitors or new predators. Competitors that invade a territory may be better adapted to a niche than the species originally occupying this niche. In this case, the population of the native species can be decimated so effectively that it is wiped out. The same thing can happen because of an invading predator superior to the defense mechanisms of the species. Similarly, new parasites can significantly reduce the population of a species and drive it to extinction.

From the species point of view, all the above cases can be subsumed under the notion of stress. A species suffers stress of various kinds, stress because of climatic changes, stress because of competition and predation etc. If the stress exceeds the level a species can sustain, it will go extinct.

We are going to develop a model in which all causes for the extinction of a species will be regarded as stress. Every species i has a threshold x_i, or in general a vector $\boldsymbol{x}_i$, against stress. If a species suffers a stress $\eta_i > x_i$, or in the general case a vector of stresses $\boldsymbol{\eta}_i$, where at least one component exceeds the corresponding component of the threshold vector $\boldsymbol{x}_i$, it dies out. So far, this is a

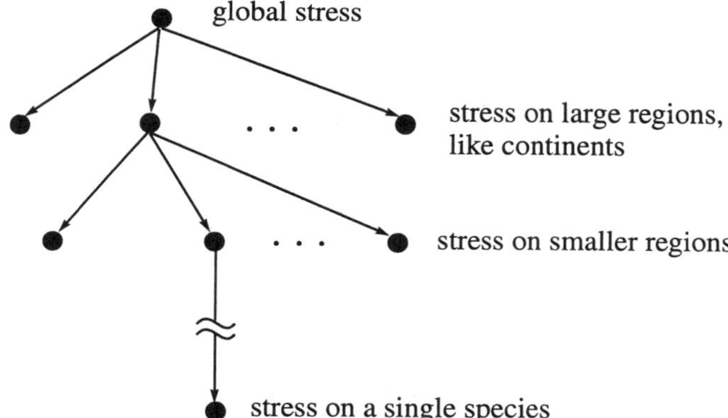

Figure 1: Stress is generated in a tree structure.

very general approach for a model in which species are the smallest units considered, i.e. a model that does not work with individuals or populations. Clearly, in such a model there will be stress on several scales. We have global stress like a global shift in temperature due to a slight change in the orbit of the Earth around the sun, or the impact of a very large meteor. Then we have stress that spans large parts of the Earth, e.g. a continent or a hemisphere, like the El Niño phenomenon that roughly spans the region about the tropical Pacific Ocean. And finally, we have stress that affects smaller regions, or only a single species. This leads us to a hierarchically ordered system of environmental stresses. The simplest way to model it is to generate stress in a tree structure, as it is shown in Fig. 1.

On all scales, the stress can be abiotic or biotic. This may sound a bit counter-intuitive, since abiotic changes are usually taken as large-scale phenomena, and biotic factors are usually taken as local phenomena. Abiotic changes happen often on a global scale, like the above mentioned examples of the orbit shift of the Earth or the meteor impact. But clearly there are more localized events. A small meteor or a small vulcano may affect only a limited number of species. If a species happens to live only in a very small territory, and this territory gets destroyed by a meteor impact, the species may be the only one that goes extinct because of the impact.

On the other hand, biotic phenomena are not necessarily localized. Although direct species competition will usually be a local phenomenon, there can be also global biotic phenomena. The composition of the atmosphere, for example, depends strongly on biotic factors, and it can change significantly due to biotic effects.

So far, we have a model which represents the biosphere as a tree, with species situated at the leafs, and environmental stress generated at the nodes. Now we have to choose the rules that determine how stress is generated and what thresholds against stress the species are given. This is the crucial part where we decide what mechanisms we want to investigate. If we were interested mainly in coevolutionary effects, we would choose rules that link the properties and actions of the species directly to the generation of the stress. In such a model, for example, the global stress at time t could be some sort of a sum over all the adaptive moves of the species at time $t-1$. In this work, however, we are mainly interested in the generic features we can expect from the hierarchical structure of the biosphere. Therefore, we will focus on a version of the model where the stresses and the species' thresholds are simply random variables. Species' interactions and abiotic effects can be so complicated and so unpredictable that in a first approximation we want to assume them to be completely random.

The model we study here is probably the simplest possible. Yet it has some intriguing features which are very similar to characteristics seen in the fossil record. To keep our model simple, we choose a homogenous tree, with l layers and n subtrees per node. In general, of course, one has to deal with inhomogenous trees. To each node of the final layer we connect exactly one leaf, where we put m species. An example of such a tree with $l=4$ and $n=2$ is displayed in Fig. 2. The total number of stresses that have to be generated in one time step is

$$N_{\text{stress}} = \sum_{i=0}^{l-1} n^i \,, \tag{1}$$

and the total number of species in the model is

$$N_{\text{species}} = mn^{l-1} \,. \tag{2}$$

Every species i has a single threshold x_i, chosen at random from the uniform distribution on the intervall $[0;1)$. At every node j, the stress η_j generated in one time step is a positive, real random variable drawn from a distribution with probability densitiy function (pdf) $p_j(x)$. It is a reasonable assumption to expect smaller stresses to happen much more often than larger stresses. Therefore, we use pdf's that fall off relatively fast with $x \to \infty$. An Exponential or Gaussian decrease should be a good choice, but the exact form of the pdf is not really important. We choose the pdf's $p_j(x)$ at the beginning of the simulation at random from some family of distribution functions and keep this choice fixed throughout the course of the simulation.

Finally, we have to fix the way a species is affected by stress generated on different levels of the tree. We simply take the maximum of all the stress values generated at nodes that lie above the species in the tree: if at any of these nodes a stress η_j is generated which exceeds the species threshold x_i, this species goes extinct. It is then immediately replaced by a new species with new random threshold.

In addition to the extinction dynamic, we introduce some sort of adaption. In agreement with our idea of a first, simple model, the adaption is a random walk: in every time step, a fraction f of the species is selected at random and given new thresholds.

There are certainly some oversimplifications in this model, such as the fixed number of species or the fact that all species have only one trait. We will return to this later and explain why we can still expect to cover the basic features of the extinction dynamic.

Analysis

The behaviour of the above introduced model can be understood to a large extent from analytical calculations. But before we begin with our analysis, we note that the mechanism for species extinction and adaption presented here is similar to the one of the so-called 'coherent-noise' models introduced by Newman and Sneppen (Newman & Sneppen 1996). These models display a distribution of extinction events that follows a power-law with exponent ≈ -2, which is in good agreement with the fossil record. For this reason, they have already been used to study macroevolutionary phenomena (Newman 1996; Wilke & Martinetz 1997). The difference to our actual approach lies in the fact that we use a multitude of stresses in a hierarchically ordered system, whereas in the coherent-noise models there is only a single stress, acting on the whole system at once. Therefore, in the previous works the idea of stress imposed on the species has been linked to external influences like meteor impacts and was opposed to coevolutionary effects.

Note that we have effectively a coherent-noise model at every leaf of the tree if the number m of species located at one leaf is large.

The effective stress-distribution at a leaf of the tree

Every leaf of the tree feels a stress-distribution which depends on the distributions of the nodes above it. Let there be N nodes above a leaf. Then the N stress values having influence on this leaf are N random variables $X_1, \dots, X_N$ with pdf's $p_1(x), \dots, p_N(x)$. We have to calculate the pdf $p_{\max}(x)$ of the random variable $X_{\max} = \max\{X_1, \dots, X_N\}$, i.e.,

$$p_{\max}(x)\,dx = P(x \le \max\{X_1, \dots, X_N\} < x + dx)\,. \tag{3}$$

With the partition theorem we can write the probability on the right-hand side as a weighted sum of conditional probabilities:

$$\begin{aligned} &P(x \le \max\{X_1, \dots, X_N\} < x + dx) \\ &\quad = \sum_{i=1}^{N} P(x \le \max\{X_1, \dots, X_N\} < x + dx \\ &\qquad\qquad \Big| \, x \le X_i < x + dx) \\ &\qquad \times P(x \le X_i < x + dx)\,. \end{aligned} \tag{4}$$

The conditional probabilities read

$$\begin{aligned} &P(x \le \max\{X_1, \dots, X_N\} < x + dx \\ &\qquad\qquad \Big| \, x \le X_i < x + dx) \\ &= \frac{1}{P(x \le X_i < x + dx)} \\ &\quad \times P(x \le \max\{X_1, \dots, X_N\} < x + dx \\ &\qquad\qquad \wedge x \le X_i < x + dx) \\ &= \frac{P(x \le X_i < x + dx) \prod_{j=1, j\ne i}^{N} P(x > X_j)}{P(x \le X_i < x + dx)} \\ &= \prod_{j=1, j \ne i}^{N} P(x > X_j)\,. \end{aligned} \tag{5}$$

After inserting Eq. (5) into Eq. (4) we find

$$\begin{aligned} &P(x \le \max\{X_1, \dots, X_N\} < x + dx) \\ &\quad = \sum_{i=1}^{N} P(x \le X_i < x + dx) \prod_{j=1, j\ne i}^{N} P(x > X_j)\,. \end{aligned} \tag{6}$$

Consequently, for the pdf $p_{\max}(x)$ we have

$$\begin{aligned} p_{\max}(x) &= \sum_{i=1}^{N} p_i(x) \prod_{j=1, j\ne i}^{N} P(x > X_j) \\ &= \sum_{i=1}^{N} p_i(x) \prod_{j=1, j\ne i}^{N} \int_0^x p_j(x')\,dx'\,. \end{aligned} \tag{7}$$

We are interested in the tail of $p_{\max}(x)$. For coherent-noise models we know that a power-law distribution of event-sizes will appear if the stress-distribution $p_{\text{stress}}(x)$ satisfies

$$\int_\eta^\infty p_{\text{stress}}(x)\,dx \approx C p_{\text{stress}}^\alpha(\eta) \quad \text{for } \eta \to \infty\,, \tag{8}$$

where C and α are positive constants which depend on $p_{\text{stress}}(x)$ (Sneppen & Newman 1997). Therefore, we assume this condition to hold also for the distributions $p_j(x)$ in Eq. (7), with constants C_j and α_j, respectively. Then we can approximate the tail of $p_{\max}(x)$ by

$$p_{\max}(x) \approx \sum_{i=1}^{N} p_i(x) \prod_{j=1, j\ne i}^{N} \left(1 - C_j p_j^{\alpha_j}(x)\right) \quad \text{for } x \to \infty\,. \tag{9}$$

We proceed further by taking only linear terms in $p_i(x)$ and obtain

$$p_{\max}(x) \approx \sum_{i=1}^{N} p_i(x) \quad \text{for } x \to \infty\,. \tag{10}$$

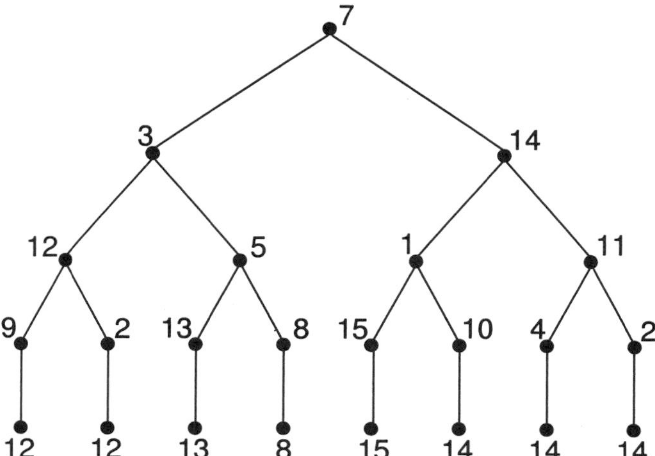

Figure 2: The tree breaks down into virtually independent parts in the limit of large stresses.

For large x, this sum will be dominated by the $p_i(x)$ that is falling off slowest. We say that distribution $p_i(x)$ falls off slower than distribution $p_j(x)$ if there exists a x_0 such that

$$p_i(x) > p_j(x) \qquad \text{for all } x > x_0. \tag{11}$$

For a set of reasonable stress-distributions it is always possible to identify one that is falling off slowest according to this definition.

The fact that the sum in Eq. (11) will asymptotically be dominated by a single term leads to the situation depicted in Fig. 2. The tree breaks down into several independent subsystems. The meaning of the numbers in the figure will be explained in detail later. In a nutshell, they indicate how slow a stress distribution is falling off. What interests us here is the breakup of the tree into several independent parts in the regime of large stresses. If these parts are not too small, they will behave like independent coherent-noise systems.

An ensemble of a finite number of independent coherent-noise systems

If the stress-distributions close to the root dominate the behaviour of the system, the tree will break down into independent coherent-noise systems, as we have mentioned above. Consequently, we proceed with the calculation of the distribution of extinction events in a system consisting of independent coherent-noise subsystems. In the calculation, however, we will deviate slightly from the actual situation in the tree model by assuming the subsystems to have each an infinite size. This allows for an easy calculation, and the main results should also hold for large but finite sizes.

In the case of an infinite system size, the event distribution of a coherent-noise model possesses a power-law tail that extends to arbitrary large events. Therefore, the task of calculating the event distribution of the compound system equals to the task of calculating the sum of a finite number of nonidentically distributed random variables with power-law tail. The latter can be treated mathematically exact under relatively weak assumptions (Wilke unpublished). But since the exact calculations are too extensive to be included in this work, we will here give only an intuitive argument about the tail behaviour of the sum.

We begin with the sum of two positive, real random variables X_1 and X_2, where the pdf's $p_1(x)$ and $p_2(x)$ have a power-law tail $x^{-\tau_1}$ and $x^{-\tau_2}$, respectively. We assume the pdf's to be continuous, non-singular, and reasonably smooth. Under these conditions, we can write $p_1(x)$ and $p_2(x)$ in the form

$$p_1(x) = \frac{f_1(x)}{(x+1)^{\tau_1}}, \tag{12}$$

$$p_2(x) = \frac{f_2(x)}{(x+1)^{\tau_2}}, \tag{13}$$

where $f_1(x)$ and $f_2(x)$ are continuous, non-singular, and reasonably smooth functions which tend towards a positive constant for $x \to \infty$. The pdf $p_{\text{sum}}(x)$ of the sum $X = X_1 + X_2$ is the convolution of $p_1(x)$ and $p_2(x)$:

$$\begin{aligned} p_{\text{sum}}(x) &= \int_0^x p_1(x')p_2(x-x')\,dx' \\ &= \int_0^x \frac{f_1(x')}{(x'+1)^{\tau_1}} \frac{f_2(x-x')}{(x-x'+1)^{\tau_2}}\,dx'. \end{aligned} \tag{14}$$

After a change of the integration variable to $z = x'/x$ we obtain

$$\begin{aligned} p_{\text{sum}}(x) &= \int_0^1 \frac{f_1(xz)}{(xz+1)^{\tau_1}} \frac{f_2(x(1-z))}{(x(1-z)+1)^{\tau_2}} x\,dx' \\ &= x^{1-\tau_1-\tau_2} \int_0^1 \frac{f_1(xz)}{(z+\frac{1}{x})^{\tau_1}} \frac{f_2(x(1-z))}{(1-z+\frac{1}{x})^{\tau_2}}\,dx'. \end{aligned} \tag{15}$$

For large x, there are two main contributions to this integral, at $z \approx 0$ and at $z \approx 1$, which stem from the first and from the second term in the denominator. Since the denominators will become arbitrarily large for large x, we can assume the other terms to be constant in the regions where the main contributions come from. Therefore, we find

$$p_{\text{sum}}(x) \approx x^{1-\tau_1-\tau_2}\Big[C_1 x^{\tau_2-1} + C_2 x^{\tau_1-1}\Big], \tag{16}$$

where C_1 and C_2 are positive constants. Obviously for large x the term with the largest exponent will dominate. Hence we have

$$p_{\text{sum}}(x) \sim x^{-\min\{\tau_1,\tau_2\}}. \tag{17}$$

This result can be easily extended to the case of an arbitrary finite number of random variables with power-law tail by iteration. Asymptotically, the tail of $p_{\text{sum}}(s)$ will always be dominated by the contribution from the term with the smallest exponent.

Back to the ensemble of infinitely large coherent-noise systems, we find that it will display power-law distributed event sizes, as its single constituents do. If the subsystems' stress-distributions are functionally different, the exponent of the compound system's event distribution will be the smallest of the subsystems' exponents.

The above result should also hold in the situation of finite coherent noise systems, as long as their total number is small compared to their typical size.

Trees with Random Stress Distributions

We argue above that in the limit of large stresses the tree will break down into subsystems, virtually independent of each other. The behaviour of our model depends heavily on the size of the parts we find. If the different parts are all very small, the system will loose its coherent-noise characteristics. Instead of a power-law distribution the extinction events will then follow a gaussian distribution because of the central-limit theorem. Therefore, in this section we will study the distribution of the subsystems' sizes that arises if we randomly assign stress distributions to the tree's nodes.

We assume that the propability for a certain stress distribution to be assigned to a certain node does not depend on the position of the node in the tree. In other words, we use the same set of stress distributions on all levels of the tree. Furthermore, we assume that for any two stress distributions we use we can identify one of the two that falls off faster than the other one. Under these conditions, we can study the structure of such trees by simply assigning integers to the nodes of the tree, where larger integers stand for distributions that are falling off slower. If the set of possible stress distributions is infinite, the probability of finding two nodes with the same distribution is zero. Consequently, in a tree with n nodes, we will assign every integer from $1 \dots n$ to exactly one node. This is displayed in Fig. 2 for a tree with 15 nodes. For every leaf i of the tree we can then define a characteristic number a_i. This number is the maximum of the nodes' numbers encountered on the way from the leaf up to the root. All the leafs with the same characteristic number belong to the same subsystem. In the example of Fig. 2, we have five subsystems in total. Three of them contain only one leaf, one contains two and one contains three leafs.

In general, we are interested in the distribution of subsystems arising in large trees. Therefore, we have done simulations in which we have several thousand times assigned random integers to the nodes of a large tree. For every single realization of the tree, we have computed a histogram of the frequency of the different parts' sizes. Finally, we have calculated the average of all the histograms. Fig. 3 shows the result of such simulations for two different trees with 10000 histograms each. We find the expected frequency $f(k)$ of large independent parts in the tree decreasing as a sawtooth function that follows approximately a power-law with exponent -2, independent of l and n. The sharp peaks in the distribution arise whenever the size of a complete subtree is reached. Therefore, we observe in Fig. 3, e.g., the peaks in the distribution of the tree with $n = 10$ appearing at powers of 10.

The power-law can be explained easily if we assume the main contributions to come from complete subtrees. The expected frequency $f(k)$ to find an independent subtree with b layers, which corresponds to a subsystem of size $k = n^b$, can be written as the number of such subtrees in the whole system, $N(b)$, times the probability that any of these subtrees will be independent of the rest, $P(b)$. Hence we write

$$f(n^b) = N(b)P(b)\,. \tag{18}$$

The number of subtrees of size n^b is $N(b) = n^{l-b}$. For the probability $P(b)$ we find

$$P(b) = \Big(l - b + \sum_{i=0}^{b-1} n^i\Big)^{-1}, \tag{19}$$

which is simply the probability for the integer assigned to the node at the root of the subtree to be larger than all the other integers which are assigned to the remaining nodes of the subtree and to the nodes above the subtree. If we increase b by one, we get $N(b+1) = n^{l-b-1} = N(b)/n$. With slightly more effort, we find also

$$\begin{aligned} P(b+1) &= \Big(l - b - 1 + \sum_{i=0}^{b} n^i\Big)^{-1} \\ &= \Big(l - b + n\sum_{i=0}^{b-1} n^i\Big)^{-1} \approx \frac{1}{n}P(b)\,. \end{aligned} \tag{20}$$

Therefore, we can write

$$f(nk) \approx \frac{N(k)}{n}\frac{P(k)}{n} = n^{-2}f(k)\,, \tag{21}$$

which implies $f(k) \sim k^{-2}$.

The peaks in Fig. 3 appear whenever the size of a complete subtree is reached, as we have noted above. This means they are connected to the extremely regular structure of the trees we use in this work. Therefore, we are currently investigating trees with irregular structure. For these trees, the spikes disappear and, in log-log plot, the function $f(k)$ becomes almost a straight line with slope -2. From the simulations we have done so far, we can say that this result is very general and seems to be independent of the special trees' properties.

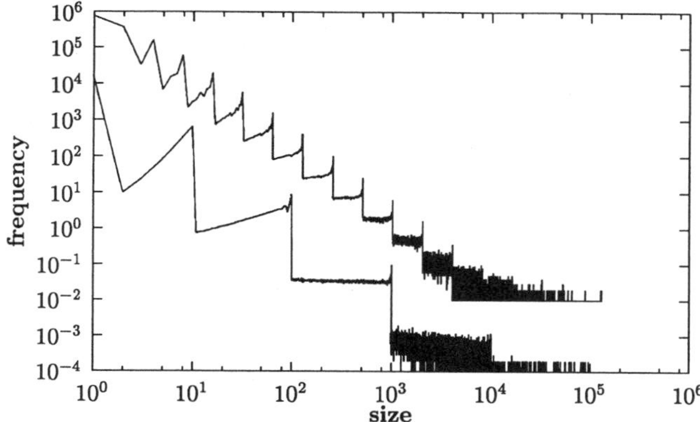

Figure 3: The expected frequency for the occurence of large independent subsystems decreases as a sawtooth function that follows approximately a power-law with exponent −2. The upper curve stems from a tree with $l = 18$ and $n = 2$. It has been rescaled by a factor of 100 so as not to overlap with the lower curve. The lower curve stems from a tree with $l = 6$ and $n = 10$.

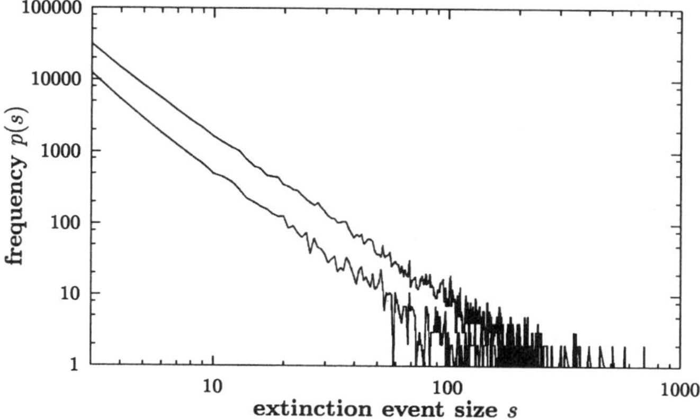

Figure 4: The frequency of extinction events in the tree model and in an ensemble of coherent-noise models. The lower curve stems from the simulation of a tree with $l = 5$, $n = 10$ and $m = 1$, which amounts to a total of 10^5 species. Stress distributions were assigned at random to the nodes of the tree. We used exponentially distributed stress with σ between 0.03 and 0.05. The upper curve corresponds to the simulation of an ensemble of coherent-noise models with a total of 10^5 species, and with the sizes k of the subsystems distributed according to k^{-2}. As stresses we used the maximum of 5 exponentially distributed random variables.

Simulation Results

Since we are interested in the typical behaviour of our model, we have to do many simulation runs with different tree sizes and different stress distributions at the tree's nodes. But the simulation of large trees is very slow, and therefore it is hard to get a good sample of the parameter-space. To overcome this difficulty we have also done simulations based on the arguments of the previous sections. As we have seen there, in the limit of large stresses it is possible to map the leafs of the tree onto a system consisting of several independent coherent-noise models, with the sizes k of these subsystems distributed according to k^{-2}.

In Fig. 4 we show a comparison between the full simulation and the approximation. To come as close as possible to the full simulation, we use the maximum of 5 independent, exponentially distributed random variables as stresses for the independent coherent-noise models, since for the tree we have likewise chosen $l = 5$ and exponential stress-distributions. Clearly the behaviour of the approximation is close to the one of the full simulation, which verifies the analytical reasoning of the previous sections. Both simulations display power-law distributed extinction events. For the full tree, we find an exponent $\tau_{\text{tree}} = 2.35 \pm 0.05$, while for the approximation, we find $\tau_{\text{approx}} = 2.30 \pm 0.05$. If we consider the high level of abstraction from the tree to an ensemble of coherent-noise systems, this agreement is excellent.

Note that in comparison to a normal coherent-noise model with only a single stress variable, the tree model produces a significantly larger exponent τ (If we run a normal coherent-noise model with the stress distribution of the approximaton in Fig. 4, we get an exponent $\tau \approx 1.8$). The increased exponent τ has its origin in the distribution of the subsystems' sizes. The sizes scale themselves, thus modifying the scale-invariant behavior of the ensemble, compared to the one of a single coherent-noise system.

Discussion

We have presented a model of large-scale evolution and extinction that combines biotic and abiotic causes for extinction within a single mathematical framework. Furthermore, the model takes into account the hierarchical structure of the biosphere. To the best of our knowledge, the implications of environmental changes happening on different scales have not been studied previously in macroevolutionary models. Despite the choice of completely random environmental changes, the model has some interesting features. The distribution of extinction events follows a power-law with exponent in the region of 2 (note that the exponent depends on the choice of the stress distribution, as it is the case with coherent-noise models). From the fossil record, a power-law distribution with exponent $\tau \approx 2$ is reported for the extinction event sizes of taxonomical families (Solé & Bascompte 1996; Newman 1996). Moreover, it is interesting to observe the breakup of the tree into subsystems with sizes k distributed according to k^{-2}. The power-law distribution of the subsytem sizes implies that even in very large trees we will find large subsystems, governed mainly by only a single stress distribution. Intuitively, we would expect the subsystems to have roughly similar sizes, and to enter the dynamic of the whole system on an equal basis. But we observe exactly the opposite. The subsystems' sizes are scale-invariant, thus producing a scale-invariant distribution of contributions to the overall system's behavior. In particular, only a small number of large subsystems produces events on large scales. This might be an explanation for the fact that in such large and complex systems like the biosphere we find usually smooth frequency distributions of typical objects or events.

The model we have studied in this work is certainly oversimplified. For that reason, we will close this paper with some remarks about extensions to the model that should be examined in a next step closer to biological reality. First of all, it is certainly a severe restriction to keep the number of species fixed throughout the simulation. Nevertheless, this is a restriction used very often in models of macroevolution (Peliti 1997). Only recently, work has been done where a change in biodiversity is considered (Head & Rodgers 1997; Wilke & Martinetz 1997). The behaviour of the model we study here is governed by the coherent-noise dynamic. For this dynamic, it has been shown that it can be generalized to include a variable system size without loss of it's main features (Wilke & Martinetz 1997). Therefore, we believe a fixed system-size can be justified in the present work. It should be possible to extend our tree model to a model with variable system size. Another severe restriction is the usage of only one trait. But here a similar argument holds as in the case of the fixed number of species. A multi-trait version of the original coherent-noise model has already been studied (Newman in press). It behaves very similar to the single-trait version.

Finally, we want to discuss the way we compute the stress on a single species out of the multitude of stress values, generated at the different levels of the tree. Throughout this paper, we have used the maximum of the stress values. This allows for an easy and very general analytical investigation. Another natural choice, however, would be to sum up all the stresses. We have also done some simulations in this fashion. The behavior of the system remains roughly the same. This happens because in a finite sum of non-identically distributed random variables, we expect large values to be dominated by a single term of the sum, similar to the case of the maximum of several random variables. For the sum of exponentially distributed random variables, an easy calculation shows that this conjecture is indeed true. With some more effort, we can prove the same for the sum of power-law distributed random variables, as we have already done in this paper. Nevertheless, in the general case with arbitrary distributions, the conjecture is hard to demonstrate.

References

Alvarez, L. W. 1987. Mass extinctions caused by large bolide impacts. *Physics Today* pp. 24–33, July 1987.

Head, D. A., and G. J. Rodgers. 1997. Speciation and extinction in a simple model of evolution. Phys. Rev. E 55: 3312.

Kauffman, S. A. 1992. *The Origins of Order*. Oxford: Oxford University Press.

Newman, M. E. J., and K. Sneppen. 1996. Avalanches, scaling and coherent noise. Phys. Rev. E 54: 6226.

Newman, M. E. J. 1996. Self-organized criticality, evolution, and the fossil extinction record. Proc. R. Soc. London B 263: 1605.

Newman, M. E. J. 1998. A model of mass extinction. J. Theor. Biol. (in press). eprint adap-org/9702003.

Peliti, L. 1997. Introduction to the statistical theory of darwinian evolution. eprint cond-mat/9712027.

Raup, D. M. 1986. Biological extinction and earth history. Science 231: 1528.

Sneppen, K., and M. E. J. Newman. 1997. Coherent noise, scale invariance and intermittency in large systems. Physica D 107: 292.

Solé, R. V., and J. Bascompte. 1996. Are critical phenomena relevant to large-scale evolution? Proc. R. Soc. Lond. B 263: 161.

Wilke, C., and Martinetz, T. 1997. Simple model of evolution with variable system size. Phys. Rev. E 56: 7128.

Wilke, C. unpublished. On the sum of random variables with power-law tail.

Evolutionary Themes

A Case Study of the Evolution of Modularity: Towards a Bridge Between Evolutionary Biology, Artificial Life, Neuro- and Cognitive Science

Raffaele Calabretta[1,2], Stefano Nolfi[2], Domenico Parisi[2] and Günter P. Wagner[1]

[1] Department of Ecology and Evolutionary Biology, Yale University
165, Prospect Street - New Haven, CT 06511, USA
e-mail: raffaele@peaplant.biology.yale.edu

[2] Department of Neural Systems and Artificial Life
Institute of Psychology, C.N.R.
Viale Marx, 15 - 00137 Rome, Italy

Abstract

The existence of modules is recognized at all levels of the biological hierarchy. In order to understand what modules are, why and how they emerge and how they change, it would be necessary to start a joint effort by researchers in different disciplines (evolutionary and developmental biology, comparative anatomy, physiology, neuro- and cognitive science). This is made difficult by disciplinary specialization. In this paper we claim that, because of the strong similarities in the intellectual agenda of artificial life and evolutionary biology and of their common grounding in Darwinian evolutionary theory, a close interaction between the two fields could easily take place. Moreover, by considering that artificial neural networks draw an inspiration from neuro- and cognitive science, an artificial life approach to the problem could theoretically enlarge the field of investigation. The present work is the first one in which an artificial life model based on neural networks and genetic algorithms is used to understand the mechanisms underlying the evolutionary origin of modularity. An interesting problem that we will address in this paper is whether modules that start as repeated elements because of genetic duplication can develop to become specialized modules. A linear regression statistical analysis performed on simulation data confirms this hypothesis and suggests a new mode for the evolution of modularity.

Introduction

Various disciplines concerned with the study of organisms and their behavior find it useful to refer to 'modules' as components that play identifiable roles in systems at various levels and tend to maintain their identity over time. Although nonmodularity may also play a part in biological structure and function, the existence of modules is recognized at all levels of the biological hierarchy. The 'modularity of mind' is a well-known assumption of symbol-manipulation models of cognition. The mind is seen as composed by a multiplicity of modules that are specialized for various behavioral capacities and areas of activity. Neuroscientists recognize in the brain various types of units above the cellular level: columns, areas, systems, etc. In fact the total architecture of the brain appears to be a mosaic of interacting components with structural and functional specialization. Geneticists subdivide the DNA chain into genes that code for proteins and control the genotype-to-phenotype mapping. Modules are also recognized at levels lower and higher than the gene level. At a lower level, genes are composed of triplets (*codons*) of bases (adenine, tymine, cytosine, guanine and uracil), each of which codifies for a specific amino acid. At a higher level, each gene codifies for a specific protein. The sequence of amino acids for each protein, as it is codified exactly in DNA, contains all the information to determine the three-dimensional structure on which the function of that protein finally depends (see for instance Creighton 1993 and Calabretta, Nolfi, and Parisi 1995). As stressed by Doolittle and Bork (1993), proteins are often composed by a limited group of modular elements (*domains*) that have spread and multiplied during evolution in ways that are starting to be understood. At the phenotypic level evolutionary biologists recognize homologous and analogous phenotypic traits in organisms belonging to different species or higher taxa, and repeated components in individual organisms, such as vertebrae in mammals (see Futuyma 1998, p. 669).

Given the postulated existence of modules at all these levels and their importance for describing and explaining both structure and process at each level, it is critical to understand what modules are, why and how they emerge, how they change, etc. To achieve this understanding it appears to be crucial to be able to coordinate modules existing at different levels of the biological hierarchy and to understand how modules at one level are related to those at other levels. This is made difficult by disciplinary specialization. The sheer amount of detailed empirical data that must be taken into consideration at each level, the heterogeneity of theoretical vocabularies and empirical methods used to study phenomena at different levels, and the great complexity of the between-level mappings, make it very difficult to clarify the relationships among modules at different levels in real organisms.

One possibility, then, is to study these problems in artificial organisms. Artificial Life studies all kinds of biological phenomena as they occur in artificial organisms and it can help us overcome many of the difficulties encountered in trying to relate modules at different levels. First, artificial organisms are simpler than real organisms. Second, simulations of biological phenomena at different levels can adopt a unified theoretical framework to facilitate inter-level conceptual dialogue. Finally, the computer is a very powerful research instrument that allows us to observe and manipulate complex phenomena and nonlinear interactions among large number of entities at each level and between levels.

In this paper we adopt an Artificial Life approach in the hope that this approach can shed some useful light on modules at different levels and how they are related to each other.

Previous Work

Research in the field of neuro- and cognitive sciences tends to assume that human cognitive process are accomplished by means of specialized modules (see e.g., Moscovitch and Umiltà 1990, Fodor 1983; for a critique of Fodor's point of view see Karmiloff-Smith 1992). Cowey (1981) and Kaas (1989) ask why the brain has so many visual areas. Ballard (1986) suggests that a limitation on the number of neurons compels the brain to adopt a modular architecture. Stevens (1994) maintains that «the complexity of human brain arises not from the complexity of its basic processing elements (the cortical module), or the richness of connections between modules, but simply in the number of the modules present». (For some connectionist simulations of modularity, see Jacobs, Jordan, and Barto 1991 and Rueckl, Cave, and Kosslyn 1989).

Even if the recognition of the existence and importance of modularity has a long historical tradition, there is little understanding of how modularity has originated. Evolutionary biologists ask whether modularity is an inherent property of organisms and thus not the result of evolution or it is the result of selection shaping the genotype-phenotype mapping function (see for instance Wagner 1995). The evolutionary implications of modular organization for development have been described by John Bonner in his book on the evolution of complexity (Bonner 1988). Modularity would allow the adaptation of different functions with little or no interference with other functions. Several population genetic models have been suggested in order to explain the evolutionary origin of modular design (e.g., Wagner and Altenberg 1996; Wagner 1996; Altenberg 1995) but our current knowledge is insufficient to assess the plausibility of these models.

In the field of Artificial Life, some researchers have tried to exploit modular design for improving the performance of various artificial systems such as artificial neural networks, evolutionary algorithms, and robots. Gruau (1994) applies a genetic algorithm to the synthesis of neural networks using cellular encoding as a new technology. This technology «can automatically and dynamically decompose a problem into a hierarchy of sub-problems, and generate a neural network solution to the problem. The structure of this network is a hierarchy of sub-networks that reflect the structure of the problem.» Snoad and Bossomaier (1995) consider «how genetic algorithms (GAs) and artificial neural networks (ANNs) (connectionist learning models) complement each other and how combining them (i.e. evolving artificial neural networks with a genetic algorithm), may give insights into the evolution of structure and modularity in biological brains.» Cho and Shimohara (1997) investigate «the emergence of structure and functionality of modular neural networks trough evolution.» The model they present is applied to a visual categorization task with handwritten digits.

In order to evolve neural controllers for mobile robots, Nolfi (1997) describes a modular neural network architecture that clearly outperforms other architectures in performing a garbage-collecting task (see below). This architecture is called an 'emergent modular architecture' because although modules are available from the beginning it is evolution that decides whether to use them or not by breaking down the required behavior into sub-components corresponding to different neural modules. In the present work we use the same simulation scenario of Nolfi (1997) but we add the genetic operator of gene duplication in order to explore the relationship between the evolutionary emergence of modularity and the phenomenon of gene duplication.

To our knowledge, the present work is the first one in which an artificial life model based on neural networks (Rumelhart and McClelland 1986) and genetic algorithms (Holland 1992) is specifically used to understand the mechanisms underlying the evolutionary origin of modularity.

Duplication-Based Modules

In the present paper we are concerned with modules that play a role in the genotype-to-phenotype mapping. More specifically, we are interested in the evolution of modules at the genetic level that map into single functions at the behavioral level of the entire organism. Mappings from genes to higher functions can be modular or nonmodular (Wagner and Altenberg 1996). The mapping is modular when there are few pleiotropic effects among characters serving different functions, with pleiotropic effects existing mainly among characters which serve one and the same function (Figure 1, right). (Pleiotropy is «the influence of the same genes on different characters», Futuyma 1998). On the contrary, we have a nonmodular mapping when there are pleiotropic effects both among characters serving different functions and among characters serving a single function (Figure 1, left). Therefore, modules can be defined as a collection of characters at different levels that are all responsible

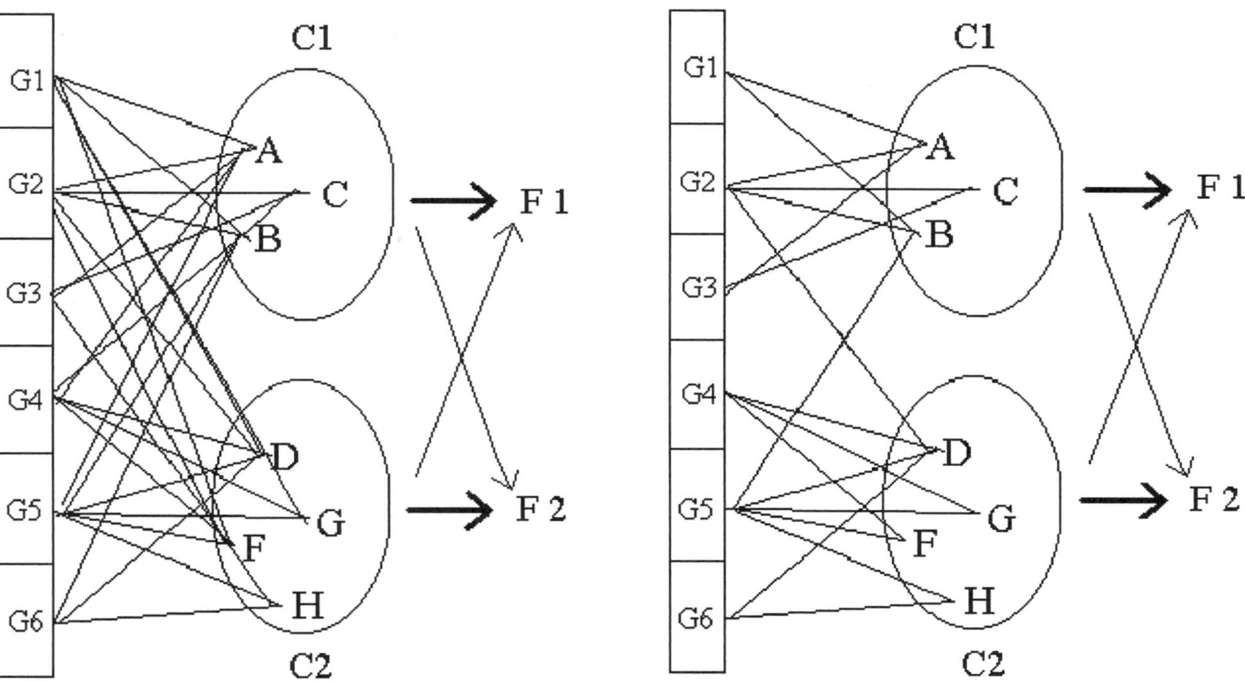

Figure 1. Examples of nonmodular and modular genotype-to-phenotypes mapping. Complexes of phenotypic characters {A, B, C} and {D, F, G, H} serve behavioral functions F1 and F2, respectively. The genetic representation is modular in the case to the right because some genes (i.e., {G1, G2, G3}) have primarily pleiotropic effects on the first set of characters (C1) supporting behavioral function F1 whereas other genes (i.e., {G4, G5, G6}) have primarily pleiotropic effects on the characters (C2) subserving function F2. The left case is nonmodular because there are about the same amount of pleiotropic effects on the characters subserving both functions. (Figure redrawn from Wagner and Altenberg 1996).

mainly for a single function. Put simply, in the genes-to-behavior mapping a module can be defined as a collection of genes which produce a set of molecules which in turn are responsible in the regulation of the nervous system serving a given behavioral function. Notice how this definition of module is more constrained than others. Neuro-physiologists, for instance, in defining a module take into account the nervous system and the higher level of organization (behavior) which is the result of the activity of the nervous system. However, they do not usually take into consideration lower levels such as the molecular and genetic level. They do not ascertain that what they have identified as a neural module is the result of a collection of genes that mainly codify for that phenotypic character. If we take an evolutionary perspective, however, the genotype level plays a very important role because it is at this level that novelties are produced through mutation, recombination, and selection.

Modules can be seen as specialized components and, therefore, different from each other, or they can be recognized as repeated identical elements. An interesting problem that we will address in this paper is how the two types of modules are related. In particular we will ask if modules that start as repeated elements because of genetic duplication can develop to become specialized modules.

Wagner and Altenberg (1996) stressed that «although modularity may sometimes be intrinsic to the mechanism of an organismal function, in many cases, especially development, modularity appears to be an evolved property.» A possible mechanism of morphological innovation is the differentiation of repeated elements (Müller and Wagner 1991; Ohno, 1970; Weiss 1990), for instance the differentiation of metameric segments at the origin of insects (see for instance Akam, Dawson, and Tear 1989). Various authors have stressed the role of genetic duplication for the emergence of evolutionary novelties, especially in complex organisms. Li (1983) claims that «gene duplication is probably the most important mechanism for generating new genes and new biochemical processes that have facilitated the evolution of complex organisms from primitives ones». Tautz (1992) argues that «redundancy of gene actions may [...] be a necessary requirement for the development and evolution of complex life forms» and in fact «redundancy seems to be widespread in genomes of higher organisms» (Nowak et al. 1997). In the neutral theory of molecular evolution (Kimura 1983), the duplication relaxes the selective constraints on one of the two copies allowing the accumulation of mutations leading to the emergence of a new function (Coissac, Maillier, and Netter 1997; see also Ohta 1989).

In the present work we present simulations of the evolution of populations of artificial organisms focusing on the evolutionarily emergence of functionally different modules at the neural-behavioral level from gene duplication.

A typical Artificial Life simulation addressing problems at the behavioral level involves a population of organisms living and reproducing in an environment. The behavior of each individual organism is controlled by a neural network that encodes the state of the local environment in its input units and some movement of the organism in its output units. Each individual has an inherited genetic code that specifies (some of) the properties of the individual's neural network and, therefore, of the individual's behavior. The individuals that inherit better neural networks tend to behave more efficiently and are more likely to leave offspring. The genetic code is inherited with random mutations and/or sexual recombination of parts of the genetic code of one parent and parts of that of the other parent. The resulting offspring are in many cases worse than their parents but, although infrequently, they can represent an improvement over their parents. The selective reproduction of the best individuals and the constant addition of variability through mutations and/or sexual recombination make it possible to observe evolutionary change in the population at three levels: genetic, neural, and behavioral (Miglino, Nolfi, and Parisi 1996).

We compare two populations. In both populations neural modules start as reduplications in the genetic code and they evolve their connection weights during the evolutionary process. In one population the genetic code is hardwired from the beginning for coding for two distinct neural modules for each separate aspect of the network's output. In principle each of the two modules can control the same network's output. In the other population the emergence of distinct modules becomes an adaptive process in the sense that the genetic code includes a 'reduplication gene' that can be turned on at some point during the evolutionary process. An important difference between the two populations is that in the first population the two alternative neural modules controlling the same network's output both start from zero, i.e., from random connection weights, and they must evolve their connection weights in parallel to become specialized for different tasks, whereas in the second population a duplicated module starts with the weights already evolved for the first module and must then adapt these weights to differentiate and specialize with respect to the first module. We will call the first type of modules «hardwired» and the second type of modules «duplication-based».

The two populations are compared with respect to how much modules at the genetic level map into meaningful units at the behavioral level. More specifically we want to test the prediction that modular architectures that originate in genetic duplication tend to have modules corresponding to meaningful behavioral units more often than architectures with hardwired modules.

Let us explain what it is for a module to correspond to a meaningful behavioral unit. Imagine a population of organisms (robots) living in a walled environment that contains a certain number of objects. The task for these organisms is to grasp the objects with their 'arms' and to release the objects over the peripheral wall outside the environment. The entire behavioral sequence that allows the organisms to accomplish this task can be divided up into a hierarchy of meaningful units. At the highest level of the hierarchy the sequence can be divided into two units: grasping an object and releasing the object beyond the wall. At the next lower level, in order to grasp an object the organism must find the object and in order to do so it must discriminate the object from the peripheral wall, approach and reach the object. At the lowest level the organism must explore the environment until it perceives an object. Also releasing the object on the other side of the wall can be divided into subsegments: avoid and ignore the other objects (since only one object can be grasped by the organism's arms), reach the wall, open the arms to release the object beyond the wall. Each of these segments is a meaningful behavioral unit. Our question is whether neural modules specialize for these units in the sense that different modules are used when a particular behavioral unit must be executed. We believe that this may be so for modules that emerge from genetic duplication and represent evolutionary specializations of already existing and functional modules whereas hardwired modules tend to be less clearly associated with meaningful behavioral segments.

Simulations

We ran a set of simulations in which two different populations of neural networks are trained to control a mobile robot designed to keep an arena clear by picking up trash objects and releasing them outside the arena. The robot has to look for 'garbage', somehow grasp it with its arms, and take it out of the arena.

The robot is a miniature mobile robot called Khepera, developed at E.P.F.L. in Lausanne (Mondada, Franzi, and Ienne 1993). The robot is supported by two wheels that allow it to move in various directions by regulating the speed of each wheel. In addition, the robot is provided with a gripper module with two degrees of freedom. The two arms of the gripper can move through any angle from vertical to horizontal while the gripper can assume only the open or closed position. The robot is also provided with six infrared proximity sensors positioned on the front of the robot and an optical barrier sensor on the gripper capable of detecting the presence of an object between the two arms of the gripper. The infrared sensors allow the robot to detect obstacles to a distance of about 4 cm. The environment is a rectangular arena 60x35 cm surrounded by walls and containing 5 objects. The walls are 3 cm in height and the objects are cylinders with a diameter of 2.3 cm and a height of 3 cm. The 5 objects are positioned randomly inside the arena. To speed up the evolutionary process a simulator of the physical robot and environment was used (see Nolfi 1997).

The basic network architecture is identical in the two populations (see Figure 2). The architecture includes 7 input units directly connected to 4 output units, each with its associated bias, for a total of (7x4)+4=32 connections. Six of the 7 input units continuously encode the activation level of the 6 infrared sensors while the seventh input unit binarily encodes whether (1) or not (0) there is an object between the two arms of the gripper. Two of the 4 output units continuously encode the speed of Khepera's two wheels. The remaining 2 output units binarily encode whether (1) or not (0) each of two procedures are executed by the robot: one output unit encodes the procedure of picking up an object and the other unit the procedure of releasing the object.

The two populations differ in the type of modularity that enriches this architecture (see Figure 2). In one population the architecture of all individual organisms includes two modules for each of the 4 output units since the beginning of evolution. More specifically, the architecture has two copies for each of the 4 output units, with each copy receiving its own set of connections from the input units. Which of the two alternative output units actually controls the robot's behavior in each particular input/output cycle is decided in the following way. Each copy of an output unit has associated with it a special unit called a 'selector' unit that receives connections from all the input units and has its own bias. In each cycle the simulator ascertains which of the two selector units is more activated and it uses the output unit corresponding to the more highly activated selector unit to determine the organism's behavior. One copy of each output unit, with its associated connections, plus its selector unit with its associated connections, constitute a module. For each output unit, therefore, there are two alternative modules that compete for controlling the organism's behavior and it is the input from the environment that ultimately decides which of the two alternative modules control the robot's behavior.

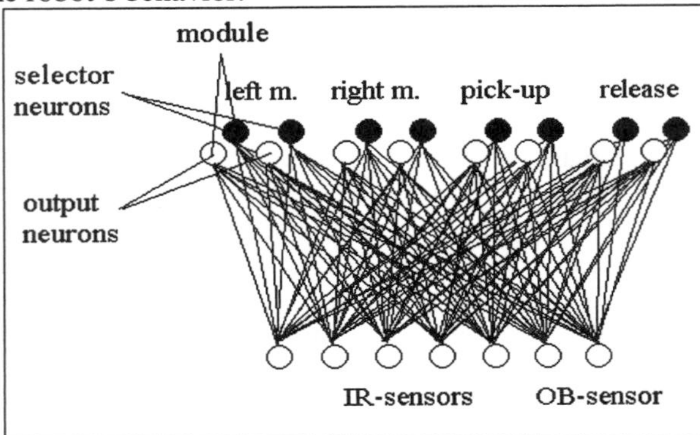

Figure 2. Modular neural network architecture of the two populations. The basic architecture is identical in the two populations. The two populations differ in the type of modularity which is added to this basic architecture. In one architecture two modules compete to gain control of each of the four actuators in all individuals since the beginning of evolution. In the second population the individuals of the initial generation have only one module for each motor. A second competing module may be added in individuals of later generations as a result of the duplication operator (see below). Another difference is that in the first population competing modules have different random weights at the beginning while in the second population when a second competing module is generated, the two competing modules have identical weights.

A genetic algorithm (Holland 1992) was used to evolve the connection weights of such neural networks. In the first population the genotype encodes the values for all the connection weights of the modular architecture. Since each module includes 7x2 connections plus 2 biases and there are 8 modules, the total number of connection weights encoded in the genotype is 128. Since each weight value is binarily encoded using 8 bits, the total genotype is a sequence of 128x8=1024 bits. The individuals of the first generation are assigned random values for these 1024 bits and then the evolutionary process progressively finds better and better genotypes on the basis of the selective reproduction of the best individuals and the addition of random mutations to inherited genotypes. Each generation includes 100 individuals. At the end of life the 20 best individuals are selected for reproduction and each of these individuals generates 5 offspring, that is, new individuals with the same genotype of their parent (reproduction is nonsexual). Genetic mutations consist in changing the value of about 10 bits in each genotype (1% mutation rate). The 20x5=100 new individuals constitute the second generation. The process is repeated for 1000 generations.

In the second population the genotypes of the initial generation encode random values for the connection weights of the single modules of the basic architecture : 32 (7x4=28 plus 4 biases) connections. However, since each of the 4 output units has associated with a nonfunctional selector unit with its 7 connection weights, the total number of connection weights encoded in the genotypes of the initial generation is 64. Notice however that until the module is not duplicated this selector unit remains completely nonfunctional and its associated connection weights are subject to random drift only. The genotype of this second population has 4 additional 'duplication genes' each associated with one of the 4 output units. When one of these duplication genes is turned on by some mutation the gene duplicates its corresponding module assigning to the duplicated module the same weight values of the original module. The duplication genes cause a duplication with some probability that we have varied in various simulations (i.e., 0.04%, 0.03% and 0.02% of the modules were duplicate in different simulations). In the generation in which the duplication of some module occurs there is no possible change in behavior since both alternative modules have the same connection weights but subsequently random mutations acting on the module's connections weights (both on those leading to the output unit and those leading to the selector unit of the module) can progressively differentiate the two alternate modules. (As in the first population, we used a mutation rate of 1%).

In conclusion, we have two populations. One population has a fixed, hardwired modular architecture since the beginning of the evolutionary process. What we can determine with respect to this first population is, first, whether the evolved individuals do actually make use of the alternate modules as a function of the circumstances or they only use a single module for all environmental inputs, and second, in the case they use alternate modules, whether or not we can attribute a functional meaning to the modules, i.e., whether or not distinct modules control meaningful behavioral units. The other population starts with a nonmodular architecture but it is free to evolve a modular architecture if that turns out to be adaptive. In the present model modules can be evolutionarily added to neural architectures (with a limit of one module for each motor output) but they cannot be deleted. Hence, because of purely random reasons the individuals in this second population will tend to approximate the modular architecture of the first population, with two alternate modules for each output unit. However, the modules of the second population have a different origin than those of the first population. Not only are they evolved rather than hardwired but while the modules of the first population all start with random weights and therefore two alternate modules for the same output unit both evolve from zero (random connection weights), the alternate modules in the second population start with the same weights of the original modules (since they duplicate these modules) and therefore with weight values that are already adapted. What we want to determine is if the different origin and evolutionary history of modules that arise out of genetic duplication results in modules endowed with a greater amount of functional meaning at the behavioral level.

Results

Both populations with modules reach a higher fitness level than a population with only the basic architecture and no modules (cf. Nolfi 1997 and Calabretta et al. 1997). However, the two populations with modules do not differ in terms of overall fitness except that fitness growth is slightly slower in the population with duplication-based modules (results not showed). In order to demonstrate that modularity plays a critical role, we varied the duplication rate in the population with duplication-based modules, with the result that both average and peak performance decreased linearly with a decreased duplication rate until the advantage of modular design was lost (see Calabretta et al. 1997).

We then examined the behavior of a typical evolved individual with hardwired modularity and a typical evolved individual with duplication-based modularity and found that an interesting difference emerged between the two individuals. While in the hardwired modular individual there was no correspondence between modules and meaningful behavioral units ('distal' description of behavior, according to Nolfi's definition), in the individual with duplication-based modularity neural modules or, better, combinations of neural modules turned out to be responsible for specific meaningful behavioral units (see Calabretta et al. 1997, Figure 5 and Figure 6).

In order to extend and reinforce this result we examined the best individual of the last generation in each of the 10 replications of the simulation for both populations and we compared the results concerning the statistical relationships between meaningful behavioral units and the use of the modules. Specifically, we considered as a meaningful behavioral unit the fact that the robot had or did not have a target object on the gripper. We tested the best individuals of the last generation in 10 different repetitions of the simulation for both populations. Each individual was allowed to live for 1 epoch consisting of 500 actions.

Seed	Hardwired modularity's chi-square values	Duplication-based modularity's chi-square values
1	11.135	368.662
2	4.679	246.374
3	425.927	495.961
4	2.747	218.359
5	21.556	190.511
6	439.391	55.947
7	16.647	55.246
8	2.348	296.993
9	29.078	32.334
10	27.081	321.769

Table 1. Chi-square values for the single best individuals of the last generation in each repetition (initial random seed) of the simulation for hardwired modularity (left) and duplication-based modularity (right).

For each action we recorded (in binary) both the state of the modules (i.e., which of the two available modules for each motor output was active) and if the meaningful behavioral unit was being executed or not. For each repetition of the simulation we calculated the linear regression between meaningful behavioral unit as a categorical dependent variable and the state of modules as a categorical independent variable. As we already have said, we wanted to test the prediction that modular architectures that originate in genetic duplication tend to have modules corresponding to meaningful behavioral units more often than architectures with hardwired modules.

Table 1 shows the chi-square values for each repetition of the simulation both in the case of hardwired modularity and of duplication-based modularity. If we look at the frequency distribution of chi-square values, two distinct pictures emerge for the two models (see Figure 3). For the hardwired modularity model chi-square values are very low in 8 out of 10 replications of the simulation; more precisely, these values are less than 20 in 5 replications and less than 30 in 3 replications (see left graph of Figure 3 and also Table 1).

In other words, there is a very low correlation between the meaningful behavioral unit we have selected for examination and the use of specific modules in 8 out of 10 replications of the simulations (in 4 replications of the simulations the correlation is not significant at all). Modules do not appear to be specialized for the specific meaningful behavioral unit we have considered. Conversely, for the duplication-based modularity model chi-square values are very high in 9 of 10 replications of the simulation; more precisely, they are higher than 100 in 7 replications and higher than 50 in 2 replications (see right graph of Figure 3 and Table 1). In statistical parlance, the dependent variable (i.e., the meaningful behavioral unit) can be said to be a function of the independent variable (i.e., the state of modules), that is, there is a significant correlation between the considered meaningful behavioral unit and the usage of modules in all the 10 replications of the simulation. (Notice that the degrees of freedom and the significance values vary in different simulations depending on how many modules are functional in particular neural networks). This means that combinations of neural modules are specialized for the specific meaningful behavioral unit we have considered and that evolved individuals tend to use different modules in different environmental situations. In other words, the prediction that modular architectures originating in genetic duplication tend to have modules corresponding to meaningful behavioral units more often than architectures with hardwired modules appears to be confirmed by the present results.

Interpretation and Conclusions

The results presented above are suggestive of a new mode of evolution for modularity. Modularity may critically depend on the duplication and subsequent divergence of units that are already partially adapted to some functional task. This proposed mechanism is thus different from the combination of directional and stabilized selection on preexisting characters proposed in Wagner (1996) as well as from the 'constructional' selection for genes with lower degrees of pleiotropy proposed by Altenberg (1995).

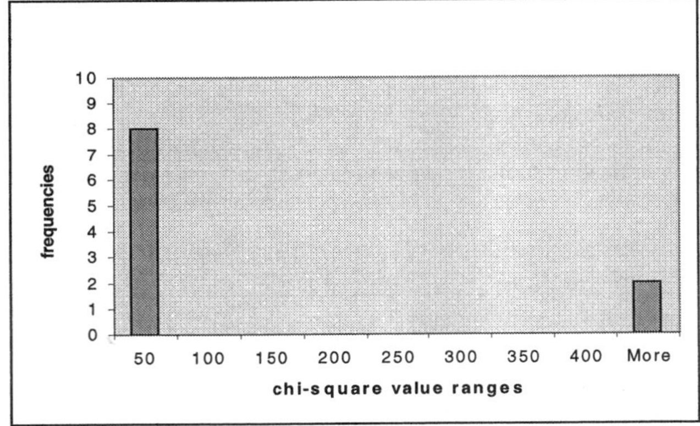

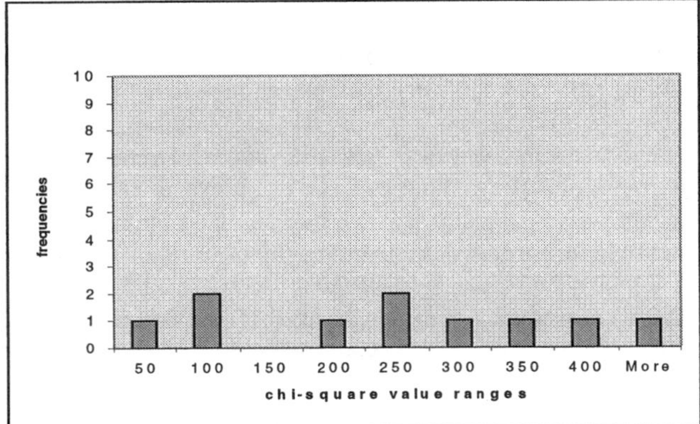

Figure 3. Frequency distribution of chi-square values shown in the Table 1, both in the case of hardwired modularity (left) and of duplication-based modularity (right).

We suggest the following scenario to explain the results of our simulations. In our model, the evolution of functional specialization depends on the partial adaptation of the units prior to the duplication event. We tested this by simulating the addition of neural units with random connection weights. The results of these simulations show that this does not lead to the origin of functionally specialized modules (results not shown). We assume that prior to duplication the units serve more than one function. We further assume that these multiple functions lead to functional conflicts in the optimization of functional performance. A duplication of a multi-functional unit then releases these constraints. Consequently the duplicated units are free to specialize for one of the functions and a modular mapping between functions and neural modules emerges. We are currently undertaking simulations to test this hypothesis.

This interpretation of our simulation results is similar to one model of evolution by gene duplication which has been proposed by Hughes (1994). The standard model, going back to Ohno (1970), assumes that the gene has only one function prior to duplication but that after duplication one copy is free to explore new functional opportunities. It has been argued that this model is problematic in assuming that new functions can be acquired by random search, i.e., mutation and random drift. An alternative model proposed by Hughes (1994) assumes that prior to duplication the gene is serving multiple functions, and that the performance of these functions is not optimal because of conflicting adaptive demands. After gene duplication, the two copies are released from the conflicting functional demands and each gene copy specializes for one of the functions of the ancestral gene. This model is supported by the preponderance of evidence about the functional history of duplicated genes (Hughes, 1994).

If correct, this interpretation about the origin of functional modularity raises important questions about the relationship between evolutionary mechanisms and evolvability. As emphasized by Bonner (1988) and Wagner and Altenberg (1996), modular genetic architectures are superior in their ability to produce functionally improved mutations. But the question remains whether these genetic architectures arise because of their impact on evolvability. There are a number of difficulties associated with the idea that evolvability arises as an adaptation to evolvability (for a recent discussion see Steward 1997). Our results further accentuate these problems, since the mechanism for the origin of modularity in our model does not derive from or is related to evolvability. Modularity appears to be a consequence of the evolution of functional specialization. Evolvability per se does not seem to be a factor in its origin. If this interpretation is correct, evolvability has to be seen as a secondary consequence of adaptation (effect selection) and not an adaptation to the evolvability of complex organisms.

Acknowledgments

Raffaele Calabretta would like to acknowledge a fellowship from the Italian National Research Council (Comitato 04), the assistantship of John W. Emerson of the Social Science Statistics Lab at Yale University for statistical analyses, the support of Jeffrey R. Powell, Valerio Sbordoni and Riccardo Galbiati, and the useful discussions with the members of the GPW's lab at Yale University during weekly meetings and with the members of the Research Group on Artificial Life (GRAL) in Rome.

References

Akam, M., Dawson, I., and Tear, G. 1989. Homeotic genes and the control of segment diversity. *Development* 104:123-133.

Altenberg, L. 1995. Genome growth and the evolution of the genotype-phenotype map. In *Evolution and Biocomputation. Computational Models of Evolution*, edited by W. Banzhaf and F. H. Eckman. Berlin-Heidelberg: Springer Verlag.

Ballard, D. H. 1986. Cortical connections and parallel processing: structure and function. *The Behavioral and Brain Sciences* 9:67-120.

Bonner, J. T. 1988. *The Evolution of Complexity*. Princeton, New Jersey: Princeton University Press.

Calabretta, R., Nolfi, S., Parisi, D., and Wagner, G. P. 1997. Evolutionary mechanisms for the origin of modular design in artificial neural networks, Technical Report, CCE-#51, Center of Computational Ecology, Yale University.

Calabretta, R., Nolfi, S., and Parisi, D. 1995. An artificial life model for predicting the tertiary structure of unknown proteins that emulates the folding process. In *Advances in artificial life. Lecture Notes in Artificial Intelligence 929:*862-875. Edited by F. Moran, A. Moreno, J.J. Merelo, and P. Chacon. Berlin-Heidelberg: Springer-Verlag.

Cho, S-B., and K. Shimohara. 1997. Emergence of structure and function in evolutionary modular neural networks. In *Fourth European Conference on Artificial Life*, edited by P. Husbands and I. Harvey. Cambridge, Mass.: MIT Press.

Coissac, E., Maillier, E., and Netter, P. 1997. A comparative study of duplications in bacteria and eukaryotes: the importance of telomeres. *Molecular Biology and Evolution* 14:1062-1074.

Cowey, A. 1981 Why are there so many visual areas? In *Models of the Visual Cortex*, edited by F. O. Schmitt, F. G. Warden, G. Adelman, and S. Dennis. New York, New York: John Wiley and Sons, p. 54-61.

Creighton, T. E. 1993. *Proteins: Structures and Molecular Properties*. New York, New York: W. H. Freeman and Company.

Doolittle, R. F. and Bork, P. 1993. La modularità delle proteine nell'evoluzione. *Le Scienze* 304:58-64.

Fodor, J. 1983. *Modularity of Mind*. Cambridge, Mass.: MIT Press.

Futuyma, D. J. 1998. *Evolutionary Biology*. Sunderland, Mass.: Sinauer.

Gruau, F. 1994. Automatic definition of modular neural networks. *Adaptive Behavior* 2:151-183.

Holland, J. H. 1992. Adaptation in Natural and Artificial Systems: An Introductory Analysis with Applications to Biology, Control, and Artificial Intelligence. Cambridge, Mass.: MIT Press.

Hughes, A. L. 1994. The evolution of functionally novel proteins after gene duplication. *Proceedings of Royal Society. Series B* 256:119-124.

Jacobs, R. A., Jordan, M. I., and Barto, A. G. 1991. Task decomposition trough competition in a modular connectionist architecture: the what and where vision task. *Cognitive Science* 15:219-250.

Kaas, J. H. 1989. Why does the brain have so many visual areas? *Journal of Cognitive Neuroscience* 1:121-135.

Karmiloff-Smith, A. 1992. *Beyond Modularity: A Developmental Perspective on Cognitive Science*. Cambridge, Mass: MIT Press.

Kimura, M. 1983. *The Neutral Theory of Molecular Evolution*. Cambridge, UK: Cambridge University Press.

Li, W-H. 1983. Evolution of duplicate genes and pseudogenes. In *Evolution of genes and proteins*, edited by M. Masatoshi and R. K. Koehn. Sunderland, Mass.: Sinauer.

Miglino, O., Nolfi, S., and Parisi, D. 1996. Discontinuity in evolution: how different levels of organization imply pre-adaptation. In *Adaptive Individuals in Evolving Populations*, edited by R. Belew and M. Mitchell. Reading, Mass.: Addison-Wesley.

Mondada, F., Franzi, E., and Ienne, P. 1993. Mobile robot miniaturisation: a tool for investigation in control algorithms. In *Proceedings of the Third International Symposium on Experimental Robotics*. Kyoto, Japan.

Moscovitch, M., and Umiltà, C. 1990. Modularity and neuropsychology: implications for the organization of attention and memory in normal and brain-demaged people. In *Modular Deficits in Alzheimer-type dementia*, edited by M. F. Schwartz. Cambridge, Mass.: MIT Press.

Müller, G. B., and Wagner, G. P. 1991. Novelty in evolution: restructuring the concept. *Annual Review of Ecology and Systematics* 22:229-256.

Nolfi, S. 1997. Using emergent modularity to develop control systems for mobile robots. *Adaptive Behavior* 5:343-363.

Nowak, M. A., Boerlijst, M. C., Cooke, J., and Maynard Smith, J. 1997. Evolution of genetic redundancy. *Nature* 388:167-171.

Ohno, S. 1970. *Evolution by Gene Duplication*. New York, New York: Springer Verlag.

Ohta, T. 1989. Role of gene duplication in evolution. *Genome* 31:304-310.

Rueckl, J. G., Cave, K. R., and Kosslyn, S. M. 1989. Why are «what» and «where» processed by separate cortical visual systems? A computational investigation. *Journal of Cognitive Neuroscience* 1:171-186.

Rumelhart, D., and McClelland, J. 1986. Parallel Distributed Processing: Explorations in the Microstructure of Cognition. Cambridge, Mass: MIT Press.

Snoad, N. and Bossomaier, T. 1995. MONSTER - the ghost in the connection machine: modularity of neural systems in theoretical evolutionary research. http://www.chg.ru/SC95PROC/531_NSNO/SC95.HTM.

Stevens, C. 1994. Complexity of brain circuits. In *Complexity: Methaphors, Models and Reality*, edited by G. A. Cowan, D. Pines, and D. Meltzer. Reading, Mass.: Addison-Wesley, p. 245-261.

Steward, J. 1997. The evolution of genetic cognition. *Journal of Social and Evolutionary Systems* 20:53-73.

Tautz, D. 1992. Redundancies, development and the flow of information. *BioEssays* 14:263-266.

Wagner, G. P. 1995. Adaptation and the modular design of organisms. In *Advances in Artificial Life. Lecture Notes in Artificial Intelligence* 929: 317-328, edited by F. Moran, A. Moreno, J. J. Merelo, and P. Chacon. Berlin-Heidelberg: Springer-Verlag.

Wagner, G. P. 1996. Homologues, natural kinds and the evolution of modularity. *American Zoologist* 36:36-43.

Wagner, G. P., and Altenberg, L. 1996. Complex adaptations and the evolution of evolvability. *Evolution* 50:967-976.

Weiss, K. 1990. Duplication with variation: metameric logic in evolution from genes to morphology. *Yearbook of Physical Anthropology* 33:1-23.

On Searching Generic Properties of Non-Generic Phenomena: An Approach to Bioinformatic Theory Formation

Paulien Hogeweg
Bioinformatics Group, Utrecht University
Padualaan 8, 3584CH Utrecht, The Netherlands.
Email ph@binf.biol.ruu.nl

Abstract

In this paper we first review the current view of the evolution of complexity and novelty in biotic evolution. Next we show that the basic processes thereof do happen automatically and are generic properties of systems including the basic mechanisms of Darwinian evolution *plus* **local**, as opposed to global, interactions. Thus we show that the multilevel evolution so generated can be studied within the paradigm 'simple rules lead to complex phenomena'. We derive some results demonstrating the power of such multilevel evolutionary processes to integrate information at multiple space and time scales.

Nevertheless, we also point out shortcomings of such an approach which necessarily uses a priori chosen and preferentially relatively simple interaction schemes. However, straightforward extensions towards more complex interaction schemes generally leads to *ad-hoc*ness and over-determinedness, rather than fundamentally new behavior of the system, and often to less understanding of that behavior. Still, biological theory formation needs a method to go beyond the generic behavior of simple interaction schemes.

We propose to use evolutionary optimization of very trivial fitness functions which are obtainable in many different ways, to push back the necessary *a priori* choices and to zoom in on interesting non-generic phenomena and their general properties. We thus derive insights into relationships between sets of derived properties at several scales. We discuss how this approach can be used in biological theory formation, focusing on information accumulation and utilization in replicator systems and immune systems.

Introduction

Reasoning from a chemical point of view, de Duve (1995) portrays *'life as a cosmic necessity'*. Maynard Smith and Szathmáry (1995b; 1995a), reconstructing the course of evolution, conclude that a limited number of major transitions shaped living systems as we know them today, and that these major transitions involved the processes of symbiogenesis, conflicts among levels of selection, division of labor, and the transition from limited inheritance to universal inheritance. Studying evolution from a bioinformatic point of view, we have shown that the first three of these major transition defining processes are generic consequences of extending basic mutation and selection with local interactions. Thus, we might also portray *'life as a* local *necessity'*.

Nevertheless, due to inheritance-based information accumulation, we can hardly study, e.g., an elephant as a generic property of matter or information: many of its properties appear to be arbitrary accidents. Even though indeed chance is an inalienable part of life, there may be stronger constraints than now appears. Biological modeling usually either focuses on those phenomena which are 'generic', or simply aims at mimicking properties observed in a particular system. For better understanding biotic systems we have to face the difficult question of how we can obtain generic theories of non-generic phenomena.

In other words, we usually study either how complex behavior is generated from simple rules, or how simple (in the sense of a priori definable) behavior is generated by complex rules. Understanding biological systems requires that we also face the difficult question of studying complex behavior generated by complex rules, without getting lost in arbitrary over-determinedness.

In this paper we present one approach for doing this. It involves focusing on 'side effects' of evolutionary optimization where the optimization criterion is extremely 'uninteresting', and can better be seen as a minimal condition than as 'goal'. We present two examples in which we employ our approach. Using diversity of entities as optimization criterion, we derive relationships between the topology of catalytic networks, self-structuring and information storage and utilization: self-structuring is a prerequisite for information storage and utilization. Using recognition of pathogens as optimization criterion, we derive a relationship between genetic operators and immune system diversity, and thus obtain a hypothesis to explain differences between vertebrate and invertebrate immune systems. In all cases the observed patterns can only be observed in the evolved systems because the 'random' initial condition of the evolutionary optimization displays none of the features which we would like to study.

Evolution of Complexity in Biotic Systems

Biotic systems are multilevel systems. Indeed, the interplay between partial independent processes at many space, time, and organizational scales appears to be the preeminent hallmark of biotic complexity. Classical population genetic and evolutionary theory does not address the generation of complexity, and indeed its occurrence does not seem to follow automatically from a 'survival of the fittest' point of view (and indeed biotic systems can also become simpler in evolutionary time). Nevertheless complex multilevel systems did arise.

Reconstructing biological evolution, Maynard Smith and Szathmáry (1995b; 1995a) conclude that such complexity arises by 'major transitions in evolution', of which the basic ingredients are:

1. Symbiogenesis, i.e., the process by which independent replicators give up their self-sufficiency and become 'parts of a whole'. Examples include eukaryotic organelles (mitochondria,chloroplasts) which evolved from prokaryote precursors, worker castes in social insects, etc.

2. Conflicts among levels of selection. In the wake of symbiogenesis, conflicts of levels of selection can arise where the parts of a whole re-evolve partial independence, and deteriorate the 'whole'. Evolution of uniparental inheritance of organelles appears as one of many 'countermeasures' to such a process,

3. Division of labor, by which 'tasks' or 'functions' initially performed by one type of entity, are later subdivided among a number of 'specialized' entities. This process occurs again at many levels: differentiation in 'germ-line' and 'soma', and again in social insects in the evolution of specialized worker casts.

4. Transition from limited inheritance to universal inheritance, and therewith the generation of 'universal' coding schemes. As examples, Maynard Smith and Szathmáry (1995b) list the evolution from autocatalytic sets to template-based replication in early stages of evolution, the evolution of a dual inheritance system in metazoans and the transition from signal-based communication to universal grammar-based languages in the later stages of evolution.

In their treatment, they recognize the universality of these processes from a chemical and natural history perspective, and discuss some of the evolutionary consequences and constraints *given* the occurrence of these processes. As one of the important premises, they take that any hypothesized intermediate structure should be selectionally advantageous *in the short run.*

Similar conclusions about major transitions were also independently (and earlier) derived by Fontana and Buss (1994b; 1994a) both on theoretical and natural history grounds. In their treatment, they stress that it is especially these processes which "would be repeated in alternate 'worlds' ". They studied random *non self-replicating* metabolic nets and show that the novel interactions are automatically created when independently evolved catalytic networks are brought into contact. Thus, they derive 'organization for free'. However, because they utilize global interactions, only one 'organization' exists and the mechanisms of Darwinian evolution are absent.

In the next section we review results of replicator networks subject to simple Darwinian mutation/selection processes in space, and show that in space the processes associated with the major transitions are an automatic consequence of mutation and selection, via the generation of higher levels of selection due to spatial self-organization. Moreoverm we show that in multilevel systems the assumption of necessary short-term fitness benefits is relaxed.

Local Interactions and the Emergence of Multiple Levels of Selection

Self-structuring is an ubiquitous property of locally interacting systems. The relationship between self-structuring and Darwinian evolutionary processes can be seen in terms of
(a) self-structuring as constraint on achievable structures
(b) self-structuring as alternative to Darwinian selection
(c) self-structuring as a substrate for Darwinian selection.
The latter point of view is, in our view, the most fruitful. We will show that through self-structuring, multiple levels of selection arise with novel interactions and novel fitness dimensions. In this sense, self-structuring enhances rather than constrains the power of Darwinian evolution. (Whether or not it does so for engineering purposes is an open question, although some examples suggest that it does (Hillis 1992; Pagie & Hogeweg 1998b)).

The simplest way of defining an evolutionary process is to define some set of predefined interactions between replicators and subject one (or a few) of the parameters of the system to mutations (selection automatically ensues from the dynamics of the system). Evolutionary systems so-defined can neither redefine their interactions nor redefine their genetic representations, both of which are important in open-ended evolution. The dynamics of the system can, however, redefine the fitness of the replicators, which is also crucial for open-ended evolution. Indeed, we have shown that because of the latter feature, even such simple evolutionary systems can give rise to processes akin to those recognized by Maynard Smith and Szathmáry (1995b) as associated with major transitions in evolution, provided that the interactions between the replicators are defined locally. This is because local interactions will lead to the formation of higher level structures (e.g., spiral waves, turbulence, patch-like structures of different sizes) which constitute new levels of selection. We have shown this in a variety of coevolutionary systems, evolving, e.g., strength of 'help' (e.g., catalysis) in cooperative systems (Boerlijst & Hogeweg 1991a; 1991b; Couwenberg & Hogeweg 1998), predation efficiency (Boerlijst, Lamers, & Hogeweg 1993; Savill & Hogeweg 1997) dispersal rate (Savill & Hogeweg 1998) or parasitoid aggregation strength (Savill, Rohani, & Hogeweg 1997). Here we summarize the major conclusions of this work.

- **Feedback of mesoscale entities on microscale entities through multilevel selection**
  The micro-scale replicators generate mesoscale entities, but, via mutation and selection, the reverse is also true: the mesoscale entities generate the microscale entitles by which they are made. This may lead to and maintain microscale entities which are non viable or less viable without the mesoscale entities. For example, the microscale entities may evolve to a shorter lifespan, or minimize the catalysis it obtains for self-replication, because this enhances the competitive strength of the mesoscale entity which they generate. This was shown in cases where oscillatory dynamics between the microscale entities leads to spiral waves in spatial systems. These spiral waves compete for space, and the fastest rotating spirals win. Shorter lifespan and less catalysis leads to faster rotating spirals and hence to microscale entities with these (seemingly) unfavorable properties. (Boerlijst & Hogeweg 1991a; 1991b).

- **Self-enhancement of mesoscale entities**
  The direction of selection enforced on the microscale entities appears to be such that it tends to favor the competitive strengths of the mesoscale entities they generate. For example, in a host-parasitoid system (Savill, Rohani, & Hogeweg 1997), regions of spiral waves and regions of turbulence occur. In the spiral-wave area, the aggregation parameter evolves to lower values which favors the formation of spiral waves over turbulence and the reverse is true in the turbulence areas: there, aggregation evolves to higher values for which spiral waves can not be formed or even maintained.

- **Symbiogenesis**
  The properties of local interacting, evolutionary systems mentioned in the items above embody a process reminiscent of 'Symbiogenesis', in that self-sufficiency is (partly) given up in favor of the larger scale entities.

- **Conflicts between levels of selection**
  Conflicts between levels of selection are inherent in this process; in fact, it is the reversal of the direction of selection which, within the system, defines the emergence of a new level of selection.

- **Division of labor**
  Division of labor is also inherent in the formation of mesoscale entities. All entities 'do only what there is to do' and for the microscale entities this depends on the position they occupy in the mesoscale entities. For example, in spiral waves, only the entities in the core of the spiral in the long run produce offspring, those in the spiral arms become extinct. Thus a kind of 'germ-line' and 'soma' differentiates.

- **Direct vs Indirect interactions**
  In contrast to globally defined ecoevolutionary system in which all replicators are interacting and competing with equal probability with all other replicators, in spatial systems with only locally interactions 'who out-competes whom' can not simply be assessed on the basis of a few of the direct links (those in which the competing entities are directly involved) of the interaction network of which they are a part: all links may play a role as they help to define the mesoscale patterns and their properties. Thus, local interactions in space generate new indirect interdependencies of the system.

- **Short term observations are insufficient to asses long term fitness**
  Short-term fitness and long-term fitness may be quite different. This is shown in Fig. 1 for the host-parasitoid system studied by (Savill, Rohani, & Hogeweg 1997). Host-parasitoid interactions are modeled by a spatial extension of the classical Nicholson Bailey equations. Parasitoid aggregation strength is the evolving parameter. Over a time-span of up to 50 generations (left panel), parasitoids with a larger aggregation tendency produce more offspring than those with less aggregation tendency, wherever they are located in space. Nevertheless, in the long run (right panel), those with the weakest aggregation tendency 'inherit the world'. It is caused by the above-mentioned property of spiral waves that only the entities in the core of spirals will give rise to offspring in the long run. Note that this is a property of the 'attractor' of the system and true for any short-term vs long-term time slice.
  Long term information integration in evolutionary processes also is strikingly apparent in experiments which use coevolving populations of 'problems' and 'solutions' for function optimization (Hillis 1992; Pagie & Hogeweg 1998b): the availability of only very sparse information per generation of the function to be optimized, even improves the chance of obtaining the globally correct solutions. Experimental biologists surely

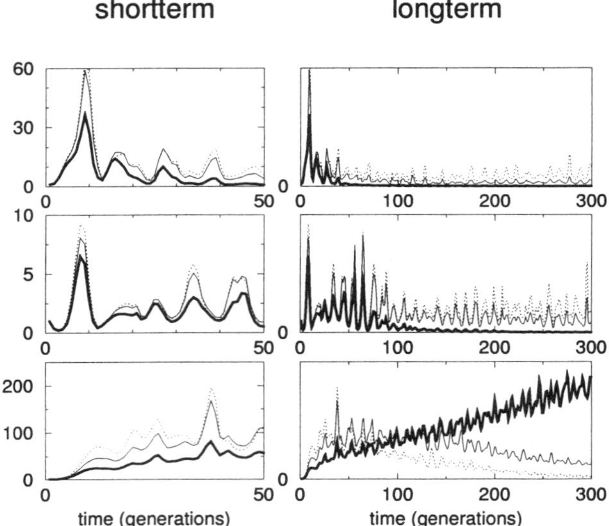

Figure 1: **Short-term and long-term fitness**
The left panels show short-term fitness (50 generations) and the right panels long-term fitness (300 generations) at 3 different locations in space (top in spiral arm, middle in chaotic region, bottom in spiral core.) The vertical axis gives average number of offspring per individual parasite with different aggregation tendency towards their host: thick line low-, thin line intermediate- and dotted line high aggregation tendency.
At all locations high aggregation tendency gives the highest number of offspring over a time slice of 50 generations. Nevertheless, in the long run the fitness of parasites with the lowest aggregation tendency is highest. Note that this is the case in the eco-evolutionary attractor of the system, i.e., for any time slice of 50 vs 300 generations.

cannot be envied: assessing inclusive fitness seems a time-consuming–and in fact impossible–task.

We conclude that even in these systems with inflexible information storage and transmission, major transitions involving the generation of new levels of selection is a basic property of mutation/selection processes *iff* interactions are local (as they indeed necessarily are!) Thus, as an addition to de Duve's assessment on chemical grounds of 'life as a global imperative', with respect to its multilevel properties we can regard 'life is a local imperative'.

We like to stress that the above listed properties all
(a) were quite unexpected from a simple minded 'survival of the fittest' point of view, and appear to enhance the 'versatility' of Darwinian selection processes in the sense that they go beyond optimization of the behavior of predefined entities by generating novel ones, and complex interactions between different levels of selection.
(b) can provide explanations for as yet not understood observations on many specific biological systems. For example, recently we have studied spatial eco-evolutionary systems which provide explanations for the shape of influenza phylogenies, which show stagnating evolution (flat phylogeny) for virus strains taken from birds, and rapid, progressive evolution (steep phylogeny) for virus strains taken from pigs or humans. Assuming a shorter lifespan, or shorter immunological memory for birds than mammals (or a larger universe) the striking difference in phyloginies arises due to self-structuring into two-armed spiral waves in birds vs chaotic waves in mammals (Hogeweg 1998). Another example is the occurrence of a large variety of toxic plasmids in bacteria and fungi which has puzzled micro-biologists and has led to hypotheses on additional (as yet unidentified) functions of those plasmids which might benefit their hosts. We have shown that such diversity of plasmid is an automatic consequence of the information integration capabilities of local interactions in spatial systems (Pagie & Hogeweg 1998a).
(c) are a direct consequence of the formation of 'generic' patterns, e.g., spiral waves, turbulence, patches of different sizes, etc.

Thus notwithstanding the novel insights in the dynamic potential Darwinian selection processes in space, they do not give us 'novel' entities, as biotic evolution undoubtedly has (e.g., elephants). Thus, we have not yet surpassed the stage for which Maynard Smith urged all evolutionary biologists to go once a year to the zoo, stand in front of the elephant and proclaim: 'elephant I believe you came about by random mutation and selection', even if now we can add 'plus local interactions creating new levels of selection'.

Beyond Generic Patterns: Complex to Complex Mappings

Simple rules may give rise to complex behavior. This was an interesting issue 10 years ago (at the first ALIFE conference) and has now become common place. In the time since then we have seen that evolutionary optimization most often leads to complex implementations when it is free to choose its implementation (as in Genetic Programming) even in the case when fairly simple coding would be possible.

Observation of biotic systems suggests a complex-to-complex mapping. Studying such complex-to-complex mappings without getting lost in over-determinedness and *ad hoc*ness therefore seems an important challenge for biological theory formation.

Obviously in the above observations, simple and complex are not well defined but can be operationalized with respect to our own (in)ability and/or willingness to a-priori conceive, make, understand or define it, although we may be able to observe it once it is there.

A complex-to-complex mapping thus means that neither the micro rules nor the macro behavior is a priori definable, whereas in the paradigms above at least one of them necessarily is a priori 'in hand', and therefore restrict us to studying complex behavior which is generic for *some (a priori chosen)* set of simple rules, or studying implementations for *some (a priori chosen)* simple functions.

The most important contribution of the simple-to-complex paradigm for bioinformatic modeling of specific systems is the possibility (and in fact necessity) of 'non goal-oriented modeling', i.e., a modeling approach in which we do not specify a priori the phenomena to be modeled. This is a necessary consequence of the simple-to-complex paradigm, as explicit modeling efforts of the complex behavior would seldom lead us to very simple rules. In a non goal-oriented modeling paradigm we therefore formulate a set of simple rules which aim to implement only some of the context in which the complex behavior that we are interested occurs. Observing the so-obtained systems we search for side-effects of the rules, which among quite expected and unexpected phenomena may also represent some (traces) of the phenomena we were interested in to begin with, and point at connections (via the simple rules) between the observed, a priori apparently independent, phenomena (Hogeweg & Hesper 1989; Hogeweg 1988). Examples are given in (Hogeweg & Hesper 1985; te Boekhorst & Hogeweg 1994a; 1994b).

The approach to complex-to-complex mapping we propose is an extension of this modeling methodology which additionally uses evolutionary optimization to zoom in on non-generic 'initial' conditions or 'not-so-simple' rules. The optimization criterion to be used in the evolutionary optimization should: (1) not represent directly the phenomena in which we are interested, but only represent some kind of boundary condition for them and (2) should be realizable in (many) different ways. Moreover, the coding used in the evolutionary optimization should be such that it is to some extent 'free' to choose a realization. We study the side effects of the 'not-so-simple' rules and 'not-so-general' initial conditions so obtained by observing the resulting systems in a similar way as above.

We have applied this idea to investigate issues related to the potential for and the role of (more or less (un)limited) inheritable information accumulation and utilization. This relates to the fourth ingredient of the major transitions in evolution listed by Maynard Smith and Szathmáry (1995b), which was not addressed in our 'simple-to-complex' experiments discussed above (which did nevertheless display the three other ingredients). We discuss these experiments and the results obtained in the next section.

Bioinformatic Theory Formation of Non-Generic Phenomena

We discuss two examples of using evolutionary optimization towards a rather 'uninteresting' target to zoom in on 'interesting' systems for bioinformatic theory formation. The background of the first example is basic bioinformatic theory related to complex replicator networks (Eigen & Schuster 1979; May 1972) and the above discussion on the role of self-structuring in evolution, whereas the second example relates to a more specific question and apart from addressing our questions about (un)limited heredity, confronts our approach to the more usual approach in theoretical biology.

The potential role of DNA in an RNA world:

unlimited inheritance needs self-organization and multiple levels of selection

In contrast to metabolic networks of non-selfreplicators (compare (Fontana & Buss 1994b; 1994a) networks of replicators generically cannot maintain high diversity. Exceptions are specific interaction topologies and systems with high mutation (or influx) rates (e.g., (Kaneko & Ikegami 1992; Forst 1997)). What are the properties of those replicator networks which can maintain high diversity, and what is the role of information storage and the occurrence of multiple levels of selection in this context? Moreover, what is the relation between information storage and multiple levels of selection? We studied these questions by evolving a population of CAs in each of which locally interacting networks of catalytic replicators compete, with species diversity in the CA as fitness criterion. We performed these experiments with and without allowing pattern formation, and with and without allowing information storage (in the form of long-lived non-catalytic counterparts of the catalytic self-replicators, i.e., in the form of DNA in an RNA world; DNA is 'transcribed' due to catalysis by the same RNAs which catalyze its RNA transcript). For more details see (Hogeweg 1994a; 1994b) The results show:

- After long evolutionary time, the temporal persistence of the evolved species diversity is indefinite, although the lifetime over which species diversity is contributing to individual fitness is relatively short. This is due to evolution towards a relatively smooth part of the landscape (Huynen & Hogeweg 1994). In other words, this mechanism results in the resolution of conflicts between levels of selection: in contrast to arbitrary sets of replicators, none of the final individual replicator species takes over in spite of the fact that the higher level selection pressure is removed.
  This indefinite persistence of the evolved networks allows us to study the evolved networks independently of the top-level evolutionary dynamics, and thus use

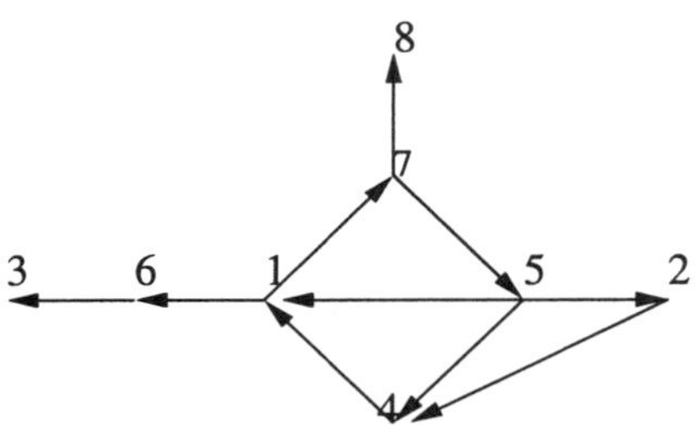

Figure 2: Evolved network. Node numbers correspond to curves in next figure (bottom to top).

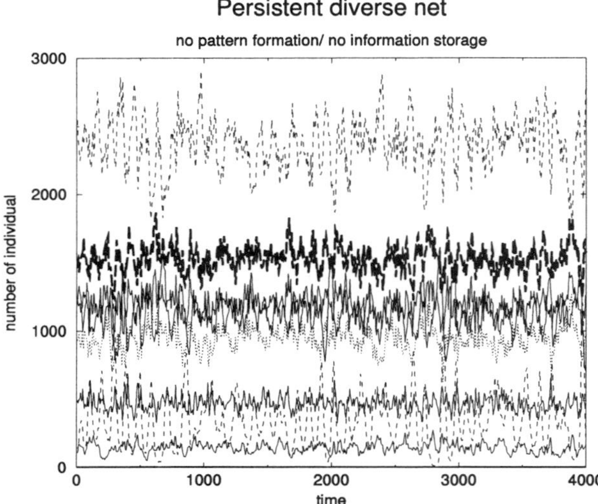

Figure 3: Attractor of the evolved network. Diversity is conserved also without information usage. Parasitic chains do not destroy the network because of strong non-linear catalysis, local interactions, and interlocked cycles (see previous figure)

the CA evolution as tool to obtain non-generic, but also non-*ad-hoc*, and interesting initial conditions for studying the diverse replicator networks and the role of information therein.

- The well-mixed systems, i.e., those without pattern formation, evolved replicator networks with the following properties:
  (1) The networks contain a few short interlocked cycles with a few 'parasitic' chains with not more than 8-10 replicators in total. (see Fig. 2);
  (2) Information storage is necessary for evolution of species diversity clearly above that occurring in random networks (because it enables the simultaneous incorporation of more then one new species in the RNA network), but
  (3) the amount of information stored is minimized. Moreover,
  (4) the stored information in almost never used and indeed not needed for the maintenance of diversity. Thus all the information available is dynamically contained as the (chaotic) attractor of the RNA network (see Fig. 3).
  (5) Such an attractor with relatively many species is rare and is not found by random initialization even of replicators interacting with this particular network topology. Evolutionary optimization is needed as a tool to find both the network and the initial conditions which lead to the attractor.

- The spatial systems with local diffusion, i.e., the systems with pattern formation, evolved replicator networks with the following properties.
  (1) The networks contain many more species and consist of (several) 2-cycles with long parasitic chains.
  (2) Information storage is not necessary to evolve diverse networks, nevertheless when information storage is allowed,
  (3) information storage is maximized. Moreover,
  (4) the stored information is regularly transcribed and thus a greater variety of RNA species is maintained then contained in an attractor of the RNA network alone.
  Fig. 5 compares the dynamics of a network which has evolved with information storage, when this information is available or not: the 'transcription' of the stored information not only increases diversity due to the temporary presence of 'transient' RNA species, but also stabilizes the competition between mesoscale patterns, and thus allows more 'permanent' RNA species in the system.

Fig. 4 contrasts the use of stored information in systems with and without pattern formation. As stated above, in the latter, diversity is maintained in the attractor of the catalytic replicators, and the stored information is not (or barely) expressed, whereas the former crucially relies for its (larger) diversity on the stored information (if and only if it is available).

The major conclusion is:

In replicator systems (i.e., in the RNA world) the transition from limited to unlimited inheritance is only evolutionary favored when multiple levels of selection develop due to spatial self-organization.

Genetic operators and immune repertoire diversity:

Somatic recombination biases evolution towards complexity 'beyond need'

How large should the immune repertoire be? And why is it much larger in vertebrates then in invertebrates: both seem to cope? Assuming random repertoires, the issue of repertoire size has previously been studied in

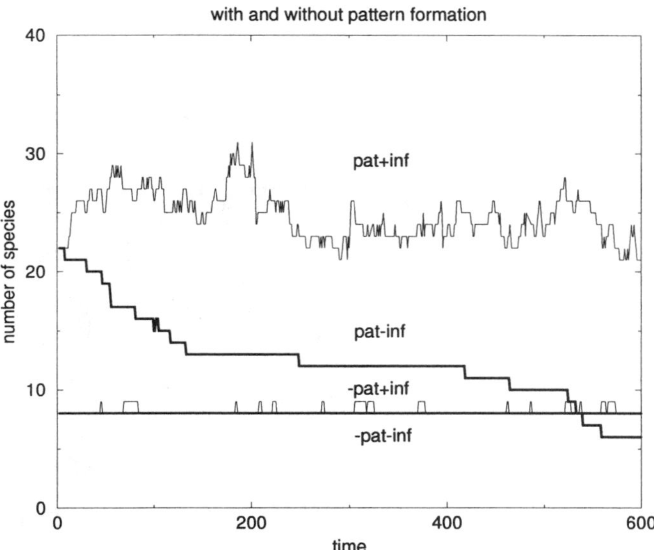

Figure 4: Dynamics of evolved networks. Information is stored during evolution, in all cases Information availability and pattern formation is as shown in figure: only in the case of pattern formation is the stored information exploited

terms of allowing optimal distinction between self and non-self antigens, focusing on evolutionary time or physiological time and including a more or less explicit structure of the (vertebrate) immune system respectively: (Percus & Perelson 1993; de Boer & Perelson 1993; Borghans & de Boer 1998). Within a partial implementation of the above-sketched modeling methodology Takumi and Hogeweg (1998) studied this question by evolving immune systems using either a genetic coding as in vertebrates (i.e., including somatic recombination) or as in invertebrates (direct encoding). Using a fixed set of pathogens to be recognized by the immune system and ignoring the issue of self/non-self discrimination we have shown:

- Vertebrates and invertebrates cope equally well with the same set of pathogens, but do so in a different way.
- The vertebrate immune system evolves large repertoires, and the invertebrate immune system evolves small repertoires.
- Moreover, the evolved repertoires cope much better with evolving or random sets of pathogens than a random repertoire does. This is true for both the vertebrate and the invertebrate case although the vertebrate case does somewhat better.

We conclude with respect to the issues of complex-to-complex mappings and limited vs unlimited inheritance:

- Answering biological questions by models which use 'random' initial conditions may lead to misleading results, because evolved systems may behave very non-random. In the case studied here:
- Questions of repertoire size (as well as immune system behavior in general) may not be answerable in terms of random repertoires: evolved repertoires behave very differently. Moreover,
- similar problems can be solved in entirely different ways. Genetic coding can determine which 'solution' is chosen, and therewith what behavior is obtained 'for free'.
- Differences in repertoire size (or other properties of biotic systems) do not necessarily reflect differences in the environment to which they adapted, but rather are also a consequence of the way genetic information is stored and retrieved.
- Somatic recombination adds coding potential to a genome of limited length. In the above example this added potential is employed without rendering direct fitness benefit, i.e., it leads to autonomic increase in complexity which is not 'needed' in the system as defined. (but may pave the way for future evolution, in this case, e.g., self/non-self discrimination.)

Discussion and Conclusions

Nowadays, we are not protected by technical limitations against formulating, and to a certain extent studying, systems including much specialized knowledge and/or many special assumptions. The behavior observed and studied in many systems formulated accordingly, does not (or barely), go beyond that observed in more simple systems where we can study and understand the behavior much better. Moreover by studying simpler systems it is easier to focus on 'generic' properties occurring in many contexts (including more complicated systems).

We have argued that in addition to studying generic properties of minimally defined systems with random initial conditions, it is possible (and seems profitable) to try to derive general properties of relatively 'rare' and complicated systems, while minimizing a priori assumptions. One way of doing this is by studying the side-effects of evolutionary optimization towards a target which describes the boundary conditions of the systems in which we are interested, rather than those aspects in which we are interested. It is the ubiquity of side effects and the existence of alternative solutions which make this method fruitful. So derived 'special' but not (entirely) 'arbitrary' systems reveal general tendencies and relations absent in most arbitrary (be it knowledge-poor or rich) systems, but important for the class of systems exhibiting the boundary conditions used in the optimization process. At the very least, as shown, such

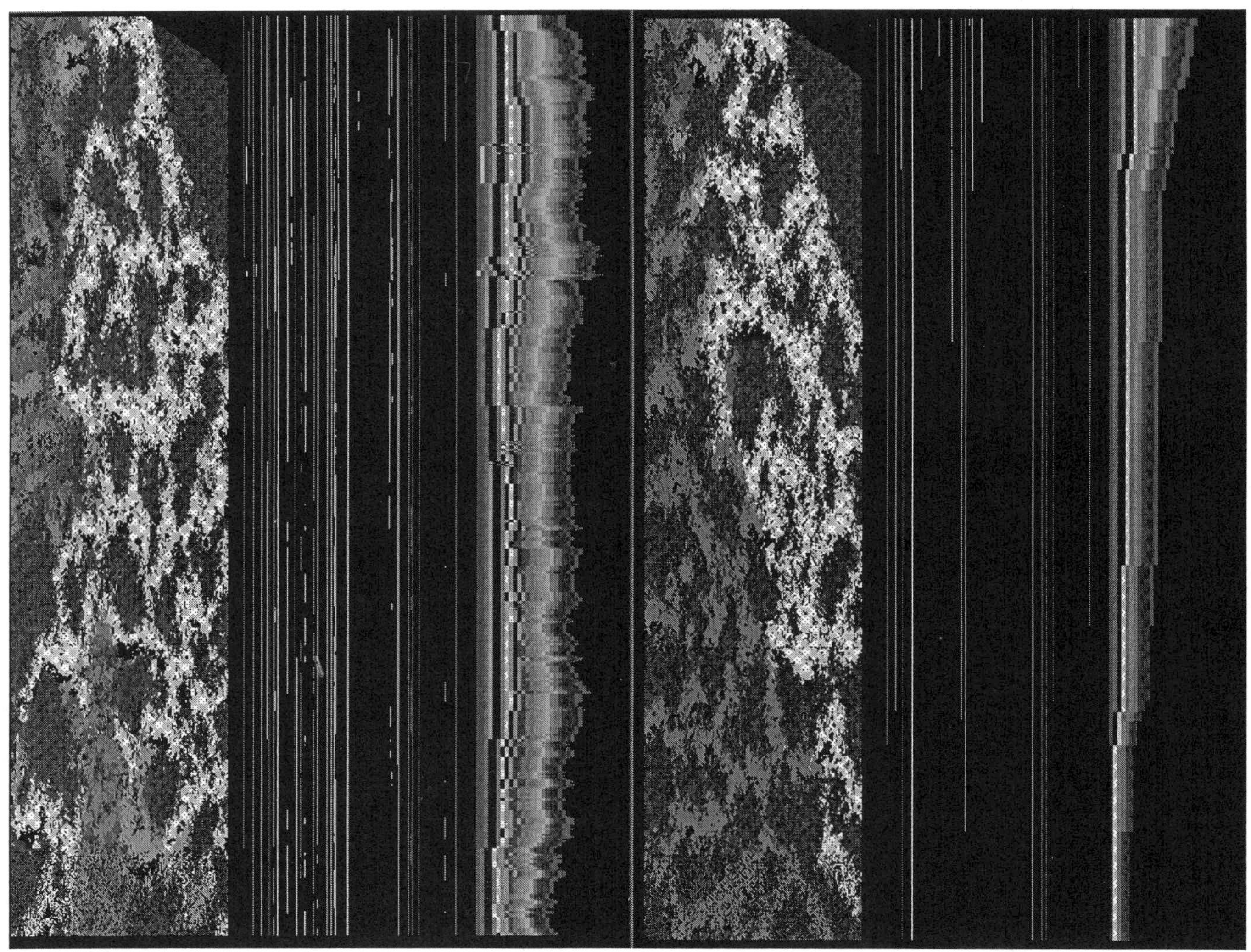

Figure 5: Spatial self-organization and the use of stored information: Interaction network evolved with pattern formation and with information storage. Three left hand panels: the stored information is available; diversity is high. Three righthand panels: the stored information is *not* available; diversity is lost. Left: space-time plot; middle: profile of RNA species present; right: number of species). A color version of this plot is available on the CD-ROM accompanying these proceedings.

systems will provide counterexamples for unquestioned assumptions, which are often implicitly or explicitly derived from random (rather than evolved) systems.

In our examples we have used this method in addition to minimally defined locally interacting evolutionary systems, to study evolution itself, in particular questions about long-term information storage, transmission, and utilization, i.e., inheritability. In this respect, our results showed that self-structuring may be a prerequisite to exploit stored information (i.e., for the transition from attractor-based ('limited') inheritance to 'storage-based' ('less limited') inheritance. Moreover, when the actual use of stored information is assumed (as it usually is in evolutionary models) self-structuring allows long-term information integration. Thus we conclude that self-structuring should neither be seen as an alternative for–nor as a constraint on–'evolution', but as the substrate on which it operates. It is the interplay between self-structuring and mutation and selection processes which create the 'major transitions' (and novelty) in evolution.

Acknowledgements

I thank Maarten Boerlijst, John Couwenberg, Martijn Huynen, Ludo Pagie and Katsuhisa Takumi for their collaboration and their contribution to the experiments presented here. I thank moreover Ben Hesper for his long-term conceptual support.

References

Boerlijst, M. C., and P. Hogeweg. 1991a. Self-structuring and selection: spiral waves as a substrate for evolution. In *Artificial Life II*, edited by C.G. Langton, C. Taylor, J. D. Farmer and S. Rasmussen. Redwood City, CA: Addison-Wesley, p. 255–276.

Boerlijst, M. C., and P. Hogeweg. 1991b. Spiral wave structure in pre-biotic evolution: hypercycles stable against parasites. *Physica* D 48: 17–28.

Boerlijst, M., M. Lamers, and P. Hogeweg. 1993. Evolutionary consequences of spiral waves in host parasitoid systems. *Proc. Roy. Soc. London* B 253: 15–18.

Borghans, J. and R. de Boer. 1998. How specific should memory be? (in prep).

Couwenberg, J. and P. Hogeweg. 1998 On the fate of cheaters in ecological and evolutionary timescales (in prep).

de Boer, R. and A. Perelson. 1993. How diverse should the immune system be? *Proc. R. Soc. London* B 252: 171–175.

de Duve, C. 1995. *Vital Dust: Life as a Cosmic Imperative.* New York: Basic Books.

Eigen, M. and P. Schuster. 1979. *The hypercycle: A Principle of Natural Self-organization.* Berlin, Heidelberg, New York: Springer-Verlag.

Fontana, W. and L. Buss. 1994a. The arrival of the fittest: Towards a theory of biological organization. *Bull. Math. Biol* 56: 1–64.

Fontana, W. and L. Buss. 1994b. What would be conserved 'if the tape were played twice'. *Proc. Nat. Acad. Sci. (USA)* 91: 757–761.

Forst, C. 1997. Molecular evolution of catalysis. In *Proceedings of ECAL IV*, edited by P. Husbands and I. Harvey, Cambridge, MA: MIT Press, p. 83–91.

Hillis, D. 1992. Coevolving parasites improve simulated evolution as an optimization process. In *Artificial Life*, edited by C. G. Langton. Redwood City, CA: Addison-Wesley, p. 313–324.

Hogeweg, P., and B. Hesper. 1989. An adaptive, selfmodifying, non goal-directed modelling approach. In *Modelling and simulation methodology: Knowledge systems paradigms*, edited by M. Elzas, T. Oren, and B. Zeigler, p. 77–92.

Hogeweg, P. and B. Hesper. 1985. Socioinformatic processes: Mirror modelling methodology. *J. Theor. Biol.* 113: 311–330.

Hogeweg, P. 1988. MIRROR beyond MIRROR, puddles of LIFE. In *Artificial Life*, edited by C. G. Langton. Redwood City, CA: Addison-Wesley, p. 297–316.

Hogeweg, P. 1994a. Multilevel evolution: replicators and the evolution of diversity. *Physica* D 75: 275–291.

Hogeweg, P. 1994b. On the potential role of DNS in an RNA world: Pattern generation and information accumulation in replicator systems. *Ber. Bunsenges. Phys. Chem.* 98: 1135–1139.

Hogeweg, P. 1998. Spatial selforganization and the shape of phylogenetic trees (in prep).

Huynen, M. and P. Hogeweg. 1994. Pattern generation in molecular evolution: exploitation of the variation in RNA landscapes. *J. Mol. Evol.* 39: 71–79.

Kaneko, K. and T. Ikegami. 1992. Homeochaos: dynamic stability of a symbiotic network with populaton dynamics and evolving mutation rates. *Physica* D 56: 406–429.

May, R. 1972. *Stability and Complexity in Model Ecosystems.* Princeton: Princeton Univ. Press.

Maynard Smith, J. and E. Szathmáry. 1995a. The major transitions in evolution. *Nature* 374: 227–232.

Maynard Smith, J. and E. Szathmáry. 1995b. *The Major Transitions in Evolution.* Oxford: Freeman.

Pagie, L. and P. Hogeweg. 1998a. Coexistence of colicines and cost of immunity (in prep.) .

Pagie, L. and P. Hogeweg. 1998b. Evolving adaptability due to coevolving targets. *Evolutionary Computation* (in press).

Percus, J. K., O. E. Percus and A. Perelson. 1993. Predicting the size of the t-cell repertoire and antibody combining region from consideration of efficient self-nonself discrimination. *Proc. Nat. Acad. Sci. USA* 90: 1691–1695.

Savill, N. J., and P. Hogeweg. 1997. Evolutionary

stagnation due to pattern-pattern interactions in a co-evolutionary predator-prey model. *Artificial Life* 3: 81–100.

Savill, N. J., and P. Hogeweg. 1998. The evolution of dispersal in predator-prey waves: Speciation prevents extinction. *Proc. Roy. Soc.* B 265: 25–32.

Savill, N. J., P. Rohani, and P. Hogeweg. 1997. Self-reinforcing spatial patterns enslave evolution in a host-parasitoid system. *J. theor. Biol.* 188: 11–20.

Takumi, K., and P. Hogeweg. 1998. Evolution of the immune repertoire with and witout somatic dna recombination. *J. Theor. Biol.* (in press).

te Boekhorst, I. J. A., and P. Hogeweg. 1994a. Effects of tree size on travelband formation in orang utans: Data analysis suggested by a model study. In *Artificial Life IV*, edited by P. Maes and R. A. Brooks. Cambridge, MA: MIT Press, p. 119–129.

te Boekhorst, I. J. A., and P. Hogeweg. 1994b. Selfstructuring in artificial 'chimps' offers new hypotheses for male grouping in chimpanzees. *Behaviour* 130: 229–252.

Evolution of Differentiated Multi-threaded Digital Organisms

Thomas S. Ray and Joseph Hart

ATR Human Information Processing Research Laboratories
2-2 Hikaridai, Seika-cho Soraku-gun, Kyoto 619-02 Japan
ray@hip.atr.co.jp jhart@hip.atr.co.jp
http://www.hip.atr.co.jp/~ray/

Abstract

Descriptive natural history of the results of evolution of differentiated multi-threaded (multi-cellular) self-replicating machine code programs (digital organisms), living in a network of computers, network Tierra. Programs are differentiated in that different threads execute different code (express different genes). The seed organism develops into a mature ten-celled form, differentiated into a two-celled reproductive tissue and an eight-celled sensory tissue. The sensory threads obtain data about conditions on the machines in the network, and then process that data to choose the best machine to migrate to or to send the daughter to. Evolution leads to a diversity of algorithms for foraging for resources, primarily CPU time, on the network.

Introduction

The work presented here consists of an exploration of the properties of evolution by natural selection in the digital medium. The evolving entities are self-replicating differentiated multi-threaded (emulated parallel) machine code programs. They live in a network of computers, and are able to sense conditions on other machines and move between machines.

This work is explicitly not about the evolutionary origin of the differentiated condition, but rather about evolution that takes place just after that threshold has been crossed. This experiment begins with the most primitively differentiated condition: two cell types.

This is an extension of the work generally known as "Tierra" (Ray 1991, 1994a, 1994b). The original Tierra was based on single-threaded (serial) machine code programs living in a single computer. The original model was extended by Thearling and Ray (1994, 1997) to include multi-threaded programs, living on a sixty-four processor connection machine. However, these multi-threaded programs were of a single "cell type", and never evolved into differentiated forms.

The seed program used by Thearling and Ray included a loop that was iterated many times. This loop was parallelized by using two threads, thus completing the work in half the time. Through evolution, the level of parallelism increased to as many as thirty-two threads. However, in the seed program and all programs that evolved from it in that experiment, all of the threads always executed the same code, thus there was no "differentiation" between threads with respect to the code executed (genes expressed). This report extends the work of Thearling and Ray by starting with multi-threaded programs which are already differentiated (into sensory and reproductive threads).

Analogies

Here we are making analogies between some features of digital organisms and organic organisms. The objective of making these analogies is not to create a digital model of organic life, but rather to use organic life as a model on which to base our better design of digital evolution.

In organic organisms, the "genome" is the complete DNA sequence, of which a copy is found in each "cell". Each cell is a membrane bound compartment, and requires its own copy of the DNA, as the genetic information is not shared across the cell membranes. The entire genome includes many "genes", which are segments of DNA that code for specific functions, mostly individual proteins. While each cell contains a complete copy of the genome, each individual cell expresses only a small subset of the genes in the entire genome. The specific subset of genes that are expressed in a cell determine the "cell type". Groups of cells of the same type form a "tissue". Different tissues are composed of cells that have "differentiated" in the sense that they express different sub-sets of the genes in the genome.

In our form of digital organisms, the genome consists of the complete sequence of executable machine code of the self-replicating computer program. Each thread of a multi-threaded process is associated with its own virtual CPU. These threads (CPUs) are considered analogous to the cells. However, the threads of a process all share a single copy of the genome, because they operate in a shared memory environment where the genetic information can easily be shared between CPUs. Duplication of the genome for each thread would be redundant, wasteful and unnecessary. In this detail, our digital system differs quite significantly from the organic system. Another difference is that here there is no spatial or geometric relationship between cells.

The genome of the digital organism includes several segments of machine code with identifiable functions, which are coherent algorithms or sub-routines of the overall program represented by the entire genome. These individual algorithms can be considered analogous to the genes. Each thread (CPU) has access to the entire genome, yet each thread will execute only a subset of the complete set of genes in the genome. The specific subset of genes executed by a single thread determine its cell type. Groups of threads of the same cell type form a tissue. Different tissues are composed of threads that have differentiated in the sense that they execute different subsets of the algorithms (genes) in the genome.

Network Tierra

The work reported here is focused on the evolution of the differentiated mutli-cellular condition. The multi-threaded digital organisms live in a networked environment where spatial and temporal heterogeneity of computational resources (most importantly CPU time) provides selective pressure to maintain a sensory system that can obtain data on conditions on various machines on the network, process the data, and make decisions about where to move within the network.

The experiment begins with a multi-threaded seed program that is already differentiated into two cell types: a sensory tissue and a reproductive tissue. The entire seed program includes about 320 bytes of executable machine code. However, no single thread executes all of this code, just as no cell in the human body expresses all of the genes in the human genome. The network ancestor genome has been somewhat arbitrarily labeled as composed of six genes, some of which have been further sub-divided (Figure 1). Two of the genes are executed only during the development from the single-celled to the mature ten-celled form (**sel**, **dif**). One gene is executed only by the reproductive tissue (**rep**), and one gene is executed only by the sensory tissue (**sen**). Two genes are executed by both tissues (**cop**, **dev**).

Figure 1: Ancestor Genome

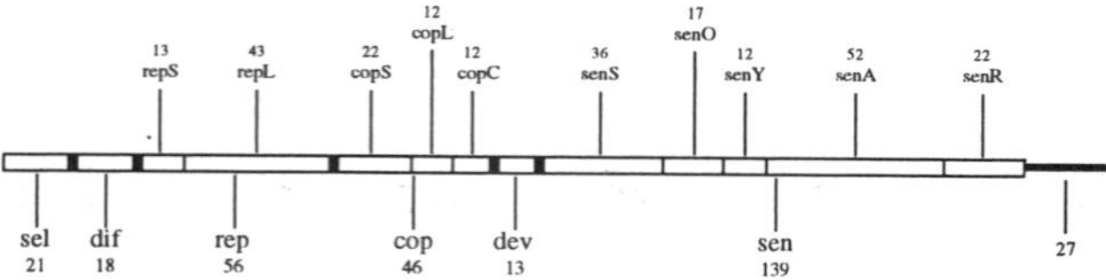

Lower labels indicate the six major genes and their sizes in bytes.
Upper labels indicate sub-divisions of the major genes, and their sizes.

Methods

The rationale for the current experiment was originally presented by Ray (1995). Technical details of the implementation have been reported in Charrel (1995) and Ray (1997, In Press). And further details are available on the web at: http://www.hip.atr.co.jp/~ray/tierra/netreport/netreport.html. Thus only a sketch of the experimental methods will be presented here.

The Tierra web

Tierra is another web on the internet. The Tierra web is created collectively as the result of running Tierra servers on many machines. The Tierra server is a piece of software written in the C language, which creates a virtual machine called Tierra. Tierra does not self-replicate, evolve, or experience mutations. Tierra does not migrate on the net. In order to run a Tierra server, someone must download the software, install it and run it.

The collection of Tierra servers creates a sub-net of the internet, within which digital organisms and Tierra browsers (Beagle) are able to move freely, accessing CPU cycles, and the block of RAM memory that is made available by the server. Note that the digital organisms and Beagle can not access other RAM on the machine, nor may they access the disk.

We can think of the web of Tierra servers as an archipelago of ''islands" (which we usually refer to as nodes or machines on the network) which can be inhabited by digital organisms. The digital organisms are mobile, and feed on CPU cycles. Therefore, selection can potentially support the evolution of network foraging strategies.

In this experiment, we must create conditions under which selection will favor more complex migratory algorithms, over small highly optimized algorithms that only reproduce locally, such as evolved in non-network Tierra. Toward this goal we introduced the "apocalypse" which at random intervals kills all organisms living on a single machine. This provides an absolute selection against non-migratory organisms, insuring that only migratory organisms can survive in the network environment.

Tierra runs as a low priority background process, like a screen saver, by using a "Nice" value of 19. This causes the CPU cycles available to Tierra to mirror the load of non-Tierra processes on the machine (the speed of Tierra is high when the load from other processes is low). Thus the speed of Tierra will vary with the load on the machine. Also, when the user of a machine touches the keyboard or the mouse, Tierra immediately sleeps for ten minutes (from the last hit). We expect the heterogeneity in available CPU cycles to provide selective forces which contribute to maintaining cell differentiation.

The work reported here is based on a small-scale experiment conducted on a local-area network of about sixty sparc stations running unix.

Sensory system

The sensory mechanism has been described previously (Ray 1997, in press), and so will be described only briefly here. Each Tierra server periodically sends a Tping data structure to all the other Tierra servers. In the current experiment, the structure contains the following entries (I32s is a 32 bit signed integer, I32u is a 32 bit unsigned integer):

```
struct TPingData /* data structure for Tping message */
{  I32s t; /* tag for message type */
   I32u address.node; /* IP address of node */
   I32u address.portnb; /* port number of socket */
   I32s cellID; /* unique identifier of organism in soup */
   I32s ranID; /* unique identifier, across network */
   I32s FecundityAvg; /* average fecundity at death */
   I32s Speed;  /* average instructions/second */
   I32s NumCells; /* number of organisms on node */
   I32s AgeAvg; /* average inst age at death */
   I32s SoupSize; /* size of memory for Tierra soup */
   I32u TransitTime; /* in milliseconds */
   I32u Fresh;  /* clock time at last refresh of this data */
   I32u Time; /* clock time at node */
   I32s InstExec; /* age of this Tierra process */
   I32s InstExecConnect; /* age while connected to net */
   I32s OS; /* operating system tag */
};
```

We will describe only those structure elements that are new in the current work, or which are mentioned elsewhere in this report.

address.node - is the 32 bit IP address of the machine from which this data came. This data is used by the organisms to specify the address of the machine that they will migrate to.

FecundityAvg - is the fecundity (number of offspring produced) at death or migration, averaged over all the organisms on the machine over the last million instructions executed.

Speed - is the speed of the virtual CPU in instructions per second executed, calculated over the last million instructions.

NumCells - is how many organisms are living on the machine at the time that the data structure is generated.

AgeAvg - is the age at death or migration, averaged over all the organisms on the machine over the last million instructions executed. The age is measured in virtual instructions executed by the individual organism.

InstExec, InstExecConnect - how many millions of instruction the Tierra process has been running, the age of the "island". InstExecConnect is how many millions of instructions the process has been running while connected to the network. The unix machines in our network are always connected to the network, so these two values are the same. They would differ on machines that are only intermittently connected to the network.

Each Tierra server maintains a "map file" which is a list of Tping data structures from all the machines on the Tierra network. Digital organisms are born with a pointer into the list of Tping structures. The location of the pointer in the list is randomly initialized at birth. Each time the organism executes the **getipp** instruction, one Tping data structure is written into the soup at a location specified by a value in a CPU register, and the pointer into the list is incremented, with wrap-around.

Genetic operators

The central problem of the Tierra experiment is to find the conditions under which evolution can generate complexity. One primary consideration is to have a highly evolvable genetic language. The evolvability of a genetic language is not determined by its structure alone, but also by the nature of the genetic operators, and the interaction between the two.

The Genetic Programming of Koza (1992, 1994) and the Genetic Images of Karl Sims (1991) have shown a very high level of evolvability, perhaps due in part to the power of their genetic operators. Both use genetic languages based on Lisp trees. The genetic operators manipulate the Lisp trees by replacing nodes in the trees (mutation), or by swapping nodes along with all their descendant branches between trees (cross-over).

The genetic operations on Lisp trees cause entire (perhaps coherent) sections of code to be moved around between genomes. Contrast this with the genetic operators of the original Tierra which do nothing more than flip bits in the linear genome. In order to enhance the power of

Table 1: Genetic Change in each gene of seven genomes

		sel	dif	rep	repS	repL	cop	copS	copL	cop C	dev	sen	senS	senO	senY	senA	senR
run	**Age**	**21**	**18**	**56**	**13**	**43**	**46**	**22**	**12**	**12**	**14**	**144**	**41**	**17**	**12**	**52**	**22**
1	11	0	0	27	0	35	11	5	25	8	7	31	22	147	17	13	9
2	6	0	0	25	0	33	28	0	100	8	0	49	22	*59	*58	*63	*55
3	8	10	6	23	0	30	20	14	17	33	0	33	46	18	42	15	59
4	9	14	0	61	8	77	13	0	50	0	0	13	17	29	33	2	9
5	6	29	6	27	15	30	50	9	158	17	0	29	34	29	33	23	32
6	6	10	0	13	0	16	4	0	8	8	0	78	22	--	--	--	--
7	14	19	0	29	0	37	35	14	50	58	0	54	34	--	--	25	--

Left columns are the run number, and age of the genome in days. Top row is the name of each of the six genes and ten sub-genes. Second row is the size of the gene in the ancestor. Remaining rows are the percentage change in the gene. * indicates that the gene is present in the genome, but is not expressed. – indicates that the gene has been lost from the genome.

genetic operators in Tierra, insertion, deletion and crossover have been added. In addition, the mutation operator has been enhanced to take two forms. One involves a bit flip, as in the original Tierra. The new form of mutation involves the replacement of a machine instruction with any other instruction chosen at random from the set of sixty-four instructions. The new genetic operations are performed on a daughter genome, just before it is born. In the runs described in this manuscript, the rates of each of the different kinds of genetic operations were all set to the same values: each class of operation affects one in thirty-two individuals born.

Results

Genetic change

Table 1 illustrates the magnitude of genetic change in each of six major genes and ten sub-genes, in each of seven genomes sampled from the end of seven runs ranging from six to fourteen days. The changes are expressed as a percentage of the original gene. For example, if ten instructions are mutated (or inserted) in a twenty byte gene, the change will be 50%. If thirty bytes are inserted into a twenty byte genome, the change will be 150%.

Table 2 summarizes the source of the genetic changes, based on the same data as Table 1. Examination of the seven genomes of Table 1 revealed the following classes of genetic changes: **Mutation** - mutations are the result of flipping one bit in the six-bit machine instruction, or of replacing a machine instruction with one of the sixty-four instructions chosen at random. This analysis did not discriminate between the two types of mutation. **Single-byte-insertion** - the insertion of a single machine instruction into the genome. This kind of genetic change may be caused as a side-effect of flaws in the increment and decrement instructions during the copying of the genome. **Single-byte-deletion** - the deletion of a single machine instruction from the genome. Like the single-byte-insertion, this may also be a side-effect of flaws. **Multiple-byte-insertion** - The insertion of a sequence of more than one machine instruction into a genome. This could be caused by the insertion genetic operation. **Multiple-byte-deletion** - The deletion of a sequence of more than one machine instruction from the genome. This could be caused by the deletion genetic operator. **Rearrangement** - A change in the order of segments of the genome. This might be caused by some combination of insertion, deletion, or crossover genetic operators. **End-loss** - A couple of examples were seen in which a segment of code was lost from the end of the genome. This might be essentially the same process as the multiple-byte-deletion, or it might be a different process.

Table 2: Sources of Genetic Change

Genetic Operation	Number of Events	Bytes Affected
Mutation	263	263
one-byte-insertion	9	9
one-byte-deletion	15	15
multi-byte-insertion	20	154
multi-byte-deletion	11	64
Rearrangement	2	83
end-loss	2	125

Mutation is by far the predominant source of genetic change (preserved by selection), in terms both of the number of genetic events, and the amount of code affected. The next most common source of genetic change is multiple-byte-insertion, with an order of magnitude fewer events, but affecting more than half as much genetic code. The distribution of the various types of genetic change within the genome is very heterogeneous. For example, the twelve byte gene **copL**, makes up 4% of the genome, but contains 55% of the multi-byte-insertion events.

Gene duplication

The insertion and cross-over genetic operations cause segments of code to be moved about within or between genomes. In some instances, this results in a duplication of a segment of code within a genome. This duplicated code might or might not correspond to our arbitrary labeling of the code as genes or sub-genes (Figure 1).

While we have observed many of these duplications, the most interesting examples have involved the complete duplication of functional algorithms which are called as sub-routines: either the **cop** gene, or the **dev** gene, or both together. We have observed instances of each of these duplications in which one copy of the duplicated gene is expressed in the reproductive tissue while the other copy is expressed in the sensory tissue (Figure 2).

Figure 2: Gene duplication

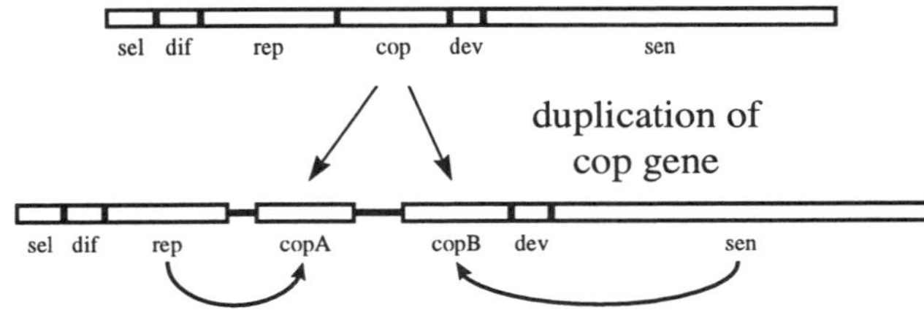

differential expression of duplicated genes

At the time of duplication, both copies of the gene are generally identical. However, when the duplicated condition survives for prolonged periods of time, the two copies do diverge substantially in their structure and function.

Reproductive algorithm

The reproductive algorithm relies on a twelve-byte copy loop (the **copL** gene) to perform a string-copy operation on the genome, resulting in the genetic code being copied from mother to daughter. The algorithm of the ancestor copies one byte for each iteration of the loop.

In the original Tierra experiments, it was observed that this algorithm sometimes evolved an optimization known as "unrolling the loop", in which efficiency is increased by copying more than one byte in each iteration. In the original Tierra, the unrolled loops copied two or three bytes (Ray 1994a). In the current experiment, we have observed loop unrollings of two, four and six bytes.

Figure 3: Developmental pattern

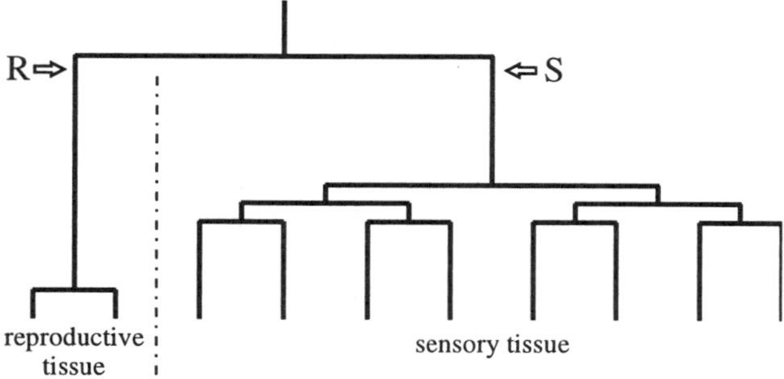

Developmental pattern

The development of the ancestor from the one-cell embryonic stage to the mature ten-cell stage is illustrated in Figure 3. The undifferentiated original cell splits into two cells. Soon after this first division, the differentiation event occurs (a conditional jump in the machine code), causing one cell to become a reproductive cell, and the other to become a sensory cell. Subsequently, the reproductive cell divides once to form a two-celled reproductive tissue. The sensory cell goes through three division cycles to form an eight-celled sensory tissue.

Figure 4: Sensory tissue developmental cycle

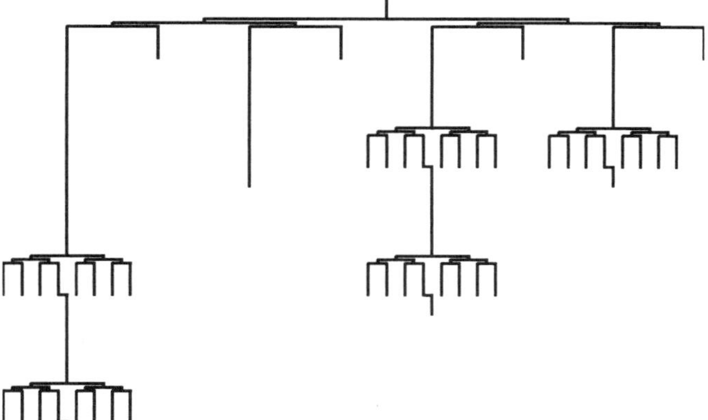

Once the sensory tissue has reached the mature eight-cell form, it exhibits further developmental changes (Figure 4). Each of the eight sensory threads executes a **getipp** instruction to obtain a Tping data structure. These are then

Table 3: Thread & decision structure

date	repro	sense	L dat	R dat	Act
960aad	2x1	8x8	S/n	s/n	Cd
960aae	2x1	8x8	f	f	Cd
960aaf	2x1	8x8	S*f	s*f	Cd
971001	256x1	0x0	-	-	-
1-971101	8x2	8x8	s/n	s/n	Cd
1-971102	16x4	8x8	s/n	s/28	Cd
1-971103	32x4	8x4	-	-	Cd
1-971104	32x4	4x4	s	0	Cd
1-971105	32x4	4x4	s	s*2	Cd
1-971106	32x4	32x4	s	0	Cd
1-971107	32x4	32x4	s	n	Cd
1-971108	32x4	32x4	s	s*2	Cd
1-971109	32x4	32x4	s	0	Cd
1-971110	32x4	32x4	s	0	Cd
1-971111	32x4	32x4	-	-	Cd
2-971112	4x1	8x8	f	f	Cd
2-971113	8x2	8x8	s	i/2	Cd
2-971114	16x4	8x8	s	s/2	Cd
2-971115	16x4	16x8	s	s/2	Cd
2-971117	16x4	1x0	-	-	1 gt
3-971118	16x4	16x8	s*5	s*6	Cd
3-971119	32x4	8x8	s*20	s*f	Cd
3-971120	32x4	8x4	s	s	Cd
3-971121	32x4	8x4	s	s	Cd
3-971122	32x4	8x4	s	s	Cd
3-971124	32x4	8x4	s	s	Cd
3-971125	32x4	8x4	s*20	s	Cd
4-971127	64x2	8x8	s*f	s*20	Cd
4-971128	64x2	8x8	s*f	s*20	Cd
4-971129	64x2	8x4	s*f	s*20	Cd
4-971201	64x2	8x8	s*f	s*20	Cd
4-971202	64x2	8x8	s*f	s*20	Cd
4-971203	64x2	8x2	s*f	s*40	Cd
4-971204	64x2	8x2	s*f	s*20	Cd
4-971205	64x2	16x8	s*f	s*40	Cd
5-971209	16x2	8x4	a	a-1	Cd
5-971210	32x2	8x4	s	s-1	Cd
5-971211	32x2	8x4	s	s-1	Cd
5-971212	32x2	16x4	s	s-1	Cd
5-971213	32x2	8x4	s	64	Cd
5-971214	32x2	8x4	s	1	Cd
6-971216	255x1	1x0	-	-	Gt
6-971217	255x1	1x0	-	-	Gt
6-971218	255x1	1x0	-	-	Gt
6-971219	255x1	1x0	-	-	Gt
6-971220	255x1	1x0	-	-	Gt
6-971221	255x1	1x0	-	-	Gt
7-971223	8x2	8x8	s n	4096 28	Cd
7-971224	8x2	1x0	s/n	28	Gt
7-971227	64x2	1x0	s/n	65	Gt
7-971230	64x2	1x0	s/n	28	Gt
7-980102	64x2	1x0	s/n	128	Gt
7-980105	64x2	1x0	s	784	Gt
7-980110	64x2	1x0	s/n	64	Gt
7-980114	64x2	1x0	s	7168	Gt

reduced to the single "best" data through a series of three pair-wise comparisons (see the Sensory Processing section below).

Just before each pair-wise comparison, half of the threads halt (half of the cells die). The cells which remain alive compare two neighboring data structures, and if the one on the right is "better" that the one on the left, the data is copied. The data is copied by calling the **cop** gene (which is also used by the reproductive tissue to copy the genome). The **cop** gene parallelizes its data copy function by splitting into multiple threads. When called from the sensory tissue, eight threads are used to copy the Tping data (if all four of the sensory threads doing the comparison should decide to copy the data, a total of thirty-two threads would be active simultaneously in the sensory tissue). After the data is copied, seven of the eight data copy threads halt.

At the end of the data reduction, only one of the eight sensory threads remains, but it splits into eight threads again to repeat the process, in an infinite loop. Similarly, after the genome has been copied by the two reproductive threads, one thread halts, and the remaining thread executes the **divide** instruction, spawning the daughter as an independent process, and potentially causing her migration. Then, the single reproductive thread splits into two threads again, and repeats the reproductive process in an infinite loop.

Table 3 presents a summary of the evolutionary changes in the configuration of the tissues. The first column lists the run number and the date of the sample in run-yymmdd format (for each of seven runs), or the name of the ancestral genome. The second column shows the configuration of the reproductive tissue, in the format: NxR, where N is the number of threads used to copy the genome, and R is the "redundancy" of the reproductive tissue.

The reproductive tissue often manifested a redundancy of function. For example, a reproductive tissue might use eight cells to copy the genome, with each cell copying one-eighth of the genome. However, this entire configuration might be duplicated, so that there are actually sixteen reproductive cells, working as two groups, with each group of eight dividing the genome into eight parts in the same way. In this case, eight of the sixteen reproductive threads would be redundant. This case would appear in column two as: 8x2.

The third column shows the configuration of the sensory tissue, in the format: SxC, where S is the number of sensory threads which obtain Tping data (right part of Figure 3), and C is the number of threads used to copy the Tping data (middle of Figure 4) if the decision conditions (columns four and five) are met.

The first three rows of Table 3 show the structure of the three ancestral organisms used to seed the run: 960aad, 960aae, and 960aaf. All three have the same configuration of tissues: 2x1 8x8. After listing the seed organisms, we show the result typical of all runs before November 1997, listed next to the date 971001.

In all runs before November 1997, the sensory tissue was completely lost, and the reproductive tissue expanded to the limit of 256 cells. In order to migrate or send daughters to other machines on the network, the digital organism must suggest the IP address of the other machine. In early runs, we allowed any suggested IP address to be mapped to a valid address by finding the closest hamming-distance match in the map file. In these runs, loss of the sensory system and expansion of the reproductive tissue resulted in the 256x1 0x0 configuration shown for the 971001 date. In later runs, we required suggested IP addresses to be valid. In these runs, loss of the sensory system and expansion of the reproductive tissue resulted in the 255x1 1x0 configuration (which also occurred in run six).

At the end of October '97 some bugs were fixed which resulted in the survival of the sensory tissue through prolonged periods of evolution. An example of a bug that led to the selective elimination of the sensory system was the resetting of the pointer into the list of Tping data structures to zero, after its original random initialization. This had the consequence that all individuals in the population (of ancestral algorithms) could only sense the first fifteen machines on the net, regardless of the number of machines actually present in the network.

After fixing the bugs in the sensory system, the sensory tissue survived through prolonged periods of evolution in most runs. The structure of the developmental pattern and the resulting relative and absolute numbers of cells in the two tissues changed to the many forms listed in columns two and three of Table 3.

Sensory processing

The ancestral organism includes a 512 byte data area where it can hold sensory data. Each cell of the eight-cell sensory tissue reads a sixty-four byte Tping data structure into one of eight offsets into the data area. Each of the Tping structures contains data about the conditions on a different machine on the network. The sensory algorithm then undertakes a series of three pair-wise comparisons (Figure 5), to select the best machine to send the daughter to at the time of its birth. At the completion of the series of comparisons, the best looking data structure will be at the left-most position (zero offset) in the data area. The reproductive algorithm looks in this location for the IP

Figure 5: Sensory processing

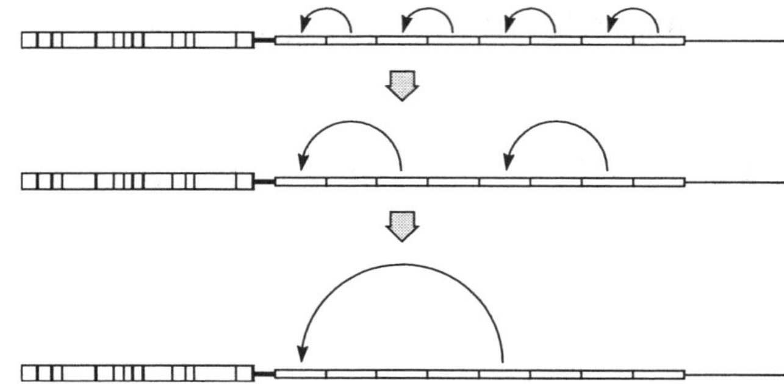

The thick box on the left is the 320 byte genome marked with the divisions into genes and sub-genes. The thin box to its right is the 512 byte data area marked with the eight 64 byte Tping data buffers.

address of the machine that it will send the daughter to.

The algorithm of the sensory tissue is an infinite loop, so that after the completion of the first cycle of three pair-wise comparisons, the entire sensory process repeats. After the first sensory cycle, only seven of the eight sensory threads write another Tping structure to the data area (the left-most data is preserved into successive cycles). During the time that it takes the reproductive tissue to copy the genome, the sensory system is able to complete two cycles, having collected and processed data from fifteen machines on the net.

The overall scheme of sensory data processing by multi-threaded sensory tissues tends to be preserved through evolution. However, there is a tendency for the reproductive algorithm to optimize, completing its function more quickly, with the result that the sensory system will be able to process less data before the results are needed by the reproductive tissue.

In some runs, the sensory processing algorithm evolved into a relatively simple form in which only a single buffer was used for storing the Tping data structure. In this case, the **getipp** instruction is used to read a structure into the buffer. Then a test such as 256 > Speed is performed, and if true, another **getipp** instruction is executed with the result that the previous data is replaced with new data.

Sensory data selection

The algorithm by which Tping data is selected is represented in columns four, five, and six of Table 3. If the value in column four is less than or equal to the value in column five, then the action in column six is performed. Two different actions are represented in column six: cd - copy the Tping data on the right over the Tping data on the left; gt - get another Tping data structure from the map file list. The values listed in columns four and five include data from the Tping structures, and constant values. The symbols used for the Tping entries are: s - Speed; n - NumCells; f - FecundityAvg; i - InstExecConnect; a - AgeAvg. In some cases two or more of these variables or constants are combined by the arithmetic operations of addition, subtraction, multiplication or division (+ - * / respectively).

In the studies reported here, all but the first of the seven runs were initiated with a mixture of three different ancestral genomes, using three different selection algorithms (top three rows of Table 3). 960aad copies the Tping data if Speed/NumCells <= Speed/NumCells; 960aae if FecundityAvg <= FecundityAvg; and 960aaf if FecundityAvg*Speed <= FecundityAvg*Speed.

It is likely that after a few generations of reproduction, an ecological process of competitive exclusion will result in a population that is entirely descended from only one of the three ancestors. Comparison of sequence similarity between the evolved organisms of Table 1 and the three ancestors reveals that in some runs, the population descended from the Speed/NumCells algorithm, and in other runs from the FecundityAvg*Speed algorithm.

Evolution has also produced a diversity of sensory data selection algorithms. The element of the Tping data structure most commonly used by these algorithms is Speed. However, the algorithms also commonly integrate data other than elements of the Tping structure, such as some constant value. For example, copy data if Speed (on the left) <= 256

The "-" symbol in columns four and five of the table indicate that the action in column six is performed unconditionally. The result in all of these cases is that the node to which the organism or its daughter migrate is chosen essentially at random. This is the situation found when the sensory system is completely lost through evolution (971001 and run 6). We call these organisms "map-file-scanners", because they constantly get new IP

Figure 6: Mob behavior

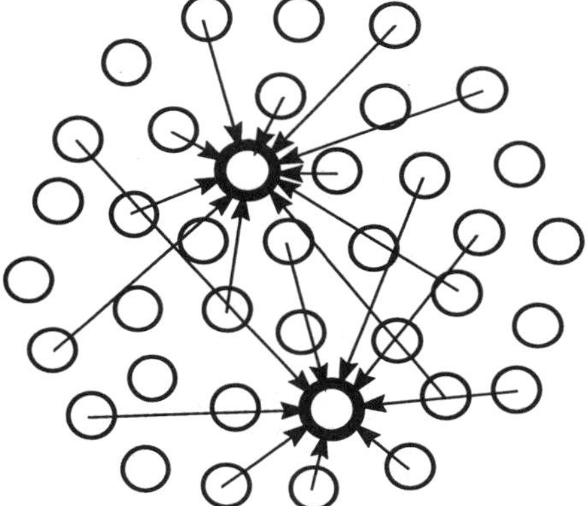

addresses from the map file, and then send the daughter (or migrate) to whatever address has been most recently accessed, by chance, when the reproductive process is completed. The notation "1 gt" in column six indicates that the program only gets one Tping data structure, and uses its IP address as the migration destination. Since the pointer into the map file is initialized at random, this is another random method of node selection.

The selection mechanism for the 7-971223 organism is unique, in that it uses two conditionals, both from the data on the left. If s <= 4096 and n <= 28, the data on the right is copied over the data on the left.

Migration patterns

At the completion of the reproductive cycle, the network ancestor causes its daughter to be sent to another machine at birth. The IP address of the target machine is taken from the Tping data analyzed by the sensory system. One change that commonly occurs through evolution is for the daughter to be born locally (on the machine where the mother lives), and for the mother to then immediately move to the machine whose IP address was recommended by the sensory system. Another common pattern is for the mother to send the daughter to another machine, and then to immediately follow the daughter to that machine.

Discussion

Genetic change

The magnitude and source of genetic change preserved by selection varies greatly between genes. For example the developmental genes **dif** and **dev** are rarely altered, while **copL** which contains the critical code for copying data, often experiences large changes. In addition, the genetic operations predominantly responsible for the genetic changes vary widely between different parts of the genome.

The **copL** gene achieved higher levels of unrolling in this experiment than in the original Tierra. The large magnitude of change in this gene can be understood in terms of strong selection pressure for efficiency of copying data, combined with an accessible pathway for change with the genetic operators available (increasing levels of loop unrolling).

The sensory genes also show a high level of genetic change, but we suggest a different interpretation. It appears that the selective pressures on the sensory system are not as intense. The organisms can survive and reproduce without the sensory system, whereas the **copL** gene is essential for reproduction. Thus the high level of genetic change in the sensory genes may be due to lower selective pressures permitting higher levels of variation to survive.

These observations seem quite significant in the context of understanding the issue of evolvability (in fact like complexity, we don't have an adequate definition of evolvability). If we were to attempt to judge the evolvability of the system described here, we would reach very different conclusions from examining the changes exclusively in different parts of the genome. For example, evolvability seems to be high in the **copL** and **sen** genes, but low in the **dif**, **dev**, and **repS** genes. At the same time, the causes of the high degree of genetic change in the **copL** and **sen** genes seem to be quite different.

Gene duplication

The phenomena of gene duplication in which both copies of the gene are expressed, but by different tissues is surprising and quite interesting. Gene duplication and subsequent divergence of the sequence and function of the two copies of the gene is believed to be a primary mechanism for the increase in the complexity of genomes in organic evolution. It appears an analogous process has occurred, or at least begun, in this experiment.

Sensory data selection

The ancestor organisms were written with sensory data selection algorithms that seem "smart" to their designers. Sometimes, apparently smart algorithms have been present in the later stages of evolution. However, it is often the case that the evolved algorithms appear to be less smart. However, they may none-the-less be good adaptations to the environment in which the organisms live.

A predominant feature of the environment is the presence of other organisms, and their behavior. One of the most difficult problems in designing a sensory data selection algorithm is that if one specific algorithm comes to dominate the network-wide population, then most organisms will tend to make the same choices. This can result in a "mob" behavior, Figure 6.

Tests with the Speed/NumCells ancestor algorithm in a four node network (with genetic operations turned off to prevent evolution) revealed a severe problem. One of the four machines had a far faster processor, resulting in a consistently high value of Speed on that machine. The high Speed caused a high Speed/NumCells ratio, making it the machine of choice for the entire network-wide population. The result was that all daughters born on all machines were sent to this one machine. In effect, there was no birth or immigration on the other three machines. Thus the original organisms on those three machines lived indefinitely, accumulating very high fecundities (and associated Darwinian fitness).

Meanwhile, on the selected machine, there was a huge influx of immigration, in addition to the local reproduction. The result was a rapid flux of organisms (for each birth or immigration, the reaper must kill an existing organism to make space) such that few if any individuals survived long enough to reproduce. Thus the average fecundity (and Darwinian fitness) on the selected machine was near zero. Because the soup size on this machine was fixed, it was not possible for growth of the population to lower the Speed/NumCells ratio to a level comparable to the slower machines.

The consequence of the use of the Speed/NumCells algorithm throughout the small network was a mob behavior that created a fitness landscape within which using the algorithm was the worst thing possible. Even random selection of machines would have been better. The severe mob behavior seen in a small network is diffused somewhat in a larger network, because the individual organism does not have time to examine data from all machines. The ancestor is able to look at fifteen machines for each reproductive cycle. Because the pointers into the list of machines are initialized at random, each organism will look at a different list. However, there remains an underlying dynamic, in which some machines tend to be chosen by any organism that looks at them, generating some mob behavior. In Figure 6 the favored machines are represented by the heavy circles.

Selection algorithms such as 256 <= Speed appear to be relatively dumb, but they may have the selective advantage of reducing the mob effect by making the choice of machines more fuzzy.

Loss or degradation of sensory system

While this experiment demonstrated that the sensory system is able to survive long periods of evolution, some of the runs showed a complete loss or a serious degradation of the sensory system (Tables 1 and 3). We believe that the primary selective factor for maintaining the sensory system is the temporal heterogeneity in the availability of CPU cycles to the Tierra process, due to the activity patterns of the human users of the machines in the Tierra network.

This experiment was conducted in a local-area network at ATR, where there are some fairly obvious patterns of human activity. ATR is in a somewhat remote location, and most researchers commute by company bus. The bus service is available from 7:40 am to 10:00 pm on weekdays only. There is no bus service on weekends or holidays. Most researchers arrive between 8:00 am and 10:00 am, and leave between 6:00 pm and 8:00 pm, on weekdays only. The data reported in this study covers the period of November 1 through January 14. In this period, weekends and holidays fell on: Nov 1-3, 8-9, 15-16, 22-24, 29-30; Dec 6-7, 13-14, 20-21, 23; Dec 27 - Jan 4; Jan 10-11.

We can expect that an important component of the selective pressure for maintaining the sensory system will be relaxed on weekends, holidays, and weekdays from mid-evening to mid-morning. We suspect that this relaxation of selective pressures may partially explain the occasions of loss of the sensory system. It is worth noting that the sensory system was lost from the outset of run six, during the business week. However, this run was initiated in the mid-evening and probably lost its sensory system before ever experiencing the relevant selective pressures. We are preparing to test the pattern of loss of the sensory system against quantitative measurements of temporal heterogeneity in human activity in the network.

Migration patterns

There is an obvious benefit to the behavior of the mother migrating after reproduction, rather than remaining on the local machine to attempt a second reproduction. When a creature moves to another machine, it enters the bottom of the reaper queue (Ray 1991). By moving after reproduction, the mother effectively delays her death.

There are however some costs to the migration of a mature organism. If the Tierra process is sleeping on the target machine (due to user activity) the migrating genome can die as a result of having its packet(s) lost in the network. Furthermore, upon arrival, the formerly mature organism reverts to an essentially embryonic, one-celled state. It must then go through the developmental process leading to the mature ten celled state, before it can begin the reproductive and sensory cycles. In addition, through migration, all sensory data is lost, whereas the mature organism which does not migrate would retain the selected sensory data in its left-most Tping data buffer.

Conclusions

The central objective of this project is to study the conditions under which evolution by natural selection leads to an increase in complexity of the replicators. For the purpose of this study, the primary quantitative measure of complexity is the level of differentiation of the multi-celled organism. The study begins with the most primitive level of differentiation: two cell types. There are two milestones in the study: 1) The differentiated state persists through prolonged periods of evolution. 2) The number of cell types increases through evolution.

In the work reported here, only the first of these two milestones has been achieved. There has been no sign of an increase in the number of cell types. However, the process of gene duplication with differential expression of the resulting genes is a kind of proto-differentiation event. This process offers some prospect of leading to new cell types.

Observations of a high degree of heterogeneity in the magnitude, source, and possible selective dynamics for genetic change in different parts of the genome provides raw data for our efforts to understand the nature of "evolvability". A practical understanding of evolvability, leading to an ability to design higher levels of evolvability into our synthetic evolving systems is crucial for progress in the area of evolutionary systems.

The ultimate imperatives in evolution are survival and reproduction. In the context of self-replicating computer programs, it is not obvious how selection can favor any behavior beyond the efficient replication of the genome. However, in this experiment we demonstrate that selection can favor the ability to gather information about conditions in the environment, analyze that data, and use the results of the analysis to control the direction of movements.

Digital organisms essentially identical to those of the original Tierra experiment, were provided with a sensory mechanisms for obtaining data about conditions on other machines on the network; code for processing that data and making decisions based on the analysis, the digital equivalent of a nervous system; and effectors in the form of the ability to make directed movements between machines in the network. This sensory-nervous-effector system required 157 bytes of genetic code, compared to 136 bytes for the reproductive system alone. In addition, the sensory system required a data area almost twice the size of the entire genome. This sensory system is not "hard-coded", in the sense that it is not essential for survival and reproduction in the network, and it can be lost if selection does not maintain it in the face of degradation by genetic operations. Yet selection maintained this large burden of additional complexity due to the selective benefits of gathering, processing, and acting upon information about the environment.

The migratory patterns of the digital organisms themselves become an important part of the fitness landscape in the network. The algorithms of the seed organisms generate an unfit (in the Darwinian sense) mob behavior by causing all individuals in the network to migrate to the "best" looking machines. Evolution resolves this problem by changing the algorithm to simply avoid poor quality machines.

References

Charrel, A. 1995. Tierra network version. ATR Technical

Report TR-H-145.
http://www.hip.atr.co.jp/~ray/pubs/charrel/charrel.pdf

Koza, John R. 1992. *Genetic Programming: On the Programming of Computers by Means of Natural Selection.* Cambridge, MA: MIT Press, p. 819

Koza, John R. 1994. *Genetic Programming II: Automatic Discovery of Reusable Programs.* Cambridge, MA: MIT Press, p. 746

Ray, T. S. 1991. An approach to the synthesis of life. In: *Artificial Life II, Santa Fe Institute Studies in the Sciences of Complexity, vol. XI*, edited by C. G. Langton, C. Taylor, J. D. Farmer, & S. Rasmussen. Redwood City, CA: Addison-Wesley, p. 371-408.
http://www.hip.atr.co.jp/~ray/pubs/tierra/tierrahtml.html

Ray, T. S. 1994a. Evolution, complexity, entropy, and artificial reality. *Physica* D 75: 239-263.
http://www.hip.atr.co.jp/~ray/pubs/oji/ojihtml.html

Ray, T. S. 1994b. An evolutionary approach to synthetic biology: Zen and the art of creating life. *Artificial Life* 1(1/2): 195-226.
http://www.hip.atr.co.jp/~ray/pubs/zen/zenhtml.html

Ray, T. S. 1995. A proposal to create a network-wide biodiversity reserve for digital organisms. ATR Technical Report TR-H-133.
http://www.hip.atr.co.jp/~ray/pubs/reserves/reserves.html

Ray, T. S. 1997. Selecting naturally for differentiation. In: *Genetic Programming 1997: Proceedings of the Second Annual Conference, July 13--16, 1997,* edited by J. R. Koza, K. Deb, M. Dorigo, D. B. Fogel, M. Garzon, H. Iba, and R.L. Riolo. San Francisco, CA: Morgan Kaufmann, p. 414-419.
http://www.hip.atr.co.jp/~ray/pubs/gp97/gp97.html

Ray, T. S. 1998. Continuing progress report on the network experiment. Published only on as a web page:
http://www.hip.atr.co.jp/~ray/tierra/netreport/netreport.html

Ray, T. S. In Press. Selecting naturally for differentiation: preliminary evolutionary results. *Complexity.*

Sims, K. 1991. Artificial evolution for computer graphics. *Computer Graphics (Siggraph '91)* 25: 319-328.

Thearling, K., and T. S. Ray. 1994. Evolving multi-cellular artificial life. In *Proceedings of Artificial Life IV*, edited by R. A. Brooks, and P. Maes. Cambridge, MA: MIT Press, p. 283-288.
http://www.hip.atr.co.jp/~ray/pubs/alife4/alife4.pdf

Thearling, K., and T. S. Ray. 1997. Evolving parallel computation. *Complex Systems* 10: 229--237.
http://www.santafe.edu/~kurt/evpar.shtml

Social Dynamics

Spatial Centrality of Dominants without Positional Preference

Charlotte K. Hemelrijk

AI Lab, Department of Computer Science, University of Zürich,
Switzerland, Fax 0041-1-363 00 35, Email: hemelrij@ifi.unizh.ch.

Abstract

In many group-living animals dominant individuals occupy the center of a group. This is generally thought to reflect a preference for locations that provide optimal protection against predators. However, in this paper I will show that such spatial-structure also emerges among artificial entities that lack preference for any spatial location.

The artificial entities dwell in a homogeneous world and are completely identical at the start of the simulation. They are gregarious and perform dominance interactions in which the effects of winning and losing are self-reinforcing. Varying essential parameters of the model revealed that: 1) Social-spatial patterns are stronger among entities that perceive each others rank directly compared to those that estimate rank of others based on personal experiences. 2) Stronger social-spatial patterns result when entities obligatory attack others than when attack-rate was negatively dependent on rank-distance. 3) Raising the intensity of attack increased the centrality of dominants for the Obligatory attack system, but weakened it for the Rank-Distance Decreasing attack system. Also, other social interaction patterns emerged, such as bi-directionality of aggression and a correlation between rank and frequency of attack. Such epi-phenomena may underlie the variation of social-spatial patterns found in real animals.

Introduction

Following Hamilton's (1971) influential model of the 'selfish herd', a spatial position in the center of a group is functionally attributed to optimal protection against predators. To test the hypothesis that animals compete for this safe location, much research has been devoted to studying nonrandom positioning of individuals and position-related fitness differences (for a review see Krause 1994). Observations on natural groupings (e.g. fish: Krause 1994), results of experiments (e.g. spiders: Rayor and Uetz 1990) and models on benefits of position preferences (e.g., Bumann, Krause, and Rubenstein 1997) have been interpreted as support for Hamilton's ideas. However, conflicting observations on spatial structure (primates: Altmann 1979, Janson 1990ab, Rhine and Westland 1981) and its fitness consequences (e.g., highest mortality in the center in groups of certain species of fishes: Parish 1989) were reported as well. These contradictory results have been suggested to be a consequence of differences in measurement methods (Collins 1984, Krause 1994) and neglect of essential variables in the optimization models.

Note that these amendments function as excuses to leave the soundness of the theoretical principles undisputed. It should be recognized, however, that the optimization approach is not without problems. Optimization models treat features as independent properties of individuals and therefore come up with a separate explanation for each trait. However, there is a growing awareness, fostered by 'Artificial Life' studies, that what are supposed to be traits actually are emergent properties from interactions between agents and their local environment (including other agents) (e.g., Pfeifer and Verschure 1995) and that such interactions may bring about more than one pattern. An example is the study on the formation of diverse spatial structure of groups of ants by Deneubourg et al. (1989). Using Monte Carlo simulations, they showed that one simple rule set of trail laying/following behavior can generate different characteristic swarm patterns of ants depending on density and distribution of food.

Similar considerations may hold for spatial-social structures with dominants in the center and subordinates at the periphery that conventionally would be associated with Hamilton's notion of the 'selfish herd'. Such a configuration was indeed found as a side effect in an artificial world in which group-living entities perform self-reinforcing dominance interactions but lack spatial preference (Hogeweg 1988). The aim of this paper is to understand the dynamics of such spatial structuring in detail in order to bring it up as an alternative to the selfish herd theory. Hereto, I have set up an artificial world comparable to that of Hogeweg, but in addition I varied the cognitive sophistication involved in dominance interactions, the tendency of entities to attack others and the impact of these interactions on their subsequent dominance position.

To examine the influence of mental sophistication on spatial patterning, I created two types of entities that differ in their way to perceive dominance of others. The simplest agents are called Perceivers, because they observe the rank of others directly and do not recognize others individually. The more sophisticated entities, the Estimators, assess a partner's dominance by recalling their last experience with them and are similar to those used by Hogeweg. Two attack systems are devised. In the simplest one, Perceivers always attack others upon encountering them. In the other, in line with a model of Bonabeau et al. (1996), I implemented the probability to attack a partner as a decreasing function of rank distance. To mirror differences in intensity of aggression (as described for primates by Thierry 1985, 1990), the impact of single acts of attack on future probabilities of winning/losing was varied. Apart from analyzing the effects of probability of attack and its impact on social-spatial structure, I will also report on other emergent social interaction patterns, such as bi-directionality of aggression and correlation between rank and frequency of attack.

Methods

In this Section I will present a description of the model and outline how spatial structure and stability of the hierarchy is measured.

The model

The model is individual-oriented and event-driven (see Hogeweg & Hesper 1979, Hogeweg 1988, Villa 1992, Judson 1994). The modeling environment (written in object-Pascal, Borland Pascal 7.0) consists of three parts:

* the 'world' (toroid) with its interacting agents,

* its visualization,

* special entities that collect and analyze data on what happens in the 'world' (cf. the 'recorders' and 'reporters' of Hogeweg 1988).

Unlike in former lattice-based models (Hemelrijk 1996, 1997), the 'world' presented here consists of a continuous space of 200 by 200 units. Therefore, agents are able to move in any direction. They have an angle of vision of 120 degrees and their maximum perception distance (MaxView) is 50 units. I will confine myself to a small ensemble of 8 entities. Agents group and perform dominance interactions according to the sets of rules described below (Figure 1).

Grouping rules

In the literature, two opposing forces affecting group structure are often postulated: on the one hand animals are attracted to one another, because being in a group provides safety. On the other hand, aggregation implies competition for resources and this drives individuals apart.

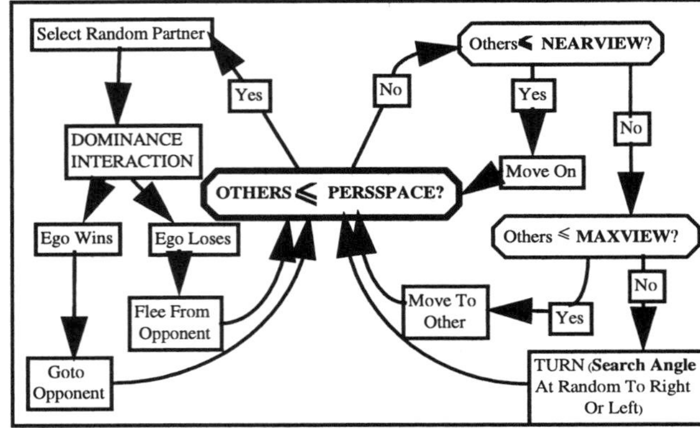

Figure 1. Flow chart for the behavioral rules of the entities

The forces leading to aggregation and spacing are realized in the model by the following set of rules (cf. Hogeweg 1988):

- If an agent sees another within a critical distance (parameter PerSpace), it performs a dominance interaction with that entity. In case several agents are within PerSpace, the interaction partner is chosen at random. If the agent wins the interaction, it moves towards its opponent, otherwise it makes a full turn and moves away from its rival.

- If nobody is in its PerSpace, but an agent perceives others within a distance of NearView, it continues moving in its original direction.

- If an agent detects it nearest neighbors outside NearView, but within its maximum range of vision (= MaxView), it moves towards them.

- If an agent does not perceive any other agent within maxView, it searches for group members by making a turn over an angle (= SearchAngle) of 90 degrees at random to the right or left.

Dominance types

Conventionally, rank-acquisition is attributed to a (possibly inherited) quality of an individual (Ellis 1994). However, experimental results from various animal species (for a listing see Bonabeau et al 1996) have shown that winning is determined by chance and self-reinforcement: once an animal has won, it has a larger chance of winning again in a subsequent fight (the so-called 'winner-effect', see Chase et al 1994). Because this study emphasizes the self-organizing properties of interactions, I confine myself to the self-enhancing effects of winning/losing by starting with completely identical entities.

About the perception of rank by others, a number of hypotheses are entertained by various authors (e.g. Barnard and Burk 1979, Hemelrijk 1996, 1997). The simplest one is that the capacity to win is directly perceived from external cues, such as pheromones in social insects (e.g., van Honk and Hogeweg 1981) and body postures in crustaceans (e.g., Copp 1986). In many species, however, dominance may not be recognized externally, but may be estimated on the basis of an individual's former encounters with a partner. Such a representation asks for more 'cognition' and was used in Hogeweg's (1988) model. Agents endowed with direct and estimated rank perception will be called Perceivers and Estimators respectively. The effects of both types of dominance perception will be compared in this paper.

Dominance interactions.

Interactions between agents with direct perception of dominance ranks (i.e. Perceivers) are modeled after Hogeweg & Hesper (1983) as follows:

1. Each entity has a variable DOM (representing the capacity to win a hierarchical interaction).

2. After meeting one another in their PerSpace, entities display and observe each other's DOM. This represents an active display and only through such a display the partner obtains information about the DOM value of its opponent. Subsequent winning and losing is determined as follows by chance and values of DOM:

$$w_i = \begin{cases} 1 & \dfrac{DOM_i}{DOM_i + DOM_j} > RND(0,1) \\ 0 & \text{else} \end{cases} \quad (1)$$

where w_i is the outcome of a dominance interaction initiated by agent i (1=winning, 0=losing). In other words, if the relative dominance value of the interacting agents is larger than a random number (drawn from a uniform distribution), then agent i wins, else it looses.

3. Updating of the dominance values is done by increasing the dominance value of the winner and decreasing that of the loser:

$$\begin{aligned} DOM_i &:= DOM_i + \left(w_i - \frac{DOM_i}{DOM_i + DOM_j} \right) * STEPDOM \\ DOM_j &:= DOM_j - \left(w_i - \frac{DOM_i}{DOM_i + DOM_j} \right) * STEPDOM \end{aligned} \quad (2)$$

The consequence of this system is that it behaves as a damped positive feedback: winning by the higher ranking agent reinforces their relative DOM-values only slightly, whereas winning by the lower ranking gives rise to a relatively large change in DOM. To keep DOM values positive, their minimum value was arbitrarily put at 0.01. STEPDOM is a scaling factor which varies between 0 and 1 and is analogous to intensity of aggression. High values imply a large change in DOM-value when updating it, and thus indicate that single interactions may strongly influence future outcomes of conflicts. Conversely, low STEPDOM-values represent low impact. Unless stated otherwise, STEPDOM is set at 0.5.

4. Winning includes chasing the opponent one unit distance and then turning randomly 45 degrees to the right or left in order to reduce the chance of repeated interactions between the same partners. The loser responds by fleeing under a small random angle over a predefined FleeingDistance.

In the case of indirect rank perception, the agents (i.e. Estimators) recognize each other individually and remember their personal experience with each partner. Dominance interactions are defined similarly as in the SKINNIES of Hogeweg (1988):

1. If an entity meets another in its PerSpace, it first consults its memory to establish whether it might win or loose a potential dominance interaction with that partner. Hereto, it performs the same dominance interaction as described in (1) and (2), but now based on the mental impressions it has of its own dominance rank and that of the other. If it looses this 'mental battle', it moves away while updating the impression of its own rank and that of the partner. If it wins, it updates and initiates a 'real' fight. Thus, unlike the Perceivers, the Estimators 'decide' whether or not to attack.

2. If it wins, a 'real' fight is initiated by displaying its expectancy to win as its updated relative dominance rank ($=D_i$) and the partner displays in return ($=D_j$). That

is:

$$D_i = \frac{DOM_{i,i}}{DOM_{i,i} + DOM_{i,j}}$$

$$D_j = \frac{DOM_{j,j}}{DOM_{j,j} + DOM_{j,i}}$$

Thus entities display their 'self-confidence'. Note that this self-confidence varies depending on the experience ego has with a particular partner. The variability of the display is not a strategic option (such as dishonest signalling in a typical game-theoretic setting), but a direct consequence of behavioral constraints.

3. Winning is decided as in (1), using D_i and D_j instead of DOM_i and DOM_j.

4. Updating of the experiences of each of both entities is done similar to (2), but involves two representations for agent i:

$$DOM_{i,i} := DOM_{i,i} + \left(w_i - \frac{DOM_{i,i}}{DOM_{i,i} + DOM_{i,j}} \right) * STEPDOM$$

$$DOM_{i,j} := DOM_{i,j} - \left(w_i - \frac{DOM_{i,i}}{DOM_{i,i} + DOM_{i,j}} \right) * STEPDOM$$

Updating for agent j is obtained by replacing $DOM_{i,.}$ by $DOM_{j,.}$.

From now on, the initiation of a dominance interaction will also be referred to as 'attack' for short.

Probability of attack.

In former versions of the model (Hemelrijk 1996, 1997) entities always engaged in dominance interactions when encountering others nearby. However, the 'Obligate attack system' may not meet certain observations on real animals. In a variety of species (e.g., chickens: Guhl 1968; primates: Kummer 1974), it has been found that some time-period after putting unacquainted individuals together, hierarchical activity subsides and non-aggressive proximity prevails. This suggests that eventually animals acknowledge the rank of others. To reflect this directly, I also implemented a version of the model in which the probability of attacking a partner decreases linearly with the rank-distance to that partner (for a comparable implementation see Bonabeau et al. 1996). This will hereafter be referred to as the Rank-Distance-Decreasing attack system. In this paper, I will compare spatial structuring and several other characteristics in the two systems.

Timing regime

Since parallel simulations cannot be run on most computers, a timing regime regulating the sequence of the activation, has to be included. The type of timing regime influences the results of a simulation. A biologically plausible timing regime must be locally controlled, i.e. by other entities and not by a monitor (e.g. Goss & Deneubourg 1988). In the timing regime used here, each entity draws a random waiting time from a uniform distribution. The entity with the shortest waiting time is activated first. The decay of waiting time is the same for each entity. However, if a dominance interaction occurs within NearView of an agent, the waiting time of this agent is reduced stronger.

Experimental setup and data collection

Because animal groupings vary in their cohesiveness, also a comparison between spacious and cohesive groups is included. Cohesive groups (Hemelrijk 1996, 1997) result from a small personal space of two units (this makes entities tolerate others very nearby before chasing them away), a small nearView (which causes entities to turn towards others soon) and a large searchAngle of 90 degrees (by which lost entities quickly find the group back). Starting from cohesive groups, I created spacious groups by enlarging personal space to 4 units and nearView from 8 to 24. Five runs were done per type of entity (Perceiver, Estimator), grouping (Cohesive, Spacious) and FleeingDistance (from one to four units), resulting in a total of 80 experiments.

The effects of attack-probability and STEPDOM were studied for Perceivers only and were evaluated on the basis of sixty runs, consisting of ten runs of each system of attack and for three values of STEPDOM (0.1, 0.5 and 1.0).

During a run, every change in spatial position and heading direction of each entity was recorded. Every time step (consisting of 160 activation) the distance between agents was calculated. Dominance interactions were continuously monitored by recording: 1) the identity of the attacker and its opponent; 2) the winner/loser; 3) the updated DOM-values of these entities.

Measures of spatial centrality of dominants and hierarchical stability

The degree with which dominants occupied the center was measured in two ways, by the spatial directions of others around ego and by the average distances of partners towards ego. Using circular statistics (Mardia 1972), for each scan the centrality of each individual was calculated by drawing a unit circle around it and projecting the direction of other group members (as seen by ego) as points on the circumference of that circle. Connecting these points with the origin gives vectors. The length of the mean vector represents the degree in which the position of group members relative to ego is clumped; longer mean vectors reflect more directedness and indicate lower centrality (i.e. 'encirclement'). Thus stronger centrality of higher ranking entities is reflected in a larger negative correlation between rank and encirclement.

The second measure is the Kendall rank correlation between dominance value and the average distance of Ego to others. Again, centrality of dominants is represented by a negative correlation. Both measures appeared to be strongly correlated and only the rank-encirclement correlation will be mentioned in the analysis.

The stability of the dominance hierarchy was expressed as the relative number of rank reversals. This was established by calculating the Kendall rank correlation between the dominance ranks of entities at successive intervals of two time steps (320 activation).

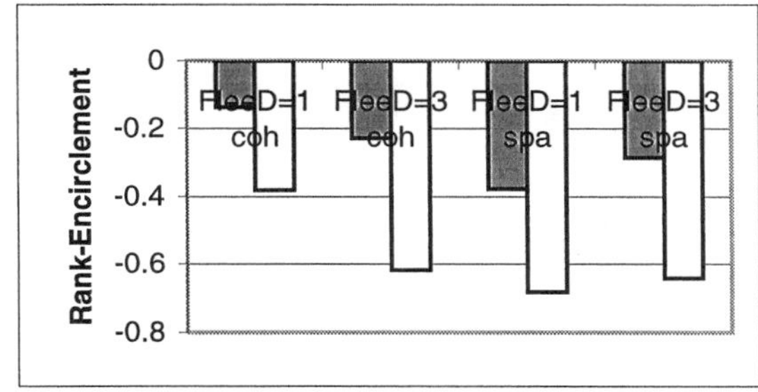

Figure 2. Kendall rank correlation between rank and encirclement for various parameter settings of groups of 8 entities. Shaded bars: Estimators, white bars: Perceivers; FleeD: FleeingDistance; coh: cohesive, spa: spacious groups.

Results

Parameters for strong social-spatial structure.

As in the previous lattice-based world, a dominance hierarchy developed among initially completely identical entities (see Figure 4 of Hemelrijk 1996). Furthermore, due to the continuous version of the world used here, a much clearer social-spatial structure (with dominants in the center and subordinates at the periphery) originated.

Rank-correlated encirclement appeared stronger among Perceivers than Estimators (Figure 2). Assuming that this type of social-spatial structure emerged because dominants chased away subordinates to the periphery, this is probably due to the Perceivers' higher frequency of aggression and clearer rank-differentiation. In the remainder, only the behavior of Perceivers will be considered; for a detailed discussion about differences between Perceivers and Estimators see Hemelrijk (1996,1997).

Social-spatial structuring appeared somewhat weaker in cohesive than in spacious groups (Figure 2). Cohesive groups have a small diameter and this implies that minor displacements suffice too bring an entity to the periphery. Thus, incidental fleeing by dominants disturbs spatial structure more in cohesive than spacious groups.

In spacious groups, the strongest social-spatial structure showed up at an intermediate FleeingDistance of two units (white bars in Figure 3).

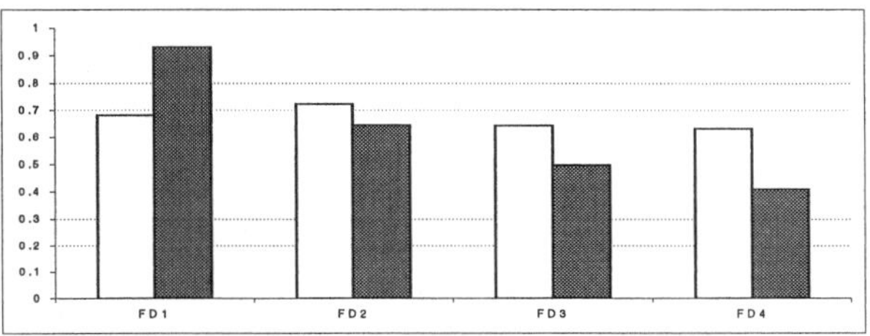

Figure 3. Frequencies of aggression and centrality of dominants for 4 FleeingDistances (FD) in spacious groups of 8 Perceivers. Shaded bars: frequency of aggression * 2000. White bars: absolute value of rank-encirclement correlation.

This may indicate the existence of two conflicting constraints: on the one hand, larger FleeingDistance brings subordinates quicker towards the periphery, thus enhancing spatial structure. On the other hand, larger FleeingDistances increase the average distance among entities thus reducing the frequency of interaction (shaded bars in Figure 3) and hence the ordering force responsible spatial structure.

From now on, the analysis will be restricted to data from runs that yielded the strongest spatial structure (i.e. from Perceivers with PersSpace=4, NearView=24 and FleeingDistance=2) (Figure 4) .

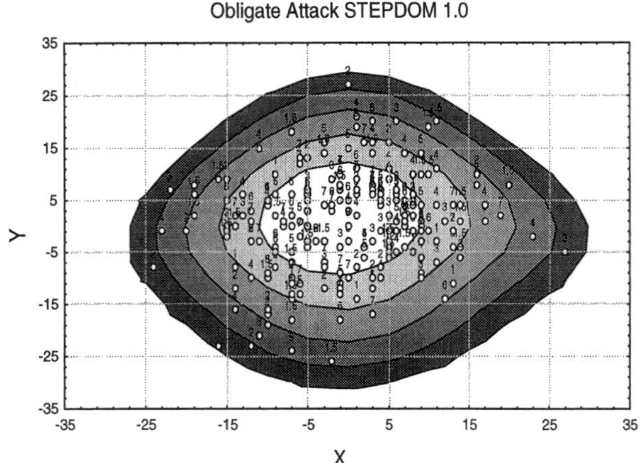

Figure 4. Visualization of social-spatial structure during the last 60 time-steps of a run. The correlation between rank-encirclement was –0.724 for this sub-period. Shown are the position of 8 entities every other time-step. Numbers indicate relative rank (from 1 to 8). Surface contours are isoclines of identical mean rank and were obtained by using a cubic spline smoothing procedure. Darker shading indicates lower mean rank.

Impact of single acts and probability of attack.

Unexpectedly, a higher STEPDOM-value led to reduced levels of aggression in both systems. In turn, this enforced the stability of the hierarchy (Figure 5).

Furthermore, a higher STEPDOM had -depending on the type of attack- opposite consequences for spatial structuring (Figure 6). For Obligatory attack, it strengthened social-spatial structure, whereas for Rank-Distance-Decreasing Attack-rates the opposite was found.

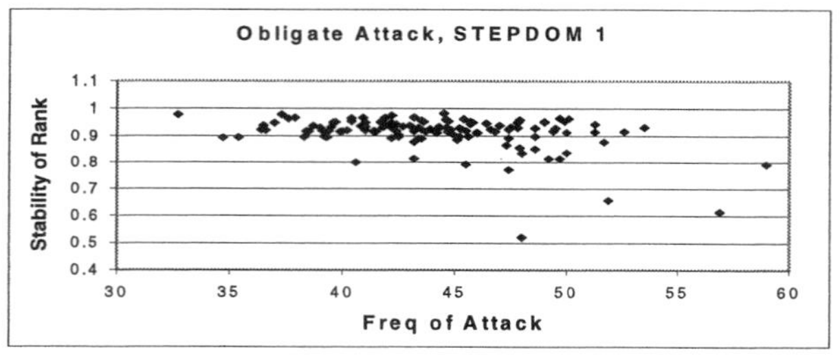

Figure 5. Relationship between frequency of aggression and stability of dominance ranks in successive periods for the Obligate Attack System and STEPDOM 1. For various parameter settings, the product-moment correlation between aggression and rank-stability was as follows: Obligate attack: at StepDom0.5, r=-0.545, at StepDom1.0, r=-0.827, N=128. Rank-Distance-decreasing Attack: N=128, StepDom0.5, r=-0.777; StepDom1.0, r=-0.829

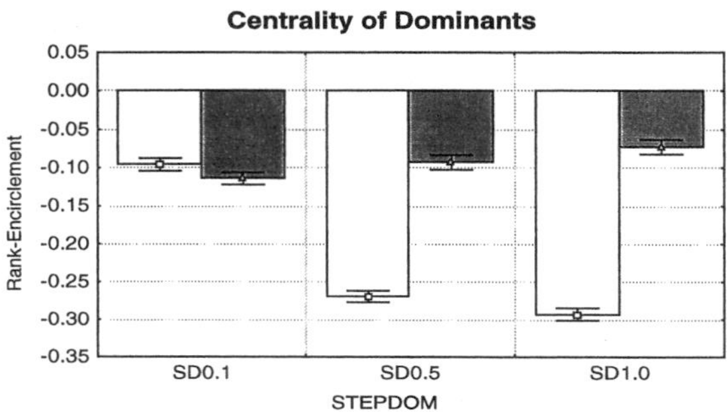

Figure 6. Intensity of aggression (STEPDOM) and centrality of dominants as measured by the rank-encirclement correlation (mean and S.E.). White bars: Obligate attack system, shaded bars: Rank-Distance Decreasing attack system. Note that the degree of rank-related encirclement is similar for both systems at STEPDOM 0.1, because under this condition no clear hierarchy forms.

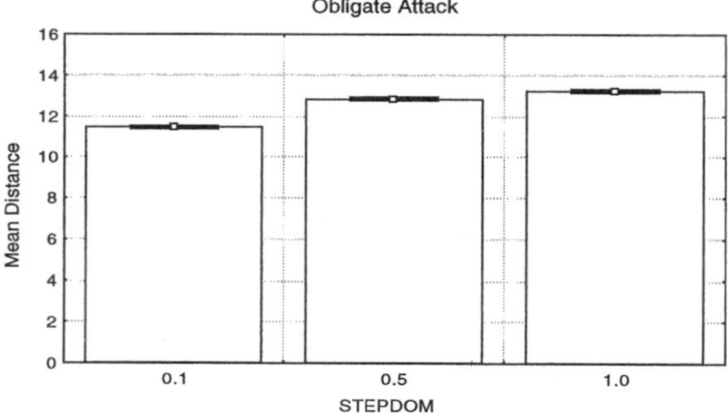

Figure 7. Average inter-individual distances and intensity of aggression (STEPDOM) of the Obligate Attack System

To explain these results, note that the higher the value of STEPDOM the stronger a single event of winning and losing influences the outcome of future interactions. Thus, starting from completely identical entities, ranks differentiate faster at higher STEPDOM. In the system with Obligatory attack, this resulted in larger average distances among entities (Figure 7): By being defeated again and again, losers moved away further and further from others. Consequently, the frequency of aggression dropped (Correlation between distance and aggression at StepDom0.5: r=-0.351, at StepDom1.0: r=-0.461, N=130) and this lowered the probability of rank-reversals (Figure 5). The thus induced higher stability and larger differentiation of ranks enhance social-spatial structure as follows. If entities are similar in rank, both partners are about as likely to chase away the other and are treated by other group-members similarly. As a consequence they remain near one another. The larger the rank-distance between two entities, however, the more subordinates will flee from dominants and in time a correspondence between rank and physical distance will develop. Obviously, when rank is not stable, the frequent rank-reversals hamper the development of a clear spatial structure.

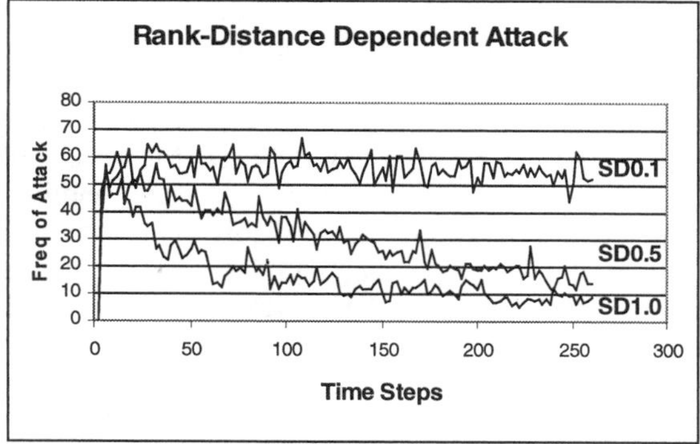

Figure 8. Intensities of aggression (STEPDOM) and decrease of frequency of attack over time in the Rank-Distance Decreasing Attack System.

The situation is different for the Rank-Distance-Decreasing Attack System. In this case, entities also reduce their attack-rate as their ranks differentiate (Figure 8). However, in contrast to the Obligate attack system, they particularly refrain from attacking partners more distant in rank. In other words, they increasingly tolerate nearby partners of more distant rank and this impairs spatial structure. However, it does not reverse the spatial configuration into one with dominants at the periphery and subordinates in the center. This is due to two forces. First, if a fight takes place, then in both systems, dominants win more often from subordinates the larger their rank-distance with these partners and second, aggressive interactions especially occur among rank-near entities. Note that in the Rank-Distance Decreasing attack system the latter is implemented a priori as a behavioral rule, whereas in the Obligate system it is due to the emergent proximity of rank-near entities.

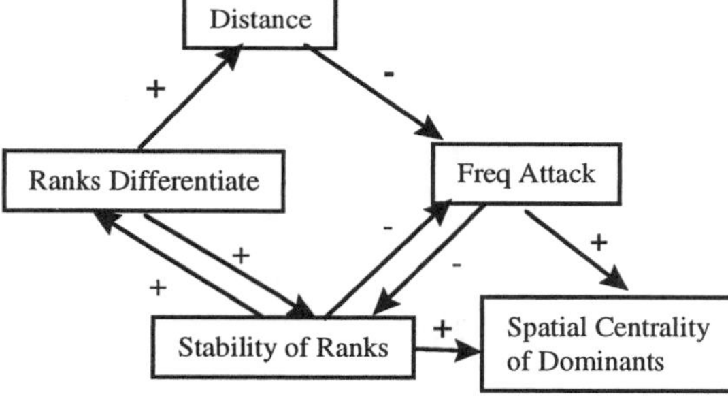

Figure 9. Summary of results for the Obligate Attack System. Arrows indicate direction of the effect.

Some other effects of spatial structure

An important property of a self-organizing system is the feedback between macro-patterns and the rules operating at the micro-level. In the Obligate attack system, this is illustrated by the reduced aggression that ensues with the growing spatial structure (which in itself arises as a consequence of dominance interactions). Lowered aggression in turn, strengthens spatial structure by decreasing the probability of rank-reversals (Figure 9).

Another example is the spontaneous development of a positive correlation between rank and aggression, as I reported before for a lattice-based artificial world (Hemelrijk 1996). In the continuous version, this correlation was found more profoundly for higher STEPDOM-values in the Obligate Attack System (being significant in respectively 0%, 30% and 60 % of the runs for STEPDOM of 0.1, 0.5 and 1.0), but was never significant for the Rank-Distance-Decreasing Attack System. This supports my previous suggestion that rank correlated aggression arises as a consequence of a spatial structure with dominants in the center. In such a configuration, others surround dominants at all sides, whereas subordinates at the periphery experience fewer encounter frequencies and therefore their opportunities to attack others are reduced.

Compared to the Obligatory Attack System, in the Rank-Distance Decreased Attack System, bidirectionality of attack was stronger, particularly so at higher STEPDOMs (Figure 10). This is understandable, because if attack rate decreases in proportion to rank-distance, this means that entities more often attack partners the nearer the rank of the partners. Since all individuals do so and rank-distance is a symmetrical characteristic, rank-nearer entities will mutually attack each other more often.

For the same reason higher STEPDOMS were associated with stronger reciprocity of non-aggressive proximity as well.

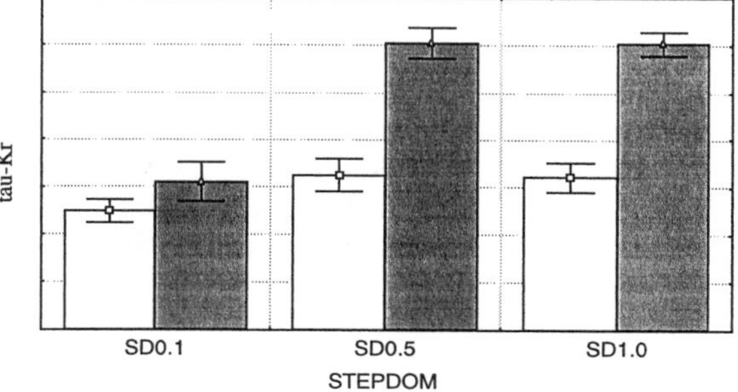

Figure 10. Bi-directionality of aggression for both systems of attack and increasing STEPDOM (mean τ_{Kr} plus/minus S. E.) Bi-directionality of attack is measured as a τ_{Kr} -correlation between an actor and receiver matrix (Hemelrijk 1990). White bars: Obligate attack system; Shaded bars: Rank-Distance decreased attack system.

Discussion

In line with Hogeweg's (1988) observations, this model clearly shows that a spatial structure with dominants in the center and subordinates located at increasingly larger distances from the core, may emerge as a side effect from self-reinforcing dominance interactions and a tendency to aggregate. Moreover, such a structure arises in the absence of any positional preference of the entities.

This implies an alternative explanation to the commonly held view that centrality of dominants reflects their positional predisposition for a safer location in the group, which in turn is assumed to be optimized by natural selection. In the model, centrality of dominants arises because dominants have a larger chance to win from (and chase away), subordinates that are more distant in rank. Provided the level of aggression is sufficiently high, this process is strengthened when dominance hierarchies are less ambiguous (because of more outspoken rank-differentiation) and more stable. Although the process is weaker in the Rank-Distance Decreasing Attack System, the pattern is generally robust; the correlation between rank and encirclement was negative for every parameter setting. Robustness was further supported by results from an extended model, in which I made FleeingDistance and SearchAngle rank dependent. As a consequence, low-ranking entities flew further (FleeingDistance of 5 versus 1 units) and returned to the group slower when lost (searchAngle of 60 instead of 90 degrees) than high-ranking ones. The resulting social-spatial structure for both attack systems and increasing STEPDOM appeared similar to vary that reported here.

The model yielded a host of other emergent effects. For instance, under the Obligate attack system, higher ranking entities aggressed others more frequently than lower-ranking ones did. This came about as a consequence of spatial structure: dominants simply have more interaction opportunities because of their central location (which itself is a result of dominance interactions). Note that this perspective is very different from the conventional one, which assumes that a rank-correlated rate of aggression is an internal characteristic of dominants. Another example is the decline of aggression due to rank-differentiation and the higher attack-rate towards rank-nearer entities. This is not only a feature of the Rank-Distance Decreasing attack system (in which it was explicitly implemented), it also originated as a self-organized feature in the Obligate attack system. In the latter, reduced aggression resulted from larger individual distances, which in turn was a consequence of dominance differentiation. Note that this feature of the Obligate attack system fulfills the original motivation for implementing the Rank-Distance Decreasing attack system, and makes them appear equally ‘natural’. Furthermore, rank-near entities were more often attacked, because they were closer than rank-distant ones.

It is especially this abundance of emergent effects that highlights the complex intertwinement of behavioral variables. This complexity hampers predictability. What, for instance, will happen when entities belong to different STEPDOM classes (compare sex-age categories in primates, Bernstein and Ehardt 1985)? Although we could expect entities of the same STEPDOM to cluster (because they react similarly to their social environment, cf. Hogeweg 1988) and within such clusters, dominants to occupy the center, it is very hard to foresee how clusters of different STEPDOM types will arrange themselves spatially relative to one another. Insight in these matters may shed light on an ongoing polemic about the spatial positioning of sex-age categories in primate groups (Altmann 1979; Rhine and Westland 1981) and is the topic of my current research. In such indecisive disputes, individual-oriented models are particularly useful, because the consequences of biologically plausible extensions can be studied directly in silica. In this context, artificial worlds may function as a kind of virtual laboratory that allow for ‘social experiments’ that are impossible in the real world (Epstein and Axtell 1996), but provide behavioral scientists with ‘tools for thought’.

Acknowledgments

I am grateful to and Rolf Pfeifer and Bob Martin for continuous support. I like to thank René te Boekhorst for improving former versions of this paper. This work is supported by the Swiss National Science Foundation by a grant from the Marie Heim-Voegtlin Foundation.

References

Altmann, S. A. 1979. Baboon progressions. Order or chaos ? A study of one-dimensional group geometry. *Animal Behaviour* 27: 46-80.

Barnard, C. J., and Burk, T. E. 1979. Dominance hierarchies and the evolution of 'individual recognition'. *Journal of theoretical Biology* 81: 65-73.

Bernstein, I. S., and Ehardt, C. L. 1985. Intragroup agonistic behavior in Rhesus monkeys (*Macaca mulatta*). *International Journal of Primatology* 6(3): 209-226.

Bonabeau, E., Theraulaz, G., and Deneubourg, J.-L. 1996. Mathematical models of self-organizing hierarchies in animal societies. *Bulletin of mathematical biology* 58(4): 661-717.

Bumann, D., Krause, J., and Rubenstein, D. 1997. Mortality risk of spatial positions in animal groups: the danger of being in the front. *Behaviour* 134: 1063-1076.

Chase, I. D., Bartelomeo, C., and Dugatkin, L. A. 1994. Aggressive interactions and inter-contest interval: how long do winners keep winning ? *Animal Behaviour* 48: 393-400.

Collins, D. A. 1984. Spatial pattern in a troop of yellow baboons (*Papio cynocepohalus*). *Animal Behaviour* 32: 536-553.

Copp, N. H. 1986. Dominance hierarchies in the crayfish Procambarus clarkii (Girard, 1852) and the question of learned individual recognition (Decapoda, Astacidea). *Crustaceana* 51(1): 9-24.

Deneubourg, J. L., and Goss, S. 1989. Collective patterns and decision-making. *Ethology, Ecology and Evolution* 1: 295-311.

Depew, D. J., and Weber, B. H. 1995. *Darwinism Evolving. Systems Dynamics and the Genealogy of Natural Selection*. The MIT Press.

Ellis, L. (Ed.). 1994. Reproductive and interpersonal aspects of dominance and status. Westport: Greenwood publishing group.

Epstein, J. M., and Axtell, R. 1996. Growing Artificial Societies. Social Science from the Bottom Up. Washinton, DC: Brookings Institution Press.

Goss, S., and Deneubourg, J. L. 1988. Autocatalysis as a source of synchronised rhythmical activity in social insects. *Insectes Sociaux* 35(3): 310-315.

Guhl, A. M. 1968. Social inertia and social stability in chickens. *Animal Behaviour* 16: 219-232.

Hamilton, W. D. 1971. Geometry for the selfish herd. *Journal of theoretical Biology* 31: 295-311.

Hemelrijk, C. K. 1990. Models of, tests for, reciprocity, unidirectionality and other social interaction patterns at a group level. *Animal Behaviour* 39: 1013-1029.

Hemelrijk, C. K. 1996. Dominance interactions, spatial dynamics and emergent reciprocity in a virtual world. In *From Animals to Animats 4: Proceedings of the fourth international conference on simulation of adaptive behavior*, edited by P. Maes, M. J. Mataric, J-A Meyer, J Pollack, and S. W. Wilson. Cambridge, MA: The MIT Press/Bradford Books, p. 545-552.

Hemelrijk, C. K. (1997). Cooperation without genes, games or cognition. *In 4th European Conference on Artificial Life,* edited by P. Husbands and I. Harvey. Cambridge, MA: MIT-Press, p. 511-520.

Hogeweg, P. 1988. MIRROR beyond MIRROR, puddles of LIFE. In *Proceedings of Artificial Life*, edited by C. G. Langton. Redwood City, California: Addison-Wesley, p. 297-316.

Hogeweg, P. and B. Hesper 1979. Heterarchical, selfstructuring simulation systems: concepts and applications in biology. In *Methodologies in Systems Modelling and Simulation.* Amsterdam: North-Holland, p. 221-231.

Hogeweg, P. and B. Hesper 1983. The ontogeny of interaction structure in bumble bee colonies: a MIRROR model. *Behavioral Ecology and Sociobiology* 12: 271-283.

Janson, C. H. 1990a. Ecological consequences of individual spatial choice in foraging groups of brown caopuchin monkeys, *Cebus apella. Animal Behaviour* 40: 922-934.

Janson, C. H. 1990b. Social correlates of individual spatial choice in foraging groups of brown capucin monkeys, *Cebus apella. Animal Behaviour* 40: 910-921.

Judson, O. P. 1994. The rise of the individual-based model in ecology. *Trends in Ecology and Evolution* 9: 9-14.

Krause, J. 1994. Differential fitness returns in relation to spatial position in groups. *Biological Reviews* 69: 187-206.

Kummer, H. 1974. Rules of dyad and group formation among captive baboons (*Theropithecus gelada*). In *Symposium 5th Congress Int'l. Primat. Soc.* Basel: S. Karger, p 129-160.

Mardia, K. V. 1972. *Statistics of Directional Data.* London and New York: Academic Press.

Parish, J. K. 1989. Re-examining the selfish herd: are central fish safer ? *Animal Behaviour* 38: 1048-1053.

Pfeifer, R., and Verschure, P. 1995. The challenge of autonomous agents: Pitfalls and how to avoid them. In *The Artificial Life Route to Artificial Intelligence: Building Embodied, Situated Agents*, edited by L. Steels and R. Brooks. Hillsdale, New Jersey: Lawrence Erlbaum Associates, p. 237-263.

Rayor, S. R., and Uetz, G. W. 1990. Trade-offs in foraging success and predation risk with spatial position in colonial spiders. *Behavioural Ecology and Sociobiology* 27: 77-85.

Rhine, R. J., and Westland, B. J. 1981. Adult male positioning in baboon progressions: order and chaos revisited. *Folia Primatologica* 35: 77-116.

Thierry, B. 1985. Patterns of agonistic interactions in three species of macaque (*Macaca mulatta, M. fascicularis, M. tonkeana). Aggressive Behavior* 11: 223-233.

Thierry, B. 1990. The state of equilibrium among agonistic behavior patterns in a group of Japanese macaques (*Macaca fuscata*). *C. R. Acad. Sci. Paris* 310(3): 35-40.

van Honk, C., and Hogeweg, P. 1981. The ontogeny of the social structure in a captive *Bombus terrestris* colony. *Behavioral Ecology and Sociobiology* 9: 111-119.

Villa, F. 1992. New computer architectures as tools for ecological thought. *Trends in Ecology and Evolution* 7: 179-183.

Generic Behavior in the Lindgren Non-Spatial Model of Iterated Two Player Games

Tad Shannon

Systems Science Program, Portland State University
PO Box 751, Portland, Oregon 97207
tads@sysc.pdx.edu

Abstract

Punctuated equilibrium is found to be a generic property of Lindgren's non-spatial model of coevolution of strategies for two player games. Macro measures of evolutionary activity and concentration within a population are introduced and used to characterize evolutionary dynamics in the model population. Punctuated equilibria are found across a wide region of parameter space, but are not found in the absence of adaptation. A variety of control experiments are introduced, including a neutral analogue that characterizes genetic drift in this model class. Finally, a model of population moving through genotype space is used to describe the punctuated equilibrium phenomenon and to introduce a taxonomy of punctuations. This classification is then applied to the observed base case model results.

Introduction

Lindgren developed several evolutionary models of simple strategies that play iterated two player games in noisy environments (Lindgren 1992, Lindgren and Nordahl 1994). In the non-spatial version, each strategy in the population plays every other strategy. A strategy's fitness in this model is an implicit function of the other strategies active in the population, thus the model performs a coevolution of strategies. Applying this model to the Iterated Prisoner's Dilemma (IPD), Lindgren found that punctuated equilibria are an endogenous behavioral mode of evolving populations. Relatively long periods of evolutionary stasis were found, followed by abrupt extinction events that lead to new periods of stasis. This behavioral pattern is encountered in many other evolving systems, and has been hypothesized to be a generic property of evolution (Langton 1992).

The term "punctuated equilibria" was introduced into evolutionary theory by Eldredge and Gould (Eldredge and Gould 1972) in the context of describing speciation events. They advanced a theory of speciation in which rapid bursts of evolutionary activity caused speciation events as punctuations between long periods of evolutionary stasis. The punctuations in Lindgren's model aren't just speciation events, but wholesale replacements of one dominant ecology with another. While the details of what is a punctuation differ, the phenomena in both cases are driven, at least in part, by the dynamics of populations diffusing in a discrete genotype space under the action of a phenotypic fitness gradient. Thus an explanation of punctuated equilibria based on population dynamics in genotype space derived from the relatively simple case of Lindgren's model applies to many other natural and artificial evolving systems. The final section of this paper attempts just such an explanation.

A measure of evolutionary activity useful for identifying punctuations in Lindgren's model is the activity statistic introduced by Bedau and Packard as a measure of useful genetic adaptation in a population (Bedau and Packard 1992). They use this measure to differentiate between population dynamics due to "meaningful" evolution and those due to the structure of the simulation methodology used. In their approach, a neutral analogue of the adaptive model is constructed, and the two behaviors compared. Consistent differences between the two can be attributed to meaningful evolution (Bedau et al. 1997).

We use their activity measure to identify punctuated equilibria across a wide region of the parameter space for Lindgren's model. We then construct several neutral analogues of the adaptive model and find no punctuated equilibrium behavior in the non-adaptive populations. Based on these observations, we proposes a model of punctuated equilibria resulting from an adaptive process moving population around in genotype space.

The Model

Lindgren's model assigns scores to different strategies based on each strategies' interaction with all the active strategies in a generation. Each strategy's percentage of the population is then adjusted based on the deviation of the strategy's score from the mean score for that generation. During this phase, the model allows for mutation of strategies, causing new strategies to enter the active population, and in some sense allowing the simulation to explore the "strategy space" of the game.

The Prisoner's Dilemma is used for the base case game. The Prisoner's Dilemma is a two person nonzero sum game in which players must choose between cooperating with their opponent or defecting. The dominant strategy for both players is defection, which leads to a non-optimal outcome for each (Axelrod 1984). The game is summarized in matrix form as:

	C	D
C	3, 3	0, 5
D	5, 0	1, 1

where in (a, b), a is the row player's payoff and b the column player's payoff, and the relation of the payoff values to one another is significant, but the absolute magnitudes are not. The dominant strategy for both players is to defect, which leads to the payoff (1, 1) that is not as desirable as the cooperative outcome (3, 3).

Strategies in the model are specifications of whether to cooperate or defect on the next play given the immediate past history of both players' actions. The length of the history considered is the memory of the strategy. The base case starts with memory 1 strategies, permits a maximum memory length of 4 and allows for both memory increasing and memory decreasing mutations. Each strategy is represented as a bit string with a one meaning cooperate, and a zero meaning defect. The length of such strings determines the memory of the strategy. A memory 1 strategy is two bits, the low order bit specifies the action given the opponent cooperated on the last play, and the high order bit specifies the action given the opponent defected on the last play. A memory 2 strategy contains 4 bits, the low order pair specifies how to respond to the opponent when the player's own last play was cooperated, while the high order pair specify the case where the player last defect. Essentially, a memory 2 strategy is two memory 1 strategies concatenated together. Larger memory strategies can be created in a like manner, a memory 3 strategy is 8 bits long, a memory 4 is 16 bits long. Note, a memory 1 strategy is phenotypically identical to a memory 2 strategy formed by concatenating it with itself, e.g. 01 is the same as 0101. These bit strings are genotypic representations in that 01, 0101, and 0101-0101 all represent the same effective strategy even though they are distinct strings.

For each generation in the simulation, the model calculates a score for the interaction of each active strategy with every other active strategy. This is done by treating the interaction, the repeated playing of the game, as a markov process with order equal to the longest memory length of the interacting strategies. The stationary distribution for this process can be solved for explicitly, and then converted to an expected score given the payoffs of the game. Each strategy accumulates a score and the population mean is found. Strategies with scores greater than the population mean have their representation in the population increased proportionally, while those with scores below the mean have their representation reduced. When a strategy's representation in the population falls below a minimum level, it is eliminated. After this population adjustment step, each surviving strategy is checked for three kinds of mutations: memory doubling, memory splitting and point mutation of individual bits. Mutations are based on the model mutation rate parameters, and result in a transfer of population percentage from the parent strategy to the mutant strategy. The mutant strategy may be a new or an existing strategy.

Macro-measures for Evolutionary Simulations

Macro population measures include the diversity or the number of distinct genotypes or phenotypes active, population uncertainty - the information theoretic uncertainty in randomly choosing a genotype from the active population, population concentration - the normalized uncertainty, and total evolutionary activity in the population.

Bedau and Packard introduced evolutionary activity as the summation over time of the continuous persistence or usage of genes, genotypes, and phenotypes. This statistic attempts to capture the presence of meaningful adaptations that make a difference to the longevity of a type. Counters are attached to each type in the population, and are incremented in proportion to the type's use or longevity and zeroed out when the type disappears.

The specific measures used are:

Simple Diversity $D(t) = \#\{i : p_i(t) > 0\}$,

Population Uncertainty

$$U(t) = -\left(\sum p_i(t) \log p_i(t)\right),$$

Population Concentration

$$C(t) = 1 - \frac{U(t)}{\log D(t)},$$

Genotypic Activity

$$a_i(t) = \sum_{\{t \geq s : p_i(s) \neq 0, p_i(s-1) = 0\}} p_i(t),$$

Total Activity

$$A(t) = \sum a_i(t),$$

where the index i is to be taken over all active genotypes in generation t, and $p_i(t)$ is the proportion of the population with genotype i in generation t.

Base Case Model Results

These current results are based on a C language implementation that closely resembles Lindgren's original Pascal code. This new implementation replicates the basic scenario reported by Lindgren, including the key strategies and epochs of parasitism, mutualism and unexploitable stability. The parameter values used by Lindgren in his original work are our base case: population size (N) = 1000, selection pressure (d) = 0.1, noise (error rate, p) =

0.01, doubling/split mutation rate ($p_d = p_s$) = 10^{-5}, point mutation rate (p_p) = $2x10^{-5}$.

The usual progression of equilibrium periods or epochs encountered in base case model runs is:

- Beginning with equal proportions of each of the four memory 1 strategies, a variety of memory 1 dynamics occur in which strategies go extinct and are reborn through point mutation. The memory 1 regime is eventually displaced by some combination of highly cooperative but exploitable memory 2 strategies. Strategies 0001 and 1001 then appear and dominate the memory 2 epoch.
- When this regime persists for long enough, 0001-0001 and 1001-1001 appear through memory doubling mutations, and then 1001-0001 and 0001-1001 appear as point mutations. These two strategies together are capable of taking over the population from the memory 2 strategies. Separately, neither plays well, thus this memory 3 epoch is characterized as mutualistic.
- Finally, 1001-0001-1001-0001 and 0001-1001-0001-1001 appear as doubling mutations of the symbiotic regime, and then mutate into 1001-0001-0001-1001 and related types (of the form 1xx1-0xxx-0xxx-x001), which take over the population and lead to an evolutionarily stable regime.

While this is the basic scenario previously reported, two important points can be added. First, this is only the general progression -- in many model runs there is a great deal of cycling between memory 1 and memory 2 regimes. Populations of memory 1 and memory 2 strategies build up only to be invaded by selfish strategies that collapse back to memory 1 dynamics. Typical long periods of stasis occur when the population crashes to all 00, which develops a significant 0000 population that introduces 0001 as a point mutation. 0001 invades the x-0 population and gets back to the memory 2 regime. Figure 2 illustrates this.

The second point is that high concentrations of any one genotype in the population lead to a build up of the memory doubled variant of that genotype, i.e. 00 leads to 0000 etc.. It is from these memory doubled variants, which are phenotypically identical to the dominant genotype(s), that point mutations can produce the next wave of dominant genotypes. This population drift to phenotypically similar but genotypically more complex types is essential for describing the mechanism that produces the punctuations.

The activity measures, together with diversity and concentration, characterize the population dynamics associated with each of the above epochs. In Figure 1, total activity exhibits two large waves (1 - 855, and 855 - 2000) a small wave (2000 - 2200) and the beginning of a fourth wave (2200 +). Each of these activity waves corresponds to an evolutionary epoch in which one or more strategies dominate the population. The first wave represents the initial period of dynamics between memory 1 strategies that is dominated by 01, and 10. The notch at the peak of the wave corresponds to 10 going extinct due to the growth of the 0101 mutant 1101. The end of this era is marked by the extinction of 01 and 1101 together, and the emergence of 1001 and then 0001 as the dominant strategies. Of these 0001 tends to dominate for most of the epoch. As memory 3 strategies emerge through gene duplication of the dominant strategies, 0001 eventually goes extinct -- the initial drop at the end of the wave, followed by 1001 at the second drop. The third, much smaller wave represents the emergence of the dominant mutualistic pair 1001-0001 and 0001-1001. The fourth wave marks the emergence of the evolutionarily stable regime of memory 4 strategies. Here the less efficient memory 3 types quickly go extinct.

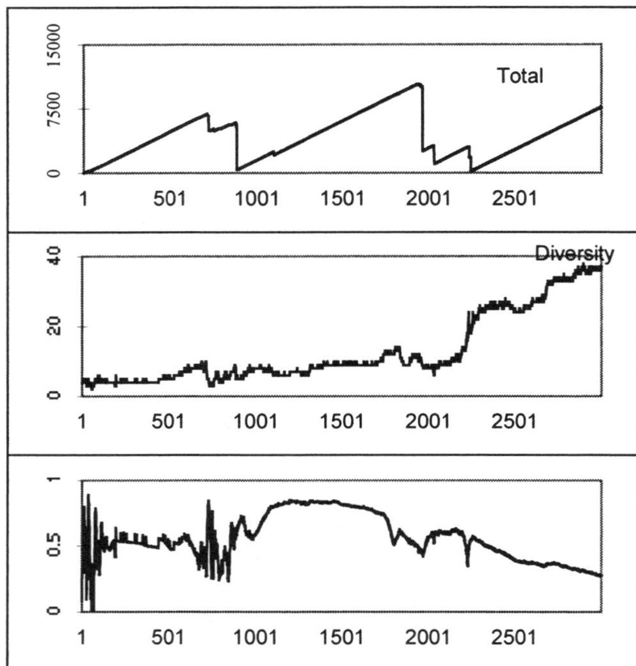

Figure 1: A(t), D(t) and C(t), base case, 30k generations.

The waves exhibited by the total activity measure summarize the punctuated equilibrium phenomena of this evolutionary simulation very well. The waves correspond to the periods of "equilibrium" while the collapse of a wave to near zero marks the "punctuation". The concentration measure roughly characterizes the nature of the dynamics within each epoch. For example, the concentration during the initial wave fluctuates during the initial memory 1 shake out, levels off during the "quiet" period of dominance by 01 and 10, then oscillates again as 1101 and then 1001 emerge and take over. During the second wave, the concentration fluctuates initially as first 1001 and then 0001 becomes dominant, and then increases for most of the epoch, corresponding to the dominance of 0001. Near the end of the wave the population becomes less concentrated as 0001 is forced out. The third wave concentration stays fairly constant during the relative stasis of 1001-0001 and 0001-1001 mutualism. Finally, after the shift to the evolutionarily stable set of memory 4 strategies, a very distinctive logarithmic decrease in concentration occurs for the rest of the simulation. This corresponds to the diffusion of population amongst the stable set of strategies. Note that the diversity of the population remains fairly low (5 to 10 types) until the emergence of the memory 4 strategies, at which point it increases.

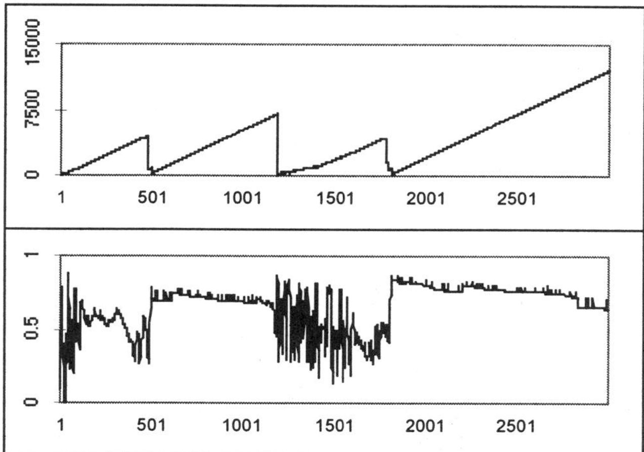

Figure 2: A(t), and C(t), base case, 30k generations. Note cycling between evolutionary epochs.

Another example in Figure 2 illustrates the cyclic nature of this evolutionary progression. Here there are four activity waves. The first exhibits typical memory 1 dynamics, the second is a period of rebuilding diversity after collapse to an entirely selfish population. The third is a period of memory 1 and 2 cycling, and the fourth is again a period of selfish dominance (00) with a slow invasion of 0001. Unlike the previous run, this one doesn't reach the stable regime of memory 4 strategies over the course of 30,000 generations.

Neutral Models

To gain a better understanding of the above dynamics, we need to see what types of behavior the model structure produces in the absence of meaningful adaptation. There are several possible approaches to shutting off adaptation. Three options investigated are: a random behavior model in which all genotypes are phenotypically identical; a random fitness model in which selection pressure is applied to the population based on fitness values randomly assigned at each generation; and the use of a payoff matrix from a game with a known, stable solution which is present in the starting population.

In the first approach, the noise level, i.e. the rate at which errors are made in the game, is set at 0.5. This produces a random behavior model in which all strategies play the same. This model amounts to a diffusion process in genotype space driven by the model mutation rates. From the initial set of memory 1 strategies with uniform concentrations, a cloud of types billows out slowly over time. Concentration remains fairly low, diversity increases slowly but steadily, and there are almost no extinction events during the first 30,000 generations. With no types going extinct, total activity increases with slope 1 over the entire simulation period. No punctuations take place. Since all genotypes are phenotypically equivalent, there is no opportunity for meaningful adaptation.

The second neutral analogue was created by driving the population dynamics of the model using a gaussian probability density. In the adaptive model, a genotype's concentration in a population changes in proportion to the deviation of the type's score from the population's mean score for the generation. This neutral model was constructed by replacing the actual score deviation with a deviation generated from a gaussian density. These random deviations were scaled and constrained to be centered and realizable based on an assumed population mean moving randomly through the interval of possible means. The standard deviations for both the movement of the population mean and the deviation distribution are definable parameters, as are the realizable limits for both the mean and the deviations. This model essentially takes a random walk in genotype space. No adaptation can take place since fitness is randomly determined at every generation. But unlike the random behavior model above, selection pressure is still exerted based on the random fitness assignments.

Analysis of neutral model runs show that after a number of generations equal to that needed for the adaptive model to reach a population of evolutionarily stable memory 4 strategies, the neutral population contains mostly memory 4 strategies that are at least somewhat related. The drift to memory 4 strategies makes sense given that there are vastly more memory 4 strategies than memory 1 through 3 strategies combined (65,536 compared to 276). This also accounts for the pattern of diversity increase seen in the adaptive simulations. Until viable memory 3 strategies get established in a population, there is little possibility of exploring most of the genotype space through the process of single point mutations. Since there are only twenty total genotypes of memory 1 and 2, its not possible to get 30 or 40 types in a population until successful memory 3 and 4 strategies appear.

In Figure 3, the activity graph for the neutral model shows that total activity initially increases, then fluctuates, but never collapses back near the zero level. The extinction events that wipe out the dominant types of an epoch are not present. The dips are much more gradual, and the over all shape of the curve is smoother. The neutral model shows a much more linear growth in diversity up to an equilibrium level.

There are significant extinction events during the course of the simulation, in which the number of types drops significantly over the course of a few hundred generations, and then rebounds to its previous level. While most of the time the concentration remains low, during these extinction episodes the concentration increases significantly.

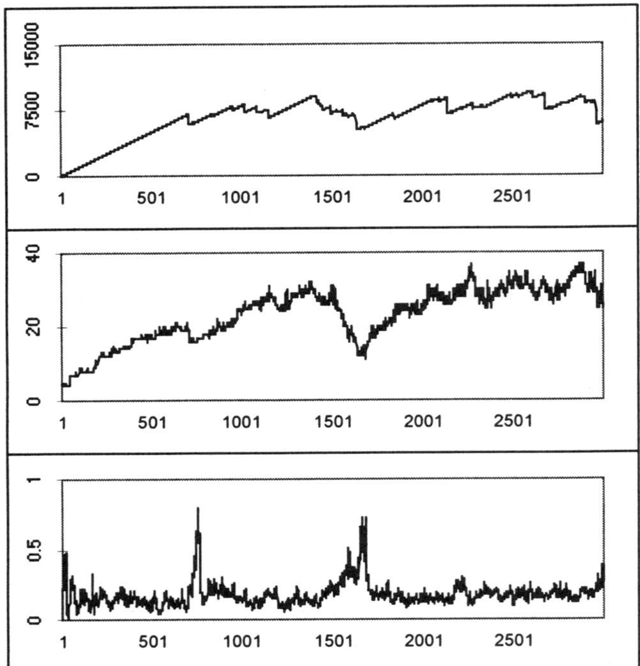

Figure 3: A(t), D(t) and C(t), base case random walk neutral model ($\sigma s = 1.0$), 30k generations.

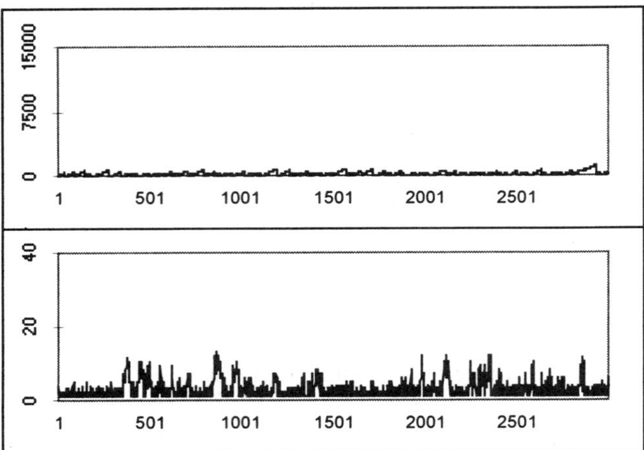

Figure 4: A(t) and D(t), random walk model with high selection pressure ($\sigma s = 1.0$, d=0.4), 30k generations.

That there are no punctuations found in either of the above neutral models strongly suggests that punctuated equilibria are products of meaningful adaptation in evolutionary processes, not products of genetic drift. However, if the selection pressure is increased sufficiently, this neutral model does produce activity waves that drop to near zero. This case is illustrated in Figure 4, note there is clearly no significant build up of activity. There are punctuations but no periods of equilibrium. We can not get both together from this neutral model -- adaptation is necessary to get punctuated equilibrium.

For the third approach, running simulations on games for which solutions are known and easily verified, we turn to the class of noncompetitive games (Rapoport, Guyer 1978). The most stable of these is:

	C	D
C	5, 5	3, 1
D	1, 3	0, 0

in which the dominant strategy for both players is to always cooperate and thus obtain the maximum payoff. When this game is used in place of the prisoner's dilemma, 11 (always cooperate) is found to dominate the population. Small populations of memory doubled 11 begin to appear with some memory 3 variations of 1111-1111 persisting for periods of time. These results are reassuring both because they agree with the game theoretic analysis, and because they show that adaptive selection can resist the drift to memory 4 strategies. While no punctuated equilibrium behavior is found in these cases, there is also no opportunity for useful innovation since the optimal strategy already exists in the starting population.

Robustness Across Parameter Values

Determining the robustness of punctuated equilibrium behavior to differing parameter values requires searching across the possible values for the three mutation rates, the population survival limit (which determines the implicit population size), the population delta (a proxy for selection pressure), the noise level of the game, the relative magnitudes of the game payoffs (3, 0, 5, 1 versus 4.9, 0, 5, 1), and the maximum memory length allowed.

Increasing the maximum memory length to five has little impact on the pattern found in the base case scenario. All the same initial epochs appear as in the base case.

Increasing the selection pressure makes the qualitative behavior of the simulation more crisp. It also seems to increase the probability of collapse back to memory 1 dynamics. The base for this parameter is 0.1. When it is increased beyond 0.5 there is a very low likelihood of arriving at the evolutionarily stable set of memory 4 strategies. The population seems to cycle indefinitely, spending most of the time with memory 1 strategies. Figure 5 illustrates a run with the parameter set at 0.4. The total activity shows four waves, while the concentration measure shows the distinctive patterns associated with the dynamics of the different memory length regimes.

Decreasing the selection pressure smoothes out the activity waves. Figure 6 illustrates this for the case where selection pressure has been decreased by a factor of ten. While the same evolutionary progression occurs, the punctuations disappear.

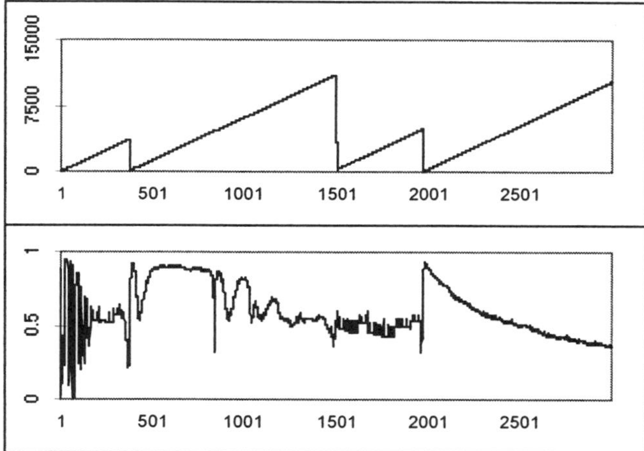

Figure 5: A(t) & C(t), high selection pressure (d=0.4), 30k generations.

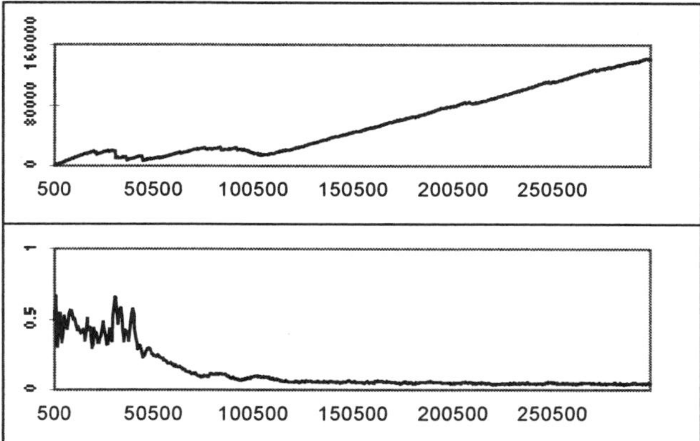

Figure 6: A(t) & C(t), low selection pressure (d=0.01), 300k generations.

Increasing the mutation rate speeds up the exploration of the genotype space. When the mutation rate is increased by a factor of ten, the evolutionary progression from memory 1 to a stable memory 4 regime is one continuous process. As Figure 7 shows no periods of stasis or punctuations appear. Decreasing the mutation rate slows down the exploration of genotype space. In Figure 8, epochs become longer lived, punctuations become very crisp, more instances of collapse are encountered, and the expected time needed to reach the stable memory 4 regime grows significantly.

The survival limit determines the size of one individual in the population, and thus both the minimum size a strategy can be in the population and survive, and the proportion of population that is transferred between genotypes when a mutation occurs. Its value thus impacts the simulation in several ways. First is the mechanism by which a cooperative strategy invades a selfish population. To be successfully, the cooperative strategy needs to attain some minimum concentration so that its gain through self interaction can offset its losses due to exploitation by the rest of the population. Since the population size of a new mutant type is determined by the survival limit, the new mutant will go extinct or become established based on whether the survival limit is less than or greater than the critical self interaction level. The general thrust of this reasoning is born out by the finding that increasing the survival limit tends to decrease the simulation time needed to reach the stable memory 4 regime and increases the rate of diffusion amongst those strategies once the regime is reached, while decreasing the survival limit tends to reverse these findings. In both cases punctuations still occur.

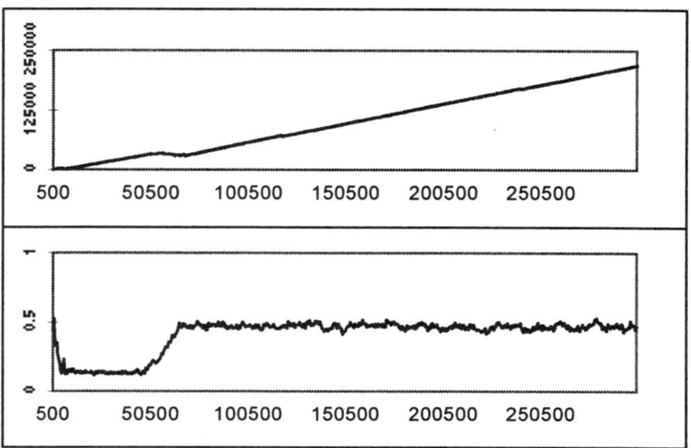

Figure 7: A(t) & C(t), high mutation (base case rates x10), 300k generations.

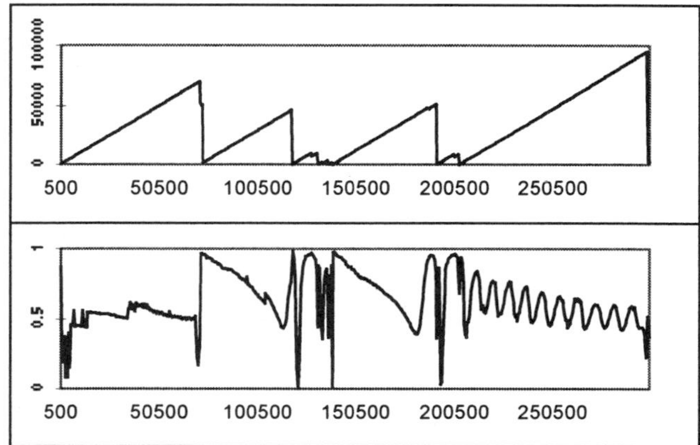

Figure 8: A(t) & C(t), low mutation (base case rates x10^{-1}), 300k generations.

Changing game parameters changes the expected payoff from each interaction. These parameters include the relative payoff structure, the absolute magnitude of the payoffs, and the noise level or error rate. The absolute magnitude of the payoffs can be considered a scaling factor that increases or decreases the variance of scores from the population mean, and thus is equivalent to selection pressure treated above. This leaves noise level and payoff structure as parameters to investigate.

A higher noise level leads to significantly different behavior. Increasing the noise level flattens out the distribution in scores. Figure 9 illustrates one extended run for an error rate of 10% instead of 1%. The dynamics differ from the base case -- they are smoother and less distinctive, but punctuations still occur. Note the epochs with much larger diversities than are ever seen in base case scenarios, and the lack of significant population concentration up until the very end of the run. A lower noise level also leads to a shift in the strategies successful in each epoch. However, the overall dynamics is still the same, the roles the strategies fill remain the same, and punctuations occur up until the emergence of the stable regime (Figure 10).

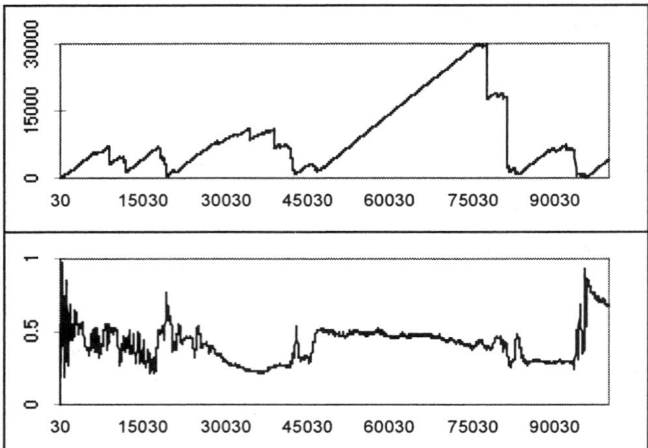

Figure 9: A(t) and C(t), high noise level (error = 0.1), 100k generations.

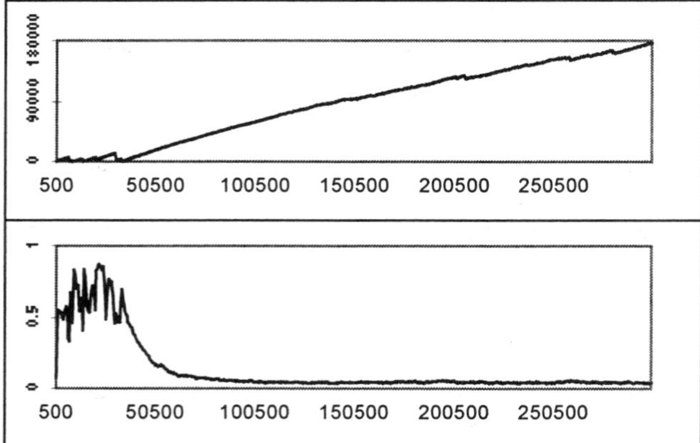

Figure 10: A(t) and C(t), low noise level (error = 0.01), 300k generations.

Perturbations to the payoff matrix produce fundamental changes in the dynamics of the simulation. Any significant increase of the jointly cooperative payoff CC above 3 (to 3.05 or greater) causes the strategy 1001 to become a more stable attractor for the population. A typical run with CC = 3.1 is shown in Figure 11. Note that there are only two distinct activity waves and that the population collapses to a highly concentrated state after 1001 becomes dominant. Through out there is a generally low level of diversity indicating that memory 3 and longer strategies are not being significantly explored. Here the evolutionary progression is merely a long period of memory 1 dynamics followed by a single punctuation, the takeover of the population by 1001 during a cooperative period of the memory 1 regime.

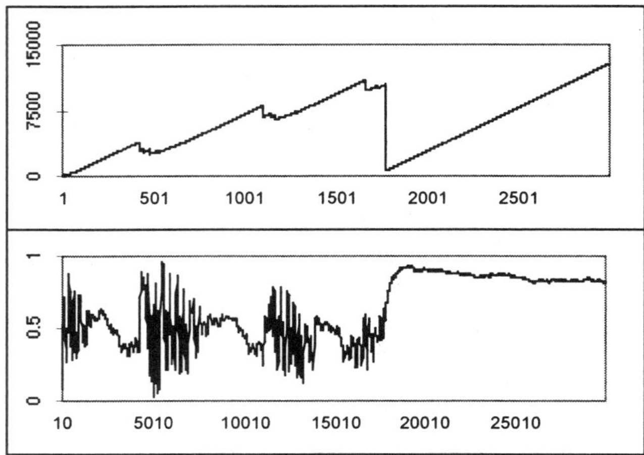

Figure 11: A(t) and C(t), payoff CC = 3.1, 30k generations.

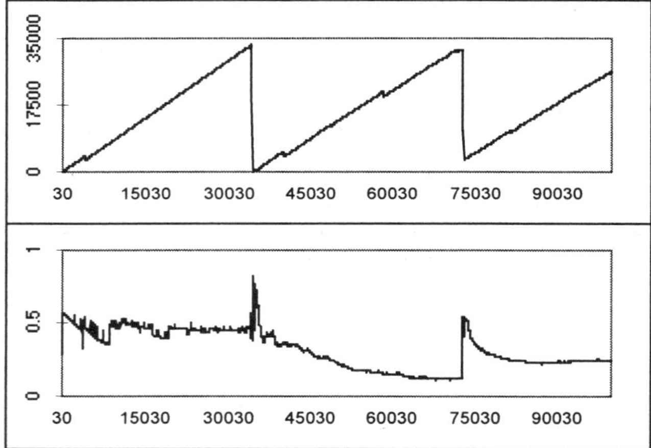

Figure 12: A(t) and C(t), game of chicken, 100k generations.

When the DD payoff is increased from 1 to 2, 01 becomes a very long lived strategy. Simulations for this case progress to memory 4 strategy sets and punctuations are still seen.

A more significant payoff structure perturbation is switching to the game of Chicken (Rapoport, Guyer, 1978):

	C	D
C	3, 3	1, 5
D	5, 1	0, 0

In Figure 12 the activity graph from a chicken run shows three activity waves and thus equilibria with two punctuations. The length of the stable epochs is much longer than in the prisoner's dilemma, and the evolutionary sequence from memory 1 through memory 3 strategies transpires during the course of the first wave. No punctuation occurs until the shift to memory 4 strategies, but a punctuation between memory 4 regimes also occurs.

Punctuated Equilibrium

We now suggest a conceptual model of the evolutionary process' implicit search through genotype space for fitter types, and how this search and ensuing population shifts generate punctuated equilibria. The basic model is that of a population density moving through genotype space based on both the fitness gradient in phenotype space and on the diffusion process associated with mutation.

The genotype space being explored by this model is the direct product of Boolean hypercubes of dimension 2^m, where m = 1, ..., max memory allowed. The memory 1 genotype space is equivalent to the corners of a square (0,0), (0,1), (1,0), and (1,1). The memory 2 genotype space is equivalent to a 4 dimensional hypercube. The phenotype space corresponds to the genotype hypercube of maximal dimension, as all shorter memory strategies are embedded in this space. A metric within each of these hypercubes is hamming distance, which can be extended into a metric for the entire genotype space by counting the minimum number of mutations of any type needed to convert one genotype into another.

The operator for exploring the genotype subspace of a particular memory length is point mutation. The likelihood of a point mutation for a given genotype is proportional to the population density at that genotype. Thus the types that are most likely to be explored are the nearest neighbors of those types with a significant proportion of the population. While multiple point mutations are possible, they are relatively unlikely in this model. So to explore types with a hamming distance greater than one from a high density type requires either low probability events or a series of nearest neighbors of relatively equal fitness extending from the dominant type. This chain of neighboring types must sustain enough population to make a point mutation at the end of the chain a likely event. The possibility of such a chain is entirely dependent on the payoff structure of the game, i.e. the ruggedness of the fitness landscape and the coupling or coevolutionary sensitivity of the landscape. For highly coupled and rugged landscapes such as that for the Prisoners Dilemma, the occurrence of such chains should be uncommon, especially at short memory lengths.

The other operator for exploration is the memory doubling/splitting mutation that moves population density between hypercubes of different dimensions. In the memory doubling case, this population transfer is phenotypically neutral and does not affect the fitness landscape. The split mutation case can shift population between phenotypes, and so may deform the fitness landscape. A memory k type has 2^k neighbors, so a memory doubling mutation increases the number of a genotype's nearest neighbors by a factor of two. Thus the memory doubled genotype has many more phenotypic possibilities to explore through single point mutations then does the phenotypically equivalent shorter memory length type. Note that types that are n mutations apart at memory length k are 2n mutations separate at memory length k+1. Thus phenotypes that are neighbors at one memory length become widely separated at longer memory lengths. Chains of phenotypically identical memory doubled genotypes will be sustained as long as the phenotype remains dominant, i.e. until a new, more fit type is found. Memory doubling is therefore a pathway to searching a larger set of types.

Given these operators, an initial population density in genotype space diffuses into adjacent types both within memory lengths and between memory lengths. Selection pressure based on fitness tends to limit this diffusion within hypercubes, but when types that are phenotypically more fit appear, selection transfers population into these types. For phenotypic fitness landscapes that are highly population coupled, these population shifts distort the fitness landscape.

Fitness landscape deformation can have three possible effects:

1) the newly discovered type may remain more fit,

2) the old dominant type(s) may become more fit,

3) some other type(s) in or neighboring the population may become more fit.

In the first case, the population density will shift to the new type and the old type(s) will go extinct. We call this a stable punctuation. In the second case there is no major extinction event, thus no punctuation. A cycle may emerge shifting population between the old and new type(s), or an equilibrium distribution including the old and new types could be reached.

In the third case, the "third party" type that becomes more fit will attract population, thus distorting the fitness landscape again. As in the second case, a cycle or equilibrium could emerge that includes the old dominant type(s); or a cycle or equilibrium that does not include the old type(s) could emerge; or the fitness gradient favoring the "third party" type could be stable with respect to the distortion. In either of the later cases, the old dominant type(s) go extinct, and the population shift is an unstable punctuation.

While these cases have been described with respect the discovery of a single new, more fit type, the general reasoning can be extended to include mutualistic pairs or sets, and clouds of phenotypically similar, genotypically related types around a dominant strategy. In any of these cases, the distinction can be made between a stable punctuation in which population flows don't distort the fitness landscape in a significant way during the punctuation, and unstable punctuations in which the landscape is distorted and the distortion causes some previously unfit type to attract the population.

A second distinction can be made between punctuations based on how they move population between memory lengths. Punctuations that result in moving population to longer memory lengths are called expanding since they increase the dimensionality of the genotype space likely to be explored. Punctuations that move population to shorter memory lengths are termed collapsing by the same reasoning. Punctuations that don't move population between memory lengths are lateral shifts within a genotypic hypercube. Thus punctuations can be classified as stable or unstable, and as expanding, collapsing, or shifting.

Table 1
Epochs observed in base case populations

1_1	Memory 1 dynamics, 01 cycling with other strategies. The starting epoch.
1_0	Selfish regime dominated by 00 and its memory double variants.
2_1	Memory 2 dynamics, characterized by cycling and usually dominated by 0001 and 1001.
3_1	Mutualistic memory 3 regime, little or no cycling, dominated by 1001-0001 and 0001-1001.
3_2	Alternate memory 3 regime, more diverse than 3_1 and characterized by 0101-1100.
4_1	Generic stable memory 4 regime, core members are of the form 1xx1-0xxx-0xxx-x001.
4_2	Alternate stable memory 4 regime whose core members are of the form 1111-0xxx-00xx-x001.
4_i	Any of several unstable memory 4 regimes encountered very infrequently.

Cycling of evolutionary epochs is likely to include at least one unstable punctuation. In a cycle, an equal number of expanding and collapsing punctuations must be included, though purely shifting cycles could occur. If the phenotypic differences between neighboring genotypes is on average greater at shorter memory lengths, one would expect to find unstable punctuations predominate until longer memory lengths develop.

To illustrate the above model, we now classify both epochs and transitions for the base case. Table 1 details a basic classification of epochs observed in base case model runs ordered by memory length of the dominant strategy or set for each epoch. These epochs correspond to periods during which population concentrations in genotype space explore the fitness of neighboring types.

Observed transitions between epochs are the result of the discovery of a significant fitness gradient and the resulting population transfer. These transitions are punctuations. Those observed in base case runs are tabulated in Table 2 by stability and their action on memory length. Unstable punctuations predominate at shorter memory lengths, while stable punctuations dominate for longer memory lengths. Shifting punctuations also don't appear for short memory lengths, and collapsing punctuations don't appear for longer memory lengths. The unstable punctuations encountered allow cycling between the memory 1 and memory 2 epochs.

We can now map out the effects of the various parameters on the movement of the population through genotype space. Mutation rate controls the speed at which the population density can move through the extended genotype space to discover new types. The doubling/split rate controls the shift between hypercubes, while the point mutation rate varies the speed of spreading within a hypercube. Survival limit regulates the minimum viable density at each point in genotype space – thus limiting or extending the boundary of the population cloud, while also controlling the speed with which population shifts due to mutation. Selection pressure regulates the speed with which population density is transferred between less fit and more fit points in genotype space. Significant selection pressure is needed for an effective fitness gradient to exist.

Table 2
Punctuations observed in base case populations

	Stable	Unstable
Expanding	$2_1 \to 3_1$ $2_1 \to 3_2$ $3_1 \to 4_1$ $3_2 \to 4_1$ $3_2 \to 4_i$	$1_1 \to 2_1$ $1_2 \to 2_1$
Collapsing	none	$1_1 \to 1_2$ $1_2 \to 1_2$ $2_1 \to 1_2$
Shifting	$3_2 \to 3_1$ $4_i \to 4_2$ $4_i \to 4_i$	none

The fitness of points in genotype space is a function of the payoff matrix structure, and the noise level. As noise increases, variations in fitness flatten out. In the extreme case of the random behavior model, all strategies play and score identically and the fitness landscape is therefore flat. Some payoff structures, such as the strongly stable noncompetitive game, may have a single smooth fitness peak. Others, such as the Prisoner's Dilemma, have rugged, highly coupled fitness landscapes, with multiple local extrema.

These observations are consistent with the exploration of the model's parameter space in the previous section. When the mutation rate is high enough to quickly find increasingly fit phenotypes, the population can move in one continuous transition to the evolutionarily stable regime without having to stop while the next positive fitness gradient is found. When selection pressure is low, the movement of population to new fitness peaks is so slow that there is no clumping while waiting for new peaks to be discovered. An effective fitness gradient in this model is the combination of a fitness difference between phenotypes with sufficient selection pressure to move population from less fit to more fit types. We get punctuations whenever we find an effective fitness gradient that causes population to shift at a rate much faster than that of the mutation driven diffusion process.

Conclusion

Activity and concentration statistics summarize many of the interesting characteristics of the models' population dynamics. Activity statistics identify equilibrium epochs and punctuations, while concentration characterizes the dynamics within epochs as stationary or cyclical. The random walk neutral model shows that there is a natural tendency in these simulations toward longer memory length strategies. However, none of the neutral models produce punctuated equilibria.

Punctuations have been found throughout a wide range of parameters for the adaptive model. While combinations of parameters exist which cause populations to shift either so smoothly or so slowly that punctuations are obscured or eliminated, the pattern of punctuated equilibrium is generic in this model when meaningful adaptation within the population is possible.

Analysis at the genotypic level explains the mechanism that produces punctuated equilibrium behavior in this particular model. The mechanism depends on the existence of a fitness gradient in genotype space. In the neutral models and the non-competitive games, there is no fitness gradient to move population around in genotype space, so no punctuations occur. Punctuated equilibria should appear whenever an evolving population moving through genotype space encounters a fitness gradient very much stronger than that induced by the mutation driven diffusion process. While the presence of punctuations suggests the presence of meaningful adaptation, the absence of punctuated equilibria does not imply the absence of adaptation. This may answer the conjecture that punctuated equilibrium is a generic feature of evolution; punctuated equilibrium is a sufficient but not necessary indicator of adaptive evolution.

The classification of punctuations and the description of the punctuation process in genotype space offered here could be applied to any evolutionary process once genotype, phenotypic fitness and genetic operators have been defined. For example, systems with fixed fitness landscapes can exhibit only stable punctuations. As the population concentration can only shift consistent with a fixed gradient field (a gradient defined on the extrema of the fitness function), no cycling of phenotypic regimes is likely. Hopefully this kind of conceptualization may lead to a more general understanding of adaptive punctuation.

Acknowledgments

Thanks to Kristian Lindgren for sharing his computer code, to Mark Bedau and Emile Snyder for a copy of that code and for the lively discussions about neutral models and punctuated equilibrium, to Marty Zwick for the helpful suggestions, to Andreas Rechtensteiner for getting me interested in diffusion processes in genotype space, and for the helpful comments of an anonymous referee.

References

Axelrod, R., 1984, *The Evolution of Cooperation*, New York, Basic Books.

Bedau, M.A., Packard, N., 1992, "Measurements of Evolutionary Activity, Teleology and Life" in *Artificial Life II*, Langton et al. eds., Redwood City, CA, Addison-Wesley.

Bedau, M.A., et al., 1997, "A Comparison of Evolutionary Activity in Artificial Evolving Systems and in the Biosphere", *Proceedings of the Fourth European Conference on Artificial Life*, Husbands, P., Harvey, I. Eds., MIT Press/Bradford Books.

Eldredge, N., Gould, S.J., 1972, "Punctuated Equilibria: An Alternative to Phyletic Gradualism", *Models in Paleobiology*, Schopf, T.J.M. Ed., San Francisco, Freeman-Cooper.

Langton, C.G., 1992, Introduction to *Artificial Life II*, Langton et al. eds., Redwood City, CA, Addison-Wesley.

Lindgren, K., 1992, "Evolutionary Phenomena in Simple Dynamics" in *Artificial Life II*, Langton et al. eds., Redwood City, CA, Addison-Wesley.

Lindgren, K., Nordahl, M.G., 1994, "Evolutionary Dynamics of Spatial Games", *Physica D*, 75., pp.292-309.

Rapoport, A., Guyer, M., 1978, "A Taxonomy of 2x2 Games", *General Systems*, vol. XXIII, pp.125-136.

TRURL: Artificial World for Social Interaction Studies

Takao Terano *
* Graduate School of Systems Management, Tsukuba University
3-29-1 Otsuka, Bunkyo-ku
Tokyo 112-0012, Japan
terano@gssm.otsuka.tsukuba.ac.jp

Setsuya Kurahashi[*,†]
† YD System Corp.,
kura@tokyo-densan.co.jp

Ushio Minami [*,‡]
‡ Hakuho-do Corp.
usshi@hakuhodo.co.jp

Abstract

TRURL is a simulation environment, which evolves artificial worlds of multi-agents to socially interact with each other. The micro-level agent activities are determined by both predetermined and acquired parameters. The former parameters have constant values during one simulation cycle, however, the latter parameters change during the interactions. Unlike conventional artificial society models, TRURL utilizes Genetic Algorithms to evolve the societies by changing the predetermined parameters to optimize macro-level socio-metric measures, which can be observed in such real societies as e-mail oriented organizations and electronic commerce markets. Thus, using TRURL, we automatically tune the parameters up and observe both micro- and macro-level phenomena grounded in the activities of real worlds. This paper first describes basic principles, architecture, and mechanisms of TRURL. Then, to investigate the features of Face-to-Face, E-Mail, Net-News, and Mass-Communication oriented societies, we have carried out intensive experiments. The results have suggested that features of evolved agents characterize each society.

Introduction

Recently, a great deal of arguments have been devoted to the study of (1) distributed information systems such as Internet applications (Kirn and O'Hare 1996, Bradshaw 1997), (2) behaviors of animats or social insects in the ALife literature (Epstein and Axtell 1996), and (3) explainable and executable models to analyze the social interaction of human organizations (Carley and Prietula 1994, Axelrod 1997). Researchers of the above categories often utilize ALife-oriented techniques including multi-agent systems and evolutionary computation. From the state-of-the-art literature, they frequently report that simple autonomous agents or artificial worlds are able to evolve global *interesting* social structures and behaviors.

However, the roles of computer simulations in organization theory have been re-evaluated in social science literature. For example, M. Cyert has described in the Foreword of Carley and Prietula (1994) that although simulations are useful to test some of the propositions in organization theory (which cannot be observed easily in the real world), the simulations become so complex that the model is as difficult to analyze as the real world, and the simulations themselves begin to appear as though they are real worlds for organization theorists. In this sense, many of the approaches seem to report too artificial results, because of the following three reasons: (I) Although many agent models are developed from the bottom-up, the functions the agents have are so simple that the models can only with difficulty to practical social interaction problems. (II) Although the functions are simple from the viewpoint of simulation experiments, the models have too many parameters that can be tuned and, therefore, it seems as if any *good* result a model builder desires is already built in. (III) The results seem to have a weak relationship with emerging phenomena in real-world activities. Thus, these studies have not yet attained a level necessary to describe the flexibility and practicability of social interactions in real organizations.

To overcome such problems, we have developed a novel multi-agent-based simulation environment TRURL [1] for social interaction analysis. In our simulation model, we have extended the ideas of artificial societies in Epstein and Axtell (1996) and computational organization theory (Carley and Prietula 1994).

In conventional artificial society models, the simulation is executed straightforwardly: Initially, many micro-level parameters and initial conditions are set, then, the simulation steps are executed, and finally the macro-level results are observed. Unlike in conventional simulation models, TRURL executes these steps in the reverse order: set a macro-level objective function, evolve the worlds to fit to the objectives, then observe the micro-level agent characteristics. Thus, TRURL solves very large inverse problems. So far, it has been considered difficult to adopt such an inverse approach to social system simulation studies, however, here we succeeded by utilizing a Genetic Algorithms (Goldberg 1989) to evolve the societies by changing the predetermined parameters to op-

[1] Trurl is a hero of science fiction: "The Seventh Sally or How Trurl's own perfection led to no good" by Stanisław Lem. Trurl developed a sophisticated micro world for an arrogant king.

timize macro-level socio-metric measures, which can be observed in such real societies as e-mail oriented organizations and electronic commerce markets. Thus, using TRURL, we automatically tune the parameters to observe both micro- and macro-level phenomena grounded in the activities of real worlds.

The basic principles of TRURL can be summarized as follows: To address point (I) above, the agents in the model have detailed characteristics with enough parameters to simulate real world decision making problems (French 1986); with respect to (II), instead of manually changing the parameters of the agents, we evolve the multi-agent worlds using GA-based techniques (Goldberg 1989); as for (III), we set some socio-metric measures which can be observed in real world phenomena as the objective functions to be optimized during evolution. Using TRURL, therefore, we are able to analyze the nature of social interactions in artificial worlds, which are based on such real-world activities as e-mail oriented organizations and electronic commerce markets.

In this paper, we first describe the design of the agent architecture, the artificial world model, and algorithms to evolve the worlds. Then, we discuss socio-metric measures which were used in a survey study to analyze activities of electronic community-based forums in Japan. Based on this discussion, we report some experimental results which reveal the nature of both micro– and macro-level phenomena which often occur in face-to-face–, e-mail–, Net-News–, and mass-communication-oriented societies. Finally, concluding remarks and future issues are given.

Agent Architecture

Agent in TRURL

Roughly, an agent in TRURL has event-action rules (Russel and Norvig 1995). Each agent exchanges knowledge and solves its own multi-attribute decision problems by interacting with the other agents. The agents move around in the world to form groups with similar attitudes in decision making. They also have the motivation or energy to send and receive messages. The messages are used to make and/or modify the decisions of each agent. To implement these functions, the agents have both predetermined and acquired parameters, by which the characteristics of micro levels of the agent activities are determined. The former parameters have constant values during one simulation cycle, and the latter parameters change during the interaction processes among the agents. Summing up the decisions of the agents, the total attitude of the artificial world is determined as the macro-level status.

More formally, agent A in TRURL is represented as the following tuples:

$$A = (\{Kd\}, D, M, C_p, C_c, P_s, P_r, P_a, P_c, \delta, \mu, n),$$

where, $\{Kd\}$ is a set of knowledge attributes, D: decision level the agent makes, M: motivation value or energy level of behaviors, C_p: physical coordinates, C_c: mental coordinates, P_s: probability of message sending, P_r: probability of message reading, P_a: probability of replying attitudes for pros-and-cons, P_c: probability of replying attitudes for comment adding, δ: metabolic rate, μ is the mutation rate of knowledge attribute values, and n is the number of knowledge attributes the agent has.

The agent usually has some subset of knowledge only which the agent can use for decision making. The knowledge the agent has is a set of knowledge attributes, defined as:

$$Kd = (N, W, E, C) \ ,$$

where N is a knowledge attribute, W its importance value, E its evaluation value; and C its credibility value.

Knowledge attributes can be exchanged among the agents via message transformation activities, however, the values of W, E, and C are changed based on the conforming behaviors determined by the agents' predetermined parameters. The decision each agent makes can be changed by changing the knowledge Kds. W and E respectively correspond to the importance factor of Bass's model and the attribute evaluation factor of the Fishbein model both in consumer behaviors of marketing sciences (see, e.g., Lilien, Kotler, and Moorthy (1992) for a definition of these models). They are used to obtain the decision D_i of agent A_i using a multi-attribute additive function:

$$D_i = \sum_{K_j \in K_{A_i}} W_j E_j .$$

C corresponds to the belief factor of the Bass model, which determines the level of the agent's belief of a given knowledge attribute. It is also used to determine comforting behaviors of the agent, which will be described below.

The motivation value M changes during the simulation to measure how strong the agent is motivated in the artificial world. If M becomes zero, the agent is retired, and a new one with random acquired parameter values participates in the world.

The metabolic rate δ is subtracted from M at every simulation step, when the agent has no messages. Also, δ is added to M per message, when the agent received it from the other agents, and $2 * \delta$ is added to M per reply-message when the agent receive it.

C_p and C_c represent where the agent is, in both the physical and mental world in decision making. The probability values P_s, P_r, P_a, and P_c are used to determine the conforming behaviors and knowledge exchange, which affect the agent decision value D. The movement and conforming behaviors are determined by the action rules described below.

Predetermined parameters of the agent

Predetermined parameters define the agents' congenital characteristics. The parameters are not changed during one simulation, but are tuned by GA operations when the world evolves. The predetermined parameters are listed below. They have values between 0.0 and 1.0.

- Physical coordinates $C_p = (X_{ip}, Y_{ip})$: The initial physical position of the agent in the artificial world; The values do not change during the simulation;

- Probability of message sending P_s: The probability that agent A_i sends messages to other agents A_js at each simulation step; The probability of selecting a specific A_j is inversely proportional to the physical or mental distance between A_i and A_j;

- Probability of message reading P_r: The probability that the agent reads messages from other agents at each simulation step;

- Parameters for conforming behavior α, β, and γ: The parameters are used to change conforming behavior of the agent; α, β, and γ are respectively used to control the importance value W, evaluation value E, and credibility value C of the knowledge attribute;

- Probability of having certain reply attitude with respect to similar or opposing opinions P_a: The probability that the agent will reply to another agent with the same opinion Kd; The value 1.0 represents the attitude of replying to only agents that have similar opinions, while the value 0.0 represents the attitude of replying to only agents that have opposing opinions. An agent with a high (resp. low) P_a value has conforming (resp. self-righteous) characteristics. In our implementation, an agent A_i gives an additional comment regarding Kd_k to another agent A_j with the following probability: $Prob = P_a - (E_{ki} - E_{kj})^2$, where E_{k*} is the evaluation value of Kd by the agent A_*;

- Probability of sending additional comments with the reply P_c: The probability that the agent will send a message containing additional comments Kd_js, when it receives message Kd_i; the value 1.0 means that the agent always replies with additional knowledge, while the value 0.0 means that the agent never sends messages with additional knowledge; The agent with high (resp. low) P_c is talkative (resp. not talkative);

- Metabolic rate δ: The metabolic rate determines the unit of change of the agent's motivation;

- Mutation rate μ: The mutation rate determines the probability of random change of the number of knowledge attributes in order to simulate the random effects of the external environment;

- Number of knowledge attributes n: The number of knowledge attributes that the agent knows. It is natural to assume each agent knows only part of the knowledge necessary for decision making; Therefore, this parameter represents the concept of "bounded rationality" of agents' knowledge; At the initial step of the simulation, for Kds which A_i does not have, we set W, E, and C to 0.0, 0.5, and 0.0, respectively.

Acquired parameters and action rules

The acquired parameters of the agents will change at each simulation step. At the initial phase of the simulation, they have random values.

- Motivation M_i: The value indicates the agent's motivational level in the artificial world;

- Mental coordinates $C_c = (X_{ic}, Y_{ic})$: The initial mental position of the agent is given at random in the artificial world; The values are changed based on the conforming behavior during the simulation; When agent A_i increases its credibility value C by exchanging knowledge Kd with another agent A_j, A_i will approach A_j by one unit distance; When C is not increased, or when A_i receives bad messages, A_i will move away from A_j with the probability of 0.5 or randomly move away for one unit distance. By this behavior, the agents will form groups with high credibility.

- Parameters for conforming behaviors: importance value w^i_{Kd}, evaluation value e^i_{Kd} and credibility value c^i_{Kd}: These parameters are changed based on the following conforming behaviors, when agent A_i makes decisions by receiving knowledge attribute Kd.

Each agent A_i interacts with another agent A_j at every (discrete) simulation step based on the constraints of the agents and the artificial world. A_j is stochastically selected by A_i proportional in terms of the physical and mental distance between them. At the interaction, a knowledge attribute Kd is transformed between A_i and A_j. When A_i receives an unknown Kd, A_i will accept Kd as it is. However, when A_i receives a Kd which it already knows, the value of the knowledge attribute will change by the following rules of conforming behavior:

$$\Delta w^i_{Kd} = \sum_{j \in S} \alpha(w^j_{Kd} - w^i_{Kd}) \cdot \max(0, c^j_{Kd} - c^i_{Kd})$$

$$\Delta e^i_{Kd} = \sum_{j \in S} \beta(e^j_{Kd} - e^i_{Kd}) \cdot \max(0, c^j_{Kd} - c^i_{Kd})$$

$$\Delta c^i_{Kd} = \sum_{j \in S} \gamma(1 - 2|e^j_{Kd} - e^i_{Kd}| \cdot \max(0, c^j_{Kd} - c^i_{Kd}))$$

,

where w^i_{Kd}, e^i_{Kd}, and c^i_{Kd} are respectively the importance value, evaluation value, and credibility value of Kd which A_i has; α, β, and γ are parameters; S is the agent from which A_i receives the message Kd at simulation time t.

Using the rules of conforming behavior, in general, if Kd of A_j has a higher credibility value than that of A_i, the attitude of A_i with respect to Kd will become similar to that of A_j. A_i's credibility value c^i_{Kd} with respect to Kd becomes higher when the evaluation value e^i_{Kd} is similar to that of A_j, and c^i_{Kd} becomes lower when e^i_{Kd} is different from e^j_{Kd} and c^j_{Kd} is higher than c^i_{Kd}. If c^i_{Kd} is higher than c^j_{Kd}, A_i does not change the credibility c^i_{Kd}.

Based on the probability Pa and Pc, A_i will reply to messages from the other A_js. The interaction activities continue. and the agents move together based on the moving rules described above.

Four Models for an Artificial Society

As a conceptual model of computer mediated social networks such as the Internet society and/or electronic commerce, we characterize the world by both physical and mental spaces (D_p and D_c). D_p and D_c consist of two-dimensional grids forming a torus structure. In D_p, the coordinates of A_j represent the physical places where A_j is. In D_c, the coordinates of A_j represent the mental positions among the agents. The movements of agents in the world are learning processes to form groups with same attitudes. In the current implementation, the size of both D_p and D_c is $50 * 50$.

We design the following four artificial societies:

1. Face-to-Face communication oriented society (FFS)
   The communication among the agents are constrained by both the physical and mental coordinates. They interact with physical and mental neighborhoods. The ratio is parameterized.

2. E-Mail oriented society (EMS)
   The communication among the agents are constrained by the mental coordinates. In this society, agents interact with each other one by one at each step.

3. Net-News oriented society (NNS)
   NNS is an extension of EMS. It has a virtual white board at the center of the world. Agents in the world send messages to the white board, and the white board distributes the messages to all the agents. The credibility value of the messages is the same as that of the senders.

4. Mass-Communication oriented society (MCS)
   MCS has one mass communication agent who gathers the decisions of all the agents at each simulation step. The decisions or attitudes are then averaged and are distributed with high credibility values. The mass communication agent acts as a monitor of the society.

Parameter Tuning of a Society by GAs

As described in the previous section, the agents, their behaviors, and the world are controlled by many parameters. Therefore it is very difficult to make them in order to properly carry out social interaction. Thus, we apply Genetic Algorithms for this purpose. The outline is shown in Figure 1.

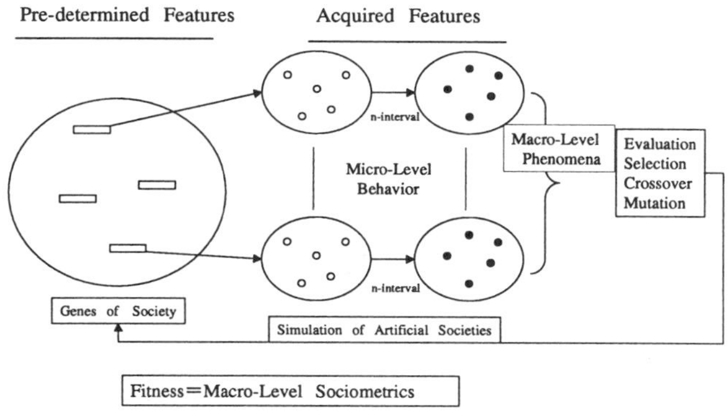

Figure 1: Evolving Artificial Societies via GAs

The predetermined 12 parameters of each agent ($C_p = (X_{ip}, Yip)$, P_s, P_r, α, β, γ, P_a, P_c, δ, μ, and n) can each be represented by integers between 0 and 9, which correspond to real numbers from 0.0 to 1.0. The predetermined characteristics of an agent are coded into a twelve integer string. Each initial world is coded into a gene, which consists of a sequence of agent codes with a fixed number specified by the user. The number represents the size of the agents.

In the simulation, we first specify the type of world (FFS, EMS, NGS, or MCS), and set the world's parameters, represented by the gene, to an initial state, then we execute simulation steps (for example, 100-200 steps) to evolve social behaviors by changing the acquired parameters. The resulting status is a phenotype of the world, which is represented by sets of both predetermined and acquired parameters of the agents.

Each world is evaluated by a specified evaluation function, which represents some of the socio-metric measures describe in the next section. Based on the function values, *good* worlds are selected. We use the size-two tournament selection method and the elitist strategy. For the reproduction, we adopt the uniform crossover operator and changing crossover rate from 10% to 0%, proportionally decreasing at each step of the reproduction.

In the current implementation, a maximum of 500 agents in each world is allowed. However, in most experiments, we evolve 100 generations for 20 worlds with

10 to 20 agents.

Discussion of Socio-Metric Measures

There are several studies in the literature that analyze social interactions among participants in computer mediated communities. Among them, an investigation carried out by our colleague (Kobayashi 1996) is very interesting because (1) he analyzed data of several network forums in Japan for several years and suggested that specific structures and leaders have evolved, and (2) he proposed five socio-metrics measures to reveal the characteristics of the network forums. These socio-metric measures can be evaluated in TRURL and reflect the characteristics of social interaction in real worlds. We adopted the proposed measures as the evaluation functions to be optimized in the evolution process of artificial societies. The definitions and brief descriptions of the measures are shown below.

Ratio of transmitters
This metric indicates the social structure where a small number of members (transmitters) sending one-way many messages to other members.

$$T = \frac{(\sum_{i=1}^{g}(Sd - rd_i) - \sum_{i=1}^{g}(Rd - rd_i) + g(g-1))Sd}{2g(g-1)^2}$$

Ratio of receivers
This metric indicates the social structure where a small number of members (receivers) receiving one-way messages from other members.

$$R = \frac{(\sum_{i=1}^{g}(Rd - rd_i) - \sum_{i=1}^{g}(Sd - sd_i) + g(g-1))Rd}{2g(g-1)^2};$$

Ratio of leaders
This metric indicates the social structure where a small number of members (leaders) acting as both transmitters and receivers. They will manage the society.

$$L = \left(\frac{\sum_{i=1}^{g}((sd_i \cdot rd_i)_{max} - sd_i \cdot rd_i)}{(g-1)((g-1)^2 - 1)}\right)^{1/2};$$

Ratio of local communication
The metric indicates the social structure where half of the members are active (they always send and receive messages) and the others are passive (they only receive messages).

$$D = \frac{\sum_{i=1}^{g}(\tilde{Sd} - sd_i)^2)}{g(g-1)^2/4};$$

Ratio of activation The metric indicates the social structure where the participants are active (they always send and receive messages)

$$A = \frac{\sum_{i=1}^{g}(sd_i + rd_i)}{2g(g-1)};$$

In the above equations, sd_i is the number of receivers to whom agent A_i sends messages, rd_i is the number of message senders to A_i, g is the number of members, Sd and Rd respectively mean the sd_i and rd_i of the agent A_i with the maximum value of $sd_i + rd_i$; and $\tilde{Sd}$, $\tilde{Rd}$ respectively mean the average values for senders and receivers. We omit the discussion on how to derive the measures. Instead, Figure 2 shows examples of the socio-metric measures applied to simple network structures to simplify understanding.

Experiments and Discussion

In this section, we describe the experimental results of social interaction by TRURL.

Validation of TRURL

In TRURL, we can set any evaluation function. For example, we can evolve such worlds where (i) only two members interact with each other, (ii) members send one-way messages, (iii) members form a hierarchical structure. Evolutions of such societies are useful to validate the simulation environment. In this subsection, we evolve societies with characteristics (i) and (iii) to validate TRURL.

Two Member Communication Society To evolve this, we use the following evaluation function:

$$Fitness = \frac{sd_{i,j} + rd_{i,j} + sd_{j,i} + rd_{j,i}}{\sum_{k \in S}(sd_k + rd_k)}; \quad \exists i, j,$$

where i and j are indices of the agent, sd_k and rd_k are traces of sending and receiving, and S is a set of senders and receivers.

Figure 3 shows the result of the evolved world and the message connections among the agents. The nodes and arcs respectively represent the agents and their message connections. Please note that the nodes do not represent where the agents are in the world. The left hand side of the figure is the initial stage and the right hand side is the final state.

	(1) 0.000 (2) 0.000 (3) 0.000 (4) 0.000 (5) 0.000		(1) 0.375 (2) 0.000 (3) 0.000 (4) 0.167 (5) 0.100
	(1) 0.500 (2) 0.500 (3) 0.000 (4) 0.000 (5) 1.000		(1) 0.313 (2) 0.094 (3) 0.342 (4) 0.167 (5) 0.150
	(1) 1.000 (2) 0.000 (3) 0.000 (4) 0.667 (5) 0.200		(1) 0.250 (2) 0.250 (3) 0.483 (4) 0.146 (5) 0.200
	(1) 0.000 (2) 1.000 (3) 0.000 (4) 0.042 (5) 0.200		(1) 0.656 (2) 0.000 (3) 0.000 (4) 0.563 (5) 0.300
	(1) 0.500 (2) 0.500 (3) 1.000 (4) 0.375 (5) 0.400		(1) 0.875 (2) 0.031 (3) 0.447 (4) 1.000 (5) 0.400

(1) Ratio of transmitters (2) Ratio of receivers
(3) Ratio of leaders
(4) Ratio of local communication
(5) Ratio of activation

Figure 2: The Characteristics of Socio-metric Measures

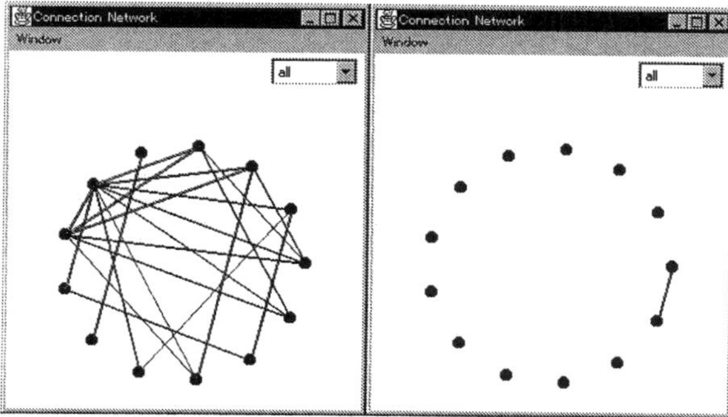

Figure 3: Two Member Communication Society

Hierarchical Society In the society with a hierarchical structure, members only communicates with the higher and lower ranking members. To evolve the world, we use the following evaluation function:

$$\text{Fitness} = sd_h + rd_h - sd_{\bar{h}} - rd_{\bar{h}},$$

where, sd_h and rd_h are the numbers of senders and receivers communicating with higher and lower members, and $sd_{\bar{h}}$ and $rd_{\bar{h}}$ are the numbers of senders and receivers communicating horizontally.

The results are shown in Figure 4. At the first stage (box in the left), the members randomly communicate each other. However, at the last stage (box in the right), they communicate only through the hierarchical structure.

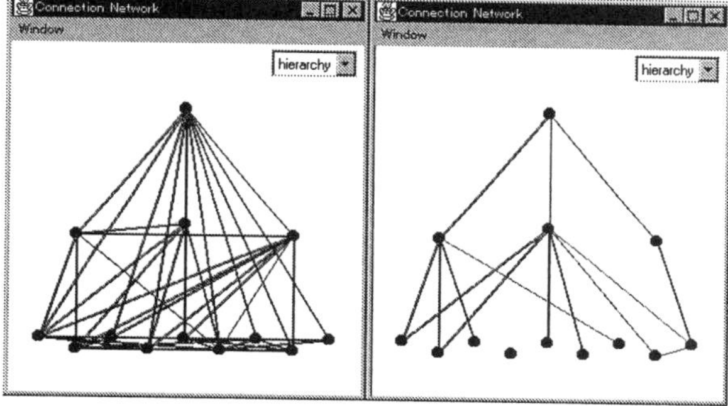

Figure 4: Society with Hierarchical Structure

From the above two preliminary experiments, we see that we can evolve any artificial worlds using TRURL, if we define appropriate evaluation functions. In the following subsections, we apply the socio-metrics in order to analyze social interactions.

Society with a leader

To analyze the characteristics of the society with leaders, which we often observe in real electronic mail based forums, we will optimize the function of ratio of leaders in EMS.

The result is summarized in Figure 5. The upper two figures shows two types of the communication among agents. The lower figure displays the intermediate screen image of the simulation.

The circles represent the location of the agents in the world. Their radii and color represent the level of motivation and the decision made, respectively. The agents moves according to the behavioral rules.

Figure 6 shows how the society evolves during the GA cycle. The upper, middle, and lower curves respectively represent the fitness of the highest, mean, and lowest values of the evaluation function. The figure suggests that the GA design works well.

We can observe there are two types of agents: those who communicate with every other agent, and those who communicate only with two other agents. We call the former types leaders and the latter types ordinary agents.

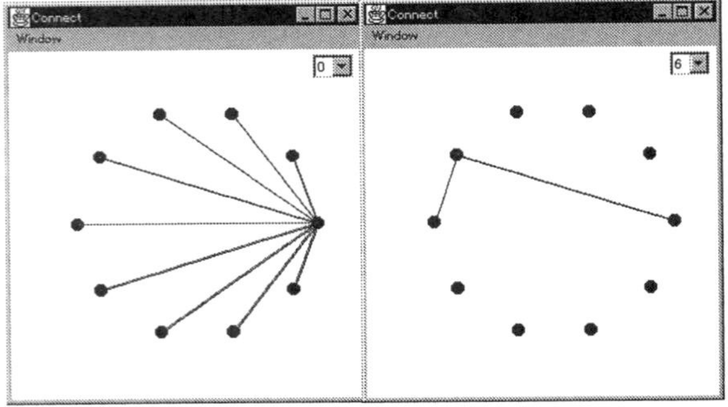

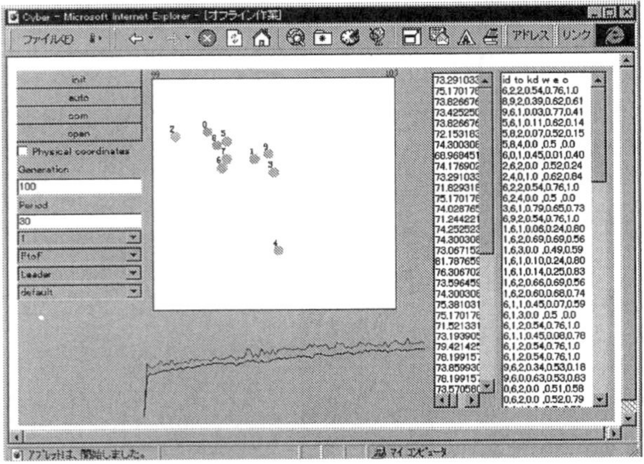

Figure 5: Evolution of the Society with a Leader

Analysis of the predetermined parameters of leader agents reveals the following characteristics:

- The leader agent usually reads messages and replies with comments;
- Leaders have larger, but not maximum number of knowledge attributes than the other agents; and
- Leaders have higher, but not maximum, credibility values with regard to the knowledge attributes.

The observations are slightly different from our original intuition that the leader should have maximum values knowledge attributes and credibility values.

Society with conforming attitudes

There are often cases where very subtle environmental changes cause a radical change of public opinions. To

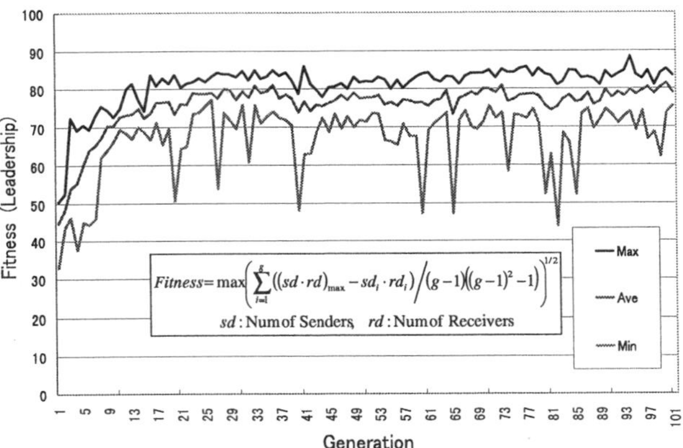

Figure 6: Changes of Fitness during the GA cycle

analyze the situation, we evolve an EMS society where the agents conform to the opinions of a single strong agent. The evaluation function is as follows:

$$Fitness = \sum_{i=1}^{n} \sum_{j=1}^{m} w_{ij} e_{ij},$$

where, n is the number of the agents and m is the number of knowledge attributes. To give an explicit chance of the conforming activities, we set the parameters so that only one agent (powerful agent) always has the decision or attitude $D_i = \sum_{K_j \in K_{A_i}} W_j E_j = 1.0$.

The characteristics or the predetermined parameters of the general agents in the world are summarized as follows:

- Evaluation parameter β of general agents is slightly higher than that of agents in other societies. This means they tend to rely upon each other;
- Probability of reply attitude P_a is nearly equal to 1.0. This means they tend to reply to the agents with similar opinions.
- They have smaller number of knowledge attributes n. This means they have interests in narrow topic areas.

The results suggest that in a conforming society, public opinion will be deflected, even if there are only a few powerful agents.

Society with a highly influential sgent

Opposite to the previous world, in this experiment, we will observe a powerful agent, which has stronger influence over the behavior of other agents. In order to evolve the world, we first evolve a conforming EMS society, and then set the predetermined parameters of the powerful agent by GA operations. The results are summarized in Figure 7.

In Figure 7, the average values of 10 simulation are shown. The predetermined parameters are classified as those of a minority of powerful agents and those of other general agents.

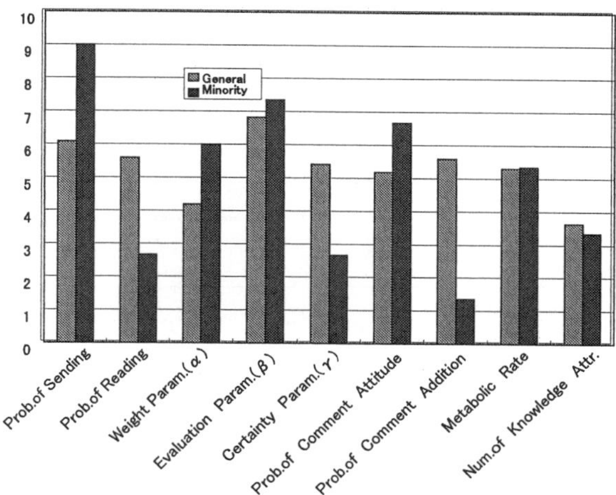

Figure 7: Characteristics of Powerful and General Agents

The remarkable characteristics of the powerful agents are as follows:

- The agents often read messages and reply to them;
- The agents have interests in various knowledge attributes;
- The agents have a lower metabolic value; and
- The agents tend to reply to the agents with different opinions.

Changes of attitudes in FFS, EMS, and NNS

This subsection describes the attitude changes or the averages for the agents' decisions, in Face-to-Face, E-mail, and Net-News oriented societies. In the experiment, we generally give random predetermined parameters and one powerful agent, and then observe the simulation processes. We do not apply GAs in the experiment, because we did not evolve any new features for the worlds.

The results are shown in Figure 8. In each graph of Figure 8, the curves represent 20 epochs with 300 simulation steps. The horizontal and vertical axes respectively represent the simulation steps and the average value of agent attitudes ($\sum evaluation_i * weight_i$).

The results are clear. Each world shows its own characteristics. In FFS, the attitudes are moderately changed. However, in EMS, the attitude change depends on the initial condition; some societies show a very rapid change while others show very little change. In the very

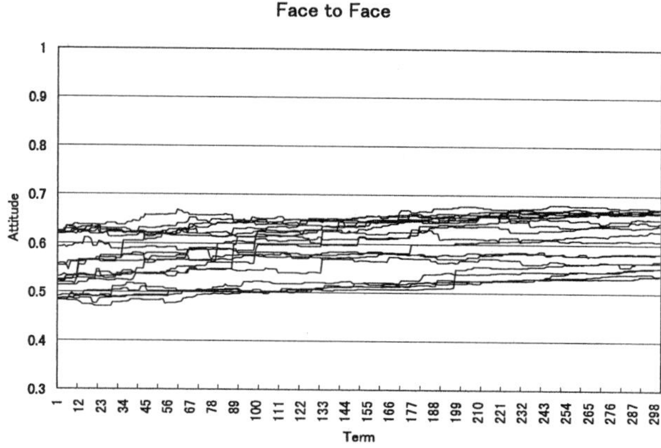

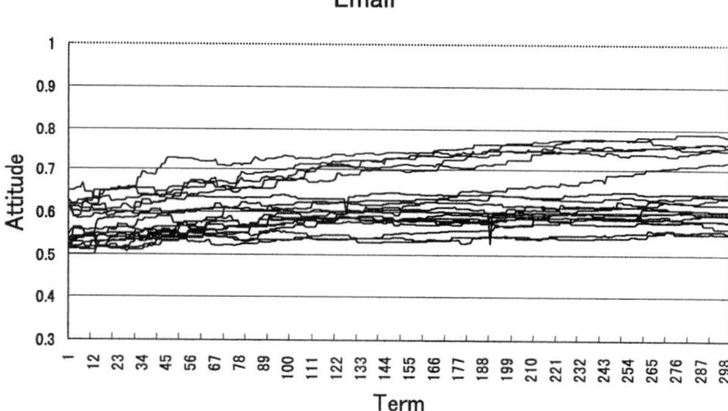

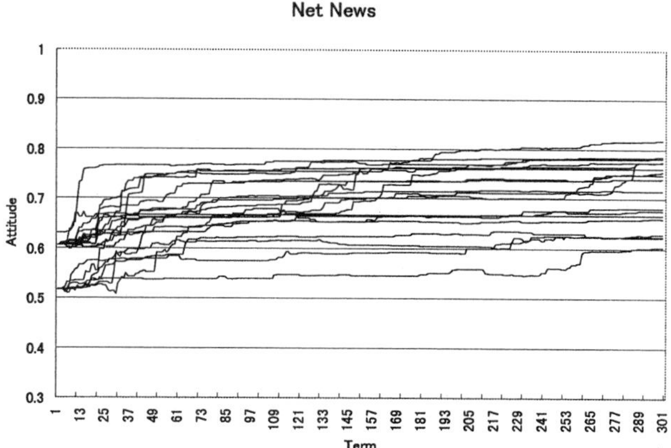

Figure 8: Changes of Attitudes in FFS, EMS, and NNS

earlier stages of the simulation for the NNS society, the attitudes are significantly changed, and then stabilized in the latter stages. This phenomenon is similar to the "techno bubble" in real electronic commerce activities that has been reported in literature.

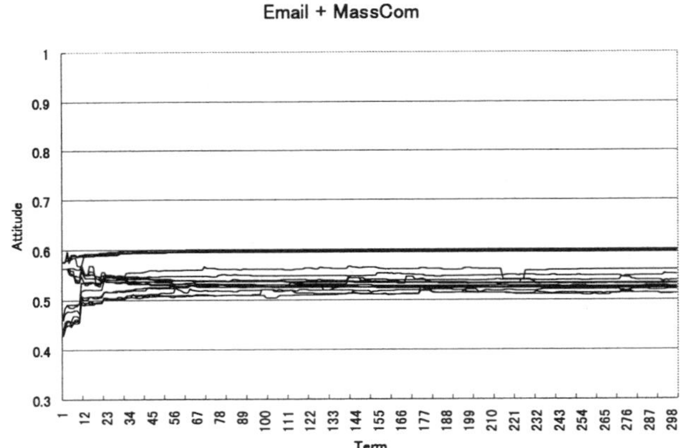

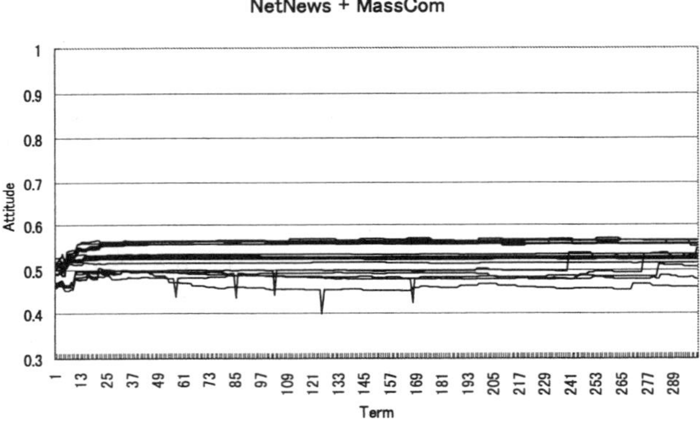

Figure 9: EMS, NNS, and Mass Communication (Upper EMS + MassCom; Lower NNS + MassCom)

Effects of mass communication

Whether we can manage the "techno babble" phenomenon particularly in consumer behavior research is a very interesting problem. To investigate the role of mass communication, in this subsection we compare two EMS worlds one with and one without mass communication. In the experiment, we do not apply GA operations.

By mass communication, in the simulation, we mean that there is a special agent which gathers all the decisions or attitudes of the agents, and then distributes the average values, or public opinions, to all the agents. The timing of gathering and distributing is stochastically determined.

The results are shown in Figure 9. The meanings of the curves are the same as in Figure 8. The upper and lower graphs respectively show the 20 epochs of simulations in EMS and NNS with mass communication. Compared with Figure 8, where there is no mass communication, it is clear that the effects of mass communication suppress conforming behaviors.

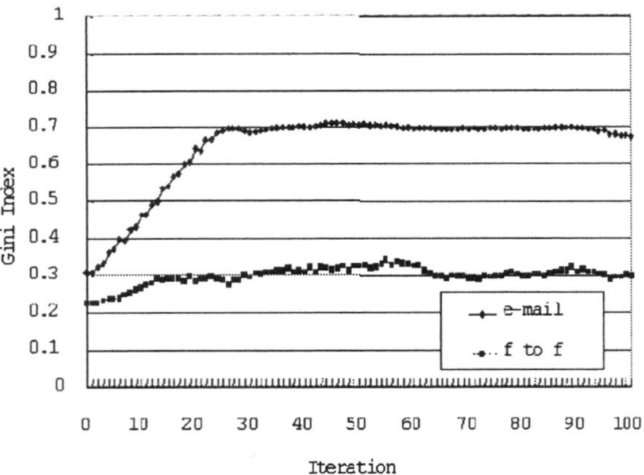

Figure 10: Changes of Gini Index in FFS and EMS

Analysis of agents' motivations

To investigate the changes in motivations of the agents during the simulation steps, we observe agent behaviors in FFS and EMS. To measure the change, we use the Gini index for the motivation value M for the agents. The Gini index is usually used in economic analyses to represent the difference of income levels. If the Gini index is near 1.0 (or 0.0), the difference is high (or low). Because the activities of the agents in TRURL is determined by the motivation value, we can use M as money in economic analyses.

The result is shown in Figure 10. The horizontal and vertical axes respectively mean simulation steps and Gini index. The upper and lower curves respectively represent the index values in EMS and FFS. Gini index in EMS is higher than that of in FFS, This means that in EMS the agents tend to form small groups and that new participants usually loose their interest or motivation within a few steps.

Concluding Remarks

This paper described a novel computational organization approach for analysis of social interaction. Although the simulation environment TRURL utilizes ALife oriented techniques, the principles are different from conventional research in the following manner: (I) the agents in the model have enough parameters to simulate real world decision making problems; (II) instead of evolving agents, GA-based techniques are applied to evolve appropriate worlds; and (III) some socio-metric measures which can be observed in the real world are defined as the objective functions to be optimized in the evolution.

Therefore, using TRURL, we can analyze various aspects of social interaction in artificial worlds, which have some grounds in the real world activities. The most remarkable feature of the approach is that it adopts an intermediate approach between mathematical models (Cyert and March 1963) and case studies (Nonaka and Takeuchi 1995). The model is rigorous in the sense that it is operational or executable on a computer and that it describes the nature of real world phenomena (Simon 1982, Russel and Norvig 1995).

However, we only began our approach a few years ago. Future work includes (i) using TRURL to carry out various social interaction experiments, (ii) analyzing micro-macro interactions between agents and societies (Kirn and O'Hare 1996, Cohen and Sproull 1991, Espejo, Schuhmann, Schwaninger and Bilello 1996), and (iii) extending our idea to general organizational problem solving and organizational learning models (Morecroft and Sterman 1994, Ishida, Gasser and Yokoo 1992, Terano 1994, Aiba and Terano 1996, Hatakama and Terano 1996).

References

Aiba, H., Terano, T. 1996. A Computational Model for Distributed Knowledge Systems with Learning Mechanisms. *Expert Systems with Applications* 10: 417–427.

Axelrod, R. 1997. *The Complexity of Cooperation: Agent-Based Models of Competition and Collaboration.* Princeton University Press.

Bradshaw, J. M., ed. 1997. *Software Agents.* AAAI/MIT Press.

Carley, K. M. and M. J. Prietula, eds. 1994. *Computational Organization Theory.* Hillsdale, N.J: Lawlence-Erlbaum Assoc..

Cohen, M. D. and L. S. Sproull, eds. 1991. Special Issue: Organizational Learning: Papers in Honor of (and by) James G. March. *Organization Science* 2(1).

Cyert, R. M., March, J. G. 1963. *A Behavioral Theory of the Firm.* Prentice-Hall.

Epstein, J. and R. Axtell. 1996. *Growing Artificial Societies.* Brookings Institution Press, The MIT Press.

Espejo, R., Schuhmann, W., Schwaninger, M., and Bilello, U. 1996. *Organizational Transformation and Learning.* John Wiley & Sons.

Fogarty, T. C., Bull. L., Carse, B. 1995. Evolving Multi-Agent Systems. In *Genetic Algorithms in Engineering and Computer Science*, edited by G. Winter,J. Periaoux, M. Galan, P. Cuesta, eds. Chichester, NY: John-Wiley, p. 3–22.

French, S. 1986. *Decision Theory: An Introduction to the Mathematics of Rationality.* John Wiley & Sons.

Goldberg, D. E. 1989. *Genetic Algorithms in Search, Optimization, and Machine Learning.* Addison-Wesley.

Hatakama, H., Terano, T. 1996. A Multi-Agent Model of Organizational Intellectual Activities for Knowledge Management. in *Knowledge Management - Organization, Competence and Methodology,* edited by J. F. Schreinemakers. Ergon Verlag, p. 143–155.

Hraber. P., T. Jones, S. and Forrest. 1997. The Ecology of Echo. *Artificial Life* 3: 165–190 .

T. Ishida, L. Gasser, and M. Yokoo. 1992. Organization Self-Design of Distributed Production Systems. *IEEE Transactions on Knowledge and Data Engineering* 4: 123–134.

Kirn, S., and G. O'Hare, eds. 1996. *Cooperative Knowledge Processing – The Key Technology for Intelligent Organizations.* Springer.

Kobayashi, Y. 1996. *Structural Analysis of Electronic Community Created by Computer Mediated Communication.* Master Thesis of Grad. Sch. Systems Management, Tsukuba University (in Japanese).

Lilien, G. L., Kotler, P., Moorthy, K. S. 1992. *Marketing Models.* Prentice-Hall.

March, J. G., Sproull, L. S. 1991. Learning from samples of one or fewer. *Organizational Science, Special Issue: Organizational Learning* 2: 1–13.

Masuch, M., and Warglien, M., eds. 1992. *Artificial Intelligence in Organization and Management Theory.* North-Holland.

Morecroft, J. D. W., and J. D. Sterman, eds. 1994. *Modeling for Learning Organizations.* Productivity-Press.

Nonaka, I., Takeuchi, H. 1995. *The Knowledge Creating Company: How Japanese Companies Create the Dynamics of Innovation.* Oxford: Oxford University Press.

Simon, H. A. 1982. *The Sciences of the Artificial, 2nd Edition.* CAmbridge, MA: MIT-Press.

Russel, S., Norvig, P. 1995. *Artificial Intelligence A Modern Approach.* Prentice Hall.

Terano, T. et. al. 1994. A Machine Learning Model for Analyzing Performance of Organizational Behaviors of Agents. *Proc. of the Third Conference of the Association of Asian-Pacific Operational Research Societies (APORS)*, p. 164–171.

Weiss, G., ed. 1997. *Distributed Artificial Intelligence Meets Machine Learning – Learning in Multi-Agent Environments.* Lecture Notes in Artificial Intelligence 1221. Heidelberg, New York: Springer-Verlag.

Language and Social Systems

A Continuous Evolutionary Simulation Model of the Attainability of Honest Signalling Equilibria

Seth Bullock
Center for Adaptive Behavior and Cognition
Max Planck Institute for Human Development
Lentzeallee 94, D-14195 Berlin (-Dahlem)
Tel: 0049-30-82406–350, Fax: 0049-30-82406-394, Email: bullock@mpib-berlin.mpg.de

Abstract

A particular game-theoretic model (Grafen 1990) of the evolutionary stability of honest signalling, which attempts a formal proof of the validity of Zahavi's 1975; 1977 handicap principle, is generalised and rendered as an evolutionary simulation model. In addition to supporting new theoretical results, this allows the effects of differing initial conditions on the attainability of signalling equilibria to be explored. Furthermore, it allows an examination of the manner in which the character of equilibrium signalling behaviour varies with the model's parameters.

It is demonstrated that (i) non-handicap signalling equilibria exist, (ii) honest signalling equilibria need not involve extravagant signals, and (iii) the basins of attraction for such equilibria are, however, relatively small. General conditions for the existence of honest signalling equilibria (which replace those offered by Zahavi) are provided, and it is demonstrated that previous theoretical results are easily accommodated by these general conditions. It is concluded that the supposed generality of the handicap principle, and the coherence of its terminology, are both suspect.

Models of the evolution of signalling have received renewed interest since the re-assessment of group selection arguments during the mid-sixties encouraged theorists to consider the worth of honest communication to the selfish individual (for a for a recent review of the literature, see Johnstone 1997). Initial claims that honest communication could not be stable outside of scenarios in which signallers and receivers enjoy a shared interest in honest information exchange (Dawkins & Krebs 1978) have been challenged by the development of Zahavi's (1975, 1977) handicap principle.

The evolution of signalling has been of interest within artificial life since its inception (e.g., (MacLennan 1991),(Werner & Dyer 1991). However, with some exceptions (e.g., (de Bourcier & Wheeler 1995; Bullock 1997), such research has not attempted to address theoretical concerns which are live within theoretical biology. Within this paper, a combination of traditional evolutionary stable strategy (ESS) modelling (Maynard Smith 1982) and evolutionary simulation modelling (Bullock 1998) will be applied to a specific theory within current evolutionary biology — the handicap principle (Zahavi 1975; 1977; Zahavi & Zahavi 1997).

The handicap principle may be presented in many forms. Indeed the multitude of scenarios which appear to admit of explanation in its terms is one of its strongest attractions. This apparent ubiquity of application has led Zahavi to suggest that his theory might usefully replace the theory of sexual selection suggested by Darwin (1871) as a means of accounting for the specific class of behavioural and morphological adaptations which arise as a result of selective pressure to accumulate mating opportunities.

Here the handicap principle will be cast in terms of courtship display — the context in which it was first described (Zahavi 1975). Assume that males vary in some respect of interest to choosy females (e.g., in their ability to forage). Females cannot ascertain this male quality directly. However, they are sensitive to an alternative trait. If this alternative trait were to systematically reflect the value of the underlying male quality, females would be selected to exploit it as a cue or advertisement upon which to base their mating choices.

Why should such an 'advertisement' accurately reflect some underlying quality? If females respond favorably to suitors with such an advertisement, what prevents every suitor from investing in this compelling signal, thus rendering it useless? In short, what might maintain the stability of a mate choice system in which males make some courtship display which reveals their quality, and females mediate their mating choices on the basis of the information gained from such a courtship display?

Zahavi's insight was to suggest that the costs incurred in producing courtship displays might enforce honesty amongst suitors if these costs were of a certain character. For example, an honest advertisement of a suitor's ability to forage might be the extent to which the suitor deliberately wastes food items which it has accrued through foraging. Since poor foragers can less afford to waste hard-won prey items than good foragers, a system in which suitors demonstrate their foraging ability through wasting food items cannot be invaded by cheats who exaggerate their foraging ability since the costs involved in such exaggeration are prohibitive of such a strategy.[1]

From this perspective, Zahavi suggests, signals should be regarded as *handicaps* which signallers must bear if they are to demonstrate their true quality. It is through suffering costs that signallers are able to convince their assessors of their status.

The validity of Zahavi's argument has proven hard to establish. However, recent game theoretic models (e.g., Grafen 1990) have suggested that the central tenets of his argument are sound. Within this paper the phrase "Zahavi's handicap condition" will be used to refer to the stipulation that as signaller quality increases, the cost of making any particular signal decreases.

Johnstone (1997) has usefully characterized the literature concerning the handicap principle as comprising two contrasting classes of account. The first class, described above, attempts to account for the evolutionary stability of the honest advertisement of *quality* as a result of the manner in which the *costs* of signalling vary with quality (e.g., Grafen 1990, Hurd 1995). The second class attempts to account for the evolutionary stability of the honest advertisement of *need* as a result of the manner in which signaller *benefits* vary with need (e.g., Godfray 1991, Maynard Smith 1991).

The latter class includes models of the kind used by Godfray (1991) to demonstrate the evolutionary stability of a strategy in which nestlings honestly advertise their hunger by varying the strength of their begging calls. Godfray showed that such a strategy is evolutionarily stable if the costs of begging are independent of a chick's hunger, but the value of any particular parental resource to a begging chick increases with the chick's hunger. In such situations no chick will exaggerate its hunger since the value of a parental resource solicited through exaggerated begging will not compensate for the increased cost of begging. Hungry chicks beg more than sated chicks because the resources are worth more to them.

Previous models (Bullock 1997) have demonstrated that the two classes identified by Johnstone (1997) are special cases of a general class of account in which the interactions between the advertised trait (quality or need) and both costs *and* benefits are such that honest signalling strategies are the best policies.

Here an evolutionary simulation model capable of addressing this superordinate class of scenarios will be implemented. The general conditions under which honest signalling may take place between parties which suffer a conflict of interests will be determined. In addition, the evolutionary attainability of such honest signalling equilibria and the character of the signalling behaviour at such equilibria will be examined.

In the following section, Grafen's (1990) continuous signalling game is presented, its implementation as an evolutionary simulation model is described, and data generated by this simulation are summarized. The satisfaction of Zahavi's handicap condition will be shown to be neither necessary nor sufficient to ensure the evolutionary stability of honest communication. Subsequently, the relationship between the simulation results and those of previous models will be discussed. It will be concluded that these previous results are accommodated as special cases of those presented here. A condition for the presence of honest signalling equilibria will be offered which replaces that proposed by Zahavi. This condition admits the existence of signalling equilibria in which (*contra* Zahavi) low-quality signallers enjoy lower signalling costs than high-quality signallers.

An Evolutionary Simulation Model of a Continuous Signalling Game

Grafen (1990) cast his model in terms of mate choice. Male fitness, w_m, was defined as a function of quality, q, level of advertisement, a, and degree of female response, p. This function was constrained such that male fitness decreased with increasing advertisement, and increased with increasing female response. Female fitness, w_f, was defined as increasing with the accuracy with which female response approximated male quality. Briefly, Grafen demonstrated that honest signalling of quality could be an ESS if the negative fitness consequences of male advertisement decrease with increasing quality, i.e., Zahavi's handicap condition is met. However, Grafen's analysis demanded one extra assumption: that the positive fitness consequences of female preference were neutral with respect to male quality, or increased with male quality.

A more general treatment of the model (Bullock 1997) demonstrated that, once Grafen's assumption concerning the manner in which male quality mediates the positive fitness consequences of female response is relaxed, Zahavi's handicap condition ceases to be either necessary or sufficient for the stability of honest signalling. Here, an evolutionary simulation model will replicate this analytic result, before allowing a more involved examination of the behaviours exhibited by signallers and receivers.

Before an evolutionary simulation model can be attempted, fitness functions which adequately capture the assumptions made during the above analysis must be defined for both signallers and receivers. Particular attention will be paid to the fitness functions' ability to capture the assumptions made by the full range of continuous signalling models under consideration here.

In addition, schemes for representing a range of continuous signalling and response strategies must be defined. They must be simple in order that the representation of strategies be amenable to manipulation by a genetic algorithm, yet they must also be able to capture an ad-

[1]This notion of waste as a signal of quality is reminiscent of the concept of "conspicuous consumption" discussed by Veblen (1899).

equate range of signalling and responding behaviours.

Fitness functions

After Grafen (1990), (female) receiver fitness, w_f, may be calculated as

$$w_f = \frac{1}{1 + |p - q|}$$

Receiver fitness increases with the accuracy with which the receiver response, p, approximates signaller quality, q.

Grafen (1990) constructed a specific function determining (male) signaller fitness with which to demonstrate how his general model worked.

$$w_m = p^r q^a$$

This fitness function allows that increases in signaller quality, q, reduce the costs incurred in making an advertisement, a, and that increases in signaller quality increase the positive fitness consequences of female preference, p. The degree to which female preference influences signaller fitness is governed by a parameter, r.[2]

As such, Grafen's function cannot accommodate the possibility that the fitness consequences of receiver responses might vary with signaller quality independently from the manner in which the negative fitness consequences of advertising vary with signaller quality. Furthermore, the function fails to accommodate the possibility that the negative fitness consequences for signallers of advertising might increase with signaller quality.

An alternative function must be constructed before an unconstrained exploration of the various possible signalling scenarios entertained within the literature can be undertaken.

$$w_m(a, p, q) = pq^R - aq^S$$

For this function, w_m, a, p, and q denote, as before, signaller fitness, level of advertising, degree of receiver preference, and level of signaller quality, respectively, whilst R and S are exponents which govern, respectively, the manner in which signaller quality mediates the positive effect of receiver responses and the manner in which signaller quality mediates the negative effect of signaller advertisement. The function is naturally understood as the sum of a positive benefit term and a negative cost term.

The first term of the fitness function, pq^R, connotes the benefit of signalling. The receiver response, p, contributes positively to signaller fitness, but the manner in which it contributes may be sensitive to signaller quality. For scenarios in which $R = 0$, the fitness consequences of receiver responses are independent of signaller quality.

[2] Grafen assumes that both q and p lie in the interval [0,1], and that both a and r are greater than or equal to unity.

For scenarios in which $R > 0$, the positive contributions of receiver responses increase with signaller quality. For scenarios in which $R < 0$, the positive contributions of receiver responses decrease with signaller quality.

The second term, aq^S, represents the cost of signalling. The signaller's level of advertisement, a, contributes negatively to signaller fitness, but the manner in which it contributes may be sensitive to signaller quality. For scenarios in which $S = 0$, the fitness consequences of advertising are independent of signaller quality. For scenarios in which $S > 0$, the cost of advertising increases with q. Conversely, for scenarios in which $S < 0$, the cost of advertising decreases with q. This last class of scenarios is asserted by Zahavi (1975, 1977; Zahavi & Zahavi, 1997) to be the only class admitting of honest signalling behaviour.

In order to derive the conditions for the existence of an honest signalling ESS we must derive the conditions under which "better males do better by advertising more" (Grafen 1990, p.520). Grafen formulated the condition thus:

$$\frac{\partial w_m / \partial a}{\partial w_m / \partial p} \text{ is strictly increasing in q.}$$

For the functions defined above, this yields,

$$(R - S)q^{S-R-1} > 0,$$

which is satisfied exclusively by $R > S$. Thus we can expect honest signalling ESSs to exist for scenarios in which $R > S$, i.e., scenarios in which, naturally enough, the manner in which quality mediates the positive fitness consequences of female preference (R) outweigh the manner in which quality mediates the negative fitness consequences of advertising (S).

Thus, through manipulation of the signaller fitness function's two free parameters, R and S, this continuous model can be made to capture the assumptions of various models within the literature. In addition, a clear prediction concerning the conditions under which honest advertisement is an ESS has been made. These ESS conditions accommodate results presented within, for example, Grafen (1990) and Godfray (1991), whilst allowing the existence of a broader class of honest signalling conditions than predicted under such models (see Figure 4). This broader class of ESS conditions includes scenarios in which Zahavi's handicap condition do not have to be met (i.e., conditions in which $S \not< 0$).

Signalling and response strategies

A population of signallers/receivers was distributed across a 25-by-25 grid. Each cell in the grid contained one signaller and one receiver. Each signaller was allocated an internal state, q, drawn at random from a uniform probability distribution in the range $[q_{min}, q_{max}]$.

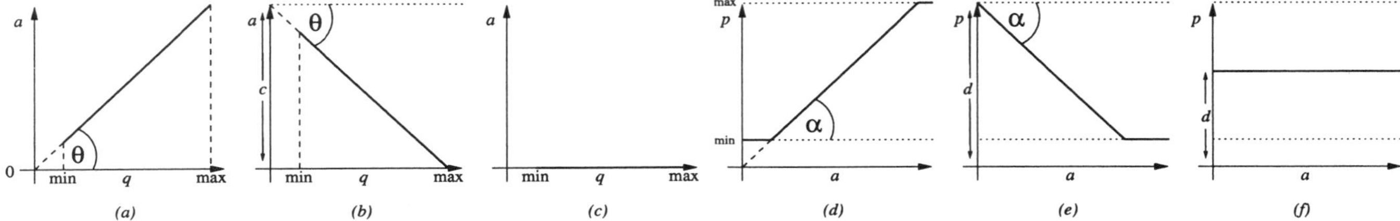

Figure 1: Examples of three continuous signalling strategies mapping signaller quality, q, onto advertisement, a, and three continuous response strategies mapping advertisement, a, onto receiver response, p. Each strategy is defined by a gradient (constrained to lie strictly within the range $[-\frac{\pi}{2}, \frac{\pi}{2}]$) and an intercept (unbounded).

In addition, each signaller inherited a signalling strategy from its parent. A signalling strategy comprised two real values, $\{\theta, c\}$. An advertisement, a, was calculated as $q \tan\theta + c$. Advertisements of below zero were truncated to zero. Similarly each receiver inherited a response strategy from its parent. A response strategy comprised two real values, $\{\alpha, d\}$. Receiver response, p, was calculated as $a \tan\alpha + d$. Responses lying outside the range $[q_{min}, q_{max}]$ were truncated to their nearest extreme. For all simulations reported here $q_{min} = 0.1$ and $q_{max} = 5.0$.

The honesty of such a signalling strategy cannot be ascertained through consideration of the strategy in isolation. Either of the signalling strategies depicted in Figures 1a and 1b could take part in an honest signalling scenario since they each provide a unique advertisement for each possible value of signaller quality. For example, Figures 1d and 1e depict response strategies which would successfully recover the value of q from advertisements made by signallers adopting the signalling strategies depicted in Figures 1a and 1b respectively. In contrast, the signalling strategy depicted in Figure 1c does not provide unique advertisements for each possible value of signaller quality. The best reply to such signalling strategies is to play the response strategy depicted in Figure 1f, which ensures that each signaller is assessed as of average quality.

Whether communication is deceitful or honest is thus contingent upon the manner in which the signalling and response strategies match up across the population. If a period of adaptation under the selection pressures implemented by the fitness functions outlined above leads to a population of signallers playing the strategy depicted in Figure 1b partnered by a population of receivers playing the strategy depicted in Figure 1e, such populations can be considered, in concert, to be taking part in an honest signalling scenario since receiver prediction error is minimized in such circumstances. In such a population, a mutant signaller playing the alternative signalling strategy depicted in Figure 1a is cheating since the quality of such a mutant would be systematically misjudged by receivers. The classification of such a signaller as a cheat must be made despite the fact that the particular signalling strategy employed by the mutant generates advertisements which are directly proportional to its internal state.

This scheme for the representation of signalling and response strategies compares favourably with alternative schemes proposed within similar models. For example, Debourcier and Wheler (1995) construct a model of aggressive signalling with which to explore the handicap principle, and propose that a signalling strategy can be represented as the (positive) gradient, m, of an advertising function of the form $a = mq$. Under such a scheme, although signallers may employ different degrees of exaggeration, no signaller is able to signal more strongly when low quality than when high, and every signaller must make an advertisement of zero when of zero quality. This overly restricts the strategy space and consequently limits the evolutionary dynamics of their model.

Algorithm and parameters

The fitnesses of signallers and receivers were calculated as per the fitness functions defined above, each interacting once with four partners chosen randomly (with replacement) from its local neighbourhood. Once each signaller and receiver had been assessed, the whole population was updated synchronously and asexually. One parent from the previous generation was chosen for each offspring cell. The location of a potential parent was chosen through perturbing both the x and y grid co-ordinates of the offspring cell by independent values drawn from a normal probability distribution with standard deviation 1.75 and mean zero. Four potential parents were chosen for each offspring signaller. An offspring signaller inherited its signalling strategy from the fittest of these four. Similarly, an offspring receiver inherited its response strategy from the fittest of four receivers chosen from the previous generation in the same manner.

A mutation operator ensured that offspring sometimes inherited a strategy which differed from that of their parents. For both signallers and receivers each of the two values comprising their inherited strategy were independently exposed to the chance of mutations, which occurred with probability 0.01. Mutations, when they occurred, consisted of perturbations drawn from a normal distribution with mean zero and standard deviation 0.05. Mutated values which lay outside the legal range for the parameter they coded for were truncated to the nearest legal value for that parameter.

Populations were simulated for 1000 generations in this manner, during which time the signalling and response strategies present in the population were recorded. The parameters R and S were varied across simulations but remained constant throughout each. The 441 possible pairs of parameter values, $\{R, S\}$, drawn from the set {-2.0, -1.8, ... 1.8, 2.0}, were exhaustively explored under each of three differing classes of initial condition. Each of the resulting 1323 (3 by 441) conditions were simulated 10 times. The pseudo-random number generator employed by the algorithm was itself seeded randomly for each simulation.

The first class of initial conditions consisted of a population of signallers sharing an 'honest' signalling strategy which mapped q directly onto a, $\{\theta = \frac{\pi}{4}, c = 0\}$, and a population of receivers sharing a 'believing' response strategy, $\{\alpha = \frac{\pi}{4}, d = 0\}$, which faithfully recovers values of q from signaller advertisements produced under the honest signalling strategy. This class of initial conditions will be termed 'Honest' since receivers are able to predict signaller quality accurately from signaller advertisements.

The second class of initial conditions consisted of a population of signallers and receivers, each with a strategy generated by drawing values for θ and α at random from a uniform distribution $[-\frac{\pi}{4}, \frac{\pi}{4}]$, and similarly drawing values for c and d at random from a uniform distribution $[-q_{max}, q_{max}]$. This class of initial conditions will be termed 'Random' since signallers' strategies and receivers' strategies are unrelated and implement a wide range of mappings.

The third class of initial conditions consisted of a population of signallers sharing a signalling strategy which mapped any value of q onto 0, i.e., $\{\theta = 0, c = 0\}$, and a population of receivers sharing a response strategy which mapped any advertisement onto 0, i.e., $\{\alpha = 0, d = 0\}$. This class of initial conditions will be termed 'Cynical' since signallers never make advertisements, whilst receivers never make responses.

Results

Results were consistent with the predictions arrived at through the analysis presented above. Two measures of performance were utilized in assessing the degree of honesty within a population. Both measures were derived from population summary statistics calculated for a particular generation. First, the average signalling strategy and response strategy were calculated. This was achieved simply by taking the population mean values of θ, c, α, and d.

From the mean signalling strategy, $\{\bar{\theta}, \bar{c}\}$, the mean strategy signal range, $\bar{r}$, was calculated as $(q_{max} - q_{min}) \tan \bar{\theta}$. The mean strategy response error, $\bar{e}$, was calculated as the absolute mean difference between signaller quality, q, and receiver response, p, for signallers using the mean signalling strategy $\{\bar{\theta}, \bar{c}\}$ and receivers using the mean response strategy $\{\bar{\alpha}, \bar{d}\}$, calculated for q ranging from q_{min} to q_{max}.

Since both these metrics are population-level summary statistics, care must be taken to appreciate that many heterogeneous populations could be responsible for any observed value. For example, a value of $\bar{e} = \frac{q_{max}+q_{min}}{4}$ may indicate a homogeneous population of receivers adopting the strategy $\{\alpha = 0, c = \frac{q_{max}+q_{min}}{2}\}$, or a heterogeneous population comprised such that, although each receiver employs a different strategy, *on average* they achieve chance levels of performance. Throughout the following sections, such ambiguity was avoided though recourse to the relevant standard deviations.

Honest Initial Conditions: The equality $R = S$ divided the parameter space into two areas (see Figure 2). The area defined by $R > S$ contained signallers which made advertisements which increased with signaller quality ($\bar{r} > 0$), and receivers which were able to recover signaller quality accurately from such advertisements ($\bar{e} \approx 0$); i.e., honest signalling obtained under these conditions. In contrast, the area defined by $R < S$ contained signallers which made advertisements which did not differ with signaller quality ($\bar{r} \approx 0$), and, as a result, receivers which were unable to accurately recover signaller quality from signaller advertisements ($\bar{e} > 0$); i.e., non-signalling obtained under these conditions.[3]

Furthermore, for scenarios in which $R > S$, mean signal range, $\bar{r}$, increased with $R - S$. For scenarios in which the difference between R and S is small, the range of signals is also small. However, for scenarios in which R far outstrips S, signals given by high quality signallers are orders of magnitude higher than those given by low quality signallers.

Random Initial Conditions: Within the area of parameter space in which honest signalling equilibria are not predicted to exist, $\bar{r} \approx 0$ whilst $\bar{e} \approx \frac{q_{max}+q_{min}}{4}$, i.e., non-signalling strategies, and response strategies which perform at the level of chance are observed.

Within the area of parameter space predicted to admit of honest signalling equilibria, both honest signalling equilibria and non-signalling equilibria were achieved. The frequency with which honest signalling equilibria were achieved from Random initial conditions increases with the magnitude of $R - S$. For simulations in which R is only slightly higher than S, honest signalling equilibria

[3]Mean response error is sometimes higher than that resulting from performance at chance levels. This is due to an artefact of the simulation design (limiting receiver response to fall within the range $[q_{min}, q_{max}]$). A full account is given in Bullock (1998).

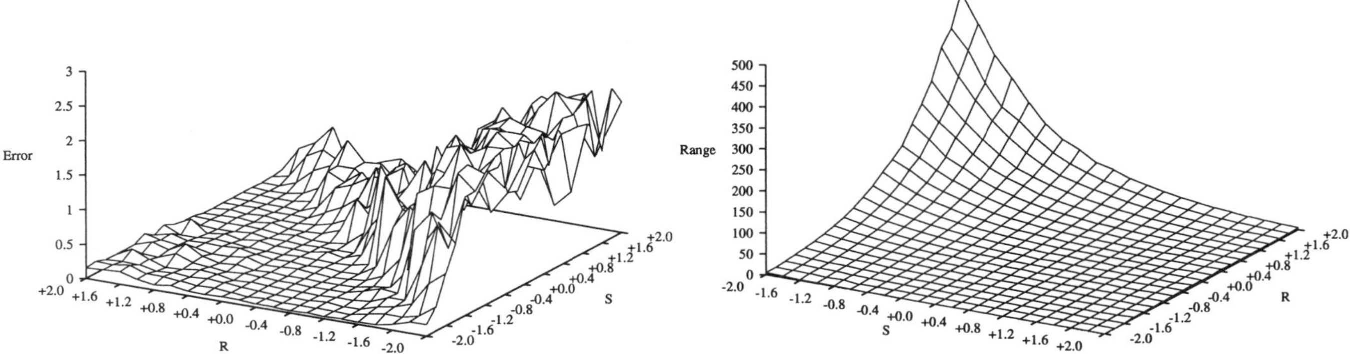

Figure 2: Mean response error (left) and signal range (right) after 1000 generations, averaged across 10 simulation runs from Honest initial conditions. For reasons of clarity the left graph has been rotated 90° anti-clockwise about the vertical axis.

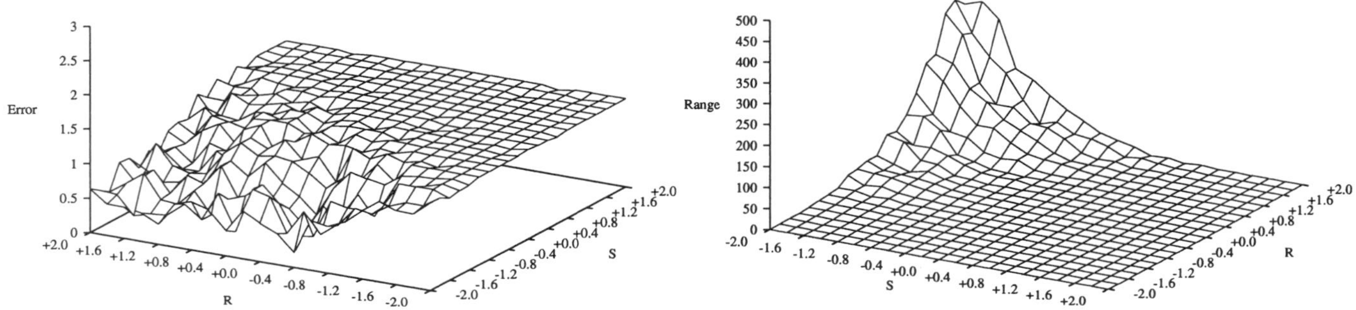

Figure 3: Mean response error (left) and signal range (right) after 1000 generations, averaged across 10 simulation runs from Random initial conditions. For reasons of clarity, the left graph has been rotated 90° anti-clockwise about the vertical axis.

are achieved only rarely. As $R - S$ increases, signalling equilibria are achieved with increasing frequency. This is reflected in the variation, across the parameter space, of both the mean values for $\bar{r}$ and $\bar{e}$ (see Figure 3) and their standard deviations.

Cynical Initial Conditions: The behaviour of the model is similar to that resulting from Random initial conditions. For simulations in which $R < S$, behaviour is indistinguishable from that resulting from Random initial conditions. For simulations in which $R > S$, signalling equilibria are sometimes attained, although the frequency with which this occurs is lower than that observed for simulations from Random initial conditions. As before, the frequency with which signalling equilibria are achieved increases with $R - S$.

A note on equilibria

At several points throughout the preceding sections use is made of the term equilibrium. The honest signalling equilibria described have the general character of point equilibria. However, the stochasticity of the tournament selection process and the allocation of signaller quality, the statistical independence of mutation events, and the co-evolutionary nature of the signaller-receiver relationship all ensure that a population of signallers or receivers will tend to move around the vicinity of its equilibrium state, rather than fix upon it rigidly, as might be expected from an idealized numerical approximation to the dynamic equations of an ESS model. Thus to call the equilibria achieved by the simulation ESSs is not strictly accurate. However, in their defence, the honest signalling equilibria achieved by the simulation are predicted by the ESS model and are characterized by approximately constant trajectories within both the signaller and receiver populations.

By contrast, what might be called the simulation's non-signalling equilibria permit significant amounts of evolutionary drift on the part of both signaller and receiver populations. There are, for example, many signalling strategies which result in signallers never making a signal. If, under certain conditions, selection favours making no signal, evolutionary drift amongst these functionally identical strategies is inevitable.

Similarly, although there is an optimal response strategy in reply to such non-signalling signallers, the relatively small sample of four signallers against which each receiver is assessed ensures that there exists a high degree of variability in fitness scores achieved by strategies in the vicinity of this optimal strategy (which is only strictly optimal if assessed on the basis of an infinite number of trials, each featuring a signaller drawn at random from the entire population). One might conceive of this situation as involving a receiver population which is subject to a rather weak negative feedback from its co-evolutionary partner. This feedback keeps the receiver population within a volume of strategy space containing strategies with fitnesses sharing a similar mean and a relatively high variance.

A related but distinct point concerns whether equilibria achieved by the simulation are repeatable, i.e., whether the same population states are always achieved from the same initial conditions under the same parameter values. For the purposes of this model no claim to this effect will be made since the simulation's stochasticity is, at times, quite capable of perturbing trajectories from one basin of attraction to another. Despite this indeterminacy, basins of attraction remain characterizable.

Considerations such as these do no damage to the generality of the results presented here, but should be borne in mind when analyzing the behaviour of any evolutionary simulation model.

Summary

These simulation results suggest that both the possibility of a stable honest signalling system, and the extravagance of signals within such a system, depends critically on the difference between the manner in which the advertised trait influences the *benefits* of signalling (R) and the manner in which it influences the *costs* of signalling (S). Where this difference is negative ($R < S$), no honest signalling is possible. Where this difference is positive ($R > S$), honest signalling equilibria exist.

Thus, honest signalling equilibria may exist for scenarios in which Zahavi's handicap condition does not hold (i.e., $S \not< 0$), and conversely honest, signalling equilibria may not exist for scenarios in which Zahavi's handicap condition does hold (i.e., $S < 0$).

Furthermore, the magnitude of the difference, $R - S$, is positively correlated with the extent of the basin of attraction for any signalling equilibrium. Thus, although under conditions in which $R - S$ is positive but small, stable signalling equilibria in which signals are relatively cheap are viable, such equilibria will seldom be attained through the evolution of non-signalling ancestral populations since the basins of attraction for such equilibria are prohibitively small. This result is derived solely from the simulation behaviour since predictions concerning the attainability of equilibria could not be made on the basis of the analytic findings reported in Bullock (1997).

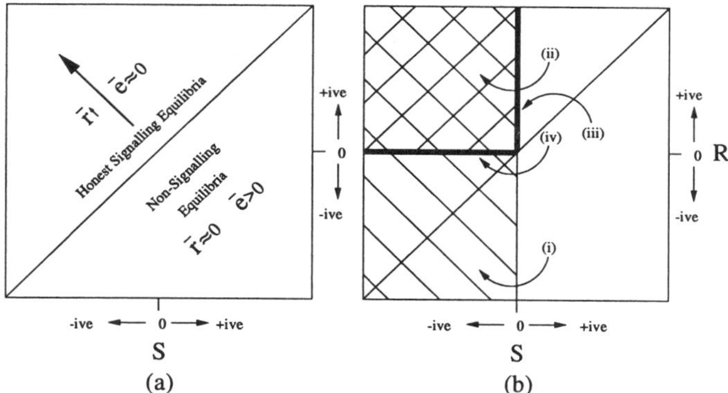

Figure 4: Showing *(a)* the conditions under which honest signalling obtain for the model presented here, and *(b)* the conditions predicted to admit of honest signalling equilibria by (i) Zahavi (1975, 1977): diagonal hatching defined by $S < 0$, (ii) Grafen (1990): cross-hatching defined by $S < 0$ and $R \geq 0$, (iii) Godfray (1991) and Maynard Smith (1991): bold vertical line defined by $R > 0$ and $S = 0$, and (iv) Hurd (1995): bold horizontal line defined by $S < 0$ and $R = 0$.

Discussion

It has been demonstrated through the use of an evolutionary simulation model that non-handicap equilibria exist for an extension to Grafen's (1990) continuous model of signal evolution. In this section, the findings reported in this paper will be compared with those reported within previous studies. These previous results are easily accommodated by those presented within this paper, which themselves provide a general formulation of the conditions governing the existence of what have been termed 'handicap' signalling scenarios.

Once this reconciliation of previous results has been described, a reconciliation of the positions which lead to their presentation will be attempted. The handicap principle will be assessed in three regards. The first issue discussed will be the various interpretations of the relationships between costs, benefits, and fitness which appear to motivate models of the handicap principle. Secondly, the validity of the term handicap itself will be considered before, finally, the implications of the results presented here for the supposed generality of the handicap principle will be addressed.

Reconciliation of results

Figure 4a depicts the broad conclusion suggested by the continuous model of signalling explored here. Honest signalling is stable for scenarios in which the manner in which the advertised trait mediates the influence of signalling benefits on signaller fitness outweighs the manner in which the advertised trait mediates the influence of signalling costs on signaller fitness, i.e., the net cost of signalling (the cost of honest signalling minus the benefit of an accurate receiver response) decreases monotonically with the advertised trait.

This result is captured graphically in Figure 4a by dividing the space of possible signalling scenarios into two halves, separated by a diagonal line along which the influence of the advertised trait on costs is exactly balanced by its influence on benefits (i.e., $R = S$). Above this line (i.e, for $R > S$), honest signalling equilibria obtain; below it (i.e., for $R < S$), no such honest signalling equilibria exist.

In Figure 4b this graphical device is used to locate previous theoretical results. For example, Zahavi's (1975, 1977; Zahavi & Zahavi, 1997) claim that honest signalling may only exist for scenarios in which the costs of signalling decrease with the trait being advertised may be represented by the area satisfying the inequality $S < 0$. It is plain from the diagram that this inequality is neither necessary nor sufficient for the existence of honest signalling equilibria. Grafen's (1990) contention is hown to be correct. Given that signaller benefits are either unaffected by the advertised trait or increase with the advertised trait ($R \geq 0$), in order that signalling be honest, signalling costs must decrease with the advertised trait ($S < 0$). However, the space of possible signalling scenarios defined by his conditions, does not exhaustively account for all honest signalling equilibria.

Models in which the negative fitness consequences of signal costs are assumed to be independent of the trait being advertised (i.e., models for which $S = 0$) have often concluded that, in order for such signalling to be honest, the positive fitness consequences for signallers of receiver behaviour must increase with the signaller's advertised trait (i.e., $R > 0$). Such models typically take the advertised trait to be signaller need (e.g., Godfray 1991, Maynard Smith 1991). They make a claim which can be recast as asserting that honest signalling may be stable for signalling systems which lie along the bold vertical line in Figure 4b.

Similarly, models in which the positive fitness consequences of the benefits accrued by signallers are assumed to be independent of the trait being advertised (i.e., models for which $R = 0$) have often concluded that, in order for such signalling to be honest, the negative fitness consequences (for signallers) of signal cost must increase with the signaller's advertised trait (i.e., $S < 0$). Such models typically take the advertised trait to be signaller quality (e.g., Hurd 1995), and make a claim which can be rephrased as asserting that honest signalling may be stable for signalling systems which lie along the bold horizontal line in Figure 4b.

Costs, benefits, and fitness

This paper opened with a description of two complementary arguments which each result from Zahavi's handicap signalling notion. The first argument suggested that honest advertisement of quality might be stabilized by differential signaller costs. The second argument suggested that the honest advertisement of need might be stabilized by differential signaller benefits. The results of the model constructed within this paper demonstrate that the honest advertisement of either quality, *or* need, may each be stabilized by differential costs, *and/or* differential benefits. This result is due to the fact that the terms 'cost' and 'benefit' may each be cashed out in the same currency — fitness. Costs are merely negative increments to fitness, whereas benefits are positive increments to fitness.

However, at a less abstract level of description, costs and benefits may come in many different forms. For example, negative fitness consequences may arise as a result of energetic costs, risks of predation, parasitism, or infection, costs of missing a high-quality mating opportunity, of mating with a sub-optimal mate, etc. Although each of these costs has negative fitness consequences, the character of these negative fitness consequences may differ radically across these different forms of cost.

Similarly there are benefits to be gained from obtaining a copulation, a food resource, a territory, an opponent's surrender, etc. Again, although each of these benefits has positive fitness consequences, the character of these positive fitness consequences may not be uniform across these different forms of benefit.

Within evolutionary models, the manner in which costs and benefits influence fitness is formalized identically. Costs, whatever their nature, influence fitness negatively, whereas benefits, whatever their nature, influence fitness positively.

However, theorists constructing models of handicap signalling are faced with a decision concerning the manner in which the influence of signalling costs (and signalling benefits) upon fitness is to *vary* with the trait which signallers are advertising. For example, how does the effect of signal production cost vary with signaller need? What will interest us here are the different decisions which may be made regarding these aspects of handicap modelling.

Consider the example of a begging nestling which is signalling in an attempt to solicit parental resources. We will assume that the trait of interest to parents is a chick's need, and that quality varies inversely with need. For this scenario Godfray (1991) models the cost of signalling as equal across all signallers. Grafen (1990), on the other hand, models cost as decreasing with signaller quality. Godfray (1991) models the benefit of soliciting a particular parental resource as increasing with need, whereas Grafen (1990) models such benefit as either independent of signaller need, or *decreasing* with signaller need.

A second example, also addressed by Grafen (1990),

involves an interloper making a signal of aggressive intent to an observing harem holder. Grafen asserts that in such a situation, the costs of signalling decrease with the increasing quality of a signaller. He further claims that the benefits for the signaller of a retreat response by a receiver increase with the quality of a signaller. In contrast, Adams and Gibbons (1995) suggest that in such situations, the benefit of eliciting a retreat response might *decrease* with increasing signaller quality. They reason that "strong animals can win many conflicts without threatening (i.e., by direct fighting), while weak animals cannot. Furthermore, weak animals have more to gain by avoiding direct fights since they are less able to defend against injury." (p. 406).

It is clear from these two examples that the authors of these models have made radically opposed assumptions with respect to the relationship between costs, benefits, and fitness (for a discussion of possible reasons for these differences, see Bullock 1997). In contrast, the model presented within this paper makes no assumptions concerning the manner in which costs and benefits influence fitness, save that costs are a negative influence, whilst benefits are a positive influence. As a result of this neutrality, a degree of generality has been gained.

Are signals handicaps?

The force of the results presented within this paper is to qualify previous statements of the conditions which must be met before honest handicap signalling may be evolutionarily stable. Rather than merely requiring *gross* signalling costs to vary with signaller quality in some manner, the model presented here requires consideration of the manner in which the *net* cost of signalling varies with signaller quality.

Although Zahavi often appears to consider the net costs involved in signalling when formulating his principle (e.g., "it is reasonable to expect a population in its optimal fitness to benefit from a handicap", and "so long as the offspring ... does not deviate to grow its handicap larger than it can afford, the handicap [may persist] as a marker of honest advertisement", p. 604, Zahavi 1977), when describing examples of natural signalling he rarely appreciates the benefits which might be accrued from signalling, and the manner in which such benefits might negate the increased costs involved in bluffing.

Zahavi's ambivalence toward the potential benefits of signalling (or bluffing) led Wiley (1983) to characterize Zahavi's (1975) claim as "signals should evolve to become a *net* handicap to signallers" (p. 176, my emphasis), whilst Adams and Gibbons (1995) reach the opposite conclusion, stating that the scenario they consider differs from that prescribed by the handicap principle in that within their model, "the net benefit for a given advertisement may not increase monotonically with the signaller's strength" (p. 406).

Furthermore, the sense of much of Zahavi's verbal argument does not seem to accord with a notion of the handicap principle couched in terms of net costs. For example, as Hurd (1995) points out, if the costs involved in signalling must be acceptable costs (i.e., they must be compensated for by consonant benefits), then in what sense are these costs a 'handicap'? Although the costs incurred by a *bluffer* might be characterized as a handicap, since these costs would not be compensated for by the receiver response, this is not the sense in which Zahavi proposed the term. For Zahavi, *honest* signallers suffer a handicap. This suffering is necessary as a means of demonstrating honesty. However, once one appreciates the role played by benefits in assuaging these costs, the notion that signallers are "suffering" becomes suspect.

The generality of the handicap principle

The inclusion of a benefit clause in the definition of the handicap principle does not preclude the existence of handicap signalling equilibria. However, it does have implications for the proposed ubiquity of the handicap principle as it has been presented by Zahavi and others.

The condition that signal cost is related to signaller quality in the manner stipulated by Zahavi (i.e., that as signaller quality increases the cost of signalling decreases) appears to be a candidate for very wide application. Indeed, Zahavi has demonstrated the breadth of this application, even going so far as to suggest that the handicap principle accounts for all natural signalling. However, the model constructed here demonstrates that the influence of benefits on signaller behaviour may ensure that despite signal cost being related to signaller quality in the manner prescribed by Zahavi, honesty may never-the-less be unstable. Similarly, some systems, despite failing to meet Zahavi's handicap condition (e.g., systems in which there is no relationship between signal cost and signaller quality) may be stable due to the influence of benefits upon signaller behaviour.

As such, the ease with which these revised conditions for the existence of evolutionarily stable handicap signalling may be confidently predicted to hold across classes of signalling scenario is much reduced. Field biologists charged with the task of establishing whether real signalling systems are handicap signalling systems must characterize both the manner in which signal cost differs with the trait being advertised *and* the manner in which signaller benefits differ with the same trait. This increased burden is compounded by the fact that, as demonstrated above, theorists' predictions concerning the manner in which costs and benefits vary with, for example, quality or need across signalling populations themselves demonstrate a lack of coherence.

From this discussion, it is clear that the model constructed within this paper, in addition to clarifying the conditions under which signalling may be honest and stable, questions the integrity of handicap terminology. It also challenges the handicap principle's supposed ubiquity through highlighting the complications which arise from a consideration of the manner in which costs *and benefits* are mediated by advertised traits.

Conclusion

In summary, the satisfaction of Zahavi's handicap condition was demonstrated to be neither necessary nor sufficient for the existence of honest signalling equilibria within a general continuous evolutionary simulation model.

It was demonstrated that in order for a signalling system to be stable, a relationship between signalling costs, signaller quality, and (*contra* Zahavi) signalling *benefits* must hold, not merely a relationship between signalling costs and signaller quality.

Stable signalling systems involving relatively cheap signals were shown to be viable under certain conditions. However, the evolutionary attainability of these equilibria was shown to be compromised by the size of their basins of attraction.

Acknowledgments

This paper was improved immeasurably through the influence of Valerie Chase, Jason Nobel, Ezequiel di Paolo, Henrietta Wilson, and the useful commentary of two anonymous referees.

References

Adams, E. S., and Mesterton-Gibbons, M. 1995. The cost of threat displays and the stability of deceptive communication. *J. Theor. Biol.* 175:405–421.

Bullock, S. 1997. An exploration of signalling behaviour by both analytic and simulation means for both discrete and continuous models. In Husbands, P., and Harvey, I., eds., *Proceedings of the Fourth European Conference on Artificial Life*, 454–463. Cambridge, MA: MIT Press.

Bullock, S. 1998. Evolutionary simulation models: On their character, and application to problems involving the evolution of natural signalling systems. Unpublished PhD Thesis, University of Sussex, England.

Darwin, C. 1871. *The Descent of Man and Selection in Relation to Sex.* London: John Murray.

Dawkins, R., and Krebs, J. R. 1978. Animal signals: Information or manipulation. In Krebs, J. R., and Davies, N. B., eds., *Behavioural Ecology: An Evolutionary Approach.* Oxford: Blackwell. 282–309.

de Bourcier, P., and Wheeler, M. 1995. Aggressive signalling meets adaptive receiving: Further experiments in Synthetic Behavioural Ecology. In Morán, F.; Moreno, A.; Morelo, J. J.; and Chacón, P., eds., *Advances in Artificial Life: Proceedings of the Third European Conference on Artificial Life.* Berlin and Heidelberg: Springer-Verlag.

Godfray, H. C. J. 1991. Signalling of need by offspring to their parents. *Nature* 352:328–330.

Grafen, A. 1990. Biological signals as handicaps. *J. Theor. Biol.* 144:517–546.

Hurd, P. L. 1995. Communication in discrete action-response games. *J. Theor. Biol.* 174:217–222.

Johnstone, R. A. 1997. The evolution of animal signals. In Krebs, J. R., and Davies, N. B., eds., *Behavioural Ecology: An Evolutionary Approach.* Oxford: Blackwell, 4th edition. 155–178.

MacLennan, B. 1991. Synthetic Ethology: An approach to the study of communication. In Langton, C. G.; Taylor, C.; Farmer, J. D.; and Rasmussen, S., eds., *Artificial Life II — SFI Studies in the Sciences of Complexity*, volume X, 631–658. Redwood City, California: Addison-Wesley.

Maynard Smith, J. 1982. *Evolution and the Theory of Games.* Cambridge: Cambridge University Press.

Maynard Smith, J. 1991. Honest signalling: The Philip Sidney game. *Anim. Behav.* 42:1034–1035.

Veblen, T. 1899. The theory of the leisure class. In Lerner, M., ed., *The Portable Veblen.* New York: Viking Press. 53–214. Collection published 1948.

Werner, G. M., and Dyer, M. G. 1991. Evolution of communication in artificial organisms. In Langton, C. G.; Taylor, C.; Farmer, J. D.; and Rasmussen, S., eds., *Artificial Life II — SFI Studies in the Sciences of Complexity*, volume X, 659–687. Redwood City, California: Addison-Wesley.

Wiley, R. H. 1983. The evolution of communication: Information and manipulation. In Halliday, T. R., and Slater, P. J. B., eds., *Communication.* Oxford: Blackwell. 156–189.

Zahavi, A., and Zahavi, A. 1997. *The Handicap Principle: A missing piece of Darwin's puzzle.* OUP.

Zahavi, A. 1975. Mate selection — A selection for a handicap. *J. Theor. Biol.* 53:205–214.

Zahavi, A. 1977. The cost of honesty (further remarks on the handicap principle). *J. Theor. Biol.* 67:603–605.

How Do Firms Transition Between Monopoly and Competitive Behavior? An Agent-Based Economic Model

Michael de la Maza
Redfire Capital Management Group
950 Massachusetts Ave., Suite 209
Cambridge, Massachusetts 02139
RedfireGrp@aol.com

Ayla Oğuş
Department of Economics
Boston College
Chestnut Hill, Massachusetts 02167
ogus@bc.edu

Deniz Yuret
Artificial Intelligence Laboratory
Massachusetts Institute of Technology
Cambridge, Massachusetts 02139
deniz@mit.edu

Abstract

Artificial life has long held out the promise of revolutionizing how scientists approach a variety of problems. In this paper we describe an application of artificial life techniques to the study of a fundamental problem in economics: How does a firm transition from monopoly behavior to competitive behavior as other firms enter the market? Solving traditional economic models provides the equilibrium, but does not give the path to equilibrium.The firms in our artificial life simulation do not have access to any global information about the market. The resulting global behavior that arises from this local price-setting behavior is the equilibrium predicted by the traditional analytical models. Hence, our simulation provides a proof by example that simple, local rules of interaction can create the global regularities observed and predicted by economists, thus providing a relatively low upper bound on how complex firm agents must be to reach equilibrium. In this paper we describe the various agents in the model–firms, consumers, capital suppliers, labor suppliers–and present the outcome of several simulations of the model.

Introduction

For over a decade, artificial life proponents have suggested that artificial life techniques will revolutionize our understanding of the way the world works. Seminal ideas, such as the notion that global regularities can arise from many local interactions, have the potential to provide theoretical underpinnings for many fields, particularly those in the social sciences.

An economic model is a set of decision-making mechanisms, organizational arrangements, and rules for allocating society's scarce resources. An economic model can be as simple as one agent on an island (a Robinson Crusoe economy), or as complex as the everyday decisions of the 5 billion people in the world, the interactions between all firms in all countries and the actions of all governments. The traditional approach to economic modeling is geared towards obtaining an equilibrium solution. This involves solving the maximization problems of all agents to yield market-clearing prices (markets clear when demand is equal to supply) for all goods and also the quantities that are exchanged at these prices. One assumption imposed for analytic tractability that rarely captures the economic phenomenon we observe is homogeneity of agents. Relaxing this assumption is not possible in a lot of economic models and, if it can be relaxed, the level of heterogeneity that can be modeled is still very restricted. Moreover, equilibrium solutions are not always very informative for policy purposes. For policy makers, the path to equilibrium is just as important as the equilibrium itself.

In this paper, we present an agent-based general equilibrium model of a simple transition economy (an economy, such as those of Poland and Hungary, that is moving from a centrally planned system to a competitive market system) that draws on methods developed in the field of artificial life. The agents in our artificial life model use only local information to arrive at the equilibrium price. The dynamics of reaching the equilibrium price are of particular interest when studying transition economies. Because of the generality of artificial life methods, our model is not restricted to homogeneous agents like most standard economic models are. As a result of these enhancements, macroeconomic outputs of our simulated economy, such as production, pricing, and profits, qualitatively resemble those of real-world transition economies.

Modeling the transition from centrally planned to market economies of former communist countries poses a particular challenge. Economies in transition are economies that are making marked changes in their market structure. Since the demise of the Soviet Union, this has become a relevant and hot research topic. Many countries have begun to move away from a centrally planned economy to a more market-based economy. The transition from communism can be analyzed in terms of four basic tasks of economic reform (Sachs 1996) :

- Systemic Transformation: The institutional, legal, political, and administrative change of the economic system from state-ownership and central planning to private ownership and market allocation of resources.
- Financial Stabilization: The end of the pre-reform monetary overhang, high inflation, and large fiscal deficits.
- Structural Adjustment: The initial reallocation of resources in the economy following the introduction of market forces.
- Implementation of a Framework to Promote Rapid Economic Growth.

The transition economies of Eastern Europe and the former Soviet Union have demonstrated that it is possible to introduce the institutions of a market economy within five years. According to Jeffrey Sachs (Sachs 1996):

> ...liberalization of the economy surely proved to be the quickest and most effective area of change. In the fastest-reform economies, currency convertibility was quickly established; prices were freed, and shortages eliminated; and international barriers were cut, resulting in significant growth of trade.
>
> ...Without question the most difficult aspect of institutional reform has been privatization.

Economic theories do not provide definite answers to the questions that are most central: What is the optimal speed of reforms and what is the best sequencing of reforms? The "shock therapy" proponents favor simultaneous reforms throughout the economy (Lipton & Sachs 1990; Boycko 1992; Frydman & Rapaczynski 1994; Sachs 1993), whereas "gradualists" emphasize the sequencing of reforms (Portes 1991; McKinnon 1991; Dewatriport & Roland 1992; Murrell 1992).

Empirical evidence shows important similarities and differences in the experiences of transitioning economies which contribute to the lack of consensus. Gross Domestic Product (GDP) in a lot of transition economies has followed a U-shaped pattern, an initial decline followed by growth. However, the severity of the fall and its duration has differed (Blanchard 1996). The private sector's share of the GDP has increased, but the increase has been anywhere from double to tenfold (Selowsky & Martin 1997). Countries that have adopted similar reform packages have differed drastically in their responses (Frye & Schleifer 1997).

Examining phenomena such as the U-shaped pattern in output requires modeling the dynamics of the economy. We adopt an artificial life methodology that lends itself with greater ease to modeling these dynamics.

Artificial life techniques hold out the promise of overcoming some of the problems associated with the traditional approach. Artificial life researchers have shown that local rules of behavior can lead to identifiable global regularities. The emphasis on exploiting local information, emergent behavior, and self-organization make artificial life techniques an ideal tool for studying transition economies.

In this paper, we take a first step towards addressing some of the vexing problems posed by transition economies. We present a general equilibrium model of a simple transition economy. It is a general equilibrium model, not because the solution assumes equilibrium, but in the traditional sense that all prices and quantities are determined within the model. We focus on the behavior of firms in a single market, but we also have markets for labor and capital. We analyze the transition from a controlled economy where production is undertaken by one state-owned enterprise (SOE) to a market economy. The agents in this economy do not have access to global information and act on simple rules. We show that equilibrium can be reached. We are also able to replicate qualitatively the U-shaped pattern of output observed in transition economies.

Model

This section describes the decision-making processes of the agents in an economy with one product market,and two input markets (capital and labor). Firms are the only agents we model explicitly and they interact with the three markets. There is a special firm, namely the state-owned enterprise (SOE), which has different constraints than the rest of the firms. All firms, including the SOE produce identical products. We do not explicitly model consumer agents but rather impose specific input supply functions and an output demand function.

This model can be solved analytically if firm agents are assumed to be homogeneous. All of the functions are differentiable, so the solution involves simultaneously solving the equilibrium conditions and all the first order conditions to the maximization problems, to get market-clearing prices and quantities. However, heterogeneous agents are a defining component of transition economies so this simplification would rob the simulation of all potential interest.

Firms

The private firms maximize profits at every period, taking prices of their output and inputs as given. The firms' objective function is:

$$\max_{K,L} \Pi = \max_{K,L} PF(K,L) - rK - wL$$

where $F(K,L) = AK^aL^b$ (Cobb-Douglas production function).

L is labor demand, K is capital demand, and, P, w and r are the market-clearing prices of output, labor services and capital services, respectively. If the parameters of the Cobb-Douglas production function (A, a, and b) are the same across firms, the firms are homogeneous.

Typically, the standard economic approach to solving such a maximization problem is to use calculus. In our simulation, the firm agents instead use local methods, drawn from the field of artificial life, which are described in the Simulation Details section. In particular, the firm agents use locally available prices instead of the market-clearing prices.

The State-Owned Enterprise (SOE)

The SOE maximizes profits at every period but it has to satisfy an employment constraint. The labor demanded in the industry has to be at least $\bar{L}$. The SOE's objective function is:

$$\max_{K,L} \Pi = \max_{K,L} PF(K,L) - rK - wL$$

subject to

$$Q_L^D \geq \bar{L}$$

where Q_L^D is industry labor demand. The production function, F, is also Cobb-Douglas, the parameters of which may be different than those of private firms.

Like the private firms, the SOE uses an optimization method that requires only local information to maximize this objective function.

Input Supply

The supply functions of inputs are increasing (at a decreasing rate) functions of the input prices.

$$Q_L^S = A_L w^p, \; p < 1 \text{ and } A_L > 0$$

$$Q_K^S = A_K r^q, \; q < 1 \text{ and } A_K > 0$$

where Q_L^S is quantity supplied in the labor market and Q_K^S is quantity supplied in the capital market.

Consumer Demand

The market demand for the firms' output is linear[1]:

$$P = A_D Q^D + D, \; D > 0 \text{ and } A_D < 0$$

As with the input suppliers' supply curves, this market demand function is provided exogenously.

Equilibrium Conditions

Demand in every market is equal to supply in every market. There are three markets: two input (capital and labor) markets and one output market. The equilibrium conditions for these three markets are:

$$\begin{aligned} Q^D &= Q^S \\ Q_L^D &= Q_L^S \\ Q_K^D &= Q_K^S \end{aligned}$$

where Q^D is the quantity demanded in the output market and the subscripts L and K refer to the labor and capital markets.

Simulation Details

In this section, we describe how the firm agents in our simulation make decisions and interact with the three markets. In contrast to traditional economic modeling where the objective functions are optimized simultaneously, our agents act in sequence. The simulation runs as follows:

- Until the stopping criterion is met:
  1. For every firm:
  (a) Labor and capital markets provide prices based on recent sales.
  (b) The firm decides the price of its product.
  (c) The product market provides quantity demanded from this firm at this price. The firm produces this amount, provided that it makes a profit. Otherwise, the firm produces the profit-maximizing amount. In doing so, the firm purchases capital and labor at the price computed in step 1a.

[1]Linear demand can also be expressed as: $Q^D = d + A_d P$, $d > 0$ and $A_d < 0$

2. Firms enter and exit the market.

One cycle through this loop is referred to as a period.

The quantity exchanged does not always have to be equal to the quantity demanded. It will be the minimum of the two: quantity produced or quantity demanded. If there is excess demand, it is left unsatisfied.

Firm Agents

Firms optimize profit by continuously changing price in small increments (1%) in the direction they think will increase profit. They only know the last change they made in price and the last change they observed in profit. If there was an increase in profits they change the price in the same direction; otherwise, they change the price in the opposite direction. This hill-climbing approach to uncovering the optimal price is successful because the firms' objective function has a single maximum.

Product Market

The quantity demanded from a single firm at a given price is computed such that the exponential average of quantity exchanged stays on the curve. Specifically, the quantity demanded is given by:

$$\max\left(\frac{P_m - D}{A_D} - q_{avg,m}(n-1), 0\right)$$

where P_m is the price submitted by the current firm, n is the number of firms and:

$$q_{avg,m} = (1 - \beta^{1/n})q + \beta^{1/n} q_{avg,m-1}$$

where q is the last quantity exchanged, m denotes the mth exchange, and β, the exponential constant, is 0.1.

Capital and Labor Markets

The rent at which a firm can purchase capital is computed as follows:

1. Total capital rented in that period is estimated using the exponential average of the capital rented.
2. The rent at which this amount of capital would be supplied is computed from the supply function.
3. If the last rent was lower the rent is increased; if the last rent was higher the rent is decreased subject to a maximum 1% change[2].

The exact formulation is:

$$r = \left(\frac{nk_{avg,m}}{A_K}\right)^{1/q}$$

where n is the number of firms and :

$$k_{avg,m} = (1 - \beta^{1/n})k + \beta^{1/n} k_{avg,m-1}$$

where k is the last capital exchange, m is the mth exchange, and β, the exponential constant, is 0.1.

The wage is determined by the same algorithm, using the average labor hired and the last wage in the following relationship:

$$w = \left(\frac{nl_{avg,m}}{A_L}\right)^{1/p}$$

where n is the number of firms and :

$$l_{avg,m} = (1 - \beta^{1/n})l + \beta^{1/n} l_{avg,m-1}$$

where l is the last labor exchanged, m is the mth exchange, and β, the exponential constant, is 0.1.

SOE agent

The SOE behaves like the firms, but with an additional employment constraint. After it decides how much labor to hire, it checks to see if its estimate of total employment is at least $\bar{L}$. If not, it hires the difference.

Results

In this section we describe four experiments of increasing complexity.

Effects of market size: This experiment attempts to reproduce well known classical results in our simulation environment. In a simple market with identical firms, we show the monopoly, the oligopoly and the competitive outcome.

Imposing minimum employment: During liberalization, the government may want to prevent unemployment by imposing a minimum employment constraint on the SOE. This experiment demonstrates that an artificially imposed employment level may reduce market efficiency.

Liberalization of the market: This experiment analyzes the effects of liberalization in a market where all firms are identical.

Introducing heterogeneous firms: This experiment analyzes the effects of liberalization in a market where firms have varying degrees of efficiency.

Effects of market size

Figure 1 shows how the market reacts to an increase in the size of the private sector. We present plots of total quantity produced in the market, average price and average profit under a monopoly ($n = 1$), an oligopoly ($n = 5$) and perfect competition ($n = 50$). We observe that quantity increases as price and profits fall when the

[2] Without this restriction, some systems are unstable. We see increasing oscillations in prices and quantities rather than convergence to equilibrium.

number of firms in the market increases. This is exactly what is predicted by economic theory: competition increases the quantity produced and decreases the average profits in the industry.

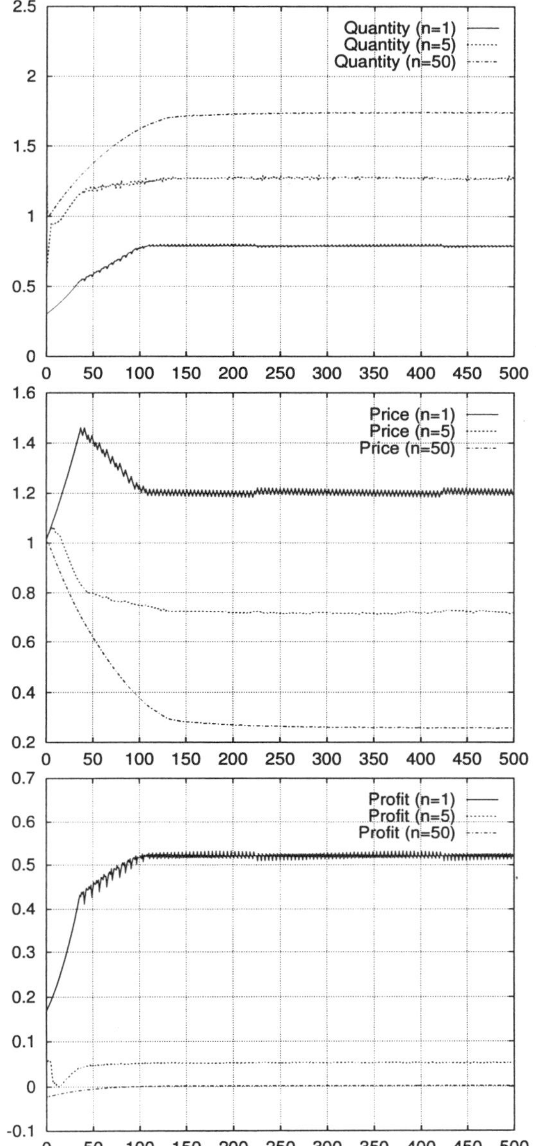

Figure 1: Dynamics of quantity, price, and profit in markets of different sizes.

Imposing minimum employment

This set of simulations shows a state owned enterprise (SOE) coexisting with a fixed number of identical firms. We observe how the behavior of the SOE, which has to maintain employment in the industry above $\bar{L}$, changes when the number of private firms in the industry changes.

Figure 2 shows how the SOE's employment constraint affects the total labor employed by the industry, total quantity and average price. Without a labor constraint, the equilibrium labor usage is approximately 0.6. When $\bar{L}$ is set to 0.8, the SOE is forced to employ more labor than it would have liked and total labor usage in the industry increases but remains below 0.8 due to averaging errors in the calculation. The labor constraint is binding which results in a less efficient outcome, illustrated by a lower equilibrium quantity and a higher equilibrium price.

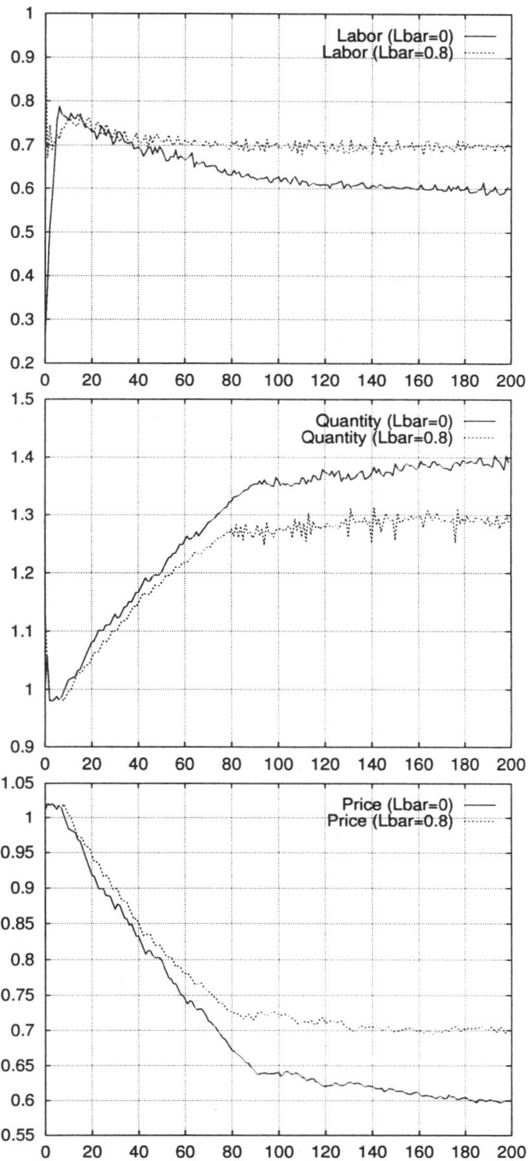

Figure 2: Imposing minimum employment decreases efficiency.

Liberalization of the market

This set of experiments differs from the first experiment in one important sense: firms are allowed to enter and exit the market.

Figure 3 shows how our simulated economy smoothly transitions from a protected environment to perfect competition. During the first 500 periods, entry into this market is prohibited and the SOE is the only firm in the industry (i.e., $n = 1$). The market is liberalized in the 501st period. High profits attract new firms and we observe an increase in the number of firms. This reduces firms' profits. In addition, quantity increases as the price declines. These findings are consistent with economic theory. All of the firms are identical to the SOE in this experiment and a minimum employment constraint is not imposed. The SOE's production can be approximated by dividing total quantity by the number of firms in the industry. The SOE's price and profit are almost identical to the average price and average profit in Figure 3.

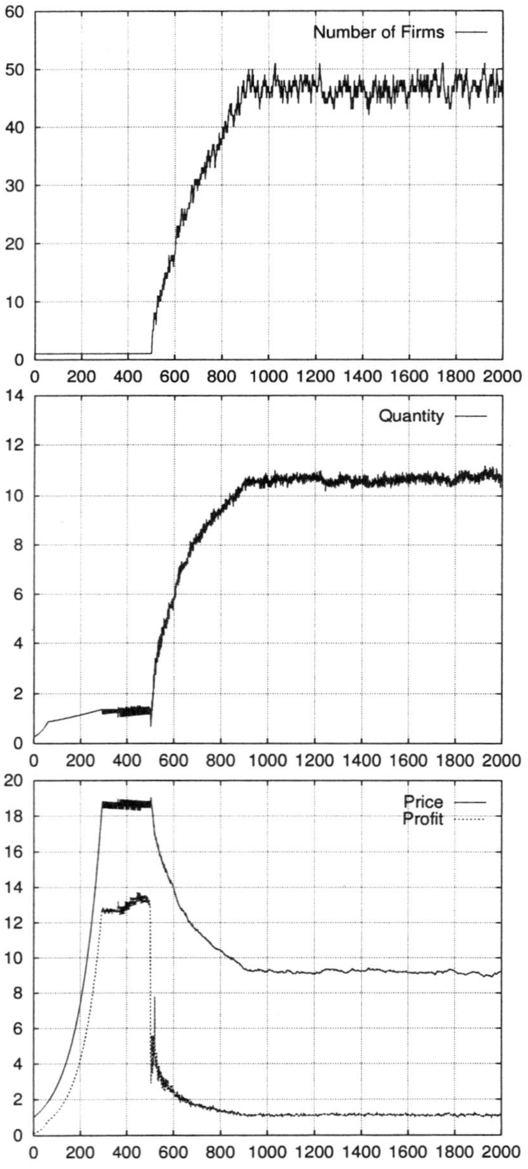

Figure 3: Liberalization in a market with identical firms at period 500.

The significance of this experiment is that the simple SOE agent exhibits monopoly and competitive behavior in an emergent and endogenous manner. The SOE's behavior rules are the same in both monopoly and competitive environments. It is the interaction with the other agents that causes the decline in average price.

Introducing heterogeneous firms

The SOE operates alone for the first 500 periods and reaches the monopoly equilibrium. These 500 periods simulate the centrally planned interval of a transition economy. After 500 periods, the market is liberalized and other firms start entering because of high profits in the industry. The probability that a new firm will want to join the market during a period is an increasing function of average profits in the market. Firms only produce in the feasible region of their supply function, so they never make negative profits. If they do not produce for two periods in a row, they exit the market. For these experiments, the SOE does not have an employment constraint because we discovered that, in the scenarios we analyzed, it was rarely binding.

In Figure 4, the heterogeneity of the firms enables us to observe how price and wage evolve as the industry becomes increasingly dominated by more efficient firms. Rent and wage follow a similar pattern so we only provide a plot for wage. Initial entrants to the market are not necessarily very efficient, because with a high profit margin even inefficient firms can survive. Competition results in lower prices, reducing profit margins so only those firms with more efficient production technologies enter the market as price declines and the inefficient firms exit. As more efficient firms enter the market, labor and capital become more productive so wage and rent are bid up.

Figure 5 shows the U-shaped output curve that immediately follows liberalization. The U-shaped pattern of output was observed in the transition economies in Eastern Europe and still puzzles economists. The simulation allows us to vary a large number of parameters, and we are able to replicate this result qualitatively for certain ranges of parameter values.

The decline in output after liberalization is due to a decline in the output of the SOE which is not offset by the output of new private firms. The initial entrants to the market are inefficient, and they lure resources away from the more efficient SOE. This is the reason for the initial decline in quantity, the corresponding fall in wage, and rent (not shown here).

Econometric evidence suggests that the start of growth is due to improved resource allocation, both within SOEs and through utilization of assets by new private firms as SOEs are downsized or liquidated (Barbone, Marchetti, & Paternostro 1996; Pinto, Belka, & Krajewski 1993).

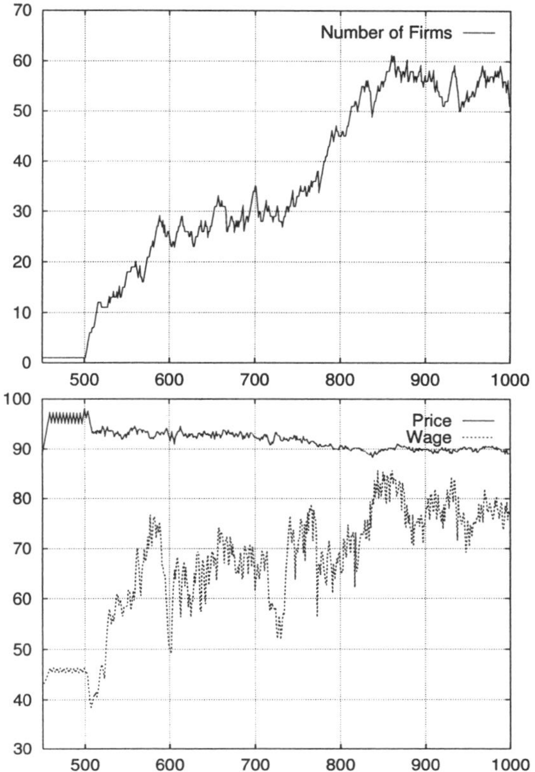

Figure 4: Competition between heterogeneous firms leads to lower price and higher wages after liberalization at period 500.

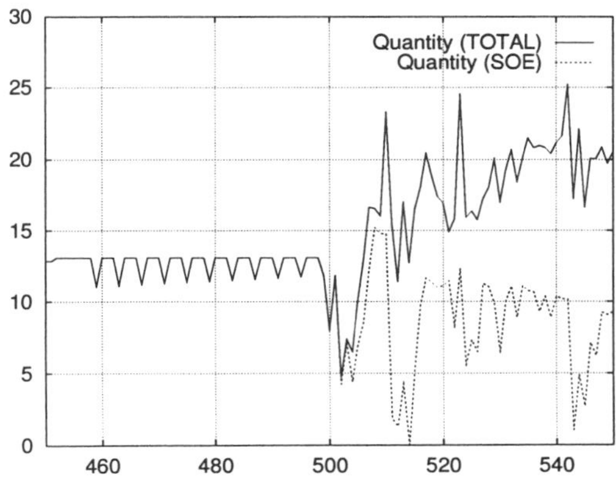

Figure 5: The U shaped output curve after liberalization at period 500.

This is illustrated here as well. The increase in quantity coincides with the increase in the efficiency of new firms. At the end of each period, one firm can enter but more than one firm can exit. As a result, n initially increases steadily because even inefficient firms can enter and survive. Later on, n declines as firms exit in large numbers and entry to the market becomes less frequent. As more efficient firms dominate the market, inefficient firms exit and the average price declines. In Figure 4, the equilibrium has not been reached yet, but the declining trend in average price is apparent. The increases in rent and quantity show that the greater efficiency in production increases the total quantity produced and the prices of the inputs.

Related Work

The field of computational economics is a young and growing field. While this paper presents the first agent-based model of transition economies, many others researchers have begun to draw on ideas from the field of artificial life to model economic phenomena. Critically, the emergent behavior exhibited by many artificial life systems has the potential to explain how large-scale economic behavior arises from local interactions among a multitude of heterogeneous agents (Arthur De Vany, personal communication).

One of the most complete artificial life models of an economy is the Aspen system developed by Richard Pryor and colleagues at Sandia National Labs (Basu *et al.* 1996). Aspen has a rich set of agents, including households, firms in four different sectors, a realtor, a capital goods producer, banks, and a government. The firms use a genetic algorithm to select a price that maximizes profits. The Aspen model duplicates several results first described by Modigliani in his research on the FMP model.

Sugarscape, a versatile system that has become a testbed for studying problems in the social sciences, has been used to examine simple trading models. In these trading models, agents in a two-dimensional landscape trade two goods (sugar and spice) that the agents then metabolize. The agents endogenously determine the prices of sugar and spice, and the quantities exchanged. This simulation replicates several findings described in standard economic literature. For example, the number of agents that can exist on a landscape increases when trading is added to the simulation. However, the Sugarscape simulations also demonstrate that, under certain conditions, prices do not converge to the general equilibrium price, a result that differs from standard economic theory.

Work by Youssefmir, Huberman, and Hogg provides a possible explanation for why markets crash, a particularly timely topic given the market gyrations of 1997 (Youssefmir, Huberman, & Hogg 1996). In their model, a set of heterogeneous agents trade in an asset market based on the agents' expectations of what future prices will be. These expectations are based on two components: the fundamental price and a trend. Each agent has a slightly different perception of the fundamental price, and a trend gets established based on the past behavior of prices. Agents differ in their belief in how long a trend will last. So a rising trend can lead to speculative bubbles since most trend followers are likely to believe strongly in the trend, and some fundamentalists will believe in the trend for a while. As prices move away from the fundamental price, fundamentalist agents will expect the trend to reverse itself and eventually some trend followers will also lose faith in the trend, and the speculative bubble will deflate. The price response to buy/sell orders and the individual trend horizon are set exogenously, and asset prices are determined endogenously. These results show that asset prices can deviate sharply from their fundamental values.

In Tesfatsion's Trade Network Game (TNG), the player set is a collection of traders consisting of pure buyers, pure sellers, and buyer-sellers (Tesfatsion 1997). Buyers repeatedly submit trade offers to sellers, who either refuse or accept these offers. If a seller accepts a trade offer from a buyer, the seller and buyer engage in a risky trade modeled as a standard prisoner's dilemma game. The iterated prisoner's dilemma strategies used by buyers and sellers to conduct their trades are evolved by means of a genetic algorithm. The fact that traders are able to choose and refuse their trading partners makes this a better model of real-world trading than standard game models in which partners are matched randomly or by round robin assignment. Simulations are run for two types of markets: Endogenous-type markets comprising only buyer-sellers; and two-sided markets comprising equal numbers of pure buyers and pure sellers. The findings illustrate how en ante capacity constraints, in the form of buyer offer quotas and seller acceptance quotas, are a primary driving force determining the evolution of trading behavior. For example, given relatively large seller acceptance quotas and relatively small buyer offer quotas, sellers tend to be parasitized by buyers in the sense that buyers are able to latch on to cooperative sellers and successfully defect against them.

Contributions and Future Work

In this paper, we applied artificial life techniques to an outstanding problem in economics. Critically, we have defined and implemented a firm agent that exhibits monopoly and competitive behavior under appropriate conditions. The development of this firm agent, an agent which relies only on local information to make pricing decisions, is the primary contribution of this work.

Our simulation provides an upper bound on the complexity of an agent required to generate the qualitative features of a transition economy. These features include a U-shaped output curve, an increasing share of the private sector in production and efficiency gains in resource allocation. These results give a proof-by-example that an approach to economics that draws on ideas from the field of artificial life may succeed in providing important insights into economic phenomena.

As the next step in developing this approach, we plan to fully model consumer agents who choose consumption and leisure. This will endogenize consumption and labor decisions thus enabling us to address labor market issues. We also plan to calibrate our simulation to a real-world transition economy, such as Poland or Hungary.

Acknowledgments

We wish to thank the anonymous ALIFE reviewers, Leigh Tesfatsion, Benedikt Stefansson, and Richard Arnott for their helpful comments.

Appendix

Parameter values for Figure 1:

$$F(K,L) = K^{0.5}L^{0.25}$$
$$F(K,L)_{SOE} = K^{0.25}L^{0.2}$$
$$Q_L^S = w^{0.5}$$
$$Q_K^S = r^{0.5}$$
$$P = 2 - Q$$

Parameter values for Figure 2:

$$F(K,L) = K^{0.5}L^{0.25}$$
$$F(K,L)_{SOE} = K^{0.25}L^{0.2}$$
$$Q_L^S = w^{0.5}$$
$$Q_K^S = r^{0.5}$$
$$P = 2 - Q$$
$$n = 10$$

Parameter values for Figure 3:

$$F(K,L) = K^{0.25}L^{0.25}$$
$$F(K,L)_{SOE} = K^{0.25}L^{0.25}$$
$$Q_L^S = w^{0.5}$$
$$Q_K^S = r^{0.5}$$
$$P = 20 - Q$$

Parameter values for Figure 4 and Figure 5:

$$F(K,L) = AK^aL^b$$
$$A \sim uniform(0.1, 2)$$
$$a \sim uniform(0.1, 0.9)$$
$$b \sim uniform(0.1, 0.9)$$
$$F(K,L)_{SOE} = 5K^{0.25}L^{0.2}$$
$$Q_L^S = w^{0.5}$$
$$Q_K^S = r^{0.5}$$
$$P = 100 - 0.25Q$$

Initial wage, rent and price are 1 for all experiments.

References

Barbone, L.; Marchetti, D.; and Paternostro, S. 1996. Structural adjustment, ownership transformation, and size in Polish industry. Policy Research Working Paper 1624, World Bank, Washington D.C.

Basu, N.; Pryor, R. J.; Quint, T.; and Arnold, T. 1996. Aspen: A microsimulation model of the economy. Technical Report 96-2459, Sandia National Laboratories.

Blanchard, O. J. 1996. Theoretical aspects of transition. In *Papers and Proceedings of the Hundredth and Eighth Annual Meeting of the American Economic Society*, 117–122.

Boycko, M. 1992. When higher incomes reduce welfare: Queues, labor supply, and macro equilibrium in socialist economies. *Quarterly Journal of Economics* 107:907–920.

Dewatripont, M., and Roland, G. 1992. The virtues of gradualism and legitimacy in the transition to a market economy. *Economic Journal* 102:291–300.

Frydman, R., and Rapaczynski, A. 1994. *Privatization in Eastern Europe: Is the State Withering Away?* London: Central University Press.

Frye, T., and Schleifer, A. 1997. The invisible hand and the grabbing hand. In *Papers and Proceedings of the Hundredth and Ninth Annual Meeting of the American Economic Society*, 354–358.

Lipton, D., and Sachs, J. 1990. Creating a market economy in Eastern Europe: The case of Poland. *Brookings Papers on Economic Activity* 1:75–133.

McKinnon, R. 1991. *The Order of Economic Liberalization.* Baltimore, Mland.: John Hopkins University Press.

Murrell, P. 1992. Conservative political philosophy and the strategy of economic transition. *East European Politics and Society* 6:3–16.

Pinto, B.; Belka, M.; and Krajewski, S. 1993. Transforming state enterprises in Poland. evidence on adjustment by manufacturing firms. *Brookings Papers on Economic Activity* 1:213–270.

Portes, R. 1991. The path of reform in central and eastern europe: An introduction. *European Economy* 2:3–15.

Sachs, J. 1993. *Poland's Jump to the Market Economy.* Cambridge, Mass.: MIT Press.

Sachs, J. 1996. The transition at mid decade. In *Papers and Proceedings of the Hundredth and Eighth Annual Meeting of the American Economic Society*, 128–133.

Selowsky, M., and Martin, R. 1997. Policy performance and output growth in the transition economies. In *Papers and Proceedings of the Hundredth and Ninth Annual Meeting of the American Economic Society*, 349–353.

Tesfatsion, L. 1997. A trade network game with endogenous partner selection. In Amman, H. M.; Rustern, B.; and Whinston, A. B., eds., *Computational Approaches to Economic Problems.* Kluwer Academic Publishers. 249–269.

Youssefmir, M.; Huberman, B. A.; and Hogg, T. 1996. Bubbles and market crashes. Technical report, Xerox Palo Alto Research Group.

Evolved Signals: Expensive Hype vs. Conspiratorial Whispers

Jason Noble
School of Cognitive and Computing Sciences
University of Sussex
BRIGHTON BN1 9QH, U.K.
jasonn@cogs.susx.ac.uk

Abstract

Artificial life models of the evolution of communication have usually assumed either cooperative or competitive contexts. This paper presents a general model that covers signalling with and without conflicts of interest between signallers and receivers. Krebs & Dawkins (1984) argued that a conflict of interests will lead to an evolutionary arms race between manipulative signallers and sceptical receivers, resulting in ever more costly signals; whereas common interests will lead to cheap signals or "conspiratorial whispers". Simple game-theoretic and evolutionary simulation models suggest that signalling will evolve only if it is in the interests of both parties. In a model where signallers may inform receivers as to the value of a binary random variable, if signalling is favoured at all, then signallers will always use the cheapest and the second-cheapest signal available. Costly signalling arms races do not get started. A more complex evolutionary simulation was constructed, featuring continuously variable signal strengths and reception thresholds. As the congruence of interests between the parties became more clear-cut, the evolution of successively cheaper signals was observed. The findings are taken to support a modified version of Krebs & Dawkins's argument.

Artificial Life Models of Communication

Artificial life (AL) models of the evolution of communication are often constructed such that honest signalling is in the interests of both signallers and receivers—any communication systems that evolve can therefore be described as cooperative. For example, Werner & Dyer (1991) postulated blind, mobile males and sighted, immobile females: the evolution of a signalling system was in the interests of both parties as it allowed mating to take place at better-than-chance frequencies. In MacLennan & Burghardt's (1994) model, signallers and receivers were rewarded if and only if they engaged in successful communicative interactions.

Other AL models (Ackley & Littman 1994; Oliphant 1996) have looked at the special case where communication would benefit receivers, but the potential signallers are indifferent. Oliphant argues that this is a good way to model the evolution of alarm calls, for example: if one bird in a flock spots an approaching hawk, it is clear that its conspecifics would benefit from an alarm call. However, why should the bird in question, considered as a product of its selfish genes, give the call? The models suggest that signalling will not evolve in these cases unless a mechanism such as reciprocal altruism or (spatially induced) kin selection is in place. Note that such mechanisms have no mystical effect: they simply shift the expected fitness payoffs for particular strategies such that communication is mutually beneficial.

Finally, some AL work considers the evolution of communication in situations where the two parties appear to have conflicting interests. Wheeler & de Bourcier (1995) modelled aggressive territorial signalling. Bullock (1997) constructed a general model in which signallers of varying degrees of quality solicited receivers for a favourable response; receivers were rewarded for responding positively only to high-quality signallers. A conclusion drawn in both studies was that if signals were sufficiently costly (e.g., long, elaborate tails or energetic ritual displays) then reliable communication could evolve and persist over time. Bullock made the more specific prediction that in order for communication to be stable, the net cost of signalling must be lower for higher-quality signallers (see also Grafen, 1990). However, it could be argued that such differential signal costs effectively render honest signalling mutually beneficial. We will return to this notion below.

One goal of the current paper is to position previous AL work in an overarching theoretical context. To this end some general models of the evolution of simple signalling systems will be presented; the models will cover situations with and without a conflict of interests between the two interacting agents.

Manipulative and Cooperative Signals

Krebs & Dawkins (1984) discuss the behavioural ecology of animal signals—they view signalling as a typically competitive affair involving mind-reading and manipulation. Mind-reading consists of one animal exploiting telltale predictors about the future behaviour of another, e.g., a dog noticing the bared teeth of an opponent, concluding that it is about to attack, and fleeing in order to avoid injury. Manipulation is what happens when those being mind-read fight back, influencing the behaviour of the mind-readers to their own advantage. For example, a dog could bare its teeth despite not having the strength or inclination to attack, and thus scare off its mind-reading opponent. The authors predict evolutionary arms races between manipulative signallers and sceptical receivers: "selection will act simultaneously to increase the power of manipulators *and* to increase resistance to it" (p. 390). The result will be increasingly costly signals.

Krebs & Dawkins admit, however, that not all interactions are competitive in nature. They suggest that when the reliable transmission of information is to the benefit of both parties (e.g., bee dances indicating the location of nectar), a different kind of signal co-evolution will result. Specifically, there will be selection for signals that are as cheap as possible while still being detectable: "conspiratorial whispers".

Krebs & Dawkins's argument has been influential but no formal justification (i.e., model) of it exists. A second goal of the current paper is to test their prediction that evolved signals will necessarily be more costly when there is a conflict of interests than when the participants have common interests. In order to do so, it will be necessary to determine whether communication should be expected *at all* when signallers and receivers have a genuine conflict of interests.

Conflicts of Interest

The first requirement in constructing a general model of communication is a classification scheme for determining when a conflict of interests exists between signallers and receivers—Figure 1 shows such a scheme, adapted from Hamilton (1964). Assume that a successful instance of communication in a particular scenario has fitness implications for both participants. The fitness effect on signallers, P_S, and the fitness effect on receivers, P_R, together define a point on the plane in Figure 1. For example, consider a hypothetical food call, by which one animal alerts another to the presence of a rich but limited food source. By calling and thus sharing the food, the signaller incurs a fitness cost; by responding to the call, the receiver benefits through obtaining food it would otherwise have missed. Thus, the call would be located in the "altruism" quadrant. The situations modelled by Ackley & Littman (1994) and Oliphant (1996), where receivers benefit but signallers are ambivalent, can be thought of as points on the positive vertical axis, i.e., where $P_S = 0$ and $P_R > 0$.

Conflicts of interest can be defined as interactions in which natural selection favours different outcomes for each participant (Trivers 1974), or in which participants place the possible outcomes in a different rank order

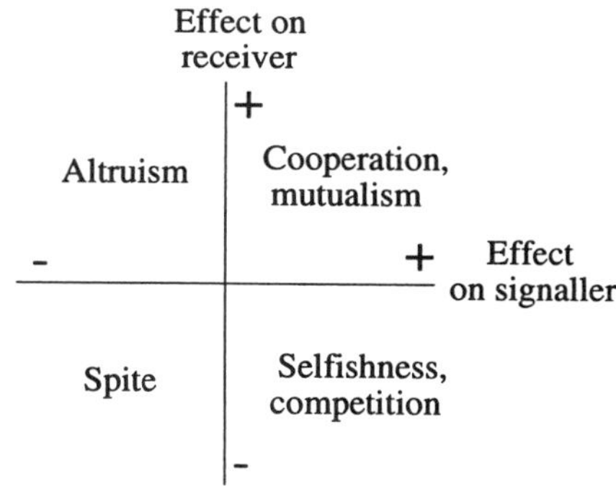

Figure 1: Possible communication scenarios classified by their effects on the fitness of each participant.

(Maynard Smith & Harper 1995). Conflicts of interest therefore exist when P_S and P_R are of opposite sign, i.e., in the upper-left and lower-right quadrants. Selection will, by definition, favour actions that have positive fitness effects. In the upper-left and lower-right quadrants, one agent[1] but not the other will be selected to participate in the communication system: their interests conflict. The "spite" quadrant does *not* represent a conflict of interests because agents will be mutually selected not to communicate.

If the specified fitness effects of participating in a communicative interaction are truly *net* values, and already include such factors as the cost of signalling and the cost of making a response (as well as inclusive fitness considerations and costs due to exploitation of the signal by predators, etc.), then predicting the evolution of the communication system is trivial. Reliable communication requires, on average, honest signallers and trusting receivers, and thus will only develop when $P_S > 0$ and $P_R > 0$, i.e., when both agents are selected to participate. However, real animals sometimes communicate despite apparent conflicts of interest (Hinde 1981). Recent models (Grafen 1990; Bullock 1997) have established that, in certain situations where communication would otherwise be unstable, increasing the production costs of the signal can lead to a prediction of evolutionarily stable signalling. Therefore, in the current model, P_S and P_R refer to gross fitness effects before the specific costs of producing the signal, C_S, and making the response, C_R, have been taken into account.

A Simple Signalling Game

If the signalling interaction is to involve information transmission, and allow for the possibilities of deception and manipulation, it must be modelled as a game of imperfect information, in which the signaller knows

[1]The term "agent" is used to refer to an entity that may be playing a signalling or a receiving role.

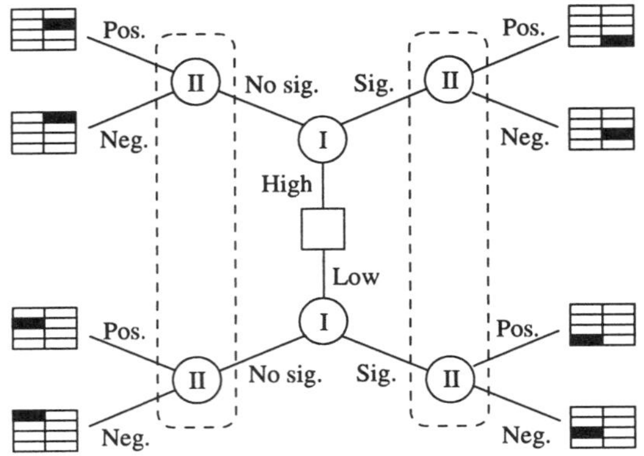

Figure 2: Extended form of the simple signalling game. Chart icons index payoffs in Table 1.

	State of environment	
	Low	High
No signal		
Neg. response	$0\ ,\ 0$	$0\ ,\ 0$
Pos. response	$0\ ,\ -C_R$	$P_S\ ,\ P_R - C_R$
Signal		
Neg. response	$-C_S\ ,\ 0$	$-C_S\ ,\ 0$
Pos. response	$-C_S\ ,\ -C_R$	$P_S - C_S\ ,\ P_R - C_R$

Table 1: Payoff matrix for the simple game. Entries in the table represent the payoff to the sender and receiver respectively.

something that the receiver does not. Figure 2 shows the extended form of a simple action-response game that fulfils this requirement. The game begins with a chance move (the central square) in which some state is randomly determined to be either "high" or "low". The signaller has access to this state, and we can suppose that it represents either a feature of the environment that only the signaller has detected (e.g., noticing an approaching predator), or a hidden internal state of the signaller (e.g., ovulation). Based on this state, the signaller (player I) must decide whether or not to send an arbitrary signal of cost C_S. The receiver (player II) is ignorant of the hidden state and only knows whether or not a signal was sent—the dashed rectangles show the receiver's information sets. The receiver can respond either positively, i.e., perform some action "appropriate" to the high state, or negatively, i.e., not respond at all. Positive responses incur a cost, C_R. If and only if the hidden state is high, a positive response results in the payoffs P_S and P_R to the signaller and receiver respectively. Table 1 specifies the payoff matrix. Hurd (1995), Oliphant (1996), and Bullock (1997) used similar games with different payoff structures.

The game models a range of possible communicative interactions. For example, suppose that the high state represents the signaller's discovery of food. Sending a signal might involve emitting a characteristic sound, while not sending a signal is to remain silent. For the receiver, a positive response means approaching the signaller and sharing the food, whereas a negative response means doing nothing. Various possibilities exist besides honest signalling of the high state: the receiver might *always* approach the signaller in the hope of obtaining food, regardless of whether a signal was sent. The signaller might be uninformative and never signal, or only signal when food was *not* present. One important feature of the game is that the signaller is ambivalent about the receiver's response in the low state—in terms of the example, this represents the assumption that when no food has been discovered, the signalling animal does not care about whether the receiver approaches or not.

The strategies favoured at any one time will depend on the relative values of P_S, P_R, C_S and C_R, as well as on what the other members of the population are doing.[2] Allowing the base fitness effects P_S and P_R to vary across positive and negative values will allow the payoff space of Figure 1 to be explored, and thus determine whether changes in signal and response cost can produce stable signalling in situations that would otherwise involve conflicts of interest. This will be a first step towards assessing Krebs & Dawkins's conspiratorial whispers theory.

Stable Strategies in the Simple Game

A signalling strategy in the simple game specifies whether to respond with no signal (NS) or a signal (Sig) to low and high states respectively. Likewise, a response strategy specifies whether to respond negatively (Neg) or positively (Pos) when faced with no signal and when faced with a signal. A strategy pair is the conjunction of a signalling and a response strategy; e.g., (NS/NS, Pos/Pos) is the strategy pair that specifies never signalling and always responding positively.

The strategy pair (NS/Sig, Neg/Pos) specifies signalling only in the high state, and responding positively only to signals—call this the honest strategy. It can be shown that honesty will be an evolutionarily stable strategy (ESS; Maynard Smith 1982) if:

$$P_S > C_S > 0$$
$$P_R > C_R > 0.$$

That is, honest signalling is stable if the costs of signalling and responding are both positive, and if the payoffs in each case outweigh the costs. The requirement that P_S and P_R must both be positive means that the

[2]Another parameter of interest in the signalling game is the relative frequency of high and low states; in the models presented here each state occurred 50% of the time.

honest strategy is only expected to be stable when the interests of the parties do not conflict.

Of the 16 possible strategy pairs, there are three besides the honest strategy that involve the transmission of information, in that the receiver responds differently to different hidden states. None of these three strategy pairs are ESSs if C_S and C_R are both positive; these two values represent energetic costs and so cannot sensibly be negative. If $C_S = 0$, i.e., if giving a signal is of negligible cost, then the reverse honesty strategy (Sig/NS, Pos/Neg) can be stable, although P_S and P_R must still be positive. It is also worth noting that any mixed strategy involving (NS/NS, Pos/Pos) and (NS/NS, Pos/Neg), both non-signalling strategies where the receiver always responds positively, can be an ESS if the payoff to the receiver is large enough, i.e., if:

$$C_S > 0$$
$$P_S > -C_S$$
$$P_R > 2C_R > 0.$$

The analysis indicates that while the cost of signalling plays some role in stabilizing the honest strategy, there are no circumstances in which stable communication is predicted when a conflict of interests exists. This is despite the fact that we have separated the costs of signalling and responding from the base fitness payoffs of a communicative interaction.

Evolutionary Simulation Model

Game theory is limited to describing equilibria; an evolutionary simulation model of the simple game was also constructed in order to determine whether communicative behaviour might sometimes be found outside the range of identified ESSs.

A straightforward genetic algorithm (GA) was used. Each individual could play both signalling and receiving roles; a strategy pair was specified by a four-bit genotype as shown in table 2. The population size was 100, the mutation rate was 0.01 per locus, and, due to the trivially small genome, crossover was not used. Each generation, 500 games were played between randomly selected opponents. An agent could therefore expect to play 5 games as a signaller and 5 as a receiver. The agent's fitness score was the total payoff from these games. For breeding purposes, the fitness scores were normalized by subtracting the minimum score from each. Proportionate selection was then applied to the normalized scores. The genetic algorithm was run in this manner for 500 generations. In the results presented below, the games played in the final, i.e., 500th, generation have been used as a snapshot of the evolved signalling strategies.

An attempt was made to investigate evolutionary dynamics, in that the initial populations were not determined randomly but started as either "honest" or "non-signalling". Honest initial populations were made up entirely of individuals who played the honest strategy, i.e., a genome of '0101'. Non-signalling populations underwent 100 generations of preliminary evolution in which their receiving strategies were free to evolve but their signalling strategies were clamped at '00', i.e., no signalling. For each class of initial conditions, a simulation run was performed for all combinations of integer values of P_S and P_R between -5 and +5, making 121 runs in all. Each run was repeated 25 times with different random seeds. The values of C_S and C_R were fixed at 1.

	Bit value	
	0	1
If low state...	No signal	Signal
If high state...	No signal	Signal
Response to no signal	Negative	Positive
Response to signal	Negative	Positive

Table 2: Genetic specification of strategies.

Communication was indexed by cross-tabulating the hidden state value with the receiver's response and calculating a chi-squared statistic. The receiver has no direct access to the hidden state, so any reliable correspondence between state and response indicates that information has been transmitted and acted upon. Values of the χ^2 statistic close to zero indicate no communication, and values close to the maximum (in this case $\chi^2_{max} = 500$, due to the 500 games played in the final, snapshot generation) indicate near-perfect communication.

Figure 3 shows the average values of the communication index for honest initial conditions. Seeding the population with honesty tests the stability of honest signalling given a particular payoff pair, much as a game-theoretic analysis does. The results are compatible with the conditions outlined in the previous section: honesty is stable when the payoffs to signalling and receiving are positive and greater than the respective costs. However, there is some suggestion of intermittent or imperfect communication when $P_R = C_R = 1$, indicating that ambivalent receivers may occasionally cooperate.

Figure 4 shows the average values of the communication index for non-signalling initial conditions. Starting the GA with a non-signalling population tests the likelihood that communication will emerge, given a particular payoff pair. Clearly the conditions for emergence and stability-once-present are not the same. If $P_S > 1$ and $P_R = 2$ communication develops but when $P_S > 1$ and $P_R > 2$ it does not. In the latter region $P_R > 2C_R$ and the population remains at the non-signalling ESS described in the previous section. Despite the fact that communication would result in a higher average fitness, the high value of P_R keeps the receivers responding positively all the time, removing any incentive for the signallers to bother signalling.

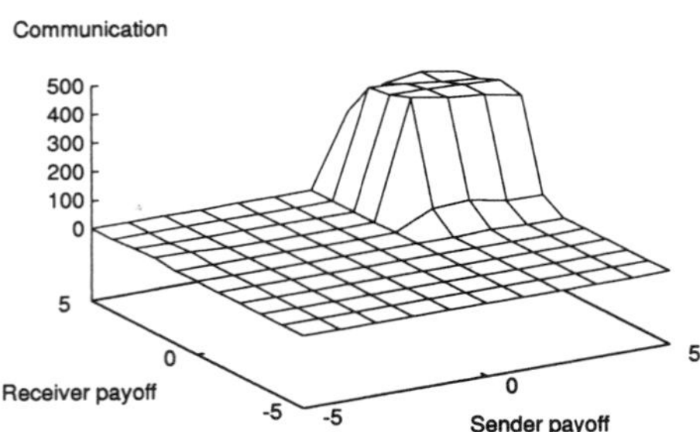

Figure 3: Mean communication index by P_S and P_R; honest initial conditions. Each point is a mean calculated over 25 runs. Mean standard error = 2.96.

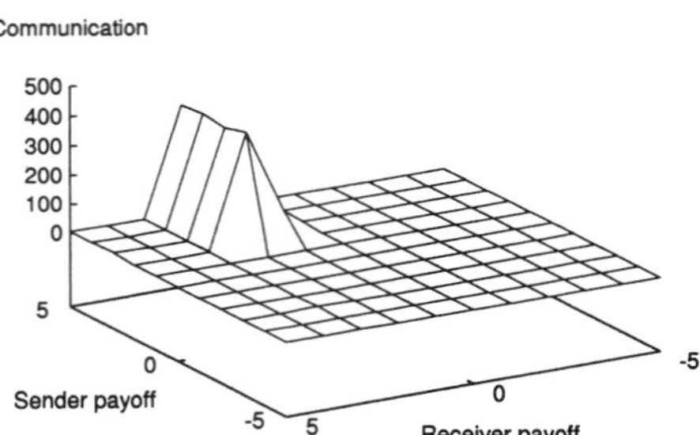

Figure 4: Mean communication index by P_S and P_R; non-signalling initial conditions. Each point is a mean calculated over 25 runs. Mean standard error = 2.75. Graph rotated for clarity.

The difference in results between the two classes of initial conditions is interesting, but should not obscure the fact that no communication was observed under conditions of conflicting interests. We must conclude that, at least in the simple model discussed so far, stable communication is only to be expected when it is in the interests of both parties.

A Game With Variable Signal Costs

In the simple signalling game, signallers can choose between a costly signal or no signal at all. The model does not allow for a range of possible signals with differing costs, and in this respect it is unrealistic. It may be that Krebs & Dawkins's implicit prediction, that signalling can occur when a conflict of interests exists, is in fact true, but can only be demonstrated in a more complex game with a range of signal costs. The simple signalling game (see Figure 2) was therefore extended to incorporate signals of differing costs.

In the extended game, the signalling player has three options: not signalling, which costs nothing; using the "soft" signal, which costs C_S, and using the "loud" signal, which costs $2C_S$. Strategies in the extended game require specifying the signal to give when the hidden state is low, the signal to give when it is high, and the response to give to each of no-signal, soft and loud. The two strategies representing conspiratorial whispers or cheap signalling are (NS/Soft, Neg/Pos/Pos) and (NS/Soft, Neg/Pos/Neg). Both strategies call for the soft signal to be used in the high state, and for positive responses to the soft signal; the strategies differ only in the response to loud signals. Neither of these strategies can strictly be considered an ESS on its own (because neutral drift can take the population from one to the other) but it can be shown that the set of all mixed strategies involving these two is an ESS under the familiar conditions:

$$P_S > C_S > 0$$
$$P_R > C_R > 0.$$

Costly signalling would involve the use of the loud signal for the high state, and either the soft signal or no signal to denote the low state, with a corresponding response strategy. None of the four strategies in this category can be an ESS. For example, (NS/Loud, Neg/Pos/Pos) cannot be an ESS assuming positive costs of signalling and responding. The similar strategy (NS/Loud, Neg/Neg/Pos) is almost stable if $P_S > 2C_S$, but can drift back to the previous strategy which can in turn be invaded by the cheap strategy (NS/Soft, Neg/Pos/Pos).

Analysis of the extended game indicates that if signalling is favoured at all, then at equilibrium the signallers will always use the cheapest and the second-cheapest signal available (i.e., no signal and the soft signal). Further extensions of the game, by adding ever more costly signalling options, do not alter this conclusion. None of the costly signalling strategies can even be an ESS, let alone support communication in the face of a conflict of interests. The possibility of expensive signalling arms races starts to look remote. However, it may be that the discrete signals used in the games presented so far have had an unwarranted effect on the results. Certainly discrete and continuous models of the same biological phenomenon can lead to different conclusions—compare Maynard Smith (1991) and Johnstone & Grafen (1992).

Simulation Model With Continuous Signal Costs and Reception Threshold

A second evolutionary simulation was constructed, in which the cost of signalling was continuously variable. Signalling strategies were represented by two positive real numbers C_{low} and C_{high}: the cost of the signals given in the low state and in the high state respectively. Response strategies were represented by a real-valued threshold T; positive responses were given to signals with costs greater than the receiver's threshold value. Note that threshold value could be negative, indicating a positive response to any signal.

A real-valued GA was used to simulate the evolution of strategies over time. Generally, the same parameters were used as in the previous simulation model, e.g., a population of 100. Mutation was necessarily a different matter: each real-valued gene in each newborn individual was always perturbed by a random gaussian value, $\mu = 0$, $\sigma = 0.05$. If a perturbation resulted in a negative cost value the result was replaced by zero. In addition, 1% of the time (i.e., a mutation rate of 0.01) a gene would be randomly set to a value between 0 and 5 for signal costs, or between -5 and +5 for the threshold value. This two-part mutation regime ensured that offspring were always slightly different from their parent, and occasionally very different.

The C_S parameter was no longer relevant, but C_R, the cost of responding, remained fixed at 1. Honest initial conditions were implemented by setting $C_{low} = 0$, $C_{high} = 1.0$ and $T = 0.5$. Non-signalling initial conditions were implemented by setting T to a random gaussian ($\mu = 0$, $\sigma = 1$) and then clamping $C_{low} = C_{high} = 0$ for 100 generations of preliminary evolution.

The use of continuous values immediately suggests the possibility of random noise, and in trial experiments gaussian noise was added to both the signalling channel (i.e., to the signal's cost value before it was "perceived" by the receiver) and to the payoff values P_S and P_R. It was felt that these measures might introduce some realistic uncertainty to the game. However, the results below were found to be robust with respect to the presence of noise; results from noise-free runs only are reported.

Figures 5 and 6 show the average values of the communication index for honest and non-signalling initial conditions respectively. The results are qualitatively similar to those of the discrete simulation model: communication occurs in both cases, but in a more limited range of the payoff space for non-signalling conditions. In neither case does communication occur outside the "cooperative" quadrant.

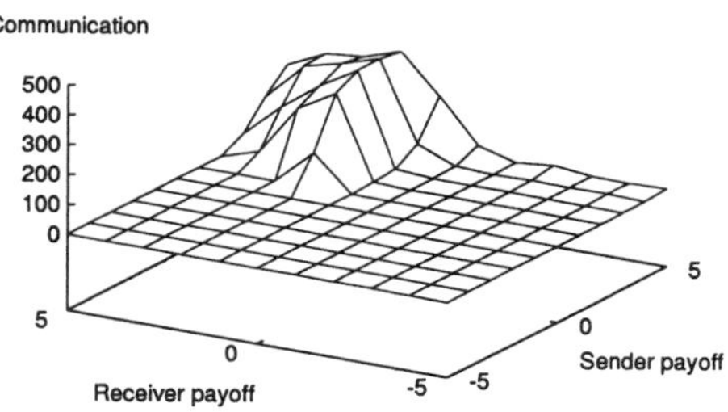

Figure 5: Mean communication index by P_S and P_R in the continuous simulation; honest initial conditions. Each point is a mean calculated over 25 runs. Mean standard error = 3.54. Graph rotated for clarity.

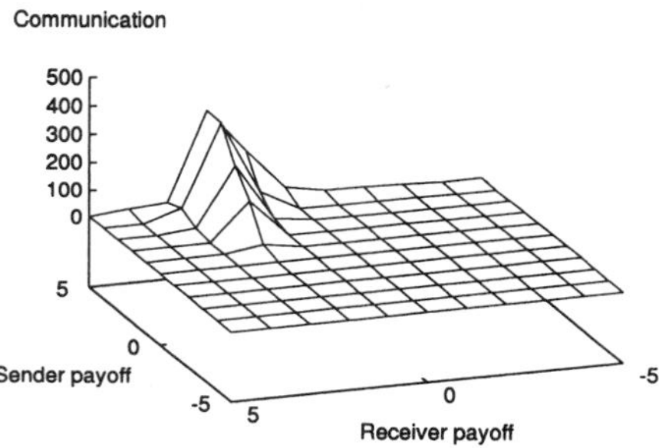

Figure 6: Mean communication index by P_S and P_R in the continuous simulation; non-signalling initial conditions. Each point is a mean calculated over 25 runs. Mean standard error = 2.81. Graph rotated for clarity.

The continuous model also allows investigation of the cost and threshold values over the payoff space. C_{low}, the cost of the signal given in response to the low state, always remained close to zero—this was unsurprising as signallers are ambivalent about the receiver's response to the low state. However, the value of C_{high} varied both inside and outside the region where communication was established: Figure 7 shows the mean values of C_{high} for honest initial conditions. The signals given in response to the high state are most costly when P_S, the payoff to the sender, is high and when the receiver's net payoff

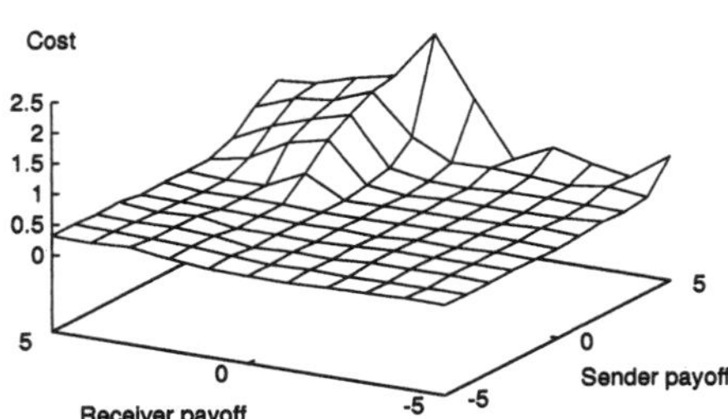

Figure 7: Mean cost of high-state signals by P_S and P_R; honest initial conditions. Each point is a mean calculated over 25 runs. Mean standard error = 0.032. Graph rotated for clarity.

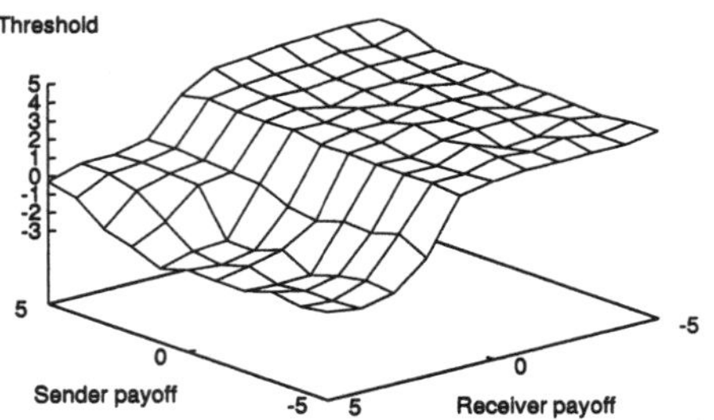

Figure 9: Mean threshold value by P_S and P_R; honest initial conditions. Each point is a mean calculated over 25 runs. Mean standard error = 0.18. Graph rotated for clarity.

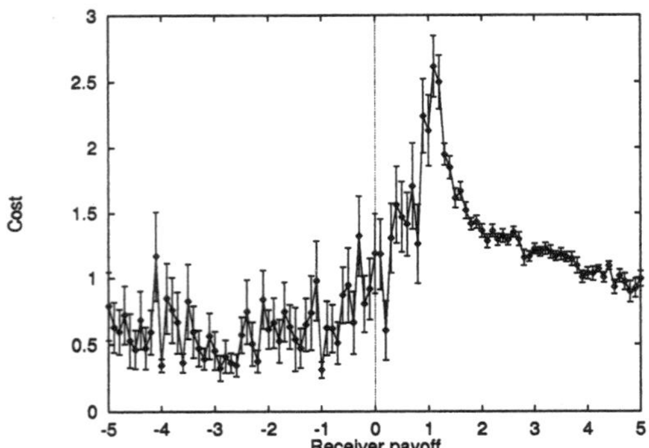

Figure 8: Cross-sectional means (±1 s.e.) for high-state signal costs with $P_S = 5$; honest initial conditions. Each point is a mean calculated over 25 runs.

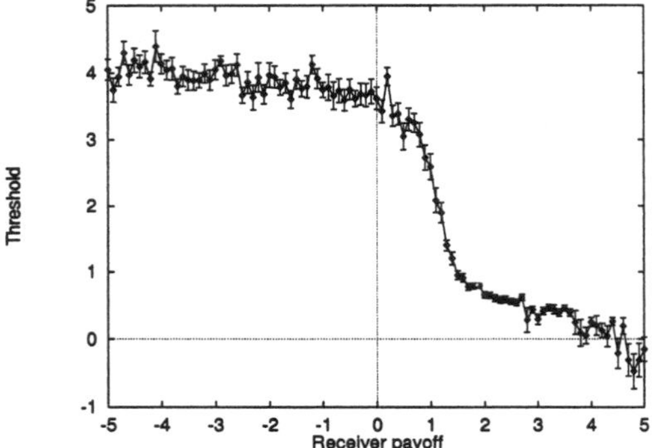

Figure 10: Cross-sectional mean threshold values (±1 s.e.) with $P_S = 5$; honest initial conditions. Each point is a mean calculated over 25 runs.

is marginal, i.e., $P_R \approx 1$. In order to study this effect more closely, additional simulation runs were performed, with P_S fixed at 5 and P_R varied between -5 and +5 in increments of 0.1. These runs can be thought of as exploring the cross section through $P_S = 5$ in Figure 7. Figure 8 shows the cross-sectional mean values of C_{high}. Note that the "energy" devoted to signalling is at a maximum around $P_R = 1$ and drops off as P_R increases—it can be seen from Figure 5 that $P_R = 1$ is approximately the point where significant communication is established. The same pattern was observed for non-signalling initial conditions (not shown for reasons of space).

The threshold values showed corresponding variation. Figure 9 shows the mean value of T across the payoff space. The threshold values are typically very high (a "never respond" strategy) or very low (an "always respond" strategy), but in the region where communication evolved, receivers become progressively less demanding, i.e., T gets lower, as P_R increases. Figure 10 shows the cross-sectional results for $P_S = 5$.

Figure 11 plots the mean cost of high and low signals and the mean reception threshold all on one graph. This makes the relationship between costs and threshold clear: at approximately $P_R = 1$, the threshold falls to a level where the mean high-state signal will generate a positive response. As P_R increases, i.e., as the two players' payoffs approach each other, the signallers become less extravagant and the receivers less "sceptical". This is *contra* the game-theoretic result of the previous section, which implies that when signals of varying costs are available, either the cheapest pair of signals will be used, or no signalling will occur—something like Figure 12 would be expected if the soft-loud signalling game accurately modelled the continuous case.

Note that the initial values of C_{high} and T under honest initial conditions were 1.0 and 0.5 respectively. For all but the highest values of P_R, C_{high} has increased on average over the 500-generation run. This rules out any

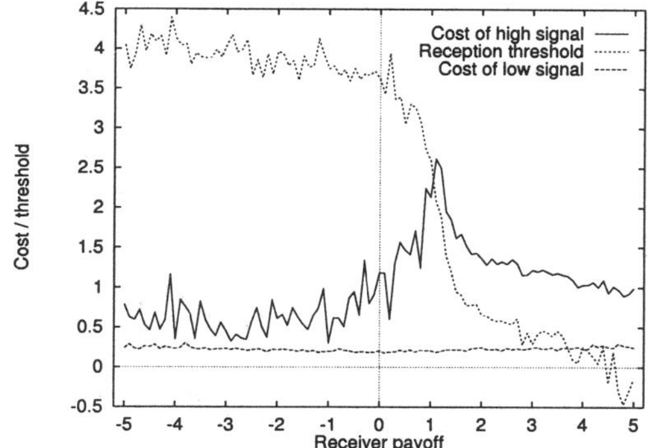

Figure 11: Cross-sectional means: cost of high and low signals, and reception threshold. $P_S = 5$, honest initial conditions. Each point is a mean calculated over 25 runs.

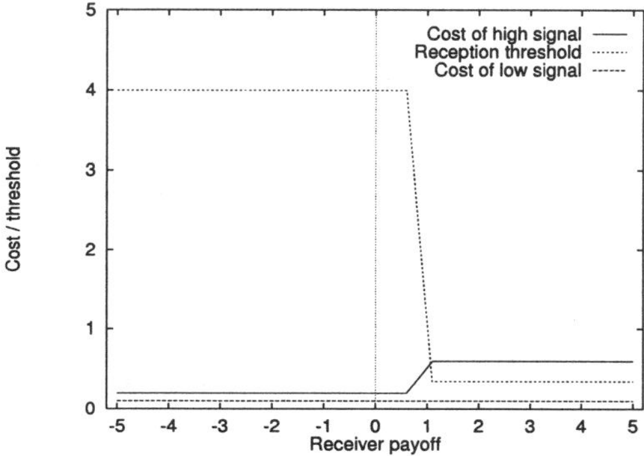

Figure 12: Approximate predicted results for Figure 11 according to discrete-cost game-theoretic model.

explanation of the results of Figure 11 in terms of there having been insufficient evolutionary time for a cheaper signalling equilibrium to have been reached when the profit for receivers ($P_R - C_R$) was marginal. Evolution has taken the populations *away* from the cheap signalling solution.

Discussion

In all of the models presented, communication evolved or was predicted to evolve only within the cooperative region of the signaller-receiver payoff space. This means that no signalling at all (costly or otherwise) was observed when the signaller and the receiver were experiencing a conflict of interests. The second game-theoretic model, in which discrete signals of varying costs are available, suggests that communication, if selected for, will involve the cheapest pair of signals available. However, the second simulation model, incorporating the more realistic assumption that signals can vary continuously in cost, implies that cheap signals will only be used when both parties stand to gain a high payoff from effective communication. When the net payoff to the receiver is marginal, evolved signals will be more costly than strictly necessary to convey the information. The relationship is not symmetrical: when the net payoff to the signaller is marginal, a non-signalling equilibrium, in which the receiver always responds positively, is likely to occur.

Krebs & Dawkins (1984) predicted that signalling would be costly if a conflict of interests existed; strictly speaking the results do not support nor contradict their prediction, as no signalling occurred in the conflict-of-interest cases. It might be the case that conflicts of interest in the context of a different signalling game would indeed result in costly signals. However, it will be argued below that the simple signalling game used in the current models is plausible, and thus the failure to evolve communication given conflicts of interest in this simple game strongly suggests that in many natural contexts (e.g., food calls, alarm calls) reliable signalling should not be expected unless it is in the interests of both parties. This conclusion is not altered by separate consideration of the specific costs of producing a signal and of making an appropriate response to that signal.

The results from the second simulation model do not confirm Krebs & Dawkins's conspiratorial whispers theory, but they definitely suggest a modification of it. As Figure 11 shows, when the net payoff to the receiver is marginal, receivers will be sceptical and express "sales-resistance" by responding only to costly signals; signallers in turn will be prepared to invest more energy in "convincing" receivers to respond positively. When communication is unambiguously good for both parties, signals are cheaper and response thresholds lower. Therefore both expensive hype and conspiratorial whispers are expected to evolve, but in a much smaller region of the payoff space than Krebs & Dawkins's theory suggests, i.e., within the cooperative region. Expensive hype is what happens when honest signalling is highly profitable to the signaller, but only marginally so to the receiver. For example, if a juvenile benefits by honestly signalling extreme hunger to its parent (because the parent responds by feeding it), but the net inclusive-fitness payoff to the parent is only slight, then costly signals by the juvenile are expected.

The evolutionary simulation models presented were unusual in their use of non-random initial conditions. The use of non-signalling initial conditions in particular can be seen as an attempt to get at the origin or emergence of communication rather than just studying the conditions for its stability, as does orthodox game theory. Non-signalling initial conditions embody the assumption that communication must emerge from a non-communicative context—the un-clamping of signalling strategies after a period of preliminary evolution can be seen as the introduction of a mutation that allows the *possibility* of signalling. To the extent that this paradigm is seen as plausible, results from the two simulations suggest that sometimes real-world signalling will not evolve despite a cooperative context: receivers may fall into blindly optimistic strategies (i.e., always responding positively) that are less efficient than the communicative equilibrium but nevertheless stable. This is particularly likely to occur when the net payoff to the receiver is high. (The expected payoff for always responding positively will of course depend on the relative frequency of high and low hidden states, a factor that was not varied in the models presented).

There are several qualifications that must be made concerning the results. Firstly, the way that conflicting and congruent interests have been defined may be too simplistic. In the simple signalling game, it is true that with positive net payoffs to the signaller and the receiver, and if the hidden state is high, both agents will benefit from a positive response, and they therefore have congruent interests. However, if we consider the moment before the hidden state has been determined, it is not clear whether the interests of the two agents conflict or not. If the signaller, for example, could somehow choose the strategy of its opponent, the receiver, it would want the opponent to play an "always respond positively" strategy—that way the signaller would always receive the payoff and would not have to expend energy in signalling. However, the receiver, if similarly allowed to determine the signaller's strategy, would prefer that the signaller used an honest strategy, precisely so that the receiver could avoid the costs of responding positively to the low hidden state. Recall that Trivers (1974) defined a conflict of interests as an interaction in which natural selection favours a different outcome for each participant. It seems that the signaller and receiver in this situation favour different strategies in their opponent, and thus have a conflict of interests, even though a high value of the hidden state would mean that their interests became congruent. If this strategy-based definition of conflicting interests were adopted, any situation in the cooperative payoff region, assuming signalling had a positive cost, would involve a conflict of interests—this would in turn mean that *all* of the signalling observed in the simulation models evolved despite a conflict of interests. The problem is perhaps that Trivers's (1974) and Maynard Smith & Harper's (1995) definitions are not specific enough about just what constitutes an "outcome" of the signalling game. The simpler definition of conflicting interests, as used in the body of the paper, is useful in isolating the cooperative region of payoff space as the place to expect signalling. It is not yet clear how the results should be interpreted if the strategy-based definition of conflicting interests was pursued.

A second limitation of the results is that the signalling game used is not likely to be a universal model of all possible communicative interactions. In particular, and despite having the same basic structure with two signals possibly used to transmit information about a binary hidden state, the signalling game is different from those employed by Hurd (1995) and Oliphant (1996). Hurd's game models sexual signalling, and the male signaller is *not* ambivalent about the female receiver's response when the hidden state is low; the signaller always prefers a positive response. A low hidden state maps to low male quality, a positive response represents a copulative episode, and even low-quality males want mating opportunities. The current signalling game, in contrast, cannot model so-called "handicap" signalling, because low-state signallers do not care about what the receiver does. Furthermore, in both Hurd's and Oliphant's games, receivers are explicitly rewarded for accuracy in discerning the hidden state, but the game presented here allows the ecologically plausible outcome that receivers simply become disinterested in the signal. The current game is a reasonable model of situations such as alarm calls[3] and food calls, in which potential signallers have no reason to care about what receivers do when no predator has been sighted or no food source has been found. Whereas Hurd's game serves as a (discrete) model of situations where signallers vary on some dimension, the current game models situations where signallers fall into two groups, only one of which is relevant to the potential response. Hurd's game has been used to model the signalling of mate quality, while the current game could be used to model the signalling of sexual maturity. Future work could certainly look at games like Hurd's, where signallers always want a positive response, in order to determine whether the apparent conflict of interests is real, and under what circumstances signalling evolves. Bullock's (1997, this volume) work considers these questions.

Finally, it must be stressed that the simple games and simulations described here are in one sense an unfair way to test Krebs & Dawkins's (1984) conspiratorial whispers hypothesis. Krebs & Dawkins were discussing the likely evolution of signals in complex real-world cases, and could therefore appeal to the effects of differing mutation rates in signallers and receivers, and the exploitation of behaviours that had originally been selected for other purposes, etc. Communication in the predicted costly signalling arms races was not expected to be stable. For example, in a real-world situation where it was not in the interests of receivers to respond positively to a particular signal from a predator, they might nevertheless continue to do so for some time if the signal was structurally similar to a mating signal made by members of the same species. The manipulative signalling

[3]Excepting those cases in which false alarm calls are given in order to frighten off other animals and give the caller a brief period of exclusive access to a food source.

system would break down as soon as an appropriate sequence of mutations resulted in organisms that could distinguish between the predator's signal and the conspecific mating signal. In the simple signalling model all this complexity is abstracted into the base fitness payoffs for signallers and receivers, and there is no guarantee that any transient, unstable evolved communication systems will be detected. The results suggest that in the long run signalling will not be stable unless it is to the mutual advantage of both parties, but this is not to deny that costly signalling arms races under conditions of conflicting interest could occur in the relatively short term. AL models of communication are uniquely equipped to investigate such issues further.

Acknowledgements

I am grateful to the Association of Commonwealth Universities and the British Council for financial support. I would also like to thank Seth Bullock and Ezequiel di Paolo for valuable discussions.

References

Ackley, D. H., and Littman, M. L. 1994. Altruism in the evolution of communication. In *Artificial Life IV*, edited by R. A. Brooks, and P. Maes. Cambridge, MA: MIT Press, p. 40–48.

Bullock, S. 1997. An exploration of signalling behaviour by both analytic and simulation means for both discrete and continuous models. In *Proceedings of the Fourth European Conference on Artificial Life*, edited by P. Husbands and I. Harvey. Cambridge, MA: MIT Press / Bradford Books, p. 454–463.

Grafen, A. 1990. Biological signals as handicaps. *Journal of Theoretical Biology* 144: 517–546.

Hamilton, W. D. 1964. The genetical evolution of social behaviour. *Journal of Theoretical Biology* 7: 1–52.

Hinde, R. A. 1981. Animal signals: Ethological and games-theory approaches are not incompatible. *Animal Behaviour* 29: 535–542.

Hurd, P. L. 1995. Communication in discrete action-response games. *Journal of Theoretical Biology* 174: 217–222.

Johnstone, R. A., and Grafen, A. 1992. The continuous Sir Philip Sydney game: A simple model of biological signalling. *Journal of Theoretical Biology* 156: 215–234.

Krebs, J. R., and Dawkins, R. 1984. Animal signals: Mind reading and manipulation. In *Behavioural Ecology: An Evolutionary Approach*, edited by J. R. Krebs and N. B. Davies. Oxford: Blackwell, second edition, p. 380–402.

MacLennan, B. J., and Burghardt, G. M. 1994. Synthetic ethology and the evolution of cooperative communication. *Adaptive Behavior* 2: 161–188.

Maynard Smith, J., and Harper, D. G. C. 1995. Animal signals: Models and terminology. *Journal of Theoretical Biology* 177 :305–311.

Maynard Smith, J. 1982. *Evolution and the Theory of Games.* Cambridge: Cambridge University Press.

Maynard Smith, J. 1991. Honest signalling: The Philip Sydney game. *Animal Behaviour* 42 :1034–1035.

Oliphant, M. 1996. The dilemma of Saussurean communication. *BioSystems* 37 :31–38.

Trivers, R. L. 1974. Parent-offspring conflict. *American Zoologist* 14: 249–264.

Werner, G. M., and Dyer, M. G. 1991. Evolution of communication in artificial organisms. In *Artificial Life II*, edited by C. G. Langton, C. Taylor, J. D. Farmer, and S. Rasmussen. Redwood City, CA: Addison-Wesley, p. 659–687.

Wheeler, M., and de Bourcier, P. 1995. How not to murder your neighbor: Using synthetic behavioral ecology to study aggressive signaling. *Adaptive Behavior* 3: 273–309.

Stochasticity as a Source of Innovation in Language Games

Luc Steels (1,2) and **Frédéric Kaplan (1,3)**
(1) Sony CSL - Paris - 6 Rue Amyot, 75005 Paris
(2) VUB AI Lab - Brussels
(3) LIP6 - UPMC - 4, Place Jussieu F-75252 Paris
E-mail: steels@arti.vub.ac.be

Abstract

Recent work on viewing language as a complex adaptive system has shown that self-organisation can explain how a group of distributed agents can reach a coherent set of linguistic conventions and how such a set can be preserved from one generation to the next based on cultural transmission. The paper continues these investigations by exploring the presence of stochasticity in the various aspects of lexical communication: stochasticity in the non-linguistic communication constraining meaning, the transmission of the message, and the retrieval from memory. We show that there is an upperbound on the amount of stochasticity which can be tolerated and that stochasticity causes and maintains language variation. Results are based on the further exploration of a minimal computational model of language interaction in a group of distributed agents, called the naming game.

Keywords: origins of language, evolution of language, self-organization.

Introduction

Exciting recent research in the origins and evolution of language (see overviews in (Hurford, Knight, & Studdert-Kennedy 1998) and (Steels 1997c)) is showing that when language is viewed as a complex adaptive system, it becomes possible to understand how a set of distributed agents is capable to reach a shared set of conventions, even if there is no global controlling agency or prior design. The main mechanism responsible for the emergence of coherence is self-organisation: A positive feedback loop causes some naturally occurring variation to propagate and eventually dominate the population. This is similar to how a product comes to dominate a market in increasing-returns economics (Arthur 1996), or how a group of social insects like an ant society can form a collective structure (Deneubourg 1977). In each of these cases, the system locks globally into specific choices based on positive feedback loops coupled to environmental conditions.

A coherent framework to study language as a complex adaptive system is to define populations of agents engaged in adaptive language games. Each game involves a linguistic as well as a non-linguistic interaction. The agents have feedback about success and failure and adapt so as to be more successful in future games. We have extensively experimented with a particular type of such a game, called the naming game, first introduced in (Steels 1996b). The game is played between a speaker and a hearer, randomly drawn from a population of agents. The speaker attempts to identify an object to the hearer, based on pointing and based on using a name. The game succeeds if the hearer guesses correctly the object chosen by the speaker. A speaker may create a new name when he does not have one yet. A hearer may adopt the name used by a speaker. Both monitor use and success and prefer in future games those names that had the highest score. This generates the desired positive feedback loop bringing the group progressively towards global coherence.

The naming game has been explored through computational simulations and is related to systems proposed and investigated by (MacLennan 1991), (Werner & Dyer 1991), and (Oliphant 1996). We have developed more complex variations of the game where the meaning consist of symbolic descriptions derived from discrimination games (Steels 1997a). The game has also been implemented on physically grounded mobile robotic agents (Steels & Vogt 1997) and on vision-based robotic 'talking heads', watching dynamically evolving scenes (Steels 1997b). Of course in natural languages both the form and the meaning are vastly more complex than the atomic forms (words) and meanings (objects) used in the naming games discussed in this paper. However, the basic properties of naming games are independent of the complexity of the forms or the meanings.

The main topic of this paper is to explore what happens when stochasticity is introduced in language games. Stochasticity means that some aspects of the game exhibit unpredictable errors. It is caused by faults in production or perception, errors in guessing meaning from the context or from pointing, or malfunctioning of memory. We have experienced this stochasticity very strongly while grounding the language games on physical robots, but want to study theoretically its consequences through software simulation. In order to cope with stochasticity, perception delivers typically several possible forms and possible meanings with various degrees of confidence. The selection and the evaluation of these forms and meanings are determined by the Tolerance level and the Focus of the Hearer. Stochasticity, Tolerance and Focus interact and are important for explaining innovation and evolution. This paper focuses on stochasticity, whereas a companion paper explores the role of tolerance, focus and stochasticity in language change (Steels & Kaplan 1998).

The rest of the paper has the following sections. First the naming game is defined. Then results are shown for the emergence of a set of conventions without any stochasticity. Next different sources of stochasticity are introduced: first in the extra-linguistic activities delimiting the context and the topic, second in terms of noise on the message being transmitted, and finally memory access. Some conclusions and suggestions for further work end the paper.

The Naming Game Model

The Naming Game, as used in the present paper, is an enriched version of a model first presented in (Steels 1996b). We assume a set of *agents* $\mathcal{A}$ where each agent $a \in \mathcal{A}$ has contact with a set of *objects*. These objects constitute a set of *meanings* to be expressed $\mathcal{M} = \{m_1, ..., m_n\}$. All the experiments in this paper involve a population of 20 agents and 10 meanings. A *form* is a sequence of letters drawn from a finite alphabet. The agents are all assumed to share the same alphabet. A *lexicon* $\mathcal{L}$ is a time-dependent relation between meanings, forms and a score. Each agent $a \in A$ has his own set of forms $F_{a,t}$ and his own lexicon $L_{a,t} \subset \mathcal{M}_a \times F_{a,t} \times \mathcal{N}$, which is initially empty. An agent a is therefore defined at a time t as a pair $a_t =< F_{a,t}, L_{a,t} >$. There is the possibility of synonymy and homonymy: an agent can associate a single form with several meanings and a given meaning with several forms. It is not required that all agents have at all times the same set of forms and the same lexicon.

Operation of the Naming Game

The Naming Game is an interaction between a Speaker and a Hearer about a Topic in a given Context. The context consists of a set of objects and both the speaker and the hearer are assumed to be capable to identify meanings to distinguish the topic from the other objects in the context, using for example mechanisms as described in (Steels 1996a).

2.1.1 Production. Let $C \subset \mathcal{M}$ with $\mathcal{M}$ the set of possible meanings. The meaning the speaker has associated with the topic is $m_s \in C$. He signals this topic using non-linguistic communication (such as through pointing). At the same time, the speaker retrieves from his lexicon all the associations indexed by m_s. This set is called the association-set of m_s. Let $m \in \mathcal{M}$ be a meaning, $a \in \mathcal{A}$ be an agent, and t a time moment, then the association-set of m is

$$A_{m,a,t} = \{< m, f, u > | < m, f, u > \in L_{a,t}\} \quad (1)$$

Each of the associations in this set suggests a form f_s to use for identifying m with a score $0.0 \leq u \leq 1.0$. The speaker chooses the association with the largest score and produces the form f_s which is part of this association to the hearer.

2.1.2 Transmission. Both linguistic and non-linguistic information are transmitted to the hearer. During the emission, transmission and reception phases, *stochasticity* (e.g. noise, unpredicable errors) can occur.

2.1.3 Comprehension. The Hearer perceives the linguistic and non-linguistic information. Because this information might have been altered during the transmission, the hearer must consider several possible forms and meanings and evaluates each of them. The form Focus FF and the Meaning Focus TF parameters determine the number of forms F_{cons} and meanings M_{cons} considered. These parameters indicate the maximum distance from the perceived information that the hearer is willing to consider:

$$M_{cons} = \{< m > | < m > \in \mathcal{M}, d(m, m') \leq TF\} \quad (2)$$

$$F_{cons} = \{f'\} \cup \{< f > | < f > \in \mathcal{F}, d(f, f') \leq FF\} \quad (3)$$

a. Meaning score. The hearer constructs a meaning-score $0.0 \leq s_m \leq 1.0$ for each possible meaning m in M_{cons} reflecting the likelihood that m is the meaning of the perceived topic m'. If there is absolute certainty, one meaning has a score of 1.0 and the others are all 0.0. If there is no non-linguistic communication, the likelihood of all meanings is the same. If there is only vague non-linguistic communication, the hearer has some idea what the topic is, but with less certainty. In our experiments, the distance $d(m', m)$ between the meaning of the perceived topic m' and the other meanings determines the meaning-score:

$$s_m = \frac{1}{1 + (\frac{d(m',m)}{\alpha})^2} \quad (4)$$

α is the tolerance factor for meaning perception.

b. Form score. The hearer constructs also a form-score $0.0 \leq s_f \leq 1.0$ for each form f of F_{cons}. The distance $d(f', f)$ between the perceived form f' and the considered form f gives a score

$$s_f = \frac{1}{1 + (\frac{d(f',f)}{\beta})^2} \tag{5}$$

β is the is the tolerance factor for form perception.

c. Decision matrix. For each form f_j in F, the hearer retrieves the association-set that contains it. He constructs a *decision-matrix* which contains for each meaning a row and for each form a column. The first column contains the meaning-scores s_{m_i}, the first row the form-scores s_{f_j}. Each cell in the inner-matrix contains the association-score for the relation between the object and the form in the lexicon of the hearer:

		f_1	f_2	...
		s_{f_1}	s_{f_2}	...
m_1	s_{m_1}	$s_{<m_1,f_1>}$	$s_{<m_1,f_2>}$	...
m_2	s_{m_2}	$s_{<m_2,f_1>}$	$s_{<m_2,f_2>}$	...
...	...	...	...	...

Obviously many cells in the matrix may be empty (and then set to 0.0), because a certain relation between a meaning and a form may not be in the lexicon of the hearer. Note also that there may be meanings identified by lexicon lookup which are not in the initial context C. They are added to the matrix, but their meaning-score is 0.0.

The final state of an inner matrix cell of the score matrix is computed by the formula:

$$score_{m_i,f_j} = w_f.s_{f_j} + w_m.s_{m_i} + w_a.s_{<m_i,f_j>} \tag{6}$$

w_f is the weight of the form information, w_m is the weight of the non-linguistic information and w_l is the weight of the lexicon. In this paper, they are by default set at 1.0 and the score is then simply the sum of the three sources of information.

One meaning-form pair will have the best score and the corresponding meaning is the topic m_h chosen by the hearer. The association in the lexicon of this meaning-form pair is called the winning association. This choice integrates extra-linguistic information (the meaning-score), form ambiguity (the form-score), and the current state of the hearer's lexicon (the association-score).

2.1.4 Adaptation. The hearer then indicates to the speaker what topic he identified. In real-world language games, this could be through a subsequent action, like handing the topic to the hearer, or through another linguistic interaction. When a decision could be made and $m_h = m_s$ the game succeeds, otherwise it fails. The following adaptations take place by the speaker and the hearer based on the outcome of the game:

a. The game succeeds This means that speaker and hearer agree on the topic. To reenforce the lexicon, the speaker increments the score s of the association that he preferred, and hence used, with a fixed quantity δ. The hearer reenforces the winning association that has led to the right comprehension. Both decrement with δ the score of all the associations that share either the meaning or the form of the winning pair. 0.0 and 1.0 remain the lower and upperbound of s. These changes implement an excitation-exhibition dynamics similar to the one used in Kohonen networks, except that the change is constant.

b. The game fails There are several cases:

1. The Speaker does not know a form

   It could be that the speaker did not have an association covering the topic. In that case, the game fails but the speaker may create a new form f' and associate this with the topic m_s in his lexicon. This happens with a form creation probability p_c.

2. The hearer does not know the form.

   In other words there is no association in the lexicon of the hearer involving the form f_h of the winning association. In that case, the game ends in failure but the hearer may extend his lexicon with a form absorption probability p_a.

3. There is a mismatch between m_h and m_s.

   In this case, both speaker and hearer have to adapt their lexicons. The speaker decrements with δ the association (m_s,f_s) and the hearer decrements with δ the association (m_h,f_h)

Macroscopic variables

The naming game model can be viewed as a complex dynamical system. The agents have a certain local behavior (an agent can only interact with one single agent, not with all agents at the same time), which is determined by their internal lexicons. Behavior changes because agents adapt their lexicon. In order to 'see' the global order in the system, we need macroscopic variables. These macroscopic variables are invisible to the agents because no agent has a complete overview of the behavior of the group. The first such variable quantifies the *average success* after n games. When average success approaches total success, this must mean that the conventions are sufficiently shared to speak of the emergence of a shared lexicon. But, because a form may have many meanings and the same meaning may be expressed by multiple forms, communicative success does not necessarily mean complete coherence. An agent can very well know a form but prefer not to use it himself.

In practice, an examination of the lexicons of the different agents shows a quite complex situation, so that it is non-trivial to extract what *the* shared language is. We determine the language of a single agent by translating his lexicon into a matrix where there is a row for every possible meaning, a column for every word, and the cells are filled by the association-scores, possibly 0.0. Based on this matrix it is possible to determine what the most preferred form is for naming a meaning, and thus what the preferred language is of the agent. Note that this represents the language for production, not for comprehension. Associations are not symmetrical. For example, in the matrix below, the agent prefers f_2 when m_1 needs to be expressed (and not f_1). When f_1 is heard, the same agent nevertheless expects m_1. The pair $< m_1, f_1 >$ is in the expected language but not in the produced language. The expected language includes the production language but not vice-versa. (See (Hurford 1989) and (Oliphant 1996) for a further exploration of the coordination between production and comprehension systems.)

	f_1	f_2
m_1	0.6	0.7
m_2	0.4	0.3

Given the preferred language for a single agent, it is straightforward to determine the language of the group as being the set of word-meaning associations that are preferred by most agents. The *coherence* of the language is equal to the average number of agents that prefer these most preferred word-meaning association.

Formation and Maintenance of Equilibrium States

We now investigate the behavior of naming games in the ideal case of closed populations of agents without any stochasticity. Agents take the information they perceive at face value ($TF = 0$ and $FF = 0$). $\delta = 0.2$ and new associations are created with an initial score of 0.2. $p_c = 0.1$ and $p_a = 1.0$.

For each experiment, it is instructive to look at the evolution of game success as well as coherence. Figure 1 shows a first simulation experiment involving a group of 20 agents. We see that very quickly coherence as well as average game success climbs up to both reach 100 %.

It is also instructive to look at the evolution of the average association-scores competing for the preferred expression of a particular form (or alternatively for the highest expectation). This is done through *competition diagrams* as the one shown in figure 2. The diagram shows that there is a winner-take-all situation. This is due to the positive feedback loop between score and use. The higher the score of an assocation, the more it is used, and the more its chances increase to be successful in further use. Such a winner-take-all situation takes place for every meaning so that a global shared lexicon emerges.

Once total game success is reached, the language does not change anymore. The only source of possible inno-

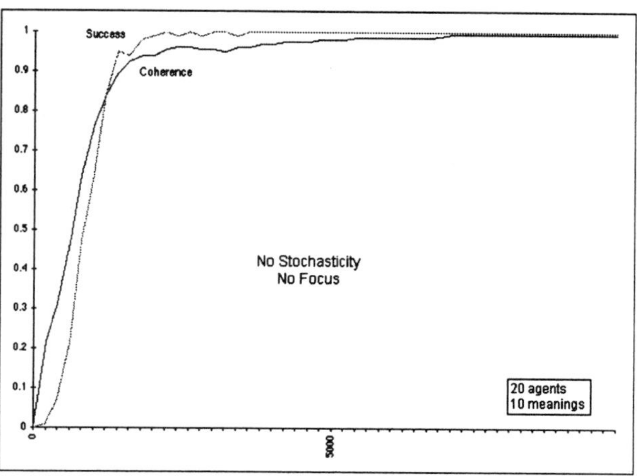

Figure 1: Evolution of average game success and coherence in a population of 20 agents for 10 objects. An equilibrium state is reached whereby the agents gain total average success and a high, stable coherence.

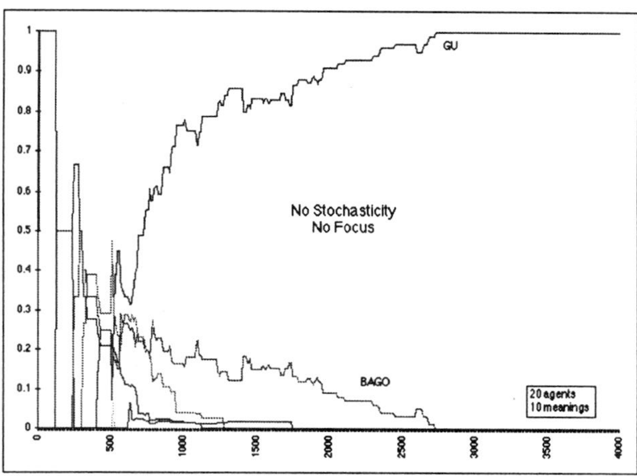

Figure 2: Competition diagram showing the competition between several forms for being the preferred way to express a certain meaning. The diagram plots the average renormalized score of the form-meaning associations of all agents for the same meaning. A winner-take-all situation emerges.

vation is the introduction of new forms, which only happens when an agent does not have a form yet, or the progressive adoption of one form by the group, which stops as soon as a winner-take-all situation has been reached.

A language is even resistent (up to a certain degree) to changes in the population. This is investigated by introducing an in- and outflux in the population. When agents leave, they take their lexicons with them. When new virgin agents enter, they have to acquire the language of the other agents in the group. They may occasionally create a new word (with a small probability the word creation probability p_c) but this new word quickly gets damped against the dominance of the preferred word. Acquisition of an existing language by a new agent happens without any addition or change to the model, as shown in figure 3 which plots also the language change. Change is quantified by comparing the state of the language at two time points and counting the number of preferred form-meaning pairs that changed. We see that the language changes rapidly in the beginning as the population moves towards total average game success. Thereafter the language remains stable. Figure 3 shows what happens when a flux is introduced in the population. When new agents come in, game success and coherence drops because the new agent has to acquire the language of the group. But if there are not too many agents coming in, the group will maintain a high rate of success. More importantly, the language itself does not change at all. It is transmitted culturally from one generation to the next. When the rate of population renewal is too high, the language disintegrates, as also shown in figure 3. There is rapid language change because the new agents start to create new word-meaning associations, but these conventions cannot propagate fast enough in the population.

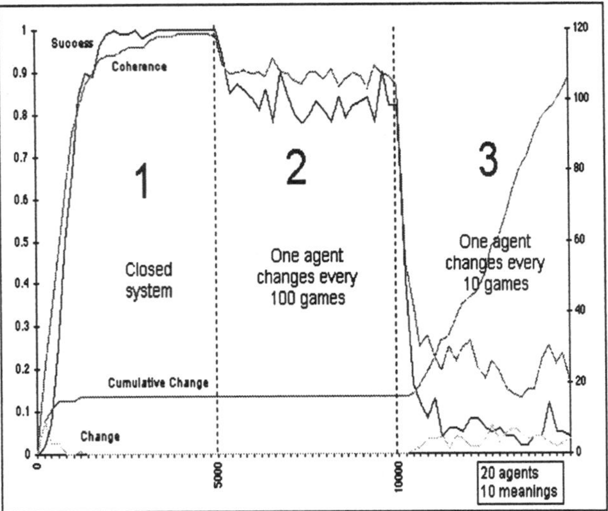

Figure 3: A language once formed remains stable even if there is an in- and outflow of agents in the population. This graph shows both language change and the average game success. In a first phase, the language forms itself in a closed population. In a second phase, an in- and outflow of agents (1 in/outflow per 100 games) is introduced, the language stays the same and success is maintained. In the third phase the flux is increased to 1 per 10 games and the language disintegrates. Average game success rapidly reaches very low levels.

We will now look at the effect of stochasticty during three steps of the Naming Game: non-linguistic communication, form transmission, and memory access. To cope with stochasticity, agents have now a large focus and a standard tolerance level ($TF = 10$, $FF = 3$, $\alpha = \beta = 1$).

Stochasticity of Non-Linguistic Communication

In the results reported so far, it is assumed that non-linguistic communication is without error. This is clearly not always the case in real-word language interactions. Stochasticity in non-linguistic communication can be investigated by probabilistically introducing a random error in the perceived attributes of the topic. The object coordinates of the meaning expressed can, for instance, be shifted by a fixed value. The probability is called the topic-recognition stochasticity E_T. Figure 4 shows the first results for an experiment exploring variations in E_T. When E_T is high (phase one), there is so much confusion that a language does not form at all. When E_T is decreased to 0.0 (phase two), a language starts to form quickly. This language maintains itself, even if E_T is again increased (third phase).

This experiment shows that there must be a minimum of reliability in non-linguistic communication at the initial phases of language formation, otherwise a language does not form. At the same time, it shows clearly that as soon as a language has bootstrapped itself, linguistic communication is capable to counteract the unreliability of non-linguistic communication.

We now investigate in how far the stochasticity of non-linguistic communication has an impact on language variation. Figure 5 shows a typical example of a competition diagram for a positive topic-recognition stochasticity. A language has already formed itself with a single winner (the form "topo") for the meaning being investigated. Stochasticity causes competition to arise, challenging - but not yet defeating - the dominating form-meaning association. Innovation is due to the fact that confusion about the topic may lead to a new form-meaning association which then starts to propagate.

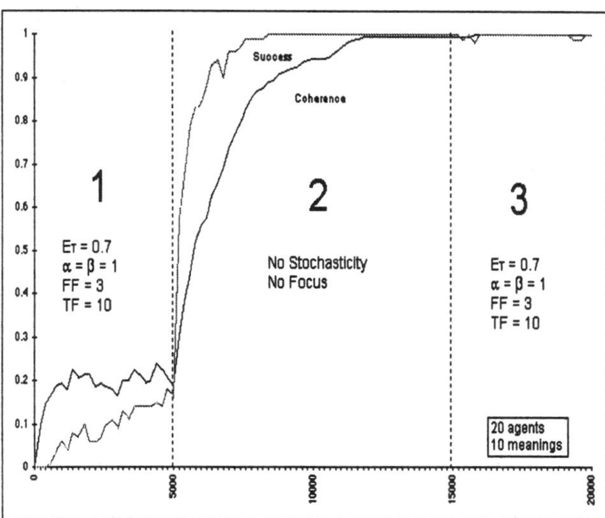

Figure 4: Exploration of variations in the stochasticity of non-linguistic communication. In the first phase stochasticity is high $E_T = 0.7$, a coherent language does not form. In the second phase stochasticity is absent, $E_T = 0.0$, a language forms. In the third phase stochasticity is increased again to $E_T = 0.7$. Communication can tolerate a high level of stochasticity, justifying linguistic communication complementary to non-linguistic communication.

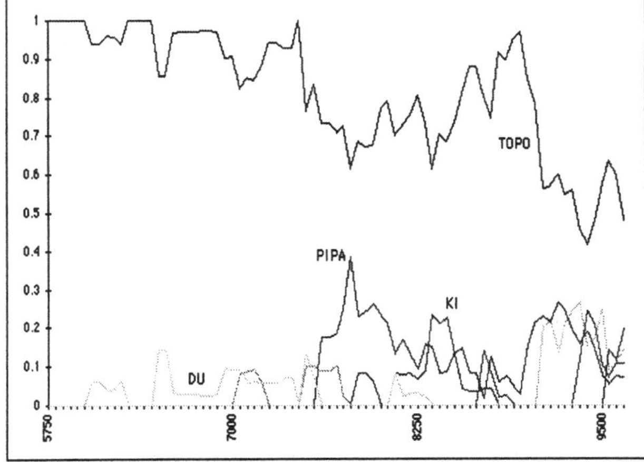

Figure 5: Example of competition diagram with $E_T =$ 0.7. There is a more complex dynamics instead of an equilibrium winner-take-all situation. New associations enter and remain in the population, even though they have not yet been able to overtake the dominating word.

Stochasticity on Form

The second source of stochasticity is in the message transmission process. So far it is assumed that a message is produced perfectly by the speaker and received perfectly by the hearer. This is well known not to be true in the case of natural languages. Speakers make a large amount of errors and blur the pronounciation to minimize energy and maximise the number of sounds transmitted in a given period of time. Hearers have a very hard time to decode speech signals, simply because the speech signal is noisy and contains only hints for some sounds. Hearers are known to partially make up for it by expectations and knowledge about the language.

In the experiment reported earlier, several forms may already be triggered due to the large focus on form reception. These are all the forms that are at a certain distance from the form produced by the speaker. This uncertainty makes it less clear what form has been used but does not yet imply mistakes. We now introduce a second stochastic operator that causes a transformation of the form transmitted. For example, the speaker may produce "moba" but the hearer may receive "mopa". The parameter controling this stochasticity is E_F, the form-recognition stochasticity: it is the probability that a character in the string of the form mutates.

Figure 6 shows results of experiments in varying this particular parameter. In the first phase $E_F = 0.5$ a language may eventually form itself but it would take a rather long time. $E_F = 0$ immediately causes the language to appear. In the third phase, we again increase the stochasticity. It is seen that the language is resilient. There are occasionally games that fail, but the language itself is not affected. As with human language users, the non-linguistic communication as well as expectations from the lexicon partially offset the problems in determining what form has been used. These experiments clearly show that once a language has formed, it counterbalances errors in message transmission.

Figure 7 investigates the impact of form-stochasticity on variation in the language. We see clearly that a positive form-recognition stochasticity $E_F = 0.3$ causes new forms to appear in the language. When $E_F = 0.0$, many of these forms disappear. Interestingly enough, competitors may still maintain themselves in the population. This is due to the large focus of the agents. "ludo" and "mudo" are words that are sufficiently close to each other that one group may have adopted one form and another slightly smaller group the other form. As uncertainty in form is tolerated, one group will always accept the form of the other even though they would not use exactly the same form themselves.

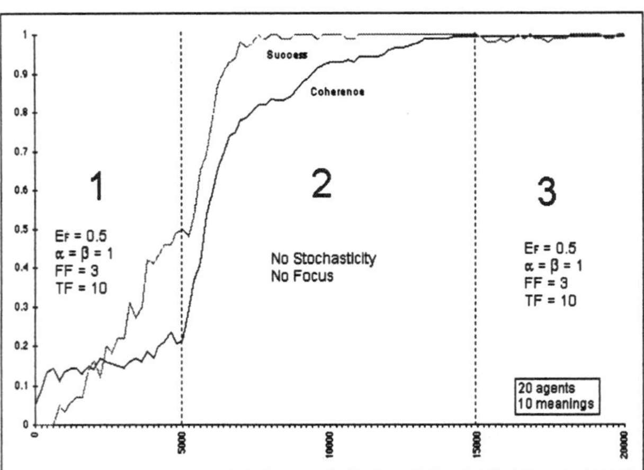

Figure 6: Exploration of variations in form stochasticity. In the first phase stochasticity is high $E_F = 0.5$. A language only slowly forms itself. In the second phase it is low $E_F = 0.0$, a language forms. Then $E_F = 0.5$. The language is resilient against a higher form stochasticity and average game success stays very high.

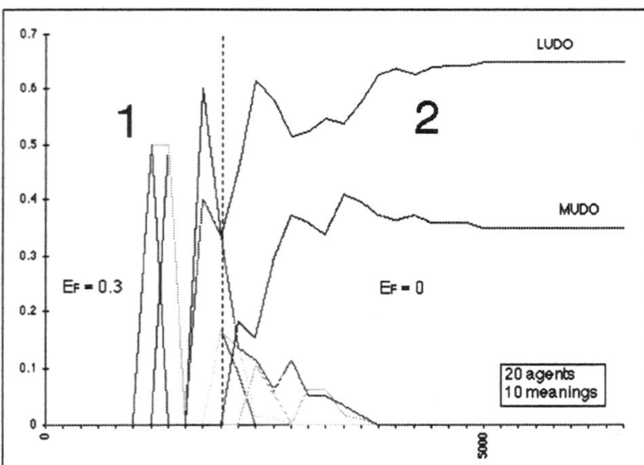

Figure 7: Competition diagram in the presence of form stochasticity. When $E_F = 0.3$ there is no clear winner-take-all situation as new forms are occasionally introduced resulting in new form-meaning associations. When $E_F = 0.0$ the innovation dies out although some form are still able to maintain themselves due to the large focus of the agents.

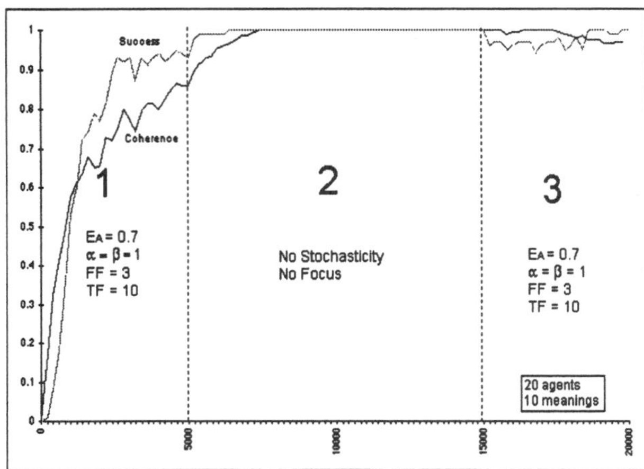

Figure 8: This figure shows the results in exploring memory malfunction. The first phase shows that a language has some difficulties forming for a positive memory-stochasticity ($E_A = 0.7$). In the second phase memory stochasticity is zero and language forms. The third phase shows resilience against positive memory stochasticity ($E_A = 0.7$)

Stochasticity on Form-Meaning Associations

The final source of stochasticity comes from the utilisation of the lexicon. It is well known that biological systems occasionally malfunction even though there is globally a robust behavior. We hypothesise that this is also the case for memory. The form-meaning association retrieved from memory may not necessarily be the way that it was first stored. Thus the speaker could accidentally retrieve the wrong form for a particular meaning, or the hearer's memory system may suggest a form-meaning association which was never stored. These errors are modeled using a third stochastic operator based on a parameter E_A, the memory stochasticity, which alters the scores of the associations in the score matrix in a probabilistic fashion. Even scores that were zero could become positive. The higher the memory stochasticity, the more likely an association score changes.

Figure 8 shows the impact of memory stochasticity on language formation. When E_A is positive, language formation is more difficult, although progress can be seen. We see also that coherence and success can be maintained even if memory is malfunctioning and yielding spurious association scores. This experiment demonstrates again that the overall language system is fault tolerant because it maximises information from three sources: non-linguistic communication, form recognition, and form-meaning conventions. The better a language is established, the more resilient it is to use in difficult circumstances.

Also in this case, we see continued language innova-

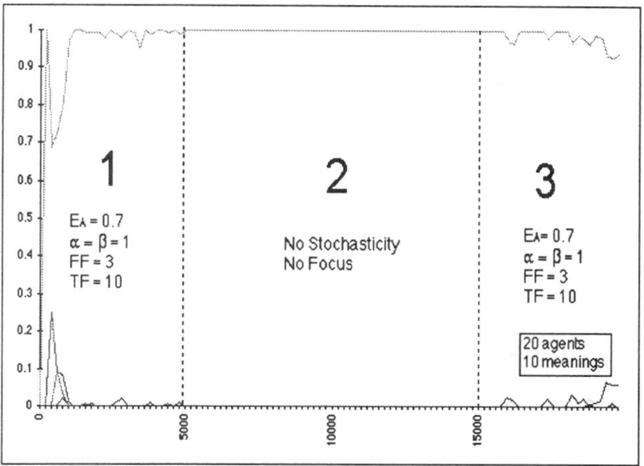

Figure 9: Typical competition diagram. First there is a positive association stochasticity $E_A = 0.7$. The language is slowly forming itself. We still see a rich competitive dynamics between the different form-meaning pairs even if one is dominating. This innovation dies out when $E_A = 0$. When $E_A = 0.7$ new associations get into the system and variation is maintained.

tion due to stochasticity. This is illustrated clearly in a competition diagram shown in figure 9, running for the same simulation as figure 8. One form ("pi") is dominant for the meaning being investigated. When the memory stochasticity becomes positive, the competition intensifies and new words ("te", "lavi") enter.

Combination of Stochasticity

The different forms of stochasticity combined lead to innovation in different areas as seen in figure 10 and figure 11.

Conclusion

This paper has investigated the effect of stochasticity on linguistic and non-linguistic communication, as it unfolds in a population of distributed agents playing adaptive language games. This was done for the three main components of a language game: the non-linguistic communication, which constrains the set of possible meanings, the message itself, and the use of the lexicon. Each of these sources of stochasticity is realistic from the viewpoint of real world language use. Human users (as well as robots) cannot be expected to guess accurately the possible meaning of an utterance purely based on non-linguistic means. The message is often errorful due to the inherent unreliability of sound-based message transmission. The brain, as many biological systems, may have unreliable components but nevertheless show global fault tolerance.

In each of the cases that were studied, the effect of stochasticity was similar and can be summarised as follows:

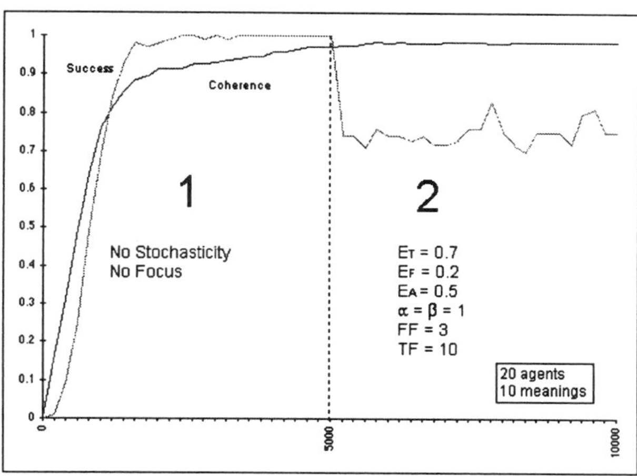

Figure 10: Average success and coherence. The three different forms of stochasticity are introduced in phase 2. We can see that average success drops because incompatibilities between non-linguistic and linguistic communication and the introduction of new forms. Notice that the language coherence remains unaffected.

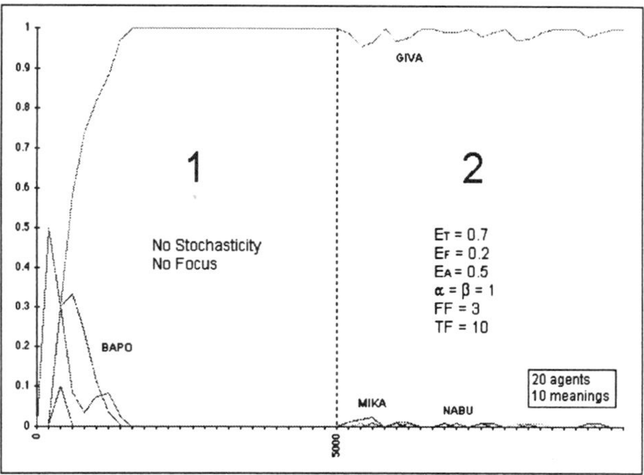

Figure 11: Competition diagram for one meaning during the same experiment as in 10. We see that there is a winner-take-all situation in the first phase and then an attack by new forms ("mika", "nabu", etc.) even though they never manage to overtake the existing word ("giva").

1. There are upper bounds on the amount of stochasticity that can be present during the initial phases of language formation. When the stochasticity is too high a language cannot self-organise.

2. Once a language has established itself, stochasticity for one component is partially counterbalanced by the other components. If the message is scrambled, non-linguistic communication and expectations from the lexicon can make up for it. If non-linguistic communication is unreliable or absent, linguistic communication can suffice. If memory is malfunctioning, clues from the environment may counterbalance.

3. Stochasticity introduces and maintains variation in the language. There is no longer a clear winner-take-all situation, whereby the language stays in an equilibrium state, even in a changing population. Instead, there is a rich dynamics where new forms appear, new associations are established, and the domination pattern of associations changes. The different sources of stochasticity each innovate in their own way: Topic stochasticity introduces new form-meaning associations for existing forms. Form stochasticity introduces new forms and hence potentially new form-meaning associations. Memory stochasticity shifts the balance among the form-meaning associations competing for the expression of the same meaning. All of these sources of stochasticity are clearly observed in real natural language use.

A complementary paper explores how stochasticity and tolerance are essential for explaining language change (Steels & Kaplan 1998).

Acknowledgement

The research described in this paper was financed and conducted at the Sony Computer Science Laboratory in Paris. The simulations presented have been built on top of the BABEL toolkit developed by Angus McIntyre (McIntyre 1998) of Sony CSL. Without this superb toolkit, it would not have been possible to perform the required investigations within the time available. We are also indebted to Mario Tokoro of Sony CSL Tokyo for continuing to emphasise the importance of stochasticity in complex adaptive systems.

References

Arthur, B., ed. 1996. *The Economy as a Complex Adaptive System.* Santa Fe Institute Series on Complexity. Menlo Park, Ca: Addison-Wesley.

Deneubourg, J.-L. 1977. Application de l'ordre par fluctuations à la description de certaines étapes de la construction du nid chez les termites. *Insectes Sociaux* 24(2):117–130.

Hurford, J.; Knight, C.; and Studdert-Kennedy, M., eds. 1998. *Evolution of Human Language.* Edinburgh: Edinburgh University Press.

Hurford, J. 1989. Biological evolution of the saussurean sign as a component of the language acquisition device. *Lingua* 77:187–222.

MacLennan, B. 1991. Synthetic ethology: An approach to the study of communication. In Langton, C., ed., *Artificial Life II.* Redwood City, Ca.: Addison-Wesley Pub. Co.

McIntyre, A. 1998. Babel: A testbed for research in origins of language. Submitted for Publication.

Oliphant, M. 1996. The dilemma of saussurean communication. *Biosystems* 1–2(37):31–38.

Steels, L., and Kaplan, F. 1998. Explaining language evolution. Submitted for Publication.

Steels, L., and Vogt, P. 1997. Grounding adaptive language games in robotic agents. In Harvey, I., and Husbands, P., eds., *Proceedings of the 4th European Conference on Artificial Life.* Cambridge, MA: The MIT Press.

Steels, L. 1996a. Perceptually grounded meaning creation. In Tokoro, M., ed., *Proceedings of the International Conference on Multi-Agent Systems.* Cambridge, Ma: The MIT Press.

Steels, L. 1996b. Self-organizing vocabularies. In *Proceeding of Alife V*, edited by C. G. Langton and T. Shimohara. Cambridge, MA: MIT Press.

Steels, L. 1997a. Constructing and sharing perceptual distinctions. In *Proceedings of the European Conference on Machine Learning*, edited by M. van Someren and G. Widmer. Berlin: Springer-Verlag.

Steels, L. 1997b. The origins of syntax in visually grounded robotic agents. In *Proceedings of the 15th International Joint Conference on Artificial Intelligence*, edited by M. Pollack. Los Angeles: Morgan Kauffman Publishers.

Steels, L. 1997c. The synthetic modeling of language origins. *Evolution of Communication Journal* 1(1):1–34.

Werner, G. M., and Dyer, M. G. 1991. Evolution of communication in artificial organisms. In *Artificial Life II, Vol.X of SFI Studies in the Sciences of Complexity*, edited by C. G. Langton, C. Taylor, and J. D. Farmer. Redwood City, CA: Addison-Wesley.

Posters

Edges and Computation in Excitable Media

Andrew Adamatzky and Owen Holland

Intelligent Autonomous Systems Laboratory, University of the West of England,
Frenchay Campus, Coldharbour Lane, Bristol BS16 1QY, United Kingdom

Abstract

Using two-dimensional cellular automata with an 8-cell neighbourhood and a ternary cell state set, we have described all possible transition rules for a class of simple lattice-based excitable media, and have carried out an exhaustive investigation of the spatio-temporal dynamics of excitation in such lattices. We have subdivided the 256 possible rules of local excitation into 11 classes as a function of the morphological characteristics of the resultant excitation configurations far beyond the transient period. Spatial factors (number and size diversity of clusters of excited states) and dynamic characteristics (length of transient period and activity level) were also examined. We present a parametrisation of the function space according to a measure equivalent to Langton's λ parameter, and offer a classification of the morphological characteristics and potential computational capabilities as a function of λ. For much of the function space, the values of λ are in accordance with Langton's predictions; in particular, some identifiable computational capabilities are located at the boundaries between order and disorder.

Introduction

A continuing theme in the exploration and understanding of cellular automata has been the investigation of the relationship between the structure of the automata and the resultant behaviour. The behaviour itself has also been subjected to examination, in respect of its morphology, its complexity, and its computational possibilities. One of the main concerns has been to discover a simple metric which, when applied to the structural characteristics, will produce similar values for structures which produce similar behaviour. The demonstration by Langton (1990) that a 1-dimensional metric, λ, appeared to be able to do just that for a range of structural types stimulated attempts to understand why the metric worked (Gutowitz and Langton 1995) and how well it worked. A further claim made by Langton was that the capacity to support universal computation would be associated with the transition from order to disorder (the 'edge of chaos'). One of the problems has been that the number of different rule sets for a given structural type is typically so large, and the computation required to produce and evaluate the behaviour of a rule set so extensive, that it has only been possible to sample a small proportion of the rule sets falling under a given value of the metric. Another problem has been the high variability of the outcomes from different rule sets with the same value of λ. Taken together, these have produced some difficulties in the interpretation of λ.

This paper describes an attempt to characterise the relevant aspects of an interesting subset of CAs, that of simple lattice based excitable media, by using an exhaustive rather than a sampling strategy, thereby avoiding some of the problems mentioned above. Excitable media are common in nature. They usually consist of sheets or volumes of cells, each of which may be stimulated by its excited neighbours into a brief excited state, after which it becomes unable to be excited again for some time (the refractory period). The typical form of activity consists of propagated waves, which may form into characteristic patterns in two or three dimensions; however, other forms of activity may occur.

Cardiac muscle is perhaps the most familiar example of a cell-based natural excitable medium. Cellular automata models of excitable media can capture the essential aspects of natural media in a computationally tractable form, while at the same time forming an intrinsically interesting subclass of cellular automata. They are particularly useful in the present context for two reasons: considered structurally, they are really a degenerate subclass of CAs, and may contain several orders of magnitude fewer distinct sets of rules than the full class; and considered functionally, they are capable not only of expressing the wave-based abilities of excitable media, but also have the potential for supporting universal computation (e.g., Adamatzky 1997).

CA Models of Excitation in a Lattice

Typical cellular automata models of excitable media take the form of a two-dimensional cellular automaton, every cell of which is connected to its closest neighbours, takes three states, and changes its states at the same discrete times. The cell state set consists of three elements written as {o,+,-} which represent the rest, excited and refractory states of a cell. The cell state transitions are as follows: a cell which is excited at one time step will be refractory at the next time step; a cell which is refractory at one time step will be at rest in the next time step; and a cell which is at rest at one time step may be either excited or at rest on the next time step, depending on which of its neighbours are currently excited. The neighbours which affect a cell are defined as its neighbourhood; all cells have the same neighbourhood u, which for the excitable media considered in this paper has 8 members:

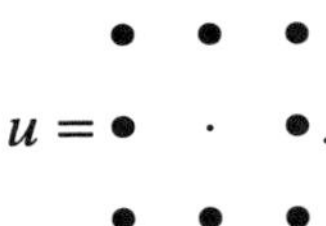

Excitable media have one overriding characteristic: the relative and absolute positions of excited cells in the neighbourhood are ignored, and it is only the *number* of excited cells which affects the state transition. (This of course means that this class of excitable media is isotropic, but it is in fact a much stronger condition than isotropy). The number of excited cells in a neighbourhood may range from 0 to 8, and so a given cell state transition rule may be defined in terms of the numbers of excited cells which will cause a cell to change from the rest state to the excited state. given range (e.g., 2, 3, or 4) or an unrestricted combination of numbers (e.g., 2, 5, or 8). The third case includes both of the others, and so we made it the basis of our investigation, using it to generate and explore all of the possible rules for an excitable medium with an 8-connected neighbourhood.

There are of course 256 possible transition functions, and they may be represented by the vectors $s = (s_j)_{1 \leq j \leq 8}$ ordered naturally by what we call the rule index

$f_1 : s = (00000000)$

$f_2 : s = (00000001)$

$f_3 : s = (00000010)$

...

$f_{256} : s = (11111111)$

In other words, if vector s has entry '1' at position j, then a resting cell becomes excited if it has j excited neighbours in its neighbourhood. Thus, in the case of the function represented by the vector (01110010), a cell at rest will become excited if it has 2, 3, 4 or 7 excited neighbours in its neighbourhood, but will not become excited if it has 0, 1, 5, 6 or 8 excited neighbours. If the neighbourhood of such a cell x at rest at time t is in state

$$u(x) = \begin{matrix} + & - & \circ \\ \circ & & \circ & + \\ + & \circ & - \end{matrix}$$

with 3 excited cells, then x will take the excited state at the next step of discrete time, t+1.

Each of these distinct transition functions may be used to generate a value for a parameter analogous to Langton's λ. In Langton's scheme, λ essentially measured the proportion of all possible input configurations (the states of the neighbourhood cells and the state of the current cell) which would produce a particular state of the current cell at the next time step. In the case of excitable media, we define the state of interest as the excited state. However, unlike Langton, we cannot manufacture rule sets with given values of λ to order; instead, we simply calculate the λ values of each of the 256 possible transition rules. The strong constraints on cell transitions in excitable media mean that fully two thirds of possible input configurations (those in which the current cell is excited or refractory) cannot produce the excited state in the next time step, and so the range over which λ can vary is rather limited, from 0 to 0.33, rather than from 0 to 1. However, if Langton's argument is correct, we should expect to see the full range of dynamic behaviour, namely from ordered to disordered and back again to ordered, as λ moves through this range. We should also find non-trivial computational capabilities at the boundaries between order and disorder.

Characterisation of Excitation Dynamics

We investigated the behaviour of all possible excitable media with 8-cell neighbourhoods by carrying out simulations on 30x30 lattices. All CAs examined had periodic boundaries, and were initialised by exciting each cell with probability p. Although we have investigated other values, p=0.3 produces a comprehensive (but incomplete) set of behaviours, and the work reported here refers to p=0.3 unless otherwise stated. 10 differently initialised runs were performed for each distinct transition rule.

To describe the behaviour in order to form a classification we used a variety of techniques. It is typical of CA to pass through a transient period τ until their behaviour settles down to some final characteristic type; we are interested in the length of this transient period, and in the final behaviour, but not in the behaviour during the transient period. After the transient period we visually examined the 2D maps of excited cells on the lattice, and also calculated various objective measures of levels and patterns of excitation. The activity level α for a function f is defined as the average number of excited cells over some sufficiently large interval after the transient period. The basic unit of analysis of patterns is the cluster. A cluster of excited states is defined as a connected subset of the lattice, every cell of which is excited and has at least one excited neighbour. We have derived two useful measures from analysing the clusters present in configurations: κ, the number of clusters, and ϑ, the size diversity of clusters.

Morphological Classification

We describe the configurations of excitation on the CA lattice using subjective phrases such as 'homogeneous', 'heterogeneous', 'fine-grained', 'coarse-grained' etc. because, thanks to the power of human visual pattern

65: 01000000 | 96: 01011111 | 97: 01100000 | 112: 01101111

113: 01110000 | 120: 01110111 | 121: 01111000 | 128: 01111111

129: 10000000 | 192: 10111111 | 193: 11000000 | 224: 11011111

225: 11100000 | 248: 11110111 | 249: 11111000 | 254: 11111101

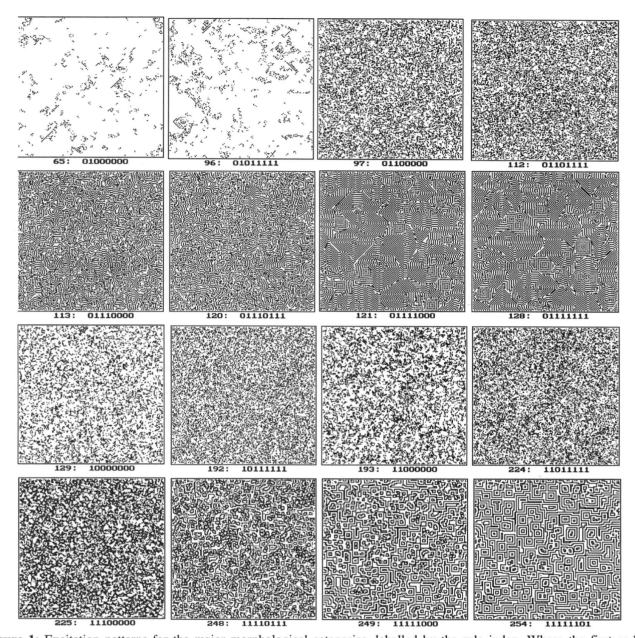

Figure 1: Excitation patterns for the major morphological categories, labelled by the rule index. Where the first and last members of a class are shown, it is possible to judge the change in character as the rules progress through the class, and also to see the clear transition between the last member of one class and the first of the next.

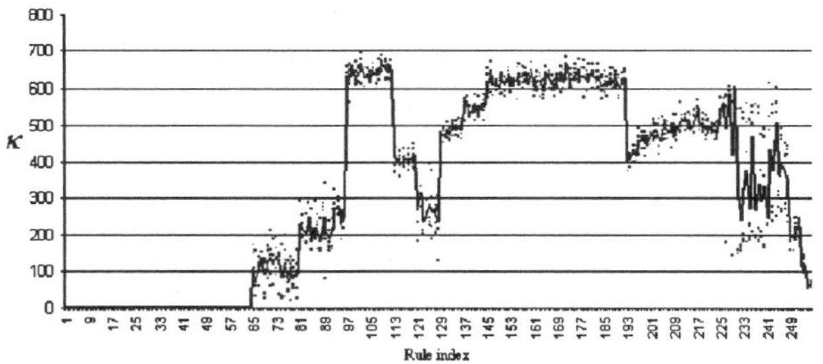

Figure 2: Number of clusters κ as a function of rule index

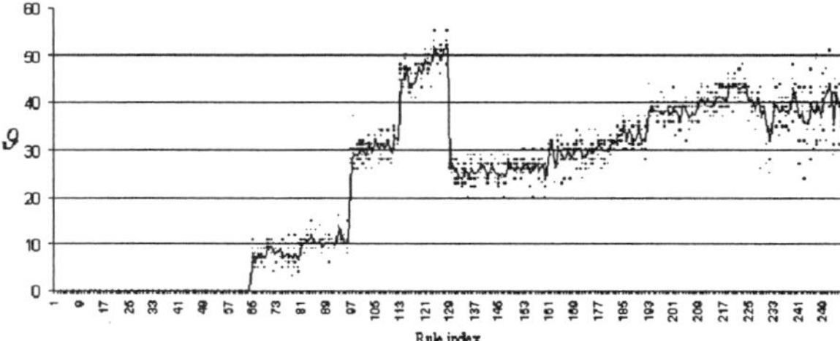

Figure 3: Size diversity of clusters ϑ as a function of rule index

perception, they are so easily characterisable and so strikingly distinct. The validity of the classifications is supported by the correspondence between the morphological classes and the objective measures. We believe that all rules can be assigned with little uncertainty to one of eleven morphological classes:

0-class: any initial configuration evolves to a state of uniform rest

2⁺-class: any initial conditions evolve to configurations comprising particle-like waves, or localised excitations, travelling around the lattice, colliding with each other, and generating new moving patterns as a result of collisions

H-class: any initial conditions produce a homogeneous activity pattern

L-class: labyrinth-like patterns appear with a large number of wave generators

F-class: fingerprint-like patterns appear, together with a small number of wave generators

CGFG-class: the members of the class exhibit a transition from coarse-grained to fine-grained patterns

HCGFG-class: the members of the class exhibit a transition from highly-coarse-grained to fine-grained patterns

CGSW-class: the members of the class pass from coarse grained patterns to saw wave patterns

SW-class: the behaviour of the members ranges from disordered wave patterns to the formation of spiral waves

Two other distinctive morphologies are also observable. Striking focused waves are seen for rule vectors (11111110) and (11111111), but the waves eventually annihilate one another. Strictly speaking, we should classify these rules in the **0**-class. However, they exhibit the longest transient periods of any rules, so we have decided to show this type of activity as the **FW**-class (Figure 4). For very high values of p, an additional morphology is seen: islands of stripe-like waves are surrounded by almost homogeneous patterns. We call this the **GW**-class (Figure 4) but do not discuss it further here.

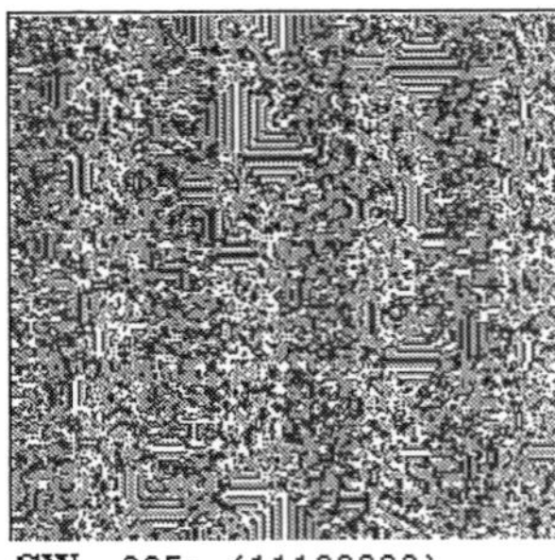

Figure 4: the GW- and FW-class

Some examples of the behaviour of the cellular automata used in the study, along with their classifications, are shown in Figure 1. But how can we be sure that the classes as revealed by our perceptions correspond to a meaningful division of the range of behaviours of excitable media? The answer is that we cannot, unless we can show that various objective measures also partition the space of behaviours in the same way. This is strikingly the case here. The key enabling device in this area is the rule vector. Consider the distribution of the above classes as a function of rule vector which is shown in Table 1. Almost all class boundaries occur as the zero in the lowest or lowest-but-one position in the function f flips to one. Within classes, as the higher bits are progressively filled, there are minor progressive qualitative changes. For example, in the **2⁺**-class the low values of f show sparser patterning than those close to the **H-class**, but these changes are slight compared with the transition between (01011111) and (01100000).

Class	Rule vectors s	Number of members
0	(00000000) ... (00111111)	64
2⁺	(01000000) ... (01011111)	34
H	(01100000) ... (01101111)	15
L	(01110000) ... (01110111)	7
F	(01111000) ... (01111111)	7
CGFG	(10000000) ... (10111111)	63
HCGFG	(11000000) ... (11011111)	31
CGSW	(11100000) ... (11110111)	23
SW	(11111000) ... (11111101)	5
FW	(11111110), (11111111)	2

Table 1: Morphological classes and rule vectors

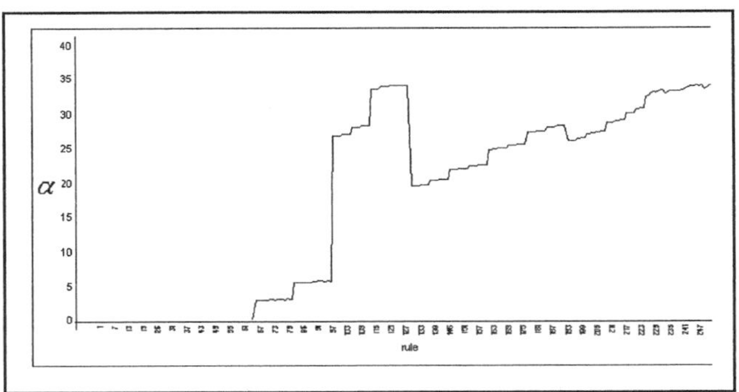

Figure 5: the activity level α as a function of rule index

Additional evidence is provided by the measures of spatial and dynamic factors. The cluster based measures examined, κ and ϑ, are most revealing; again, the discontinuities mark the morphological class boundaries. Figures 2 and 3 show κ and ϑ as functions of the rule index. The activity α of the sample configurations generated by the excitation rules is shown in Figure 5, and the values of τ in Figure 6. Note again that, wherever there are sharp discontinuities in either of these graphs, there is a morphological class boundary.

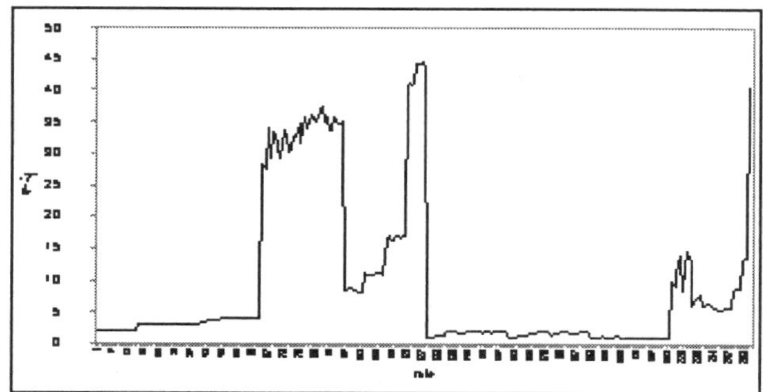

Figure 6: the transient period τ as a function of rule index

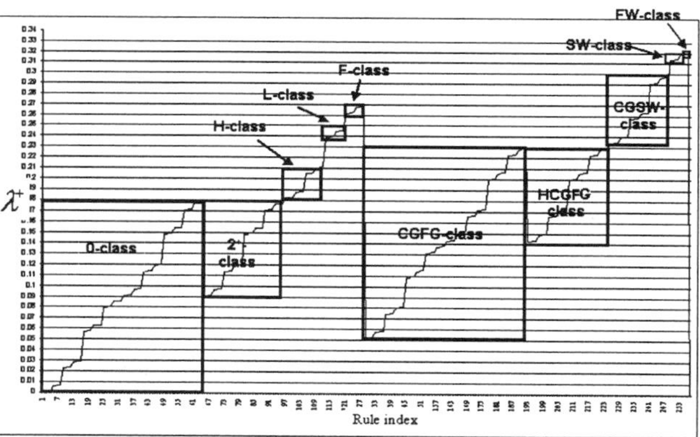

7: the values of λ plotted against the rule index, with morphological classifications

λ, the Morphological Classification, and Computational Capability

The values of λ plotted against the rule index are shown in Figure 7, along with the morphological classification. We look first of all at the way order and disorder vary as λ is increased from the minimum to the maximum. From 0 to 0.08, there is only order - the **0**-class. As λ increases to 0.09, there is both order and disorder, as the **CGFG**-class appears. Continuing up to 0.18, there is at first also the possibility of universal computation in the **2**$^+$-class, with further disorder possible from the **HCGFG**-class for higher values. However, from 0.18 to 0.23 there is only disorder, as the **H**-class is added to the **CGFG** and **HCGFG** classes, and the **2**$^+$-class drops out.

Up to this point, everything has followed Langton's predictions very neatly: there is a gradual increase from completely ordered to completely disordered behaviour, with the possibility of universal computation occurring between the two extremes. However, things become less clear as we increase λ further. First, as **H**, **CGFG**, and **HCGFG** are left behind, the ambiguous **CGSW** appears, with its overtones of both order and disorder. But as the **L**- and **F**-classes appear, we are again in a regime with long transients, propagated structures, and high visual complexity – all characteristics associated with potential computational ability. Finally, the simpler wave structures of **SW** appear, followed by the rigidity of **FW**, if we decide to admit the class.

It could therefore be argued that we do indeed see a transition in the reverse direction, from disorder to order. However, at the boundary between order and disorder we see no behaviour known to support universal computation, but we do see the potential for wave-based computation which is characteristic of excitable media. (This is no longer of merely theoretical interest - real excitable media have recently been used to build specialised computational devices (Tolmachev and Adamatzky 1996). Langton **Figure** (1990) regarded such specialised computational abilities as trivial; Mitchell *et al* (1993) acknowledged their potential importance; but neither made any attempt to locate them in λ-space, and we find it interesting to see where they sit.

Conclusions

We have carried out an exhaustive search of an interesting but degenerate subclass of cellular automata, a 2D excitable medium. It has been possible to classify the behaviours beyond the transient period on a number of subjective and objective grounds. A variant of Langton's λ parameter tracks the transitions from order to disorder and back to order adequately; at the edges of these regions we find one morphological class which is able to support universal computation, and another class which constitutes the essence of excitable media, the wave processing functions. This may indicate that an extension of this approach may assist in the understanding of both natural and artificial excitable media.

References

Adamatzky A. 1997. Universal computation in excitable media: the 2$^+$-medium. *Adv. Mater. Opt. Electron.* 7: 263-272.

Gutowitz H.A. and C. G. Langton. 1995. Mean field theory of the edge of chaos. *Proc. 3rd European Conf. On Artificial Life*. Lect. Notes in Artif. Intell. 929. Springer.

Langton C.G. 1990. Computation at the edge of chaos: phase transitions and emergent computation. *Physica D* 42: 12-27.

Mitchell M., Hraber P.T. and Crutchfield J.P. 1993. Revisiting the edge of chaos: evolving cellular automata to perform computation. *Complex Systems* 7: 89-130.

Tolmachev D. and A. Adamatzky. 1996. Chemical processor for computation of Voronoi diagram. *Adv. Mater. Opt. Electron.* 6: 191-196.

Evolving Novel Behaviors via Natural Selection

A.D. Channon and **R.I. Damper**
Image, Speech & Intelligent Systems Research Group
University of Southampton, Southampton, SO17 1BJ, UK
http://www.soton.ac.uk/~adc96r
adc96r@soton.ac.uk rid@ecs.soton.ac.uk

Abstract

The traditional fitness function based methodology of artificial evolution is argued to be inadequate for the construction of entities with behaviors novel to their designers. Evolutionary emergence via natural selection (without an explicit fitness function) is the way forward. This paper further considers the question of what to evolve, the focus being on principles of developmental modularity in neural networks. To develop and test the ideas, an artificial world containing autonomous organisms has been created and is described. Results show the developmental system to be well suited to long-term incremental evolution. Novel emergent strategies are identified both from an observer's perspective and in terms of their neural mechanisms.

How to Evolve Novel Behaviors

The Artificial Life goal presents us with the problem that we do not understand (natural) life well enough to specify it to a machine. Therefore we must either increase our understanding of it until we can, or create a system which outperforms the specifications we can give it. The first possibility includes the traditional top-down methodology, which is clearly as inappropriate for ALife as it has proved to be for AI. It also includes manual incremental (bottom-up) construction of autonomous systems with the aim of increasing our understanding and ability to model life by building increasingly impressive systems, retaining functional validity by testing them within their destination environments.

The second option is to create systems which outperform the specifications given them and which are open to producing behaviors comparable with those of (albeit simple) natural life. Evolution in nature has no (explicit) evaluation function. Through organism-environment interactions, including interactions between similarly-capable organisms, certain behaviors fare better than others. This is how the non-random cumulative selection works without any long-term goal. It is why novel structures and behaviors emerge.

As artificial evolution is applied to increasingly complex problems, the difficulty in specifying satisfactory evaluation functions is becoming apparent – see (Zaera, Cliff & Bruten 1996), for example. At the same time, the power of natural selection is being demonstrated in prototypal systems such as Tierra (Ray 1991) and PolyWorld (Yaeger 1993). Artificial selection involves the imposition of an artifice crafted for some cause external to a system beneath it while natural selection does not. Natural selection is necessary for evolutionary emergence but does not imply sustained emergence (evermore new emergent phenomena) and the question "what should we evolve?" needs to be answered with that in mind (Channon & Damper 1998). This paper sets out to answer that question. Further discussion concerning evolutionary emergence can be found in (Channon & Damper 1998), along with evaluations of other natural selection systems. Note that an explicit fitness landscape is not a requirement for artificial selection and so an implicit fitness landscape does not imply natural selection.

General issues concerning long-term evolution have been addressed by Harvey's 'Species Adaptation Genetic Algorithm' (SAGA) theory (Harvey 1993). He demonstrates that changes in genotype length should take place much more slowly than crossover's fast mixing of chromosomes. The population should be nearly-converged, evolving as species. Therefore the fitness landscape (actual or implicit) must be sufficiently correlated for mutation to be possible without dispersing the species in genotype space or hindering the assimilation by crossover of beneficial mutations into the species.

What to Evolve

Neural networks are the clear choice because of their graceful degradation (high degree of neutrality). But how should the network structure be specified? The evolutionary emergence of novel behaviors requires new neural structures. We can expect most to be descended from neural structures which once had different functions. There are many known examples of neural structures that serve a purpose different from a previous use.

Evidence from gene theory tells us that genes are used like a recipe, not a blueprint. In any one cell, at any one stage of development, only a tiny proportion of the genes will be in use. Further, the effect that a gene has depends upon the cell's local environment – its neighbors.

The above two paragraphs are related: For a type of module to be used for a novel function (and then to continue to evolve from there), without loss of current function, either an extra module must be created or there must be one 'spare' (to alter). Either way, a duplication system is required. This could be either by gene duplication or as part of a developmental process.

Gene duplication can be rejected as a sole source of neural structure duplication, because the capacity required to store all connections in a large network without a modular coding is genetically infeasible. Therefore, for the effective evolutionary emergence of complex behaviors, a modular developmental process is called for. For the sake of research validity (regarding long-term goals), this should be included from the outset.

Gruau's cellular encoding: Gruau used genetic programming (GP) (Koza 1992) to evolve his 'cellular programming language' code (Gruau 1996) to develop modular artificial neural networks. The programs used are trees of graph-rewrite rules whose main points are cell division and iteration.

The crucial shortcoming is that modularity can only come from either gene duplication (see objections above) or iteration. But iteration is not a powerful enough developmental backbone. Consider, for example, the cerebral cortex's macro-modules of hundreds of mini-columns. These are complicated structures that cannot be generated with a 'repeat one hundred times: mini-column' rule. There are variations between modules.

Cellular automata: Many investigators have used conventional cellular automata (CA) for the construction of neural networks. However, such work is more at the level of neuron growth than the development of whole networks. Although CA *rules* are suited to the evolution of network development in principle, the amount of work remaining makes this a major research hurdle.

Diffusion models: While there are a number of examples of work involving the evolution of neural networks whose development is determined by diffusion along concentration gradients, the resulting network structures have (to date) been only basic. So as to concentrate on the intended area of research, these models have also been passed over.

Lindenmayer systems: Kitano used a context-free L-system (Lindenmayer 1968) to evolve connectivity matrices (Kitano 1990). The number of rules in the genotype was variable. Boers and Kuiper used a context-sensitive L-system to evolve modular feed-forward network architectures (Boers & Kuiper 1992). Both these works used backpropagation to train the evolved networks. Also, the resulting structures were fully-connected clusters of unconnected nodes (i.e. no links within clusters and if one node in cluster A is linked to one node in cluster B then all nodes in A are linked to all in B). It may be that the results achieved reflect the workings of backpropagation more than evolution. However, these works demonstrated the suitability of L-systems to 'non-iterative modular' network development.

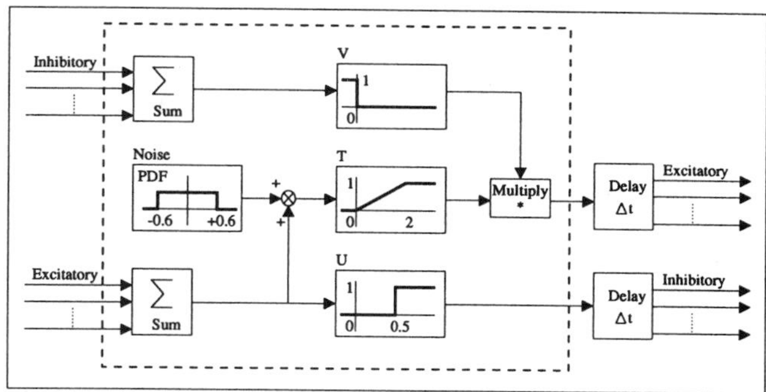

Figure 1: Schematic block diagram of a neuron, from (Cliff, Harvey & Husbands 1992).

The Neural and Development Systems

The artificial neural networks used here are recurrent networks of nodes as used successfully by Cliff, Harvey and Husbands in their evolutionary robotics work.

Developmental system: A context-free L-system was designed for the evolution of networks of these neurons. Specific attention was paid to producing a system in which children's networks resemble aspects of their parents'. Each node has a bit-string 'character' (label) associated with it, initialized at construction and modifiable during development. These characters may be of any non-zero length. A node may be a network input, a network output, or neither, as determined by an axiom (birth) network and development.

A production rule matches a node if its predecessor is the start of the node's character. The longer the matching predecessor, the better the match; the best matching rule (if any) is applied. Thus ever more specific rules can evolve from those that have already been successful.

The production rules have the following form:

$$\mathcal{P} \rightarrow \mathcal{S}_r, \mathcal{S}_n \; ; b_1, b_2, b_3, b_4, b_5, b_6 \quad \text{where:}$$

$\mathcal{P}$	Predecessor (initial bits of node's character)
$\mathcal{S}_r$	Successor 1: *replacement* node's character
$\mathcal{S}_n$	Successor 2: *new* node's character
bits:	link details [0=no,1=yes]:
(b_1, b_2)	reverse types [inhibitory/excitatory] of (input, output) links on $\mathcal{S}_n$
(b_3, b_4)	(inhibitory, excitatory) link from $\mathcal{S}_r$ to $\mathcal{S}_n$
(b_5, b_6)	(inhibitory, excitatory) link from $\mathcal{S}_n$ to $\mathcal{S}_r$

If a successor has no character (0 length) then that node is not created. Thus the predecessor node may be replaced by 0, 1 or 2 nodes. The 'replacement' successor (if it exists) is just the old (predecessor) node, with the same links but a different character. The 'new' successor (if it exists) is a new node. It inherits a copy of the old node's input links unless it has a link from the old node (b_3 or b_4). It inherits a copy of the old node's output links unless it has a link to the old node (b_5 or b_6).

New network input nodes are (only) produced from network input nodes and new network output nodes are (only) produced from network output nodes. Character-based matching of network inputs and outputs ensures that the addition or removal of nodes later in development or evolution will not damage the relationships of previously adapted network inputs and outputs.

Genetic decoding of production rules: The genetic decoding is loosely similar to that in (Boers & Kuiper 1992). For every bit of the genotype, an attempt is made to read a rule that starts on that bit. A valid rule is one that starts with 11 and has enough bits after it to complete a rule.

To read a rule, the system uses the idea of 'segments'. A segment is a bit string with its odd-numbered bits (1st, 3rd, 5th, ...) all 0. Thus the reading of a segment is as follows: read the current bit; if it is a 1 then stop; else read the next bit – this is the next information bit of the segment; now start over, keeping track of the information bits of the segment. Note that a segment can be empty (have 0 information bits).

The full procedure to (try to) read a rule begins with reading a segment for each of the predecessor, the first successor (replacement node) and the second successor (new node). Then, if possible, the six link-details bits are read. For example:

```
Genotype: 1 1 1 0 1 1 0 0 1 0 1 1 1 0 0 0 0 0
Decoding: +++ ->_1_ * _0_ * 0 1 1 1 0 0
            +++ _1_ ->_0_ * _1_ * 1 0 0 0 0 0
Rules: 1.  P   -> Sr  ,  Sn  , link bits
          any -> 1   ,  0   , 0 1 1 1 0 0
       2.         P   -> Sr  ,  Sn  , link bits
                  1   -> 0   ,  1   , 1 0 0 0 0 0
```

Experimental World

To develop and validate the above, a simple ALife system has been created. 'Geb' (after the Egyptian god of the earth) is a two-dimensional toroidal world of artificial organisms each controlled by a neural network using the developmental system above. Evolution is strictly by natural selection. There are no global system rules that delete organisms; this is under their own control.

Geb's world (figure 2) is divided into a grid of squares; usually 20 × 20 of them. No two individuals may be within the same square at any one time. This gives the organisms a 'size' and puts a limit on their number. They are otherwise free to move around the world, within and between squares. As well as a position, each organism has a forward (facing) direction, set randomly at birth. Organisms are displayed as filled arcs, the sharp points of which indicate their direction.

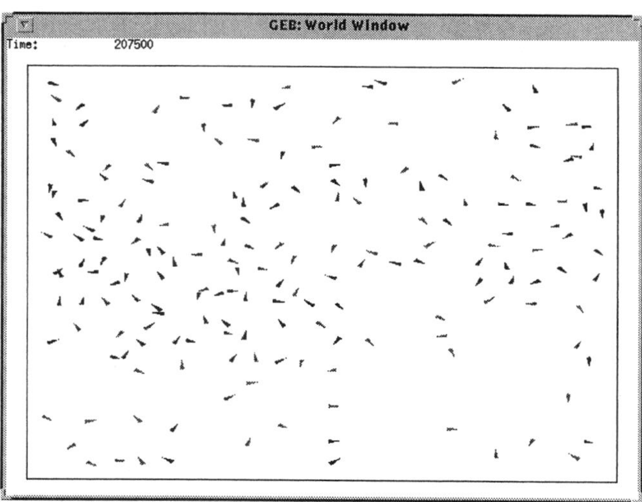

Figure 2: Geb's world.

Initialization
Every square in the world has an individual with a single-bit genotype '0' born into it.

Main Loop
In each time step (loop), every individual alive at the start of the cycle is processed once. The order in which the individuals are processed is otherwise random.
These are the steps involved for each individual:

- Network inputs are updated.
- Development – one iteration.
- Update all neural activations, including network outputs.
- Actions associated with certain network outputs are carried out according to those outputs. These actions are reproduce, fight, turn anti-clockwise, turn clockwise, and move forward.

Neural network details: The axiom network consists of three nodes with two excitatory links:

$$\text{network input } 001 \longmapsto 000 \longmapsto 01 \text{ network output}$$

The network output node's character (01) matches reproduction. The network input node's character (left input 01) matches this, without matching any of the other action characters. Finally, the hidden node's character neither matches nor is matched by the other nodes' or the action characters.

Development takes place throughout the individual's life, although necessary limits on the number of nodes and links are imposed.

Organism ⟷ environment interactions: Five built-in actions are available to each organism. Each is associated with network output nodes whose characters start with a particular bit-string:

- `01*` Try to *reproduce* with organism in front
- `100*` *Fight*: Kill organism in front (if there is one)
- `101*` *Turn anti-clockwise*
- `110*` *Turn clockwise*
- `111*` *Move forward* (if nothing in the way)

For example, if a network output node has the character 1101001, the organism will turn clockwise by an angle proportional to the node's excitatory output. If an action has more than one matching network output node then the relevant output is the sum of these nodes' excitatory outputs, bounded by unity as within any node. If an action has no output node with a matching character, then the relevant output is noise, at the same level as in the (other) nodes.

Both *reproduce* and *fight* are binary actions. They are applied if the relevant output exceeds a threshold and have no effect if the square in front is empty. *Turn* and *move forward* are done in proportion to output.

When an organism reproduces with a mate in front of it, the child is placed in the square beyond the mate if that square is empty. If it is not, the child replaces the mate. An organism cannot reproduce with an individual that is fighting if this would involve replacing that individual. Reproduction involves crossover and mutation. Geb's crossover always offsets the cut point in the second individual by one gene, with equal probability either way – which is why the genotype lengths vary. Mutation at reproduction is a single gene-flip (bit-flip).

An organism's network input nodes have their excitatory inputs set to the weighted sum of 'matching' output nodes' excitatory outputs from other individuals in the neighborhood. If the first bit of an input node's character is 1 then the node takes its input from individuals to the right hand side (including forward- and back-right), otherwise from individuals to the left. An input node 'matches' an output node if the rest of the input node's character is the same as the start of the character of the output node. For example, an input node with character 10011 matches (only) output nodes with character's starting with 0011 in the networks of individuals to the right. Weighting is inversely proportional to the Euclidean distances between individuals. Currently the input neighborhood is a 5×5 area centered on the relevant organism.

Results

Kin similarity and convergence: When two Geb organisms (with networks developed from more than just a couple of production rules each) reproduce, the child's network almost always resembles a combination of the parents' networks. Examination of networks from Geb's population at any time shows similarities between many of them. The population remains nearly-converged, in small numbers of species, throughout the evolution. The criterion of a sufficiently correlated (implicit) fitness landscape has been met by the developmental system, making it suitable for long-term evolution.

Emergence of increasing complexity: Once Geb has started, there is a short period while genotype lengths increase until capable of containing a production rule. For the next ten to twenty thousand time steps (in typical runs), networks resulting in very simple strategies such as 'do everything' and 'always go forwards and kill' dominate the population. Some networks do better than others but not sufficiently well for them to display a dominating effect.

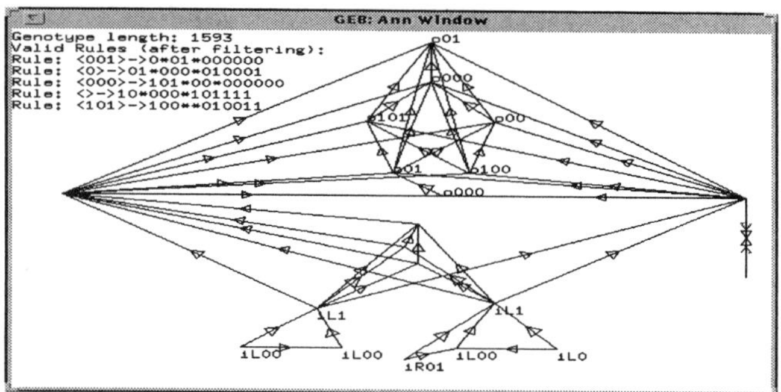

Figure 3: A dominant organism

In every run to date, the first dominant species that emerges has been one whose individuals turn in one direction while trying to fight and reproduce at the same time. Figure 3 shows an example of such an individual, after the user had dragged the nodes apart to make detailed examination possible. Note the outputs o101, o01 [x2] and o100 (turn anti-clockwise, reproduce and fight). Note also the large number of links necessary to pass from inputs to outputs, and the input characters which match non-action output characters of the same network (o000 [x2], o00). Individuals of this species use nearby members, who are also turning in circles, as sources of activation (so keeping each other going).

Although a very simple strategy, watching it in action makes its success understandable. Imagine running around in a small circle stabbing the air in front of you. Anyone trying to attack would either have to get their timing exactly right or approach in a faster spiral – both relatively advanced strategies. These individuals also mate just before killing. The offspring (normally) appear beyond the individual being killed, away from the killer's path.

Because of the success of this first dominant species, the world always has enough space for other organisms to exist. Such organisms tend not to last long; almost any movement will bring them into contact with one of the dominant organisms. Hence these organisms share some of the network morphology of the dominant species. However, they can make some progress: Individuals have emerged that are successful at turning to face the dominant species and holding their direction while trying to kill and reproduce. An example of such a 'rebel' (from the same run as figure 3) is shown in figure 4.

Running averages of the number of organisms reproducing and killing (figure 5) suggest that further species

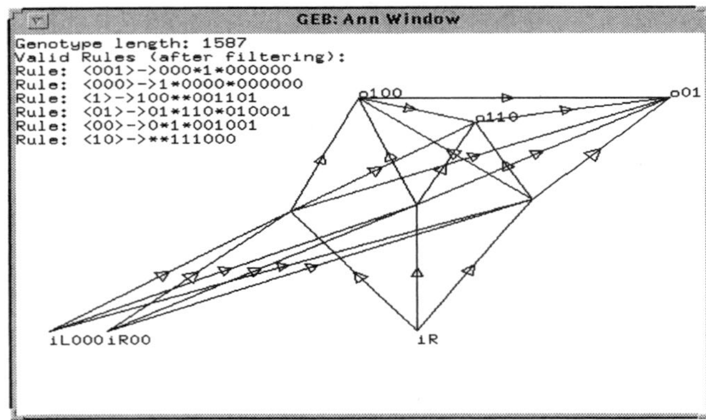

Figure 4: A rebel

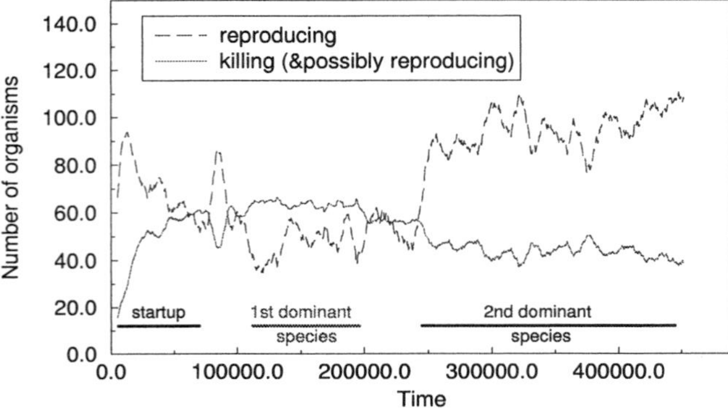

Figure 5: Typical run (running averages).

emerge. However, organisms have proved difficult to analyze beyond the above, even at the behavioral level. All that can currently be said is that they share characteristics of the previous species but are different.

Conclusions

The main conclusion is that the proposed approach is viable. Although the behaviors that emerged are very low-level, they are encouraging nonetheless, for the increases in complexity were in ways not specified by the design. It is difficult to evaluate any ongoing emergence, because of the difficulty in analyzing later organisms. Either tools to aid in such analysis will have to be constructed, or a more transparent system created.

In work involving pure natural selection, the organisms' developmental and interaction systems are analogous to the fitness functions of conventional genetic algorithms. While the general aim involves moving away from such comparisons, the analogy is useful for recognizing how the epistasis of fitness landscape issue transfers across: Certain ontogenetic and interaction systems can result in individuals with similar genotypes but very different phenotypes. The results show that Geb's developmental system does not suffer from this problem, making it suitable for long-term incremental evolution. This alone is a significant result for a modular developmental system.

This work has made it clear that the *specification* of 'actions', even at a low-level, results in the organisms being constrained around these actions and limits evolution. Alternatives in which the embodiment of organisms is linked to their actions need to be investigated.

Acknowledgements

This work is supported by an award from the United Kingdom's Engineering and Physical Sciences Research Council to author ADC. It is a continuation of previous work also supported by an award from the EPSRC (supervisor Inman Harvey, University of Sussex).

References

Boers, E. J., and Kuiper, H. 1992. Biological metaphors and the design of modular artificial neural networks. Master's thesis, Departments of Computer Science and Experimental Psychology, Leiden University.

Channon, A., and Damper, R. 1998. Perpetuating evolutionary emergence. In *Proceedings of SAB98*. MIT Press. http://www.soton.ac.uk/~adc96r/.

Cliff, D.; Harvey, I.; and Husbands, P. 1992. Incremental evolution of neural network architectures for adaptive behaviour. Technical Report CSRP256, University of Sussex School of Cognitive and Computing Sciences.

Gruau, F. 1996. Artificial cellular development in optimization and compilation. Technical report, Psychology department, Stanford University, Palo Alto, CA.

Harvey, I. 1993. Evolutionary robotics and SAGA: the case for hill crawling and tournament selection. In Langton, C. G., ed., *Artificial Life III.*

Kitano, H. 1990. Designing neural networks using genetic algorithms with graph generation system. *Complex Systems* 4:461–476.

Koza, J. R. 1992. *Genetic Programming.* Cambridge, MA: MIT Press/ Bradford Books.

Lindenmayer, A. 1968. Mathematical models for cellular interaction in development. *Journal of Theoretical Biology* 18:280–315. Parts I and II.

Ray, T. S. 1991. An approach to the synthesis of life. In Langton, C.; Taylor, C.; Farmer, J.; and Rasmussen, S., eds., *Artificial Life II*, 371–408. Redwood City, CA: Addison-Wesley.

Yaeger, L. 1993. Computational genetics, physiology, metabolism, neural systems, learning, vision, and behavior or polyworld: Life in a new context. In Langton, C. G., ed., *Artificial Life III*, 263–298.

Zaera, N.; Cliff, D.; and Bruten, J. 1996. (Not) evolving collective behaviours in synthetic fish. In Maes, P.; Mataric, M.; Meyer, J.-A.; Pollack, J.; and Wilson, S., eds., *Proceedings of SAB96*, 635–644. MIT Press Bradford Books.

Why Gliders Don't Exist: Anti-Reductionism and Emergence

Joe Faith
School of Cognitive and Computing Sciences
University of Sussex, Brighton, UK.
josephf@cogs.susx.ac.uk

Abstract

ALife has always been centrally concerned with the nature and origins of emergent phenomena and their anti-reductionist implications for our understanding of complex systems. I argue that the traditional approach to understanding emergent phenomena in physical systems is still fundamentally reductionist, and outline an anti-reductionist alternative.

Keywords: philosophy; philosophy of artificial life; anti-reductionism; emergence

Contemporary debate about emergence can only be understood as part of the much older debate about reductionism. Indeed much of the importance of, and interest in, the question of emergence in Artificial Life is because of the light that it can shed on this much wider issue.

The central point of this paper is that the usual arguments against reductionism are too weak, that they concede a crucial part of the reductionist case, and that a more radical approach is required. When we apply these arguments to the question of emergence we find that the usual models of emergent phenomena are flawed, and that an alternative is needed.

Pragmatic Anti-Reductionism

The central claim of reductionism is that if all phenomena are on every occasion physically realised, then the laws governing those phenomena are determined by, and derivable from, the laws governing their constituent parts. Does a materialist have any alternative but to accept this priority of lower level entities over those they comprise?

The usual alternative to reductionism is some form of *pragmatic anti-reductionism* which argues that although reductionism may be correct in principle, it can rarely be used in practise: it is simply not feasible to collect all the data, and perform the calculations necessary, for all but the most trivial of systems. In other words, that the properties of the whole may be *determined* by those of the parts, but it is (usually) impossible for us to *derive* them.

Basic pragmatic anti-reductionism can be strengthened in various ways. We can borrow from chaos theory and argue that aggregate properties of the system may be sensitive to some properties of a part, such as the infamous sensitivity of weather systems to a butterfly's wing. If this is the case then an accurate derivation of a higher level description would require that the properties of the parts are known with unbounded accuracy, and there are various reasons, such as the Uncertainty Principle, why this is not possible.

A pragmatic anti-reductionist can also argue that just knowing the properties of the parts is not enough to derive higher level properties; we also have to know the composition of the higher level entities that we are interested in, i.e. a set of bridging laws. Thus although the set of valid higher level descriptions may be *determined* by the lower level properties, they cannot be *discovered* or *derived* without additional knowledge. Thus we find that there is not a single case in the history of science in which a higher level scientific law or description has been derived from laws governing its constituent parts; rather such phenomena are discovered by investigation at the appropriate level and only subsequently related to lower level properties.

The problem with pragmatic anti-reductionism is that it implies that as soon as we can discover some systematic relationship between phenomena at higher and lower levels of organisation, then the status of the former is threatened. They become *potentially* reducible, or reducible *in principle.* Pragmatic anti-reductionism fails to rebut the central reductionist claim that higher properties are determined by, even whilst they may not be derivable from, the lower. Is there an alternative anti-reductionism that can?

Principled Anti-Reductionism

Let us consider the particular example of the gas laws. This is a *locus classicus* of emergent behaviour and exemplifies many of the properties found in the more complex models used in ALife. Understanding the relationship between the bulk gas laws and the collisions of individual particles was a triumph of reductionism, so hopefully by questioning this example I can cast doubt on reductionism as a whole.

The reductionist picture of how gases behave is that a property such as pressure is an intrinsic property of the gas as a whole that rises with temperature and produces a force exerted on the container wall. This latter property is supervenient upon the set of molecular momenta, each of which is a prior property, intrinsic to each molecule, and determining the course of its collisions. The pressure is then equal to, and determined by, the mean of the set of momenta of molecules in a given volume.

The pragmatic anti-reductionist would argue that we cannot measure the momentum of every single molecule in practise. However they would (probably) concede that the derivations on which statistical thermodynamics are based are theoretically sound. Therefore the pragmatic anti-reductionist must agree with reductionist that the properties of the whole gas are not only determined by, but also derivable from, those of the molecular parts in this case. Therefore the gas laws are a case in which the reductionist and pragmatic anti-reductionist agree.

However there are two key differences between the reductionist idealisation and how things work in real life.

The first is that in real life gas molecules do not behave like atomistic billiard balls, but are complex structured entities. Van der Waals forces between adjacent electron clouds mean that the molecular collisions are not perfectly elastic, but instead are slightly 'lossy', with the exact behaviour being dependent on the particular physical characteristics of the molecules, and on the velocity and direction of the collision. Indeed, as the temperature drops, the molecules can stop rebounding at all and instead form weak bonds as the gas condenses or even crystallises. The gas laws are an approximation, describing 'ideal' gases whose molecules collide perfectly elastically under all conditions. In short, the pressure of a real gas is *not* equal to its mean molecular momentum.

The second problem is that, in real life, volumes of gas are not in static, isolated, thermal equilibrium. As Feynman puts it,

> we shall find that we can derive all kinds of things–marvelous things–from the kinetic theory, and it is most interesting that we can apparently get so much from so little. ... How do we get so much out? The answer is that we have been perpetually making a certain important assumption, which is that if a system is in thermal equilibrium at some temperature, it will also be in thermal equilibrium with *anything else* at the same temperature. (Feynman 1963, p40-1)

So what happens if the system is *not* in equilibrium?[1]

[1]The study of non-equilibirum systems has been largely neglected, with the notable exception of Prigogine (1962).

The easiest way to find out is to compress it. As soon as we do this the measured pressure will rise. As we continue to push we do work in compressing the gas, and this energy diffuses through the gas and raises the mean molecular momentum per unit volume. The properties of the parts are therefore *causally dependent* on those of the wholes. The constituent molecules have the momentum that they do *because* of the pressure on the whole. The dependency only appears to run the other way when the system is static.

The purpose in these examples is not nit pick, or to criticise the classical reductionist understanding of the gas laws *per se*, but to make explicit the assumptions that it depends on. In particular it is only accurate to say that properties of parts determine those of wholes when the entire system is in a narrow range of thermal equilibria. Outside of these specific cases it is equally true to say that *the properties of parts are determined by those of the whole*, in contrast to both reductionism and pragmatic anti-reductionism. Therefore the 'upward' dependency on which reductionism depends is an artefact of how we choose to model a system, *not* a property of the system itself.

Reductionism (including pragmatic anti-reductionism) is often seen as a necessary implication of physicalism (Melnyk 1995). After all, if every object is instantiated in a set of lower-level parts, then it seems obvious and necessary that the properties of those parts will determine those of the whole. But this statement of physicalism neglects that every object is also *situated* in an overall context, and that it will only have the properties it does because of that context. The causal dependence between parts and wholes goes down, as well as up.

Emergence

Following Nagel (Nagel 1961) the relationship between levels of organisation in nature has increasingly been described in terms of emergence, and more recently the sciences of complexity and artificial life have made emergent phenomena their special area of concern. Within ALife, emergent phenomena have usually been understood in terms of what Casti and others have called *complex adaptive systems*, indeed Langton has described such systems as the "distilled essence of artificial life"(Langton 1988). Such systems start with a collection of well-defined objects each with intrinsic individual properties and governed by laws. These interact, producing an overall behaviour which is then described as emergent since it is not explicitly defined in any of the rules governing any part, but rather is the novel product of the interaction of them all. A typical example is the higher level behaviours of gliders and blinkers in Conway's Game of Life. A great deal of energy is then spent trying to define precisely what sort of higher order entities should count as emergent and which as reducible, usually by trying to pin down the intuitive notions of "explicit" or "novel".

Understood this way, emergent phenomena fit a category-theoretic commutativity diagram:

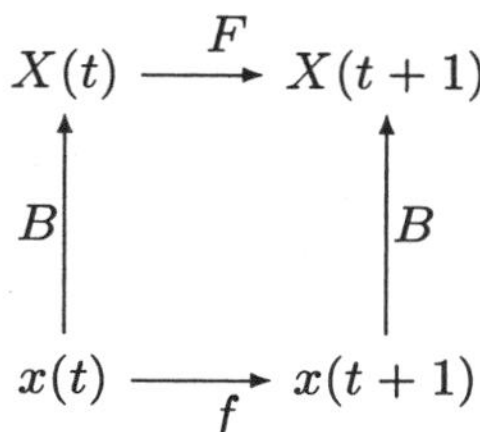

in which the states of the lower and upper levels are described by $x(t)$ and $X(t)$ respectively, the trajectory of the lower level is described by the state equation $x(t+1) = f(x(t))$, the upper by $X(t+1) = F(X(t))$, and the synchronic bridging law describing the composition of the higher entities in terms of the lower by $X(t) = B(x(t))$. In some cases, such as Life, the lower state equation is exact, quantitative and deterministic, whereas the higher level rules, such as "eaters tend to destroy blinkers", are statistical and qualitative. In other cases, such as the model of an ideal gas used to derive the gas laws, the higher will also be exact.

The commutativity of the diagram is ensured by the fact that F is determined by B and f, since it is that mapping that satisfies $FB = Bf$–though F will only be formally derivable if B is invertible. In other words, if there are a set of laws governing the behaviour of the objects at the lower level then, given the composition of an aggregate, the behaviour of that aggregate is determined. Therefore higher-level behaviours produced in this way can *never* count as truly emergent, but rather are determined by the properties of the atomistic objects. Many aspects of the higher behaviour may not be analytically derivable from those of the parts, and must be discovered through empirical computer experiments; but this is just a failure of our analysis and does not mean that they are not determined by the lower properties. Such higher level behaviours are emergent in only an epistemic sense; only for a pragmatist, such as Dennett, will they also be ontologically emergent (Dennett 1991).

I do not wish to make this a terminological dispute: if we wish to describe phenomena such as gliders as emergent, then so be it. However, in this case we can no longer associate *emergent* with *non-reducible*, and if we want to be anti-reductionist about physical phenomena, then we have to find a different way of understanding them than emergence as it is traditionally used. Also note that this is not a criticism of the study of systems such as Life *per se*; after all they are a fascinating class of formal system, and can give us clues about the origins of much natural pattern and order. The problem comes when they are used as the sole intuition pump and model for understanding emergence, reductionism, and the relationship between levels of organisation in natural systems. But what is the alternative?

Consider this example. Every cell in an organism carries exactly the same genome as every other. However in, say, a mammal, there will be around 300 different types of cells–blood cells, hair cells, liver cells, and so on–depending on which genes are expressed. When a new cell is produced, why does it become one type of cell rather than another? There are two sorts of answer. The first points to the particular biochemical mechanisms in the new cell's environment that caused particular genes to switch on. The second identifies the cause at a higher level: a cell becomes a liver cell because it is born in a liver, and so on. Both of these stories are correct. There is no conflict between them and which one we choose to tell depends on what aspects of development we want to understand. The latter explains how the body maintains a stable overall structure despite individual cell death. The former explains how this is achieved in a particular case. The lower level story is not 'more right' than the higher, and nor is the higher assymetrically dependent on the latter. The reductionist intuition is to say that given the range of biomolecular mechanisms, then the effects of the liver context are fixed. But this misses the fact that if it were not for the presence of the entire liver, then those mechanisms would not be produced in the first place. Indeed it was precisely the problem of restoring the totipotency of differentiated cells–and so neutralising the effect of the context upon them–that made the cloning of adult mammals seemingly impossible. Even now that it has been done with a particular group of cells taken from the udder of a sheep we still have very little idea of how the process works, how to make it reliable, or whether the technique will generalise to cells taken from other contexts.

In the case of Life, the rules governing the fate of a cell are written in lower level terms such as "a cell will not survive into the next generation if it has no neighbours". In practise the fate of a particular cell will be instrumentally dependent on its context, but this dependence is derived from the more fundamental dependence expressed in formal atomistic terms. In other words, the fate of a particular cell will be dependent on its position within a glider or blinker, but only because the future state of a cell is a function of the number of neighbours that it has, and gliders and blinkers are made from different arrangements of cells. The future of a cell is not affected by its position within a glider *qua* glider.

In general the reductionist approach is to start with a set of deterministic laws governing the atoms of the system expressed as functions of atomistic properties. We can then derive–if not formally then at least empirically–qualitative, statistical, rules governing higher level objects expressed only in terms of higher level properties. However, if we accept that these latter rules are real, then we should also accept that distal rules that describe the fate of cells in terms of the properties that they are part of, are also real. For example "a cell that is part of a blinker will tend to go into the reverse state in the next generation", "a cell that is part of an aggregate that is attacked by an eater will soon die" (or "cells born in livers become liver cells"). These downward rules, which attribute the cause of the fate of the part to the properties of the whole, may be qualitative and non-deterministic, but no more so than the derived higher level rules that we all wish to defend; and they should be accorded the same status.

In the case of physical systems we are not presented with a set of laws, but with a set of empirical regularities: the job of the scientist is then to find accurate ways to describe and account for those regularities in descriptive laws. If we want to describe a physical system in such a way that preserves the non-reducible and non-eliminable nature of its emergent phenomena we should therefore include three sorts of laws: atomistic laws that describe the interactions of parts; 'bridging' laws that describe the composition of higher order entities in terms of their parts; *and* 'downwards' laws that describe how properties of those entities act as contexts to affect their parts.

We also need to be careful how we individuate the parts, as this too can be dependent on the context. In Life, for example, 'a cell' usually refers to a value ascribed to a fixed coordinate position; 'the fate of a cell' then refers to what happens at that position in the future. However we could also refer to a cell by reference to the higher order object that it is part of. For example, we could refer to 'the cell' at the nose of a glider even as it traverses the grid, occupying a series of positions. If we individuate the parts of the system in this way–a way which is irreducibly dependent on prior individuation of higher level objects–then a whole new type of order is revealled. The fixed coordinate positions only seem like the 'real' cells compared with the 'virtual' mobile ones because of the way the formal system is defined. In nature there are no such given formal rules.

Conclusion

The starting-point of reductionism is that wholes are dependent on parts, but not *vice versa.* This assumption is also carried over into traditional models of emergent phenomena, such as the Game of Life. Pragmatic anti-reductionism agrees with this starting point but denies some of the implications that a reductionist draws, such that there are higher properties and behaviours of a system that cannot be analytically derived from those of the parts.

A more principled anti-reductionism holds that properties are held by objects in, and because of, their context; which implies that the dependence relation between levels of organisation is symmetrical. According to this reductionism is not just wrong in practise, but wrong in principle.

New assumptions about the relationship between levels of organisation in nature require new models to describe them. Therefore if we want to understand emergent phenomena in nature, then we will need models in which ontological symmetry between levels is built into their formal definition.

Acknowledgement

Thanks to members of the E-Intentionality discussion group at the University of Sussex for comments on an earlier draft of this paper.

References

Dennett, D. 1991. Real patterns. *The Journal of Philosophy* 88(3): 27–51.

Feynman, R. 1963. *The Feynman Lectures on Physics,* Volume 1. Reading, MA: Addison Wesley.

Langton, C., ed. 1988. *Artificial Life: Proceedings of the workshop on artificial life,* Santa Fe Institute studies in the sciences of complexity. Redwood City, CA: Addison-Wesley.

Melnyk, A. 1995. Two cheers for reductionism: or, the dim prospects for non-reductive materialism. *Philosophy of Science* 62:370–388.

Nagel, E. 1961. *The Structure of Science.* New York: Harcourt, Brace & World.

Prigogine, I. 1962. *Non-Equilibrium Statistical Mechanics.* New York: Interscience Publishers.

Artificial Evolution of Visually Guided Foraging Behaviour

Ben Hutt and Dave Keating

Department of Cybernetics,
The University of Reading, Whiteknights,
PO Box 225, Reading, RG6 6AY, UK.
B.D.Hutt@rdg.ac.uk & D.A.Keating@rdg.ac.uk

Abstract

A population of visually guided agents has been evolved to forage for food pellets using an extended genetic algorithm. Each agent is equipped with an artificial neural network that controls its behaviour and a simple eye that provides input from the environment. The genetic algorithm is responsible for the positioning of light sensitive cells on the retina of the eye and also the design of the neural network. This includes the number, size and sensitivity of the light sensitive cells and also the number of neurons, connectivity and weights contained within the neural network. The system produces complicated and highly recurrent neural network controlled agents that can successfully forage for food pellets.

Introduction

Many organisms in the natural world exhibit complex visually guided behaviours, these systems have not been designed but have arisen over many millions of years throughout the course of biological evolution. Creatures with simple visual and nervous systems have given rise to creatures with more sophisticated visual and nervous systems. Although it is difficult to see exactly how these systems have evolved it is apparent that these systems must have evolved together in order to produce viable visually guided behaviours (Reynolds 1994).

Classically, AI vision systems have used high bandwidth images consisting of many hundreds of thousands of pixels. Such systems are difficult to design, as it is not always obvious how to translate the visual information into the desired behaviour. We therefore advocate using an incremental evolutionary approach to develop simple visual systems as in Cliff, Husbands and Harvey (1993). Instead of starting with high bandwidth vision systems each agent starts life with only a very simple visual system and controlling neural network. As evolution proceeds the neural networks and visual systems co-evolve and can become more complex until the agents reach a sufficient level of proficiency. It is also possible that agents may become less complex and still become better at the given task. In this way, it is the complexity of the task that dictates the complexity of the visual system and the size of the neural network required.

Foraging Task

In the experiments, described below, we evolve a population of visually guided fish-like agents whose task is to collect as many food pellets as possible from their aquatic environment. Each agent in the population must evolve to be able to gather relevant visual information from the environment and suitably co-ordinate its behaviour in order to collect food pellets. Each agent receives sensory input from the environment through a single 180 degree field of vision eye. An internal neural network processes this visual information in order to control two side-mounted thrusters with which an agent is able to propel itself through the environment. A simple schematic of an agent within the environment is shown in Figure 1.

The environment consists of a shallow pond containing agents that are free to roam about and collect food pellets. This is effectively a 2-D plane within which all objects are subject to viscous damping. Collisions between an agent and a food pellet cause the agent to pick up and 'eat' that food pellet. Every time an agent eats a food pellet, a new food pellet is placed at a random location in the pond, this prevents the agents from consuming all the food pellets in the environment, leaving room for agents to improve their foraging behaviour.

For the purposes of agent vision all objects in the environment, including other agents, are considered to be circular. Objects are rendered in order of distance so that closer objects obscure more distant ones. The intensity of the object to be rendered is determined by an inverse square relationship to range. The size and position of the region of retina illuminated by the object is dependent on the apparent angle and angular width of the object.

Genetic Representation

In order to evolve agents in an incremental and open-ended manner, the representation must be able to specify both simple and complex visual and neural structures, such that the evolutionary process can gradually build up these structures so as to produce the desired behaviour.

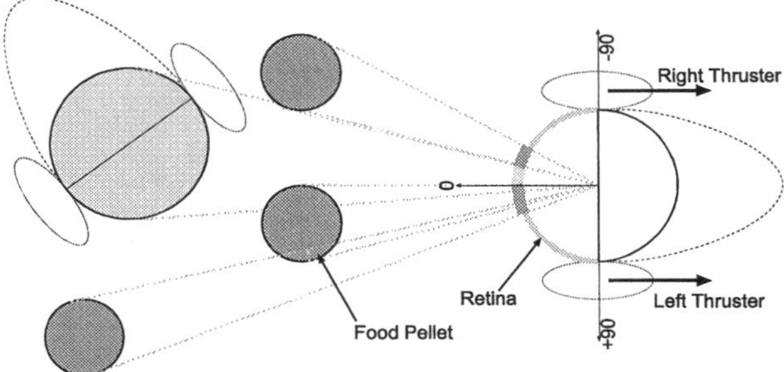

Figure 1: *Agents propel themselves through the environment using two side mounted thrusters, all objects in the environment are considered to be circular for the purposes of agent vision and are projected onto each agents retina.*

Visual morphologies

The image mapped onto the retina is sub sampled by a number of light sensitive cells, whose size, position and sensitivity are determined by the agents' genotype (Harvey, Husbands and Cliff 1994). Each cell calculates the mean intensity of red, green and blue light falling on it and returns a weighted sum as the input to its associated neuron. The structure of a light sensitive cell definition is shown below.

Cell definition:

<expressed><position><size><Rs,Gs,Bs>

where:

expressed	-controls gene expression i.e. gene on/off
position	-position of cell on retina
size	-size of cell
Rs,Gs,Bs	-weights controlling sensitivity of cell to red, green and blue light respectively.

Neural networks

The neural networks that control the behaviour of each agent are effectively 'hard wired', since the morphology and weights of the network do not change during the lifetime of an agent. Each neuron in the network calculates a weighted sum of its inputs and subjects this to a standard sigmoid function. The output of a neuron is thus given by:

$$o_i(t) = sig\left(\sum_{j=1}^{N} o_j(t-1).w_{j,i} + s_i(t) + b_i \right)$$

where:

$o_i(t)$ is the output of neuron i at time t.
$w_{j,i}$ is the weight that connects the output of neuron j to the input of neuron i.
$s_i(t)$ is a possible external input into neuron i from a light sensitive cell.
b_i is the bias (effectively a weight connected to a permanently active neuron) of neuron i.
The function $sig(x)$ is a standard sigmoid function given by:

$$sig(x) = \frac{1}{1+e^{-x}}$$

Connections are made in these networks by matching key values of weights with the key values of neurons, a connection being made to the neuron with the closest key value. This is done using a similar method to that of Fullmer and Miikkulainen (1991). The structure of a neuron definition is shown below.

Neuron definition:

<key><bias><w_0,k_0><w_1,k_1>...<w_n,k_n>

where:

key	-Node identification value used in making connections.
bias	-is the bias of the node.
$\mathbf{w_i}$	-specifies the weight of a connection.
$\mathbf{k_i}$	-specifies the target of the connection. The connection will be made to the node whose key value is closest to this value.

Overall representation

The genetic representation used consists of a variable number of chromosomes, each of which is allowed to change in length. Each chromosome consists of a string of real valued numbers and specifies a neuron, its output connections and an associated light sensitive cell that may provide input to that neuron.

Extending the Genetic Algorithm

In order to evolve agents in a truly incremental manner, it is necessary to make several modifications to the standard genetic algorithm. Our implementation borrows many ideas from Harvey's SAGA (Species adaption genetic algorithms) artificial evolution techniques, more information can be found in Harvey (1992a).

Similarities to a standard GA

The general principles underlying SAGA are much the same as those of a standard GA. Potential solutions to a problem are encoded on strings of data called *chromosomes*, this encoded version of a solution is referred to as the *genotype*. A genetic algorithm operates on a legion of genotypes, the *population*, containing numerous potential solutions to a problem. Each genotype in the population is initialised with random data and the algorithm begins its main loop. First, each genotype is decoded into the actual solution to the problem, the *phenotype*, in our case this is a specific visual morphology and neural network. The phenotype is then evaluated to see how well it solves the problem and is assigned a *fitness*, as defined by some objective function, a *fitness function*, that defines the problem to be solved. Once all members have been evaluated and assigned a fitness, those genotypes in the population with the best fitness scores are randomly selected to be recombined in order to form a new population. Small random changes or mutations may also modify the genotypes of the new population members. Each iteration of this loop is referred to as a *generation*. The basic idea of a GA is that genotypes that led to good phenotypes in previous generations can be recombined and modified in order to produce new and hopefully better phenotypes in subsequent generations. A good introduction to standard genetic algorithms is Goldberg (1989).

Differences from a standard GA

Whilst SAGA is very similar in concept to a standard GA it also contains some important differences. A standard GA operates in a search space of fixed dimensionality, whereas SAGA also allows for the dimensionality of the search space to change, as evolution proceeds. This allows the complexity of a solution to change dependent on the fitness function. It is worth noting that SAGA may increase or decrease the size of a genotype in order to increase fitness.

In a standard GA, measures are normally taken to prevent or slow convergence of the population, however SAGA searches problem spaces with a relatively converged homogenous population or species. In the case of the evolution of cognitive structures there is often no simple correlation between the genotype and the behaviour of the phenotype. It is therefore argued in Harvey (1993) that it is only when a population is nearly converged that recombination is likely to be beneficial.

Recombination

In our implementation recombination is performed in a rather different fashion to that advocated in Harvey (1992b). However, the basic underlying concept is the same, namely that like genes are exchanged with like genes in order to produce viable offspring with a full complement of genes. In our implementation the genotype consists of a variable number of variable length chromosomes that together specify a complete visual morphology and neural network. Recombination is achieved by matching the homogenous chromosomes from both parents and allowing crossover only within matching genes.

Mutation

After recombination, the offspring may undergo a mutation, this may take the form of a point mutation or of a more radical type that causes entire chromosomes to be deleted from or inserted into the genotype. In the case of point mutation a small random gaussian number is added to one of the real numbers that constitute the genotype. On average one such point mutation will occur every time a new genotype is generated through recombination.

More radical mutations that add or remove entire genes from the Genotype are much less likely, each gene in the genotype stands a small probability of being removed or replicated.

Multiple species evolution

SAGA typically has a single focus around which members of the population search. Such a population will follow a single line of descent, unlike the branching structures produced by biological evolution.

In a multimodal search space, peaks can be thought of as niches, capable of supporting a certain number of individuals from the population. Each peak is then populated according to its fitness relative to other niches within the population. The number of individuals found within any niche reflect the amount of computational effort the GA is currently spending attempting to improve that niche. This is known as niche proportional selection.

One method of niche formation is sharing, first introduced by Holland (1975) and extended by Goldberg and Richardson (1987). Fitness sharing causes similar individuals to share fitness with each other. Sharing reduces the fitness of members of the population that have a high degree of similarity to others in the population, this effectively rewards those members of the population that are able to exploit unique areas of a search space. Sharing creates a selection pressure that acts to increase population diversity and also causes members of the population to focus on local optima. Such a population will be fairly diverse, however it will be relatively converged within each niche, thus the individuals within each niche constitute a separate species. To prevent recombination of very different species, which would be likely to generate unviable offspring, a breeding restriction scheme is also implemented that makes it improbable for dissimilar genotypes to be recombined, whereas similar genotypes stand a high probability of recombination.

The genetic algorithm evolves several different species concurrently, these different species can be thought of as different *prototype* solutions, those prototypes which seem more promising (according to the fitness function) will have more members of the population searching that particular species' niche, attempting to modify and improve the species. Poorly performing species, that are unable to be improved will eventually become extinct as population resources are allocated to better performing species.

Overall strategy

The selection scheme used is tournament selection with a tournament size of 2. This provides a uniform, weak, selection pressure across the population.

The fitness function consists of two parts. The first term relates to the task at hand, i.e., picking up as many food pellets as possible within the 3 minutes of simulated time. The second term penalises genotypes that do not perform as well as smaller genotypes, this controls the growth of genotypes and causes the algorithm to optimise neural networks for efficiency. Without this term genotype lengths were found to increase uncontrollably. It is only significant within a converged species, as within a species N_i will be approximately equal.

The fitness function is given by:

$$F_i = N_i - \frac{L_i}{\max(L)}$$

where:

N_i is the number of food pellets consumed by agent i during its lifetime. This is always a whole number.
L_i is the length of genotype of agent i.
$\max(L)$ is the longest genotype in the population.

Evolved Systems

Behaviours

The simulation was allowed to run for 500 generations, with a population of 100 agents. The resulting evolved behaviours are dependent on the dynamics of the agents and the environment containing them. Namely the maximum force produced by the thrusters, the viscosity of the fluid and the density of food within the environment.

Two types of efficient foraging behaviours were evolved. The first type of behaviour causes an agent to move fairly slowly through the environment, this allows an agent the time to turn towards and collect any food pellets that may be within its visual field. This will often involve stopping and changing direction in order to acquire a food pellet.

The second type of behaviour causes an agent to move through its environment rapidly, agents will not stop in order to eat food pellets, and they will attempt only to steer towards a food pellet, without slowing down significantly. This behaviour is viable since an agent will be likely to encounter another food pellet which it can easily collect in less time than it would take to stop, turn and collect a pellet that is off course.

Evolved structures

An example of an evolved visual morphology and neural network is shown in Figure 2; the network has been simplified by pruning weak connections. As can be seen, the network is complicated and has many recurrent connections. It is fairly easy to see how feed-forward connections specify certain aspects of the observed

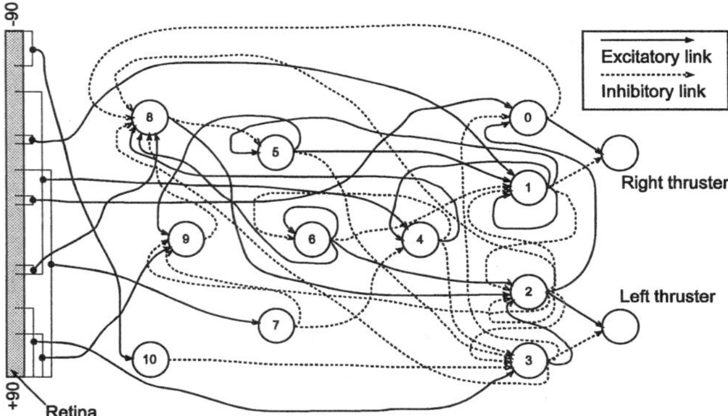

Figure 2: Evolved neural network and visual morphology. Light sensitive cell sample positions and widths are shown by square brackets.

behaviour, the small light sensitive cells at the edges of the retina cause turning behaviour. The cell at the right edge of the retina excites node 10, which in turn inhibits node 3, which causes the left thruster to increase its thrust, turning the agent to the right. In addition a direct excitatory connection from the left of the retina is connected to node 3, this causes the left thruster to decrease its thrust, turning the agent towards the left. Connections between the output nodes cause the agent to steer more effectively.

Within sections of the network that contain many recurrent connections, however it soon becomes very difficult to work out exactly how the observed behaviours are generated. This is because feedback due to recurrent connections causes time delays, so the network must be considered as a dynamic system that interacts with the environment (Beer 1996). The structure of such a control network is only likely to make sense within the context of the agents environment.

Genotype lengths

As can be see from Figure 3, the mean genotype length stays fairly constant for the majority of the time, and never drops below a lower limit; genotypes below this value are unviable.

The large spike that occurs at generation 300 is due to the emergence of a new neutral species with a longer genotype, as can be seen it is accompanied by a large increase in population diversity. Since there is no noticeable increase in the mean fitness of the population, this strongly indicates that this is a result of a neutral recombination where the genotypes of two individuals were fused together. The redundant sections of this longer genotype are quickly removed by the action of the optimising criterion in the fitness function.

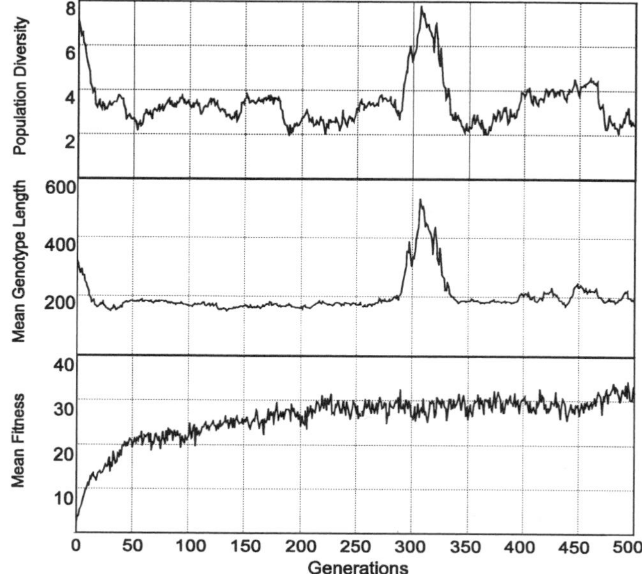

Figure 3: Evolution of mean fitness, mean genotype length, and population diversity.

Discussion

The experiments successfully evolved some simple visually guided behaviour. The same two basic strategies were evolved in successive simulation runs, an example of convergent evolution. The networks generating these similar behaviours were, however, very different.

Reasonable visually guided behaviours can be evolved in a relatively small number of generations. This opens up the possibility of evolving real world, visually guided, autonomous robots. This will be a topic of future research, we intend the robots to have real hardware analogue neural networks rather than an on board microprocessor.

Future work will also focus on predator prey co-evolutionary systems in order to evolve more interesting and complex visually guided behaviours.

References

Beer, R. 1996. Toward the evolution of dynamical neural networks for minimally cognitive behavior. In *Proceedings of the fourth International Conference on Simulation of Adaptive Behaviour (SAB96),* edited by P. Maes, M. Mataric, J. Meyer, J. Pollack and S. Wilson. Cambridge, MA: MIT Press - Bradford Books, p. 421-429.

Cliff, D., P. Husbands, and I. Harvey. 1993. Evolving visually guided robots. In *Proceedings of the Second International Conference on Simulation of Adaptive Behaviour (SAB92)*, edited by J. Meyer, H. Roitblat and S. Wilson. Cambridge, MA: MIT Press-Bradford Books, p. 374-383

Fullmer, B., and R. Miikkulainen. 1991. Using marker-based genetic encoding of neural networks to evolve finite-state behaviour. In *Towards a Practice of Autonomous Systems: Proceedings of the First European Conference on Artificial Life (ECAL91),* edited by F.J. Varela and P. Bourgine. Cambridge, MA: MIT Press - Bradford Books.

Goldberg, D., and J. Richardson. 1987. Genetic algorithms with sharing for multimodal function optimization. In *Proceedings of the Second International Conference on Genetic Algorithms*, edited by J. J. Grefenstette. Hillsdale, NJ: Lawrence Erlbaum Associates, p. 41-49.

Goldberg, D. 1989. *Genetic Algorithms in Search, Optimization, and Machine Learning.* Addison Wesley.

Harvey, I. 1992a. Species adaption genetic algorithms: A basis for a continuing SAGA. In *Towards a Practice of Autonomous Systems: Proceedings of the First European Conference on Artificial Life (ECAL91),* edited by F.J. Varela and P. Bourgine. Cambridge, MA: MIT Press - Bradford Books, p. 346-354

Harvey, I. 1992b. The SAGA cross: The mechanics of crossover for variable-length genetic algorithms. In *Parallel Problem Solving From Nature 2*, edited by R. Manner and B. Manderick, North Holland, p. 269-278.

Harvey, I. 1993. Evolutionary robotics and SAGA: the case for hill crawling and tournament selection. In *Proceedings of Artificial Life III*, Santa Fe Institute Studies in the Sciences of Complexity, edited by C. G. Langton. Redwood, CA: Addison-Wesley.

Harvey, I., P. Husbands, and D. Cliff. 1994. Seeing the light: Artificial evolution, real vision. In *Proceedings of the Third International Conference On Simulation of Adaptive Behaviours (SAB94),* edited by D. Cliff, P. Husbands, J. Meyer and S. Wilson. Cambridge, MA: MIT Press - Bradford Books, p. 392-401.

Holland, J. 1975. *Adaption in Natural and Artificial Systems.* Ann Arbor: University of Michigan Press.

Reynolds, C. 1993. An evolved, vision-based model of obstacle avoidance behaviour. In *Proceedings of Artificial Life III*, Santa Fe Institute Studies in the Sciences of Complexity, edited by C. G. Langton. Redwood, CA: Addison Wesley, p. 327-346.

Emergent Phenomena in a Foreign Exchange Market: Analysis Based on an Artificial Market Approach

Kiyoshi Izumi and **Kazuhiro Ueda**
Graduate School of Arts and Sciences, University of Tokyo
3-8-1 Komaba, Meguro-ku, Tokyo 153-8902, JAPAN
Fax: +81 3 3465 2896, E-mail: kiyoshi@game.c.u-tokyo.ac.jp

Abstract

In this study we propose an artificial market approach, which is a new agent-based approach to foreign exchange market studies. Using this approach, emergent phenomena of markets were explained. This approach consists of fieldwork, construction of a multi-agent model, and computer simulation of a market. The simulation results show that the emergent phenomena can be explained by a phase transition of forecast variety. This approach therefore integrates fieldwork and a multi-agent model, and provides a quantitative explanation of micro-macro relations in markets.

Introduction

Recently, large economic changes have brought to our attention the behavioral aspects of economic phenomena. One example is that large fluctuations in exchange rates are said to be mainly caused by 'bandwagon expectations'[1]. This fact shows that an exchange market has the features of multi-agent systems: autonomous agents, interaction, and emergence.

These features are related to the micro-macro problem in economics. Most conventional market models in economics, however, ignore the multi-agent features by assuming a Rational Expectations Hypothesis (REH). REH assumes that all agents are homogeneous and forbids essential differences of agents' forecasts. Recently, this assumption has been criticized and the multi-agent features have been said to be important for analysis of the micro-macro relation in markets.

Among several alternative approaches, there are *multi-agent* models. These model the market with artificial adaptive agents and conduct computer simulations. There are, however, two problems in the multi-agent models constructed up to now. First, they do not reflect the results of fieldwork studies about behavioral aspects of agents. Second, they do not use actual data series about economic fundamentals and political news. They can not, therefore, investigate the actual exchange rate dynamics quantitatively.

[1]The word "bandwagon" here means that many agents in a market ride along with the recent trend.

The purpose of this study is to propose a new agent-based approach of foreign exchange market studies, an *artificial market approach.* This approach integrates fieldwork and multi-agent models in order to provide a quantitative explanation of the micro and macro relation in markets.

Framework of the Artificial Market Approach

The artificial market approach is divided into three steps. First, *fieldwork;* field data of actual dealers' behavior are gathered by interviews. As a result of analysis, hypotheses are proposed about the dealers' behavioral pattern. Second, *construction of a multi-agent model;* a multi-agent model of the market is implemented based on these hypotheses. The model provides linkage between the behavioral pattern of agents at the micro level and the rate dynamics at the macro level. Third, *analysis of emergent phenomena;* in order to evaluate the model, we conduct simulations using actual data of economic fundamentals. Based on the simulation results, we verify whether the model can explain emergent phenomena of an actual market.

This approach has two advantages over previous studies. First, a multi-agent model in this approach reflects the results of fieldwork, because the model is constructed on the basis of observations of dealers' behavior, and because actual data about economic fundamentals and news are used in the simulation. Next, the model is evaluated at both the micro and macro level. At the micro level, the behavioral patterns of agents in the model are compared with those of the actual dealers in the field data. At the macro level, it is verified whether the model can simulate the emergent phenomena of rate dynamics in the real world. These advantages of the artificial market approach are necessary for a quantitative analysis of the micro-macro relation the actual markets.

Fieldwork

We observed the actual dealers' behavior by interviews and proposed a hypothesis of dealers' learning, which is used in the construction of the multi-agent model.

Interview Methods We held interviews with two dealers who usually engaged in yen-dollar exchange transactions in Tokyo foreign exchange market. We asked each dealer to do the following with respect to the rate dynamics from January 1994 to November 1995: To divide these two years into several periods according to their recognition of the market situations, to talk about which factors they regarded as important in their rate forecasts in each period, to rank the factors in order of weight (importance), and to explain the reasons for their ranking. When they changed the ranking between periods, to explain the reasons for the reconsideration.

Results From the interview data, we found three basic features in the acquisition of prediction methods in the market. First, there are fashions in the interpretation of factors in the markets, which are called *market consensus.* Second, the dealers communicated with other dealers to infer a new market consensus, and replaced (part of) their prediction method with that of other dealers which better explained recent rate dynamics, when switching prediction method. Finally, large differences between forecasts and actual rates promoted a change of each dealer's opinion. For example, in July 1995, when the rate reached the level of 92 yen, one dealer suddenly recognized that the trend had changed. He then discarded his old opinions about factors and adopted new opinions.

From the above features, we propose the following hypothesis at the micro level in markets. *When the forecasts based on a dealer's own opinion markedly differs from the actual rates, each dealer replaces (part of) their opinions about factors with other dealers' successful opinions.* This hypothesis implies that the learning pattern of actual dealers is similar to the adaptation in ecosystem. In our multi-agent model, the adaptation of agents in the market will be described with genetic algorithm, which based on ideas of population genetics.

Construction of a Multi-agent Model

Using weekly actual data, the proposed model iteratively executes the five steps (Fig.1 and Fig.2).

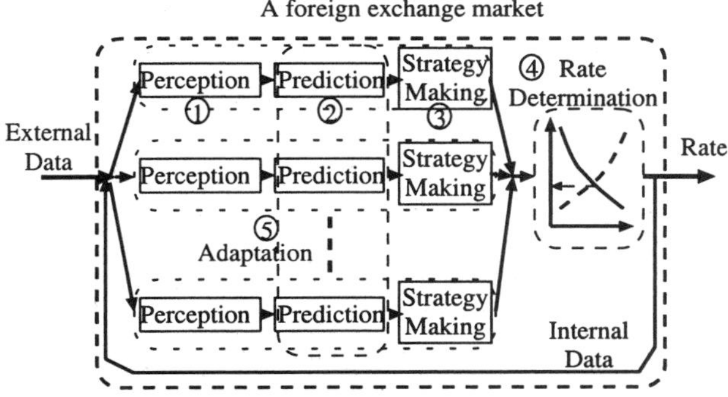

Figure 1: Framework of model.

STEP 1: Perception Each agent first interprets raw data and perceives news about factors affecting the yen-dollar exchange rate. The news data are made by coding the weekly change in 17 data streams[2]. Those values range discretely from -3 to $+3$[3]. *External data* are defined as the data of economic fundamentals or political news (No.1-14). *Internal data* are defined as data of short-term or long-term trends of the chart (No.15-17).

STEP 2: Prediction Each agent has his own weights of the 17 data, whose values range among nine discrete values $\{\pm3, \pm1, \pm0.5, \pm0.1, 0\}$. After receiving the data, each agent predicts the rate fluctuation of the coming week by using the weighted average of the news data in this week as well as equations (1) and (2) in Fig. 2.

STEP 3: Strategy Making Each agent has dollar assets and yen assets. Each agent decides, on the basis of his or her own prediction, the trading strategy (order to buy or sell dollar) according to Equations (3), (4), and (5) in Fig. 2. The trader then maximizes his negative exponential utility function[4] of his expected return of the following week.

STEP 4: Rate Determination After the submission of orders, the demand (resp., supply) curve is made by the aggregation of orders of all agents who want to buy (resp., sell). The demand and supply then determine the equilibrium rate, where supply and demand just balance.

STEP 5: Adaptation In our model, different agents have different prediction methods (combinations of weights). After the rate determination, each agent improves his prediction method using other agents' predictions. Our model uses GAs to describe the interaction between agents in learning.

A chromosome is a string of all weights of one agent, that is, the trader's prediction method. The fitness value reflects the forecast accuracy of each prediction method as per Equation (7) in Fig. 2. Our model is based on Goldberg's simple GA[5]. The selection operator is economically interpreted as the propagation of successful prediction methods. The crossover operator works like the agent's communication with other agents, and the mutation operator works like independent changes of each agent's prediction method.

[2]The 17 data are 1. Economic activities, 2. Price, 3. Interest rates, 4. Money supply, 5. Trade, 6. Employment, 7. Consumption, 8. Intervention, 9. Announcement, 10. Mark, 11. Oil, 12. Politics, 13. Stock, 14. Bond, 15. Short-term Trend 1 (Change in the last week), 16. Short-term Trend 2 (Change of short-term Trend 1), and 17. Long-term Trend (Change through five weeks).

[3]Plus (minus) values indicate that the data change causes dollar depreciation (appreciation) according to traditional economic theories.

[4]Equation (3) is calculated by using this function.

[5]The percentage of selection is called the *generation gap*, G. A single-point crossover (mutation) operation occurs with probabilities p_{cross} (p_{mut}).

Example (Week t, Logarithm of last week's rate = 5.20)

STEP 1: Perception

This week's news data (common to all agents).

Interest	Trade	Stock	Trend
++	−	− − −	++

STEP 2: Prediction

Agents **i**'s weights.

+0.5	−0.5	+0.1	+3.0

Agent **i**'s forecast:

Mean = trunc{$\sum$(Weight × News)} × scale ...(1)

=trunc{(+2)×(+0.5)+(−1)×(−1.0)+(−3)×(+0.1)+(+2)×(+3.0)}×0.02 = +7×0.02 = **+0.14** ← Rise from 5.20

$\textbf{Variance}^{-1}$ =

$$\sqrt{\{\sum(\text{Weight} \times \text{News} > 0)\}^2 - \{\sum(\text{Weight} \times \text{News} < 0)\}^2} \quad ...(2)$$

$$= \sqrt{\{2 \times +0.5 + (-1) \times (-1.0) + 3 \times 2.0\}^2 - \{-2 \times 0.1\}^2}$$

= **8.00**

STEP 3: Strategy Making

Optimal amount of agent **i**'s dollar asset

= (Forecast mean) / (Forecast variance) ...(3)

= +0.14× 8.00 = +1.12

Agent **i**'s order quantity

= (Optimal amount) − (Last week's amount) ...(4)

= +1.12 − (−0.74) = +1.86 (Buy)

(+ : Order to buy, − : Order to sell.)

Agent **i**'s strategy

$$= \begin{cases} 1.86 \text{ (Buy)} & \text{(If rate} \leq +0.14) \\ \text{No Action} & \text{(If rate} > +0.14) \end{cases} \quad ...(5)$$

Each agent orders to buy (resp., sell) when the rate is lower (resp., higher) than his forecast mean.

STEP 4: Rate Determination

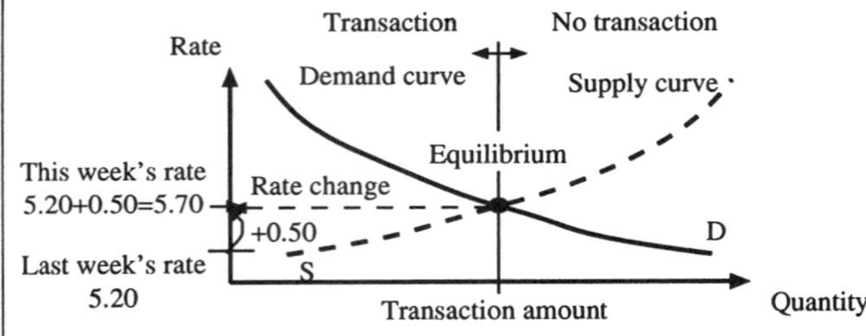

STEP 5: Adaptation

Agent **i**'s Chromosome ={**+0.5, −1.0, +0.1, +3.0**} ...(6)

Agent **i**'s Fitness

= −| (Forecast mean)−(Rate change)| ...(7)

= −|(+0.14) − (+0.50)| = **−0.36**

⇓ **GAs** (Selection,Crossover,Mutation)

New weights

⇓

STEP 1 in the Next Week t+1

Figure 2: Algorithm.

After the Adaptation Step, the week ends and our model proceeds to the next week's Perception Step.

Analysis of Emergent Phenomena

In order to examine the emergent phenomena of markets, we conducted extrapolation simulations of the rate dynamics from January 1994 to December 1995.

Simulation Methods

We repeated the following procedure a hundred times in order to generate a hundred simulation paths[6] First, the initial population is a hundred agents whose weights are randomly generated. Second, we trained our model by using the 17 real world data streams from January 1992 to December 1993[7]. During this *training period*, we skipped the Rate Determination Step and used the cumulated value of differences between the forecast mean and the *actual rate* as the fitness in the Adaptation Step. Finally, for the period from January 1994 to December 1995 we conducted the extrapolation simulations. In this *forecast period*, our model forecasted the rates in the Rate Determination Step by using only external data. We did not use any actual rate data, and both the internal data and the fitness were calculated on the basis of the rates generated by our model.

Overview of Results

The simulation paths are divided into two groups: the *bubble group*, in which the paths have a quick fall and a rise (a rate bubble) (Fig. 3a), and the *non-bubble group*, in which the paths don't have such a bubble (Fig. 3b)[8]. The movement of the actual path is similar to that of the mean path of the bubble group. On the other hand, the path extracted by linear regression using the external data of our model moves in a way similar to that in which the mean path of the non-bubble group moves.

Phase Transition of Forecast Variation

In order to analyze any emergent phenomena, we examine a phase transition in the agents' forecast variability (variation) in the simulated paths. We analyze five simulation paths randomly selected from the bubble group. Because the pattern of these results are common among the selected five paths, we illustrates the results of one typical path.

Flat Phase and Bubble Phase Each simulated path in the bubble group is divided into two phases: The period with small fluctuations(Mar.'94 - Dec.'94) is termed

[6]We used the parameter sets (p_{cross}=0.3, p_{mut} =0.003, G=0.8). The simulation suffered from the smallest forecast errors by using this set in our previous study.

[7]Each weekly time series was used a hundred times, so in this training period there were about ten thousand generations.

[8]The bubble group occupies 25% of all the simulation paths. The non-bubble group occupies 75%.

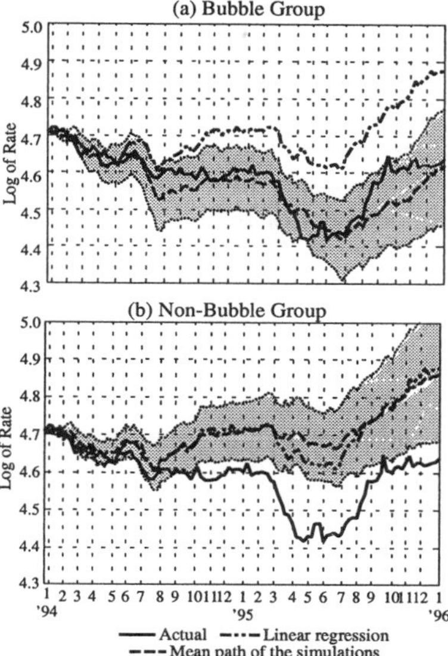

The dotted areas denote the mean ± one standard deviations.

Figure 3: Distribution of simulation paths.

the *flat phase* while the period with large fluctuations (Jan.'95 - Dec.'95) is termed the *bubble phase*.

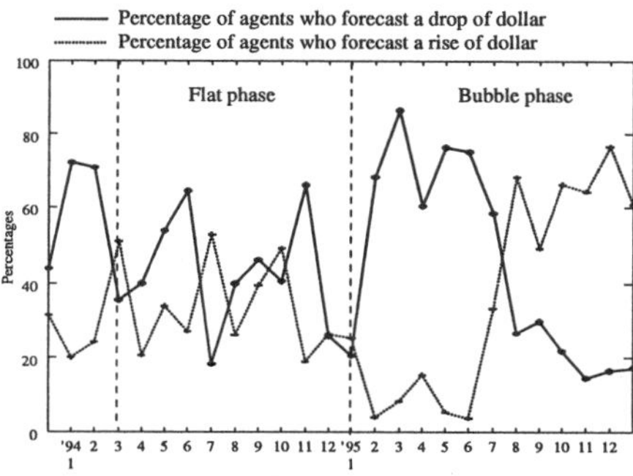

Figure 4: Percentages of agents' forecasts

Fig. 4 shows the percentage of forecasts of rise and drop of the dollar, in the form of four weeks averages. In the flat phase, the variation among forecasts is rich because there are forecasts on both sides. In the bubble phase, the variation among forecasts is poor because most agents agree.

In the flat phase, because there is sufficient supply and demand at or around last week's rate, supply and demand tend to meet around the the last week's rate, (i.e., the rate fluctuation is small), and the trading amounts are larger at the equilibrium point. In contrast, during the bubble phase, the supply and demand are one-sided, so the trading amounts are smaller at the equilibrium point. Supply and demand tend to meet away from the previous week's point because there are not enough opposite orders at last week's equilibrium rate. Hence, the rate fluctuation tend to get larger.

Mechanism of Phase Transition In order to determine the mechanism behind the phase transition, we need to investigate the dynamic patterns of the agent's weights.

First, the weights are classified by a factor analysis. The matrix which is analyzed is a list of 12 weights[9] of 100 agents every 10 weeks. As a result, six factors are extracted[10]. Weights of Economic activities and Price data have the largest loading value of the first factor. We call the first factor *Price monetary* factor, because these two data are used by the price monetary The second factor has relation to Short-term trends and Stock data, so we call it *Short-term* factor. The third, to Trade and Interest rate data, which are included in the portfolio balance approach in econometrics, so we call it *Portfolio balance* factor. The forth, to Announcement and Employment data, so we call it *Announcement* factor. The fifth, to Intervention, Politics, and Employment data, so we call it *Politics* factor. The sixth, to Long-term trend data, so we call it *Long-term* factor. Moreover, according to their meanings we divide these six factors into the three categories. Price monetary and Portfolio balance factor are classified into *Econometrics category*. Announcement and Politics factor, into *News category*. Short-term and Long-term factor, into *Trend category*.

Next, for each category, the dynamics of its weight is examined. First, the weights of Econometric category are relatively stable, however, its absolute value is so small that the influence on rates is not so large. Only Portfolio balance factor has large absolute values during the bubble phase. Second, the very strong market consensus about News category is established just before the bubble phase started. Finally, because of the large correlation before the bubble started, the weights of the trend category got larger in the bubble phase. The plus weights of Trend category mean that agents forecast that the trend in the future will be the same as the recent trend. Therefore, the upward (downward) trend of dollar makes demand (supply) of dollar. The demand (supply) makes the following upward (downward) trend, and so on. It is defined as *positive feedback*. However, at the end of the bubble phase, this positive feedback weakened because the weight of the long-term data changed into negative territory. After the rate passed its lowest point in May '95, the correlation coefficients became much smaller. A lack of opposing orders thus led the forecasts using the trend data to fail.

In summary, we propose the following mechanism to explain the transition between phases. First, in the flat phase, there are varying opinions with respect to the News and Trend category. This leads to large trading

[9]Five time series are discarded because they are alway zero or both their market average and variance are too small.

[10]The proportion of explanation is 67.0 %.

amounts and small exchange rate fluctuations. Second, in the later half of the flat phase, many agents focus on Trade, Announcement, and Politics data. Third, a convergence of opinions with respect to these data and a positive feedback of Trend factors ushered in the bubble phase, which leads to small trading amounts and large rate fluctuations. Fourth, in May 1995, almost all forecasts in the market converged. Because there were no opposing orders in the market, the downward trend vanished. Finally, after the rate passed its lowest point in May 1995, the weight of the long-term data became negative, and the positive feedback was weakened. Thus, the bubble phase ended.

Departure from Normality Many statistical studies reveal that the distribution of rate changes is different from normal distribution. The rate changes in the simulations of the bubble group also have peaked, long tailed (i.e., leptokurtic) distributions not unlike the actual rate. In fact, the kurtosis of a typical simulation in the bubble group (0.477) is close to that of actual rate changes (0.564)[11]. The mechanism giving rise to such a leptokurtosis can be explained by the phase transition. The distribution of rate changes in the bubble phase has a large variance (long tailed distribution), while the flat phase has a small variance (peaked distribution). Combining these two distributions gives rise to a distribution of rate changes that is peaked and long tailed.

Volume and Fluctuation Previous statistical studies also show that there is negative correlation between trading volume and rate fluctuation. Namely, when the rate fluctuates more, the volume is smaller. Contrariwise, when the rate turns flat, the volume becomes larger. Also, a typical simulation shows a significant negative correlation, −0.2800. This negative correlation can be explained as follows: In the bubble phase, many agents forecast changes in the same direction. The rate movement continues in that direction for many weeks and rate fluctuations are amplified. However, the transaction amount drops because the order quantity in the other direction is small. In contrast, in the flat phase, because there is a sustaining amount of both supply and demand around last week's equilibrium rate, trading amounts are larger at equilibrium, but rates fluctuate less.

Contrary Opinions Phenomenon Many dealers and their books say, " If almost all dealers have the same opinion, the contrary opinion will win." In fact, field data sometimes show that convergence of dealers' forecasts leads to an unexpected result in the rate change. Also in typical simulations, in May 1995, when almost all the agents' forecasts converged to the same forecast in the same direction, the rate did not move in that direction. As mentioned, this is caused by the fact that there are no orders in the opposite direction and no transactions can occur.

[11]The kurtosis is 0.0 for a normal distribution.

Conclusions

We proposed an artificial market approach and analyzed three emergent phenomena in markets. First, the a transition between phases of agents' forecast variety (variation among forecasts) in the simulations was examined. As a result, a mechanism for these transitions was proposed: convergence of opinions about news factors and trade factors, and positive feedback by trend factors caused the phase transition. Second, based on these concepts, we explained certain emergent phenomena. The long-tailed and peaked distribution of rate changes was explained by combining the long-tailed distribution in the bubble phase and the peaked distribution in the flat phase. Negative correlation between trading volume and rate fluctuations was explained by their negative relation in the two phases. The phenomenon of 'Contrary opinions' was explained by the lack of opposite orders when all agents' forecasts converged.

The artificial market approach therefore explained the mechanisms of the emergent phenomena at the macro level by a hypothesis about the learning rules at the micro level, that is, this approach provides a quantitative explanation of the micro-macro relation in markets both by integration of fieldwork and a multi-agent model, and by using actual data about economic fundamentals and news.

References

de la Maza, M. and D. Yuret. 1994. A futures market simulation with non-rational participants. In *Artificial Life IV*, edited by R.A. Brooks and P. Maes. Cambridge, MA: MIT Press, p. 325–330.

Goldberg, D. E. 1989. *Genetic Algorithms in Search, Optimization, and Machine Learning.* Addison-Wesley Publishing Company.

Izumi, K. and T. Okatsu. 1996. An artificial market analysis of exchange rate dynamics. In *Evolutionary Programming V*, edited by L.J. Fogel, P.J. Angeline, and T. Bäck. Cambridge, MA: MIT Press, p. 27–36.

Palmer, R. G., W. B. Arthur, J. H. Holland, B. LeBaron, and P. Taylor. 1994. Artificial economic life: A simple model of a stock market. *Physica D*, 75: 264–265.

Symbiotic Intelligence: Self-Organizing Knowledge on Distributed Networks Driven by Human Interaction

Norman L. Johnson[a], Steen Rasmussen[a,b], Cliff Joslyn[a], Luis Rocha[a], Steven Smith[a], and Marianna Kantor[a].

[a]Los Alamos National Laboratory, Los Alamos, New Mexico, 87545
[b]Santa Fe Institute, 1399 Hyde Park Road, Santa Fe, New Mexico, 87501

Abstract

Through conceptual examples and demonstrations, we argue that the symbiotic combination of the Internet and humans will result in a significant enhancement of the previously existing, self-organizing social structure of humans. The combination of the unique capabilities of intelligent, distributed information systems (the relatively loss-less transmission and capturing of detailed signatures) with the unique capabilities of humans (processing and analysis of complex, but limited, systems) will enable essential problem solving within our increasingly complex world. The capability may allow solutions that are not achievable directly by individuals, organizations or governments.

Introduction

The premise of our work is presented in this section. We acknowledge that the following ideas are still somewhat controversial within their own fields of relevance, but we are encouraged also by the growing integration of these ideas across many disciplines and are confident that the viewpoint presented here will be demonstrated and generally accepted.

The argument follows the path of (1) the evolution of human social behavior, (2) the effect of technology on social dynamics and structures, and (3) the relationship of system complexity and traditional problem solving within these social structures. These arguments lead us to our beginning point of the technology of the Internet (Net) and how it will change how humans solve problems.

We use "problem solving" in a broader context than the traditional usage of finding a solution to a problem by analysis. We include the ability of a dynamical system to "find" a new "solution" upon a change of state. While the usage can be problematic, no existing words/language seems suitable to cover both applications. The need of this inclusion will be apparent.

We start with the premise that we have evolved social structures, and the supporting dynamics, which enabled us to "solve" problems that threaten our existence (Joslyn, et al. 1995, Byron 1998). Unlike biological evolution, social change has the distinct advantage of enabling us to adapt within our own lifetime. Although possibly different in detail, social and biological evolution use the same dynamical processes and exhibit the same properties, inherent to self-organizing systems (see, e.g., Babloyantz 1991, Forrest 1990 and the Artificial Life Proceedings I-V):

- "Solutions" arise as a selection by the system dynamics, driven by local processes, from a diversity of potential solutions. Selection does not typically reduce diversity, but only shifts the relative prevalence of the subsystems.
- These systems have the properties of distributed "control" (control from the bottom up), redundancy and persistent non-equilibrium.
- The global properties are: functionality greater than the individual subsystems, the capability to find solutions in the presence of conflicting needs, and scalability without loss of viability.

The view of human society as an adaptive, collective organism is not new. George Dyson (1997) in *Darwin Among the Machines* surveys the works of thinkers (e.g., Hobbes and Leibnitz to Margulous) who have touched on this vision of society during the past five centuries. Despite the long history of interest in these ideas, it has only been in the last decades that there is now promise of a quantitative theory of social dynamics. This new foundation was driven by the dramatic success of the application of complex systems methods to biological problems as expressed, for example, in the Artificial Life movement. In the last two decades there has been a virtual explosion of interpretations or dynamical theories of social and economic systems (e.g., citations in Abraham 1994).

Evidence of our social evolution in action is easily seen in how we have adapted to the significant changes in technology, even though we are biologically unchanged for many millennia. The changes are most apparent in the dramatic increase in the maximum size of a social group as a result of technology advances in transportation, communication and knowledge storage. With each advance, the maximum size of a functioning social group has increased from initially tribes, to city-states, to nations, to regional coalitions, to finally global coalitions. These major societal shifts have occurred by processes similar to biological evolution without centralized planning, often with extreme diversity of capabilities and goals, and with solutions often far beyond the ability or understanding of any individual.

An central question at this juncture is "what is the role of individual or organizational problem solving within the context of self-organizing social dynamics?" Certainly many important societal shifts have resulted from the work or influence of a single individual, organization or government. Arguably these contributions may be necessary components to the overall dynamics, representing the actions of a mostly autonomous entity in a hierarchical self-organizing system.

But what is more important is that the capability of the individual, organization or government will falter, and possibly fail, if centralized problem solving is applied to a system that is not understandable. Without the understanding, there cannot be the analysis and prediction necessary for an effective and timely solution; there can only be trial and error. Humans are premiere problem solvers in systems with heterogeneous data of limited quantity, but we are overwhelmed by vast amounts of homogenous data. Obversely our computer processing counterparts are overwhelmed by complex data of any extent. Furthermore, we are limited in our ability to combine individual resources to solve problems of greater complexity, such as is observed in the limit on the maximum size of a useful committee.

If organizations or societies were to rely on just centralized control to solve problems, we would expect these efforts to fail as our society or the domain of our organizations becomes too complex. Social structures that take advantage of our inherent, self-organizing social dynamics will be best enabled to cope with our increasingly complex world (Abraham 1994). Indeed, we argue that this has happened in modern, overly centralized governments, such as the USSR, and is the reason that democracy and capitalism provide the most robust solutions in modern times (Slater and Bennis 1964 and 1990). There are also trends towards decentralized corporate management (Anderson and Arrow 1988, Youngblood 1996).

Herein lies our proposition and starting point. Self-organizing social dynamics has been an unappreciated positive force in our social development and has been significantly extended, at least in scope, by new technologies. At the same time, our culture and society are facing greater challenges due to the increasing complexity of our world, both in vastness and heterogeneity, possibly to the point of global disfunction. We argue that the Internet (Net) will change and enhance our social dynamics, to the point of becoming a significant resource for organizations and society as a whole. Once better understood, the consequence for management and governments will be an emphasis on encouraging diversity, increased access to information, and decentralized control.

The Unique Capabilities of the Net and its Effect on Social Dynamics

The Net has three significant, arguably unique, capabilities beyond prior human-technological systems:

(1) <u>*The Net integrates the breadth of diverse systems*</u>. It has the ability within one hyper-system to integrate (Schement and Lievrouw 1987):

a. *Information storage*, both in the form of simple data and complex text and images. This was done earlier in off-line libraries and a variety of data banks.

b. *Communication*. Communication was done earlier either by the relatively slow movement of people or documents or, in recent times, by telephone or other electronic technologies. However, complex documents, simple data and images can now be transported instantaneously and close to cost-free from anywhere to everywhere. Geographical barriers are virtually gone.

c. *Traditional computing*: the automated (simple) information processing of huge amounts of data.

d. *Human processing*. The human ability to analyze, understand and process limited, but highly complex information.

Until very recently (a), (b) and (c) were physically separated processes, all combined by human intervention (d). Now (a), (b) and (c) are integrated in a more standardized medium. Thus, the time scale for knowledge organization and creation using traditional, non-self-organizing methods, is drastically shorter. The new integration has been overwhelming to humans, but tools are readily evolving in this infant hyper-structure to overcome the initial shortcoming [e.g., firefly.net, amazon.com, alexa.com].

(2) <u>*The Net captures the depth of systems.*</u> It can capture the complexity of how information is associated by retaining all references between data on the network. A simple example of how much of this relational information is currently lost is in the use of scientific publications. While papers contain citations that connect a paper with other papers, the information about the numbers and types of readers of the papers could be only obtained in the past at great expense. With the advent of on-line publications, such information is explicitly available at effectively no cost. In general, the Net can capture all traces of the use of information. These traces represent implicit knowledge of how we interact and how new knowledge is created. As (1) above is better realized, these traces will capture the full complexity of our interactions.

(3) <u>*The Net has accuracy of communication.*</u> Traditional human-to-human communication results in a rapid loss of information a bit removed from its creator (the children's game of whispering a phrase around a circle is a telling example of the high noise-to-signal ratio of verbal communication). By contrast, information exchanged or

related on the Net suffers minimal loss of information during transmission or linking, in the same way that the content of a book is not altered when exchanged. We do note that we sacrifice bandwidth using current technologies because of the elimination of vocal, facial and gestural expressions. In this discussion, we do not include the misinterpretation that can still occur in understanding of exchanged information; this source of miscommunication occurs regardless of the mechanism of exchange.

With the stronger presence of these unique capabilities of the Net in human dynamics, we propose that minimally the creation, manipulation and rejection of knowledge can be captured for the first time, encompassing the full complexity of the cognition process in our society. More importantly, the processes of our social dynamics, which previously relied on slower, spatially concentrated, and noisy forms of communication, now has the potential to form a symbiotic relationship between humans and the Net, enabling our prior self-organizing capabilities to operate at a significantly enhanced functionality. In the next section we give two examples of demonstrations of how this symbiosis might be possible. Furthermore, in the same manner as to how society self-organized to solve problems of survival, the same processes on the Net will result in self-organization of knowledge. Because self-organizing knowledge arises from diverse contributions and can encompass knowledge greater than the contribution of any individual, there is the arguable potential of creating knowledge that will contribute to solutions that are not understandable within our current processes. In the next section, we will also give a suggestive example of this capability.

Self-Organizing Systems Demonstrations

We now present two studies that demonstrate collective knowledge development: the first demonstrating knowledge formation from humans interacting on a network and the second examining how many individual solutions can combine to solve a global problem in an idealized system without human involvement.

Self-organization on networks: adaptive hypertext experiment

A simple experiment was conducted by Bollen and Heylighen (1996a) of the Free University of Brussels under the Principia Cybernetica Project's goal to explore the "brain metaphor" (Gaines 1994; Heylighen and Bollen 1996) to make hypertext webs more intelligent (Drexler 1991, Bollen and Heylighen 1996b). This metaphor led them to consider hypertext links like neural associations in the brain according to a Hebbian dynamics: "The strength of the links, like the connection strength of synapses, can change depending on the frequency of use of the link. This allows the network to 'learn' automatically from the way it is used" (Ibid.), which illustrates the concept of emergent knowledge through human interaction.

The experiment was set up by first constructing a list of the 150 most common words in newspaper English. When a user initially enters the system, a target word is displayed on a web page, followed by a list of 10 more randomly chosen words from the list (more words were available from the list without replacement at the user's request, to the point of potentially exhausting the list). The user is then asked to pick the word from the list that most closely is associated with the header word. Upon choosing a word, the order of the list is recalculated based on the frequency of selection according to a Hebbian rule, with weight added to the initial link, the reflexive link backwards, and the transitive link across two pairs of words. The user is then taken to a new page corresponding to the selected word, and the process is repeated. The researchers found that the lists stabilized to a fixed order after about 4000 selections in a site.

The resulting ordered lists determined a common semantics despite the heterogeneity of users. This simple task of ordering is easy for an individual but of little utility due to large individual variation in semantic differences between individuals. The network solution actively constructed useful collective knowledge representing a consensual semantics, but with minimal instruction and effort from the collective group of individuals. This example captures the essence of developing a self-organizing knowledge system that combines the advantages of both human and computer networks to quickly solve a syntactically complex problem. From this example, one can imagine a host of previously challenging, if not intractable, problems that could be addressed once the methodology is developed.

Simulation of collective decision making

The second demonstration is not an example of self-organization on an existing network, but a demonstration (Johnson 1998) that supports some of the fundamental assumptions of the present argument and illustrates desirable features of a large and diverse self-organizing system. We want to answer the following question: "what is the effect of noise or information loss on a collective decision involving many individuals."

The system that was examined was a maze (a connected, undirected graph) which has one or more solutions (paths) between two nodes (one being the starting point and the other being the end or goal). Solutions to the maze were found for a large (100s) number of independent "individuals" (no information is shared between individuals as in the prior demonstration). All individuals initially use the same set of "Learning Rules" that (1) determine their movement through the maze as based only on local information, and (2) how they modify their own path "preference" at each node. The restriction to using only local information means that they have no "global" sense of the maze and explore the maze until they just happen to reach the end node.

The set of "Nodal Path Preferences" is a weighted, directed graph overlaying the maze and is retained for each individual for later use. Basically the Learning Rules select a link that has not been tried and then sets the Path Preference of this choice to be larger than the other links at this node. After the Learning phase is completed, another set of rules, the "Application Rules," are used. These apply, but do not modify, the nodal preferences to find the "optimal" path of each individual. Basically the Application Rules select the preferred link at a node with minor additional logic to prevent infinite loops. Because random choices are made in the rules between equal preference, a diversity of preferred paths through the maze and a diversity of total lengths of paths ("performance") are created. Once the individual nodal preferences are found from the Learning Phase, these can be combined at each node in various ways to create a collective nodal preference, and then the same set of the Application Rules are used to determine the collective solution.

For a demonstration maze of 35 nodes with 14 paths of a minimum path length of 9 (see Fig. 1), the average number of steps to "solve" the problem of 100 individuals is 34.3 with a standard deviation of 24.5 in the Learning phase. The average performance of the individuals using the Application Rules is 12.8 with a standard deviation of 3.1. There is no correlation observed between the performance in the Learning and Application phases: a slow learner is not necessarily a poor performer. For the reference simulation, a simple average of the individual nodal preferences is used to create a collective nodal preference. Its application using the identical Application Rules results in solution of 9-11 steps when more than 20 individuals are included, most often sampling one of the minimum path lengths. Figure 2 shows the change in path length as the numbers of individuals in the collective solution increases. Note the effect of randomness, even though the identical individuals contribute to each collective decision. The average random walk solution is 138 with a standard deviation of 101. We note that the primary source of variation at larger contributors is due to the multiple minimum paths. Had there been only one minimum path, the solution is much more stable.

Figure 1. The "maze" used for the demonstration problem. Two of the 14 paths of minimum length are highlighted.

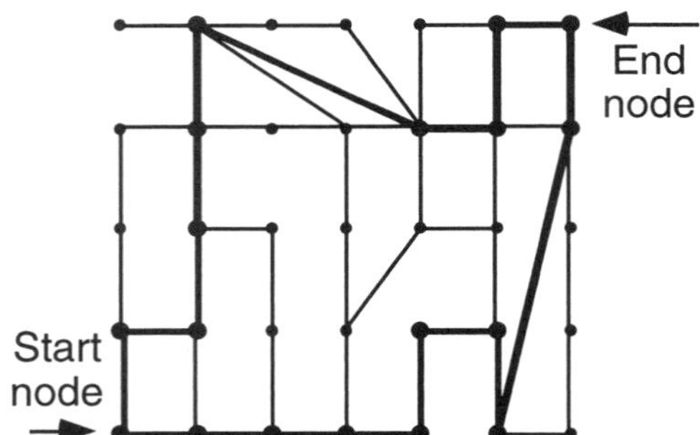

A few properties of the system illustrate some of the fundamental assumptions and arguments presented earlier. The significant improvement of the collective solution over the average individual solution (9 versus 12.8) illustrates that information can be combined from uncoupled individual solutions using only local information to achieve an optimal global solution to a problem. This emergent property of the collective system was generally observed on all mazes, even ones of higher complexity, with only difference being that different numbers of individuals are needed in the collective solutions to achieve the same performance.

In general, the collective solution was remarkably robust. Degradation of the individual's contribution, however implemented, generally had no effect or just postponed the collective convergence to the minimal solution. A few effects were found to significantly degrade the collective solution. One was the random selection and use of the nodal preference of one of the contributing individuals, with a different individual selected at each node. The resulting average path length was about 45 steps (3.5 normalized), independent of the number of individuals contributing to the solution. This illustrates how the change of a dominant individual during a solution process can yield results much worse than that of an average individual. A second degradation of the collective solution was achieved by the random addition of noise (the random replacement of a nodal preference by a small value) to the collective solution, in an attempt to model miscommunication of the individual contribution to the whole. At moderate random addition, around half of the time and greater, the collective solution does worse than the average individual performance. These results support the argument proposed in the prior section: many more individuals can contribute to a collective decision when sources of noise and loss are reduced.

Figure 2. Plot of normalized path lengths of the collective solutions versus the number of individuals contributing to the collective for two initial random seeds in the Application phase. The normalization is by the average individual path or about 12.8 steps.

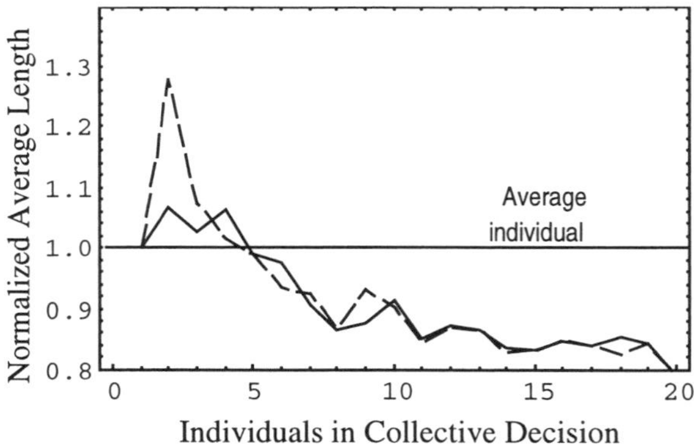

Another observation was that a collective solution from a diverse population is more flexible and performs better in changing goals than the average, more narrowly-focused individuals. For example, it was observed that the collective solution is degraded if only the "better" individuals (those with shorter path lengths in the Application Phase) contribute to the collective solution, illustrating that even a diversity of performance is important to a collective solution. Another example is to apply the Learning Phase to more than one goal (i.e., each individual learns with one goal out of many) or to change the goal after learning with different goal, measuring the robustness of the solution. In both of these simulations, the collective decision performed significantly better with a normalized path of about 0.5.

There are obvious similarities between the processes we are describing here and what is being studied under the terms *Genetic Algorithms* and *Programming* (Koza 1994, Mitchell 1996). However, there are also some significant differences, perhaps the most important being that these agents do not evolve, but learn and create knowledge as they share information among themselves. The key to performance in these systems is diversity and not selection.

Conclusions

This paper presents preliminary arguments on the possible future of "problem solving" or collective decision making in our society and organizations. We have argued that a dynamic process underlies all life: the ability of self-organizing systems to "solve" essential problems, will take on new functionality as our society increasingly utilizes the Net for human interaction. The symbiotic intelligence of the combined human-Net system is believed to be able to operate at a level of functionality, both in numbers of individuals and the complexity of capability, higher than previously possible.

To support this argument, we have described two demonstrations of collective intelligence. The hypertext example of ordering word lists captures the creation of self-organizing knowledge by the interaction of humans processing complex semantic content, facilitated by the Net. This example illustrates the ease of solution to a problem that would be difficult using traditional approaches. The Los Alamos simulation demonstrates (1) the potential for more individuals to contribute to a collective solution, (2) the collective solution has better performance and is more robust than an average individual's solution, and (3) more complex problems can be solved with larger numbers of contributing individuals.

References

Abraham, R. 1994. *Chaos, Gaia, Eros*. San Francisco: Harper.

Anderson, P.H. & Arrow, K.A. 1988. *The Economy as an Evolving Complex System.* Addison-Wesley.

Babloyantz, A. (Ed.) 1991. *Reviews and Commentary for Self-Organization, Emerging Properties, and Learning.* Portland, Or.: Book News, Inc.

Bollen, J. and Heylighen, F. 1996a. Algorithms for the self-organization of distributed, multi-user networks, Possible application to the future World Wide Web. *Cybernetics and Systems '96.* R. Trappl (Ed.). Austrian Society For Cybernetics Press :911-916.

Bollen J, & Heylighen, F. 1996b. *Learning, "Brain-like" Webs.* http://pespmc1.vub.ac.be.

Byron, M. 1998. Crisis-Driven Evolutionary Learning: Conceptual Foundations and Systematic Modeling. *World Congress on Sociology '98.* Montreal. Forthcoming.

Drexler, K.E. 1991. Hypertext publishing and the evolution of knowledge. *Social Intelligence* 1:2-22.

Dyson, G. 1997. *Darwin among the Machines: The Evolution of Global Intelligence*. Reading, Mass.: Addison-Wesley Publishing.

Forrest, S. (Ed.) 1990. *Emergent Computation.* Cambridge, MA: MIT Press. (Special issue of Physica D)

Gaines, B.R. 1994. The Collective Stance in Modeling Expertise in Individuals and Organizations. *International Journal of Expert Systems* 7(1):22-51.

Heylighen, F. & J. Bollen 1996. The World-Wide Web as a super-brain: from metaphor to model. *Cybernetics and Systems '96.* R. Trappl (Ed.). Austrian Society for Cybernetics Press: 917-922.

Johnson, N. L. 1998. *Effects of Complexity, Noise and Loss in Collective Decision Making*. Forthcoming.

Joslyn, C., Turchin V. , & Heylighen, F. 1995. *Social Evolution*, http://pespmc1.vub.ac.be/SOCEVOL.html.

Koza, J. 1994. *Genetic programming II*. Cambridge, MA: MIT Press.

Mitchell, M. 1996. *An Introduction to Genetic Algorithms*. Cambridge, MA: MIT Press.

Schement, J.R., & Lievrouw, L.A. (Eds.) 1987. *Competing Visions, Complex Realities: Social Aspects of the Information Society*. Norwood, NJ: Ablex.

Slater, P. & W. Bennis 1964. Democracy is inevitable. *Harvard Business Review*: March-April (reissued September–October 1990).

Youngblood, M. 1996. *Life at the Edge of Chaos*, New York: John Wiley & Sons.

Simulating Multiple Emergent Phenomena - Exemplified in an Ant Colony

Franziska Kluegl and Frank Puppe

Dep. for Artificial Intelligence, University of Wuerzburg
Am Hubland, 97074 Wuerzburg

{kluegl, puppe}@informatik.uni-wuerzburg.de

Ulrich Raub and Juergen Tautz

Dep. for Behavioral Physiology and Sociobiology,
University of Wuerzburg
Am Hubland, 97074 Wuerzburg
{raub, tautz}@biozentrum.uni-wuerzburg.de

Abstract

Modeling the activity of an ant community based on the individual behavior of a single ant is a very modern approach, but until now the modeling has often been restricted to single phenomenon, e.g., foraging or recruiting. But these activities can not be seen independently from other necessary abilities. For example foraging, breeding, building a nest or defending a territory from enemies are all dependent on each other. In this paper we want to present a model of an ant community that unifies different activities during a complete life cycle of a colony. We present experiments with a simulated ant colony that exhibits concurrently
- foraging and recruiting
- storing energy and distributing it inside of the anthill
- breeding and individual development
- mass recruitment for defending the colony's territory

For modeling the behavior of an ant we use the SeSAm-architecture. This is a discrete, rule-based multi-agent simulation system that allows easy graphical modeling. Because of its simple structure and powerful graphical editors the large, unifying ant-model is easily accessible.

Introduction

How can complex and seemingly organized behavior of a group of agents result from simple behavioral rules of the individual agents without central control? Answers to this question may not only help in better understanding social animal or human behavior, but also in computational approaches for reducing complexity. For studying such emergent phenomena, a sophisticated multi-agent simulation shell is necessary, which allows straightforward modeling of the behavior of single agents and the environment as well as offers sophisticated tools for recording the behavior of the group. A typical example is the organization of an ant colony with emergent phenomena like effective foraging or recruiting. Currently, most approaches have studied such phenomena in isolation and shown that they can be reached with simple individual rules. The next step is to study them in combination. Is it necessary to completely redesign the local behavior of the agents or reassemble the single emergent phenomena more like modules in software engineering with nice integration opportunities? In the following we report about the experiences of modeling a broad range of behaviors of an ant colony with SeSAm (**She**ll for **S**imulated **A**gent Syste**m**s). This system provides a generic environment for modeling agent-based systems and experimenting with these models. We specially focused on providing a framework for the easy construction of complex models. Besides several graphical tools for animating and evaluating the simulation experiments, the modeler may use a rule-based activity selection paradigm that is also supported by a graphical modeling tool (for further information see Kluegl, 1998).

There are four categories for modeling the behavior of single agents related to the stimulus-response paradigm which is easily translated using rule-based mechanisms. They vary in different degrees of flexibility:

1. Strict caste-controlled agents: they perform only activities associated with their role
2. Less strict caste-controlled agents: they perform activities associated with their role, but can execute other activities on very strong stimuli.
3. Unspecialized, activity-bounded agents: they perform activities which may last over some time, but can be interrupted on certain stimuli.
4. Unspecialized agents: Their actions are determined from one basic time-step to another dependent only on external stimuli and internal state.

All four of these paradigms can be found in the simple behavioral rules that form the basis for the development of several individual based stochastic models, specially modeling task allocation. Sees for example (Pacala et. al. 1996), who use the following simplified rule to develop stochastic processes for task allocation: Ants that don't encounter a task-specific resource during a certain time interval, switch their task or become inactive. The problem with all these analytic simulation models is that they cannot formulate the complex situation the ant is confronted with. Neither spatial structures, nor complex, interacting stimuli or activities can be considered without an essential reduction to very simplified assumptions.

For our aim of modeling different interacting phenomena the approach of multi-agent simulation seems more promising. The behavior of an ant is modeled explicitly using the rule-based paradigms above. The first (strict caste-like system) is - as it excludes task switching - not very useful for modeling. The second paradigm provides the standard action selection paradigm used in SeSAm. For flexibility there is also the possibility to introduce stimuli which can interrupt all activities. Therefore a modeler is provided with an additional (3)-like paradigm. This third paradigm corresponds to some of the „classical" task competition approaches (e.g. Maes 1991). For the selection of the next action, possible tasks, including the specially treated current activity are rated and the best one is chosen to determine the next action of the agent. Dependencies between the different tasks are taken into account, therefore the modeling of many different behaviors becomes rather costly. The last category where the selection of the next action is only based on the currently perceived stimuli is for example used in the MANTA model (Drogoul and Ferber 1994).
In the next section, we generally describe the natural behavior of ant colonies. Thereafter models of the behavior of individual ants sufficient for single emergent phenomena like foraging, recruiting, storing and distributing energy, breeding, and defending territory are given, followed by a report on our experiments with combining them. The last section discusses the results and describes open questions.

Ant Behavior

The natural behavior of ants is enormous variable and perfectly fitted to the environment the colony lives in. The ecological range of the nearly 9000 described ant species is form the arctic circle to the rain forests of south America (for review see Hölldobler & Wilson 1990). The very common feature of ant societies is „eusociality". This term describes three behavioral characteristics that are the main reasons for the success of the ants: 1. Reproductive division of labor with one or more queens responsible for the reproduction and non-reproductive workers helping the queens 2. Cooperation of the workers in caring for the young and 3. the overlap of two or more generations living in one colony capable to contribute to the colony labor.
Next to eusociality, the potential of most of the members of a colony to switch from one task to another guarantees the functioning of a colony. Doing so, the colony has the ability to divide their capacities among the routine tasks or, if necessary adjust it to the actual situation. One example is the use of foragers to look for food supply outside the nest. Usually food items are distributed in an unpredictable way in the environment. So it is very important to concentrate the workers available for searching and exploiting a food source in a efficient way. This problem is solved by employing subgroups of ants, called foragers, to go out to look for these items. Successful foragers run back to the nest and recruit unemployed workers to exploit this food source in a fast and effective way.

Simulated Ant Behavior

In ant colonies several self-organizing behaviors can be observed, each is in itself an interesting phenomenon. Therefore several separated approaches to simulate it were already undertaken. The following aspects are part of our model (Kluegl et al. 1996), (Raub and Kluegl 1997).

Foraging and recruiting

The emerging cooperation of ants in order to exploit a food source is one of the most famous and probably most often modeled and simulated self-organizing pattern. It even supplies a model for emergent cooperation (Steels 1990). Dispersed food resources are exploited very effectively using a chemical trail for information about the position and the quality of the source.
We constructed a simple model for the behavior of a forager: depending on its individual energy level the worker leaves the nest searching for food. When it perceives a pheromone trail, the modeled worker chooses to follow it with a high probability. When discovering a food particle, it transports it back to the nest thereby refreshing the trail. For modeling the „exact" pattern of behavior, some questions arise: For example, when a worker perceives more than one trail, which one does it follow? In our model the ant chooses always the strongest, but with a small probability it does not follow a perceived trail at all, but starts searching for new food sources. Figure 1 shows a typical situation during a simulation experiment.

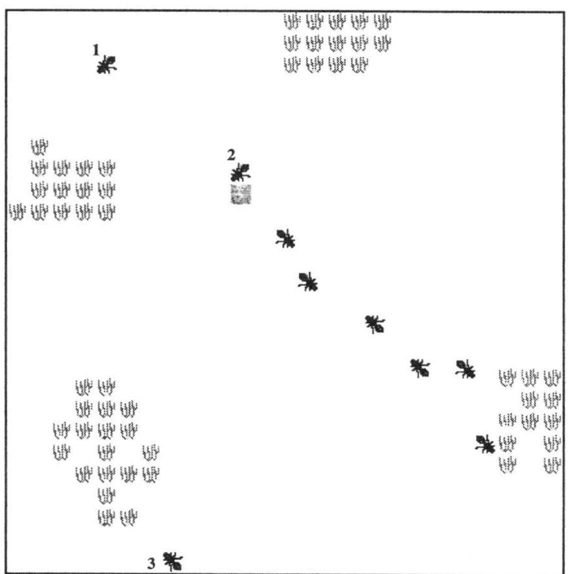

Figure 1: Situation during an animated simulation experiment: Foraging ants are exploiting a food source, whereas the numbered ant search for new patches.

There are many reports about models examining the distribution of foraging ants between several food sources, often developed from experiments with real ants. The asymmetric, most effective foraging between two food sources could be reproduced using logistic equations (Pasteels et al. 1987) or stochastic processes (Fletcher et al. 1995). They also consider the question, whether ants could loose the trail and state that there may be a relation between the length and the concentration of the pheromone and the probability to leave it. In our model an agent only leaves a selected trail, when it arrives at the end and no food is perceived. Then it starts searching. (Millonas 1994) focuses still more on the way ants follow trails. He uses microscopic dynamics described by an pheromone energy function to describe how ants follow trails.

Development inside of the nest

The activity inside of an anthill is strongly depending on the queen. She produces eggs that become new workers via several stages of development.

In our model the queen produces eggs and feeds them with her own energy until the first workers hatch and take over this job. The time she needs for producing an egg increases with falling energy. When she has used up her energy she has to be fed by other agents, otherwise she stops production and finally starves. We subsumed all stages of development into one of the following agent types: "brood" and "sexual brood". When the colony reaches a certain size, the queen starts producing sexual brood, that become new queens representing the next generation of ant colonies. Thus the number of produced sexual animals determines the overall success of an ant colony.

A critical question in modeling the behaviors of ants concerning the growth of a colony is the mechanism how the queen decides, when to produce what kind of brood. In our model we designed simple rules like: If the queen perceives more than 30 brood agents with enough energy inside a restricted radius, it starts producing sexual brood entities.

In the MANTA project (Drogoul and Ferber 1994) the activities inside of an anthill are modeled based on agents that purely react on stimuli that spread on the spatial structure of the nest. They incorporate the different stages of development requiring different caring activities, but do not consider other than brood that becomes workers.

Additional to the explicit feeding of the queen and the brood there is another mechanism to share energy between the workers committed to tasks beyond foraging (and thus information about the complete energy supply in the nest). We combined two mechanisms as can be found in real ants (Hölldobler and Wilson 1990). One is a central storage in form of ants (e.g., the "honeypot ants" of the American desert ant Myrmecocystus mimicus) representing a reserve for the dry season. A second mechanism is a decentralized distribution. Every time one ant meets another, the one with more energy gives some amount of energy to the other ("trophallaxis").

As the colony grows, the nest itself will become too small thus the nest size has to be adjusted dynamically. Although in our model the number of ants on the same grid is not yet restricted, we modeled nest building, as the size of the nest generally determines the amount of social contact inside of the anthill. In the modeled colony the motivation of a nestworker to dig out a part of the nest is coupled with the amount of social contact during a certain time (see Figure 2 for an example of nest enlargement during a simulation experiment). A piece of soil is deposited outside the nest. With the simple rule "if another piece of soil is perceived, add it to it" it was possible to establish a waste deposit site.

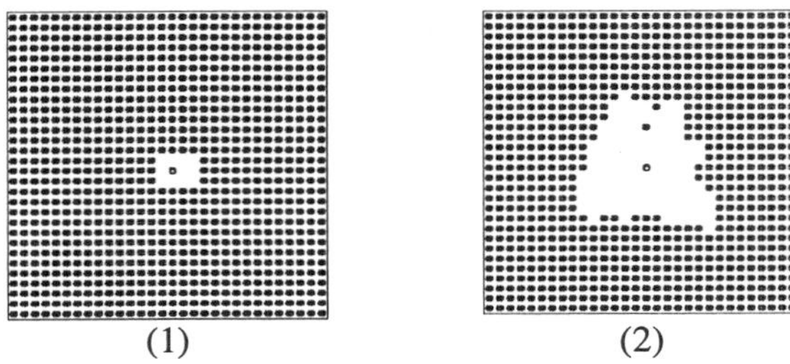

Figure 2: Structure of the nest at the start of the simulation (1) and after 2000 time-steps (2). The circle in the middle of the maps depicts the connection to the outside world.

A simple form of nest building behavior was also reproduced by (Deneubourg et al. 1991). They compared the construction of nest-structures by social insects (termite or wasp colonies) using different, very simple, fixed behavioral patterns for agents filling the cells they occupy and moving to neighboring cells.

Mass recruitment for defending the territory

One of the biggest competitors of an ant colony is another colony, therefore a mechanism for interacting with ants from other colonies is necessary.

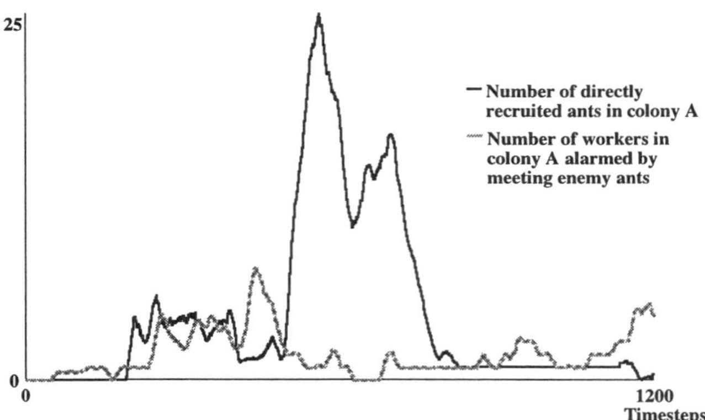

Figure 3: Recruitment of workers in reaction to contact with ants from another colony

We modeled the interaction pattern that is exhibited by ants of the species Myrmecocystus mimicus, that assess in "tournaments" the strength of the other colony. We incorporated one of the explaining hypotheses for their emergence (Hölldobler 1983) in our model: Having contact to a foreign ant, the ant checks the number of foreign animals in an area by running in circles for a short time. If a certain number of foreign ants is counted the ants runs back and recruits other nest mates to this area. If additional ants encounter foreign ants there will be a exponential increase of alerted ants. By this it is guaranteed that a single ant is not sufficient to alert the whole colony. This is exemplified in figure 3.

Issues in Combinability

An ant colony in reality must perform all the above-described behavioral processes concurrently, as they are strongly associated. For example foraging is useless, when there is no effective mechanism for distributing energy to ants busy with other tasks. An attempt to recruit ants for a tournament is futile, when all workers are foraging and no waiting reserve can be found in the nest. Only a effective foraging mechanism supplies sufficient energy for feeding the brood. Many more of these interconnected tasks can be found.

In principle the integration of several separate phenomena raises problems of two categories: A complete model must be carefully calibrated to exhibit a functioning task allocation and on the other side energy consumption and gain must be balanced. Thus combining several processes is not trivial: Both time and energy balance is disturbed when adding a further process, as ants that are committed to the new task can not perform others, but nevertheless consume energy.

Our rules for switching from one task to another mostly represent priorities between the different behaviors. The most critical issues can be associated with the workers: They can stop being inactive (resting) and start foraging at any time with a rather low probability, which is increasing when their energy falls beneath a certain value and any honey-pot ant cannot provide enough new energy. An ant always performs trophallaxis-behavior when it has contact to another of its own colony, and continues its former work after that. When a worker encounters a foreign ant, it starts immediately with the alarmed counting behavior, independent form what it has done before.

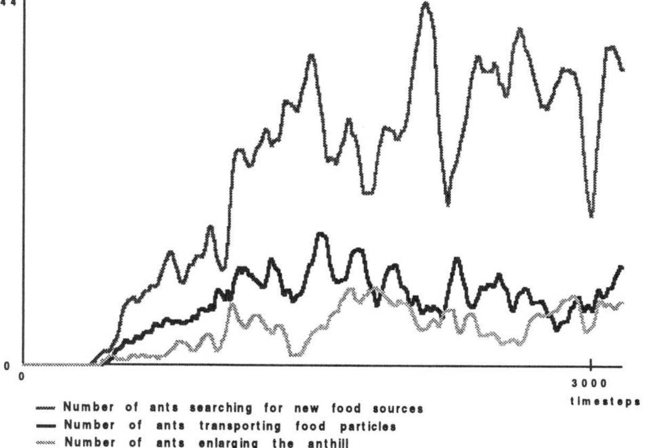

Figure 4: Number of workers committed to different tasks.

Figures 4 and 5 show clarifying example results of simulation experiments for the functioning of the combination of the behaviors. In figure 4 the number of workers committed to different tasks, like the different phases of foraging or enlarging the nest, are presented. After about 1000 time-steps constantly more than 200 workers are available, between 30 and 50 of them are busy with caring for brood and queen. In figure 5 the distribution of different behavioral roles during a simulation experiment is presented. At the beginning of the colony's life–starting with just one queen, only brood exists. The queen feeds the brood, until its own energy level decreases–some brood starves. After nest workers have developed, they start feeding the hungry brood. When a certain amount of brood can be maintained, the colony starts crowing.

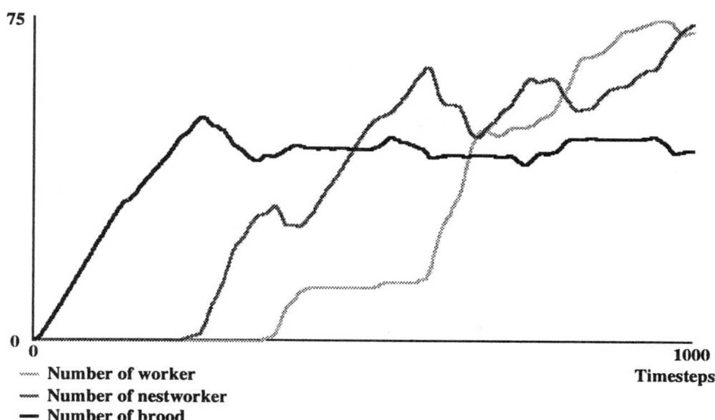

Figure 5: Number of ants belonging to certain developmental states or behavioral roles.

Thus we generated in principle an explicit, rather sophisticated task allocation model. In the real world social insects distribute workers on tasks quite optimally, but how this is accomplished based on pure self-organization is not completely known. Reproducing it is therefore a very attractive research area. In contrast to the work of for example (Pacala et al. 1996), we modeled the stimuli that lead to task switching explicitly, not translating them into abstract probabilities and transition rates. The behavior and situation of a single ant can be pursued and recognized directly in the model, and is not hidden in decision matrices for a small number of different tasks (Gordon et al. 1992). We can directly model spatial properties, feed back loops, etc. without simplifying in order to cope with large equation systems (Lachmann and Selly 1995). Using multi-agent simulation we can directly translate the results of observing the individual ants into the model and thus produce plausible over all behavior of an ant colony without restrictions that must be taken into account when modeling mathematically.

Conclusions and Further Work

Examining different phenomena and integrating them into one unified model, we gain results that mirror better the fragile balance between different aspects of a colony's life than previous simulations. There are no structural problems combining different emerging phenomena, but the critical issue is finding out the overall optima of the combined behavior. Although we have managed to built a model that leads to plausible behavior of the colony, we have to do controlled experiments to find out whether the model is both realistic compared to external field data and optimal with respect to internal parameter adjustments. Evaluating the experiments based on animation, statistics and the genetical fitness measure of produced sexual animals, we can gain more evidence about the quality of our model. Currently the model can already be used as a basis for testing specialized hypotheses about, e.g., different counting mechanisms during a tournament.

The most important result of our attempt to integrate several phenomena in one model consists of the questions arisen during the model construction: What mechanisms are responsible for the optimal distribution of ants in nest - workers, forager exploiting known resources or looking for new resources, lazy colonist numbers, etc.? How can an ant gain reliable information about important aspects of the colony state (e.g., the details of the counting mechanism in tournaments, see Section 3.3)? And, after all, how does the queen decide, how many eggs she should produce?

References

Deneubourg, J.-L., Theraulaz, G. and Becker, R. 1991. Swarm-made architectures. In *Towards a Practice of Autonomous Agents. Proceedings of the first European Conference on Artificial Life*, p. 123-133.

Drogoul, A. and J. Ferber. 1994. Multi-agent simulation as a tool for modeling societies: Application to social differentiation in ant colonies. In *Artificial Social Systems, Proceedings of the MAAMAW'92*. Berlin: Springer-Verlag, p. 3-23.

Fletcher. R. P., C. Cannings and P. G. Blackwell. 1995. Modeling foraging behavior of ant colonies In *Advances in Artificial Life, Proceedings of the Third European Conference on Artificial Life*, edited by . F. Morán, A. Moreno, J. J. Merelo and P. Chacón. Berlin, Heidelberg: Springer-Verlag, p. 772-783.

Gordon, D. M., B. C. Goodwin, and L. E. H. Trainor. 1992. A parallel distributed model of the behavior of ant colonies. *Journal of Theoretical Biology*. 156: 293-307.

Hölldobler, B. and E. O. Wilson. 1990. *The Ants*. Heidelberg: Springer-Verlag.

Hölldobler, B. 1983. Chemical manipulation, enemy specification and intercolony communication in ant communities. In *Neuroethology and Behavioral Physiology*, dited by F. Huber and H. Markl, H. Berlin: Springer-Verlag.

Kluegl, F. 1998. The multi-agent simulation environment SeSAm. Forthcoming.

Kluegl, F., Puppe, F., Raub U. and Tautz, J. 1996. A simulation system for the representation of emergent behavior. In *Proceedings of the Conference Simulation and Animation 1996* (ASIM, ed.). Magdeburg (in German)

Lachmann, M. and Selly, G. 1995. The computationally complete ant colony: Global coordination in a system with no hierarchy. In *Advances in Artificial Life, Proceedings of the Third European Conference on Artificial Life*, edited by F. Morán, A. Moreno, J. J. Merelo and P. Chacón. Berlin, Heidelberg: Springer, p. 785-800

Maes, P. 1991. A bottom-up mechanism for behavior selection in an artificial creature. In *From Animals to Animats: Proceedings of the First International Conference on Simulation of Adaptive Behavior,* edited by J. A Meyer and S. W. Wilson. Cambridge, MA: MIT Press, p. 238-246.

Millonas, M. 1994. Swarms, phase transitions, and collective intelligence. In *Artificial Life III*, edited by C. G. Langton. Redwood City, CA: Addison-Wesley, p. 417-445.

Pacala S. W., Gordon, D. M. and Godfray, H. D. J. 1996. Effects of social group size on information transfer and task allocation. *Evolutionary Ecology* 10: 127-165.

Pasteels, J. M., Deneubourg, J.-L. and Goss, S. 1987. Self-organization mechanisms in ant societies (1) Trail recruitment to newly discovered food sources. In *Form Individual to Collective Behavior in Social Insects,* edited by J. B. Pasteels, and J. L. Deneubourg., p. 155-176.

Raub, U. and F. Kluegl. 1997. A new technique to simulate ant-colonies. *In Social Insects, Proceedings of IUSSI-Conference,* edited by K. Crailsheim and A. Stubentheiner Graz: Eigenverlag.

Steels, L. 1990. Cooperation between distributed agents through self-organization. In *Decentralized A. I.*, edited by Y. Demazeau and J.-P. Mueller. North Holland, p. 175-196.

Evolution of Places: Intentionality in the Built Environment

Joseph Lambke

Animate Research Group, 954 Washington, Chicago, IL 60607
lambke@animate.org

Abstract

Within the evolution of places including metropolises, cities, towns and neighborhoods, human beings and human organizations are the actors that make *deals* resulting in architectural changes to the built environment. The patterns that evolve are intentional at two levels: at a simple level, the actors (city planners) in the system directly intend to create certain features; and at more complex levels, the interactions of many autonomous actors (developers, transportation officials, financiers, etc.) indirectly give rise to yet different patterns, notably metropolitan sprawl. This paper proposes an organizational mechanism intending to evolve the built environment into a highly correlated fitness landscape of human *deal* centers that reflect actual building densities and land values. The final section considers the implications of this mechanism relative to the human limitations of structuring the built environment.

Context/Fitness Landscape

Technological advances in the past 300 years have prompted a variety of means and methods to manipulate building and construction within cities, towns, metropolises and neighborhoods. Theoretical debates range from absolute generalization and self-sufficiency, i.e., Walden Pond types, to absolute specialization and system dependence, such as Brave New World types. The current paradigm for manipulating places, Zoning-by-Function, was an intentional response to a fitness landscape defined by the industrial conditions affecting places 50-150 years ago.

Cities such as Brasilia and Canberra have been built strictly according to this paradigm and have demonstrated the limitations of changing fitness landscapes. Unable to predict the viability of businesses and industries over many years makes it impossible to layout a city based on clearly identified areas for different functions. However these intentions are still visible in most communities' Master Plan. Alternatively many places have simply evolved without any governmental guidance such as shanty towns which can be witnessed in many economically stressed places; others such as the city of Houston, have evolved with a minimum of governmental guidance on a large scale.

Recent technological advances define a new fitness landscape, one that is more sensitive to transportation and communication networks. The resulting increased mobility of people, goods and services, dramatically limits the effect of direct intentions by municipalities because people and organizations move from place to place much more frequently. However the effect of indirect intentions, those patterns that emerge due to the interactions between many different organizations, are substantially changing the way places are built. Within this fitness landscape many different organizations are building and re-locating according to their own needs and desires.

This research is developing an organizational mechanism for manipulating the built environment at the level of indirect intentions. The goal is to direct the evolution towards a highly correlated, multi-scaled network of distinct places. It is suggested that on such a fitness landscape, places are most suitable for human living. The organizational mechanism coordinates the range of possible interactions such that places maintain a balance point between extremes, i.e., the edge of chaos. Near this balance point, places are stable enough to maintain a sense of community and build history; and yet, also open enough to accommodate significant changes in the operating environment, whether developed internally or pressured by the fitness landscape. To understand the patterns that emerge in the built environment, this paper reviews three influences on the built environment: *historical chance*, *self-organization*, and *selective pressures*.

Historical Chance. The operating environment for places is rooted in chance events occurring in three areas: physical features, human actions, and natural stress. Places are defined by strong differentiation, or contrast in the physical features: water and land, forest and fields, mountains and valleys. Great examples of differentiated environments are harbor cities such as Hong Kong, which emerged because the physical features were the most suitable for land/water shipping within an entire region.

Human actions first emerged in places where there was easy availability of food, water and shelter. Subsequently organizational structures for groups of people exceeding 2500 also began to shape places because physical structures were required for the operation of the community. Archeologists studying these early villages built by humans in many parts of the world, have identified patterns of open spaces associated with different scales which supported the need for human interactions.

Also natural stress continually changes the built environment in unpredictable ways. From meteors to plagues to economic swings, nature itself is constantly changing the character of a place with the passing of time. The discovery of gold in California and the abandonment of the Yucatan Peninsula are intriguing examples of natural stresses which dramatically changed the built environment.

An example of the interplay between these three types of chance events can be illustrated through the brief 200 year history of Chicago. Geographically situated at the crossroads of land, river and Great Lakes trading routes gave it a reason in 1831, for existing. In the 1870's, St. Louis was forecast to be the biggest Midwestern city due to its location on the Mississippi as well as the gate way to the west. However human actions like the opening of the St. Lawrence seaway, the emergence of railroads, and the invention of refrigeration changed the fitness landscape substantially. Additionally the natural stress of the enormous 1887 Chicago Fire, presented huge opportunities to update the underlying infrastructure preparing the city for the 20th century. In a matter of 50 years, Chicago's population far out paced St. Louis' and the city became the hub of the midwest.

Self-Organization. Through time humans and human organizations continually make *deals* between each other to accomplish individual objectives. In this research, deals include all human interactions, recreational activities as well as actual monetary transactions. Additionally the actors are considered to be entities such as developers and land owners in the real estate industry, entities creating regulations in the government, and entities needing spaces for deal-making of any reason. Notably any specific deal requires three events: two or more actors come together at a specific place; they exchange ideas, goods, or services; and then they depart.

Through these interactions buildings such as homes, offices, arenas, factories, exhibition halls, schools, etc. are built to facilitate deal-making activities. High-density environments reflect a higher quantity of deal-making, and the diversity of buildings reflects the kinds of deals being made. In places with a long history of deal-making and stability of location, buildings are built to endure longer periods of time. By contrast in places where the location is unstable, and deal-making is temporary or swings dramatically, buildings are built cheaply reflecting a temporary character of place.

The value of a place is determined by how effective it is at facilitating deals. Places therefore are extremely sensitive to the actor's mobility and to the facilities available for making deals. In varied cultures and many different places throughout history plazas, squares and open urban spaces supported deal-making with a few minor amenities: water and open space. These spaces were typically surrounded by high-density buildings for every functional purpose, and were accessed on foot or by animals and carts. They became the center of community life with boundaries defined by a reasonable walking distance, after which agricultural open spaces were required to provide necessary amenities. In today's global marketplace the scale has grown tremendously and a similar phenomenon can be seen, as large exhibition halls are located within close proximity to airports. In addition to water and open space, these new deal centers provide power, telecommunications and climate control, but basically the same underlying deals are being made.

Selective Pressures. Identifying the focal level is necessary to assess which selective pressures occurring at higher levels are influencing patterns at the level of interest. This research primarily focuses on the level of multiple municipalities, but can be extended both to smaller levels such as neighborhoods and towns; as well as higher levels such as metropolises and regions. The level of multiple municipalities is where runaway patterns of sprawling autocentric development are evident. If these patterns are to be addressed in any intentional manner, we will have to look at higher levels of events for solutions.

Selective pressures change the population dynamics, and therefore the underlying evolution of a place and its corresponding ability to facilitate deals. Pressures at the focal level of multiple municipalities include: warfare and political organization, major economic transformations, environmental devastation, and radical change in the beliefs of society. Population in the city of Detroit rose and fell substantially between 1910 and 1970. It grew rapidly in the effort to produce automobiles, which once established as the primary means of transportation expanded people's mobility. Then many different selection pressures left the cities built form obsolete: built for a different way of life people equipped with economical automobiles and new beliefs preferred to live in the suburbs.

Organizational Mechanism

The organizational mechanism utilizes five features to effect changes in the built environment. Two are used to specify conditions at the focal level of multiple municipalities, *Levels of Mobility* and *Access Points*; and two features specify conditions locally within municipalities, *Urban Open Space* and *Degrees of Freedom*; and then the *Parameters* relates all conditions together. The two operational features are demonstrated through a Starlogo simulation, and the two local level issues are explained relative to functioning communities. The organizational mechanism does not specify how communities should build, but coordination of these features would effectively change the way developers play the game of building projects and assessing risk

Levels of Mobility. Today there is a huge variety of modes for traveling, however it is possible to identify distinct levels of mobility that are independent of specific modes. It is essential to consider mobility without reference to a particular mode of travel. This allows the organizational mechanism to be open to new technologies, and open to the most efficient modes of travel for any purpose. Early engineering studies have provided an analysis of the energy efficiencies of different modes relative to rates of travel. Using this as a starting point we can identify the following distinct levels of mobility, using the existing network of travel for reference:

Level 0	• pedestrians	5mph
Level 1	• small streets, mostly residential access	20mph
Level 2	• busy roads, mostly commercial access	40mph
Level 3	• highways, mostly local distribution	80mph
Level 4	• high speed rail, mostly between regions	200mph
Level 5	• airports, mostly between continents	600mph

These levels exist relative to each other and have energy efficient rates with respect to various technologies. Specific modes of transportation vehicles are better suited than others are for certain ranges, capacities and rates of travel. Also within a particular level, there are a variety of transportation modes such as Level 1 including bicycles, scooters and delivery vans; and Level 2 including ferries, light rail, trucks and cars.

Access Points. The mechanism limits the distribution of access points to a particular level of mobility based upon the distance that level of mobility travels with no access. An example might be that a Level 3 interstate highway would have to run 10.5 mi. with no access, which could then be followed by 1 mi. of unlimited access points, and again followed by 12 mi. of no access. Similarly a Level 2 "busy road" might run 3 mi. with no access, followed by 0.3 mi. of unlimited access, and then another 3.2 mi. of no access. It is essential to note that since capacity is variable, the restriction on *distribution* of access does not affect the rate of flow, allowing transportation networks to accommodate the traffic potential for any particular route.

Urban Open Space. When a community decides to add access or a new level of transit, a specified amount of urban open space is required. Simply, these are area requirements for plazas or squares that are located immediately adjacent to the access points to transportation. Although this may seem unnecessary when most financial transactions today are electronic, as stated previously, deals are simply meetings between people or organizations and the subsequent exchange of ideas, goods or services and therefore encompass all of human activities. These activity centers provide a focal point for public life and the opportunity for people to interact in planned and spontaneous ways.

Local Degrees of Freedom. When the access to mobility is coordinated across a network, it becomes possible to ensure the stability of place, because really large-scale activities can only occur where there is support for equally large scaled mobility. Therefore as a part of the organizational mechanism, municipalities would eliminate density restrictions, setbacks and functional restrictions imposed on the changing needs for buildings that facilitate deal making. This gives actors in a community the ability to shape things according to locally determined need, both direct intentions and indirect intentions are open to evolve to selective pressures.

Rather than separate activities by function, the network created by the organizational mechanism filters mixed-use places by level. Large-scale activities occur with other large scale activities, and small scale activities occur with other small scaled activities. Previous strategies have yielded performance regulations that restricted noise levels and traffic within certain districts of a municipality unfortunately they cannot go beyond a municipal jurisdiction to address multi-municipality auto-centric sprawl. Additionally performance regulations are still tied to arbitrarily defining districts on a Zoning Map of a community by planners, rather than accommodating the evolution of the built environment.

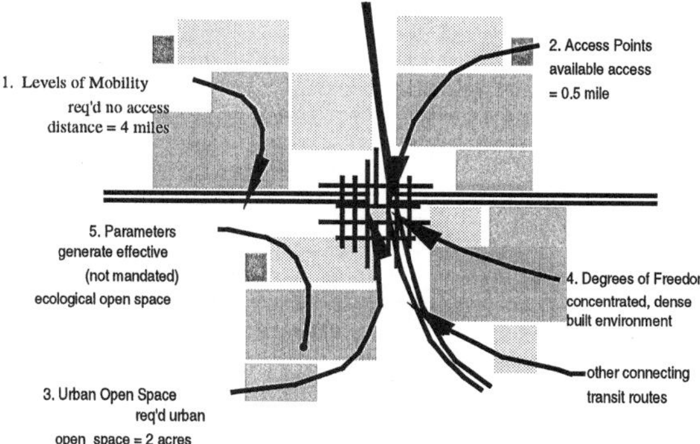

Figure 1 : Mechanism Features - Example @ Level 2

Parameters. Levels of Mobility and Access Points are focused on operational features that coordinate transportation between places. The Urban Open Space and Local Degrees of Freedom are focused on physical features that facilitate deal making within places. All of these features are interconnected by a intricate web of relationships, or the Parameters. Calibrating the ratios between these features is the artful and intentional task of building a highly correlated fitness landscape that successfully allows the built environment to evolve at that point between chaos and stasis.

Observed values used to determine the levels of the mechanism are populations and rate of travel. Sociological literature is filled with observations of optimum populations for communities based on stable patterns that have evolved over millenniums. These observations include many different organizational methods in history and culture. The observed values indicating rates of travel for various levels of mobility have emerged in the relatively short period of a few hundred years. Similar to other complex adaptive systems, these values are clearest at the focal level and slowly become less precise as one tries to apply them to levels further from the focal level. This condition is not a problem because it is the few levels closest to the focal level that are most important to the functioning of the mechanism.

Effects

A simulation of Levels of Mobility and Access Points was developed to demonstrate the effects of deal making activities on the landscape. Five stages of the simulation using Starlogo from MIT, illustrate the fundamental approach towards the development of the mechanism.

Initialization. A number of agents are randomly located on the landscape, each selects a random direction (360°) and begins moving at a rate of 1 space per time step.

Deals. Agents make deals with other agents when they meet in the same location, and then add value to that place. Additionally, after completing a deal each agent selects a new random direction and continues moving.

Levels of Mobility. At the third stage agents are given the ability to utilize a second level of mobility allowing them to travel at the rate of approximately 12 spaces per time step. This occurs only for one time step and after they complete a deal, i.e., they leave quickly.

Motivation. The next stage gives agents the ability to see the value of the landscape and the motivation to seek places of high value.

A Network of Places. Finally when all of these features are combined, the agents proceed to build a loosely structured network of high valued places approximately 12 spaces apart according to the rate of travel for the second level of mobility. The value of the landscape becomes highly contrasted with spaces in-between being of substantially lower value. Abstractly, the random directions selected by the agents as they run around the landscape are essential because it frees the system from physical tracks or routes. Even though today many forms of transport are "track based" some are not, and air travel is reducing the need for physical routes to determine which directions are possible.

Evolution of Landscape Value. Stuart Kauffman's notion about highly correlated fitness landscapes being more robust for evolution is related to the need for increased spatial contrast between places and therefore increased land value contrast. In this context, smooth landscapes are exemplified by suburban environments and extremely rugged landscapes can be seen in urban areas where neighborhoods can change value by crossing a street. He states in <u>At Home in the Universe:</u>

Since selection faces an error catastrophe on very smooth landscapes and can become excessively trapped in small regions of the space of possibilities on very rugged landscapes, we must also begin to suspect that selection seeks 'good' landscapes. We do not as yet know in any detail what kinds of landscapes are 'good,' although it seems safe to conclude that such landscapes must be highly correlated, not random.

Figure 2 : Types of Fitness Landscapes

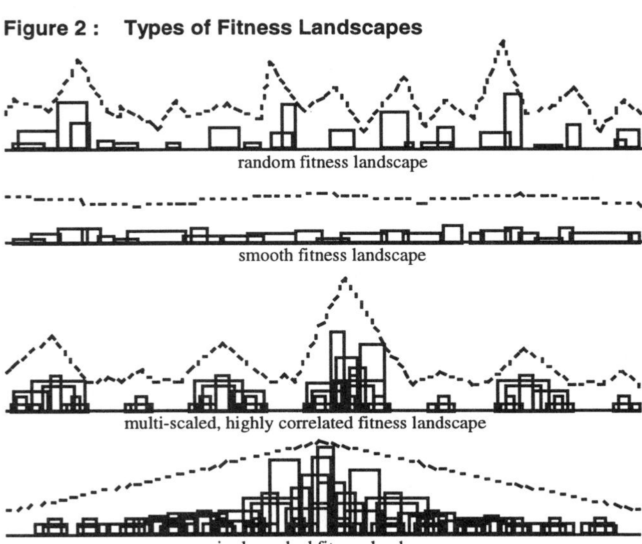

The organizational mechanism is an attempt to provide a highly correlated and multi-leveled fitness landscape where peaks and valleys of land value are related to a system for distributing access to levels of mobility. Developers compete for projects based on a generally defined fitness landscape, where land value is high near access points, also due to the relative stability in the location of access to mobility, they are also challenged to create projects uniquely tailored to a specific place.

Nested Levels of Places. Patterns of mixed-use pedestrian supported, amenity saturated, higher density places will instigate much greater integration of community functions visible to people living in a place. By contrast Zoning-by-Function induces formal patterns with each function in its logical but necessarily effective location.

The following diagrams indicate levels of places that are nested within each other. T, the double ended arrow, represents the transportation level; SO, the small grid, represents the Urban Open Space requirement; SS, the small circle, represents the nested smaller scaled spaces, and the curving arrow represents the direction towards the next larger level.

Figure 3 : Nested Levels of Places

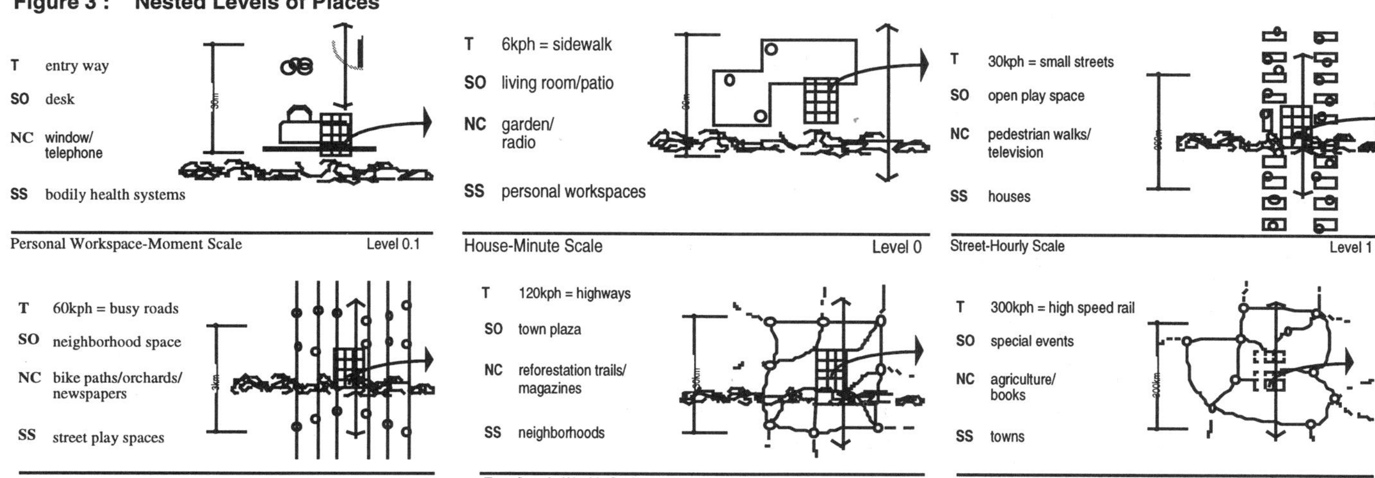

Boundedness. The idea of boundedness is essential in creating a cooperative environment which can support the dynamics of living systems. Boundedness for human beings and the communities we live in consist of two aspects: activity centers and spatial perimeters. Activity centers such as plazas or squares, and perimeters including the Great Wall, nation-state borders, and garden fences work together to create a sense of boundedness.

The Urban Open Space parameter is included to instigate the formation of activity centers. The large distances without access points to transportation provides a sense of perimeter by incorporating ecological open spaces between activity centers, defined by openness rather than property lines.

Recent actions by some metropolises strive for a sense of boundedness by defining a city perimeter beyond which no more development can occur, or by identifying certain lands as "Preservation Areas" and then allowing developers to build as they see fit on the remaining lands. These strategies involve a high-level government agency determining which portions of the landscape will be used for which types of activities. They have an arbitrary and non-adaptive character.

Considerations

The prevailing operating system of places determines a range of possible lifestyles for the people living within those places, e.g., it is pretty difficult to live in a large suburban metropolis and not drive a car. Many do not perceive these as limits, and yet they strongly influence the patterns of how we live. To what extent can or should humans direct the system? Indeed intentions do exist both direct and indirect, the difference is simply our awareness of them as actors within the system.

Sustainability one often heard goal, seems contrary to evolution which is more about survival. Can we develop organizational tools that direct our human evolution? Or should we develop organizational tools that ensure the stability of where we are? The organizational mechanism is open for evolution to a number of unpredictable perturbations, however it also attempts to evolve toward a built environment that supports human interactions gracefully. Thus it is an attempt to intend patterns at a more complex level than humans have been able to manipulate in the past.

References

Giddens, A. 1990. *The Consequences of Modernity.* Stanford, California: Stanford University Press.

Kelso, J. A. S. 1995. *Dynamic Patterns: The Self-Organization of Brain and Behavior.* Cambridge Massachusetts: The MIT Press.

Rusk, D. 1993. *Cities without Suburbs.* Washington D.C.: Woodrow Wilson Center Press.

Buss, L., W. Fontana, and G. Wagner. 1993. Beyond digital naturalism. *Artificial Life* 1:2.

Langton, C. G.. 1990. Life at the edge of chaos. In *Proceedings of the Workshop on Artificial Life*, edited by C. G. Langton. Redwood City, CA: Addison-Wesley. .

Lekson, S. H. 1989. The community in Anasazi archaeology. In *Proceedings of the 21st Annual Chacmool Conference*. University of Calgary.

Investigating Forest Growth Model Results on Evolutionary Time Scales

Holger Lange[1], Birgit Thies[1], Alois Kastner-Maresch[1], Walter Dörwald[1], Jan T. Kim[2] and Michael Hauhs[1]

[1]BITÖK, University of Bayreuth
D-95440 Bayreuth, Germany
[2] Max-Planck-Institut für Züchtungsforschung Carl-von-Linné-Weg 10
D- 50829 Köln, Germany
holger.lange@bitoek.uni-bayreuth.de

Abstract

The output time series from the individual-based tree growth model TRAGIC++ are characterized by measures quantifying their randomness and complexity and by power spectra. TRAGIC++ provides, in addition to spatially very explicit tree stand representations, annual values for biomass production, root development, tree height and many others, for arbitrarily long simulation periods. Site conditions are translated into external growth constraints affecting the aggregated ecosystem level in the form of long-term nutrient input fluxes. Evolutionary effects are included by random mutations of parameters related to height growth strategies of individual trees. Genealogies are being traced to reconstruct evolutionary paths of successful strategies. Long-range correlations for some of the output variables are observed. At the ecosystem level, the nutrient budget remains stationary and uneffected by mutations. Tree strategies, however, appear to show long-term "genetic" drift. Different phenotypes appear to cluster relative independently of mutation rates and resemble adaptation within real forest ecosystems and experiences in forestry.

Introduction to the problem

Traditional AL investigations substitute real world systems ("Life as it is") by artificial ones, sharing a few features considered essential with life and unrestricted otherwise ("Life as it could be"). In most cases, these alternative life forms are realized on a closed finite state machine, i.e. a computer. However, we consider the openness of a living system to its non-living environment a necessary condition for open-ended evolution: Turing machines and their relatives are not capable of simulating "true" evolutionary phenomena. Here, we focus on the computational aspects of learning about the resource distributions in an abiotic environment. A closed evolving system with a given learning capacity will ultimately exploit the prevailing environmental structures exhaustively. After that, nothing happens from an outside perspective. In most situations of natural evolution, feedbacks between ecosystems and the external abiotic resources (exploitable thermodynamic gradients) occur at time scales different from those of internal feedbacks, e.g. by competition among organisms. Evolution shapes the environment of biological systems as much as these are shaped by their abiotic surrounding. This kind of "true" openess has not yet been translated into computational models of life.

Considering ecosystem reactions to (slowly) changing (abiotic) environmental conditions is the main topic of current ecosystem research. In this context, the phrase "Life as it could be" refers to exploration of seminatural managed ecosystems (e.g. forests "as they are") by controlled experiments. Modeling the responses of such ecosystems requires knowledge on the relevant potential (growth) reactions of the biota to input. However, the task of predicting an ecosystem response to a changing abiotic environment is not determined by observations of current phenotypes alone. A key referent of such potential responses is the genotype level. The relevant phenotype level effects can at best be identified in retrospective. Well-documented examples of potential behavior are available from long-term experiences in ecosystem management (e.g. German forestry). We consider *height growth strategies* of trees as such a candidate where the potential behavior to changing abiotic factors (light, nutrients) is sufficiently known to explore its reconstruction through modelling.

Forest ecosystems have the advantage that external resources can be idealized to a few and simple input fluxes of energy and nutrients. Even at the time scales considered here, external feedbacks can be neglected (probably with the prize of sacrificing open-ended evolution). The corresponding learning task for trees that explore these resources is thus easy to pose (at the ecosystem level) but difficult to solve (at the tree level). This work was motivated by the idea that AL on a computer may be a simpler task for *situations* that are **computational** simple rather than for *systems* that are simple biologically.

Contrary to most artificial ecology investigations (e.g. `tierra` (Ray 1992)), our model is biologically detailed. We parametrized the phenotypic appearance and growth of trees in detail, as the range of growth strategies is only partially determined by these building blocks. Furthermore, spatial constraints and relations are explicitly given.

Contrary to most other models, our model is "realistic" *and* simple in its description of external resources. The abiotic environment consists of only two spatially homogeneous input fluxes (energy and a growth-limiting nutrient). In practical forestry, it has repetitively been shown that the mean stand height reflects the relation between these two.

Key elements of this learning task are specified in the growth simulator TRAGIC++. The parametrization, however, is subject to evolution. In a larger perspective we seek a model to reconstruct growth potentials inferred in practical ecosystem management. Here we run the model over evolutionary time-scales under stationary environmental constraints to study the relation between evolutionary paths of strategies and growth-related variables in an artificial ecosystem. We quantify the behavior of output variables of the model by time series analysis, comprising spectral and information-theoretic methods as well as usual statistics.

The model TRAGIC++

The forest growth model TRAGIC++ (Hauhs, Kastner-Maresch and Rost-Siebert 1995) was designed to support silvicultural evaluation tasks in an intuitive manner through a visualized interface. In TRAGIC++ the actual growth of each individual tree is derived from local competition for two abstract and stationary resources: energy and nutrients. The ecosystem constraints on resource availability are transformed into local probability density functions. Only the latter are "visible" to organisms competing locally for these resources. Light extinction through the local shading biomass is simulated by a Lambert-Beer law approach. In the case of nutrients, which come in small discrete portions called "wusels", a simple random walk is used. The majority of the nutrient resource is recycled through "mineralization" determined by litter quality. This release rate to the soil is controlled by a model of the decomposer community (Ågren and Bosatta 1987).

In TRAGIC++, trees maximize instantaneous growth rates as they seek a balance between the efficiency of shoot and root organs by dynamically partitioning their internal resources for biomass growth. Energy and wusels are taken up in yearly time steps. Besides the balanced biomass growth of tree compartments, the respective growth *forms* are regulated by species-specific rules. The aboveground growth of shoots is controlled by a simple L-Grammar, whereas the growth of fine roots is opportunistic and occurs at points of recent wusel uptake. A minimum external wusel input is necessary to account for leaching losses from the soil, or to realize possible scenarios for long-term trends of external input to the system.

Trees compete for space above- and belowground. A detailed description of every tree w.r.t. spatial relationships of five different tree tissues (roots, stems, segments, branches and leaves) is updated in each time step. The height growth of the current year is determined by the potential height growth at that tree's age and its current root uptake efficiency. Thus, the leading shoot requires minimal biomass investment in the year it is built. However, it may largely change the dynamic biomass allocation in later years.

The death of trees is triggered by the internal energy budget. Trees not capable of matching the respiration losses by photosynthesis are removed and their biomass added to the decomposing organic matter pool. Only trees older than 110 years may in addition die randomly due to senescence. Fitness is thus fully implicit to the competitional growth process. *There is no explicit fitness functional provided.*

Evolution of the potential height growth function is modeled by assigning the parameters of this function individually to each "try" (newly built tree). These sets of four real parameters constitute the "genotype" of trees:

$$h(t) = \varsigma \exp(a_0 + a_1 \ln(t / t_0) + a_2 (\ln(t / t_0))^2) \quad (1)$$

where $h(t)$ is potential height growth, ζ is root to height ratio, and t_0 is one year. The sensitivity of realized growth strategies to the parameters ζ, a_1 and a_2 will be discussed below. The a_0 term may be absorbed into a redefined ζ and has no independent meaning. It was kept constant for all simulations. At each reproduction event, one of these three parameters may randomly change within a given range of mutational steps. By varying the rate of nutrient inputs at the ecosystem level, the range of height growth observed in Norway spruce stands (*Picea abies* Karst.) can be reproduced (Hauhs, Kastner-Maresch and Rost-Siebert 1995).

Introduction to complexity measures

It is obvious that a complex model such as TRAGIC++ defeats analytical treatment. Further on, the relationship between model input and simulation results is far from being obvious or trivial. Here, an abstract characterization of behavioral patterns rather than a detailed description of observables is seeked for, as the specific realization of a single simulation is considered unimportant. A byproduct of this analysis is a classification of output variables according to their overall behavior (e.g., to distinguish between random, complex, and deterministic variables).

Besides statistical techniques, we consider power spectra and a collection of complexity measures. To this end, we transform the model output time series to a sequence of the symbols 0 and 1 via *partitioning*. It is advantageous to choose the median of the value distribution as threshold parameter (Lange et al. 1997).

From the symbol sequence $\{s_i\}$, ($i=1,...,N$, $s_i = 0$ or 1), subsequences of fixed length $L \ll N$, called *words*, are considered and their probability distribution $p(s_i)$ analysed. We show results for two representative measures:

The information contained in the symbol sequence at word length L, i.e. the *mean information gain* (Wackerbauer et al. 1994) is derived as an entropy-like variable in the following way:

$$H_L = -\sum_i p(s_i) \log_2 p(s_i)$$

$$MIG(L) = H_{L+1} - H_L$$

By construction, MIG is a quantity in the range [0,1], giving the amount of information gained when enlarging the word length one step. For perfectly random sequences, MIG equals 1; for constant or periodic sequences with period smaller than word length, it is 0.

The complexity of a symbol sequence can be characterized by its *fluctuation complexity* (Bates and Shephard 1993):

$$FC = \sum_{i,j} p_{ij} (\log_2 (p_i / p_j))^2$$

where the sum is over all occurring words of a given length, p_i and p_j their respective relative frequencies, and p_{ij} is the joint (conditional) probability. FC is zero for constant as well as perfectly random sequences and exhibits a maximum in between.

Power spectra give insight into the correlational structure of the data set. Periodic parts are exhibited, as well as possible long-range correlations, which are present if the spectrum shows power-law behavior.

Figure 1: Screenshot of a running TRAGIC++ simulation. This 40 m x 40 m plot contains about 130 trees.

Setting

Setting Up Virtual Evolution with TRAGIC++

The site conditions that will ultimately decide the competition among trees were kept constant throughout all runs presented here. Internal recycling dominates the nutrient supply after a start-up phase in which organic matter is accumulated. After an initial phase of soil formation, the nutrient input level is diminished by 50% after 600 years.

In this paper, we focus on the overall effect of mutation on long-term behavior, randomness and complexity of key output variables. In addition, we investigate how the evolutionary paths depend on mutation rates, and whether phenotypic or genotypic clustering occurs.

The Simulations

All scenarios are based on a parameter set calibrated against a spruce stand at Lange Bramke (Germany). The parameters characterizing the decomposer community are typical for coniferous stands. More than 10000 years or approx. 120 tree generations were simulated with an initial population of trees with identical parameters. Three different scenarios were investigated: without mutating parameters, with small mutation rates ("single mutation") and with large ones ("double mutation"). For single mutation, variation of one of the three parameters ζ (by a maximum of 3%), a_1 or a_2 (maximal 0.3%) takes place at each reproduction event.

Due to performance requirements, the size (40m x 40m, Fig. 1) is limited, but beyond correlation lengths due to shading and root competition which define a *patch*. However, due to spatial interactions among patches, the simulated stand nevertheless partially synchronizes in generation cycles. We thus show **time series** of a variable characterizing the whole stand rather than individual trees. The biomass-weighted mean of all a_1 values shows a long-term declining trend depending on the mutation rate, which also is related to its variability: *nonzero mutation rates introduce non-stationarity*. This is also clearly visible from the time series of the decreasing maximal tree height (Fig. 2), and the increasing total foliage weight (not shown). Under the imposed limiting nutrient supply, long-term drift seems to preferentially select smaller and thicker trees.

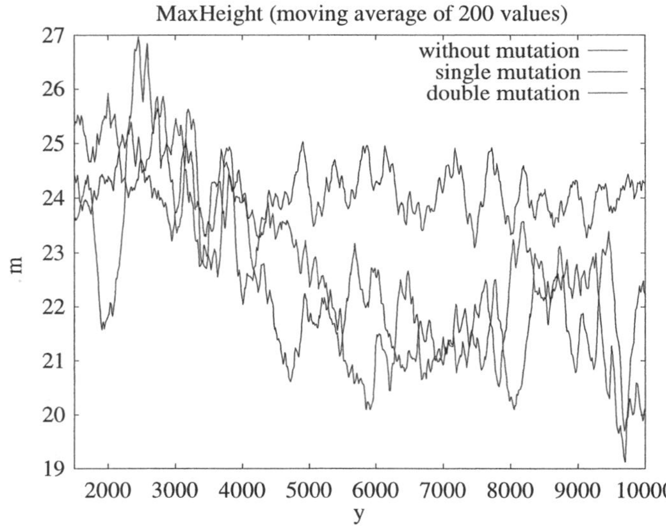

Figure 2: A typical output time series for the three evolutionary scenarios. Mutation leads to a declining maximum height.

After reducing the nutrient input at year 600, a transient

phase in biomass variables is observed. We start our inspection of the runs only after simulation of 1500 years; after that time spurious synchronization effects are absent.

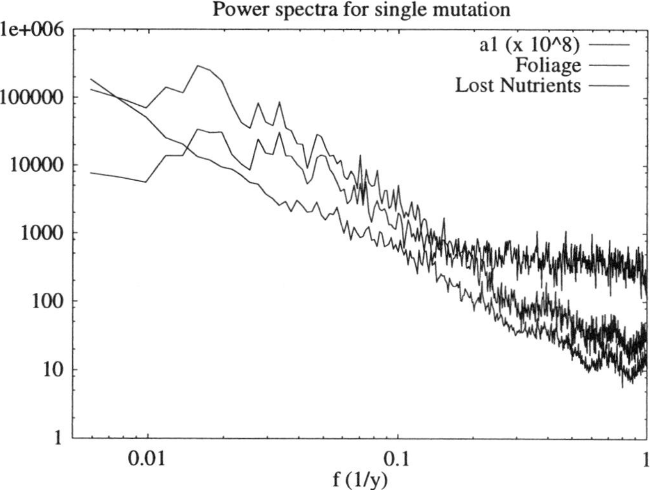

Figure 3: Power spectra in the case of single mutation rate. a1 is close to a random walk without pronounced periodicity. Foliage weight is well approximated by $1/f^2$ at higher frequencies; lost nutrients are also periodic with the same frequency but have no significant structure (close to white noise) at frequencies above 1/(10 y).

The **power spectra** show a clear maximum at the mean generation time of approx. 75 years for biomass-related parameters. As an example, the total foliage weight is shown in Fig. 3.

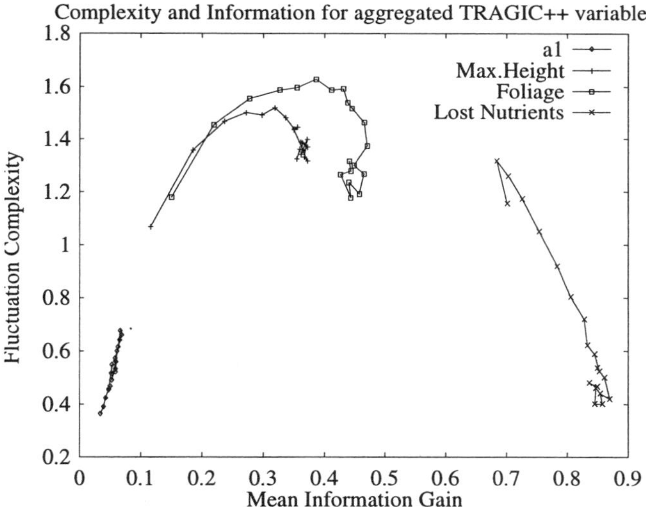

Fig. 4: The curves for randomness and complexity for key variables for single mutation rate were obtained by aggregating up to 20 consecutive values of the original time series.

At time scales below mean generation times, the slope indicates a deterministic process (controlled by the growth, operating under current constraints), whereas at longer time scales foliage weight behaves randomly. The nutrients leaching out of the system share the "generation peak" with biomass variables, but show white noise behavior at shorter time scales, reflecting the random walk of "wusel" nutrients in the root zone. The mutating parameters, exemplified by a_1, exhibit pure Brownian motion over several orders of magnitude.

A comparison of **short-range patterns** (up to 20 years) is illustrated in Fig. 4. Aggregation of values in general makes signals more random, unless the investigation methods detect significant longer correlations. Whereas mutating parameters have very low complexity and randomness values, maximal height and foliage weight show intermediate randomness at high complexity; at least the latter also contains long-term structure. The leaching of nutrients is near random, compatible with the high-frequency behavior of the power spectrum (Fig. 3).

In contrast to these ecosystem-scale (aggregated) variables **evolutionary paths** of height growth strategies at the tree level are affected by mutation rates. In general, trees with similar parameter values and similar phenotypes are "relatives" (exemplified in Fig. 5).

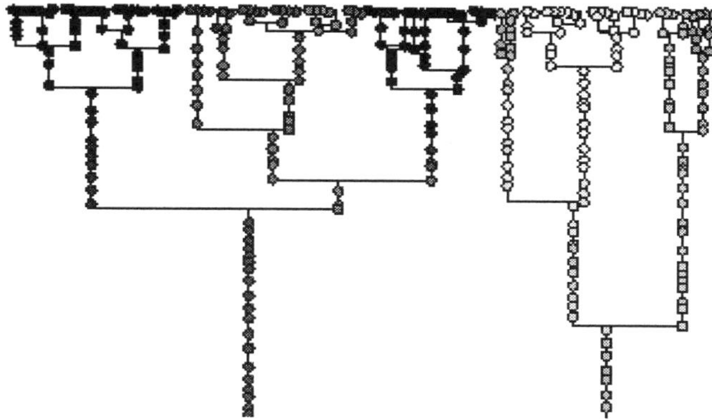

Figure 5: Mutating parameter genealogy: Grey levels indicate values. All branches without surviving members are pruned. The inheritance relations correspond to parameter regimes.

The impact of varying genotypic parameters on phenotypic performance is investigated using **correlograms** (Fig. 6). To that end, the potential height h at a fixed age is calculated from Eq. (1) (the actual height may differ because fitness is fully implicit). Whereas a_2 and ζ are almost uncorrelated to potential height, a_1 shows significant correlations which, however, depend on mutation rate. This poses the question how the distribution of a_1 and height differ for the two mutation scenarios. The respective **histograms** (Fig. 7) show that the effect of doubling the mutation rate is quite different for the two variables: whereas the h distribution has a larger spreading for double mutation, but covers the single mutation case, the a_1 (Fig. 7) and ζ distributions are nearly distinct; a_2 remains unaffected.

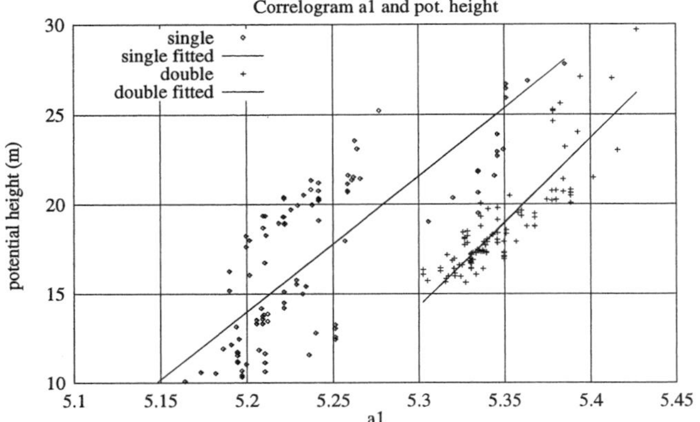

Figure 6 : Correlation diagram for two evolutionary scenarios.

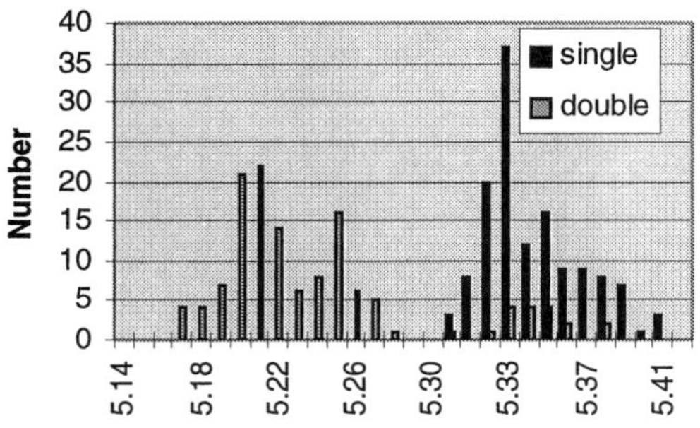

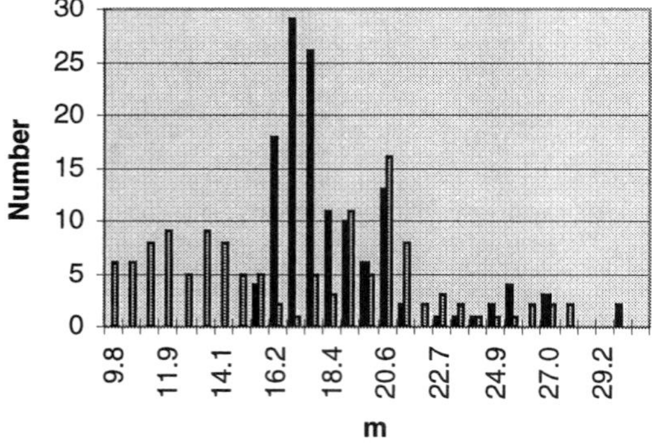

Figure 7: Histograms for two evolutionary scenarios.

Discussion

An artificial forest was exposed to a learning task in which growth strategies had to adapt to a global nutrient constraint. In the two mutating scenarios height growth becomes subject to long-term trends, and a tendency to form clusters could be observed for both scenarios after 120 generations. Thus, the height growth strategy appears to affect fitness and has been exposed to selection in these simulations. The trends in the tree population appear very differently when inspected at different scales. At the "microscopic" scale of genotypes all changes can be characterized as random walks. Due to the over-parameterization of phenotypes, genotypes show different sorts of clustering into common genealogies, without effect on the phenotype. At the "macroscopic" scale of the ecosystem the overall budget of the limiting nutrient remains unaffected and in all runs the leaching losses vary randomly around their long-term means. Thus complexity does only appear at the level of sub-populations and tree related variables, whereas higher or lower levels of aggregation behave deterministically or randomly. Even though these simulations allow to reconstruct growth strategies inferred from forest management, they do not show "true" open-ended evolution. Clearly the next step is to confront this evolving system with a varying pool of invading strategies. Some of which may be cheating (mixed forests). An interactive visualization (Fig. 1) tool is currently developed to allow intuitive user interference ("flight simulator for foresters"), possibly leading to a *truly* open system.

Acknowledgments. The complexity calculations were performed with a program written by F. Wolf, to whom we express our gratitude. This work was financed by the German Ministry of Research (BMBF) under contract no. PT BEO 51-0339476B.

References

Ågren, G.I. and Bosatta, E. 1987. Theoretical analysis of the long-term dynamics of carbon and nitrogen dynamics in soils. *Ecology* 68: 1181-1189.

Bates, J. E., and Shepard, H. K. 1993. Measuring complexity using information fluctuation. *Phys. Lett. A* 172: 416-425.

Hauhs, M., A. Kastner-Maresch, and K. Rost-Siebert. 1995. A model relating forest growth to ecosystem-scale budgets of energy and nutrients. *Ecol. Mod.* 83: 229-243.

Hauhs, M., W.Dörwald, A.Kastner-Maresch, and H.Lange. 1997. The role of visualization in forest growth modeling. Submitted.

Lange, H., J. Newig, and F. Wolf. 1997. Comparison of complexity measures for time series from ecosystem research. *Bayreuther Forum Ökologie* 52: 99-116.

Ray, T.S. 1992. In *Proceedings of Artificial Life II*, edited by C. G. Langton et al. Redwood, CA: Addison-Wesley, p. 371.

Toquenaga, Y., T. Saruwatari, and T. Hoshino. 1997. Repairing genetic algorithm and diversity in artificial ecosystems. In *Proceedings of Artificial Life V*, edited by C. G. Langton and K. Shimohara. Cambridge, MA: MIT Press, p. 300-307

Wackerbauer, R., A. Witt, H. Atmanspacher, J. Kurths and H. Scheingraber. 1994. A comparative classification of complexity measures. *Chaos, Solitons and Fractals* 4: 133-173.

Models in Evolutionary Ecology and the Validation Problem

C. C. Maley*
MIT Artificial Intelligence Laboratory
545 Technology Sq.
Cambridge, MA 02139
cmaley@ai.mit.edu

Abstract

If Alife is ever to contribute significantly to biology, we must find methods by which we can build confidence in our models. One alternative to experimental tests of a model is to validate it against previously verified theory. I have applied a series of ecological and evolutionary validation tests to a model of species diversification. Examination of the predator-prey dynamics, trophic cascades, competitive exclusion, adaptation, and the species-area curve in the model has shown that a course grained spatial structure was inadequate to capture the realistic dynamics of an ecosystem. Only when spatial structure was extended to the local patch dynamics did the model begin to behave realistically under a wide range of parameters. Validation of the ecological dynamics of the model provides indirect support for the evolutionary behavior of the species within the ecosystem. Counterintuitively, under parameter settings that restrict predation, predator biomass rises. Furthermore, the implementation of species resulted in realistic growth rates in the species-area curve.

The Problem of Validation

Traditionally we can try to disprove the validity of the model by collecting data from the real system and comparing it to the predictions of the model. In artificial life we rarely have that luxury. Artificial life models tend to be highly abstract and general because the field is striving to discover general properties of life. Experimental validation extremely difficult due to the time scale of evolution as well as the complexity and size of ecosystems.

An alternative form of validation can be pursued indirectly through reference to ecological and evolutionary theory. Instead of asking if the model matches the experimental data, we can ask if the model matches our understanding of the dynamics of ecology and evolution. Then, to the extent that the theories of ecology and evolution have been validated by experimental observations, we can disprove the validity of a model when it fails to match those theories. What follows is an example of this technique applied to a model designed to examine the factors that impact the origin and maintenance of species diversity. While the purpose of this model is to explore new theoretical ground in biology, the ecological and evolutionary dynamics in the model have been validated against theories of predation, competition, adaptation and island biogeography.

The Evolution of Species Diversity

Why has life diversified so dramatically over the last four billion years (Benton 1995)? Or more specifically, what are the most important factors that have influenced speciation and extinction in the history of life?

Investigations into the dynamics of species diversity depend fundamentally upon the concept of a species. Unfortunately, there does not exist a species definition that unambiguously partitions organisms into mutually exclusive groups (Mayr 1942; 1982; Paterson 1985; Simpson 1961; Wiley 1978; Valen 1976; Cracraft 1983; Baum & Donoghue 1995). The predominate species definition, the "biological species concept," or more appropriately the "reproductive species concept," defines two organisms as belonging to the same species if they can potentially mate and produce fertile offspring (Mayr 1982).

Previous work on diversity has generally substituted genotype diversity for species diversity and so has not addressed the issues surrounding speciation (Hraber & Milne 1997; Jones, Hraber, & Forrest 1997; Bedau, Ronneburg, & Zwick 1992). Hypotheses for the origination and survival of a species typically hinge on both abiotic factors like geographic isolation of a subpopulation, and biotic factors like expansion into new ecological niches through evolutionary innovations. A

*This research was supported in part by NDSEG grant DAAH04-95-1-0557. I would like to thank Rod Brooks, Michael Donoghue, and Hal Caswell for their guidance and support.

model to examine species diversity grounded in our knowledge of microevolutionary dynamics must include representations of organisms, species, geography, sexual reproduction, mutation, migration, death, and predation. Geography and migration are necessary to model allopatric speciation in the isolation and divergence of subpopulations. Mutation, reproduction with inheritance, and death are necessary conditions for the process of evolution, assuming an environment with finite space. Furthermore, reproduction must be sexual for the reproductive species concept to be relevant. And finally, predation, with the concomitant dynamics of specialization and generalization, introduces ecological niches to the model and so allows testing of hypotheses that make reference to ecological niches.

An instantiation

One possible instantiation[1] of these requirements has been implemented. All italicized terms below are parameters to the model. Their experimental settings are generally parenthesized. For a full description see (Maley 1998).

Geography: Space is organized into a two-dimensional grid of "patches." Each patch may contain many (2K) organisms.

Organisms and Predation: To set up a food web, we use three 32-bit genes. *Phenotype*, a bit pattern representing the characteristics of the organism relevant to predator-prey interactions. *Prey template*, a bit pattern specifying the phenotype of an organism that can serve as food. And *generalism*, a bit pattern mask specifying which bits in the prey template are not necessary for the selection of a prey organism. These bits indicate "wild-card" positions. The prey template with wild card positions is compared to the prey's phenotype gene and the number of mismatching bits determines the probability of prey consumption (e^{-n}). The bottom of the food web is populated by autotrophs, organisms that synthesize their own food, which I will call plants. Instead of matching their prey template and generalism genes against a prey organism's phenotype, plants match them against the climate of their environment. The climate of a patch is represented by another 32-bit pattern. A partial match results in the consumption of an energy unit with probability equal to the match. Energy is modeled by a particular number of meals granted to the plant.

Reproduction: Once *energy-conversion* number of meals (3) have been consumed a reproduction attempt is triggered. If an organism can locate a viable mate in its patch, they will produce a new organism. The new organism's genes are constructed by forming the parent's genes by two-point crossover. The new organism's genome then undergoes mutation. Reproductive barriers are implemented by giving the organisms a fourth gene called the reproduction gene, representing phenotypic characters that influence reproduction. Organisms may only mate if their reproductive genes differ in at most one bit.

Species: Consider a graph of the potential mating relationships with nodes representing the states of the reproductive genes in the populations and links between the nodes represent potential mates. Then the dangling cluster (connected component) you would get if you picked up one of the nodes in this graph represents a gene pool and thus a species. The reproduction gene has twice as many (64) bits as the other genes. If there were only a few bits in the reproductive gene, then the probability of two lineages randomly evolving to within a single bit would be relatively high. Conventional wisdom in Biology assumes that it is highly unusual for two species to coalesce into one.

Topology: The random walk in the migration of a newborn organism is modified by the topological barrier value of each location. This value is the probability that the new born organism fails to enter the patch and must remain at is current location for that step of the random walk.

Life in a patch proceeds by working through the stack of living organisms from youngest to oldest, giving each a chance to locate and consume one prey organism in the patch. If there are no edible prey in the patch, the predator starves to death. However, if the predator does find and consume a prey organism, the number of meals it has consumed may trigger a reproduction attempt.

Theoretical Validation

The problems of speciation include both ecological and evolutionary dynamics, and so both dynamics should be validated.

Predator-prey oscillations

The Lotka-Volterra equations were an early abstraction of the dynamics of predator and prey populations. Predator and prey population sizes tend to oscillate. At a minimum, a model of an ecosystem should exhibit these oscillations. The model specified above doesn't. As written, a predator can automatically find a prey organism in its patch. This means that even when prey organisms are rare, the predators can still find them. The prey are driven to extinction and the predator

[1] The current model was written in CILK, a parallel extension of C, and run on the Xolas cluster of Sun Ultra symmetric multiprocessors. See `http://xolas.lcs.mit.edu/` for information on the processors and links to the CILK distribution pages.

population crashes shortly thereafter.

A *prey-location* probability was introduced to the model to represent the chance that a particular predator might find a particular prey organism in its patch. However, a predator still gets one attempt for every potential prey organism in its patch. This results in stable herbivore-plant oscillations across a wide range of parameters ($0.15 \lessapprox$ *prey-location* $\lessapprox 0.3$).

Trophic cascades

While the introduction of the *prey-location* probability stabilized the two-trophic level dynamics, the difficulties multiply when we move to three trophic levels by the addition of a carnivore species. All three trophic levels could only be sustained by lowering the *energy-conversion* parameter to the unrealistic levels, requiring the consumption of only two prey organisms to produce a new predator organism.

For a prey organism to survive during a time step, it must evade location by *every* predator in the patch. The spatial structure of the real world tends to soften intense predation. A prey organism is generally not directly threatened by all the predators in the patch. The model was elaborated with an additional form of spatial structure. A prey organism that survives an encounter with a predator, because of the *prey-location* probability, becomes more difficult to find by other predators. Specifically, the *prey-location* probability is multiplied by $e^{-(\text{number of encounters} \times \textit{predation-distribution})}$. When the *predation-distribution* is 0, there is effectively no spatial structure, and the model behaves as it did before. However, when the *predation-distribution* is positive, a form of spatial structure is imposed on the patch, and a small prey population has a better chance of surviving intense predation.

Booth has attempted to validate the ecological dynamics of a dramatically modified version of ECHO (Holland 1993), called Gecko (Booth 1997). She demonstrated that the model exhibits a "trophic cascade." This is the phenomena that plant biomass first drops and then partially recovers as herbivores and then carnivores are added to the ecosystem.

Results As long as the carnivores were able to survive, a trophic cascade was found. The addition of the *search-radius* had little effect. Both herbivore and carnivore populations were stable with a *predation-distribution* ≥ 0.8. In fact, the average biomass of both herbivores and carnivores increased with the *predation-distribution*, up to the maximum value that was examined (2.0), as seen in the lower graph of Figure 1.

A similarly counter-intuitive result can be seen if we look at the effect of the *prey-location* probability on the

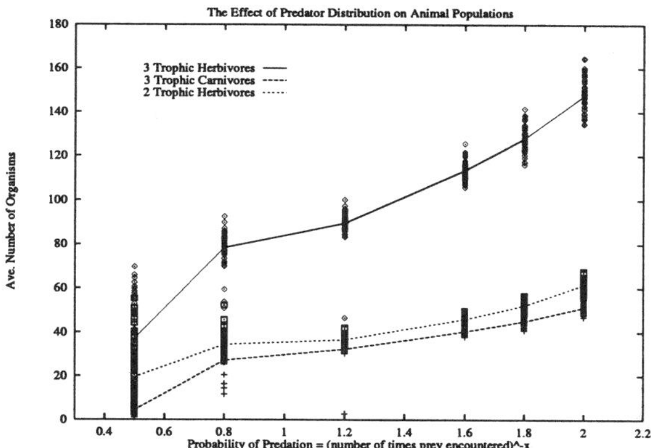

Figure 1: The biomass of the herbivores and carnivores in the two and three trophic level ecosystems. A trophic cascade was found whenever the carnivores survived. Each data point indicates an independent run of the model, and the lines show the mean for all the runs. There are at least 40 data points for each parameter value.

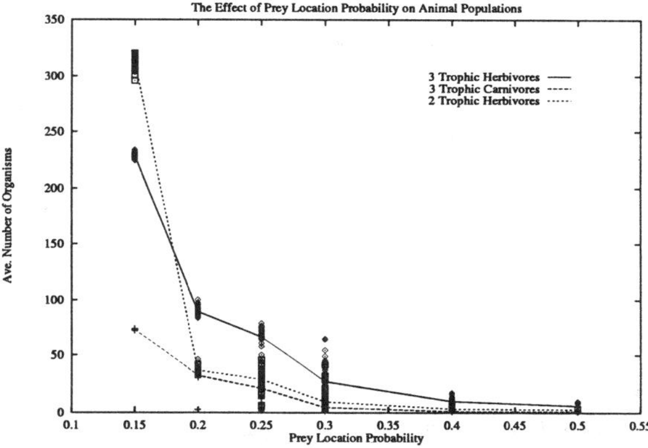

Figure 2: The effect of the prey location probability on the population sizes of animals.

populations of herbivores and carnivores as shown in Figure 2. The most dramatic trophic cascade appears when the *prey-location* probability is 0.2 (the setting used for future experiments). Once again, as the parameter values make predation more difficult, the average predator populations expand. This is probably due to a more efficient allocation of resources to the predators. The average maximum and minimum population sizes of the predators are shown in Figure 3 along with the means. When predation is easy, the predator populations can expand rapidly, reaching higher values than the maximum population sizes attained when predation is hard. However, the success of the predators has a dramatic effect on the prey, and so the predator populations collapse, reaching lower minima as compared to the minima in the runs where predation is more difficult. Ease of predation tends to destabilize the populations, causing larger fluctuations and resulting in lower average predator populations over time.

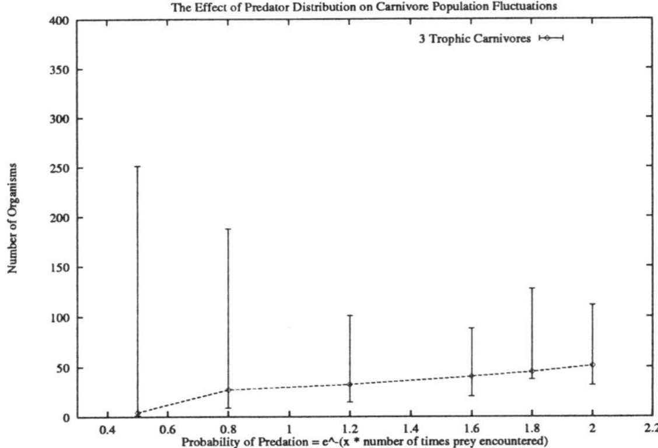

Figure 3: The average maximum and average minimum population sizes have been added to the carnivore curve from Figure 1.

Competitive exclusion

A series of competitive exclusion experiments were designed wherein the environment was seeded with equal numbers of two species of plant. The "climate" of the environment had all its bits set to 0 and the prey template genes of the plant species differed by only one bit. That is, one of the two species was exactly one bit better adapted to the environment than the other. This should result in a slightly better energy absorption and a consequent slightly higher reproduction rate in the species with fewer bits set. A species was considered to have excluded the other species when it had expanded to 90% of the carrying capacity of the environment. 100 trials were run with 1, 4, 8, 16, 24, and 31 bits set to 1 in prey template gene of the inferior species. Mutation was turned off for these experiments. The superior species excluded the inferior in all the trials.

Adaptation

A model of evolution should at least demonstrate that, all other things being constant, organisms evolve to be better adapted to their environment. This can be tested in the model when mutation is introduced into the dynamics. Consider a plant species evolving in the conditions of the competitive exclusion experiments. The optimal genotype matches the climate bit pattern of all 0's. If the prey template and generalism genes were evolving neutrally, with no natural selection, then we would expect one in four bits in the plant's prey template to have a 1 not masked by the generalism gene. We can thus detect natural selection in any significant reduction in that proportion of unmasked 1's.

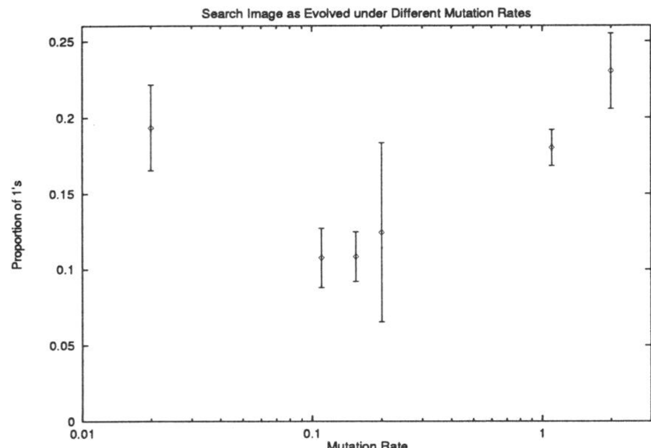

Figure 4: The normalized distance (with standard deviations) of plant populations from the optimal genotype under different mutation rates. In all cases the null hypothesis of neutral evolution can be rejected.

The model was initialized with a plant species with exactly 8 out of 32 positions in its prey template set to 1 and no wild-card positions. After 5000 time steps the proportion of unmasked 1's was counted and averaged. The data for at least 32 runs in each setting of the *mutation-rate* parameter is shown in Figure 4. For all mutation rates, the resulting data is significantly below a mean of 25% unmasked 1's as tested by a one-sided t-test ($p < 0.001$ in all cases). There can be little doubt that the plant species have adapted to their environment.

The species-area curve

The previous experiments were conducted within a single patch. To investigate the relationship of species diversity to area, we must move to multiple patch experiments. The central result of island biogeography is that the number of species (S) on an island is a power law of the area (A) of the island (MacArthur & Wilson 1967). Specifically, $S = cA^z$, where c is a constant and the exponent z is particular to the group of organisms being studied. Begon et al. (1990, p.778) have summarized observed values for z which range from a low of $z = 0.10$ for English flowering plants to a high of $z = 0.43$ for mountainous mammals in the USA, with an outlier of $z = 0.72$ for cave dwelling invertebrates.

The model was run in four spatial configurations, 1 by 2, 2 by 2, 2 by 4, and 4 by 4 patches. The climates of the patches were made to differ by randomly flipping 2 of their 32 bits. There were topological barriers to migration of 0.9 between all patches. Species diversity data were collected after 5000 time steps for 50 runs of the model under each spatial configuration. A linear regression of the $\log_2$ species as determined by the $\log_2$ area gives $z = 0.44$ ($p < 0.001$, standard error $= 0.05$). While this is on the high end of the range found in nature, most island biogeographical studies have focused on a single group of organisms, such as birds, ants, or land plants, and do not look at diversity across multiple trophic levels, and so miss coevolutionary diversification effects. Furthermore, the species-area curve is based on the origination of species by colonization from some source pool, not by speciation events, as in the model. The z of 0.44 compares well to the values (0.7–0.95) found by Jones et al. (1997) for genotype diversity.

Conclusions

The initial failure of the model and subsequent elaboration of the predation algorithms illustrates an important benefit of validation studies. Failure in a validation study helps to sharpen our understanding of the essential features of the system and so helps to guide the further development of the model. It is also important to note that even when there exists a paucity of theory that can be used to verify the central results of a model, there generally exists a rich field of theory that impacts upon the dynamics of the model. In this case, a model of species diversification was designed for the very reason that there is a lack of established theory covering the topic. However, such a model must include both ecological and evolutionary dynamics and so we have validated it against both ecological and evolutionary theory. Because the dynamic of diversification intimately depends upon ecological and evolutionary interactions, these validation studies can help to support the end results of the model.

This model suggests that obstacles to predation can actually boost predator biomass by curtailing population oscillations. In addition, the use of species rather than genotype diversity results in realistic growth rates in the species-area curve. The fact that a model passes a series of validation tests against theory does not guarantee the quality of its results. The above model is only one instantiation of the requirements for modeling species diversity, and so stands as a single data point for theory. This perspective on models is particularly important to artificial life where seemingly trivial implementation details often manifest in artefactual results. In the end, the model does not provide Truth but rather a hypothesis that should be experimentally verified, similar to any other theoretical result. Although, it must be granted that such experimental verification is difficult. Meanwhile, by testing our models against theory, we may at least make progress toward significant theoretical insight.

References

Baum, D. A., and Donoghue, M. J. 1995. Choosing among alternative "phylogenetic" species concepts. *Systematic Botany* 20:560–573.

Bedau, M. A.; Ronneburg, F.; and Zwick, M. 1992. Dynamics of diversity in an evolving population. In Männer, R., and Manderick, B., eds., *Parallel Problem Solving from Nature, 2.* Amsterdam, The Netherlands: Elsevier Science Publishers. 95–104.

Begon, M.; Harper, J. L.; and Townsend, C. R. 1990. *Ecology.* London: Blackwell Scientific Publications.

Benton, M. J. 1995. Diversification and extinction in the history of life. *Science* 268:52–58.

Booth, G. 1997. Gecko: A continuous 2-d world for ecological modeling. *Artificial Life* 3:147–164.

Cracraft, J. 1983. Species concepts and speciation analysis. *Current Ornithology* 1:159–187.

Holland, J. H. 1993. Echoing emergence: Objectives, rough definitions, and speculations for echo-class models. Technical Report 93-04-023, Santa Fe Institute.

Hraber, P. T., and Milne, B. T. 1997. Community assembly in a model ecosystem. *Ecological Modelling.*

Jones, T.; Hraber, P. T.; and Forrest, S. 1997. The ecology of echo. *Artificial Life* 3:165–190.

MacArthur, R. H., and Wilson, E. O. 1967. *The Theory of Island Biogeography.* Princeton, NJ: Princeton University Press.

Maley, C. C. 1998. *The Evolution of Biodiversity: A Simulation Approach.* Ph.D. Dissertation, Massachusetts Institute of Technology, Cambridge, MA.

Mayr, E. 1942. *Systematics and the Origin of Species.* New York: Columbia University Press.

Mayr, E. 1982. *The growth of biological thought : diversity, evolution, and inheritance.* Cambridge, MA: Belknap Press.

Paterson, H. E. H. 1985. The recognition concept of species. In Vrba, E. S., ed., *Species and Speciation.* Pretoria: Transvaal Museum Monograph No. 4. 21–29.

Simpson, G. G. 1961. *Principles of Animal Taxonomy.* New York: Columbia University Press.

Valen, L. V. 1976. Ecological species, multispecies, and oaks. *Taxon* 25:223–239.

Wiley, E. O. 1978. The evolutionary species concept reconsidered. *Systematic Zoology* 27:17–26.

A Framework for Sensor Evolution in a Population of Braitenberg Vehicle-like Agents

Alexandra Mark, Daniel Polani, and Thomas Uthmann

Institut für Informatik
Johannes Gutenberg-Universität
D-55099 Mainz, Germany
{polani,uthmann}@informatik.uni-mainz.de

Abstract

We introduce a framework for the study of sensor evolution in a continuous 2-dimensional virtual world (XRAPTOR) populated by agents with Braitenberg vehicle-like capabilities. The agents have a fixed or a varying number of "eyes" as sensors and are controlled by simple neural networks. Results of runs evolving characteristics of sensors and networks are presented.

Introduction

In nature a rich variety of new sensor channels evolved during the development of life. There are, e.g., weakly electric fish using electroreceptors (Heiligenberg 1991), chameleon eyes with a telephoto lens effect (Ott 1995) or flies that can hear (Lakes-Harlan & Heller 1992). v. Salvini-Plawen and Mayr (1977) show morphological sequences of eye differentiation of still existing species from simple light-sensitive cells over pinhole eyes to highly differentiated lenticular eyes. Nilsson & Pelger (1994) simulate such a sequence to estimate the time required for an eye to evolve in Nature: less than 400,000 years. Sometimes synesthesia, mixing of several senses, occurs: stimulation of one sensory modality causing perceptions in different senses (Cytowic 1995).

But what about artificial or simulated new sensor channels? (Cariani 1992) considers the construction of new sensors in real devices and (Pask 1959) provides an example by constructing an artificial ear. (Lund, Hallam, & Lee 1997) evolve ears for the Khepera robot and (Lee, Hallam, & Lund 1996) simulate an agent acquiring distance information from any number of sensors. There also exist several approaches coding some sensor parameters genetically (Cliff, Harvey, & Husbands 1993); (Menczer & Belew 1994); (Todd & Wilson 1993) or switching off given sensors (Balakrishnan & Honavar 1996); (Nolfi, Miglino, & Parisi 1994). (Vaario, Hori, & Ohsuga 1995) introduce a complex model forming agents and sensors by production rules.

Since the simulation of sensor evolution is a very complex task that cannot be solved satisfactorily with the currently available computer power, our aim is to concentrate on the simulation of the evolution of two eye parameters of Braitenberg vehicle-like agents (Braitenberg 1984). Here we evolve *eye width* described in Sec. 2 and the eye number within a wide range. For agents with fixed sensors we earlier performed GA evolution of general population behavior (Uthmann & Polani 1997). After introducing our simulation scenario in Sec. 2, two models for agent control are presented in Sec. 3, followed by a description of GA and network coding. We test two different environments, one of them with increasing difficulty. The latter serves to obtain an environment difficult enough to achieve a selective pressure toward higher eye numbers. Often it proves to be impossible to start at once with a very difficult task (cf. Gomez and Miikkulainen (1997). Results and outlook are presented in Sec. 4.

Scenario

For the simulations we used the simulation environment XRAPTOR (Mössinger *et al.* 1997). It provides a model for a 2-dimensional continuous world, in which the agents can move. The agent body contains only the sensory and motoric equipment of the agent. Agent control obtains its world information filtered through the sensors and performs actions via the motoric interface. A freshly created agent is provided with an initial life energy, which is used up during lifetime, modeling *aging*. An agent dies when its life energy drops below a given threshold. Energy is gained by dwelling in *lamps*, and heavily lost by collisions with other agents. Collisions with *obstacles* immediately kill an agent. This life energy balance establishes the selection mechanism needed for the GA discussed in Sec. 3.

The agent dynamics used in our simulations is similar to that of Braitenberg vehicles (Braitenberg 1984). Each agent operates in a 2-dimensional world and has two motors left and right from its orientation axis (Fig. 1) which can each be operated with intensities between -1 and 1. If both motors are activated with the same positive (negative) intensity, the agent moves forward (backward). A difference in the motor intensities leads to rotation in addition to a possible net movement.

The agent sensors ("eyes") detect the presence of other

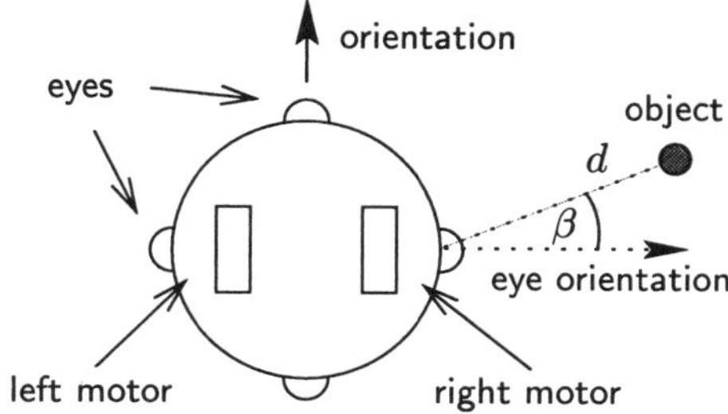

Figure 1: Agent with 8 eyes (4 eye positions)

agents or objects. They are placed at the periphery of the agent body (Fig. 1 shows an agent with 4 eye pairs, see below). Eye orientation is perpendicular to the agent periphery, in Fig. 1 the eyes are oriented outwards. They possess an orientation characteristics, i.e. the intensity I of a signal induced in an eye by the presence of an object depends on the object distance d and on the angle β (Fig. 1): $I_b(d,\beta) = \max\left(\log\left(c \cdot \frac{\max(0,1-\frac{\beta^2}{2b^2})}{d^2+\delta^2}\right), 0\right)$, $b > 0$ being the *eye width*, c a scaling constant and $\delta > 0$ a regularization term (details in Mark (1998).

Similarly to *Vehicle 3c* from Braitenberg (1984) our agents are equipped with 2 types of eyes, detecting either other agents and lamps or obstacles and lamps. At each eye position in Fig. 1 there is an eye pair of two different eye types. The number of an agent's eyes can be chosen at creation time and is not modified afterwards. The pairs are located at equally spaced angles and are more densely placed for a larger eye number.

Evolution Model

As we are primarily interested in evolution of sensors, the design of a particular control structure has not been the main objective of this paper. However an agent's control is required to evaluate the performance of its sensors w.r.t. the tasks in the virtual world, is therefore closely linked to its sensors and has to be evolved together with them.

We used different kinds of simple agent control models, particularly simple neural network models. First we examined a linear network mapping the input vector (one neuron for each eye) linearly to the 2-dimensional output which is then scaled between -1 and 1 via a squashing function and directly used as motor activation. *Direct weight coding* was used to code the weights directly into the GA chromosome. This approach requires a mechanism to increase the chromosome length for variable eye number (see below).

In a second approach we applied Sanger's unsupervised specialization of Plumbley's rule (Plumbley 1991) to a one-layer linear net with inputs observed during the agent's life as training signal. This unsupervised rule essentially performs a PCA on the input data such that the output neurons become feature detectors for the first few principal components. A second linear layer (with two outputs for the motor and a typically small number of neurons), is appended to the first; its weights are generated by the GA (Fig. 2) and determine how the detected features are to be translated into motor activations. The genome information required for the GA in this approach is much smaller than with direct weight coding and the chromosome size does not depend on the number of eyes. The computational effort for the online-learning involved is very high for this model, thus at this point we only present preliminary results for task 1, which is described below.

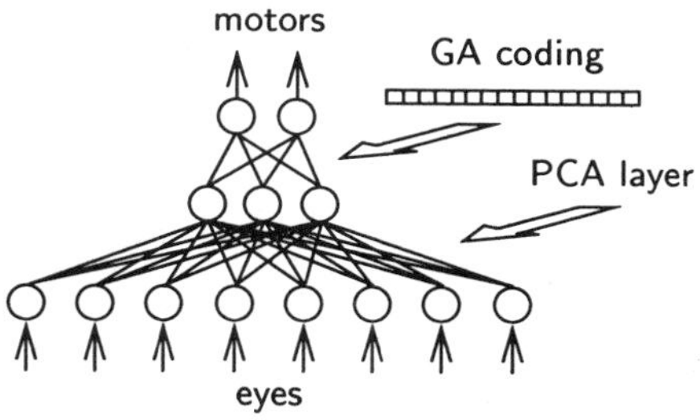

Figure 2: Plumbley network

Motivated from the idea to overcome the linearity restrictions of the simple linear and the Plumbley network, we also studied further network models closely related to vector quantization and Self-Organizing Maps as control structure (for details on models and results see (Mark 1998)).

To determine whether certain eye numbers yield significant advantage, a sequence of GA runs optimizing eye width and control was used. Another also allowed eye numbers to vary. At the beginning of a generation population size is 60, which may drop to 40 before the population is refilled by new agents resulting from recombination of survivor chromosomes, mutated clones of survivors or "immigrants" with new chromosomes. Chromosomes determine sensor parameters like eye width and eye number and adjustable weights of the neural networks. Eye width (range $[0,3]$) and weights are real numbers, coded by one byte each, eye number is an integer in $\{0,2,4,\ldots,100\}$.

For fixed-number eyes, the GA-process is canonical, but becomes more subtle when the number of eyes is varying, because for the direct weight coding the number of weights (and thus chromosome length) scales with the number of eyes. Since recombination of varying length chromosomes cannot be expected to conserve building blocks (Goldberg 1989), we introduce *families*, sets of agents with the same eye number, and forbid interbreeding between members of different families. A new family is created reducing or extending a chromosome by one eye position (i.e., two eyes) and a slight mutation. The motivation is that switching from one eye number to a neighboring one the eye positions do not shift too far and thus sensory input will not change too strongly, enabling the GA to adapt itself to the new eye number. Since all chromosomes have the same length in the Plumbley model, we did not apply any interbreeding restriction, but inclusion of the family concept is planned for the future.

Two tasks are to be solved by the agent population. In task 1 agents have to find lamps and to avoid other agents. Entering lamps is rewarded by energy and collisions between agents are punished. The two types of agent eyes can distinguish between other agents and lamps.

Task 2 studies sensor evolution in a more difficult and controlled environment. The agents have to get to a light source, every agent being alone in its world. Task 2 is made increasingly difficult by introducing obstacles. The two agent eye types detect lamps and obstacles. An agent starts at a random position in the grey shaded rectangular region denoted in Fig. 3, the lamp is denoted by the grey shaded circle. The obstacles are inserted into the world on completing different levels given by certain performance conditions. Fig. 3 shows the obstacles for the different levels. The run starts with level 0. When completed, the obstacles of level 1 are introduced and so forth. Thereby the task becomes gradually more challenging and the GA is forced to search for increasingly better solutions.

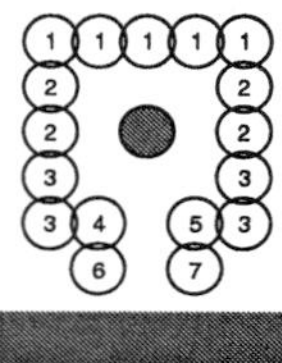

Figure 3: Setting for task 2.

Results and Outlook

The results presented here have been obtained mainly using Sun Ultra 1 workstations. A typical 5000 generation run took between 1 or 2 weeks of computation time. Consequently, the number of runs we could perform was strongly restricted and limited our capability of making statements of statistical nature. However some tendencies are quite prominent and warrant some preliminary interpretation and further investigation.

The results of the GA runs (5000 generations) using the linear net with fixed eye number are shown in Tab. 1. The numbers in the table denote the generations needed to get to the current task level. The runs show clearly that getting to task level 5 is achieved for all eye numbers, but the introduction of obstacle 5 poses a very strong impediment. Reaching task level 6 (getting to the lamp after obstacle 5 has been inserted) seems to be clearly harder for agents with smaller eye numbers (< 32) and task level 7 is only reached by agents with 32 or 100 eyes. Of course the significance of these results will have to be improved by further runs; however they are corroborated by further 1000 generation runs which we performed to improve statistics of the initial phase of the runs. For every eye number we ran 10 such GAs. Nearly all reached task level 5. Only the 32-eyed achieved task level 6 (in 5 runs), indicating strongly that the larger number of sensors is an advantage to solve the problem. The GA for the 100-eyed agents is of course slower because of the larger search space.

eyes	lev. 1	lev. 2	lev. 3	lev. 4	lev. 5	lev. 6	lev. 7
4	10	17	17	59	123	–	–
4	8	12	12	19	88	–	–
4	9	13	14	20	99	–	–
6	9	19	30	67	409	–	–
6	6	16	19	36	510	4756	–
6	10	16	19	68	230	–	–
8	10	19	24	66	496	4139	–
8	8	20	22	45	258	–	–
8	7	14	23	38	106	–	–
32	6	25	29	49	312	1504	–
32	8	15	18	42	524	792	963
32	8	22	31	71	1122	2486	–
100	5	15	22	60	64	1492	–
100	8	17	19	96	210	–	–
100	7	27	36	67	547	708	2256

Table 1: Number of generations for reaching given level

The runs using the Plumbley networks were restricted to task 1. Fig. 4 shows the behavior of clones from well-performing agents in the GA run at different ages, learning their way to the lamp. The agent is denoted by a small diamond, lines indicating its movement vector, small circles denoting starting positions and the large circle the lamp. The untrained agent (not shown here) performs weakly and never reaches the lamp. After 10^4 time steps living in the population it had learned to move to the lamp from most initial positions, and, when older (e.g., 10^6), to extend and smooth its path. Interestingly,

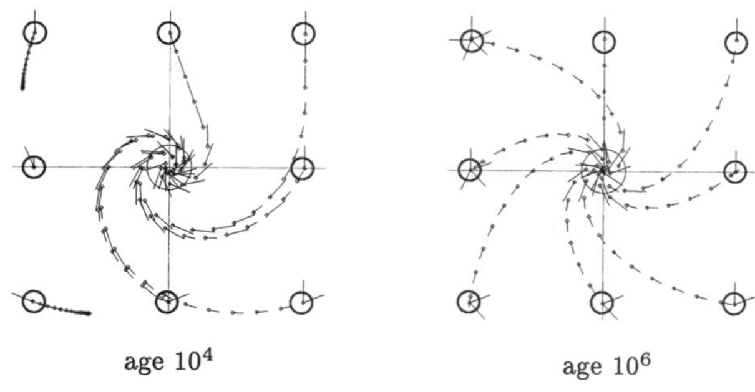

Figure 4: Plumbley learning

from the point of view of sensory evolution these runs did not indicate any selection advantage to a particular number of eyes. This could be due to the fact that interbreeding of completely different eye numbers was allowed in these runs. To clarify this point, inclusion of the family concept from Sec. 3 is indicated for these runs.

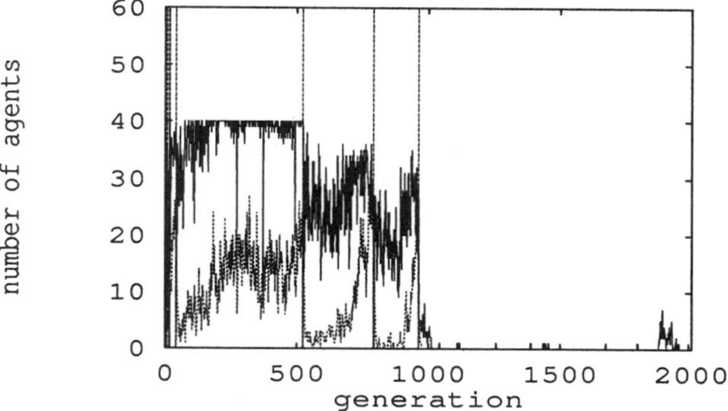

Figure 5: Agents in lamps

Now we have a closer look at the run with 32 eyes that reached level 7 after 963 generations (Tab. 1). Fig. 5 shows the performance of that run. This picture is typical for *all* runs (even with different models). The vertical lines mark the generations in which a new task level is reached. The x-axis shows the generations from 0 to 2000. The last 3000 generations are cut off because the plot does not show any relevant development. The y-axis shows the number of agents (pop. size 60). The solid line indicates the number of agents that spend more than 50% of generation time in a lamp. Note that each agent is placed back at a new random start position every 2000 simulation steps. The dotted line shows the number of agents older than 10,000 simulation steps possessing an energy higher than their initial energy plus an offset. If this value reaches 30 (half the full pop. size) it is assumed that a satisfactory fitness level is reached and a new task level is introduced. As can be seen the solid line grows much earlier than the dotted one after the introduction of each new task level; it represents a global dynamical property of the system since it is not necessarily calculated for the same agents in succeeding generations. 40 is an upper limit for all lines because a new generation starts when less than 40 agents are alive and all data are generated at the end of each generation. All agents are set back to a new random start position and get a new start energy when a new task level is introduced. Thus the solid line shows that on average a relatively high part of the agents reaches the lamps quickly at the earlier levels and slower at the later levels. The dotted line increases much slower, mainly because of the condition that the agents have to be older than 10,000, i.e.

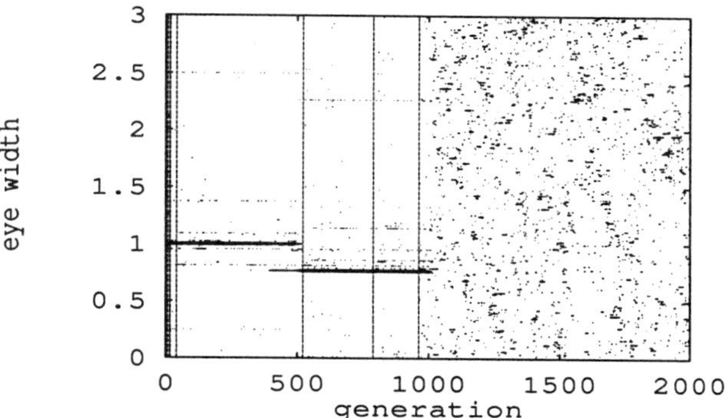

Figure 6: Eye width statistics

individual agents have to reach a lamp several times in succession. Level 7 seems to be very difficult as almost no agent reaches the lamp.

As mentioned in Sec. 3, we evolved the parameter eye-width. In Fig. 6 (same run as in Fig. 5) at every generation (x-axis) a splotch marks an eye width (y-axis) that is attained at least twice within the population. The radius of each splotch is proportional to the number of agents possessing the corresponding eye width in the current generation. Until reaching a certain level (in above case 7 in generation 1000), few eye widths are dominant. After that the eye widths spread out over the full interval $[0, 3]$. This is typical for all runs performed with the linear model and fixed eye number, indicating that at a certain level the task becomes difficult and the GA search gets unspecific.

In all runs to the linear network we find clear indications that agents with higher eye numbers develop lower eye widths (except for 100 eyes, probably because 1000 generations were not enough to evolve better solutions). These results, however, show a relatively high standard deviation because of the small number of runs (see Mark (1998). Nevertheless this indicates that agents with more eyes achieve a better image resolution and therefore can navigate better. This phenomenon deserves further investigation.

As mentioned in Sec. 3, we did some prototypic runs with variable eye numbers. We introduced sensor noise (added to eye signal) to get a selective pressure toward higher eye numbers. In Fig. 7 we show a run where the dominant number of eyes (y-axis) increased strongly. The x-axis shows the number of generations. The simulation starts with a population of agents possessing 2 eyes. The eye number increases to 6 and stays at that level until the first five task levels are reached. Specific noise and GA settings consistently lead to increasing eye numbers in a sequence of several runs.

For a more detailed presentation and discussion of the results see (Mark 1998). Future work will include a sub-

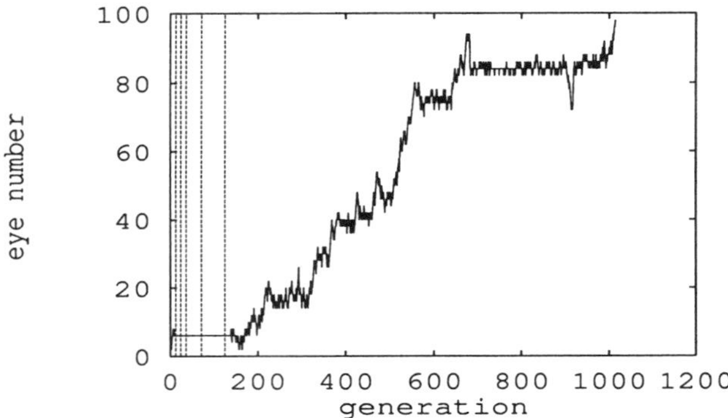

Figure 7: Most frequent eye number

stantial increase of the statistical basis, additional runs with variable eye numbers and study of different levels of sensor noise to increase selection pressure toward larger eye numbers as well as fixed-length variable eye number approaches using unsupervised on-line learning (e.g., Plumbley networks). To be better able to evaluate the success of the GA runs it would be important to introduce a measure of visual acuity adequate to describe the improvements; we did not want to preassume such a measure for our GA selection, as our interest was to study simulated sensor evolution driven by the requirements of world tasks and not by the optimization of abstract quantities.

Acknowledgements

We would like to thank the anonymous reviewers for helpful comments.

References

Balakrishnan, K., and Honavar, V. 1996. On sensor evolution in robotics. In Koza; Goldberg; Fogel; Riolo., eds., *Proc. of GP-96*, 455–460. MIT.

Braitenberg, V. 1984. *Vehicles.* Cambridge: MIT.

Cariani, P. 1992. Some epistemological implications of devices which construct their own sensors and effectors. In Varela; Bourgine, eds., *Proc. of ECAL 1*, 484–493.

Cliff, D.; Harvey, I.; and Husbands, P. 1993. Explorations in evolutionary robotics. *Adaptive Behavior* 2(1):73–110.

Cytowic, R. E. 1995. Synaesthesia: Phenomenology and neuropsychology. *Psyche* 2(10).

Goldberg, D. E. 1989. *Genetic Algorithms in Search, Optimization and Machine Learning.* Addison-Wesley.

Gomez, F., and Miikkulainen, R. 1997. Incremental evolution of complex general behavior. *Adaptive Behavior* 5(3-4):317–342.

Heiligenberg, W. 1991. *Neural Nets in Electric Fish.* Cambridge MA: MIT.

Lakes-Harlan, R., and Heller, K.-G. 1992. Ultrasound-sensitive ears in a parasitoid fly. *Naturwissenschaften* 79:224–226.

Lee, W.-P.; Hallam, J.; and Lund, H. H. 1996. A hybrid gp/ga approach for co-evolving controllers and robot bodies to achieve fitness-specified tasks. In *Proc. IEEE 3rd Int. Conference on Evolutionary Computation.* NJ: IEEE.

Lund, H. H.; Hallam, J.; and Lee, W.-P. 1997. Evolving robot morphology. In *Proc. IEEE 4th Int. Conference on Evolutionary Computation.* NJ: IEEE.

Mark, A. 1998. Sensorielle Evolution. Diploma Thesis (`ftp://ftp.informatik.uni-mainz.de/pub/publications/thesis/mark_diplom_98`).

Menczer, F., and Belew, R. K. 1994. Evolving sensors in environments of controlled complexity. In Brooks; Maes, eds., *Artificial Life IV: Proc.*, 210–221. MIT.

Mössinger, P.; Polani, D.; Spalt, R.; and Uthmann, T. 1997. A virtual testbed for analysis and design of sensorimotoric aspects of agent control. *Simulation Practice and Theory* 5(7-8):671–687.

Nilsson, D.-E., and Pelger, S. 1994. A pessimistic estimate of the time required for an eye to evolve. In *Proc. Royal Soc. London*, vol. 256 of *Series B*, 53–58.

Nolfi, S.; Miglino, O.; and Parisi, D. 1994. Phenotypic plasticity in evolving neural networks. In Gaussier; Nicoud, eds., *Proc. of first Int. Conference From Perception to Action.* Los Alamitos, CA: IEEE.

Ott, M. 1995. A negatively powered lens in the chameleon. *Nature* 373:692–694.

Pask, G. 1959. Physical analogues to the growth of a concept. In *Mechanisation of Thought Processes: Proc. of Symposium held at Nat. Physical Lab. (No. 10)*, vol. II, 877–928. London: Her Majesty's Stationary Office.

Plumbley, M. D. 1991. On information theory and unsupervised neural networks. TR 78 CUED/F-INFENG, Cambridge Univ. Engineering Dep., UK.

Todd, P. M., and Wilson, S. W. 1993. Environment structure and adaptive behavior from the ground up. In *From Animal to Animats 2: Proc.*, 11–20. MIT.

Uthmann, T., and Polani, D. 1997. Investigations of the dynamics of an evolving agent population. In *Proc. 2nd German Workshop on Artificial Life.* Univ. of Dortmund.

v. Salvini-Plawen, L., and Mayr, E. 1977. On the evolution of photoreceptors and eyes. In Hecht et al., eds., *Evolutionary Biology*, vol. 10. NY: Plenum. 207–263.

Vaario, J.; Hori, K.; and Ohsuga, S. 1995. Toward evolutionary design of autonomous systems. *Int. Journal in Computer Simulation* 5:187–206.

A Gene Network Model of Resource Allocation to Growth and Reproduction

George Marnellos
Sloan Center for Theoretical Neurobiology,
The Salk Institute, La Jolla, CA 92037, USA

Eric Mjolsness
Machine Learning Systems Group,
Jet Propulsion Laboratory,
Pasadena, CA 91109, USA

Abstract

We present a model of optimal allocation of resources to reproduction and growth in a simple multicellular organism with limited lifespan, using a gene network formalism to simulate gene interactions within cells. The model is compatible with more conventional approaches to allocation problems in life history and in addition provides connections between processes at the gene and cell levels on one hand and life history strategies on the other. The model may offer an example of how a genotype orchestrating development imposes constraints on the optimal solutions that evolution can reach.

Introduction

How an organism uses energy and other resources extracted from the environment to promote its survival and growth, produce offspring or store for future needs is crucial for the organism's fitness. Life-history traits of an organism, that determine when and in what proportions the organism allocates resources during its lifetime, include age and size at first reproduction, number and size of offspring and life-span; all these traits and others have been studied both theoretically and experimentally (Roff 1992; Stearns 1992). A particular line of theoretical work in this area has explored optimal allocation of resources to maintenance, storage, growth and reproduction (Gadgil & Bossert 1970; Cohen 1971; Vincent & Pulliam 1980; Kozłowski 1992). Analytical models on this question have relied largely on methods from optimal control theory (Perrin & Sibly 1993) to locate the sought optima. In these models the state variables are high level phenotypic traits like amount of reserves, size of vegetative and reproductive parts and other such subsystems of an organism, and what is optimized is the proportion of resources allocated to each subsystem at each age. Stochastic optimization techniques have also been used in optimal allocation models (Blarer & Doebeli 1996).

Although such models have dealt with growth of organisms, they have not considered the effects of development and the constraints it might impose on the evolution of life-history traits. In order to address questions about how development determines what life-history strategies are reachable by optimization, and about what influence cell-level events during development may have on evolution towards optimal phenotypes, we have constructed a model of optimal allocation of resources in a simple multicellular organism with limited lifespan. Our model deals explicitly with life history questions as have been formulated in the evolutionary biology literature and uses a fitness measure from this literature to evaluate the organism's strategy for growth and reproduction. The genetic and cellular interactions of the model are based on the modeling framework which was introduced in (Mjolsness, Sharp, & Reinitz 1991) to simulate developmental processes through the use of regulatory gene networks; this framework has been previously used in a preliminary attempt to explore the effects of developmental gene interactions on the evolution of a multicellular phenotype (Mjolsness *et al.* 1995).

Model

Our model examines growth and reproduction of a simple multicellular organism with limited lifespan; the organism starts as a single cell (equipped with a certain amount of resource reserves) and grows by cell divisions; cells may differentiate into propagule cells which are considered to be the progeny of the organism. No specific geometry has been assumed for the organism: the cells can be thought to form an aggregate of non-interacting units.

Gene net framework. The modeling approach which we have used to represent gene regulation, and which we will be referring to as the *gene net framework*, uses recurrent neural nets to represent state variable dynamics, and a set of rules, a grammar, to represent interactions within and between cells. Our model has five rules: one for non-dividing vegetative cells (e.g. cells in phase G1 of interphase), one for vegetative cells entering mitosis, two rules for cell division (symmetric and asymmetric partitioning of gene products to daughter cells) and one for differentiation from vegetative cell to reproductive propagule. For a detailed description of the gene net framework see (Mjolsness, Sharp, &

Reinitz 1991) and for shorter versions (Marnellos 1997; Marnellos & Mjolsness 1998).

Resource production and allocation. Gene product concentrations are state variables in our model and, through the control of cell divisions, determine how organism size (S), another state variable, changes over time. They thus determine events like resource extraction from the environment and also propagule formation, and consequently control allocation of resources to vegetative growth and reproduction. *Surplus energy* (E), i.e. energy and other resources not used for maintenance, is an allometric function of size $E = \alpha S^{\gamma}$, where $\alpha = 0.12$ and $\gamma = 0.80$; we refer to surplus energy also as *production*. Surplus energy is added to the *reserves* (R) of the organism, another state variable; every time the organism increases by a certain number of cells, an amount proportional to that number is subtracted from the reserves; the same occurs when a propagule leaves the organism equipped with an amount of resources, this amount being a parameter of the model that may be thought of as offspring size. The currency unit used to measure reserve and production amounts in these transactions is the amount of resources needed to make one cell, so one cell "costs" one reserve unit.

Mortality and fecundity. The maximum lifespan of an organism is a number Ω of time steps over which we examine its growth and reproduction (and integrate the differential equations describing the changes in state variables); in our simulations this is $\Omega = 100$. There are two sources of mortality in the model: *extrinsic* and *intrinsic*. Extrinsic mortality μ_e at age (time) t is the probability that the organism will die at that age due to external factors and in our simulations is constant with age; intrinsic mortality is a decreasing sigmoid function of reserve levels (the lower the reserves, the higher the mortality) and is given by

$$\mu_i(t) = \frac{e^{-bR_s(t)}}{1 + e^{-bR_s(t)}} \tag{1}$$

where $R_s(t)$ is the quantity of reserves per cell at time t and b is a positive constant. With these mortalities the *survival* function $l(t)$, i.e. the probability that an organism will survive to a certain age t, is given by the decreasing function

$$l(t) = \prod_{\tau=1}^{t}(1-\mu_e(\tau))(1-\mu_i(\tau)) = (1-\mu_e)^t \prod_{\tau=1}^{t}(1-\mu_i(\tau)) \tag{2}$$

for constant extrinsic mortality μ_e.

Fecundity $m(t)$ is given by the number of propagules that are produced at age t. Propagules survive and give rise to a new organism with probability Pr that is an increasing function of propagule size S_p, i.e. the amount of reserves that a propagule is equipped with when it leaves the parent organism (S_p is the same for all propagules and constant in time),

$$Pr(S_p) = \frac{C_1}{1 + e^{-S_p}} - C_2, \tag{3}$$

where C_1 and C_2 are positive constants — we have used $C_1 = 1.8$ and $C_2 = 0.8$, but any values that result in a concave increasing function with range between 0 and 1 would do. Thus effective fecundity $\tilde{m}$ at age t is taken to be the product of number of propagules produced at that age times propagule survival probability

$$\tilde{m}(t) = m(t)Pr(S_p). \tag{4}$$

The amount of propagule reserves becomes the initial amount of reserves of the organism that the propagule gives rise to. We allow negative reserve levels up to 30% of an organism's size; this would correspond to an organism under severe resource shortage that has started using up components of its cells as nutrients. When reserves fall below –30% of size, mortality becomes 1 and the organism is not considered further.

Fitness and objective functions. The fitness measure we maximize by optimization is the lifetime offspring production of the organism $R_0 = \sum_{t=1}^{\Omega} l(t)\tilde{m}(t)$, where Ω is maximum lifespan, $l(t)$ survival to time t (Eq. 2) and $\tilde{m}(t)$ effective fecundity at time t (Eq. 4). The objective function of this problem also contains a quadratic penalty term which is minimized and tends to make all propagules of the organism have gene product concentrations identical to those of all the other propagules and of the founder spore cell that gave rise to the organism; this term we refer to as *identical propagule cost*, I:

$$I = \sum_{i}^{propagules} \sum_{j}^{genes} (v_j^i - v_j^F)^2 \tag{5}$$

where v_j^i is concentration of gene product j in propagule i and v_j^F is concentration of the same gene product in the founder cell of the organism. Finally there is a quadratic penalty term P (a sum of the squares of all the parameters we optimize on) that prevents the parameters from getting excessively large (in our runs they rarely grow beyond order of magnitude 10^1). All terms of the objective function are weighted, and in our runs we have tuned these weights so as to achieve the best results with the optimization methods used. The objective function we maximize is therefore

$$\max J = w_{R_0}R_0 - w_I I - w_P P \tag{6}$$

where the weights w_{R_0}, w_I, w_P are positive numbers.

The parameters we optimize on are: propagule size, S_p (i.e. the amount of reserves invested in each propagule); initial concentrations of gene products in the founder cell (spore) of the organism (which, if identical propagule cost I is very small, should be almost identical to those of the propagules that the organism produces); and parameters of the gene network, like gene interaction strengths, thresholds for gene activation, decay rates of gene products, parameters that govern the triggering of grammar rules, and so on. In the case of runs with two (2) genes there are 27 parameters that are optimized on. We have used stochastic optimization techniques to maximize Eq. 6, namely simulated annealing with an efficient temperature schedule and a genetic algorithm implemented in parallel — for a description of these algorithms, as well as a more detailed description of the parameters optimized on, see (Marnellos 1997; Marnellos & Mjolsness 1998).

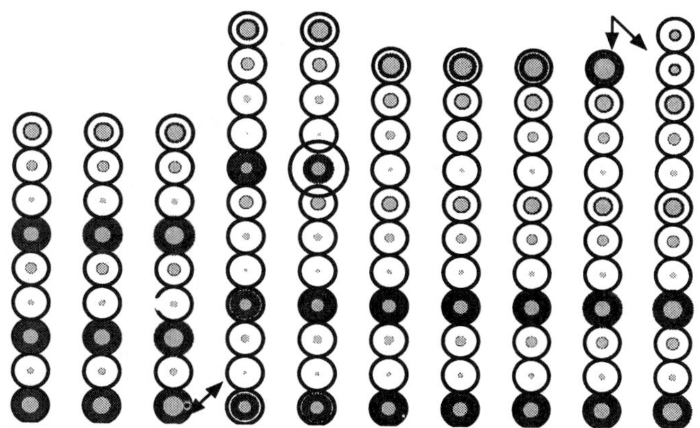

Figure 1: Simulation based on parameters derived by an optimization run, with frames (columns of cells) showing an organism at successive points in time (here are shown time points 51 to 60 out of a maximum lifespan of $\Omega = 100$ time points). The organism has two genes; sizes of the two disks within each cell represent levels of gene products. The larger cell in the 5th column represents a propagule with its reserves. The arrows at the bottom of the 3rd and 4th columns point to an asymmetric cell division: on the left the mother cell and on the right the two daughter cells; the daughter at the bottom receives most of both gene products of the mother (there are other instances of asymmetric division in this Figure which we have not indicated by arrows). The arrows at the top of the 9th and 10th columns point to a symmetric cell division: the daughter cells on the right each receive equal amounts of the two gene products from the mother cell. Note that levels and proportions of gene products are distinct for the cell differentiating into a propagule, for the cell dividing asymmetrically and for the cell dividing symmetrically; gene product levels determine which of these rules is triggered in each instance. In this figure the organism is represented as a column of cells for illustration purposes only (to better illustrate changes in organism size, cell divisions, etc.); in the simulations no specific organism geometry has been assumed and organism cells can be thought to form an aggregate of non-interacting units.

Results

We have carried out optimization runs with two-gene networks for various strengths of extrinsic mortality μ_e. Illustrations of model simulations using parameter values derived by optimization appear in Figs. 1 and 2. The best solutions (in terms of fitness) obtained in these runs are presented in Table 1. The life history features, apart from fitness, of the solutions listed in this Table are: age at maturity, i.e. age at first reproduction; life expectancy at birth (LE) which is given by $LE = \sum_{t=1}^{\Omega} l(t)$, where Ω is maximum lifespan and $l(t)$ is probability of survival to age t as determined by Eq. 2; *intrinsic life expectancy* which is due to intrinsic factors only, i.e. is calculated as LE but with μ_e assumed to be zero; propagule reserves (or propagule size) S_p; total number of propagules produced during the organism's lifetime; and finally, total reproductive effort, which is the total number of propagules multiplied by the reserves S_p of each propagule.

Solutions of higher fitness tend to produce more propagules but make a smaller reproductive effort. It appears that, because of intrinsic mortality (which increases when reserves fall), the strategy adopted in these solutions is to maintain high reserves throughout and release them in reproductive events towards the end of the maximum lifespan; as a consequence, growth rates are kept low, but intrinsic life expectancies are high for all solutions (in all cases higher than 93, out of a maximum of 100, see Table 1) . However, these solutions are not well adapted to the different levels of extrinsic mortality: reproduction does not shift to earlier times with increasing extrinsic mortality — as has been for instance observed in an analytical model quite close to ours in high level structure (Kozłowski & Wiegert 1987) — or, at least, there is no clear relation between age at maturity and level of extrinsic mortality. In fact, in all but one of the solutions, age at maturity is greater than life expectancy (see Table 1).

In connection with age at maturity, it is interesting to observe that solutions fall into two phenotypes: one with older age at maturity and smaller propagule size, as is in the solutions in the first column of Table 1 and the top of the second column, and another with earlier age at maturity and larger propagule size, as in the rest of the solutions (see also Fig. 2). This trade-off between propagule size and development time to maturity is a consequence of the fact that, on one hand, a larger size propagule costs more reserves to produce and so tends to reduce future growth and reproduction of the parent and thus fitness, but, on the other, leads to higher growth rates, higher production and so earlier reproduction and higher fitness; conversely, smaller propagule size costs less but leads to slower growth, later reproduction and decrease in fitness. Related to this trade-off is another trade-off between propagule size and propagule number (the smaller the size, the larger the number, and vice versa) which is clearly evident in the solutions of Table 1. These trade-offs are affected by the propagule sur-

μ_e		1	2	3
0.010	**Fitness (R_0)**	**13.7**	**12.4**	**11.7**
	Age at Maturity	88	86	48
	Life Expectancy (LE)	62.3	61.4	59.3
	Intrinsic LE	99.3	97.3	93.8
	Propagule Reserves	1.36	1.21	3.80
	Propagules	58	64	33
	Reproductive Effort	78.9	77.4	125.4
0.013	**Fitness (R_0)**	**10.0**	**9.4**	**8.7**
	Age at Maturity	75	61	64
	Life Expectancy (LE)	54.0	53.7	53.3
	Intrinsic LE	97.4	96.2	95.4
	Propagule Reserves	1.96	2.79	3.99
	Propagules	46	34	30
	Reproductive Effort	90.1	95.0	119.8
0.015	**Fitness (R_0)**	**9.1**	**9.1**	**8.0**
	Age at Maturity	86	64	58
	Life Expectancy (LE)	48.9	48.6	49.2
	Intrinsic LE	94.7	93.6	95.1
	Propagule Reserves	2.26	3.89	3.41
	Propagules	49	39	34
	Reproductive Effort	110.7	151.7	115.9
0.017	**Fitness (R_0)**	**8.0**	**6.7**	**6.5**
	Age at Maturity	89	61	71
	Life Expectancy (LE)	46.4	45.2	45.2
	Intrinsic LE	97.5	94.5	93.4
	Propagule Reserves	1.28	3.84	3.96
	Propagules	72	32	34
	Reproductive Effort	92.2	122.9	134.6

Table 1: Life-history features of the 3 best optimization solutions obtained for various strengths of extrinsic mortality μ_e.

vival function (Eq. 3), which determines how much an increase in propagule size will increase the propagule's chances of survival and thus fitness.

Another salient feature is that life histories in the solutions presented here often include what is called a *bang-bang* switch: after an initial period of exclusive allocation of resources to growth, the organism ceases to grow in size and completely switches to investment in reproduction. This is true for the majority of solutions obtained apart from a few where the switch is more gradual. Both modes of switching have been reported in previous theoretical work (Cohen 1971; Vincent & Pulliam 1980; King & Roughgarden 1982).

All solutions presented in Table 1 differ in the signs and magnitudes of their optimized parameters, which is true even for solutions that are similar in their life-history features (like solutions 1 and 2 for $\mu_e = 0.010$, or solution 3 for $\mu_e = 0.010$ and 2 for $\mu_e = 0.015$). This may indicate that the objective function of this problem (Eq. 6) has many similar optima. The similar life histories that result from different optimization solutions can be considered instances of "phenotypic convergence".

Finally, identical propagule cost, which is not considered in previous resource allocation work, has turned out to be an important component of our model: growth and fecundity in our simulations can be very sensitive to initial concentrations of gene products in the founder cell of the organism. Identical propagule cost may correspond, to a certain extent, to maternal effects described in work on state-dependent life histories (McNamara & Houston 1996).

Discussion

In this paper we have tried to make a connection between the gene network approach and previous optimal resource allocation models and have probed the role of cell-level events during development in shaping the life histories of organisms.

Solutions found by our optimization runs have features in common with previous work in resource allocation and life history: such features are the bang-bang switch from growth to reproduction and the trade-offs between propagule size and time of development to maturity and between propagule size and number. An advantage of our approach in comparison with previous work is that, through the use of lower level state variables, our model encompasses many life history characters in a natural way; for instance, in our model the form of fecundity as a function of age, organism size or reserves, falls out naturally from the underlying physiology of cell differentiation. In previous work relations between fecundity, survival, size, surplus energy and so on have been based upon reasonable assumptions but differ substantially across models; it is not always clear what these differences imply or how they map to real physiological processes in an organism. Our model goes some way towards addressing this problem.

Our approach has additionally provided a reductionist window into the lower level workings of the solutions: it has, for instance, revealed the phenotypic convergence of solutions that differ in their low level parameters, the importance of regulating tightly gene product concentrations in propagules, and the correlation of propagule size, a cell-level feature, to the two kinds of phenotypes observed in our solutions.

Finally, as was mentioned in the Results, our life history solutions can respond to certain features of the selective environment, like the presence of intrinsic mortality, but cannot adapt to others, like increases in the level of extrinsic mortality. This may be due to constraints imposed by the number of genes and other parameters, as well as the genotypic structure of the model, and can be viewed as an illustration of the phylogenetic constraints within which selection has to move in order to optimize life histories; with the fixation of traits within lineages and other such lineage specific effects some the-

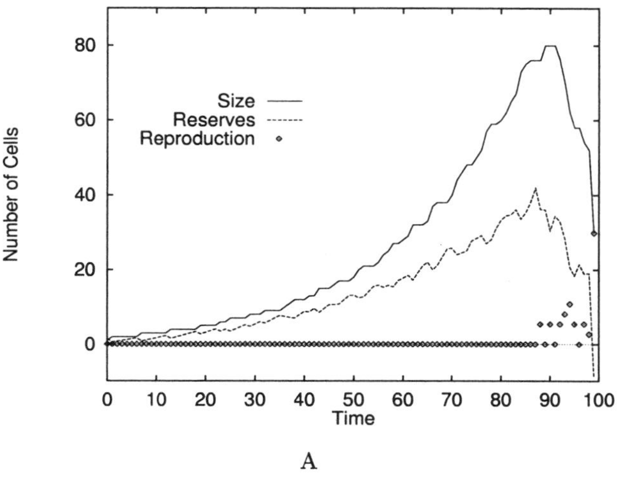

A

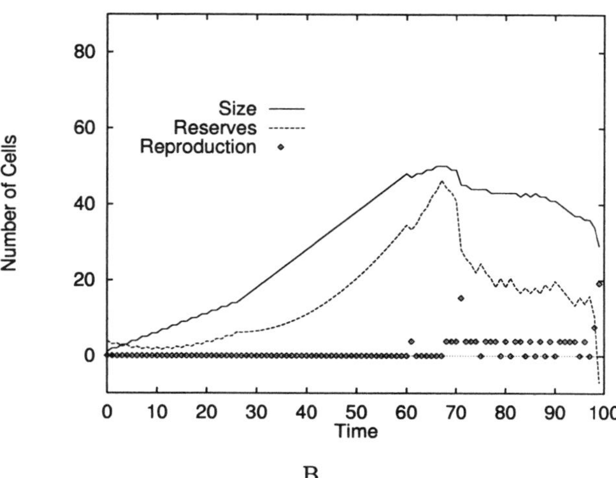

B

Figure 2: Solutions obtained by optimization fall into two life-history phenotypes: (A) older age at maturity and smaller propagule size, and (B) earlier age at maturity and larger propagule size. Illustrations (A) and (B) in this figure correspond to solution 1 for $\mu_e = 0.010$ and solution 2 for $\mu_e = 0.017$ of Table 1, respectively. Organism size, amount of reserves and reproductive effort (i.e. number of propagules produced times propagule size) are plotted against time (age); all three quantities are measured in the same currency used in the model, namely number of cells (see text for more details).

oretical optima may not be reachable.

Acknowledgements

Supported in part by the Yale Institute for Biospheric Studies (Center for Computational Ecology), and the Yale Center for Parallel Supercomputing, and by an Office of Naval Research grant (number N00014-97-1-0422).

References

Blarer, A., and Doebeli, M. 1996. Heuristic optimization of the general life history problem: A novel approach. *Evolutionary Ecology* 10:81–96.

Cohen, D. 1971. Maximizing final yield when growth is limited by time or by limiting resources. *Journal of Theoretical Biology* 12:19–29.

Gadgil, M., and Bossert, W. 1970. Life historical consequences of natural selection. *American Naturalist* 104:1–24.

King, D., and Roughgarden, J. 1982. Graded allocation between vegetative and reproductive growth for annual plants in growing seasons of random lengths. *Theoretical Population Biology* 22:1–16.

Kozłowski, J., and Wiegert, R. G. 1987. Optimal age and size at maturity in annuals and perennials with determinate growth. *Evolutionary Ecology* 1:231–244.

Kozłowski, J. 1992. Optimal allocation of resources to growth and reproduction: Implications for age and size at maturity. *Trends in Ecology and Evolution* 7:15–19.

Marnellos, G., and Mjolsness, E. 1998. A model of optimal resource allocation to growth and reproduction using gene networks. Technical Report CS97-568, Computer Science and Engineering, UCSD.

Marnellos, G. 1997. *Gene Network Models Applied to Questions in Development and Evolution.* Ph.D. Dissertation, Yale University.

McNamara, J., and Houston, A. 1996. State-dependent life histories. *Nature* 380:215–221.

Mjolsness, E.; Garrett, C.; Reinitz, J.; and Sharp, D. 1995. Modeling the connection between development and evolution: Preliminary report. In Banzhaf, W., and Eeckman, F., eds., *Evolution and Biocomputation, Computational Models of Evolution*, volume 899 of *Lecture Notes in Computer Science.* Berlin: Springer. 429–453.

Mjolsness, E.; Sharp, D.; and Reinitz, J. 1991. A connectionist model of development. *Journal of Theoretical Biology* 152:429–453.

Perrin, N., and Sibly, R. 1993. Dynamic models of energy allocation and investment. *Annual Review of Ecology and Systematics* 24:379–410.

Roff, D. 1992. *The Evolution of Life Histories.* New York: Chapman and Hall.

Stearns, S. 1992. *The Evolution of Life Histories.* Oxford: Oxford University Press.

Vincent, T., and Pulliam, H. 1980. Evolution of life history strategies for an asexual annual plant model. *Theoretical Population Biology* 17:215–231.

Emergence and Maintenance of Relationships among Agents

Shin I. Nishimura and Takashi Ikegami

Institute of Physics, The Graduate School of Arts and Sciences,
University of Tokyo,
3-8-1 Komaba, Meguro-ku, Tokyo 153, Japan

Abstract

We study the emergence and maintenance of relationships among individual agents based on simulations of a model ecosystem. Usually an ecosystem is modeled as an ensemble of individuals, whose interactions are given as direct couplings among individuals. In this paper, a new type of coupling and coupling dynamics are introduced. Here, each individual is seen as *not* directly interacting with other individuals, but rather with the relationships among the individuals (e.g., relationships such as "one agent follows the other"). We study the dynamics of individuals moving on a 2-dimensional plane, where they are making/breaking the relationships constructed between them. In practice, these relationships are assumed to be spatial patterns of more than two individuals. When certain patterns appear, each individual is forced to one of the locations where the pattern has emerged. Some patterns will be lost immediately, but some can be sustained dynamically. For example, we found that a relationship, such as "one individual follows the other", is dynamically sustained by the motions induced by the relationship. Examples of possible relationships and the induced dynamics which hold the relationships together will be discussed.

Introduction

For the simulation of animal behavior, we have two extreme approaches. One is to simulate it as a dynamic system (e.g., animal behavior obeys the Newtonian equations of motion) (Breder 1954; Sannomyia et al. 1996; Reynolds 1987; Shimoyama et al. 1996). The other is to simulate it as a finite automaton (e.g., behavior is pre-programmed as a table of states and transitions).

These approaches are also referred to respectively as bottom-up and top-down approaches. In the bottom-up approach, the higher functions of animal behavior are expected to be explained by the dynamics of the lowest. In the top-down approach, the underlying dynamics are inversely restricted by the higher functions, which are often more easily described as functions of a finite automaton. These two approaches are seen as complementary, and a goal of the present study, especially as a study of artificial life, is to reconcile these two (Hogeweg 1988). In doing so, we present a novel framework for studying animal behavior.

We first take the bottom-up approach; motions of each individual are determined by a simple set of equations. But to produce animation of the group motions of individuals, we must introduce some quasi-top-down elements. That is, interactions between individuals are not given as a simple function of their positions, since we assume that each individual cannot directly sense the locations and speed of other individuals. Any individual can only sense the relationship established among other individuals. There exist some ethological studies whose findings correspond to this assumption. McDonald and Potts (1994) reported that long-tailed manakins display dual-male courtship; males form multi-male teams, which include an "alpha" and "beta" male that do the bulk of the obligate dual-male unison song duets and dual-male dance displays. A female comes to the perfect team, from which only the alpha individual mates with the female. We emphasize that a female is not attracted to a single male but to the synergistic dancing.

In the present paper, we show how the relationship that we describe is dynamically sustained by the group of motions induced by the given relationship, and we try to show how behaviors can be "discretized" in the sense that the whole behavior can be decomposed into some basic units of behavior. The existence of such units of behavior is experimentally suggested by Csànyi (1993).

We must take relationship dynamics into account for the following reason. There exist "how" and "why" questions about animal behavior, such as: how do animals behave? (e.g. what does their navigation trajectory look like?); and why do animals behave in that way? (e.g. what motivates their behavior?). To describe animal behavior, i.e., to answer the "how" questions, we construct a simple mathematical model, as minimal as possible. To discuss motivations for animal behavior, i.e., to answer "why" questions, a simple model does not suffice. Uexküll (1950) pointed out that surrounding objects have different meanings depending on the internal state of the animals that see the objects. Since we cannot definitively know the internal state of individuals, we always have to speculate on the cause of an action only after the action is executed.

However, if some events always cause the same action, we can refer to these events as "motivations" for that action. There must exist some dynamic feedback mechanisms to repetitively reinforce the events as motivations. This is one way to capture the motivations behind animal behavior. We thus ask the "why" question in the following way; "what kinds of motivations can be sustained in a society of agents ranging from ants colony to human society". Behaviors can be motivated either by internal or external events. Hunger, anger, sorrow, etc. are examples of internal events. Environmental changes, changes in the spatial structures of individuals or in sensory patterns are examples of external events. In this study, we neglect internal events and focus on external events. Practically speaking, we study the spatio-temporal relationship between two individuals as an external event which motivates individual behavior.

A Model Equation

We first introduce the basic equations of motion for individual navigation, then we introduce some relationships between two individuals that act as target patterns.

In the world we simulate, individuals live on a 2-dimensional plane. They each have their own positions ($\vec{r}$) and headings ($\vec{n} = (cos(\theta), sin(\theta))$). The equations of motion involve these two variables. The heading movement is navigated according to the discrepancy between the velocity ($\frac{d\vec{r}}{dt} = |\frac{d\vec{r}}{dt}|(cos(\psi), sin(\psi))$) and the heading direction. Hence the equation of motion for the $i-th$ individual is given by,

$$\frac{d\vec{r}_i}{dt} = g \cdot \vec{E}_i/|E_i| + \vec{n}_i, \tag{1}$$

$$\frac{d\theta_i}{dt} = \sin(\psi_i - \theta_i). \tag{2}$$

The introduction of heading dynamics has recently been recognized as an important factor in bringing diversity into grouping behavior (see, e.g., Sannomyia et al., 1996, Nishimura and Ikegami 1998). If the term ($g\vec{E}_i/|E_i|$) in Eq. (1) can be neglected, in other words if no event is sensed by the individual i, that individual thus moves freely along its heading direction. We call this freely moving state an ideal gas state.

When the term ($g\vec{E}_i/|E_i|$) in Eq. (1) exists, this means that the individual can sense the event, which in turn attracts the individual to it. No individual can directly sense other individuals' positions or headings. But individuals can sense the relationships established among individuals. In this paper, relationships are given as spatial patterns of a pair of individuals. These relationships are also called "target patterns", since they tend to attract other agents. Although we prepare those patterns in advance, it is not obvious whether they can be sustained in a system. If target patterns exist, it is clear that each individual is attracted to them.

If the jth and the kth individuals form a target pattern, $\vec{E}_i$ in the first term of Eq. (1) is given as follows:

$$\vec{E}_i = \vec{n}_{ijk} - \vec{r}_i \tag{3}$$

$$i \neq j \neq k \neq i, \tag{4}$$

where $\vec{n}_{ijk}$ is the position that the ith individual is attracted to. If many target patterns appear, the ith individual moves to the nearest pattern that she finds. The inequality (4) is introduced in order to exclude self-interaction. No individual can recognize a pattern which includes herself.

We give two examples of the relationship below.

The Relationships and the Induced Dynamics

In the following, we introduce examples of two different target patterns and their resulting dynamics. The system contains a fixed number of individuals N, which in this simulation we fix at 15. The 2-dimensional world where the individuals live has periodic boundaries.

Case 1

It is a matter of controversy whether a single agent leads a whole group in general in animal groups. Menzel (1974) says that this is so for chimpanzees, but Partridge (1982) holds that no such leader exists in fish schools, where a leader and follower emerge only if no more than two fish are enclosed in a tank (Partridge 1982).

On the basis of those discussions, we speculate that agents do not see one specific agent as a leader, but rather are aware of some dynamical pattern between agents that may indicate a direction to follow. Therefore, as a simplest possible case, we here adopt a pair that includes a leader and a follower as a target pattern in our simulation. Formally, it is described as follows:

$$\phi_j < \delta \tag{5}$$

$$\phi_k < \delta \tag{6}$$

$$|\vec{r}_j - \vec{r}_k| < D, \tag{7}$$

where ϕ_j (ϕ_k) is the angle between the heading direction of the jth (kth) individual and $\vec{r}_k - \vec{r}_j$. δ and D are constant. Eqs. (5) and (6) indicate that the discrepancies between the heading directions of each individual and the line from the kth to jth individual is defined to be less than δ. Eq. (7) states that two individuals should neighbor within a distance of D. As is expected, a target pattern is regarded as a linear pattern (see Fig. 1). The j th individual is called a *leader*, and the k th individual is called a *follower*.

Here, the vector $\vec{n}_{ijk}$ in Eq. (3) is given as the "follower's" position in the target pattern.

This linear formulation is less likely to be sustained if we have smaller values of δ and D. Note that although

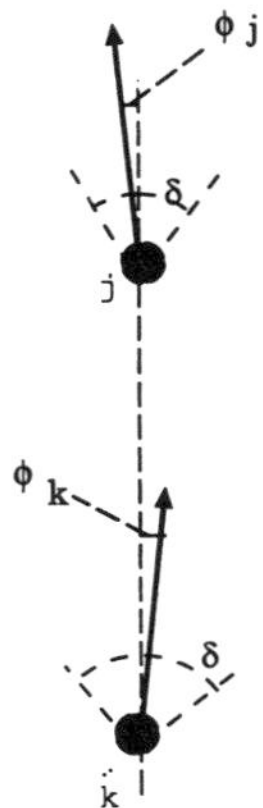

Figure 1: Black colored discs indicate the locations of individuals and the arrows represent their heading directions. This pattern is called *Target Pattern.* The jth individual is called a leader and the i th individual is called a follower.

we explicitly defined the target pattern, it is not obvious whether it emerges or not. In order to avoid an instant response to the emergence of the target pattern, we assume that individuals can only be attracted to a target pattern that persists more than τ time steps. Here, as in case 2 below, τ is set at 2000.

- **Results**

The strength with which each individual is attracted to the target pattern is controlled by a parameter g. By changing the value of g, we obtain different sizes of groupings. Also, the parameters τ, D and δ determine the size and the number of isolated groupings. Here we choose the parameters so that we will have only one or two groupings within a system. Over the wide range of parameter regions that satisfy this restriction, we see the dynamics which stabilize the linear formation of groupings.

The snapshots of the grouping and its dynamics are shown in Fig. 2. When a pair happens to form a *target pattern* at a certain location, it attracts many other individuals. The new individuals approaching the follower of the target will form a new linear formation. If the new target pattern does not contain the members of the initial target pattern, both leader and follower of the initial target pattern are attracted to the new pattern. Therefore the first target pattern will be lost. But often the first pattern continues to produce new target patterns as in Fig. 2, where it can be seen that the individuals easily aggregate and the number of target patterns will decrease. At a certain point, however, a new pair of individuals will escape from the aggregation and attract the others. According to this scenario, the linear target pattern is maintained.

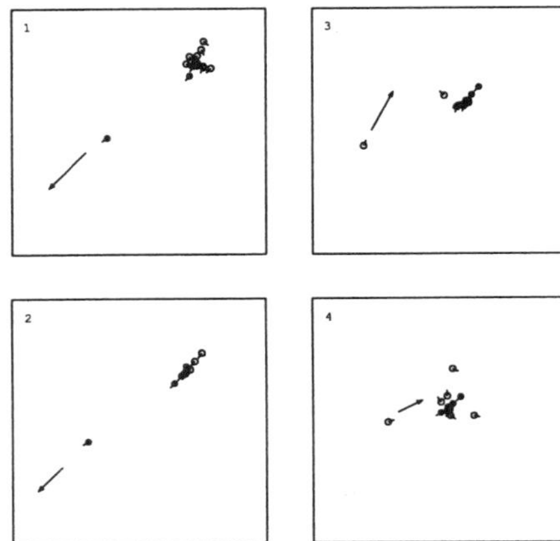

Figure 2: Snapshots of the simulation are illustrated. A disc and a small spike denote an individual's position and a heading direction, respectively. A black colored disc indicates individuals forming *target patterns.* The arrow indicates the direction of motion of a whole group. (1) One target pattern emerges and attracts others. (2) New target patterns are created. (3) The leader of the first target pattern changes its heading direction toward the new target pattern. (4) Every individual aggregates at the center. The number of target patterns decreases and situation (1) appears again. The parameters g, τ, D and δ are set to 0.007, 8333, 3000 and 0.3176, respectively.

Case 2

For our second example, we take the target pattern to be two individuals with opposite headings. This differs from the case 1 situation in that two kinds of target patterns occur in this case; i.e., two individuals either move closer together or move apart. These two target patterns are depicted in Figs. 3a and b. We have no natural reference for these patterns.

The formal descriptions of the patterns are as follows. Fig. 3a is described by,

$$\phi_j < \delta \tag{8}$$

$$\phi_k < \delta \tag{9}$$

$$|\vec{r}_j - \vec{r}_k| < D, \tag{10}$$

where D, δ and τ are the parameters, as in case 1. The new variable ϕ_j is the angle from $\vec{r}_j - \vec{r}_k$ to $\vec{n}_j$, and ϕ_k is the angle from $\vec{r}_k - \vec{r}_k$ to $\vec{n}_j$.

Fig. 3b is described as follows:

$$\phi_j > \pi - \delta \tag{11}$$

$$\phi_k > \pi - \delta \tag{12}$$

$$|\vec{r}_j - \vec{r}_k| < D, \tag{13}$$

The location of these target patterns is defined as being halfway between the jth and kth individuals. Hence

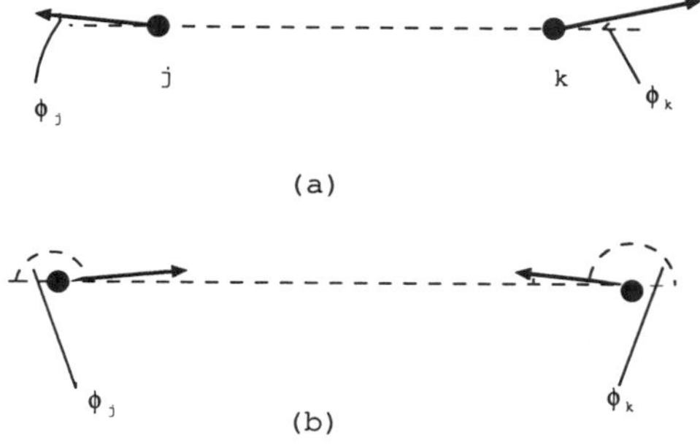

Figure 3: *Target Patterns* (a) and (b) are illustrated. Black discs indicate the positions of individuals and arrows represent the individuals' heading directions. (a) ϕ_j and $\pi - \phi_k$ must be less than δ. (b) $\pi - \phi_j$ and ϕ_k must be less than δ.

individuals who sense either of the target patterns will approach the middle of the space between the individuals who form the target pattern. Below, we discuss how these two target patterns can be stabilized.

- **Results**

Figs. 4 (1) and (2) show snapshots of the dynamics where target patterns (a) and (b) respectively emerge. When either of the target patterns emerge, other individuals aggregate to its middle point except for the individuals that initially formed the target pattern. These individuals are marked in black. Unlike in case 1, we seldom have more than two targets coexisting at one time. A single pair of individuals can participate in forming the target pattern. Depending on the parameter values, the speed of the aggregation changes, but the basic picture of the induced dynamic is that a pair of individuals will go straight and the rest will aggregate.

We notice that these two patterns can seldom coexist at one time but one pattern subsequently induces the other one. So temporalily, we have a sequential changes of target pattern a) and b) in turn. Further, one pattern is followed by the other. To acount for this observation, we compute the order parameters for those two target patterns as:

$$I_a = \sum_{l \in C_a} cos(\phi_l) / \sum_{l \in C_a} 1, \quad (14)$$

$$I_b = \sum_{l \in C_b} cos(\phi_l) / \sum_{l \in C_a} 1. \quad (15)$$

The sets C_a and C_b each represent a set of individuals that satisfy target pattern conditions (a) and (b), respectively. If no target pattern is present, those order parameters give null values. Therefore, $I_a > 0$ and $I_b < 0$ imply the emergence of target patterns (a) and (b), respectively.

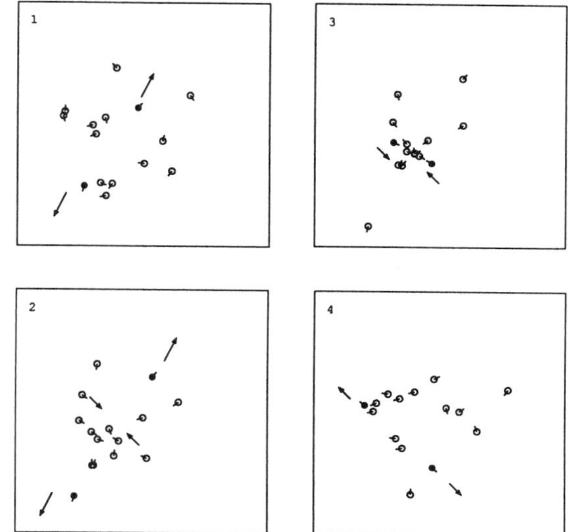

Figure 4: Snapshots of spatio-temporal patterns of individual movements are illustrated. A disc with a small spike denotes an individual's position and heading direction. A black colored disc indicates a pair of individuals forming *target patterns.* Arrows represent the moving directions of those individuals forming the target pattern. (1) One target pattern a) emerges. (2) Other individuals aggregate to the middle point of the target pattern. The direction of this aggregation is denoted again by the arrow. (3) Target pattern a) was lost as the two individuals which originally composed it went too far apart, failing to form the target pattern. Target Pattern b) subsequently emerges. (4) Target pattern b) reverts to target pattern a) when the agents which form target pattern b) exchange their position at the middle point of target pattern b). The parameters g, T, D and δ are set at 0.007, 8333, 3000 and 0.432, respectively.

In Fig. 5, I_a and I_b are plotted. This figure shows that two states iteratively emerge, so that we cannot observe both of the patterns at one time. This confirms our observations derived from the snapshots. The emergence of one target pattern suppresses the other.

Discussions

How individuals interact with other individuals should not be taken as a given but should rather be treated as a phenomenon that emerges from simple dynamics. We call the interaction an emergent phenomenon because whether it is sustained or not is decided by the actions of agents of the system. This is what we have shown in this paper, although still at a primitive level.

An initial ideal gas state changes to a state where interaction takes place. Individuals are attracted to an event, which emerges merely by chance. If the event

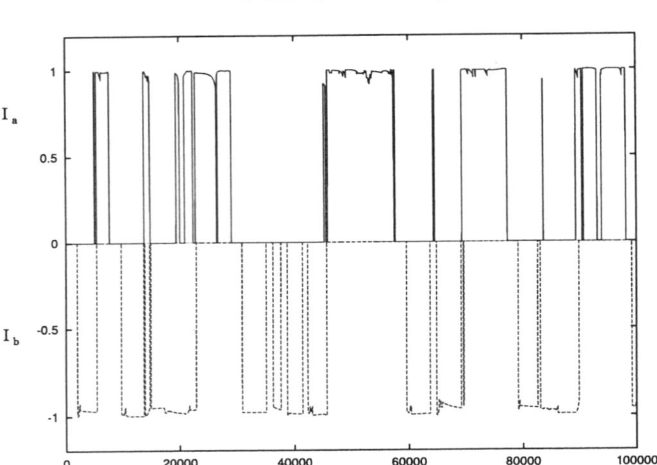

Figure 5: Order parameters for the target patterns a and b are depicted. By definition, the order parameter for pattern a) satisfies $I_a > 0$ and that for pattern b) satisfies $I_b < 0$.

subsequently disappears, again by chance, it can be regarded as a mere perturbation of the system. But if the event is recursively generated by the dynamics which are triggered by the event itself, that event becomes more than a perturbation, and we thus can treat the event as the definitive cause for the individuals' behavior. In the example we referred to as case 2), we saw that two target patterns a) and b) can coexist. The dynamics induced by pattern a) can solely sustain pattern a) without being additionally supported by pattern b). On the other hand, the dynamics induced by pattern b) cannot solely stabilize pattern b). Soon or later, pattern b) will drop out of the system, and can only be retrieved accidentally. For example, since we use a periodic boundary condition, two agents who go in the opposite direction will meet each other by accrossing the boundary. However, if individuals can recognize both patterns a) and b), pattern b) could be retrieved in the system by the dynamics induced by pattern a). The dynamics induced by pattern b) are now, in turn, able to generate pattern a). Therefore a sequential appearance of patterns a) and b) emerges.

Behavior patterns a) and b) can be seen as examples of the behavior units induced by the target pattern in case 2). More studies on the classification of target patterns and their accompanying behavior units will be performed.

Acknowledgments

This work was partially supported by the Grants-in-Aid (No.07243102) for Scientific Research under the priority of "System Theory of Function Emergence" from the Japanese Ministry of Education, Science and Culture.

References

Breder, C. M. 1954. Equations ascriptive of fish school and other animal aggregations. *Ecology* 35: 211–129.

Csànyi, V. 1993. How genetics and learning make a fish and individual: A case study on the paradise fish. In *Perspectives in Ethology*, edited by P. P. G. Bateson et al. Plenum, p. 1–51.

Hogeweg, P. 1988. Mirror beyond mirror, puddles of life. In *Artificial Life, SFI Studies in the Sciences of Complexity*, edited by C. G. Langton. Redwood City: Addison-Wesley.

McDonald, D. B. and W. K. Potts. 1994. Cooparative display and relatedness among males in a Lek-Mating bird. *Science* 266: 1030–1032.

Menzel, E. W. 1974. A group of young chimpanzees in a 1-acre field: Leadership and communication. In *Perspectives in ethology*, edited by A. M. Schrier and F. Stollnitz, volume 5. New York: Academic Press.

Nishimura, S. I. and T. Ikegami. 1998. Emergence of collective strategies in a prey-predator game model. *Artif. Life* 3 (to appear).

Partridge, B. L. The structure and function of fish schools. *Sci. Am.* 246(6): 114.

Reynolds, C. W. 1987. Flocks, herds, and schools: A distributed behavioral model. *Computer Graphics* 21: 25–34.

Sannomiya, N., K. Nagano, and M. Kuramitsu. 1996. A behavior model of fish school with three individuals. *SICE*, 32: 948–956.

Shimoyama, N, K. Sugawara, T. Mizuguchi, Y. Hayakawa, and M. Sano. 1996. Collective motion in a system of motile elements. *Physical Review Letters* 76: 3870–3873.

von Uexküll, J. 1950. *Das Allmächtige Leben.* Hamburg: Christian Wegner Verlag.

A Preliminary Investigation of Evolution as a Form Design Strategy

Una-May O'Reilly *
Artificial Intelligence Lab
Massachusetts Institute of Technology
545 Technology Square
Cambridge, MA, 02143
unamay@ai.mit.edu

Girish Ramachandran
School of Architecture
Massachusetts Institute of Technology
77 Massachusetts Avenue
Cambridge, MA 02139
girish@mit.edu

Abstract

We describe the preliminary version of our investigative software, GGE – Generative Genetic Explorer, in which genetic operations interact with AutoCAD to generate novel 3D forms for the architect. GGE allows us to asess how evolutionary algorithms should be tailored to suit Architecture CAD tasks.

Introduction

An evolutionary process exemplifies the "explore, evaluate and refine" subprocesses of architectural design and its overall non-linear nature. We report on Generative Genetic Explorer (GGE), an evolution-based software system that we have developed and interfaced with AutoCAD (Autocad 1995). Presently, GGE is an investigative platform for assessing Alife CAD tool issues. Ultimately GGE is intended to be used during the initial stages of the design process when form is being explored through the use of visual models. Its goal is the active generation and suggestion of new designs by means of a computational evolutionary process that sensitively interacts with the creative process of an architect.

An evolutionary algorithm typically requires the designation of a genotype, genotype-phenotype mapping, and a fitness function. To suit its architectural domain, the genotype of GGE is expressed in a vocabulary that an architect can relate to and understand. The architect is led to intuitively think of an initial form as a skeleton and its covering skin. The genotype is a sequence of visual-based, "manual" transformations that will be applied to the skeleton and skin. For example, a form undergoes a sequence of lifts and folds to parts of its extent. The result (i.e. the phenotype) in GGE is an AutoCAD graphical entity which the architect simply views and assesses. At the system level, i.e. below the graphics level, the phenotype is specified in terms of vertices and faces. It is mapped from the genotype by the programming in GGE of the transformations. Transformations are coded at the level of vertex and face manipulation. However, this mapping and the gritty details of the transformation are hidden from the architect.

Because form design stresses exploration, GGE does not have a programmed fitness function. Instead, it leaves selection to the architect. This choice is well suited to our desire to make the architect an "architectural geneticist". This desire has also instigated a GGE feature that is not typically considered to be part of an evolutionary algorithm: because architects do not want too much randomness GGE's transformations are parameterized over all their degrees of freedom and the architect is allowed to constrain which parameters are subject to mutation. The architect can also control the sequence of transformations to some degree, in some sense, manually directing crossover. This capability provides an effective compromise between the execution of random crossovers and mutations and the design process proceeding too deterministically.

The paper proceeds as follows: It starts by relating GGE to other projects which also use evolution and morphogenesis as a process for generating architectural designs or structures. With this context established, GGE is described and its design motivations discussed. We conclude with a list of future work and a summary of the contributions of GGE in its current state.

Work Related to GGE

Many interesting projects are similar in respects to GGE and, indeed, are far more developed and investigated. Because of limitations of space, we can only briefly mention some of them and their pertinent features. Biormorphs by Dawkins (1986) allows forms to evolve under ranked selection where the user provides the ranking. In this way GGE follows Biomorph's initiative in using an user-based fitness function.

Frazer (1995) is a key proponent of making the architectural design process follow a model of nature. Rather than seek expression by focusing on *output* (i.e., space, structure or form), Frazer proposes that architecture should focus on a process that parallels morphogenesis

U.M.O'R.'s research was supported in part by Canada's Natural Sciences and Engineering Research Council and the U.S. Office of Naval Research (contract No. N00014-95-1-1600)

and evolution in the natural world. He proposes "Evolutionary Architecture". GGE, like Evolutionary Architecture, is an attempt to exploit evolution, though in its present form, it lacks the complex morphogenesis process of Evolutionary Architecture. Another related example is Rosenman (1996).

An example of an Alife CAD tool in the architectural domain is Bucci (1997). This genetic algorithm system evolves virtual spaces. Two structural elements of the 3D space are parameterized in terms of volume and location. Two other structural elements of the space are not evolved but are part of the environment. The system searches through spatial and volumetric configurations of the evolved forms to find a space in which one form is maximized for volume and the other one is closely positioned to the center of the space.

The Bucci system and similar work not directly from the architectural domain, e.g., (Bentley and Wakefield 1996; Funes and Pollack 1998) show how an Evolutionary Algorithm can pragmatically assist design by satisfying objective constraints. These systems do not share GGE's focus on creativity and discovery. They are employed to solve a problem rather than generate suggestions. Usually, the task is one-shot rather than a design process. These systems tend to exclude the designers. They reduce them to programmers who have to specify a fitness function. GGE has a clear goal of integrating the architect and the Evolutionary Algorithm into one seamless design process.

Generative Genetic Explorer

The genotype in GGE

In GGE the representation for a genotype is a combination of data and instructions. It is:

- an initial form, and
- a sequence of transformations

Initial Form: To generate the initial form, the architect computationally generates (e.g., using trigonometric functions in a procedure) or hand draws a 3D line segment (vertices with X,Y,Z orientation) in AutoCAD. She then repeatedly copies the segment and changes the new segment's location in 3D space using the mouse. Optionally the angles or vertex distances are modified. The final set of segments is termed a "profile set". From the architect's point of view, the line segments constitute a skeleton over which a "skin" (or a polygonal "face" or surface) will be stretched. She then saves the profile set to a file with an AutoCAD command written for GGE. GGE is actually implemented in LISP (Steele 1990).

Transformation sequence: The remainder of the genotype is a sequence of transformations. To create the phenotype these are applied to the initial form in sequence. First, we shall describe the transformation language and second, we shall describe how a sequence is chosen for a genotype:

1. **Transformation Language** We chose the vocabulary of transformation by analyzing an architect's verbal description of changes she observed to a form. The architect spoke in terms of actions that changed the appearance of the form. Concentrating on the verbs, we developed a small example set of transformations based on visual adaptations: insert, delete, fold, punch-hole and lift.

   Concentrating on the nouns the architect used, we realized the same transformation (from the architect's viewpoint) could act upon data at multiple scales: coordinate, vertex, profile or profile set and for a range of quantities (1 or more vertices, profiles, etc.). This led us to code the transformations with extensive parameter lists when implementing them. Most parameters were optional. If a parameter was optional and was not specified in the call to the transformation, its value was determined randomly. For example, if the parameter denoting the number of vertices to be lifted was not specified in a call to the lift transformation, the routine randomly determined how many vertices would be lifted. If the parameter was specified, it acted as a restraint on the randomness of the outcome of the transformation.

   In addition, adjectives were very important. The architect spoke using terms like "sharp bend", "gentle slope", "symmetrical", "regular", "curved". At this stage we have neglected these adjectives but plan to integrate them as parameterizations later.

   A great number of interesting forms are possible with just the five transformations we implemented because of the great extent to which each was parameterized.

   - **Insert** The insert transformation adds one or more profiles to the profile set of the initial form. These profiles can be randomly generated, randomly selected from a database of profiles or specified by the architect. The relative position of the new profile(s) in the current profile set can be randomly determined or specified by the architect. When a profile is added, the skeleton is essentially extended and the skin that formerly spanned the profiles that have been separated by the new profile's insertion is "repaired" to now stretch to the new profile.

     We found that totally randomized insert transformations were unacceptable to the architect. While they were complicated and unanticipated, they were far too irregular and "crazy". However, the architect responded to inserts that were slightly random in only one or two degrees of freedom (e.g., insertion of an existing, but randomly selected profile, insertion of a given profile into a random location).

- **Delete** The delete operation is essentially the opposite of the insert operation. It is capable of removing equal numbers of vertices (an optional parameter) from a profile subset in the profile set.
- **Fold** Fold is a planar operation. Given an angle, a group of vertices in a plane are rotated. The parameters of the fold oeration control the angles, plane, the number and rank of the vertices and which subset of profiles are folded.

  Like Insert, Fold needed to be constrained. In particular, a fold of either just one vertex or of just one angle provided sufficient novel and surprising variation without creating excessive irregularity.

  Our implementation of Fold is limited. The architect wants a fold transformation that also creates enclosures with curved boundaries or twists. It may prove more useful to subclassify folds and make them distinct transformations.
- **Lift**

  The lift transformation increments (or decrements) a subset of vertices in a subset of axes for a subset of profiles by either one constant quantity or by different quantities. Lift was very popular, particularly when it was applied with a fixed increment to only one axis (specified by the architect) but left to decide randomly upon the subsets of vertices and profiles.
- **Poke-Hole** This transformation was the only one we implemented that adapted the surface or skin of the profile. GGE assumes the initial form is completely surfaced. The Poke-Hole action removed skin from the skeleton leaving (as the name suggests) a hole. It was controlled by parameters dictating how much skin was removed and where it was removed from.

2. **Determining an Initial Transformation Sequence:** The phenotype results from applying the transformation sequence of the genotype to its initial form. When GGE was allowed to specify an initial transformation sequence by drawing transformations from the vocabulary at random and by randomly determining each parameter value of the sequence, the resulting phenotype was almost always unacceptable to the architect except, perhaps, as a radical surprise. A more acceptable initial transformation sequence to the architect was one that she provided. The architect chose the sequence of transformations (with explorative intentions) and then set a range for each parameter of each transformation. The actual value of the parameter was then randomly determined but only from within the range specified by the architect. In some cases, the architect completely specified a parameter of a transformation in order to indicate that no exploration was desired in the domain of the parameter.

   This approach i.e. allowing the architect to partially control the specification of the initial genotype, addresses a problem we think is likely not unique to GGE. In general, the architect wants a high degree of control over what aspects of a design are explored and what aspects are controlled. In GGE we gave such power to the architect and facilitated the architect's sense of control by using a transformation language that the architect understood.

Genotype coding: Following the genetic programming (GP) style (Koza 1992), in GGE a transformation is a primitive program element. It consists of a name and a list of the actual parameters for invoking the transformation. The initial form portion of the genotype is never subject to genetic variation (i.e. crossover or mutation) but the transformation sequence is. It, like a GP-style program, is a variable length, linear and ordered collection of transformation program elements. GGE crosses over two transformation sequences by selecting a crossover point between any two transformation program elements and swapping material between the parents at this point. It does not allow crossover to take place at a point within a transformation primitive. Mutation takes place within a transformation. The actual parameters to the transformation are randomly changed within their operative ranges.

Fitness function and selection

We found the architect quite imprecise regarding an aesthetic for forms. This suggested that GGE include a component that allowed the architect indicate preferences (e.g., by ranking or choosing). The solution curently implemented in GGE is far from perfect. GGE relies on the architect choosing whether a form should be propagated to the next generation. At present, we have only used crossover and mutation manually (that is, we crossover profile sets or transformation sequences and mutate transformation parameters by setting up a genotype). So, GGE actually blurs the evolutionary algorithm steps of first judging fitness and then selecting. This is not necessarily recommended. We simply wanted to learn a bit more about how GGE performed before we made commitments to selection. Every transformation is logged to record the values of parameters that defaulted randomly. This lets the architect understand what happened.

The rest of the evolutionary algorithm

GGE does not yet support automatic population initialization nor does it execute an automated generation loop which includes a selection routine. These components are not yet implemented because they are not the primary issues of GGE's investigation into Alife CAD tools. In lieu of them, we have encouraged the architect to build an ancestry of forms and to hand guide GGE through generations and very small populations (1 to 3 forms) at present. This has proved somewhat adequate. If we were to remain with the ancestry guiding metaphor, GGE would need a tracking interface which shows the forms and their associated transformations. We do expect to implement the remaining components of the evolutionary algorithm in the next version of GGE. We also intend to design an interface by which to inspect the population. This will be useful for form ranking and it could link into the automated selection procedure.

Figure 1: Initial Form: plane-0

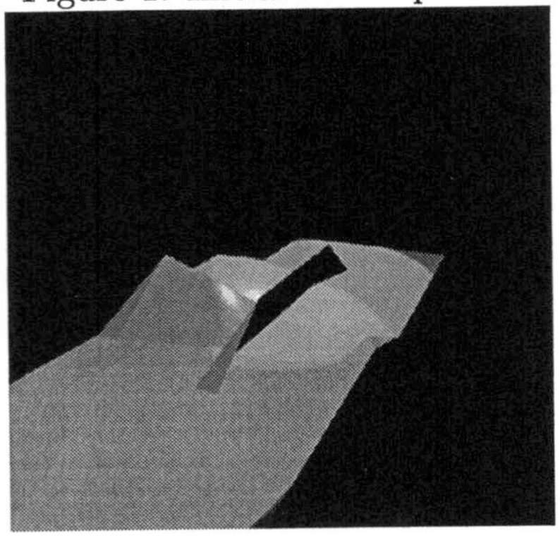

Figure 2: plane-1, transformation of plane-0

Figure 3: plane-2, transformation of plane-1

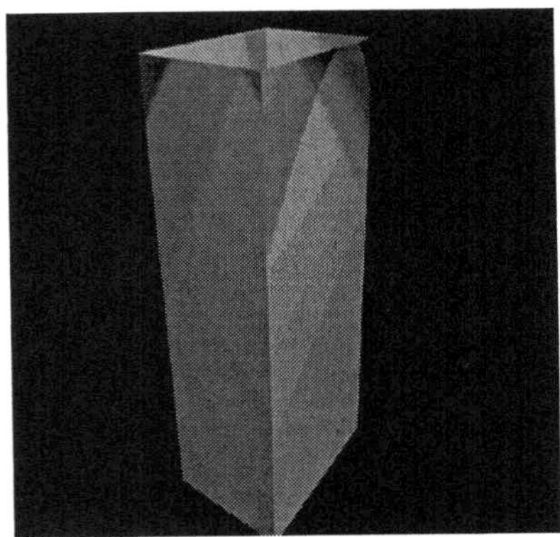

Figure 4: Initial Form: cube-0

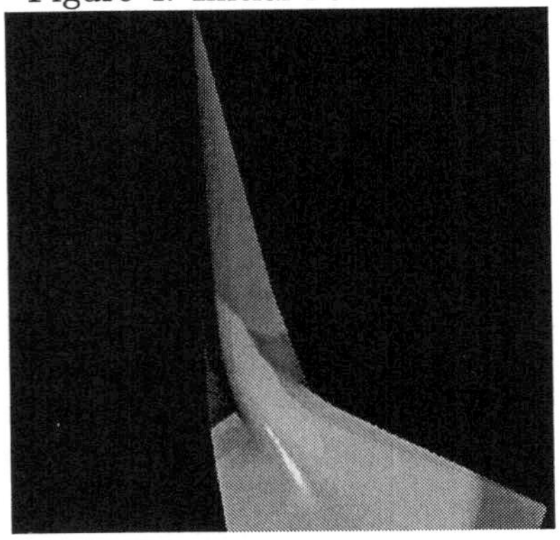

Figure 5: Cube-1, transformation of cube-0

Figure 6: Cube-2, transformation of cube-1

Examples

Some examples of GGE are helpful. Figure 1 shows an initial form. Figure 2 is the genetic offspring of Figure 1. The transformation sequence consisted of 4 Lift transformations. The first two acted on the Z axis and the final two acted on the X and Y axes respectively. Figure 3 is the offspring of Figure 2. The transformation sequence included an Insert of a random profile, then two Lifts.

Exchanging the planar form for a more cubic form, Figures 4, 5, and 6 have the same ancestral chain as Figures 1,2 and 3. The transformation sequence of Figure 5 exchanged the X,Y and Z coordinates of a subset of vertices in 3 profiles of the form. This resulted in a radical twist and a radical change to the original regular, cubic form. Figure 6 demonstrates how quickly even a small number of transformations can lead to a very complicated form. Two profiles were deleted from Figure 5 and portions of the X and Y axes of another set of (the same) profiles were lifted.

Summary

GGE comprises some innovative system design choices. For example, GGE's genotype representation consists of an "embryonic" initial form (data) and a sequence of form transformations that are based on visual actions and which are applied to the initial form. Forms undergo lifts, folds, insertions or deletions. This vocabulary allows the architect to understand what adaptation has occurred between a timestep of evolution. This helps her with proceeding like a architectural geneticist. In effect, in GGE the architect can guide evolution but not totally control it.

GGE illustrates that fewer degrees of freedom in a transformation lead to more acceptable forms. Plus, in using GGE we noticed that the architect desires a high degree of control over a smaller number of degrees of freedom. These facts were not initially obvious to us. (In fact, the behaviour of the transformations was not at all initially obvious.) Perhaps, higher degrees of freedom are a good strategy in fully automated evolutionary algorithm systems where many generations can be executed quickly or large population sizes can quickly eliminate extremely random forms.

Watching the architect subjectively select forms for her ancestory chain revealed that regularity, to some degree, is clearly a form aesthetic. This indicates a potential factor for a programmed fitness function. However, it still seems far from unclear how to specify regularity. Perhaps, it could be induced in a fitness function learning session in which the architect provides a ranking of various forms.

Because not all of its evolutionary algorithm's components are not yet implemented, GGE can not conclusively demonstrate that artificial evolution is well suited to guide the architectural design process. However, given what it *can* do, GGE lends support to this hypothesis.

Future work

We have a long list of future proof of concept investigations for GGE. In the upcoming academic term, our hope is that architecture graduate students in a studio design course will experiment with extending GGE in the following ways:

- Provide larger sized population processing.
- Implement new transformation actions.
- Link the output of GGE to a 3D printer.
- Extend the user interface and seamlessly integrate GGE with AutoCAD.

Conclusions

At this initial stage of its implementation GGE has shown that:

- Evolutionary algorithms are well suited as CAD tools for architecture though they need to be quite constrained in terms of random variation.
- the architect *must* be able to interact with the Alife CAD tool at opportunities during its execution, not solely before it runs.
- A genotype representation in the architect's vocabulary supports a better understanding of the tool's actions. This brings stronger user acceptance. It also makes the tool easier for the architect to guide.

References

Autocad. *Release 13 Reference Manual.* AutoDesk Inc., 1995.

Bentley, P. J. and J. P. Wakefield. '996. The evolution of solid object designs using genetic algorithms. In *Modern Heuristic Search Methods*, chapter 12, pages 197–211. John Wiley and Sons.

Bucci, E. J. 1997. Genetic algorithms and evolving virtual spaces. In *Designing Digital Space, An architect's guide to virtual reality*, edited by Daniela Bertol. New York: John Wiley and Sons.

Dawkins, R. 1986. *The Blind Watchmaker.* Longman Scientific and Technical Publications.

Frazer, J. 1995. *Evolutionary Architecture.* London: Architectural Association.

Funes, P. and J. Pollack. 1998. Computer evolution of buildable objects. http://www.demo.cs.brandeis.edu/papers/other/cs-97-191.html.

Koza, J. R. 1992. *Genetic Programming: On the Programming of Computers by Means of Natural Selection.* Cambridge, MA: MIT Press.

Rosenman, M. A. 1996. A growth model for form generation using a hierarchical evolutionary approach. *Microcomputers in Civil Engineering* 11: 163–174.

Steele, G. 1990. *Common LISP: the language.* Bedford, MA: Digital Press.

Merging the Energetic and the Relational-Constructive Logic of Life

Kepa Ruiz-Mirazo[1], Alvaro Moreno[1] and Federico Morán[2]

[1] University of the Basque Country Post Box 1249 / 20080 Donostia (Spain)
[2] University Complutense of Madrid 28040 Madrid (Spain)

Abstract

In this paper we criticize a theoretical standpoint, common in the field of Artificial Life (ALife), which assumes that the energetic and material aspects of living organization are contingent and irrelevant to define its logical essence. We argue, instead, that the relational-constructive logic of a basic biological system and the logic of its physical (thermodynamic) implementation are intertwined. Therefore, this must be taken into account to establish a universal definition of life.

Introduction: Metabolism and Alife

The community of "alifers" has searched for the organizational principles of possible life in the context of relational or formal systems, inspired by some abstract chemistry, rather than in the physics of self-organization or thermodynamics. Computational models conceive the *basic living organization*[1] as an operationally closed network of component production, independent of aspects related to energy and specific materiality, which are regarded as contingent. Then, a minimal living being appears as a particular (hierarchical) organization, thoroughly established by the formal rules of component production and transformation. Of course, it is presumed that the implementation of this type of organization requires flows of matter and energy; yet, in these models material aspects are invariably abstracted and energetic constraints tend to be assimilated to the constructive relationships themselves. As a consequence, the energetic and material problems (dissipation, irreversibility...) of the physical realization of the system tend to be completely disregarded. Kauffman´s *autocatalytic sets* (Farmer et al. 1986; Kauffman 1986), the computational models of *autopoiesis* (Varela, et al. 1974; McMullin and Varela 1997) or Fontana´s work on 'algorithmic chemistries' (Fontana 1992; Fontana et al. 1994) are good examples of the approach we criticize.

However, from a different ('thermodynamic') standpoint the basic living organization can be considered as a complex web of energy flows (understandable in terms of heat and work transactions) supported by a component production machinery -a chemical reaction network. In this context, the concept of metabolism becomes central; metabolism taken as the material-energetic expression of the basic organization of life, realized through the continuous structural, constructive and functional transformations that take place in the system. This perspective forces us to reconsider some features of the abstract-relational logic of computational models; a natural question will be whether this logic should be geared in with the set of requirements arising from the physical realization of the system.

Hence, the attempt to find out if, and how, a link can be established between these two distinct theoretical approaches seems worthwhile. This will enhance the significance of metabolism for the definition of life. The discussion on the role of metabolism is precisely motivated by the challenge embraced by ALife when it intends to extend biology by producing a universal science of *life as it could be* (Langton 1989). The goal is, then, to find a more general notion of metabolism in the framework of an 'extended biochemistry', based on different chemical components or even on virtual "biochemical" entities in some computational universe. In the following pages, we shall argue that the concept of metabolism is rich enough to accommodate what we call basic living organization. In other words, the analysis of the full implications of the notion of metabolism may discover a new avenue of research where matter and energy are necessary ingredients of a universal definition of the living.

Why Take Thermodynamics Into Account

Relational or computational models of the basic organization of life articulate the structural elements of the system

---

[1] By '*basic* living or biological organization' we mean the minimal organization necessary for an individual biological system to self-constitute and operate in its environment; the wider concept of 'biological organization' includes evolutionary aspects related to a collective and historical dimension, which we will not discuss in depth here.

according to rules of combination that ignore thermodynamic requirements. However, when energetic considerations are included, the framework of description of the system needs to be significantly modified: a new relationship between micro/macro levels must be considered, together with the establishment of some additional conditions on the rules of production and transformation of components (conditions involving couplings, energy currencies, intrinsic rates of reaction, etc.).[2]

In principle, all these new requirements could be captured in the formal terms of computational systems, but the motivations behind them are grounded on physical -rather than formal- considerations. As said in the previous section, the complex physical and chemical levels underlying biological organization are usually ignored in most computational models.

However, the fundamental question is the following one: how can we study life as it could be? Obviously, starting from life as we actually know it. It would not make any sense at all to try to universalize biology in AL making proposals which are contradictory or inconsistent with our basic knowledge of terrestrial biology. Of course, one could abstract or ignore many energetic and material aspects and study only certain formal properties of the system like, for instance, its operational closure. Yet, the material implementation of such mathematical or formal properties implies some additional requirements. Therefore, investigating lifelike systems in computational media should be consistent with the *complete* logic of this material organization, namely, with the implications of its physical implementation.

Even assuming the idea of life just in terms of 'organization', this must be instantiated in some type of material system. Life is a phenomenon exhibited by certain complex material systems, even though -so far- we only know a particular way of expression of it. In this sense, it is difficult to determine which biological principles established at present are contingent and which are general laws of all possible forms of life. Nevertheless, since we are considering living systems as a material phenomena, all biological laws should be consistent with the universal laws of physics and in particular, of thermodynamics (Moreno et al, 94). Now, how could we decide which are the universal laws for life? This question should be investigated by specifying the physico-chemical laws underlying the material realization of the organizational features abstracted from the analysis of terrestrial life (as well as by exploring formal computational models).

[2] This point is developed further in (A. Moreno & K. Ruiz-Mirazo, submitted). The paper also addresses some difficulties to include thermodynamic constraints in computational models of basic living organization.

Hence, thermodynamic constraints cannot be contingent elements of life understood as a material phenomenon. Besides, our basic view of the physical universe would have to change if thermodynamic requirements were taken as contingent. Of course, one can ignore these requirements in purely virtual universes, but this is not possible to do in a material one. Therefore, let us try to determine which are the fundamental requirements of the basic living organization from an energetic perspective.

The Problem of Autonomy

In the thermodynamic or energetic study of biological systems a central question is how an open system far from equilibrium becomes self-maintaining and able to *manage* the flow of matter and energy through it. The pattern generated by a self-organizing physico-chemical dissipative system may contribute to its own energetic sustenance, but not in an independent or minimally robust way. The self-organizing phenomenon may disappear out of small variations in the external constraints or boundary conditions -like the temperature gradient or the inward flow of some substrate. All this kind of dissipative phenomena (Bénard thermal convection, Belousov-Zhabotinski chemical reactions, or simply a candle or a whirl) depend on external constraints not controlled by the system.

In contrast, biological systems -although they are also subject to external constraints- present two distinctive features: first, they are able to store energy and thus maintain their characteristic organization for a relatively long time, even if external resources are insufficient; second, they take part in the construction and reconstruction of their internal constraints, the ones which actually define them and make them viable (Morán et al. 1997). Probably the best example to illustrate this is the cellular membrane, whose selective permeability and active role in metabolic processes cannot be understood unless it has been internally generated and maintained. In turn, it constitutes the physical border necessary to distinguish the system from its environment, to determine its limits and identity.

Therefore, the living organization is a network of mechanisms constraining matter and energy conversion, so that the system *itself* controls when, where, and how to use of the resources needed for its continuous realization as a whole. In other words, metabolism implies a set of processes of *autonomous* management of energetic flows and transformation of components with some global functionality (i.e., the problem of autonomy is at the heart of the meaning of metabolism (Boden 1997)). Now, whereas in the context of relational-constructive theoretical models the term 'autonomous' stands for an organization that builds itself up through its closure or recursivity properties (Varela 1979), what is the notion of 'autonomy' arising from a thermodynamic perspective?

Atkins (1984) defends that the thermodynamic organization of a biological system is based on its capability to generate work. Following this idea, the thermodynamic notion of autonomy takes the living as a complex network of constraints making possible to capture, conduct and transform energy, so that it can do useful work within its environment. The details of the ways in which organisms actually carry out such an efficient management of energy flows can get very complicated but, in essence, they involve the cooperative accomplishment of ***endo-exo-ergonic couplings***. This requires, at least, two important conditions: On the one hand, the presence of *energetic intermediaries* which make possible that the exergonic drive of some processes is invested in carrying through endergonic ones -a fact clearly supported by the common use of a few 'energy-currencies' in all known forms of life (Skulachev 1992). On the other hand, the presence of some specific components which modify the reaction rates so that coupling processes are suitably *synchronized* -role played by enzymes in all present metabolisms.

Constraints are necessary to generate work, to harness flows of energy coherently. Now, in a self-generated and self-producing system these constraints cannot be assumed as given: the actual system must construct them. Therefore, the system needs to avail itself of energy in the form of work precisely to produce constraints, constraints which in turn allow it to cyclically generate more work, and so on. Kauffman (1996) has recently introduced the idea of 'work-constraint (W-C) cycle' to argue that this recursive relationship underlies the achievement of real autonomy by a system.

It is important to notice that in this new context, the concepts of 'work' and 'constraint' may be defined *internally*, i.e., they acquire sense for the system itself. Work is any form of energy which contributes to the maintenance of the system, through the production of components that facilitate a suitable coupling among exergonic and endergonic processes. Similarly, we can define (functional) constraints as those components or aggregates of components within a network whose macroscopic action permits the renewal of useful forms of energy. In a relational-constructive type of approach, constraints contribute to the production of new components of the network; in this energetic perspective, they recursively maintain the W-C cycle by means of an effective control on energetic flows.

Hence, this notion of autonomy takes place in a domain different from that of the purely relational-constructive one. It is a dimension including theoretical elements connected with the energetic viability of the system, with its physical realization. Besides, the introduction of the W-C cycle entails a new energetic logic in the system. Although somewhat different, this logic is not completely independent or separated from the thermodynamic implications of the second law in its multiple formulations. After all, to stay alive, that is to say, far from equilibrium, living beings require an income of matter and energy: i.e., both 'to take in from a source' and 'give away into a sink' is necessary to keep the flows running and cycling (Morowitz 1992). In this sense, the energetic autonomy of living will always be *relative*. Yet, as we said before, another -possibly more important- side of the idea of autonomy is related to the self-construction and self-repair capabilities of the system. Thus, autonomy as an internal management of energy (control upon energy flows) is achieved only if the system can reinvest a big deal of the absorbed energy to generate and maintain these constraints.

Merging Two Characteristic Logics of the Living

As stated above, a system properly called autonomous must be able to constrain flows of energy so that the generated organization is functional and significant for the system itself. Yet,, the introduction of the W-C cycle implies that this is impossible without the intermediation of (functional) constraints. To be more precise, the cycle is maintained through the action of high-level structures (like enzymes) on the dynamics of lower-level elements (simple reactants). Thus, the structural (constructive) organization of a component production system must be somehow taking part in the energy flow control that its own maintenance requires.

Then, in order to grasp the *whole* logical essence of the living we need both things: a material autonomous apparatus of energy management (i.e., a set of devices constraining energy flows in a self-maintaining way); and a relational-constructive system of production and transformation of components operationally closed.

Although in the study of the basic organization of biological systems, these two conceptions have been traditionally unattached, we defend the necessity to establish a connection between them. For, in fact, there is a tight interweaving between the energetic and the relational logic of a living being, and metabolism (in its deepest and most universal sense) is the result of it. Accordingly, metabolism would be any material-organizational apparatus of energy management which can implement an operationally closed constructive-relational system, so that the network of component production relations recursively maintains and renews the aforementioned apparatus.

This new and integrating definition conveys that:

a) neither the energetic conditions or rules governing the system, nor the operational closure of its component production network can be taken separately; both aspects are causally dependent on each other. Thermodynamic requirements modify the logic of component production and, inversely, the type of functional components generated is crucial, for instance, to accomplish the W-C cycle, which constitutes the key for the energetic autonomy of the system.

b) the concept of metabolism proves powerful enough to capture all what is to be captured behind the idea of '(universal) basic living organization'.

Final Remarks

Establishing a real -and universal- characterization of metabolism appears to be a crucial point to understand a minimal living organization. According to the new definition proposed here, metabolism is grounded on the recursive self-maintenance of controls upon energy flows necessary for the physical realization of an operationally closed component production system, and, in turn, these components make the control upon the energy flows possible.

In principle, any chemical system able to realize this kind of organization is a possible candidate for constituting a metabolism. Therefore, this definition is not linked to a specific chemistry; we think that it provides an answer to the question of what metabolism consists in, not only 'as we know it', but also 'as it could be'. We put the emphasis on reminding that the "grammar" of any chemistry subject to physical realization must include some specifically energetic and material rules, rules without which the level of abstraction of the model is simply too big.

Nevertheless, our answer to the challenge of universalization of the basic living organization does not follow from the presumption (taken up by Langton and the 'strong' AL program) which splits 'organization conceived in purely logical-formal terms' and 'materiality conceived as something concomitant or accessory, passive with respect to that organization'. Rather, the contrary: it stands on their mutual interweaving. The origin of this interweaving is found, ultimately, in the intrinsic causal activity of matter, which does not allow us to dissociate or discern the relational-constructive properties from the thermodynamic ones in the domain explored here.

Unlike in a computational universe, matter in the physical world always performs some intrinsic activity; and the concept of energy is precisely the appropriate one to express that inherent capacity of matter to generate spontaneous actions. Then, not surprisingly, adding the thermodynamic dimension of a living system does not only mean including some new rules or conditions in a metabolism built according to a relational-constructive scheme. These conditions implicitly redefine the whole system, because they are entangled in its constructive logic, i.e., they substantially transform any (purely formal) abstraction of it.

Therefore, one of the essential features of living systems is the capability to use autonomously the intrinsic activity of matter to constrain itself. This autonomous causal power constitutes the main difference between a real natural system (in which the thermodynamic phenomenology arises spontaneously) and virtual lifelike organizations, which are the result of the operation of an externally constrained material system.

Acknowledgments

Authors acknowledge funding from the Research Project Number PB95-0502 from the DGICYT-MEC, and from the Research Project Number BIO96-0895, from the CICYT. Kepa Ruiz-Mirazo was supported by a Ph. D. Research Grant of the University of The Basque Country (UPV/EHU). We also want to thank A. Etxeberria for her critical comments on a previous draft of the paper.

References

Atkins, P. W. 1984. *The Second Law.* New York: Freeman & Co. Chapters 2, 8 and 9.

Boden, M. 1997. Is metabolism necessary? Oral presentation in the First Workshop on Philosophy of Artificial Life (PAL), Oxford (March, 97).

Farmer, J., Kauffman, S. & Packard, N. 1986. *Physica* D 22: 50.

Fontana, W. 1992. In *Artificial Life II*, edited by C. G. Langton, C. Taylor, J.D. Farmer & S. Rasmussen. Redwood City: Addison-Wesley, p. 159.

Fontana, W., Wagner, G. & Buss L.W. 1994. *Artificial Life* 1: 211.

Kauffman, S. 1986. *J. Theor. Biol.* 119:1.

Kauffman, S. 1996. Investigations. Santa Fe Institute Working Paper. Chapters 3 and 4.

Langton, C.G. 1989. In *Artificial Life I*, edited by C. G. Langton. Redwood City: Addison-Wesley, p. 1.

McMullin, B. & Varela, F. 1997. In *Fourth European Conference on Artificial Life*, edited by P. Husbands and I. Harvey. Cambridge, MA: MIT Press, p. 38.

Morán, F., Moreno, A., Montero, F. & Minch, E. 1997. In *Artificial Life V*, edited by Langton, C. G. & Shimohara, K. London: MIT Press, p. 255.

Moreno, A., Etxeberria, A. & Umerez, J. 1994. In *Artificial Live IV*, edited by R. A. Brooks & P. Maes. MIT Press, p. 406.

Moreno, A. & Ruiz-Mirazo, K. 1998. (Submitted)

Morowitz, H.J. 1992. *Beginnings of Cellular Life.* Binghamton, New York: Yale University Press. Chapter 9.

Skulachev, V.P. 1992. *Eur. J. Biochem.* 208: 203.

Varela, F., Maturana, H. & Uribe, R. 1974. *BioSystems* 5: 187.

Varela, F. 1979. *Principles of Biological Autonomy.* New York: Elsevier.

Model Predictions of an Origin of Life Hypothesis Based on Sea Spray

William Seffens
Department of Biological Sciences and
Center for Theoretical Study of Physical Systems
Clark Atlanta University
223 Brawley Dr., S.W.
Atlanta, GA 30314
wseffens@cau.edu

Abstract

According to geological evidence life arose in the sea no more than several hundred million years following earth formation. A new sea spray model for the origin of life is developed here to calculate the time of appearance of the first living cell, termed a protocell. The model proposes that life arose from sea spray that concentrated organic materials from a dilute primordial sea, and this spray became suspended in the atmosphere for several days and dehydrated to the extent of forming polymers. Each dehydrated sea spray droplet then became an experiment or trial of the mixture of biochemical activities (e.g., enzymes) contained in each droplet. If the dehydrated spray contains a certain minimal set of essential biochemical activities, and returns to the ocean intact, it is considered a successful protocell in this model termed the sea spray hypothesis. A range of values is assigned to all model parameters and median values are used to calculate the time of appearance of the first protocell to have been 2.7 million years. If the sea spray hypothesis is correct for primordial Earth, the model predicts that life could appear in less time on Mars or Titan under similar processes.

Introduction

The process leading to the origin of life was the result of the establishment of distinct physical and chemical conditions that lead from the formation of simple organic compounds on the primitive earth (Dyson 1985). These simple compounds combined together to give increasingly complex chemical structures until the first living cell termed a protocell was formed with the ability to metabolize and divide. The mechanism responsible for the origin of protocells must have taken place at such a rate that within no more than a few hundred million years successful protocells were formed. This time frame is demonstrated from microfossil and geological evidence (Schop 1983). The hypothesis advanced in this work is that protocells were generated as sea spray suspended in the atmosphere by winds (Seffens 1980, and also Lerman 1986). The marine bubble bursting process, which generates aerosol spray enriched in organic material, is proposed as the source of polypeptide and protocell synthesis. As organic compounds formed and accumulated in the cooling oceans of the Archaean era (2.8 billion years ago) bursting sea bubbles would concentrate surface-active material into ejected droplets of spray. Those droplets, which became suspended in the atmosphere by winds, would lose water through evaporation. If this process of evaporation is given sufficient time, of the order of several days depending upon temperature, the dehydration could cause amino and nucleic acids to condense and polymerize. Each of these dehydrated spray droplets, of the size of contemporary bacteria, is potentially protocellular and each would be an individual experiment in evolution. Within no more than several hundred million years one or more of these protocells could have ended up with a sufficient mixture of various enzymes to be able to exhibit metabolic and replicative activities. Success would be the formation of a metabolically active cellular entity that is capable of forming other similar entities. A most probable time of appearance of successful protocells can be estimated from this hypothesis based on contemporary ocean spray production rates.

Model Development

A calculation of the time of appearance of protocells can be formulated using an estimate of the rate of protocell production and the probability of finding a successful protocell. Estimates of protocell production can be based on current oceanographic data. The probability model of protocell success is built upon the following calculations or estimates: (1) number of enzymes expected per dehydrated droplet, and (2) the probability that a droplet contains at least one subset of required enzymes for the protocell to exhibit life-like properties. For any origin of life hypothesis, the number of enzymes in each protocell would depend upon the protocell volume, and the concentration of polymers within that compartment. The model-input variables needed to calculate the number of enzymes per droplet include droplet radius, ocean monomer concentration, monomer enrichment factor, monomer-to-polymer fraction, polymer length, and fraction of polymers with enzyme activity. A probability model of protocell success is then constructed considering all possible enzyme activities and a subset of required activities that must be present in the protocell for success. An analysis of errors arising from these parameters helps to delimit the conditions that generated life on earth under this sea spray hypothesis (Abdu 1997).

This model development is based on amino acid enzyme activity due to the greater knowledge of protein chemistry. The basis of the model is invariant with respect to what is causing the activity within each droplet. Enzymatic activity within the droplets could be caused by amino acid polymers (enzymes), nucleic acid polymers (ribozymes), or some other repeated structure such as clay or minerals. Therefore, with sufficient knowledge of ribozyme chemistry, this sea spray model could be reformulated to consider an RNA origin of life (Joyce 1989). The following sections explain each model parameter and how values are assigned.

Droplet radius (r). Contemporary aerosols of the undisturbed marine environment are composed of sea spray, tropospheric particles, and mineral dust with a spectrum of radii larger than 20 microns (μm) spanning smaller than 0.03 μm (Toba 1965). The sea spray component of tropospheric particles is present only within 1 to 2 kilometers above the sea surface, and with the exception of particles larger than 10 μm have lifetimes of several days (Junge 1972). From oceanographic data, sea spray has a statistically normal distribution of sizes (Wu 1981). Droplet radius is predominately in the range 15 to 25 μm. Using a mean value of 20 μm gives a mean droplet volume of 3.4 x10^{-8} cm^3. It is proposed that protocells came from this most numerous fraction of sea spray which is of the same size as bacteria and which also remains suspended in the atmosphere long enough to promote polymerization reactons (Seffens 1980).

Monomer concentration (C_m). Primordial seawater organic composition depends upon prebiotic synthesis mechanisms. Organic synthesis was demonstrated by Stanley Miller in 1953 with his fundamental experiment using prebiotic atmosphere conditions. The concentration of compounds that could be labeled as monomers in Miller's experiment was typically 10^{-3} M (Miller and Orgel 1974). This concentration probably represents an upper limit because the electrical discharges were done in a closed system; whereas the ocean is practically an open system thermodynamically. Another estimate for the concentration of organic material is suggested by Miller and Stribling (1987) to be 10^{-4} M. Thus, with an estimated range of 10^{-4} M to 10^{-3} M, the mean value would be 6 x10^{-4} M. In this model, organic compounds that can participate in polymerization reactions are labeled as monomers.

Monomer enrichment factor (E_m). Surface active organic material in the sea tends to concentrate at the surface due to hydrophobicity. The concentration of organic material in spray has been measured to be greater than the content in bulk seawater (Blanchard 1974). A monomer enrichment factor is needed to calculate the actual concentration of organic material in each spray droplet. Each chemical compound has some enrichment factor due to bubble fractionation that depends mostly upon hydrophobicity. Dissolved organic carbon, carbohydrates, and adenosine triphosphate have been found to be significantly enriched in the upper 150 μm surface layer of the ocean compared to subsurface water, with mean enrichment factors being 1.5, 2.0, 2.5, respectively (Sieburth et al. 1976). From the above data 2.0 is estimated as the mean value for this factor.

Monomer concentration (6 x 10^{-4}M) times the enrichment factor (=2.0) gives the expected concentration of monomers in each droplet to be 1.2 x 10^{-3}M, so that each droplet would be expected to contain 2.4 x 10^{10} monomers. This large number of compounds may participate in polymerization reactions as the droplet dehydrates in the atmosphere.

Monomer-to-polymer fraction (P_m). Polymerization of monomers is hypothesized to take place in this model when sea spray suspended in the atmosphere by winds is dehydrated. Amino acid polymers have been prepared in the laboratory using heat. These thermal proteinoids were found to have many of the properties of proteins (Fox, 1964). Typical reaction conditions are 170°C for 6 hours, yet the minimum temperature for polymerization can be as low as 65°C (Fox, 1965). Yield of proteinoids depends on conditions of the reaction and typically range between 5% and 40% (Fox, 1965). Therefore the lower estimate for monomer-to-polymer fraction is 0.05, the upper estimate is 0.4, with an assumed mean value of 0.2.

Polymer length (L_p). The thermal method of Fox has yielded polymers of amino acids with mean molecular weights of 3000 to 10000 Daltons (Fox and Harada 1960). That molecular weight range would represent polypeptides with 30 to 100 amino acids, with a mean of 65. Monomer-to-polymer fraction and polymer length are used to calculate the number of polymers expected per droplet, which is equal to the number of monomers per droplet multiplied by the monomer-to-polymer fraction and divided by polymer length. Using mean values the expected number of polymers per droplet in this model is 7.4 x 10^7 polymers.

Fraction of polymers with activity (F_p). The fraction of polymers with activity is a parameter that estimates the enzymatic activity resulting from a collection of random polymers. In order to determine this parameter the probability that a randomly chosen sequence of amino acids has enzymatic activity must be determined. Estimates range from 10^{-20}, if 10 residues are essential (Hoyle and Wickeramasinghe 1981), to 2.1 x 10^{-65}, based on sequence variation in cytochrome c (Yockey 1977). The action of cytochrome must be very specific to prevent damage to the cell from side reactions. Therefore the function of cytochrome c would be a poor choice as a model of typical enzyme functioning.

Thermal proteinoids have been prepared experimentally and compared to pure enzyme (Rohlfing, 1967). Rohlfing's data suggests that only one in a thousand proteinoid molecules had enzyme activity for reducing oxaloacetate. This may have been a common or easy to find enzyme type among random thermal proteinoids. Assume then that rarer activities are no more than ten thousand times less frequent than common activities for the sake of argument. The parameter value will span 10^{-3} to 10^{-7}, the greatest range in this model. In this regard this study considered three values of the parameter estimate 10^{-3}, 10^{-5}, 10^{-7} (upper, middle, and lower, respectively). Combining the parameters above to calculate the number of activities expected per droplet, A, yields:

$$A = (4/3\pi r^3) \cdot C_m \cdot E_m \cdot P_m \cdot F_p / L_p \qquad (1)$$

Using the three different estimates for the parameter F_p (10^{-3}, 10^{-5}, 10^{-7}) resulted in a wide range of values for the number of activities per droplet ($A = 7.4 \times 10^4$, 7.4×10^2, and 7.4, respectively). The calculations for the time of appearance in this model use the middle value.

Probability Model

To estimate a time of appearance of a protocell it is necessary to calculate the probability of finding a successful collection of enzymes given the number of activities in a spray droplet. The probability would depend upon the total number of possible enzymes given all prebiotic molecules. A probability model can be constructed that considers some set of required activities necessary for "success". Success would mean a protocell able to perform life-like properties including growth and division. The required activities are a subset of all possible activities. The number of members in this required set is labeled R. The number of all possible activities is labeled as T.

Total activities (T). This parameter is defined as the sum of all possible activities, resulting from thermal polymerization, that could be found in the droplet. Let the total number of possible enzymes be equal to the number of possible substrates multiplied by the number of transformations for each substrate, divided by two since enzymes are reversible. For example, the enzyme that catalyzes the reaction A -> B will also catalyze B -> A. The number of substrates in the primordial environment depends upon chemical complexity. If pre-biotic molecules had less than eight carbons, then the number of possible substrate molecules is about 10000. This estimate is based on lists of known chemicals (Lide 1995). Assume that eight possible transformations are expected for each substrate in this model. Therefore, the total number of enzymes would be equal to 10000 x 8/2 = 40000 (upper estimate). If pre-biotic molecules had less than six carbons, then the number of substrate molecules would be approximately 5000. Therefore, with a lower estimate of 20000 enzymes, the mean value would be 30000 activities.

Required activities (R). This parameter counts the activities needed for metabolism (catabolism and anabolism) and replication, which would be essential for a successful protocell. Several studies using different lines of reasoning have suggested that the first cell could have needed a very small number of activities.

A recent study (Fraser et al. 1995) on a bacterium called *Mycoplasma genitalium*, which has one of the smallest genomes of a free living organism, suggests it is close to being a model minimal cell. DNA sequencing of *M. genitalium* has shown that this organism has 482 genes. It is estimated that its minimal translation pathway requires nearly 90 different proteins, while the complete DNA replication process requires only about 30 proteins. It has only 44 genes associated with metabolic pathways. Therefore, the three essential model pathways (catabolism, anabolism, and division) in this organism requires a total of 164 genes. The first cell could have had a much lower number of required activities than this number and could have been very inefficient.

Studies of the computer Game of Life indicate that a very small number of rules can give rise to complex and growing structures (Conway et al. 1982). If each computer rule needs only a small number of biochemical activities to encode the rule, then the total number of required activities in a protocell could be small. Assume three pathways encoding catabolism, anabolism, and division are necessary for a successful protocell. If only a few activities are needed for each pathway, and all three pathways are equally complex, then each pathway will require an equal number of activities. Since the first organism was unicellular, not complicated, and could be very inefficient, it is assumed in this model that 7 activities are needed for each pathway (catabolism, anabolism, and division). This makes a total number of 21 required activities.

The parameters T and R are used to calculate the probability of finding the set of required activities in a droplet. The probability of finding this set in a droplet can be estimated from the following probability model. Consider a box that contains A numbered balls (A = activities per droplet). Any ball can have a number from 1 to T (T = total activities). We need to find the probability that the box contains at least one ball of each of the set of numbers N_1, N_2, ... N_R, where R is the number of elements in this set (R = required activities). There are a total of T^A different configurations. A combinatorial argument shows that for each of R given activities to be present at least once, we have a probability of:

$$P = \bullet (-1)^k \cdot \text{Binomial}(R/k) \cdot [\,1-(k/T)]^A \qquad (2)$$

where "k" is a summation index integer going from zero to R (Abebe 1995).

From Equation (2) the protocell probability of success is equal to 1.2 x 10^{-34} using the values 10^{-5} for fraction with activity, 745 for activities per droplet, 30,000 for total possible activities, and 21 for required activities.

Spray production rate. The spray production rate from whitecap bubbles has been estimated to be 10^{18} to 10^{20} per second over the ocean worldwide at present time (MacIntryre 1972). The primitive atmosphere probably had higher temperatures and consequently greater winds than now (Hoyle and Wickeramasinghe 1981). Therefore, the spray production rate could easily have been higher than 10^{20} droplets per second. Assume 10^{20} droplets per second as mean value. Therefore the primordial production rate would be equal to 3 x 10^{27} droplets per year.

The time of appearance is equal to the total number of droplets needed (to find a success) divided by the spray production rate, which is as a result of all the above calculations using mean values is equal to 2.7 x 10^6 years. This is the number of years of spray generation required to find at least one successful protocell.

Discussion

In this work we have examined several parameters that may have been involved in the appearance of the first living cells termed protocells. The values assigned to all of the parameters are estimates used to test the possibility of obtaining solutions that are geologically reasonable. For a spray production rate of $3\text{x}10^{27}$ droplets per year and a probability of success $P=10^{-36}$ yields a time of appearance of 300 million years. Figure (1) shows the number of activities that must be present in each droplet to yield the above time of appearance for various parameter values of required activities (R) and total activities (T). As the number of required activities increases, the number of activities per droplet increases greatly. Therefore to find successful protocells within geologically realistic time frames, R and T must take on low values.

The calculations above are only meant to demonstrate that a time of appearance can be estimated. The result of the calculations gives a time of appearance of 2.7 x 10^6 years. This period does not include the time for the protocell to reproduce and eventually appear in microfossils. A range of parameter values produces times that are less than or equal to one billion years (Seffens 1997). Evidence from microfossils demonstrates that bacteria-like life was present within a billion years after earth formation. Since the time of appearance from the model calculations is within the time estimated from geological records, the model supports a plausible hypothesis. If this hypothesis is correct for primordial Earth, then various parameters in the model can be established to predict a time of appearance on other planets. Under a lesser gravitational field, larger spray droplets will be able to remain suspended in the atmosphere for longer times. Hence in this model "r" will be greater, which will yield a greater number of activities per droplet "A". From equation (2), this will yield a greater probability value, and hence for equal spray production rates, will yield a smaller time of appearance.

Acknowledgement

This work was supported (or partially supported) by NIH grant GM08247, Research Centers in Minority Institutions award G12RR03062 from the Division of Research Resources, National Institutes of Health and NSF CREST Center for Theoretical Studies of Physical Systems (CTSPS) Cooperative Agreement #HRD-9632844.

References

Abdu, S. 1997, Sea spray model study of an origin of life hypothesis". Masters Thesis, Clark Atlanta University, Atlanta, GA.

Abebe, 1995. Clark Atlanta University, Mathematical department (personal communication).

Blanchard, D. C. 1974. Bubble scavenging and the water-to-air transfer of organic material in the sea. *Applied Chemistry at Protein Interfaces* 18: 360-376.

Conway, J., E. Berlekamp, and R. Guy. 1982. *The Recursive Universe*. New York: Academic Press.

Dyson, F. 1985. *Origins of Life*. Cambridge, UK: Cambridge University Press, p.18.

Fox, S. 1964. Thermal polymerization of amino acids and production of formed microparticles on lava. *Nature* 201: 336.

Fox, S. 1965. A theory of macromolecular and cellular origins. *Nature* 205: 328-340.

Fox, S., and K.J. Harada. 1960. The thermal copolymerization of amino acids common to protein. *Amer. Chem. Soc.* 82: 3745-3751.

Fox, S., K. Harada, G. Krampitz, and G. Muller. 1970. Chemical origins of cells. *Bioscience* 20: 5.

Fraser, C.M. 1995. The minimal gene complement of *Mycoplasme genitalium* . *Science* 270: 397-402.

Hoyle, F., and C. Wickeramasinghe. 1981. *Evolution from*

Space: A Theory of Cosmic Creationism. New York: Simon and Schuster, p. 24.

Joyce, G.F. 1989. RNA evolution and the origin of life. *Nature* 338: 217-224.

Junge, C.E. 1972. Our knowledge of the pysico-cemistry of arosols in the udisturbed mrine evironment. *Journal of Geophysical Research* 77: 3183-5200.

Lerman, L. 1986. Potential role of bubbles and droplets in primordial and planetary chemistry: Exploration of the liquid gas interface as a reaction zone for condensation processes. *Origins of Life* 16: 201-202.

Lide, D. R. 1995. *Handbook of Chemistry and Physics.* 74th edition, Boca Raton, Fl: CRC Press.

MacIntryre, F. 1972. Flow patterns in breaking bubbles. *Journal of Geophysical Research* 77: 5211-5228.

Miller, S., and L. Orgel. 1974. *The Origins of Life on the Earth.* Englewood Cliffs, NJ: Prentice Hall.

Miller, S., and R. Stribling. 1987. Formaldehyde synthesis, the HCN and amino acids concentration in the primitive ocean. *Origins of Life Evolution Biosphere* 17: 261-273.

Rohlfing, D. L. 1967. The catalytic decarboxylation of oxaloacetic acid by thermally prepared poly-alpha amino acids". *Archives of Biochemistry and Biophysics* 118: 468-474.

Schopf, J. W. and M. R. Walter. 1983. In *Earth's Earliest Biosphere: Its Origin and Evolution*, edited by J.W. Schopf. Princeton, New Jersey: Princeton University Press, p. 214-239.

Seffens, W. 1980. A hypothesis of the origin of cells concerning the dehydration of sea spray aerosol. Lecture given at University of Texas at El Paso and unpublished manuscript.

Seffens, W. 1997. Sea spray model calculation of the origin of life using Mathematica. *Mathematica Journal* July 1997.

Sieburth, J., P. Willis, and K. Johnson. 1976. Dissolved organic matter and heterotrophic microneuston in the surface microlayers of the North Atlantic. *Science* 194: 1415-1418. Toba, Y. 1965. The giant sea-salt articles in the atmosphere, 1. General features of the distribution. *Tellus* 7: 131-195.

Wu, J. 1981. Evidence of sea spray produced by bubbles. *Science* 212: 324-326.

Yockey, H. 1977. A calculation of the probability of spontaneous biogenesis by information theory. *Journal of Theoretical Biology* 67: 377-398.

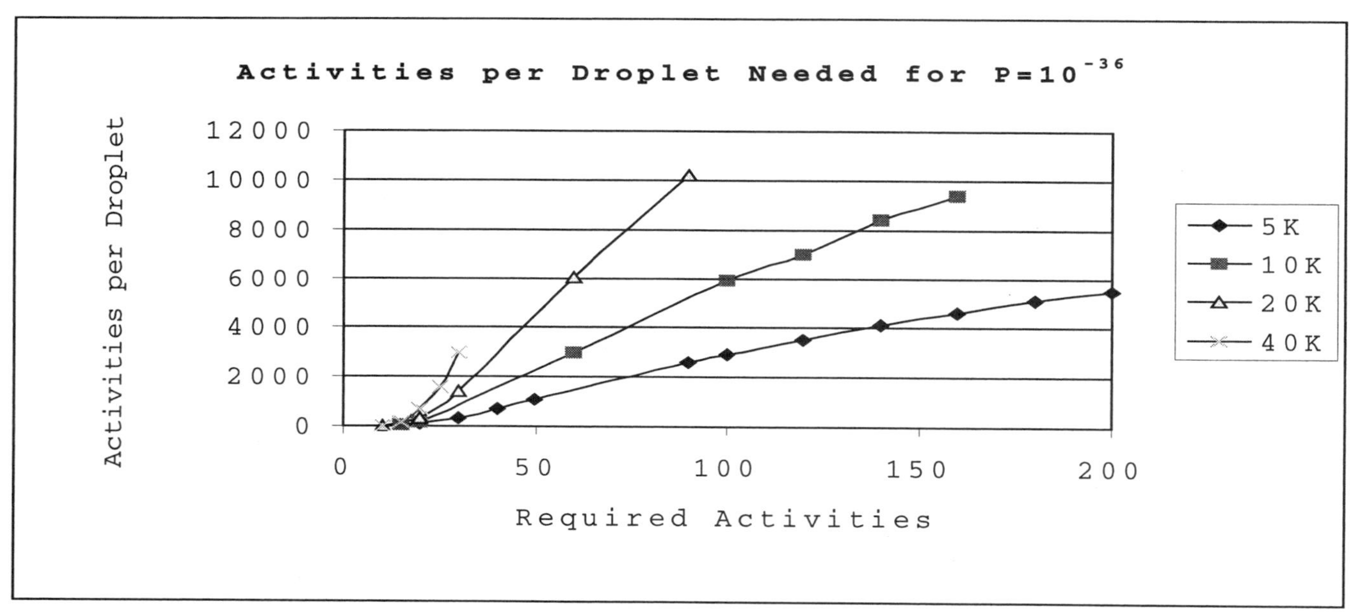

Tom Thumb Robots Revisited : Self-Regulation as the Basis of Behavior

Elpida S. Tzafestas

Intelligent Robotics and Automation Laboratory
Electrical and Computer Engineering Department
National Technical University of Athens
Zographou Campus
Athens 15773, GREECE
brensham@softlab.ece.ntua.gr

Abstract

We analyze the problem of the Tom Thumb robots, i.e., of robots that forage in a closed world and communicate the position of sources using a crumb laying technique. We demonstrate that past solutions to the problem suffer from physical instability, due to crumb exhaustion for individual robots, and we propose as solution a self-regulating mechanism. On a second level, we demonstrate that the introduction of an additional self-regulation loop, parallel to the first, improves the performance of the system. A number of theoretical conclusions are drawn, the most prominent being that the actual collaborative behavior of the system is the by-product of a self-regulation process within each of the agents and that the second regulation loop concerns the parameters that define the temporal dynamics of behavior.

Introduction

One classical problem on the intersection of artificial life and behavior-based robotics is the robot foraging problem, where one or more robots forage locally for some source of interest, such as food or minerals. In the usual version of the problem (Steels 1990, Mataric 1992, Drogoul and Ferber 1992) there are a few large sources distributed in the world, while in (Tzafestas 1995) we have tackled the case of more or less uniform source distribution. The solution to the usual case consists in allowing a robot to lay down trails or “crumbs” while carrying a source sample to a home base, that another robot or itself may follow to arrive to the source quickly. A variant of the problem considers that trails laid down by the robots evaporate slowly, in the same way as pheromone quantities laid down by real ants in the physical world (Deneubourg et al. 1990, Nakamura and Kurumatani 1996).

We reexamine the usual version of the problem from a different point of view, in an attempt to identify or specify the conditions of validity of the solution found in the literature. The most complete solution to date has been given in (Drogoul and Ferber 1992), where a number of increasingly complex and increasingly satisfactory solutions have been analyzed. The Tom Thumb robot is able to successfully build, reinforce and correctly use trails from the home base to the source, while the Docker robot (Drogoul and Ferber 1992) uses an additional mechanism of sample “theft” from neighbors, which allows robots to build chains resembling harbor Dockers. The motivation for our work has been our feeling that the Tom Thumb robot as defined is not stable because it assumes unbounded numbers of “crumbs”, which is not physically possible, and which would show in a real robotic implementation.

Why Tom Thumb Robots Fail

The Tom Thumb robot’s behavioral diagram as described in (Drogoul and Ferber 1992) is depicted in Figure 1.

If (carrying samples)
If (back home) lay down samples
Else {go home, lay down 2 crumbs}
Else
If (found samples) pick up samples
Else
If (crumb or stimulus sensed)
{follow stimulus, pick up 1 crumb}
Else move randomly

Figure 1. The behavioral diagram of the Tom Thumb robot (cf. Drogoul & Ferber 1992, p. 455). In the Docker robot, the condition (crumb or stimulus sensed) is replaced by (crumb or stimulus or loaded robot sensed).

The Tom Thumb robot lays down two crumbs while homing, and picks up one crumb while following crumbs or stimuli. Unless otherwise stated, all simulations reported below use a 30x30 grid world with the home base in the center emitting an orientation signal, a large source at one of the corners and a population of 10 robots starting with 50 crumbs each. Robots may sense a sample or crumb from a distance of up to three grid cells.

We have simulated first the behavior of the system as is, by measuring the quantities of crumbs deposited in the world or owned by individual agents. The results are given in figures 2 and 3. As was expected, the quantities of crumbs owned by robots generally fall below zero, while the quantity of crumbs deposited in the world may rise without limit. The exact values of these quantities depend on the problem parameters (distance from source to home base, number of robots and source size) that define the expected number of robot trips source-base necessary to complete the task.

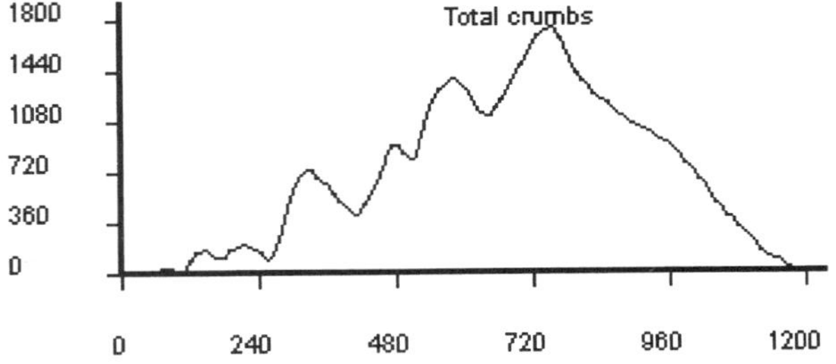

Figure 2. Quantity of crumbs in the world in a typical run (the maximum is around 1400 crumbs, which is much more than the total number of crumbs owned by all robots). The job is over when the source is exhausted and all crumbs are collected, i.e., when the path to the source has vanished.

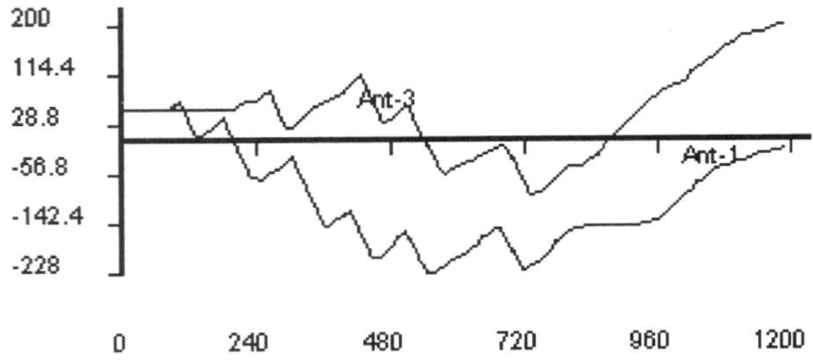

Figure 3. Quantities of crumbs owned by two robots in the above run. Both fall below zero.

An apparent question arising at this point is, "what if we just constrain robot behavior so as not to lay down crumbs when it does not have any ? aren't crumbs deposited so far enough ?" We have been able to see in several experiments that, first, depending on the problem parameters, the total quantity of crumbs might not be sufficient, in which case the path to the source will be disconnected, and, second, when it is sufficient — for instance if we start the above experiment with 1000 crumbs per agent — the total number of crumbs deposited in the world may rise tremendously. This last condition generates an important problem : the robots will continue being attracted for a long time to an empty source, that is, the surplus crumbs will be misleading. This observation brings us to the actual formulation of the above trailing problem :

We are seeking a laydown-pickup mechanism such that a trail to a source is built quickly and reinforced while the source exists and vanishes shortly after the source is exhausted.

The Solution : Self-Regulation

The problem of agent crumb exhaustion lends itself to a simple solution. Every time a robot needs to lay down or pick up crumbs, it should do it in a way so as to preserve its own quantity of crumbs within some desired bounds $crumbs_{min}$ and $crumbs_{max}$, by using the following laws :

For laydown (1a)

$$crumbs(t+1) = crumbs(t) + r_l * (crumbs_{min} - crumbs(t))$$

For pickup (1b)

$$crumbs(t+1) = crumbs(t) + r_p * (crumbs_{max} - crumbs(t))$$

This simple regulation mechanism ensures that no agent will ever run out of crumbs completely. However, the absolute (real-valued) quantity of crumbs deposited or collected at each cycle will depend on the state of the agent : an agent with many crumbs will lay down more and pick up less than an agent with just a few crumbs remaining. This arrangement allows for trails to be built rapidly (because agents in the beginning have a statistically medium number of crumbs, so they tend to lay down large quantities of crumbs) and to vanish quickly (because agents toward the end of the task have statistically only a few crumbs, so they tend to pick up large quantities of crumbs). In what follows it will be assumed that $crumbs_{min}$=10 and $crumbs_{max}$ = 100, for all agents.

Meta-Regulation : Temporal Dynamics

While we can certainly fix r_l and r_p to two values and get the system running, it is an important concern to identify proper values for these parameters, i.e., values that will ensure a "statistically optimal" performance, according to the problem formulation given at the end of section 2. Intuitively, and all other things being equal, we expect to have different "optimal" values of r_l and r_p, for different environmental conditions. In figure 4 we give the comparative results of a typical simulation run with r_l = 0.12 and r_p=0.06 for three cases of a small, a medium and a large source size (20, 50 and 80 samples, respectively).

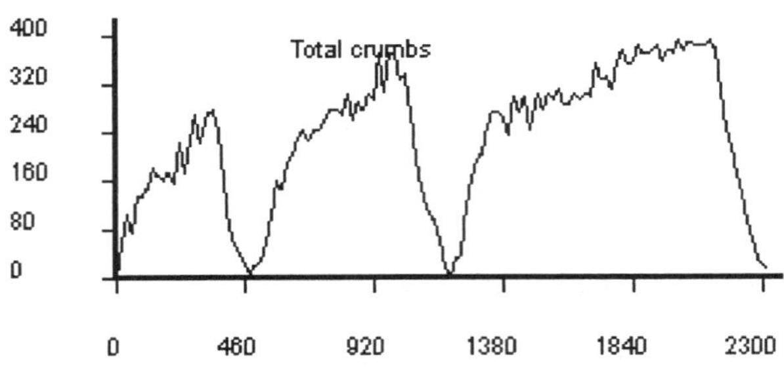

Figure 4. Comparative performance for a typical simulation run with r_l=0.12, r_p=0.06 in three environments where the source size is 20, 50 and 80, respectively. The duration of the task is 488, 696 and 1105 cycles, respectively.

We have conducted experiments with various parameter settings in various environmental conditions and we have obtained results that differ both quantitatively and qualitatively. However, all of these parameter settings share the essential characteristic of uniform laydown or pickup rates. A large laydown rate will be beneficial in the start and middle of the task, when the agents would like to build and reinforce a trail quickly, while a large pickup rate would be beneficial toward the end of the task, when the agents would like to destroy the trail to the exhausted source as quickly as possible. While a given parameter setting would be more desirable than another one in a particular context, our goal as designers should be to ensure the better behavior *globally*, i.e., to ensure that the system will "discover" or identify the proper parameter setting in each situation.

Consequently, what we really want is *not* a particular parameter setting, but a mechanism that will allow a robot to lay down more and pick up less crumbs at the beginning of the task (so as to build and reinforce the path) and vice versa toward the end (so as to destroy it quickly). To this end, a measure of the state of the task must be available. The only such measure that a robot may have is the number of the crumbs in the world. However, since this quantity cannot be directly perceivable, we have used an estimate of it, simply the number of crumbs at the current position of the robot. This estimate is used as follows :

For laydown

If crumbs(t) >= world_crumbs_estimate (2)

$$r_l(t+1) = r_l(t) + r_{rl} * (r_{lmax} - r_l(t))$$

else

$$r_l(t+1) = r_l(t) + r_{rl} * (r_{lmin} - r_l(t))$$

For pickup

If crumbs(t) >= world_crumbs_estimate (3)

$$r_p(t+1) = r_p(t) + r_{rp} * (r_{pmin} - r_p(t))$$

else

$$r_p(t+1) = r_p(t) + r_{rp} * (r_{pmax} - r_p(t))$$

As is obvious from the formulae, the rate of crumb laying increases when the robot owns more crumbs than may be found in its current position and decreases otherwise. Inversely, the rate of crumb picking increases when the robot owns less crumbs than may be found in its current position and decreases otherwise.

Figure 5 gives the result of the application of the above model in the three environmental settings used in figure 4. Surprisingly enough, the self-regulation of the laydown and pickup rates not just does change the shape of the curves, i.e., the qualitative behavior of the agents (the quantity of crumbs in the world rises quickly to a fairly high value, stays close to it during the task, and falls back quickly to zero when the source is exhausted, while showing far less fluctuations than in the previous case), but it improves results quantitatively as well : in all runs, including the one depicted, the duration of the task has been shorter than with the previous model.

Figure 6 gives the curves of the r_l and r_p parameters of one of the agents in the above run. It is clearly seen that r_l is high at the beginning and during foraging, while r_p is high toward the end of the task.

This improvement is more pronounced in harder environments where the regulation needs are more urgent, for example in the case of longer distances from home base to source or in the case of more agents. Also, figure 7 gives comparative results without and with meta-regulation for the case of Docker robots. Note that the performance is inferior to the one of Tom Thumb robots (middle curve of figure 5). This result is most probably statistically insignificant, but the actual comparative performances for Tom Thumb robots and Dockers in the case of meta-regulated behavior remain to be investigated. Note also that in this last setting there are more fluctuations in the shape of the path than in the previous ones, because since Dockers "steal" samples from one another the crumbs path are generally neither continuous nor persistent.

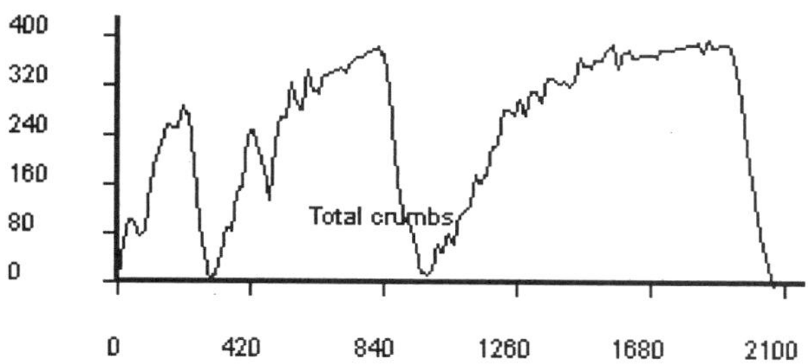

Figure 5. The same experiment as in figure 4 but with meta-regulation of r_l and r_p, between 0.06 and 0.12 for each one of them ($r_{rl} = r_{rp} = 0.1$). The task duration is 302, 676 and 1063 cycles, respectively. The maximum number of crumbs in the world is approximately the same in all three cases, because they are laid down quickly enough, and on average higher than in the previous cases.

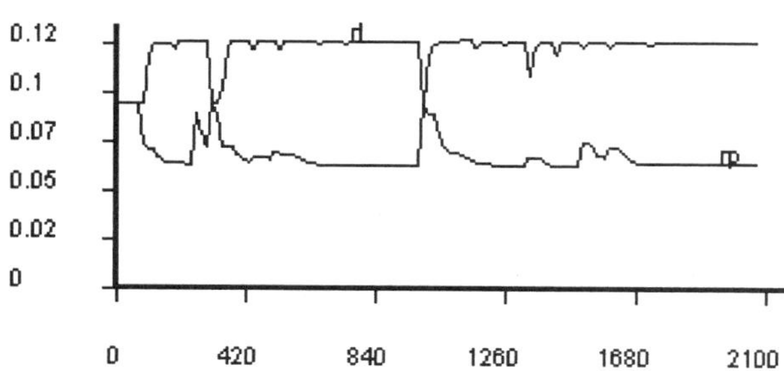

Figure 6. Curves of r_l and r_p, for an agent in the run of the previous figure. Local peaks of r_p correspond to situations where the agent has had to return to the home base while the trail was temporarily disrupted. However, the agent has been able to return to the correct behavior quickly. Similar observations may be drawn for r_l. Notice that the value of r_l only changes during the beginning of the task, when agents collect samples and need to lay down crumbs.

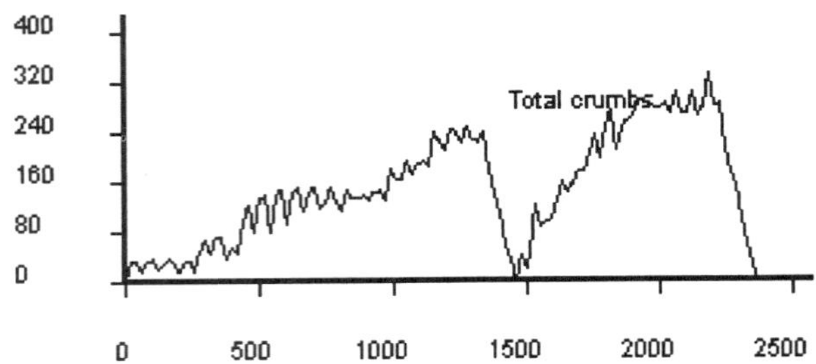

Figure 7. Comparative results without and with meta-regulation for the case of the agents having the Docker behavior as described in (Drogoul and Ferber 1992). The task duration is 1440 and 1021 cycles, respectively.

Theoretical Discussion

We have shown above that the agent's behavior is based on a critical variable (the individual crumb quantity) that drives its motivation to participate in the crumb laying and picking process. This variable is coupled with the actual quantity of crumbs in the environment through the agent's behavior. By regulating its own variable, an agent tries to bring the corresponding world variable to 0. In (Tzafestas 1995) we have called this property of the agent-world system "*operational coupling*", since it defines a coupling between agent and world such that the agent's behavior is qualitatively operational, that is, it responds to the environmental perturbations in a uniform way. Furthermore, this variable has *cognitive value*, since it represents the agent's idea about the state of the environment (a low value of the agent variable most probably means a world where a source exists). Seen this way, the agent may be thought of as trying to approach or approximate the world variable, i.e., as trying to adapt to its environment.

The operationality of the behavior is ensured through an additional self-regulation mechanism acting on the adaptation rates. This is an important observation, since it is compatible with the dynamical approach to cognition (van Gelder and Port 1995), stating that the most important factor in cognitive mechanisms is the nature of dynamics involved. Mechanisms like the ones developed here may be also regarded as a first step toward the realization of autopoietic systems :

> "... an autopoietic system is a homeostat ... the critical variable is *the system's own organization.* It does not matter, it seems, whether every measurable property of that organizational structure changes utterly in the system's process of continuing adaptation. *It* survives." (Maturana and Varela 1980, p. 66, authors' emphasis)

Of course, we have explored many unsuccessful regulation variants as well, the most important being the inverse regulation scheme, where in formulae (2) and (3) the inequalities are inversed. A comparison of the two mechanisms showed that the inverse mechanism is unsuccessful because agents then take the environment's state into account negatively, so that they appear non cooperative to other agents. For instance, an agent possessing many more crumbs than there are in its environment will try to give away as little or possible or pick up as many as possible, so as to maintain this difference, hence hiding information from other agents. Of course, this kind of behavior will have a negative impact on itself as well, because if other agents do not find a path to a source, he won't either. This is another demonstration of the well-known principle that cooperative behavior is first of all selfish (Axelrod 1984).

The final observation concerns the point of view taken to analyze this problem. While it has been traditionally tackled as an engineering problem, where the goal has been to solve a primitive problem of communication between agents, in this work we are proposing an inverse point of view, where the agent may be thought of as trying to regulate within bounds some internal variables (the regulated variables appear to be critical for an agent's survival or operationality, so that Ashby (1960) calles them *essential variables*). The buildup and reinforcement of the communication means, i.e., of the trail, is a by-product of agent self-regulation when a perturbation occurs, i.e., when sample sources exist. The driving force of the agent's behavior is thus the state of its essential variables, whereas the picking and laying components constitute the metabolic part of the overall mechanism.

It is noteworthy that exactly the same qualitative conclusions have been drawn in the case of agents exploring an environment with more or less uniform distribution of sources (Tzafestas 1995), though with a different cognitive variable and a different type of first-level adaptation.

Conclusions and Perspectives

We have investigated the classical robot exploration problem in the case of a few large localized sources and we have shown that the fundamental Tom Thumb solution is not complete from a physical and stability point of view, since individual agents run out of crumbs or the world gets overwhelmed with unnecessarily large quantities of them. What is necessary is a regulation mechanism that ensures that no agent will fall out of bounds as far as its own quantity of crumbs is concerned. The regulation model yields a better performance than the original Tom Thumb solution. On top of that, a second regulation loop is introduced that acts on the rates of the first one. The meta-regulation mechanism improves the performance of the agents and this improvement is more pronounced in harder problems where the regulation needs are more urgent, such as longer distances home-source, or larger numbers of agents, or Docker behavior. Theoretically, the overall model relies on the definition of a *cognitive variable* for each agent, that is coupled with an environmental variable and is adapted by the agent throughout the job. The adaptation rates that define the dynamics of the system are themselves regulated within bounds and this constitutes the meta-regulation loop. Overall, the agents may be regarded as self-regulating some internal "essential" variables, with the by-product being the communication with other agents through trails and the completion of the task.

The linear regulation model is by no means new. It is a fundamental model in early cybernetics research and it is also widely used in reinforcement learning work. Note, however, that our problem is *not* a learning one, in the usual sense of the term. To our opinion, this is an indication that the basic mechanisms underneath learning (be it linear regulation or others) preexist in an agent for some other reason, namely to solve some more primitive adaptation problems before true learning becomes necessary.

In the past, our approach has been already validated for the exploration problem in a uniform source distribution and the same principles have been found to apply. The next step is to formulate and solve in the same way a few other classical artificial life problems, such as robot cooperation in a closed ecosystem (Steels 1994) and action selection (Tyrrell 1993,1994). We hope that the comparative study of the results and conclusions for each of these problems will reveal a few secret principles for engineering or understanding regulation mechanisms.

Acknowledgments

Most of the ideas presented in this paper emerged while I was with the LAFORIA-IBP at Université Pierre et Marie Curie, Paris, France. I wish to thank Professor Jacques Ferber, as well as Claude Delaye, Steffen Lalande and Stéphane Bura, for inspiring discussions.

References

Ashby, W.R. 1960. *Design for a brain - The Origin of Adaptive Behaviour.* 2nd revised edition, London: Chapman & Hall.

Axelrod, R. 1984. *The Evolution of Cooperation.* Basic Books.

Deneubourg, J.-L., Aron, S. Goss, S. and Pasteels, J.M. 1990. The self-organizing exploratory pattern of the Argentine Ant. *Journal of Insect Behavior* 3:159-168.

Drogoul, A. and Ferber, J. 1992. From Tom Thumb to the Dockers : Some experiments with foraging robots. In *Proceedings Simulation of Adaptive Behavior 1992.* p. 451-459.

Mataric, M. 1992. Designing emergent behaviors : From local interactions to collective intelligence. In *Proceedings Simulation of Adaptive Behavior 1992.* p. 432-441.

Maturana, H.R., and Varela, F. 1980. *Autopoiesis and cognition — The realization of the living.* Dordrecht/ Boston: D. Reidel Publishing.

Nakamura, M. and Kurumatani, K. 1996. Formation mechanism of pheromone pattern and control of foraging behavior in an ant colony model. In *Proceedings Artificial Life V*, edited by C. G. Langton and K. Shimohara. Cambridge, MA: MIT Press, p. 67-74.

Steels, L. 1990. Towards a theory of emergent functionality. In *Proceedings Simulation of Adaptive Behavior 1990*, p. 451-461.

Steels, L. 1994. A case study in the behavior-oriented design of autonomous agents. In *Proceedings Simulation of Adaptive Behavior 1994*, p. 445-452.

Tyrrell, T. 1993. The use of hierarchies for action selection. *Adaptive Behavior* 1:387-420.

Tyrrell, T. 1994. An evaluation of Maes' bootom-up mechanism for behavior selection. *Adaptive Behavior* 2:307-348.

Tzafestas, E. 1995. Vers une systémique des agents autonomes : Des cellules, des motivations et des perturbations. Ph.D. diss., LAFORIA-IBP, Univ. Pierre et Marie Curie, Paris.

van Gelder, T., and Port, R. 1995. It's about time : An overview of the dynamical approach to cognition, in *Mind as Motion : Explorations in the Dynamics of Cognition*, edited by T. van Gelder and R. Port. Cambridge, Mass.: MIT Press.

A Generalized Reaction-Diffusion Simulator for Studying the Molecular Basis of Pattern Formation in Biological Systems

Hiroki Ueda
University of Tokyo, Medical School
7-3-1 Hongo, Bunkyo-ku,
Tokyo 113 Japan
m61016@hongo.ecc.u-tokyo.ac.jp

Hiroaki Kitano
Sony Computer Science Laboratory
3-14-13 Higashi-Gotanda, Shinagawa-ku,
Tokyo 141 Japan
kitano@csl.sony.co.jp

Abstract

The Generalized Reaction-Diffusion simulator enables us to experiment with various reaction-diffusion processes, and their spatio-temporal pattern formations. Such processes include the Turing Wave, Limit Cycle and Progressive Wave. The user can define a number of the factors involved and their interactions, boundary conditions, perturbation patterns, and other critical parameters. The power of such a simulator is demonstrated by creating patterns that simulates various steps of *Drosophila* eye formation.

Introduction

Rapidly increasing amounts of gene expression data are becoming available. But the complexity of the expression patterns and their underlying gene expression networks have made intuitive analysis difficult. One strategy for dealing with such complexity is to use a computer to simulate such biological systems.

Various biological systems are modeled with a reaction-diffusion system, in which chemical substances react with each other and diffuse though a cell or a tissue. In this paper, these chemical substances are known as factors. In 1952, Alan Turing suggested that a reaction-diffusion system is adequate to account for the main phenomena of morphogenesis (Turing 1952). In the same year, Hodgkin and Huxley developed the *gate model* of action potential on a neural membrane. Hodgkin and Huxley's model is based on the diffusion of ions and the interaction of ions and ionic channels (Hodgkin and Huxley 1952).

Such networks in biological reaction-diffusion systems are complex because of these reasons.

- There are many factors and interaction among them.
- Each factor and reaction is different from others.
- The initial conditions of factors vary.
- The spatial boundary of a reaction-diffusion system is typically irregular.

To simulate such a complex system, one needs a simulator, which can handle these issues. Expression patterns resulting from such networks are also complex because of these reasons.

- The temporal pattern is not constant.
- The spatial pattern is not homogeneous.

Likewise, a simulator is useful for dealing with complex expression patterns.

A major focus of our recent work has been to develop a Generalized Reaction-Diffusion simulator satisfying all these criteria. The Generalized Reaction-Diffusion simulator was developed as a part of the Virtual Biology Project, and proved a flexible simulation system for the reaction-diffusion process. We have to augment the core of the system to simulate various genetic and metabolic cascades and to be compatible with the single-cell modules of the Virtual Drosophila, Virtual Cell Laboratory, and Perfect C. elegans projects (Kitano et al. 1997).

The work reported here is an application of the Generalized Reaction-Diffusion simulator to actual biological systems, namely, various processes involved in *Drosophila* compound eye formation.

System Organization

Simulation kernel

The Generalized Reaction-Diffusion simulator program deals with the production, decay and diffusion of factors. As a simplification, the rate of production is given lower and upper bounds and is assumed to be a linear function of regulatory factors between these limits.

In biological systems, it is known that production rates of factors are influenced by regulatory factors not only in the same cell but also in neighboring cells. The same-cell process is called *intracellular signaling* and the neighboring-cell case is called *lateral signaling*. The Generalized Reaction-Diffusion simulator can deal with both processes.

The concentration of factor i is calculated by the formula:

$$\frac{dC_{i,k}}{dt} = \sum_j R_{i,j} C_{j,k} + \sum_j \sum_l L_{i,j} C_{j,l} - G_i C_{i,k} + D_i \nabla^2 C_{i,k}$$

$$0 \le \sum_j R_{i,j} C_{j,k} + \sum_j \sum_l L_{i,j} C_{j,l} \le P_{\max}$$

The first and second terms represent the intracellular signaling part and the lateral signaling part of the production rate. The third and forth terms represent the diffusion and decay. $C_{i,k}$ is concentration of factor i at position k. D_i and G_i are the diffusion rate and decay rate of factor *i*. $R_{i,j}$ and $L_{i,j}$ are the reaction rate and the lateral signaling rate from factor *j* to factor *i*. Indexes *j* and *l* represent a factor and a neighboring cell, respectively.

As mentioned above, the production rate of factor *i* is given upper and lower bounds(P_{max} and 0).

User interface

Reaction-diffusion parameters. For interactive simulation, the Generalized Diffusion Reaction simulator has various windows. The first window sets diffusion-reaction parameters such as diffusion constants, decay constants, intracellular signaling and lateral signaling parts of production rates and the maximum rates of production. The user can change parameters at any time, even if the simulation is running.

Initial condition and boundary condition. Another window defines the initial concentration of factors and the boundary condition of the system. Here the user can assign different initial concentrations to different factors. If the user wants to assign different concentrations at different spatial positions of the same factor, the user can choose a gaussian or uniform distribution mode instead of a constant distribution mode. In a gaussian or uniform distribution mode, concentrations of a factor are chosen at random, and different values are assigned to different positions in the system.

The user can also define the boundary condition of the system. The user can choose a von Neumann condition, Dirichlet condition or periodical condition as appropriate. If the spatial layout of the biological system is a ring or cylinder, the user can choose the periodical condition. If the system has no gradient of concentration of factors, the user can choose the von Neumann condition. If the system has fixed concentration of factors, the user can set the boundary condition to the Dirichlet condition.

Boundary and perturbation shapes. The third window sets boundary and perturbation shapes. Here the user can define the shape of a system boundary, or of an area where the concentration of various factors is to be perturbed. The user can draw any boundary or perturbation shape by combining circles, squares and lines. This is important for biological simulation, because a system is likely to have an irregular boundary and irregular pattern of initial conditions.

Visualization

Spatial pattern visualization. The results of a simulation are often homogeneous and constant. But if appropriate parameters are chosen, simulation results can be otherwise. To analyze such results, the Generalized Reaction-Diffusion simulator has four views, two for spatial analysis and two for temporal analysis.

The first and second views analyze the spatial pattern of concentration. The first is for grasping the global pattern of concentration while the second is for understanding more local patterns of concentration.

The first view is a contour plot in which concentrations of factors are represented in gray scale. The X axis and Y axis are both spatial axes. With this view, the user grasps the spatial distribution of a single factor.

The second view is a "slice" of the first view in which concentrations of factors are represented on the Y axis while the X axis represents the position of several factors together. With this view, the user grasps the detailed spatial pattern of and relationship among factors.

Temporal pattern visualization. The third and fourth views are for analyzing the temporal pattern of concentrations of factors in a chosen cell. The third is for visualizing temporal pattern of concentration of all factors, while the fourth is for visualizing detailed relationship between two factors.

The third view is a "Time Course" plot, in which concentrations of factors are represented on the Y axis while the X axis represents time. The present time is represented by line at X=0; past time instances flow out to the right.

The fourth view is a "Concentration" plot where the X axis represents the concentration of one factor and the Y axis represents the concentration of another. With this window, the user can visualize the detailed relationship between two factors.

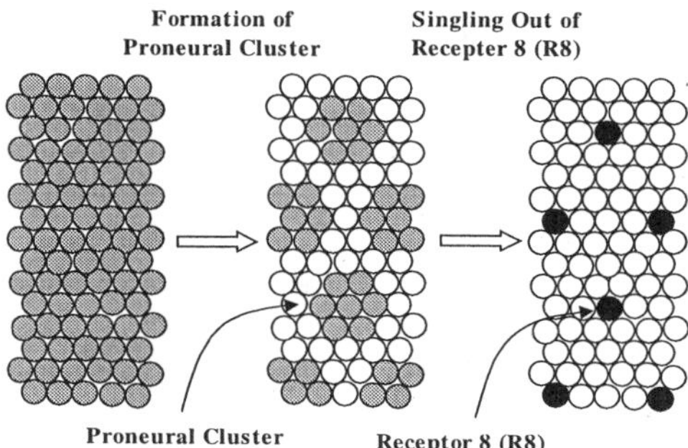

Figure 1. Two steps in Neural Pattern Formation of Drosophila Compounds Eye

Application to Actual Biological Systems

As an example of the power of the Generalized Reaction-Diffusion simulator, we will demonstrate that the Generalized Reaction-Diffusion simulator can generate patterns in various steps of *Drosophila* eye formation. This biological system is a popular example and has been well-investigated (Bate et al. 1993)

Eye development in *Drosophila*

The *Drosophila* compound eye represents a regular

hexagonal array of approximately 750 facets, the lenses of the eye.

In this section, we briefly discuss the cellular mechanisms controlling eye formation. This mechanism is similar to other biological systems in *Drosophila*, such as embryonic neurogenesis and the development of progenitor cells of mechano-sensory organs (Campos-Ortega et al. 1990; Cabrera et al. 1992; Jan et al. 1995; Artavanis-Tsakonas et al. 1991).

Like other systems, there are two distinct steps in the neural pattern formation of the *Drosophila* compound eye (Figure 1). First, small groups of four to six cells form *proneural clusters*. Second, one of these cells is arbitrarily chosen to become photoreceptor (R8), the precursor cell of a single eye lens. R8 then inhibits other cells in the proneural cluster from becoming precursor cells as well.

Proneural cluster formation

Real genetic circuit and expression pattern. Proneural cluster formation is the key step in forming the hexagonal symmetry of a single eye lens, or *ommatidia*. Two genes involving this step have been isolated: *Scabrous* and *Atonal.*

Atonal belongs to the "proneral gene" family that makes a cell able to become a neuronal precursor. *Atonal* is a transcription factor that activates production of other factors as well as its own production; activation produces proneural activity (Jarman et al. 1993). For this reason, *Atonal*'s precise spatial position of concentration to precise position is thought to be one of the key elements in *Drosophila* eye formation.

Scabrous is necessary to localize *Atonal* to only proneural clusters. Without *Scabrous* spacing between ommatidia is irregular. The protein product of *Scabrous* belongs to a secreted protein, fibrinogen (Mlozik et al. 1990).

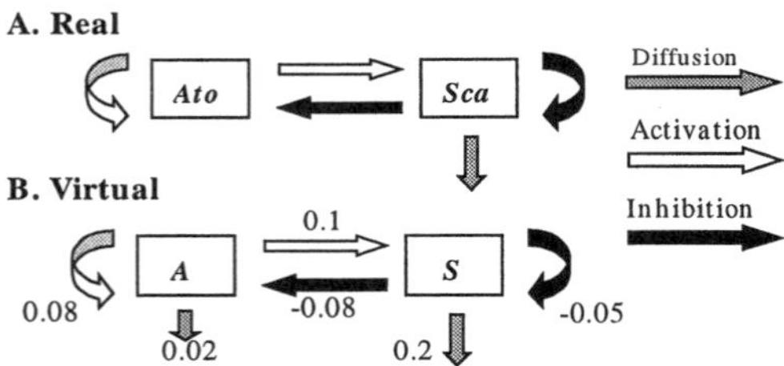

Figure 2. Real and Virtual Genetic Circuit in Proneural Cluster Formation

Interactions between *Atonal* and *Scabrous* and their properties are described Figure2A. This genetic circuit is based on various experiments (Mlodzik et al. 1990, Ellis et al. 1994).

The expression patterns of *Atonal* and *Scabrous* are coincident with each other. Initially, *Atonal* and *Scabrous* both are expressed in proneural clusters. This expression then becomes confined to isolated, regularly spaced columns of R8.

Virtual genetic circuit. In the virtual (simulated) genetic circuit, factor A in Figure 2B corresponds to *Atonal* and factor S to *Scabrous.* Factor A activates the production rate of factor S and A. Factor S represses production rates of factor S and A. Factor S and factor A are both diffusive, but Factor S is more diffusive than factor A.

The difference between real genetic circuit and virtual genetic circuit is the diffusion process of factor A (Figure 2A and 2B). In an actual biological system, *Atonal* (factor A) is not a secreted molecule but a nuclear factor; that is, it is not diffusive.

Comparison between real and virtual expression patterns. The Simulation result is shown in Figure3B.

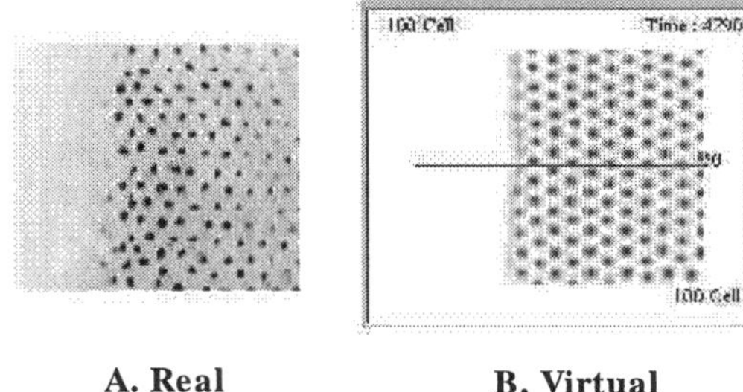

A. Real **B. Virtual**

Figure 3. Real and Virtual Expression Pattern in Proneural Formation(Mlodzik et al. 1990)

Concentrations of factor A and factor S are co-localized (data not shown) and form a hexagonal pattern (Figure3B.)

The system based on the interactions and properties described in Figure 2B is a Turing System, proposed by Alan Turing in 1952. The Turing system is composed of an activator and an inhibitor. The activator activates the production of itself and the inhibitor. The inhibitor represses the production of the activator and itself. Furthermore, the inhibitor is much more diffusive than an activator. Various biological systems are proposed to be Turing systems (Murray 1989, Kondo and Asai 1995) but the factors of the system (the activators and the inhibitors) have not been determined.

Our simulation results (which we will give in a future paper) suggest a specific mechanism whereby the *Atonal/Scabrous* Turing System results in proneural cluster formation. But to prove this proposition, the difference between virtual and actual genetic circuits must be explained with further biological and/or computational research.

Singling out of R8

The singling out of the R8 cell follows the formation of proneural clusters. During this step, cell-to-cell interactions result in a single cell within the group differentiating into R8. It is currently unknown how one cell of the cluster becomes singled out to form R8, although a stochastic model has been proposed. In the model, once some cell starts to differentiate, it prevents adjacent cells from doing so. This process is called *lateral inhibition* and is mediated by the "neurogenic genes".

Genetic circuit based on experiment. The neurogenic genes include *Notch, Delta, big brain, mastermind, neuralized* , the *Enhancer of split* complex (E[spl]-C) and *Suppressor of Hairless* (Su[H]) (These *really* are the gene names!). Figure 4A describes the known circuit involving these genes, which results in lateral inhibition. *Notch* and *Delta* genes encode membrane proteins that mediate lateral inhibition (Wharton et al. 1985). *Atonal* again activates the production rates of various factors, including itself.

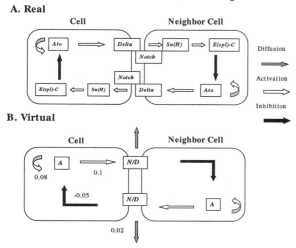

A. Real

Cell
Neighbor Cell
Ato
Delta
Su(H)
E(spl)-C
Notch
Notch
E(spl)-C
Su(H)
Delta
Ato
Diffusion
Activation
Inhibition

B. Virtual

Cell
Neighbor Cell
A
N/D
0.08
0.1
-0.05
N/D
A
0.02

Figure 4. Real and Virtual Genetic Circuit in Singling Out of R8

Real expression pattern. The expression pattern of *Atonal* and *Delta* are coincident with each other. As described above, *Atonal* is expressed only in proneural clusters. This expression then becomes confined to isolated, regularly spaced columns of R8 cells. Without *Scabrous,* proneural cluster formation does not take place, and a broader region has the potential to become a R8 cell. Figure 5A is the R8 pattern in the *Scabrous* mutant (Baker et al. 1995.) In this mutant, only the step of singling out R8 has occurred. The R8 pattern in the *Scabrous* mutant is not precisely spaced compared with the wild type.

Virtual genetic circuit. In the virtual (simulated) genetic circuit, factor A in Figure 4B corresponds to *Atonal* and factor N/D to *Notch/Delta* complex. Factor A activates the production rate of factor N/D and A in the same cell. Factor N/D represses production rates of factor A in neighboring cells.

The difference between real genetic circuit and virtual genetic circuit is the diffusion process of factor N/D (Figure 4A and 4B).

Comparison between real and virtual expression patterns. Simulation results are shown in Figure 5B. Factor A and factor N/D are co-localized (data not shown) and the expression pattern of factor A resembles that of *Atonal* in that that is not regular. *Notch* and *Delta* are membrane proteins and it is not reported that either protein is diffusive. Our simulation results do not directly suggested that *Notch* or *Delta must* have a diffusive process because other genetic circuit presenting the same results may exist. But the striking similarity between the actual expression pattern and the simulation result suggest that current knowledge based on experiments are not sufficient, and processes equivalent to N/D diffusion may exist.

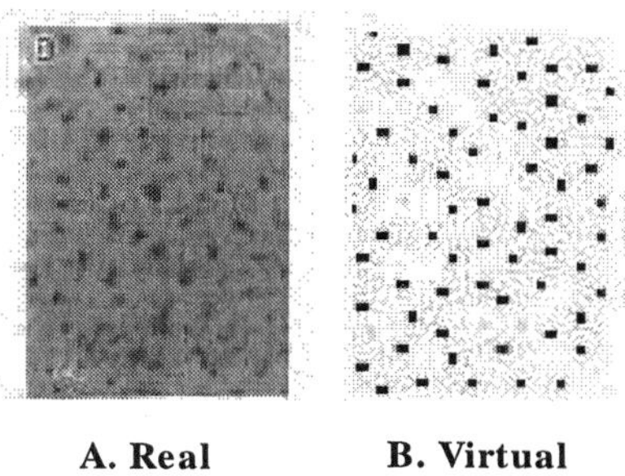

A. Real B. Virtual

Figure 5. Real and Virtual Pattern of R8(Baker and Zitron 1995)

Conclusion

In this paper, we have reported on the Generalized Reaction–Diffusion simulator, which enables us to simulate various biological systems based on reaction and diffusion processes and to analyze the spatio-temporal pattern of simulation results. The power of the Generalized Reaction-Diffusion simulator is demonstrated by actually generating the expression patterns of key factors in various steps of *Drosophila* eye development. In the proneural formation step, the striking similarities between the actual and virtual expression patterns of *Scabrous* suggest the possibility that *Atonal* and *Scabrous* are activators and inhibitors in a Turing System. During the R8 differentiation step, the remarkable similarities between the actual R8 pattern and the virtual expression pattern of *Atonal* suggest that a diffusive process exists in the *Notch/Delta* pathway.

Reference

Artavanis-Tsakonas, S., C. Delidakis, and R. G. Fehon. 1991. The *Notch* locus and the cell biology of neuroblast segregation. *Annu. Rev. Cell Biology* 7:427-52.

Baker, N. E., and A. E. Zitron. 1995. *Drosophila* eye development: *Notch* and *Delta* amplify a neurogenic pattern conferred on the morphogenetic furrow by *scabrous. Mechanisms of Development* 49: 173-189.

Cabrera C. V. 1992. The generation of cell diversity during early neurogenesis in *Drosophila. Development* 115: 893-901.

Campos-Ortega, J. A., and E. Knust. 1990. Genetics of early neurogenesis in *Drosophila melanogaster. Annu. Rev. Genet.* 24:387-407.

Ellis, M. C., U. Weber, V. Wiersdorff, and M. Mlodzik. 1994. Confrontation of *scabrous* expressing and non-expressing cells is essential for normal ommatidial spacing in the *Drosophila* eye. *Development* 120: 1959-69.

Hodgkin, A. L., and A. F. Huxley. 1952. A quantitative description of membrane current and its application to conduction and excitation in nerve. *J. Physiol. (Lond.)* 117: 500-544.

Jan, Y. N., and L. Y. Jan. 1995. Maggot's hair and bug's eye: Role of cell interactions and intrinsic factors in cell fate specification. *Neuron* 14:1-5.

Jarman, A. P., Y. Grau, L. Y. Jan, and Y. N. Jan. 1993. *Atonal* is the proneural gene that directs chordotonal organ formation in the *Drosophila* peripheral nervous system. *Cell* 73: 1307-21.

Kitano, H., S. Hamahashi, J. Kitazawa, K. Takao, and S. Imai. 1997. Virtual Biology Laboratories: A new approach of computational biology. In *Proceedings of Fourth European Conference on Artificial Life*, edited by P. Husbands and I. Harvey. Cambridge, MA: MIT Press, p. 274-283.

Kondo , S. and Asai, R. 1995. A reaction-diffusion wave on the skin of the marine angelfish *Pomacanthus. Nature* 376: 765-768

Mlodzik, M., N. E. Baker, and G. M. Rubin. 1990. Isolation and expression of *scabrous,* a gene regulating neurogenesis in *Drosophila. Genes and Development* 4: 1848-1861.

Murray, J. D. 1989. *Mathematical Biology*. Berlin, New York: Springer-Verlag, p. 360-468.

Turing, A. M. 1952. *Phil. Trans. R. Soc.* B 237: 37-72.

Wharton, K.A., K. M. Johansen, T. Xu, and S. Artavanis-Tsakonas. 1985. Nucleotide sequence from the neurogenic locus Notch implies a gene product that shares homology with proteins containing EGF-like repeats. *Cell* 43: 567-81.

Evolution of a Botanical Development System in 3D Euclidean Space

Tatsuo Unemi and **Takeshi Koike**
Dept. of Info. Sys. Sci., Soka University
1-236 Tangi-machi, Hachioji, Tokyo 192-8577, JAPAN
email: unemi@iss.soka.ac.jp
URL: http://www.intlab.soka.ac.jp/~unemi/

Abstract

This paper describes an alternative trial to simulate evolutionary and developmental process of multi-cellular plants in 3D Euclidean space. Starting from a seed on the surface of the ground, each individual grows by spawning daughter cells of each active cells. The rule set of growth is encoded as a gene on the chromosome that indicates the orientation of daughter cell and state transition. The model is very simple but includes a type of metabolism for absorbing water at the root underground and photosynthesis at the cells above the ground. Through the computer simulation of evolutionary process by a genetic algorithm with a fitness measure given by the number of cells, a variety of phenotypic shapes which are similar to moss have emerged.

Introduction

It is a feasible view that the growth of multi-cellular plants is realized by an iteration of cell division, cohesion, enlargement, reformation, and death. These activities are triggered by some chemical and physical events on the cell itself guided by the genetic information on the chromosomes it contains. Through a lot of efforts of biologists, some details of species-specific developmental process have been revealed, and the wide variety of complicated strategies of development are sometimes surprising. To deepen our understanding of the foundations of life, it is also important to build mathematical models of biological activities on a more abstract level, while investigating concrete organisms in more detail.

One of the remarkable mathematical models of growth of multi-cellular plants is the *L-system* (Lindenmayer 1989), which provides a formal method with a type of *rewrite rule set* to describe recursive processes such as growth. It has been widely used to draw computer graphics images of many types of plants of both real and imaginary species. L-system and its extended framework are very useful not only for drawing but also for understanding formal aspects of morphology by clarifying how wide a variety of shapes a simple rule set can generate.

In real biological organisms, the rule set for developmental processes is encoded on the chromosomes: the genotype, which has changed from simple to sophisticated through billions of years of evolutionary processes by adapting to its environment. It will be helpful to combine models of evolution and development from the stand point of *Artificial Life* in which we move towards the intrinsics of life through synthesis. We designed a model of the evolution of the development process, and examined it via computer simulation.

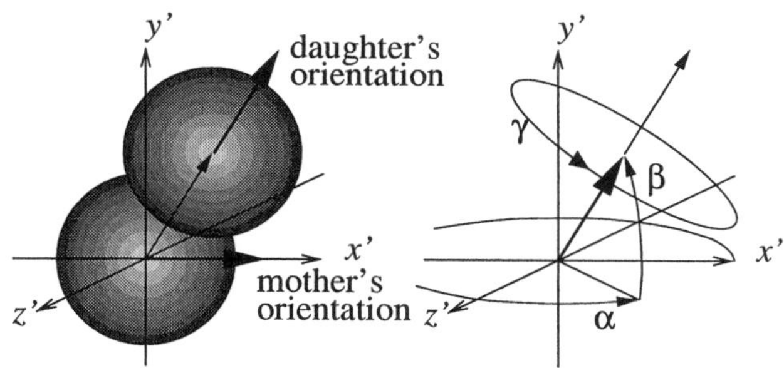

Figure 1: Spawning a daughter cell in 3D space.

For real natural organisms, various types of features of physical and chemical entities and events affect the cell activities. To avoid the complicated task to build a realistic model, many types of physical features are ignored such as gravity, shade, weather, seasons, and so on. Our model presented below does not use a discrete grid world, but a continuous three-dimensional Euclidean space because it theoretically provides an infinite number of degrees of freedom to form a shape. This feature is important to investigate evolution of sophisticated strategies, although it consumes more computational resources.

In the following sections, we examine morphology, metabolism, and evolution of our proposed model, and then describe experimental simulations, the results and close with some remarks.

Morphology

At an abstract level in the developmental process, each cell decides its action according to the rules on the gene conditioned by its own status. For a mathematical model of cell division, we assume that the orientation of division is determined by two kinds of information: the internal state, and the genetic information the cell contains. Because of the difficulty of simulating all of these complicated features, we assumed that

(1) the cell shape is a sphere,
(2) the cell size is constant,
(3) cells do not split but spawn daughter cells at an adjoining side,
(4) cells do not move from the original position where they were born,
(5) cells spawn daughter cell only if there is enough empty space, and
(6) each cell has its own direction as one of the attributes.

Each cell has an attribute indicating whether it is active or inactive. An active cell intends to spawn its daughter cell at an adjoining side where the gene corresponding to the current state designates the relative orientation. The internal states are represented by four bit integers of which the most significant bit indicates active (=0) or inactive (=1). The conditional part of the development rule contains the current internal state. The action part contains the relative orientation from the cell's direction to spawn a daughter cell, the daughter's initial internal state, and next internal state of itself. Each information to decide the orientation of a daughter cell requires a triplet of angles in 3D space as shown in Figure 1. The total action part of each rule includes two more four-bit integers and three eight-bit integers, that is, $4 \times 2 + 8 \times 3 = 32$ bits. Thus, one genome consists of $32 \times 8 = 256$ bits. Actually, we employ a look-up table to represent these rules as shown in Figure 2.

On the initial seed, the state is zero, and the orientation is vertically upward.

Metabolism

The above model is very simple, but we added a type of metabolism to

(1) absorb water from root,
(2) photosynthesize glucose for cells above ground,
(3) evaporate water from cells above ground,
(4) move water and glucose between mother and daughter cell, and
(5) consume an amount of water and glucose when spawning.

Each cell keeps track of the amount of water W and glucose G it contains. These parameters are normalized and range from zero to one. A cell under ground absorbs water according to

$$\Delta W = P_w(1.0 - W) \quad (1)$$

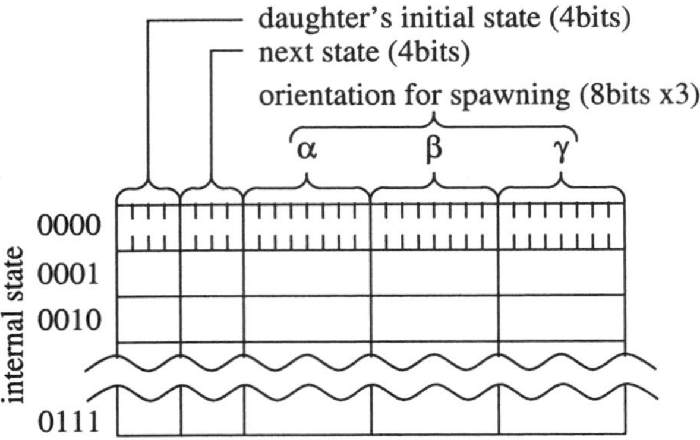

Figure 2: Form of chromosome and gene.

for each step, where P_w is a constant. A cell above ground looses water through evaporation by

$$\Delta W = -P_v W \quad (2)$$

for each step, where P_v is a constant. It also increases glucose content through photosynthesis by

$$\Delta G = P_g(1.0 - G) \quad (3)$$

for each step, where P_g is a constant. Both water and glucose move between mother cell and daughter cell according to

$$\Delta W_m = -\Delta W_d = M_w(W_d - W_m) \quad (4)$$
$$\Delta G_m = -\Delta G_d = M_g(G_d - G_m) \quad (5)$$

for each step, where M_w and M_g are constants, W_m and G_m are the values of the mother's parameters and W_d and G_d are the daughter's parameters. Each cell can spawn its daughter cell only when it is active, if it has enough water and glucose ($W > \theta_w, G > \theta_g$), and if there is enough empty space for the daughter. After spawning the daughter, water and glucose decrease by

$$\Delta W = -\theta_w \quad (6)$$
$$\Delta G = -\theta_g \quad (7)$$

where θ_w and θ_g are threshold values.

Photosynthesis of glucose consumes water via its chemical reaction

$$6CO_2 + 12H_2O \rightarrow C_6H_{12}O_6 + 6O_2 + 6H_2O\,. \quad (8)$$

However we ignore this phenomenon here because a decrease of water through evaporation can account for this. We also ignored other materials such as nitrogen and other essential elements, because they will not affect the shape as the result of the development process in this simple model.

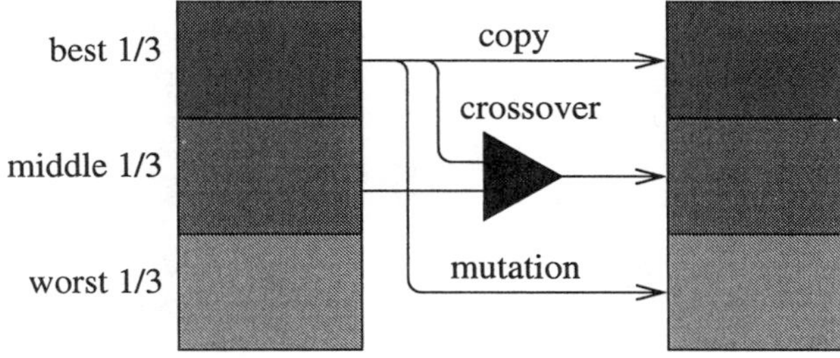

Figure 3: *1/3 selection.*

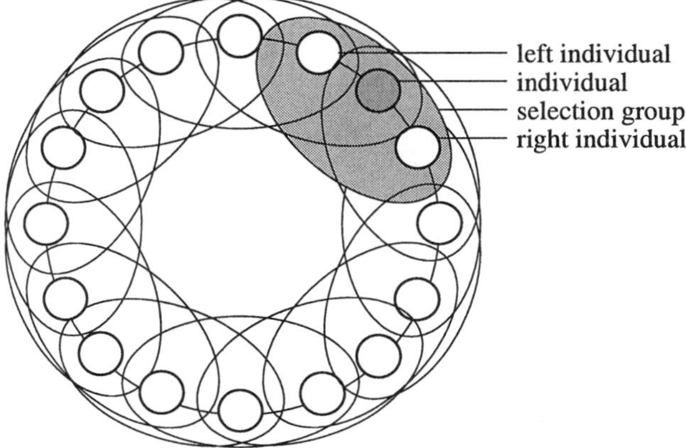

Figure 4: Local selection using ring.

Evolution

The evolutionary process of natural organisms strongly depends on inter-species interactions such as the food web. Starting from the simplest settings, we examined evolution by a Genetic Algorithm (GA) (Goldberg 1989) with pre-defined fitness function.

We use two types of generational GA in which every individual in the population is initialized by a random genotype and is tested through selection process to decide whether it remains in the next generation or not. First, to accelerate the evolutionary process, we did not employ ordinary selection algorithms widely used in GAs (such as roulette-wheel selection, ranking selection, or any other probability-based selection mechanism) but instead used a *1/3 selection* algorithm as shown in Figure 3. In this algorithm:

(1) The best third of the population remains in the next generation without any modification of genotype,

(2) the middle third of the population is replaced with individuals generated using crossover operation between the best third individuals and the middle third individuals, and

(3) the worst third of the population is replaced with mutants of the best third individuals.

In our second type of GA, we use a type of local selection where individuals are arranged along a ring as shown in Figure 4. The algorithm is similar to the 1/3-selection described above, but selection is done among local neighbors, that is:

(1) after evaluating the fitness, each individual obtains for comparison the values of its nearest (left and right) neighbors.

(2) it remains in the next generation without any modification if it is the best among these three individuals,

(3) it is replaced with the one generated by crossover with the best one; and

(4) it is replaced with a mutant of the best one if it is the worst.

As some researchers pointed out, GAs with local selection have an advantage to approach the global optimal solution because they can keep more diversity in the population than global selection (Sarma 1997). It is better not only as an optimization algorithm but also as a model of natural selection, because the competition among real organisms must always be local.

Experiments

Using as fitness measure the number of cells after allowing growth for a constant number of steps, the results of our simulations showed a wide variety of phenotypic shapes as shown in Figure 5.

State transition networks of development rules for individuals can be drawn as shown in Figure 6, viewing the active part of gene as an automaton. Networks in Figure 6 correspond to phenotypes shown in Figure 5. From this figure, we can see that the genotype of larger phenotypes includes cyclic transitions which can produce a recursive structure of development.

Evolutionary processes using fifty distinct random number sequences for each selection strategy are shown in Figure 7. It is clear that local selection leads to better fitness more often than global 1/3-selection.

Conclusion

We designed a model to study the evolution of botanical development in 3D Euclidean space and a simple metabolism, and examined the evolution with two types of selection algorithms. Via experiments described above, we observed that a variety of phenotypic shapes reflecting effective strategies for efficient body growth have emerged. These shapes resemble a kind of moss because they tend to spread on the ground. Comparing two different strategies for selection, local selection appears to be better than global selection for reaching better solutions.

The results of the simulations presented above are only a sample of forms we found. Though one might conclude that this provides possible evidence for the diversity of forms that emerged through evolution, we should investigate more thoroughly the effects that different parame-

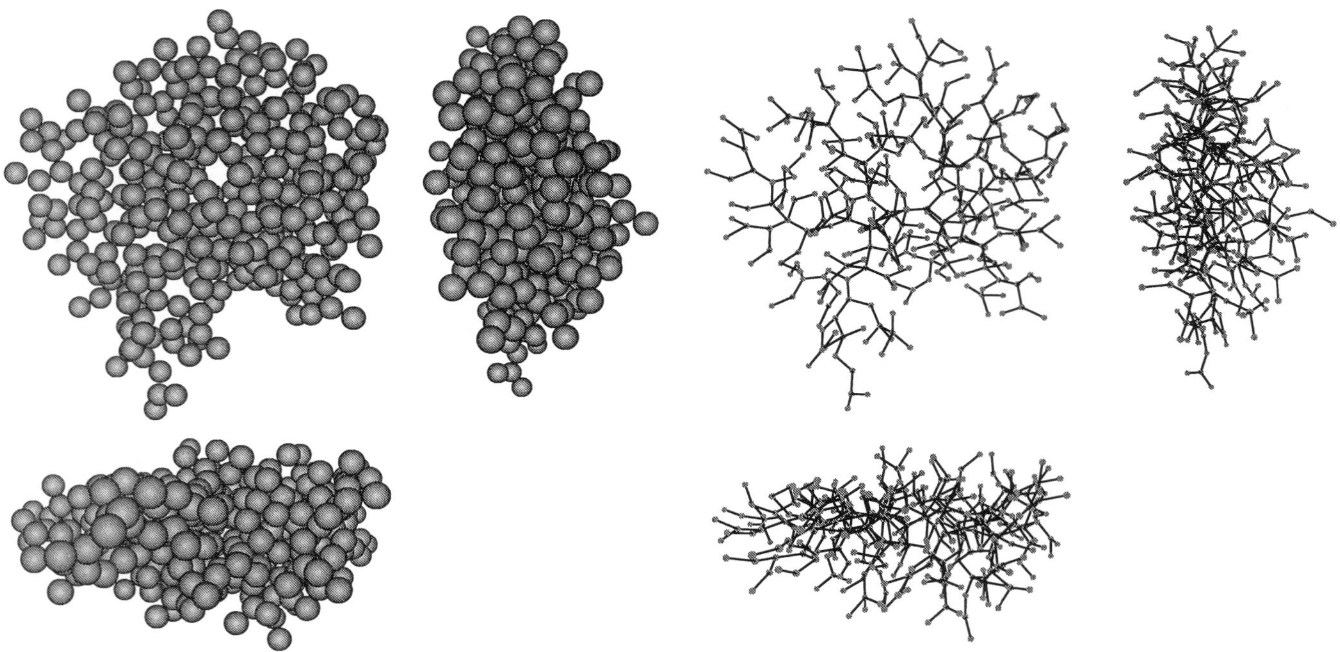

Global 1/3 selection, 378 cells.

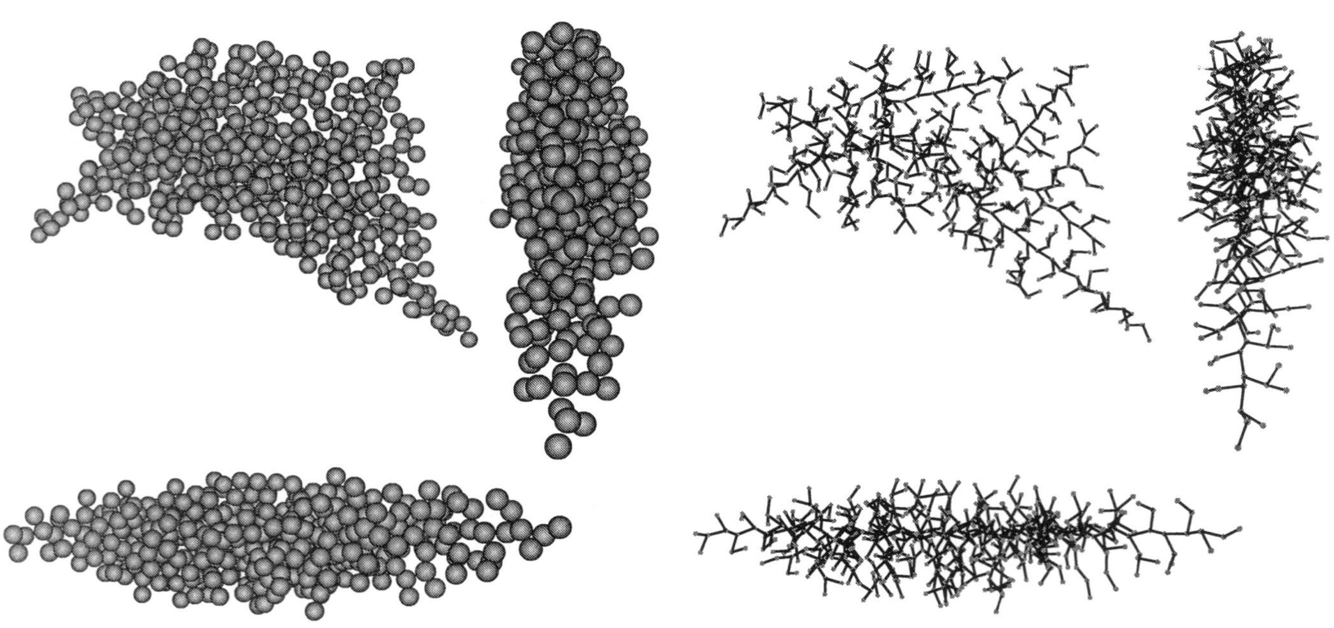

Local selection, 542 cells

Figure 5: Typical phenotypes that emerged from evolution through 500 generations in 400 steps per one generation, with a population size 36. Cells are drawn as spheres in the left hand figure, while line segments between the centers of mothers and daughters are drawn in the right hand figure. The upper left figure of each is the top view, the right figure is the right view, and the lower figure is the front view. The parameter settings are: $P_w = 0.1, P_v = 0.01, P_g = 0.1, M_w = 0.02, M_g = 0.02, \theta_w = 0.2, \theta_g = 0.2$.

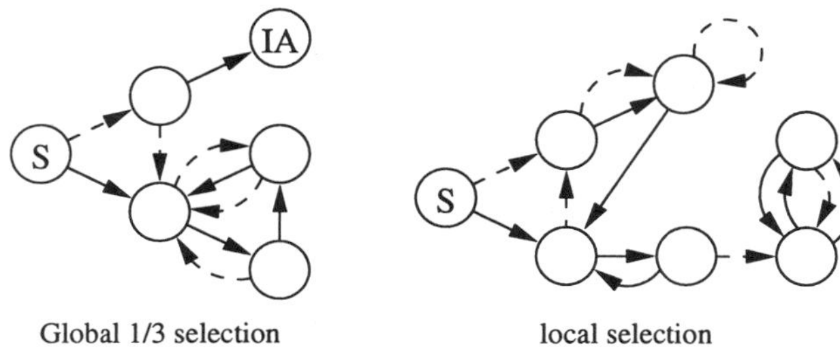

Figure 6: State transition networks of development rules produced through evolution. S indicates the initial seed, and IA indicates inactive. Dashed arrows indicate transitions from mother to daughter. These networks are generated for the phenotypes shown in Figure 5.

ters have on the process of evolution, before more fruitful results can be obtained from the point of view of biology.

We are also considering some directions to extend the model described above, such as physical interaction, chemical diffusion, differentiation, life cycle and ecology. A combination of this research with other morphological research such as (Fleischer 1996) and (Onitsuka 1996), and artificial botany such as (Colasanti 1997) might provide the inspiration for progress with this research in the near future.

References

Colasanti, R. L., and R. Hunt. 1997. Real botany with artificial plants: A dynamic, self-Assembling, plant mode for individuals and populations. In *Proc. of the Fourth European Conf. on Artificial Life*, edited by P. Husbands and I. Harvey. Cambridge, MA: MIT Press, p. 266–273.

Fleischer, K. 1996. Investigations with a multicellular developmental model. In *Artificial Life V*, edited by C. G. Langton and K. Shimohara. Cambridge, MA: MIT Press, p. 229–236.

Goldberg, D. E. 1989. *Genetic Algorithms in Search, Optimization and Machine Learning.* Addison-Wesley.

Lindenmayer, A., and P. Prusinkiewicz. 1989. Developmental models of multicellular organisms: A computer graphics perspective. In *Artificial Life*, edited by C. G. Langton. Redwood City, CA: Addison-Wesley, p. 221–249.

Onitsuka, A., J. Vaario, and K. Ueda. 1996. Structural formation by enhanced diffusion limited aggregation mode. In *Artificial Life V*, edited by C. G. Langton and K. Shimohara. Cambridge, MA: MIT Press, p. 237–251.

Sarma, J. and K. de Jong. 1997. An analysis of local selection algorithms in a spatially structured evolutionary algorithm. In *Proc. of the Seventh Intl. Conf. on Genetic Algorithms*, edited by T. Bäck. Morgan Kaufmann, p. 181–186.

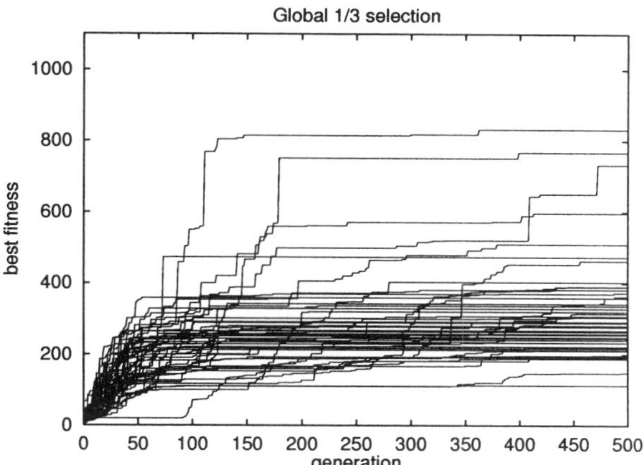

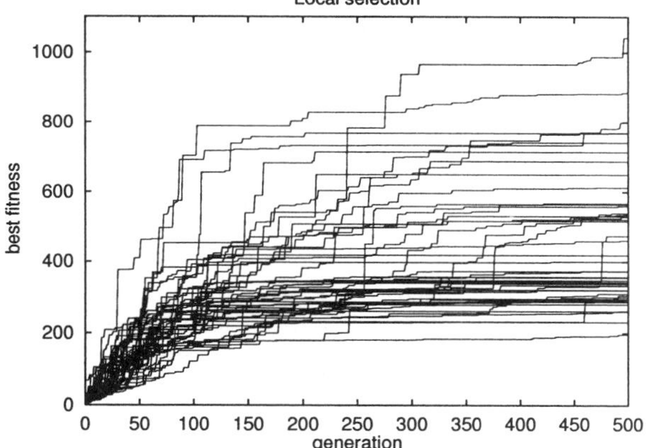

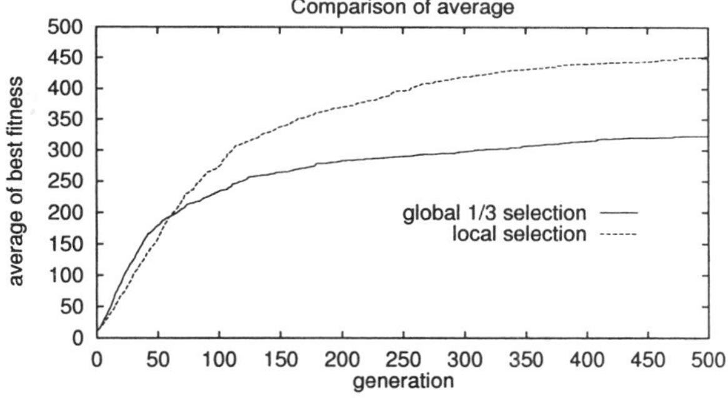

Figure 7: Evolutionary processes of fifty distinct random number sequences, and comparison between average values of best fitness of global and local selection.

Co-evolving Pursuit-Evasion Strategies in Open and Confined Regions

Mattias Wahde
Nordita,
Blegdamsvej 17,
DK-2100 Copenhagen,
Denmark

Mats G. Nordahl
Institute of Theoretical Physics,
Chalmers University of Technology,
S-412 96 Gothenburg, Sweden,
and
Santa Fe Institute, 1399 Hyde Park Road,
Santa Fe, NM 87501, USA

Abstract

We have studied pursuit-evasion games where the players can move in the plane or in a square region. Confining the pursuer and evader to a restricted region, or making them different, makes the problem more complex, and excludes simple solutions such as running straight towards infinity as fast as possible. In particular we study the case when the pursuer is made faster but less maneuverable. A steady improvement in performance measured against a fixed set of strategies is often found. We study the how the behavior changes with the parameters in the problem, such as the degree of asymmetry, and investigate the occurrence of unpredictable (protean) evasion behavior.

Introduction

Coevolution of strategies has been studied fairly extensively for simple discrete games, both in the case of two-person games, such as the Prisoner's Dilemma (Lindgren 1991, Lindgren & Nordahl 1994a, 1994b), and multi-person games (e.g., Akiyama and Kaneko 1995). Continuous strategies for differential games (Isaacs 1965), such as pursuit-evasion, require more elaborate strategy representations, and have so far been less investigated.

A large number of interesting problems can be formulated as games with continuous actions. Pursuit-evasion problems with multiple players can address both the evolution of flocking behavior and coordination in collective problem solving. Interesting two-person games with continuous actions include the Cournot game for pricing strategies in oligopolies, and signaling games with applications to sexual selection and the occurrence of deception in nature.

In this contribution, we study the coevolution of strategies for two-player pursuit and evasion games. Pursuit and evasion is omnipresent in nature, and an important concept in (evolutionary) robotics. Evolution of pursuit and evasion strategies has been studied both in simulations (Cliff & Miller 1996) and with real robots (Floreano & Nolfi 1997).

In cases where the evader and pursuer have identical properties, a good strategy for the evader is to move as fast as possible on a straight line away from the pursuer. To provide for more interesting dynamics, the pursuer and the evader can be given different properties by, for instance, making the pursuer faster but less maneuverable. In order to escape, the evader must then turn in an unpredictable way to avoid the pursuer. Rapid, unpredictable changes in direction and speed are referred to as *protean behavior* and occur frequently in nature (e.g., Miller and Cliff 1994).

Another more interesting game places the pursuers and evaders in a confined space. In this case, the evader can never use the strategy of escaping with full speed along a straight line, even if the pursuers and the evaders have identical properties.

In this contribution, we study the coevolution of pursuit-evasion strategies, and in particular begin a study of the effects of asymmetries between the pursuer and evader. These are either confined to a square or allowed to move freely in the plane.

Methods

Dynamics and genetic representation

The artificial creatures used in the simulations are controlled by recurrent neural networks, described by the equation

$$\tau \frac{\mathrm{d}x_i}{\mathrm{d}t} = -x_i + \sigma\left(\sum w_{i,j} x_j\right) + I_i, \qquad (1)$$

where x_i is the activation level of neuron i, I_i is the visual input, τ is a time constant, and σ is the neuron activation function. Information about the surroundings of a creature propagate from the visual input neurons through the network and produce motor signals, which control muscles that determine the movements of the creature.

The equations of motion for the creatures are

$$m\frac{\mathrm{d}v}{\mathrm{d}t} + c_l v = k_l \frac{(M_\mathrm{l} + M_\mathrm{r})}{2}, \qquad (2)$$

$$\frac{\mathrm{d}s}{\mathrm{d}t} = v, \qquad (3)$$

$$I\frac{\mathrm{d}\dot{\theta}}{\mathrm{d}t} + c_a\dot{\theta} = k_a \frac{(M_\mathrm{l} - M_\mathrm{r})}{2}, \qquad (4)$$

where m, c_l, k_l, I, c_a, and k_a are constants. M_l and M_r are the left and right motor signals. s denotes the curvilinear coordinate along the direction of motion, which is denoted by θ.

The neurons are arranged in layers, with arbitrary connections, which allows the network to have nontrivial internal dynamical behavior. Both pursuers and evaders are generated through a growth process from chromosomes consisting of 13 genes (which take integer values between 0 and 9) per neuron. The first bit codes for the layer of the neuron, and bits 2-4 determine its horizontal position. For input neurons, bits 5-6 code for the opening angle, i.e. the circle sector in which the neuron receives visual input. The visual input equals the fraction of the circle sector which is occupied. The visual neurons are situated along a line around the circular body of the creature, and can point in any direction.

For non-input neurons, bits 5-6 code for the direction of neural growth (vertical for input neurons). Bits 7-8 code for the opening angle of the neural growth cone, where the neuron makes connections to other neurons (centered on the growth direction defined by bits 5-6). The connection weight at distance r is given by the parameters w_0 (bits 9-11) and l_{scale} (bits 12-13) according to $w = w_0 e^{-r/l_{\mathrm{scale}}}$. Thus, the weights of the network are *not* coded in the chromosome. Instead, they result from the growth process.

The simulations

Initially, two populations of typically 50-100 creatures with random genomes with at most 30 neurons were generated. The individuals were then evaluated in pairs, i.e., each pursuer was paired with a member of the evader population and these were evaluated by simulating the pair for $N_{\mathrm{step}} = 30,000$ time steps. The evader fitness was the time averaged value distance between the two creatures; the pursuer fitness was the inverse of the average distance.

When all pairs had been evaluated, the next generation was created using a genetic algorithm with fitness-proportional selection and mutation. In the first N_{start} generations of each run, the nth member of the pursuer population was paired with the nth member of the evader population. In subsequent generations all pursuers were evaluated against the best evader of the previous generation and vice versa.

The simplest topology for the world of the creatures is an infinite plane. Coevolution of pursuers and evaders in the plane was studied by Cliff and Miller (1994), who used pursuers and evaders with identical properties. Thus, a successful strategy for an evader would be to run as fast as possible straight away from the pursuer. To avoid this, Cliff and Miller introduced an energy variable, which decreased rapidly with increasing strength of the motor signals. Pursuers were given more initial energy than evaders.

We consider other changes to the game itself more fundamental from a game theoretic point of view (and possibly more open to analysis). For instance, the space can be made finite by introducing walls, or the pursuer and evader can have different properties. In this paper, both motion on an infinite plane and in a finite square are considered. In the simulations, the creatures were not able to see the walls. At wall collisions, the velocity normal to the wall was reversed, and the speed of the creature was reduced by 50%.

Results

Symmetric and asymmetric creatures in a finite world

Since the creatures in our simulations moved in a finite space, interesting strategies could be obtained even with pursuers and evaders with identical properties.

We carried out one such symmetric simulation (Run 1), in which two populations of size $n_{\mathrm{pop}} = 100$ were evaluated for 700 generations. The creatures moved in a square of 20×20 units. No strong trend in fitness for either evader or pursuer was found in this case. This is expected, since even though evolution can improve the creatures, it does so without preference for either pursuers or evaders, and the result is an 'arms race' in which neither can gain a permanent advantage.

To study the effects of making the pursuers different from the evaders, 8 additional runs were carried out with the creatures confined to a square. The parameter values of the pursuers were varied in order to study the effects of differences in speed and maneuverability between pursuers and evaders. In this case, the population size was 50 individuals, and the simulations extended over 200 generations each.

Under these conditions, successful evaders often tried to stay close to the walls. By bouncing against the walls, they were able to confuse the pursuers. Unfortunately, this strategy was rather easy to achieve: Once the evader had reached a wall, it only needed to keep on turning without changing direction. The pursuers displayed more interesting behavior, often involving sharp turns to keep the target in sight and occasional 360-degree turns to re-acquire a lost target. Some examples of pursuit strategies are shown in Fig. 1. In all figures showing trajectories, the pursuer and the evader start close to the origin.

The relative importance of speed and maneuverability was also investigated. In Fig. 2, averages (over all individuals, generations, and runs) of the pursuer fitness values are shown. Maneuverability appears to be more important than speed when pursuing a target in a confined space.

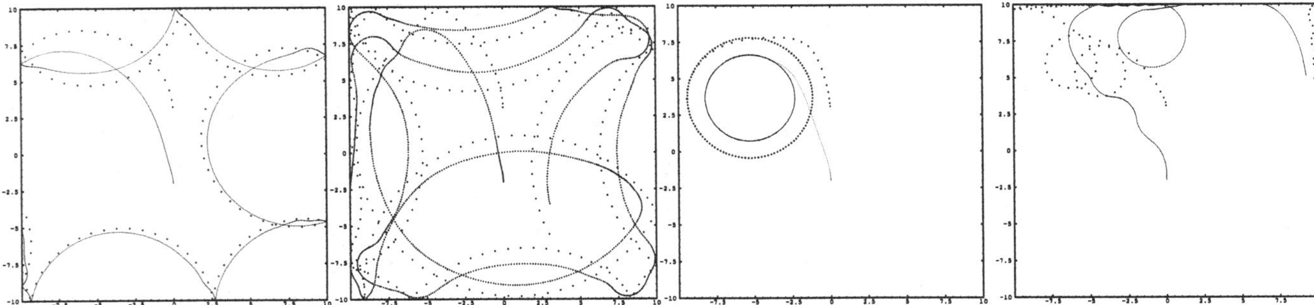

Figure 1: Pursuit strategies from various runs. The evader orbit is indicated by a dotted line, and the pursuer orbit by a solid line.

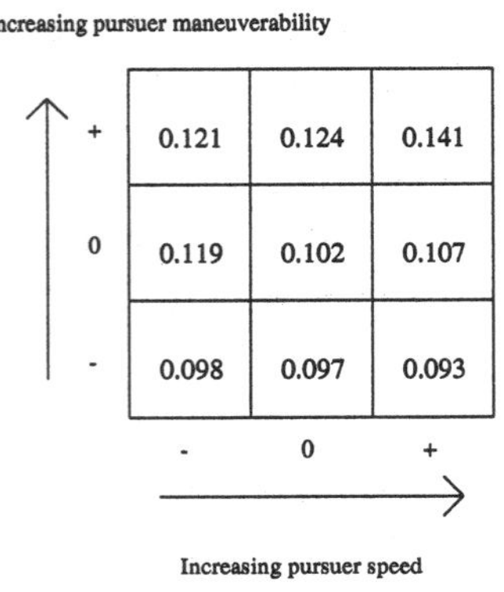

Figure 2: Average (over all individuals and 200 generations) of pursuer fitness.

Asymmetric creatures in an infinite world

We also carried out a set of simulations in an infinite world, but with asymmetries between pursuer and evader.

Some evader strategies sampled from different generations of one of the runs are shown in Fig. 3, where the evaders are evaluated against the best pursuer of the preceding generation.

The co-evolutionary process tended to evolve networks with high complexity. In the early generations, the networks only performed a simple input-output mapping. The pursuer and evader are essentially Braitenberg vehicles (Braitenberg 1984), where sensory inputs map directly to motor units. In later generations, backward connections started appearing, and more complex dynamical behavior became possible. The connectivity of the network also showed an increasing trend, albeit a very weak one (a linear fit to the data yields a connectivity varying as $1.56 + 0.18(g/100)$, where g denotes the generation number), see Fig. 4.

Co-evolutionary progress

An interesting issue is that of co-evolutionary progress. Presumably, in the co-evolutionary arms race an improved pursuer strategy is followed (through selective pressure) by a better evader strategy which, in turn, leads to stronger selective pressure on the pursuers, and so on. However, it is difficult to measure co-evolutionary progress, since both pursuers and evaders improve simultaneously.

We used a very simple method: In every generation of Run 1, the best pursuer was re-evaluated against an evader on a fixed orbit. The resulting fitness curve is displayed in Fig. 5. Despite the noise, the curve shows that co-evolutionary progress occurs.

Protean behavior

In the simulations of pursuit and evasion in confined spaces (Runs 1-9), the evaders displayed very little active protean behavior, presumably because the wall-bouncing technique was sufficiently successful to make protean behavior unnecessary. From the point of view of the pursuers, however, the wall-bouncing evader strategy is equivalent to protean behavior, and, as can be seen in Fig. 1, our best pursuers were able to cope with it.

In Runs 10-11, in which the pursuit-evasion contests took place in an infinite space, some of the evaders display (seemingly) unpredictable behavior. Two examples are shown in Fig. 6. In both cases, the evader managed to shake off the pursuer by making rapid, unexpected turns. The pursuer in the upper panel was of the fixed strategy type, and was therefore able to re-acquire the target, whereas the neural network pursuer in the lower panel completely lost track of its target.

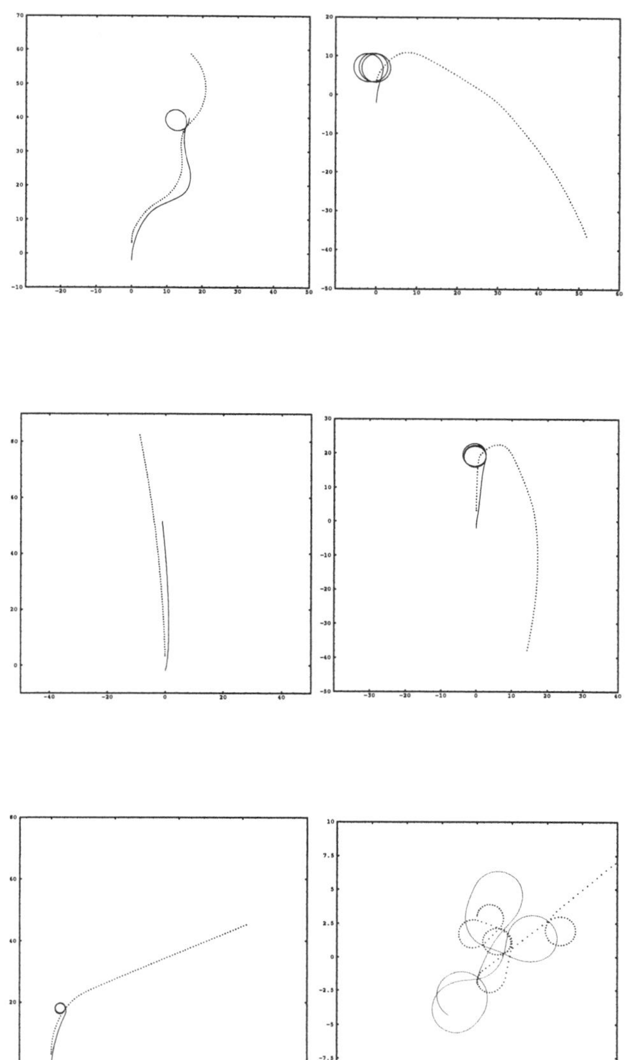

Figure 3: The best evaders in generation 109, 114, 217, 334, 371, and 456 of Run 10 evaluated against their respective pursuer.

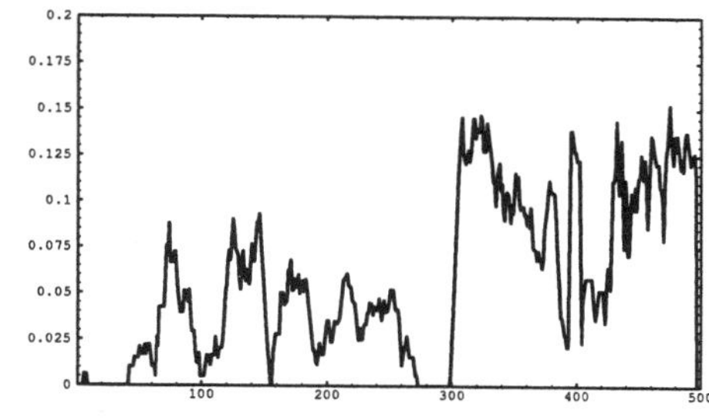

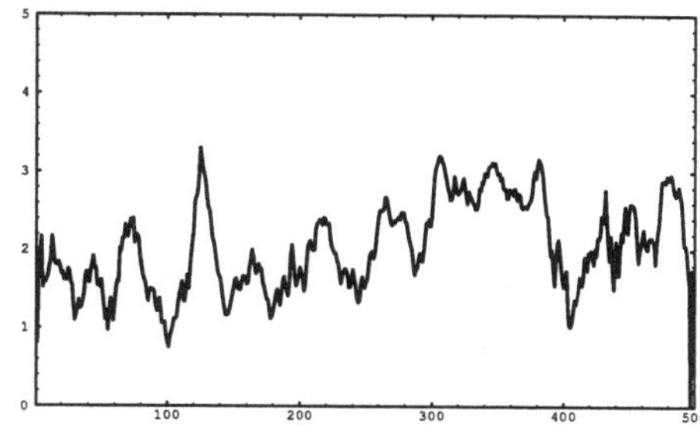

Figure 4: Number of backward connections per neuron and network connectivity (connections per neuron) of the best evader as a function of generation for Run 10.

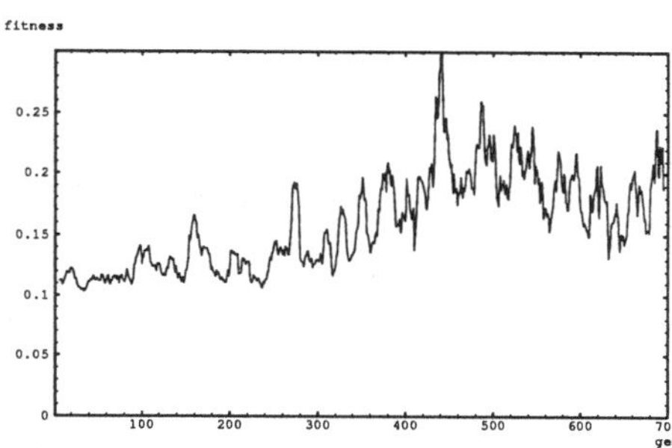

Figure 5: The fitness of the best pursuer in each generation evaluated against identical evader orbits.

Conclusions and Directions for Further Work

We have studied the dynamics of pursuit-evasion contests in finite regions and on infinite planes. Our results suggest that coevolution slowly improves the performance of pursuers: In a simulation over several hundred generations, pursuers in later generations are generally able to follow any evader moving on a simple (e.g., straight-line) trajectory, whereas early pursuers are not.

Coevolution in a confined space gave rise to interesting pursuit behavior, but the evaders evolved only very little–the simple strategy of bouncing against the walls sufficed against most pursuers. On the infinite plane, the evaders evolved more advanced behavior, including rapid turns which confused the pursuers. A trend towards more complex network architecture was found, both for the connectivity and the amount of feedback in the neural networks.

An important issue for further work is the internal dynamics of the networks: As the number of feedback

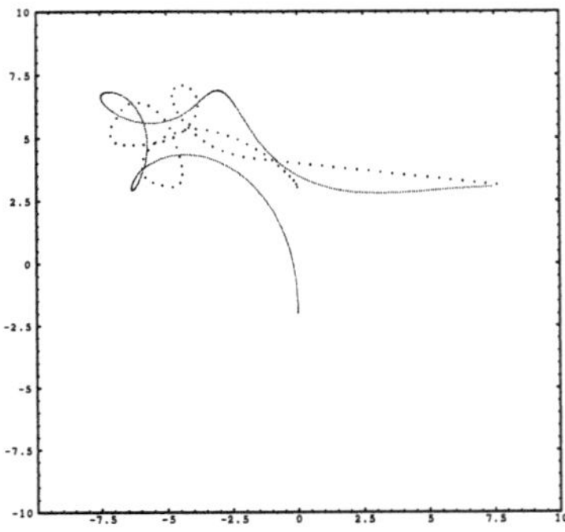

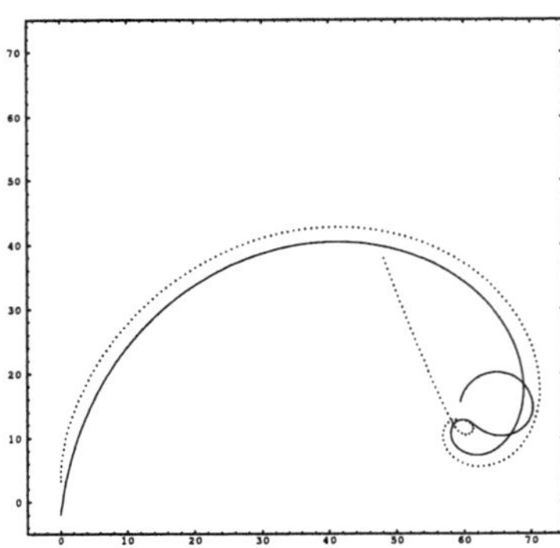

Figure 6: The orbit of two advanced evaders from Runs 10 and 11.

connections increase, the possibility of chaotic oscillations increases as well. One should attempt to characterize the neural circuits that give rise to protean behavior as dynamical systems, and study the role of chaos as a generator of unpredictable behavior further. We are at present investigating the matter through a detailed analysis of the neural networks obtained in co-evolutionary simulations.

Another important issue is that of representations for strategies in continuous games. The neural networks used in this contribution are very far from the pleasant degree of interpretability of the strategies for discrete games in Lindgren (1991), Lindgren and Nordahl (1994a, 1994b). While one cannot hope for that kind of simplicity, it may still be possible to find representations that allow some degree of theoretical interpretation.

It is also important to develop ways of characterizing behavior in a more quantitative way. Characterizing the structure of the networks is straight-forward, but finding good quantities to characterize their behavior is more difficult. The degree of unpredictability could be characterized using methods from nonlinear dynamics, but this would then still be a property of a pair of players, rather than a single evader or pursuer.

References

Akiyama, E., and K. Kaneko. 1995. Evolution of cooperation, differentiation, complexity, and diversity in an iterated three-person game. *Artificial Life* 2: 293–304.

Braitenberg, V. 1984. *Vehicles: Experiments in Synthetic Psychology.* Cambridge, MA: MIT Press.

Cliff, D., and G. F. Miller. 1996. Co-evolution of pursuit and evasion II: Simulation methods and results. In *From Animals to Animats 4*, edited by P. Maes et al. Cambridge, MA: MIT Press, p. 506–515,

Floreano, D. and S. Nolfi. 1997. God save the Red Queen! Competition in co-evolutionary robotics. In *Genetic Programming 1997: Proceedings of the Second Annual Conference*, edited by J. R. Koza et al. Morgan Kaufmann, p. 398-406.

Isaacs, R. 1965. *Differential Games: A Mathematical Theory with Applications to Warfare and Pursuit, Control and Optimization.* New York: John Wiley.

Lindgren, K. 1991. Evolutionary phenomena in simple dynamics. In *Artificial Life II*, edited by C. G. Langton, C. Taylor, J. D. Farmer, and S. Rasmussen. Redwood City, CA: Addison-Wesley, p. 295-312.

Lindgren, K. and M. G. Nordahl. 1994. Cooperation and community structure in artificial ecosystems. *Artificial Life* 1: 15–39.

Lindgren, K., and M. G. Nordahl. 1994. Evolutionary dynamics of spatial games. *Physica D* 75: 292–309.

Miller, G. F. and D. Cliff. 1994. Co-Evolution of pursuit and evasion I: Biological and game-theoretic foundation, Technical Report CSRP311, University of Sussex.

A Morpho-Functional Machine: An Artificial Amoeba Based on the Vibrating Potential Method

Hiroshi Yokoi, Wenwei Yu, Jun Hakura, and Yukinori Kakazu

Laboratory of Autonomous Systems Engineering, Graduate School of Engineering, Hokkaido University
Kita-13, Nishi-8, Kita-ku, Sapporo,

Hokkaido 060, JAPAN

{ yokoi, hakura, yu, kakazu}@complex.eng.hokudai.ac.jp

Abstract

We discuss the design of flexible deformation and adaptive motion in a mechanical system. This paper describes a Morpho-Functional Machine that is an amoeba-like deformable system. A remarkable characteristic of an amoeba is that it can transform from a unicellular mode to a multi-cellular mode depending on the state of the environment. This paper proposes using the Vibrating Potential Method to control the Artificial Amoeba, and uses goal acquisition as an example of searching the environment spatially. The proposed model consists of the new field technique named Vibrating Potential Field and a new parameter tuning method inspired by thermodynamics. The field model creates self organizing gathering behaviors through the physical interaction of potential fields. The computer simulation shows the emergence of typical characteristics, such as gathering toward energy, thermotaxis, obstacle avoidance, and swarm intelligence. Those characteristics are designed and built as an SMA structured Artificial Amoeba based on a physical system, the so-called Morpho-Functional Machine.

Introduction

The A-Life research area discovered evolutionary social competition, self-organized system design, flexible deformable groups, and adaptive complex behaviors. This paper describes one approach to realize flexible deformable functions based on adaptive computation techniques. The A-Life world consists of the interaction of many functional elements and mutual scrambling of limited resources: for example, competitive agents, cooperative agents, neural network, and swarm systems often achieve Nash's equilibrium. However, A-Life research has contributed little towards the development of functional emergence in the physical world. Functional emergence discovered from the interaction of many functional elements with mutual access to limited resources should be useful technology for physical systems in the real world.

Our approach to an A-Life system has been to imitate amoeba-like behavior. We especially focus on flexible motion emerging from the competitive life game of amoeba cells. Artificial cells are designed to be adapted into energy utilization; each such artificial cell is called a unit. The unit consists of sensor(s), controller(s), indicator(s) and actuator(s); how to select and find the suitable set is our chosen problem. For this problem, we have described a mathematical model of mutual action of units as well as a parameter tuning method for each unit. To approximate the dynamics of cell interaction, sensing and indications are mediated by a vibrating potential field. Actuation is described by a kinematics equation. The strength, stiffness, and density of sensors are all parameters. Such parameters are tuned to get more energy than neighbors, as well as improving energy access in general. This paper shows the hardware design and control rules taken from living NC4 (the most famous species of amoeba) for flexible motion. Computer simulation also shows the adaptation process of obstacle avoidance.

Related Works on Artificial Amoeba

Unit-based modeling is a convenient approach for the systematic description of multi-cellular organisms. That is, "Cells are unit of the structure and functionality of all organisms, and, in a sense, are first-order elements of organisms." Fleischer (1994) made developmental models that can represent some characteristic behaviors of cells. Agarwal (1995) made the Cell Programming Language (CPL) to model and simulate biological phenomena, e.g., slime mold aggregation.

For the field technique, the theory of cellular automata (CA) is a basic model used to generate or calculate field patterns from local interactions between cells. Turing's morphogen model is also a more basic model of the field technique. Ueda's work, concerned with a model of intelligence of Physarum, concluded that self-organizing chemical patterns at the molecular level cause intelligent behavior (Ueda 1993). However, Unit-based modeling must consist of sensor(s), controller(s), indicator(s) and actuator(s). All information propagated from the indicator is mediated by suitable fields, and picked up by the sensors. Such simulation technique of propagating information is a so-called field technique. The field technique and movable phenomena of particles is derived from the VPM (vibrating potential method) proposed by (Yokoi 1996). VPM is applied both to imitating cell movement and to engineering problems.

Aspects of real slug to be modeled

Slime mold is a colony of unicellular amoeba, during one period in the amoeba's life cycle. Cells are rather shapeless unicellular organisms that move by extending contractile portions of themselves (pseudopods). If the food supply becomes exhausted, the amoeba begin to aggregate at a number of collection points. After aggregation has been completed, the amoebae that have collected at a given point form a multi-cellular slug. Fig. 1 shows that cells in the slime-mold state exhibit searching and walking behavior using flexible arms (pseudopodia of Dictyostelium Discoideum) stretched from the cell membrane.

From microscopic and chemical analysis of the biological system, the mechanism of amoeba motions are classified as follows:

- Chemo-taxis and Thermotaxis.
- Cells respond to information in chemical field through a grouping and searching process.
- Expansion and contraction of internal fiber causes the deformation and flexible motion of the whole body.
- As an assumption, an amoeba cell consists of Motor Units that interact with the other units. Through self-organization of a local group of motor units, whole cell motion and deformation can be obtained.

Figure 1. Photo-Image of Dictyostelium

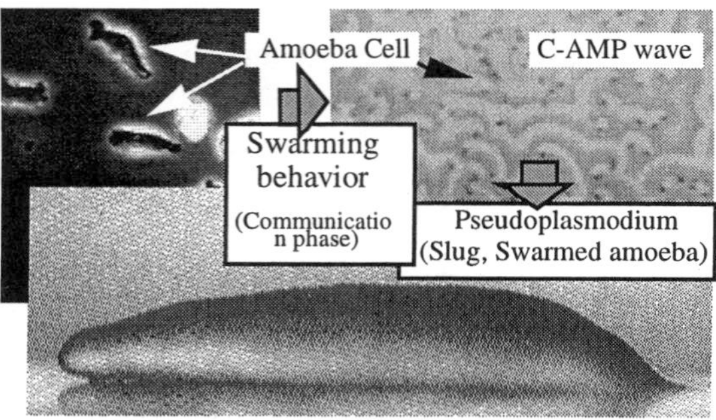

Information in a biological medium

The spatial movement of an amoeba cell is driven by cAMP. The detail of cell motion is shown in Varnum (1984 and 1987). Flexible motion is controlled by the spatial pattern of cAMP waves. The morphogenesis of amoebae is adaptive in an environment based on chemotaxis and thermotaxis, as shown in Siegert (1992) and Steinbock (1993).

Amoeba Model

The mathematical design of the amoeba model consists of four distinct parts: "Sensors", "Actuators", "Indicators", and "Controllers". A sensor picks up information, and an indicator performs a function. Those two functions are described by "Field" and "Potential functions". An actuator physically interacts with the environment causing "Unit Motion". A controller makes decisions, and includes an adaptive parameter tuning mechanism.

{ **H** } = { **Force** } + { **Signal** } + { **Energy** }
Field Physical interaction Information Reward

{ **P** } = { O(**H**) } {**Parameter**} { **Energy** }
Actuation Sensor System Parameter Consumption

{ **K** } = Opt{ **Internal Entropy** }
Parameter Optimization of System Parameter

Figure 2. Concept of Chemotaxis using field information

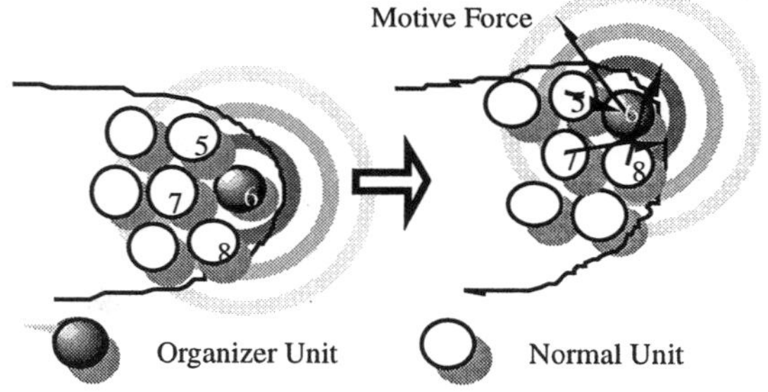

Field (sensor and indication)

As the model of a biological medium, we propose a single virtual field. The whole field **H** (the VPF) consists of summing up individual fields generated by units. The interactions among units are obtained by the interaction between one unit and the VPF, as two body interaction problems. Two body interaction offers the special feature that a unit observes the status of other units without any knowledge of the relationship between them. The VPF is mathematically described using potential functions (h,w,E,hl) on individual fields (ψ, χ, τ, φ). In the equation, the information is defined only as a propagating wave, and described using a potential function on a spatial and temporal interval.

Thus,

$$\mathbf{H}(\boldsymbol{r},\phi,t) = \sum_{i}^{\text{Unit number}} \Big\{ \mathbf{h}_i(\boldsymbol{r},t)\,\psi(\phi) + \mathbf{w}_i(\boldsymbol{r},t)\,\chi(\phi) + \sum_{i}^{\text{Unit number}} \mathbf{hl}_{ij}(\boldsymbol{r},t)\,\varphi_i(\phi)\varphi_j(\phi) \Big\} + \mathbf{E}(\boldsymbol{r},t)\,\tau(\phi) \tag{1}$$

where $\mathbf{H}(r,\phi,t)$ is the vibrating potential field (whole field). The ϕ is the total coordinate axis; the i is the unit number. $\mathbf{E}(r,t)$ is energy function of environment. $\mathbf{h}i(r,t)$, $\mathbf{w}i(r,t)$, and $\mathbf{hl}ij(r,t)$ are information propagated from unit i (the potential function). r is the position vector. From $H(\boldsymbol{r}, \phi, t)$, a unit interacts with other units via $\psi(\phi)$, $\chi(\phi)$, $\tau(\phi)$, $\varphi(\phi)$ depending on the amplitude of each individual field. The diffusion of each field is mathematically described using partial differential equation $u=u(r,t)$ for each field parameters $\{\alpha,\beta,\gamma,\delta,\varepsilon\}$ as in Eq.(2).

$$\alpha\frac{d^2u}{dt^2} + \beta\frac{du}{dt} + \gamma\nabla^2 u + \delta\nabla u + \varepsilon u = 0 \tag{2}$$

Unit communication is mediated by the multiple VPF **H** in Eq. (1). The sensors and indicators are described by the wave equation shown in Eq. (3). Selection of the type of sensor and indicator is defined by the System Parameter vector $K(t)=(K\psi\ K\chi,\ K\tau,\ K\varphi)$. Boundary conditions should be different for each property to avoid confusion.

$$\frac{\mathbf{K}(t)}{2}\frac{d^2\zeta(\phi)}{d\phi^2} + \mathbf{E}_{env}(\boldsymbol{r}_i, t)\,\zeta(\phi) = 0$$

$$(\ \zeta(\phi) = \psi(\phi),\ \chi(\phi),\ \varphi(\phi),\ \tau(\phi)\ ) \tag{3}$$

$\psi(\phi)$, $\chi(\phi)$, $\varphi(\phi)$, $\tau(\phi)$ are the unit coordinate axes, and $\mathbf{E}_{env}(r_i,t)$ is the interaction energy in Eq. (4),

$$d\mathbf{E}_{env} = \sum_{i}^{\text{Unit number}} \mathbf{E}_{out}(\mathbf{r}_i, \mathbf{t})\,dt \tag{4}$$

Figure 3. Fundamental movement of unit group.

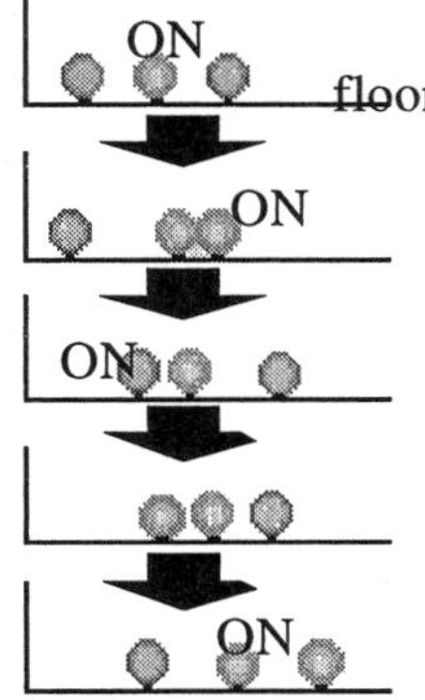

Movement of unit group driven by phase shift of attractive potential function. The gravity center of unit group is advanced. Where ON" means active unit of attractive/repulsive potential functions. Friction of floo set as 0.1 (in case unit velocity equal 0), and (velocity not equal

Unit motion (actuation)

Unit motion is defined according to the field information and the unit's stored energy, and is realized as a result of external stimuli on unit internal parameters. In Eq. (5), the unit motion p(t) is derived by Lagrange equations of motion with regard to $\mathbf{H}(r,\phi,t)$, Eout, and K(t) as the potential function. The integral $\mathbf{H}(r,\phi,t)$ is the observation of field information, Eout is the outflowing energy from the unit to environment, K(t) is the unit parameter. Fig. 3 shows one example of unit motion, where the sign "ON" means active input from field. The computation shows that reciprocal activation input causes movement of the center of gravity of the units through an attractive/repulsive potential function.

$$\dot{P}(t) = M\cdot\nabla\oint \mathbf{H}(r,\phi,t\ \ \zeta(\phi))\{\varphi(\phi)\ d\phi\cdot\mathbf{E}\ \ \cdot\mathbf{K}(t) \tag{5}$$

Unit information (potential functions)

The unit information in this paper deals with amplitude of propagating information in a field. Two types of information are applied: one is a density type that simply diffuses; the other is a wave that propagates and gradually declines. Depending on the boundary conditions of the field, it undergoes resonance, reflection and refraction. The unit outputs this information, and influences surrounding units according to the distance between them. This information is realized by setting a suitable value on the individual field, and also those defined by Strength, Delay, Frequency , and Direction for each piece of information $\mathbf{h}i(r,t)$, $\mathbf{w}i(r,t)$, $\mathbf{hl}ij(r,t)$, and $\mathbf{E}(r,t)$. Fig. 4 shows the reciprocal activation according to the wave input for neighboring units.

Figure 4. Wave propagation from unit. (Time delay of activation drives reciprocal action of wavy field)

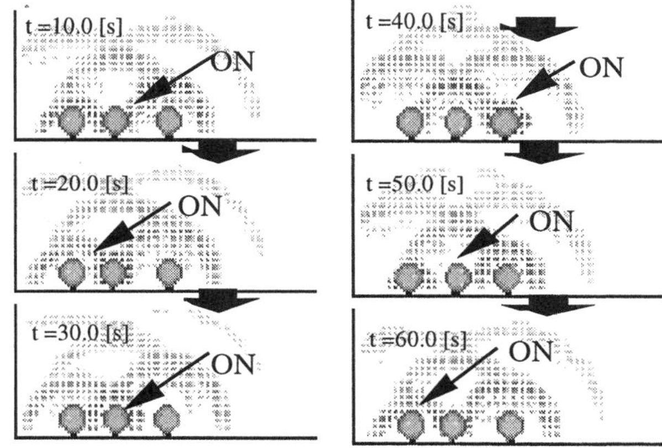

The propagating wave pattern is output from the speaker in the Indicator, and is deformed by tuned delay timing of each unit.

Objective function

Adaptive behavior of units using local information requires an objective function for decentralized control. An ideal objective function of a decentralized system leads the units to an orderly configuration dependent on the environment. In this section, the objective function for the system parameter **K**(t) is set by the concept of adaptive mechanics of living creatures. According to statistical mechanics, each unit conserves order by minimizing the differential calculated gain of entropy ds. The ds is derived by input-output relation of environment energy. State inputs and outputs on each unit i are: inflowing heat **E**in=**E**in(ri,t), stored energy **Q**=**Q**i(t), work **W**=**W**i(t), **E**out=**E**out(ri,t), and spatial heat environment **E**env=**E**env(r,t). The inflowing heat **E**in is input energy from environment that is transmitted through wave propagation and threshold TH as shown in Eq. (6)

$$\mathbf{E}_{in} = \oint \mathbf{H}(\boldsymbol{r}, \phi, t)\chi(\phi)\, d\phi - TH \tag{6}$$

The stored energy of each unit **Q** is:

$$d\mathbf{Q} = (\mathbf{E}_{in} - \mathbf{E}_{out} - \mathbf{W})\, dt \tag{7}$$

W is energy given by the unit to the environment; it is defined for each velocity **v**(t) in Eq. (8).

$$\mathbf{W} = \frac{1}{2}M\mathbf{v}(t)^2 \tag{8}$$

The outflowing heat **E**out from each unit is a function of **Q** and **E**env in Eq. (9).

$$d\mathbf{E}_{out} = (\mathbf{Q} - \mathbf{E}_{env})dt \tag{9}$$

Since such state values are connected with the other state values, numerical computation is applied to obtain. Now, the differential calculated gain of entropy ds is define as Eq. (10) using state values **E**in, **E**out, and **E**env.

$$ds = \frac{d\mathbf{E}_{out} - d\mathbf{E}_{in}}{T(\mathbf{E}_{env})} \tag{10}$$

The system parameter **K**(t) is derived by Eq. (11) for minimize ds.

$$\frac{\partial \mathbf{K}(t)}{\partial t} = -\frac{\partial\, ds}{\partial \mathbf{K}(t)} \tag{11}$$

Where the system parameter K(t) consists of the Sensor part, Indicator part and Actuator part shown in Fig. 5. The sensor part has Kψ Kχ, Kτ, Kφ (boundary condition of individual field), Kg (gravity), and Kt (temperature). The indicator part has Kw (Speaker). The actuator part has Kh (magnetic potential) and Khl (elastic potential). Each parameter has 4 degree of freedom {Strength, Delay, Frequency, Direction}.

Using Eq. (11), the adaptive behavior of unit groups is shown in Fig. 6. The number of unit groups is 30, 15, 9, 6, 3 and 2. Goal searching behavior was acquired except in the case of only 2 unit groups. Fig. 7 shows the acquired delay parameter for the 30 unit group case. Fig. 8 is a picture of the search goal.

Figure 5. System parameters K(t)

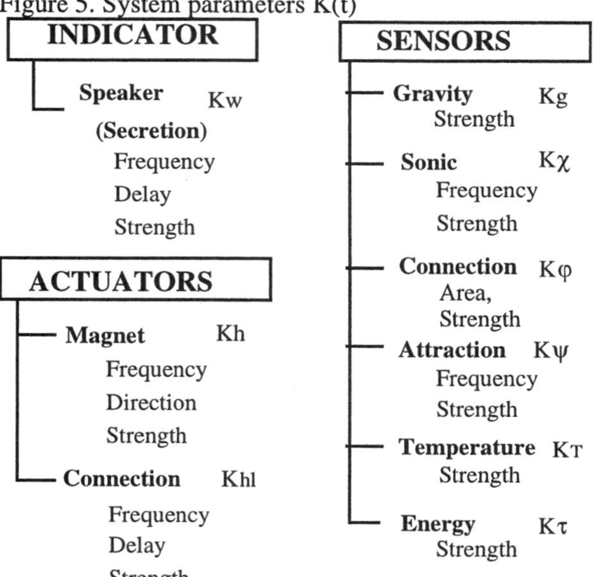

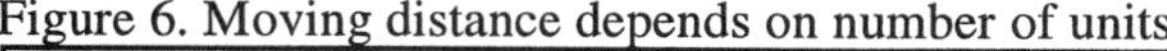

Figure 6. Moving distance depends on number of units

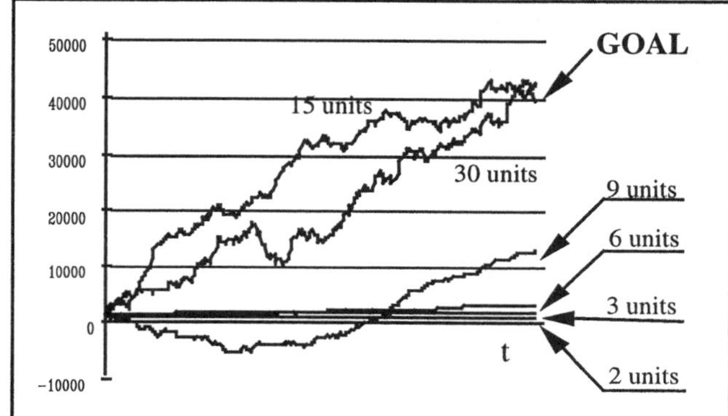

Figure 7. Adapted delay parameters of actuation for 30 units

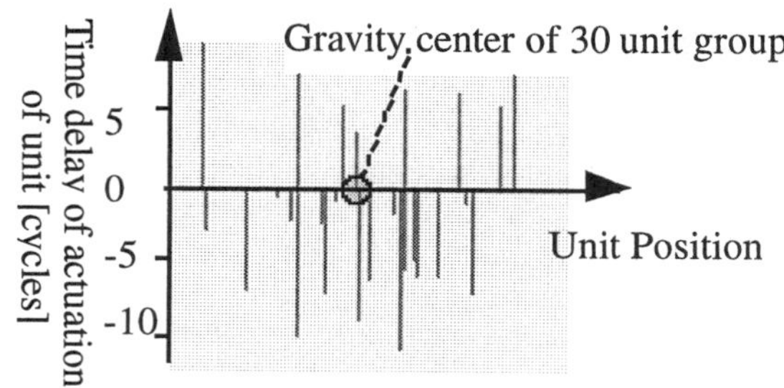

Figure 8. Mutual action of 30 units group.

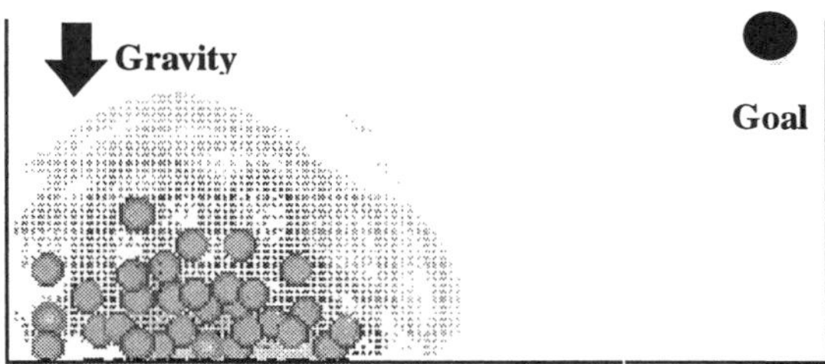

Computer Simulations and Hardware Design of Artificial Amoeba.

Computer simulation shows the functionality of mathematical representation of the amoeba model, and the experiment shows that collective behavior of the unit group is realized through interaction of the potential function as communication between units. Fig. 9 shows the result of parameter tuning process. Initially, the unit group acquired ability to climb steps. However, they fell down to the floor below the goal. Therefore, they found the standing up function next, and finally achieved the goal.

Figure 9. Simulation of the amoeba model (Climbing Step motion)

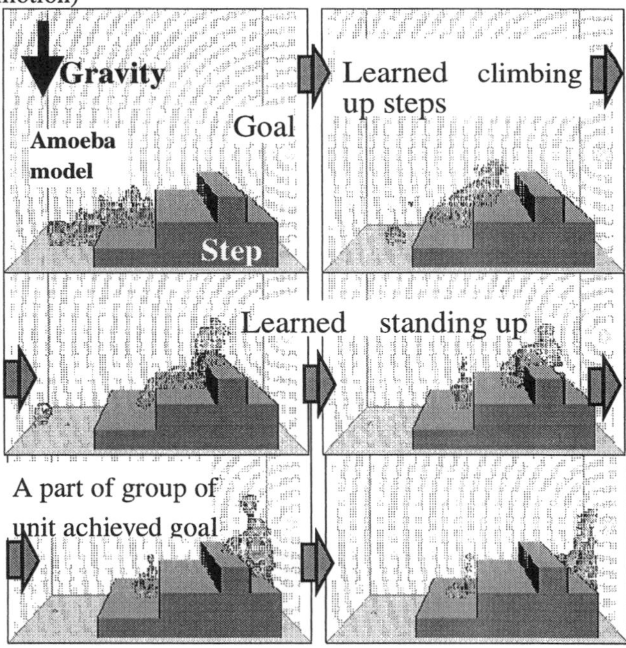

The flexible function of the amoeba model is applied to the hardware design of an Artificial Amoeba. The unit has CPU, photo and sonic sensors, as well as an actuator. Each unit has the learning mechanism of sensor-actuator mapping that is tuned according to energy consumption. The SMA Net type consists of a lattice structure of Shape Memory Array as the actuator. This Artificial Amoeba established loop-like creeping motion through the mutual action of the SMA net. Such Artificial Amoebas are structured as collective unit groups that realize a distributed autonomous system.

Figure 10. Hardware approach for the SMA Net type Artificial Amoeba (Each node of SMA lattice has CPU and sensors. This mechanism can move to the direction of photo and sonic inputs.)

Summary

This paper tries to use the morpho-functional machine to achieve deformable system design. For this purpose, an Artificial Amoeba is proposed based on the amoeba model structure of collective unit groups. The amoeba model describes a competitive adaptation mechanism through the mutual action of units on the vibrating potential method. The results show that competitive learning causes reciprocal adaptation, and that autonomous synchronization of phase delay derives both a creeping motion and walking behavior.

This work was supported in part by Grant-In-Aid for Scientific Research on Germination Area No.08875052, Ministry of Education, Science and Culture.

References

Agarwal, P. 1995. The Cell Programming Language. *Artificial Life* 2: 37-77.

Barbara, J., Varnum, F., Voss, E., and Soll D. R. 1987. Frequency and orientation of pseudopod formation of Dictyostelium discoideum amoeba chemotaxing in a spatial gradient: Further evidence for a temporal mechanism, Alan R. Liss, Inc., *Cell Motility and the Cytoskeleton* 8: 18-26.

Barbara, J., and Soll D. R. 1984. Effects of cAMP on single cell motility in Dictyostelium. *Journal of Cell*

Biology 99: 1151-1155.

Fleischer, K. and A. H. Barr. 1994. A simulation test bed for the study of multicellular development: The multiple mechanisms of morphogenesis. In *Artificial Life III*, edited by C. G. Langton. Reading, MA: Addison-Wesley, p. 389-416.

Steinbock, O., Siegert, F., Muller, S. C., and Weijer, C. J. 1993. Three-dimensional waves of excitation during Dictyostelium morphogenesis. *Proc. Natl. Acad. Sci. USA* 90:7332-7335.

Siegert F., and Weijer C. J. 1992. Three-dimensional scroll waves organize Dictyostelium slugs. *Proc. Natl. Acad. Sci. USA* 89: 6433-6437.

Ueda, T. 1993. Controlling perception and behavior of the cell (in Japanese). Nikkei Science, pp. 32-39.

Yokoi, H., Mizuno, T., Takita, M., Hakura, J., and Kakazu, Y., 1996. Amoeba like self-organization model using vibrating potential field. In *Proceedings of Artificial Life V*, edited by C. G. Langton and K. Shimohara. Cambridge, MA: MIT Press, p. 32-39.

Self-organized Complexity in a Computer Program Ecosystem

Shinichiro Yoshii, Satoshi Ohashi, and Yukinori Kakazu

Complex Systems Engineering, Hokkaido University
N-13, W-8, Kita-ku, Sapporo 060, Japan
{yoshii, ohhashi, kakazu}@complex.eng.hokudai.ac.jp

Abstract

This paper describes self-organized complexity of an ecosystem consisting of computer programs that exhibit life-like behavior. As an artificial life approach to simulating the life-like behavior on a computer, attention should be given to the emergent dynamics by which a new action is brought forth. In considering how to implement such a notion onto a computer, it could be interpreted as the generation of a new algorithm, or the generation of a new code establishing a mapping between a symbol and an information. This paper discusses complex behaviors in our artificial-life system named PROTEAN, that is an ecological model consisting of Turing machines as a platform on which to simulate the emergent dynamics of computer programs. Although the system is not provided with any particular mechanism for self-reproduction, the system is self-organized so that the system constituents can utilize their environments for survival. For the approaches emphasizing simulations on a computer, it is important to understand an emergent process from the viewpoint of computational complexity. Using this ecosystem model, this paper demonstrates how computer programs may be able to achieve life-like behavior, and discusses the relation with their self-organized complexity.

Introduction

Even if we don't have a strict definition of life, we can observe life-like properties in various phenomena, such as increase of complexity, adaptiveness, and emergence. In fact, the notion of emergence itself is also difficult to define in a way that distinguishes simply quantitative changes from those cases where something really new emerges. In this paper, we should formalize it as the appearance of a new action or agent as the realization of that action.

In this context, most simulation models for life-like behavior are unable to realize the emergence of new actions. Rather than modeling a process whereby something really new emerges, those models seem to focus on the implementation and simulation of particular aspects of life-like adaptive behavior. This arises from the process by which these systems are modeled to meet a specific purpose. On the other hand, to further our understanding of mechanisms that exhibit truly life-like behavior, attention should be given to the modeling of an emergent process whereby new actions may be brought forth. Life-like behavior should be understood as the result of complex relations brought about by the emergence of new actions, rather than beginning with the application of a specific scheme designed to simulate a certain phenomenon.

In implementing this onto a computer, it could be interpreted as the generation of a new algorithm within a computer program and the generation of a new code, establishing a mapping between a symbol and information. This paper discusses life-like adaptive behaviors of an ecological model consisting of computer programs described by Turing machines. A Turing machine is a mathematical model of computing or algorithms, enabling any computational procedure that we know today to be described. In particular, we use a universal Turing machine (UTM), that, depending on its program, can simulate any other Turing machine's operation. In PROTEAN, computer programs are decoded onto the UTM, where they interact with each other by performing their various functions. Through computer simulations, this paper demonstrates how computer programs may be able to achieve self-organization, resulting in life-like behavior. Furthermore, in order to understand those behaviors of computer programs, we have to take their computational complexity into account. This paper discusses unpredictable population dynamics from the viewpoint of the computational complexity, that would be correspondent to those behaviors bounded with energy in the physical systems.

PROTEAN: Turing Machine Ecosystem

PROTEAN (Platform on Recursive Ontogenetic Turing-machine Ecosystem for Autopoietic Networks) is an emergent system aimed at simulating autopoietic behaviors of computer programs described in a form of Turing machine. In PROTEAN, survival games take place on the UTM, with ecological resources being competed for. The essential features of PROTEAN are the representation of a UTM, the interaction procedure between constituents, and the constitution of the system as a whole. For more details about PROTEAN, refer to (Yoshii and Kakazu 1998) or our web site at http://junji.complex.eng.hokudai.ac.jp/export/yoshii/WWW/index.html.

Universal encoding of algorithms for UTM

Conceptually speaking, PROTEAN has the capability of describing and producing any kind of computer program in the form of Turing machines due to the utilization of a UTM that reads bit strings. A tape for the UTM is nothing more than the coded version of a Turing machine that performs the task desired of the UTM. We can regard a tape as a genotype that encodes the Turing machine's functionality.

Ecological resources

Figure 1 shows the ecosystem, which consists of the description tapes of the Turing machines. Its total resource is a static volume of memory, while a Turing machine itself can make use of an almost infinite memory capacity in its functioning. Each Turing machine occupies its own memory block, dependent on its description length.

Figure 1: Ecological Resource.

Interaction between Turing machines

First, a genotype g_n is decoded into a phenotype, that is, a specific Turing machine T_n, through interpretation by the UTM. Next, the decoded Turing machine, T_n, reads and operates on another genotypic machine description, g_m. The newly generated genotype will dictate a new Turing machine, or in other words, a new algorithm. This means that such an interaction can realize a process whereby a program can directly operate on the description of another program to generate a new algorithm.

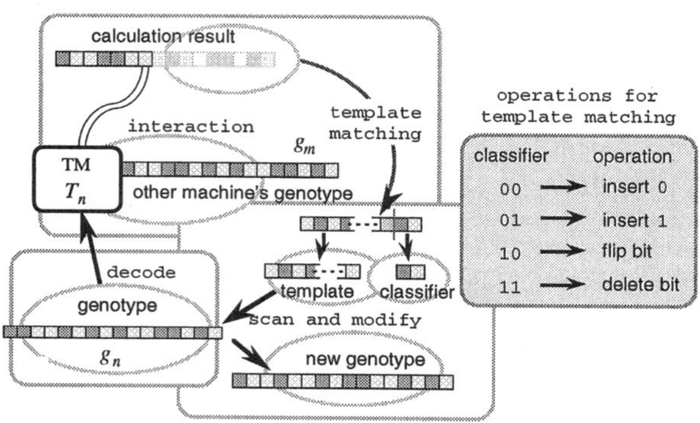

Figure 2: Interaction between Turing machines.

Parallel processing against halting problem

The way interaction takes place in PROTEAN is based on the technical assumption that an algorithm is a definite step-by-step procedure guaranteed to terminate after a finite number of steps. However, in fact, there is no way to tell in advance whether a Turing machine will accept its input tape or not. In order to avoid this insoluble problem, known as the halting problem, PROTEAN adopts parallel processing and compulsory termination: Each Turing machine reads the other machines' descriptions chosen at random. When a Turing machine accepts a tape and some partition is vacant, the parent Turing machine allocates a memory block for its child there. On the other hand, if another machine or machines have already occupied that memory block, the parent can terminate their interaction process and rewrite the memory. As a result, those machines that face the halting problem are eliminated from the ecosystem.

Characteristics of the model

Some of the properties of our model may be regarded as being similar to those of Tierra (Ray 1991) or other evolutionary models which use bit strings (Banzhaf 1994) (Ikegami and Hashimoto 1995). However, the following points make PROTEAN stand out from former works:

First, there are no arbitrary rules for self-organization or self-reproduction, as well as no special metaphor. Even how an interaction is interpreted, and what kind of result will be obtained, are not predictable beforehand, but deterministically dependent on the interaction between Turing machines. Furthermore, the interaction takes place independent of the location at the ecological resource, unlike avida (Adami and Brown 1994) and COSMOS (Taylor and Hallam 1997) that simulate life-like behaviors of computer programs on 2D cellular environment. Second, there are no explicit parameters to control the

Figure 3: Turing machines in 100-adic notation in simulation.

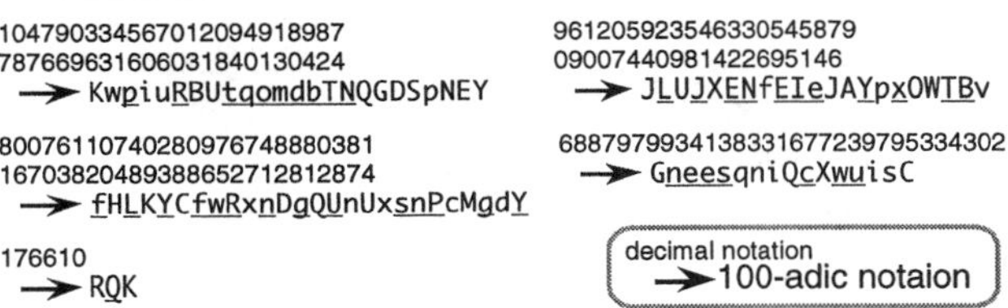

Figure 4: Emergence of self-assembling network.

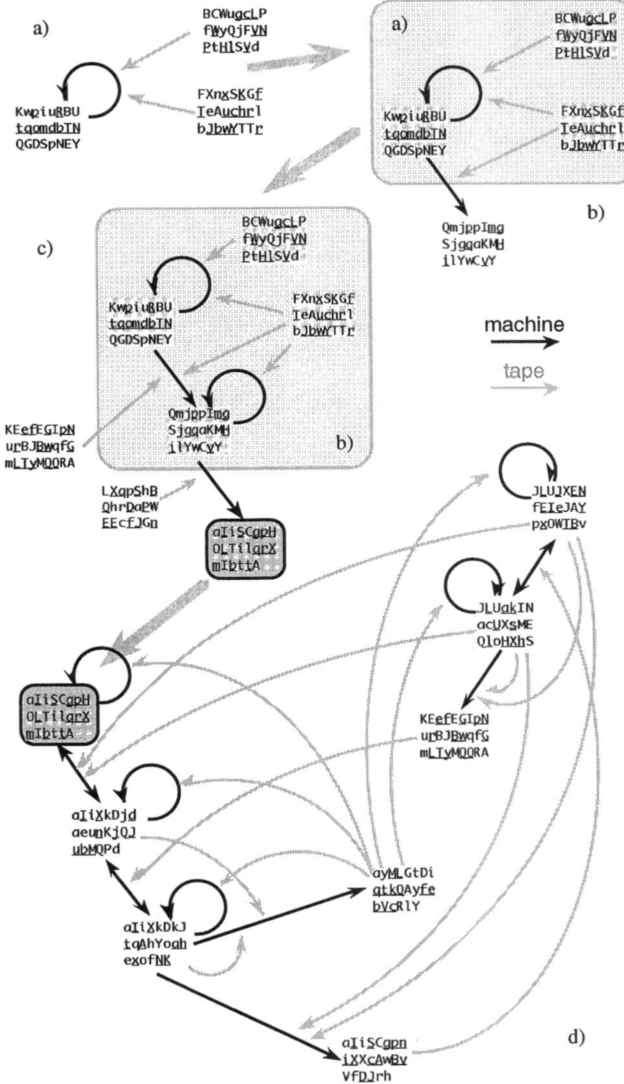

dynamics, such as, a parameter which would reap constituent machines in the system if the memory filled up to some specified level. The sole condition for a Turing machine to survive is its being able to accept its local resource more effectively than the others, and self-reproduce, where possible. Consequently, the fitness of each machine is dependent dynamically on its relation to the others within the system and the consequent global environment thereof. Thus, the problem of ill-defined machines becoming stuck is also left up to the system's dynamics, by which they will be eliminated from the ecosystem.

Computer Simulations

Emergence of Self-assembling Network

This section simulates the self-reproductive dynamics that resulted in the emergence of self-assembling network of the Turing machines. The first computer simulation started from a configuration with the five kinds of description tape described in Figure 3, and adopted a 100-adic notation system for their long descriptions, using 100 characters such as "A, ◡ ,Y,a, ◡ ,y,A, ◡ ,Y,a, ◡ ,y", as their length didn't allow representation in decimal notation.

Figure 4 illustrates the reaction pathways between the Turing machines. These figures are abbreviations as their total size doesn't allow full inclusion here. Each number in this figure is the description tape of a Turing machine described in the 100-adic notation. Figure 4 a) shows Turing machine $T_{\mathrm{KwpiuRBUtqomdbTNQGDSpNEY}}$ reproduced itself by reading the description tapes, such as BCWugcLPfWyQjFVNPtHlSVd, that had been generated from other interactions. On the other hand, these Turing machines generated new description tapes dictating new Turing machines, one after another. It should be noted here that almost all kinds of Turing machines shown in Figure 4 are those that didn't originally exist in the initial configuration, but were newly generated through interactions.

Look at the reaction networks, such as Figure 4 a), b), and c). These denote the growth of altruistic networks, where the initial Turing machines generated new Turing machines, one after another, through their interactions. "Altruistic", here, means that the growth of these networks was of no benefit to their generators. From the exoscopic viewpoint, they seem to self-assemble into these subsequent networks by their accepting the changing ecological resources. Thus, Turing machine $T_{\mathrm{KwpiuRBUtqomdbTNQGDSpNEY}}$, for example, disappeared because of its accepting the resource and generating other machines that could utilize the resource more effectively, as seen from Figure 5. Figure 5 shows a change in the number of certain specific representative Turing machines, concentrating on the earlier dynamics of the ecosystem where more interesting behavior was observed.

Figure 5: Change in number of constituent Turing machines in self-assembling network.

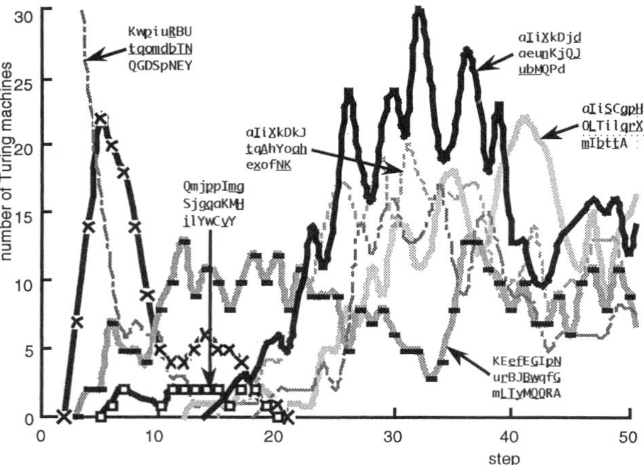

Up to about the 20th step, various Turing machines appeared and disappeared. Finally, the reaction network shown in Figure 4 d) emerged in the ecosystem. This reaction network is very interesting in respect to the following points: first, it consists of various kinds of self-reproductive network; and, second, the constituent Turing machines also behaved as tapes that were made use of by other interactions. Thus, in total, the self-assembling network forms a large and complicated hypercycle (Eigen and Schuster 1977) consisting of various Turing machines.

Self-organized complexity in ecosystem

It is important to see the behavior simulated, from the viewpoint of the complexity in an algorithm. This section examines how the complexity of the system may be able to self-organize.

It is possible to define the degree of complexity of a Turing machine by measuring the amount of resources required to execute its function, even though this is based on the assumption that a difficult computation will require more resources than a less difficult one. According to one definition (Brookshear 1989), complexity of a Turing machine is characterized by the following properties: *time complexity* means the amount of time required to perform a computation, which will correspond to the steps of a head moving in the case of a Turing machine. On the other hand, *space complexity* refers to the amount of storage space required by a computation. The space complexity of a Turing machine is defined as the number of tape cells required.

Figure 6: Self-organized complexity of Turing machines.

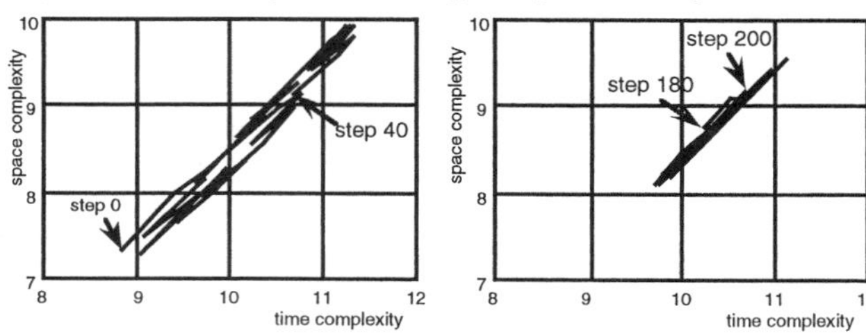

Thus, Figure 6 shows the transition of correlation between both complexities, with respect to the average number of constituent Turing machines in the above simulation. These figures indicate that the averaged complexity of constituent Turing machines increases and self-organizes to a certain attractor. Finally, as long as there emerges a stable self-reproductive hypercycle, the complexity of the system will not expand ad infinitum, or rather it will fluctuate within a certain boundary. This helps us to predict to what kind of point the system will reach. Moreover, such a measurement of the complexity enables us to understand an unpredictable behavior.

Population dynamics dependent on calculation complexity

Interactions based on the complexity in calculation, sometimes, bring about phenomena contrary to our expectations. This section examines how the calculation complexity in Turing machine affects the population dynamics of self-reproductive hypercycle network.

The computer simulation here utilized two Turing machines shown in Figure 7. In order to simplify their description, we call the left Turing machine, T_{8524}, while the right one is called T_{1812}, after the numbers of lower four figures in their decimal genotypic descriptions. These Turing machines are characterized by the following point: both Turing machines can self-reproduce by reading its description tape as well as the other's description, as shown in Figure 8. Therefore, the interaction between these Turing machines forms such a mutually self-reproductive network.

Figure 7: Decoded programs of Turing machines.

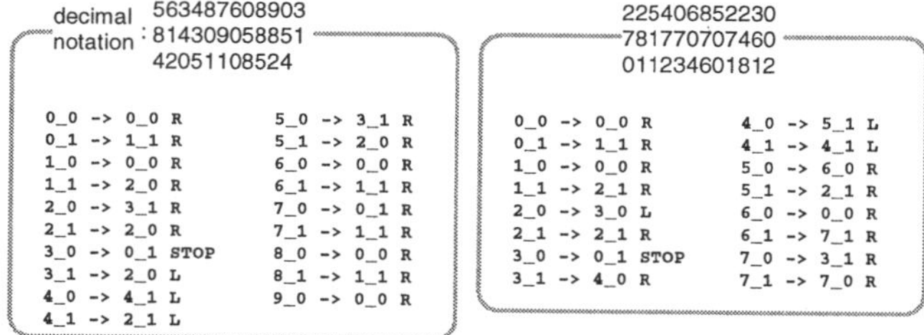

Figure 8: Mutually self-reproductive hypercycle.

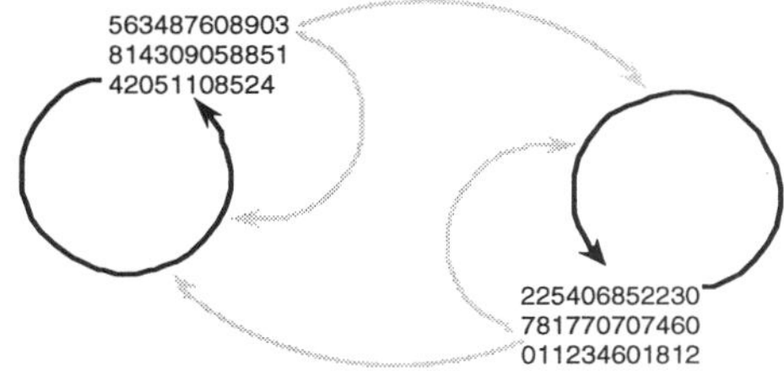

Figure 9: Population dynamics on change in number.

initial condition: $T_{1812} : T_{8524} = 1.5 : 1$ $\quad T_{1812} : T_{8524} = 2 : 1$

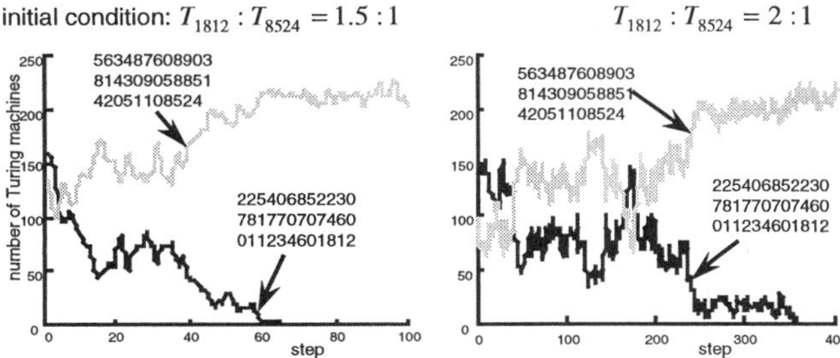

The left diagram in Figure 9 indicates a change in the number of these Turing machines in the case where the numbers of T_{1812} and T_{8524} are in the ratios 1.5:1; while the right in Figure 9 in the ratios 2:1. As the simulation time steps proceed, T_{8524} superseded the other Turing machine T_{1812} in both cases. These results didn't necessarily occur accidentally. Table 1 indicates the percentage of victories of T_{8524}, to the total number of matches. As can be seen from Table 1, Turing machine T_{8524} dominated the ecological resource with the considerably high possibilities, even if there were more Turing machines T_{1812} than T_{8524} in the initial condition. Such situations are related with the calculation complexity of constituent Turing machines. Table 2 indicates the costs required for each interaction. For example, when Turing machine T_{8524} operates on the description tape for T_{1812}, Turing machine T_{8524} makes use of 4 states within its 19 states, and it takes 15 steps to accept that tape.

It follows from these results that a Turing machine whose time complexity is larger is disadvantageous for its survival in our ecological model. The reason for that is a Turing machine with larger time complexity is more likely to be terminated by other Turing machines during its

Table 1: Domination ratio by Turing machine T_{8524}.

initial population ratio 225406852230 : 563487608903 781770707460 : 814309058851 011234601812 : 42051108524	domination ratio 563487608903 814309058851 42051108524	
1:1	4/4	100%
2:1	3/4	75%
5:1	2/6	33%

Table 2: All the costs concerning interaction.

machine \ tape	225406852230 781770707460 011234601812				563487608903 814309058851 42051108524			
225406852230 781770707460 011234601812	16	8	34	23	16	8	21	14
563487608903 814309058851 42051108524	19	4	15	10	19	4	15	10
	number of state	number used in interaction	time complexity	space complexity	number of state	number used in interaction	time complexity	space complexity

operation. As a result, such a Turing machine loses a chance for self-reproduction. This kind of situation is unpredictable beforehand, because no one can tell in advance whether a Turing machine will accept its input tape or not. In fact, the time complexity defines a kind of adaptivity to each Turing machine, from the viewpoint of speed of tape acceptance.

On the other hand, the space complexity becomes important when the ecological resource contains many kinds of constituent Turing machine. The space complexity is correlative with the length of a tape of the calculation output. It means a Turing machine, whose space complexity is smaller, outputs a shorter output tape. Therefore, such a machine tends to modify its reproduced description tape during the pattern matching procedure after its interaction, resulting in generating a genotype different from its own genotypic description tape. Even if it can accept its input tape, there is a less possibility where it can self-reproduce. Although this simulation didn't explicitly show such a relation between self-reproduction and the space complexity, a Turing machine has to accept many kinds of tape with a smaller time complexity and a larger space complexity in order to self-reproduce for its survival. Thus, from these discussions, one general point regarding the adaptivity becomes clear: the small time complexity is necessary for the short-term adaptation, and, on the other hand, the large space complexity tends to benefit the long-term adaptation.

Discussion and Conclusion

This section discusses the obtained simulation results from the viewpoint of the life-like behavior of computer programs. PROTEAN has nothing special added whatsoever for achieving either self-reproduction or self-organization. Nevertheless, we were able to observe some interesting behavior in the computer simulations.

These Turing machines behaved as real computer programs, processing information, or, as data, providing information. Although their description tapes as data showed altruistic behavior, they could survive when a parasitic relation, in which they were produced from other reactions, was possible. However, in PROTEAN where there is no static fitness function, such a relation is actually fragile, as their fitness is dynamically dependent on their relations to others and the consequent environment thereof. Thus, the system continues to transit up to a certain point where stable self-reproductive networks may be achieved. The constituent Turing machines are highly adaptive from the viewpoint of their capability to utilize and accept their surrounding resources. The Turing machines read, stored, and interpreted information in their environment, and then, exhibited autopoietic dynamics. Macroscopically, "autopoietic" means those dynamics that result from the transformation of self-reproductive networks. This self-assembling aspect is of central importance in understanding of life-like behavior.

Since there is no mutative operation in our ecological model in its present form, the final version of this self-reproductive network shows no further change. However, it might be possible to realize boundless evolution, if a mutative process was being operated. In this paper, we didn't examine such a situation as we intended to discuss an emergent system consisting of computer programs representing the step-by-step deterministic procedure of an algorithm.

This paper also discussed these dynamics from the viewpoint of the complexity in calculation. In fact, there is room for further investigation. However, we think it is necessary to simulate life-like behavior, taking the complexity in calculation into account. Although a simulated phenomenon on a computer is usually free from energy unlike the real physical systems, we believe the nature of life lies in the relations between information and the calculation complexity. Our future work will aim at studying the relation between emergent behaviors and their complexity for processing information in PROTEAN.

References

Adami, C. and Brown, T. 1994. Evolutionary learning in the 2D Artificial Life system 'Avida'. In *Artifical Life IV,* edited by R. A. Brooks and P. Maes. Cambridge, MA: MIT Press, p. 377-381.

Banzhaf, W. 1994. Self-organization in a system of binary strings. . In *Artifical Life IV,* edited by R. A. Brooks and P. Maes. Cambridge, MA: MIT Press, p.109-118.

Eigen, M. and Schuster, P. 1977. The hypercycle: A principle of natural self-organization. *Naturwissenschaften* 64.

Ikegami, T and Hashimoto, T. 1995. Coevolution of machines and tapes. In *Advances in Artificial Life. Proceedings of the3rd European Conference on Artificial Life*. Berlin, Heidelberg: Springer-Verlag, p. 234-245.

Ray, T. S. 1991. An approach to the synthesis of life. In *Artificial Life II,* edited by C. G. Langton, J. D. Farmerr, C. Taylor, and S. Rasmussen. Redwood City, CA: Addison-Wesley, p. 371-408.

Taylor, T. and Hallam, J. 1997. Studying evolution with self-replicating computer programs. In *Fourth European Conference on Artificial Life*, edited by P. Husbands and I. Harvey. Cambridge, MA: MIT Press, p. 550-559.

Yoshii, S. and Kakazu, Y. 1998. Self-assembling networks of computer programs. *Journal of Robotics and Autonomous Systems.* Elsevier (to appear)

AUTHOR INDEX

KEYWORD INDEX

Complex Adaptive Systems
John H. Holland, Christopher G. Langton, and Stewart W. Wilson, advisors

Adaptation in Natural and Artificial Systems: An Introductory Analysis with Applications to Biology, Control, and Artificial Intelligence, John H. Holland

Toward a Practice of Autonomous Systems: Proceedings of the First European Conference on Artificial Life, edited by Francisco J. Varela and Paul Bourgine

Genetic Programming: On the Programming of Computers by Means of Natural Selection, John R. Koza

Genetic Programming: The Movie, John R. Koza and James P. Rice

From Animals to Animats 2: Proceedings of the Second International Conference on Simulation of Adaptive Behavior, edited by Jean-Arcady Meyer, Herbert L. Roitblat, and Stewart W. Wilson

Intelligent Behavior in Animals and Robots, David McFarland and Thomas Bösser

Advances in Genetic Programming, edited by Kenneth E. Kinnear, Jr.

Genetic Programming II: Automatic Discovery of Reusable Programs, John R. Koza

Genetic Programming II Video: The Next Generation, John R. Koza

Turtles, Termites, and Traffic Jams: Explorations in Massively Parallel Microworlds, Mitchel Resnick

From Animals to Animats 3: Proceedings of the Third International Conference on Simulation of Adaptive Behavior, edited by Dave Cliff, Philip Husbands, Jean-Arcady Meyer, and Stewart W. Wilson

Artificial Life IV: Proceedings of the Fourth International Workshop on the Synthesis and Simulation of Living Systems, edited by Rodney A. Brooks and Pattie Maes

Comparative Approaches to Cognitive Science, edited by Herbert L. Roitblat and Jean-Arcady Meyer

Artificial Life: An Overview, edited by Christopher G. Langton

Evolutionary Programming IV: Proceedings of the Fourth Annual Conference on Evolutionary Programming, edited by John R. McDonnell, Robert G. Reynolds, and David B. Fogel

An Introduction to Genetic Algorithms, Melanie Mitchell

Catching Ourselves in the Act: Situated Activity, Interactive Emergence, and Human Thought, Horst Hendriks-Jansen

Toward a Science of Consciousness: The First Tucson Discussions and Debates, edited by Stuart R. Hameroff, Alfred W. Kaszniak, and Alwyn C. Scott

Genetic Programming: Proceedings of the First Annual Conference, edited by John R. Koza, David E. Goldberg, David B. Fogel, and Rick L. Riolo

Evolutionary Programming V: Proceedings of the Fifth Annual Conference on Evolutionary Programming, edited by Lawrence J. Fogel, Peter J. Angeline, and Thomas Bäck

Elements of Artificial Neural Networks, Kishan Mehrotra, Chilukuri K. Mohan, and Sanjay Ranka

From Animals to Animats 4: Proceedings of the Fourth International Conference on Simulation of Adaptive Behavior, edited by Pattie Maes, Maja J. Mataric, Jean-Arcady Meyer, and Stewart W. Wilson

Advances in Genetic Programming, Volume 2, edited by Peter J. Angeline and Kenneth E. Kinnear, Jr.

Growing Artificial Societies: Social Science from the Bottom Up, Joshua M. Epstein and Robert Axtell

Artificial Life V: Proceedings of the Fifth International Workshop on the Synthesis and Simulation of Living Systems, edited by Christopher G. Langton and Katsunori Shimohara

An Introduction to Natural Computation, Dana H. Ballard

Fourth European Conference on Artificial Life, edited by Phil Husbands and Inman Harvey

Toward a Science of Consciousness 2: The 1996 Tucson Discussions and Debates, edited by Stuart R. Hameroff, Alfred W. Kaszniak, and Alwyn C. Scott

An Introduction to Fuzzy Sets: Analysis and Design, Witold Pedrycz and Fernando Gomide

The Simple Genetic Algorithm: Foundations and Theory, Michael D. Vose

From Animals to Animats 5: Proceedings of the Fifth International Conference on Simulation of Adaptive Behavior, edited by Bruce Blumberg, Jean-Arcady Meyer, Rolf Pfeifer, and Stewart W. Wilson

Artificial Life VI: Proceedings of the Sixth International Conference, edited by Christoph Adami, Richard K. Belew, Hiroaki Kitano, and Charles E. Taylor